Preface

The *Uniform Building Code*™ is dedicated to the development of better building construction and greater safety to the public by uniformity in building laws. The code is founded on broad-based principles that make possible the use of new materials and new construction systems.

The *Uniform Building Code* was first enacted by the International Conference of Building Officials at the Sixth Annual Business Meeting held in Phoenix, Arizona, October 18-21, 1927. Revised editions of this code have been published since that time at approximate three-year intervals. New editions incorporate changes approved since the last edition.

The *Uniform Building Code* is designed to be compatible with related publications to provide a complete set of documents for regulatory use. See the publications list following this preface for a listing of the complete family of Uniform Codes and related publications.

Code Changes. The ICBO code development process has been suspended by the Board of Directors and, because of this action, changes to the *Uniform Building Code* will not be processed. For more information, write to the International Conference of Building Officials, 5360 Workman Mill Road, Whittier, California 90601-2298. An analysis of changes between editions is published in the *Analysis of Revisions to the Uniform Codes*.

Marginal Markings. Solid vertical lines in the margins within the body of the code indicate a change from the requirements of the 1994 edition except where an entire chapter was revised, a new chapter was added or a change was minor. Where an entire chapter was revised or a new chapter was added, a notation appears at the beginning of that chapter. The letter **F** repeating in line vertically in the margin indicates that the provision is maintained under the code change procedures of the International Fire Code Institute. Deletion indicators (◆) are provided in the margin where a paragraph or item listing has been deleted if the deletion resulted in a change of requirements.

Three-Volume Set. Provisions of the *Uniform Building Code* have been divided into a three-volume set. Volume 1 accommodates administrative, fire- and life-safety, and field inspection provisions. Chapters 1 through 15 and Chapters 24 through 35 are printed in Volume 1 in their entirety. Any appendix chapters associated with these chapters are printed in their entirety at the end of Volume 1. Excerpts of certain chapters from Volume 2 are reprinted in Volume 1 to provide greater usability.

Volume 2 accommodates structural engineering design provisions, and specifically contains Chapters 16 through 23 printed in their entirety. Included in this volume are design standards that have been added to their respective chapters as divisions of the chapters. Any appendix chapters associated with these chapters are printed in their entirety at the end of Volume 2. Excerpts of certain chapters from Volume 1 are reprinted in Volume 2 to provide greater usability.

Volume 3 contains material, testing and installation standards.

Metrication. The *Uniform Building Code* was metricated in the 1994 edition. The metric conversions are provided in parenthesis following the English units. Where industry has made metric conversions available, the conversions conform to current industry standards.

Formulas are also provided with metric equivalents. Metric equivalent formulas immediately follow the English formula and are denoted by "For **SI**:" preceding the metric equivalent. Some formulas do not use dimensions and, thus, are not provided with a metric equivalent. Multiplying conversion factors have been provided for formulas where metric forms were unavailable. Tables are provided with multiplying conversion factors in subheadings for each tabulated unit of measurement.

1997

UNIFORM

BUILDING

CODE™

VOLUME 3

MATERIAL, TESTING AND INSTALLATION STANDARDS

Third Printing

Publication Date: April 1997

ISSN 0896-9655
ISBN 1-884590-91-8 (soft cover edition)
ISBN 1-884590-92-6 (loose leaf edition)
ISBN 1-884590-93-4 (3-vol. set—soft cover)
ISBN 1-884590-94-2 (3-vol. set—loose leaf)

CODES AND RELATED PUBLICATIONS

The International Conference of Building Officials (ICBO) publishes a family of codes, each correlated with the *Uniform Building Code*™ to provide jurisdictions with a complete set of building-related regulations for adoption. Some of these codes are published in affiliation with other organizations such as the International Fire Code Institute (IFCI) and the International Code Council (ICC). Reference materials and related codes also are available to improve knowledge of code enforcement and administration of building inspection programs. Publications and products are continually being added, so inquiries should be directed to Conference headquarters for a listing of available products. Many codes and references are also available on CD-ROM or floppy disk. These are denoted by (*). The following publications and products are available from ICBO:

CODES

*Uniform Building Code, Volumes 1, 2 and 3. The most widely adopted model building code in the United States, the performance-based *Uniform Building Code* is a proven document, meeting the needs of government units charged with the enforcement of building regulations. Volume 1 contains administrative, fire- and life-safety and field inspection provisions; Volume 2 contains structural engineering design provisions; and Volume 3 contains material, testing and installation standards.

*Uniform Mechanical Code™. Provides a complete set of requirements for the design, construction, installation and maintenance of heating, ventilating, cooling and refrigeration systems; incinerators and other heat-producing appliances.

International Plumbing Code™. Provides consistent and technically advanced requirements that can be used across the country to provide comprehensive regulations of modern plumbing systems. Setting minimum regulations for plumbing facilities in terms of performance objectives, the IPC provides for the acceptance of new and innovative products, materials and systems.

International Private Sewage Disposal Code™. Provides flexibility in the development of safety and sanitary individual sewage disposal systems and includes detailed provisions for all aspects of design, installation and inspection of private sewage disposal systems.

International Mechanical Code™. Establishes minimum regulations for mechanical systems using prescriptive and performance-related provisions. It is founded on broad-based principles that make possible the use of new materials and new mechanical designs.

Uniform Zoning Code™. This code is dedicated to intelligent community development and to the benefit of the public welfare by providing a means of promoting uniformity in zoning laws and enforcement.

*Uniform Fire Code™, Volumes 1 and 2. The premier model fire code in the United States, the *Uniform Fire Code* sets forth provisions necessary for fire prevention and fire protection. Published by the International Fire Code Institute, the *Uniform Fire Code* is endorsed by the Western Fire Chiefs Association, the International Association of Fire Chiefs and ICBO. Volume 1 contains code provisions compatible with the *Uniform Building Code*, and Volume 2 contains standards referenced from the code provisions.

*Urban-Wildland Interface Code™. Promulgated by IFCI, this code regulates both land use and the built environment in designated urban-wildland interface areas. This newly developed code is the only model code that bases construction requirements on the fire-hazard severity exposed to the structure. Developed under a grant from the Federal Emergency Management Agency, this code is the direct result of hazard mitigation meetings held after devastating wildfires.

Uniform Housing Code™. Provides complete requirements affecting conservation and rehabilitation of housing. Its regulations are compatible with the *Uniform Building Code*.

Uniform Code for the Abatement of Dangerous Buildings™. A code compatible with the *Uniform Building Code* and the *Uniform Housing Code* which provides equitable remedies consistent with other laws for the repair, vacation or demolition of dangerous buildings.

Uniform Sign Code™. Dedicated to the development of better sign regulation, its requirements pertain to all signs and sign construction attached to buildings.

Uniform Administrative Code™. This code covers administrative areas in connection with adoption of the *Uniform Building Code*, *Uniform Mechanical Code* and related codes. It contains provisions which relate to site preparation, construction, alteration, moving, repair and use and occupancies of buildings or structures and building service equipment, including plumbing, electrical and mechanical regulations. The code is compatible with the administrative provisions of all codes published by the Conference.

Uniform Building Security Code™. This code establishes minimum standards to make dwelling units resistant to unlawful entry. It regulates swinging doors, sliding doors, windows and hardware in connection with dwelling units of apartment houses or one- and two-family dwellings. The code gives consideration to the concerns of police, fire and building officials in establishing requirements for resistance to burglary which are compatible with fire and life safety.

Uniform Code for Building Conservation™. A building conservation guideline presented in code format which will provide a community with the means to preserve its existing buildings while achieving appropriate levels of safety. It is formatted in the same manner as the *Uniform Building Code*, is compatible with other Uniform Codes, and may be adopted as a code or used as a guideline.

Dwelling Construction under the Uniform Building Code™. Designed primarily for use in home building and apprentice training, this book contains requirements applicable to the construction of one- and two-story dwellings based on the requirements of the *Uniform Building Code*. Available in English or Spanish.

Dwelling Construction under the Uniform Mechanical Code™. This publication is for the convenience of the homeowner or contractor interested in installing mechanical equipment in a one- or two-family dwelling in conformance with the *Uniform Mechanical Code*.

Supplements to UBC and related codes. Published in the years between editions, the Supplements contain all approved changes, plus an analysis of those changes.

Uniform Building Code—1927 Edition. A special 60th anniversary printing of the first published *Uniform Building Code*.

One and Two Family Dwelling Code. Promulgated by ICC, this code eliminates conflicts and duplications among the model codes to achieve national uniformity. Covers mechanical and plumbing requirements as well as construction and occupancy.

Application and Commentary on the One and Two Family Dwelling Code. An interpretative commentary on the *One and Two Family Dwelling Code* intended to enhance uniformity of interpretation and application of the code nationwide. Developed by the three model code organizations, this document includes numerous illustrations of code requirements and the rationale for individual provisions.

Model Energy Code. This code includes minimum requirements for effective use of energy in the design of new buildings and structures and additions to existing buildings. It is based on American Society of Heating, Refrigeration and Air-conditioning Engineers Standard 90A-1980 and was originally developed jointly by ICBO, BOCA, SBCCI and the National Conference of States on Building Codes and Standards under a contract funded by the United States Department of Energy. The code is now maintained by ICC and is adopted by reference in the *Uniform Building Code*.

National Electrical Code®. The electrical code used throughout the United States. Published by the National Fire Protection Association, it is an indispensable aid to every electrician, contractor, architect, builder, inspector and anyone who must specify or certify electrical installations.

TECHNICAL REFERENCES AND EDUCATIONAL MATERIALS

Analysis of Revisions to the Uniform Codes™. An analysis of changes between the previous and new editions of the Uniform Codes is provided. Changes between code editions are noted either at the beginning of chapters or in the margins of the code text.

*Handbook to the Uniform Building Code. The handbook is a completely detailed and illustrated commentary on the *Uniform Building Code,* tracing historical background and rationale of the codes through the current edition. Also included are numerous drawings and figures clarifying the application and intent of the code provisions. Also available in electronic format.

*Handbook to the Uniform Mechanical Code. An indispensable tool for understanding the provisions of the current UMC, the handbook traces the historical background and rationale behind the UMC provisions, includes 160 figures which clarify the intent and application of the code, and provides a chapter-by-chapter analysis of the UMC.

*Uniform Building Code Application Manual. This manual discusses sections of the *Uniform Building Code* with a question-and-answer format, providing a comprehensive analysis of the intent of the code sections. Most sections include illustrative examples. The manual is in loose-leaf format so that code applications published in *Building Standards* magazine may be inserted. Also available in electronic format.

*Uniform Mechanical Code Application Manual. As a companion document to the *Uniform Mechanical Code,* this manual provides a comprehensive analysis of the intent of a number of code sections in an easy-to-use question-and-answer format. The manual is available in a loose-leaf format and includes illustrative examples for many code sections.

*Uniform Fire Code Applications Manual. This newly developed manual provides questions and answers regarding UFC provisions. A comprehensive analysis of the intent of numerous code sections, the manual is in a loose-leaf format for easy insertion of code applications published in IFCI's *Fire Code Journal.*

Quick-Reference Guide to the Occupancy Requirements of the 1997 UBC. Code requirements are compiled in this publication by occupancy groups for quick access. These tabulations assemble requirements for each occupancy classification in the code. Provisions, such as fire-resistive ratings for occupancy separations in Table 3-B, exterior wall and opening protection requirements in Table 5-A-1, and fire-resistive ratings for types of construction in Table 6-A, are tabulated for quick reference and comparison.

Plan Review Manual. A practical text that will assist and guide both the field inspector and plan reviewer in applying the code requirements. This manual covers the nonstructural and basic structural aspects of plan review.

Field Inspection Manual. An important fundamental text for courses of study at the community college and trade or technical school level. It is an effective text for those studying building construction or architecture and includes sample forms and checklists for use in the field.

Building Department Administration. An excellent guide for improvement of skills in departmental management and in the enforcement and application of the Building Code and other regulations administered by a building inspection department. This textbook will also be a valuable aid to instructors, students and those in related professional fields.

Building Department Guide to Disaster Mitigation. This new, expanded guide is designed to assist building departments in developing or updating disaster mitigation plans. Subjects covered include guidelines for damage mitigation, disaster-response management, immediate response, mutual aid and inspections, working with the media, repair and recovery policies, and public information bulletins. This publication is a must for those involved in preparing for and responding to disaster.

Building Official Management Manual. This manual addresses the unique nature of code administration and the managerial duties of the building official. A supplementary insert addresses the budgetary and financial aspects of a building department. It is also an ideal resource for those preparing for the management module of the CABO Building Official Certification Examination.

Legal Aspects of Code Administration. A manual developed by the three model code organizations to inform the building official on the legal aspects of the profession. The text is written in a logical sequence with explanation of legal terminology. It is designed to serve as a refresher for those preparing to take the legal module of the CABO Building Official Certification Examination.

Illustrated Guide to Conventional Construction Provisions of the UBC. This comprehensive guide and commentary provides detailed explanations of the conventional construction provisions in the UBC, including descriptive discussions and illustrated drawings to convey the prescriptive provisions related to wood-frame construction.

Introduction to the Uniform Building Code. A workbook that provides an overview of the basics of the UBC.

Uniform Building Code Update Workbook. This manual addresses many of the changes to the administrative, fire- and life-safety, and inspection provisions appearing in the UBC.

UMC Workbook. Designed for independent study or use with instructor-led programs based on the *Uniform Mechanical Code,* this comprehensive study guide consists of 16 learning sessions, with the first two sessions reviewing the purpose, scope, definitions and administrative provisions and the remaining 14 sessions progressively exploring the requirements for installing, inspecting and maintaining heating, ventilating, cooling and refrigeration systems.

UBC Field Inspection Workbook. A comprehensive workbook for studying the provisions of the UBC. Divided into 12 sessions, this workbook focuses on the UBC combustible construction requirements for the inspection of wood-framed construction.

Concrete Manual. A publication for individuals seeking an understanding of the fundamentals of concrete field technology and inspection practices. Of particular interest to concrete construction inspectors, it will also benefit employees of concrete producers, contractors, testing and inspection laboratories and material suppliers.

Reinforced Concrete Masonry Construction Inspector's Handbook. A comprehensive information source written especially for masonry inspection covering terminology, technology, materials, quality control, inspection and standards. Published jointly by ICBO and the Masonry Institute of America.

You Can Build It! Sponsored by ICBO in cooperation with CABO, this booklet contains information and advice to aid "do-it-yourselfers" with building projects. Provides guidance in necessary procedures such as permit requirements, codes, plans, cost estimation, etc.

Guidelines for Manufactured Housing Installations. A guideline in code form implementing the *Uniform Building Code* and its companion code documents to regulate the permanent installation of a manufactured home on a privately owned, nonrental site. A commentary is included to explain specific provisions, and codes applying to each component part are defined.

Accessibility Reference Guide. This guide is a valuable resource for architects, interior designers, plan reviewers and others who design and enforce accessibility provisions. Features include accessibility requirements, along with detailed commentary and graphics to clarify the provisions; cross-references to other applicable sections of the UBC and the Americans with Disabilities Act Accessibility Guidelines; a checklist of UBC provisions on access and usability requirements; and many other useful references.

Educational and Technical Reference Materials. The Conference has been a leader in the development of texts and course material to assist in the educational process. These materials include vital information necessary for the building official and subordinates in carrying out their responsibilities and have proven to be excellent references in connection with community college curricula and higher-level courses in the field of building construction technology and inspection and in the administration of building departments. Included are plan review checklists for structural, nonstructural, mechanical and fire-safety provisions and a full line of videotapes and automated products.

Table of Contents—Volume 1
Administrative, Fire- and Life-Safety, and Field Inspection Provisions

Table of Contents—Volume 2
Structural Engineering Design Provisions

Table of Contents—Volume 3
Material, Testing and Installation Standards

Volume 3

UNIFORM BUILDING CODE STANDARD 2-1
NONCOMBUSTIBLE MATERIAL—TESTS

**Based on Standard Method of Test E 136-79 of the American Society for Testing and Materials.
Extracted, with permission, from the *Annual Book of ASTM Standards,* copyright
American Society for Testing and Materials, 100 Barr Harbor Drive, West Conshohocken, PA 19428**

**See Sections 201.2 and 215, *Uniform Building Code*; Section 216,
Uniform Mechanical Code; and Section 211, *Uniform Sign Code***

SECTION 2.101 — SCOPE

This standard describes a procedure for the determination of noncombustibility of elementary materials of which building materials are composed, to indicate those materials which do not act to aid combustion or add appreciable heat to an ambient fire. It is not intended to apply to laminated or coated materials.

SECTION 2.102 — APPARATUS

The apparatus shall consist primarily of the following:

Refractory tubes. Two 10-inch-long (254 mm), concentric refractory tubes, 3 inches (76 mm) and 4 inches (102 mm) in inside diameter, with axes vertical and with heat applied by electric heating coils outside of the larger tube. A controlled flow of air is admitted tangentially near the top of the annular space between the tubes and passes to the bottom of the inner tube. The outer tube rests on a refractory bottom and the inner tube rests on three spacer blocks so as to afford a total opening under the inner tube equal to or greater than that of the annular space. The refractory bottom plate has a removable plug for cleaning.

Transparent cover. A transparent cover of heat-resisting glass or other transparent material shall be provided over the top of the inner tube with a 1-inch square (645 mm^2) opening over the axis of the tubes. This cover may be in two movable parts.

Thermocouples or other temperature-measuring devices, preferably automatically recording, shall be provided, one for the air in the lower part of the inner tube, another on the specimen in the approximate center of the space, and a third within the interior of the specimen. A thermocouple may be provided in the region of the heating coils for better regulation of the temperature of the air in the furnace space. The two specimen thermocouples shall have a time constant [time to reach 63.2 percent of the furnace air temperature of 1382°F (750°C)] of five to 10 seconds.

SECTION 2.103 — TEST SPECIMENS

All test specimens shall be $1^1/_2$ inches (38 mm) wide by $1^1/_2$ inches (38 mm) thick in cross section perpendicular to the air flow in the furnace and 2 inches (51 mm) long with tolerances on the dimensions of plus or minus $^1/_{10}$ inch (2.5 mm). The specimens shall be dried at 140°F plus or minus 5°F (60°C ± 3°C) for not less than 24 hours nor more than 48 hours before being tested.

Specimens in granular or powder form may be contained in thin-wall, open-top vessels of inert materials whose outside dimensions conform to the specimen shape and maximum size specified in this section. These vessels may have solid walls or be of mesh.

Not less than four identical specimens shall be tested.

SECTION 2.104 — PROCEDURE

Prepare the furnace by bringing the temperature (at the approximate position to be occupied by the center of the specimen) of the air in the furnace tube to 1382°F plus or minus 10°F (750°C ± 6°C), maintaining the furnace setting long enough to ascertain that it will remain at constant temperature in the unloaded furnace for at least 15 minutes while air passes at a velocity of 10 feet per minute (3 m/min.) plus or minus 20 percent past a loaded specimen in the tube, computed on the basis of air supply and velocity at room temperature and pressure.

As rapidly as possible, insert the test specimen into the furnace, with a thermocouple attached to the side surface of the specimen and a thermocouple inserted from the top of the specimen to its approximate volumetric center. Close the top cover to the 1-square-inch (645 mm^2) opening immediately after insertion of the specimen. Readings for the specimen thermocouples shall be made at intervals not to exceed 10 seconds during the first five minutes, and as often afterwards as necessary to produce a smooth curve. Do not change the regulation of the current through the heating coils and the air flow during the test.

Continue the test until the temperatures at the specimen thermocouples have reached maxima or until it is clearly evident that the specimen does not pass this test.

Throughout the test make and record visual observations on the specimens, noting quality, quantity or intensity and duration of flaming or smoking, or both, and change of state.

Weigh each specimen before and after testing and record the weight loss to the nearest 1 percent.

SECTION 2.105 — INTERPRETATION OF RESULTS

Materials subjected to the test described in this method shall be reported as noncombustible if, for three or more of the four specimens tested, (1) the recorded temperatures of the surface and interior thermocouples do not at any time during the test rise to more than 54°F (30°C) above the furnace air temperature at the beginning of the test, (2) if there is no flaming from the specimen after the first 30 seconds and (3) when the weight loss of the specimen during testing exceeds 50 percent, the recorded temperature of the surface and interior thermocouples do not at any time during the test rise above the furnace air temperature at the beginning of the test and there is no flaming of the specimen.

UNIFORM BUILDING CODE STANDARD 4-1
PROSCENIUM FIRESAFETY CURTAINS
Installation Standard of the International Conference of Building Officials
See Sections 303.8 and 405.3.4, *Uniform Building Code*

SECTION 4.101 — GENERAL REQUIREMENTS

Proscenium curtains, when required, shall be made of approved materials constructed and mounted so as to intercept hot gases, flames and smoke, and to prevent a glow from a severe fire on the stage from showing on the auditorium side within a period of 30 minutes. The closing of the curtain from the full-open position shall be effected in less than 30 seconds, but the last 8 feet (2438 mm) of travel shall not require less than five seconds.

SECTION 4.102 — DEFINITIONS

Curtain styles regulated by this standard are defined as follows:

BRAILLE PROSCENIUM FIRESAFETY CURTAIN is a curtain that folds up and stores in a very limited space above the proscenium opening. (See Figure 4-1-1.)

FRAME PROSCENIUM FIRESAFETY CURTAIN is a curtain that has a rigid frame, and stores over the proscenium opening in one flat panel.

MODIFIED FRAME PROSCENIUM FIRESAFETY CURTAIN is a curtain made of various components of both the frame and straight-lift-style curtains, and stores over the proscenium opening in one flat panel.

STRAIGHT-LIFT PROSCENIUM FIRESAFETY CURTAIN is a curtain which stores over the proscenium opening in one flat panel.

SECTION 4.103 — CURTAIN FABRICS

4.103.1 General. A proscenium curtain shall be constructed and installed as specified in this standard.

4.103.2 Fabrics.

4.103.2.1 Asbestos. When not prohibited by federal, state or local law, an existing installed curtain may be made of one or more thicknesses of not less than $2^3/_4$-pound-per-square-yard (1.5 kg/m^2) AAA grade wire-inserted asbestos fabric, or of another wire-inserted asbestos fabric obviously of greater fire resistance than this $2^3/_4$-pound (1.5 kg/m^2) AAA grade wire-inserted fabric. Nonasbestos portions of these fabrics, if any, shall be flame-resistant treated so as not to support combustion.

4.103.2.2 Other fabrics. Curtains not meeting the above criteria shall be made of one or more thicknesses of a noncombustible fabric, or a fabric with a noncombustible base material which may be given a coating provided the modified fabric meets the criteria detailed in this section.

Curtain fabrics shall not weigh less than $2^3/_8$ pounds per square yard (1.3 kg/m^2) unless it can be substantiated by approved tests that the fabric is equivalent in strength and durability.

4.103.3 Tensile Strength. Curtain fabric shall have tensile strength of not less than 400 pounds per inch (70 kN/mm) in both the warp and fill directions.

4.103.4 Wire-insertion Reinforcement. Curtain fabric shall be reinforced with noncorrosive wire intertwined with the base fiber at a minimum rate of one wire per yarn. Wire may be omitted if it can be substantiated by approved tests that it is equivalent in strength and durability.

4.103.5 Fire Test. A sample curtain with a minimum of two vertical seams shall be subjected to the standard fire test specified in UBC Standard 7-1 as applicable to nonbearing walls and partitions for a period of 30 minutes. Surface temperature measurements need not be taken and the hose stream exposure need not be made. The curtain shall overlap the furnace edges an appropriate amount to seal the top and sides. It shall have a bottom pocket containing a minimum 4 pounds per linear foot (5.94 kg/m) of batten. The unexposed surface of the curtain shall not glow, and neither flame nor smoke shall penetrate the curtain during the test period.

4.103.6 Smoke Test. Curtain fabrics shall have a smoke density of no greater than 25 when tested in accordance with UBC Standard 8-1. The curtain fabric shall be tested in the condition in which it is intended to be used.

SECTION 4.104 — DESIGN AND CONSTRUCTION

4.104.1 General. The various style curtains detailed below shall all be acceptable for use, except when the fly space above the stage is sufficient to allow the straight-lift, frame or modified frame styles to be used.

When the fly space is sufficient for these above-mentioned full-lift-style curtains, the straight-lift, frame or modified frame styles shall be used for proscenium openings 50 feet (15 240 mm) wide or less and 30 feet (9144 mm) high or less; and the frame or modified frame styles shall be used for openings over 50 feet (15 240 mm) in width or 30 feet (9144 mm) in height.

Curtain installations in new facilities with openings over 50 feet (15 240 mm) in width or 30 feet (9144 mm) in height shall be the frame or modified frame construction.

Regardless of curtain style, the curtain shall be made of continuous strips of fabric as specified above, sewn together vertically using minimum 1-inch-wide (25 mm) double-needled overlap seams. These vertical seams and all other functional stitching on the curtain shall consist of two rows of lockstitch stitching using flame-resistant thread, conforming to the test requirements of Section 4.103.

The curtain shall overlap the sides of the opening at least 18 inches (457 mm) and the top of the opening at least 24 inches (610 mm).

All style curtains, except the frame style and the modified frame style (unless it has batten pockets and vertical side edge hems), shall have minimum 6-inch (153 mm) flat [12-inch (305 mm) circumference] single-thickness pockets at the top and bottom of the curtain to hold the pipe battens, and double-thick vertical side edge hems each a minimum of $^1/_2$ inch (13 mm) wider than the length of side edge guide brackets being used and width of the metal hem reinforcing pieces being used, if any, except that hems shall not be less than 4 inches (102 mm) in width. Should the curtain fabric being used be an acceptable nonwire-inserted (nonwire reinforced) fabric, batten pockets shall be double thick and vertical side edge hems shall be triple thick or faced with wire-inserted (wire reinforced) webbing or fabric (raw edges turned under). Pockets and vertical side edge hems shall be sewn as specified above. Minimum $1^1/_2$-inch (38 mm) inside diameter metal battens shall be placed in the top and bottom curtain pockets when the proscenium opening height is 18 feet (5486 mm) or less and width is 34 feet (10 363 mm) or less. For openings 50 feet (15 240 mm) or less in width [but more than 34 feet (10 363 mm)], and 30 feet (9144 mm) or less in height [but more than 18 feet [5486 mm]], the top and bottom metal battens shall not be less than 2 inches (51 mm) inside diameter. Metal battens shall be Schedule 40 steel pipe, Schedule 80 steel pipe or other metallic tubing meeting or exceeding the tensile strength and performance standards of Schedule 40 steel pipe. All batten joints shall be reinforced with minimum 18-inch (457 mm) sections of said pipes or tubing internally and shall be riveted.

A minimum 3-inch-thick (76 mm) yield pad made with an outer covering of the curtain fabric, filled with fiberglass or other noncombustible materials, in such a manner so as to achieve a minimum 3-pound-per-cubic-foot (48 kg/m^3) density, shall be sewn beneath the bottom batten pocket with four rows of flame-resistant thread (two on each side of the pocket) in such a manner so as to force the bottom batten to compress the yield pad firmly against the stage floor, producing the best possible seal when the curtain is lowered.

4.104.2 Straight-lift Style. The straight-lift-style curtain shall meet the general requirements detailed above with vertical side edge hems reinforced with one piece of 0.064-inch-thick (1.63 mm) (16 gauge) plated or painted sheet metal on each side of the hem on each side of the curtain for its full vertical height so that both faces are covered 5^1/$_2$ inches (140 mm) deep, or with minimum 2-inch-wide by 1^1/$_2$-inch (51 mm by 38 mm) projection by ^{1}/$_8$-inch-thick (3.2 mm) steel angle/2-inch-wide (51 mm) by ^{1}/$_8$-inch-thick (3.2 mm) steel flat piece set (plated or painted) clamped on both edges for the curtain's full height. Either edge-reinforcement system shall be fastened to the side edge hems with pairs of minimum ^{3}/$_{16}$-inch (4.8 mm) plated tubular or solid steel rivets, or bolts spaced not more than 6 inches (153 mm) on center vertically.

Curtains for proscenium openings, 50 feet (15 240 mm) or less in width and 30 feet (9144 mm) or less in height, shall use a roller guide/metal track side edge guide system, using guides with at least two roller or ball bearing steel wheels each, and 0.079-inch-thick (2 mm) (14 gage) galvanized steel tracks (installed rigidly in place so that roller guides will operate smoothly with a wind load of 2 pounds per square foot (95.8 Pa) over entire area of curtain). Each guide shall be attached to the curtain's metal stiffened edges by way of three or more minimum ^{3}/$_{16}$-inch (4.8 mm) plated tubular or solid steel rivets, or bolts through a plated steel strap assembly [0.064-inch-thick (1.63 mm) sheet metal stiffening system], a minimum ^{3}/$_8$-inch (9.5 mm) machine screw assembly (attached to the projecting flange of the angle iron/flat steel edge stiffening system), or an equivalent attachment system. Guides shall be on maximum 18-inch (457 mm) vertical centers.

Curtains for proscenium openings 42 feet (12 802 mm) or less in width and 22 feet (6706 mm) or less in height may have a bronze-alloy, oil-impregnated wood, or other spool-type guide wire side edge system, where the guide wires are at least ^{1}/$_4$-inch (6.4 mm) diameter 7 by 19 galvanized aircraft cable installed securely using at least ^{3}/$_8$-inch (9.5 mm) locked turnbuckles, thimbles and three forged wire rope clips (or one swagged fitting) at the end of each guide wire; or the roller guide system with either hem reinforcing/stiffening system as detailed above. Guides shall not be more than 18 inches (457 mm) on vertical centers.

Curtains for proscenium openings less than 34 feet (10 363 mm) in width and less than 18 feet (5486 mm) in height may have a spool-type guide wire side guide system, as detailed in the paragraph above, except neither edge reinforcing/stiffening system is required. Guides shall be on maximum 18-inch (457 mm) vertical centers.

An approximate 3-inch-diameter (76 mm) smoke seal made of the curtain fabric and filled with fiberglass insulation or other noncombustible materials, to a density of not less than 3 pounds per cubic foot (48 kg/m^3), shall be attached to the upstage side of the proscenium wall, above the proscenium opening. The seal shall contact with the curtain's top batten pocket, and compress against it when the curtain is in its deployed position to make as smoke-tight a seal as practical.

4.104.3 Braille Style. The dead hung braille-style curtain shall meet the requirements detailed above in Sections 4.104.1 and 4.104.2, except for the following:

1. Curtain shall have minimum 5 percent fullness in the height only.

2. Side edge guide system shall be bronze spool guides on a maximum 18-inch (457 mm) vertical centers on both of the curtain's vertical edges, without any type of edge reinforcing/stiffening system.

3. Galvanized minimum ^{1}/$_4$-inch (6.4 mm) diameter 7 by 19 aircraft cable vertical life lines shall be located on maximum 10-foot (3048 mm) horizontal centers with the outermost two cables a maximum of 3 feet (914 mm) from either of the curtain's vertical edges. Each life line shall operate on a path reinforced with a layer of the curtain's fabric (raw edges turned under) or equivalent webbing, with plated steel D (dee) rings on maximum 18-inch (457 mm) vertical centers.

4. Seven by 19 aircraft cable for ^{3}/$_8$-inch-diameter (9.5 mm) or smaller sized and 6 by 19 or other flexible independent wire rope core, wire rope for larger sizes, sized using a minimum 8 to 1 safety factor, shall be used for the drive lines which connect the winch to the cable clew.

5. In lieu of the approximate 3-inch-diameter (76 mm) smoke seal detailed in Section 4.104.2 above, an attached fill piece smoke seal made of the curtain fabric, spanning the gap from the curtain to the upstage portion of the proscenium opening's wall above the opening, shall be installed.

The lift lines detailed above in conjunction with the D (dee) rings create an accordion-fold-type storage arrangement.

4.104.4 Frame and Modified Frame Style.

4.104.4.1 Frame-style curtain. The frame-style curtain shall consist of a rigid steel or metallic alloy frame, with a frame thickness not less than ^{1}/$_{120}$ of the width, and ^{1}/$_{96}$ of the height of the proscenium opening, but in no case less than 4 inches (102 mm) in thickness, complete with interior steel or metallic alloy members, such that when the required single thickness is battened to the downstage side (audience side) of the frame, the assembly will operate smoothly, and perform as required, when subjected to a lateral load of 2 pounds per square foot (95.8 N/m^2) over the entire area of the curtain.

The side edge guide system shall consist of vertical steel flat edges parallel to the face of the curtain with bronze bushings on this vertical steel edge on both upstage and downstage surfaces, or in the grooves traveled by these vertical steel edges located in the vertical steel smoke pockets on each side of the proscenium opening.

A separate yield pad, the cross section of which shall be square with each edge measuring approximately the same as the thickness of the frame, shall be made of the curtain fabric and filled with fiberglass or other noncombustible materials to a density of not less than 3 pounds per cubic foot (48 kg/m^3). The yield pad shall be attached beneath the bottom frame member so that it will compress and seal when the curtain is lowered.

A separate upper smoke seal, the same as detailed in Section 4.104.2 above, except that the seal shall be approximately 5 inches (127 mm) in diameter, shall be attached to the top of the frame on the downstage edge (edge facing the audience), and rigged so that the smoke seal is forced to compress against a steel or metallic alloy angle or other solid noncombustible material protruding from the proscenium wall above the opening (optionally, seal may be mounted above the proscenium opening on the upstage side and rigged to force the smoke seal to compress against a steel or metallic alloy member protruding downstage from the top member of the curtain's frame).

This curtain style is rigged like and operates like a straight-lift curtain except that the lift lines, blocks and all other involved operating equipment, shall be sized to accommodate the size and weight of the assembly with a minimum 8 to 1 safety margin.

4.104.4.2 Modified frame-style curtain. The modified frame-style curtain shall be any variation or combination of the frame style immediately above, and the straight-lift-style curtain that minimizes the horizontal movement or bowing of a curtain to a point where the curtain assembly will operate smoothly and perform as required when subjected to a lateral load of 2 pounds per square foot (95.8 N/m^2) over the entire area of the curtain.

This curtain style, like the frame style, is rigged like and operates like a straight-lift curtain, except that the lift lines, blocks and all other involved operating equipment shall be sized to accommodate the size and weight of the assembly with a minimum 8 to 1 safety margin.

SECTION 4.105 — OPERATING EQUIPMENT

Vertical smoke pockets which contain the curtain's vertical edges and guide system shall be fabricated of minimum $1/4$-inch-thick (6.4 mm) structural steel shapes and plates (plated or painted), with a bolted construction using minimum $3/8$-inch (9.5 mm) diameter Grade 5 bolts spaced not more than 4 feet (1219 mm) on center to attach plates to the steel shapes for the entire height of the smoke pockets, or at least for removable sections at the bottom of each smoke pocket (plate portions only), at least the height of the opening plus 4 feet (1219 mm) for frame and modified frame styles of semirigid construction, or at least 6 feet (1829 mm) for all other styles. These smoke pockets shall extend vertically from the stage floor to a point 1 to 3 feet (305 to 914 mm) above the top of the raised curtain and shall be securely fastened to the upstage side (side away from audience) of the proscenium wall, with minimum $1/2$-inch-diameter (13 mm) Grade 5 anchors or bolts in concrete spaced not more than 4 feet (1219 mm) on center, with minimum $3/8$-inch-diameter (9.5 mm) Grade 5 anchors or bolts in concrete spaced not more than 2 feet (610 mm) on center, or an anchoring system equivalent in strength on concrete or other surfaces. The smoke pockets may vary in depth and width, depending on the style of curtain and the distance the smoke pockets are set back from the vertical edges. Straight-lift curtains shall not have less than 6-inch-deep (153 mm) pockets, braille curtains shall not have less than 8-inch-deep (203 mm) pockets, and frame and modified frame curtains shall have pockets at least 4 inches (102 mm) deeper than the thickest batten or frame member; the pockets shall be at least 11 inches (279 mm) wide set back a minimum of 6 inches (153 mm) from the vertical edges (stage left/stage right) of the proscenium opening, and contain at least 8 inches (203 mm) of the curtain's vertical edges.

The curtain's side edge guide system shall be as specified in Section 4.104.

Straight-lift and braille curtains for proscenium openings 50 feet (15 240 mm) or less in width and 30 feet (9144 mm) or less in height shall not have less than $1/4$-inch-diameter (6.4 mm) 7 by 19 galvanized aircraft cable life lines 10 feet (3048 mm) or less on center, with the end overhang not more than 3 feet (914 mm). Attachment to battens shall be accomplished through the use of two-piece pipe clamps made of minimum 0.105-inch-thick (2.7 mm) (12 gage) steel, or equivalent material (plated or painted) with corners rounded and the entire assembly deburred.

The clamps shall attach to the battens using two minimum $3/8$-inch (9.5 mm) Grade 5 bolts, one under the batten and one over the batten, with the lift cable securely attached using a thimble and three forged wire rope clips (or one swagged-type fitting). Other methods of attachment that can be shown to be equivalent shall be acceptable as long as the lift lines are not tied in a clove hitch, and they do not require cutting the curtain fabric and leaving exposed cut edges. Frame and modified frame curtains may require larger diameter lift lines to meet the requirements in Section 4.104.4; galvanized cable or wire rope, 7 by 19 aircraft cable for $3/8$-inch (9.5 mm) diameter or smaller sizes, and 6 by 19 or other flexible independent wire rope core rope for larger sizes shall be used.

Straight-lift-style curtains for openings 34 feet (10 363 mm) or less in width and 18 feet (5486 mm) or less in height, and braille-style curtains of all sizes, may be designed to operate using properly sized manual and electric winches of various styles, all with adjustable hydraulic-assisted, speed-governing devices; any model with handles shall be so designed that the handle is removable, with an appropriate sign in English and other languages prevalent to the facility's area, stating DANGER! REMOVE HANDLE AFTER USE! prominently displayed near the location of the winch.

Curtain lift lines shall pass through sheaves in or under the gridiron, over to the counterweight guides or winch clew. Cables shall fasten to the curtain's top batten as detailed above. Connections to the braille curtain's bottom batten shall be accomplished by a loop at the end of each lift line secured with three forged wire rope clips, or minimum $3/16$-inch-thick (4.8 mm) clam-shell-type steel pipe clamps, and to the counterweight guides or winch drive line clew, using $3/8$-inch (9.5 mm) locked turnbuckles, thimbles and three forged wire rope clips (each lift line cable). Swagged-type fittings (one per connection) may be used in lieu of three forged wire rope clips. Clove hitches shall not be used and the batten pocket shall not be cut to facilitate the installation of the lift lines.

Straight-lift- and braille-style curtains shall have safety stay chains of a straight-welded link minimum $1/4$-inch (6.4 mm) proof coil chain fastened securely to the curtain's top batten. Frame and modified frame-style curtains shall also have the same type safety stay chains, except they shall be sized to support safely the weight of the curtain. There shall be one more stay chain than the number of supporting cables and, except for the stay chains at the ends of the curtain, all stay chains shall be centered between the supporting cables. One end of each stay chain shall be securely attached to the curtain's top batten (or top of a frame), with the other to the gridiron, if of steel construction; otherwise, the upper stay chain ends shall be fastened to $3/4$-inch (19 mm) bolts bolted through the proscenium wall. Safety chains shall be so adjusted that they support the curtain when it is lowered and the bottom batten is resting on the yield pad and supported by the floor. In the case of the braille-style curtain, the safety chains will also be the method of holding the curtain's top batten in its stationary position.

All cables shall be carried overhead using head and loft blocks fitted with precision ball or tapered roller bearings of ample capacity to accommodate the weight at the speeds required. Grooves in the blocks shall be machined properly to cradle and protect the cable. All blocks supporting the proscenium firesafety curtain shall be supported on the proscenium wall by means of steel brackets of suitable size to safely carry the weight, or shall be mounted on structural steel beams and other steel shapes that may be added.

Head and loft blocks shall be installed so as to prevent cable fouling.

For all style curtains using $1/4$-inch-diameter (6.4 mm) 7 by 19 galvanized aircraft cable lift lines, the minimum diameter of loft blocks shall be 8 inches (203 mm) when the height of the proscenium is 20 feet (6096 mm) or less, and 12 inches (305 mm) for all others. Curtains using larger diameter lift lines shall use loft blocks with a minimum diameter 38 times the diameter of the cable. Head blocks shall be at least 4 inches (102 mm) greater in diameter than the loft blocks.

The mechanism and devices for controlling the curtain shall be of simple design and positive in operation. Normal day-to-day operation of straight-lift, braille curtains installed on proscenium openings of 1,500 square feet (139.4 m^2) or less may be by manual means as long as operation can be accomplished with relative ease by a single person. Curtains meeting the size criteria in the previous sentence that are difficult for a single person to operate and other curtains not meeting the size criteria shall be operated by electric devices.

Automatic emergency release shall be by gravity obtained by overbalancing the curtain. The emergency control line shall be of minimum $3/8$-inch-diameter (9.5 mm) manila rope, or $3/32$-inch-diameter (2.38 mm) 7 by 19 galvanized aircraft cable, fitted with not less than four 165°F (74°C) or less nonelectric fusible links. One of these fusible links shall be located on each side of the stage and two overhead. When any link in the series separates, or the emergency control line is burned, the curtain shall automatically lower properly to its deployed position (see Section 4.101). This emergency control line shall extend up both sides and above the proscenium opening. As is the case with the manual emergency tripping mechanism detailed below, any attachment to the hand line on any operation machine or device that must be disconnected from the hand line or device for proper curtain deployment shall be a mechanical quick-release device that is easily resettable. The fire curtain emergency-release system shall not be interconnected mechanically, electromechanically, electrically or electronically with the emergency ventilator release system, unless a time delay is incorporated to assure that, in the event of a fire, the fire curtain will be fully deployed before the vents open. The building's fire alarm system shall not be interconnected with the fire curtain emergency-release system.

Manual emergency deployment of the fire curtain shall be accomplished by the activation of one of two mechanical quick-release assemblies (one on each side of the proscenium opening). Activation of either assembly shall be by pulling a minimum $1^1/_2$-inch-diameter (38 mm) red (color) ring, attached to a quick-release pin that is normally pinned through two steel plates housing a minimum 1-inch-diameter (25 mm) ring that is securely attached to the emergency-release line; these quick-release mechanisms shall be such that they can quickly (within a few minutes) and easily be reset in the event of erroneous activations. Other similar activation assemblies that are positive in nature and meet the basic criteria of the quick-release system detailed above may be used. Knife, axe and other emergency-release systems shall be allowable only until a new fire curtain is installed.

Appropriate signs in English and other languages prevalent to the facility's area, shall be prominently displayed near the location of the emergency control line quick-release mechanisms. For the release assembly detailed above, the sign would read IN CASE OF FIRE, PULL RED RING TO LOWER FIRE CURTAIN AUTOMATICALLY! with an arrow pointing to the location of the ring. There shall also be a less prominent sign or instruction pamphlet located on the main control side of the opening only, detailing the procedure required to properly and quickly reset the fire curtain in its raised position (this would include the mechanical quick-release mechanisms mentioned in this paragraph and the paragraph above).

Electric operation shall be from a single station located on either side of the proscenium opening and shall consist of two hold-to-operate-style push buttons, one labeled "Up" and one labeled "Down." Alternately, three push buttons that function from a single push of a button; one button shall be labeled "Up" for raising the curtain, one labeled "Down" for lowering the curtain, and one labeled "Stop" for stopping the curtain at the point it is located when the button is pushed; a sign stating NONEMERGENCY FIRE CURTAIN OPERATION shall be adjacent to the push-button station. Buttons and sign shall be labeled in English only.

All manually rigged counterweight curtains shall have their minimum $3/4$-inch (19 mm) manila endless operation hand line securely fastened to both the top and bottom of the counterweight arbor and shall pass under a minimum 12-inch-diameter (305 mm) floor block which is adjustable for tension.

The top and bottom counterweight sections of the arbor shall be of steel, sufficiently heavy to safely accommodate the loads. The top and bottom sections shall be connected with rods not less than $3/4$ inch (19 mm) in diameter, with one tie plate for every 4 feet (1219 mm) of rod. Counterweights may be cast iron or flame cut steel with edges deburred. There shall be smooth grooves on the ends of the top and bottom weights which engage the steel guides. The arbor top and bottom shall be provided with an oilless-type bushing.

Counterweight guide tracks shall be structural tees or angles properly tied together and securely anchored to the proscenium wall. All joints where the counterweight travels shall be ground smooth. These guide tracks shall be caged their entire length.

All proscenium firesafety curtains shall have an approved adjustable checking device or system, whether it be a counterweight arrangement, a hydraulic speed-governing system, a hydraulic dash pot shock-absorbing unit, or some other equivalent device or system that will enable the installation to meet the automatic-closing requirements detailed in Section 4.101.

SECTION 4.106 — TESTS

The complete installation of every proscenium firesafety curtain shall be subjected to a minimum of two successful emergency-type operating tests triggered by release of the end of the emergency control line away from the hand line, winch or motor, and an on-site review of specifications by the building official prior to a new facility being issued an occupancy permit, and an existing facility being allowed the use of the newly renovated facilities.

SECTION 4.107 — NEW DESIGNS

A water curtain or deluge system complying with UBC Standard 9-1 may be used in conjunction with an automatically closing opaque noncombustible curtain in lieu of the proscenium firesafety curtain described in UBC Standard 4-1. Both the deluge system and curtain closure shall be actuated by combination rate-of-temperature-rise and temperature devices located on the stage. The water system shall be designed to completely wet the entire curtain.

Curtains of other designs and materials, when not obviously of greater fire resistance than specified in this standard, shall, before acceptance, be subjected to the standard fire test specified in Chapter 7 of the Building Code as applicable to nonbearing partitions, except that such tests shall be continued only for a period of five minutes unless failure shall have occurred previously. The unexposed face of the curtain shall not glow within a period of 30 minutes nor shall there be any passage of smoke or flame through the curtain.

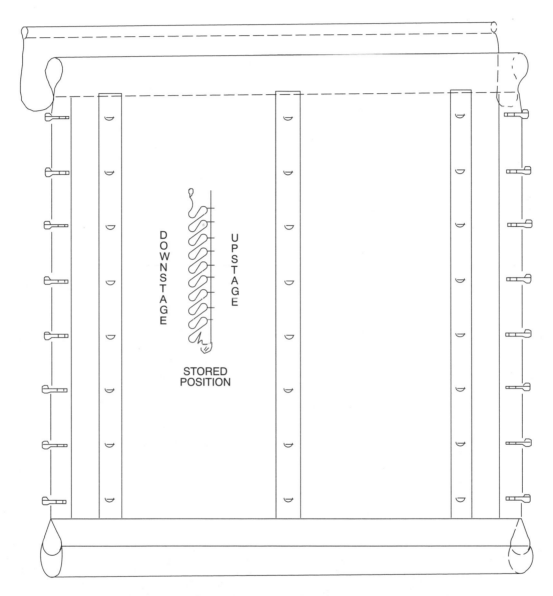

FIGURE 4-1-1—BRAILLE-STYLE PROSCENIUM FIRESAFETY CURTAIN

UNIFORM BUILDING CODE STANDARD 7-1

FIRE TESTS OF BUILDING CONSTRUCTION AND MATERIALS

**Based on Standard Methods E 119-83 of the American Society for Testing and Materials.
Extracted, with permission, from the *Annual Book of ASTM Standards,* copyright American Society for Testing and Materials, 100 Barr Harbor Drive, West Conshohocken, PA 19428**

**See Sections 405.1.1, 601.3, 703.2, 703.4, 706, 709.3.2.2,
709.5, 709.6, 709.7, 710.2, 2602.5.2 and Table 7-A, *Uniform Building Code***

SECTION 7.101 — SCOPE

This standard for fire tests is applicable to assemblies of masonry units and to composite assemblies of structural materials for buildings, including bearing and other walls and partitions, columns, girders, beams, slabs, and composite slab and beam assemblies for floors and roofs. They are also applicable to other assemblies and structural units that constitute permanent integral parts of a finished building.

It is the intent that classifications shall register performance during the period of exposure and shall not be construed as having determined suitability for use after fire exposure.

Control of Fire Tests

SECTION 7.102 — TIME-TEMPERATURE CURVE

The conduct of fire tests of materials and construction shall be controlled by the standard time-temperature curve shown in Figure 7-1-1. The points on the curve that determine its character are:

1,000°F (538°C)	at 5 minutes
1,300°F (704°C)	at 10 minutes
1,550°F (843°C)	at 30 minutes
1,700°F (927°C)	at 1 hour
1,850°F (1010°C)	at 2 hours
2,000°F (1093°C)	at 4 hours
2,300°F (1260°C)	at 8 hours or over

SECTION 7.103 — FURNACE TEMPERATURES

The temperature fixed by the curve shall be deemed to be the average temperature obtained from the readings of not less than nine thermocouples for a floor, roof, wall or partition and not less than eight thermocouples for a structural column symmetrically disposed and distributed to shown the temperature near all parts of the sample, the thermocouples being enclosed in protection tubes of such materials and dimensions that the time constant of the protected thermocouple assembly lies within the range from 5.0 to 7.2 minutes. The exposed length of the pyrometer tube and thermocouple in the furnace chamber shall not be less than 12 inches (305 mm). Other types of protecting tubes or pyrometers may be used that, under test conditions, give the same indications as the above standard within the limit of accuracy that applies for furnace-temperature measurements. For floors and columns, the junction of the thermocouples shall be placed 12 inches (305 mm) away from the exposed face of the sample at the beginning of the test and, during the test, shall not touch the sample as a result of its deflection. In the case of walls and partitions, the thermocouples shall be placed 6 inches (152 mm) away from the exposed face of the sample at the beginning of the test, and shall not touch the sample during the test in the event of deflection.

The temperatures shall be read at intervals not exceeding five minutes during the first two hours, and thereafter the intervals may be increased to not more than 10 minutes.

The accuracy of the furnace control shall be such that the area under the time-temperature curve, obtained by averaging the results from the pyrometer readings, is within 10 percent of the corresponding area under the standard time-temperature curve shown in Figure 7-1-1 for fire tests of one hour or less duration, within 7.5 percent for those over one hour and not more than two hours, and within 5 percent for tests exceeding two hours in duration.

SECTION 7.104 — TEMPERATURES OF UNEXPOSED SURFACES OF FLOORS, WALLS AND PARTITIONS

Temperatures at unexposed surfaces shall be measured with thermocouples or thermometers placed under flexible, dry, felted asbestos pads 6 inches square, 0.4 inch (152 mm square, 10.2 mm) in thickness and weighing not less than 1 nor more than 1.4 pounds per square foot ($9.6 kg/m^2$). The pads shall be sufficiently soft so that, without breaking, they may be shaped to contact over the whole surface against which they are placed. The wire leads of the thermocouple or the stem of the thermometer shall have an immersion under the pad and be in contact with the unexposed surface for not less than $3^1/_2$ inches (88.9 mm). The hot junction of the thermocouple or the bulb of the thermometer shall be placed approximately under the center of the pad. The outside diameter of protecting or insulating tubes, and of thermometer stems, shall not be more than $^5/_{16}$ inch (7.9 mm). The pad shall be held firmly against the surface and shall fit closely about the thermocouples or thermometer stems. Thermometers shall be of the partial-immersion type with a length of stem between the end of the bulb and the immersion mark of 3 inches (76.2 mm). The wires for the thermocouple in the length covered by the pad shall not be heavier than No. 18 B.&S. gage [0.04 inch (1.02 mm)] and shall be electrically insulated with heat-resistant and moisture-resistant coatings.

Temperature readings shall be taken at not less than nine points on the surface; five of these shall be symmetrically disposed, one to be approximately at the center of the specimens and four at approximately the center of quarter sections. The other four should be located at the discretion of the testing agency to obtain representative information on the performance of the construction under tests. None of the thermocouples shall be located nearer to the edges of the test specimen that one and one-half times the thickness of the construction or 12 inches (305 mm). An exception can be made in those cases where there is an element of the construction that is not otherwise represented in the remainder of the test specimen. None of the thermocouples shall be located opposite or on top of beams, girders, pilasters or other structural members if temperatures at such points will obviously be lower than at more representative locations. None of the thermocouples shall be located opposite or on top of fasteners such as screws, nails or staples that will be obviously higher or lower in temperature than at more representative locations if the aggregate area of any part of such fasteners projected to the unexposed surface is less than 0.8 percent of the area within any 5-inch square (127 mm). Such fasteners shall not extend through the assembly.

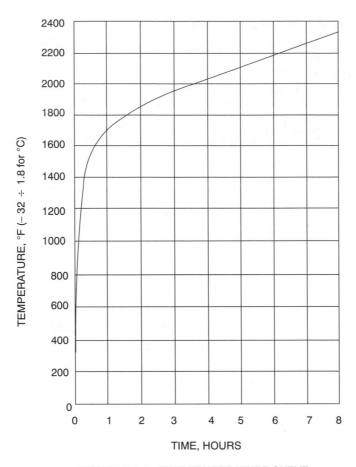

FIGURE 7-1-1—TIME-TEMPERATURE CURVE

Temperature readings shall be taken at intervals not exceeding 15 minutes until a reading exceeding 212°F (100°C) has been obtained at any one point. Thereafter the readings may be taken more frequently at the discretion of the testing body, but the intervals need not be less than five minutes.

Where the conditions of acceptance place a limitation on the rise of temperature of the unexposed surface, the temperature end point of the fire-endurance period shall be determined by the average of the measurements taken at individual points; except that if a temperature rise 30 percent in excess of the specified limit occurs at any one of these points, the remainder shall be ignored and the fire-endurance period judged as ended.

Classification as Determined by Test

SECTION 7.105 — REPORT OF RESULTS

Results shall be reported in accordance with the performance in the tests prescribed in this standard. They shall be expressed in time periods of resistance to the nearest integral minute. Reports shall include observations of significant details of the behavior of the material or construction during the test and after the furnace fire is cut off, including information on deformation, spalling, cracking, burning of the specimen or its component parts, continuance of flaming and production of smoke.

Reports of tests involving wall, floor, beam or ceiling constructions in which restraint is provided against expansion, contraction or rotation of the construction shall describe the method used to provide this restraint.

Reports of tests in which other than maximum load conditions are imposed shall fully define the conditions of loading used in the test and shall be designated in the title of the report of the test as a restricted load condition.

When the indicated resistance period is one-half hour or over, and determined by the average or maximum temperature rise on the unexposed surface or within the test sample, or by failure under load, a correction shall be applied for variation of the furnace exposure from that prescribed where it will affect the classification by multiplying the indicated period by two thirds of the difference in area between the curve of average furnace temperature and the standard curve for the first three fourths of the period and dividing the product by the area between the standard curve and a base line of 68°F (20°C) for the same part of the indicated period, the latter area increased by 54 Fahrenheit-hours (30 centigrade-hours) [3,240 Fahrenheit-minutes (1800 centigrade-minutes)], to compensate for the thermal lag of the furnace thermocouples during the first part of the test. For fire exposure in the test higher than standard, the indicated resistance period shall be increased by the amount of the correction and be similarly decreased for fire exposure below standard.

NOTE: The correction can be expressed by the following formula:

$$C = \frac{2I\,(A - A_s)}{3\,(A_s + L)}$$

WHERE:

A = area under the curve of indicated average furnace temperature for the first three fourths of the indicated period.

A_s = area under the standard furnace curve for the same part of the indicated period.

C = correction in the same units as I.

I = indicated fire-resistance period.

L = lag correction in the same units as A and A_s [54 Fahrenheit-hours (30 centigrade-hours) (3,240 Fahrenheit-minutes {1800 centigrade-minutes})].

Walls and partitions of nonsymmetrical construction shall be tested with both faces exposed to the furnace and the report shall indicate the fire-endurance classification applicable to each side. Subject to the approval of the building official based on data submitted by the applicant justifying a single-side test only, unsymmetrical wall assemblies may be tested with the least fire-resistive side exposed in the furnace.

SECTION 7.106 — TEST SPECIMEN

The test sample shall be truly representative of the construction for which classification is desired, as to materials, workmanship, and details such as dimensions of parts, and shall be built under conditions representative of those obtained as practically applied in building construction and operation. The physical properties of the materials and ingredients used in the test sample shall be determined and recorded.

The size and dimensions of the test sample specified herein are intended to apply for rating constructions of dimensions within the usual general range employed in buildings. If the conditions of use limit the construction to smaller dimensions, a proportionate reduction may be made in the dimensions of the samples for a test qualifying them for such restricted use.

When it is desired to include a built-up roof covering, the test specimen shall have a roof covering of three-ply, Type 15 felt not in excess of 120 pounds per square (100 square feet) (6.04 kg/m^2) of hot-mopping asphalt without gravel surfacing. Tests of assemblies with this covering do not preclude the field use of other built-up roof coverings.

Fire Test Procedures

SECTION 7.107 — FIRE-ENDURANCE TEST

The fire-endurance test on the sample with its applied load, if any, shall be continued until failure occurs, or until the sample has withstood the test conditions for a period equal to that herein specified in the conditions of acceptance for the given type of construction.

For the purpose of obtaining additional performance data, the test may be continued beyond the time the fire-endurance classification is determined.

SECTION 7.108 — HOSE STREAM TEST

7.108.1 General. Where required by the conditions of acceptance, a duplicate sample shall be subjected to a fire-exposure test for a period equal to one half of that indicated as the resistance period in the fire-endurance test, but not for more than one hour, immediately after which the sample shall be subjected to the impact, erosion and cooling effects of a hose stream directed first at the middle and then at all parts of the exposed face, changes in direction being made slowly.

7.108.2 Exemption. The hose stream test shall not be required in the case of constructions having a resistance period, indicated in the fire-endurance test, of less than one hour.

7.108.3 Optional Program. The submitter may elect, with the advice and consent of the testing body, to have the hose stream test made on the sample subjected to the fire-endurance test and immediately following the expiration of the fire-endurance test.

7.108.4 Stream Equipment and Details. The stream shall be delivered through a $2^1/_2$-inch (64 mm) hose discharging through a National Standard Playpipe of corresponding size equipped with a $1^1/_8$-inch (28.6 mm) discharge tip of the standard-taper smooth-bore pattern without shoulder at the orifice. The water pressure and duration of application shall be as prescribed in Table 7-1-A.

7.108.5 Nozzle Distance. The nozzle orifice shall be 20 feet (6096 mm) from the center of the exposed surface of the test sample if the nozzle is so located that when directed at the center, its axis is normal to the surface of the test sample. If otherwise located, its distance from the center shall be less than 20 feet (6096 mm) by an amount equal to 1 foot (305 mm) for each 10 degrees of deviation from the normal.

SECTION 7.109 — TIME OF TESTING

The material or construction shall not be tested until a large proportion of its final strength has been attained and, if it contains moisture, until the excess has been removed to achieve an air-dry condition in accordance with the requirements given in this section. Protect the testing equipment and sample undergoing the fire test from any condition of wind or weather that might lead to abnormal results. The ambient air temperature at the beginning of the test shall be within the range of 50°F to 90°F (10°C to 32°C) The velocity of air across the unexposed surface of the sample, measured just before the test begins, shall not exceed 4.4 feet per second (1.3 m/s) as determined by an anemometer placed at right angles to the unexposed surface. If mechanical ventilation is employed during the test, an airstream shall not be directed across the surface of the specimen.

TABLE 7-1-A—CONDITIONS FOR HOSE STREAM TEST

RESISTANCE PERIOD	WATER PRESSURE AT BASE OF NOZZLE (pounds per square inch)	DURATION OF APPLICATION (minutes per 100 square feet) EXPOSED AREA
	× 6.89 for kPa	× 0.0108 for min./m^2
8 hours and over	45	6
4 hours and over if less than 8 hours	45	5
2 hours and over if less than 4 hours	30	$2^1/_2$
$1^1/_2$ hours and over if less than 2 hours	30	$1^1/_2$
1 hour and over if less than $1^1/_2$ hours	30	1
Less than 1 hour, if desired	30	1

Prior to fire test, condition constructions with the objective of providing, within a reasonable time, a moisture condition within the specimen approximately representative of that likely to exist in similar construction in buildings. For purposes of standardization, this condition is to be considered as that which would be established at equilibrium resulting from drying in an ambient atmosphere of 50 percent relative humidity at 73°F (23°C) However, with some constructions, it may be difficult or impossible to achieve such uniformity within a reasonable period of time. Accordingly, where this is the case, specimens may be tested when the dampest portion of the structure, the portion at 6 inches (152 mm) depth below the surface of massive constructions, has achieved a moisture content corresponding to drying to equilibrium with air in the range of 50 to 75 percent relative humidity at 73°F ± 5°F (20°C ± 3°C) In the event that specimens dried in a heated building fail to meet these requirements after a 12-month conditioning period, or in the event that the nature of the construction is such that it is evident that drying of the specimen interior will be prevented by hermetic sealing, these requirements may be waived, except as to attainment of a large portion of final strength, and the specimen tested in the condition in which it then exists.

If during the conditioning of the specimen it appears desirable or is necessary to use accelerated drying techniques, it is the responsibility of the laboratory conducting the test to avoid procedures which will significantly alter the structural or fire-endurance characteristics of the specimen or both from those produced as the result of drying in accordance with procedures given in this section.

Within 72 hours prior to the fire test, information on the actual moisture content and distribution within the specimen shall be obtained. Include this information in the test report.

Tests of Bearing Walls and Partitions

SECTION 7.110 — SIZE OF SAMPLE

The area exposed to fire shall not be less than 100 square feet (9.3 m^2), with neither dimension less than 9 feet (2743 mm). The test specimen shall not be restrained on its vertical edges.

For construction joints, the area of the test specimen may be less than 100 square feet (9.3 m^2) provided the length of the joint is not less than 9 feet (2743 mm). The test specimen shall be of sufficient size so as to produce a representative construction joint for which evaluation is desired.

SECTION 7.111 — LOADING

Throughout the fire-endurance and fire and hose stream tests, apply a constant superimposed load to simulate a maximum load condition. The applied load shall be as nearly as practicable the maximum load allowed by design under design criteria set forth in the Building Code. The tests may also be conducted by applying to the specimen a load less than the maximum. Such tests shall be identified in the test report as having been conducted under restricted load conditions. The applied load, and the applied load expressed as a percentage of the maximum allowable design load, shall be included in the report. A double-wall assembly shall be loaded during the test to simulate field-use conditions, with either side loaded separately or both sides together. (Note: The method used shall be reported.)

The choice depends on the intended use and whether the load on the exposed side, after it has failed, will be transferred to the unexposed side. If, in the intended use, the load from the structure above is supported by both walls as a unit and would be or is transferred to the unexposed side in case of collapse of the exposed side, both walls shall be loaded in the test by a single unit. If in the intended use the load from the structure above each wall is supported by each wall separately, the walls shall be loaded separately in the test by separate load sources. If the intended use of the construction system being tested involved situations of both loading conditions described above, the walls shall be loaded separately in the test by separate load sources. In tests conducted with the walls loaded separately, the condition of acceptance requiring the walls to maintain the applied load shall be based on the time at which the first of either of the walls fails to sustain the load.

SECTION 7.112 — CONDITIONS OF ACCEPTANCE

The test shall be regarded as successful if the following conditions are met:

1. The wall or partition shall have sustained the applied load during the fire-endurance test without passage of flame or gases hot enough to ignite cotton waste, for a period equal to that for which classification is desired.

2. The wall or partition shall have sustained the applied load during the fire and hose stream test as specified in Section 7.108, without passage of flame, of gases hot enough to ignite cotton waste, or of the hose stream. The assembly shall be considered to have failed the hose stream test if an opening develops that permits a projection of water from the stream beyond the unexposed surface during the time of the hose stream test.

3. Transmission of heat through the wall or partition during the fire-endurance test shall not have been such as to raise the temperature on its unexposed surface more than 250°F (139°C) above its initial temperature.

Tests of Nonbearing Walls and Partitions

SECTION 7.113 — SIZE OF SAMPLE

The area exposed to fire shall not be less than 100 square feet (9.3 m^2), with neither dimension less than 9 feet (2734 mm). The test specimen shall be restrained on all four edges.

For construction joints, the area of the test specimen may be less than 100 square feet (9.3 m^2) provided the length of the joint is not less than 9 feet (2734 mm). The test specimen shall be of sufficient size so as to produce a representative construction joint for which evaluation is desired.

SECTION 7.114 — CONDITIONS OF ACCEPTANCE

The test shall be regarded as successful if the following conditions are met:

1. The wall or partition shall have withstood the fire-endurance test without passage of flame or gases hot enough to ignite cotton waste, for a period equal to that for which classification is desired.

2. The wall or partition shall have withstood the fire and hose stream test as specified in Section 7.108, without passage of flame, of gases hot enough to ignite cotton waste, or of the hose stream. The assembly shall be considered to have failed the hose stream test if an opening develops that permits a projection of water from the stream beyond the unexposed surface during the time of the hose stream test.

3. Transmission of heat through the wall or partition during the fire-endurance test shall not have been such as to raise the temperature on its unexposed surface more than 250°F (139°C) above its initial temperature.

Tests of Columns

SECTION 7.115 — SIZE OF SAMPLE

The length of the column exposed to fire shall, when practicable, approximate the maximum clear length contemplated by the design, and for building columns shall not be less than 9 feet (2734 mm). The contemplated details of connections, and their protection, if any, shall be applied according to the methods of acceptable field practice.

SECTION 7.116 — LOADING

During the fire endurance test, the column shall be exposed to fire on all sides and shall be loaded in a manner calculated to develop theoretically, as nearly as practicable, the working stresses contemplated by the design. Provision shall be made for transmitting the load to the exposed portion of the column without unduly increasing the effective column length.

If the submitter and the building official jointly so decide, the column may be subjected to one and three-fourths times its designed working load before the fire-endurance test is undertaken. The fact that such a test has been made shall not be construed as having had a deleterious effect on the fire-endurance test performance.

SECTION 7.117 — CONDITION OF ACCEPTANCE

The test shall be regarded as successful if the column sustains the applied load during the fire-endurance test for a period equal to that for which classification is desired.

Alternate Test of Protection for Structural Steel Columns

SECTION 7.118 — APPLICATION

This test procedure does not require column loading at any time and may be used at the discretion of the testing laboratory to evaluate steel column protections that are not required by design to carry any of the column load.

SECTION 7.119 — SIZE AND CHARACTER OF SAMPLE

The size of the steel column used shall be such as to provide a test specimen that is truly representative of the design, materials and workmanship for which classification is desired. The protection shall be applied according to the methods of acceptable field practice. The length of the protected column shall be at least 8 feet (2438 mm). The column shall be vertical during application of the protection and during the fire exposure.

The applied protection shall be restrained against longitudinal temperature expansion greater than that of the steel column by rigid steel plates or reinforced concrete attached to the ends of the steel column before the protection is applied. The size of the plates or amount of concrete shall be adequate to provide direct bearing for the entire transverse area of the protection.

The ends of the specimen, including the means for restraint, shall be given sufficient thermal insulation to prevent appreciable direct heat transfer from the furnace.

SECTION 7.120 — TEMPERATURE MEASUREMENT

The temperature of the steel in the column shall be measured by at least three thermocouples located at each of four levels. The upper and lower levels shall be 2 feet (610 mm) from the ends of the steel column, and the other two intermediate levels shall be equally spaced. The thermocouples at each level shall be so placed as to measure significant temperatures of the component elements of the steel section.

SECTION 7.121 — EXPOSURE TO FIRE

During the fire-endurance test the specimen shall be exposed to fire on all sides for its full length.

SECTION 7.122 — CONDITIONS OF ACCEPTANCE

The test shall be regarded as successful if the transmission of heat through the protection during the period of fire exposure for which classification is desired does not raise the average (arithmetical) temperature of the steel at any one of the four levels above 1,000°F (538°C), or does not raise the temperature above 1,200°F (649°C) at any one of the measured points.

Tests of Floors and Roofs

SECTION 7.123 — APPLICATION

This procedure is applicable to floor and roof assemblies with or without attached, furred or suspended ceilings and requires application of fire exposure to the underside of the specimen under test.

Two fire-endurance classifications shall be developed for assemblies restrained against thermal expansion, a restrained assembly classification based upon the conditions of acceptance specified in Section 7.127 and an unrestrained assembly classification based upon the conditions of acceptance specified in Section 7.128.

One fire-endurance classification shall be developed from tests of assemblies not restrained against thermal expansion based upon the conditions of acceptance specified in Section 7.128, Items 1 and 2.

Individual unrestrained classifications may be developed for beams tested in accordance with this test method using the conditions of acceptance specified in Section 7.136.

SECTION 7.124 — SIZE AND CHARACTERISTICS OF SPECIMEN

The area exposed to fire shall not be less than 180 square feet (16.7 m^2) with either dimension less than 12 feet (3658 mm). Structural members, if a part of the construction under test, shall lie within the combustion chamber and have a side clearance of not less than 8 inches (203 mm) from its walls.

For construction joints, the area of the test specimen may be less than 180 square feet (16.7 m^2) provided the length of the joint is not less than 12 feet (3658 mm). The test specimen shall be of sufficient size so as to produce a representative construction joint for which evaluation is desired.

The specimen shall be installed in accordance with recommended fabrication procedures for the type of construction and shall be representative of the design for which classification is desired. Where a restrained classification is desired, specimens representing forms of construction in which restraint to thermal expansion occurs shall be reasonably restrained in the furnace.

SECTION 7.125 — LOADING

Throughout the fire-endurance test, apply a superimposed load to the specimen. This load, together with the weight of the specimen, shall be as nearly as practicable the maximum theoretical dead and live loads permitted by this code. A fire-endurance test may be conducted applying a restricted load condition to the specimen which shall be identified for a specific load condition other than the maximum allowed load condition.

SECTION 7.126 — TEMPERATURE MEASUREMENT

For specimens employing structural members (beams, open-web steel joists, etc.) spaced at more than 4 feet (1219 mm) on centers, measure the temperature of the steel in these structural members by thermocouples at three or more sections spaced along the length of the members with one section preferably located at midspan, except that in cases where the cover thickness is not uniform along the specimen length, at least one of the sections at which temperatures are measured shall include the point of minimum cover.

For specimens employing structural members (beams, open-web steel joists, etc.) spaced at 4 feet (1219 mm) on center or less, measure the temperature of the steel in these structural members by four thermocouples placed on each member, except that no more than four members shall be so instrumented. Place the thermocouples at significant locations, such as at midspan, over joints in the ceiling, and over light fixtures, etc.

For steel structural members, there shall be four thermocouples at each section, except that where only four thermocouples are required on a member, the thermocouples may be distributed along the member at significant locations as provided for in the preceding paragraph. Locate two on the bottom of the bottom flange or chord, one on the web at the center, and one on the top flange or chord. The recommended thermocouple distribution at each section is shown in Figure 7-1-2.

For reinforced or prestressed concrete structural members, locate thermocouples on each of the tension-reinforcing elements, unless there are more than eight such elements, in which case place thermocouples on eight elements selected in such a manner as to obtain representative temperatures of all the elements.

For steel floor or roof units, locate four thermocouples on each section (a section to comprise the width of one unit), one on the bottom plane of the unit at an edge joint, one on the bottom plane of the unit remote from the edge, one on the side wall of the unit, and one on the top plane of the unit. The thermocouples should be applied, where practicable, to the surface of the units remote from fire and spaced across the width of the unit. No more than four or less than two sections need be so instrumented in each representative span. Locate the groups of four thermocouples in representative locations. Typical thermocouple locations for a unit section are shown in Figure 7-1-3.

SECTION 7.127 — CONDITIONS OF ACCEPTANCE—RESTRAINED ASSEMBLY

In obtaining a restrained assembly classification, the following conditions shall be met:

1. The specimen shall have sustained the applied load during the classification period without developing unexposed surface conditions which will ignite cotton waste.

2. Transmission of heat through the specimen during the classification period shall not have been such as to raise the average temperature on its unexposed surface more than 250°F (139°C) above its initial temperature.

3. For specimens employing steel structural members (beams, open-web joists, etc.) spaced more than 4 feet (1219 mm) on centers, the assembly shall achieve a fire-endurance classification on the basis of the temperature criteria specified in Section 7.128,

Item 3, for assembly classifications up to and including one hour. For classifications greater than one hour, the above temperature criteria shall apply for a period of one half the classification of the assembly or one hour, whichever is greater.

4. For specimens employing steel structural members (beams, open-web steel joists, etc.) spaced 4 feet (1219 mm) or less on centers, the assembly shall achieve a fire-endurance classification on the basis of the temperature criteria specified in Section 7.128, Item 4, for assembly classifications up to and including one hour. For classifications greater than one hour, the above temperature criteria shall apply for a period of one half the classification of the assembly or one hour, whichever is greater.

5. For specimens employing conventionally designed concrete beams, spaced more than 4 feet (1219 mm) on centers, the assembly shall achieve a fire-endurance classification on the basis of the temperature criteria specified in Section 7.128, Item 5, for assembly classifications up to and including one hour. For classifications greater than one hour, the above temperature criteria shall apply for a period of one half the classification of the assembly or one hour, whichever is greater.

SECTION 7.128 — CONDITIONS OF ACCEPTANCE—UNRESTRAINED ASSEMBLY

In obtaining a unrestrained assembly classification, the following conditions shall be met:

1. The specimen shall have sustained the applied load during the classification period without developing unexposed surface conditions which will ignite cotton waste.

2. The transmission of heat through the specimen during the classification period shall not have been such as to raise the average temperature on its unexposed surface more than 250°F (139°C) above its initial temperature.

3. For specimens employing steel structural members (beams, open-web steel joists, etc.) spaced more than 4 feet (1219 mm) on centers, the temperature of the steel shall not have exceeded 1,300°F (704°C) at any location during the classification period nor shall the average temperature recorded by four thermocouples at any section have exceeded 1,100°F (593°C) during the classification period.

4. For specimens employing steel structural members (beams, open-web steel joists, etc.) spaced 4 feet (1219 mm) or less on center, the average temperature recorded by all joist or beam thermocouples shall not have exceeded 1,100°F (593°C) during the classification period.

5. For specimens employing conventionally designed concrete structural members (excluding cast-in-place concrete roof or floor slabs having spans equal to or less than those tested), the average temperature of the tension steel at any section shall not have exceeded 800°F (427°C) for cold-drawn prestressing steel or 1,100°F (593°C) for reinforcing steel during the classification period.

6. For specimens employing steel floor or roof units intended for use in spans greater than those tested, the average temperature recorded by all thermocouples located on any one span of the floor or roof units shall not have exceeded 1,100°F (593°C) during the classification period.

SECTION 7.129 — REPORT OF RESULTS

The fire-endurance classification of a restrained assembly shall be reported as that developed by applying the conditions of acceptance specified in Section 7.127.

The fire-endurance classification of an unrestrained assembly shall be reported as that developed by applying the conditions of acceptance specified in Section 7.128 to a specimen tested in accordance with this test procedure.

Tests of Loaded Restrained Beams

SECTION 7.130 — APPLICATION

An individual classification of a restrained beam may be obtained by this procedure and based upon the conditions of acceptance specified in Section 7.133. The fire-endurance classification so derived shall be applicable to the beam when used with a floor or roof construction which has a comparable or greater capacity for heat dissipation from the beam than the floor or roof with which it was tested. The fire-endurance classification developed by this method shall not be applicable to sizes of beams smaller than those tested.

SECTION 7.131 — SIZE AND CHARACTERISTICS OF SPECIMEN

Install the test specimen in accordance with recommended fabrication procedures for the type of construction. It shall be representative of the design for which classification is desired. The length of beam exposed to the fire shall not be less than 12 feet (3658 mm) and the member shall be tested in its normal horizontal position. A section of a representative floor or roof construction not more than 7 feet (2134 mm) wide, symmetrically located with reference to the beam, may be included with the test specimen and exposed to the fire from below. Restrain the beam including that part of the floor or roof element forming the complete beam as designed (such as composite steel or concrete construction) against longitudinal thermal expansion in a manner simulating the restraint in the construction represented. Do not support or restrain the perimeter of the floor or roof element of the specimen, except that part which forms part of a beam as designed.

SECTION 7.132 — LOADING

Throughout the fire-endurance tests, apply a superimposed load to the specimen. This load, together with the weight of the specimen, shall be as nearly as practicable the maximum theoretical dead and live loads permitted by this code.

SECTION 7.133 — CONDITIONS OF ACCEPTANCE

The following conditions shall be met:

1. The specimen shall have sustained the applied load during the classification period.

2. The specimen shall have achieved a fire-endurance classification on the basis of the temperature criteria specified in Section 7.128, Item 3 or 4, of one half the classification of the assembly, or one hour, whichever is greater.

Alternative Classification Procedure for Loaded Beams

SECTION 7.134 — APPLICATION

Individual unrestrained classifications may be developed for beams tested as part of a floor or roof assembly as described in Sections 7.123 through 7.126 (except for the fourth paragraph of Section 7.123) or for restrained beams tested in accordance with the procedure described in Sections 7.130 through 7.132. The fire-endurance classification so derived shall be applicable to beams when used with a floor or roof construction which has a comparable or greater capacity for heat dissipation from the beam than the

floor or roof with which it was tested. The fire-endurance classification developed by this method shall not be applicable to sizes of beams smaller than those tested.

SECTION 7.135 — TEMPERATURE MEASUREMENT

Measure the temperature of the steel in structural members by thermocouples at three or more sections spaced along the length of the members with one section preferably located at midspan, except that in cases where the cover thickness is not uniform along the specimen length, at least one of the sections at which temperatures are measured shall include the point of minimum cover.

For steel beams, there shall be four thermocouples at each section; locate two on the bottom of the bottom flange, one on the web at the center, and one on the bottom of the top flange.

For reinforced or prestressed concrete structural members, locate thermocouples on each of the tension-reinforcing elements unless there are more than eight such elements, in which case place thermocouples on eight elements selected in such a manner as to obtain representative temperatures of all the elements.

SECTION 7.136 — CONDITIONS OF ACCEPTANCE

In obtaining an unrestrained beam classification, the following conditions shall be met:

1. The specimen shall have sustained the applied load during the classification period.

2. For steel beams, the temperature of the steel shall not have exceeded 1,300°F (704°C) at any location during the classification period nor shall the average temperature recorded by four thermocouples at any section have exceeded 1,100°F (593°C) during this period.

3. For conventionally designed concrete beams, the average temperature of the tension steel at any section shall not have exceeded 800°F (427°C) for cold-drawn prestressing steel or 1,100°F (593°C) for reinforcing steel during the classification period.

Alternate Test of Protection for Solid Structural Steel Beams and Girders

SECTION 7.137 — APPLICATION

Where the loading required in Section 7.125 is not feasible, this alternate test procedure may be used to evaluate the protection of steel beams and girders without application of design load, provided that the protection is not required by design to function structurally in resisting applied loads. The conditions of acceptance of this alternate test are not applicable to tests made under design load as provided under tests for floors and roofs in Sections 7.124, 7.127 and 7.128.

SECTION 7.138 — SIZE AND CHARACTER OF SAMPLE

The size of the steel beam or girder shall be such as to provide a test specimen that is truly representative of the design, materials and workmanship for which classification is desired. The protection shall be applied according to the methods of acceptable field practice and the projection below the ceiling, if any, shall be representative of the conditions of intended use. The length of beam or girder exposed to the fire shall not be less than 12 feet (3658 mm) and the member shall be tested in horizontal position. A section of a representative floor construction not less than 5 feet (1524 mm) wide, symmetrically located with reference to the beam or girder and extending its full length, shall be included in the test assembly and exposed to fire from below. The rating of performance shall not be applicable to sizes smaller than those tested.

The applied protection shall be restrained against longitudinal expansion greater than that of the steel beam or girder by rigid steel plates or reinforced concrete attached to the ends of the member before the protection is applied. The ends of the member, including the means for restraint, shall be given sufficient thermal insulation to prevent appreciable direct heat transfer from the furnace to the unexposed ends of the member or from the ends of the member to the outside of the furnace.

SECTION 7.139 — TEMPERATURE MEASUREMENT

The temperature of the steel in the beam or girder shall be measured with not less than four thermocouples at each of four sections equally spaced along the length of the beam and symmetrically disposed and not nearer than 2 feet (610 mm) from the inside face of the furnace. The thermocouples at each section shall be symmetrically placed so as to measure significant temperatures of the component elements of the steel section.

SECTION 7.140 — CONDITIONS OF ACCEPTANCE

The test shall be regarded as successful if the transmission of heat through the protection during the period of fire exposure for which classification is desired does not raise the average (arithmetical) temperature of the steel at any one of the four sections above 1,000°F (649°C), or does not raise the temperature above 1,200°F (649°C) at any one of the measured points.

Determining Conditions of Restraint for Floor and Roof Assemblies and for Individual Beams

SECTION 7.141 — GENERAL

Construction tested in accordance with this standard shall be classified as restrained or unrestrained.

A restrained condition in fire tests, as used in this standard, is one in which expansion at the supports of a load-carrying element resulting from the effects of the fire is resisted by forces external to the element. An unrestrained condition is one in which the load-carrying element is free to expand and rotate at its supports.

For the purpose of this section, restraint in buildings is defined as follows: floor and roof assemblies and individual beams in buildings shall be considered restrained when the surrounding or supporting structure is capable of resisting the thermal expansion throughout the range of anticipated elevated temperatures. Construction not complying with this definition is assumed to be free to rotate and expand and shall be considered as unrestrained.

Restraint may be provided by the lateral stiffness of supports for floor and roof assemblies and intermediate beams forming part of the assembly. In order to develop restraint, connections must adequately transfer thermal thrusts to such supports. The rigidity of adjoining panels or structures shall be considered in assessing the capability of a structure to resist thermal expansion.

Performance of Protective Membranes in Wall, Partition, Floor or Roof Assemblies

SECTION 7.142 — APPLICATION

When the thermal protection afforded by membrane elements in wall, partition, floor or roof assemblies is to be determined, the nonstructural performance of protective membranes shall be obtained by the following procedure. The performance of protective membranes as determined by this procedure is not a substitute for the fire-endurance classification determined by Sections 7.110 through 7.141 of this standard.

SECTION 7.143 — SIZE AND CHARACTER OF SAMPLE

The sample shall conform to the provisions specified in Section 7.106. The size of the sample shall also conform to the provisions specified in Section 7.110 for bearing walls and partitions, Section 7.113 for nonbearing walls and partitions, or Section 7.124 for floors or roofs.

SECTION 7.144 — TEMPERATURE PERFORMANCE OF PROTECTIVE MEMBRANES

The temperature performance of protective membranes shall be measured with thermocouples, the measuring junctions of which are in intimate contact with the exposed surface of the elements being protected. The diameter of the wires used to form the thermo-junction shall not be greater than the thickness of sheet metal framing or panel members to which they are attached, and in no case greater than No. 18 B.&S. gage [0.040 inch (1.02 mm)]. The lead shall be electrically insulated with heat-resistant and moisture-resistant coatings.

For each class of elements being protected, temperature readings shall be taken at not less than five representative points. Thermocouples shall not be located nearer to the edges of the test assembly than 12 inches (305 mm). An exception may be made in those cases when there is an element or feature of the construction that is not otherwise represented in the test assembly. Thermocouples shall not be located opposite, on top of or adjacent to fasteners such as screws, nails or staples when such locations are excluded for thermocouple placement on the unexposed surface of the test assembly as specified in the second paragraph of Section 7.104.

Thermocouples shall be located to obtain representative information on the temperature of the interface between the exposed membrane and the substrate or element being protected.

Temperature readings shall be taken at intervals not exceeding five minutes, but the intervals need not be less than two minutes.

SECTION 7.145 — CONDITIONS OF PERFORMANCE

Unless otherwise specified, the performance of protective membranes shall be determined as the time at which the following conditions occur:

1. The average temperature rise of any set of thermocouples for each class of element being protected is more than 250°F (139°C) above the initial temperature, or

2. The temperature rise of any one thermocouple of the set for each class of element being protected is more than 325°F (181°C) above the initial temperature.

SECTION 7.146 — REPORT OF RESULTS

The protective membrane performance for each class of element being protected shall be reported to the nearest integral minute.

The test report shall identify each class of elements being protected and shall show the location of each thermocouple.

The test report shall show the time-temperature data recorded for each thermocouple and the average temperature for the set of thermocouples on each element being protected.

The test report shall state any visual observations recorded that are pertinent to the performance of the protective membrane.

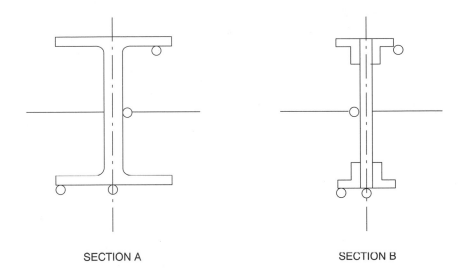

SECTION A   SECTION B

FIGURE 7-1-2—RECOMMENDED THERMOCOUPLE DISTRIBUTION

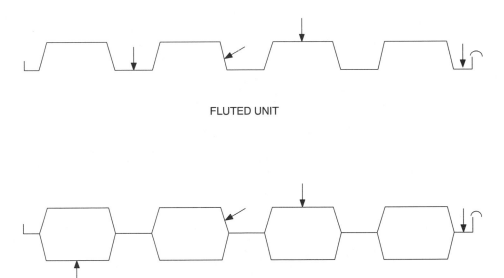

FLUTED UNIT

CELLULAR UNIT

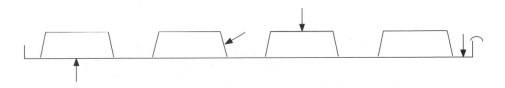

CELLULAR UNIT

FIGURE 7-1-3—TYPICAL LOCATION OF THERMOCOUPLES

UNIFORM BUILDING CODE STANDARD 7-2
FIRE TESTS OF DOOR ASSEMBLIES
See Sections 302.4, 703.4, 713.5, 713.9, 1004.3.4.3.2 and 1005.3.3.5, *Uniform Building Code*

Part I—Based on Underwriters Laboratories Inc. Standard 10B-1988, Fire Tests of Door Assemblies

SECTION 7.201 — SCOPE

These methods of fire test are applicable for door assemblies of various materials and types of construction, for use in wall openings to retard the passage of fire.

Tests made in conformity with these test methods will register performance during the test exposure; but such tests shall not be construed as determining suitability for use after exposure to fire.

SECTION 7.202 — TIME-TEMPERATURE CURVE

The fire exposure of door assemblies shall be controlled to conform to the applicable portion of the standard time-temperature curve shown in Figure 7-1-1 of UBC Standard 7-1. The points on the curve that determine its character are:

1,000°F (538°C)	at 5 minutes
1,300°F (704°C)	at 10 minutes
1,462°F (794°C)	at 20 minutes
1,550°F (843°C)	at 30 minutes
1,638°F (892°C)	at 45 minutes
1,700°F (927°C)	at 1 hour
1,792°F (978°C)	at $1^1/_2$ hours
1,850°F (1010°C)	at 2 hours
1,925°F (1052°C)	at 3 hours

SECTION 7.203 — FURNACE TEMPERATURES

7.203.1 Test Exposure. The temperatures of the test exposure shall be deemed to be the average temperature obtained from the readings of not less than nine thermocouples symmetrically disposed and distributed to show the temperature near all parts of the test assembly. The thermocouples shall be protected by sealed porcelain tubes having $3/_4$-inch (19.1 mm) outside diameter and $1/_8$-inch (3.2 mm) wall thickness; or, as an alternate, in the case of base metal thermocouples shall be protected by $1/_2$-inch (12.7 mm) wrought steel or wrought-iron pipe of standard weight. The junction of the thermocouples shall be 6 inches (152 mm) from the exposed face of the test assembly or from the masonry in which the assembly is installed during the entire test exposure.

7.203.2 Reading Intervals. The temperatures shall be read at intervals not exceeding five minutes during the first two hours, and thereafter the intervals may be increased to not more than 10 minutes.

7.203.3 Accuracy of Control. The accuracy of furnace control shall be such that the area under the time-temperature curve, obtained by averaging the results from the thermocouple readings, is within 10 percent of the corresponding area under the standard time-temperature curve for fire tests of one hour or less duration, within 7.5 percent of those over one hour and not more than two hours and within 5 percent for tests exceeding two hours in duration.

SECTION 7.204 — UNEXPOSED SURFACE TEMPERATURES

If unexposed surface temperatures are recorded other than for single-layer metal doors, they shall be determined in the following manner:

1. Unexposed surface temperatures shall be taken at not less than three points with at least one thermocouple in each 16-square-foot (1.5 m^2) area of the door.

Thermocouples shall not be located over reinforcements extending through the door, over vision panels or nearer than 12 inches (305 mm) from the edge of the door.

2. Unexposed surface temperatures shall be measured with thermocouples placed under flexible, oven-dry pads, $6^1/_8$ inches square (156 mm square), 0.40 inch ± 0.05 inch (10.2 mm ± 1.3 mm) thick and weighing not less than 1.0 (4.9 kg/m^2) or more than 1.4 pounds per square foot (6.8 kg/m^2). The pads shall be held firmly against the surface of the door and shall fit closely about the thermocouples. The thermocouple leads shall be positioned under the pad for a distance of not less than $3^1/_2$ inches (88.9 mm) with the hot junction under the center of the pad. The thermocouple leads under the pads shall not be heavier than No. 18 AWG [0.04 inch (1.02 mm)] and shall be electrically insulated with heat-resistant and moisture-resistant coatings.

3. Unexposed-surface temperatures shall be read at the same intervals as those for furnace temperatures in Section 7.203.2.

4. The thermocouples and pads shall be removed from the surface of the test assembly after the first 30 minutes of the fire exposure.

> **EXCEPTION:** The thermocouples and pads are permitted to remain if additional temperature rise information beyond the initial 30 minutes of exposure is being sought.

SECTION 7.205 — TEST ASSEMBLIES

7.205.1 Construction and Size. The construction and size of the test door assembly, consisting of single doors or doors in pairs, special purpose doors (such as dutch doors, double egress doors, etc.) or multisection doors shall be representative of that for which classification or rating is desired.

7.205.2 Sills. A floor structure shall be provided as part of the opening to be protected except where such sill interferes with the operation of the door. The sill shall be of noncombustible material and project into the furnace to a distance approximately twice the thickness of the test door or to the limit of the frame, whichever is greater.

SECTION 7.206 — MOUNTING

7.206.1 Side to Be Exposed. Swinging doors shall be mounted so as to open into the furnace chamber.

Sliding and rolling doors, except passenger-elevator shaft doors, shall be mounted on the exposed side of the opening in the wall closing the furnace chamber.

Horizontal slide-type elevator shaft doors shall be mounted on the unexposed side of the opening in the wall closing the furnace chamber.

Access-type doors and chute-type doors and frame assemblies shall be mounted so as to have one assembly open into the furnace chamber and another assembly open away from the furnace chamber.

Dumbwaiter and service-counter doors and frame assemblies shall be mounted on the exposed side of the opening in the wall.

7.206.2 Frames. Door frames shall be evaluated when mounted so as to have the doors open either away from, or into, the furnace chamber at the discretion of the testing agency, to obtain representative information on the performance of the construction under test.

7.206.3 Hardware. Surface-mounted hardware (fire-exit devices) for use on fire doors shall be evaluated by being installed on one door assembly swinging into the furnace chamber and another door assembly swinging away from the furnace chamber.

7.206.4 Anchors. Door frame wall anchors, when used, shall be acceptable for the wall or partition construction.

7.206.5 Fit. The mounting of all doors shall be such that they fit snugly within the frame, against the wall surfaces, or in guides, but such mounting shall not prevent free and easy operation of the test door.

7.206.6 Clearances. Clearances for swinging doors shall be as follows: With a minus $^1/_{16}$-inch (1.6 mm) tolerance—$^1/_8$ inch (3.2 mm) along the top, $^1/_8$ inch (3.2 mm) along the hinge and latch jambs, $^1/_8$ inch (3.2 mm) along the meeting edge of doors in pairs, and $^3/_8$ inch (9.5 mm) at the bottom edge of a single swing door, and $^1/_4$ inch (6.4 mm) at the bottom of a pair of doors.

Clearances for horizontal sliding doors not mounted within guides shall be as follows: With a minus $^1/_8$-inch (3.2 mm) tolerance—$^1/_2$ inch (12.7 mm) between door and wall surfaces, $^3/_8$ inch (9.5 mm) between door and floor structure, and $^1/_4$ inch (6.4 mm) between the meeting edges of center-parting doors. A maximum lap of 4 inches (101.6 mm) of the door over the wall opening at sides and top shall be provided.

Clearances for vertical sliding doors moving within guides shall be as follows: With a minus $^1/_8$-inch (3.2 mm) tolerance—$^1/_2$ inch (12.7 mm) between door and wall surfaces along top and/or bottom door edges with guides mounted directly to the wall surface and $^3/_{16}$ inch (4.8 mm) between meeting edges of biparting doors or $^3/_{16}$ inch (4.8 mm) between door and floor structure or sill.

Clearances for horizontal slide-type elevator doors shall be as follows: With a minus $^1/_8$-inch (3.2 mm) tolerance—$^3/_8$ inch (9.5 mm) between door and wall surfaces, $^3/_8$ inch (9.5 mm) between multisection door panels and $^3/_8$ inch (9.5 mm) from the bottom of the panel to the sill. Multisection door panels shall overlap $^3/_4$ inch (19.1 mm). Door panels shall lap the wall opening $^3/_4$ inch (19.1 mm) at sides and top.

SECTION 7.207 — CONDUCT OF TEST

7.207.1 Time of Testing. Masonry settings shall have sufficient strength to retain the assembly securely in position throughout the fire and hose stream tests.

7.207.2 Fire-endurance Test. After five minutes into the test, the neutral pressure level in the furnace shall be established at 40 inches (1016 mm) or less above the sill for side-hinged or pivoted swinging doors. For other types of doors, including swinging elevator doors, the pressure in the furnace shall be maintained as nearly equal to the atmosphere's pressure as possible. The pressure shall be maintained during the entire test period.

The test shall be continued until the exposure period of the desired classification or rating is reached unless the conditions of acceptance specified in Section 7.209 are exceeded in a shorter period.

7.207.3 Hose Stream Test. Immediately following the fire-endurance test, the test assembly shall be subjected to the impact, erosion and cooling effects of a hose stream directed first at the middle and then at all parts of the exposed surface, changes in direction being made slowly.

The hose stream shall be delivered through a $2^1/_2$-inch (63.5 mm) hose discharging through a National Standard Playpipe of corresponding size equipped with a $1^1/_8$-inch (28.6 mm) discharge tip of standard-taper smoothbore pattern without shoulder at the orifice. The water pressure at the base of the nozzle and the duration of application in seconds per square foot (square meter) of exposed area shall be as set forth in Table 7-2-A.

The tip of the nozzle shall be located 20 feet (6096 mm) from and on a line normal to the center of the test door. If impossible to be so located, the nozzle may be on a line deviating not to exceed 30 degrees from the line normal to the center of the test door.

When so located, the distance from the center shall be less than 20 feet (6096 mm) by an amount equal to 1 foot (305 mm) for each 10 degrees of deviation from the normal.

7.207.4 Cotton Pad Test. For doors rated for a temperature rise of 650°F (361°C) or less, a cotton pad test shall be required during and at the end of the first 30 minutes of fire test. This test, for the passage of gases hot enough to ignite a cotton pad (absorbent cotton U.S.P. sterilized dried at 100°C for 24 hours) 4 inches by 4 inches (100 mm by 100 mm) in size, $^3/_4$ inch (19 mm) thick, weighing not less than 3 nor more than 4 grams. The pad shall be mounted in a steel device which will hold the pad parallel to, and 1 inch (25.4 mm) away from, the unexposed surface of the door. The cotton pad is to be held in position on the door for a minimum period of 20 seconds at such locations where cracks, seams or similar openings appear to have developed.

SECTION 7.208 — REPORT AND LABELING

7.208.1 Report. Results shall be reported in accordance with the performance in the tests prescribed in these test methods. The report shall show the performance under an exposure period chosen from the following: 20 minutes, 30 minutes, three-fourths hour, one hour, one and one-half hours, or three hours. The report shall include the temperature measurements of the furnace and, if determined, of the unexposed side of the test assembly. It shall also contain a record of all observations having a bearing on the performance of the test assembly including:

1. Any flaming on the unexposed surface of the door leaf.

2. The amount of movement of any portion of the edges of the door adjacent to the door frame from the original position.

3. The materials and construction of the door and frame and the details of the installation, hardware, hangers, guides, trim, finish and clearance or lap shall also be recorded or appropriately referenced to provide positive identification or duplication in all respects.

4. It shall also contain pressure measurements relative to the elevation of the top of the door.

7.208.2 Label. The classification marking or label on the door shall indicate the temperature rise developed on the unexposed surface of the door after the first 30 minutes of fire exposure as follows:

250°F (138°C) maximum
450°F (250°C) maximum

650°F (361°C) maximum
More than 650°F (361°C)

All doors with glass lights in excess of 100 square inches (64 516 mm²) are not eligible for a temperature rise rating.

SECTION 7.209 — CONDITIONS OF ACCEPTANCE

7.209.1 General. A door assembly shall be considered as meeting the requirements for acceptable performance when it remains in the opening during the fire-endurance test and hose stream test within the following limitations:

1. The movement of swinging doors shall not result in any portion of the edges adjacent to the door frame moving from the original position in a direction perpendicular to the plane of the door more than the thickness of the door, during the entire classification period or more than $1^1/_2$ times the door thickness as a result of the hose stream test.

2. An assembly consisting of a pair of swinging doors shall not separate more than $^3/_4$ inch (19.1 mm) or a distance equal to the throw of the latch bolt at the latch location.

3. An assembly consisting of a single swinging door shall not separate more than $^1/_2$ inch (12.7 mm) at the latch location.

4. The lap edges of passenger (horizontal slide-type) elevator doors, including the lap edges of multisection doors, shall not move from the wall or adjacent panel surfaces sufficiently to develop a separation of more than $2^7/_8$ inches (73.0 mm) during the entire classification period, or immediately following the hose stream test. The meeting edges of center-parting elevator door assemblies, for a fire and hose stream exposure of one and one-half hours or less, shall not move apart more than $1^1/_4$ inches (31.8 mm) as measured in any horizontal plane during the entire classification period or immediately following the hose stream test.

5. Doors mounted in guides shall not release from guides and guides shall not loosen from fastenings.

6. The test assembly shall have withstood the fire-endurance test and the hose stream test without developing openings anywhere through the assembly; except that dislodging of small portions of glass by the hose stream and within the limits specified in these requirements shall remain in place.

7. An opening is defined as a through hole in the assembly that can be seen from the unexposed side when viewed from the direction perpendicular to the plane of the assembly at the location of the suspected opening.

8. Ignition of the cotton pad shall be considered as failure.

7.209.2 Specific, All Doors.

1. Light intermittent flaming not exceeding 10-second duration and 6 inches (152 mm) in length shall be permitted during the first 30 minutes of the classification period.

2. After 30 minutes, some intermittent light flames [approximately 6 inches (152.4 mm) long], for periods not exceeding five-minute intervals, may occur along the edges of doors.

3. Light flaming may occur during the last 15 minutes of the classification period on the unexposed surface area of the door, provided it is contained within a distance of $1^1/_2$ inches (38.1 mm) from a vertical door edge and within 3 inches (76.2 mm) from the top edge of the door and within 3 inches (76.2 mm) from the top edge of the frame of a vision panel.

4. When hardware is to be evaluated for use on fire doors, it shall hold the door closed in accordance with the conditions of acceptance for the intended door assembly classification period and, in addition, the latch bolt shall remain projected and shall be intact after the test. The hardware need not be operable after test.

5. The door itself shall not emit excessive amounts of smoke during the fire test.

7.209.3 Swinging Doors. The movement of swinging doors shall not result in any portion of the door edges adjacent to the door frame moving from the original position in a direction perpendicular to the plane of the door more than the thickness of the door during the entire classification period, or more than one and one-half times the door thickness as a result of the hose stream test.

An assembly consisting of a pair of swinging doors incorporating an astragal shall not separate in a direction parallel to the plane of the doors more than $^3/_4$ inch (19.1 mm) or a distance equal to the throw of a latch bolt at the latch location.

An assembly consisting of a pair of swinging doors, without an overlapping astragal, for a fire and hose stream exposure of one and one-half hours or less, shall not separate along the meeting edges more than $^3/_8$ inch (9.5 mm), including the initial clearance between doors.

An assembly consisting of a single swinging door shall not separate more than $^1/_2$ inch (12.7 mm) at the latch location.

Door frames to be evaluated with doors shall remain securely fastened to the wall on all sides and shall not permit through openings between frame and doors or between frame and adjacent wall.

7.209.4 Sliding Doors. Doors mounted on the face of the wall shall not move from the wall sufficiently to develop a separation of more than $2^7/_8$ inches (73.0 mm) during the entire classification period or as a result of the hose stream test.

Doors mounted in guides shall not release from the guides, and the guides shall not loosen from fastenings.

The bottom bar of rolling steel doors shall not separate from the floor structure more than $^3/_4$ inch (19.1 mm) during the entire classification period or as a result of the hose stream test.

The meeting edge of center-parting horizontal sliding doors and biparting vertical sliding doors shall not separate more than the door thickness in a direction perpendicular to the plane of the doors. The meeting edges of center-parting horizontal sliding doors and biparting vertical sliding doors without an overlapping astragal, for a fire and hose stream exposure of one and one-half hours or less, shall not separate in a direction parallel to the plane of the doors more than $^3/_8$ inch (9.5 mm) along the meeting edges, including the initial clearance between doors.

The meeting edges of center-parting horizontal sliding doors incorporating an astragal shall not separate in a direction parallel to the plane of the doors more than $^3/_4$ inch (19.1 mm) nor a distance equal to the throw of the latch bolt along the meeting edges.

The bottom edge of service-counter doors or single-slide dumbwaiter doors shall not separate from the sill more than $^3/_8$ inch (9.5 mm).

A resilient astragal, if provided, shall not deteriorate sufficiently to result in through openings during the fire-endurance test, but small portions may be dislodged during the hose stream test.

TABLE 7-2-A—WATER PRESSURE AT BASE OF NOZZLE AND DURATION OF APPLICATION

DESIRED RATING	WATER PRESSURE AT BASE OF NOZZLE (pounds per square inch)	DURATION OF APPLICATION (seconds per square foot of exposed area)
	× 6.89 for kPa	× 10.76 for sec./m²
3 hrs.	45	3
1½ hrs. and over, if less than 3 hrs.	30	1.5
1 hr. and over, if less than 1½ hrs.	30	0.9
Less than 1 hr.	30	0.6

Part II—Test Standard for Smoke- and Draft-control Assemblies of the International Conference of Building Officials

SECTION 7.210 — SMOKE- AND DRAFT-CONTROL DOOR ASSEMBLIES

7.210.1 Scope. This method of test measures air leakage through door assemblies to determine the resistance of the door assembly in the closed position to the passage of smoke. The door assembly does not include a transom or sidelights.

7.210.2 Fire-endurance Test. The method of test for 20-minute smoke- and draft-control assemblies shall be as required for swinging doors under Part I of this standard. The fire-endurance test for these door assemblies shall be for an exposure period of not less than 20 minutes, except that the hose stream test required by Section 7.207.3 need not be applied.

7.210.3 Mounting.

7.210.3.1 Test chamber. The air leakage test chamber shall consist of a well-sealed chamber or box with an opening large enough to accommodate the test sample. A means of access into the chamber shall be permitted to facilitate adjustments and observations of the installed test sample.

At least one static pressure tap shall be provided to measure the chamber pressure. It shall be located so that readings are unaffected by the velocity of the air supplied to, or existing from, the chamber.

7.210.3.2 Test sample. The test sample shall be representative of production design. It shall be installed in accordance with manufacturers' instructions.

Test samples shall be tested swinging away from the positive pressure of the test chamber, or swinging toward the positive pressure, depending on which direction causes the most air infiltration for the type of door tested. Where representative test data exists to verify the ambient temperature results in higher leakage rates, additional tests for warm temperature measurements need not be conducted.

7.210.3.3 Conditioning. Test samples containing hygroscopic materials or other materials that can be affected by moisture shall be conditioned in an environment having a dry bulb temperature of 77 ± 5°F (25 ± 3°C) and a relative humidity of 40 to 65 percent until reaching equilibrium.

7.210.3.4 Gasketing. Gasketing may or may not not be installed in the test sample.

7.210.3.5 Bottom seal. An artificial bottom seal shall be installed across the full width of the bottom of the assembly.

7.210.4 Conduct of Test.

7.210.4.1 Chamber leakage test. Prior to the air leakage test, the clearances between the test sample and the chamber opening shall be measured at three points on each vertical and horizontal edge. Extraneous chamber leakage shall be measured using an air-impermeable sheet to cover the entire test sample. It shall be mea-

sured prior to the ambient temperature exposure tests specified in Section 7.210.4.2 and after the elevated temperature tests specified in Section 7.210.4.3 after the temperatures at the face of the test sample have returned to within 20°F (11°C) of their temperatures prior to the test. Chamber leakage shall be subtracted from the measured test sample leakage.

7.210.4.2 Ambient temperature test. The temperature of the exposed face of the test sample shall be 75 ± 20°F (24 ± 11°C), and each door face shall be ± 5°F (± 3°C) of each other prior to the conduct of the test. The air flow in the chamber shall be adjusted to provide a positive test pressure differential of 0.05-inch water (12.5 Pa) between the test chamber and the area immediately outside the chamber. The difference shall be within a tolerance of ± 0.005-inch water (1.25 Pa). After test conditions are stabilized, the air flow through the air flow metering system and the test pressure difference shall be measured and recorded. This measured air flow is designated the total metered air flow. The total measured air flow is then determined and recorded at test pressure differentials of 0.10-inch water (25 Pa), 0.20-inch water (50 Pa) and 0.30-inch water (75 Pa).

7.210.4.3 Elevated temperature test. The temperature of the exposed face of the test sample shall be 75 ± 20°F (24 ± 11°C), and each door face shall be ± 5°F (± 3°C) of each other prior to the conduct of the test. The test at ambient temperatures in Section 7.210.4.2 shall be repeated at a test chamber temperature of 400 ± 10°F (204 ± 5°C). The chamber temperature is to be increased so that it reaches 350°F (177°C) within 15 minutes and 400°F (204°C) within 30 minutes. When stabilized at 400°F ± 10°F (204 ± 5°C), metered air flow is determined and recorded to exceed 30 minutes.

7.210.5 Report. The air flow through the test sample shall be determined with an error not greater than ± 5 percent when the air flow equals or exceeds 2 cubic feet per minute (cfm) (9.44 × 10⁻⁴ m³), or 10 percent when the air flow is less than 2 cfm (9.44 × 10⁻⁴ m³) but more than 0.5 cfm (2.36 × 10⁻⁴ m³). At lower rates, a greater percentage of error is acceptable.

The barometric pressure, temperature and relative humidity of the supply air shall be measured at the test sample and recorded. The air supply flow values shall be corrected to normal temperature and pressure standard conditions for reporting purposes.

7.210.6 Conditions of Acceptance. A smoke- and draft-control door meeting the requirements of Section 7.209.2 as modified herein shall be considered as meeting the requirements for acceptable performance when the air leakage rate of the door assembly does not exceed 3.0 cfm (14.16 × 10⁻⁴ m³) per square foot of door opening at 0.10-inch water (25 Pa).

7.210.7 Marking. Door assemblies shall bear fire-rating labels issued by a listing agency showing compliance with this part. The hourly fire rating shall be followed by the letter "S." Label markings shall include the following:

1. Name and address of the listee.

2. Model number of type.

3. Symbol, serial or issue number of the listing agency.

UNIFORM BUILDING CODE STANDARD 7-3
TINCLAD FIRE DOORS
Based on Tinclad Fire Doors Standard ANSI/UL 10 A-1979 (R 1985)
See Sections 703.4, Item 1 and 713.5, *Uniform Building Code*

Part I—General

SECTION 7.301 — SCOPE

This standard covers the design and construction of tinclad fire doors which have been shown by fire tests to possess sufficient fire-retardant values to warrant classification as three, one and one-half or three-fourths-hour assemblies, when tested in accordance with the Standard Specification for Fire Tests of Door Assemblies. Doors complying with these requirements are classified in two temperature-rise groups:

1. Temperature rise on the unexposed side at the end of 30 minutes, 250°F (139°C) maximum.

2. Temperature rise on the unexposed side at the end of 30 minutes in excess of 650°F (361°C).

SECTION 7.302 — REQUIREMENTS

A door conforming to these specifications consists essentially of a core made up of layers of boards nailed to each other, encased in terne or zinc-coated steel in the form of sections jointed together at their edges and nailed through the seams to the core.

SECTION 7.303 — SIZES AND RATINGS

The sizes and ratings for three-ply and two-ply doors are given in Table 7-3-A.

Doors exceeding the sizes in Table 7-3-A have not been subjected to standard fire tests, and certificates on such doors indicate that the units conform to construction requirements of this standard, except in size.

It should be noted that Table 7-3-A pertains to maximum size of opening. Doors limited in size by this table fall into two categories: (1) swinging doors intended to be installed within an opening, and (2) all sliding doors and those swinging doors intended for surface mounting outside of the opening. Swinging doors in the first category are limited in size to the maximum dimensions specified for the opening. Doors in the second category must be larger than the maximum opening dimensions to provide the minimum 4-inch (101.6 mm) lap at each side and the top of the door. Doors exceeding these two basic dimension considerations are termed "Oversize," the design and construction of which are not necessarily fully covered in these requirements.

Part II—Materials

SECTION 7.304 — LUMBER

7.304.1 Species and Condition. The following soft woods may be used, provided only one kind of lumber is used in the assembly of a single core:

Cedars—All classes	Redwood
Cypress—All classes	Sitka Spruce
Douglas Fir	Tupelo Gum
Eastern Spruce	Yellow Poplar
Northern White Pine	Western White Pine

Other kinds of lumber may be added to the foregoing list, provided the kind of wood to be used has properties equivalent to the above species with respect to low resin content, light weight, resistance to fungus and decay, and ability to withstand nailing without splitting or splintering.

Lumber shall have a moisture content of 19 percent or less at the time of manufacturing door cores. Tests for moisture content shall be made using the oven-drying or the electrical meter method in accordance with approved methods for tests for moisture content of wood.

Stocks of lumber shall be stored under cover in the premises of the fire-door manufacturer for at least one month before being used in the manufacture of fire-door cores and, while in storage, shall be piled in such a manner that the air has free access to all surfaces of each board. Kiln drying will be accepted for the 30-day drying period.

7.304.2 Size. The boards shall be nominal 1-inch (25 mm) lumber, surfaced on two sides and matched. They shall be without beading, beveling, painting or other treatment.

The actual thickness of the boards shall not be less than $^3/_4$ inch (19.1 mm).

The boards shall not be less than 4 inches (102 mm) or more than 8 inches (203 mm) in nominal width.

The nominal width (or stock width) is greater than the actual width over the tongue and groove.

7.304.3 Grading. The boards shall be free from wane (bark), decay, knots or other holes, loose knots, unsound knots or knots exceeding $2^1/_2$ inches (63.5 mm) in any dimension.

Lumber of a No. 2 Common or Construction grade or better will generally meet these requirements. However, because some pieces of No. 2 grade could be unacceptable, the kind of lumber used and its condition shall be judged from characteristic properties of the wood as commonly known. These characteristics include:

1. **Decay**—Destruction of the wood substance due to the action of wood destroying fungi.

> **NOTE:** "Dote" and "rot" are synonymous with "decay" and are any form of decay which may be evident either as a dark red discoloration, not found in the sound wood, or the presence of white or red rotten spots.

2. **Advanced (typical decay)**—The older stage of decay in which the destruction is readily recognized because the wood has become punky, soft and spongy, stringy, ring shaped, pitted or crumbly.

3. **Incipient decay**—The early stage of decay which has not proceeded far enough to soften or otherwise perceptibly impair the hardness of the wood.

4. **Knot**—That portion of a branch which has become incorporated in the body of a tree.

5. **Loose knot**—A knot which is not firmly held in place by growth or position.

6. **Tight knot**—A knot so fixed by growth or position that it will firmly retain its place in the wood piece.

7. **Hollow knot**—A hollow knot is an apparently sound knot except it contains a hole over $1/4$ inch (6.4 mm) in diameter or a void area behind the knot.

8. **Check**—A separation along the grain, the greater part of which occurs across the rings of annual growth.

9. **Wane**—The lack of wood from any cause, or bark on the surface of lumber.

To permit judging of the several characteristics of knots, oval and circular knots are to be measured across their lines of growth. For spike knots, the measurement is to be parallel to the lines of growth. In all cases, the measured distance is to be the visible portion of the knot which is normally darker or lighter than the coloring of the board.

The following characteristics are to be judged as unacceptable:

1. Oval, circular or spike knots exceeding $2^1/_2$ inches (63.5 mm) in any direction.

2. Loose knots, open knots or any knot over 1 inch (25.4 mm) in any direction located on the tongue or lip.

3. Loose knots, open knots, through holes and surface pits [deeper than $1/_{16}$ inch (1.6 mm)] in the central portion of the boards.

4. Hollow and decayed knots.

5. Checks, advanced (typical) and incipient decay.

6. Warpage which would prevent the boards from being nailed flat or which would affect the flatness of the nailed core.

7. Cluster knots or knots in groups [less than $5/_8$ inch (15.9 mm) apart].

Tight knots on the lips or tongue of a board may be judged acceptable if, due to manufacturing, the lips or tongue have been chipped, but only to the extent that (1) the dimensions of the damage do not exceed $3/_8$ inch (9.5 mm) in length and $3/_{16}$ inch (4.8 mm) in diameter, and (2) the lip or tongue with a chip cannot be easily broken, such as upon exerting direct hand pressure.

SECTION 7.305 — METAL COVERINGS

7.305.1 General. The terne or zinc-coated steel sections shall have straight edges and square corners. A deviation of $1/_{32}$ inch per foot (2.6 mm per meter) from square shall be accepted, provided the door manufacturer is able to obtain true, straight joints and to avoid patching the rows of sheets in the covering.

7.305.2 Terne-coated Sheet Steel. Only prime terne plate shall be used. For the purpose of these requirements, "terne" shall be understood as indicating an alloy of tin and lead in the proportion of 80 percent lead and 20 percent tin, hot-dipped applied. The terne coating shall be uniformly applied on both sides of sheet steel having an uncoated thickness of not less than 0.010 inch (0.254 mm). The terne coating shall not crack, peel or flake when formed.

The sheet steel shall be coated with not less than 0.55 ounce per square foot (0.168 kg/m^2) average of terne coating (total both sides) by triple spot test and not less than 0.40 ounce per square foot (0.122 kg/m^2) of terne coating (total both sides) by the single spot test, with not less than 40 percent of the coating of any side, by the single spot test requirement. The weight of terne coating shall be determined by approved nationally recognized methods.

A determination for percent tin shall be made on a portion of the solution containing the stripped terne coating, using standard laboratory analytical methods. The amount of tin in the coating shall not be less than 20 percent.

A determination for percent lead may be made on a portion of the solution containing the stripped terne coating, using standard laboratory analytical methods, or the percent of lead in coating may be determined by subtracting the percent of tin from 100 percent.

7.305.3 Zinc-coated (Galvanized) Sheet Steel. Zinc-coated sheet steel shall have an uncoated thickness of not less than 0.010 inch (0.254 mm). The zinc coating shall not crack or flake when formed.

Finished doors shall be painted with a good grade of corrosion-resisting paint before shipment. Before painting, zinc surfaces shall be thoroughly cleaned and pretreated to provide for adherence of the paint coating.

The protective coating of zinc shall be as applied to hot-dipped, mill galvanized sheet steel, with not less than 40 percent of the zinc on any side, based on the single spot requirement. The weight of zinc coating, minimum 0.5 oz./ft.^{2} (0.153 kg/m^2), shall be determined by approved nationally recognized methods.

SECTION 7.306 — NAILS

Core nails shall be cut nails of the clinch type or duck-bill point-type power-driven nails that clinch. For three-ply cores, the nails shall not be less than $2^7/_8$ inches (73 mm) or more than 3 inches (76.2 mm) long. For two-ply cores, the nails shall not be less than $1^{11}/_{16}$ inches (42.9 mm) or more than 2 inches (50.8 mm) long. The shank diameters of duckbill-point nails shall be 0.130 inch to 0.140 inch (3.3 mm to 3.6 mm) for three-ply doors and 0.100 inch to 0.110 inch (2.5 mm to 2.8 mm) for two-ply doors.

Nails for applying the metal covering shall be wire nails with flat heads. The shank of the nails shall not be less than 0.091 inch (2.3 mm) nor more than 0.109 inch (2.8 mm) in diameter. The nails for three-ply cores shall be 2 inches (50.8 mm) long, and for two-ply cores shall not be less than $1^1/_4$ inches (31.8 mm) or more than $1^1/_2$ inches (38.1 mm) long.

Part III—Construction

SECTION 7.307 — ASSEMBLY OF BOARDS

The details for the assembly of boards are shown in Figures 7-3-1 and 7-3-2.

Only one stock width of board shall be used in any one core, except that the edge board and the stock board immediately adjacent to the edge board may differ in width from the remaining stock boards. Edge boards shall not finish less than 3 inches (76.2 mm) in width and the exposed edges shall not be tongued or grooved.

Boards shall not be less than 1 foot (305 mm) in length, with ends cut square. Not more than two pieces shall be used in any continuous strip in any outside layer of a two-ply or three-ply core, nor more than three pieces in any middle layer strip of a three-ply core. At least alternate strips in outside layers shall be full-length boards.

If glass panels are provided and the panel opening is of such a size that the distance between the opening and the edges of the door is less than 2 feet (609.6 mm), all boards bordering the vertical edges of the opening may be laid vertically, and all boards bordering the horizontal edges of the opening may be laid horizontally.

If glass panels are provided, the boards in the normally vertical layers bordering the sides of the panel opening shall be continuous from top to bottom of the door, and boards in the normally horizontal layer bordering the top or bottom of the panel opening shall be continuous from side to side of the door. The distance between the panel opening and the side of the door shall not be less than 7 inches (177.8 mm). See Figure 7-3-2.

Outside layers in a three-ply core and one layer of a two-ply core shall be vertical, and the other layer horizontal. The several boards in each layer and the ends of pieces of boards in strips shall make tight joints at edges and ends of boards.

The top edge for a sliding door designed to close by gravity shall conform to an incline of $^3/_4$ inch per foot (62.5 mm per meter). The minimum face width of the top horizontal board of a core having the top edge inclined shall not be less than 3 inches (76.2 mm). See Figures 7-3-3, 7-3-4 and 7-3-5.

SECTION 7.308 — NAILING OF CORES

7.308.1 General. The boards shall be nailed so that the several layers are fastened tightly together, with the points of the nails turning back and clinching thoroughly in the face of the core and with no portion of the nails projecting beyond the surfaces of the core. See Figure 7-3-6.

7.308.2 Two-ply and Three-ply Cores of Boards 3 Inches to 4 Inches (76.2 mm to 101.6 mm) (Inclusive) Stock Width. The details for nailing of boards 3 inches to 4 inches (76.2 mm to 101.6 mm), inclusive, stock width are shown in Figure 7-3-3.

Horizontal rows of nails shall be about the center of each horizontal layer board. Vertical rows of nails shall be about the center of each vertical layer of board. Nails in horizontal and vertical rows shall be spaced not more than five times the face width of each board. Rows of nails at edges of core shall be about $1^1/_2$ inches (38 mm) from each edge. Nails in vertical edge rows shall be placed not more than the face width of each board and shall be about the center of each horizontal board. Nails in horizontal edge rows shall be spaced not more than the face width of each board and shall be about the center of each vertical board.

7.308.3 Two-ply and Three-ply Cores of Boards $4^1/_2$ Inches to 8 Inches (114.3 mm to 203.2 mm) (Inclusive) Stock Width. The details for nailing of boards $4^1/_2$ inches to 8 inches (114.3 mm to 203.2 mm), inclusive, stock width are shown in Figure 7-3-4.

Horizontal rows of nails shall be about 1 inch (25 mm) from each edge of each horizontal layer board (two horizontal rows of nails through each horizontal board). Vertical rows of nails shall be about 1 inch (25 mm) from each edge of each vertical layer board (two vertical rows of nails through each vertical board). Nails in horizontal and vertical rows shall be spaced not more than twice the face width of each board.

Rows of nails at edges of core shall be about $1^1/_2$ inches (38 mm) from each edge. Nails in vertical-edge rows shall be spaced not more than the face width of each board and shall be about the center of each horizontal board. Nails in horizontal edge rows shall be spaced not more than the face width of each board and shall be about the center of each vertical board, except that the nails in the top edge row of a core having the top edge inclined shall be spaced not more than $4^1/_2$ inches (114.3 mm).

7.308.4 Three-ply Cores Only of Boards $4^1/_2$ Inches to 8 Inches (114.3 mm to 203.2 mm) (Inclusive) Stock Width. The details for nailing of boards $4^1/_2$ inches to 8 inches (114.3 mm to 203.2 mm), inclusive, stock width for three-ply core only are shown in Figure 7-3-5.

Horizontal rows of nails shall be about the center of each horizontal layer board. Vertical rows of nails shall be about 1 inch (25 mm) from each edge of each vertical layer board (two vertical rows of nails through each vertical board). Nails in horizontal rows shall be spaced not more than the face width of each board.

Nails in vertical rows shall be spaced not more than twice the face width of each board.

Rows of nails at edges of core shall be about $1^1/_2$ inches (38 mm) from each edge. Nails in vertical edge rows shall be spaced not more than the face width of each board and shall be about the center of each horizontal board. Nails in horizontal edge rows shall be spaced about 1 inch (25 mm) from each edge of each vertical board, except that each vertical edge board shall have only one nail, which should be placed about the center of the board.

SECTION 7.309 — FINISHED CORES

A finished three-ply core shall not be less than $2^1/_4$ inches (57.2 mm) nor more than $2^5/_8$ inches (66.7 mm) in thickness, and a finished two-ply core shall not be less than $1^1/_2$ inches (38.1 mm) nor more than $1^3/_4$ inches (44.5 mm) in thickness.

   EXCEPTION: A finished three-ply core door which is less than $2^1/_4$ inches (57.2 mm) thick may be marked in accordance with the schedule for two-ply doors.

The cores shall have true corners. All edges shall be finished smooth and square, except that meeting edges of swinging doors may be beveled $^1/_4$ inch (6.4 mm) (not rabbeted).

SECTION 7.310 — SIZES OF STEEL SECTIONS

Coated steel sections shall not be larger than the 14- by 20-inch (355.6 mm by 508 mm) size. Corner sections shall not be over 14 inches (355.6 mm) wide and of any length that will avoid joints with edge sections coming under miter fold. Edge sections (excepting "cap" sections) shall be of the same width as corner sections and of any convenient length. Cap sections shall be of any convenient length and equal in width to thickness of core plus $3^1/_2$ inches (88.9 mm).

SECTION 7.311 — FORMING OF STEEL SECTIONS

Turned edges of coated steel sections shall be parallel to cut edges. Turned-up portions of all sections shall be of uniform width.

Face sections, excepting the face sections used in the row forming the closure, shall have one vertical edge turned $^5/_8$ inch (15.9 mm) and the other vertical edge doubled under $1^3/_{16}$ inches (30.2 mm) and the doubled edge then turned up $^5/_8$ inch (15.9 mm) from cut edge as shown in Figure 7-3-7, Section A-B.

Face sections, excepting face sections forming top horizontal seams, shall have both horizontal seams, shall have both horizontal edges turned $^5/_8$ inch (15.9 mm) to lock with edge and other face sections shown in Figure 7-3-7, Section C-D.

Face sections forming top horizontal seams, excepting seams formed with a cap, shall have the lower horizontal edge turned $^5/_8$ inch (15.9 mm) to lock with other face sections, and the other horizontal edge doubled under $1^3/_{16}$ inches (30.2 mm) and the doubled edge then turned up $^5/_8$ inch (15.9 mm) from cut edge.

Face sections forming top horizontal seams with a cap shall have both horizontal edges turned up $^5/_8$ inch (15.9 mm) to lock with cap and other face sections.

Corner sections shall have all edges turned $^5/_8$ inch (15.9 mm) so as to lock with edge and face sections as shown in Figure 7-3-8.

Edge sections, excepting cap sections, shall have all edges turned $^5/_8$ inch (15.9 mm) so as to lock with corner, face and other edge sections as shown in Figure 7-3-9.

Cap sections shall have edges forming seams with other cap sections turned $^5/_8$ inch (15.9 mm). Cap sections shall have edges forming top horizontal seams with face and edge sections doubled under $1^3/_{16}$ inches (30.2 mm) and the portion next to the cut edge turned down $^5/_8$ inch (15.9 mm) so as to lap the edge and face sections as shown in Figure 7-3-10.

SECTION 7.312 — APPLICATION OF STEEL SECTIONS

The sections shall fit the core as flatly and tightly as practicable. Any air space created as the result of bulging shall not exceed $^3/_{16}$ inch (4.8 mm).

The sections shall be locked together not less than $^1/_2$ inch (12.7 mm). Both faces of the core shall be covered with sections laid with their longer sides vertical, except that the sections in one vertical row on each face of the core may be laid horizontally.

Vertical seams formed with face sections shall be hook seams with the upper section having a fold for covering the heads of the nails in the seam as shown in Figure 7-3-11.

Horizontal seams formed with face sections, excepting top horizontal seams, shall be hook seams as shown in Figure 7-3-12. Top horizontal seams, excepting seams formed with a cap, shall have a fold for covering the heads of the nails in the seam as shown in Figure 7-3-11. Top horizontal seams formed with a cap shall be lock seams with the locking portion of the cap having a fold for covering the heads of the nails in the seam as shown in Figure 7-3-10.

The upper ends of vertical seams shall be covered by the doubled edges of the top horizontal seams.

Each bottom corner of the core shall be covered with a section bent over the edges of the core and lapped an equal distance on both faces of the core, making a miter fold (without cutting) on each face, the folds on a door for use at an opening in an exterior wall being arranged to shed water as shown in Figure 7-3-8.

Each upper corner shall be covered the same as bottom corners if a cap is not used for covering the top edge of the core.

The bottom edge and the vertical edges of the core shall be covered with sections bent over edges of the core and lapped an equal distance on both faces. The sections shall be joined to each other and to the corners with hook seams, the seams being made so as to shed water when the door is for use at an opening in an exterior wall as shown in Figures 7-3-7 and 7-3-9.

The top edge of the core shall be covered the same as the bottom and vertical edges if a cap is not used. The top edge of a core shall be covered with a cap when the door is for use at an opening in an exterior wall or when the door has a segmental head. The cap shall be formed of sections joined to each other with hook seams as shown in Figure 7-3-13.

If glass panels are provided and band or angle iron reinforcement for glass grooves is used, the vertical edges of the panel openings shall be covered with terne or zinc-coated steel secured to the face sections by vertical seams. The covering at the horizontal edges of the opening shall be cap seams as shown in Figure 7-3-14.

SECTION 7.313 — NAILING OF STEEL SECTIONS

The nails shall pass straight into the core and as near as possible through the center of the lock in the seams as shown in Figures 7-3-10, 7-3-11 and 7-3-12.

Full-sized face sections shall be held to the core by 18 nails in the seams, with nails near but not in the corners, and with four nails along each short side and five along each long side of each section.

Face sections smaller than 14- by 20-inch (355.6 mm by 508 mm) size shall be held to the core by nails in the seams placed near but not in the corners, with at least two nails along each side and

with nails spaced not over 3 inches (76.2 mm) apart in horizontal seams and not over 4 inches (101.6 mm) apart in vertical seams.

Vertical seams formed with face sections shall have nails through two thicknesses of each section as shown in Figure 7-3-11.

Horizontal seams formed with face sections, except top horizontal seams, shall have nails through two thicknesses of lower sections and one thickness of upper section forming the seams as shown in Figure 7-3-12. Top horizontal seams, except seams made with a cap, shall have nails through two thicknesses of each section forming the seams as shown in Figure 7-3-11. Top horizontal seams formed with a cap shall have nails through one thickness of each plate forming the seams as shown in Figure 7-3-10.

Each corner section shall be held to the core with two nails on each side near the edge of the core as shown in Figure 7-3-8.

If glass panels are provided and band or angle-iron reinforcement for glass grooves is used, nails securing seams between face sections and strips covering edges of panel opening shall be spaced at intervals not exceeding 3 inches (76.2 mm) in horizontal seams and 4 inches (101.6 mm) in vertical seams, with one nail near but not in each corner.

SECTION 7.314 — PROTECTION OF NAILHEADS

Heads of nails in vertical seams formed with face sections shall be covered by the doubled edges of face sections as shown in Figure 7-3-11. Heads of nails in horizontal seams formed with face sections, except top horizontal seams, shall be covered by the face sections as shown in Figure 7-3-12. Heads of nails in top horizontal seams formed with face sections shall be covered by the doubled edges of face sections or cap as shown in Figures 7-3-10 and 7-3-11. Heads of nails in corner sections shall be covered by the miter fold as shown in Figure 7-3-8.

SECTION 7.315 — ASTRAGALS

Swinging doors to be mounted in pairs shall be provided with at least one astragal extending the full height of the doors. Sliding doors to be mounted in pairs shall be provided with only one astragal extending to within 4 inches (101.6 mm) of the top and bottom of the doors. Astragals shall be of steel not less than $^3/_{16}$ inch (4.8 mm) thick and 3 inches (76.2 mm) wide. The astragal shall be fastened to the door, when installed, by not less than $^1/_4$-inch (6.4 mm) carriage or stove bolts spaced at intervals not exceeding 12 inches (304.8 mm). Top bolts shall not be over 5 inches (127 mm) from the end of the astragal and bottom bolts not over 3 inches (76.2 mm). Bolts shall pass through the astragal and be secured by nuts on the opposite side of the door. Washers shall be used under nuts. Bolt holes in the astragal and door shall be located so that the astragal will extend at least $^3/_4$ inch (19.1 mm) beyond the edge of the door to which it is attached.

In case the astragal is to be attached in the field, the bolt holes in the astragal shall be drilled by the manufacturer to ensure proper spacings, fit, etc. In such case it will not be necessary to drill the door for the bolts.

SECTION 7.316 — GLASS PANELS

7.316.1 General. The construction details for any one of the following types of glass panel construction shall not be used in or combined with any of the other types described.

7.316.2 Reinforcements for Grooves. In all doors provided with grooves constructed of angles, the opening shall be reinforced either by means of a band-iron strip not less than $^1/_8$ inch

(3.2 mm) in thickness and equal in width to the thickness of the core or by means of $1/8$-by-$1^3/8$-by-$7/8$-inch (3.2 mm by 34.9 mm by 22.2 mm) angles bolted together through the door. See Figures 7-3-14, 7-3-16 and 7-3-15.

The band-iron strip shall be secured to the inner edges of the panel opening by not less than two wood screws and shall be provided with threaded holes for receiving the bolts which secure the angles forming the glass grooves.

The $1/8$-by-$1^3/8$-by-$7/8$-inch (3.2 mm by 34.9 mm by 22.2 mm) angles shall be bolted together through the door by $3/16$-inch (4.8 mm) stove bolts spaced at intervals not exceeding 12 inches (304.8 mm) and not more than 2 inches (50.8 mm) from each end. They shall be provided with threaded holes for receiving the bolts which secure angles forming the glass groove.

7.316.3 Glass Grooves Constructed of Angles. The angles used in forming the glass grooves shall not be less than $1/8$ inch (3.2 mm) in thickness and shall be of such other dimensions as to provide a groove not less than $3/4$ inch (19.1 mm) deep by $3/8$ inch (9.5 mm) wide as shown by Figures 7-3-14, 7-3-15 and 7-3-16.

Rivets or screws used to secure the groove angles to the reinforcement shall be spaced at intervals not exceeding 12 inches (304.8 mm) and not more than 2 inches (50.8 mm) from each end.

7.316.4 Grooves Constructed of Formed Sheet Metal. Grooves of this type shall be formed of a single piece of galvanized or terne-coated sheet steel having an uncoated thickness of not less than 0.020 inch (0.508 mm) as shown by Figures 7-3-17, 7-3-18 and 7-3-19 and shall not be less than $3/4$ inch (19.1 mm) deep by $3/8$ inch (9.5 mm) wide.

The edges of this formed strip shall be secured to the face sections of the door by vertical seams at the vertical edges of the opening as shown by Figure 7-3-19, Section B-B, and by cap seams at the horizontal edges of the opening as shown by Figure 7-3-19, Section D-D.

The edges of this formed strip shall be secured to the face plates of the door by vertical seams at the vertical edges of the opening as shown by Figure 7-3-19, Section B-B, and by cap seams at the horizontal edges of the opening as shown by Figure 7-3-19, Section D-D.

In the case of glass openings employing only one light, the sheet-metal glass groove may be constructed as shown by Figure 7-3-19, Section A-A. In this type of glass groove the reinforcing strip shall be $1/8$-inch (3.2 mm) band iron and shall either be continuous for the full length of the groove or consist of individual reinforcing strips not less than 1 inch (25 mm) long for each screw securing the removable molding. The reinforcing strip shall be secured to the fixed part of the glass groove by rivets or screws, independent of the screws fastening the removable molding. Rivets or screws used to secure the reinforcing strip or the removable molding shall be spaced at intervals not exceeding 12 inches (304.8 mm) and not more than 2 inches (50.8 mm) from each end.

Nails securing seams between molding strips and face sections shall be spaced at intervals not exceeding 3 inches (76.2 mm) in horizontal seams and 4 inches (101.6 mm) in vertical seams, with one nail near, but not in, each corner.

7.316.5 Muntins. Muntins may be of any of the constructions shown by Figures 7-3-12 through 7-3-19. In all cases, fixed parts of muntins shall be firmly secured to glass moldings at ends and at intersections with each other. Rivets, screws, welds or clips may be employed. Rivets, screws, etc., shall be spaced at intervals not exceeding 12 inches (304.8 mm).

When muntins are formed of sheet metal, the reinforcing plate shall be $1/8$-inch (3.2 mm) band iron which may be either continuous for the full length of the muntin or may consist of individual reinforcing strips not less than 1 inch (25 mm) long for each screw securing the removable part of the muntin.

7.316.6 Screws and Rivets. Screw sizes shall be $3/16$ inch (4.8 mm) (10-24) spaced 10 inches (254 mm) on centers; $1/8$ inch (3.2 mm) (either 6-32 or 8-32) spaced 8 inches (203.2 mm) on centers. Rivets shall not be less than $1/8$ inch (3.2 mm) in diameter.

7.316.7 Glass Sizes. Individual lights in doors bearing the marking "Rating: $3/4$-Hr. (C) or (E)" shall not exceed 1,296 square inches (0.836 m^2) in exposed area or 54 inches (1371.6 mm) in either dimension.

Area of exposed glass light per door leaf in doors bearing the marking "Rating: $1^1/2$-Hr. (B), Temp. Rise—30 Min.—250°F (139°C) Max." shall not exceed 100 square inches (0.064 m^2), neither length nor width to exceed 12 inches (304.8 mm).

Glass lights shall not be used in doors bearing the marking "Rating: 3-Hr. (A) or $1^1/2$-Hr. (D)."

SECTION 7.317 — SPLICING OF DOORS MADE IN SECTIONS

If doors are made in sections to be assembled as a single unit in the field, each section shall be constructed and marked in accordance with the requirements for a completed door.

Sections less than 10 feet (3048 mm) in height (not more than two) shall be joined together vertically by attaching to each face of the completed door a strip of galvanized sheet steel having a minimum thickness of not less than 0.056 inch (1.42 mm), not less than 6 inches (152.4 mm) in width and of a length corresponding to the height of the door. The splice metal sections shall be attached to each section of the door by not less than $1/4$-inch (6.4 mm) through bolts spaced on not more than 12-inch (304.8 mm) centers and not to exceed 3 inches (76.2 mm) from the top and bottom edges of the door. Through bolts shall extend through both splice plates and the door body and shall thread into nuts.

Sections over 10 feet (3048 mm) in height (not more than two) may be joined together vertically by attaching to each face of the completed door not more than two strips of sheet steel having a minimum thickness of 0.12 inch (3.05 mm), painted on both sides, or galvanized sheet steel having a minimum thickness of 0.126 inch (3.20 mm) not less than 6 inches (152.4 mm) in width and of a length corresponding to the height of the door. The meeting edges of such splice sections on one side of the door section shall be at least 2 feet (610 mm) higher or lower than those on the opposite side.

On three-ply doors, 2-by-2-by-$3/16$-inch (50.8 mm by 50.8 mm by 4.8 mm) angles or $2^1/2$-by-$5/8$-by-$3/16$-inch (63.5 mm by 15.9 mm by 4.8 mm) channels shall be attached horizontally across the width of the door and not to exceed 18 inches (457.2 mm) from the bottom edge and the lowest corner of the top edge by not less than $3/8$-inch (9.5 mm) through bolts spaced on not more than 18-inch (457.2 mm) centers and at not more than 6 inches (152.4 mm) from each edge of the assembled door. On two-ply doors, 2-by-$1^1/2$-by-$3/16$-inch (50.8 mm by 38.1 mm by 4.8 mm) angles or $1^1/2$-by-$5/8$-by-$3/16$-inch (38.1 mm by 15.9 mm by 4.8 mm) channels shall be attached in a like manner.

Angle- and channel-iron reinforcements and both splice plates may be shipped separately, but through bolts shall be secured to them before shipment. Both sections of the door shall be drilled at the factory to receive through bolts for attachment of splice metal sections and angle- and channel-iron reinforcements.

SECTION 7.318 — WICKETS

Doors or door sections shall not be provided with wickets or openings for same.

SECTION 7.319 — APPLIED METALS

Doors or door sections shall not be provided with kick plates or metals applied over the standard construction.

Part IV—Marking

SECTION 7.320 — MARKING

7.320.1 Content. Each door shall be marked with:

1. The manufacturer's or vendor's name or identifying symbol.

2. The words "Tinclad Fire Door."

3. The appropriate hourly rating and temperature rise for the classification and any glass panels.

If a door has been provided with edge notches to clear conveyor rails, for example, it becomes ineligible to carry the marking outlined in Section 7.320, Item 3; but it shall be otherwise identified with the following statement:

> "This door(s) violates one of the fundamental principles of wall opening protection in that it (they) does not provide for a continuous lap of the door over the edge of the opening to oppose the passage of flame and therefore cannot be provided with an hourly classification."

If a manufacturer produces doors at more than one factory, each door shall have a distinctive marking to identify it as the product of a particular factory.

7.320.2 Application. Markings shall be permanent to the degree afforded by a lithographed metal plate, a pressure-sensitive label, or stamping. All markings on one door shall be grouped in one location.

TABLE 7-3-A—SIZES AND RATINGS

TYPE, METHOD OF OPERATION AND MAXIMUM SIZE OF OPENING	RATING AND CLASS OF OPENING	MAXIMUM EXPOSED GLASS AREA × 645 for mm^2
Three-ply Swinging single 6′ 0″ × 12′ 0″ (1829 × 3658 mm) Swinging in pairs 10′ 0″ × 12′ 0″ (3048 × 3658 mm) Sliding single and center-parting 120 square feet (11.15 m^2) with maximum dimension 12′ 0″ (3658 mm) Vertically sliding 80 square feet (7.43 m^2) with maximum dimension 10′ 0″ (3048 mm)	3-hr. (A)[1] $1^{1}/_{2}$-hr. (B)[1] $^{3}/_{4}$-hr. (C)[2] $1^{1}/_{2}$-hr. (D)[1] $^{3}/_{4}$-hr. (E)[2]	None 100 square inches per door 1,296 square inches per light None 1,296 square inches per light
Two-ply Swinging single 6′ 0″ × 10′ 0″ (1829 × 3048 mm) Swinging in pairs 10′ 0″ × 10′ 0″ (3048 × 3048 mm) Sliding single and 80 square feet (7.43 m^2) with maximum dimension 10′ 0″ (3048 mm)	$1^{1}/_{2}$-hr. (B)[1] $^{3}/_{4}$-hr. (C)[2] $1^{1}/_{2}$-hr. (D)[1] $^{3}/_{4}$-hr. (E)[2]	100 square inches per door 1,296 square inches per light None 1,296 square inches per light

[1]Three-hour (A), one- and one-half-hour (B) and one- and one-half hour (D) doors have a temperature rise of 250°F (139°C) maximum at 30 minutes.

[2]Three-fourths-hour (C) and three-fourths-hour (E) doors with large glass lights may permit a temperature rise in excess of 650°F (361°C) on the unexposed side at 30 minutes.

FIGURE 7-3-1—ASSEMBLY OF BOARDS IN THREE-PLY CORE

7 IN. MIN.
(177.8 mm)

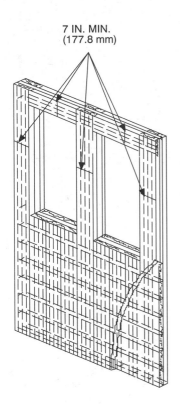

**FIGURE 7-3-2—ASSEMBLY OF BOARDS IN THREE-PLY CORE
WITH GLASS OPENINGS**

3 IN. MIN.
(76.2 mm)

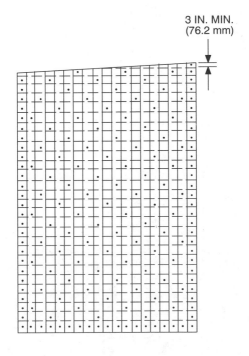

**FIGURE 7-3-3—NAILING FOR 3- TO 4-INCH
(76.2 to 101.6 mm) STOCK**

3 IN. MIN. (76.2 mm)

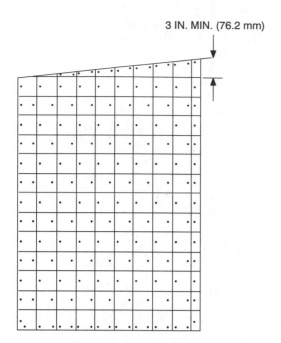

**FIGURE 7-3-4—NAILING FOR 4$^1/_2$- TO 8-INCH
(114.3 to 203.2 mm) STOCK**

3 IN. MIN. (76.2 mm)

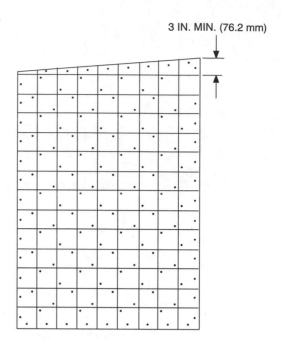

**FIGURE 7-3-5—NAILING FOR THREE-PLY
CORES ONLY 4$^1/_2$- TO 8-INCH
(114.3 to 203.2 mm) STOCK**

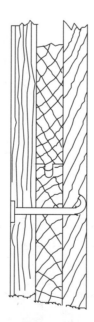

**FIGURE 7-3-6—NAILING IN THREE-PLY
CORE SHOWING CLINCHING**

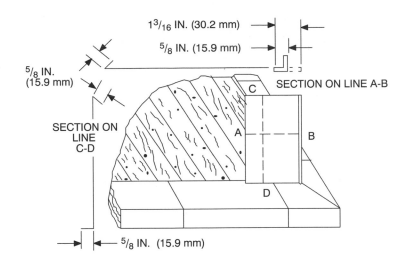

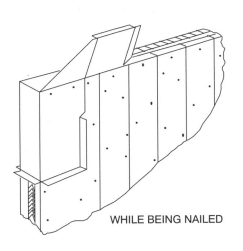

WHILE BEING NAILED

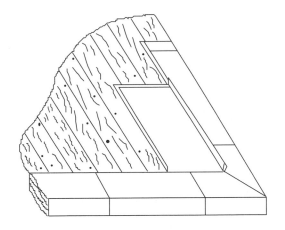

**FIGURE 7-3-7—APPLICATION OF METAL
SECTIONS ON FACE OF CORE**

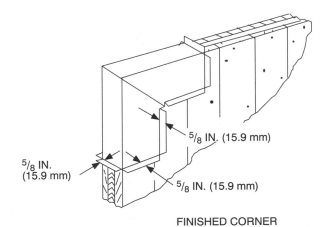

FINISHED CORNER

**FIGURE 7-3-8—APPLICATION OF METAL
SECTIONS AT CORNER OF CORE**

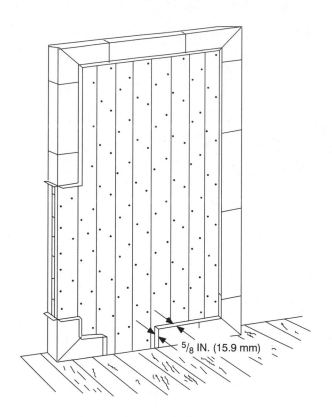

**FIGURE 7-3-9—APPLICATION OF METAL
SECTIONS AT EDGES OF CORE**

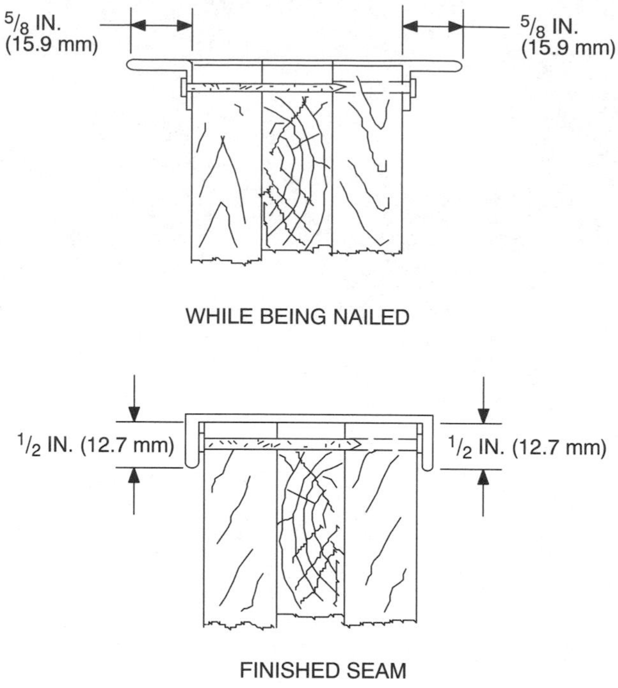

WHILE BEING NAILED

FINISHED SEAM

**FIGURE 7-3-10—APPLICATION OF CAP
METAL SECTIONS AT TOP EDGE OF CORE**

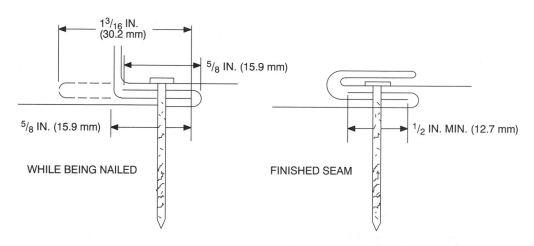

WHILE BEING NAILED

FINISHED SEAM

FIGURE 7-3-11—VERTICAL SEAMS OF FACE SECTIONS (TOP VIEW)

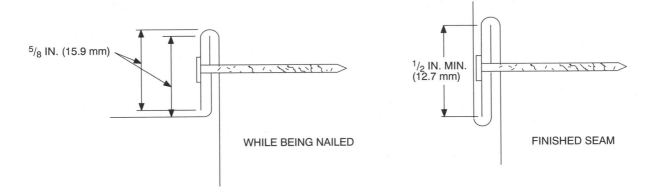

5/8 IN. (15.9 mm)

WHILE BEING NAILED

1/2 IN. MIN. (12.7 mm)

FINISHED SEAM

FIGURE 7-3-12—HORIZONTAL SEAMS OF FACE SECTIONS (SIDE VIEW)

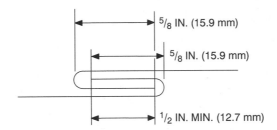

5/8 IN. (15.9 mm)

5/8 IN. (15.9 mm)

1/2 IN. MIN. (12.7 mm)

FIGURE 7-3-13—SEAMS BETWEEN CORNER AND EDGE SECTIONS

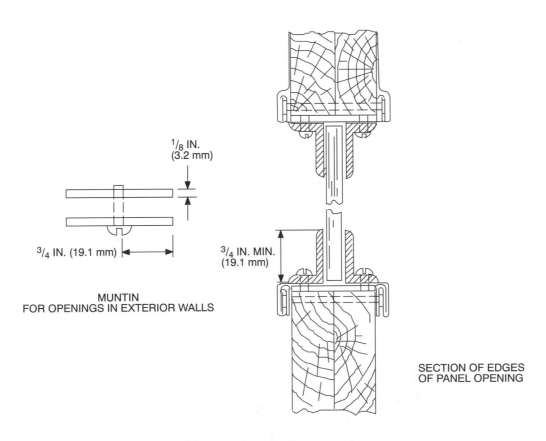

1/8 IN. (3.2 mm)

3/4 IN. (19.1 mm)

MUNTIN
FOR OPENINGS IN EXTERIOR WALLS

3/4 IN. MIN. (19.1 mm)

SECTION OF EDGES
OF PANEL OPENING

FIGURE 7-3-14—GLASS OPENING DETAILS

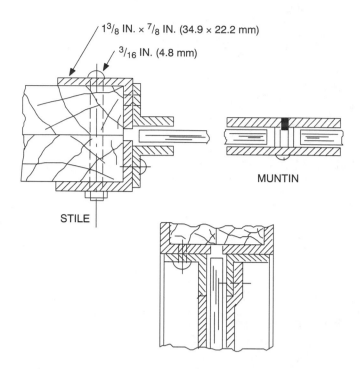

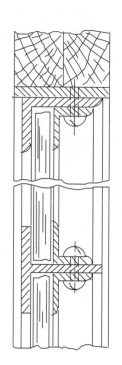

FIGURE 7-3-15—GLASS OPENING DETAILS

FIGURE 7-3-16—GLASS OPENING DETAILS

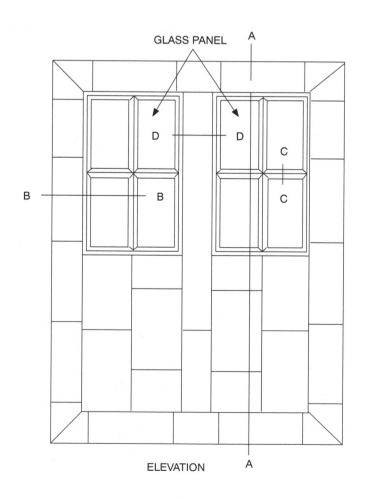

FIGURE 7-3-17—ASSEMBLY—GLASS GROOVES, FORMED SHEET METAL

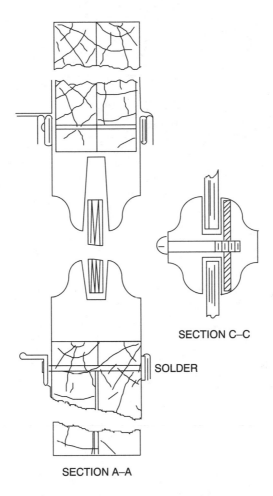

SECTION C–C

SOLDER

SECTION A–A

FIGURE 7-3-18—GLASS OPENING DETAILS

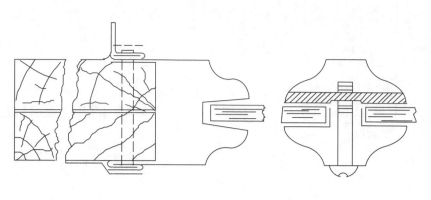

SECTION B–B

NOTE: For sash having more than one light in width.

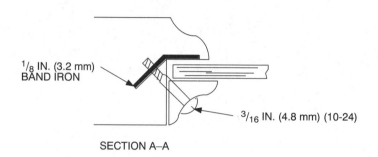

$^1/_8$ IN. (3.2 mm) BAND IRON

$^3/_{16}$ IN. (4.8 mm) (10-24)

SECTION A–A

NOTE: For sash having one light in width.

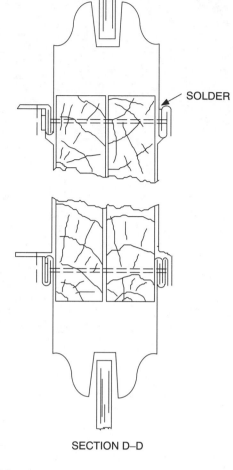

SOLDER

SECTION D–D

FIGURE 7-3-19—GLASS OPENING DETAILS

UNIFORM BUILDING CODE STANDARD 7-4
FIRE TESTS OF WINDOW ASSEMBLIES

Based on Standard Methods E 163-76 of the American Society for Testing and Materials.
Extracted, with permission, from the *Annual Book of ASTM Standards,* copyright American Society for Testing and Materials, 100 Barr Harbor Drive, West Conshohocken, PA 19428

See Sections 703.4, 713.5 and 713.9, *Uniform Building Code*

SECTION 7.401 — SCOPE

These methods of fire tests are applicable to window assemblies, including glass block and other light-transmitting assemblies, for use in wall openings to retard the passage of fire. Test methods in this standard are intended to evaluate the ability of a window or other light-transmitting assembly to remain in an opening during a predetermined test exposure of 45-minute duration.

Tests made in conformity with these test methods will register performance during the test exposure and develop data to determine the suitability of window assemblies for use in wall openings where fire protection is required. Such tests shall not be construed as determining suitability of window assemblies for continued use after fire exposure.

SECTION 7.402 — CONTROL OF FIRE TESTS

7.402.1 Time-temperature Curve. The fire exposure of window assemblies shall be controlled to conform to the standard time-temperature curve shown in Figure 7-1-1.

7.402.2 Furnace Temperatures. The temperatures of the test exposure shall be the average temperature obtained from the readings of not less than nine thermocouples symmetrically disposed and distributed to show the temperature near all parts of the test assembly. The thermocouples shall be protected by sealed porcelain tubes having $^3/_4$-inch (19.1 mm) outside diameter and $^1/_8$-inch (3.2 mm) wall thickness or, as an alternate, in the case of base metal thermocouples, protected by sealed $^1/_2$-inch (12.7 mm) wrought-steel or wrought-iron pipe of standard weight. The exposed length of the thermocouple protection tube in the furnace chamber shall not be less than 12 inches (304.8 mm). The junction of the thermocouples shall be 6 inches (152.4 mm) from the exposed face of the test assembly or from the masonry in which the assembly is installed during the entire test exposure.

The temperature shall be read at intervals not exceeding five minutes.

The furnace shall be controlled so that the maximum temperature at individual points shall not exceed 1,650°F* (899°C) and the area under the time-temperature curve, obtained by averaging the results from the temperature readings, is within 10 percent of the corresponding area under the standard time-temperature curve.

SECTION 7.403 — TEST ASSEMBLIES

7.403.1 Construction and Size. The design, construction, material, workmanship and hardware of the test window assembly shall be representative of that for which approval is desired. A record of materials and construction details adequate for identification shall be made.

The area of the test assembly shall not be less than 100 square feet (9.29 m²), with neither dimension less than 9 feet (2743 mm). If the conditions of use limit the construction to smaller dimensions, a proportionate reduction may be made in the dimensions of the test assembly for tests qualifying them for such restricted use.

7.403.2 Mounting. The test assembly shall be installed in the manner in which it is to be used. It shall be mounted so that the latches and fasteners other than hinges shall be on the unexposed side, and the mounting shall not prevent the free and easy operation of all openable components such as ventilators and sash.

SECTION 7.404 — CONDUCT OF TESTS: TIME OF TESTING

Masonry settings shall be allowed to season at least seven days, and reinforced concrete settings at least 28 days, before fire tests are made.

SECTION 7.405 — FIRE-ENDURANCE TEST

The pressure in the furnace shall be so managed that the upper two thirds of the test specimen is above the neutral pressure plane.

The test shall be continued for 45 minutes unless the conditions of acceptance specified in Section 7.407 are exceeded in a shorter period.

SECTION 7.406 — HOSE STREAM TEST

Immediately following the fire-endurance test and within one and one-half minutes, the fire exposed side of the test assembly shall be subjected to the impact, erosion and cooling effects of the hose stream.

The hose stream shall be delivered through a $2^1/_2$-inch (63.5 mm) hose discharging through a National Standard Playpipe of corresponding size equipped with a $1^1/_8$-inch (28.6 mm) discharge tip of the standard-taper, smooth-bore pattern without shoulder at the orifice.

The tip of the nozzle shall be located 20 feet (6.1 m) from and on a line normal to the center of the test assembly. If impossible to be so located, the nozzle may be on a line deviating not to exceed 30 degrees from the line normal to the center of the test assembly. When so located, the distance from the plane of the surface of the test assembly shall be less than 20 feet (6.1 m) by an amount equal to 1 foot (304.8 mm) for each 10 degrees of deviation from the normal.

The hose stream shall be directed around the periphery of the test assembly starting upward from a lower corner. When the circuit is about 1 foot (304.8 mm) from the starting point, the hose stream shall be applied in paths about 1 foot (304.8 mm) apart up and down the assembly across the entire width and then back and forth horizontally across the entire height.

The water pressure at the base of the nozzle shall be 30 psi (207 kPa) and the hose stream shall be applied $^6/_{10}$ second for each square foot (0.0929 m²) of area of the test assembly.

---

* In case the temperature at any point does exceed 1,650°F (899°C), the performance of the glass in that area shall be disregarded.

SECTION 7.407 — CONDITIONS OF ACCEPTANCE

7.407.1 Window Assemblies. A window assembly shall be considered as meeting the requirements for acceptable performance when it remains in the opening during the fire-endurance and hose stream tests within the following limitations:

1. The window assembly shall not be loosened from its fastenings.

2. Movement at the perimeter of openable components, from the initial closed position, shall not exceed the thickness of the frame member at any point.

3. At least 70 percent of the edges of each individual glass light shall remain in position through the hose stream test. The dislodging of small fragments from the central areas of individual lights shall be disregarded.

7.407.2 Glass Block Assemblies. A glass block assembly shall be considered as meeting the requirements for acceptable performance when it remains in the opening during the fire-endurance and hose stream tests within the following limitations:

1. The glass block assembly shall not be loosened from the frame.

2. At least 70 percent of the glass blocks shall not develop through openings.

UNIFORM BUILDING CODE STANDARD 7-5
FIRE TESTS OF THROUGH-PENETRATION FIRE STOPS

Based on Standard Method E 814-88 of the American Society for Testing and Materials.
Extracted, with permission, from the *Annual Book of ASTM Standards,* copyright American Society for Testing and Materials, 100 Barr Harbor Drive, West Conshohocken, PA 19428

See Section 714, *Uniform Building Code*

Part I—General

SECTION 7.501 — SCOPE

This method is applicable to penetration fire stops as defined in this code. Part I of this standard is applicable to both through-penetration and membrane-penetration fire stops. Part II contains additional criteria applicable to through-penetration fire stops.

In addition to evaluating the fire-resistive characteristics of penetration fire stops, this test method considers the resistance of penetration fire stops to an external force simulated by a hose stream. However, this method shall not be construed as determining the performance of the fire stop during actual fire conditions when subjected to forces such as failure of support systems and falling debris.

SECTION 7.502 — SIGNIFICANCE AND USE

This method is used to determine the performance of a penetration fire stop with respect to exposure to a standard temperature-time fire test and hose stream test. The performance of a penetration fire stop is dependent upon the specific assembly of materials tested, including the number, type and size of penetrations and the floors or walls in which it is installed.

SECTION 7.503 — DEFINITIONS

For the purpose of this standard, certain terms are defined as follows:

TEST ASSEMBLY is the wall or floor into which the test sample is mounted or installed.

TEST SAMPLE is the fire stop being tested.

SECTION 7.504 — CONTROL OF FIRE TESTS

7.504.1 Temperature-time Curve. The fire environment within the furnace shall be in accordance with the standard temperature-time curve shown in UBC Standard 7-1, Figure 7-1-1. The points on the curve that determine its character are set forth in Section 7.504.2.

7.504.2 Furnace Temperatures. The temperature fixed by the curve shall be the average temperature obtained from the readings of thermocouples symmetrically disposed and distributed within the test furnace to show the temperature near all parts of the assembly. Use a minimum of three thermocouples, with not fewer than five thermocouples per 100 square feet ($9.29 \ m^2$) of floor surface, and not fewer than nine thermocouples per 100 square feet ($9.29 \ m^2$) of wall specimen surface.

Enclose the thermocouples in sealed protection tubes of such materials and dimensions that the time constant of the protected thermocouple assembly lies within the range from 300 to 400 seconds. The exposed length of the pyrometer tube and thermocouple in the furnace chamber shall not be less than 12 inches (300 mm). Other types of protection tubes of pyrometers may be used, provided that temperature measurements obtained in

accordance with Figure 7-1-1 are within the limit of accuracy that applies for furnace temperature measurements.

For floors, place the junction of the thermocouples 12 inches (300 mm) away from the exposed face of the assembly. In the case of walls, place the thermocouples 6.0 inches (150 mm) away from the exposed face.

Read the temperature at intervals not exceeding five minutes during the first 120 minutes. Thereafter, the intervals may be increased to not more than 10 minutes.

The accuracy of the furnace control shall be such that the area under the temperature-time curve, obtained by averaging the results from the pyrometer or thermoelectric device readings, is within 10 percent of the corresponding area under the standard temperature-time curve shown in Figure 7-1-1 for fire tests of 60 minutes or less duration; within 7.5 percent for those over 60 minutes and not more than 120 minutes; and within 5 percent for tests exceeding 120 minutes in duration.

7.504.3 Unexposed Surface Temperatures. Measure temperatures on the unexposed surface of the test sample and assembly with thermocouples placed under flexible pads.

The pads shall be of suitable inorganic material and shall exhibit the following properties:

1. **Length and width:** 2.00 ± 0.04 inch (50 ± 1.02 mm).

2. **Thickness:** 0.04 ± 0.05 inch (10.2 ± 1.27 mm).

3. **Density:** 31.2 ± 0.6 pounds/cubic feet ($499.2 \pm 9.6 \ kg/m^3$).

4. **Thermal conductivity (k) at 150°F (65.6°C):** 0.380 ± 0.027 Btu × inches/hour × square feet °F [0.0548 ± 0.0039 W/(m·k)].

The pads shall be sufficiently soft so that, without breaking, they may be shaped to contact over the whole surface against which they are placed.

The pads shall be held firmly against the surface; they shall fit closely about the thermocouples. The thermocouple junction shall be located under the center of the pads. The thermocouple leads under the pads shall not be heavier than No. 18 B.&S. gage (0.040 inches) (1.02 mm) and shall be electrically insulated with heat-resistant, moisture-resistant coverings.

Read temperatures at intervals not exceeding 15 minutes until a reading exceeding 212°F (100°C) has been obtained at any one point. Thereafter, the readings may be taken more frequently, but the intervals need not be less than five minutes.

For specific locations of thermocouples, see Part II.

Additional temperature measurements may be made at the discretion of the testing agency to obtain representative information on the performance of the test sample.

7.504.4 Differential Pressure. Measure the pressure differential between the exposed and unexposed surfaces of the test assembly required in Section 7.507.2 at three points 0.78 inch (20 mm) from the surface and locate as follows:

1. **Walls**—At the center and quarter points on the vertical center line.

2. **Floors**—At the center and quarter points along the longitudinal center line.

The pressure-measuring probe tip shall be as shown in Figure 7-5-2, manufactured from stainless steel or other suitable material.

Measure the pressure by means of a manometer or equivalent transducer. The manometer or transducer shall be capable of reading 0.01-inch of water (2.5 Pa) increments.

SECTION 7.505 — TEST SAMPLE

The construction of the test sample shall be of sufficient size and include all conduits, pipes, cables (jacket types, sizes, conductor types, percent fills), required supports or other penetrating items so as to produce a representative penetration fire stop for which evaluation is desired. Penetration fire stops shall be installed and tested in each representative construction for which ratings are desired.

The periphery of the test sample shall not be closer than one and one-half times the thickness of the test assembly or a minimum of 12 inches (300 mm) to the furnace edge, whichever is greater.

The distance between test sample periphery and furnace edge may be reduced if the testing agency demonstrates and reports that the edge effects do not affect the results.

SECTION 7.506 — PROTECTING AND CONDITIONING

Prior to fire test, condition the floor or wall assembly and test samples to provide, within a reasonable time, a moisture condition approximately representative of that likely to exist in similar construction in buildings. This moisture condition is considered as that which would be established at equilibrium resulting from drying in an ambient atmosphere of 50 percent relative humidity at 73°F (23°C). However, with some assemblies and test samples it may be difficult or impossible to achieve the equilibrium moisture condition within a reasonable period of time. Therefore, floor or wall assemblies and test samples may be tested when their dampest portion has achieved a moisture content corresponding to drying to equilibrium with air in the range from 50 to 75 percent relative humidity at 73°F ± 5°F (23°C ± 3°C). If the assembly or test sample dried in a heated building fails to meet these requirements after a 12-month conditioning period, or if the nature of the construction is such that drying of the assembly or test sample interior will be prevented by hermetic sealing, these requirements may be waived, except as to attainment of the required strength as described in Section 7.507.1, and the assembly or test sample may be tested in the condition in which it then exists.

Protect the testing equipment, sample and assembly undergoing the fire test from any condition of wind or weather that might lead to abnormal results. The ambient air temperature at the beginning of the test shall be within the range from 50°F to 90°F (10°C to 32°C). The velocity of air across the unexposed surface measured just before the test begins shall not exceed 4.4 feet/seconds (1.3 m/s) as determined by an anomometer placed at right angles to the unexposed surface. If mechanical ventilation is employed during the test, an airstream shall not be directed across the surface of the sample.

SECTION 7.507 — CONDUCT OF TESTS

7.507.1 Time of Testing. The test sample shall not be tested until the test assembly has developed sufficient strength to retain the test sample securely in position.

7.507.2 Fire Test. After the first 10 minutes, the test sample shall be subject to a minimum positive pressure differential of 0.01 inch of water (2.5 Pa).

Continue the test until the desired evaluation period is reached or until the rating criteria are satisfied.

7.507.3 Hose Stream Test. Subject a duplicate test sample to a fire exposure test for a period equal to one half of that indicated as the resistance period in the fire test, but not more than 60 minutes, immediately after which subject the sample to the impact, erosion and cooling effects of a hose stream as described in Table 7-5-A directed first at the middle and then at all parts of the exposed face, with changes in direction being made slowly.

The test sponsor may elect, with the advice and consent of the testing body, to have a hose stream test made on the sample subjected to the fire test immediately following the fire test.

The stream shall be delivered through a 2$^1/_2$-inch (63.5 mm) hose and discharged through a National Standard Playpipe of corresponding size equipped with a 1$^1/_8$-inch (28.6 mm) discharge tip of the standard-taper, smooth-bore pattern without a shoulder at the orifice. The water pressure shall be 30 psi ± 2 psi as (207 kPa ± 13.8 kPa) measured at the base of the nozzle.

The nozzle orifice shall be 20 feet (6096 mm) from the center of the exposed surface of the test sample if the nozzle is so located that when directed at the center its axis is normal to the surface of the test sample. If otherwise located, its distance from the center shall be less than 20 feet (6096 mm) by an amount equal to 1 foot (300 mm) for each 10 degrees of deviation from the normal.

SECTION 7.508 — REPORT

Results expressed as F and T ratings, as appropriate, shall be reported in accordance with the performance in the tests prescribed in this method. They shall be expressed in hours and minutes to the nearest integral minute. Reports shall include the following:

1. The assembly, materials and penetrating items of the tested penetration fire stop, clearly identified and described. Drawings depicting geometry, exact size (length, width, thickness) and location of penetration fire stops within the test assembly.

2. The relative humidities of the test assembly and test sample materials, if applicable.

3. The furnace and the unexposed side temperatures for the duration of the standard fire test.

4. The measurement of differential pressure between the exposed and unexposed test assembly surface during the fire test.

5. Observations of significant details of the behavior of the test sample during the test and after the furnace fire is extinguished. These shall include cracks, deformation, flaming and smoke issuance. Also, these include continued burning within the test sample after termination of the fire test.

When the indicated, penetration fire-stop rating period is 60 minutes or over, a correction shall be applied for variation of the furnace exposure from that prescribed, where it will affect the rating, by multiplying the indicated period by two thirds of the difference in area between the curve of average furnace temperature and the standard curve for the first three fourths of the period, and dividing the product by the area between the standard curve above a base line of 68°F (20°C) for the same part of the indicated period, the latter areas increased by 54°F × hours (30°C × hours) [3,240°F × minutes (1800°C × minutes)], to compensate for the thermal lag of the furnace thermocouples during the first part of the test. For higher-than-standard fire exposure in the test, the indicated rating period shall be increased by the amount of the correction and similarly decreased for fire exposure below surface. The correction can be expressed as follows:

$$C = \frac{2I(A - A_s)}{3(A_s + L)}$$

WHERE:

A = area under the curve of indicated average furnace temperature for the first three fourths of the indicated period.

A_s = area under the standard furnace curve for the same part of the indicated period.

C = correction in the same units as I.

I = indicated fire-resistance period.

L = lag correction in the same units as A and A_s [54°F × hours (30°C × hours); 3,240°F × minutes (1800°C × minutes)].

Part II—Through-penetration Fire Stops

SECTION 7.509 — SCOPE

This part of this standard contains specific criteria for testing and rating through-penetration fire stops.

Two ratings are established for each through-penetration fire stop. An F rating is based on flame occurrence on the unexposed surface, while the T rating is based on the temperature rise on the unexposed side of the through-penetration fire stop.

SECTION 7.510 — UNEXPOSED SURFACE AND PENETRATION TEMPERATURES

Measurements shall be made at the locations on the unexposed surface of the test sample and floor or wall assembly as shown in Figure 7-5-1 and as described in the following:

Measure temperatures of each type and size of penetrating item with at least one thermocouple located 1 inch (25.4 mm) from the unexposed surface of the test sample. Where a thermal protection assembly is used to wrap around the penetrating items on the unexposed side, an additional thermocouple shall be located on the penetrating items 1 inch (25.4 mm) from the end of the thermal-protection assembly. The thermocouple lead shall be held firmly against the penetrating item. The thermocouple leads shall not be heavier than No. 22 B.&S. gage (0.0253 inches) (300 mm) and shall be electrically insulated with heat-resistant and moisture-resistant coverings. The pads as described in Part I shall be held firmly against the penetrating item and shall fit closely about the thermocouples.

SECTION 7.511 — INSTALLATION OF PENETRATING ITEMS

Penetrating items shall be installed so that they extend a minimum of 12 inches (300 mm) on the exposed side and a minimum of 36 inches (900 mm) on the unexposed side. The extended portion of the penetrating items on the unexposed side shall be supported in the same manner as methods employed in field installation. When the end use of the penetrating items precludes the minimum projections specified, the penetrating items shall be installed in the end-use configuration.

Individual ends of the penetrating items shall be covered and sealed by suitable means on the exposed side to prevent excessive transfer of gases through the test sample. When the penetrating item is intended to be representative of a closed system that is not normally vented or open to the atmosphere, the penetrating item may also be capped or sealed on the unexposed side. Otherwise, the penetrating items shall not be capped or sealed on the unexposed side.

SECTION 7.512 — RATING CRITERIA

7.512.1 F Rating. A through-penetration fire stop shall be considered as meeting the requirements for an F rating when it remains in the test assembly during the fire test and hose stream test within the following limitations:

1. The through-penetration fire stop shall have withstood the fire test for the rating period without permitting the passage of flame through openings or the occurrence of flaming on any element of the unexposed side of the test sample.

2. During the hose stream test, the test sample shall not develop any opening that would permit a projection of water from the stream beyond the unexposed side.

7.512.2 T Rating. A through-penetration fire stop shall be considered as meeting the requirements for a T rating when it remains in the test assembly during the fire test and hose stream test so as to meet the requirements for an F rating and it performs within the following limitations:

1. The transmission of heat through the test sample during the rating period shall not have been such as to raise the temperature of any thermocouple on the unexposed surface of the test sample or any penetrating item more than 325°F (181°C) above its initial temperature.

SECTION 7.513 — REPORT

In addition to the information required in Section 7.508, the following shall be included in the report:

1. The F and T ratings for each through-penetration fire stop in the time period of resistance.

TABLE 7-5-A—HOSE STREAM TEST PRESSURE AND DURATION

RESISTANCE PERIOD	DURATION OF APPLICATION (seconds per square foot of exposed area[1])
	× 10.76 for sec./m²
120 minutes and over	1.5
90 minutes and over if less than 120 minutes	0.9
Less than 90 minutes	0.6

[1]The exposed area shall be calculated using the area of the wall or floor assembly in which the penetration fire stop is mounted.

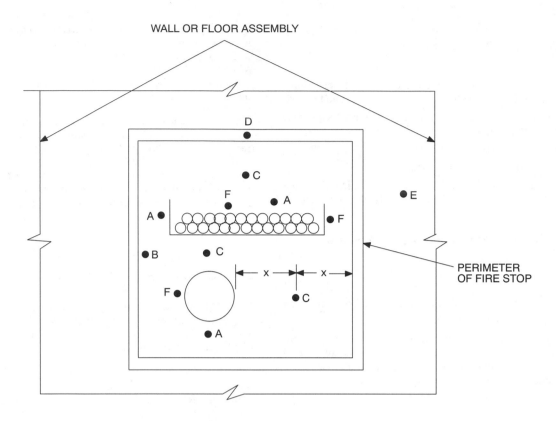

FLOOR ASSEMBLY—PLAN
WALL ASSEMBLY—ELEVATION

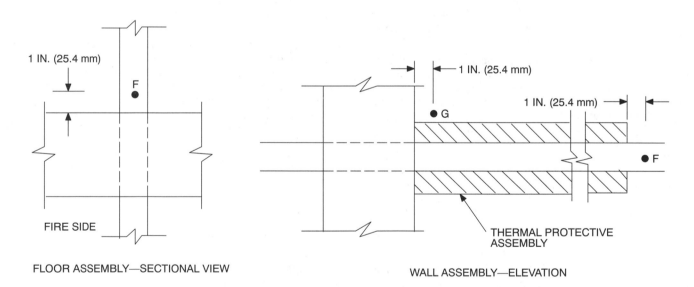

FLOOR ASSEMBLY—SECTIONAL VIEW

WALL ASSEMBLY—ELEVATION

FIGURE 7-5-1—TEMPERATURE MEASUREMENT LOCATIONS

LEGEND:

A—At a point on the surface of the fire stop 1 inch (25.4 mm) from one through-penetrating item for each type of penetrating item employed in the field of the fire stop. If the grouping of penetrating items through the test sample prohibits placement of the thermocouple pad, the thermocouple shall not be required.

B—At a point on the fire stop surface at the periphery of the fire stop.

C—At a minimum of three points on the fire stop surface approximately equidistant from a penetrating item or group of penetrating items in the field of the fire stop and the periphery.

D—At one point on any frame that is installed about the perimeter of the opening.

E—At one point on the unexposed surface of the wall or floor that is not less than 12 inches (300 mm) from any opening.

F—At one point on each type of through-penetrating item, 1 inch (25.4 mm) beyond test sample or thermal protective assembly.

G—At one point on the surface of thermal protective assembly, 1 inch (25.4 mm) beyond test sample.

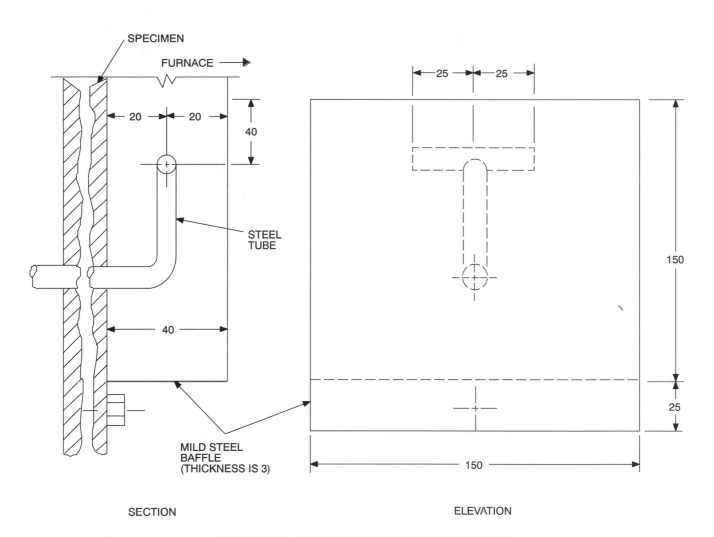

SECTION

ELEVATION

**FIGURE 7-5-2—STATIC PRESSURE-MEASURING DEVICE
DIMENSIONS IN MILLIMETERS**

UNIFORM BUILDING CODE STANDARD 7-6
THICKNESS, DENSITY DETERMINATION AND COHESION/ADHESION FOR SPRAY-APPLIED FIRE-RESISTIVE MATERIAL

Test Standard of the International Conference of Building Officials

See Sections 703.4, 704.6 and 1701.4, *Uniform Building Code*

SECTION 7.601 — SCOPE

These methods cover procedures for obtaining the thickness, density and cohesion/adhesion for sprayed fibrous and cementitious fire-resistive materials. In addition, provisions for field inspection procedures by a special inspector employed by an approved agency on a random basis are included.

SECTION 7.602 — APPLICATIONS

These test methods require that the application of the field-applied, sprayed, fire-resistive material be in accordance with the manufacturer's published instructions. The apparatus, materials and procedure used to apply the fire-resistive material shall be the same as the procedure used to prepare the test specimens which were subjected to the fire tests set forth in UBC Standard 7-1.

SECTION 7.603 — TEST METHODS FOR THICKNESS

7.603.1 General. The following tests, based on samplings as described in this standard, shall be conducted by a special inspector employed by an approved agency.

7.603.2 Substrate Condition. The condition of the substrate on each floor shall be inspected prior to application of the spray-applied fire-resistive material. The substrate shall be prepared in accordance with the manufacturer's instructions and shall be free of dirt, grease, oil, loose scale, loose paint or primer and other materials which may prevent adequate adhesion.

7.603.3 Thickness Measurement and Acceptance Criteria. The thickness of the spray-applied fire-resistive material shall be measured by either of the following methods:

1. A steel rule graduated in at least $1/16$-inch (1.6 mm) increments, a depth gage consisting of a movable needle or pin and a disc perpendicular to the needle as shown in Figure 7-6-1.

The pin shall be of sufficient length to penetrate the material to be measured. The disc shall be perpendicular to the needle at all times and shall have a friction device to grip the pin unless purposely moved. The disc shall have a diameter of $1^1/8$ inches (28.6 mm) to permit complete contact with the surface of the specimen to be measured. In materials not readily penetrated by the depth gage, other suitable approved measuring devices may be used.

The thickness shall be determined by inserting the penetrating pin of the depth gage perpendicular to and through the sprayed fire-resistive material to the substrate. When the point of the pin touches the substrate, the disc shall be moved against the fire-resistive material with sufficient force on the disc to register the average plane of the surface. The gage shall be withdrawn to read the thickness in $1/16$-inch (1.6 mm) increments as shown by the position of the sliding clip indicator. The acceptance of measurements with a minus tolerance greater than $1/4$ inch (6.4 mm) shall not be permitted. If design thickness is less than 1 inch (25.4 mm), no more than 25 percent less thickness shall be permitted. Measurements greater than $1/4$ inch (6.4 mm) for thickness over 1 inch (25.4 mm), or 25 percent for thickness less than 1 inch (25.4 mm) above the required thickness, shall not be used to determine the thickness average.

2. As an alternate to the method described above, the thickness of the spray-applied fire-resistive material may be measured by a fixed probe with a $1^1/8$-inch-diameter (28.6 mm) disc set to the required thickness. If any measurement is less than that required, the thickness shall be increased or measurement shall be taken as required in Method 1.

Where thickness is less than that required, the condition shall be corrected. The location of any uncorrected areas shall be reported to the building official.

7.603.4 Thickness Determination for Structural Frame Members. Twenty-five percent of the structural frame, columns and beams as defined in Section 601.4 of this code in each story shall be inspected for thickness determination. Five measurements at a single cross section shall be made and averaged on structural frame beams, and six measurements shall be made and averaged at a single cross section on columns as shown in Figure 7-6-2.

Where open flutes or valley of steel deck sections occur over beams, they shall be filled solid unless the flutes were unfilled in the fire-tested assembly.

7.603.5 Thickness Determination for Beams Other than Structural Frame. Ten percent of beams (other than structural frame members) on each floor shall be selected at random and shall be measured for thickness as required for structural frame members in Section 7.603.4.

7.603.6 Thickness Determination for Floor Sections. Ten floor thickness measurements for each prescribed thickness shall be made on a random basis for each 10,000 square feet (929 m^2). At each area selected, a rectangle having an area of 144 square inches (0.0929 m^2) and a minimum width of 6 inches (152.4 mm) where possible shall be laid out, and a thickness measurement shall be taken at the center and at each corner. The five measurements shall be averaged and shall be reported as a single measurement of the area. The average thickness as determined by Section 7.603.3, Item 1, shall not be less than that specified. If the method for thickness determination as described in Section 7.603.3, Item 2 is used, the thickness at any location shall not be less than the required thickness.

SECTION 7.604 — TEST METHODS FOR DENSITY

7.604.1 General. The test to determine the density of spray-applied fire-resistive material shall be conducted by a special inspector employed by an approved agency.

7.604.2 Density Sample Groups. There shall be density test specimens taken from a column, a beam and a deck for each 10,000 square feet (929 m^2) of floor area or fraction thereof, or from each floor if the floor area is smaller than 10,000 square feet (929 m^2).

7.604.3 Density Determination. The density of each sample shall be determined as follows:

1. Utilizing a rectangular template as described in Section 7.603.6, a known area of the test sample shall be marked off.

2. Utilizing the procedure described in Section 7.603.6 and Section 7.603.3, Method 1, at least five thickness measurements

shall be taken. One measurement shall be taken at the center of the specimen and one at each of the four corners approximately $1^1/_2$ (38 mm^2) inches from adjacent sides. The thickness measurement shall be determined prior to removing the sample, and the average of these five measurements shall be considered as the thickness of the specimen.

3. The specimen shall be cut along the perimeter of the template. All of the in-place material shall be carefully removed from the substrate and dried at 120°F (49°C) at a relative humidity of not less than 50 percent until a constant weight is obtained. The constant weight of the dried material shall be measured.

4. The density shall be calculated in accordance with the following formula:

Density in pounds per cubic foot:

$$\frac{W \times 1,728}{l \times w \times t}$$

For **SI:** (Density in kilograms per cubic meter)

$$\frac{W \times (10^9)}{l \times w \times t}$$

WHERE:

l = length of the specimen, inches (mm).

t = thickness of the specimen, inches (mm).

W = weight of the dried material, pounds (kg).

w = width of the specimen, inches (mm).

7.604.4 Alternative Density Displacement Method.

1. This is an alternative method for determining the in-place density of specimens with irregular surfaces or dimensions or for specimens that are difficult to remove from the substrate.

2. The minimum sample size recommended is 131 cm^3 (8 in.^{3}).

3. The sample shall be cut to a uniform size, removing all uneven edges.

4. Cure the specimen in accordance with Section 7.604.3.3.

5. Determine weight.

6. Use the following apparatus to determine volume:

   6.1 Unexpanded polystyrene beads, 500 mL—Designation C bead with a nominal diameter of 1.0 mm (0.04 in.) (preferred) or lead shot-size No. 8 (alternate).

   6.2 Graduated cylinders, two 250 cm^3 (15 in.^{3}).

   6.3 Funnel—Polypropylene funnel having a top diameter of 150 mm (6 in.) and a bottom diameter of 28 mm (1.1 in.).

   6.4 Beaker, 400 mL smooth wall type.

   6.5 Screed, minimum 150 mm (6 in.) long rigid straight edge.

   6.6 Pan—Two flat pans minimum 150 mm (6 in.) diameter with minimum 150 mm (6 in.) high rim.

7. Determine volume as follows:

   7.1 Place the empty 400 mL beaker in the center of the flat pan and pour the unexpanded polystyrene beads or shot through the funnel until the excess beads (shot) fall over the rim of the beaker.

   7.2 Hold the screed perpendicular to the rim or the beaker. Begin at the edge opposite the spout and screed off the excess beads (shot). Only one pass is needed.

   7.3 Discard the overflow that collects in the pan.

   7.4 Pour all the beads (shot) remaining in the beaker into the graduated cylinders.

   7.5 Return the empty beaker into the center of the pan and pour about 100 mL of beads (shot) poured from the graduated cylinder(s) into the beaker. Do not shake the beaker in any way.

   7.6 Place the sample to be tested in the center of the beaker, making sure no edge touches the side of the glass. Gently twist the sample if required.

   7.7 Pour the remainder of the beads from the graduated cylinders over the sample, letting the excess beads (shot) flow over the top of the beaker into the pan. Do not leave any beads (shot) in the graduated cylinders.

   7.8 Screed the excess beads (shot) off the top of the beaker (8.3.7.a) and remove the beaker from the pan.

   7.9 Using the funnel, pour the beads (shot) collected in the pan into the empty graduated cylinder and read the volume displaced by the sample. Do not tap or shake the graduated cylinder when reading.

8. Calculate density as follows:

$$D = W \times 62.43/V$$

For **SI:** 1 pcf = 16.0 kg/m^3.

WHERE:

D = density in pounds per cubic foot (kg/m^3).

V = volume of sample dried in cm^3 (equal to the volume of beads displaced by the sample).

W = constant weight of dried material, g.

7.604.5 Density Acceptance Criteria. No sample shall have a density less than 5 percent below the specified density. Where the density is less than the 5 percent tolerance allowed above, the work shall be corrected to the satisfaction of the building official.

SECTION 7.605 — TEST METHOD FOR COHESION/ADHESION

7.605.1 General. The test to determine the cohesion/adhesion of spray-applied fire-resistive material shall be conducted by an approved agency.

7.605.2 Adhesive/Cohesive Samples. There shall not be less than one cohesion/adhesion test taken from a column, a beam and a deck for each 10,000 square feet (929 m^2) of floor area or fraction thereof, or from each floor if the floor is smaller than 10,000 square feet (929 m^2).

7.605.3 Adhesive/Cohesive Determination.

1. Use the following equipment:

   1.1 Bottle screw cap, metal or rigid plastic 51 mm to 83 mm (2 inches to $3^1/_4$ inches) in diameter and 12 mm ($^1/_2$ inch) in nominal depth. A hook shall be attached at the center. Where deck profile does not allow the use of an 83 mm ($3^1/_4$ inch) diameter cap, a smaller cap shall be used.

   1.2 Adhesive, single or two component, suitable for adhering cap to the spray-applied fire-resistive material.

   1.3 Weighing scale, spring-type (fish hook), with a capacity suitable for the spray-applied fire-resistive material being tested [typically 12 kg to 30 kg (26 to 66 pounds) capacity]. The accuracy shall be within 0.1 kg ($^1/_4$ pound).

2. The test specimen shall be the in-place spray-applied fire-resistive material as applied to any field condition surface. Where

a 300-by-300 mm (12 by 12 inch) area is not available, such as on beams and fluted deck, use the width of the beam or the width of a flute by 300 mm (12 inch) length. The area shall be at least 100 by 300 mm (4 by 12 inches). See Item 1.1 for exceptions.

3. Condition the specimen at atmospheric conditions or in accordance with the manufacturer's recommendations for a period sufficient to be considered dry.

4. Apply adhesive sufficient to fill the metal or plastic cap, and immediately place the cap against the surface of the spray-applied fire-resistive material.

5. Support the cap at the surface until the adhesive has adequately cured. Wipe away any excess adhesive around the cap before it cures or carefully cut it away after it cures.

6. Engage the scale with the hook and exert an increasing force at a minimum uniform or incremental rate of approximately 5 kg (11 pounds)/minutes perpendicular to the surface.

7. Force shall be applied until failure occurs, a predetermined value is reached, or until the capacity of the scale is reached.

8. Record the force in newtons or points-force at the time failure occurs or other end point is reached.

9. A field test may be performed by replacing the scale (Item 1.3) with a fixed weight sufficient to exert the minimum force specified in Section 7.605.4. The weight must be supported for a minimum one minute duration.

10. Calculate the cohesive/adhesive force (bond strength) as follows:

$$CA = F/A$$

WHERE:

A = area of the cap, m^2 (ft.^{2}).

CA = cohesive/adhesive force, Pa (lbs./ft.^{2}).

F = recorded force, N (lbs.).

7.605.4 Cohesive/Adhesive Acceptance Criteria. No sample shall have a cohesive/adhesive force of less than 150 pounds per square foot (7.18 kN/m^2). Where the cohesive/adhesive force is less than 150 pounds per square foot (7.18 kN/m^2), the work shall be corrected to the satisfaction of the building official.

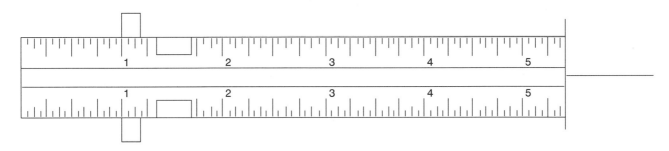

FIGURE 7-6-1—THICKNESS GAGE

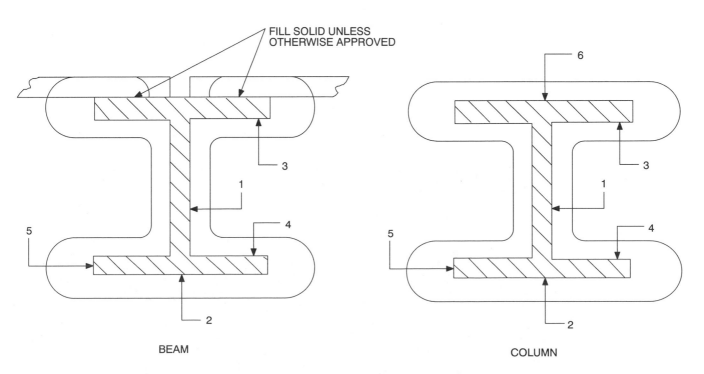

BEAM

COLUMN

FIGURE 7-6-2—THICKNESS MEASUREMENT LOCATIONS

UNIFORM BUILDING CODE STANDARD 7-7

METHODS FOR CALCULATING FIRE RESISTANCE OF STEEL, CONCRETE, WOOD, CONCRETE MASONRY AND CLAY MASONRY CONSTRUCTION

Standard of the International Conference of Building Officials

Part I—Method for Calculating the Fire Resistance of Steel Construction

See Sections 703.3 and 703.4, *Uniform Building Code*

SECTION 7.701 — SCOPE

This part of this standard contains procedures by which the fire resistance of steel columns, beams, girders and trusses protected by specific materials or combinations of materials can be established by calculations. These procedures apply to the material contained in this part only.

SECTION 7.702 — DEFINITION

CERAMIC FIBER BLANKET is a mineral wool insulation material made of alumina-silica fibers and weighing 4 to 10 pounds per cubic foot (64 to 160 kg/m^3).

SECTION 7.703 — STRUCTURAL STEEL COLUMN PROTECTION

7.703.1 Procedures. These procedures establish a basis for determining the fire resistance of column assemblies as a function of the thickness of fire-resistive material, the weight (W) or cross-sectional area (A) of steel columns and the heated perimeter (D or P) of steel columns. As used in these sections, W is the average weight of a structural steel column in pounds per linear foot (kg/m) and A is the cross-sectional area of a structural steel column in square inches (mm^2). The heated perimeter (D) is the inside perimeter of the fire-resistive material in inches (mm) as illustrated in Figure 7-7-S-1.

Application of these procedures shall be limited to column assemblies in which the fire-resistive material is not designed to carry any of the load acting on the column. In the absence of substantiating fire-endurance test results, ducts, conduit, piping and similar mechanical, electrical and plumbing installations shall not be embedded in any required fire-resistive materials of assemblies designed in accordance with this standard. Table 7-7-S-A1 contains weight-to-heated-perimeter ratios (W/D) for both contour and box fire-protection profiles for the wide-flange shapes most often used as columns. For different fire-resistive design profiles or column cross sections, the weight-to-heated-perimeter ratios (W/D) and cross-sectional-area-to-heated-perimeter ratios (A/P) shall be determined in accordance with the definitions given in this section.

7.703.2 Gypsum Wallboard (Wide-flange, Pipe and Tubular Columns). The fire resistance of structural steel columns with weight-to-heated-perimeter ratios (W/D) less than or equal to 3.65 (0.215) and which are protected with Type X gypsum wallboard may be determined from the following expression:

$$R = 130 \left[\frac{h(W'/D)}{2} \right]^{0.75}$$

For **SI:**
$$R = 96 \left[\frac{h(W'/D)}{2} \right]^{0.75}$$

WHERE:

D = heated perimeter of the structural steel column, inches (mm).

h = total thickness of gypsum wallboard, inches (mm).

R = fire resistance (minutes).

W' = total weight of the structural steel column and gypsum wallboard protection, pounds per linear foot (kg/m).

$$= W + \frac{50\,h\,D}{144}$$

For **SI:** = $W + 0.0008\,hD$

The gypsum wallboard shall be supported and fastened as illustrated in either Figure 7-7-S-2 for fire-resistance ratings of four hours or less, or Figure 7-7-S-3 for fire-resistance ratings of three hours or less. The fire resistance of structural steel columns can be determined from Figure 7-7-S-4 for various thicknesses of gypsum wallboard as a function of the weight-to-heated-perimeter ratio (W/D) of the column. For structural steel columns with weight-to-heated- perimeter ratios (W/D) greater than 3.65 (0.215), the thickness of gypsum wallboard required for specified fire-resistance ratings shall be the same as the thickness determined for a W14 × 233-wide (W 360 × 347) flange shape.

7.703.3 Spray-applied Fire-resistive Materials (Wide-flange Columns). The fire resistance of wide-flange structural steel columns protected with spray-applied fire-resistive materials, as illustrated in Figure 7-7-S-5, may be determined from the following expression:

$$R = \left(C_1 \frac{W}{D} + C_2 \right) h$$

WHERE:

C_1 and

C_2 = material-dependent constants.

D = heated perimeter of the structural steel column, inches (mm).

h = thickness of spray-applied fire-resistive material, inches (mm).

R = fire resistance, minutes.

W = average weight of steel column, pounds per linear foot (kg/m).

The material-dependent constants, C_1 and C_2, shall be determined for specific spray-applied fire-resistive materials on the basis of standard fire-endurance tests in accordance with Section 703.2. These constants shall be determined from results of at least four fire-endurance tests in accordance with requirements set forth in UBC Standard 7-1. At least two tests shall be conducted on the largest and two on the smallest columns which establish the limits of applicability to the resulting equation. Test data shall be evaluated with respect to the assumption that the ratio of fire endurance to fire-resistive material thickness (R/h) is reasonably constant for a given column shape (W/D ratio). The tests conducted on columns of the same shape shall be designed so that the resulting fire-endurance times are approximately one and one-half hours and three and one-half hours. In evaluating the R/h ratios resulting from tests on the same column shape, differences in the range of 10 percent are typical. Differences greater than 20 percent may, however, suggest that the equation is not applicable to the specific fire-resistive material under consideration and further examination of the test data is warranted.

Unless evidence is submitted to the building official substantiating a broader application, this expression shall be limited to determining the fire resistance of structural steel columns with weight-to-heated-perimeter ratios (*W/D*) between the largest and smallest columns for which standard fire-endurance test results are available.

7.703.4 Spray-applied Fire-resistive Materials (Pipe and Tubular Columns). The fire resistance of pipe and tubular steel columns protected with spray-applied fire-resistive materials may be determined from the following expressions:

$$R = C_3 (A/P) h + C_4$$

WHERE:

A = cross-sectional area of the structural steel column, square inches (mm^2).

C_3 and
C_4 = material-dependent constants.

h = thickness of spray-applied fire-resistive material, inches (mm).

P = heated perimeter of the structural steel column, inches (mm).

R = fire resistance, hours.

The material-dependent constants (C_3 and C_4) shall be determined for specific spray-applied fire-resistive materials on the basis of standard fire-resistance tests in accordance with Section 703.2. These constants shall be determined from the results of at least four fire-endurance tests in accordance with requirements set forth in UBC Standard 7-1. At least two tests shall be conducted on each of two different column sizes as follows:

1. For the smaller of the two columns, one of the test specimens shall be protected so as to develop the minimum desired fire-resistance rating, and the second specimen shall be protected with the maximum intended thickness of fire-resistive material.

2. For the larger of the two columns, one of the test specimens shall be protected with the minimum intended thickness of fire-resistive material, and the second specimen shall be protected so as to develop the maximum desired fire-resistance rating.

These four tests shall establish limits governing the use of the resulting equation. These limits shall define the minimum and maximum permitted thicknesses of the fire-resistive material and the minimum and maximum fire-resistance ratings. Additional tests may be conducted to modify any of these four limits and these additional tests may involve different column sizes. The material-dependent constants shall be determined based on all applicable test data using a linear, least-squares curve-fitting technique or similar statistical analysis.

Unless evidence is submitted to the building official substantiating a broader application, this expression shall be limited to determining the fire resistance of structural steel columns with cross-sectional-area-to-heated-perimeter ratios (*A/P*) between the largest and smallest columns for which standard fire-endurance test results are available.

Table 7-7-S-A2 contains area-to-heated-perimeter ratios (*A/P*) for circular, square and rectangular tubes most often used as columns.

7.703.5 Concrete. The fire-resistance rating of structural steel columns protected with concrete, as illustrated in Figure 7-7-S-6, may be determined from the following expression:

$$R = R_o (1 + 0.03m)$$

$$R_o = 10\left(\frac{W}{D}\right)^{0.7} + 17\,\frac{h^{1.6}}{k_c^{\,0.2}}\left[1 + 26\left(\frac{H}{\rho_c\,c_c h(L + h)}\right)^{0.8}\right]$$

For **SI:** $R_o = 73\left(\frac{W}{D}\right)^{0.7} +$

$$0.16\,\frac{h^{1.6}}{k_c^{\,0.2}}\left[1 + 30984\left(\frac{H}{\rho_c\,c_c h(L + h)}\right)^{0.8}\right]$$

WHERE:

c_c = ambient temperature specific heat of concrete, Btu/lb.°F (KJ/kg·K).

D = heated perimeter of the steel column, inches (mm).

H = ambient temperature thermal capacity of the steel column.

   = 0.11W, Btu/ft.°F [0.46W(kJ/m·k)].

h = thickness of the cover for concrete, inches (mm).

k_c = ambient temperature thermal conductivity of the concrete, Btu/hr. ft.°F (W/m·K).

L = interior dimension of one side of a square concrete, inches (mm).

m = equilibrium moisture content of the concrete by volume, percentage.

R = fire endurance at equilibrium moisture conditions, minutes.

R_o = fire endurance at zero moisture content, minutes.

W = average weight of the steel column, pounds per linear foot (kg/m).

ρ_c = concrete density, pounds per cubic foot (kg/m^3).

For wide-flange steel columns completely encased in concrete with all reentrant spaces filled (Figure 7-7-S-6, Detail C), the thermal capacity of the concrete with the reentrant spaces may be added to the thermal capacity of the steel column, and the total thermal capacity may be determined by the expression:

$$H = 0.11W + \frac{\rho_c\,c_c\,(b_f d - A_s)}{144}$$

For **SI:** $\qquad H = 0.46W + \dfrac{\rho_c\,c_c\,(b_f d - A_s)}{1,000,000}$

WHERE:

A_s = cross-sectional area of the steel column, square inches (mm^2).

b_f = flange width of the steel column, inches (mm).

d = depth of the steel column, inches (mm).

If specific data on the properties of concrete or concrete masonry are not available, the values given in Table 7-7-S-B may be used.

For structural steel columns encased in concrete with all reentrant spaces filled (Figure 7-7-S-6, Detail C), Tables 7-7-S-C and 7-7-S-D give the thickness of concrete cover required for various fire-resistance ratings for typical wide-flange sections. The thicknesses of concrete given in these tables also apply to structural steel columns larger than those listed.

For structural steel columns protected with precast concrete column covers (Figure 7-7-S-6, Detail A), Tables 7-7-S-E and 7-7-S-F give the thickness of the column covers required for various fire-resistance ratings for typical wide-flange shapes. The thicknesses of concrete given in these tables also apply to structural steel columns larger than those listed.

For structural steel columns protected with concrete masonry (Figure 7-7-S-7), Tables 7-7-S-G and 7-7-S-H give the equivalent thickness of concrete masonry required for various fire-resistance ratings for typical wide-flange shapes. The equivalent thicknesses given in these tables also apply to structural steel columns larger than those listed.

Head and bed joints shall be fully mortared. Design and anchorage of concrete masonry shall be in accordance with Chapter 21. The thickness of column units (Figure 7-7-S-7) shall not be less than $1^1/_2$ inches (38 mm). The nominal thickness of hollow or solid units (Figure 7-7-S-7) shall not be less than 4 inches (102 mm).

7.703.6 Concrete Masonry. The fire-resistance rating of structural steel columns protected with concrete masonry, as illustrated in Figure 7-7-S-7, may be determined in accordance with the following expression:

$$R = 0.401(A_s/p_s)^{0.7} + 0.285(T_{ea}^{1.6}/K^{0.2}) \times$$
$$[1.0 + 42.7\{(A_s/DT_{ea})/(0.25p + T_{ea})\}^{0.8}]$$

For SI:

$$R = 0.042(A_s/p_s)^{0.7} + 0.0018(T_{ea}^{1.6}/K^{0.2}) \times$$
$$[1.0 + 384\{(A_s/DT_{ea})/(0.25p + T_{ea})\}^{0.8}]$$

WHERE:

A_s = cross-sectional area of the steel column, square inches (mm^2).

D = density of the concrete masonry protection, pounds per cubic foot (kg/m^3).

K = ambient thermal conductivity of concrete masonry. See Table 7-7-S-J, Btu/hr.ft.°F (W/m·k).

p = inner perimeter of concrete masonry protection, inches (mm).

p_s = heated perimeter of steel column, inches (mm).

R = fire-resistance rating of the column assembly, hours.

T_{ea} = equivalent thickness of concrete masonry protection assembly, inches (mm).

SECTION 7.704 — PROTECTED STEEL BEAMS, GIRDERS AND TRUSSES

7.704.1 Beams and Girders.

7.704.1.1 General. These procedures establish a basis for determining the fire resistance of structural beams and girders which differ in size from that specified in approved fire-resistant assemblies as a function of the thickness of fire-resistive material and the weight W and heated perimeter D of the beam or girder. The use of the methodology in this section is limited to unrestrained conditions. As used in these sections, W is the average weight of a structural steel member in pounds per linear foot (kg/m). The heated perimeter D is the inside perimeter of the fire-resistive material in

inches (mm) as illustrated in Figure 7-7-S-8. The weight-to-heated-perimeter ratios (W/D) for both contour and box fire-resistive design profiles for the wide-flange shapes most often used as beams or girders are given in Table 7-7-S-I. For different shapes, the weight-to-heated-perimeter ratios (W/D) shall be determined in accordance with the definitions given in this section. Except as provided for in Section 7.704.1, structural steel beams in approved fire-resistant assemblies shall be considered the minimum permissible size. Other beam or girder shapes may be substituted, provided that the weight-to-heated-perimeter ratio (W/D) of the substitute beam is equal to or greater than that of the beam specified in the approved assembly.

7.704.1.2 Spray-applied fire-resistive materials. The provisions in this section apply to unrestrained structural steel beams and girders protected with spray-applied cementitious or mineral fiber materials. Larger or smaller unrestrained beam and girder shapes may be substituted for beams specified in approved unrestrained fire-resistant assemblies, provided that the thickness of fire-resistive materials is adjusted in accordance with the following expression:

$$h_2 = \left[\frac{W_1/D_1 + 0.60}{W_2/D_2 + 0.60}\right] h_1$$

For SI:
$$h_2 = \left[\frac{W_1/D_1 + 0.036}{W_2/D_2 + 0.036}\right] h_1$$

WHERE:

D = heated perimeter of the structural steel beam or girder, in inches (mm).

h = thickness of spray-applied fire-resistive material, in inches (mm).

W = weight of the structural steel beam or girder in pounds per linear foot (kg/m).

Subscript 1 refers to the beam and fire-resistive material thickness in the approved assembly.

Subscript 2 refers to the substitute beam or girder and the required thickness of fire-resistive materials.

This equation is limited to beams with a weight-to-heated-perimeter ratio (W/D) of 0.37 (0.022) or greater. The thickness of protection shall not be less than $^3/_8$ inch (9.5 mm).

7.704.2 Structural Steel Trusses. The fire resistance of structural steel trusses protected with cementitious or mineral fiber materials spray applied to each of the individual truss elements may be determined in accordance with this section. The thickness of the fire-resistive material shall be determined in accordance with Section 7.703.3. The weight-to-heated-perimeter ratio (W/D) of truss elements which can be simultaneously exposed to fire on all sides shall be determined on the same basis as columns, as specified in Section 7.703.1. The weight-to-heated-perimeter ratio (W/D) of truss elements which directly support floor or roof construction shall be determined on the same basis as beams and girders, as specified in Section 7.704.1, Item 1.

TABLE 7-7-S-A1—WEIGHT-TO-HEATED-PERIMETER RATIOS (W/D)
FOR TYPICAL STRUCTURAL STEEL WIDE FLANGE COLUMNS

STRUCTURAL SHAPE	STRUCTURAL SHAPE	CONTOUR PROFILE (W/D)	BOX PROFILE[1] (W/D)
in. × lb./ft.	mm × kg/m	× 0.059 for metric W/D	
W14 × 730	W360 × 1086	6.62	9.05
W14 × 665	W260 × 990	6.14	8.46
W14 × 605	W360 × 900	5.69	7.89
W14 × 550	W360 × 818	5.26	7.35
W14 × 500	W360 × 744	4.86	6.83
W14 × 455	W360 × 677	4.49	6.35
W14 × 426	W360 × 634	4.24	6.02
W14 × 398	W360 × 592	4.00	5.71
W14 × 370	W360 × 551	3.76	5.38
W14 × 342	W360 × 509	3.51	5.04
W14 × 311	W360 × 463	3.23	4.66
W14 × 283	W360 × 421	2.97	4.31
W14 × 257	W360 × 382	2.72	3.97
W14 × 233	W360 × 347	2.49	3.65
W14 × 211	W360 × 314	2.28	3.35
W14 × 193	W360 × 287	2.10	3.09
W14 × 176	W360 × 262	1.93	2.85
W14 × 159	W360 × 237	1.75	2.60
W14 × 145	W360 × 216	1.61	2.39
W14 × 132	W360 × 196	1.52	2.25
W14 × 120	W360 × 179	1.39	2.06
W14 × 109	W360 × 162	1.27	1.88
W14 × 99	W360 × 147	1.16	1.72
W14 × 90	W360 × 134	1.06	1.58
W14 × 82	W360 × 122	1.20	1.68
W14 × 74	W360 × 110	1.09	1.53
W14 × 68	W360 × 101	1.01	1.41
W14 × 61	W360 × 91	0.91	1.28
W14 × 53	W360 × 79	0.89	1.21
W14 × 48	W360 × 72	0.81	1.10
W14 × 43	W360 × 64	0.73	0.99
W12 × 336	W310 × 500	4.02	5.56
W12 × 305	W310 × 454	3.70	5.16
W12 × 279	W310 × 415	3.44	4.81
W12 × 252	W310 × 375	3.15	4.43
W12 × 230	W310 × 342	2.91	4.12
W12 × 210	W310 × 313	2.68	3.82
W12 × 190	W310 × 283	2.46	3.51
W12 × 170	W310 × 253	2.22	3.20
W12 × 152	W310 × 226	2.01	2.90
W12 × 136	W310 × 202	1.82	2.63
W12 × 120	W310 × 179	1.62	2.36
W12 × 106	W310 × 158	1.44	2.11
W12 × 96	W310 × 143	1.32	1.93
W12 × 87	W310 × 129	1.20	1.76
W12 × 79	W310 × 117	1.10	1.61
W12 × 72	W310 × 107	1.00	1.48
W12 × 65	W310 × 97	0.91	1.35
W12 × 58	W310 × 86	0.91	1.31
W12 × 53	W310 × 79	0.84	1.20
W12 × 50	W310 × 74	0.89	1.23
W12 × 45	W310 × 67	0.81	1.12
W12 × 40	W310 × 60	0.72	1.00
W10 × 112	W250 × 167	1.78	2.57
W10 × 100	W250 × 149	1.61	2.33
W10 × 88	W250 × 131	1.43	2.08
W10 × 77	W250 × 115	1.26	1.85
W10 × 68	W250 × 101	1.13	1.66
W10 × 60	W250 × 89	1.00	1.48
W10 × 54	W250 × 80	0.91	1.34
W10 × 49	W250 × 73	0.83	1.23
W10 × 45	W250 × 67	0.87	1.24
W10 × 39	W250 × 58	0.76	1.09
W10 × 33	W250 × 49	0.65	0.93
W8 × 67	W200 × 100	1.34	1.94
W8 × 58	W200 × 86	1.18	1.71
W8 × 48	W200 × 71	0.99	1.44
W8 × 40	W200 × 59	0.83	1.23
W8 × 35	W200 × 52	0.73	1.08
W8 × 31	W200 × 46	0.65	0.97
W8 × 28	W200 × 42	0.67	0.96
W8 × 24	W200 × 36	0.58	0.83
W8 × 21	W200 × 31	0.57	0.77
W8 × 18	W200 × 27	0.49	0.67

(Continued)

TABLE 7-7-S-A1—WEIGHT-TO-HEATED-PERIMETER RATIOS (W/D)
FOR TYPICAL STRUCTURAL STEEL WIDE FLANGE COLUMNS—(Continued)

STRUCTURAL SHAPE	STRUCTURAL SHAPE	CONTOUR PROFILE (W/D)	BOX PROFILE[1] (W/D)
in. × lb./ft.	mm × kg/m	× 0.059 for metric W/D	
W6 × 25	W150 × 37	0.69	1.00
W6 × 20	W150 × 30	0.56	0.82
W6 × 16	W150 × 24	0.57	0.78
W6 × 15	W150 × 22	0.42	0.63
W6 × 12	W150 × 18	0.43	0.60
W6 × 9	W150 × 13	0.33	0.46
W5 × 19	W130 × 28	0.64	0.93
W5 × 16	W130 × 24	0.54	0.80
W4 × 13	W130 × 19	0.54	0.79

[1]See Section 7.703.2 for *W/D* limitations for gypsum wallboard protected assemblies.

TABLE 7-7-S-A2—AREA-TO-HEATED-PERIMETER RATIOS (A/P)
FOR TYPICAL ROUND AND SQUARE STRUCTURAL TUBING

ROUND PIPE COLUMNS STANDARD STEEL PIPE				
Nominal Diameter (inches)	Thickness (inches)	A/P Ratio (× 25.4 for metric A/P)	Nominal Diameter (mm)	Thickness (mm)
12	0.375	0.36	310	9.52
10	0.365	0.35	254	9.27
8	0.322	0.31	203	8.18
6	0.280	0.27	152	7.11
5	0.258	0.25	127	6.55
4	0.237	0.22	102	6.02
3.5	0.226	0.21	89	5.74
3	0.216	0.20	75	5.49
EXTRA-STRONG STEEL PIPE COLUMNS				
Nominal Diameter (inches)	Thickness (inches)	A/P Ratio (× 25.4 for metric A/P)	Nominal Diameter (mm)	Thickness (mm)
12	0.500	0.48	310	12.70
10	0.500	0.48	254	12.70
8	0.500	0.47	203	12.70
6	0.432	0.40	152	10.97
5	0.375	0.35	127	9.52
4	0.337	0.31	102	8.56
3.5	0.318	0.29	89	8.08
3	0.300	0.27	75	7.62
DOUBLE EXTRA-STRONG STEEL PIPE COLUMNS				
Nominal Diameter (inches)	Thickness (inches)	A/P Ratio (× 25.4 for metric A/P)	Nominal Diameter (mm)	Thickness (mm)
8	0.875	0.79	203	22.23
6	0.864	0.75	152	21.95
5	0.750	0.65	127	19.05
4	0.647	0.57	102	17.12
3	0.600	0.50	75	15.24
SQUARE STRUCTURAL TUBING				
Nominal Size Each Side (inches)	Thickness (inches)	A/P Ratio (× 25.4 for metric A/P)	Nominal Size Each Side (mm)	Thickness (mm)
16	5/8	0.58	406	15.9
16	1/2	0.48	406	12.7
14	5/8	0.58	356	15.9
14	1/2	0.47	356	12.7
14	3/8	0.36	356	9.5
12	5/8	0.57	305	15.9
12	1/2	0.47	305	12.7
12	3/8	0.36	305	9.5
10	5/8	0.56	254	15.9
10	9/16	0.51	254	14.3
10	1/2	0.46	254	12.7
10	3/8	0.35	254	9.5
10	5/16	0.30	254	7.9

(Continued)

TABLE 7-7-S-A2—AREA-TO-HEATED-PERIMETER RATIOS (A/P)
FOR TYPICAL ROUND AND SQUARE STRUCTURAL TUBING—(Continued)

SQUARE STRUCTURAL TUBING				
Nominal Size Each Side (inches)	Thickness (inches)	A/P Ratio (× 25.4 for metric A/P)	Nominal Size Each Side (mm)	Thickness (mm)
9	5/8	0.55	229	15.9
9	9/16	0.51	229	14.3
9	1/2	0.46	229	12.7
9	3/8	0.35	229	9.5
9	5/16	0.29	229	7.9
8	5/8	0.54	203	15.9
8	9/16	0.50	203	14.3
8	1/2	0.45	203	12.7
8	3/8	0.35	203	9.5
8	5/16	0.29	203	7.9
8	1/4	0.24	203	6.4
7	9/16	0.49	178	14.3
7	1/2	0.44	178	12.7
7	3/8	0.34	178	9.5
7	5/16	0.29	178	7.9
7	1/4	0.24	178	6.4
6	9/16	0.48	152	14.3
6	1/2	0.43	152	12.7
6	3/8	0.34	152	9.5
6	5/16	0.29	152	7.9
6	1/4	0.23	152	6.4
6	3/16	0.18	152	4.8
5	1/2	0.42	127	12.7
5	3/8	0.33	127	9.5
5	5/16	0.28	127	7.9
5	1/4	0.23	127	6.4
5	3/16	0.18	127	4.8
4	1/2	0.40	102	12.7
4	3/8	0.32	102	9.5
4	5/16	0.27	102	7.9
4	1/4	0.22	102	6.4
4	3/16	0.17	102	4.8
3	5/16	0.26	76	7.9
3	1/4	0.22	76	6.4
3	3/16	0.17	76	4.8

RECTANGULAR STRUCTURAL TUBING				
Nominal Size (inches)	Thickness (inches)	A/P Ratio (× 25.4 for metric A/P)	Nominal Size (mm)	Thickness (mm)
16 × 12	5/8	0.58	406 × 305	15.9
16 × 12	1/2	0.47	406 × 305	12.7
16 × 8	1/2	0.47	406 × 203	12.7
14 × 10	5/8	0.57	356 × 254	15.9
14 × 10	1/2	0.47	356 × 254	12.7
14 × 10	3/8	0.36	356 × 254	9.5
12 × 8	5/8	0.56	305 × 203	15.9
12 × 8	9/16	0.51	305 × 203	14.3
12 × 8	1/2	0.46	305 × 203	12.7
12 × 8	3/8	0.35	305 × 203	9.5
12 × 6	5/8	0.55	305 × 152	15.9
12 × 6	9/16	0.51	305 × 152	14.3
12 × 6	1/2	0.46	305 × 152	12.7
12 × 6	3/8	0.35	305 × 152	9.5
10 × 8	5/8	0.55	254 × 203	15.9
10 × 8	9/16	0.51	254 × 203	14.3
10 × 8	1/2	0.46	254 × 203	12.7
10 × 8	3/8	0.35	254 × 203	9.5
10 × 8	5/16	0.29	254 × 203	7.9
10 × 8	1/4	0.24	254 × 203	6.4

(Continued)

TABLE 7-7-S-A2—AREA-TO-HEATED-PERIMETER RATIOS (A/P)
FOR TYPICAL ROUND AND SQUARE STRUCTURAL TUBING—(Continued)

RECTANGULAR STRUCTURAL TUBING				
Nominal Size (inches)	Thickness (inches)	A/P Ratio (× 25.4 for metric A/P)	Nominal Size (mm)	Thickness (mm)
10 × 6	5/8	0.54	254 × 152	15.9
10 × 6	9/16	0.50	254 × 152	14.3
10 × 6	1/2	0.45	254 × 152	12.7
10 × 6	3/8	0.35	254 × 152	9.5
10 × 6	5/16	0.29	254 × 152	7.9
10 × 5	5/8	0.54	254 × 127	15.9
10 × 5	9/16	0.49	254 × 127	14.3
10 × 5	1/2	0.45	254 × 127	12.7
10 × 5	3/8	0.34	254 × 127	9.5
10 × 5	5/16	0.29	254 × 127	7.9
9 × 7	5/8	0.50	229 × 178	15.9
9 × 7	9/16	0.45	229 × 178	14.3
9 × 7	1/2	0.35	229 × 178	12.7
9 × 7	3/8	0.29	229 × 178	9.5
9 × 7	5/16	0.24	229 × 178	7.9
9 × 6	5/8	0.54	229 × 152	15.9
9 × 6	9/16	0.49	229 × 152	14.3
9 × 6	1/2	0.45	229 × 152	12.7
9 × 6	3/8	0.34	229 × 152	9.5
9 × 6	5/16	0.29	229 × 152	7.9
9 × 5	9/16	0.49	229 × 127	14.3
9 × 5	1/2	0.44	229 × 127	12.7
9 × 5	3/8	0.34	229 × 127	9.5
9 × 5	5/16	0.29	229 × 127	7.9

RECTANGULAR STRUCTURAL TUBING				
Nominal Size (inches)	Thickness (inches)	A/P Ratio (× 25.4 for metric A/P)	Nominal Size (mm)	Thickness (mm)
8 × 6	9/16	0.49	203 × 152	14.3
8 × 6	1/2	0.44	203 × 152	12.7
8 × 6	3/8	0.34	203 × 152	9.5
8 × 6	5/16	0.29	203 × 152	7.9
8 × 6	1/4	0.24	203 × 152	6.4
8 × 4	9/16	0.48	203 × 102	14.3
8 × 4	1/2	0.43	203 × 102	12.7
8 × 4	3/8	0.34	203 × 102	9.5
8 × 4	5/16	0.29	203 × 102	7.9
8 × 4	1/4	0.23	203 × 102	6.4
7 × 5	1/2	0.43	178 × 127	12.7
7 × 5	3/8	0.34	178 × 127	9.5
7 × 5	5/16	0.29	178 × 127	7.9
7 × 5	1/4	0.23	178 × 127	6.4
6 × 5	1/2	0.43	152 × 127	12.7
6 × 5	3/8	0.33	152 × 127	9.5
6 × 5	5/16	0.28	152 × 127	7.9
6 × 5	1/4	0.23	152 × 127	6.4
6 × 5	3/16	0.18	152 × 127	4.8
6 × 4	1/2	0.42	152 × 102	12.7
6 × 4	3/8	0.33	152 × 102	9.5
6 × 4	5/16	0.28	152 × 102	7.9
6 × 4	1/4	0.23	152 × 102	6.4
6 × 4	3/16	0.18	152 × 102	4.8
6 × 3	3/8	0.32	152 × 76	9.5
6 × 3	5/16	0.28	152 × 76	7.9
6 × 3	1/4	0.23	152 × 76	6.4
6 × 3	3/16	0.17	152 × 76	4.8
5 × 3	1/2	0.40	127 × 76	12.7
5 × 3	3/8	0.32	127 × 76	9.5
5 × 3	5/16	0.27	127 × 76	7.9
5 × 3	1/4	0.22	127 × 76	6.4
5 × 3	3/16	0.17	127 × 76	4.8
4 × 3	5/16	0.27	102 × 76	7.9
4 × 3	1/4	0.22	102 × 76	6.4
4 × 3	3/16	0.17	102 × 76	4.8
4 × 2	5/16	0.26	102 × 51	7.9
4 × 2	1/4	0.22	102 × 51	6.4
4 × 2	3/16	0.17	102 × 51	4.8
3.5 × 2.5	1/4	0.22	89 × 64	6.4
3.5 × 2.5	3/16	0.17	89 × 64	4.8
3 × 2	1/4	0.21	76 × 51	6.4
3 × 2	3/16	0.16	76 × 51	4.8

TABLE 7-7-S-B—PROPERTIES OF CONCRETE

PROPERTIES OF CONCRETE AND CONCRETE MASONRY				
	Concrete		Concrete Masonry	
Thermal Conductivity Metric W/m•k	Normal-Weight	Structural Lightweight	Normal-Weight	Structural Lightweight
Thermal conductivity, k_c (Btu/h ft. °F) (× 1.73 for KJ/kg·K)	0.95	0.35	0.51	0.33
Specific heat, c_c (Btu/h/lb. °F) (× 4.187 for KJ/kg·K)	0.20	0.20	0.20	0.20
Density, p_c (pcf) (× 16 for kg/m^3)	145	110	125	105
Equilibrium (free) moisture content, m, percent by volume	4	5	4	5

TABLE 7-7-S-C—THICKNESS OF NORMAL-WEIGHT CONCRETE[1] FOR VARIOUS FIRE-RESISTANCE RATINGS FOR TYPICAL WIDE-FLANGE STRUCTURAL STEEL COLUMNS ENCASED IN CONCRETE [Inches (mm)] (Figure 7-7-S-6, Detail C)

STRUCTURAL STEEL COLUMN SHAPES			FIRE-RESISTANCE RATING (hours)			
(mm)		(kg/m)	1	2	3	4
W14X (W360)	233	347			1½	2
	176	262		1		
	132	196				2½
	90	134	1		2	
	61	91		1½		
	48	72				3
	43	64			2½	
W12X (W310)	152	226		1		
	96	143			2	2½
	65	97	1			
	50	74		1½		3
	40	60			2½	
W10X (W250)	88	131			2	
	49	73		1½		3
	45	67	1			
	39	58			2½	
	33	49		2		3½
W8X (W200)	67	100				3
	58	86		1½	2½	
	48	71				
	31	46	1			3½
	21	31		2		
	18	27			3	4
W6X (W150)	25	37				3½
	20	30		2	3	
	16	24	1			
	15	22		2½		4
	9	13	1½		3½	

[1]The tabulated thicknesses are based on the assumed properties of normal-weight concrete given in Table 7-7-S-B.

TABLE 7-7-S-D—THICKNESS OF LIGHTWEIGHT CONCRETE[1] FOR VARIOUS FIRE-RESISTANCE RATINGS FOR TYPICAL WIDE-FLANGE STRUCTURAL STEEL COLUMNS ENCASED IN CONCRETE [Inches (mm)] (Figure 7-7-S-6, Detail C)

<table>
<tr><th colspan="3">STRUCTURAL STEEL COLUMN SHAPES</th><th colspan="4">FIRE-RESISTANCE RATING (hours)</th></tr>
<tr><th>(mm)</th><th></th><th>(kg/m)</th><th>1</th><th>2</th><th>3</th><th>4</th></tr>
<tr><td rowspan="5">W14X
(W360)</td><td>233</td><td>347</td><td rowspan="5">1</td><td rowspan="4">1</td><td>1</td><td rowspan="2">1½</td></tr>
<tr><td>193</td><td>287</td><td rowspan="3">1½</td></tr>
<tr><td>74</td><td>110</td><td>2</td></tr>
<tr><td>61</td><td>91</td><td rowspan="2">2½</td></tr>
<tr><td>43</td><td>64</td><td>1½</td><td>2</td></tr>
<tr><td rowspan="3">W12X
(W310)</td><td>65</td><td>97</td><td rowspan="3">1</td><td rowspan="2">1</td><td>1½</td><td>2</td></tr>
<tr><td>53</td><td>79</td><td rowspan="2">2</td><td rowspan="2">2½</td></tr>
<tr><td>40</td><td>60</td><td>1½</td></tr>
<tr><td rowspan="4">W10X
(W250)</td><td>112</td><td>167</td><td rowspan="4">1</td><td rowspan="3">1</td><td rowspan="2">1½</td><td rowspan="2">2</td></tr>
<tr><td>88</td><td>131</td></tr>
<tr><td>60</td><td>89</td><td rowspan="2">2</td><td rowspan="2">2½</td></tr>
<tr><td>33</td><td>49</td><td>1½</td></tr>
<tr><td rowspan="4">W8X
(W200)</td><td>35</td><td>52</td><td rowspan="4">1</td><td rowspan="4">1½</td><td rowspan="2">2</td><td>2½</td></tr>
<tr><td>28</td><td>42</td><td rowspan="3">3</td></tr>
<tr><td>24</td><td>36</td><td rowspan="2">2½</td></tr>
<tr><td>18</td><td>27</td></tr>
</table>

[1]The tabulated thicknesses are based on the assumed properties of structural lightweight concrete given in Table 7-7-S-B.

TABLE 7-7-S-E—THICKNESS OF NORMAL-WEIGHT CONCRETE[1] PRECAST CONCRETE COVERS FOR VARIOUS FIRE-RESISTANCE RATINGS FOR TYPICAL WIDE-FLANGE STRUCTURAL STEEL COLUMNS [Inches (mm)] (Figure 7-7-S-6, Detail A)

<table>
<tr><th colspan="3">STRUCTURAL STEEL COLUMN SHAPES</th><th colspan="4">FIRE-RESISTANCE RATING (hours)</th></tr>
<tr><th>(mm)</th><th></th><th>(kg/m)</th><th>1</th><th>2</th><th>3</th><th>4</th></tr>
<tr><td rowspan="8">W14X
(W360)</td><td>233</td><td>347</td><td rowspan="8">1½</td><td rowspan="2">1½</td><td rowspan="3">2½</td><td>3</td></tr>
<tr><td>211</td><td>314</td><td rowspan="3">3½</td></tr>
<tr><td>176</td><td>262</td><td rowspan="3">2</td></tr>
<tr><td>145</td><td>216</td><td rowspan="3">3</td></tr>
<tr><td>109</td><td>162</td><td rowspan="3">4</td></tr>
<tr><td>99</td><td>147</td><td rowspan="3">2½</td></tr>
<tr><td>61</td><td>91</td><td rowspan="2">3½</td></tr>
<tr><td>43</td><td>64</td><td>4½</td></tr>
<tr><td rowspan="7">W12X
(W310)</td><td>190</td><td>283</td><td rowspan="7">1½</td><td>1½</td><td rowspan="2">2½</td><td rowspan="3">3½</td></tr>
<tr><td>152</td><td>226</td><td rowspan="3">2</td></tr>
<tr><td>120</td><td>179</td><td rowspan="3">3</td></tr>
<tr><td>96</td><td>143</td><td rowspan="3">4</td></tr>
<tr><td>87</td><td>129</td><td rowspan="3">2½</td></tr>
<tr><td>58</td><td>86</td><td rowspan="2">3½</td></tr>
<tr><td>40</td><td>60</td><td>4½</td></tr>
<tr><td rowspan="5">W10X
(W250)</td><td>112</td><td>167</td><td rowspan="5">1½</td><td rowspan="2">2</td><td rowspan="3">3</td><td>3½</td></tr>
<tr><td>88</td><td>131</td><td rowspan="3">4</td></tr>
<tr><td>77</td><td>115</td><td rowspan="3">2½</td></tr>
<tr><td>54</td><td>80</td><td rowspan="2">3½</td></tr>
<tr><td>33</td><td>49</td><td>4½</td></tr>
<tr><td rowspan="6">W8X
(W200)</td><td>67</td><td>100</td><td rowspan="6">1½</td><td>2</td><td>3</td><td rowspan="3">4</td></tr>
<tr><td>58</td><td>86</td><td rowspan="3">2½</td><td rowspan="4">3½</td></tr>
<tr><td>48</td><td>71</td></tr>
<tr><td>28</td><td>42</td><td rowspan="3">4½</td></tr>
<tr><td>21</td><td>31</td><td rowspan="2">3</td></tr>
<tr><td>18</td><td>27</td><td>4</td></tr>
<tr><td rowspan="5">W6X
(W150)</td><td>25</td><td>37</td><td rowspan="3">1½</td><td>2½</td><td rowspan="2">3½</td><td rowspan="4">4½</td></tr>
<tr><td>20</td><td>30</td><td rowspan="4">3</td></tr>
<tr><td>16</td><td>24</td><td rowspan="3">4</td></tr>
<tr><td>12</td><td>18</td><td rowspan="2">2</td></tr>
<tr><td>9</td><td>13</td><td>5</td></tr>
</table>

[1]The tabulated thicknesses are based on the assumed properties of normal-weight concrete given in Table 7-7-S-B.

TABLE 7-7-S-F—THICKNESS STRUCTURAL OF LIGHTWEIGHT[1] PRECAST CONCRETE COVERS FOR VARIOUS FIRE-RESISTANCE RATINGS FOR TYPICAL WIDE-FLANGE STRUCTURAL STEEL COLUMNS [Inches (mm)] (Figure 7-7-S-6, Detail A)

STRUCTURAL STEEL COLUMN SHAPES			FIRE-RESISTANCE RATING (hours)			
(mm)		(kg/m)	1	2	3	4
W14X (W360)	233	347		$1\frac{1}{2}$		$2\frac{1}{2}$
	176	262			2	
	145	216		$1\frac{1}{2}$		
	132	196				3
	109	162	$1\frac{1}{2}$			
	99	147			$2\frac{1}{2}$	
	68	101		2		
	43	64			3	$3\frac{1}{2}$
W12X (W310)	190	283		$1\frac{1}{2}$		
	152	226			2	$2\frac{1}{2}$
	136	202				
	106	158		$1\frac{1}{2}$		
	96	143	$1\frac{1}{2}$		$2\frac{1}{2}$	3
	87	129				
	65	97				
	40	60		2	3	$3\frac{1}{2}$
W10X (W250)	112	167			2	
	100	149		$1\frac{1}{2}$		
	88	131			$2\frac{1}{2}$	3
	77	115	$1\frac{1}{2}$			
	60	89				
	39	58		2		$3\frac{1}{2}$
	33	49			3	
W8X (W200)	67	100		$1\frac{1}{2}$		3
	48	71			$2\frac{1}{2}$	
	35	52	$1\frac{1}{2}$	2		$3\frac{1}{2}$
	28	42			3	
	18	27		$2\frac{1}{2}$		4
W6X (W150)	25	37		2		$3\frac{1}{2}$
	15	22	$1\frac{1}{2}$		3	
	9	13		$2\frac{1}{2}$	$3\frac{1}{2}$	4

[1]The tabulated thicknesses are based on the assumed properties of structural lightweight concrete given in Table 7-7-S-B.

TABLE 7-7-S-G—EQUIVALENT THICKNESS OF NORMAL-WEIGHT CONCRETE MASONRY FIRE PROTECTION FOR TYPICAL WIDE-FLANGE STRUCTURAL STEEL COLUMNS[1, 2] [Inches (mm)] (See Figure 7-7-S-7)

STRUCTURAL STEEL COLUMN SHAPES			FIRE-RESISTANCE RATING (hours)			
(mm)		(kg/m)	1	2	3	4
W14X (W360)	233	347	0.4	1.1	1.8	2.5
	176	262	0.6	1.4	2.1	2.8
	145	216	0.7	1.5	2.3	3.0
	132	196	0.7	1.6	2.4	3.1
	109	162	0.8	1.7	2.5	3.3
	99	147	0.9	1.8	2.6	3.4
	68	101	1.0	2.0	2.9	3.6
	43	64	1.2	2.3	3.1	3.9
W12X (W310)	190	283	0.4	1.2	1.9	2.6
	152	226	0.6	1.4	2.1	2.8
	136	202	0.6	1.5	2.2	2.9
	106	158	0.8	1.7	2.5	3.2
	96	143	0.8	1.7	2.5	3.3
	87	129	0.9	1.8	2.6	3.4
	65	97	1.0	2.0	2.8	3.6
	40	60	1.0	2.2	3.1	3.8
W10X (W250)	112	167	0.6	1.5	2.3	3.0
	100	149	0.7	1.6	2.4	3.1
	88	131	0.8	1.7	2.5	3.2
	77	115	0.8	1.8	2.6	3.3
	60	89	1.0	1.9	2.8	3.5
	39	58	1.2	2.2	3.0	3.8
	33	49	1.2	2.3	3.1	3.9
W8X (W200)	67	100	0.8	1.7	2.6	3.3
	48	71	1.0	2.0	2.8	3.6
	35	52	1.1	2.2	3.0	3.8
	28	42	1.2	2.3	3.1	3.9
	18	27	1.4	2.3	3.3	4.0
W6X (W150)	25	37	1.2	2.2	3.1	3.8
	15	22	1.4	2.4	3.3	4.0
	9	13	1.5	2.6	3.4	4.2

[1]The tabulated thicknesses are based on the assumed properties of normal-weight concrete masonry given in Table 7-7-S-B.
[2]The thicknesses of concrete masonry units shall not be less than set forth in Section 7.703.4.

TABLE 7-7-S-H—EQUIVALENT THICKNESS OF LIGHTWEIGHT CONCRETE MASONRY FIRE PROTECTION FOR TYPICAL WIDE-FLANGE STRUCTURAL STEEL COLUMNS[1, 2] [Inches (mm)] (See Figure 7-7-S-7)

STRUCTURAL STEEL COLUMN SHAPES			FIRE-RESISTANCE RATING (hours)			
(mm)		(kg/m)	1	2	3	4
W14X (W360)	233	347	0.3	0.9	1.5	2.1
	176	262	0.4	1.1	1.8	2.4
	145	216	0.5	1.3	1.9	2.6
	132	196	0.6	1.3	2.0	2.7
	109	162	0.7	1.5	2.2	2.9
	99	147	0.7	1.5	2.3	2.9
	68	101	0.9	1.8	2.5	3.2
	43	64	1.1	2.0	2.8	3.5
W12X (W310)	190	283	0.3	0.9	1.5	2.1
	152	226	0.4	1.1	1.8	2.4
	136	202	0.5	1.2	1.9	2.5
	106	158	0.6	1.4	2.1	2.8
	96	143	0.7	1.5	2.2	2.8
	87	129	0.7	1.5	2.3	2.9
	65	97	0.8	1.7	2.5	3.2
	40	60	1.1	2.0	2.8	3.5
W10X (W250)	112	167	0.5	1.2	1.9	2.5
	100	149	0.5	1.3	2.0	2.7
	88	131	0.6	1.4	2.1	2.8
	77	115	0.7	1.5	2.2	2.9
	60	89	0.8	1.7	2.4	3.1
	39	58	1.0	1.9	2.7	3.4
	33	49	1.1	2.0	2.8	3.5
W8X (W200)	67	100	0.6	1.5	2.2	2.9
	48	71	0.8	1.7	2.5	3.2
	35	52	1.0	1.9	2.7	3.4
	28	42	1.1	2.0	2.8	3.5
	18	27	1.2	2.2	3.0	3.7
W6X (W150)	25	37	1.0	2.0	2.7	3.4
	15	22	1.2	2.2	3.0	3.7
	9	13	1.4	2.3	3.1	3.8

[1]The tabulated thicknesses are based on the assumed properties of normal-weight concrete masonry given in Table 7-7-S-B.

[2]The thicknesses of concrete masonry units shall not be less than set forth in Section 7.703.4.

TABLE 7-7-S-I—WEIGHT-TO-HEATED-PERIMETER RATIOS *W/D*
FOR TYPICAL WIDE-FLANGE BEAM AND GIRDER SHAPES

STRUCTURAL SHAPE		CONTOUR PROFILE	BOX PROFILE
in. × lb./ft.	mm × kg/m	× 0.059 for metric *W/D*	
W36 × 300	W920 × 446	2.47	3.33
× 280	× 417	2.31	3.12
× 260	× 387	2.16	2.92
× 245	× 365	2.04	2.76
× 230	× 342	1.92	2.61
× 210	× 313	1.94	2.45
× 194	× 289	1.80	2.28
× 182	× 271	1.69	2.15
× 170	× 253	1.59	2.01
× 160	× 238	1.50	1.90
× 150	× 223	1.41	1.79
× 135	× 201	1.28	1.63
W33 × 241	W840 × 359	2.11	2.86
× 221	× 329	1.94	2.64
× 201	× 299	1.78	2.42
× 154	× 226	1.51	1.94
× 141	× 210	1.41	1.80
× 130	× 193	1.31	1.67
× 118	× 176	1.19	1.53
W30 × 211	W760 × 314	2.00	2.74
× 191	× 284	1.82	2.50
× 173	× 257	1.66	2.28
× 132	× 196	1.45	1.85
× 124	× 185	1.37	1.75
× 116	× 173	1.28	1.65
× 108	× 161	1.20	1.54
× 99	× 147	1.10	1.42
W27 × 178	W690 × 265	1.85	2.55
× 161	× 240	1.68	2.33
× 146	× 217	1.53	2.12
× 114	× 170	1.36	1.76
× 102	× 152	1.23	1.59
× 94	× 140	1.13	1.47
× 84	× 125	1.02	1.33
W24 × 162	W610 × 241	1.85	2.57
× 146	× 217	1.68	2.34
× 131	× 195	1.52	2.12
× 117	× 174	1.36	1.91
× 104	× 155	1.22	1.71
× 94	× 140	1.26	1.63
× 84	× 125	1.13	1.47
× 76	× 113	1.03	1.34
× 68	× 101	0.92	1.21
× 62	× 92	0.92	1.14
× 55	× 82	0.82	1.02
W21 × 147	W530 × 219	1.83	2.60
× 132	× 196	1.66	2.35
× 122	× 182	1.54	2.19
× 111	× 165	1.41	2.01
× 101	× 150	1.29	1.84
× 93	× 138	1.38	1.80
× 83	× 123	1.24	1.62
× 68	× 101	1.03	1.35
× 62	× 92	0.94	1.23
× 57	× 85	0.93	1.17
× 50	× 74	0.83	1.04
× 44	× 66	0.73	0.92

(Continued)

TABLE 7-7-S-I—WEIGHT-TO-HEATED-PERIMETER RATIOS *W/D*
FOR TYPICAL WIDE-FLANGE BEAM AND GIRDER SHAPES—(Continued)

STRUCTURAL SHAPE		CONTOUR PROFILE	BOX PROFILE
in. × lb./ft.	mm × kg/m	× 0.059 for metric *W/D*	
W18 × 119	W460 × 177	1.69	2.42
× 106	× 158	1.52	2.18
× 97	× 144	1.39	2.01
× 86	× 128	1.24	1.80
× 76	× 113	1.11	1.60
× 71	× 106	1.21	1.59
× 65	× 97	1.11	1.47
× 60	× 89	1.03	1.36
× 55	× 82	0.95	1.26
× 50	× 74	0.87	1.15
× 46	× 68	0.86	1.09
× 40	× 60	0.75	0.96
× 35	× 52	0.66	0.85
W16 × 100	W410 × 149	1.56	2.25
× 89	× 132	1.40	2.03
× 77	× 114	1.22	1.78
× 67	× 100	1.07	1.56
× 57	× 85	1.07	1.43
× 50	× 75	0.94	1.26
× 45	× 67	0.85	1.15
× 40	× 60	0.76	1.03
× 36	× 53	0.69	0.93
× 31	× 46	0.65	0.83
× 26	× 39	0.55	0.70
W14 × 132	W360 × 196	1.83	3.00
× 120	× 179	1.67	2.75
× 109	× 162	1.53	2.52
× 99	× 147	1.39	2.31
× 90	× 134	1.27	2.11
× 82	× 122	1.41	2.12
× 74	× 110	1.28	1.93
× 68	× 101	1.19	1.78
× 61	× 91	1.07	1.61
× 53	× 79	1.03	1.48
× 48	× 72	0.94	1.35
× 43	× 64	0.85	1.22
× 38	× 58	0.79	1.09
× 34	× 51	0.71	0.98
× 30	× 44	0.63	0.87
× 26	× 39	0.61	0.79
× 22	× 33	0.52	0.68
W12 × 87	W310 × 129	1.44	2.34
× 79	× 117	1.32	2.14
× 72	× 107	1.20	1.97
× 65	× 97	1.09	1.79
× 58	× 86	1.08	1.69
× 53	× 79	0.99	1.55
× 50	× 74	1.04	1.54
× 45	× 67	0.95	1.40
× 40	× 60	0.85	1.25
× 35	× 52	0.79	1.11
× 30	× 45	0.69	0.96
× 26	× 39	0.60	0.84
× 22	× 33	0.61	0.77
× 19	× 28	0.53	0.67
× 16	× 24	0.45	0.57
× 14	× 21	0.40	0.50

(Continued)

TABLE 7-7-S-I—WEIGHT-TO-HEATED-PERIMETER RATIOS *W/D*
FOR TYPICAL WIDE-FLANGE BEAM AND GIRDER SHAPES—(Continued)

STRUCTURAL SHAPE		CONTOUR PROFILE	BOX PROFILE
in. × lb./ft.	mm × kg/m	× 0.059 for metric *W/D*	
W10 × 112	W250 × 167	2.14	3.38
× 100	× 149	1.93	3.07
× 88	× 131	1.72	2.75
× 77	× 115	1.52	2.45
× 68	× 101	1.35	2.20
× 60	× 89	1.20	1.97
× 54	× 80	1.09	1.79
× 49	× 73	0.99	1.64
× 45	× 67	1.03	1.59
× 39	× 58	0.90	1.40
× 33	× 49	0.77	1.20
× 30	× 45	0.79	1.12
× 26	× 39	0.69	0.98
× 22	× 33	0.59	0.84
× 19	× 28	0.59	0.78
× 17	× 25	0.54	0.70
× 15	× 22	0.48	0.63
× 12	× 18	0.38	0.51
W8 × 67	W200 × 100	1.61	2.55
× 58	× 86	1.41	2.26
× 48	× 71	1.18	1.91
× 40	× 59	1.00	1.63
× 35	× 52	0.88	1.44
× 31	× 46	0.79	1.29
× 28	× 42	0.80	1.24
× 24	× 36	0.69	1.07
× 21	× 31	0.66	0.96
× 18	× 27	0.57	0.84
× 15	× 22	0.54	0.74
× 13	× 19	0.47	0.65
× 10	× 15	0.37	0.51
W6 × 25	W150 × 37	0.82	1.33
× 20	× 30	0.67	1.09
× 16	× 24	0.66	0.96
× 15	× 22	0.51	0.83
× 12	× 18	0.51	0.75
× 9	× 13	0.39	0.57
W5 × 19	W130 × 28	0.76	1.24
× 16	× 24	0.65	1.07
W4 × 13	W100 × 19	0.65	1.05

TABLE 7-7-S-J—THERMAL CONDUCTIVITY OF CONCRETE MASONRY UNITS AT 70°F (21°C)

DENSITY (*D*) (pcf)	THERMAL CONDUCTIVITY *(K)* (Btu/hr.ft .°F)
× 16 for kg/m³	× 1.73 for W/m•K
80	0.207
85	0.228
90	0.252
95	0.278
100	0.308
105	0.340
110	0.376
115	0.416
120	0.459
125	0.508
130	0.561
135	0.620
140	0.685
145	0.758
150	0.837

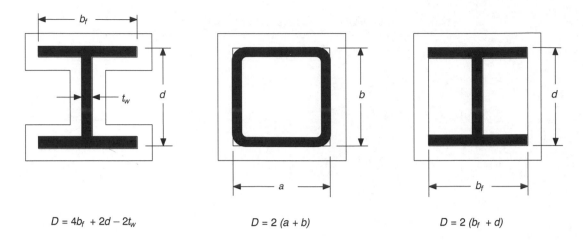

$D = 4b_f + 2d - 2t_w$ $D = 2\,(a + b)$ $D = 2\,(b_f + d)$

FIGURE 7-7-S-1—DETERMINATION OF THE HEATED PERIMETER OF STRUCTURAL STEEL COLUMNS

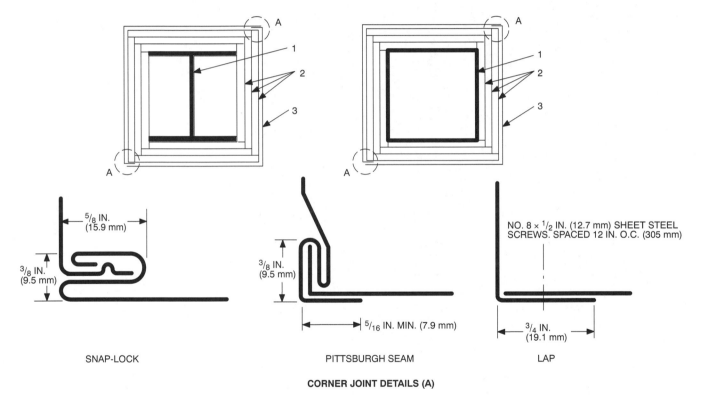

CORNER JOINT DETAILS (A)

NOTES:

1. Structural steel column, either wide-flange or tubular shapes.

2. Type X gypsum wallboard. For single-layer applications, the wallboard shall be applied vertically with no horizontal joints. For multiple-layer applications, horizontal joints are permitted at a minimum spacing of 8 feet (2438 mm), provided that the joints in successive layers are staggered at least 12 inches (305 mm). The total required thickness of wallboard shall be determined on the basis of the specified fire-resistance rating and the weight and heated perimeter of the column. For fire-resistance ratings of two hours or less, one of the required layers of gypsum wallboard may be applied to the exterior of the sheet steel column covers with 1-inch-long (25.4 mm) Type S screws spaced 1 inch (25.4 mm) from the wallboard edge and 8 inches (203.2 mm) on center. For such installations, 0.016-inch-minimum-thickness (0.4 mm) galvanized steel corner beads with $1^1/_2$-inch (38.1 mm) legs shall be attached to the wallboard with Type S screws spaced 12 inches (305 mm) on center.

3. For fire-resistance ratings of three hours or less, the column covers shall be fabricated from 0.024-inch-minimum-thickness (0.6 mm) galvanized or stainless steel. For four-hour fire-resistance ratings, the column covers shall be fabricated from 0.024-inch-minimum-thickness (0.6 mm) stainless steel. The column covers shall be erected with the snap lock or Pittsburgh joint details.

    For fire-resistance ratings of two hours or less, column covers fabricated from 0.027-inch-minimum-thickness (0.7 mm) galvanized or stainless steel may be erected with lap joints. The lap joints may be located anywhere around the perimeter of the column cover. The lap joints shall be secured with $^1/_2$-inch-long (12.7 mm) No. 8 sheet metal screws spaced 12 inches (305 mm) on center.

    The column covers shall be provided with a minimum expansion clearance of $^1/_8$ inch (10.4 mm) per linear foot (m) between the ends of the cover and any restraining construction.

**FIGURE 7-7-S-2—GYPSUM WALLBOARD PROTECTED STRUCTURAL STEEL COLUMNS
WITH SHEET STEEL COLUMN COVERS (FOUR HOURS OR LESS)**

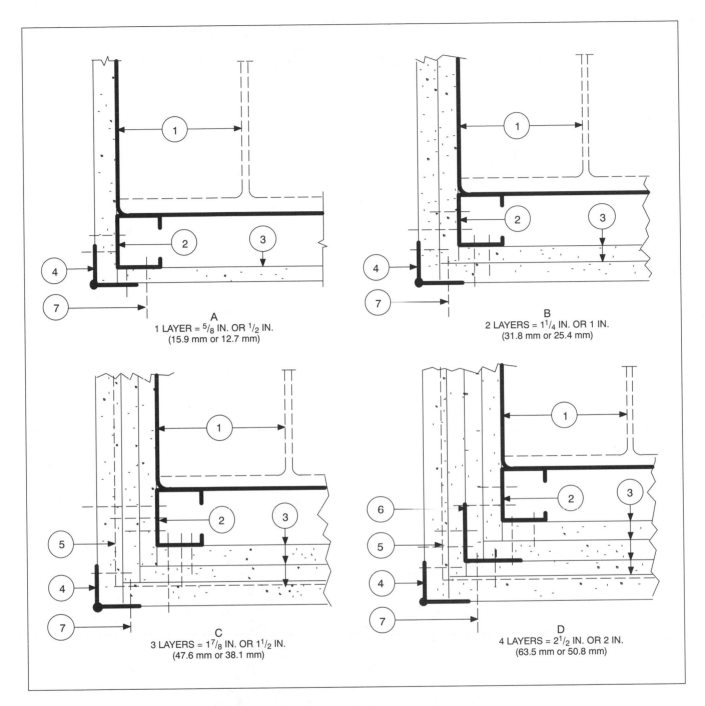

A
1 LAYER = $^5/_8$ IN. OR $^1/_2$ IN.
(15.9 mm or 12.7 mm)

B
2 LAYERS = $1^1/_4$ IN. OR 1 IN.
(31.8 mm or 25.4 mm)

C
3 LAYERS = $1^7/_8$ IN. OR $1^1/_2$ IN.
(47.6 mm or 38.1 mm)

D
4 LAYERS = $2^1/_2$ IN. OR 2 IN.
(63.5 mm or 50.8 mm)

**FIGURE 7-7-S-3—GYPSUM WALLBOARD PROTECTED STRUCTURAL STEEL COLUMNS WITH
STEEL STUD/SCREW ATTACHMENT SYSTEM (THREE HOURS OR LESS)**

NOTES:

1. Structural steel column, either wide-flange or tubular shapes.
2. One and five-eighths-inch-deep (41.3 mm) studs fabricated from 0.021-inch-minimum-thickness (0.5 mm) galvanized steel with $1^5/_{16}$- or $1^7/_{16}$-inch (33.3 mm or 36.5 mm) legs and $^1/_4$-inch (6.4 mm) stiffening flanges. The length of the steel studs shall be $^1/_2$ inch (12.7 mm) less than the height of the assembly.
3. Type X gypsum wallboard. For single-layer applications, the wallboard shall be applied vertically with no horizontal joints. For multiple-layer applications, horizontal joints are permitted at a minimum spacing of 8 feet (2438 mm), provided that the joints in successive layers are staggered at least 12 inches (305 mm). The total required thickness of wallboard shall be determined on the basis of the specified fire-resistance rating and the weight and heated perimeter of the column.
4. Galvanized steel corner beads [0.016-inch (0.4 mm) minimum thickness] with $1^1/_2$-inch (38.1 mm) legs attached to the wallboard with 1-inch-long (25.4 mm) Type S screws spaced 12 inches (305 mm) on center.
5. No. 18 SWG steel tie wires spaced 24 inches (610 mm) on center.
6. Sheet metal angles with 2-inch (50.8 mm) legs fabricated from 0.021-inch-minimum-thickness (0.5 mm) galvanized steel.
7. Type S screws 1-inch (25.4 mm) long shall be used for attaching the first layer of wallboard to the steel studs and the third layer to the sheet metal angles at 24 inches (610 mm) on center. Type S screws $1^3/_4$ inches (44.5 mm) long shall be used for attaching the second layer of wallboard to the steel studs and the fourth layer to the sheet metal angles at 12 inches (305 mm) on center. Type S screws $2^1/_4$ inches (57.1 mm) long shall be used for attaching the third layer of wallboard to the steel studs at 12 inches (305 mm) on center.

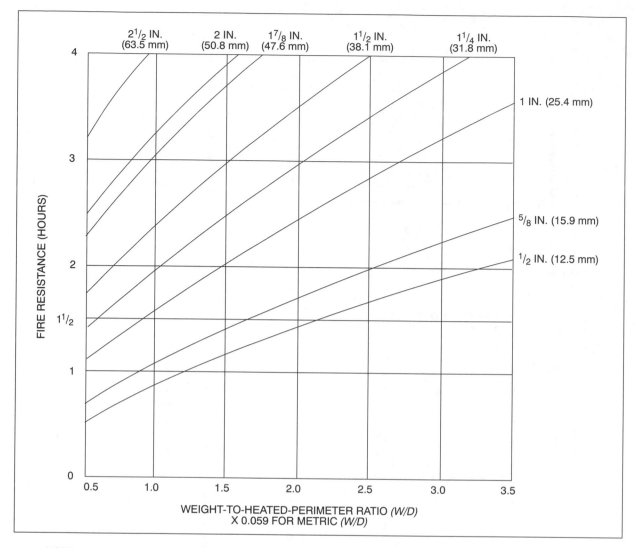

NOTE: The *W/D* ratios for typical wide-flange columns are listed in Table 7-7-S-A1. For other column shapes, the *W/D* ratios shall be determined in accordance with Section 7.703.

FIGURE 7-7-S-4—FIRE RESISTANCE OF STRUCTURAL STEEL COLUMNS PROTECTED WITH VARIOUS THICKNESSES OF TYPE X GYPSUM WALLBOARD

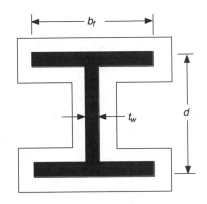

**FIGURE 7-7-S-5—WIDE FLANGE STRUCTURAL STEEL COLUMN
WITH SPRAY-APPLIED FIRE-RESISTIVE MATERIAL**

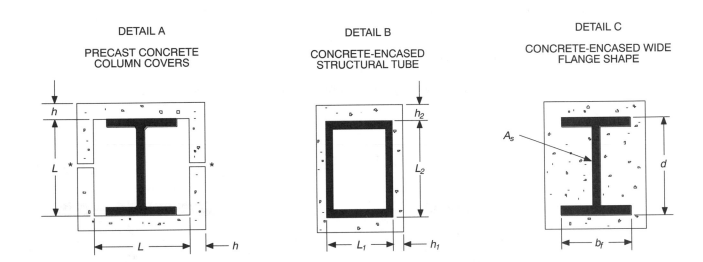

DETAIL A

PRECAST CONCRETE
COLUMN COVERS

DETAIL B

CONCRETE-ENCASED
STRUCTURAL TUBE

DETAIL C

CONCRETE-ENCASED WIDE
FLANGE SHAPE

NOTE: When the inside perimeter of the concrete protection is not square, L shall be taken as the average of L_1 and L_2.
When the thickness of concrete cover is not constant, h shall be taken as the average of h_1 and h_2.
*Joints shall be protected with a minimum 1 inch (25.4 mm) thickness of ceramic fiber blanket, but in no case less
than one half the thickness of the column cover. The joint width shall not exceed 1 inch (25.4 mm) maximum.

FIGURE 7-7-S-6—CONCRETE-PROTECTED STRUCTURAL STEEL COLUMNS

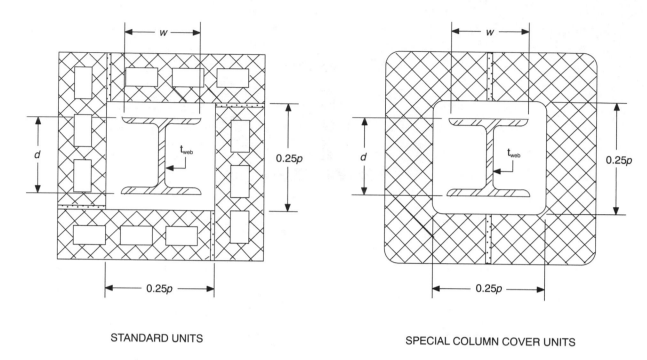

STANDARD UNITS

SPECIAL COLUMN COVER UNITS

FIGURE 7-7-S-7—CONCRETE MASONRY PROTECTED STRUCTURAL STEEL COLUMNS

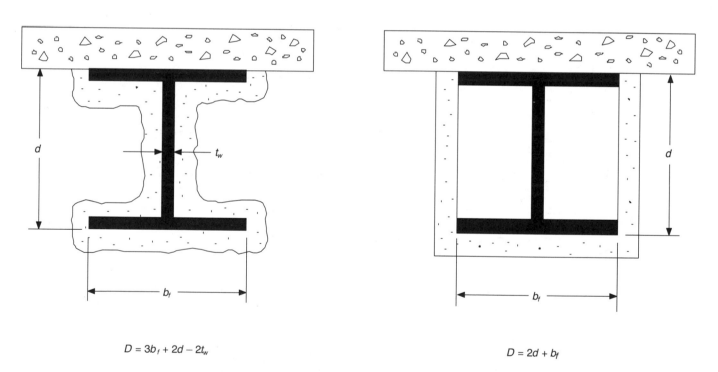

$D = 3b_f + 2d - 2t_w$

$D = 2d + b_f$

**FIGURE 7-7-S-8—DETERMINATION OF THE HEATED PERIMETER
OF STRUCTURAL STEEL BEAMS AND GIRDERS**

Part II—Method for Calculating the Fire Resistance of Concrete Construction

See Section 703.3, *Uniform Building Code*

SECTION 7.705 — SCOPE

This part of this standard contains procedures by which the fire resistance of concrete of specific materials or combinations of materials can be established by calculations. These procedures apply to the material contained in this part only. Procedures shown in this standard for calculating the fire resistance of concrete construction shall apply to all cast-in-place and precast concrete, conventionally reinforced or prestressed. The procedures shall not apply to single or double "T" precast, prestressed (pretensioned) units in wall or floor-roof assemblies.

SECTION 7.706 — DEFINITIONS

CARBONATE AGGREGATE CONCRETE is concrete made with aggregates consisting mainly of calcium or magnesium carbonate, e.g., limestone or dolomite.

CELLULAR CONCRETE is a lightweight insulating concrete made by mixing a preformed foam with portland cement slurry and having a dry unit weight of approximately 30 pounds per cubic foot (pcf).

CERAMIC FIBER BLANKET is a mineral wool insulation material made of alumina-silica fibers and weighing 4 to 10 pcf (64 to 160 kg/m^3).

GLASS FIBER BOARD is fibrous glass roof insulation consisting of inorganic glass fibers formed into rigid boards using a binder. The board has a top surface faced with asphalt and kraft paper reinforced with glass fibers.

LIGHTWEIGHT AGGREGATE CONCRETE is concrete made with aggregates of expanded clay, shale, slag or slate or sintered fly ash and weighing 85 to 115 pcf (1362 to 1842 kg/m^3).

MINERAL BOARD is a rigid felted thermal insulation board consisting of either felted mineral fiber or cellular beads of expanded aggregate formed into flat rectangular units.

PERLITE CONCRETE is a lightweight insulating concrete having a dry unit weight of approximately 30 pcf (482 kg/m^3) made with perlite concrete aggregate. Perlite aggregate is produced from a volcanic rock which, when heated, expands to form a glass-like material of cellular structure.

SAND-LIGHTWEIGHT CONCRETE is concrete made with a combination of expanded clay, shale, slag or slate or sintered fly ash and natural sand. Its unit weight is generally between 105 and 120 pcf (1682 to 1930 kg/m^3).

SILICEOUS AGGREGATE CONCRETE is concrete made with normal-weight aggregates consisting mainly of silica or compounds other than calcium or magnesium carbonate.

VERMICULITE CONCRETE is a lightweight insulating concrete made with vermiculite concrete aggregate, which is laminated micaceous material produced by expanding the ore at high temperatures. When added to a portland cement slurry, the resulting concrete has a dry unit weight of approximately 30 pcf (482 kg/m^3).

SECTION 7.707 — CONCRETE WALLS

7.707.1 Walls, Cast-in-place or Precast.

1. The minimum equivalent thicknesses of cast-in-place or precast concrete walls for fire-resistance ratings from one to four hours are shown in Table 7-7-C-A. For solid walls with flat vertical surfaces, the equivalent thickness is the same as the thickness. The values in Table 7-7-C-A apply to plain, reinforced or prestressed concrete walls.

2. For hollow-core precast concrete wall panels in which the cores are of constant cross section throughout the length, the equivalent thickness may be calculated by dividing the net cross-sectional area (the gross cross section minus the area of the cores) of the panel by its width.

3. Where all of the core spaces of hollow-core wall panels are filled with loose-fill material, such as expanded shale, clay or slag, or vermiculite or perlite, the fire-resistance rating of the wall is the same as that of a solid wall of the same concrete type and of the same overall thickness.

4. The thickness of panels with tapered cross sections shall be that determined at a distance $2t$ or 6 inches (152 mm), whichever is less, from the point of minimum thickness, where t is the minimum thickness.

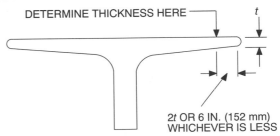

5. The equivalent thickness of panels with ribbed or undulating surfaces shall be determined by one of the following expressions, whichever is applicable:

for $s \geq 4t$, the thickness to be used shall be t

for $s \leq 2t$, the thickness to be used shall be t_e

for $4t > s > 2t$, the thickness to be used shall be

$$t + \left(\frac{4t}{s} - 1\right)(t_e - t)$$

WHERE:

s = spacing of ribs or undulations.

t = minimum thickness.

t_e = equivalent thickness of the panel calculated as the net cross-sectional area of the panel divided by the width in which the maximum thickness used in the calculation shall not exceed $2t$.

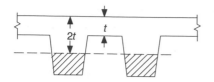

NEGLECT SHADED AREA
IN CALCULATION OF
EQUIVALENT THICKNESS

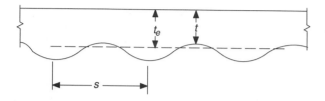

7.707.2 Multiwythe Walls.

1. For walls which consist of two wythes of different types of concrete, the fire-resistance ratings may be determined from Figure 7-7-C-1.

2. The fire-resistance rating for wall panels consisting of two or more wythes may be determined by the formula:

$$R = (R_1^{0.59} + R_2^{0.59} + \ldots R_n^{0.59})^{1.7} \qquad (7\text{-}1)$$

Formula (7-1) can also be expressed as:

$$R^{0.59} = R_1^{0.59} + R_2^{0.59} + \ldots \; R_n^{0.59}$$

WHERE:

R = the fire endurance of the assembly, minutes.

R_1,
R_2
and

R_n = the fire endurances of the individual wythes, minutes.

Values of $R_n^{0.59}$ for use in Formula (7-1) are given in Table 7-7-C-B.

R_1 MINUTES	$R^{0.59}$
60	11.20
90	14.22
120	16.85
180	21.41
240	25.37

3. The fire-resistance ratings of precast concrete wall panels consisting of a layer of foam plastic insulation sandwiched between two wythes of concrete may be determined by use of Formula (7-1). Foam plastic insulation with a total thickness of less than 1 inch (25 mm) shall be disregarded. The R_n value for thickness of foam plastic insulation of 1 inch (25 mm) or greater, for use in the calculation, is five minutes; therefore, $R_n^{0.59} = 2.5$.

7.707.3 Joints between Precast Concrete Wall Panels.
Where openings in exterior walls are required to be protected, or where openings are not permitted in walls, the provisions of this section shall be used to determine the amount of joint insulation required.

Figure 7-7-C-2 shows thicknesses of ceramic fiber blankets to be used to protect joints between precast concrete wall panels for various panel thicknesses. For joint widths of $^3/_8$ inch and 1 inch (10 mm and 25 mm) for fire-resistance ratings of one hour to four hours for joint widths between $^3/_8$ inch and 1 inch (10 mm and

25 mm), the thickness of ceramic fiber blanket may be determined by direct interpolation. Other approved tested and labeled materials may be used in place of ceramic fiber blankets.

SECTION 7.708 — CONCRETE FLOOR AND ROOF SLABS

7.708.1 Reinforced and Prestressed Concrete Floor and Roof Slabs.

1. The minimum thickness of reinforced and prestressed concrete floor or roof slabs for fire-resistance ratings from one to four hours are shown in Table 7-7-C-C.

2. For hollow-core prestressed concrete slabs in which the cores are of constant cross section throughout the length, the equivalent thickness may be obtained by dividing the net cross-sectional area of the slab, including grout in the joints, by its width.

3. The thickness of slabs with sloping soffits shall be determined at a distance of 2t or 6 inches (152 mm), whichever is less, from the point of minimum thickness, where t is the minimum thickness.

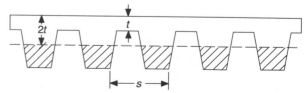

DETERMINE THICKNESS HERE

2t OR 6 IN. (152 mm)
WHICHEVER IS LESS

4. The thickness of slabs with ribbed or undulating soffits shall be determined by one of the following expressions, whichever is applicable:

for $s \geq 4t$, the thickness to be used shall be t

for $s \leq 2t$, the thickness to be used shall be t_e

for $4t > s > 2t$, the thickness to be used shall be

$$t + \left(\frac{4t}{s} - 1 \right)(t_e - t)$$

WHERE:

s = spacing of ribs or undulations.

t = minimum thickness.

t_e = equivalent thickness of the panel calculated as the net cross-sectional area of the panel divided by the width in which the maximum thickness used in the calculation shall not exceed 2t.

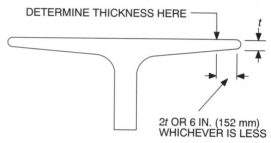

NEGLECT SHADED AREA
IN CALCULATION OF
EQUIVALENT THICKNESS

7.708.2 Multicourse Floors and Roofs.

1. Figure 7-7-C-3A gives information on the fire-resistance ratings of floors which consist of a base slab of concrete with a topping (overlay) of a different type of concrete.

2. Figure 7-7-C-3B gives information on the fire-resistance ratings of roofs which consist of a base slab of concrete with a topping (overlay) of an insulating concrete or with an insulating board and built-up roofing. Three-ply built-up roofing contributes 10 minutes to the fire-resistance rating; therefore, 10 minutes can be added to the assemblies shown in Figure 7-7-C-3B, Details (a), (b) and (c), but not to those shown in Figure 7-7-C-3B, Details (d) and (e).

7.708.3 Joints in Precast Slabs. Joints between adjacent precast concrete slabs may be ignored in calculating the slab thickness, provided that a concrete topping at least 1 inch (25 mm) thick is used. Where no concrete topping is used, joints must be grouted to a depth of at least one third the slab thickness at the joint, but not less than 1 inch (25 mm), or the joints must be made fire resistive by other approved methods.

SECTION 7.709 — MINIMUM CONCRETE COVER REQUIREMENTS

7.709.1 Slabs. The minimum thickness of concrete cover to the positive moment reinforcement is given in Table 7-7-C-D for reinforced concrete and Table 7-7-C-E for prestressed concrete. Tables 7-7-C-D and 7-7-C-E are applicable for solid- or hollow-core one-way or two-way slabs with flat undersurfaces. Slabs may be cast-in-place or precast.

7.709.2 Beams.

1. The minimum thickness of concrete cover to the positive moment reinforcement (bottom steel) for reinforced concrete beams is shown in Table 7-7-C-F for fire-resistance ratings from one to four hours.

2. The minimum thickness of concrete cover to the positive moment prestressing tendon (bottom steel) for prestressed concrete beams is shown in Table 7-7-C-G for fire-resistance ratings from one to four hours.

SECTION 7.710 — CONCRETE COLUMNS

7.710.1 Minimum Size. Table 7-7-C-H shows the minimum overall dimensions of reinforced concrete columns for fire-resistance ratings from one to four hours.

7.710.2 Minimum Cover for Reinforced Concrete Columns. The minimum cover to the main reinforcement in columns for fire-resistance ratings of one hour, one and one-half hours, two hours and three hours shall be $1^1/_2$ inches (38 mm); for a four-hour rating, the minimum cover to the main reinforcement shall be 2 inches (51 mm) for siliceous aggregate concrete and $1^1/_2$ inches (38 mm) for carbonate aggregate concrete or sand-lightweight concrete.

TABLE 7-7-C-A—MINIMUM EQUIVALENT THICKNESS, INCHES, OF CAST-IN-PLACE OR PRECAST CONCRETE WALLS, LOAD BEARING OR NONLOAD BEARING

CONCRETE TYPE	MINIMUM WALL THICKNESS (INCHES) FOR FIRE-RESISTANCE RATING OF				
	× 25.4 for mm				
	1 Hr.	1½ Hr.	2 Hr.	3 Hr.	4 Hr.
Siliceous[1]	3.5	4.3	5.0	6.2	7.0
Carbonate	3.2	4.0	4.6	5.7	6.6
Sand-lightweight	2.7	3.3	3.8	4.6	5.4
Lightweight concrete	2.5	3.1	3.6	4.4	5.1

[1]The equivalent thickness may include the thickness of portland cement plaster or 1.5 times the thickness of gypsum plaster applied in accordance with the requirements of Chapter 25.

TABLE 7-7-C-B—VALUES OF $R_n^{0.59}$ FOR USE IN FORMULA 1

TYPE OF MATERIAL	VALUES OF $R_n^{0.59}$ FOR USE IN EQUATION 1 FOR THICKNESS OF											
	1½ In. (38 mm)	2 In. (51 mm)	2½ In. (64 mm)	3 In. (76 mm)	3½ In. (89 mm)	4 In. (102 mm)	4½ In. (114 mm)	5 In. (127 mm)	5½ In. (140 mm)	6 In. (152 mm)	6½ In. (165 mm)	7 In. (178 mm)
Siliceous aggregate concrete	5.3	6.5	8.1	9.5	11.3	13.0	14.9	16.9	18.8	20.7	22.8	25.1
Carbonate aggregate concrete	5.5	7.1	8.9	10.4	12.0	14.0	16.2	18.1	20.3	21.9	24.7	27.2[3]
Sand-lightweight concrete	6.5	8.2	10.5	12.8	15.5	18.1	20.7	23.3	26.0[3]	3	3	3
Lightweight concrete	6.6	8.8	11.2	13.7	16.5	19.1	21.9	24.7	27.8[3]	3	3	3
Insulating concrete[1]	9.3	13.3	16.6	18.3	23.1	26.5[3]	3	3	3	3	3	3
Air space[2]	—	—	—	—	—	—	—	—	—	—	—	—

[1]Dry unit weight of 35 pcf (563 kg/m³) or less and consisting of cellular, perlite or vermiculite concrete.
[2]The $R_n^{0.59}$ value for ½ inch to 3½ inches (13 mm to 89 mm) air space is 3.3. The $R_n^{0.59}$ value for 2½ inches to 3½ inches (64 mm to 89 mm) air space is 6.7.
[3]The fire-resistance rating for this thickness exceeds four hours.

TABLE 7-7-C-C—MINIMUM SLAB THICKNESS FOR CONCRETE FLOORS OR ROOFS

CONCRETE TYPE	MINIMUM WALL THICKNESS (INCHES) FOR FIRE-RESISTANCE RATING OF				
	× 25.4 for mm				
	1 Hr.	1½ Hr.	2 Hr.	3 Hr.	4 Hr.
Siliceous[1]	3.5	4.3	5.0	6.2	7.0
Carbonate	3.2	4.0	4.6	5.7	6.6
Sand-lightweight	2.7	3.3	3.8	4.6	5.4
Lightweight	2.5	3.1	3.6	4.4	5.1

[1]The equivalent thickness may include the thickness of portland cement plaster or 1.5 times the thickness of gypsum plaster applied in accordance with the requirements of Chapter 25.

TABLE 7-7-C-D—COVER THICKNESS FOR REINFORCED CONCRETE FLOOR OR ROOF SLABS

CONCRETE AGGREGATE TYPE	THICKNESS OF COVER (INCHES) FOR FIRE-RESISTANCE RATING OF									
	× 25.4 for mm									
	Restrained[1]					Unrestrained[1]				
	1 Hr.	1^1/$_2$ Hr.	2 Hr.	3 Hr.	4 Hr.	1 Hr.	1^1/$_2$ Hr.	2 Hr.	3 Hr.	4 Hr.
Siliceous	^{3}/$_4$	^{3}/$_4$	^{3}/$_4$	^{3}/$_4$	^{3}/$_4$	^{3}/$_4$	^{3}/$_4$	1	1^1/$_4$	1^5/$_8$
Carbonate	^{3}/$_4$	^{3}/$_4$	^{3}/$_4$	^{3}/$_4$	^{3}/$_4$	^{3}/$_4$	^{3}/$_4$	^{3}/$_4$	1^1/$_4$	1^1/$_4$
Sand-lightweight	^{3}/$_4$	^{3}/$_4$	^{3}/$_4$	^{3}/$_4$	^{3}/$_4$	^{3}/$_4$	^{3}/$_4$	^{3}/$_4$	1^1/$_4$	1^1/$_4$
Lightweight	^{3}/$_4$	^{3}/$_4$	^{3}/$_4$	^{3}/$_4$	^{3}/$_4$	^{3}/$_4$	^{3}/$_4$	^{3}/$_4$	1^1/$_4$	1^1/$_4$

[1]See Section 7.141 of UBC Standard 7-1 for guidance on restrained and unrestrained assemblies.

TABLE 7-7-C-E—COVER THICKNESS FOR PRESTRESSED CONCRETE FLOOR OR ROOF SLABS

CONCRETE AGGREGATE TYPE	THICKNESS OF COVER (INCHES) FOR FIRE-RESISTANCE RATING OF									
	× 25.4 for mm									
	Restrained[1]					Unrestrained[1]				
	1 Hr.	1^1/$_2$ Hr.	2 Hr.	3 Hr.	4 Hr.	1 Hr.	1^1/$_2$ Hr.	2 Hr.	3 Hr.	4 Hr.
Siliceous	^{3}/$_4$	^{3}/$_4$	^{3}/$_4$	^{3}/$_4$	^{3}/$_4$	1^1/$_8$	1^1/$_2$	1^3/$_4$	2^3/$_8$	2^3/$_4$
Carbonate	^{3}/$_4$	^{3}/$_4$	^{3}/$_4$	^{3}/$_4$	^{3}/$_4$	1	1^3/$_8$	1^5/$_8$	2^1/$_8$	2^1/$_4$
Sand-lightweight	^{3}/$_4$	^{3}/$_4$	^{3}/$_4$	^{3}/$_4$	^{3}/$_4$	1	1^3/$_8$	1^1/$_2$	2	2^1/$_4$
Lightweight	^{3}/$_4$	^{3}/$_4$	^{3}/$_4$	^{3}/$_4$	^{3}/$_4$	1	1^3/$_8$	1^1/$_2$	2	2^1/$_4$

[1]See Section 7.141 of UBC Standard 7-1 for guidance on restrained and unrestrained assemblies.

TABLE 7-7-C-F—MINIMUM COVER TO MAIN REINFORCING BARS FOR REINFORCED CONCRETE BEAMS (APPLICABLE TO ALL TYPES OF STRUCTURAL CONCRETE)

RESTRAINED OR UNRESTRAINED[1]	BEAM WIDTH[2] (inches)	COVER THICKNESS (INCHES) FOR FIRE-RESISTANCE RATING OF				
	× 25.4 for mm	× 25.4 for mm				
		1 Hr.	1^1/$_2$ Hr.	2 Hr.	3 Hr.	4 Hr.
Restrained	5	^{3}/$_4$	^{3}/$_4$	^{3}/$_4$	1[1]	1^1/$_4$[1]
Restrained	7	^{3}/$_4$	^{3}/$_4$	^{3}/$_4$	^{3}/$_4$	^{3}/$_4$
Restrained	≥ 10	^{3}/$_4$	^{3}/$_4$	^{3}/$_4$	^{3}/$_4$	^{3}/$_4$
Unrestrained	5	^{3}/$_4$	1	1^1/$_4$	—	—
Unrestrained	7	^{3}/$_4$	^{3}/$_4$	^{3}/$_4$	1^3/$_4$	3
Unrestrained	≥ 10	^{3}/$_4$	^{3}/$_4$	^{3}/$_4$	1	1^3/$_4$

[1]See Section 7.141 of UBC Standard 7-1 for guidance on restrained and unrestrained assemblies. Tabulated values for restrained assemblies apply to beams spaced more than 4 feet (1219 mm) on centers; for restrained beams spaced 4 feet (1219 mm) or less on centers, minimum cover of ^{3}/$_4$ inch (19.1 mm) is adequate for ratings of four hours or less.

[2]For beam widths between the tabulated values, the minimum cover thickness can be determined by direct interpolation.

TABLE 7-7-C-G—MINIMUM COVER FOR PRESTRESSED CONCRETE BEAMS[1]

RESTRAINED OR UNRESTRAINED[2]	CONCRETE AGGREGATE TYPE[3]	BEAM WIDTH[4] (inches)	COVER THICKNESS[5] (INCHES) FOR FIRE-RESISTANCE RATING OF				
		× 25.4 for mm	× 25.4 for mm				
			1 Hr.	1^1/$_2$ Hr.	2 Hr.	3 Hr.	4 Hr.
Restrained	Carb or Sil	8	1^1/$_2$	1^1/$_2$	1^1/$_2$	1^3/$_4$[2]	2^1/$_2$[2]
Restrained	Carb or Sil	≥ 12	1^1/$_2$	1^1/$_2$	1^1/$_2$	1^1/$_2$	1^7/$_8$[2]
Restrained	Sand LW	8	1^1/$_2$	1^1/$_2$	1^1/$_2$	1^1/$_2$	2[2]
Restrained	Sand LW	≥ 12	1^1/$_2$	1^1/$_2$	1^1/$_2$	1^1/$_2$	1^5/$_8$[2]
Unrestrained	Carb or Sil	8	1^1/$_2$	1^3/$_4$	2^1/$_2$	5[6]	—
Unrestrained	Carb or Sil	≥ 12	1^1/$_2$	1^1/$_2$	1^7/$_8$	2^1/$_2$	3
Unrestrained	Sand LW	8	1^1/$_2$	1^1/$_2$	2	3^1/$_4$	—
Unrestrained	Sand LW	≥ 12	1^1/$_2$	1^1/$_2$	1^5/$_8$	2	2^1/$_2$

[1]This table shall not apply to I-shaped beams.

[2]See Section 7.141 of UBC Standard 7-1 for guidance on restrained and unrestrained assemblies. Tabulated values for restrained assemblies apply to beams spaced more than 4 feet on center.

[3]Carb = carbonate aggregate concrete; Sil = siliceous aggregate concrete; Sand LW = sand lightweight concrete.

[4]For beam widths between 8 inches and 12 inches (203 mm and 305 mm), minimum cover thickness can be determined by direct interpolation.

[5]The cover for an individual tendon is the minimum thickness of concrete between the surface of the tendon and the fire-exposed surface of the beam, except that the ungrouted ducts the assumed cover thickness is the minimum thickness of concrete between the surface of the duct and the surface of the beam. For beams in which several tendons are used, the cover is assumed to be the average of the minimum cover of the individual tendons. The cover for any individual tendon must not be less than one half of the value given in this table or less than 1 inch (25 mm).

[6]Not practical for 8-inch-wide (203 mm) beam, but shown for purposes of interpolation.

TABLE 7-7-C-H—MINIMUM SIZES OF CONCRETE COLUMNS

	MINIMUM COLUMN DIMENSION (INCHES) FOR FIRE-RESISTANCE RATING OF				
	× 25.4 for mm				
TYPE OF CONCRETE	1 Hr.	1½ Hr.	2 Hr.	3 Hr.	4 Hr.
Siliceous	8	8	10	12	14
Carbonate	8	8	10	12	14
Sand-lightweight	8	8	9	10.5	12

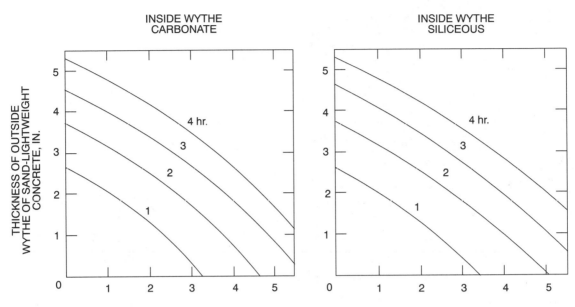

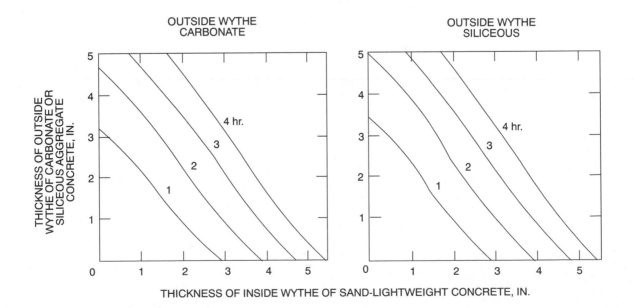

For **SI:** 1 inch = 25.4 mm.

**FIGURE 7-7-C-1—FIRE-RESISTANCE RATINGS OF TWO-WYTHE CONCRETE WALLS
CONSISTING OF WYTHES OF DIFFERENT TYPES OF CONCRETE**

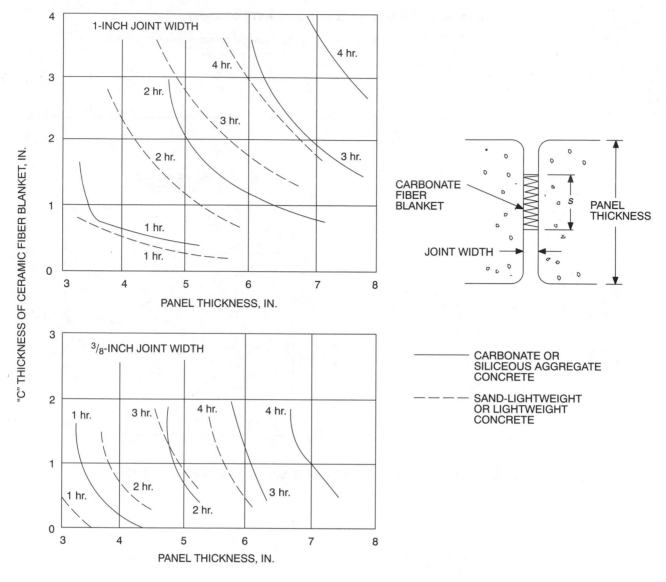

For SI: 1 inch = 25.4 mm.

FIGURE 7-7-C-2—MINIMUM THICKNESS OF CERAMIC FIBER BLANKET REQUIRED BETWEEN PRECAST CONCRETE WALL PANELS TO PROVIDE FIRE-RESISTANCE RATINGS OF ONE HOUR TO FOUR HOURS

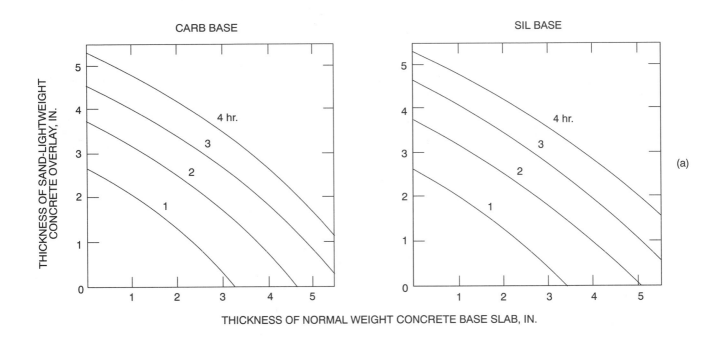

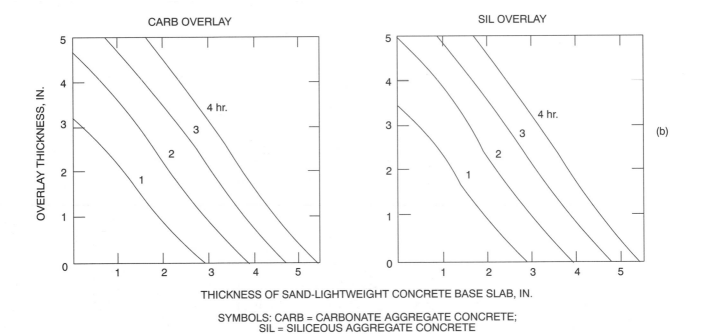

SYMBOLS: CARB = CARBONATE AGGREGATE CONCRETE;
SIL = SILICEOUS AGGREGATE CONCRETE

For **SI:** 1 inch = 25.4 mm.

FIGURE 7-7-C-3A—FIRE-RESISTANCE RATINGS FOR TWO-COURSE CONCRETE FLOORS

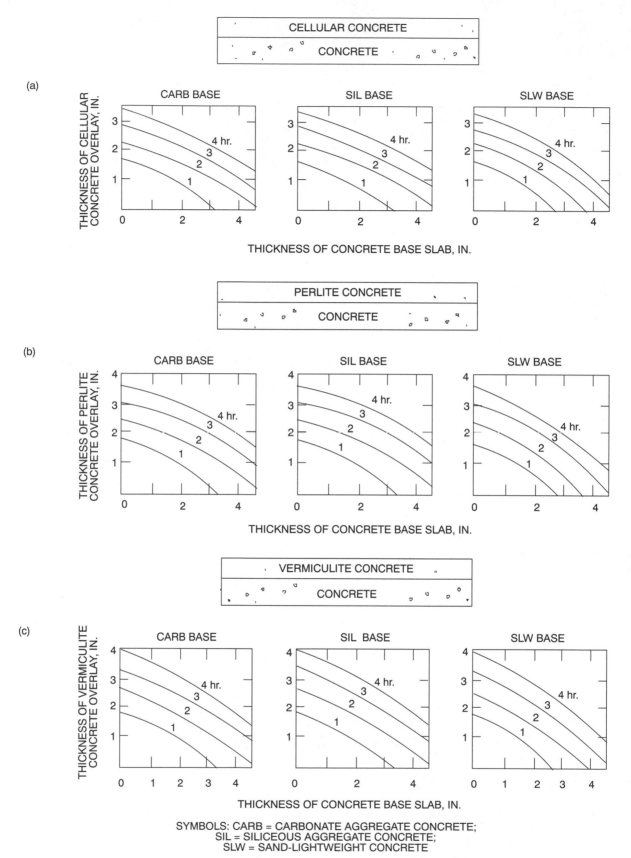

SYMBOLS: CARB = CARBONATE AGGREGATE CONCRETE;
SIL = SILICEOUS AGGREGATE CONCRETE;
SLW = SAND-LIGHTWEIGHT CONCRETE

For **SI:** 1 inch = 25.4 mm.

FIGURE 7-7-C-3B—FIRE-RESISTANCE RATINGS FOR CONCRETE ROOF ASSEMBLIES

(Continued)

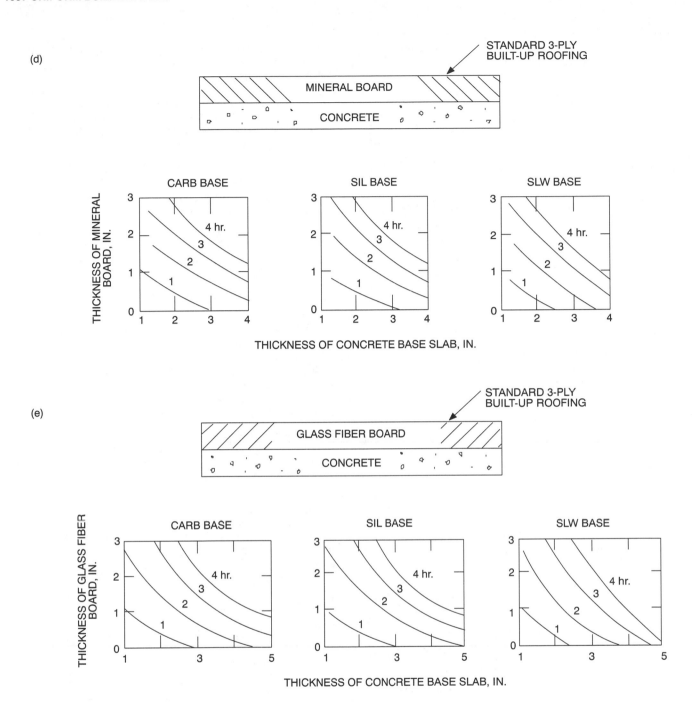

For **SI:** 1 inch = 25.4 mm.

FIGURE 7-7-C-3B—FIRE-RESISTANCE RATINGS FOR CONCRETE ROOF ASSEMBLIES—(Continued)

Part III—Methods for Calculating the Fire-resistance Rating of Concrete Masonry

SECTION 7.711 — SCOPE

This part of this standard contains procedures by which the fire-resistance rating of concrete masonry assemblies can be established by calculations. It is applicable to concrete masonry walls, concrete masonry columns, concrete masonry lintels and steel columns protected with concrete masonry.

SECTION 7.712 — MATERIAL REQUIREMENTS

Materials used in accordance with this standard shall comply with the following:

7.712.1 Concrete Masonry Units.

UBC Standard 21-2, Standard Specification for Calcium Silicate Face Brick (Sand-lime Brick)

UBC Standard 21-3, Standard Specification for Concrete Building Brick

UBC Standard 21-4, Standard Specification for Hollow and Solid Load-bearing Concrete Masonry Units

UBC Standard 21-5 Standard Specification for Nonload-bearing Concrete Masonry Units

7.712.2 Mortar.

UBC Standard 21-15, Standard Specifications for Mortar for Unit Masonry and Reinforced Masonry Other Than Gypsum

7.712.3 Grout.

UBC Standard 21-19, Standard Specification for Grout for Masonry

7.712.4 Material for Filling Cells of Units.

Sand or slag having a maximum particle size of $^3/_8$ inch (9.5 mm).

ASTM C 33-86, Standard Specification for Aggregate

ASTM C 144-89, Standard Specification for Aggregate for Masonry Mortar

ASTM C 330-85 and C 332-83, Standard Specifications for Lightweight Aggregates for Structural and Insulating Concrete

ASTM C 549-81, Perlite Loose-fill Insulation (Type II)

ASTM C 516-80, Vermiculite Loose-fill Insulation (Type I and Type II)

7.712.5 Material for Surface Coverings.

ASTM C 28-76a, Gypsum Plasters

ASTM C 36-76a, Gypsum Wallboard

SECTION 7.713 — CONCRETE MASONRY WALLS

7.713.1 General.
The fire-resistance rating of concrete masonry walls shall be determined in accordance with this section. The wall shall have the minimum equivalent thickness for the desired fire-resistive rating as specified in Table 7-7-M-A. The equivalent thickness of the wall may be increased by adding finishes in accordance with Section 7.713.3 and may be modified by combining more than one type of aggregate in the manufacture of the concrete masonry units in accordance with Section 7.713.4.

7.713.2 Determining Equivalent Thickness.
Equivalent thickness of concrete masonry walls shall be determined in accordance

with Formula (13-1) for units composed of a single aggregate and by Formula (13-2) for units composed of combined aggregates. When a plaster or gypsum wallboard finish material is applied over an entire face of a concrete masonry wall, the equivalent thickness of the wall assembly shall be determined in accordance with Formula (13-1). Equivalent thickness of units filled with grout or 100 percent solid units shall be the specified thickness.

$$T_E = \frac{V}{(L \times H)} + T_F \qquad (13\text{-}1)$$

WHERE:

H = height of block or brick using specified dimensions as defined in Chapter 21, inches (mm).

L = length of block or brick using specified dimensions as defined in Chapter 21, inches (mm).

T_E = equivalent thickness of wall, inches (mm).

T_F = equivalent thickness of finishes in Table 7-7-M-B.

V = net volume of unit, cubic inch (mm^3) (See ASTM C 140).

7.713.3 Finishes.
When a plaster or gypsum wallboard finish is applied over an entire face of the concrete masonry wall, the equivalent thickness of finish shall be determined in accordance with Table 7-7-M-B. The calculated equivalent thickness of the finish can then be added to the calculated equivalent thickness of the concrete masonry wall to determine the total equivalent thickness in accordance with Formula (13-1).

7.713.4 Minimum Required Equivalent Thickness for a Combination of Aggregates.
The fire-resistance rating of concrete masonry units composed of a combination of aggregate types shall be based on equivalent thickness values determined as follows:

Determine equivalent thickness values for each tabular column of the desired fire-resistance rating in Table 7-7-M-A by interpolating between equivalent thickness values for aggregate types in proportion to the percentage by volume of each aggregate used in accordance with Formula (13-2).

$$T_R = T_1 \times V_1 + T_2 \times V_2 \ldots T_n \times V_n \qquad (13\text{-}2)$$

WHERE:

$T_1, T_2 \ldots$

$\quad T_n$ = equivalent thickness for each aggregate Type 1, 2, ... n, respectively, used as indicated in Table 7-7-M-A for the desired fire-resistance rating.

T_R = minimum required equivalent thickness corresponding to the desired fire-resistance rating as listed in Table 7-7-M-A for concrete masonry units manufactured with a particular combination of aggregate types.

$V_1, V_2, \ldots$

$\quad V_n$ = percentage by volume of each aggregate Type 1, 2, ... n, respectively, which is used in the manufacture of the concrete masonry unit.

7.713.5 Fire-resistance Increase.
When the calculated fire-resistance rating of the concrete masonry wall without fill materials or finishes is not less than two hours, the fire-resistance rating may be increased to four hours provided the cells are completely filled with any of the materials specified in the Building Code and the minimum specified thickness of the concrete masonry units is $7^5/_8$ inches (193.7 mm) as determined in accordance with Chapter 21 of the Building Code.

7.713.6 Framing into Wall.
Combustible members framed into a wall shall be protected at their ends by not less than one half the required equivalent thickness of such wall.

7.713.7 Multiwythe. The fire-resistance rating of multiwythe walls, such as illustrated in Figure 7-7-M-1, shall be based on the fire-resistance rating of each wythe and the continuous air space between each wythe in accordance with Formula (13-3).

$$R = (R_1^{0.59} + R_2^{0.59} + R_n^{0.59} + A_1, + A_2 + \ldots A_n)^{1.7} \quad (13\text{-}3)$$

WHERE:

$A_1, A_2, \ldots$
$\quad A_n$ = 0.30, factor for each continuous air space $(1, 2, \ldots n$, respectively) having a depth of $^1/_2$ inch or more between wythes.

$R_1, R_2, \ldots$
$\quad R_n$ = fire-resistance rating of wythe $1, 2, \ldots n$ (hours), respectively.

SECTION 7.714 — CONTROL JOINTS

7.714.1 Design. Control joints installed in fire-resistance-rated concrete masonry walls may be designed in accordance with this section to maintain the fire-resistance rating of the wall in which they are installed.

7.714.2 Materials. The control joints shall be sealed with approved caulk, grout or gaskets in accordance with the details provided in Figure 7-7-M-2.

SECTION 7.715 — STEEL COLUMNS PROTECTED BY CONCRETE MASONRY

7.715.1 The fire-resistance rating of steel columns illustrated in Figure 7-7-S-7, protected by concrete masonry shall be determined in accordance with Part I of this standard.

SECTION 7.716 — CONCRETE MASONRY COLUMNS

7.716.1 Concrete masonry columns shall be designed and reinforced in accordance with the requirements of this code. The fire-resistance rating of concrete masonry columns shall be determined based on the least dimension of the column faces in accordance with the requirements of Table 7-7-M-C.

SECTION 7.717 — CONCRETE MASONRY LINTELS

7.717.1 The fire-resistance rating of concrete lintels shall be determined based on the nominal thickness of the lintel and the minimum thickness of concrete or concrete masonry or any combination thereof, covering the reinforcing steel as determined in accordance with Table 7-7-M-D.

TABLE 7-7-M-A—FIRE-RESISTANCE RATING OF CONCRETE MASONRY WALLS

AGGREGATE TYPE	MINIMUM REQUIRED EQUIVALENT THICKNESS, T_R (inches)			
	× 25.4 for mm			
	4 Hours	3 Hours	2 Hours	1 Hour
Calcareous or siliceous gravel	6.2	5.3	4.2	2.8
Limestone, cinders or slag	5.9	5.0	4.0	2.7
Expanded clay, shale or slate	5.1	4.4	3.6	2.6
Expanded slag or pumice	4.7	4.0	3.2	2.1

NOTE: The minimum required equivalent thickness of concrete masonry units made with a combination of aggregates shall be determined by linear interpolation of the values shown for each aggregate type in accordance with Formula (13-2) and Section 7.713.4.

TABLE 7-7-M-B—EQUIVALENT THICKNESS FOR EACH INCH OF FINISH THICKNESS (inches)

FINISH	AGGREGATE TYPE			
	Siliceous or Calcareous Gravel	Limestone Cinders or Slag	Expanded Shale, Clay or Slate	Expanded Slag or Pumice
	× 25.4 for mm			
Portland cement-sand plaster	1.00	0.75	0.75	0.50
Gypsum-sand plaster or gypsum wallboard	1.25	1.00	1.00	1.00
Gypsum-vermiculite or perlite plaster	1.75	1.50	1.25	1.25

TABLE 7-7-M-C—MINIMUM SIZES OF CONCRETE MASONRY COLUMNS

MINIMUM COLUMN DIMENSIONS, INCHES, FOR FIRE-RESISTANCE RATING OF			
1 Hour	2 Hours	3 Hours	4 Hours
× 25.4 for mm			
8	10	12	14

**TABLE 7-7-M-D—MINIMUM COVER ON MAIN REINFORCING BARS
FOR REINFORCED CONCRETE MASONRY LINTELS**

LINTEL THICKNESS (inches) (Nominal)	COVER THICKNESS (inches) FOR FIRE-RESISTANCE RATING OF			
× 25.4 for mm	× 25.4 for mm			
× 25.4 for mm	1 Hour	2 Hours	3 Hours	4 Hours
6	1	$1^1/_4$	—	—
8	1	1	$1^3/_4$	3
10 or more	1	1	1	$1^3/_4$

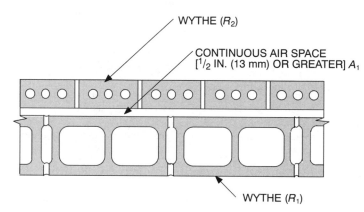

WYTHE (R_2)

CONTINUOUS AIR SPACE
[$^1/_2$ IN. (13 mm) OR GREATER] A_1

WYTHE (R_1)

A_1 = FIRE-RESISTANCE RATING FACTOR OF AIR SPACE
R_1 = FIRE-RESISTANCE RATING OF WYTHE 1
R_2 = FIRE-RESISTANCE RATING OF WYTHE 2

FIGURE 7-7-M-1—MULTIWYTHE WALL

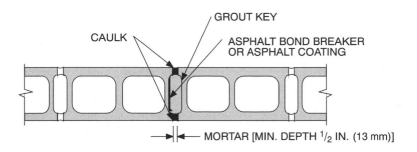

FOR RATINGS UP TO AND INCLUDING 4 HOURS

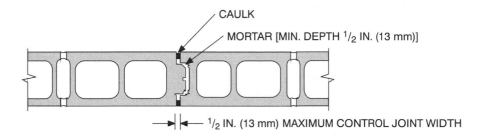

FOR RATINGS UP TO AND INCLUDING 4 HOURS

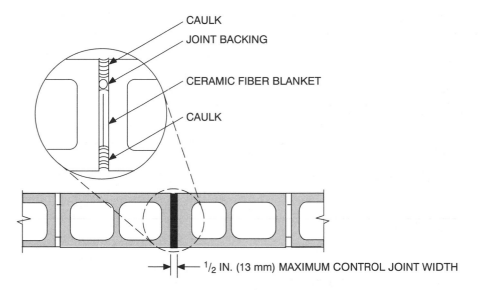

FOR RATINGS UP TO AND INCLUDING 4 HOURS

**FIGURE 7-7-M-2—TYPES OF CONTROL JOINTS FOR
FIRE-RESISTANCE-RATED CONCRETE MASONRY WALLS**

(Continued)

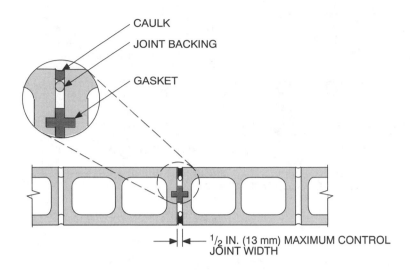

FOR RATINGS UP TO AND INCLUDING 2 HOURS

**FIGURE 7-7-M-2—TYPES OF CONTROL JOINTS FOR
FIRE-RESISTANCE-RATED CONCRETE MASONRY WALLS—(Continued)**

Part IV—Methods of Calculating the Fire-resistance Rating of Clay Masonry

SECTION 7.718 — SCOPE

This standard provides methods for calculating the fire-resistance-rating periods of clay and shale masonry. This standard is applicable to clay and tile masonry walls.

SECTION 7.719 — GENERAL

Clay masonry construction shall comply with the applicable requirements of this code.

SECTION 7.720 — CLAY MASONRY WALLS

7.720.1 General. The rated fire-resistive period of clay masonry walls shall be determined in accordance with this section. The fire-resistance periods of clay masonry units shall be determined from Tables 7-7-B-A, 7-7-B-B and 7-7-B-C. When sanded gypsum plaster is applied over the entire face of the clay masonry wall, the rated fire-resistive period shall be determined in accordance with Section 7.720.2. When continuous air spaces separate multiwythe walls, the rated fire-resistive period shall be determined in accordance with Section 7.720.4. The rated fire-resistive period of multiwythe walls shall be determined in accordance with Section 7.720.4. Hollow clay masonry walls shall have a minimum equivalent thickness for the desired fire-resistive rating as specified in Section 7.720.5.

7.720.2 Plaster Finishes. The fire-resistive rating period of sanded gypsum plastered clay masonry walls shall be based in accordance with Formula (20-1).

$$R = (R_n^{0.59} + Pl)^{1.7} \qquad (20\text{-}1)$$

WHERE:

Pl = thickness coefficient of sanded gypsum plaster.

R = fire-resistive rating of the assembly, hours.

R_n = fire-resistive period of wythe, hours.

Coefficients for thickness of sanded gypsum plaster shall be selected from Table 7-7-B-D, based on the actual thickness of plaster applied to the clay masonry wall and whether one or two sides of the wall are plastered.

7.720.3 Continuous Air Spaces. The fire-resistive rating period of multiwythe clay masonry walls separated by a continuous air space between each wythe shall be based in accordance with Formula (20-2).

$$R = (R_1^{0.59} + R_2^{0.59} + \ldots R_n^{0.59} + A_s)^{1.7} \qquad (20\text{-}2)$$

WHERE:

A_s = 0.30 factor for each continuous air space having a depth of $1/2$ inch to $3^1/2$ inches (12.7 mm to 88.9 mm) between wythes.

R = fire-resistive rating of the assembly, hours.

$R_1, R_2,$

R_n = fire-resistive period of each individual wythe, hours.

7.720.4 Multiwythe Walls. The fire-resistive rating period of multiwythe walls consisting of two or more dissimilar wythes shall be based on the fire-resistive periods of each wythe and shall be based in accordance with Formula (20-3).

$$R = (R_1^{0.59} + R_2^{0.59} + R_n^{0.59})^{1.7} \qquad (20\text{-}3)$$

WHERE:

R = fire-resistive rating of the assembly, hours.

$R_1, R_2, \ldots$

R_n = fire-resistive period of each individual wythe, hours.

For walls which consist of two or more wythes of dissimilar materials (concrete or concrete masonry units) in combination with clay masonry units, the fire-resistive period of the dissimilar materials shall be based in accordance with Table 7-7-C-B for concrete, Table 7-7-M-A for concrete masonry units or Table 7-7-B-A, 7-7-B-B or 7-7-B-C for clay masonry units.

7.720.5 Hollow Clay Masonry Walls. The rated fire-resistive period of hollow clay masonry units shall be based on the equivalent thickness in accordance with Formula (20-4).

$$T_E = \frac{V_n}{L \times H} \qquad (20\text{-}4)$$

WHERE:

H = height of brick using the specified dimensions as defined in Chapter 21 of the Building Code, inches (mm).

L = length of brick using the specified dimensions as defined in Chapter 21 of the Building Code, inches (mm).

T_E = equivalent thickness of wall, inches (mm).

V_n = net volume of unit, cubic inches (mm^3).

The fire-resistive rating for hollow clay brick shall be determined from Table 7-7-B-C based on the equivalent thickness. The fire-resistive rating determined from Table 7-7-B-C may be used in the calculated fire-resistance procedure of Sections 7.720.1, 7.720.2, 7.720.3 and 7.720.4.

TABLE 7-7-B-A—FIRE-RESISTIVE PERIODS FOR NONLOAD-BEARING AND LOAD-BEARING CLAY MASONRY WALLS[1]

WALL OR PARTITION ASSEMBLY, MINIMUM NOMINAL THICKNESS ×25.4 for mm ×0.093 for m²	FIRE-RESISTIVE PERIOD (hours)
CLAY OR SHALE, SOLID 4-inch brick 6-inch brick 8-inch brick	1.25 2.55 4.00
CLAY OR SHALE, HOLLOW 8-inch brick, 71% solid 12-inch brick, 64% solid 8-inch brick, 60% solid, cells filled with loose fill insulation	3.00 4.00 4.00
CLAY OR SHALE, ROLOK 8-inch Hollow Rolok 12-inch Hollow Rolok	2.50 4.00
CAVITY WALLS, CLAY OR SHALE 8-inch wall; two 3-inch (actual) brick wythes separated by 2-inch air space; masonry joint reinforcement spaced 16 inches on center vertically 10-inch wall; two nominal 4-inch wythes separated by 2-inch air space; 1/4-inch metal ties for each 3 square feet of wall area	3.00 4.00
CLAY OR SHALE BRICK, METAL FURRING CHANNELS 5-inch wall, 4-inch nominal brick (75% solid) backed with a hat-shaped metal furring channel 3/4 inch thick formed from 0.021 inch sheet metal attached to brick wall on 24 inch centers with approved fasteners; and 1/2-inch Type X gypsum board attached to the metal furring strips with 1-inch-long Type S screws spaced 8 inches on center	2.00
HOLLOW CLAY TILE, BRICK FACING 8-inch wall; 4-inch units (40% solid)[2] plus 4-inch solid brick 12-inch wall; 8-inch units (40% solid)[2] plus 4-inch solid brick	3.50 4.00

[1]Units shall comply with the requirements of UBC Standard 21-1 or ASTM C 126.
[2]Units shall comply with the requirements of ASTM C 34.

TABLE 7-7-B-B—FIRE-RESISTIVE PERIODS FOR
NONLOAD-BEARING AND LOAD-BEARING CLAY TILE MASONRY WALLS[1]

WALL OR PARTITION ASSEMBLY, MINIMUM NOMINAL THICKNESS	FIRE-RESISTIVE PERIOD (hours)
× 25.4 for mm	
HOLLOW CLAY TILE	
8-inch unit; 2 cells in wall thickness, 40% solid	1.25
8-inch unit; 2 cells in wall thickness, 43% solid	1.50
8-inch unit; 2 cells in wall thickness, 46% solid	1.75
8-inch unit; 2 cells in wall thickness, 49% solid	2.00
8-inch unit; 3 or 4 cells in wall thickness, 40% solid	1.75
8-inch unit; 3 or 4 cells in wall thickness, 43% solid	2.00
8-inch unit; 3 or 4 cells in wall thickness, 48% solid	2.50
8-inch unit; 3 or 4 cells in wall thickness, 53% solid	3.00
12-inch unit; 3 cells in wall thickness, 40% solid	2.50
12-inch unit; 3 cells in wall thickness, 45% solid	3.00
12-inch unit; 3 cells in wall thickness, 49% solid	3.50
12-inch wall; 2 units with 3 or 4 cells in wall thickness, 40% solid	3.50
12-inch wall; 2 units with 3 or 4 cells in wall thickness, 45% solid	4.00
12-inch wall; 2 units with 3 or 4 cells in wall thickness, 53% solid	4.00
16-inch wall; 2 or 3 units with 4 or 5 cells in wall thickness, 40% solid	4.00
CLAY TILE	
4-inch unit; 1 cell in wall thickness, 40% solid[2,3]	1.25
6-inch unit; 1 cell in wall thickness, 30% solid[2,3]	2.00
6-inch unit; 2 cell in wall thickness, 45% solid[4]	1.00
4-inch unit; 1 cell in wall thickness, 40% solid[3,4]	1.25
6-inch unit; 1 cell in wall thickness, 40% solid[3,4]	2.00
HOLLOW STRUCTURAL CLAY TILE	
8-inch unit; 2 cells in wall thickness, 40% solid	1.25
8-inch unit; 2 cells in wall thickness, 49% solid	2.00
8-inch unit; 3 or 4 cells in wall thickness, 53% solid	3.00
8-inch unit; 2 cells in wall thickness, 46% solid	1.75
12-inch unit; 3 cells in wall thickness, 40% solid	2.50
12-inch wall; 2 units, with 3 cells in wall thickness, 40% solid	3.50
12-inch wall; 2 units with 3 or 4 cells in wall thickness, 45% solid	4.00
12-inch unit, 3 cells in wall thickness, 45% solid	3.00
12-inch unit, 3 cells in wall thickness, 49% solid	3.50
16-inch wall, 2 units with 4 cells in wall thickness, 43% solid	4.00
16-inch wall; 2 or 3 units with 4 or 5 cells in wall thickness, 40% solid	4.00

[1]Units shall comply with the requirements of ASTM C 34, C 56, C 212 or C 530.
[2]Ratings are for dense hard-burned clay or shale tile.
[3]Cells filled with tile, stone, slag, cinders or sand mixed with mortar.
[4]Ratings are for medium-burned clay tile.

TABLE 7-7-B-C—MINIMUM EQUIVALENT THICKNESS[1] (inches) OF LOAD-BEARING
OR NONLOAD-BEARING HOLLOW CLAY MASONRY WALLS[2,3,4]

TYPE OF MATERIAL	FIRE-RESISTIVE PERIOD (hours)			
	1	2	3	4
	× 25.4 for mm			
Brick of clay or shale, unfilled	2.3	3.4	4.3	5.0
Brick of clay or shale, grouted or filled with perlite, vermiculite or expanded shale aggregate	3.0	4.4	5.5	6.6

[1]Equivalent thickness as determined for UBC Standard 7-7, Section 7.720.5.
[2]Values between those shown can be determined by direct interpolation.
[3]Where combustible members are framed in the wall, the thickness of solid material between the end of each member and the opposite face of the wall, or between members set in from opposite sides, shall not be less than 93 percent of the thickness shown in the table.
[4]Units shall comply with the requirements of UBC Standard 21-1, Section 21.107.

TABLE 7-7-B-D—COEFFICIENTS FOR PLASTER (PI)[1]

THICKNESS OF PLASTER (inch)	ONE-SIDE	TWO-SIDE
× 25.4 for mm		
$1/2$	0.30	0.60
$5/8$	0.37	0.75
$3/4$	0.45	0.90

[1]Values listed are for 1:3 sanded gypsum plaster.

Part V—Methods for Calculating One-hour Fire-resistive Ratings of Wood-framed Walls, Floors and Roofs

See Section 703.3, *Uniform Building Code*

SECTION 7.721 — SCOPE

This part establishes acceptable calculation methods for determining the fire-resistive classification of structural parts, walls and partitions and floor-ceiling or roof-ceiling assemblies. It is intended for use in cases where fire test results specified in UBC Standard 7-1 are not available and the specific assembly of materials is not among those listed in Tables 7-A, 7-B and 7-C.

Wood-framed Walls, Floors and Roofs

SECTION 7.722 — GENERAL

These procedures apply to both load-bearing and nonbearing construction. The calculated fire-resistive ratings shall only apply to one-hour construction. When the wall construction is nonsymmetrical, the provisions of Section 709.5 of the Building Code apply.

SECTION 7.723 — PROCEDURES

The fire-resistive rating of wood-framed construction is equal to the sum of the time assigned to the membrane on the fire-exposed side (Table 7-7-W-A), the time assigned to the framing members (Table 7-7-W-C), and the time assigned for other protective measures, such as insulation (Table 7-7-W-D). The membrane on the unexposed side shall not be included in determining the fire resistance of the assembly. When more than one membrane is installed on the wall surface exposed to fire, ratings of each membrane may be added.

SECTION 7.724 — WALLS AND PARTITIONS

Table 7-7-W-A lists the time of fire resistance accredited to the materials used on the fire-exposed side of walls and partitions.

SECTION 7.725 — ROOF-CEILING AND FLOOR-CEILING ASSEMBLIES

Table 7-7-W-B specifies the various acceptable membranes and limits the structural frame to wood joists installed on no more than 16-inch (406 mm) spacings. Ratings for roof-ceiling and floor-ceiling assemblies are based on the membranes listed in Table 7-7-W-A being installed on the fire-exposed side in combination with membranes listed in Table 7-7-W-B being installed on the side not exposed to furnace temperatures.

SECTION 7.726 — MEMBRANE FASTENING

Fastening the membrane to the supporting construction shall be as specified in Tables 7-B, 7-C and 23-II-B-1 of the Building Code for corresponding membrane materials.

TABLE 7-7-W-A—TIME ASSIGNED TO WALLBOARD MEMBRANES[1, 2, 3]

DESCRIPTION OF FINISH	TIME, MINUTES
$^3/_8$-inch (9.5 mm) Exterior-glue plywood	5
$^1/_2$-inch (12.7 mm) Exterior-glue plywood	10
$^5/_8$-inch (15.9 mm) Exterior-glue plywood	15
$^3/_8$-inch (9.5 mm) gypsum wallboard	10[4]
$^1/_2$-inch (12.7 mm) gypsum wallboard	15
$^5/_8$-inch (15.9 mm) gypsum wallboard	30
$^1/_2$-inch (12.7 mm) Type X gypsum wallboard	25
$^5/_8$-inch (15.9 mm) Type X gypsum wallboard	40
Double $^3/_8$-inch (9.5 mm) gypsum wallboard	25
$^1/_2 + ^3/_8$-inch (12.7 + 9.5 mm) gypsum wallboard	35
Double $^1/_2$-inch (12.7 mm) gypsum wallboard	40

[1]All wall panels shall be installed with the long dimension parallel to framing members or shall be backed with at least 2-inch-thick (51 mm) framing and gypsum panels.

[2]These values apply only when framing members are spaced a maximum of 16 inches (406 mm) on center.

[3]Plywood membranes shall be limited to nonbearing applications. Other membranes shall be limited to the design stress for studs shown by Footnote 19 to Table 7-B.

[4]Membrane rating combined with stud rating is 25.

TABLE 7-7-W-B—FLOORING OR ROOFING OVER WOOD FRAMING

ASSEMBLY	STRUCTURAL MEMBERS	SUBFLOOR OR ROOF DECK	FINISH FLOORING OR ROOFING
Floor	Wood joists	$^1/_2$-inch (12.7 mm) plywood or $^{11}/_{16}$-inch (17.5 mm) tongue-and-groove softwood	Hard or softwood flooring on building paper.
			Resilient flooring, parquet floor, felted-synthetic-fiber floor coverings, carpeting or ceramic tile on $^5/_8$-inch-thick (15.9 mm) panel-type underlay
			Ceramic tile on $1^1/_4$-inch (32 mm) mortar bed.
Roof	Wood joists	$^1/_2$-inch (12.7 mm) plywood or $^{11}/_{16}$-inch (17.5 mm) tongue-and-groove softwood	Finish roofing material with or without insulation. See Section 710.1 for the addition of insulation.

TABLE 7-7-W-C—TIME ASSIGNED FOR CONTRIBUTION OF WOOD FRAME[1, 2]

DESCRIPTION OF FRAME	TIME ASSIGNED TO FRAME, MINUTES
Wood studs 16 inches (406 mm) on center	20
Wood floor and roof joists 16 inches (406 mm) on center	10

[1]This table does not apply to studs or joists spaced more than 16 inches (406 mm) on center.

[2]All studs shall be nominal 2 inches by 4 inches (51 mm by 102 mm) and all joists shall have a nominal thickness of at least 2 inches (51 mm).

TABLE 7-7-W-D—TIME ASSIGNED FOR ADDITIONAL PROTECTION

DESCRIPTION OF ADDITIONAL PROTECTION	FIRE RESISTANCE, MINUTES
Add to the fire-resistance rating of wood stud walls if the spaces between the studs are filled with rock-wool batts weighing not less than 1.0 lb./ft.^{2} (4.9 kg/m^2) [3.3 lb.ft.^{3} (52.8 kg/m^3)] or glass-wool batts at 0.6 lb./ft.^{2} (2.9 kg/m^2) [2.0 lb./ft.^{3} (32 kg/m^3)] wall surface.	15

Part VI—Method for Design of One-hour Fire-resistive Exposed Wood Member [6-inch (152 mm) Nominal or Greater]

See Section 703.3, *Uniform Building Code*

SECTION 7.727 — SCOPE

Part IV of this standard applies to the design of one-hour fire-resistive exposed solid-sawn and glued-laminated timbers described in Chapter 23. The timbers shall have a minimum nominal thickness of 6 inches (152 mm).

This design method for one-hour fire-resistive exposed wood members is an accepted method of determining fire-resistive construction as specified in Section 703.3 of the Building Code.

SECTION 7.728 — DESIGN PROCEDURES

Design procedures, loads and allowable design stresses shall be as specified in Chapters 16 and 23. In addition, the column or beam shall be analyzed to determine the size required to sustain the design load at the end of a one-hour fire. This design procedure is specified in Section 7.729.

SECTION 7.729 — CALCULATION OF TIMBER SIZE

The following procedure shall be used to establish the fire rating of columns or beams and to determine the size required to be treated as one hour.

The fire-resistance rating, in minutes, of timber beams and columns with a minimum nominal dimension of 6 inches (152 mm) is equal to:

Beams—

1. $2.54\,Zb\,[4 - 2(b/d)]$ {For **SI**: $0.10\,Zb\,[4 - 2(b/d)]$} for beams which may be exposed to fire on four sides.
2. $2.54\,Zb\,[4 - (b/d)]$ {For **SI**: $0.10\,Zb\,[4 - (b/d)]$} for beams which may be exposed on three sides.

Columns—

3. $2.54\,Zd\,[3 - (d/b)]$ {For **SI**: $0.10\,Zd\,[3 - (d/b)]$} for columns which may be exposed to fire on four sides.

4. $2.54\,Zd\,[4 - (d/2b)]$ {For **SI**: $0.10\,Zd\,[4 - (d/2b)]$} for columns which may be exposed on three sides. (Applies only when the smaller side of the column is the exposed face.)

WHERE:

b = the breadth (width) of a beam or larger side of a column before exposure to fire, inches (mm).

d = the depth of a beam or smaller side of a column before exposure to fire, inches (mm).

K_e = the effective length factor (Figure 7-7-2).

l = the unsupported length of column, inches (mm) (Figure 7-7-1).

Z = the load factor (Figure 7-7-1).

If a column is recessed into a wall and protected, its minimum dimension need not be calculated using this procedure.

SECTION 7.730 — ACCEPTANCE CRITERIA OF CONSTRUCTION

In addition to sizing the timber, the following conditions shall be met:

1. The minimum nominal width or thickness is 6 inches (152 mm).

2. Connectors and fasteners relating to the support of the member shall be protected for equivalent fire resistance. When the minimum one-hour fire resistance is required, connectors and fasteners shall be protected from fire exposure by not less than $1^1/_2$ inches (38 mm) of wood, appropriate thickness or layers of Type X gypsum board, or any coating approved for one-hour rating.

3. For structural integrity of glued-laminated timbers, one additional lamination of 2-inch (51 mm) thickness shall be placed on the tension face of the beam and shall be equivalent in quality to that required by the design for the outer tensile lamination. The additional lamination n the tension face shall replace a core lamination to maintain the same design depth required in Section 7.729.

4. Glued-laminated timber shall be marked "Fire-rated One-hour" by the manufacturer to indicate compliance with Item 3.

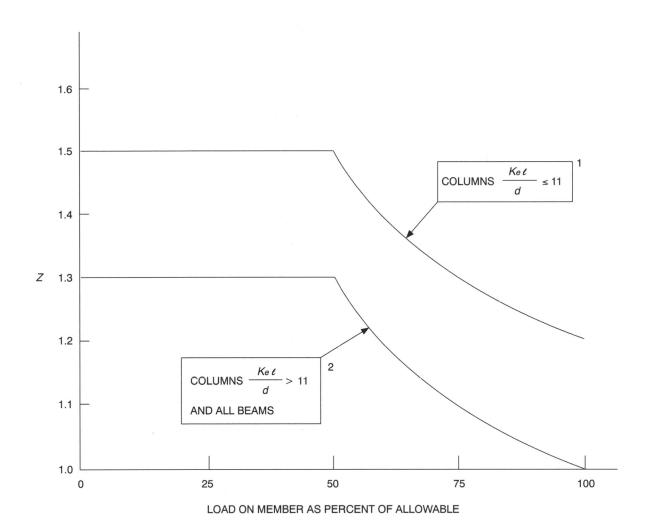

FIGURE 7-7-1—LOAD FACTOR

[1] For columns having a $K_e\ell/d \le 11$, Z shall be determined as follows:
Where the ratio of applied load to allowable load is equal to or less than 50, $Z = 1.5$.
Where the ratio of applied load to allowable load is greater than 50, Z shall be determined in accordance with the following formula.
$Z = 0.9 + 30/r$, where r = ratio of applied load to allowable load expressed as a percent of allowable.

[2] For columns having a $K_e\ell/d > 11$ and all beams, Z shall be determined as follows:
Where the ratio of applied load to allowable load is equal to or less than 50, $Z = 1.3$.
Where the ratio of applied load to allowable load is greater than 50, Z shall be determined in accordance with the following formula:
$Z = 0.7 + 30/r$, where r = ratio of applied load to allowable load expressed as a percent of allowable.

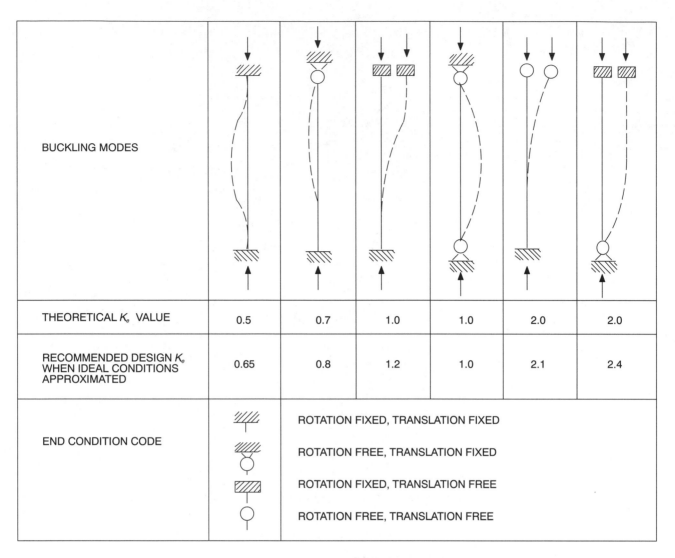

BUCKLING MODES						
THEORETICAL K_e VALUE	0.5	0.7	1.0	1.0	2.0	2.0
RECOMMENDED DESIGN K_e WHEN IDEAL CONDITIONS APPROXIMATED	0.65	0.8	1.2	1.0	2.1	2.4
END CONDITION CODE		ROTATION FIXED, TRANSLATION FIXED				
		ROTATION FREE, TRANSLATION FIXED				
		ROTATION FIXED, TRANSLATION FREE				
		ROTATION FREE, TRANSLATION FREE				

FIGURE 7-7-2—EFFECTIVE COLUMN LENGTH

UNIFORM BUILDING CODE STANDARD 7-8
HORIZONTAL SLIDING FIRE DOORS USED IN A MEANS OF EGRESS
Test Standard of the International Conference of Building Officials
See Sections 308.2.2.1 and 1004.3.4.3.2, Uniform Building Code

SECTION 7.801 — SCOPE

This standard covers performance criteria and conditions for horizontal sliding fire doors in means of egress.

SECTION 7.802 — APPLICATION

Compliance with these conditions permits use of horizontal fire doors in areas specifically authorized by the code.

SECTION 7.803 — GENERAL

Installation shall be in accordance with manufacturer's instructions and nationally recognized standards.

SECTION 7.804 — CONSTRUCTION

Door assemblies shall be fire rated in accordance with UBC Standard 7-2, and shall have a Class I interior finish rating. The door's power operating system shall be approved and listed. The power operating system shall be housed in a fire-resistive enclosure of the same rating as the door.

SECTION 7.805 — OPERATION

The door shall be power operated, be capable of manual operation in the event of power failure and be self-closing or smoke-detector-activated automatic closing. The door's power supply shall be capable of being electrically supervised at a constantly attended location and the door shall have an emergency power supply. Actuating devices shall be installed on both sides of the door and shall be inhibited from opening the door if the temperature on either side exceeds 500°F (260°C). The door shall be equipped with sensors capable of detecting obstructions in its closing path and of signaling such detection at the door location or at a constantly attended location. Automatic closing of the door or trouble conditions shall cause an audible alarm to be sounded at the door location. The alarm shall also be capable of being sounded at a constantly attended location. Operation of the activating device while the door is opening shall cause it to return to the closed position.

SECTION 7.806 — PERFORMANCE

7.806.1 Power Operation. The power operating system shall be examined in accordance with nationally recognized standards and shall be listed. The test report shall contain engineering data relative to tests for normal operation, electrical supervision, input and output, jarring, temperature, charging current, battery charger, undervoltage and overvoltage, standby operating power, variable ambient temperature, humidity, leakage current, transient, overload, endurance, dielectric withstand and abnormal operation. The report shall describe the mechanical operation of the power operating system in sequence as the door opens and closes under both normal and emergency conditions. It shall set forth the tests performed in accordance with nationally recognized standards and the results thereof. Additionally, the report shall contain an analysis comparing each feature of the design against the performance test procedures.

7.806.2 Automatic-closing Test. Upon receipt of the initiating device signal, the power operating system shall move the door to the closed position. The door shall begin closing within 10 seconds of receiving the signal. Closing speed shall not be less than 6 inches (152 mm) or more than 24 inches (610 mm) per second.

7.806.3 Ease of Operation Test. Manufacturers shall provide a test report from an approved independent authority that the door is easily recognized and operable for its intended usage without a key, special knowledge or effort.

The actuating device shall be subjected to a measurable force load. The force shall be applied to the actuating device in the direction of egress travel (perpendicular to the door). The force causing the actuating device to signal the power operating system to open the door shall not be more than 15 pounds (67 N).

7.806.4 Self-contained Power Test. Doors equipped with a self-contained power supply shall be subjected to cycle testing. One cycle shall be defined as the time to completely close the door from the open position and return it to the open position. The self-contained power supply shall have sufficient capacity to operate the door 50 cycles without the aid of outside power.

7.806.5 Manual Operation Test. With all power disconnected, and with the door in the closed position, 30 pounds (134 N) of force or less shall be applied in the direction of door travel to initiate the door opening. With a sustained force of 15 pounds (67 N) or less, the door shall open to the specified open distance but not less than 44 inches (1118 mm).

7.806.6 Temperature Override Test. The door shall include temperature-sensing devices installed at the leading edge approximately 12 inches (305 mm) from the top of the door. These devices shall be subjected to a measurable temperature. When the temperature exceeds 500°F (260°C), the actuating devices shall be deactivated and shall not cause the door to open.

7.806.7 Lateral Load Test. A lateral load shall be applied to the door in the direction of egress travel. The total load shall be equivalent to 250 pounds (1113 N) of force distributed over a minimum of five points over the total area of the closed door at locations at least 3 feet (914 mm), but not more than 6 feet (1829 mm), from the floor. Under this condition, the door must meet the conditions of the ease of operation test outlined in Section 7.806.3.

7.806.8 Opening Speed. The door shall open to a distance of 88 inches (2235 mm) within 10 seconds after activation of the actuating device.

SECTION 7.807 — CONDITIONS OF ACCEPTANCE

A door shall be considered as meeting the requirements for acceptable performance when it conforms to the tests under Section 7.806.

SECTION 7.808 — MARKING

7.808.1 Label. Doors shall bear fire-rating labels issued by a listing agency showing compliance with UBC Standards 7-2 and

7-8. The label shall be of metal attached to the assembly by welding, brazing, riveting or contact adhesive.

7.808.2 Label Markings. The markings on the label shall include the following:

1. Name and address of the listee.

2. Model number or type.

3. Symbol, serial or issue number issued by the listing agency.

UNIFORM BUILDING CODE STANDARD 8-1
TEST METHOD FOR SURFACE-BURNING
CHARACTERISTICS OF BUILDING MATERIALS

**Based on Standard Test Method E 84-84 of the American Society for Testing and Materials.
Extracted, with permission, from the *Annual Book of ASTM Standards,* copyright American Society for
Testing and Materials, 100 Barr Harbor Drive, West Conshohocken, PA 19428**

**See Sections 201.2; 207; 215; 217; 405.1; 405.3.4; 601.3; 707.2; 707.3; 801.1, Items 1 and 2;
802.2; 2602.3; 2602.5.2 and 2602.6, *Uniform Building Code;* Section 216, Table 3-A, and
Section 1201.1, *Uniform Mechanical Code;* and Sections 202 and 211, *Uniform Sign Code***

SECTION 8.101 — SCOPE

This method for surface-burning characteristics of building materials is applicable to any type of building material that, by its own structural quality or the manner in which it is applied, is capable of supporting itself in position or may be supported in the test furnace to a thickness comparable to its recommended use.

> **EXCEPTION:** This test method shall not apply to cellulose loose-fill insulation.

The purpose of the test is to determine the comparative burning characteristics of the material under test by evaluating the flame spread over its surface when exposed to a test fire and thus to establish a basis on which surface-burning characteristics of different materials may be compared, without specific consideration of all the end-use parameters that might affect the surface-burning characteristics.

Smoke density as well as the flame-spread rate are recorded in this test. However, there is not necessarily a relationship between these measurements.

It is the intent of this method to register performance during the period of exposure, and not to determine suitability for use after the test exposure.

This standard shall be used to measure and describe the properties of materials, products or assemblies in response to heat and flame under controlled laboratory conditions and is not to describe or appraise the fire hazard or fire risk of materials, products or assemblies under actual fire conditions. However, results of this test may be used as elements of a fire risk assessment which takes into account all of the factors which are pertinent to an assessment of the fire hazard of a particular end use.

This method is intended to provide only comparative measurements of surface flame-spread and smoke-density measurements with that of Select grade red oak and asbestos-cement board surfaces under the specific fire exposure conditions described herein.

The test exposes a nominal 24-foot-long (7315 mm) by 20-inch-wide (508 mm) specimen to a controlled airflow and flaming fire exposure adjusted to spread the flame along the entire length of the Select grade red oak specimen in $5^1/_2$ minutes.

The test method does not provide for the following:

Measurement of heat transmission through the tested surface.

The effect of aggravated flame-spread behavior of an assembly resulting from the proximity of combustible walls and ceilings.

Classifying or defining a material as noncombustible, by means of a flame-spread index by itself.

SECTION 8.102 — FIRE TEST CHAMBER

The fire test chamber, Figures 8-1-1 and 8-1-2, shall consist of a horizontal duct having an inside width of $17^3/_4$ inches $\pm$ $^1/_4$ inch (451 mm $\pm$ 6.3 mm) measured at ledge location along side walls and $17^5/_8$ inches $\pm$ $^3/_8$ inch (448 mm $\pm$ 10 mm) at all other points; a

depth of 12 inches $\pm$ $^1/_2$ inch (305 mm $\pm$ 13 mm) measured from the bottom of the test chamber to the ledge of the inner walls on which the sample is supported [including the $^1/_8$-inch (3.2 mm) thickness of asbestos fabric gasketing tape]; and a length of 25 feet (7620 mm). The sides and base of the duct are to be lined with insulating masonry as illustrated in Figure 8-1-2 consisting of A. P. Green, G-26 refractory firebrick. The operation and calibration of this equipment is based on the use of A. P. Green Refractories. One side is to be provided with a double window with the inside pane flush mounted (see Figure 8-1-2) pressure tight as described in Section 8.104. Exposed inside glass shall be $2^3/_4$ inches $\pm$ $^3/_8$ inch by 11 inches plus 1 inch minus 2 inches (70 mm $\pm$ 10 mm by 279 mm + 25 mm – 50 mm). The center line of the exposed area of the inside glass shall be in the upper half of the furnace wall, with the upper edge not less than 2.5 inches (63 mm) below the furnace ledge. The window shall be located such that not less than 12 inches (305 mm) of the specimen width can be observed. Multiple windows shall be located along the tunnel so that the entire length of the test sample may be observed from outside the fire chamber.

The ledges shall be fabricated of structural material capable of withstanding the abuse of continuous testing, level with respect to length and width of the chamber and each other and maintained in a state of repair commensurate with the frequency, volume and severity of testing occurring at any time.

To provide air turbulance for proper combustion, turbulence baffling is to be provided as necessary by positioning six A. P. Green, G-26, refractory firebricks [long dimension vertical $4^1/_2$-inch (114 mm) dimension along the wall] along the sidewalls of the chamber at distances of 7 feet, 12 feet and 20 feet $\pm$ 0.5 foot (2.1 m, 3.7 m and 6.1 m $\pm$ 0.2 m) on the window side and $4^1/_2$ feet, $9^1/_2$ feet and 16 feet $\pm$ 0.5 foot (1.3 m, 2.9 m and 4.9 m $\pm$ 0.2 m) on the opposite side.

The top shall consist of a removable noncombustible (metal and mineral composite) structure, insulated with nominal 2-inch-thick (51 mm) mineral composition material as shown in Figure 8-1-2 and of a size necessary to completely cover the fire test chamber and the test samples. The mineral composition material shall have physical characteristics comparable to the following:

Maximum effective temperature—1,200°F (650°C)

Bulk density—12.5 $\pm$ 1.5 lb/ft.^{3} (200 $\pm$ 24 kg/m^3)

Thermal conductivity—0.45-0.65 Btu in./h. ft.^{2} °F at 300-700°F (0.065 – 0.094 W/m·k at 149 – 371°C)

The entire lid assembly shall be protected with flat sections of high density [nominal 110 lb./ft.^{3} (1761 kg/m^3)] $^1/_4$-inch (6.3 mm) asbestos-cement board maintained in an unwarped and uncracked condition through continued replacement. When in place, the top is to be completely sealed against the leakage of air into the fire test chamber during the test.

One end of the test chamber, designated as the "fire end," shall be provided with two gas burners delivering flames upward against the surface of the test sample. The burners are to be spaced

12 inches (305 mm) from the fire end of the test chamber sample and $7^1/_2$ inches ± $^1/_2$ inch (190 mm ± 13 mm) below the under surface of the test sample. The air intake shutter is to be located 54 inches ± 5 inches (1372 mm ± 127 mm) upstream of the burner, as measured from the burners' center line to the outside surface of the shutter. Gas to the burners shall be provided through a single inlet pipe, distributed to each port burner through a tee section. The outlet shall be a $^3/_4$-inch (19 mm) elbow. The plane of the port shall be parallel to the furnace floor, such that the gas is directed upward toward the specimen. Each part shall be positioned transversely approximately 4 inches ± $^1/_2$ inch (102 mm ± 13 mm) on each side of the center line of the furnace so that the flame is evenly distributed over the width of the exposed sample surface. See Figure 8-1-2. The controls used to assure constant flow of gas to the burners during periods of use are to consist of a pressure regulator, a gas meter calibrated to read in increments of not more than 0.1 ft.^{3} (2.8 L), a manometer to indicate gas pressure in inches of water, a quick-acting gas shutoff valve, a gas-metering valve and an orifice plate in combination with a water manometer to assist in maintaining uniform gas-flow conditions. An air intake fitted with a vertically sliding shutter extending the entire width of the test chamber is to be provided at the fire end. The shutter is to be positioned so as to provide an air-inlet port 3 inches ± $^1/_{16}$ inch (76 mm ± 2 mm) high measured from the floor level of the test chamber at the air-intake point.

The other end of the test chamber, designated as the "vent end," is to be fitted with a gradual rectangular-to-round transition piece, not less than 20 inches (508 mm) in length with a minimum cross-sectional area of 200 square inches (0.129 m^2) at any point. The transition piece shall in turn be fitted to a 16-inch-diameter (406 mm) flue pipe. The movement of air is to be by induced draft system, and the draft-inducing system is to have a total draft capacity of at least 0.15-inch (3.8 mm) water column with the sample in place, the shutter at the fire end open to normal 3 inches ± $^1/_{16}$ inch (76 mm ± 2 mm), and the damper in the wide-open position. A draft gage tap to indicate static pressure shall be inserted through the top at the midwidth of the tunnel, 1 inch ± 0.5 inch (25 mm ± 12 mm) below the ceiling, 15 inches ± 0.5 inch (381 mm ± 13 mm) downstream from the inlet shutter.

A light source shall be mounted on a horizontal section of the 16-inch-diameter ± (406 mm) horizontal vent pipe at a point where it will be preceded by a straight run of pipe [at least 12 diameters or 16 feet (4880 mm) and not more than 30 diameters or 40 feet (12 190 mm)], from the vent end of the chamber, with the light beam directed upward along the vertical axis of the vent pipe. The vent pipe is to be insulated with at least 2 inches (51 mm) of high-temperature mineral composition material from the vent end of the chamber to the photometer location. A photoelectric cell of which the output is directly proportional to the amount of light received is to be mounted over the light source and connected to a recording device for indicating changes in the attenuation of incident light by passing smoke, particulate and other effluent. The distance between the light source lens and the photocell lens shall be 36 inches ± 4 inches (914 mm ± 102 mm). The cylindrical light beam shall pass through 3-inch-diameter (76 mm) openings at the top and bottom of the 16-inch-diameter (406 mm) duct, with the resultant light beam centered on the photocell.

Linearity of the photometer system shall be verified periodically by interrupting the light beam with calibrated neutral density filters. The filters shall cover the full range of the recording instrument. Transmittance values measured by the photometer, using neutral density filters, shall be within ± 3 percent of the calibrated value for each filter.

An automatically controlled damper to regulate the draft pressure shall be installed in the vent pipe downstream of the smoke-indicating attachment. The damper shall be provided with a manual override.

Other manual or automatic draft regulation devices, or both, may be incorporated to maintain fan characterization and airflow control throughout test periods.

A No. 18 AWG (1.02 mm) thermocouple, with $^3/_8$ inch ± $^1/_8$ inch (9.5 mm ± 3.2 mm) of the junction exposed in the air, shall be inserted through the floor of the test chamber so that the tip is 1 inch ± $^1/_{32}$ inch (25.4 mm ± 0.8 mm) below the top surface of the asbestos gasketing tape and 23 feet ± $^1/_2$ inch (7010 mm ± 13 mm) from the center line of the burner ports at the center of its width.

A No. 18 AWG (1.02 mm) thermocouple embedded $^1/_8$ inch (3.2 mm) below the floor surface of the test chamber is to be mounted in refractory or portland cement carefully dried to avoid cracking at distances of 13 feet ± $^1/_2$ inch (3962 mm ± 13 mm) and $23^1/_4$ feet ± $^1/_2$ inch (7087 mm ± 13 mm) from the center line of the burner ports.

The room in which the test chamber is located is to have provision for a free inflow of air during test to maintain the room at atmospheric pressure during the entire test run.

SECTION 8.103 — TEST SPECIMENS

The test specimen shall be at least 2 inches (51 mm) wider [nominally $20^1/_4$ inches ± $^3/_4$ inch (514 mm ± 19 mm)] than the interior width of the tunnel and total 24 feet ± $^1/_2$ inch (7315 mm ± 13 mm) in length. The specimen may consist of a continuous, unbroken length or of sections joined end-to-end. A 14-inch ± $^1/_8$-inch (356 mm ± 3 mm) length of uncoated 16-gage (0.053-inch to 0.060-inch) steel sheet shall be placed on specimen mounting ledge in front of and under the specimen in the upstream end of the tunnel. Specimens shall truly represent the materials for which classification is desired. Properties adequate for identification of the materials or ingredients, or both, of which the test specimen is made are to be determined and recorded.

The test specimen shall be conditioned to a constant weight at a temperature of 73.4°F ± 5°F (23°C ± 2.8°C) and at a relative humidity of 50 ± 5 percent.

SECTION 8.104 — CALIBRATION OF TEST EQUIPMENT

A $^1/_4$-inch (6.3 mm) asbestos-cement board shall be placed on the ledge of the furnace chamber. The removable top of the test chamber shall be placed in position.

With the $^1/_4$-inch (6.3 mm) asbestos-cement board in position on top of the ledge of the furnace chamber, and with the removable top in place, the draft is to be established so as to produce a 0.15-inch (3.8 mm) water-column reading on the draft manometer, with the fire-end shutter open 3 inches ± $^1/_{16}$ inch (76 mm ± 1.6 mm) by manually setting the damper as a characterization of fan performance. The fire-end shutter shall be closed and sealed without changing the damper position. The manometer reading shall increase to at least 0.375-inch (9.53 mm) water column, indicating that no excessive air leakage exists.

In addition, a supplemental leakage test is to be conducted periodically with the fire shutter and exhaust duct beyond the differential manometer tube sealed, by placing a smoke bomb in the chamber. The bomb shall be ignited and the chamber pressurized to 0.375 inch ± 0.15-inch (9.53 mm ± 3.18 mm) water column. All points of leakage observed in the form of escaping smoke particles shall be sealed.

A draft reading shall be established within the range 0.055-inch to 0.100-inch (1.40 to 2.54 mm) water column. The required draft gage reading shall be maintained by the automatic damper. Record the air velocity at seven points, 23 feet (7010 mm) from the center line of the burner ports, 6 inches ± $^1/_4$ inch (168 mm ± 7 mm) below the plane of the specimen mounting ledge. Determine these seven points by dividing the width of the tunnel into seven equal sections and recording the velocity at the geometrical center of each section. During the measurement of velocity, remove the turbulence bricks and exposed 23-foot (7010 mm) thermocouple and place 24-inch-long (670 mm) straightening vanes between 16 feet and 18 feet (4876 mm and 5486 mm) from the burner. The straightening vanes shall divide the furnace cross section into nine uniform sections. Determine the velocity with furnace air temperature at 73.4°F ± 5°F (23°C ± 2.8°C) using a velocity transducer. The velocity, determined as the arithmetic average of the seven readings, shall be 240 feet ± 5 feet (7.32 m ± 1.5 m) per minute.

Maintain the air supply at a temperature of 73.4°F ± 5°F (23°C ± 2.8°C) and a relative humidity of 50 ± 5 percent.

The fire test chamber shall be suppled with natural (city) or methane (bottled) gas fuel of uniform quality with a heating value of nominally 1,000 Btu/ft^3 (37.3 MJ/m^3). The gas supply is to be initially adjusted at approximately 5,000 Btu/min. (5.3 MJ/min.) The gas pressure, the pressure differential across the orifice plate and the volume of gas used shall be recorded in each test. Unless otherwise corrected for, when bottled methane is employed, a length of coiled copper tubing is to be inserted into the gas line between the supply and metering connection to compensate for possible errors in the flow indicated due to reductions in gas temperature associated with the pressure drop and expansion across the regulator. With the draft and gas supply adjusted as indicated in this section, the test flame is to extend downstream to a distance of $4^1/_2$ feet (1372 mm) over the specimen surface, with negligible upstream coverage.

The test chamber shall be preheated with the $^1/_4$-inch (6.3 mm) asbestos-cement board and the removable top in place and with the fuel supply adjusted to the required flow. The preheating shall be continued until the temperature indicated by the floor thermocouple at $23^1/_4$ feet (7087 mm) reaches 150°F ± 5°F (66°C ± 2.8°C). During the preheat test, the temperatures indicated by the thermocouple at the vent end of the chamber shall be recorded at 15-second intervals and compared to the preheat temperature shown in the time-temperature curve, Figure 8-1-3. The preheating is for the purpose of establishing the conditions that will exist following the successive tests and to indicate the control of the heat input into the test chamber. If the appreciable variation from the temperatures shown in the representative preheat curve is observed, because of variation in the characteristics of the gas used, adjustments in the fuel supply may be made prior to proceeding with the red oak calibration tests.

The furnace shall be allowed to cool after each test. When the floor thermocouple at 13 feet (3962 mm) shows a temperature of 105°F ± 5°F (40.5°C ± 2.8°C), the next specimen shall be placed in position for test.

With the test equipment adjusted and conditioned as described in this section, a test or series of tests shall be made, using nominal $^{23}/_{32}$-inch (18.3 mm) Select grade red oak flooring as the sample, conditioned to 6 to 8 percent moisture content as determined by the 221°F (105°C) oven-dry method in accordance with approved nationally recognized standards. Observations shall be made at distance intervals of not more than 2 feet (610 mm) and time intervals of not more than 30 seconds and the time recorded when the flame reaches the end of the specimen, that is, $19^1/_2$ feet (5944 mm) from the end of the ignition fire. The end of the ignition fire shall be considered as being $4^1/_2$ feet (1372 mm) from the burners. The flame shall reach the end point in five and one-half minutes ± 15 seconds. The temperature measured by the thermocouple near the vent end shall be automatically recorded at least every 15 seconds. The photoelectric cell output shall be automatically recorded immediately prior to the test and at least every 15 seconds during the test.

The results of tests of Select grade red oak flooring in which the flame spreads $19^1/_2$ feet (5944 mm) from the end of the igniting flame in five and one-half minutes shall be considered as representing a classification of 100. Plot the flame spread distance, temperature, and change in photoelectric cell readings separately on suitable coordinate paper. Figures 8-1-4, 8-1-5 and 8-1-6 are representative curves for red oak flame spread distance, time-temperature development, and smoke density, respectively. Flame-spread distance shall be determined as the observed distance minus $4^1/_2$ feet (1372 mm).

Following the calibration tests for red oak, a similar test(s) is to be conducted on samples of $^1/_4$-inch (6.3 mm) asbestos-cement board. The results are to be considered as representing a classification of zero. The temperature readings shall be plotted separately on coordinate paper. Figure 8-1-7 is a representative curve for fuel contribution of asbestos-cement board.

SECTION 8.105 — MOUNTING METHODS

8.105.1 General.

8.105.1.1 Purpose. The methods specified in this section have been compiled as an aid in selecting a means for mounting and supporting various building materials in the fire test chamber for test method uniformity and convenience. They are not meant to imply restriction in the specific details of field installation.

8.105.1.2 Application. These methods shall apply to (i) materials that, in and of themselves, are not self-supporting when installed in the test chamber in accordance with Section 8.106, and (ii) materials that are self-supporting as indicated herein, but which become dislodged from their mounting position or otherwise separate or distort so that they fall to the floor of the test chamber during the test. Materials that are installed and perform as described in (ii) above shall be retested when mounted and supported in accordance with the applicable method specified in this section.

8.105.1.3 Alternates. For some building materials, none of the methods described may be applicable. In such cases, other means of mounting and support shall be devised to minimize the effect of the mounting and support method on the performance of the material when tested in accordance with this standard.

8.105.1.4 Format. These mounting methods are grouped according to building materials to be tested, which are broadly described either by usage or by form of the material.

8.105.1.5 Cement board backing. Whenever inorganic reinforced cement board is specified as a backing in this section, the material shall be nominal $^1/_4$-inch (6.3 mm) thick, high density [110 ± 5 lb./ft.^{3} (1792 ± 80 kg/m^3)] and uncoated.

8.105.1.6 Use of metal rods. When metal rods or bars are specified in this section as supports, they shall be:

Steel rods, $^1/_4$-inch (6.3 mm) diameter
Steel bars, $^3/_{16}$ inch by 2 inches (5 mm by 51 mm)

The rods or bars shall span the width of the tunnel. Rods shall be placed approximately 2 inches (51 mm) from each end of each panel and at approximately 2-foot (610 mm) intervals starting with the fire end of each panel.

Bars shall be used instead of rods only when they are required to support the sample. The bars shall be placed approximately 2 inches (51 mm) from each end of each panel and at approximately 2-foot (610 mm) intervals starting with the fire end of each panel.

8.105.1.7 Use of netting. Whenever netting is specified as a support in this section, the material shall be 20-gage, 2-inch (51 mm), hexagonal galvanized steel netting (chicken wire).

8.105.2 Acoustical and Other Similar Panel Products Less Than 20 Inches (508 mm).

8.105.2.1 For acoustical materials and other similar panel products whose maximum dimension is less than 20 inches (508 mm), metal splines or wood furring strips and metal fasteners shall be used.

8.105.2.2 Steel tee splines for mounting kerfed-acoustical tile shall be nominal $^1/_2$-inch (13 mm) web by $^3/_4$-inch (19 mm) flange, formed No. 24 gage [0.021-inch (0.53 mm) minimum thickness] sheet metal.

8.105.2.3 Wood furring frames for mounting acoustical materials and other similar panel products whose maximum dimension is less than 20 inches (508 mm) shall be nominal 1-inch-by-2-inch (25 mm by 51 mm) wood furring joined with corrugated-metal fasteners. Use two frames as shown in Figure 8-1-9.

8.105.3 Adhesives. To determine the surface-burning characteristics of adhesives, they shall be mixed as specified in the manufacturer's instructions and shall be applied to inorganic reinforced cement board in the thickness or at the coverage rate recommended by the manufacturer. The adhesive application shall be cured prior to testing.

8.105.4 Batt or Blanket-type Insulating Materials. Batt or blanket materials that do not have sufficient rigidity or strength to support themselves shall be supported by metal rods inserted through the material and positioned such that the bottom of the rod is approximately $^1/_4$ inch (6.3 mm) from the surface to be exposed to the flame. Batt or blanket materials less than 1-inch (25.4 mm) thick shall not be mounted for testing in this manner.

8.105.5 Coating Materials, Cementitious Mixtures and Sprayed Fibers. Coating materials, cementitious mixtures and sprayed fibers shall be mixed and applied as specified in the manufacturer's instructions.

8.105.6 Loose-fill Insulation. Loose-fill insulation, other than cellulose loose-fill insulation, shall be placed on the floor of the tunnel at an approximate thickness of 2 inches (51 mm) by length of the tunnel, packed to the density specified by the manufacturer. Ceramic paper with a nominal density of 0.7 kg/m^2 shall be laid on the floor of the tunnel beneath the insulation, with appropriate cutouts being made to accommodate the burners and thermocouple.

The following modifications to the tunnel shall be made:

Inside windows shall be removed, leaving only the outside windows.

The burners shall be capable of vertical movement upwards and adjusted so that their center line is 2 inches ± $^1/_8$ inch (50.8 mm ± 3.2 mm) above the nominal level of the top of the test sample. The elbows constituting the burner ports shall be rotated until they are pointed downwards at an angle of 45 degrees to the horizontal in the direction of the air flow (see Figure 8-1-12).

To reduce (air) eddies and possible ablation of low-density materials in the burner vicinity, an air ramp (see Figure 8-1-13) shall be placed as shown with the downstream end of the ramp terminating beneath the center line of the burner tee and overlapping the specimen 1 inch (25.4 mm). The ramp shall be made of No. 304 stainless steel, minimum thickness $^1/_{16}$ inch (1.6 mm), 26 inches (660 mm) long and sized to fit within $^1/_8$ inch (3.2 mm) of the furnace width.

Flame Spread Index shall be determined as follows:

If the total area (A_T) is less than or equal to 97.5 feet·min., the Flame Spread Index shall be 0.564 times the total area (FSI = 0.564_T) (For SI: If $A_T \le 29.7$ m·min., FSI = 1.85 A_T).

If the total area (A_T) is greater than 97.5 feet·min., the Flame Spread Index shall be 5363, divided by the difference of 195 minus the total area (A_T). [FSI = 5363/(195 – A_T)] [For SI: If $A_T >$ 29.7 m·min., FSI = 1640/(59.4 – A_T)].

Smoke developed is determined as stated in Section 8.104.

8.105.7 Plastics. Plastics shall be supported by metal rods or bars, or by netting supported with metal bars or rods, spanning the width of the tunnel in accordance with Section 8.105.1.6.

8.105.8 Thin Membranes. Single-layer membranes or thin laminates consisting of a limited number of similar or dissimilar layers shall be supported on netting placed on metal rods in accordance with Section 8.105.1.6.

8.105.9 Wall Coverings. Wall coverings of various types intended for application directly to a noncombustible wall surface shall be mounted to $^1/_4$-inch (6.4 mm) inorganic-cement board with the adhesive specified by the manufacturer in a manner consistent with field practice.

If intended to be applied over gypsum wallboard, the wall coverings shall be tested on that substrate.

If intended for application over a combustible substrate, the wall coverings shall be tested on that substrate.

Wall coverings not intended to be adhered directly to a wall surface, but hung or otherwise supported by framing or a track system, shall be mounted for test in a manner that is representative of their installation. Where this is not practical, the sample shall be supported on netting placed on metal rods as provided.

8.105.10 Mounting Method for Heavy Textile Materials. When the surface-burning characteristics of the material itself are required, specimens shall be mounted on inorganic reinforced cement board with high-temperature bonding mortar or the equivalent.

The application shall be determined by a $^3/_{32}$-inch (2.4 mm) notched trowel held at an 80-degree to 90-degree angle using a random pattern. The adhesive shall be applied only to the specimen back. The specimen shall then be placed on the smooth side of the inorganic reinforced-cement board and rolled using a 100-pound (45.4 kg) roller [nominal 5-inch (127 mm) diameter, three 5-inch-long (127 mm) sections placed end-to-end for a total length of 15 inches (381 mm)]. The prepared samples can be dead stacked overnight but should be transferred to separate storage racks until tested. Each sample shall be vacuumed prior to test.

SECTION 8.106 — TEST PROCEDURE

With the furnace draft operating, the test specimen shall be placed on the test chamber ledges which have been completely covered with nominal $^1/_8$-inch-thick (3.2 mm) by $1^1/_2$-inch-wide (38 mm) woven asbestos tape. The removable top shall be placed in position over the specimen.

The completely mounted specimen is to remain in position in the chamber with the furnace draft operating for 120 ± 15 seconds prior to application of the test flame.

The igniting flame shall be lighted and adjusted. The distance and time of maximum flame front travel is to be observed and recorded. The test shall be continued for a 10-minute period unless the sample is completely consumed in the fire area before that time, in which case the test is to be ended after no further progressive burning is evident and the photoelectric cell reading has returned to the base line.

The photoelectric cell output shall be recorded immediately prior to the test and at least every 15 seconds during test.

The gas pressure, the pressure differential across the orifice plate and the volume of gas used shall be recorded in each test.

When the test is ended, the gas supply shall be shut off. Smoldering and other conditions within the test duct are to be observed and the sample removed for further examination.

The temperature, flame-spread distance and change in photoelectric cell readings shall be plotted separately on the same coordinate paper as used for those graphs required in Section 8.104 for use in determining the flame-spread and smoke-developed indexes as outlined in Section 8.106. Flame front advancement shall be recorded at the time of occurrence or at least every 30 seconds if no advancement is noted. Flame-spread distance shall be determined as the observed distance minus $4^1/_2$ feet (1372 mm).

SECTION 8.107 — INTERPRETATION OF RESULTS

The flame-spread index (FSI) shall be the value as determined below rounded to the nearest multiple of 5 points:

In plotting the flame-spread distance-time relationship, all progressive flaming as previously recorded shall be included at the time of occurrence. A straight line shall be used to connect successive points. The total area (A_T) under the flame-spread distance-time plot shall be determined by ignoring any flame front recession. For example, in Figure 8-1-8 the flame spreads 10 feet (3048 mm) in $2^1/_2$ minutes and then recedes. The area is calculated as if the flame had spread to 10 feet (3048 mm) in $2^1/_2$ minutes and then remained at 10 feet (3048 mm) for the remainder of the test or until the flame front again passed 10 feet (3048 mm). This is shown by the dashed line in Figure 8-1-8. The area (A_T) used for calculating the flame-spread index is the sum of areas A_1 and A_2 in Figure 8-1-8.

If this total area (A_T) is less than or equal to 97.5 feet·min., the flame-spread index shall be 0.515 times the total area (FSI = 0.515 A_T) (For **SI:** If $A_T \le$ 29.7 m·min., FSI = 1.85 A_T).

If this total area (A_T) is greater than 97.5 feet·min., the flame-spread index shall be 4,900 divided by the difference of 195 minus the total area (A_T). [FSI = 4,900/(195 − A_T)] [For **SI:** If $A_T >$ 29.7 m·min., FSI = 1640/(59.4 − A_T)].

The test results for smoke shall be plotted, using the same coordinates as in Section 8.104. The area under the curve shall be divided by the area under the curve for red oak, and multiplied by 100, and rounded to the nearest multiple of 5 points to establish a smoke-developed index by which the performance of the material may be compared with that of inorganic reinforced cement board and Select grade red oak flooring, which has been arbitrarily established as 0 and 100, respectively. For smoke-developed indexes 200 or over, the calculated value shall be rounded to the nearest 50 points.

When multiple test data are provided, the flame-spread index and smoke-developed index shall be determined as follows:

Flame-spread Index (FSI)

The individual flame-spread data values shall be rounded to the nearest multiple of 5 points. If the rounded values do not exceed a 10-point range, the original values shall be averaged and the resultant average shall be rounded to the nearest multiple of 5 points and considered as the FSI.

Where the individual rounded values do exceed a 10-point range, the highest individual value shall be rounded to the nearest multiple of 5 points and considered as the FSI.

Smoke-developed Index (SDI)—All Rounded Smoke Values 200 or under

The individual smoke-developed data values shall be each rounded to the nearest multiple of 5 points. If the rounded values do not exceed a 20-point range, the original values shall be averaged and the resultant average shall be rounded to the nearest multiple of 5 points and considered as the SDI.

Where the individual rounded values do exceed a 20-point range, the highest individual value shall be rounded to the nearest multiple of 5 points and considered as the SDI.

Smoke-developed Index (SDI)—All Rounded Smoke Values 200 or over

The individual smoke-developed data values shall be each rounded to the nearest multiple of 5 points. If the rounded values do not exceed a 50-point range, the original values shall be averaged and the resultant average shall be rounded to the nearest multiple of 50 points and considered as the SDI.

Where the individual rounded values do exceed a 50-point range, the highest individual value shall be rounded to the nearest multiple of 50 points and considered as the SDI.

Rounded Smoke Values both under and over 200

The calculated smoke-developed data values shall each be rounded to the nearest multiple of 5 points. If the rounded values do not exceed a 20-point range, the SDI value shall be considered as 200.

Where the individual rounded values do exceed a 20-point range, the highest individual value shall be rounded to the nearest multiple of 50 points and considered as the SDI.

SECTION 8.108 — ANALYSIS OF PRODUCTS OF COMBUSTION

Samples for combustion product analysis, when analysis is requested, shall be taken downstream from the photometer, or shall consist of not more than 1 percent of the total flow. It should be noted that analysis of the products of combustion is not required in this method.

SECTION 8.109 — REPORT

The report shall include the following:

1. Description of the material being tested,

2. Test results as calculated in Section 8.106,

3. Details of the method used in placing the specimen in the test chamber,

4. Observations of the burning characteristics of the specimen during test exposure, such as delamination, sagging, shrinkage, fallout, etc., and

5. Graphical plots of flame-spread and smoke-developed data.

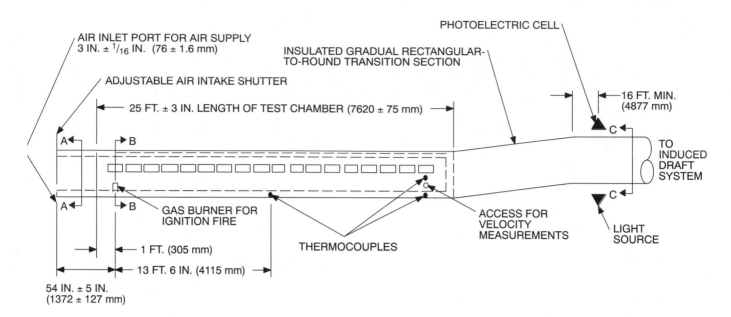

FIRE END

VENT END

PHOTOELECTRIC CELL

AIR INLET PORT FOR AIR SUPPLY
3 IN. ± $^1/_{16}$ IN. (76 ± 1.6 mm)

INSULATED GRADUAL RECTANGULAR-
TO-ROUND TRANSITION SECTION

ADJUSTABLE AIR INTAKE SHUTTER

16 FT. MIN.
(4877 mm)

25 FT. ± 3 IN. LENGTH OF TEST CHAMBER (7620 ± 75 mm)

A

B

C

TO
INDUCED
DRAFT
SYSTEM

A

B

C

GAS BURNER FOR
IGNITION FIRE

ACCESS FOR
VELOCITY
MEASUREMENTS

LIGHT
SOURCE

1 FT. (305 mm)

THERMOCOUPLES

13 FT. 6 IN. (4115 mm)

54 IN. ± 5 IN.
(1372 ± 127 mm)

17$^3/_4$ IN. ± $^1/_4$ IN.
(451 ± 6.4 mm)

12 IN. ± $^1/_2$ IN.
(305 ± 13 mm)

16 IN. I.D. (406 mm)

AUTOMATICALLY
CONTROLLED
DAMPER

2 IN. (51 mm) MINIMUM,
HIGH-TEMPERATURE
MINERAL COMPOSITION
MATERIAL

SECTION A-A

SECTION C-C

FIGURE 8-1-1—DETAILS OF TEST FURNACE

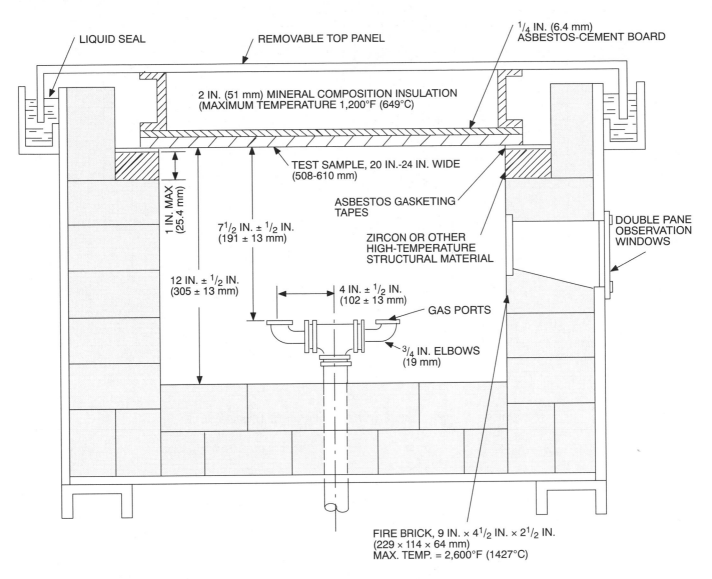

FIGURE 8-1-2—SECTION B-B

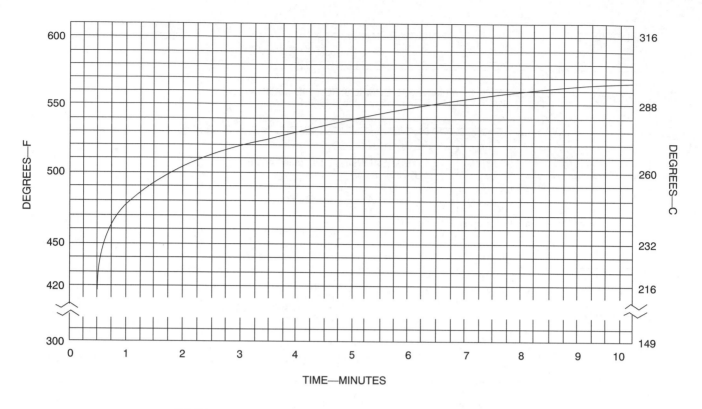

FIGURE 8-1-3—TIME-TEMPERATURE FOR PREHEAT TEMPERATURE

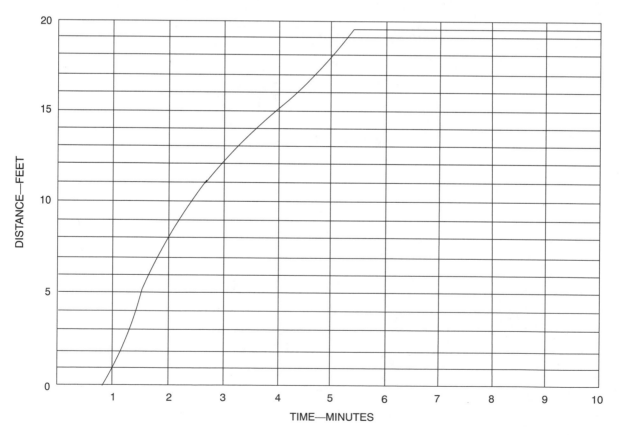

For **SI:** 1 foot = 0.3048 m.

FIGURE 8-1-4—REPRESENTATIVE TIME-DISTANCE CURVE FOR FLAME SPREAD OF RED OAK

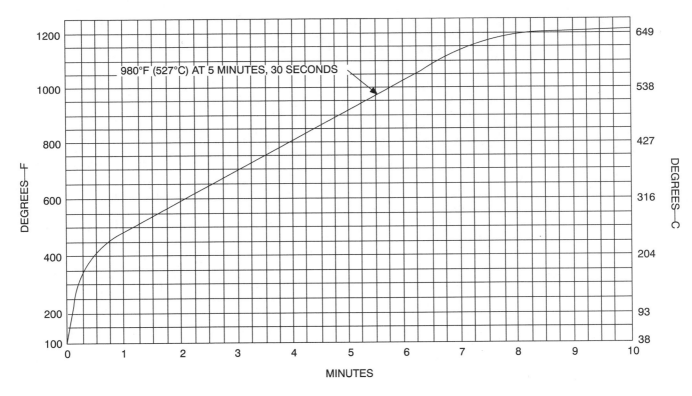

FIGURE 8-1-5—TIME-TEMPERATURE CURVE FOR FUEL CONTRIBUTION OF RED OAK

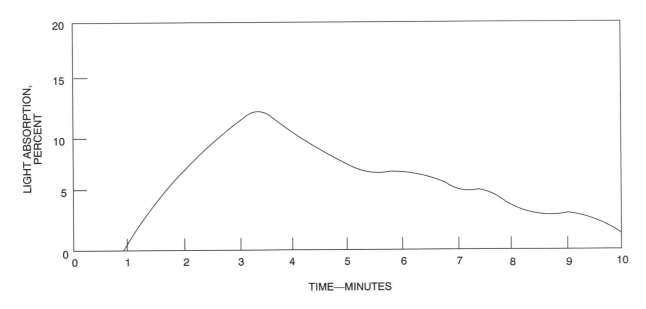

FIGURE 8-1-6—SMOKE DENSITY—RED OAK

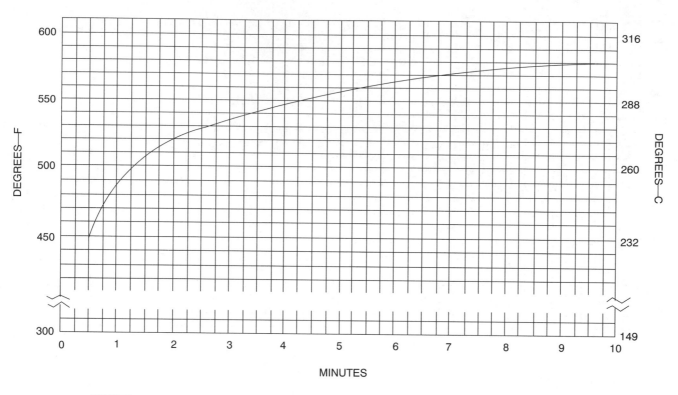

FIGURE 8-1-7—TIME-TEMPERATURE CURVE FOR FUEL CONTRIBUTION ASBESTOS-CEMENT BOARD

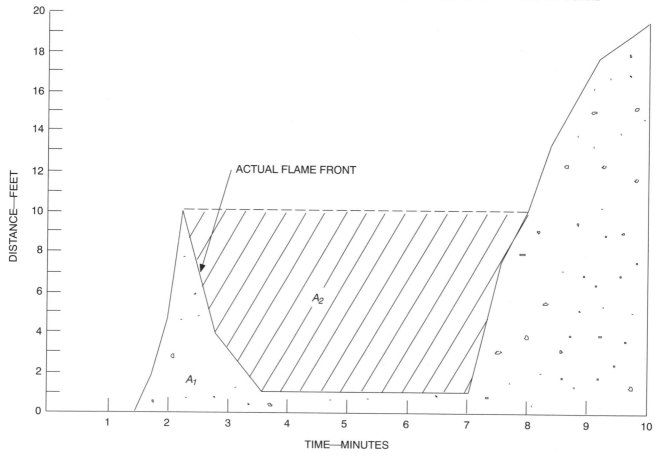

For **SI:** 1 foot = 0.3048 m.

FIGURE 8-1-8—EXAMPLE OF TIME-DISTANCE RELATIONSHIP
WITH FLAME FRONT RECESSION
(Total Area, $A_T = A_1 + A_2$)

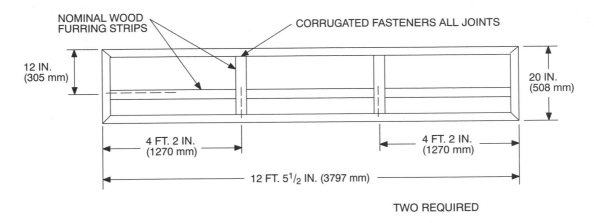

FIGURE 8-1-9—WOOD FRAME FOR ACOUSTICAL MATERIALS AND OTHER
SIMILAR PANEL PRODUCTS LESS THAN 20 INCHES (508 mm)

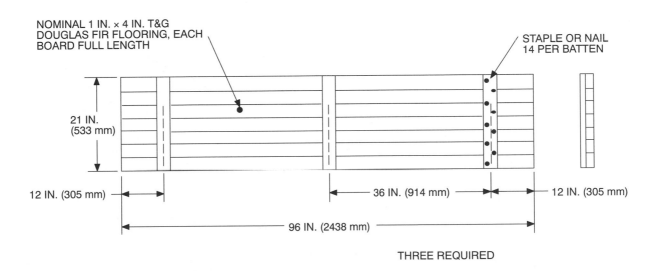

FIGURE 8-1-10—WOOD DECK FOR COATING MATERIAL

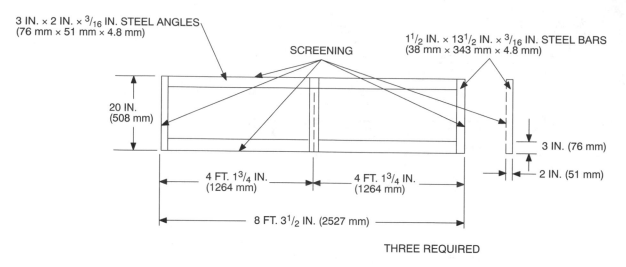

FIGURE 8-1-11—STEEL FRAME FOR LOOSE FILL MATERIALS

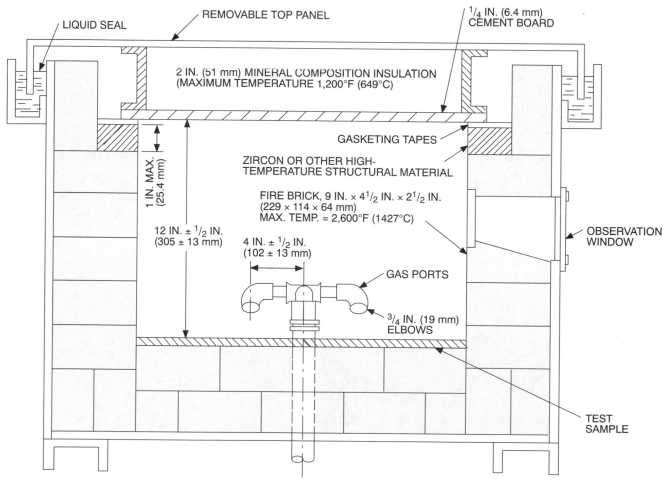

FIGURE 8-1-12—SECTION B-B

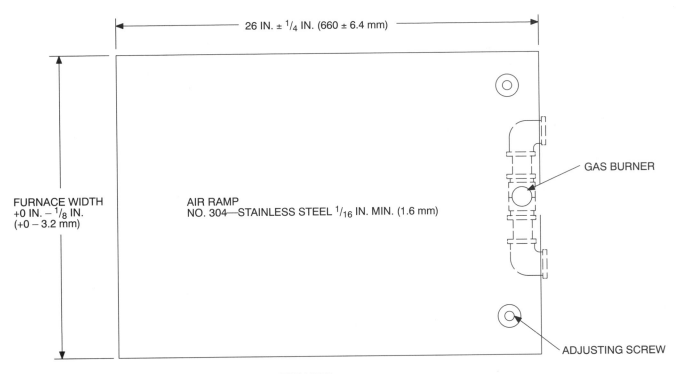

TOP VIEW

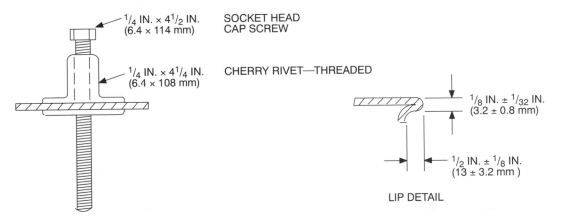

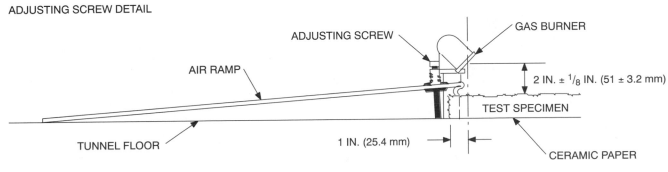

SIDE VIEW

FIGURE 8-1-13—AIR RAMP

UNIFORM BUILDING CODE STANDARD 8-2
STANDARD TEST METHOD FOR EVALUATING ROOM FIRE GROWTH CONTRIBUTION OF TEXTILE WALL COVERING
Test Method of the International Conference of Building Officials
See Sections 801.2 and 805, *Uniform Building Code*

SECTION 8.201 — SCOPE

This standard describes a method for determining the contribution of textile wall covering to room fire growth during specified fire exposure conditions. This method is not intended to evaluate the fire endurance of assemblies, nor is it able to evaluate the effect of fires originating within the wall assembly. The method is not intended for the evaluation of floor or ceiling finishes.

This method is to be used to evaluate the flammability characteristics of textile wall coverings when such materials constitute the exposed interior surfaces of buildings. This test method does not apply to fabric covered less than ceiling height; freestanding, prefabricated panel furniture systems; or demountable, relocatable, full-height partitions used in open building interiors. Freestanding panel furniture systems include all freestanding panels that provide visual and/or acoustical separation and are intended to be used to divide space and may support components to form complete work stations. Demountable, relocatable, full-height partitions include demountable, relocatable, full-height partitions that fill the space between the finished floor and the finished ceiling.

This method is to be used to evaluate the flammability characteristics of textile wall coverings when required by this code.

SECTION 8.202 — SIGNIFICANCE AND USE

This fire test measures certain fire performance characteristics of textile wall covering materials in an enclosure under specified fire exposure conditions. It determines the extent to which the textile wall covering materials may contribute to fire growth in a room and the potential for fire spread beyond the room under the particular conditions simulated. The test indicates the maximum extent of fire growth in a room, the rate of heat release, and if they occur, the time to flashover and the time to flame extension beyond the doorway following flashover. It does not measure the fire growth in, or the contribution of, the room contents. Time to flashover is defined herein as either the time when the radiant flux onto the floor reaches 20 kW/m^2 or the temperature of the upper air reaches 600°C. A crumpled single sheet of newspaper shall be placed on the floor 3 feet (914 mm) out from the center of the rear wall. The spontaneous ignition of this newspaper provides the visual indication of flashover.

The potential for spread of fire to other objects in the room, remote from the ignition source, is evaluated by measurements of:

1. The total heat flux incident on the center of the floor.

2. A characteristic upper-level gas temperature in the room.

3. Instantaneous net peak rate of heat release.

The potential for the spread of fire to objects outside the room of origin is evaluated by the measurement of the total heat release of the fire.

Measurements of the rate of production of carbon monoxide and carbon dioxide are taken.

The overall performance of the test specimen is to be visually documented by full-color photographic records. Videotaping of the complete fire test may be done as an alternative to the photographic record. Such records shall show when each area of the test specimen becomes involved in the fire.

SECTION 8.203 — SUMMARY OF METHOD

The test method has two types of protocols. One is a "screening test" protocol and the second is the "fully lined test" protocol. The "screening test" protocol utilizes a corner test exposure of relatively small specimens mounted on the walls of the test compartment. The "fully lined test" protocol involves the same test in a compartment having three fully lined walls.

This method uses a gas burner to produce a diffusion flame to expose the walls in the corner of an 8- by 12- by 8-foot-high (2348 mm by 3658 mm by 2438 mm) room. The burner produces a prescribed rate of heat output of 40 kW for five minutes followed by 150 kW for 10 minutes, for a total exposure period of 15 minutes. The contribution of the textile wall covering to fire growth is measured via constant monitoring of the incident heat flux on the center of the floor, the temperature of the gases in the upper part of the room, the rate of heat release and the time to flashover. The test is conducted with natural ventilation to the room provided through a single doorway 30 inches by 80 inches (762 mm by 2032 mm) in width and height. The combustion products are collected in a hood feeding into a plenum connected to an exhaust duct in which measurements are made of the gas velocity, temperature, and concentrations of selected gases.

SECTION 8.204 — IGNITION SOURCE

The ignition source for the test shall be a gas burner with a nominal 12-inch-by-12-inch (305 mm by 305 mm) porous top surface of a refractory material. See Figure 8-2-1. A burner may be constructed with 1-inch-thick (25.4 mm) porous ceramic-fiberboard over a 6-inch (152 mm) plenum, or, alternatively, a minimum 4-inch (102 mm) layer of Ottawa sand can be used to provide the horizontal surface through which the gas is supplied.

The top surface of the burner through which the gas is applied shall be 12 inches (305 mm) above the floor, and the burner enclosure shall be located such that the edge of the diffusion surface is located 2 inches (51 mm) from both walls in the left corner of the room opposite from the door. See Figure 8-2-3.

The gas supply to the burner (see Figure 8-2-1) shall be of C.P. grade propane (99 percent purity). The burner shall be capable of producing a gross heat output of 40 ± 1 kW for five minutes followed by 150 ± 5 kW for 10 minutes. The flow rate shall be metered throughout the test. Flow rates may be calculated using propane's gross heat of combustion as 2,480 Btu/foot^3 (92.5 MJ/m^3) at 68°F (20°C) and 14.70 psia (101.4 kPa). The burner design shall permit switching from 40 kW to 150 kW within 10 seconds. Burner controls should be provided for automatic shutoff of the gas supply if flameout occurs. Two arrangements for gas supply that have been used are shown in Figures 8-2-2A and 8-2-2B.

The burner shall be ignited by a pilot burner or a remotely controlled spark igniter.

SECTION 8.205 — COMPARTMENT GEOMETRY AND CONSTRUCTION

The interior dimensions of the floor of the fire room, when the specimens are in place, shall measure 8 feet ± 1 inch by 12 feet ± 1 inch (2438 mm ± 25 mm by 3658 mm ± 25 mm). The finished ceiling shall be 8 feet ± 0.5 inch (2438 mm ± 13 mm) above the floor. There shall be four walls at right angles defining the compartment.

There shall be a (30- ± 0.25- by 80- ± 0.25-inch) (762 mm ± 6 mm by 2032 mm ± 6 mm) doorway in the center of one of the 8-foot-by-8-foot (2438 mm by 2438 mm) walls, and no other wall, floor or ceiling openings that allow ventilation.

The inside surface of the wall containing the door shall be of calcium-silicate board of 46 pounds per cubic foot (737 kg/m³) density and 0.5 inch (12.7 mm) in nominal thickness or 0.5-inch (12.7 mm) gypsum wallboard. The door frame shall be constructed to remain unchanged during the test period to a tolerance of ± 1 percent in height and width.

The test compartment may be framed or a concrete block structure. If self-supporting panels are tested, a separate exterior frame or block compartment may not be required.

The floor, ceiling and walls of the test compartment shall be covered by calcium-silicate board or by gypsum wallboard.

SECTION 8.206 — SPECIMEN MOUNTING

Test specimens shall be mounted on a framing or support system comparable to that intended for their actual use, using backing materials, insulation or air gaps as appropriate to the intended application and representing a typical value of thermal resistance for the wall system. Where a manufacturer specifies use of an adhesive, specimens shall be mounted using the adhesive and application rate as recommended by the manufacturer and comparable to actual field installations. The adhesive utilized shall be the same as that intended for actual use.

Where a textile wall covering has a distinct directionality, the sample shall be mounted such that the machine direction is vertical unless the manufacturer indicates a different method of mounting will be used in actual installations.

For the screening test protocol, specimens shall be mounted on the left side and rear walls (as viewed from the room door) and as illustrated in Figure 8-2-3. Vertically mounted portions of test specimens shall extend 2 feet (610 mm) from the room corner on the left side and rear walls. Horizontally mounted specimens on the rear and left sidewalls shall extend 2 feet (610 mm) down from the ceiling and be installed for the full 8-foot (2438 mm) width of the rear wall and the full 12-foot (3658 mm) wall length of the left sidewall.

In the fully lined room protocol test, specimens shall be mounted to fully cover both 8-foot-by-12-foot (2438 mm by 3658 mm) walls and the 8-foot-by-8-foot (2438 mm by 2438 mm) wall, which does not have a door in it.

SECTION 8.207 — FIRE ROOM ENVIRONMENT

8.207.1 General. The test building in which the fire room is located shall have vents for the discharge of the combustion products and have provisions for fresh air intake so that no oxygen-deficient air shall be introduced into the fire room during the test. Prior to the start of the test, the ambient air at the mid-height entrance to the compartment shall have a velocity in any direction of less than 100 feet per minute (30.5 m/min.). The building shall be of adequate size so that there shall be no smoke accumulation in the building below the level of the top of the fire compartment.

8.207.2 Ambient Conditions in Test Building. The ambient temperature in the test building at locations around the fire compartment shall be above 40°F (4.4°C) and the relative humidity shall be less than 75 percent for the duration of the test.

8.207.3 Ambient Conditions in Fire Room. If test samples are installed within the test room two or more hours prior to test, the following ambient conditions shall be maintained:

1. The ambient temperature in the fire room measured by one of the thermocouples in Section 42.208 shall be from 65°F to 75°F (18.3°C to 23.9°C).

2. The ambient relative humidity in the fire room shall be within the range of 50 ± 5 percent.

8.207.4 Specimen Conditioning. Prior to testing, mounted specimens shall be conditioned for a minimum of seven days and until the sample reaches a rate of weight change of less than 0.1 percent per day at a temperature of 70°F ± 5°F (21.1°C ± 2.8°C) and at a relative humidity of 50 ± 5 percent.

SECTION 8.208 — INSTRUMENTATION

The following are minimum requirements for instrumentation for this test:

8.208.1 Total Heat Flux Gage.

8.208.1.1 Location. A gage shall be mounted a maximum of 2 inches (51 mm) above the floor surface, facing upward in the geometric center of the test room (see Figure 8-2-4).

8.208.1.2 Specification. The gage shall be of the Gardon type, with a flat black surface, and a 180 degree view angle. In operation, it shall be maintained at a constant temperature [within ± 5 percent °F (± 2.8 percent °C)] above the dew point by water supplied at a temperature from 120°F to 150°F (48.9°C to 65.6°C). This will normally require a flow rate of at least 0.1 gallon per minute (6.31 mL/s). The full-scale output range shall be 50 kW/m² for the gage.

8.208.2 Gas Temperature Thermocouples.

8.208.2.1 Specification. Bare chromel-alumel thermocouples 20 mil in diameter shall be used at each required location. The thermocouple wire, within 0.5 inch (13 mm) of the bead, should be run along expected isotherms to minimize conduction errors. The insulation between the chromel and alumel wires shall be stable to at least 2,000°F (1093°C) or the wires shall be separated. Metal-clad thermocouples with ceramic-powder filling shall be used.

8.208.2.2 Location in doorway. A thermocouple shall be located in the interior plane of the door opening on the door center line, 4 inches (102 mm) down from the top. (See Figure 8-2-5.)

8.208.2.3 Locations for room. Thermocouples shall be located 4 inches (102 mm) below the ceiling at the center of the ceiling, the center of each of the four ceiling quadrants and directly over the center of the ignition burner. The thermocouples shall be mounted on supports or penetrate through the ceiling with their junctions 4 inches (102 mm) away from a solid surface. (See Figure 8-2-5.) Any ceiling penetration shall be just large enough to permit passage of the thermocouples. Spackling compound or ceramic fiber insulation shall be used to backfill the holes around the thermocouple wires.

8.208.2.4 Location in canopy hood and duct system. One pair of thermocouples shall be placed a minimum of 8.25 exhaust duct diameters downstream of the entrance to the horizontal duct. The pair of thermocouples shall straddle the center of the duct and be separated 2 inches (51 mm) from each other. (See Figure 8-2-6.)

8.208.3 Canopy Hood and Exhaust Duct.

8.208.3.1 Location and design. A hood shall be installed immediately adjacent to the door of the fire room. The bottom of the hood shall be level with the top surface of the room. The face dimensions of the hood shall be at least 8 feet by 8 feet (2438 mm by 2438 mm) and the depth shall be 3.5 feet (1067 mm) minimum. The hood shall feed into a plenum having a 3-foot-by-3-foot (914 mm by 914 mm) cross-section minimum. The plenum shall have a minimum height of 3 feet (914 mm) and a maximum height of 6 feet (1829 mm). The exhaust duct connected to the plenum shall be at least 16 inches (406 mm) in diameter, horizontal, and shall have a circular aperture of between one-half and three-fourths of the duct diameter at its entrance. (See Figures 8-2-6 and 8-2-7.)

8.208.3.2 Draft. The hood shall have sufficient draft to collect all of the combustion products leaving the room. [This draft should be capable of moving up to 7,000 standard cubic feet per minute (3303 L/s) equivalent to 16,000 acfm at 750°F (7550 L/s at 399°C) during the test.] Provisions shall be made so that the draft can operate at either 1,000 or 7,000 standard cubic feet per minute (472 L/s or 3303 L/s). Mixing vanes may also be required in the duct if concentration gradients are found to exist.

8.208.3.3 Alternate exhaust system. An alternative exhaust system design may be used if it has been shown to produce equivalent results. (Equivalency may be shown in meeting the requirements of Section 8.209.)

8.208.4 Duct Gas Velocity. A bidirectional probe or an equivalent measuring system shall be used to measure gas velocity in the duct. The probe shown in Figure 8-2-8 consists of a short stainless steel cylinder 1.75 inches (44 mm) long and 0.875 inch (22.2 mm) inside diameter with a solid diaphragm in the center. The pressure taps on either side of the diaphragm support the probe. The axis of the probe shall be along the center line of the duct a minimum of 8.25 duct diameters downstream from the entrance. The taps shall be connected to a pressure transducer that shall be able to resolve pressure differences of 0.001-inch water (0.25 Pa). Capacitance transducers have been found to be most stable for this application.

8.208.5 Oxygen-depletion Measurements.

8.208.5.1 Determination of rate of heat release. A stainless steel gas sampling tube shall be located 2 feet (610 mm) downstream from the bidirectional probe at the geometric center of the duct $\pm$ $^1/_2$ inch ($\pm$ 13 mm) to obtain a continuously flowing sample for determining the oxygen concentration of the exhaust gas as a function of time. A suitable filter and cold trap shall be placed in the line ahead of the analyzer to remove particulates and water. The oxygen analyzer shall be of the paramagnetic or polarographic type and shall be capable of measuring the oxygen concentration in the range from 21 percent down to 15 percent with a relative accuracy of $\pm$ 2 percent in this concentration range. The signal from the oxygen analyzer shall be within 5 percent of its final value in 30 seconds after introducing a step change in composition of the gas stream flowing past the inlet to the sampling tube.

8.208.5.2 Duct carbon dioxide concentration: specification. The gas-sampling tube described in Section 8.208 may be used to provide a continuous sample for the measurement of the carbon dioxide concentration using an analyzer with a range of not more than 0 to 6 percent (vol.), with a maximum relative error of 2 percent of full scale. The total system response time between the sampling inlet and the meter shall be no greater than 30 seconds.

8.208.5.3 Duct carbon monoxide concentration: specification. The gas-sampling tube defined in Section 8.208 shall provide a continuous sample for the measurement of the carbon monoxide concentration using an analyzer with a range from not more than 0 to 1 percent (vol.) with a maximum relative error of 2 percent of full scale. The signal from the analyzer shall be within 5 percent of its final value in 30 seconds after introducing a step change in composition of the gas stream flowing past the inlet to the sampling tube.

8.208.6 Photographic Records. Photographic or video equipment shall be used to record the fire spread in the room and the fire projection from the door of the room. The location of the camera shall avoid interference with the air inflow. The interior wall surfaces of the test room, adjacent to the corner in which the burner is located, shall be clearly marked with a 12-inch (305 mm) grid. A clock shall appear in all photographic records, giving time to the nearest 1 second or 0.01 minimum from the start of the test. This clock shall be accurately synchronized with all other measurements, or other provisions shall be made to correlate the photo record with time. Color slides shall be taken at 30-second intervals from the duration of the test or a continuous video recording shall be made.

SECTION 8.209 — CALIBRATION AND DOCUMENTATION OF IGNITION SOURCE AND TEST EQUIPMENT

A calibration test shall have been performed prior to and within 30 days of any fire test. The calibration test, to last for 15 minutes, shall use the standard ignition source with inert wall and ceiling materials [calcium-silicate board of 46 pounds per cubic foot (737 kg/m^3) density, 0.50 inch (12.7 mm) in thickness]. The following data shall be reported:

1. The output as a function of time, after the burner is activated, of all instruments normally used for the standard fire test.

2. The maximum extension of the burner flame, as recorded by still photographs taken at 30-second intervals or continuous video recording.

3. The calibration constant shall be determined as follows:

   3.1   Estimate the initial calibration constant for C in the Heat Release Rate Equations using the product 22.1 $\times$ A, where A is the area of the duct (in m^2). This gives a good estimation (generally within about 20 percent) of the final value one can expect for C.

   3.2   Burn 99 percent purity propane or methane fuel at a constant rate corresponding to 150 kW for 10 minutes. Measure the heat release rate using oxygen consumption calorimetry and the "initial" value for C estimated in Item 3.1. Use the appropriate constants for the fuel being used as follows:

Procedure	α	E
Methane calibration	1.105	12.5 MJ/kg
Propane calibration	1.084	12.8 MJ/kg

   3.3   Calculate the total heat released from the mass loss of the fuel and its heat of combustion. The heat of combustion for 99 percent purity propane is 46.5 MJ/kg. The heat of combustion for 99 percent purity methane is 50.0 MJ/kg.

   3.4   Adjust the calibration constant C so that the total rate of heat released, as determined by the oxygen consumption calculation, agrees with that from the mass of fuel consumed to within 5 percent.

$$C_{new} = \left[\frac{A(\text{MJ/kg}) \times B(\text{kg})}{\int_0^T \dot{q}(t) (\text{MW})^{dt}} \right] \times C_{old} \pm 5\%$$

A is the heat of combustion of the fuel being used and B is the total mass of fuel burned in the period T. Use the new constant for subsequent tests for calculation of the heat release rate and flow rate.

3.5   **Example:** An initial value of 6.6 is assigned to C. A 10-minute calibration burn uses 1.80 kg of methane (50 MJ/kg), which corresponds to a burning rate of 150 kW. The oxygen consumption calculations reveal an average heat release rate of 160 kW during the burn period. Integrating the the heat release rate curve over the 10-minute burn period, one calculates the total heat released as 96.0 MJ. Applying the formula above, one finds

$$C_{new} = [0.94] \times C_{old}$$

SECTION 8.210 — PROCEDURE

The screening test protocol and the fully lined test protocol, except for specimen mounting, follow the same test procedure. Where indicated by Section 8.211, the fully lined test protocol shall be followed.

Establish an initial volumetric flow rate of 1,000 cubic feet per minute (472 L/s) through the duct and increase the volume flow rate to 7,000 cubic feet per minute (3303 L/s) when the oxygen content falls below 14 percent.

Turn on all sampling and recording devices, and establish steady-state baseline readings for at least three minutes.

Ignite the gas burner and simultaneously start the clock and increase gas flow rate to provide a rate of heat release of 40 kW ± 1 kW by the burner. Continue the exposure at the 40 kW ± 1 kW level for five minutes. Within 10 seconds following the five-minute exposure, increase the gas flow to provide a rate of heat release by the burner of 150 kW ± 5 kW exposure for 10 minutes.

Take 35mm color photographs at 30-second intervals or provide a continuous video recording to document the growth of the fire.

Provide a continuous voice or written record of the fire, which will give times of all significant events, such as time of ignition, flames out the doorway, flashover, etc.

The ignition burner shall be shut off at 15 minutes after start of the test and the test terminated at that time, unless safety considerations dictate an earlier termination.

Document damage after the test, using words, pictures and drawings.

SECTION 8.211 — ACCEPTANCE CRITERIA

Textile wall coverings shall be considered as demonstrating satisfactory performance if, during the screening test protocol, the following conditions are met:

Flame shall not spread to the ceiling during the 40 kW exposure.

During the 150 kW exposure, the following criteria shall be met:

1. Flame shall not spread to the outer extremity of the sample on the 8-foot-by-12-foot (2438 mm by 3658 mm) wall.

2. The specimen shall not burn to the outer extremity of the 2-foot-wide (610 mm) samples mounted vertically in the corner of the room.

3. Burning droplets shall not be formed and drop to the floor which are judged to be capable of igniting the textile wall covering or which persist in burning for 30 seconds or more.

4. Flashover shall not occur. Flashover may be judged to occur when heat flux at floor level exceeds 20 kW/m^2, upper-level air temperatures within the room exceed 1,100°F (593°C) or flames project out the room door opening.

5. The maximum instantaneous net peak rate of heat release shall not exceed 300 kW. Textile wall coverings in the screening test protocol developing a maximum, instantaneous net peak rate of heat release of 300 kW may or may not cause flashover in a fully lined room. A fully lined room test protocol shall be used to judge acceptability of such products. The maximum instantaneous net peak rate of heat release shall be derived by taking the measured maximum rate of heat release and subtracting the burner output.

Textile wall coverings which fail to meet the criteria of Section 8.211 may be judged to perform satisfactorily when tested following the fully lined test protocol and when meeting the following criteria:

A. Flame shall not spread to the ceiling during the 40 kW exposure.

During the 150 kW exposure, the following criteria shall be met:

(i) Flame shall not spread to the outer extremities of the samples on the 8-foot-by-12-foot (2438 mm by 3658 mm) walls.

(ii) Flashover shall not occur. Flashover shall be judged to have occurred when heat flux at floor level exceeds 20 kW/m^2, upper-level air temperatures exceed 1,100°F (593°C) or flames project out the room door opening.

SECTION 8.212 — REPORT

The report shall include the following:

8.212.1 Materials:

1. **Material description.** The name, thickness, density and size of the material to be listed, along with other identifying characteristics or labels.

2. Materials mounting and conditioning.

3. Layout of specimens and attachments in test room (include appropriate drawings).

4. Relative humidity and temperature of the room and the test building prior to and during the test.

8.212.2 Burner Gas Flow. The fuel gas flow to the ignition burner and its calculated rate of heat output.

8.212.3 Time History of the Total Heat Flux to Floor. The total incident heat flux at the center of the floor for the heat flux gage as a function of time starting three minutes prior to the test.

8.212.4 Time History of the Gas Temperature. The temperature of gases in the room, the doorway, and in the exhaust duct for each thermocouple as a function of time starting three minutes prior to the test.

8.212.5 Time History of the Total Rate of Heat Production of the Fire. The total of heat production shall be calculated from the measured oxygen and carbon monoxide concentrations or measured oxygen, carbon monoxide and carbon dioxide concentrations and the temperature and volumetric flow rate of the gas in the duct. The calculations shall be based on the method shown in Section 8.213.

8.212.6 Time History of the Fire Growth. A transcription of the visual, photographic, audio and written records of the fire test. The records shall indicate the time of ignition of the wall finish, the approximate location of the flame front most distant from the ignition source, at intervals not exceeding 15 seconds during the fire test, the time of flashover, and the time at which flames extend outside the doorway. In addition, still photographs taken at intervals not exceeding 30 seconds or continuous video recordings shall be supplied. Drawings and photographs or video recordings showing the extent of the damage of the materials after the test shall also be supplied.

8.212.7 Discussion of Performance. Complete discussion of sample performances related to acceptance criteria within Section 8.211.

SECTION 8.213 — CALCULATIONS

Calculate mass flow rate using Formula (13-1), using the calibration constant C as described in Section 8.209 — Calibration and Documentation of Ignition Source and Test Equipment.

$$\dot{m} = C \sqrt{\frac{\Delta P}{T}} \qquad (13\text{-}1)$$

The heat release formulas are a function of the oxygen depletion factor ϕ. Three cases exist for calculating ϕ depending on the gas analysis equipment being used. Use the formula below for Case 1 or 2 to calculate the heat release rate.

$$\dot{q} = E \left(\frac{M_{O_2}}{M_a} \right) \left(\frac{\phi}{1 + \phi(\alpha-1)} \right) \dot{m} X^0{}_{O_2} \qquad (13\text{-}2)$$

Case 1: Only O_2 measurements are made.

Use:

$$\phi = \frac{X^O{}_{O_2} - X_{O_2}}{(1 - X_{O_2})X^O{}_{O_2}} \qquad (13\text{-}3)$$

NOTE: Water vapor and CO_2 must be removed before introducing the sample air into the O_2 analyzer. Use a water trap and desiccant to remove water and use soda lime to remove the CO_2. The concentration range of CO in most fires is a small fraction of the concentration range of CO_2, hence, the correction for the heat release rate is generally less than 5 percent. Therefore, CO measurements can be ignored.

Case 2: O_2 and CO_2 measurements are made.

Use:

$$\phi = \frac{X^0{}_{O_2}(1-X_{CO_2})-X_{O_2}(1-X^O{}_{CO_2})}{X^O{}_{O_2}(1-X_{O_2}-X_{CO_2})} \qquad (13\text{-}4)$$

NOTE: Water vapor must be removed before introducing the sample air into the O_2 analyzer. Use a water trap and desiccant to remove water. The concentration range of CO in most fires is a small fraction of the concentration range of CO_2, hence, the correction for the heat release rate is generally less than 5 percent. Therefore, CO measurements can be ignored.

In Case 3, the heat release rate is calculated using the following formula:

$$\dot{q} = \left[E\phi-(E_{CO}-E)\frac{(1-\phi)}{2}\frac{X_{CO}}{X_{O_2}} \right] \left(\frac{M_{O_2}}{M_a} \right) \left(\frac{\dot{m}}{1 + \phi(\alpha-1)} \right) X^O{}_{O_2}$$

$$(13\text{-}5)$$

Case 3: O_2, CO_2 and CO_0 measurements are made.

Use:

$$\phi = \frac{X^O{}_{O_2}(1-X_{CO_2}-X_{CO})-X_{O_2}(1-X^O{}_{CO_2})}{X^O{}_{O_2}(1-X_{O_2}-X_{CO_2}-X_{CO})} \qquad (13\text{-}6)$$

NOTE: Water vapor must be removed before introducing the sample air into the O_2 analyzer. Use a water trap and desiccant to remove water.

It is important that one choose the correct constants for calculating heat release rates.

Note that the formulas incorporate α (the chemical expansion factor) and E (net heat released for complete combustion per unit of oxygen consumed). Use $\alpha = 1.105$ and $E = 13.1$ MJ/kg for testing.

WHERE:

C = calibration factor for orifice plate or bidirectional probe.

E = average heat released for complete combustion per unit of oxygen consumed (13.1 MJ/kg).

E_{CO} = heat released for complete combustion per unit of oxygen consumed, for CO (17.6 MJ/kg).

M_{O_2} = molecular weight of oxygen (32 kg/kmol).

M_a = molecular weight of air (29 kg/kmol).

$\dot{m}$ = mass flow rate in the duct (kg/s).

$\dot{q}$ = heat release rate (MW).

T = temperature of air near measurement probe (K.).

X_{CO} = measured mole fraction of carbon monoxide.

X_{CO_2} = measured mole fraction of carbon dioxide.

X_{O_2} = measured mole fraction of oxygen.

$X^O{}_{O_2}$ = ambient mole fraction of oxygen (0.2095).

α = chemical expansion factor.

ΔP = pressure across orifice plate or bidirectional probe (Pa).

ϕ = oxygen depletion factor.

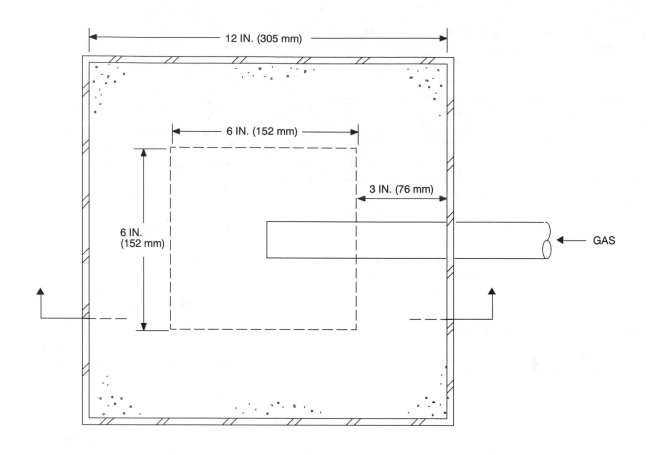

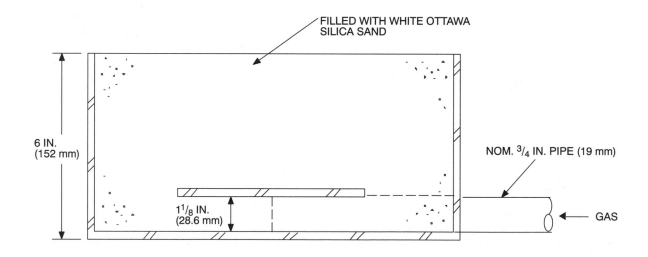

FIGURE 8-2-1—GAS BURNER

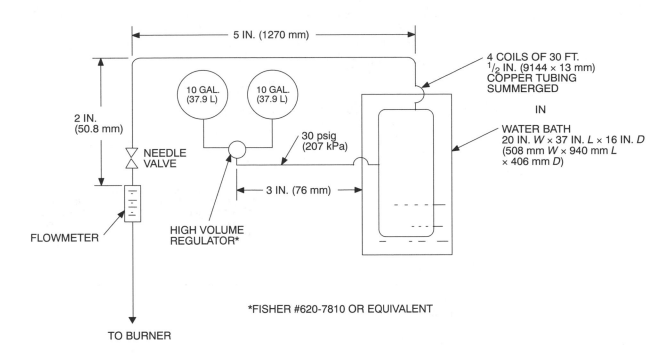

FIGURE 8-2-2A—TYPICAL GAS FLOW REGULATION SYSTEM

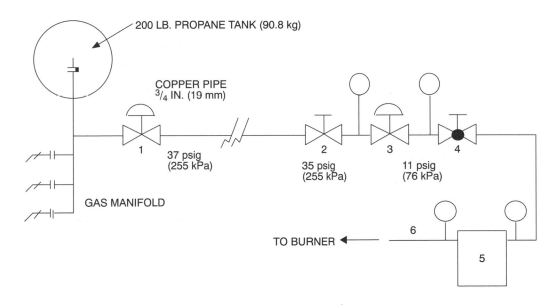

1—PROPANE GAS REGULATOR (HIGH PRESSURE)
    (MAIN GAS SUPPLY)
2—SHUTOFF VALVE
3—REGULATOR (LOW PRESSURE)
4—ADJUSTABLE VALVE FOR FLOW IMPENDANCE
5—VOLUME METER
6—STEEL BRAID OVER TUBING TO BURNER
*—LINE PRESSURES ARE SHOWN

FIGURE 8-2-2B—TYPICAL GAS FLOW REGULATION SYSTEM

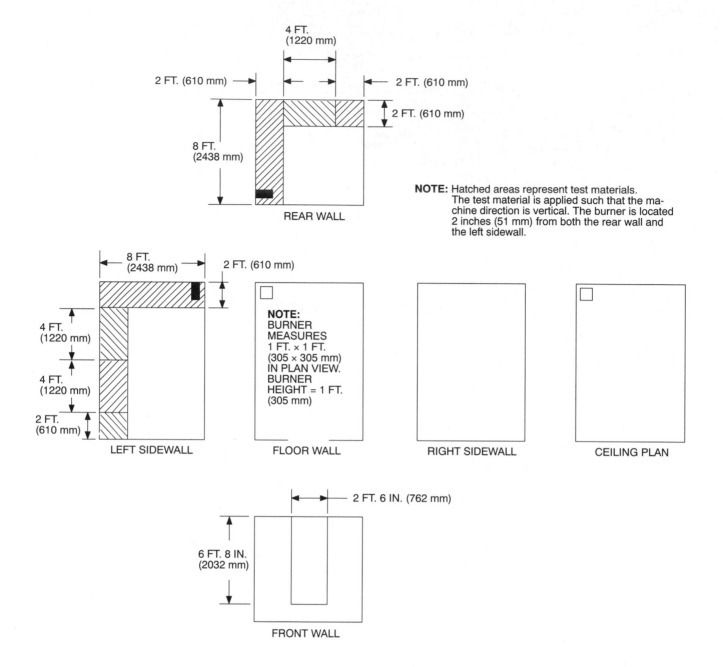

NOTE: Hatched areas represent test materials. The test material is applied such that the machine direction is vertical. The burner is located 2 inches (51 mm) from both the rear wall and the left sidewall.

NOTE: BURNER MEASURES 1 FT. × 1 FT. (305 × 305 mm) IN PLAN VIEW. BURNER HEIGHT = 1 FT. (305 mm)

FIGURE 8-2-3—MOUNTING OF SPECIMEN

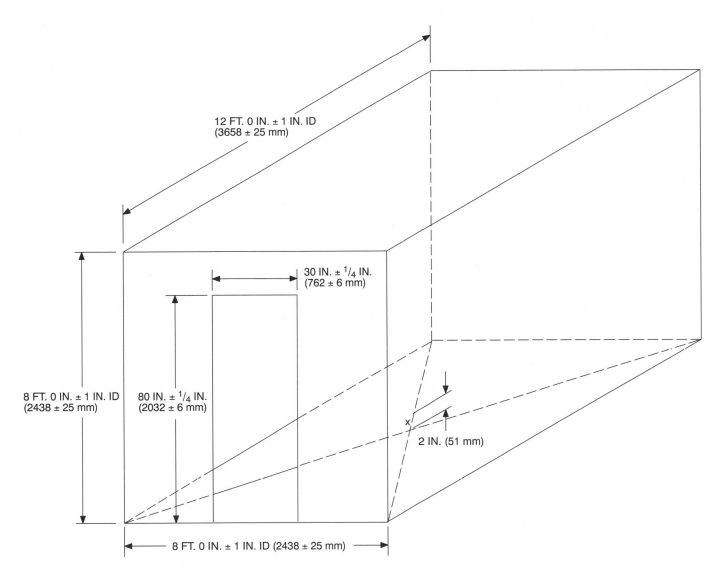

12 FT. 0 IN. ± 1 IN. ID
(3658 ± 25 mm)

30 IN. ± $^1/_4$ IN.
(762 ± 6 mm)

8 FT. 0 IN. ± 1 IN. ID
(2438 ± 25 mm)

80 IN. ± $^1/_4$ IN.
(2032 ± 6 mm)

2 IN. (51 mm)

x

8 FT. 0 IN. ± 1 IN. ID (2438 ± 25 mm)

FIGURE 8-2-4—ROOM RADIOMETER LOCATION

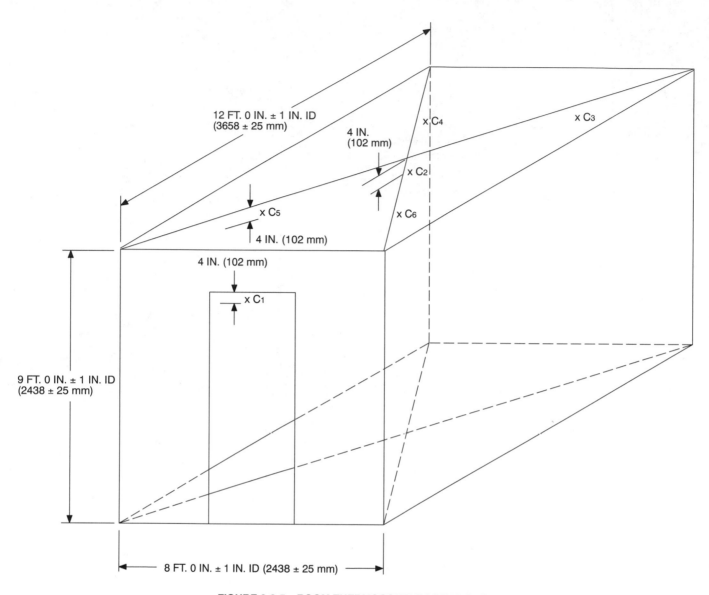

12 FT. 0 IN. ± 1 IN. ID
(3658 ± 25 mm)

4 IN.
(102 mm)

x C4

x C3

x C2

x C5

x C6

4 IN. (102 mm)

4 IN. (102 mm)

x C1

9 FT. 0 IN. ± 1 IN. ID
(2438 ± 25 mm)

8 FT. 0 IN. ± 1 IN. ID (2438 ± 25 mm)

FIGURE 8-2-5—ROOM THERMOCOUPLE LOCATIONS

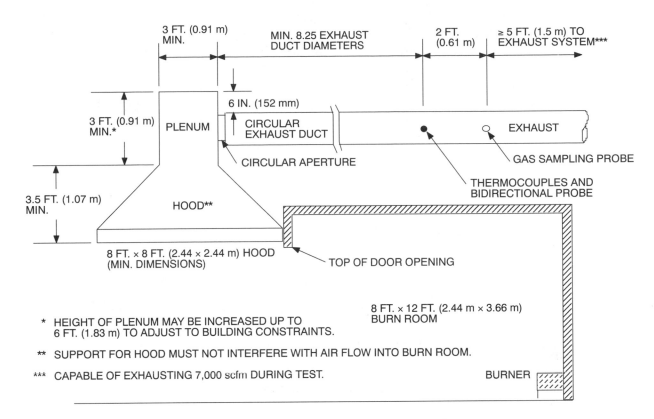

FIGURE 8-2-6—CANOPY HOOD AND EXHAUST DUCT

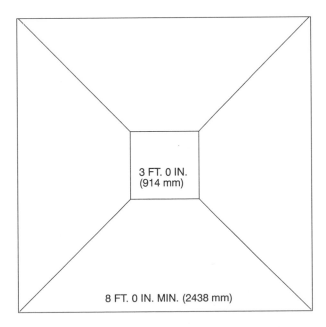

FIGURE 8-2-7—PLAN VIEW OF CANOPY HEAD

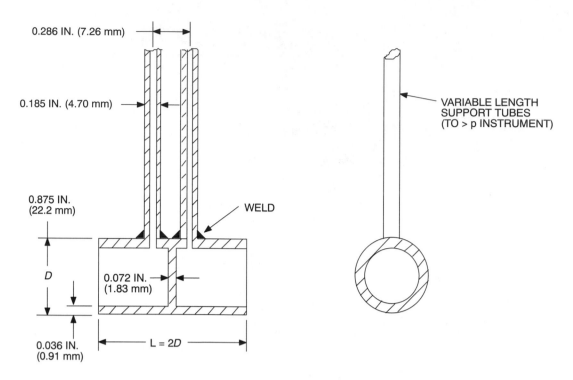

FIGURE 8-2-8—BIDIRECTIONAL PROBE

UNIFORM BUILDING CODE STANDARD 9-1
INSTALLATION OF SPRINKLER SYSTEMS

See Sections 307.11.3; 404.3.1; 405.1.1; 405.3.4; 804.1; 902; 904.1.2; 904.1.3; 904.2.6.3; 904.2.8; 904.2.9; 2603.7.1; 2603.8.1, Item 4; Appendix 327.2, *Uniform Building Code*

This standard, with certain exceptions, is based on the National Fire Protection Association Standard for the Installation of Sprinkler Systems, NFPA 13-1991[1].

Part I of this standard contains the exceptions to NFPA 13-1991[1]. Part II of this standard contains NFPA 13-1991[1] reproduced in its entirety with permission of the publisher.

[1]The current edition is NFPA 13-1996.

Part I

SECTION 9.101 — AMENDMENTS

The National Fire Protection Association standard adopted by this standard applies to the selection, installation, acceptance inspection and acceptance testing of sprinkler systems, except as follows:

1. Sec. 1-1 is amended by changing the note to read as follows:

Consult other recognized and accepted standards for additional requirements relating to water supplies.

2. Sec. 1-4 is amended by changing the definition of "authority having jurisdiction" to read as follows:

Authority Having Jurisdiction is the building official.

The definitions of "approved" and "listed" shall be as set forth in Volume 1 of this code.

Sec. 1-4.1 is amended by deleting the definitions of the terms "limited combustible material," "noncombustible material," "should" and "standard;" by deleting the note following the definition of "sprinkler system;" and by adding definitions for "acceptance," "building official" and "thermal barrier" to read as follows:

Acceptance is acceptance by the building official.

Building Official is the officer or other designated authority charged with the administration and enforcement of this standard, or the officer's or other designated authority's duly authorized representative.

Thermal Barrier is a material that will limit the average temperature rise of the unexposed surface to not more than 250°F (121°C) after 15 minutes of fire exposure complying with nationally recognized standards.

3. Sec. 1-4.7 is amended to read as follows:

1-4.7. For the purpose of determining the level of protection to be provided by required sprinkler system installations, Table 1.4.7 shall be used.

For hazard classifications other than those indicated, see appropriate nationally recognized standards for design criteria.

When fire sprinkler systems are required in buildings of undetermined use, they shall be designed and installed to have a sprinkler density of not less than that required for an Ordinary Hazard Group 2 use with a minimum design area of 3,000 square feet (279 m[2]).

Use is considered undetermined if not specified at time permit is issued.

Where a subsequent occupancy requires a system with greater capability, it shall be the responsibility of the occupant to upgrade the system to the required density for the new occupancy.

Other Uniform Codes or standards contain sprinkler system design criteria for fire control or suppression of specific hazards.

TABLE 1.4.7—HAZARD CLASSIFICATION

OCCUPANCY OF BUILDING OR PORTION THEREOF	HAZARD CLASSIFICATION
Group A Occupancies used as meeting rooms, library reading rooms, restaurant seating areas, clubs, theaters, museums, health clubs, educational classrooms and churches. Group B Occupancies used as offices, data processing areas, colleges and universities. Group E Occupancies other than shops and laboratories. Group I Occupancy living and sleeping areas. Group R, Division 1 Occupancies.[1] Typically these uses are such that the quantity and combustibility of contents is such that relatively low-rate-of-heat-release fires would be expected.	Light
Groups B, F and S Occupancies used for light manufacturing, commercial kitchens, laundries, automobile parking garages, bakeries, canneries, electronic plants, beverage manufacturing and glass products manufacturing plants not producing dust or fibers. Typically these uses are such that the quantity of combustibles is relatively low, the combustibility of contents is moderate, storage does not exceed 8 feet (2438 mm) in height, and moderate-rate-of-heat-release fires would be expected.	Ordinary Group 1
Groups B, F, M and S Occupancies used for chemical plant laboratories, mercantile, machine shops, printing, plants, library stack areas, metal working, wood product assembly, textile manufacturing, confectionary products, cold storage warehouses,[2] cereal mills, service stations and repair garages. Typically these uses are such that the quantity of combustibles is moderate. The combustibility of contents is moderate, storage does not exceed 12 feet (3658 mm) in height[2] and moderate-rate-of-heat-release fires would be expected. **Also:** Group A Occupancies such as exhibition halls. Groups B, F and S Occupancies used as to tobacco products manufacturing, paper and pulp mills, piers and wharfs, and warehousing[2] of higher combustible contents (including packaging). Group H Occupancies used as fee mills, tire manufacturing, chemical plants, repair garages and woodworking. Group H, Division 6 Occupancies (except extra-hazard areas). Typically these uses are such that high-rate-of-heat-release fires would be expected and the spread of fire would be rapid.	Ordinary Group 2
Group H Occupancies used for printing [using inks with flash points below 100°F (38°C)], combustible hydraulic fluid-use areas such as die casting and metal extruding, upholstering with plastic foam, rubber reclaiming, compounding, drying, milling, vulcanizing, plywood and particle board manufacturing, saw mills, textile picking, opening, blending, garnetting, carding and combining of cotton, synthetics, wool shoddy or burlap. Typically these uses are such that a significant fire hazard exists.	Extra Hazard Group 1
Group H Occupancies used as asphalt saturating, flammable liquids spraying, flow coating, open oil quenching, varnish and paint dipping, solvent cleaning, and manufactured home or modular building manufacturing (where the finished building enclosure is present and has combustible interiors). These uses are such that a severe fire hazard exists.	Extra Hazard Group 2[3]

[1]See also Section 5-3.2
[2]For high-piled storage, see UFC Article 81.
[3]For additional or more stringent criteria, see UFC Article 79 or 80.

4. Sec. 2-1.1 is revised to read as follows:

2-1.1 All materials and devices shall be listed and approved.

5. Sec. 2-3.5 is revised to read as follows:

2-3.5. Other types of pipe or tube, such as plastic, may be used if it is investigated and found to be listed for this service.

6. Sec. 2-8.1 is revised to read as follows:

2-8.1. The fire department connection(s) shall be internal swivel fittings having national standard hose thread or as approved by the chief.

7. Sec. 2-9.1 is revised by changing the last line as follows: "on the premises within two minutes after such flow begins."

8. Sec. 2-9.5.1 is revised to read as follows:

Electrically operated alarm attachments forming part of an auxiliary, proprietary, remote station or local signalling system shall be installed in accordance with Uniform Fire Code Standard 10-2.

9. Sec. 3-9.1 is revised by deleting the last sentence.

10. Sec. 4-2-1 is revised by changing the last item to read as follows:

Storage—High piled storage (as defined in *Uniform Fire Code*)—40,000 square feet (3716 m^2).

(Exception to remain unchanged.)

11. Table 4-2.2 is revised by substituting "Uniform Fire Code Standards 81-1 and 81-2" for "NFPA 231 and 231C" in Footnote 6, Item 1, and by deleting "NFPA" in Footnote 6, Item 2.

12. Sec. 4-3.6.1 is revised by substituting "UBC Standard 9-3" for "NFPA 13R, Standard for the Installation of Sprinkler Systems in Residential Occupancies up to and including Four Stories in Height," and by deleting references to NFPA 13D.

13. Sec. 4-4.1.4.2 is revised by adding Exception 3 to read as follows:

Exception No. 3: Where sprinklers are installed under composite wood joists less than 16 inches (406 mm) in depth, sprinkler deflectors shall be a minimum of 1 inch (25 mm) and a maximum of 6 inches (152 mm) below the bottom of the composite wood joist and the joist channels shall be fire-stopped the full depth of the joist with a material equivalent to the web construction so that individual channel areas do not exceed 300 square feet (27.9 m^2). Where the depth of the composite wood joist is 16 inches (406 mm) or greater, protection shall be provided by using one or more of the following methods:

(a) Provide a sprinkler in each joist channel. The distance between sprinklers within the joist channel shall not exceed 15 feet (4572 mm).

(b) Protect the composite wood joist with $^5/_8$-inch (16 mm) Type X gypsum wallboard attached directly to the bottom of the composite wood joist. Joist channels shall be fire-stopped the full depth of the joist with a material equivalent to the web construction so that the volume of individual channels do not exceed 160 cubic feet (4.53 m^3).

(c) Completely fill the channel with noncombustible insulation. The insulation shall be secured to prevent the insulation from falling. Joist channels shall be fire-stopped the full depth of the joist with a material equivalent to the web construction so that the volume of individual channels does not exceed 160 cubic feet (4.53 m^3).

14. Sec. 4-4.1.7.17 is revised to read as follows:

Rack Storage. For sprinklers in rack storage, see Uniform Fire Code Standard 81-2.

15. Sec. 4-5.2.1.2 is revised to read as follows:

When sprinkler piping is installed in storage racks as defined in UFC Standard 81-2, piping shall be substantially supported from the storage rack structure or building in accordance with all applicable provisions of Sections 4-5.2 and 4-5.4.3.

16. Sec. 4-6.1.1.1 is revised to read as follows:

Local water-flow alarms shall be provided on each sprinkler system having more than five sprinklers and shall be located in an area approved by the chief.

17. Sec. 5-2.3.1.1 is revised by substituting "nationally recognized" for "NFPA" in the first line of Exception 1.

18. Sec. 5-2.3.1.3 (e) is revised by substituting the phrase *"Uniform Building Code"* for "NFPA 14, Standard for the Installation of Standpipe and Hose Systems" in the fourth line of the text and where located in the two exceptions.

19. Sec. 5-3.4.1 is revised by substituting "nationally recognized" for "NFPA" in the second line of the text.

20. Sec. 6-1.1.1.1 (l) is revised to read as follows:

6-1.1.1.1 (l). Manufacturing data sheets for sprinkler head which contain at least the following information:

-Make

-Type

-K-factor

-Nominal office size

-Temperature rating

-Minimum operating pressures and discharge rates for proposed area of coverage.

21. Sec. 7-2.1 is revised by deleting "See NFPA 24, Standard for the Installation of Private Fire Service Mains and Their Appurtenances."

22. Sec. 7-2.2.1 is revised by substituting "nationally recognized standards" for "NFPA 20, Standard for the Installation of Centrifugal Pumps."

23. Sec. 7-2.3.1.1 is revised by substituting "nationally recognized standards" for "NFPA 22, Standard for Water Tanks for Private Fire Protection."

24. Sec. 7-2.4 is revised by substituting "nationally recognized standards" for "NFPA 22, Standard for Water Tanks for Private Fire Protection."

25. Sec. 8-2.2.5 is revised by substituting "nationally recognized standards" for "NFPA 24, Standard for the Installation of Private Fire Service Mains and their Appurtenances" in the first sentence.

26. Sec. 8-2.2.5 is revised by substituting "nationally recognized standards" for "NFPA 24, Standard for the Installation of Private Fire Service Mains and Their Appurtenances" in the first sentence and by deleting "by NFPA 24 and" from the second sentence.

27. Sec. 8-4.1 is revised to read as follows:

8-4.1. The installer of the system shall provide the owner with written instructions and information relating to the care and maintenance of the sprinkler system, with special attention given to the sprinkler system devices.

Subsections (a) and (b) are deleted.

28. Sec. 9-1.1 is revised to read as follows:

9-1.1. A sprinkler system installed under this standard shall be maintained in accordance with the UFC Article 10.

29. Sec. 9-3.1 is revised by deleting "(See NFPA 24, standard for the installation of private Fire Service Mains and Their Appurtenances.)"

30. Chapter 10 is deleted.

Part II

Reproduced with permission from the Standard for Installation of Sprinkler Systems, NFPA 13, copyright © 1991[1], National Fire Protection Association, Batterymarch Park, Quincy, Massachusetts 02269. Persons desiring to reprint in whole or part any portion of the Standard for Installation of Sprinkler Systems, NFPA 13, copyright © 1991[1], must secure permission from the National Fire Protection Association. The following standard is not necessarily the latest revision used by NFPA. If the reader desires to compare with that version, the same is available from NFPA.

[1]The current edition is NFPA 13-1996.

NOTE: See page 3–239 for errata to NFPA 13-1991.

Contents

NFPA 13

Standard for the

Installation of Sprinkler Systems

1991 Edition

NOTICE: An asterisk (*) following the number or letter designating a paragraph indicates explanatory material on that paragraph in Appendix A.

Information on referenced publications can be found in Chapter 10 and Appendix C.

Chapter 1   General Information

1-1 Scope. This standard provides the minimum requirements for the design and installation of automatic fire sprinkler systems and exposure protection sprinkler systems, including the character and adequacy of water supplies and the selection of sprinklers, piping, valves, and all materials and accessories, but not including the installation of private fire service mains and water supplies.

NOTE: Consult other NFPA standards for additional requirements relating to water supplies.

NOTE: See Tentative Interim Amendment on page 131.

1-2 Purpose. The purpose of this standard is to provide a reasonable degree of protection for life and property from fire through standardization of design, installation, and testing requirements for sprinkler systems based upon sound engineering principles, test data, and field experience. This standard endeavors to continue the excellent record that has been established by sprinkler systems while meeting the needs of changing technology. Nothing in this standard is intended to restrict new technologies or alternate arrangements, providing the level of safety prescribed by this standard is not lowered. Materials or devices not specifically designated by this standard shall be utilized in complete accord with all conditions, requirements, and limitations of their listings.

NOTE 1: A sprinkler system is a specialized fire protection system and requires knowledgeable and experienced design and installation.

NOTE 2: Since its inception, this document has been developed on the basis of standardized materials, devices, and design practices. However, certain paragraphs, such as 2-3.5, 4-3.2, and this one, allow the use of materials and devices not specifically designated by this standard, provided such use is within parameters established by a listing organization. In using such materials or devices, it is important that all conditions, requirements, and limitations of the listing be fully understood and accepted and that the installation is in complete accord with such listing requirements.

1-3 Retroactivity Clause. The provisions of this document are considered necessary to provide a reasonable level of protection from loss of life and property from fire. They reflect situations and the state of the art at the time the standard was issued.

Unless otherwise noted, it is not intended that the provisions of this document be applied to facilities, equipment, structures, or installations that were existing or approved for construction or installation prior to the effective date of this document.

Exception: In those cases where it is determined by the authority having jurisdiction that the existing situation involves a distinct hazard to life or property, this standard shall apply.

1-4 Definitions.

1-4.1 NFPA Definitions.

Approved.   Acceptable to the "authority having jurisdiction."

NOTE: The National Fire Protection Association does not approve, inspect or certify any installation, procedures, equipment, or materials nor does it approve or evaluate testing laboratories. In determining the acceptability of installations or procedures, equipment or materials, the authority having jurisdiction may base acceptance on compliance with NFPA or other appropriate standards. In the absence of such standards, said authority may require evidence of proper installation, procedure or use. The authority having jurisdiction may also refer to the listings or labeling practices of an organization concerned with product evaluations which is in a position to determine compliance with appropriate standards for the most current production of listed items.

Authority Having Jurisdiction.   The "authority having jurisdiction" is the organization, office or individual responsible for "approving" equipment, an installation or a procedure.

NOTE: The phrase "authority having jurisdiction" is used in NFPA documents in a broad manner since jurisdictions and "approval" agencies vary as do their responsibilities. Where public safety is primary, the "authority having jurisdiction" may be a federal, state, local or other regional department or individual such as a fire chief, fire marshal, chief of a fire prevention bureau, labor department, health department, building official, electrical inspector, or others having statutory authority. For insurance purposes, an insurance inspection department, rating bureau, or other insurance company representative may be the "authority having jurisdiction." In many circumstances the property owner or his designated agent assumes the role of the "authority having jurisdiction"; at government installations, the commanding officer or departmental official may be the "authority having jurisdiction."

Listed.   Equipment or materials included in a list published by an organization acceptable to the "authority having jurisdiction" and concerned with product evaluation, that maintains periodic inspection of production of listed equipment or materials and whose listing states either that the equipment or material meets appropriate standards or has been tested and found suitable for use in a specified manner.

NOTE: The means for identifying listed equipment may vary for each organization concerned with product evaluation, some of which do not recognize equipment as listed unless it is also labeled. The "authority having jurisdiction" should utilize the system employed by the listing organization to identify a listed product.

Shall. Indicates a mandatory requirement.

Should. Indicates a recommendation or that which is advised but not required.

Standard. A document containing only mandatory provisions, using the word shall to indicate requirements. Explanatory material may be included only in the form of fine print notes, in footnotes, or in an appendix.

1-4.2 General Definitions.

Compartment. As used in 4-3.6.3 and 6-4.4.4, a space completely enclosed by walls and a ceiling. The compartment enclosure may have openings to an adjoining space if the openings have a minimum lintel depth of 8 in. (203 mm) from the ceiling.

Drop-Out Ceiling. A suspended ceiling system with listed translucent or opaque panels that are heat sensitive and fall from their setting when exposed to heat. This ceiling system is installed below the sprinklers.

Dwelling Unit. One or more rooms arranged for the use of one or more individuals living together as in a single housekeeping unit normally having cooking, living, sanitary, and sleeping facilities.

For purposes of this standard, dwelling unit includes hotel rooms, dormitory rooms, apartments, condominiums, sleeping rooms in nursing homes, and similar living units.

Fire Control. Limiting the size of a fire by distribution of water so as to decrease the heat release rate and pre-wet adjacent combustibles, while controlling ceiling gas temperatures to avoid structural damage.

Fire Suppression. Sharply reducing the heat release rate of a fire and preventing its regrowth by means of direct and sufficient application of water through the fire plume to the burning fuel surface.

High Challenge Fire Hazard. A fire hazard typical of that produced by fires in combustible high-piled storage.

High-Piled Storage. Solid piled, palletized, rack storage, bin box, and shelf storage in excess of 12 ft (3.7 m) in height. (*See 5-2.3.1.1.*)

Hydraulically Designed System. A calculated sprinkler system in which pipe sizes are selected on a pressure loss basis to provide a prescribed water density, in gallons per minute per square foot [(L/min)/m²], or a prescribed minimum discharge pressure or flow per sprinkler, distributed with a reasonable degree of uniformity over a specified area.

Limited-Combustible Material. As applied to a building construction material, a material, not complying with the definition of noncombustible material, that, in the form in which it is used, has a potential heat value not exceeding 3500 Btu per lb (8141 kJ/kg) and complies with one of the following paragraphs, (a) or (b). Materials subject to increase in combustibility or flame spread rating beyond the limits herein established through the effects of age, moisture, or other atmospheric condition shall be considered combustible.

(a) Materials having a structural base of noncombustible material, with a surfacing not exceeding a thickness of 1/8 in. (3.2 mm) that has a flame spread rating not greater than 50.

(b) Materials, in the form and thickness used, other than as described in (a), having neither a flame spread rating greater than 25 nor evidence of continued progressive combustion and of such composition that surfaces that would be exposed by cutting through the material on any plane would have neither a flame spread rating greater than 25 nor evidence of continued progressive combustion.

Miscellaneous Storage.* Storage that does not exceed 12 ft (3.7 m) in height and is incidental to another occupancy use group as defined in 1-4.7 (see 5-2.3.1.1). Protection criteria for miscellaneous storage are within the scope of this standard.

Noncombustible Material. A material that, in the form in which it is used and under the conditions anticipated, will not ignite, burn, support combustion, or release flammable vapors when subjected to fire or heat. Materials that are reported as passing ASTM E136, *Standard Test Method for Behavior of Materials in a Vertical Tube Furnace at 750°C*, shall be considered noncombustible materials.

Pipe Schedule System. A sprinkler system in which the pipe sizing is selected from a schedule that is determined by the occupancy classification. A given number of sprinklers are allowed to be supplied from specific sizes of pipe.

Small Rooms. Rooms of light hazard occupancy classification having unobstructed construction and floor areas not exceeding 800 sq ft (74.3 m²). (*See 1-4.7.1.*)

Sprinkler System.* For fire protection purposes, an integrated system of underground and overhead piping designed in accordance with fire protection engineering standards. The installation includes one or more automatic water supplies. The portion of the sprinkler system aboveground is a network of specially sized or hydraulically designed piping installed in a building, structure, or area, generally overhead, and to which sprinklers are attached in a systematic pattern. The valve controlling each system riser is located in the system riser or its supply piping. Each sprinkler system riser includes a device for actuating an alarm when the system is in operation. The system is usually activated by heat from a fire and discharges water over the fire area.

NOTE: The design and installation of water supply facilities such as gravity tanks, fire pumps, reservoirs or pressure tanks, and underground piping are covered by the following NFPA standards: NFPA 22, *Standard for Water Tanks for Private Fire Protection*; NFPA 20, *Standard for the Installation of Centrifugal Fire Pumps*; and NFPA 24, *Standard for the Installation of Private Fire Service Mains and Their Appurtenances*.

Thermal Barrier. A material that will limit the average temperature rise of the unexposed surface to not more than 250°F (121°C) after 15 minutes of fire exposure complying with the standard time-temperature curve of NFPA 251, *Standard Methods of Fire Tests of Building Construction and Materials*.

1-4.3 Sprinkler System Type Definitions.

Wet Pipe System. A sprinkler system employing automatic sprinklers attached to a piping system containing water and connected to a water supply so that water discharges immediately from sprinklers opened by heat from a fire.

Dry Pipe System. A sprinkler system employing automatic sprinklers attached to a piping system containing air or nitrogen under pressure, the release of which (as from the opening of a sprinkler) permits the water pressure to open a valve known as a dry pipe valve. The water then flows into the piping system and out the opened sprinklers.

Preaction System. A sprinkler system employing automatic sprinklers attached to a piping system containing air that may or may not be under pressure, with a supplemental detection system installed in the same areas as the sprinklers. Actuating means of the valve are described in 3-3.2.1. Actuation of the detection system opens a valve that permits water to flow into the sprinkler piping system and to be discharged from any sprinklers that may be open.

Deluge System. A sprinkler system employing open sprinklers attached to a piping system connected to a water supply through a valve that is opened by the operation of a detection system installed in the same areas as the sprinklers. When this valve opens, water flows into the piping system and discharges from all sprinklers attached thereto.

Combined Dry Pipe-Preaction System. A sprinkler system employing automatic sprinklers attached to a piping system containing air under pressure with a supplemental detection system installed in the same areas as the sprinklers. Operation of the detection system actuates tripping devices that open dry pipe valves simultaneously and without loss of air pressure in the system. Operation of the detection system also opens listed air exhaust valves at the end of the feed main, which usually precedes the opening of sprinklers. The detection system also serves as an automatic fire alarm system.

Antifreeze System. A wet pipe sprinkler system employing automatic sprinklers attached to a piping system containing an antifreeze solution and connected to a water supply. The antifreeze solution is discharged, followed by water, immediately upon operation of sprinklers opened by heat from a fire.

Circulating Closed-Loop System. A wet pipe sprinkler system having non-fire-protection connections to automatic sprinkler systems in a closed-loop piping arrangement for the purpose of utilizing sprinkler piping to conduct water for heating or cooling. Water is not removed or used from the system, but only circulated through the piping system.

1-4.4* System Component Definitions.

Branch Lines. The pipes in which the sprinklers are placed, either directly or through risers.

Cross Mains. The pipes supplying the branch lines, directly or through risers.

Feed Mains. The pipes supplying risers or cross mains.

Risers. The vertical supply pipes in a sprinkler system.

Supervisory Devices. Devices arranged to supervise the operative condition of automatic sprinkler systems.

System Riser. The aboveground supply pipe directly connected to the water supply.

1-4.5 Sprinkler Definitions.

1-4.5.1 Sprinklers defined according to design and performance characteristics:

Spray Sprinkler. A type of sprinkler listed for its capability to provide fire control for a wide range of fire hazards.

Old-Style/Conventional Sprinkler. Sprinklers that direct from 40 to 60 percent of the total water initially in a downward direction and that are designed to be installed with the deflector either upright or pendent.

Fast Response Sprinkler. A type of sprinkler with a high level of thermal sensitivity, enabling it to respond at an early stage of fire development. This includes ESFR, QR, QREC, QRES, and residential sprinklers.

Residential Sprinkler. A type of fast response sprinkler specifically listed for use in protection against the fire hazards typically found in dwelling units.

Extended Coverage (EC) Sprinkler. A type of spray sprinkler listed as a special sprinkler with extended maximum protection area.

Quick-Response (QR) Sprinkler. A type of sprinkler that is both a fast response and a spray sprinkler.

Quick-Response Extended Coverage (QREC) Sprinkler. Sprinklers that are listed as both quick-response and extended coverage sprinklers.

Quick-Response Early Suppression (QRES) Sprinkler.* Fast response sprinklers that are listed for their capability to provide fire suppression of specific fire hazards.

Large-Drop Sprinkler. A type of sprinkler that is capable of producing characteristic large water droplets and that is listed for its capability to provide fire control of specific high challenge fire hazards.

Early Suppression Fast Response (ESFR) Sprinkler.* A type of fast response sprinkler listed for its capability to provide fire suppression of specific high challenge fire hazards.

Open Sprinkler. Sprinklers from which the heat responsive and actuating elements have been removed.

Nozzles. Devices for use in applications requiring special water discharge patterns, directional spray, or other unusual discharge characteristics.

Special Sprinkler. Sprinklers that have been tested and listed as prescribed in 4-3.2.

1-4.5.2 Sprinklers defined according to orientation:

Concealed Sprinkler. Recessed sprinklers with cover plates.

Flush Sprinkler. Sprinklers in which all or part of the body, including the shank thread, is mounted above the lower plane of the ceiling.

Pendent Sprinkler. Sprinklers designed to be installed in such a way that the water stream is directed downward against the deflector.

Recessed Sprinkler. Sprinklers in which all or part of the body, other than the shank thread, is mounted within a recessed housing.

Sidewall Sprinkler. Sprinklers having special deflectors that are designed to discharge most of the water away from the nearby wall in a pattern resembling one quarter of a sphere, with a small portion of the discharge directed at the wall behind the sprinkler.

Upright Sprinkler. Sprinklers designed to be installed in such a way that the water spray is directed upwards against the deflector.

1-4.5.3 Sprinklers defined according to special application or environment:

Corrosion-Resistant Sprinkler. Sprinklers fabricated with corrosion-resistant material or with special coatings or platings to be used in an atmosphere that would normally corrode sprinklers.

Dry Sprinkler.* Sprinklers secured in an extension nipple that has a seal at the inlet end to prevent water from entering the nipple until the sprinkler operates. Dry sprinklers are intended to extend into an unheated area from a wet pipe system or (for dry-pendent sprinklers) to be used on a dry pipe system in the pendent position.

Intermediate Level Sprinkler/Rack Storage Sprinkler. Sprinklers equipped with integral shields to protect their operating elements from the discharge of sprinklers installed at higher elevations.

Ornamental/Decorative Sprinkler. Sprinklers that have been painted or plated by the manufacturer.

1-4.6* Construction Definitions.

Obstructed Construction. Construction where beams, trusses, or other members impede heatflow or water distribution in a manner that materially affects the ability of sprinklers to control or suppress a fire.

Unobstructed Construction. Construction where beams, trusses, or other members do not impede heatflow or water distribution in a manner that materially affects the ability of sprinklers to control or suppress a fire. Unobstructed construction has horizontal structural members that are not solid, where the openings are at least 70 percent of the cross section area, and the depth of the member does not exceed the least dimension of the openings, or all construction types where the spacing of structural members exceed 7 1/2 ft (2.3 m) on center.

For descriptions of construction types, see A-1-4.6(a) and (b).

1-4.7* Classification of Occupancies. Occupancy classifications for this standard relate to sprinkler installations and their water supplies only. They are not intended to be a general classification of occupancy hazards.

1-4.7.1* Light Hazard Occupancies. Occupancies or portions of other occupancies where the quantity and/or combustibility of contents is low and fires with relatively low rates of heat release are expected.

1-4.7.2 Ordinary Hazard Occupancies.

1-4.7.2.1* Ordinary Hazard (Group 1). Occupancies or portions of other occupancies where combustibility is low, quantity of combustibles is moderate, stockpiles of combustibles do not exceed 8 ft (2.4 m), and fires with moderate rates of heat release are expected.

1-4.7.2.2* Ordinary Hazard (Group 2). Occupancies or portions of other occupancies where quantity and combustibility of contents is moderate to high, stockpiles do not exceed 12 ft (3.7 m), and fires with moderate to high rates of heat release are expected.

1-4.7.3 Extra Hazard Occupancies.

1-4.7.3.1* Occupancies or portions of other occupancies where quantity and combustibility of contents is very high and flammable and combustible liquids, dust, lint, or other materials are present, introducing the probability of rapidly developing fires with high rates of heat release.

1-4.7.3.2 Extra hazard occupancies involve a wide range of variables that may produce severe fires. The following shall be used to evaluate the severity of Extra Hazard Occupancies:

Extra Hazard (Group 1) includes occupancies described in 1-4.7.3.1 with little or no flammable or combustible liquids.

Extra Hazard (Group 2) includes occupancies described in 1-4.7.3.1 with moderate to substantial amounts of flammable or combustible liquids or where shielding of combustibles is extensive.

1-4.7.4 Special Occupancy Hazards.

1-4.7.4.1* Other NFPA standards contain sprinkler system design criteria for fire control or suppression of specific hazards. These are listed in Chapter 10 and include but are not limited to NFPA 30, *Flammable and Combustible Liquids Code*; NFPA 30B, *Code for the Manufacture and Storage of Aerosol Products*; NFPA 40, *Standard for the Storage and Handling of Cellulose Nitrate Motion Picture Film*, NFPA 58, *Standard for the Storage and Handling of Liquefied Petroleum Gases*; NFPA 81, *Standard for Fur Storage, Fumigation and Cleaning*; NFPA 231, *Standard for General Storage*; NFPA 231C, *Standard for Rack Storage of Materials*; NFPA 231D, *Standard for Storage of Rubber Tires*; NFPA 231E, *Recommended Practice for the Storage of Baled Cotton*; NFPA 231F, *Standard for the Storage of Roll Paper*; NFPA 232, *Standard for the Protection of Records*; and NFPA 409, *Standard on Aircraft Hangars*.

1-4.7.4.2 Miscellaneous storage as defined herein shall be classified as to occupancy group in accordance with Table 1-4.7.4.2.

Table 1-4.7.4.2 Occupancy Group Classification for Miscellaneous Storage 12 ft (3.7 m) or Less in Height

Commodity Classification	Palletized and Bin Box	Rack
I	OH-1	OH-1
II	OH-1	OH-1
III	OH-2	OH-2
IV	OH-2	OH-2
Group A Plastic	EH-1	EH-2

NOTE: See Tentative Interim Amendment on page 131.

1-4.7.4.2.1 The commodity classifications and storage characteristics in Table 1-4.7.4.2 shall be as defined in NFPA 231 and NFPA 231C.

1-5 Abbreviations. The standard abbreviations in Table 1-5 shall be used on the hydraulic calculation form.

Table 1-5

Symbol or Abbreviation	Item
p	Pressure in psi
gpm	U.S. Gallons per minute
q	Flow increment in gpm to be added at a specific location
Q	Summation of flow in gpm at a specific location
P_t	Total pressure in psi at a point in a pipe
P_f	Pressure loss due to friction between points indicated in location column
P_e	Pressure due to elevation difference between indicated points. This can be a plus value or a minus value. Where minus, the (−) shall be used; where plus, no sign need be indicated
P_v	Velocity pressure in psi at a point in a pipe
P_n	Normal pressure in psi at a point in a pipe
E	90° Ell
EE	45° Ell
Lt.E	Long Turn Elbow
Cr	Cross
T	Tee—flow turned 90°
GV	Gate Valve
BV	Butterfly (Wafer) Check Valve
Del V	Deluge Valve
ALV	Alarm Valve
DPV	Dry Pipe Valve
CV	Swing Check Valve
WCV	Butterfly (Wafer) Check Valve
St	Strainer
psi	Pounds per square inch
v	Velocity of water in pipe in feet per second

1-6 Level of Protection.

1-6.1 A building, when protected by an automatic sprinkler system installation, shall be provided with sprinklers in all areas.

Exception: Where specific sections of this standard permit the omission of sprinklers.

1-6.2 Limited Area Systems. When partial sprinkler systems are installed, the requirements of this standard shall be used insofar as they are applicable. The authority having jurisdiction shall be consulted in each case.

Chapter 2 System Components and Hardware

2-1 General. This chapter provides requirements for correct use of sprinkler system components.

2-1.1* All materials and devices essential to successful system operation shall be listed.

Exception No. 1: Equipment as permitted in Table 2-3.1, Table 2-4.1, and the Exceptions to 2-6.1 and 2-6.1.1 need not be listed.

Exception No. 2: Components that do not affect system operation such as drain valves and signs need not be listed. The use of reconditioned valves and devices other than sprinklers as replacement equipment in existing systems shall be permitted.

2-1.2 System components shall be rated for the maximum working pressure to which they are exposed but not less than 175 psi (12.1 bars).

2-2 Sprinklers.

2-2.1 Only new sprinklers shall be installed.

2-2.2 Sprinkler Discharge Characteristics. The K factor, relative discharge, and identification for sprinklers having different orifice sizes shall be in accordance with Table 2-2.2 on the following page.

Exception: Listed sprinklers having pipe threads different from those shown in Table 2-2.2 shall be permitted.

2-2.2.1 For Light Hazard Occupancies not requiring as much water as is discharged by a nominal 1/2-in. (12.7-mm) orifice sprinkler operating at 7 psi (0.5 bar), sprinklers having a smaller orifice shall be permitted subject to the following restrictions:

(a) The system shall be hydraulically calculated. (See Chapter 6.)

(b) Small orifice sprinklers shall be installed in wet systems only.

Exception: Small orifice outside sprinklers for protection from exposure fires installed in conformance with Section 3-7 shall be permitted.

(c) A listed strainer shall be provided on the supply side of sprinklers having orifices smaller than 3/8 in. (9.5 mm).

2-2.2.2 Sprinklers having orifice sizes exceeding 1/2 in. (12.7 mm) and having 1/2 in. NPT shall not be installed in new sprinkler systems.

2-2.3* Temperature Characteristics.

2-2.3.1 The standard temperature ratings of automatic sprinklers are shown in Table 2-2.3.1 on the following page. Automatic sprinklers shall have their frame arms colored in accordance with the color code designated in Table 2-2.3.1.

Exception No. 1: A dot on the top of the deflector, or the color of the coating material, or colored frame arms shall be permitted for color identification of corrosion-resistant sprinklers.

Table 2-2.2   Sprinkler Discharge Characteristics Identification

Nominal Orifice Size (in.)	Orifice Type	K Factor[1]	Percent of Nominal 1/2 in. Discharge	Thread Type	Pintle	Nominal Orifice Size Marked On Frame
1/4	Small	1.3-1.5	25	1/2 in. NPT	Yes	Yes
5/16	Small	1.8-2.0	33.3	1/2 in. NPT	Yes	Yes
3/8	Small	2.6-2.9	50	1/2 in. NPT	Yes	Yes
7/16	Small	4.0-4.4	75	1/2 in. NPT	Yes	Yes
1/2	Standard	5.3-5.8	100	1/2 in. NPT	No	No
17/32	Large	7.4-8.2	140	3/4 in. NPT or 1/2 in. NPT	No	No
5/8	Extra Large	11.0-11.5	200	1/2 in. NPT or 3/4 in. NPT	Yes	Yes
5/8	Large-Drop	11.0-11.5	200	1/2 in. NPT or 3/4 in. NPT	Yes	Yes
3/4	ESFR	13.5-14.5	250	3/4 in. NPT	Yes	No

[1]K factor is the constant in the formula $Q = K\sqrt{p}$
Where Q = Flow in gpm
    p = Pressure in psi

For SI Units: $Q_m = K_m\sqrt{p_m}$
Where Q_m = Flow in L/min
    P_m = Pressure in bars
    K_m = 14 K

Exception No. 2:   Color identification shall not be required for ornamental sprinklers such as factory plated or factory painted sprinklers or for recessed, flush, or concealed sprinklers.

Exception No. 3:   The frame arms of bulb type sprinklers need not be color coded.

2-2.3.2   The liquid in bulb type sprinklers shall be color coded in accordance with Table 2-2.3.1.

2-2.4 Special Coatings.

2-2.4.1*   Listed corrosion-resistant sprinklers shall be installed in locations where chemicals, moisture, or other corrosive vapors sufficient to cause corrosion of such devices exist.

2-2.4.2*   Corrosion-resistant coatings shall be applied only by the manufacturer of the sprinkler.

Exception: Any damage to the protective coating occurring at the time of installation shall be repaired at once using only the coating of the manufacturer of the sprinkler in the approved manner so that no part of the sprinkler will be exposed after installation has been completed.

2-2.4.3*   Unless applied by the manufacturer, sprinklers shall not be painted, and any sprinklers that have been

painted shall be replaced with new listed sprinklers of the same characteristics, including orifice size, thermal response, and water distribution.

Exception: Factory-applied paint or coating to sprinkler frames in accordance with 2-2.3.1 shall be permitted.

2-2.4.4   Ornamental finishes shall not be applied to sprinklers by anyone other than the sprinkler manufacturer, and only sprinklers listed with such finishes shall be used.

2-2.5 Escutcheon Plates.

2-2.5.1   Nonmetallic escutcheon plates shall be listed.

2-2.5.2*   Escutcheon plates used with a recessed or flush type sprinkler shall be part of a listed sprinkler assembly.

2-2.6* Guards and Shields.   Sprinklers subject to mechanical injury shall be protected with listed guards.

2-2.7 Stock of Spare Sprinklers.

2-2.7.1   A supply of spare sprinklers (never less than 6) shall be maintained on the premises so that any sprinklers that have operated or been damaged in any way can be

Table 2-2.3.1   Temperature Ratings, Classifications, and Color Codings

Max. Ceiling Temp. °F	°C	Temperature Rating °F	°C	Temperature Classification	Color Code	Glass Bulb Colors
100	38	135 to 170	57 to 77	Ordinary	Uncolored or Black	Orange or Red
150	66	175 to 225	79 to 107	Intermediate	White	Yellow or Green
225	107	250 to 300	121 to 149	High	Blue	Blue
300	149	325 to 375	163 to 191	Extra High	Red	Purple
375	191	400 to 475	204 to 246	Very Extra High	Green	Black
475	246	500 to 575	260 to 302	Ultra High	Orange	Black
625	329	650	343	Ultra High	Orange	Black

promptly replaced. These sprinklers shall correspond to the types and temperature ratings of the sprinklers in the property. The sprinklers shall be kept in a cabinet located where the temperature to which they are subjected will at no time exceed 100°F (38°C).

2-2.7.2 A special sprinkler wrench shall also be provided and kept in the cabinet to be used in the removal and installation of sprinklers.

2-2.7.3 The stock of spare sprinklers shall include all types and ratings installed and shall be as follows:

(a) For systems with not over 300 sprinklers, not less than 6 sprinklers.

(b) For systems with 300 to 1000 sprinklers, not less than 12 sprinklers.

(c) For systems with over 1000 sprinklers, not less than 24 sprinklers.

2-3 Pipe and Tube.

2-3.1 Pipe or tube used in sprinkler systems shall meet or exceed one of the standards in Table 2-3.1 or be in accordance with 2-3.2 through 2-3.5.

Table 2-3.1 Pipe or Tube Materials and Dimensions

Materials and Dimensions	Standard
Ferrous Piping (Welded and Seamless)	
† Spec. for Black and Hot-Dipped Zinc Coated (Galvanized) Welded and Seamless Steel Pipe for Fire Protection Use	ASTM A795
† Spec. for Welded and Seamless Steel Pipe	ANSI/ ASTM A53
Wrought Steel Pipe	ANSI B36.10M
Spec. for Elec.-Resistance Welded Steel Pipe	ASTM A135
Copper Tube (Drawn, Seamless)	
† Spec. for Seamless Copper Tube	ASTM B75
† Spec. for Seamless Copper Water Tube	ASTM B88
Spec. for General Requirements for Wrought Seamless Copper and Copper-Alloy Tube	ASTM B251
Brazing Filler Metal (Classification BCuP-3 or BCuP-4)	AWS A5.8
Solder Metal, 95-5 (Tin-Antimony-Grade 95TA)	ASTM B32

† Denotes pipe or tubing suitable for bending (see 2-3.6) according to ASTM standards.

2-3.2* When steel pipe listed in Table 2-3.1 is used and joined by welding as referenced in 2-5.2 or by roll grooved pipe and fittings as referenced in 2-5.3, the minimum nominal wall thickness for pressures up to 300 psi (20.7 bars) shall be in accordance with Schedule 10 for sizes up to 5 in. (127 mm); 0.134 in. (3.40 mm) for 6 in. (152 mm); and 0.188 in. (4.78 mm) for 8 and 10 in. (203 and 254 mm) pipe.

Exception: Pressure limitations and wall thickness for steel pipe listed in accordance with 2-3.5 shall be in accordance with the listing requirements.

2-3.3 When steel pipe listed in Table 2-3.1 is joined by threaded fittings referenced in 2-5.1 or by fittings used with pipe having cut grooves, the minimum wall thickness shall be in accordance with Schedule 30 [in sizes 8 in. (203 mm) and larger] or Schedule 40 [in sizes less than 8 in. (203 mm)] pipe for pressures up to 300 psi (20.7 bars).

Exception: Pressure limitations and wall thickness for steel pipe specially listed in accordance with 2-3.5 shall be in accordance with the listing requirements.

2-3.4* Copper tube as specified in the standards listed in Table 2-3.1 shall have a wall thickness of Type K, L, or M where used in sprinkler systems.

2-3.5* Other types of pipe or tube investigated for suitability in automatic sprinkler installations and listed for this service, including but not limited to polybutylene, chlorinated polyvinyl chloride (CPVC), and steel differing from that provided in Table 2-3.1, shall be permitted when installed in accordance with their listing limitations, including installation instructions. Pipe or tube shall not be listed for portions of an occupancy classification.

2-3.6 Pipe Bending. Bending of Schedule 40 steel pipe and Types K and L copper tube shall be permitted when bends are made with no kinks, ripples, distortions, reductions in diameter, or any noticeable deviations from round. The minimum radius of a bend shall be 6 pipe diameters for pipe sizes 2 in. (51 mm) and smaller, and 5 pipe diameters for pipe sizes 2½ in. (64 mm) and larger.

2-4 Fittings.

2-4.1 Fittings used in sprinkler systems shall meet or exceed the standards in Table 2-4.1 or be in accordance with 2-4.2.

Table 2-4.1 Fittings Materials and Dimensions

Materials and Dimensions	Standard
Cast Iron	
Cast Iron Threaded Fittings, Class 125 and 250	ANSI B16.4
Cast Iron Pipe Flanges and Flanged Fittings	ANSI B16.1
Malleable Iron	
Malleable Iron Threaded Fittings, Class 150 and 300	ANSI B16.3
Steel	
Factory-made Wrought Steel Buttweld Fittings	ANSI B16.9
Buttwelding Ends for Pipe, Valves, Flanges, and Fittings	ANSI B16.25
Spec. for Piping Fittings of Wrought Carbon Steel and Alloy Steel for Moderate and Elevated Temperatures	ASTM A234
Steel Pipe Flanges and Flanged Fittings	ANSI B16.5
Forged Steel Fittings, Socket Welded and Threaded	ANSI B16.11
Copper	
Wrought Copper and Bronze Solder-Joint Pressure Fittings	ANSI B16.22
Cast Bronze Solder-Joint Pressure Fittings	ANSI B16.18

2-4.2* Other types of fittings investigated for suitability in automatic sprinkler installations and listed for this service, including but not limited to polybutylene, chlorinated polyvinyl chloride (CPVC), and steel differing from that provided in Table 2-4.1, shall be permitted when installed in accordance with their listing limitations, including installation instructions.

2-4.3 Fittings shall be extra-heavy pattern where pressures exceed 175 psi (12.1 bars).

Exception No. 1: Standard weight pattern cast-iron fittings 2 in. (51 mm) in size and smaller shall be permitted where pressures do not exceed 300 psi (20.7 bars).

Exception No. 2: Standard weight pattern malleable iron fittings 6 in. (152 mm) in size and smaller shall be permitted where pressures do not exceed 300 psi (20.7 bars).

Exception No. 3: Fittings shall be permitted for system pressures up to the limits specified in their listings.

2-4.4* Couplings and Unions. Screwed unions shall not be used on pipe larger than 2 in. (51 mm). Couplings and unions of other than screwed-type shall be of types listed specifically for use in sprinkler systems.

2-4.5 Reducers and Bushings. A one-piece reducing fitting shall be used wherever a change is made in the size of the pipe.

Exception No. 1: Hexagonal or face bushings shall be permitted in reducing the size of openings of fittings when standard fittings of the required size are not available.

Exception No. 2: Hexagonal bushings as permitted in 4-4.1.7.21.1 are acceptable.

2-5 Joining of Pipe and Fittings.

2-5.1 Threaded Pipe and Fittings.

2-5.1.1 All threaded pipe and fittings shall have threads cut to ANSI/ASME B1.20.1.

2-5.1.2* Steel pipe with wall thicknesses less than Schedule 30 [in sizes 8 in. (203 mm) and larger] or Schedule 40 [in sizes less than 8 in. (203 mm)] shall not be joined by threaded fittings.

Exception: A threaded assembly investigated for suitability in automatic sprinkler installations and listed for this service shall be permitted.

2-5.1.3 Joint compound or tape shall be applied only to male threads.

2-5.2* Welded Pipe and Fittings.

2-5.2.1 Welding methods that comply with all of the requirements of AWS D10.9, *Specification for Qualification of Welding Procedures and Welders for Piping and Tubing*, Level AR-3, are acceptable means of joining fire protection piping.

2-5.2.2* Sprinkler piping shall be shop welded.

Exception: Welding of sprinkler piping in place inside new buildings under construction shall be permitted only when the construction is noncombustible and no combustible contents are present and when the welding process is performed in accordance with NFPA 51B, Standard for Fire Prevention in Use of Cutting and Welding Processes.

2-5.2.3 Fittings used to join pipe shall be listed fabricated fittings or manufactured in accordance with Table 2-4.1. Such fittings joined in conformance with a qualified welding procedure as set forth in this section are an acceptable product under this standard, provided that materials and wall thickness are compatible with other sections of this standard.

Exception: Fittings are not required when pipe ends are buttwelded.

2-5.2.4 No welding shall be performed if there is impingement of rain, snow, sleet, or high wind on the weld area of the pipe product.

2-5.2.5 When welding is performed:

(a)* Holes in piping for outlets shall be cut to the full inside diameter of fittings prior to welding in place of the fittings.

(b) Discs shall be retrieved.

(c) Openings cut into piping shall be smooth bore, and all internal slag and welding residue shall be removed.

(d) Fittings shall not penetrate the internal diameter of the piping.

(e) Steel plates shall not be welded to the ends of piping or fittings.

(f) Fittings shall not be modified.

(g) Nuts, clips, eye rods, angle brackets, or other fasteners shall not be welded to pipe or fittings.

Exception: Only tabs welded to pipe for longitudinal earthquake braces shall be permitted. (See 4-5.4.3.5.1.)

2-5.2.6 When reducing the pipe size in a run of piping, a reducing fitting designed for that purpose shall be used.

2-5.2.7 Torch cutting and welding shall not be permitted as a means of modifying or repairing sprinkler systems.

2-5.2.8 Qualifications.

2-5.2.8.1 A welding procedure shall be prepared and qualified by the contractor or fabricator before any welding is done. Qualification of the welding procedure to be used and the performance of all welders and welding operators is required and shall meet or exceed the requirements of American Welding Society Standard AWS D10.9, Level AR-3.

2-5.2.8.2 Contractors or fabricators shall be responsible for all welding they produce. Each contractor or fabricator shall have an established written quality assurance procedure ensuring compliance with the requirements of 2-5.2.5 available to the authority having jurisdiction.

2-5.2.9 Records.

2-5.2.9.1 Welders or welding machine operators shall, upon completion of each weld, stamp an imprint of their identification into the side of the pipe adjacent to the weld.

2-5.2.9.2 Contractors or fabricators shall maintain certified records, which are available to the authority having jurisdiction, of the procedures used and the welders or welding machine operators employed by them along with their welding identification imprints. Records shall show the date and the results of procedure and performance qualifications.

2-5.3 Groove Joining Methods.

2-5.3.1 Pipe joined with grooved fittings shall be joined by a listed combination of fittings, gaskets, and grooves. Grooves cut or rolled on pipe shall be dimensionally compatible with the fittings.

2-5.3.2 Grooved fittings including gaskets used on dry pipe systems shall be listed for dry pipe service.

2-5.4* Brazed and Soldered Joints. Joints for the connection of copper tube shall be brazed.

Exception No. 1: Solder joints shall be permitted for exposed wet pipe systems in Light Hazard Occupancies where the temperature classification of the installed sprinklers is ordinary or intermediate.

Exception No. 2: Solder joints shall be permitted for wet pipe systems in Light Hazard and Ordinary Hazard (Group 1) Occupancies where the piping is concealed, irrespective of sprinkler temperature ratings.

2-5.4.1* Highly corrosive fluxes shall not be used.

2-5.5 Other Types. Other joining methods investigated for suitability in automatic sprinkler installations and listed for this service shall be permitted when installed in accordance with their listing limitations, including installation instructions.

2-5.6 End Treatment. After cutting, pipe ends shall have burrs and fins removed.

2-5.6.1 Pipe used with listed fittings and its end treatment shall be in accordance with the fitting manufacturer's installation instructions and the fitting's listing.

2-6 Hangers.

2-6.1* General. Types of hangers shall be in accordance with the requirements of Section 2-6.

Exception: Hangers certified by a registered professional engineer to include all of the following shall be acceptable:

(a) Hangers are designed to support five times the weight of the water-filled pipe plus 250 lb (114 kg) at each point of piping support.

(b) These points of support are adequate to support the sprinkler system.

(c) Hanger components shall be ferrous.

Detailed calculations shall be submitted, when required by the reviewing authority, showing stresses developed both in hangers and piping and safety factors allowed.

2-6.1.1 The components of hanger assemblies that directly attach to the pipe or to the building structure shall be listed.

Exception: Mild steel hangers formed from rods need not be listed.

2-6.1.2 Hangers and their components shall be ferrous.

Exception: Nonferrous components that have been proven by fire tests to be adequate for the hazard application, that are listed for this purpose, and that are in compliance with the other requirements of this section shall be acceptable.

2-6.1.3 Sprinkler piping shall be substantially supported from the building structure, which must support the added load of the water-filled pipe plus a minimum of 250 lb (114 kg) applied at the point of hanging.

2-6.1.4 When sprinkler piping is installed below ductwork, piping shall be supported from the building structure or from the ductwork supports, provided such supports are capable of handling both the load of the ductwork and the load specified in 2-6.1.3.

2-6.1.5* For trapeze hangers, the minimum size of steel angle or pipe span between purlins or joists shall be such that the available section modulus of the trapeze member from Table 2-6.1.5(b) equals or exceeds the section modulus required in Table 2-6.1.5(a). (*See following pages.*)

Any other sizes or shapes giving equal or greater section modulus shall be acceptable. All angles shall be used with the longer leg vertical. The trapeze member shall be secured to prevent slippage. When a pipe is suspended from a pipe trapeze of a diameter less than the diameter of the pipe being supported, ring, strap, or clevis hangers of the size corresponding to the suspended pipe shall be used on both ends.

2-6.1.6 The size of hanger rods and fasteners required to support the steel angle iron or pipe indicated in Table 2-6.1.5(a) shall comply with 2-6.4.

2-6.1.7* Sprinkler piping or hangers shall not be used to support nonsystem components.

2-6.2 Hangers in Concrete.

2-6.2.1 The use of listed inserts set in concrete to support hangers shall be permitted.

2-6.2.2 Listed expansion shields for supporting pipes under concrete construction shall be permitted to be used in a horizontal position in the sides of beams. In concrete

Table 2-6.1.5(a)   Section Modulus Required for Trapeze Members (in.^{3})

Span of Trapeze	1 in.	1¼ in.	1½ in.	2 in.	2½ in.	3 in.	3½ in.	4 in.	5 in.	6 in.	8 in.	10 in.
1 ft 6 in.	.08	.09	.09	.09	.10	.11	.12	.13	.15	.18	.24	.32
	.08	.09	.09	.10	.11	.12	.13	.15	.18	.22	.30	.41
2 ft 0 in.	.11	.12	.12	.13	.13	.15	.16	.17	.20	.24	.32	.43
	.11	.12	.12	.13	.15	.16	.18	.20	.24	.29	.40	.55
2 ft 6 in.	.14	.14	.15	.16	.17	.18	.20	.21	.25	.30	.40	.54
	.14	.15	.15	.16	.18	.21	.22	.25	.30	.36	.50	.68
3 ft 0 in.	.17	.17	.18	.19	.20	.22	.24	.26	.31	.36	.48	.65
	.17	.18	.18	.20	.22	.25	.27	.30	.36	.43	.60	.82
4 ft 0 in.	.22	.23	.24	.25	.27	.29	.32	.34	.41	.48	.64	.87
	.22	.24	.24	.26	.29	.33	.36	.40	.48	.58	.80	1.09
5 ft 0 in.	.28	.29	.30	.31	.34	.37	.40	.43	.51	.59	.80	1.08
	.28	.29	.30	.33	.37	.41	.45	.49	.60	.72	1.00	1.37
6 ft 0 in.	.33	.35	.36	.38	.41	.44	.48	.51	.61	.71	.97	1.30
	.34	.35	.36	.39	.44	.49	.54	.59	.72	.87	1.20	1.64
7 ft 0 in.	.39	.40	.41	.44	.47	.52	.55	.60	.71	.83	1.13	1.52
	.39	.41	.43	.46	.51	.58	.63	.69	.84	1.01	1.41	1.92
8 ft 0 in.	.44	.46	.47	.50	.54	.59	.63	.68	.81	.95	1.29	1.73
	.45	.47	.49	.52	.59	.66	.72	.79	.96	1.16	1.61	2.19
9 ft 0 in.	.50	.52	.53	.56	.61	.66	.71	.77	.92	1.07	1.45	1.95
	.50	.53	.55	.59	.66	.74	.81	.89	1.08	1.30	1.81	2.46
10 ft 0 in.	.56	.58	.59	.63	.68	.74	.79	.85	1.02	1.19	1.61	2.17
	.56	.59	.61	.65	.74	.82	.90	.99	1.20	1.44	2.01	2.74

For SI Units: 1 in. = 25.4 mm; 1 ft = 0.3048 m.
Top values are for Schedule 10 pipe; bottom values are for Schedule 40 pipe.
Note: The table is based on a maximum allowable bending stress of 15 KSI and a midspan concentrated load from 15 ft of water-filled pipe, plus 250 lb.

having gravel or crushed stone aggregate, expansion shields shall be permitted to be used in the vertical position to support pipes 4 in. (102 mm) or less in diameter.

2-6.2.3 For the support of pipes 5 in. (127 mm) and larger, expansion shields, if used in the vertical position, shall alternate with hangers connected directly to the structural members, such as trusses and girders, or to the sides of concrete beams. In the absence of convenient structural members, pipes 5 in. (127 mm) and larger shall be permitted to be supported entirely by expansion shields in the vertical position, but spaced not over 10 ft (3 m) apart.

2-6.2.4 Expansion shields shall not be used in ceilings of gypsum or similar soft material. In cinder concrete, expansion shields shall not be used except on branch lines where they shall alternate with through bolts or hangers attached to beams.

2-6.2.5 When expansion shields are used in the vertical position, the holes shall be drilled to provide uniform contact with the shield over its entire circumference. Depth of the hole shall not be less than specified for the type of shield used.

2-6.2.6 Holes for expansion shields in the side of concrete beams shall be above the center line of the beam or above the bottom reinforcement steel rods.

2-6.3 Powder-Driven Studs and Welding Studs.

2-6.3.1* Powder-driven studs, welding studs, and the tools used for installing these devices shall be listed. Pipe size, installation position, and construction material into which they are installed shall be in accordance with individual listings.

2-6.3.2* Representative samples of concrete into which studs are to be driven shall be tested to determine that the studs will hold a minimum load of 750 lb (341 kg) for 2-in. (51-mm) or smaller pipe, 1000 lb (454 kg) for 2½-, 3-, or 3½-in. (64-, 76-, or 89-mm) pipe, and 1200 lb (545 kg) for 4- or 5-in. (102- or 127-mm) pipe.

2-6.3.3 Increaser couplings shall be attached directly to the powder-driven studs or welding studs.

2-6.3.4 Welding studs or other hanger parts shall not be attached by welding to steel less than U.S. Standard, 12 gauge.

2-6.4 Rods and "U" Hooks.

2-6.4.1 Hanger rod size shall be the same as that approved for use with the hanger assembly, and the size of rods shall not be less than that given in Table 2-6.4.1.

Exception: Rods of smaller diameter shall be permitted when the hanger assembly has been tested and listed by a testing laboratory and installed within the limits of pipe sizes expressed in individual listings. For rolled threads, the rod size shall not be less than the root diameter of the thread.

2-6.4.2 U-Hooks. The size of the rod material of U-hooks shall not be less than that given in Table 2-6.4.2. Drive screws shall be used only in a horizontal position as in the side of a beam in conjunction with U-hangers only.

2-6.4.3 The size of the rod material for eye rods shall not be less than specified in Table 2-6.4.3. When eye rods are fastened to wood structural members, the eye rod shall be backed with a large flat washer bearing directly against the structural member, in addition to the lock washer.

Table 2-6.1.5(b) Available Section Moduli of Common Trapeze Hangers

Pipe	Modulus	Angles					Modulus
Schedule 10							
1 in.	.12	$1\frac{1}{2}$	×	$1\frac{1}{2}$	×	$\frac{3}{16}$	.10
$1\frac{1}{4}$ in.	.19	2	×	2	×	$\frac{1}{8}$	.13
$1\frac{1}{2}$ in.	.26	2	×	$1\frac{1}{2}$	×	$\frac{3}{16}$	.18
2 in.	.42	2	×	2	×	$\frac{3}{16}$	.19
$2\frac{1}{2}$ in.	.69	2	×	2	×	$\frac{1}{4}$	.25
3 in.	1.04	$2\frac{1}{2}$	×	$1\frac{1}{2}$	×	$\frac{3}{16}$	.28
$3\frac{1}{2}$ in.	1.38	$2\frac{1}{2}$	×	2	×	$\frac{3}{16}$	.29
4 in.	1.76	2	×	2	×	$\frac{5}{16}$	.30
5 in.	3.03	$2\frac{1}{2}$	×	$2\frac{1}{2}$	×	$\frac{3}{16}$	.30
6 in.	4.35	2	×	2	×	$\frac{3}{8}$	.35
		$2\frac{1}{2}$	×	$2\frac{1}{2}$	×	$\frac{1}{4}$	.39
		3	×	2	×	$\frac{3}{16}$	.41
Schedule 40		3	×	$2\frac{1}{2}$	×	$\frac{3}{16}$	.43
1 in.	.13	3	×	3	×	$\frac{3}{16}$	.44
$1\frac{1}{4}$ in.	.23	$2\frac{1}{2}$	×	$2\frac{1}{2}$	×	$\frac{5}{16}$	.48
$1\frac{1}{2}$ in.	.33	3	×	2	×	$\frac{1}{4}$	.54
2 in.	.56	$2\frac{1}{2}$	×	2	×	$\frac{3}{8}$	.55
$2\frac{1}{2}$ in.	1.06	$2\frac{1}{2}$	×	$2\frac{1}{2}$	×	$\frac{3}{8}$	.57
3 in.	1.72	3	×	3	×	$\frac{1}{4}$	.58
$3\frac{1}{2}$ in.	2.39	3	×	3	×	$\frac{5}{16}$	.71
4 in.	3.21	$2\frac{1}{2}$	×	$2\frac{1}{2}$	×	$\frac{1}{2}$	.72
5 in.	5.45	$3\frac{1}{2}$	×	$2\frac{1}{2}$	×	$\frac{1}{4}$	.75
6 in.	8.50	3	×	$2\frac{1}{2}$	×	$\frac{3}{8}$	.81
		3	×	3	×	$\frac{3}{8}$	.83
		$3\frac{1}{2}$	×	$2\frac{1}{2}$	×	$\frac{5}{16}$	.93
		3	×	3	×	$\frac{7}{16}$	.95
		4	×	4	×	$\frac{1}{4}$	1.05
		3	×	3	×	$\frac{1}{2}$	1.07
		4	×	3	×	$\frac{5}{16}$	1.23
		4	×	4	×	$\frac{5}{16}$	1.29
		4	×	3	×	$\frac{3}{8}$	1.46
		4	×	4	×	$\frac{3}{8}$	1.52
		5	×	$3\frac{1}{2}$	×	$\frac{5}{16}$	1.94
		4	×	4	×	$\frac{1}{2}$	1.97
		4	×	4	×	$\frac{5}{8}$	2.40
		4	×	4	×	$\frac{3}{4}$	2.81
		6	×	4	×	$\frac{3}{8}$	3.32
		6	×	4	×	$\frac{1}{2}$	4.33
		6	×	4	×	$\frac{3}{4}$	6.25
		6	×	6	×	1	8.57

For SI Units: 1 in. = 25.4 mm; 1 ft = 0.3048 m.

2-6.4.3.1 Eye rods shall be secured with lock washers to prevent lateral motion.

2-6.4.4 Threaded sections of rods shall not be formed or bent.

2-6.4.5 Screws. For ceiling flanges and U-hooks, screw dimensions shall not be less than those given in Table 2-6.4.5.

Exception: When the thickness of planking and thickness of flange do not permit the use of screws 2 in. (51 mm) long, screws $1\frac{3}{4}$ in. (44 mm) long shall be permitted with hangers spaced not over 10 ft (3 m) apart. When the thickness of beams or joists does not permit the use of screws $2\frac{1}{2}$ in. (64 mm) long, screws 2 in. (51 mm) long shall be permitted with hangers spaced not over 10 ft (3 m) apart.

Table 2-6.4.1 Hanger Rod Sizes

Pipe Size	Diam. of Rod in.	mm	Pipe Size	Diam. of Rod in.	mm
Up to and including 4 in.	$\frac{3}{8}$	9.5	5, 6, and 8 in.	$\frac{1}{2}$	12.7
			10 and 12 in.	$\frac{5}{8}$	15.9

For SI Units: 1 in. = 25.4 mm.

Table 2-6.4.2 U-Hook Rod Sizes

Pipe Size	Hook Material Diameter in.	mm
Up to 2 in.	$\frac{5}{16}$	7.9
$2\frac{1}{2}$ in. to 6 in.	$\frac{3}{8}$	9.5
8 in.	$\frac{1}{2}$	12.7

For SI Units: 1 in. = 25.4 mm.

Table 2-6.4.3 Eye Rod Sizes

Pipe Size	Diameter of Rod With Bent Eye in.	mm	With Welded Eye in.	mm
Up to 4 in.	$\frac{3}{8}$	9.5	$\frac{3}{8}$	9.5
5-6 in.	$\frac{1}{2}$	12.7	$\frac{1}{2}$	12.7
8 in.	$\frac{3}{4}$	19.1	$\frac{1}{2}$	12.7

For SI Units: 1 in. = 25.4 mm.

Table 2-6.4.5 Screw Dimensions for Ceiling Flanges and U-Hooks

Pipe Size	2 Screw Flanges
Up to 2 in.	Wood Screw No. 18 × $1\frac{1}{2}$ in.
Pipe Size	**3 Screw Flanges**
Up to 2 in.	Wood Screw No. 18 × $1\frac{1}{2}$ in.
$2\frac{1}{2}$ in., 3 in., $3\frac{1}{2}$ in.	Lag Screw $\frac{3}{8}$ in. × 2 in.
4 in., 5 in., 6 in.	Lag Screw $\frac{1}{2}$ in. × 2 in.
8 in.	Lag Screw $\frac{5}{8}$ in. × 2 in.
Pipe Size	**4 Screw Flanges**
Up to 2 in.	Wood Screw No. 18 × $1\frac{1}{2}$ in.
$2\frac{1}{2}$ in., 3 in., $3\frac{1}{2}$ in.	Lag Screw $\frac{3}{8}$ in. × $1\frac{1}{2}$ in.
4 in., 5 in., 6 in.	Lag Screw $\frac{1}{2}$ in. × 2 in.
8 in.	Lag Screw $\frac{5}{8}$ in. × 2 in.
Pipe Size	**U-Hooks**
Up to 2 in.	Drive Screw No. 16 × 2 in.
$2\frac{1}{2}$ in., 3 in., $3\frac{1}{2}$ in.	Lag Screw $\frac{3}{8}$ in. × $2\frac{1}{2}$ in.
4 in., 5 in., 6 in.	Lag Screw $\frac{1}{2}$ in. × 3 in.
8 in.	Lag Screw $\frac{5}{8}$ in. × 3 in.

For SI Units: 1 in. = 25.4 mm.

2-6.4.6 The size bolt or lag (coach) screw used with an eye rod or flange on the side of the beam shall not be less than specified in Table 2-6.4.6.

Exception: When the thickness of beams or joists does not permit the use of screws 2¹/₂ in. (64 mm) long, screws 2 in. (51 mm) long shall be permitted with hangers spaced not over 10 ft (3 m) apart.

Table 2-6.4.6   Minimum Bolt or Lag Screw Sizes

	Size of Bolt or Lag Screw		Length of Lag Screw Used with Wood Beams	
Size of Pipe	in.	mm	in.	mm
Up to and including 2 in.	³/₈	9.5	2¹/₂	64
2¹/₂ to 6 in. (inclusive)	¹/₂	12.7	3	76
8 in.	⁵/₈	15.9	3	76

2-6.4.7 Wood screws shall be installed with a screwdriver. Nails are not acceptable for fastening hangers.

2-6.4.8 Screws in the side of a timber or joist shall be not less than 2¹/₂ in. (64 mm) from the lower edge when supporting branch lines and not less than 3 in. (76 mm) when supporting main lines.

Exception: This requirement shall not apply to 2 in. (51 mm) or thicker nailing strips resting on top of steel beams.

2-6.4.9 The minimum plank thickness and the minimum width of the lower face of beams or joists in which lag screw rods are used shall be as given in Table 2-6.4.9.

Table 2-6.4.9   Minimum Plank Thicknesses and Beam or Joist Widths

	Nominal Plank Thickness		Nominal Width of Beam or Joist Face	
Pipe Size	in.	mm	in.	mm
Up to 2 in.	3	76	2	51
2¹/₂ in. to 3¹/₂ in.	4	102	2	51
4 in. and 5 in.	4	102	3	76
6 in.	4	102	4	102

2-6.4.10 Lag screw rods shall not be used for support of pipes larger than 6 in. (152 mm). All holes for lag screw rods shall be predrilled ¹/₈ in. (3.2 mm) less in diameter than the maximum root diameter of the lag screw thread.

2-7 Valves.

2-7.1 Types of Valves to Be Used.

2-7.1.1 All valves controlling connections to water supplies and to supply pipes to sprinklers shall be listed indicating valves. Such valves shall not close in less than 5 seconds when operated at maximum possible speed from the fully open position.

Exception No. 1: A listed underground gate valve equipped with a listed indicator post shall be permitted.

Exception No. 2: A listed water control valve assembly with a reliable position indication connected to a remote supervisory station shall be permitted.

Exception No. 3: A nonindicating valve, such as an underground gate valve with approved roadway box complete with T-wrench, accepted by the authority having jurisdiction, shall be permitted.

2-7.1.2 When water pressures exceed 175 psi (12.1 bars), valves shall be used in accordance with their pressure ratings.

2-7.1.3 Wafer type valves with components that extend beyond the valve body shall be installed in a manner that does not interfere with the operation of any system components.

2-7.2 Drain Valves and Test Valves. Drain valves and test valves shall be approved.

2-7.3 Identification of Valves. All control, drain, and test connection valves shall be provided with permanently marked weather-proof metal or rigid plastic identification signs. The sign shall be secured with corrosion-resistant wire, chain, or other approved means.

2-8 Fire Department Connections.

2-8.1 The fire department connection(s) shall be internal threaded swivel fitting(s) having threads compatible with those of the local fire department.

2-8.2 Connections shall be equipped with listed plugs or caps.

2-9 Waterflow Alarms.

2-9.1 Waterflow alarm apparatus shall be listed for the service and so constructed and installed that any flow of water from a sprinkler system equal to or greater than that from a single automatic sprinkler of the smallest orifice size installed on the system will result in an audible alarm on the premises within 5 minutes after such flow begins.

2-9.2 Waterflow Detecting Devices.

2-9.2.1 Wet Pipe Systems. The alarm apparatus for a wet pipe system shall consist of a listed alarm check valve or other listed waterflow detecting alarm device with the necessary attachments required to give an alarm.

2-9.2.2 Dry Pipe Systems. The alarm apparatus for a dry pipe system shall consist of listed alarm attachments to the dry pipe valve. When a dry pipe valve is located on the system side of an alarm valve, connection of the actuating device of the alarms for the dry pipe valve to the alarms on the wet pipe system is permitted.

2-9.2.3 Preaction and Deluge Systems. The alarm apparatus for deluge and preaction systems shall consist of alarms actuated independently by the detection system and the flow of water.

2-9.2.4* Paddle-type waterflow alarm indicators shall be installed in wet systems only.

2-9.3 Attachments — General.

2-9.3.1* An alarm unit shall include a listed mechanical alarm, horn, or siren or a listed electric gong, bell, speaker, horn, or siren.

2-9.3.2* Outdoor water motor operated or electrically operated bells shall be weatherproofed and guarded.

2-9.4 All piping to water motor operated devices shall be galvanized or brass or other corrosion-resistant material acceptable under this standard and of a size not less than ³⁄₄ in. (19 mm).

2-9.5 Attachments — Electrically Operated.

2-9.5.1* Electrically operated alarm attachments forming part of an auxiliary, central station, local protective, proprietary, or remote station signaling system shall be installed in accordance with the following applicable NFPA standards:

(a) NFPA 71, *Standard for the Installation, Maintenance, and Use of Signaling Systems for Central Station Service,*

(b) NFPA 72, *Standard for the Installation, Maintenance, and Use of Protective Signaling Systems.*

Exception: Sprinkler waterflow alarm systems that are not part of a required protective signaling system need not be supervised and shall be installed in accordance with NFPA 70, National Electrical Code,® Article 760.

2-9.5.2 Outdoor electric alarm devices shall be listed for outdoor use.

2-9.6 Drains from alarm devices shall be so arranged that there will be no overflowing at the alarm apparatus, at domestic connections, or elsewhere with the sprinkler drains wide open and under system pressure. *(See 4-5.3.6.1.)*

Chapter 3   System Requirements

3-1 Wet Pipe Systems.

3-1.1 Pressure Gauges. A listed pressure gauge conforming to 4-6.3.2 shall be installed in each system riser. Pressure gauges shall be installed above and below each alarm check valve when such devices are present.

3-1.2 Relief Valves. A gridded wet pipe system shall be provided with a relief valve not less than ¹⁄₄ in. (6.4 mm) in size set to operate at pressures not greater than 175 psi (12.1 bars).

Exception No. 1: When the maximum system pressure exceeds 165 psi (11.4 bars), the relief valve shall operate at 10 psi (0.7 bars) in excess of the maximum system pressure.

Exception No. 2: When auxiliary air reservoirs are installed to absorb pressure increases, a relief valve shall not be required.

3-1.3 Auxiliary Systems. A wet pipe system shall be permitted to supply an auxiliary dry pipe, preaction, or deluge system, provided the water supply is adequate.

3-2* Dry Pipe Systems.

3-2.1 Pressure Gauges. Listed pressure gauges conforming to 4-6.3.2 shall be connected:

(a) On the water side and air side of the dry pipe valve,

(b) At the air pump supplying the air receiver where one is provided,

(c) At the air receiver where one is provided,

(d) In each independent pipe from air supply to dry pipe system, and

(e) At exhausters and accelerators.

3-2.2 Dry-Pendent Sprinklers. Automatic sprinklers installed in the pendent position shall be of the listed dry-pendent type.

Exception: Pendent sprinklers installed on return bends are permitted when both the sprinklers and the return bends are located in a heated area.

3-2.3* Size of Systems.

3-2.3.1 Volume Limitations. Not more than 750 gal (2839 L) system capacity shall be controlled by one dry pipe valve.

Exception: Piping volume may exceed 750 gal (2839 L) for nongridded systems if the system design is such that water is delivered to the system test connection in not more than 60 seconds, starting at the normal air pressure on the system and at the time of fully opened inspection test connection.

3-2.3.2 Gridded dry pipe systems shall not be installed. *(See 4-5.3.5.3.3.)*

3-2.4 Quick-Opening Devices.

3-2.4.1 Dry pipe valves shall be provided with a listed quick-opening device when system capacity exceeds 500 gal (1893 L).

Exception: A quick-opening device shall not be required if the requirements of 3-2.3.1 Exception can be met without such a device.

3-2.4.2 The quick-opening device shall be located as close as practical to the dry pipe valve. To protect the restriction orifice and other operating parts of the quick-opening device against submergence, the connection to the riser shall be above the point at which water (priming water and back drainage) is expected when the dry pipe valve and quick-opening device are set, except where design features of the particular quick-opening device make these requirements unnecessary.

3-2.4.3 A soft disc globe or angle valve shall be installed in the connection between the dry pipe sprinkler riser and the quick-opening device.

3-2.4.4 A check valve shall be installed between the quick-opening device and the intermediate chamber of the dry pipe valve. If the quick-opening device requires pressure feedback from the intermediate chamber, a valve type that will clearly indicate whether it is opened or closed shall be permitted in place of that check valve. This valve shall be constructed so that it may be locked or sealed in the open position.

3-2.4.5 A listed antiflooding device shall be installed in the connection between the dry pipe sprinkler riser and the quick-opening device.

Exception: Where the quick-opening device has built-in anti-flooding design features.

3-2.5* Location and Protection of Dry Pipe Valve.

3-2.5.1 The dry pipe valve and supply pipe shall be protected against freezing and mechanical injury.

3-2.5.2 Valve rooms shall be lighted and heated. The source of heat shall be of a permanently installed type. Heat tape shall not be used in lieu of heated valve enclosures to protect the dry pipe valve and supply pipe against freezing.

3-2.5.3 The supply for the sprinkler in the dry pipe valve enclosure shall be from the dry side of the system.

3-2.5.4 Protection against accumulation of water above the clapper shall be provided for a low differential dry pipe valve. An automatic high water level signaling device or an automatic drain device is acceptable.

3-2.6 Air Pressure and Supply.

3-2.6.1 Maintenance of Air Pressure. Air or nitrogen pressure shall be maintained on dry pipe systems throughout the year.

3-2.6.2* Air Supply. The compressed air supply shall be from a source available at all times and having a capacity capable of restoring normal air pressure in the system within 30 minutes.

3-2.6.3 Air Filling Connection. The connection pipe from the air compressor shall not be less than $\frac{1}{2}$ in. (13 mm) in diameter and shall enter the system above the priming water level of the dry pipe valve. A check valve shall be installed in this air line, and a shutoff valve of the renewable disc type shall be installed on the supply side of this check valve and shall remain closed unless filling the system.

3-2.6.4 Relief Valve. A listed relief valve shall be provided between the compressor and controlling valve, set to relieve at a pressure 5 psi (0.3 bars) in excess of maximum air pressure carried in the system.

3-2.6.5 Shop Air Supply. When the air supply is taken from a shop system having a normal pressure greater than that required for dry pipe systems and an automatic air maintenance device is not used, the relief valve shall be installed between two control valves in the air line, and a small air cock, which is normally left open, shall be installed in the fitting below the relief valve. (*See Figure 3-2.6.5.*)

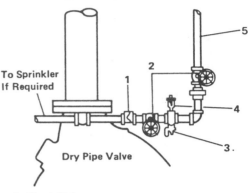

1. Check Valve
2. Control Valve (Renewable Disc Type)
3. Small Air Cock (Normally Open)
4. Relief Valve
5. Air Supply

Figure 3-2.6.5 Air supply from shop system.

3-2.6.6 Automatic Air Compressor. When a dry pipe system is supplied by an automatic air compressor or plant air system, any device or apparatus used for automatic maintenance of air pressure shall be of a type specifically listed for such service and capable of maintaining the required air pressure on the dry pipe system. Automatic air supply to more than one dry pipe system shall be connected to enable individual maintenance of air pressure in each system. A check valve or other positive backflow prevention device shall be installed in the air supply to each system to prevent air- or waterflow from one system to another.

3-2.6.7 System Air Pressure. The system air pressure shall be maintained in accordance with the instruction sheet furnished with the dry pipe valve, or 20 psi (1.4 bars) in excess of the calculated trip pressure of the dry pipe valve, based on the highest normal water pressure of the system supply. The permitted rate of air leakage shall be as specified in 8-2.3.

3-2.6.8 Nitrogen. When used, nitrogen shall be introduced through a pressure regulator set to maintain system pressure in accordance with 3-2.6.7.

3-3 Preaction Systems and Deluge Systems.

3-3.1* General.

3-3.1.1 All components of pneumatic, hydraulic, or electrical systems shall be compatible.

3-3.1.2 The automatic water control valve shall be provided with manual means for operation that is independent of detection devices and of the sprinklers.

3-3.1.3 Pressure Gauges. Listed pressure gauges conforming to 4-6.3.2 shall be installed as follows:

(a) Above and below preaction valve and below deluge valve.

(b) On air supply to preaction and deluge valves.

3-3.1.4 A supply of spare fusible elements for heat-responsive devices, not less than two of each temperature rating, shall be maintained on the premises for replacement purposes.

3-3.1.5 Hydraulic release systems shall be designed and installed in accordance with manufacturer's requirements and listing for height limitations above deluge valves or deluge valve actuators to prevent water column.

3-3.1.6 Location and Spacing of Detection Devices. Spacing of detection devices, including automatic sprinklers used as detectors, shall be in accordance with their listing and manufacturer's specifications.

3-3.1.7 Devices for Test Purposes and Testing Apparatus.

3-3.1.7.1 When detection devices installed in circuits are located where not readily accessible, an additional detection device shall be provided on each circuit for test purposes at an accessible location and shall be connected to the circuit at a point that will assure a proper test of the circuit.

3-3.1.7.2 Testing apparatus capable of producing the heat or impulse necessary to operate any normal detection device shall be furnished to the owner of the property with each installation. Where explosive vapors or materials are present, hot water, steam, or other methods of testing not involving an ignition source shall be used.

3-3.1.8 Location and Protection of System Water Control Valves.

3-3.1.8.1 System water control valves and supply pipes shall be protected against freezing and mechanical injury.

3-3.1.8.2 Valve rooms shall be lighted and heated. The source of heat shall be of a permanently installed type. Heat tape shall not be used in lieu of heated valve enclosure rooms to protect preaction and deluge valves and supply pipe against freezing.

3-3.2 Preaction Systems.

3-3.2.1 Preaction systems shall operate by one of the means described in (a) through (c) below.

(a) Systems that admit water to sprinkler piping upon operation of detection devices.

(b) Systems that admit water to sprinkler piping upon operation of detection devices or automatic sprinklers.

(c)* Systems that admit water to sprinkler piping upon operation of both detection devices and automatic sprinklers.

3-3.2.2 Size of Systems. Not more than 1000 automatic sprinklers shall be controlled by any one preaction valve.

Exception: For preaction system types described in 3-3.2.1(c), system volume shall not exceed 750 gal (2839 L) controlled by one preaction valve unless the system is designed to deliver water to the system test connection in not more than 60 seconds, starting at the normal air pressure on the system with the detection system operated and at the time of fully opened inspection test connection. Air pressure and supply shall comply with 3-2.6.

3-3.2.3 Supervision. Sprinkler piping and fire detection devices shall be automatically supervised when there are more than 20 sprinklers on the system.

3-3.2.4 Pendent Sprinklers. Automatic sprinklers on preaction systems installed in the pendent position shall be of the listed dry-pendent type.

Exception: Pendent sprinklers installed on return bends are permitted when both the sprinklers and the return bends are located in a heated area.

3-3.3* Deluge Systems.

3-3.3.1 The detection devices or systems shall be automatically supervised.

3-3.3.2 Deluge systems shall be hydraulically calculated.

3-4 Combined Dry Pipe and Preaction Systems.

3-4.1* General.

3-4.1.1* Combined automatic dry pipe and preaction systems shall be so constructed that failure of the detection system shall not prevent the system from functioning as a conventional automatic dry pipe system.

3-4.1.2 Combined automatic dry pipe and preaction systems shall be so constructed that failure of the dry pipe system of automatic sprinklers shall not prevent the detection system from properly functioning as an automatic fire alarm system.

3-4.1.3 Provisions shall be made for the manual operation of the detection system at locations requiring not more than 200 ft (61 m) of travel.

3-4.1.4 Dry-Pendent Sprinklers. Automatic sprinklers installed in the pendent position shall be of the listed dry-pendent type.

Exception: Pendent sprinklers installed on return bends are permitted when both the sprinklers and the return bends are located in a heated area.

3-4.2 Dry Pipe Valves in Combined Systems.

3-4.2.1 Where the system consists of more than 600 sprinklers or has more than 275 sprinklers in any fire area, the entire system shall be controlled through two 6-in. (152-mm) dry pipe valves connected in parallel and shall feed into a common feed main. These valves shall be checked against each other. (*See Figure 3-4.2.*)

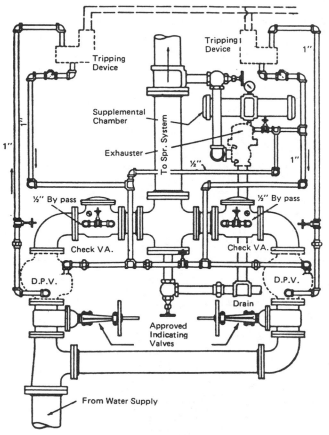

Tubing or Wiring to Fire Detection System

For SI Units: 1 in. = 25.4 mm.

Figure 3-4.2 Header for dry pipe valves installed in parallel for combined systems, standard trimmings not shown.

3-4.2.2 Each dry pipe valve shall be provided with a listed tripping device actuated by the detection system. Dry pipe valves shall be cross-connected through a 1-in. (25.4-mm) pipe connection to permit simultaneous tripping of both dry pipe valves. This 1-in. (25.4-mm) pipe connection shall be equipped with an indicating valve so that either dry pipe valve can be shut off and worked on while the other remains in service.

3-4.2.3 The check valves between the dry pipe valves and the common feed main shall be equipped with ½-in. (13-mm) bypasses so that a loss of air from leakage in the trimmings of a dry pipe valve will not cause the valve to trip until the pressure in the feed main is reduced to the

tripping point. An indicating valve shall be installed in each of these bypasses so that either dry pipe valve can be completely isolated from the main riser or feed main and from the other dry pipe valve.

3-4.2.4 Each combined dry pipe and preaction system shall be provided with listed quick-opening devices at the dry pipe valves.

3-4.3* Air Exhaust Valves. One or more listed air exhaust valves of 2-in. (51-mm) or larger size controlled by operation of a fire detection system shall be installed at the end of the common feed main. These air exhaust valves shall have soft-seated globe or angle valves in their intakes; also, approved strainers shall be installed between these globe valves and the air exhaust valves.

3-4.4 Subdivision of System Using Check Valves.

3-4.4.1 Where more than 275 sprinklers are required in a single fire area, the system shall be divided into sections of 275 sprinklers or less by means of check valves. If the system is installed in more than one fire area or story, not more than 600 sprinklers shall be supplied through any one check valve. Each section shall have a 1¼-in. (33-mm) drain on the system side of each check valve supplemented by a dry pipe system auxiliary drain.

3-4.4.2 Section drain lines and dry pipe system auxiliary drains shall be located in heated areas or inside of heated cabinets to enclose drain valves and auxiliary drains for each section.

3-4.4.3 Air exhaust valves at the end of a feed main and associated check valves shall be protected against freezing.

3-4.5 Time Limitation. The sprinkler system shall be so constructed and the number of sprinklers controlled shall be so limited that water shall reach the farthest sprinkler within a period of time not exceeding 1 minute for each 400 ft (122 m) of common feed main from the time the heat-responsive system operates. Maximum time permitted shall not exceed 3 minutes.

3-4.6 System Test Connection. The end section shall have a system test connection as required for dry pipe systems.

3-5 Antifreeze Systems.

3-5.1* Where Used. The use of antifreeze solutions shall be in conformity with state and local health regulations.

3-5.2* Antifreeze Solutions.

3-5.2.1 When sprinkler systems are supplied by potable water connections, the use of antifreeze solutions other than water solutions of pure glycerine (C.P. or U.S.P. 96.5 percent grade) or propylene glycol shall not be permitted. Suitable glycerine-water and propylene glycol-water mixtures are shown in Table 3-5.2.1.

Table 3-5.2.1   Antifreeze Solutions to Be Used if Potable Water Is Connected to Sprinklers

Material	Solution (by Volume)	Specific Gravity at 60°F (15.6°C)	Freezing Point °F	Freezing Point °C
Glycerine	50% Water	1.133	−15	−26.1
C.P. or U.S.P. Grade*	40% Water	1.151	−22	−30.0
	30% Water	1.165	−40	−40.0
Hydrometer Scale 1.000 to 1.200				
Propylene Glycol	70% Water	1.027	+ 9	−12.8
	60% Water	1.034	− 6	−21.1
	50% Water	1.041	−26	−32.2
	40% Water	1.045	−60	−51.1
Hydrometer Scale 1.000 to 1.200 (Subdivisions 0.002)				

*C.P.—Chemically Pure.   U.S.P.—United States Pharmacopoeia 96.5%.

3-5.2.2   If potable water is not connected to sprinklers, the commercially available materials indicated in Table 3-5.2.2 (*see page 25*) are permitted for use in antifreeze solutions.

3-5.2.3*   An antifreeze solution shall be prepared with a freezing point below the expected minimum temperature for the locality. The specific gravity of the prepared solution shall be checked by a hydrometer with suitable scale or refractometer having a scale calibrated for the antifreeze solution involved. [*See Figures 3-5.2.3(a) and (b)*.]

3-5.3*   Arrangement of Supply Piping and Valves.   Sprinklers shall be below the interface between the water and antifreeze solutions.

Exception: Sprinklers are permitted to be above the water/antifreeze interface when a check valve with a 1/32-in. (0.8-mm) hole in the clapper is provided in a U-loop. In most cases, this necessitates the use of a 5-ft (1.5-m) drop pipe or U-loop as illustrated in Figure 3-5.3.

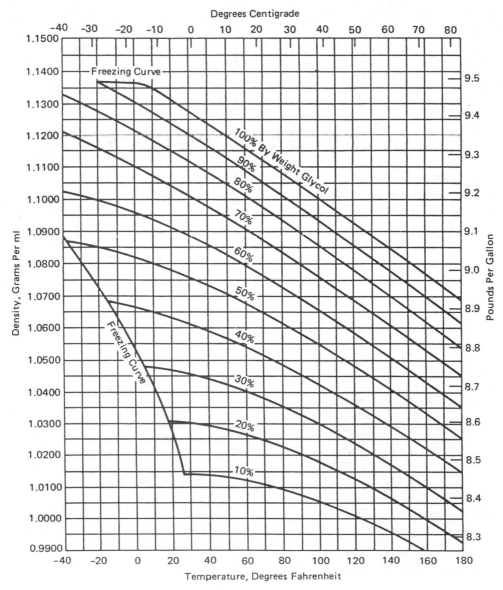

Figure 3-5.2.3(a)   Densities of aqueous ethylene glycol solutions (percent by weight).

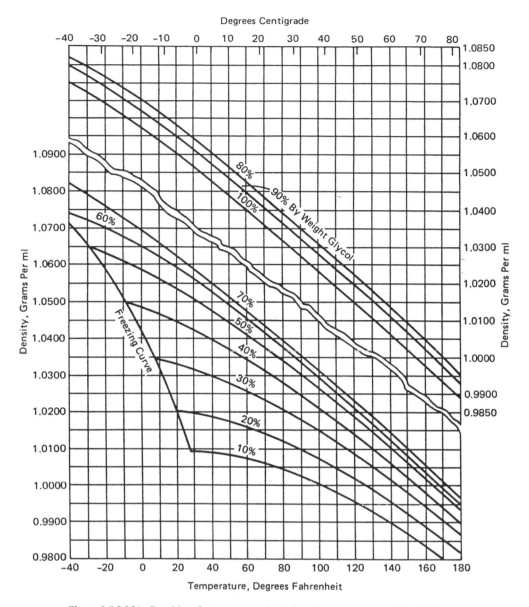

Figure 3-5.2.3(b)   Densities of aqueous propylene glycol solutions (percent by weight).

Table 3-5.2.2   Antifreeze Solution to Be Used if Nonpotable Water Is Connected to Sprinklers

Material	Solution (by Volume)	Specific Gravity at 60°F (15.6°C)	Freezing Point °F	Freezing Point °C
Glycerine	If glycerine is used, see Table 3-5.2.1			
Diethylene Glycol	50% Water	1.078	−13	−25.0
	45% Water	1.081	−27	−32.8
	40% Water	1.086	−42	−41.1
Hydrometer Scale 1.000 to 1.120 (Subdivisions 0.002)				
Ethylene Glycol	61% Water	1.056	−10	−23.3
	56% Water	1.063	−20	−28.9
	51% Water	1.069	−30	−34.4
	47% Water	1.073	−40	−40.0
Hydrometer Scale 1.000 to 1.120 (Subdivisions 0.002)				
Propylene Glycol	If propylene glycol is used, see Table 3-5.2.1			
Calcium Chloride 80% "Flake"	lb CaCl$_2$ per gal of Water			
Fire Protection Grade†	2.83	1.183	0	−17.8
Add corrosion inhibitor	3.38	1.212	−10	−23.3
of sodium bichromate	3.89	1.237	−20	−28.9
$\frac{1}{4}$ oz per gal water	4.37	1.258	−30	−34.4
	4.73	1.274	−40	−40.0
	4.93	1.283	−50	−45.6

† Free from magnesium chloride and other impurities.

3-5.3.1 A water control valve and two small solution test valves shall be provided as illustrated in Figure 3-5.3.

Exception: When the connection between the antifreeze system and the wet pipe system incorporates a backflow prevention device, an expansion chamber shall be provided to compensate for the expansion of the antifreeze solution.

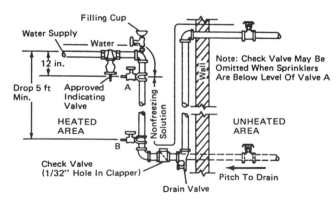

NOTE: The $\frac{1}{32}$-in. (0.8-mm) hole in the check valve clapper is needed to allow for expansion of the solution during a temperature rise and thus prevent damage to sprinklers.

For SI Units: 1 in. = 25.4 mm; 1 ft = 0.3048 m.

Figure 3-5.3   Arrangement of supply piping and valves.

3-6 Automatic Sprinkler Systems with Nonfire Protection Connections.

3-6.1 Circulating Closed-Loop Systems.

3-6.1.1 System Components.

3-6.1.1.1 A circulating closed-loop system is primarily a sprinkler system and shall comply with all provisions of this standard such as those for control valves, area limitations of a system, alarms, fire department connections, sprinkler spacing, etc.

Exception: Items as specifically detailed within 3-6.1.

3-6.1.1.2 Piping, fittings, valves, and pipe hangers shall meet requirements specified in Chapter 2.

3-6.1.1.3 A dielectric fitting shall be installed in the junction where dissimilar piping materials are joined, e.g., copper to steel.

Exception: Dielectric fittings are not required in the junction where sprinklers are connected to piping.

3-6.1.1.4 It is not required that other auxiliary devices be listed for sprinkler service; however, these devices, such as pumps, circulating pumps, heat exchangers, radiators, and luminaries, shall be pressure rated at 175 or 300 psi (12.1 or 20.7 bars) (rupture pressure of 5 times rated water working pressure) to match the required rating of sprinkler system components.

3-6.1.1.5 Auxiliary devices shall incorporate materials of construction and be so constructed that they will maintain their physical integrity under fire conditions to avoid impairment to the fire protection system.

3-6.1.1.6 Auxiliary devices, where hung from the building structure, shall be supported independently from the sprinkler portion of the system, following recognized engineering practices.

3-6.1.2* Hydraulic Characteristics. Piping systems for attached heating and cooling equipment shall have auxiliary pumps or an arrangement made to return water to the piping system in order to assure the following:

(a) Water for sprinklers shall not be required to pass through heating or cooling equipment. At least one direct path shall exist for waterflow from the sprinkler water supply to every sprinkler. Pipe sizing in the direct path shall be in accordance with design requirements of this standard.

(b) No portions of the sprinkler piping shall have less than the sprinkler system design pressure regardless of the mode of operation of the attached heating or cooling equipment.

(c) There shall be no loss or outflow of water from the system due to or resulting from the operation of heating or cooling equipment.

(d) Shutoff valves and a means of drainage shall be provided on piping to heating or cooling equipment at all points of connection to sprinkler piping and shall be installed in such a manner as to make possible repair or removal of any auxiliary component without impairing the serviceability and response to the sprinkler system. All auxiliary components, including the strainer, shall be installed on the auxiliary equipment side of the shutoff valves.

3-6.1.3 Water Temperature.

3-6.1.3.1 Maximum. In no case shall maximum water temperature flowing through the sprinkler portion of the system exceed 120°F (49°C). Protective control devices listed for this purpose shall be installed to shut down heating or cooling systems when temperature of water flowing through the sprinkler portion of the system exceeds 120°F (49°C). When water temperature exceeds 100°F (37.8°C), intermediate or higher temperature rated sprinklers shall be used.

3-6.1.3.2 Minimum. Precautions shall be taken to ensure that temperatures below 40°F (4°C) are not permitted.

3-6.1.4 Obstruction to Discharge. Automatic sprinklers shall not be obstructed by auxiliary devices, piping, insulation, etc., from detecting fire or from proper distribution of water.

3-6.1.5 Signs. Caution signs shall be attached to all valves controlling sprinklers. The caution sign shall be worded as follows:

"This valve controls fire protection equipment. Do not close until after fire has been extinguished. Use auxiliary valves when necessary to shut off supply to auxiliary equipment.

CAUTION: Automatic alarm will be sounded if this valve is closed."

3-6.1.6 Water Additives. Materials added to water shall not adversely affect the fire fighting properties of the water and shall be in conformity with any state or local health regulations. Due care and caution shall be given to the use of additives that may remove or suspend scale from older piping systems. When additives are necessary for proper system operation, due care shall be taken to ensure that additives are replenished after alarm testing or whenever water is removed from the system.

3-6.1.7 Waterflow Detection. The supply of water from sprinkler piping through auxiliary devices, circulatory piping, and pumps shall not under any condition or operation, transient or static, cause false sprinkler waterflow signals.

3-6.1.7.1 A sprinkler waterflow signal shall not be impaired when water is discharged through an opened sprinkler or through the system test connection while auxiliary equipment is in any mode of operation (on, off, transient, stable).

3-7 Outside Sprinklers for Protection against Exposure Fires.

3-7.1 Applications. Exposure protection systems shall be permitted on buildings regardless of whether the building's interior is protected by a sprinkler system.

3-7.2 Water Supply and Control.

3-7.2.1* Sprinklers installed for protection against exposure fires shall be supplied from a standard water supply as outlined in Chapter 7.

Exception: When approved, other supplies, such as manual valves or pumps or fire department connections, shall be acceptable.

3-7.2.2 When fire department connections are used for water supply, they shall be so located that they will not be affected by the exposing fire.

3-7.3 Control.

3-7.3.1 Each system of outside sprinklers shall have an independent control valve.

3-7.3.2 Manually controlled open sprinklers shall be used only where constant supervision is present.

3-7.3.3 Sprinklers may be of the open or automatic type. Automatic sprinklers in areas subject to freezing shall be on dry pipe systems conforming to Section 3-2 or antifreeze systems conforming to Section 3-5.

3-7.3.4 Automatic systems of open sprinklers shall be controlled by the operation of fire detection devices designed for the specific application.

3-7.4 System Components.

3-7.4.1 Drain Valves. Each system of outside sprinklers shall have a separate drain valve installed on the system side of each control valve.

Exception: Open sprinkler-top fed systems arranged to facilitate drainage.

3-7.4.2 Check Valves. When sprinklers are installed on two adjacent sides of a building, protecting against two separate and distinct exposures, with separate control valves for each side, the end lines shall be connected with check valves located so that one sprinkler around the corner will operate. The intermediate pipe between the two check valves shall be arranged to drain. As an alternate solution, an additional sprinkler shall be installed on each system located around the corner from the system involved.

3-7.4.3 System Arrangement. When one exposure affects two sides of the protected structure, the system shall not be subdivided between the two sides, but rather shall be arranged to operate as a single system.

3-7.5 Pipe and Fittings. Pipe and fittings installed on the exterior of the building shall be corrosion resistant.

3-7.6 Strainers. A listed strainer shall be provided in the riser or feed main that supplies sprinklers having orifices smaller than 3/8 in. (9.5 mm).

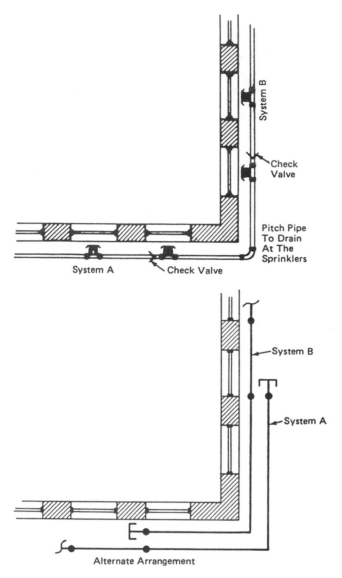

Figure 3-7.4.2 Arrangement of check valves.

3-7.7 Gauge Connections. A listed pressure gauge conforming to 4-6.3.2 shall be installed immediately below the control valve of each system.

3-7.8 Sprinklers. Only sprinklers of such type as are listed for window, cornice, sidewall, or ridge pole service shall be installed for such use except where adequate coverage by use of other types of listed sprinklers and/or nozzles has been demonstrated. Small orifice or large orifice sprinklers shall be permitted.

3-8* Cold Storage Rooms.

3-8.1* Fittings for visual internal inspection of piping in cold storage rooms shall be provided whenever the following occurs:

(a)* A cross main connects to a riser or feed main,

(b)* Feed mains change direction,

(c)* A riser or feed main passes through a wall or floor from a warm room to a cold room.

3-8.2 A local low air-pressure alarm shall be installed on sprinkler systems supplying freezer sections.

3-8.3 Piping in cold storage rooms shall be installed with pitch, as outlined in 4-5.3.3.

3-8.4* The air supply for systems shall be taken from the room of lowest temperature, or through a chemical dehydrator, to eliminate introducing moisture. Compressed nitrogen gas from cylinders shall be acceptable in lieu of air.

3-9 Commercial-Type Cooking Equipment and Ventilation.

3-9.1 In cooking areas protected by automatic sprinklers, additional sprinklers or automatic spray nozzles shall be provided to protect commercial-type cooking equipment and ventilation systems that are designed to carry away grease-laden vapors unless otherwise protected. (See NFPA 96, Standard for the Installation of Equipment for the Removal of Smoke and Grease-Laden Vapors from Commercial Cooking Equipment.)

3-9.2* Standard sprinklers or automatic spray nozzles shall be so located as to provide for the protection of exhaust ducts, hood exhaust duct collars, and hood exhaust plenum chambers.

Exception: Sprinklers or automatic spray nozzles in ducts, duct collars, and plenum chambers may be omitted when all cooking equipment is served by listed grease extractors.

3-9.3 Exhaust ducts shall have one sprinkler or automatic spray nozzle located at the top of each vertical riser and at the midpoint of each offset. The first sprinkler or automatic spray nozzle in a horizontal duct shall be installed at the duct entrance. Horizontal exhaust ducts shall have such devices located on 10-ft (3-m) centers beginning no more than 5 ft (1.5 m) from the duct entrance. Sprinkler(s) or automatic spray nozzle(s) in exhaust ducts subject to freezing shall be properly protected against freezing by approved means. (See 4-5.4.1.)

Exception: Sprinklers or automatic spray nozzles may be omitted from a vertical riser located outside of a building provided the riser does not expose combustible material or provided the interior of a building and the horizontal distance between the hood outlet and the vertical riser is at least 25 ft (7.6 m).

3-9.4 Each hood exhaust duct collar shall have one sprinkler or automatic spray nozzle located 1 in. minimum to 12 in. maximum (25.4 mm min. to 305 mm max.) above the point of duct collar connection in the hood plenum. Hoods that have listed fire dampers located in the duct collar shall be protected with a sprinkler or automatic spray nozzle located on the discharge side of the damper and be so positioned as not to interfere with damper operation.

3-9.5 Hood exhaust plenum chambers shall have one sprinkler or automatic spray nozzle centered in each chamber not exceeding 10 ft (3 m) in length. Plenum chambers greater than 10 ft (3 m) in length shall have two sprinklers or automatic spray nozzles evenly spaced with the maximum distance between the two sprinklers not to exceed 10 ft (3 m).

3-9.6 Sprinklers or automatic spray nozzles being used in duct, duct collar, and plenum areas shall be of the extra high temperature classification [325 to 375°F (163 to 191°C)] and have orifice sizes not less than $1/4$ in. (6.4 mm) and not more than $1/2$ in. (13 mm).

Exception: When use of a temperature measuring device indicates temperatures above 300°F (149°C), a sprinkler or automatic spray nozzle of higher classification shall be used.

3-9.7 Access must be provided to all sprinklers or automatic spray nozzles for examination and replacement.

3-9.8 Cooking Equipment.

3-9.8.1 Cooking equipment (such as deep fat fryers, ranges, griddles, and broilers) that may be a source of ignition shall be protected in accordance with the provisions of 3-9.1.

3-9.8.2 A sprinkler or automatic spray nozzle used for protection of deep fat fryers shall be listed for that application. The position, arrangement, location, and water supply for each sprinkler or automatic spray nozzle shall be in accordance with its listing.

3-9.8.3 The operation of any cooking equipment sprinkler or automatic spray nozzle shall automatically shut off all sources of fuel and heat to all equipment requiring protection. Any gas appliance not requiring protection but located under ventilating equipment shall also be shut off. All shutdown devices shall be of the type that requires manual resetting prior to fuel or power being restored.

3-9.9 A listed indicating valve shall be installed in the water supply line to the sprinklers and spray nozzles protecting the cooking and ventilating system.

3-9.10 An approved line strainer shall be installed in the main water supply preceding sprinklers or automatic spray nozzles having orifices smaller than $3/8$ in. (9.5 mm).

3-9.11 A system test connection shall be provided to verify proper operation of equipment specified in 3-9.8.3.

3-9.12 Sprinklers and automatic spray nozzles used for protecting commercial-type cooking equipment and ventilating systems shall be replaced annually.

Exception: When automatic bulb-type sprinklers or spray nozzles are used and annual examination shows no build-up of grease or other material on the sprinklers or spray nozzles.

Chapter 4   Installation Requirements

4-1* Basic Requirements.

4-1.1* The requirements for spacing, location, and position of sprinklers are based on the following principles:

(a) Sprinklers installed throughout the premises,

(b) Sprinklers located so as not to exceed maximum protection area per sprinkler,

(c) Sprinklers positioned and located so as to provide satisfactory performance with respect to activation time and distribution.

Exception No. 1: For locations permitting omission of sprinklers see 4-4.1.7.1, 4-4.1.7.2, 4-4.1.7.7.

Exception No. 2: When sprinklers are specifically tested and test results demonstrate that deviations from clearance requirements to structural members do not impair the ability of the sprinkler to control or suppress a fire, their positioning and locating in accordance with the test results shall be permitted.

Exception No. 3: Clearance between sprinklers and ceilings exceeding the maximum specified in 4-4.1.4 shall be permitted provided that tests or calculations demonstrate comparable sensitivity and performance of the sprinklers to those installed in conformance with 4-4.1.4.

4-2 Protection Area Limitations.

4-2.1 Systems. The maximum floor area on any one floor to be protected by sprinklers supplied by any one sprinkler system riser or combined system riser shall be as follows:

Light Hazard	52,000 sq ft (4831 m²)
Ordinary Hazard	52,000 sq ft (4831 m²)
Extra Hazard	
Pipe Schedule	25,000 sq ft (2323 m²)
Hydraulically Calculated	40,000 sq ft (3716 m²)
Storage — High-piled storage	40,000 sq ft (3716 m²)
(as defined in 1-4.2) and storage covered by other NFPA standards	

Exception No. 1: The floor area occupied by mezzanines shall not be included in the above area.

Exception No. 2: When single systems protect extra hazard, high-piled storage, or storage covered by other NFPA standards and ordinary or light hazard areas, the extra hazard or storage area coverage shall not exceed the floor area specified for that hazard and the total area coverage shall not exceed 52,000 sq ft (4831 m²).

4-2.2* Sprinklers. The maximum protection area per sprinkler shall comply with Table 4-2.2.

4-2.2.1 The protection area per sprinkler shall be determined as follows:

4-2.2.1.1 Along Branch Lines. Determine distance to next sprinkler (or to wall or obstruction in case of end sprinkler on branch line) upstream and downstream. Choose the larger of either twice the distance to the wall or the distance to the next sprinkler. Call this *S*.

Table 4-2.2   Maximum Sprinkler Protection Areas (sq ft)[8]

	Light Hazard	Ordinary Hazard	Extra Hazard[5]	High-Piled Storage[6]	Large-Drop Sprinklers[7]	Early Suppression Fast Response Sprinklers[7]
Unobstructed Construction[1] Noncombustible	225[2]	130	100	100	130	100
Obstructed Construction Combustible	225[2]	130	100	100	130	100
Obstructed Construction	168[3,4]	130	100	100	100	N/A

Note 1: Wood truss construction as defined in A-1-4.6(b)(v) is classified as obstructed construction for the purpose of determining sprinkler protection areas.
Note 2: For Light Hazard Occupancies, the protection area per sprinkler for pipe schedule systems shall not exceed 200 sq ft per sprinkler.
Note 3: For light combustible framing members spaced less than 3 ft on center, maximum spacing is 130 sq ft [for examples, see A-1-4.6(a)(ii), A-1-4.6(a)(v), and A-1-4.6(b)(v)].
Note 4: For heavy combustible framing members spaced 3 ft or more on center, maximum spacing is 225 sq ft [for examples, see A-1-4.6(a)(i)].
Note 5: For Extra Hazard Occupancies:
  1) The protection area per sprinkler for pipe schedule systems shall not exceed 90 sq ft.
  2) The protection area per sprinkler for hydraulically designed systems with densities below 0.25 gpm/ft^2 may exceed 100 sq ft, but shall not exceed 130 sq ft.
Note 6: For high-piled storage occupancies:
  1) The protection area per sprinkler may exceed 100 sq ft but shall not exceed 130 sq ft for systems hydraulically designed in accordance with NFPA 231 and 231C for densities below 0.25 gpm/sq ft.
  2) Where protection areas are specifically indicated in the design criteria of other portions of this standard or other NFPA standards, those protection areas shall be used.
  3) For protection involving large-drop sprinklers use the large-drop sprinkler column in the table.
Note 7: For large-drop and ESFR sprinklers, the minimum spacing is 80 sq ft per sprinkler.
Note 8: For special sprinkler protection areas see 4-3.2.
N/A Denotes data not available in current standard.
For SI Units: 1 sq ft = 0.0929 m^2; 1 ft = 0.3048 m; 1 gpm/ft^2 = 40.746 L/min/m^2.

4-2.2.1.2 Between Branch Lines. Determine perpendicular distance to sprinkler on branch lines (or to wall or obstruction in the case of the last branch line) on each side of the branch line on which the subject sprinkler is positioned. Choose the larger of either twice the distance to the wall or obstruction or the distance to the next sprinkler. Call this L.

4-2.2.1.3 Protection area of the sprinkler = $S \times L$.

Exception: In a small room as defined in 1-4.2, the protection area of each sprinkler in the small room shall be the area of the room divided by the number of sprinklers in the room.

4-3 Use of Sprinklers.

4-3.1 General.

4-3.1.1* Sprinklers shall be installed in accordance with their listing.

Exception: When construction features or other special situations require unusual water distribution, listed sprinklers shall be permitted to be installed in positions other than anticipated by their listing to achieve specific results.

4-3.1.2* Upright sprinklers shall be installed with the frame arms parallel to the branch line.

4-3.1.3 Temperature Ratings.

4-3.1.3.1 Ordinary-temperature rated sprinklers shall be used throughout buildings.

Exception No. 1: Where maximum ceiling temperatures exceed 100°F (38°C), sprinklers with temperature ratings in accordance with the maximum ceiling temperatures of Table 2-2.3.1 shall be used.

Exception No. 2: Intermediate- and high-temperature sprinklers shall be permitted to be used throughout Ordinary and Extra Hazard Occupancies.

Exception No. 3: Sprinklers of intermediate and high temperature classifications shall be installed in specific locations as required by 4-3.1.3.2.

4-3.1.3.2 The following practices shall be observed to provide sprinklers of other than ordinary temperature classification unless other temperatures are determined or unless high-temperature sprinklers are used throughout [see Tables 4-3.1.3.2(a) and (b) and Figure 4-3.1.3.2 on the following pages].

(a) Sprinklers in the heater zone shall be of the high temperature classification, and sprinklers in the danger zone of the intermediate temperature classification.

(b) Sprinklers located within 12 in. (305 mm) to one side or 30 in. (762 mm) above an uncovered steam main, heating coil, or radiator shall be of the intermediate temperature classification.

(c) Sprinklers within 7 ft (2.1 m) of a low-pressure blow-off valve that discharges free in a large room shall be of the high temperature classification.

(d) Sprinklers under glass or plastic skylights exposed to the direct rays of the sun shall be of the intermediate temperature classification.

(e) Sprinklers in an unventilated, concealed space, under an uninsulated roof, or in an unventilated attic shall be of the intermediate temperature classification.

(f) Sprinklers in unventilated show windows having high powered electric lights near the ceiling shall be of the intermediate temperature classification.

(g) Sprinklers protecting commercial-type cooking equipment and ventilation systems shall be of the high or

Table 4-3.1.3.2(a)   Temperature Ratings of Sprinklers Based on Distance from Heat Sources

Type of Heat Condition	Ordinary Degree Rating	Intermediate Degree Rating	High Degree Rating
1. Heating Ducts (a) Above	More than 2 ft 6 in.	2 ft 6 in. or less	—
(b) Side and Below	More than 1 ft 0 in.	1 ft 0 in. or less	—
(c) Diffuser Downward Discharge Horizontal Discharge	Any distance except as shown under Intermediate	*Downward:* Cylinder with 1 ft 0 in. radius from edge, extending 1 ft 0 in. below and 2 ft 6 in. above *Horizontal:* Semi-cylinder with 2 ft 6 in. radius in direction of flow, extending 1 ft 0 in. below and 2 ft 6 in. above	—
2. Unit Heater (a) Horizontal Discharge	—	*Discharge Side:* 7 ft 0 in. to 20 ft 0 in. radius pie-shaped cylinder [see Figure 4-3.1.3.2] extending 7 ft 0 in. above and 2 ft 0 in. below heater; also 7 ft 0 in. radius cylinder more than 7 ft 0 in. above unit heater	7 ft 0 in. radius cylinder extending 7 ft 0 in. above and 2 ft 0 in. below unit heater
(b) Vertical Downward Discharge [Note: For sprinklers below unit heater, see Figure 4-3.1.3.2.]	—	7 ft 0 in. radius cylinder extending upward from an elevation 7 ft 0 in. above unit heater	7 ft 0 in. radius cylinder extending from the top of the unit heater to an elevation 7 ft 0 in. above unit heater
3. Steam Mains (Uncovered) (a) Above	More than 2 ft 6 in.	2 ft 6 in. or less	—
(b) Side and Below	More than 1 ft 0 in.	1 ft 0 in. or less	—
(c) Blowoff Valve	More than 7 ft 0 in.	—	7 ft 0 in. or less

For SI Units: 1 in. = 25.4 mm; 1 ft = 0.3048 m.

Table 4-3.1.3.2(b)   Ratings of Sprinklers in Specified Locations

Location	Ordinary Degree Rating	Intermediate Degree Rating	High Degree Rating
Skylights	—	Glass or plastic	—
Attics	Ventilated	Unventilated	—
Peaked Roof: Metal or thin boards; concealed or not concealed; insulated or uninsulated	Ventilated	Unventilated	—
Flat Roof: Metal, not concealed; insulated or uninsulated	Ventilated or unventilated	Note: For uninsulated roof, climate and occupancy may necessitate Intermediate sprinklers. Check on job.	—
Flat Roof: Metal; concealed; insulated or uninsulated	Ventilated	Unventilated	—
Show Windows	Ventilated	Unventilated	—

Note: A check of job condition by means of thermometers may be necessary.

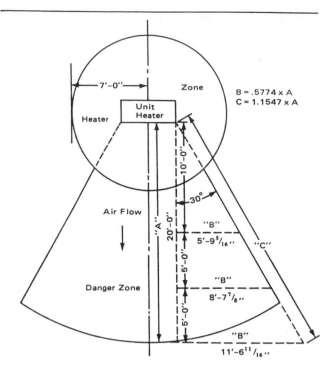

For SI Units: 1 in. = 25.4 mm; 1 ft = 0.3048 m.

Figure 4-3.1.3.2   Heater and danger zones at unit heaters.

extra high temperature classification as determined by use of a temperature measuring device. (*See 3-9.6.*)

4-3.1.3.3 In case of occupancy change involving temperature change the sprinklers shall be changed accordingly.

4-3.2 Special Sprinklers. Installation of special sprinklers with protection areas, locations, and distances between sprinklers differing from those specified in Table 4-2.2 and Section 4-4 shall be permitted when found suitable for such use based on: fire tests related to the hazard category; tests to evaluate distribution, wetting of floors and walls, and interference to distribution by structural elements; and tests to characterize response sensitivity.

Exception No. 1:   The maximum protection area for special sprinklers shall not exceed 400 sq ft (36 m²) per sprinkler.

Exception No. 2:   Maximum area of coverage for individual extended coverage pendent and upright sprinklers shall be limited to areas having equal-sided dimensions.

4-3.3 Old-Style Sprinklers. Old-style sprinklers shall not be used in a new installation.

Exception No. 1:   Old-style sprinklers shall be installed in fur storage vaults. See 4-4.1.7.15.

Exception No. 2:   Use of old-style sprinklers shall be permitted when construction features or other special situations require unique water distribution.

4-3.4 Sidewall Spray Sprinklers. Sidewall sprinklers shall be installed only in Light Hazard Occupancies.

Exception:· Sidewall sprinklers shall be permitted to be used in Ordinary Hazard Occupancies when specifically listed for such use.

4-3.5 Open Sprinklers. Open sprinklers shall be permitted to protect special hazards, for protection against exposures, or in other special locations.

4-3.6 Residential Sprinklers.

4-3.6.1* Residential sprinklers shall be permitted in dwelling units and their adjoining corridors located in any occupancy provided they are installed in conformance with their listing and the positioning requirements of NFPA 13D, *Standard for the Installation of Sprinkler Systems in One- and Two-Family Dwellings and Mobile Homes*, or NFPA 13R, *Standard for the Installation of Sprinkler Systems in Residential Occupancies up to and Including Four Stories in Height.*

4-3.6.2 Residential sprinklers shall be used only in wet systems.

Exception: Residential sprinklers shall be permitted for use in dry systems if specifically listed for such service.

4-3.6.3 When residential sprinklers are installed within a compartment as defined in 1-4.2, all sprinklers shall be from the same manufacturer and have the same heat-response thermal characteristic.

4-3.7 Early Suppression Fast Response (ESFR) Sprinklers.

4-3.7.1 ESFR sprinklers shall be used only in wet pipe systems.

4-3.7.2 ESFR sprinklers shall be installed only in buildings with roof or ceiling slope not exceeding 1 in. per ft (84 mm/m).

4-3.7.3 ESFR sprinklers shall be permitted for use in buildings with the following types of construction:

(a) Smooth ceiling, joists consisting of steel truss shaped member, wood truss shaped members that consist of wood top and bottom chord members not exceeding 4 in. (102 mm) in depth with steel tube or bar web.

(b) Wood beams of 4 in. by 4 in. (102 mm by 102 mm) or greater nominal dimension, concrete or steel beams spaced 3½ to 7½ ft (0.9 to 2.3 m) on centers and either supported on or framed into girders. Ceiling panels formed by members capable of trapping heat to aid the operation of sprinklers with members spaced greater than 7½ ft (2.3 m) and limited to a maximum of 300 sq ft (27.9 m²) in area.

(c) Paragraphs (a) and (b) apply to construction with noncombustible or combustible roof or decks.

(d) Construction with ceiling panels formed by members capable of trapping heat to aid the operation of sprinklers with members spaced greater than 7½ ft (2.3 m) and limited to a maximum of 300 sq ft (27.9 m²) in area.

4-3.7.4 Temperature Rating. Sprinkler temperature ratings shall be nominal 165°F (74°C).

Exception: Sprinklers of intermediate and high temperature ratings shall be installed in specific locations as required by 4-3.1.3.

4-3.8 Large-Drop Sprinklers.

4-3.8.1 Large-drop sprinklers shall be permitted to be used in wet, dry, or preaction systems.

4-3.8.2* In preaction and dry pipe systems, piping materials shall be limited to internally galvanized steel or copper.

Exception: Nongalvanized fittings shall be permitted.

4-3.8.3 Sprinkler temperature ratings shall be the same as those indicated in Tables 4-3.1.3.2(a) and (b) or those used in large scale fire testing to determine the protection requirements for the hazard involved.

Exception: Sprinklers of intermediate and high temperature ratings shall be installed in specific locations as required by 4-3.1.3.

4-3.9 Quick Response Early Suppression (QRES) Sprinklers. (Reserved)

4-4 Sprinkler Spacing and Location.

4-4.1 Upright and Pendent Spray Sprinkler.

4-4.1.1 Sprinkler Spacing Limitations. The maximum distance between sprinklers, either on branch lines or between branch lines, shall be as follows:

Light Hazard Occupancies	15 ft
Ordinary Hazard Occupancies	15 ft
Extra Hazard Occupancies	12 ft
High-Piled Storage	12 ft

When sprinklers are spaced less than 6 ft (1.8 m) on center see 4-4.1.7.8.

Exception No. 1: For Extra Hazard Occupancies and high-piled storage in bays 25 ft (7.6 m) wide, a spacing of 12 ft 6 in. (3.8 m) shall be permitted.

Exception No. 2: For densities less than 0.25 gpm per sq ft [10.2 (L/min)/m²)] spacing of 15 ft (4.6 m) shall be permitted.

4-4.1.2 Distance from Walls.

4-4.1.2.1 The distance from sprinklers to walls shall not exceed one-half of the allowable distance between sprinklers.

Exception*: Within small rooms, sprinklers shall be permitted to be located not more than 9 ft (2.7 m) from any single wall. Sprinkler spacing limitations of 4-4.1.1 and area limitations of Table 4-2.2 shall not be exceeded.

4-4.1.2.2 Sprinklers shall be located a minimum of 4 in. (102 mm) from a wall.

4-4.1.3 Obstructions to Sprinkler Discharge

4-4.1.3.1* Obstructions Located at the Ceiling. Noncontinuous obstructions at the ceiling or roof such as columns, bar joists, truss webs, and light fixtures shall be treated as vertical obstructions.

Exception: Obstructions that can meet the separation requirements for horizontal obstructions in 4-4.1.3.1.2.

4-4.1.3.1.1 Vertical Obstructions. The minimum separation between vertical obstructions and a sprinkler shall be as shown in Table 4-4.1.3.1.1 and Figures 4-4.1.3.1.1(a), (b), (c), and (d).

Exception: Sprinklers shall be permitted to be spaced on opposite sides of the obstruction providing the distance from the centerline of the obstruction to the sprinklers does not exceed one-half the allowable distance between sprinklers.

Table 4-4.1.3.1.1   Minimum Distance from Vertical Obstructions

Maximum Dimension of Obstruction	Minimum Horizontal Distance
½ – 1 in.	6 in.
>1 in. – 4 in.	12 in.
>4 in.	24 in.

For SI Units: 1 in. = 25.4 mm.

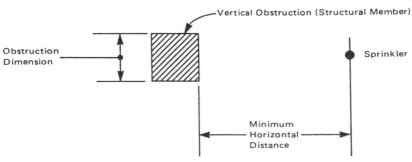

Figure 4-4.1.3.1.1(a).

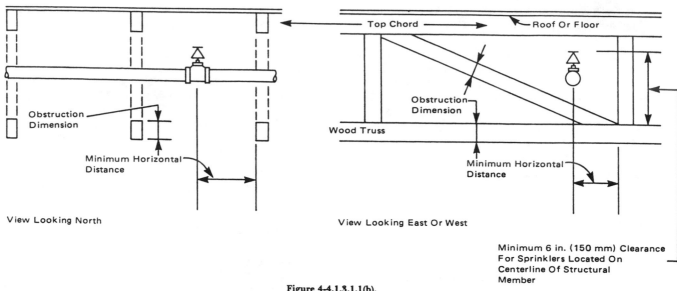

Figure 4-4.1.3.1.1(b).

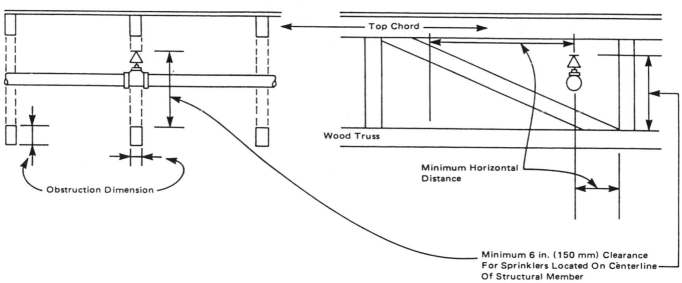

Figure 4-4.1.3.1.1(c).

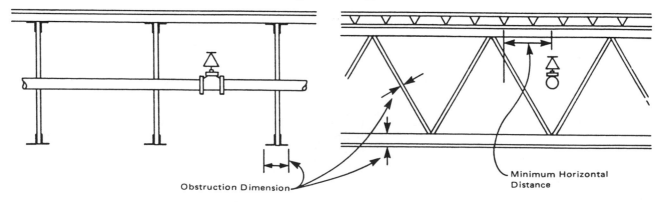

Figure 4-4.1.3.1.1(d).

4-4.1.3.1.2 Horizontal Obstructions. The minimum separation of a sprinkler from a horizontal obstruction shall be determined by the height of the deflector above the bottom of the obstruction as shown in Table 4-4.1.3.1.2 and Figure 4-4.1.3.1.2.

Exception: Sprinklers shall be permitted to be spaced on opposite sides of the obstruction providing the distance from the centerline of the obstruction to the sprinklers does not exceed one-half the allowable distance between sprinklers.

Table 4-4.1.3.1.2 Position of Deflector when Located above Bottom of Obstruction

Distance from Sprinkler to Side of Obstruction	Maximum Allowable Distance Deflector above Bottom of Obstruction
Less than 1 ft	0 in.
1 ft to less than 2 ft	1 in.
2 ft to less than 2 ft 6 in.	2 in.
2 ft 6 in. to less than 3 ft	3 in.
3 ft to less than 3 ft 6 in.	4 in.
3 ft 6 in. to less than 4 ft	6 in.
4 ft to less than 4 ft 6 in.	7 in.
4 ft 6 in. to less than 5 ft	9 in.
5 ft to less than 5 ft 6 in.	11 in.
5 ft 6 in. to less than 6 ft	14 in.

For SI Units: 1 in. = 25.4 mm; 1 ft = 0.3048 m.

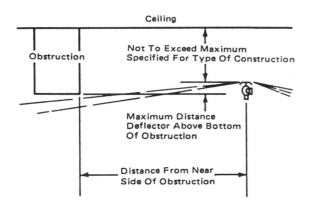

Figure 4-4.1.3.1.2 Position of deflector, upright, or pendent sprinkler when located above bottom of obstructions.

4-4.1.3.2 Obstructions Located below Sprinklers

4-4.1.3.2.1* Sprinklers shall be installed under ducts, decks, and other obstructions over 4 ft (1.2 m) wide.

Exception: Ceiling sprinklers shall be permitted to be spaced in accordance with Table 4-4.1.3.1.2.

4-4.1.3.2.2 Sprinklers installed under open gratings shall be of the intermediate level/rack storage type or otherwise shielded from the discharge of overhead sprinklers.

4-4.1.3.2.3 Sprinklers shall be permitted to be installed on the centerline of a truss or directly above a beam provided the truss chord or beam dimension is not more than 8 in. (203 mm) and the sprinkler deflector is located at least 6 in. (152 mm) above the structural member.

4-4.1.3.3* Suspended or Floor Mounted Vertical Obstructions. The distance from sprinklers to privacy curtains, free-standing partitions, room dividers, and similar obstructions in Light Hazard Occupancies shall be as shown in Table 4-4.1.3.3 and Figure 4-4.1.3.3.

Table 4-4.1.3.3 Horizontal and Minimum Vertical Distances for Sprinklers

Horizontal Distance	Minimum Vertical Distance below Deflector
6 in. or less	3 in.
More than 6 in. to 9 in.	4 in.
More than 9 in. to 12 in.	6 in.
More than 12 in. to 15 in.	8 in.
More than 15 in. to 18 in.	9½ in.
More than 18 in. to 24 in.	12½ in.
More than 24 in. to 30 in.	15½ in.
More than 30 in.	18 in.

For SI Units: 1 in. = 25.4 mm.

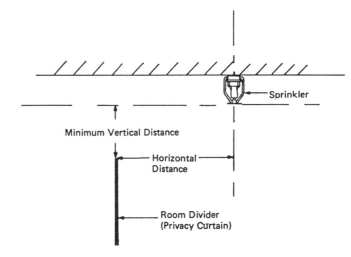

Figure 4-4.1.3.3 Sprinklers installed near privacy curtains, free-standing partitions, or room dividers.

4-4.1.3.4 Double Joist Obstructions. Where there are two sets of joists under a roof or ceiling, and there is no flooring over the lower set, sprinklers shall be installed above and below the lower set of joists where there is a clearance of 6 in. (152 mm) or more between the top of the lower joist and the bottom of the upper joist. (*See Figure 4-4.1.3.4.*)

Exception: Sprinklers are permitted to be omitted from below the lower set of joists where at least 18 in. (457 mm) is maintained between the sprinkler deflector and the top of the lower joist.

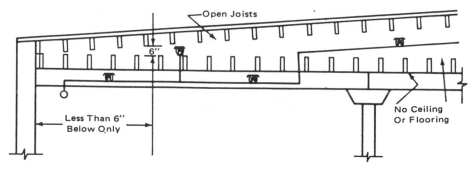

For SI Units: 1 in. = 25.4 mm.

Figure 4-4.1.3.4   Arrangement of sprinklers under two sets of open joists — no sheathing on lower joists.

4-4.1.4 Distance below Ceilings.

4-4.1.4.1   Under unobstructed construction, the distance between the sprinkler deflector and the ceiling shall be a minimum of 1 in. (25.4 mm) and a maximum of 12 in (305 mm).

Exception: Special ceiling-type sprinklers (concealed, recessed, and flush types) shall be permitted to have the operating element above the ceiling and the deflector located nearer to the ceiling when installed in accordance with their listing.

4-4.1.4.2   Under obstructed construction, the sprinkler deflector shall be located 1 to 6 in. (25.4 to 152 mm) below the structural members and a maximum distance of 22 in. (559 mm) below the ceiling/roof deck.

Exception No. 1:   Sprinklers shall be permitted to be installed with the deflector at or above the bottom of the structural member to a maximum of 22 in. (559 mm) below the ceiling/roof deck when the sprinkler is installed in conformance with 4-4.1.3.1.2.

Exception No. 2:   Where sprinklers are installed in each bay of obstructed construction, deflectors shall be a minimum of 1 in. (25.4 mm) and a maximum of 12 in. (152 mm) below the ceiling.

4-4.1.4.3   Deflectors of sprinklers under concrete tee construction with stems spaced less than 7½ ft (2.3 m) but more than 3 ft (0.9 m) on centers shall, regardless of the depth of the tee, be located at or above the plane 1 in. (25.4 mm) below the bottom of the stems of the tees and shall comply with Table 4-4.1.3.1.2.

4-4.1.5* Position of Deflectors.   Deflectors of sprinklers shall be parallel to ceilings, roofs, or the incline of stairs.

Exception No. 1:   When sprinklers are installed in the peak of a pitched roof, the sprinkler shall be installed with the deflector horizontal.

Exception No. 2:   Pitched roofs having slopes less than 1 in. per ft (83 mm/m) are considered level in the application of this rule, and sprinklers shall be permitted to be installed with deflectors horizontal.

4-4.1.6* Clear Space below Sprinklers.   A minimum of 18 in. (457 mm) clearance shall be maintained between top of storage and ceiling sprinkler deflectors.

Exception: Where other standards specify greater minimums, they shall be followed.

4-4.1.7 Special Situations.

4-4.1.7.1 Concealed Spaces.

4-4.1.7.1.1*   All concealed spaces enclosed wholly or partly by exposed combustible construction shall be protected by sprinklers.

Exception No. 1:   Concealed spaces formed by studs or joists with less than 6 in. (152 mm) between the inside or near edges of the studs or joists. (See Figure 4-4.1.3.4.)

Exception No. 2:   Concealed spaces formed by bar joists with less than 6 in. (152 mm) between the roof or floor deck and ceiling.

Exception No. 3:   Concealed spaces formed by ceilings attached directly to or within 6 in. (152 mm) of wood joist construction.

Exception No. 4:   Concealed spaces formed by ceilings attached directly to the underside of composite wood joist construction, provided the joist channels are fire-stopped into volumes each not exceeding 160 cu ft (4.53 m³) using materials equivalent to the web construction.

Exception No. 5:   Concealed spaces entirely filled with noncombustible insulation.

Exception No. 6:   Concealed spaces within wood joist construction and composite wood joist construction having noncombustible insulation filling the space from the ceiling up to the bottom edge of the joist of the roof or floor deck, provided that in composite wood joist construction the joist channels are fire-stopped into volumes each not exceeding 160 cu ft (4.53 m³). The joists shall be fire-stopped to the full depth of the joist with material equivalent to the web construction.

Exception No. 7:   Concealed spaces over isolated small rooms not exceeding 55 sq ft (4.6 m²) in area.

Exception No. 8: When the exposed surfaces have a flame spread rating of 25 or less and the materials have been demonstrated not to propagate fire in the form in which they are installed in the space.

Exception No. 9: Noncombustible concealed spaces having exposed combustible insulation when the heat content of the facing and substrate of the insulation material does not exceed 1000 Btu per sq ft (11 356 kJ/m^2).

4-4.1.7.1.2 Sprinklers in concealed spaces having no access for storage or other use shall be installed in accordance with requirements of Light Hazard Occupancy.

4-4.1.7.1.3 When heat-producing devices such as furnaces or process equipment are located in the joist channels above a ceiling attached directly to the underside of composite wood joist construction that would not otherwise require sprinkler protection of the spaces, the joist channel containing the heat-producing devices shall be sprinklered by installing sprinklers in each joist channel, on each side, adjacent to the heat-producing device.

4-4.1.7.2 Vertical Shafts.

4-4.1.7.2.1 One sprinkler shall be installed at the top of shafts.

Exception No. 1: Noncombustible, nonaccessible vertical duct shafts.

Exception No. 2: Noncombustible, nonaccessible vertical electrical shafts.

Exception No. 3: Noncombustible, nonaccessible vertical pipe shafts.

4-4.1.7.2.2* Where vertical shafts have combustible surfaces, one sprinkler shall be installed at each alternate floor level. Where a shaft having combustible surfaces is trapped, an additional sprinkler shall be installed at the top of each trapped section.

4-4.1.7.2.3 Where accessible vertical shafts have noncombustible surfaces, one sprinkler shall be installed near the bottom.

4-4.1.7.2.4 Where vertical openings are not protected by fire rated enclosures, sprinklers shall be placed so as to fully protect the openings.

4-4.1.7.3 Stairways.

4-4.1.7.3.1 Sprinklers shall be installed beneath all stairways of combustible construction.

4-4.1.7.3.2 In noncombustible stair shafts with noncombustible stairs, sprinklers shall be installed at the top of the shaft and under the first landing above the bottom of the shaft.

Exception: Sprinklers shall be installed beneath landings or stairways when the area beneath is used for storage.

4-4.1.7.3.3* Sprinklers shall be installed in the stair shaft at each floor landing serving two or more separate fire divisions located at the same level as the landing.

4-4.1.7.3.4* Where moving stairways, staircases, or similar floor openings are unenclosed, the floor openings involved shall be protected by closely spaced sprinklers in combination with draft stops.

The draft stops shall be located immediately adjacent to the opening, shall be at least 18 in. (457 mm) deep, and shall be of noncombustible or limited-combustible material that will stay in place before and during sprinkler operation. Sprinklers shall be spaced not more than 6 ft (1.8 m) apart and placed 6 to 12 in. (152 to 305 mm) from the draft stop on the side away from the opening. When sprinklers are closer than 6 ft (1.8 m), cross baffles shall be provided in accordance with 4-4.1.7.8.

Exception: Closely spaced sprinklers and draft stops are not required around large openings such as those found in shopping malls, atrium buildings, and similar structures where all adjoining levels and spaces are protected by automatic sprinklers in accordance with this standard and where the openings have all horizontal dimensions between opposite edges of 20 ft (6 m) or greater and an area of 1000 sq ft (93 m^2) or greater.

4-4.1.7.4* Building Service Chutes. Building service chutes (linen, rubbish, etc.) shall be protected internally by automatic sprinklers. A sprinkler shall be provided above the top service opening of the chute, above the lowest service opening, and above service openings at alternate levels in buildings over two stories in height. The room or area into which the chute discharges shall also be protected by automatic sprinklers.

4-4.1.7.5 Spaces under Ground Floors, Exterior Docks, and Platforms. Sprinklers shall be installed in spaces under all ground floors, exterior docks, and platforms.

Exception: Sprinklers shall be permitted to be omitted when all of the following conditions prevail:

(a) The space is not accessible for storage purposes and is protected against accumulation of wind-borne debris;

(b) The space contains no equipment such as steam pipes, electric wiring, or conveyors;

(c) The floor over the space is of tight construction;

(d) No combustible or flammable liquids or materials that under fire conditions may convert into combustible or flammable liquids are processed, handled, or stored on the floor above the space.

4-4.1.7.6* Exterior Roofs or Canopies.

4-4.1.7.6.1 Sprinklers shall be installed under roofs or canopies over areas where combustibles are stored or handled.

Exception: Sprinklers are permitted to be omitted where construction is noncombustible and areas under the roofs or canopies are not used for storage or handling of combustibles.

4-4.1.7.6.2 Sprinklers shall be installed under exterior combustible roofs or canopies exceeding 4 ft (1.2 m) in width.

4-4.1.7.7 Dwelling Units.

4-4.1.7.7.1 Sprinklers are not required in bathrooms that are located within dwelling units, that do not exceed 55 sq ft (5.1 m²), and that have walls and ceilings of noncombustible or limited-combustible materials with a 15 minute thermal barrier rating including the walls and ceilings behind fixtures.

Exception: Sprinklers are required in bathrooms of nursing homes and in bathrooms opening directly onto public corridors or exitways.

4-4.1.7.7.2 Sprinklers are not required in clothes closets, linen closets, and pantries within dwelling units in hotels and motels where the area of the space does not exceed 24 sq ft (2.2 m²), the least dimension does not exceed 3 ft (0.9 m), and the walls and ceilings are surfaced with noncombustible or limited-combustible materials.

4-4.1.7.8 Baffles. Baffles shall be installed whenever sprinklers are less than 6 ft (1.8 m) apart to prevent operating sprinklers from wetting adjacent sprinklers, thus delaying or preventing their operation. Baffles shall be located midway between sprinklers and arranged to protect the actuating elements. Baffles shall be of noncombustible or limited-combustible material that will stay in place before and during sprinkler operation. The baffles shall be approximately 8 in. (203 mm) wide and 6 in. (152 mm) high. The tops of baffles shall extend 2 to 3 in. (51 to 76 mm) above the deflectors of upright sprinklers. The bottoms of baffles shall extend downward to a level at least even with the deflectors of pendent sprinklers. (*See A-4-4.1.7.3.4.*)

Exception No. 1: For in-rack sprinklers, see NFPA 231C, Standard for Rack Storage of Materials.

Exception No. 2: Baffles are not required for old-style sprinklers protecting fur storage vaults.

4-4.1.7.9 Spacing under Pitched Surfaces.

4-4.1.7.9.1 The distance between sprinklers either on the branch lines or between the branch lines, running up or down the slope of a pitched surface, shall be measured along the slope.

4-4.1.7.9.2* Sprinklers under or near the peak shall have deflectors located not more than 3 ft (0.9 m) vertically down from the peak. [*See Figures 4-4.1.7.9.2(a) and 4-4.1.7.9.2(b).*]

Exception No. 1: Under saw-toothed roofs, sprinklers at the highest elevation shall not exceed a distance of 3 ft (0.9 m) measured down the slope from the peak.

Exception No. 2: Under a steeply pitched surface, the distance from the peak to the deflectors shall be permitted to be increased to maintain a horizontal clearance of not less than 2 ft (0.6 m) from other structural members. [See Figure 4-4.1.7.9.2(c).]

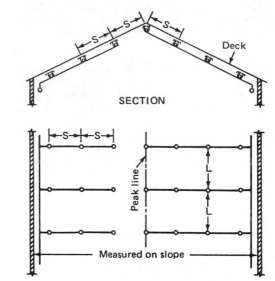

For SI Units: 1 in. = 25.4 mm; 1 ft = 0.3048 m.

Figure 4-4.1.7.9.2(a)   Sprinklers at pitched roofs; branch lines run up the slope.

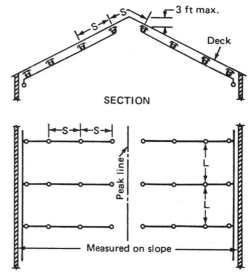

For SI Units: 1 in. = 25.4 mm; 1 ft = 0.3048 m.

Figure 4-4.1.7.9.2(b)   Sprinklers at pitched roofs; branch lines run up the slope.

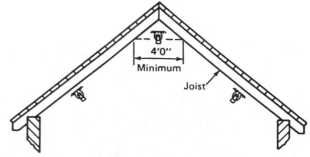

For SI Units: 1 in. = 25.4 mm; 1 ft = 0.3048 m.

Figure 4-4.1.7.9.2(c)   Desirable horizontal clearance for sprinklers at peak of pitched roof.

4-4.1.7.10 Spacing of Sprinklers under Curved Roof Buildings.

4-4.1.7.10.1 Under curved surfaces, the horizontal distance measured at the floor level from the wall to the nearest sprinkler shall not be greater than one-half the allowable distance between sprinklers.

4-4.1.7.10.2 Deflectors of sprinklers shall be parallel with the curve of the surface.

4-4.1.7.10.3 When Extra Hazard Occupancy spacing of sprinklers is used under curved ceilings of other than fire resistive construction, the sprinkler spacing as projected on the floor shall not be greater than that required for Extra Hazard Occupancies, but in no case shall the spacing at the roof or ceiling be wider than that required for Ordinary Hazard Occupancies.

4-4.1.7.11 Library Stack Rooms. Sprinklers shall be installed in every aisle and at every tier of stacks with distance between sprinklers along aisles not to exceed 12 ft (3.6 m). [See Figure 4-4.1.7.11(a).]

Exception No. 1: When vertical shelf dividers are incomplete and allow water distribution to adjacent aisles, sprinklers are permitted to be omitted in alternate aisles on each tier. Where ventilation openings are also provided in tier floors, sprinklers shall be staggered vertically. [See Figure 4-4.1.7.11(b).]

Exception No. 2: Sprinklers are permitted to be installed without regard to aisles when there is 18 in. (457 mm) or more clearance between sprinkler deflectors and tops of racks.

4-4.1.7.12 Electrical Equipment. When sprinkler protection is provided in generator or transformer rooms, hoods or shields installed to protect important electrical equipment from sprinkler discharge shall be noncombustible.

4-4.1.7.13* Open-Grid Ceilings. Open-grid ceilings shall not be installed beneath sprinklers.

Exception No. 1: Open-grid ceilings in which the openings are ¼ in. (6.4 mm) or larger in the least dimension, when the thickness or depth of the material does not exceed the least dimension of the opening, and when such openings constitute 70 percent of the area of the ceiling material. The spacing of the sprinklers over the open grid ceiling shall then comply with the following:

(a) In Light Hazard Occupancies when sprinkler spacing (either spray or old-style sprinklers) is less than 10 ft by 10 ft (3 m by 3 m), a minimum clearance of at least 18 in. (457 mm) shall be provided between the sprinkler deflectors and the upper surface of the open-grid ceiling. When spacing is greater than 10 ft by 10 ft (3 m by 3 m) but less than 10 ft by 12 ft (3 m by 3.7 m), a clearance of at least 24 in. (610 mm) shall be provided from spray sprinklers and at least 36 in. (914 mm) from old-style sprinklers. When spacing is greater than 10 ft by 12 ft (3 m by 3.7 m), a clearance of at least 48 in. (1219 mm) shall be provided.

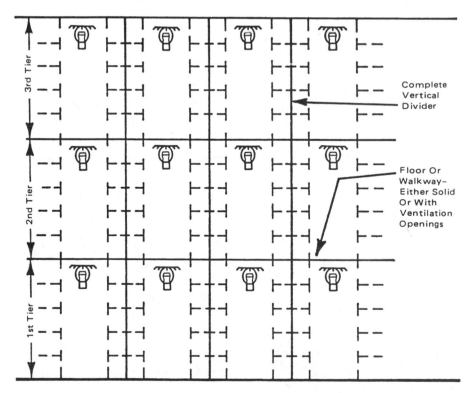

Figure 4-4.1.7.11(a) Sprinklers in multitier library bookstacks with complete vertical dividers.

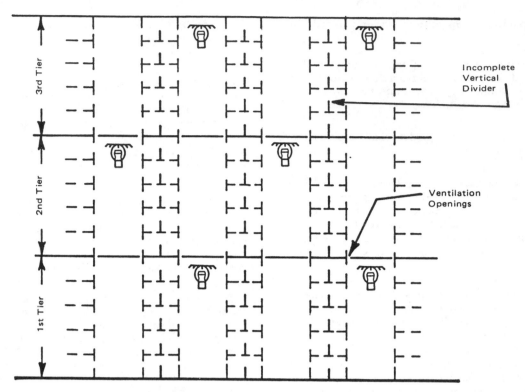

Figure 4-4.1.7.11(b)   Sprinklers in multitier library bookstacks with incomplete vertical dividers.

(b) *In Ordinary Hazard Occupancies, open-grid ceilings shall be permitted to be installed beneath spray sprinklers only. When sprinkler spacing is less than 10 ft by 10 ft (3 m by 3 m), a minimum clearance of at least 24 in. (610 mm) shall be provided between the sprinkler deflectors and the upper surface of the open-grid ceiling. When spacing is greater than 10 ft by 10 ft (3 m by 3 m), a clearance of at least 36 in. (914 mm) shall be provided.*

Exception No. 2: Other types of open-grid ceilings shall not be installed beneath sprinklers unless they are listed for such service and are installed in accordance with instructions contained in each package of ceiling material.

4-4.1.7.14 Drop-Out Ceilings.

4-4.1.7.14.1 Drop-out ceilings shall be permitted to be installed beneath sprinklers when ceilings are listed for that service and are installed in accordance with their listings.

Exception: Special sprinklers shall not be installed above drop-out ceilings unless specifically listed for this purpose.

4-4.1.7.14.2 Drop-out ceilings shall not be considered ceilings within the context of this standard.

4-4.1.7.14.3* Piping installed above drop-out ceilings shall not be considered concealed piping (*see 2-5.4, Exception No. 2*).

4-4.1.7.14.4* Sprinklers shall not be installed beneath drop-out ceilings.

4-4.1.7.15* Fur Vaults.

4-4.1.7.15.1 Sprinklers shall be listed old-style having orifice sizes selected to provide as closely as possible but not less than 20 gal per min (76 L/min) per sprinkler, for four sprinklers, based on the water pressure available.

4-4.1.7.15.2 Sprinklers in fur storage vaults shall be located centrally over the aisles between racks and shall be spaced not over 5 ft (1.5 m) apart along the aisles.

4-4.1.7.15.3 When sprinklers are spaced 5 ft (1.5 m) apart along the sprinkler branch lines, pipe sizes shall be in accordance with the following schedule:

1 in.	4 sprinklers	2 in.	20 sprinklers
1¼ in.	6 sprinklers	2½ in.	40 sprinklers
1½ in.	10 sprinklers	3 in.	80 sprinklers

4-4.1.7.16 Stages. Sprinklers shall be installed under the roof at the ceiling, in spaces under the stage either containing combustible materials or constructed of combustible materials, and in all adjacent spaces and dressing rooms, storerooms, and workshops.

4-4.1.7.16.1 When proscenium opening protection is required, a deluge system shall be provided with open sprinklers located not more than 3 ft (0.9 m) away from the stage side of the proscenium arch and spaced up to a maximum of 6 ft (1.8 m) on center. (*See Chapter 5 for design criteria.*)

4-4.1.7.17 Rack Storage. For sprinklers in storage racks see NFPA 231C, *Standard for Rack Storage of Materials.*

4-4.1.7.18 Provision for Flushing Systems. All sprinkler systems shall be arranged for flushing. Readily removable fittings shall be provided at the end of all cross mains. All cross mains shall terminate in 1¼-in. (33-mm) or larger pipe. All branch lines on gridded systems shall be arranged to facilitate flushing.

4-4.1.7.19 Stair Towers. Stairs, towers, or other construction with incomplete floors, if piped on independent risers, shall be treated as one area with reference to pipe sizes.

4-4.1.7.20 Return Bends. Return bends shall be used when pendent sprinklers are supplied from a raw water source, mill pond, or from open-top reservoirs. Return bends shall be connected to the top of branch lines in order to avoid accumulation of sediment in the drop nipples.

Exception No. 1: Return bends are not required for deluge systems.

Exception No. 2: Return bends are not required when dry-pendent sprinklers are used.

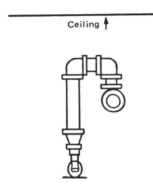

Figure 4-4.1.7.20   Return bend arrangement.

4-4.1.7.21 Piping to Sprinklers below Ceilings.

4-4.1.7.21.1 In new installations expected to supply sprinklers below a ceiling, minimum 1 in. (25 mm) outlets shall be provided.

Exception: Hexagonal bushings may be used to accommodate temporary sprinklers and shall be removed with the temporary sprinklers when the permanent ceiling sprinklers are installed.

4-4.1.7.21.2 In revamping existing systems, a nipple not exceeding 4 in. (102 mm) in length and of the same pipe thread size as the sprinkler being removed shall be permitted to be installed in the branch line fitting. All other piping shall be 1 in. (25 mm) where it supplies a single sprinkler in an area.

Exception: When it is necessary to pipe two new ceiling sprinklers from an existing outlet in an overhead system, the use of a nipple not exceeding 4 in. (102 mm) in length and of the same pipe thread size as the existing outlet shall be permitted, provided that a hydraulic calculation verifies that the design flow rate will be achieved.

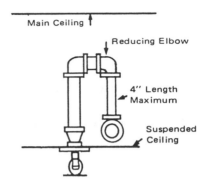

Figure 4-4.1.7.21.2(a)   Nipple and reducing elbow supplying sprinkler below ceiling.

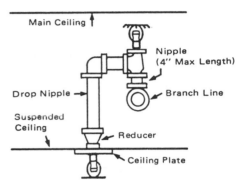

Figure 4-4.1.7.21.2(b)   Sprinklers in concealed space and below ceiling.

4-4.1.7.22 Dry Pipe Underground. When necessary to place pipe that will be under air pressure underground, the pipe shall be protected against corrosion (*see 4-5.4.2*), or unprotected cast or ductile iron pipe may be used when joined with a gasketed joint listed for air service underground.

4-4.1.7.23* One and One-Half-Inch Hose Connections. One and one-half-inch [1½-in. (38-mm)] hose used for fire purposes only shall be permitted to be connected to wet sprinkler systems only, subject to the following restrictions:

(a) Hose station's supply pipes shall not be connected to any pipe smaller than 2½ in. (64 mm).

Exception: For hydraulically designed loops and grids the minimum size pipe between the hose station's supply pipe and the source shall be permitted to be 2 in. (51 mm).

(b) For piping serving a single hose station, pipe shall be minimum 1 in. (25 mm) for horizontal runs up to 20 ft (6.1 m), minimum 1¼ in. (33 mm) for the entire run for runs between 20 and 80 ft (6.1 and 24.4 m), and minimum 1½ in. (38 mm) for the entire run for runs greater than 80 ft (24.4 m). For piping serving multiple hose stations, runs shall be a minimum of 1½ in. (38 mm) throughout.

(c) Piping shall be at least 1 in. (25 mm) for vertical runs.

(d) When the pressure at any hose station outlet exceeds 100 psi (6.9 bars), an approved device shall be installed at the outlet to reduce the pressure at the outlet to 100 psi (6.9 bars).

4-4.1.7.24* Hose Connections for Fire Department Use.
In buildings of Light or Ordinary Hazard Occupancy, 2½ in. (64 mm) hose valves for fire department use may be attached to wet pipe sprinkler system risers. [See 5-2.3.1.3(d).] The following restrictions shall apply:

(a) Sprinklers shall be under separate floor control valves.

(b) The minimum size of the riser shall be 4 in. (102 mm) unless hydraulic calculations indicate a smaller size riser will satisfy sprinkler and hose stream demands.

(c) Each combined sprinkler and standpipe riser shall be equipped with a riser control valve to permit isolating a riser without interrupting the supply to other risers from the same source of supply.

(d) For fire department connections serving standpipe and sprinkler systems, refer to Section 2-8.

4-4.1.7.25* When individual floor/zone control valves are not provided, a flanged joint or mechanical coupling shall be used at the riser at each floor for connections to piping serving floor areas in excess of 5000 sq ft (465 m²).

4-4.2 Sidewall Spray Sprinklers.

4-4.2.1 Distance between Sprinklers on Branch Lines.
Sidewall sprinklers shall be installed along the length of a single wall of rooms or bays not exceeding the width dimension specified in Table 4-4.2.1.

Exception: Where the width of the room or bay exceeds the maximum allowed, up to 30 ft (9.1 m) for Light Hazard Occupancy, or 20 ft (6.1 m) for Ordinary Hazard Occupancy, sidewall sprinklers on a staggered basis shall be provided on two opposite walls or sides of bays with spacing as required by Table 4-4.2.1. (See Figure 4-4.2.1.)

4-4.2.2 Protection Area Limitations.

4-4.2.2.1* Protection area limitations for sidewall sprinklers shall be in conformity with Table 4-4.2.1.

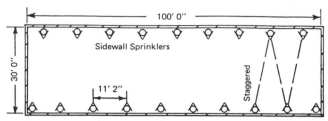

For SI Units: 1 in. = 25.4 mm; 1 ft = 0.3048 m.

Figure 4-4.2.1   Spacing of sidewall sprinklers under unobstructed construction in Light Hazard Occupancies.

4-4.2.2.2 The distance from a sidewall sprinkler to an end wall shall not exceed one-half the allowable distance between sidewall sprinklers.

4-4.2.3 Position of Sidewall Sprinklers.

4-4.2.3.1 Sidewall sprinklers shall only be installed along walls, lintels, or soffits where the distance from the ceiling to the bottom of the lintel or soffit is at least 2 in. (51 mm) greater than the distances from the ceiling to sidewall sprinkler deflector.

4-4.2.3.2 Sidewall sprinklers shall not be installed back to back without being separated by a continuous lintel or soffit.

4-4.2.3.3 Sidewall sprinkler deflectors (vertical type) shall be located not more than 6 in. (152 mm) or less than 4 in. (102 mm) from walls and ceilings.

Exception No. 1:   Horizontal sidewall sprinklers are permitted to be located 6 to 12 in. (152 to 305 mm) below noncombustible ceilings when listed for these positions.

Exception No. 2:   Horizontal sidewall sprinklers are permitted to be located with their deflectors less than 4 in. (102 mm) from the wall on which they are mounted.

Table 4-4.2.1   Dimensions for Sidewall Sprinkler Installation for Various Ceiling Types

	Light Hazard Occupancy			Ordinary Hazard Occupancy	
	Combustible sheathing	Combustible construction with noncombustible or limited combustible sheathing, wood lath and plaster	Noncombustible construction with non-combustible or limited combustible sheathing	Combustible sheathing	Noncombustible or limited combustible sheathing
Maximum distance between sprinklers on branch line	14	14	14	10	10
Maximum room width for single branch line along wall (ft)	12	12	14	10	10
Maximum area coverage (ft²)	120	168	196	80	100

For SI Units: 1 ft = 0.3048 m; 1 ft² = 0.0929 m².

4-4.2.3.4 Sidewall sprinklers, when installed under a sloped ceiling, shall be located at the high point of the slope and positioned to discharge downward, and the deflector shall be parallel to the sloped ceiling.

4-4.2.3.5 When soffits are used for the installation of sidewall sprinklers, they shall not exceed 8 in. (203 mm) in width or projection from the wall.

Exception: When soffits exceed 8 in., additional sprinklers shall be installed below the soffit.

4-4.2.4 Obstructions to Sidewall Sprinklers. Sidewall sprinklers shall be installed where no beams or similar obstructions are located closer than 4 ft (2.3 m) from the sprinkler. Beams or similar obstructions located greater than 4 ft (2.3 m) from the sprinkler shall be in conformity with Table 4-4.2.4.

Table 4-4.2.4　Sidewall Sprinkler Clearance

Distance from Sidewall Sprinkler to Side of Obstruction	Maximum Allowable Distance of Deflector above Bottom of Obstruction (In.)
Less than 4 ft	0
4 ft to less than 5 ft	1
5 ft to less than 5 ft 6 in.	2
5 ft 6 in. to less than 6 ft	3
6 ft to less than 6 ft 6 in.	4
6 ft 6 in. to less than 7 ft	6
7 ft to less than 7 ft 6 in.	7
7 ft 6 in. to less than 8 ft	9
8 ft to less than 8 ft 6 in.	11
8 ft 6 in. to less than 9 ft	14

For SI Units: 1 in. = 25.4 mm; 1 ft = 0.3048 m.

4-4.3　Large-Drop Sprinklers.

4-4.3.1* Spacing. The distance between sprinklers shall be limited to not more than 12 ft (3.7 m) or less than 8 ft (2.4 m).

Exception: Under obstructed combustible construction, the maximum distance shall be limited to 10 ft (3.0 m).

4-4.3.2 Clear Space below Sprinklers. A minimum of 36 in. (914 mm) shall be maintained between the top of storage and ceiling sprinkler deflectors.

4-4.3.3* Distance below Ceiling.

4-4.3.3.1 Under unobstructed construction, the distance between the sprinkler deflector and the ceiling shall be a minimum of 6 in. and a maximum of 8 in.

4-4.3.3.2 Under obstructed construction, the distance between the sprinkler deflector and the ceiling shall be a minimum of 6 in. and a maximum of 12 in.

Exception: Under wood joist or composite wood joist construction, the sprinklers shall be located 1 to 6 in. below the structural members to a maximum distance of 22 in. below the ceiling/roof or deck.

4-4.3.4* Obstructions to Distribution.

4-4.3.4.1 Obstructions Located at the Ceiling. When sprinkler deflectors are located above the bottom of obstructions such as beams, girders, ducts, fluorescent lighting fixtures, etc., located at the ceiling, the sprinklers shall be positioned so that the maximum distance from the bottom of the obstruction to the deflectors does not exceed the values specified in 4-4.1.3.

4-4.3.4.2 Obstructions Located below the Sprinklers.

4-4.3.4.2.1 Sprinklers shall be positioned with respect to fluorescent lighting fixtures, ducts, and obstructions more than 24 in. (610 mm) wide and located entirely below the sprinklers so that the minimum horizontal distance from the near side of the obstruction to the center of the sprinkler is not less than the value specified in Table 4-4.3.4.2.1. (*See Figure 4-4.3.4.2.1.*)

Table 4-4.3.4.2.1　Position of Sprinklers in Relation to Obstruction Located Entirely Below the Sprinklers

Distance of Deflector above Bottom of Obstruction	Minimum Distance to Side of Obstruction, ft (m)
Less than 6 in. (152 mm)	1½ (0.5)
6 in. (152 mm) to less than 12 in. (305 mm)	3 (0.9)
12 in. (305 mm) to less than 18 in. (457 mm)	4 (1.2)
18 in. (457 mm) to less than 24 in. (610 mm)	5 (1.5)
24 in. (610 mm) to less than 30 in. (660 mm)	6 (1.8)

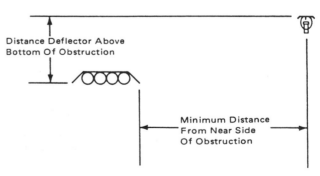

Figure 4-4.3.4.2.1　Position of sprinklers in relation to obstructions located entirely below the sprinklers. (To be used with Table 4-4.3.4.2.1.)

4-4.3.4.2.2 When the bottom of the obstruction is located 24 in. (610 mm) or more below the sprinkler deflectors:

(a) Sprinklers shall be positioned so that the obstruction is centered between adjacent sprinklers. (*See Figure 4-4.3.4.2.2.*)

(b) The obstruction shall be limited to a maximum width of 24 in. (610 mm). (*See Figure 4-4.3.4.2.2.*)

Exception: When obstruction is greater than 24 in. (610 mm) wide, one or more lines of sprinklers shall be installed below the obstruction.

(c) The obstruction shall not extend more than 12 in. (305 mm) to either side of the midpoint between sprinklers. (*See Figure 4-4.3.4.2.2.*)

Exception: When the extensions of the obstruction exceed 12 in. (305 mm), one or more lines of sprinklers shall be installed below the obstruction.

(d) At least 18 in. (457 mm) clearance shall be maintained between the top of storage and the bottom of the obstruction. (*See Figure 4-4.3.4.2.2.*)

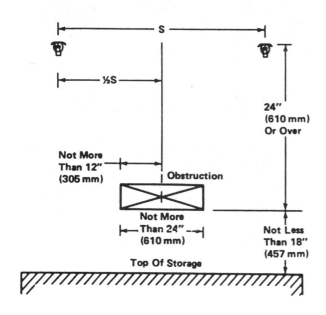

Figure 4-4.3.4.2.2   Position of sprinklers in relation to obstructions located 24 in. (610 mm) or more below deflectors.

4-4.3.4.2.3 Obstructions Parallel to and Directly below Branch Lines.   In the special case of an obstruction running parallel to and directly below a branch line:

(a) The sprinkler shall be located at least 36 in. (914 mm) above the top of the obstruction. (*See Figure 4-4.3.4.2.3.*)

(b) The obstruction shall be limited to a maximum width of 12 in. (305 mm). (*See Figure 4-4.3.4.2.3.*)

(c) The obstruction shall be limited to a maximum extension of 6 in. (152 mm) to either side of the center line of the branch line. (*See Figure 4-4.3.4.2.3.*)

4-4.4 Quick Response Early Suppression (QRES) Sprinklers.   (Reserved)

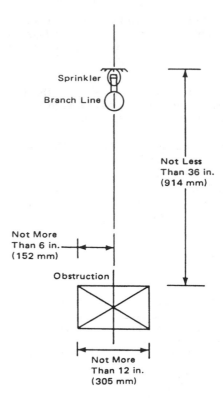

Figure 4-4.3.4.2.3   Position of sprinklers in relation to obstructions running parallel to and directly below branch lines.

4-4.5 Early Suppression Fast Response (ESFR) Sprinklers.

4-4.5.1 Spacing.   The distance between sprinklers shall be limited to not more than 12 ft (3.7 m) or less than 8 ft (2.4 m).

4-4.5.2 Distances.

4-4.5.2.1 Distance from Walls.   The distance from walls to sprinklers shall not exceed one-half of the allowable distance between sprinklers.

4-4.5.2.2 Clear Space below Sprinklers.   At least 36 in. (914 mm) shall be maintained between sprinkler deflectors and the top of storage.

4-4.5.2.3 Distances below Ceiling.   Sprinklers shall be positioned so that deflectors are a maximum 14 in. (356 mm) and a minimum 6 in. (152 mm) below the ceiling.

4-4.5.3 Location of Sprinklers in Obstructed Construction.   With obstructed construction, the branch lines shall be permitted to be installed across the beams, but sprinklers shall be located in the bays and not under the beams.

4-4.5.4 Obstruction to Discharge.

4-4.5.4.1 Obstructions Located at or near the Ceiling. When sprinkler deflectors are located above the bottom of beams, girders, ducts, fluorescent lighting fixtures, or other obstructions located at the ceiling, the sprinklers shall be positioned so that the maximum distance from the bottom of the obstruction to the deflector does not exceed the value specified in 4-4.1.3.

4-4.5.4.2 Obstructions Located Entirely below the Sprinklers. Sprinklers shall be positioned with respect to any fluorescent lighting fixtures, ducts, or any other obstruction more than 12 in. (305 mm) wide and located entirely below the sprinklers so that the minimum horizontal distance from the near side of the obstruction to the center of the sprinkler is not less than the value specified in Table 4-4.3.4.2.1. (*See Figure 4-4.3.4.2.1.*)

4-5 Piping Installation.

4-5.1 Valves.

4-5.1.1* Valves Controlling Sprinkler Systems. (*See 2-7.1.*)

4-5.1.1.1* Each system shall be provided with a listed indicating valve in an accessible location, so located as to control all automatic sources of water supply.

4-5.1.1.2 At least one listed indicating valve shall be installed in each source of water supply.

Exception: There shall be no shutoff valve in the fire department connection.

4-5.1.1.3 Valves on connections to water supplies, sectional control valves, and other valves in supply pipes to sprinklers shall be supervised open by one of the following methods:

  (a) Central station, proprietary, or remote station signaling service.

  (b) Local signaling service that will cause the sounding of an audible signal at a constantly attended point.

  (c) Valves locked in the open position.

  (d) Valves located within fenced enclosures under the control of the owner, sealed in the open position, and inspected weekly as part of an approved procedure.

Floor control valves in high-rise buildings and valves controlling flow to sprinklers in circulating closed loop systems shall comply with (a) or (b) above.

Exception: Supervision of underground gate valves with roadway boxes shall not be required.

4-5.1.1.4 When there is more than one source of water supply, a check valve shall be installed in each connection.

4-5.1.1.5 Check valves shall be installed in a vertical or horizontal position in accordance with their listing.

4-5.1.1.6* When a single wet pipe sprinkler system is equipped with a fire department connection, the alarm valve is considered a check valve and an additional check valve shall not be required.

4-5.1.1.7* In a city connection serving as one source of supply, the city valve in the connection shall be acceptable as one of the required valves. A listed indicating valve or an indicator post valve shall be installed on the system side of the check valve required in 4-5.1.1.4.

Exception: When a wet pipe sprinkler system is equipped with an (alarm) check valve, a gate valve is not required on the system side of the (alarm) check valve.

4-5.1.2 Pressure Reducing Valves.

4-5.1.2.1 In portions of systems where all components are not listed for pressure greater than 175 psi (12.1 bars) and the potential exists for normal (nonfire condition) water pressure in excess of 175 psi (12.1 bars), a listed pressure reducing valve shall be installed and set for an outlet pressure not exceeding 165 psi (11.4 bars) at the maximum inlet pressure.

4-5.1.2.2 Pressure gauges shall be installed on the inlet and outlet sides of each pressure reducing valve.

4-5.1.2.3* A relief valve of not less than $1/2$ in. (13 mm) in size shall be provided on the discharge side of the pressure reducing valve set to operate at a pressure not exceeding 175 psi (12.1 bars).

4-5.1.2.4 A listed indicating valve shall be provided on the inlet side of each pressure reducing valve.

Exception: A listed indicating valve is not required where the pressure reducing valve meets the listing requirements for use as an indicating valve.

4-5.2 Pipe Support.

4-5.2.1 General

4-5.2.1.1 Sprinkler piping shall be supported independently of the ceiling sheathing.

Exception: Toggle hangers shall be permitted only for the support of pipe $1 1/2$ in. (38 mm) or smaller in size under ceilings of hollow tile or metal lath and plaster.

4-5.2.1.2 When sprinkler piping is installed in storage racks as defined in NFPA 231C, *Standard for Rack Storage of Materials*, piping shall be supported from the storage rack structure or building in accordance with all applicable provisions of 4-5.2 and 4-5.4.3.

4-5.2.2 Maximum Distance between Hangers.

4-5.2.2.1* The maximum distance between hangers shall not exceed that in Table 4-5.2.2.1.

Exception No. 1: The maximum distance between hangers for steel pipe and copper tube shall be modified as specified in 4-5.2.1 and 4-5.2.2.

Exception No. 2: The maximum distance between hangers for CPVC pipe and polybutylene pipe shall be modified as specified in the individual product listings.

Table 4-5.2.2.1   Maximum Distance between Hangers (ft - in.)

Nominal Pipe Size (in.)	3/4	1	1 1/4	1 1/2	2	2 1/2	3	3 1/2	4	5	6	8
Steel Pipe Except Threaded Light-wall	N/A	12-0	12-0	15-0	15-0	15-0	15-0	15-0	15-0	15-0	15-0	15-0
Threaded Light-wall Steel Pipe	N/A	12-0	12-0	12-0	12-0	12-0	12-0	N/A	N/A	N/A	N/A	N/A
Copper Tube	8-0	8-0	10-0	10-0	12-0	12-0	12-0	15-0	15-0	15-0	15-0	15-0
CPVC	5-6	6-0	6-6	7-0	8-0	9-0	10-0	N/A	N/A	N/A	N/A	N/A
Polybutylene (IPS)	N/A	3-9	4-7	5-0	5-11	N/A	N/A	N/A	N/A	N/A	N/A	N/A
Polybutylene (CTS)	2-11	3-4	3-11	4-5	5-5	N/A	N/A	N/A	N/A	N/A	N/A	N/A

For SI Units: 1 in. = 25.4 mm; 1 ft = 0.3048 m.

Exception No. 3: *Holes through concrete beams shall be acceptable for the support of steel pipe as a substitute for hangers.*

4-5.2.3 Location of Hangers on Branch Lines. This subsection applies to the support of steel pipe or copper tube as specified in 2-3.1 and subject to the provisions of 4-5.2.2.

4-5.2.3.1 There shall be not less than one hanger for each section of pipe.

Exception No. 1*: *When sprinklers are spaced less than 6 ft (1.8 m) apart, hangers spaced up to a maximum of 12 ft (3.7 m) shall be permitted.*

Exception No. 2: *Starter lengths less than 6 ft (1.8 m) shall not require a hanger, unless on the end line of a sidefeed system or where an intermediate cross main hanger has been omitted.*

4-5.2.3.2 The distance between a hanger and the centerline of an upright sprinkler shall not be less than 3 in. (76 mm).

4-5.2.3.3* The unsupported length between the end sprinkler and the last hanger on the line shall not be greater than 36 in. (914 mm) for 1-in. (2.5-cm) pipe or 48 in. (1219 mm) for 1 1/4-in. (3.2-cm) pipe, and 60 in. (15.2 cm) for 1 1/2-in. (3.8-cm) or larger pipe. When any of these limits is exceeded, the pipe shall be extended beyond the end sprinkler and shall be supported by an additional hanger.

Exception No. 1*: *When the maximum pressure at the sprinkler exceeds 100 psi (6.9 bars), and a branch line above a ceiling supplies sprinklers in a pendent position below the ceiling, the hanger assembly supporting the pipe supplying an end sprinkler in a pendent position shall be of a type that prevents upward movement of the pipe.*

Exception No. 2*: *When the maximum pressure at the sprinkler exceeds 100 psi (6.9 bars), the unsupported length between the end sprinkler in a pendent position or drop nipple and the last hanger on the branch line shall not be greater than 12 in. (305 mm) for steel pipe or 6 in. (152 mm) for copper pipe. When this limit is exceeded, the pipe shall be extended beyond the end sprinkler and supported by an additional hanger. The hanger closest to the sprinkler shall be of a type that clamps to and prevents upward movement of the piping.*

4-5.2.3.4* The length of an unsupported armover to a sprinkler shall not exceed 24 in. (610 mm) for steel pipe or 12 in. (305 mm) for copper tube.

Exception*: *When the maximum pressure at the sprinkler exceeds 100 psi (6.9 bars) and a branch line above a ceiling supplies sprinklers in a pendent position below the ceiling, the length of an unsupported armover to a sprinkler and drop nipple shall not exceed 12 in. (305 mm) for steel pipe and 6 in. (152 mm) for copper tube.*

When the limits of the unsupported armover lengths of 4-5.2.3.4 or this Exception are exceeded, the hanger closest to the sprinkler shall be of a type that prevents upward movement of the piping.

4-5.2.3.5 Wall mounted sidewall sprinklers shall be restrained to prevent movement.

4-5.2.4 Location of Hangers on Cross Mains. This subsection applies to the support of steel pipe only as specified in 4-5.2.3, subject to the provisions of 4-5.2.2.

4-5.2.4.1 On cross mains there shall be at least one hanger between each two branch lines.

Exception No. 1: *In bays having two branch lines, the intermediate hanger shall be permitted to be omitted provided that a hanger attached to a purlin is installed on each branch line located as near to the cross main as the location of the purlin permits. Remaining branch line hangers shall be installed in accordance with 4-5.2.3.*

Exception No. 2: *In bays having three branch lines, either side or center feed, one (only) intermediate hanger shall be permitted to be omitted provided that a hanger attached to a purlin is installed on each branch line located as near to the cross main as the location of the purlin permits. Remaining branch line hangers shall be installed in accordance with 4-5.2.3.*

Exception No. 3: *In bays having four or more branch lines, either side or center feed, two intermediate hangers shall be permitted to be omitted provided the maximum distance between hangers does not exceed the distances specified in 4-5.2.2.1 and a hanger attached to a purlin on each branch line is located as near to the cross main as the purlin permits.*

4-5.2.4.2 Intermediate hangers shall not be omitted for copper tube.

4-5.2.4.3 At the end of the cross main, intermediate trapeze hangers shall be installed unless the cross main is extended to the next framing member with a hanger installed at this point, in which event an intermediate hanger shall be permitted to be omitted in accordance with 4-5.2.4.1, Exceptions No. 1, No. 2, and No. 3.

4-5.2.5 Support of Risers.

4-5.2.5.1 Risers shall be supported by pipe clamps or by hangers located on the horizontal connections close to the riser.

4-5.2.5.2 Clamps supporting pipe by means of setscrews shall not be used.

4-5.2.5.3 In multistory buildings, riser supports shall be provided at the lowest level, at each alternate level above, above and below offsets, and at the top of the riser. Supports above the lowest level shall also restrain the pipe to prevent movement by an upward thrust when flexible fittings are used. Where risers are supported from the ground, the ground support constitutes the first level of riser support. Where risers are offset or do not rise from the ground, the first ceiling level above the offset constitutes the first level of riser support.

4-5.2.5.4 Risers in vertical shafts, or in buildings with ceilings over 25 ft (7.6 m) high, shall have at least one support for each riser pipe section.

4-5.3 Drainage.

4-5.3.1* All sprinkler pipe and fittings shall be so installed that the system can be drained.

4-5.3.2 On wet pipe systems, sprinkler pipes shall be permitted to be installed level. Trapped piping shall be drained in accordance with 4-5.3.5.

4-5.3.3 In dry pipe systems and portions of preaction systems subject to freezing, branch lines shall be pitched at least $1/2$ in. per 10 ft (4 mm/m) and mains shall be pitched at least $1/4$ in. per 10 ft (2 mm/m).

Exception: Mains shall be pitched at least $1/2$ in. per 10 ft (4 mm/m) in refrigerated areas.

4-5.3.4 System, Main Drain, or Sectional Drain Connections. [*See Figures 4-5.3.4 and A-4-6.4.2(b).*]

4-5.3.4.1 Provisions shall be made to properly drain all parts of the system.

4-5.3.4.2 Drain connections for systems supply risers and mains shall be sized as shown in Table 4-5.3.4.2.

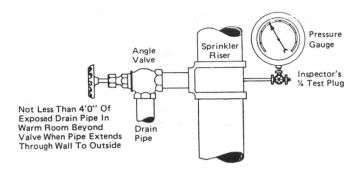

For SI Units: 1 in. = 25.4 mm; 1 ft = 0.3048 m.

Figure 4-5.3.4   Drain connection for system riser.

Table 4-5.3.4.2

Riser or Main Size	Size of Drain Connection
Up to 2 in.	$3/4$ in. or larger
$2^1/2$ in., 3 in., $3^1/2$ in.	$1^1/4$ in. or larger
4 in. and larger	2 in. only

4-5.3.4.3 When interior sectional or floor control valve(s) are provided, they shall be provided with a drain connection sized as shown in Table 4-5.3.4.2 to drain that portion of the system controlled by the sectional valve. Drains shall discharge outside or to a drain connection. [*See Figure A-4-6.4.2(b).*]

4-5.3.4.4 The test connections required by 4-6.4.1 shall be permitted to be used as main drain connections.

Exception: When drain connections for floor control valves are tied into a common drain riser, the drain riser shall be one pipe size larger than the largest size drain connection tying into it.

4-5.3.5 Auxiliary Drains.

4-5.3.5.1 Auxiliary drains shall be provided when a change in piping direction prevents drainage of system piping through the main drain valve.

4-5.3.5.2 Auxiliary Drains for Wet Pipe Systems and Preaction Systems in Areas Not Subject to Freezing.

4-5.3.5.2.1 When the capacity of trapped sections of pipes in wet systems is less than 5 gal (18.9 L), the auxiliary drain shall consist of a nipple and cap or plug not less than $1/2$ in. (12 mm) in size.

Exception: Auxiliary drains are not required for system piping that can be drained by removing a single pendent sprinkler.

4-5.3.5.2.2 When the capacity of isolated trapped sections of pipe is more than 5 gal (18.9 L) and less than 50 gal (189 L), the auxiliary drain shall consist of a valve $3/4$ in. or larger and a plug or a nipple and cap.

4-5.3.5.2.3* When the capacity of isolated trapped sections of pipe is 50 gal (18.9 L) or more, the auxiliary drain shall consist of a valve not smaller than 1 in. (25.4 mm), piped to an accessible location.

4-5.3.5.2.4 Tie-in drains are not required on wet pipe and preaction systems.

4-5.3.5.3 Auxiliary Drains for Dry Pipe Systems and Preaction Systems in Areas Subject to Freezing.

4-5.3.5.3.1 When capacity of trapped sections of pipe is less than 5 gal (18.9 L), the auxiliary drain shall consist of a valve not smaller than ¹/₂ in. (12 mm) and a plug or a nipple and cap.

Exception: *Auxiliary drains are not required for pipe drops supplying dry-pendent sprinklers installed in accordance with 3-2.2.*

4-5.3.5.3.2 When the capacity of isolated trapped sections of system piping is more than 5 gal (18.9 L), the auxiliary drain shall consist of two 1-in. (25-mm) valves and one 2-in. by 12-in. (51-mm by 305-mm) condensate nipple or equivalent, accessibly located. *(See Figure 4-5.3.5.3.2.)*

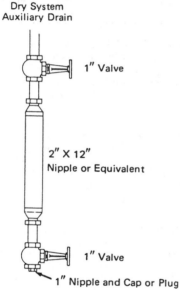

Dry System
Auxiliary Drain

1″ Valve

2″ X 12″
Nipple or Equivalent

1″ Valve

1″ Nipple and Cap or Plug

For SI Units: 1 in. = 25.4 mm; 1 ft = 0.3048 m.

Figure 4-5.3.5.3.2 Dry system auxiliary drain.

4-5.3.5.3.3 Tie-in drains shall be provided for multiple adjacent trapped branch pipes and shall only be 1 in. (25.4 mm). Tie-in drain lines shall be pitched a minimum of ¹/₂ in. per 10 ft (4 mm/m).

4-5.3.6 Discharge of Drain Valves.

4-5.3.6.1* Direct interconnections shall not be made between sprinkler drains and sewers. The drain discharge shall conform to any health or water department regulations.

4-5.3.6.2 When drain pipes are buried underground, approved corrosion-resistant pipe shall be used.

4-5.3.6.3 ·Drain pipes shall not terminate in blind spaces under the building.

4-5.3.6.4 When exposed to the atmosphere, drain pipes shall be fitted with a turned down elbow.

4-5.3.6.5 Drain pipes shall be arranged to avoid exposing any part of the sprinkler system to freezing conditions.

4-5.4 Protection of Piping.

4-5.4.1 Protection of Piping against Freezing.

4-5.4.1.1 When portions of systems are subject to freezing and temperatures cannot reliably be maintained at or above 40°F (4°C), sprinklers shall be installed as a dry pipe or preaction system.

Exception: *Small unheated areas are permitted to be protected by antifreeze systems or by other systems specifically listed for this purpose. (See 3-5.2.)*

4-5.4.1.2 When water-filled supply pipes, risers, system risers, or feed mains pass through open areas, cold rooms, passageways, or other areas exposed to freezing, the pipe shall be protected against freezing by insulating coverings, frostproof casings, or other reliable means capable of maintaining a minimum temperature of 40°F (4°C).

4-5.4.2 Protection of Piping against Corrosion.

4-5.4.2.1* When corrosive conditions are known to exist due to moisture or fumes from corrosive chemicals or both, special types of fittings, pipes, and hangers that resist corrosion shall be used or a protective coating shall be applied to all unprotected exposed surfaces of the sprinkler system. *(See 2-2.4.)*

4-5.4.2.2 When water supplies are known to have unusual corrosive properties and threaded or cut groove steel pipe is to be used, wall thickness shall be in accordance with Schedule 30 [in sizes 8 in. (203 mm) or larger] or Schedule 40 [in sizes less than 8 in. (203 mm)].

4-5.4.2.3 Steel pipe, when exposed to weather, shall be externally galvanized or otherwise protected against corrosion.

4-5.4.2.4 When steel pipe is used underground the pipe shall be protected against corrosion.

4-5.4.3 Protection of Piping against Damage Where Subject to Earthquakes.

4-5.4.3.1* General. Sprinkler systems shall be protected to prevent pipe breakage where subject to earthquakes in accordance with the requirements of 4-5.4.3.

Exception: *Alternative methods of providing earthquake protection of sprinkler systems based on a dynamic seismic analysis certified by a registered professional engineer such that system performance will be at least equal to that of the building structure under expected seismic forces.*

4-5.4.3.2* Couplings. Listed flexible pipe couplings joining grooved end pipe shall be provided as flexure joints to allow individual sections of piping 3½ in. (89 mm) or larger to move differentially with the individual sections of the building to which it is attached. Couplings shall be arranged to coincide with structural separations within a building. They shall be installed:

(a) Within 24 in. (610 mm) of the top and bottom of all risers.

Exception No. 1: In risers less than 3 ft (0.9 m) in length flexible couplings are permitted to be omitted.

Exception No. 2: In risers 3 to 7 ft (0.9 to 2.1 m) in length, one flexible coupling is adequate.

(b) Within 12 in. (305 mm) above or below the floor in multistory buildings.

(c) On one side of concrete or masonry walls within 3 ft (0.9 m) of the wall surface.

(d)* At or near building expansion joints.

(e) Within 24 in. of the ceiling at the top of drops to hose lines, rack sprinklers, and mezzanines, regardless of pipe size.

(f) Within 24 in. of the ceiling at the top of drops exceeding 15 ft (4.6 m) in length to portions of systems supplying more than one sprinkler, regardless of pipe size.

4-5.4.3.3* Seismic Separation Assembly. Seismic separation assemblies with flexible fittings shall be installed where sprinkler piping, regardless of size, crosses building seismic separation joints above ground level.

4-5.4.3.4* Clearance. Clearance shall be provided around all piping extending through walls, floors, platforms, and foundations, including drains, fire department connections, and other auxiliary piping.

(a) Minimum clearance on all sides shall be not less than 1 in. (25 mm) for pipes 1 in. (25 mm) through 3½ in. (89 mm), and 2 in. (51 mm) for pipe sizes 4 in. (102 mm) and larger.

Exception No. 1: When clearance is provided by a pipe sleeve, a nominal diameter 2 in. (51 mm) larger than the nominal diameter of the pipe is acceptable for pipe sizes 1 in. (25 mm) through 3½ in. (89 mm), and the clearance provided by a pipe sleeve of nominal diameter 4 in. (102 mm) larger than the nominal diameter of the pipe is acceptable for pipe sizes 4 in. (102 mm) and larger.

Exception No. 2: No clearance is necessary for piping passing through gypsum board or equally frangible construction that is not required to have a fire-resistance rating.

Exception No. 3: No clearance is necessary if flexible couplings or swing joints are located within 1 ft (0.3 m) of each side of a wall.

(b) When required the clearance shall be filled with a flexible material such as mastic.

4-5.4.3.5 Sway Bracing.

4-5.4.3.5.1* Both lateral and longitudinal sway braces shall be sized and fastened to the structure such that the horizontal loads assigned to the braces in Table 4-5.4.3.5.1(a) do not exceed the allowable loads on the braces as shown in Table 4-5.4.3.5.1(b) and the allowable loads on fasteners as shown in Table 4-5.4.3.5.1(c). Sway bracing shall be tight and concentric. All parts and fittings of a brace shall lie in a straight line to avoid eccentric loadings on fittings and fasteners. For longitudinal braces only, the brace shall be permitted to be connected to a tab welded to the pipe in conformance with 2-5.2. The structural component shall be capable of carrying the added applied loads.

Exception: In lieu of using Table 4-5.4.3.5.1(a), horizontal loads for braces shall be permitted to be determined by analysis. Sway braces shall be designed to withstand a force in tension or compression equivalent to not less than half the weight of water-filled piping. For lateral braces, the load shall include all branch lines and mains within the zone of influence of the brace. For longitudinal braces, the load shall include all mains within the zone of influence of the brace. For individual braces the slenderness ratio l/r shall not exceed 200, where l is the length of the brace and r is the least radius of gyration, both in inches.

Table 4-5.4.3.5.1(a)   Assigned Load Table (Based on half the weight of the water-filled pipe)

Spacing of Lateral Braces (ft)	Spacing of Longitudinal Braces** (ft)	Assigned Load for Pipe Size to Be Braced (lb)						
		2	2½	3	4	5	6	8
10	20	380	395	410	435	470	655	915
20	40	760	785	815	870	940	1305	1830
25	50	950	980	1020	1090	1175	1630	2290
30	60	1140	1180	1225	1305	1410	1960	2745
40	80	1515	1570	1630	1740	1880	2610	3660
50*		1895	1965	2035	2175	2350	3260	4575

*Permitted only under Exception No. 4 to 4-5.4.3.5.4.
**If branch lines are provided with lateral bracing or hung with U-hooks bent out at least 30 degrees from vertical, half the assigned load may be used for longitudinal braces.

TABLE 4-5.4.3.5.1(b)

Shape and Size	Least Radius of Gyration	Maximum Length for l/r = 200	Maximum Horizontal Load (lb)		
			30° Angle from Vertical	45° Angle from Vertical	60° Angle from Vertical
Pipe (Schedule 40)	$= \dfrac{\sqrt{r_0^2 + r_i^2}}{2}$				
1 in.	.42	7 ft 0 in.	1767	2500	3061
$1\frac{1}{4}$ in.	.54	9 ft 0 in.	2393	3385	4145
$1\frac{1}{2}$ in.	.623	10 ft 4 in.	2858	4043	4955
2 in.	.787	13 ft 1 in.	3828	5414	6630
Pipe (Schedule 10)	$= \dfrac{\sqrt{r_0^2 + r_i^2}}{2}$				
1 in.	.43	7 ft 2 in.	1477	2090	2559
$1\frac{1}{4}$ in.	.55	9 ft 2 in.	1900	2687	3291
$1\frac{1}{2}$ in.	.634	10 ft 7 in.	2194	3103	3800
2 in.	.802	13 ft 4 in.	2771	3926	4803
Angles					
$1\frac{1}{2} \times 1\frac{1}{2} \times \frac{1}{4}$	.292	4 ft 10 in.	2461	3481	4263
$2 \times 2 \times \frac{1}{4}$	.391	6 ft 6 in.	3356	4746	5813
$2\frac{1}{2} \times 2 \times \frac{1}{4}$	.424	7 ft 0 in.	3792	5363	6569
$2\frac{1}{2} \times 2\frac{1}{2} \times \frac{1}{4}$	.491	8 ft 2 in.	4257	6021	7374
$3 \times 2\frac{1}{2} \times \frac{1}{4}$	.528	8 ft 10 in.	4687	6628	8118
$3 \times 3 \times \frac{1}{4}$	.592	9 ft 10 in.	5152	7286	8923
Rods	$= \dfrac{r}{2}$				
$\frac{3}{8}$	.094	1 ft 6 in.	395	559	685
$\frac{1}{2}$	.125	2 ft 6 in.	702	993	1217
$\frac{5}{8}$	.156	2 ft 7 in.	1087	1537	1883
$\frac{3}{4}$	.188	3 ft 1 in.	1580	2235	2737
$\frac{7}{8}$	.219	3 ft 7 in.	2151	3043	3726
Flats	= 0.29 h (where h is smaller of two side dimensions)				
$1\frac{1}{2} \times \frac{1}{4}$	.0725	1 ft 2 in.	1118	1581	1936
$2 \times \frac{1}{4}$ in.	.0725	1 ft 2 in.	1789	2530	3098
$2 \times \frac{3}{8}$	.109	1 ft 9 in.	2683	3795	4648

Table 4-5.4.3.5.1(c) Maximum Loads for Various Types of Structure

Maximum Loads for Various Types of Fasteners to Structure

NOTE: Loads (given in pounds) are keyed to vertical angles of braces and orientation of connecting surface. These values are based on concentric loadings of the fastener. Use figures to determine proper reference within table. For angles between those shown, use most restrictive case. Braces should not be attached to light structure members.

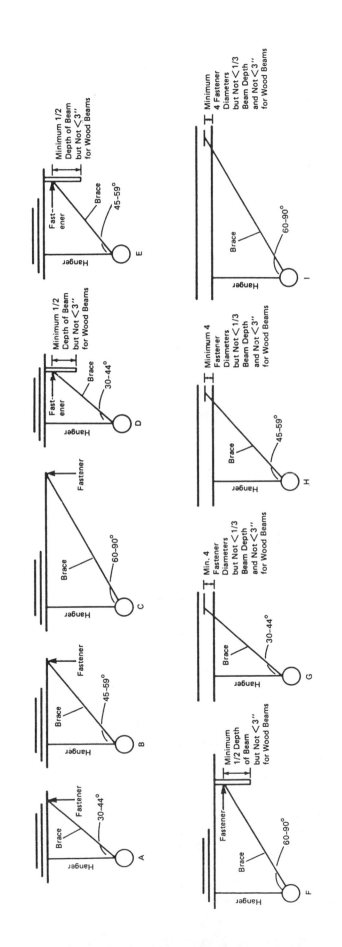

Lag Screws in Wood (load perpendicular to grain—holes predrilled using good practice)

Shank Diameter of Lag (in.)

Length Under Head (in.)	3/8									1/2									5/8									7/8								
	A	B	C	D	E	F	G	H	I	A	B	C	D	E	F	G	H	I	A	B	C	D	E	F	G	H	I	A	B	C	D	E	F	G	H	I
3	304	325	292	168	325	526	230	324	400	366	—	—	—	—	834	—	—	626	410	—	—	—	—	716	—	—	—	487	—	—	—	—	843	—	—	—
4	392	354	317	183	354	678	250	352	435	473	509	456	264	509	818	360	507	670	538	—	—	—	—	532	—	—	—	548	—	—	—	—	1122	—	—	—
5	476	375	336	194	375	824	265	373	461	582	545	488	282	545	1008	385	542	687	687	728	653	277	728	1154	515	725	896	813	—	—	—	—	1407	—	—	—
6	564	382	342	196	382	976	270	380	470	689	559	501	209	559	1192	395	556	687	791	778	697	403	778	1360	550	775	957	971	—	1223	685	1365	1630	—	—	—
8	—	—	—	—	—	—	—	—	—	905	573	513	296	573	1586	405	570	704	1044	806	723	416	806	1807	570	803	991	1297	1365	1223	685	1365	2244	965	1359	1678

Table 4-5.4.3.5.1(c) Maximum Loads for Various Types of Structure (cont.)

Through Bolts in wood (load perpendicular to grain)
Diameter of Bolt (in.)

3/8

Length of Bolt in Timber (in.)	ABCE	D	F	G	H	I
1½	300	173	519	150	211	261
2	370	214	641	185	261	322
2½	460	266	796	230	324	400
3	480	277	831	240	338	417
3⅞	460	268	797	230	324	400
5½	—	—	—	—	—	—

1/2

Length of Bolt in Timber (in.)	ABCE	D	F	G	H	I
1½	340	197	589	170	239	296
2	420	243	727	210	296	365
2½	550	318	952	275	387	478
3	630	364	1091	315	444	548
3⅞	720	416	1247	360	507	626
5½	680	393	1177	340	479	591

5/8

Length of Bolt in Timber (in.)	ABCE	D	F	G	H	I
1½	390	225	675	195	275	339
2	470	272	814	235	331	409
2½	620	358	1074	310	437	539
3	710	410	1229	355	500	617
3⅞	850	491	1472	425	599	739
5½	1020	590	1766	510	718	887

7/8

Length of Bolt in Timber (in.)	ABCE	D	F	G	H	I
1½	470	272	614	235	331	409
2	580	335	1004	290	408	504
2½	760	439	1316	380	535	661
3	870	503	1506	435	613	757
3⅞	1050	607	1818	525	739	913
5½	1580	913	2736	790	1113	1374

Expansion Shields in Concrete
Diameter of Bolt (in.)

3/8

Min. Depth of Hole (in.)	A	B	C	D	E	F	G	H	I
2½	498	962	1173	678	962	962	925	1303	1609
3¼	-	-	-	-	-	-	925	1303	1609
3¾	-	-	-	-	-	-	925	1303	1609
4½	-	-	-	-	-	-	925	1303	1609

1/2

Min. Depth of Hole (in.)	A	B	C	D	E	F	G	H	I
2½	-	-	-	-	-	-	1638	2306	2848
3¼	923	1782	2076	1200	1782	1597	1638	2306	2848
3¾	-	-	-	-	-	-	1638	2306	2848
4½	-	-	-	-	-	-	1638	2306	2848

5/8

Min. Depth of Hole (in.)	A	B	C	D	E	F	G	H	I
2½	-	-	-	-	-	-	2080	2930	3617
3¼	-	-	-	-	-	-	2080	2930	3617
3¾	1480	2857	2637	1524	2857	2581	2080	2930	3617
4½	-	-	-	-	-	-	2080	2930	3617

7/8

Min. Depth of Hole (in.)	A	B	C	D	E	F	G	H	I
2½	-	-	-	-	-	-	2470	4113	5078
3¼	-	-	-	-	-	-	2970	4113	5078
3¾	-	-	-	-	-	-	2970	4113	5078
4½	3070	4130	3702	2139	4130	5312	2970	4113	5078

Connections to Steel (values assume bolt perpendicular to mounting surface)
Diameter of Unfinished Steel Bolt (in.)

Diameter	A	B	C	D	E	F	G	H	I
1/4	400	500	600	300	500	650	325	458	565
3/8	900	1200	1400	800	1200	1550	735	1035	1278
1/2	1600	2050	2550	1450	2050	2850	1300	1830	2260
5/8	2500	3300	3950	2250	3300	4400	2045	2880	3557

For SI Units: 1 in. = 25.4 mm.

4-5.4.3.5.2 Longitudinal sway bracing spaced at a maximum of 80 ft (24 m) on center shall be provided for feed and cross mains.

4-5.4.3.5.3* Tops of risers shall be secured against drifting in any direction, utilizing a four-way sway brace.

4-5.4.3.5.4 Lateral sway bracing spaced at a maximum of 40 ft (12 m) on center shall be provided for feed and cross mains.

Exception No. 1: Lateral sway bracing shall be permitted to be omitted on pipes individually supported by rods less than 6 in. (152 mm) long.

Exception No. 2: Wraparound U-type hangers used to support the mains shall be permitted to be used to satisfy the requirements for lateral sway bracing provided the legs are bent out at least 30 degrees from the vertical and the maximum length of each leg satisfies the conditions of Table 4-5.4.3.5.1(b).

Exception No. 3: When flexible couplings are installed on mains other than as required in 4-5.4.3.2, a lateral brace shall be provided within 24 in. (610 mm) of every other coupling, but not more than 40 ft (12 m) on center.

Exception No. 4: When building primary structural members exceed 40 ft (12 m) on center, lateral braces shall be permitted to be spaced up to 50 ft (15.2 m) on center.

4-5.4.3.5.5 Bracing shall be attached directly to feed and cross mains.

4-5.4.3.5.6 A length of pipe shall not be braced to sections of the building that will move differentially.

4-5.4.3.5.7 The last length of pipe at the end of a feed or cross main shall be provided with a lateral brace. Lateral braces may also act as longitudinal braces if they are within 24 in. (610 mm) of the center line of the piping braced longitudinally.

4-5.4.3.5.8* Sway bracing is not required for branch lines.

Exception No. 1: The end sprinkler on a line shall be restrained against excessive movement by use of a wraparound U-hook (see Figure A-2-6.1) or by other approved means.

Exception No. 2: Branch lines 2¹/₂ in. (64 mm) or larger shall be provided with lateral bracing in accordance with 4-5.4.3.5.4.

Exception No. 3: Where upward or lateral movement of sprinklers would result in an impact against the building structure, equipment, or finish materials, branch lines shall be provided at intervals not exceeding 30 ft (9 m) with a wraparound U-hook, lateral sway brace, or #12, 440 lb (200 kg) splayed seismic brace wire installed at least 45 degrees from the vertical plane and anchored on both sides of the pipe. This bracing shall be located within 2 ft (610 mm) of a hanger. The hanger closest to a splayed wire restraint shall be of a type that resists upward movement of a branch line.

4-5.4.3.5.9 C-type clamps (including beam and large flange clamps) used to attach hangers to the building structure in areas subject to earthquakes shall be equipped with a retaining strap or other approved means to prevent movement. (*See Figure A-2-6.1.*)

4-5.4.3.5.10 C-type clamps (including beam and large flange clamps), with or without retaining straps, shall not be used to attach braces to the building structure.

4-6 System Attachments.

4-6.1 Sprinkler Alarms.

4-6.1.1* Waterflow Alarms.

4-6.1.1.1 Local waterflow alarms shall be provided on all sprinkler systems having more than 20 sprinklers.

4-6.1.1.2 On each alarm check valve used under conditions of variable water pressure, a retarding device shall be installed. Valves shall be provided in the connections to retarding devices to permit repair or removal without shutting off sprinklers; these valves shall be so arranged that they may be locked or sealed in the open position.

4-6.1.1.3 Alarm, dry pipe, preaction, and deluge valves shall be fitted with an alarm bypass test connection for an electric alarm switch, water motor gong, or both. This pipe connection shall be made on the water supply side of the system and provided with a control valve and drain for the alarm piping. A check valve shall be installed in the pipe connection from the intermediate chamber of a dry pipe valve.

4-6.1.1.4 An indicating control valve shall be installed in the connection to pressure-type contactors or water-motor-operated alarm devices. Such valves shall be locked or sealed in the open position. The control valve for the retarding chamber on alarm check valves shall be accepted as complying with this paragraph.

4-6.1.1.5* Attachments — Mechanically Operated. For all types of sprinkler systems employing water-motor-operated alarms, a listed ³/₄-in. (19-mm) strainer shall be installed at the alarm outlet of the waterflow detecting device.

Exception: When a retarding chamber is used in connection with an alarm valve, the strainer shall be located at the outlet of the retarding chamber unless the retarding chamber is provided with an approved integral strainer in its outlet.

4-6.1.1.6* Alarm Attachments — High-Rise Buildings. When a fire must be fought internally due to the height of a building, the following additional alarm apparatus shall be provided:

(a) When each sprinkler system on each floor is equipped with a separate waterflow device, it shall be connected to an alarm system in such a manner that operation of one sprinkler will actuate the alarm system and the location of the operated flow device shall be indicated on an annunciator and/or register. The annunciator or register shall be located at grade level at the normal point of fire department access, at a constantly attended building security control center, or at both locations.

Exception: When the location within the protected buildings where supervisory or alarm signals are received is not under constant supervision by qualified personnel in the employ of the owner, a connection shall be provided to transmit a signal to a remote central station.

(b) A distinct trouble signal shall be provided to indicate a condition that will impair the satisfactory operation of the sprinkler system.

4-6.2* Fire Department Connections.

4-6.2.1* A fire department connection shall be provided as described in this section. (See Figure 4-6.2.1.)

Exception No. 1: Omission of the fire department connection shall be permitted for systems having 20 sprinklers or less.

Exception No. 2: Omission of the fire department connection shall be permitted when approved by the authority having jurisdiction.

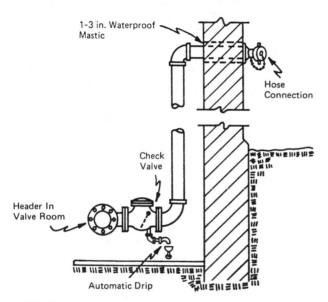

For SI Units: 1 in. = 25.4 mm.

Figure 4-6.2.1   Fire department connection.

4-6.2.2 Size. Pipe size shall be 4 in. (102 mm) for fire engine connections and 6 in. (152 mm) for fire boat connections.

Exception No. 1: For hydraulically calculated systems, fire department connection pipe as small as the system riser shall be permitted when serving one system riser.

Exception No. 2: A single outlet fire department connection shall be acceptable when piped to a 3-in. (76-mm) or smaller riser.

4-6.2.3* Arrangement. (See Figure 4-6.2.1.)

4-6.2.3.1 The fire department connection shall be on the system side of the water supply check valve.

4-6.2.3.2 For single systems, the fire department connection shall be installed as follows:

(a) *Wet System.* On the system side of system control, check, and alarm valves. (See Figure A-4-5.1.1.)

(b) *Dry System.* Between the system control valve and the dry pipe valve.

(c) *Preaction System.* Between the preaction valve and the check valve on the system side of the preaction valve.

(d) *Deluge System.* On the system side of the deluge valve.

Exception: Connection of the fire department connection to underground piping is acceptable.

4-6.2.3.3 For multiple systems, the fire department connection shall be connected between the supply control valves and the system control valves.

Exception: Connection of the fire department connection to underground piping is acceptable.

4-6.2.3.4 Fire department connections shall be located and arranged so that hose can be readily and conveniently attached.

Each fire department connection to sprinkler systems shall be designated by a sign having raised letters at least 1 in. (25.4 mm) in height cast on plate or fitting reading service design, e.g., "AUTOSPKR.," "OPEN SPKR. AND STANDPIPE."

4-6.2.3.5 Fire department connections shall not be connected on the suction side of fire pumps.

4-6.2.4 Valves.

4-6.2.4.1 A listed check valve shall be installed in each fire department connection.

4-6.2.4.2 There shall be no shutoff valve in the fire department connection piping.

4-6.2.5 Drainage. The piping between the check valve and the outside hose coupling shall be equipped with an approved automatic drip.

Exception: An automatic drip is not required in areas not subject to freezing.

4-6.3 Gauges.

4-6.3.1 A pressure gauge with a connection not smaller than $1/4$ in. (6.4 mm) shall be installed at the system main drain, at each main drain associated with a floor control valve, and on the inlet and outlet side of each pressure reducing valve. Each gauge connection shall be equipped with a shutoff valve and provisions for draining.

4-6.3.2 The required pressure gauges shall be listed and shall have a maximum limit not less than twice the normal working pressure at the point where installed. They shall be installed to permit removal and shall be located where they will not be subject to freezing.

4-6.4 System Test Connections.

4-6.4.1 Waterflow Test Connections. Waterflow test connections shall be provided at locations that will permit flow tests of water supplies and connections. They shall be so

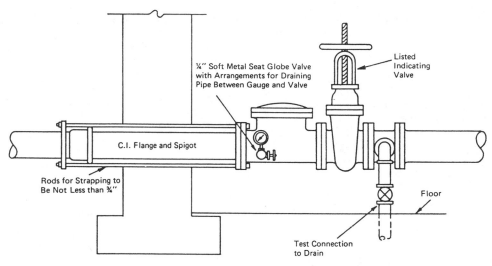

For SI Units: 1 in. = 25.4 mm.

Figure 4-6.4.1 Water supply connection with test connection.

installed that the valve may be opened wide for a sufficient time to assure a proper test without causing water damage. (See 4-5.3.4 and 4-5.3.6.)

4-6.4.2* Wet Pipe Systems. A test connection not less than 1 in. (25 mm) in diameter, terminating in a smooth bore corrosion-resistant orifice, giving a flow equivalent to one sprinkler of a type having the smallest orifice installed on the particular system, shall be provided to test each waterflow alarm device for each system. The test connection valve shall be readily accessible. The discharge shall be to the outside, to a drain connection capable of accepting full flow under system pressure, or to another location where water damage will not result.

4-6.4.3* Dry Pipe Systems. A test connection not less than 1 in. (25 mm) in diameter, terminating in a smooth bore corrosion-resistant orifice, to provide a flow equivalent to one sprinkler of a type installed on the particular system, shall be installed on the end of the most distant sprinkler pipe in the upper story and be equipped with a readily accessible 1-in. (22-mm) shutoff valve and plug, at least one of which shall be brass. In lieu of a plug, a nipple and cap shall be acceptable.

4-6.4.4 Preaction Systems. A test connection shall be provided on a preaction system using supervisory air. The connection used to control the level of priming water is adequate to test the operation of the alarms monitoring the supervisory air pressure.

4-6.4.5 Deluge Systems. A test connection is not required on a deluge system.

Chapter 5   Design Approaches

5-1 General. Water demand requirements shall be determined from the occupancy hazard fire control approach of Section 5-2.

Exception: Special design approaches shall be permitted for specific hazards in Section 5-3.

5-2 Occupancy Hazard Fire Control Approach.

5-2.1 Occupancy Classifications.

5-2.1.1 Occupancy classifications for this standard relate to sprinkler installations and their water supplies only. They shall not be used as a general classification of occupancy hazards.

5-2.1.2 Occupancies or portions of occupancies shall be classified according to the quantity and combustibility of contents, the expected rates of heat release, the total potential for energy release, the heights of stockpiles, and the presence of flammable and combustible liquids, using the definitions contained in 1-4.7. Classifications are as follows:

Light Hazard

Ordinary Hazard (Groups 1 and 2)

Extra Hazard (Groups 1 and 2)

Special Occupancy Hazard

5-2.2 Water Demand Requirements—Pipe Schedule Method.

5-2.2.1 Table 5-2.2 shall be used in determining the minimum water supply requirements for Light and Ordinary Hazard Occupancies protected by systems with pipe sized according to the pipe schedules of Section 6-5. Pressure and flow requirements for Extra Hazard Occupancies shall be based on the hydraulic calculation methods of 5-2.3. The pipe schedule method shall be permitted only for new installations of 5000 sq ft (465 m²) or less or for additions or modifications to existing pipe schedule systems.

Exception No. 1:   The pipe schedule design method shall be permitted for use in systems exceeding 5000 sq ft (465 m²) when the flows required in Table 5-2.2 are available at a minimum residual pressure of 50 psi (3.4 bar) at the elevation of the highest sprinkler.

Exception No. 2:   The pipe schedule method shall be permitted for additions or modifications to existing extra hazard pipe schedule systems if the pressures and flows are determined to be acceptable to the authority having jurisdiction.

5-2.2.2   The lower duration value of Table 5-2.2 shall be acceptable only where remote station or central station waterflow alarm service is provided.

5-2.2.3*   The residual pressure requirement of Table 5-2.2 shall be met at the elevation of the highest sprinkler. *(See the Exceptions to 5-2.2.1.)*

5-2.2.4   The lower flow figure of Table 5-2.2 shall be permitted only where the building is of noncombustible construction or the potential areas of fire are limited by building size or compartmentation such that no open areas exceed 3000 sq ft (279 m²) for Light Hazard or 4000 sq ft (372 m²) for Ordinary Hazard.

Table 5-2.2   Water Supply Requirements for Pipe Schedule Sprinkler Systems

Occupancy Classification	Minimum Residual Pressure Required	Acceptable Flow at Base of Riser	Duration in Minutes
Light Hazard	15 psi	500-750 gpm	30-60
Ordinary Hazard	20 psi	850-1500 gpm	60-90

For SI Units: 1 gpm = 3.785L/min; 1 psi = 0.0689 bar.

5-2.3 Water Demand Requirements—Hydraulic Calculation Methods.

5-2.3.1 General.

5-2.3.1.1*   The minimum water supply requirements for a hydraulically designed occupancy hazard fire control sprinkler system shall be determined by adding the hose stream demand from Table 5-2.3 to the water supply for sprinklers determined in 5-2.3.1.2. This supply shall be available for the minimum duration specified in Table 5-2.3.

Exception No. 1:   Where other NFPA standards have developed sprinkler system area/density or other design criteria and water supply requirements appropriate for fire control or suppression of Special Occupancy Hazards, they shall take precedence.

Exception No. 2:   An allowance for inside and outside hose shall not be required when tanks supply sprinklers only.

Exception No. 3:   When pumps taking suction from a private fire service main supply sprinklers only, the pump need not be sized to accommodate inside and outside hose. Such hose allowance shall be considered in evaluating the available water supplies.

5-2.3.1.2   The water supply for sprinklers only shall be determined either from the area/density curves of Figure 5-2.3 *(see following page)* in accordance with the method of 5-2.3.2 or be based upon the room design method in accordance with 5-2.3.3, at the discretion of the designer. For special areas under consideration, as described in 5-2.3.4, separate hydraulic calculations shall be required in addition to those required by 5-2.3.2 or 5-2.3.3.

Table 5-2.3   Hose Stream Demand and Water Supply Duration Requirements

Hazard Classification	Inside Hose (gpm)	Total Combined Inside and Outside Hose (gpm)	Duration in Minutes
Light	0, 50, or 100	100	30
Ordinary	0, 50, or 100	250	60-90
Extra Hazard	0, 50, or 100	500	90-120

For SI Units: 1 gpm = 3.785L/min.

5-2.3.1.3   Regardless of which of the two methods is used, the following restrictions apply:

(a) For areas of sprinkler operation less than 1500 sq ft (139 m²) used for Light and Ordinary Hazard Occupancies, the density for 1500 sq ft (139 m²) shall be used. For areas of sprinkler operation less than 2500 sq ft (232 m²) for Extra Hazard Occupancies, the density for 2500 sq ft (232 m²) shall be used.

(b)* For buildings having unsprinklered combustible concealed spaces (as described in 4-4.1.7.1.1) the minimum area of sprinkler operation shall be 3000 sq ft (279 m²).

Exception No. 1:   Combustible concealed spaces filled entirely with noncombustible insulation.

Exception No. 2:   Light or Ordinary Hazard Occupancies where noncombustible or limited combustible ceilings are directly attached to the bottom of solid wood joists so as to create enclosed joist spaces 160 cu ft (4.8 m³) or less in volume.

Exception No. 3:   *Concealed spaces where the exposed surfaces have a flame spread rating of 25 or less and the materials have been demonstrated to not propagate fire in the form in which they are installed in the space.*

(c) Water demand of sprinklers installed in racks or water curtains shall be added to the ceiling sprinkler water demand at the point of connection. Demands shall be balanced to the higher pressure. (See Chapter 6.)

Water demand of sprinklers installed in concealed spaces or under obstructions such as ducts and cutting tables need not be added to ceiling demand.

(d) When inside hose stations are planned or are required by other standards, a total water allowance of 50 gpm (189 L/min) for a single hose station installation or 100 gpm (378 L/min) for a multiple hose station installation shall be added to the sprinkler requirements. The water allowance shall be added in 50 gpm (189 L/min) increments beginning at the most remote hose station, with each increment added at the pressure required by the sprinkler system design at that point.

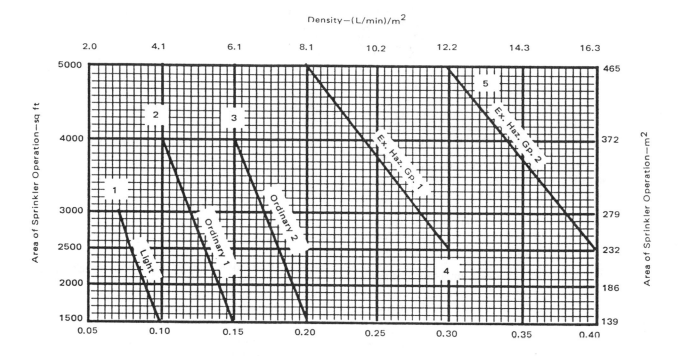

For SI Units: 1 sq ft = 0.0929 m², 1 gpm/sq ft = 40.746 (L/min)/m².

Figure 5-2.3   Area/density curves.

(e) When hose valves for fire department use are attached to wet pipe sprinkler system risers in accordance with 4-4.1.7.24, the water supply need not be added to standpipe demand as determined from NFPA 14, *Standard for the Installation of Standpipe and Hose Systems.*

Exception No. 1:   When the combined sprinkler system demand and hose stream allowance of Table 5-2.3 exceeds the requirements of NFPA 14, Standard for the Installation of Standpipe and Hose Systems, this higher demand shall be used.

Exception No. 2:   For partially sprinklered buildings, the sprinkler demand, not including hose stream allowance, as indicated in Table 5-2.3 shall be added to the requirements given in NFPA 14, Standard for the Installation of Standpipe and Hose Systems.

(f) Water allowance for outside hose shall be added to the sprinkler and inside hose requirement at the connection to the city water main, or a yard hydrant, whichever is closer to the system riser.

(g) The lower duration values in Table 5-2.3 shall be permitted where remote station or central station water-flow alarm service is provided.

(h) When pumps, gravity tanks, or pressure tanks supply sprinklers only, requirements for inside and outside hose need not be considered in determining the size of such pumps or tanks.

5-2.3.1.4   Total system water supply requirements shall be determined in accordance with the hydraulic calculation procedures of Section 6-4.

5-2.3.2   Area/Density Method.

5-2.3.2.1   The water supply requirement for sprinklers only shall be calculated from the area/density curves in Figure 5-2.3. The calculations shall satisfy any single point on the appropriate area/density curve as follows:

(a) Light Hazard	Area/Density Curve 1
(b) Ordinary Hazard (Group 1)	Area/Density Curve 2
(c) Ordinary Hazard (Group 2)	Area/Density Curve 3
(d) Extra Hazard (Group 1)	Area/Density Curve 4
(e) Extra Hazard (Group 2)	Area/Density Curve 5

It is not necessary to meet all points on the selected curve.

5-2.3.2.2   The densities and areas provided in Figure 5-2.3 are for use only with spray sprinklers. For use with other types of sprinklers see Section 5-3.

Exception No. 1:   Quick-response sprinklers shall be permitted for use with Area/Density Curve 1 (Light Hazard) and Curves 2 and 3 (Ordinary Hazard) of Figure 5-2.3.

Exception No. 2:   Sidewall spray sprinklers shall be permitted for use with Area/Density Curve 1 (Light Hazard) and, if specifically listed, with Area/Density Curves 2 or 3 (Ordinary Hazard).

5-2.3.2.3   For dry pipe systems, the area of sprinkler operation shall be increased by 30 percent without revising the density.

5-2.3.2.4 When high temperature sprinklers are used for Extra Hazard Occupancies, the area of sprinkler operation shall be permitted to be reduced by 25 percent without revising the density, but to not less than 2000 sq ft (186 m²).

5-2.3.3 Room Design Method.

5-2.3.3.1* The water supply requirements for sprinklers only shall be based upon the room that creates the greatest demand. The density selected shall be that from Figure 5-2.3 corresponding to the room size. To utilize this method, all rooms shall be enclosed with walls having a fire-resistance rating equal to the water supply duration indicated in Table 5-2.3.

5-2.3.3.2 If the room is smaller than the smallest area shown in the applicable curve in Figure 5-2.3, the provisions of 5-2.3.1.3(a) shall apply.

5-2.3.3.3 Minimum protection of openings shall be as follows:

(a) Light Hazard — automatic or self-closing doors.

Exception: When openings are not protected, calculations shall include the sprinklers in the room plus two sprinklers in the communicating space nearest each such unprotected opening unless the communicating space has only one sprinkler, in which case calculations shall be extended to the operation of that sprinkler. The selection of the room and communicating space sprinklers to be calculated shall be that which produces the greatest hydraulic demand.

(b) Ordinary and Extra Hazard — automatic or self-closing doors with appropriate fire resistance ratings for the enclosure.

5-2.3.4 Special Design Methods.

5-2.3.4.1 When the design area consists of a building service chute supplied by a separate riser, the maximum number of sprinklers that needs to be calculated is 3.

5-2.3.4.2 When the room design method is used, and the area under consideration is a corridor protected by one row of sprinklers, the maximum number of sprinklers that needs to be calculated is 5. (See 5-2.3.1.)

Exception: Where the area under consideration is a corridor protected by a single row of sprinklers and the openings are not protected, the design area shall include all sprinklers in the corridor to a maximum of 7.

5-3 Special Design Approaches.

5-3.1 General. All special design approaches utilize the hydraulic calculation procedures of Section 6-4 except as specified.

5-3.2 Residential Sprinklers.

5-3.2.1 Sprinkler discharge rates shall be provided in accordance with minimum flow rates indicated in individual residential sprinkler listings, both for the single sprinkler discharge and the multiple sprinkler discharge of the design sprinklers.

5-3.2.2* The design area shall be that area that includes the 4 hydraulically most demanding sprinklers.

5-3.2.3 When areas such as attics, basements, or other types of occupancies are outside of dwelling units but within the same structure, these areas shall be protected in accordance with the provisions of this standard, including appropriate design criteria of 5-2.3.

5-3.2.4 Hose stream demand and water supply duration requirements shall be in accordance with those for Light Hazard Occupancies in Table 5-2.3.

5-3.3 Quick Response Early Suppression (QRES) Sprinklers. (Reserved) (*See 1-4.5.1 and A-1-4.5.1.*)

5-3.4* Large-Drop Sprinklers.

5-3.4.1 Protection shall be provided as specified in Table A-5-3.4 or appropriate NFPA standards in terms of minimum operating pressure and the number of sprinklers to be included in the design area.

5-3.4.2 Large-drop sprinkler systems shall be designed such that the minimum operating pressure is not less than 25 psi (170 kPa).

Exception: Lower pressures shall be permitted if proven successful by large-scale fire testing for a particular hazard.

5-3.4.3 For design purposes, 95 psi (650 kPa) shall be the maximum discharge pressure at the hydraulically most remote sprinkler.

5-3.4.4 The nominal diameter of branch line pipes (including riser nipples) shall be not less than 1¼ in. (33 mm) or greater than 2 in. (51 mm).

Exception No. 1: Starter pieces shall be permitted to be 2½ in. (64 mm).

Exception No. 2: When branch lines are larger than 2 in. (51 mm), the sprinkler shall be supplied by a riser nipple to elevate the sprinkler 13 in. (330 mm) for 2½-in. (64-mm) pipe and 15 in. (380 mm) for 3-in. (76-mm) pipe. These dimensions are measured from the centerline of the pipe to the deflector. In lieu of this, sprinklers may be offset horizontally a minimum of 12 in. (305 mm).

5-3.4.5 Hose stream demand and water supply duration requirements shall be in accordance with those for extra hazard occupancies in Table 5-2.3.

5-3.5* Early Suppression Fast Response (ESFR) Sprinklers.

5-3.5.1 ESFR sprinklers are suitable for use with the hazards listed in Table A-5-3.5 and may be used in other specific hazard classifications and configurations only when proven by large-scale or other suitable fire testing.

5-3.5.2 ESFR sprinkler systems shall be designed such that the minimum operating pressure is not less than 50 psi (340 kPa).

5-3.5.3 The design area shall consist of the most hydraulically demanding area of 12 sprinklers, consisting of 4 sprinklers on each of 3 branch lines. Design shall include a minimum of 960 sq ft (89 m^2).

5-3.5.4 Small hose stations shall be provided. Hose stream water demand is not required to be added to total water demand.

5-3.5.5 Water supply duration shall be at least 60 minutes.

5-3.6 Exposure Protection.

5-3.6.1* Piping shall be hydraulically calculated in accordance with Section 6-4 to furnish a minimum of 7 psi (48 kPa) at any sprinkler with all sprinklers facing the exposure operating.

5-3.6.2 When the water supply feeds other fire protection systems, it shall be capable of furnishing total demand for such systems as well as the exposure system demand.

5-3.7 Water Curtains. Sprinklers in a water curtain as described in 4-4.1.7.3.4 shall be hydraulically designed to provide a discharge of 3 gpm per lineal foot [37 (L/min)/m] of water curtain, with no sprinklers discharging less than 15 gpm (56.8 L/min). The number of sprinklers calculated in this water curtain shall be the number in the length corresponding to the length parallel to the branch lines in the area determined by 6-4.4.1(a). The water supply for these sprinklers shall be added to the water supply required for the area of operation in hydraulically designed systems or to the water supply required as determined in accordance with Table 5-2.2. Supplies shall be balanced to the higher pressure demand in either case.

Chapter 6   Plans and Calculations

6-1* Working Plans.

6-1.1* Working plans shall be submitted for approval to the authority having jurisdiction before any equipment is installed or remodeled. Deviation from approved plans will require permission of the authority having jurisdiction.

6-1.1.1 Working plans shall be drawn to an indicated scale, on sheets of uniform size, with a plan of each floor, and shall show those items from the following list that pertain to the design of the system.

(a) Name of owner and occupant.

(b) Location, including street address.

(c) Point of compass.

(d) Full height cross section, or schematic diagram, if required for clarity; including ceiling construction and method of protection for nonmetallic piping.

(e) Location of partitions.

(f) Location of fire walls.

(g) Occupancy class of each area or room.

(h) Location and size of concealed spaces, closets, attics, and bathrooms.

(i) Any small enclosures in which no sprinklers are to be installed.

(j) Size of city main in street and whether dead-end or circulating; and, if dead-end, direction and distance to nearest circulating main. City main test results and system elevation relative to test hydrant (*see A-7-2.1*).

(k) Other sources of water supply, with pressure or elevation.

(l) Make, type, and nominal orifice size of sprinklers.

(m) Temperature rating and location of high-temperature sprinklers.

(n) Total area protected by each system on each floor.

(o) Number of sprinklers on each riser per floor.

(p) Total number of sprinklers on each dry pipe system, preaction system, combined dry pipe-preaction system, or deluge system.

(q) Approximate capacity in gallons of each dry pipe system.

(r) Pipe type and schedule of wall thickness.

(s) Nominal pipe size and cutting lengths of pipe (or center to center dimensions).

NOTE: Where typical branch lines prevail, it will be necessary to size only one typical line.

(t) Location and size of riser nipples.

(u) Type of fittings and joints and location of all welds and bends. The contractor shall specify on drawing any sections to be shop welded and the type of fittings or formations to be used.

(v) Type and locations of hangers, sleeves, braces, and methods of securing sprinklers when applicable.

(w) All control valves, check valves, drain pipes, and test connections.

(x) Make, type, model, and size of alarm or dry pipe valve.

(y) Make, type, model, and size of preaction or deluge valve.

(z) Kind and location of alarm bells.

(aa) Size and location of hose outlets, hand hose, and related equipment.

(bb) Underground pipe size, length, location, weight, material, point of connection to city main; the type of valves, meters, and valve pits; and the depth that top of the pipe is laid below grade.

(cc) Piping provisions for flushing (*see 9-3.2*).

(dd) When the equipment is to be installed as an addition to an existing system, enough of the existing system indicated on the plans to make all conditions clear.

(ee) For hydraulically designed systems, the information on the hydraulic data nameplate.

(ff) A graphic representation of the scale used on all plans.

(gg) Name and address of contractor.

(hh) Hydraulic reference points shown on the plan shall correspond with comparable reference points on the hydraulic calculation sheets.

(ii) The minimum rate of water application (density), the design area of water application, in-rack sprinkler demand, and the water required for hose streams both inside and outside.

(jj) The total quantity of water and the pressure required noted at a common reference point for each system.

(kk) Relative elevations of sprinklers, junction points, and supply or reference points.

(ll) If room design method is used, all unprotected wall openings throughout the floor protected.

(mm) Calculation of loads for sizing, and details of, sway bracing.

(nn) The setting for pressure reducing valves.

(oo) Information about backflow preventers (manufacturer, size, type).

(pp) Information about antifreeze solution used (type and amount).

6-1.1.2* Working plans for automatic sprinkler systems with nonfire protection connections. Special symbols shall be used and explained for auxiliary piping, pumps, heat exchangers, valves, strainers, and the like, clearly distinguishing these devices and piping runs from those of the sprinkler system. Model number, type, and manufacturer's name shall be identified for each piece of auxiliary equipment.

6-2 Hydraulic Calculation Forms.

6-2.1 General. Hydraulic calculations shall be prepared on form sheets that include a summary sheet, detailed work sheets, and a graph sheet. (*See copies of typical forms, Figures A-6-2.2(a), A-6-2.3, and A-6-2.4.*)

6-2.2* Summary Sheet. The summary sheet shall contain the following information, where applicable:

(a) Date

(b) Location

(c) Name of owner and occupant

(d) Building number or other identification

(e) Description of hazard

(f) Name and address of contractor or designer

(g) Name of approving agency

(h) System design requirements

1. Design area of water application, sq ft

2. Minimum rate of water application (density), gpm per sq ft

3. Area per sprinkler, sq ft

(i) Total water requirements as calculated including allowance for inside hose, outside hydrants, and water curtain and exposure sprinklers

(j) Allowance for in-rack sprinklers, gpm

(k) Limitations (dimension, flow, and pressure) on extended coverage or other listed special sprinklers.

6-2.3* Detailed Work Sheets. Detailed work sheets or computer printout sheets shall contain the following information:

(a) Sheet number

(b) Sprinkler description and discharge constant (K)

(c) Hydraulic reference points

(d) Flow in gpm

(e) Pipe size

(f) Pipe lengths, center to center of fittings

(g) Equivalent pipe lengths for fittings and devices

(h) Friction loss in psi per ft of pipe

(i) Total friction loss between reference points

(j) In-rack sprinkler demand balanced to ceiling demand

(k) Elevation head in psi between reference points

(l) Required pressure in psi at each reference point

(m) Velocity pressure and normal pressure if included in calculations

(n) Notes to indicate starting points, reference to other sheets, or to clarify data shown

(o)* Diagram to accompany gridded system calculations to indicate flow quantities and directions for lines with sprinklers operating in the remote area

(p) Combined K-factor calculations for sprinklers on drops, armovers, or sprigs where calculations do not begin at sprinkler.

6-2.4* Graph Sheet. A graphic representation of the complete hydraulic calculation shall be plotted on semilogarithmic graph paper ($Q^{1.85}$) and shall include the following:

(a) Water supply curve

(b) Sprinkler system demand

(c) Hose demand (where applicable)

(d) In-rack sprinkler demand (where applicable).

6-3 Water Supply Information. The following information shall be included:

(a) Location and elevation of static and residual test gauge with relation to the riser reference point

(b) Flow location

(c) Static pressure, psi

(d) Residual pressure, psi

(e) Flow, gpm

(f) Date

(g) Time

(h) Test conducted by or information supplied by

(i) Other sources of water supply, with pressure or elevation.

6-4 Hydraulic Calculation Procedures.

6-4.1* General. A calculated system for a building, or a calculated addition to a system in an existing sprinklered building, supersedes the rules in the sprinkler standard governing pipe schedules, except that all systems continue to be limited by area, and pipe sizes shall be no less than 1 in. (25.4 mm) nominal for ferrous piping and ¾ in. (19 mm) nominal for copper tubing or nonmetallic piping listed for fire sprinkler service. The size of pipe, number of sprinklers per branch line, and number of branch lines per cross main are otherwise limited only by the available water supply. However, sprinkler spacing and all other rules covered in this and other applicable standards shall be observed.

6-4.2 Formulas.

6-4.2.1 Friction Loss Formula. Pipe friction losses shall be determined on the basis of the Hazen-Williams formula.

$$p = \frac{4.52 \, Q^{1.85}}{C^{1.85} \, d^{4.87}}$$

where p is the frictional resistance in pounds pressure per square inch per foot of pipe, Q is the gallons per minute flowing, and d is the actual internal diameter of pipe in inches with C as the friction loss coefficient.

For SI Units: $P_m = 6.05 \times \dfrac{Q_m^{1.85}}{C^{1.85} \, d_m^{4.87}} \times 10^5$

Where P_m is the frictional resistance in bars per meter of pipe, Q_m is the flow in L/min, d_m is the actual internal diameter in mm and C is the friction loss coefficient.

6-4.2.2 Velocity Pressure Formula. Velocity pressure shall be determined on the basis of the formula

$$P_v = 0.001 \, 123 \, Q^2 D^4$$

P_v = velocity pressure in psi.

where:

Q = flow in gpm

D = the inside diameter in inches.

For SI units: 1 in. = 25.4 mm; 1 gal = 3.785 L; 1 psi = 0.0689 bar.

6-4.2.3 Normal Pressure Formula. Normal pressure (P_n) shall be determined on the basis of the formula

$$P_n = P_t - P_v$$

where:

P_t = total pressure in psi (bars)

P_v = velocity pressure in psi (bars)

6-4.2.4 Hydraulic Junction Points. Pressures at hydraulic junction points shall balance within 0.5 psi (0.03 bar). The highest pressure at the junction point, and the total flows as adjusted, shall be carried into the calculations.

6-4.3 Equivalent Pipe Lengths of Valves and Fittings.

6-4.3.1 Table 6-4.3.1 shall be used to determine the equivalent length of pipe for fittings and devices unless manufacturer's test data indicate that other factors are appropriate. For saddle-type fittings having friction loss greater than that shown in Table 6-4.3.1, the increased friction loss shall be included in hydraulic calculations.

6-4.3.2 Table 6-4.3.1 shall be used with Hazen-Williams C = 120 only. For other values of C, the values in Table 6-4.3.1 shall be multiplied by the factors indicated in Table 6-4.3.2.

Table 6-4.3.2

Value of C	100	130	140	150
Multiplying Factor	0.713	1.16	1.33	1.51

NOTE: This is based upon the friction loss through the fitting being independent of the C factor available to the piping.

Table 6-4.3.1 Equivalent Pipe Length Chart

Fittings and Valves	Fittings and Valves Expressed in Equivalent Feet of Pipe													
	¾ in.	1 in.	1¼ in.	1½ in.	2 in.	2½ in.	3 in.	3½ in.	4 in.	5 in.	6 in.	8 in.	10 in.	12 in.
45° Elbow	1	1	1	2	2	3	3	3	4	5	7	9	11	13
90° Standard Elbow	2	2	3	4	5	6	7	8	10	12	14	18	22	27
90° Long Turn Elbow	1	2	2	2	3	4	5	5	6	8	9	13	16	18
Tee or Cross (Flow Turned 90°)	3	5	6	8	10	12	15	17	20	25	30	35	50	60
Butterfly Valve	-	-	-	-	6	7	10	-	12	9	10	12	19	21
Gate Valve	-	-	-	-	1	1	1	1	2	2	3	4	5	6
Swing Check*	-	5	7	9	11	14	16	19	22	27	32	45	55	65

For SI Units: 1 ft = 0.3048 m.

*Due to the variations in design of swing check valves, the pipe equivalents indicated in the above chart are considered average.

NOTE: This table applies to all types of pipe listed in Table 6-4.4.5

6-4.3.3 Specific friction loss values or equivalent pipe lengths for alarm valves, dry pipe valves, deluge valves, strainers, and other devices shall be made available to the authority having jurisdiction.

6-4.4* Calculation Procedure.

6-4.4.1* For all systems the design area shall be the hydraulically most demanding based on the criteria of 5-2.3.

Exception: Special design approaches in accordance with 5-3.3.

(a) When the design is based on area/density method, the design area shall be a rectangular area having a dimension parallel to the branch lines at least 1.2 times the square root of the area of sprinkler operation (A) used. This may include sprinklers on both sides of the cross main. Any fractional sprinkler shall be carried to the next higher whole sprinkler.

Exception: In systems having branch lines with an insufficient number of sprinklers to fulfill the 1.2 $\sqrt{A}$ requirement, the design area shall be extended to include sprinklers on adjacent branch lines supplied by the same cross main.

(b) When the design is based on the room design method, see 5-2.3.3. The calculation shall be based on the room and communicating space, if any, that is the hydraulically most demanding.

6-4.4.2* For gridded systems, the designer shall verify that the hydraulically most demanding area is being used. A minimum of two additional sets of calculations shall be submitted to demonstrate peaking of demand area friction loss when compared to areas immediately adjacent on either side along the same branch lines.

Exception: Computer programs that show the peaking of the demand area friction loss shall be acceptable based on a single set of calculations.

6-4.4.3 System piping shall be hydraulically designed using design densities and areas of operation in accordance with Figure 5-2.3 as required for the occupancies involved.

(a)* The density shall be calculated on the basis of area of sprinkler operation. The area covered by any sprinkler for use in hydraulic design and calculations shall be determined in accordance with 4-2.2.1.

(b)* When sprinklers are installed above and below a ceiling or in a case where more than two areas are supplied from a common set of branch lines, the branch lines and supplies shall be calculated to supply the largest water demand.

6-4.4.4* Each sprinkler in the design area and the remainder of the hydraulically designed system shall discharge at a flow rate at least equal to the stipulated minimum water application rate (density) multiplied by the area of sprinkler operation. Begin calculations at the hydraulically most remote sprinkler. Discharge at each sprinkler shall be based on the calculated pressure at that sprinkler.

Exception No. 1: When area of application is equal to or greater than 1500 sq ft, sprinkler discharge in closets, washrooms, and similar small compartments requiring only one sprinkler shall be permitted to be omitted from hydraulic calculations within the area of application. Sprinklers in these small compartments shall, however, be capable of discharging minimum densities in accordance with Figure 5-2.3.

Exception No. 2: When sprinklers are provided above and below obstructions such as wide ducts or tables, the water supply for one of the levels of sprinklers shall be permitted to be omitted from the hydraulic ceiling design calculations within the area of application. In any case, the most hydraulically demanding arrangement shall be calculated.

6-4.4.5 Calculate pipe friction loss in accordance with the Hazen-Williams formula with C values from Table 6-4.4.5.

(a) Include pipe, fittings, and devices such as valves, meters, and strainers, and calculate elevation changes that affect the sprinkler discharge.

Exception: Tie-in drain piping shall not be included in the hydraulic calculations.

(b) Calculate the loss for a tee or a cross where flow direction change occurs based on the equivalent pipe length of the piping segment in which the fitting is included. The tee at the top of a riser nipple shall be included in the branch line; the tee at the base of a riser nipple shall be included in the riser nipple; and the tee or cross at a cross main-feed main junction shall be included in the cross main. Do not include fitting loss for straight-through flow in a tee or cross.

(c) Calculate the loss of reducing elbows based on the equivalent feet value of the smallest outlet. Use the equivalent feet value for the standard elbow on any abrupt 90-degree turn, such as the screw-type pattern. Use the equivalent feet value for the long-turn elbow on any sweeping 90-degree turn, such as a flanged, welded, or mechanical joint-elbow type. (*See Table 6-4.3.1.*)

(d) Friction loss shall be excluded for the fitting directly connected to a sprinkler.

(e) Losses through a pressure-reducing valve shall be included based on the normal inlet pressure condition. Pressure loss data from the manufacturer's literature shall be used.

Table 6-4.4.5   Hazen-Williams C Values

Pipe or Tube	C Value*
Unlined Cast or Ductile Iron	100
Black Steel (Dry Systems including Preaction)	100
Black Steel (Wet Systems including Deluge)	120
Galvanized (all)	120
Plastic (listed)—All	150
Cement Lined Cast or Ductile Iron	140
Copper Tube or Stainless Steel	150

*The authority having jurisdiction may recommend other C values.

6-4.4.6* Orifice plates or sprinklers of different orifice sizes shall not be used for balancing the system.

Exception No. 1: Sprinklers with different orifice sizes shall be acceptable for special use such as exposure protection, small rooms or enclosures, or directional discharge. (See 1-4.2 for definition of small rooms.)

Exception No. 2: Sprinklers with different orifice sizes shall be acceptable in light hazard occupancies that utilize extended coverage sprinklers for part of the protection area.

6-4.4.7* Velocity pressure (P_v) may or may not be included in the calculations at the discretion of the designer. If velocity pressures are used, they shall be used on both branch lines and cross mains where applicable.

6-4.4.8 Minimum operating pressure of any sprinkler shall be 7 psi (0.5 bar).

Exception: When different minimum operating pressure for the desired application is specified in the listing of the sprinkler.

6-5 Pipe Schedules. Pipe schedules shall not be used, except in existing systems and in new systems or extensions to existing systems described in Chapter 5. Water supplies shall conform to 5-2.2.

6-5.1* General. The pipe schedule sizing provisions shall not apply to hydraulically calculated systems. Sprinkler systems having sprinklers with orifices other than 1/2 in. (13 mm) nominal, listed piping material other than that covered in Table 2-3.1, Extra Hazard Groups 1 and 2 systems, and exposure protection systems shall be hydraulically calculated.

6-5.1.1 The number of automatic sprinklers on a given pipe size on one floor shall not exceed the number given in 6-5.2, 6-5.3, or 6-5.4 for a given occupancy.

6-5.1.2* Size of Risers. Each system riser shall be sized to supply all sprinklers on the riser on any one floor as determined by the standard schedules of pipe sizes in 6-5.2, 6-5.3, or 6-5.4.

6-5.1.3 Slatted Floors, Large Floor Openings, Mezzanines, and Large Platforms. Buildings having slatted floors, or large unprotected floor openings without approved stops, shall be treated as one area with reference to pipe sizes, and the feed mains or risers shall be of the size required for the total number of sprinklers.

6-5.1.4 Stair Towers. Stairs, towers, or other construction with incomplete floors, if piped on independent risers, shall be treated as one area with reference to pipe sizes.

6-5.2 Schedule for Light Hazard Occupancies.

6-5.2.1 Branch lines shall not exceed 8 sprinklers on either side of a cross main.

Exception: When more than 8 sprinklers on a branch line are necessary, lines may be increased to 9 sprinklers by making the two end lengths 1 in. (25.4 mm) and 1 1/4 in. (33 mm), respectively, and the sizes thereafter standard. Ten sprinklers may be placed on a branch line making the two end lengths 1 in. (25.4 mm) and 1 1/4 in. (33 mm), respectively, and feeding the tenth sprinkler by a 2 1/2-in. (64-mm) pipe.

6-5.2.2 Pipe sizes shall be in accordance with Table 6-5.2.2.

Exception: Each area requiring more sprinklers than the number specified for 3 1/2-in. (89-mm) pipe in Table 6-5.2.2 and without subdividing partitions (not necessarily fire walls) shall be supplied by mains or risers sized for Ordinary Hazard Occupancies.

Table 6-5.2.2   Light Hazard Pipe Schedules

Steel		Copper	
1 in.	2 sprinklers	1 in.	2 sprinklers
1 1/4 in.	3 sprinklers	1 1/4 in.	3 sprinklers
1 1/2 in.	5 sprinklers	1 1/2 in.	5 sprinklers
2 in.	10 sprinklers	2 in.	12 sprinklers
2 1/2 in.	30 sprinklers	2 1/2 in.	40 sprinklers
3 in.	60 sprinklers	3 in.	65 sprinklers
3 1/2 in.	100 sprinklers	3 1/2 in.	115 sprinklers
4 in.	See 4-2.1	4 in.	See 4-2.1

For SI Units: 1 in. = 25.4 mm.

6-5.2.3 When sprinklers are installed above and below ceilings [*see Figures 6-5.2.3(a), (b), and (c)*] and such sprinklers are supplied from a common set of branch lines or separate branch lines from a common cross main, such branch lines shall not exceed 8 sprinklers above and 8 sprinklers below any ceiling on either side of the cross main. Pipe sizing up to and including 2 1/2 in. (64 mm) shall be as shown in Table 6-5.2.3 utilizing the greatest number of sprinklers to be found on any two adjacent levels.

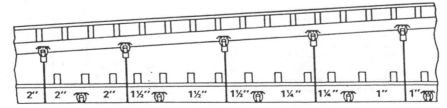

For SI Units: 1 in. = 25.4 mm.

Figure 6-5.2.3(a)   Arrangement of branch lines supplying sprinklers above and below a ceiling.

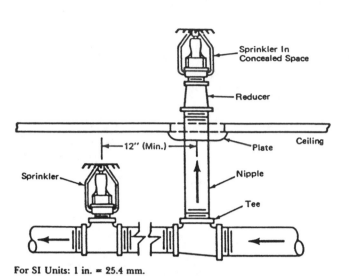

For SI Units: 1 in. = 25.4 mm.

Figure 6-5.2.3(b) Sprinkler on riser nipple from branch line in lower fire area.

6-5.2.3.1* When the total number of sprinklers above and below a ceiling exceeds the number specified in Table 6-5.2.3 for 2½-in. (64-mm) pipe, the pipe supplying such sprinklers shall be increased to 3 in. (76 mm) and sized thereafter according to the schedule shown in Table 6-5.2.2 for the number of sprinklers above or below a ceiling, whichever is larger.

Table 6-5.2.3   Number of Sprinklers above and below a Ceiling

Steel		Copper	
1 in.	2 sprinklers	1 in.	2 sprinklers
1¼ in.	4 sprinklers	1¼ in.	4 sprinklers
1½ in.	7 sprinklers	1½ in.	7 sprinklers
2 in.	15 sprinklers	2 in.	18 sprinklers
2½ in.	50 sprinklers	2½ in.	65 sprinklers

6-5.3 Schedule for Ordinary Hazard Occupancies.

6-5.3.1 Branch lines shall not exceed 8 sprinklers on either side of a cross main.

Exception: When more than 8 sprinklers on a branch line are necessary, lines may be increased to 9 sprinklers by making the two end lengths 1 in. (25.4 mm) and 1¼ in. (33 mm), respectively, and the sizes thereafter standard. Ten sprinklers may be placed on

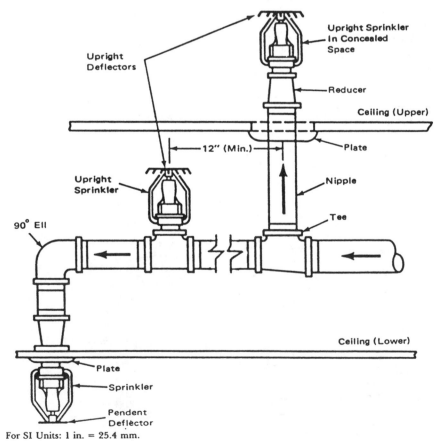

For SI Units: 1 in. = 25.4 mm.

Figure 6-5.2.3(c) Arrangement of branch lines supplying sprinklers above and below ceilings.

a branch line making the two end lengths 1 in. (25.4 mm) and 1¼ in. (33 mm), respectively, and feeding the tenth sprinkler by a 2½-in. (64-mm) pipe.

6-5.3.2 Pipe sizes shall be in accordance with Table 6-5.3.2(a).

Table 6-5.3.2(a)   Ordinary Hazard Pipe Schedule

Steel		Copper	
1 in.	2 sprinklers	1 in.	2 sprinklers
1¼ in.	3 sprinklers	1¼ in.	3 sprinklers
1½ in.	5 sprinklers	1½ in.	5 sprinklers
2 in.	10 sprinklers	2 in.	12 sprinklers
2½ in.	20 sprinklers	2½ in.	25 sprinklers
3 in.	40 sprinklers	3 in.	45 sprinklers
3½ in.	65 sprinklers	3½ in.	75 sprinklers
4 in.	100 sprinklers	4 in.	115 sprinklers
5 in.	160 sprinklers	5 in.	180 sprinklers
6 in.	275 sprinklers	6 in.	300 sprinklers
8 in.	See 4-2.1	8 in.	See 4-2.1

For SI Units: 1 in. = 25.4 mm.

Exception: When the distance between sprinklers on the branch line exceeds 12 ft (3.7 m), or the distance between the branch lines exceeds 12 ft (3.7 m), the number of sprinklers for a given pipe size shall be in accordance with Table 6-5.3.2(b).

Table 6-5.3.2(b)   Number of Sprinklers—Greater than 12 ft Separations

Steel		Copper	
2½ in.	15 sprinklers	2½ in.	20 sprinklers
3 in.	30 sprinklers	3 in.	35 sprinklers
3½ in.	60 sprinklers	3½ in.	65 sprinklers
For other pipe and tube sizes, see Table 6-5.3.2(a).			

For SI Units: 1 in. = 25.4 mm.

6-5.3.3 When sprinklers are installed above and below ceilings and such sprinklers are supplied from a common set of branch lines or separate branch lines supplied by a common cross main, such branch lines shall not exceed 8 sprinklers above and 8 sprinklers below any ceiling on either side of the cross main. Pipe sizing up to and including 3 in. (76 mm) shall be as shown in Table 6-5.3.3 [*see Figures 6-5.2.3(a), (b), and (c)*] utilizing the greatest number of sprinklers to be found on any two adjacent levels.

Table 6-5.3.3   Number of Sprinklers above and below a Ceiling

Steel		Copper	
1 in.	2 sprinklers	1 in.	2 sprinklers
1¼ in.	4 sprinklers	1¼ in.	4 sprinklers
1½ in.	7 sprinklers	1½ in.	7 sprinklers
2 in.	15 sprinklers	2 in.	18 sprinklers
2½ in.	30 sprinklers	2½ in.	40 sprinklers
3 in.	60 sprinklers	3 in.	65 sprinklers

For SI Units: 1 in. = 25.4 mm.

6-5.3.3.1* When the total number of sprinklers above and below a ceiling exceeds the number specified in Table 6-5.3.3 for 3-in. (76-mm) pipe, the pipe supplying such sprinklers shall be increased to 3½ in. (89 mm) and sized thereafter according to the schedule shown in Table 6-5.2.2 or Table 6-5.3.2(a) for the number of sprinklers above or below ceiling, whichever is larger.

Exception: When the distance between the sprinklers protecting the occupied area exceeds 12 ft (3.7 m) or the distance between the branch lines exceeds 12 ft (3.7 m), the branch lines shall be sized in accordance with either Table 6-5.3.2(b), taking into consideration the sprinklers protecting the occupied area only, or paragraph 6-5.3.3, whichever requires the greater size of pipe.

6-5.4*   Extra Hazard Occupancies shall be hydraulically calculated.

Exception: For existing systems, see A-6-5.4.

6-5.5 Deluge Systems.   Open sprinkler and deluge systems shall be hydraulically calculated according to applicable standards.

6-5.6* Exposure Systems.   Exposure sprinklers shall be hydraulically calculated using Table 6-5.6 and a relative classification of exposures Guide Number.

Chapter 7   Water Supplies

7-1 General.   Every automatic sprinkler system shall have at least one automatic water supply.

7-1.1 Capacity.   Water supplies shall be reliable and be capable of providing the required flow and pressure for the recommended duration as specified in Chapter 5 (Design Approaches).

7-1.2 Arrangement.

7-1.2.1 Underground Supply Pipe.   For pipe schedule systems, the underground supply pipe shall be at least as large as the system riser.

7-1.2.2 Connection between Underground and Aboveground Piping.   The connection between the system piping and underground piping shall be made with a suitable transition piece and shall be properly strapped or fastened by approved devices. The transition piece shall be protected against possible damage from corrosive agents, solvent attack, or mechanical damage.

7-1.2.3* Connection Passing through or under Foundation Walls.   When system piping pierces a foundation wall below grade or is located under the foundation wall, clearance shall be provided to prevent breakage of the piping due to building settlement.

7-1.3 Meters.   Where meters are required by other authorities, they shall be listed.

Table 6-5.6   Exposure Protection

SECTION A—WINDOW SPRINKLERS

Guide Number	Level of Window Sprinkler	Window Sprinkler Orifice Size	Discharge Coefficient (K Factor)	Flow Rate (Q)	Application Rate over 25 ft^2 of Window Area
1.50 or less	Top 2 levels	3/8 in.	2.8	7.4 gpm	0.30 gpm/ft^2
	Next lower 2 levels	5/16 in.	1.9	5.0 gpm	0.20 gpm/ft^2
	Next lower 2 levels	1/4 in.	1.4	3.7 gpm	0.15 gpm/ft^2
1.51 to 2.20	Top 2 levels	1/2 in.	5.6	14.8 gpm	0.59 gpm/ft^2
	Next lower 2 levels	7/16 in.	4.2	11.1 gpm	0.44 gpm/ft^2
	Next lower 2 levels	3/8 in.	2.8	7.4 gpm	0.30 gpm/ft^2
2.21 to 13.15	Top 2 levels	5/8 in.	11.2	29.6 gpm	1.18 gpm/ft^2
	Next lower 2 levels	17/32 in.	8.0	21.2 gpm	0.85 gpm/ft^2
	Next lower 2 levels	1/2 in.	5.6	14.8 gpm	0.59 gpm/ft^2

SECTION B—CORNICE SPRINKLERS

Guide Number	Cornice Sprinkler Orifice Size	Application Rate per Lineal Foot
1.50 or less	3/8 in.	0.75 gpm
1.51 to 2.20	1/2 in.	1.50 gpm
2.21 to 13.15	5/8 in.	3.00 gpm

7-2   Types.

7-2.1* Connections to Water Works Systems. A connection to a reliable water works system shall be an acceptable water supply source. The volume and pressure of a public water supply shall be determined from waterflow test data. (*See NFPA 24, Standard for the Installation of Private Fire Service Mains and Their Appurtenances.*) The authority having jurisdiction shall be permitted to require an adjustment to the waterflow test data to account for daily and seasonal fluctuations, possible interruption by flood or ice conditions, large simultaneous industrial use, future demand on the water supply system, or any other condition that could affect the water supply.

7-2.2   Pumps.

7-2.2.1* Acceptability. A single automatically controlled fire pump installed in accordance with NFPA 20, *Standard for the Installation of Centrifugal Fire Pumps*, shall be an acceptable water supply source.

7-2.2.2* Supervision. When a single fire pump constitutes the sole sprinkler supply, it shall be provided with supervisory service from an approved central station, proprietary, or remote station system or equivalent.

7-2.3   Pressure Tanks.

7-2.3.1   Acceptability.

7-2.3.1.1 A pressure tank installed in accordance with NFPA 22, *Standard for Water Tanks for Private Fire Protection*, shall be an acceptable water supply source.

7-2.3.1.2 Pressure tanks shall be provided with an approved means for automatically maintaining the required air pressure. When a pressure tank is the sole water supply, there shall also be provided an approved trouble alarm to indicate low air pressure and low water level with the alarm supplied from an electrical branch circuit independent of the air compressor.

7-2.3.1.3 Pressure tanks shall not be used to supply other than sprinklers and hand hose attached to sprinkler piping.

7-2.3.2 Capacity. In addition to the requirements of 7-1.1, the water capacity of a pressure tank shall include the extra capacity needed to fill dry pipe or preaction systems when installed. The total volume shall be based on the water capacity, plus the air capacity required by 7-2.3.3.

7-2.3.3* Water Level and Air Pressure. Pressure tanks shall be kept two-thirds full of water, and an air pressure of at least 75 psi (5.2 bars) by the gauge shall be maintained. When the bottom of the tank is located below the highest sprinklers served, the air pressure by the gauge shall be at least 75 psi (5.2 bars) plus three times the pressure caused by the column of water in the sprinkler system above the tank bottom.

7-2.4 Gravity Tanks. An elevated tank installed in accordance with NFPA 22, *Standard for Water Tanks for Private Fire Protection*, shall be an acceptable water supply source.

Chapter 8   System Acceptance

8-1 Approval of Sprinkler Systems. The installing contractor shall:

(a) Notify the authority having jurisdiction and owner's representative of the time and date testing will be performed.

(b) Perform all required acceptance tests. (*See Section 8-2.*)

(c) Complete and sign the appropriate Contractor's Material and Test Certificate(s) [*see Figures 8-1(a) and 8-1(b)*].

CONTRACTOR'S MATERIAL & TEST CERTIFICATE FOR **A**BOVEGROUND PIPING

PROCEDURE

Upon completion of work, inspection and tests shall be made by the contractor's representative and witnessed by an owner's representative. All defects shall be corrected and system left in service before contractor's personnel finally leave the job.

A certificate shall be filled out and signed by both representatives. Copies shall be prepared for approving authorities, owners, and contractor. It is understood the owner's representative's signature in no way prejudices any claim against contractor for faulty material, poor workmanship, or failure to comply with approving authority's requirements or local ordinances.

PROPERTY NAME	DATE

PROPERTY ADDRESS

PLANS	ACCEPTED BY APPROVING AUTHORITIES (NAMES)	
	ADDRESS	
	INSTALLATION CONFORMS TO ACCEPTED PLANS	☐ YES ☐ NO
	EQUIPMENT USED IS APPROVED	☐ YES ☐ NO
	IF NO, EXPLAIN DEVIATIONS	
INSTRUCTIONS	HAS PERSON IN CHARGE OF FIRE EQUIPMENT BEEN INSTRUCTED AS TO LOCATION OF CONTROL VALVES AND CARE AND MAINTENANCE OF THIS NEW EQUIPMENT? IF NO, EXPLAIN	☐ YES ☐ NO
	HAVE COPIES OF THE FOLLOWING BEEN LEFT ON THE PREMISES:	☐ YES ☐ NO
	1. SYSTEM COMPONENTS INSTRUCTIONS	☐ YES ☐ NO
	2. CARE AND MAINTENANCE INSTRUCTIONS	☐ YES ☐ NO
	3. NFPA 13A	☐ YES ☐ NO
LOCATION OF SYSTEM	SUPPLIES BUILDINGS	

	MAKE	MODEL	YEAR OF MANUFACTURE	ORIFICE SIZE	QUANTITY	TEMPERATURE RATING
SPRINKLERS						

PIPE AND FITTINGS	Type of Pipe _____
	Type of Fittings _____

	ALARM DEVICE			MAXIMUM TIME TO OPERATE THROUGH TEST CONNECTION	
ALARM VALVE OR FLOW INDICATOR	TYPE	MAKE	MODEL	MIN.	SEC.

	DRY VALVE			Q.O.D.		
	MAKE	MODEL	SERIAL NO.	MAKE	MODEL	SERIAL NO.
DRY PIPE OPERATING TEST						

	TIME TO TRIP THRU TEST CONNECTION*		WATER PRESSURE	AIR PRESSURE	TRIP POINT AIR PRESSURE	TIME WATER REACHED TEST OUTLET*		ALARM OPERATED PROPERLY	
	MIN.	SEC.	PSI	PSI	PSI	MIN.	SEC.	YES	NO
Without Q.O.D.									
With Q.O.D.									

IF NO, EXPLAIN

* MEASURED FROM TIME INSPECTOR'S TEST CONNECTION IS OPENED.
85A (10-88)   PRINTED IN U.S.A.   (OVER)

Figure 8-1(a).

DELUGE & PREACTION VALVES	OPERATION					
	☐ PNEUMATIC ☐ ELECTRIC ☐ HYDRAULIC					
	PIPING SUPERVISED ☐ YES ☐ NO		DETECTING MEDIA SUPERVISED		☐ YES	☐ NO
	DOES VALVE OPERATE FROM THE MANUAL TRIP AND/OR REMOTE CONTROL STATIONS				☐ YES	☐ NO
	IS THERE AN ACCESSIBLE FACILITY IN EACH CIRCUIT FOR TESTING		IF NO, EXPLAIN			
	☐ YES ☐ NO					

	MAKE	MODEL	DOES EACH CIRCUIT OPERATE SUPERVISION LOSS ALARM		DOES EACH CIRCUIT OPERATE VALVE RELEASE		MAXIMUM TIME TO OPERATE RELEASE	
			YES	NO	YES	NO	MIN.	SEC.

TEST DESCRIPTION	HYDROSTATIC: Hydrostatic tests shall be made at not less than 200 psi (13.6 bars) for two hours or 50 psi (3.4 bars) above static pressure in excess of 150 psi (10.2 bars) for two hours. Differential dry-pipe valve clappers shall be left open during test to prevent damage. All aboveground piping leakage shall be stopped.
	PNEUMATIC: Establish 40 psi (2.7 bars) air pressure and measure drop which shall not exceed 1-1/2 psi (0.1 bars) in 24 hours. Test pressure tanks at normal water level and air pressure and measure air pressure drop which shall not exceed 1-1/2 psi (0.1 bars) in 24 hours.

TESTS	ALL PIPING HYDROSTATICALLY TESTED AT _____ PSI FOR _____ HRS.		IF NO, STATE REASON
	DRY PIPING PNEUMATICALLY TESTED ☐ YES ☐ NO		
	EQUIPMENT OPERATES PROPERLY ☐ YES ☐ NO		
	DO YOU CERTIFY AS THE SPRINKLER CONTRACTOR THAT ADDITIVES AND CORROSIVE CHEMICALS, SODIUM SILICATE OR DERIVATIVES OF SODIUM SILICATE, BRINE, OR OTHER CORROSIVE CHEMICALS WERE NOT USED FOR TESTING SYSTEMS OR STOPPING LEAKS? ☐ YES ☐ NO		
	DRAIN TEST	READING OF GAGE LOCATED NEAR WATER SUPPLY TEST CONNECTION: _____ PSI	RESIDUAL PRESSURE WITH VALVE IN TEST CONNECTION OPEN WIDE _____ PSI
	UNDERGROUND MAINS AND LEAD IN CONNECTIONS TO SYSTEM RISERS FLUSHED BEFORE CONNECTION MADE TO SPRINKLER PIPING.		
	VERIFIED BY COPY OF THE U FORM NO. 85B ☐ YES ☐ NO	OTHER EXPLAIN	
	FLUSHED BY INSTALLER OF UNDERGROUND SPRINKLER PIPING ☐ YES ☐ NO		

BLANK TESTING GASKETS	NUMBER USED	LOCATIONS	NUMBER REMOVED

WELDING	WELDED PIPING ☐ YES ☐ NO		
	IF YES...		
	DO YOU CERTIFY AS THE SPRINKLER CONTRACTOR THAT WELDING PROCEDURES COMPLY WITH THE REQUIREMENTS OF AT LEAST AWS D10.9, LEVEL AR-3	☐ YES	☐ NO
	DO YOU CERTIFY THAT THE WELDING WAS PERFORMED BY WELDERS QUALIFIED IN COMPLIANCE WITH THE REQUIREMENTS OF AT LEAST AWS D10.9, LEVEL AR-3	☐ YES	☐ NO
	DO YOU CERTIFY THAT WELDING WAS CARRIED OUT IN COMPLIANCE WITH A DOCUMENTED QUALITY CONTROL PROCEDURE TO INSURE THAT ALL DISCS ARE RETRIEVED, THAT OPENINGS IN PIPING ARE SMOOTH, THAT SLAG AND OTHER WELDING RESIDUE ARE REMOVED, AND THAT THE INTERNAL DIAMETERS OF PIPING ARE NOT PENETRATED	☐ YES	☐ NO

CUTOUTS (DISCS)	DO YOU CERTIFY THAT YOU HAVE A CONTROL FEATURE TO ENSURE THAT ALL CUTOUTS (DISCS) ARE RETRIEVED?	☐ YES	☐ NO

HYDRAULIC DATA NAMEPLATE	NAME PLATE PROVIDED ☐ YES ☐ NO	IF NO, EXPLAIN

REMARKS	DATE LEFT IN SERVICE WITH ALL CONTROL VALVES OPEN:

SIGNATURES	NAME OF SPRINKLER CONTRACTOR		
	TESTS WITNESSED BY		
	FOR PROPERTY OWNER (SIGNED)	TITLE	DATE
	FOR SPRINKLER CONTRACTOR (SIGNED)	TITLE	DATE

ADDITIONAL EXPLANATION AND NOTES

Figure 8-1(a) (cont.).

CONTRACTOR'S MATERIAL & TEST CERTIFICATE FOR NDERGROUND PIPING

PROCEDURE

Upon completion of work, inspection and tests shall be made by the contractor's representative and witnessed by an owner's representative. All defects shall be corrected and system left in service before contractor's personnel finally leave the job.

A certificate shall be filled out and signed by both representatives. Copies shall be prepared for approving authorities, owners, and contractor. It is understood the owner's representative's signature in no way prejudices any claim against contractor for faulty material, poor workmanship, or failure to comply with approving authority's requirements or local ordinances.

PROPERTY NAME	DATE

PROPERTY ADDRESS

PLANS	ACCEPTED BY APPROVING AUTHORITIES (NAMES)		
	ADDRESS		
	INSTALLATION CONFORMS TO ACCEPTED PLANS	☐ YES	☐ NO
	EQUIPMENT USED IS APPROVED	☐ YES	☐ NO
	IF NO, STATE DEVIATIONS		

INSTRUCTIONS	HAS PERSON IN CHARGE OF FIRE EQUIPMENT BEEN INSTRUCTED AS TO LOCATION OF CONTROL VALVES AND CARE AND MAINTENANCE OF THIS NEW EQUIPMENT? IF NO, EXPLAIN	☐ YES	☐ NO
	HAVE COPIES OF APPROPRIATE INSTRUCTIONS AND CARE AND MAINTENANCE CHARTS BEEN LEFT ON PREMISES? IF NO, EXPLAIN	☐ YES	☐ NO

LOCATION	SUPPLIES BUILDINGS		

UNDERGROUND PIPES AND JOINTS	PIPE TYPES AND CLASS	TYPE JOINT		
	PIPE CONFORMS TO _____ STANDARD		☐ YES	☐ NO
	FITTINGS CONFORM TO _____ STANDARD		☐ YES	☐ NO
	IF NO, EXPLAIN			
	JOINTS NEEDING ANCHORAGE CLAMPED, STRAPPED, OR BLOCKED IN		☐ YES	☐ NO
	ACCORDANCE WITH _____ STANDARD			
	IF NO, EXPLAIN			

TEST DESCRIPTION	FLUSHING. Flow the required rate until water is clear as indicated by no collection of foreign material in burlap bags at outlets such as hydrants and blow-offs. Flush at flows not less than 390 GPM (1476 L/min) for 4-inch pipe, 880 GPM (3331 L/min) for 6-inch pipe, 1560 GPM (5905 L/min) for 8-inch pipe, 2440 GPM (9235 L/min) for 10-inch pipe, and 3520 GPM (13323 L/min) for 12-inch pipe. When supply cannot produce stipulated flow rates, obtain maximum available. HYDROSTATIC. Hydrostatic tests shall be made at not less than 200 psi (13.8 bars) for two hours or 50 psi (3.4 bars) above static pressure in excess of 150 psi (10.3 bars) for two hours. LEAKAGE. New pipe laid with rubber gasketed joints shall, if the workmanship is satisfactory, have little or no leakage at the joints. The amount of leakage at the joints shall not exceed 2 qts. per hr. (1.89 L/h) per 100 joints irrespective of pipe diameter. The leakage shall be distributed over all joints. If such leakage occurs at a few joints the installation shall be considered unsatisfactory and necessary repairs made. The amount of allowable leakage specified above may be increased by 1 fl oz per in. valve diameter per hr. (30 mL/25 mm/h) for each metal seated valve isolating the test section. If dry barrel hydrants are tested with the main valve open, so the hydrants are under pressure, an additional 5 oz per minute (150 mL/min) leakage is permitted for each hydrant.

	NEW UNDERGROUND PIPING FLUSHED ACCORDING TO _____ STANDARD		☐ YES	☐ NO
	BY (COMPANY) IF NO, EXPLAIN			

FLUSHING TESTS	HOW FLUSHING FLOW WAS OBTAINED ☐ PUBLIC WATER ☐ TANK OR RESERVOIR ☐ FIRE PUMP	THROUGH WHAT TYPE OPENING ☐ HYDRANT BUTT. ☐ OPEN PIPE		
	LEAD-INS FLUSHED ACCORDING TO _____ STANDARD		☐ YES	☐ NO
	BY (COMPANY) IF NO, EXPLAIN			
	HOW FLUSHING FLOW WAS OBTAINED ☐ PUBLIC WATER ☐ TANK OR RESERVOIR ☐ FIRE PUMP	THROUGH WHAT TYPE OPENING ☐ Y CONN. TO FLANGE & SPIGOT ☐ OPEN PIPE		

85B(10-88)   PRINTED IN USA   (OVER)

Figure 8-1(b).

HYDROSTATIC TEST	ALL NEW UNDERGROUND PIPING HYDROSTATICALLY TESTED AT _____ PSI FOR _____ HOURS		JOINTS COVERED ☐ YES ☐ NO
LEAKAGE TEST	TOTAL AMOUNT OF LEAKAGE MEASURED _____ GALS. _____ HOURS		
	ALLOWABLE LEAKAGE _____ GALS. _____ HOURS		
HYDRANTS	NUMBER INSTALLED	TYPE AND MAKE	ALL OPERATE SATISFACTORILY ☐ YES ☐ NO
CONTROL VALVES	WATER CONTROL VALVES LEFT WIDE OPEN IF NO, STATE REASON		☐ YES ☐ NO
	HOSE THREADS OF FIRE DEPARTMENT CONNECTIONS AND HYDRANTS INTERCHANGEABLE WITH THOSE OF FIRE DEPARTMENT ANSWERING ALARM		☐ YES ☐ NO
REMARKS	DATE LEFT IN SERVICE		
SIGNATURES	NAME OF INSTALLING CONTRACTOR		
	TESTS WITNESSED BY		
	FOR PROPERTY OWNER (SIGNED)	TITLE	DATE
	FOR INSTALLING CONTRACTOR (SIGNED)	TITLE	DATE

ADDITIONAL EXPLANATION AND NOTES

Figure 8-1(b) (cont.).

8-2 Acceptance Requirements.

8-2.1* Flushing of Piping. Underground mains and lead-in connections to system risers shall be completely flushed before connection is made to sprinkler piping. The flushing operation shall be continued for a sufficient time to ensure thorough cleaning. The minimum rate of flow shall be not less than:

(a) The hydraulically calculated water demand rate of the system including any hose requirements, or

(b) That flow necessary to provide a velocity of 10 ft per second (3 m/s), or

(c) The maximum flow rate available to the system under fire conditions.

Table 8-2.1 Flow Required to Produce a Velocity of 10 ft per second (3 m/s) in Pipes

Pipe Size (in.)	Flow Rate (gpm)	Flow Rate (L/min)
4	390	1476
6	880	3331
8	1560	5905
10	2440	9235
12	3520	13323

8-2.2 Hydrostatic Tests.

8-2.2.1* All interior piping and attached appurtenances subjected to system working pressure shall be hydrostatically tested at 200 psi (13.8 bars) and shall maintain that pressure without loss for 2 hours. Loss shall be determined by a drop in gauge pressure or visual leakage.

Exception No. 1: Portions of systems normally subjected to working pressures in excess of 150 psi (10.4 bars) shall be tested as described above at a pressure of 50 psi (3.5 bars) in excess of normal working pressure.

Exception No. 2: When cold weather will not permit testing with water, an interim air test may be conducted as described in 8-2.3.

The test pressure shall be read from a gauge located at the low elevation point of the system or portion being tested.

8-2.2.2 Additives. Additives, corrosive chemicals such as sodium silicate or derivatives of sodium silicate, brine, or other chemicals shall not be used while hydrostatically testing systems or for stopping leaks.

8-2.2.3 Piping between the exterior fire department connection and the check valve in the fire department inlet pipe shall be hydrostatically tested in the same manner as the balance of the system.

8-2.2.4 When hydrostatically testing deluge systems, plugs shall be installed in fittings and replaced with open sprinklers after the test is completed, or the operating elements of automatic sprinklers shall be removed after the test is completed.

8-2.2.5 All underground piping shall be hydrostatically tested in accordance with NFPA 24, *Standard for the Installation of Private Fire Service Mains and Their Appurtenances.* The allowable leakage shall be within the limits prescribed by NFPA 24 and shall be recorded on the test certificate.

8-2.2.6 Provision shall be made for proper disposal of water used for flushing or testing.

8-2.2.7* Test blanks shall have painted lugs protruding in such a way as to clearly indicate their presence. The test blanks shall be numbered, and the installing contractor shall have a record-keeping method ensuring their removal after work is completed.

8-2.2.8 Differential Type Valves. The clapper of a differential type valve when subject to hydrostatic test pressures shall be held off its seat to prevent damaging the valve.

8-2.3 Dry System Air Test. In addition to the standard hydrostatic test, an air pressure leakage test at 40 psi (2.8 bars) shall be conducted for 24 hours. Any leakage that results in a loss of pressure in excess of $1\frac{1}{2}$ psi (0.1 bar) for the 24 hours shall be corrected.

8-2.4 System Operational Tests

8-2.4.1 Waterflow detecting devices including the associated alarm circuits shall be flow tested through the inspector's test connection to result in an alarm on the premises within 5 minutes after such flow begins.

8-2.4.2 A working test of the dry pipe valve alone, and with a quick-opening device, if installed, shall be made by opening the inspector's test connection. The test shall measure the time to trip the valve and the time for water to be discharged from the inspector's test connection. All times shall be measured from the time the inspector's test connection is completely opened. The results shall be recorded using the Contractor's Material and Test Certificate for Aboveground Piping.

8-2.4.3 The automatic operation of a deluge or preaction valve shall be tested in accordance with the manufacturer's instructions. The manual and remote control operation, when present, shall also be tested.

8-2.4.4 Main Drain Flow Test. The main drain valve shall be opened and remain open until the system pressure stabilizes. The static and residual pressures shall be recorded on the contractor's test certificate.

8-2.5 Each pressure reducing valve shall be tested upon completion of the installation to ensure proper pressure reduction at both maximum and normal inlet pressures.

8-2.6 Operating tests shall be made of exposure protection systems upon completion of the installation, when such tests do not risk water damage to the building on which it is installed or to adjacent buildings.

8-3 Circulating Closed Loop Systems. For sprinkler systems with nonfire protection connections, additional information shall be appended to the Contractor's Material and Test Certificate shown in Figure 8-1(a) as follows:

(a) Certification that all auxiliary devices, such as heat pumps, circulating pumps, heat exchangers, radiators, and luminaries, if a part of the system, have a pressure rating of at least 175 psi or 300 psi if exposed to pressures greater than 175 psi (12.1 or 20.7 bars).

(b) All components of sprinkler system and auxiliary system have been pressure tested as a composite system in accordance with 8-2.2.

(c) Waterflow tests have been conducted and waterflow alarms have operated while auxiliary equipment is in each of the possible modes of operation.

(d) With auxiliary equipment tested in each possible mode of operation and with no flow from sprinklers or test connection, waterflow alarm signals did not operate.

(e) Excess temperature controls for shutting down the auxiliary system have been properly field tested.

8-4 Instructions.

8-4.1 The installing contractor shall provide the owner with:

(a) All literature and instructions provided by the manufacturer describing proper operation and maintenance of any equipment and devices installed.

(b) Publication titled NFPA 13A, *Recommended Practice for the Inspection, Testing and Maintenance of Sprinkler Systems.*

8-5* Hydraulic Design Information Sign. The installing contractor shall identify a hydraulically designed sprinkler system with a permanently marked weatherproof metal or rigid plastic sign secured with corrosion resistant wire, chain, or other approved means. Such signs shall be placed at the alarm valve, dry pipe valve, preaction valve, or deluge valve supplying the corresponding hydraulically designed area. The sign shall include the following information:

(a) Location of the design area or areas.

(b) Discharge densities over the design area or areas.

(c) Required flow and residual pressure demand at the base of riser.

(d) Hose stream demand included in addition to the sprinkler demand.

8-6 Circulating Closed Loop Systems. Discharge tests of sprinkler systems with nonfire protection connections shall be conducted using system test connections described in 2-7.2. Pressure gauges shall be installed at critical points and readings taken under various modes of auxiliary equipment operation. Waterflow alarm signals shall be responsive to discharge of water through system test pipes while auxiliary equipment is in each of the possible modes of operation.

Chapter 9   System Maintenance

9-1 General.

9-1.1* A sprinkler system installed in accordance with this standard shall be properly maintained to provide at least the same level of performance and protection as designed. The owner shall be responsible for maintaining the system and keeping the system in good operating condition. (Guidance for maintaining the system is provided in NFPA 13A, *Recommended Practice for Inspection and Maintenance of Sprinkler Systems.*)

9-1.2 When the sprinkler system has been subjected to adverse conditions such as freezing conditions in wet sprinkler systems, structural damage, severe earthquakes, or fire exposure, the sprinkler system, including hangers, piping, alarms, and sprinklers, shall be inspected and repaired or replaced if damaged. Sprinklers in the fire area shall be replaced.

9-1.3* When the sprinkler piping is given any kind of coating, such as whitewash or paint, care shall be exercised to see that no automatic sprinklers are coated.

9-2 Replacement of Sprinklers.

9-2.1 When sprinklers are replaced, the replacement sprinkler shall be of the same type, orifice, and temperature rating unless conditions require a different type sprinkler be installed. The replacement sprinkler shall then be of a type, orifice, and temperature rating to suit the new conditions.

9-2.2 Old-style sprinklers may be replaced with old-style sprinklers or with the appropriate pendent or upright sprinkler.

9-2.3 Old-style sprinklers shall not be used to replace pendent or upright sprinklers.

9-2.4 Extreme care shall be exercised when replacing horizontal sidewall and extended coverage sprinklers to assure the correct replacement sprinkler is installed.

9-2.5 Sprinklers that have been painted or coated, except by the manufacturer, shall be replaced and shall not be cleaned by use of chemicals, abrasives, or other means. (*See 2-2.4.3.*)

9-2.6 Sprinkler or spray nozzles used in commercial cooking equipment shall be replaced as specified in 3-9.12.

9-3 Obstruction in Piping.

9-3.1 Screens located in the inlet piping directly connected to rivers, lakes, ponds, reservoirs, uncovered tanks, and similar sources shall be cleaned annually and after work has been performed on fire protection water supplies. (*See NFPA 24, Standard for the Installation of Private Fire Service Mains and Their Appurtenances.*)

9-3.2 Visual or flushing investigation shall be conducted of all systems for presence of foreign material at intervals not exceeding 5 years.

9-3.3* The main drain shall be tested quarterly.

9-4 Testing of Antifreeze Systems. Before freezing weather each year, the solution in the entire system shall be emptied into convenient containers and brought to the proper specific gravity by adding concentrated liquid as needed. The resulting solution may be used to refill the system.

Chapter 10   Referenced Publications

10-1 The following documents or portions thereof are referenced within this standard and shall be considered part of the requirements of this document. The edition indicated for each reference is the current edition as of the date of the NFPA issuance of this document.

10-1.1 NFPA Publications. National Fire Protection Association, 1 Batterymarch Park, P.O. Box 9101, Quincy, MA 02269-9101.

NFPA 13D, *Standard for the Installation of Sprinkler Systems in One- and Two-Family Dwellings and Mobile Homes*, 1991 edition

NFPA 13R, *Standard for the Installation of Sprinkler Systems in Residential Occupancies up to and Including Four Stories in Height*, 1991 edition

NFPA 14, *Standard for the Installation of Standpipe and Hose Systems*, 1990 edition

NFPA 20, *Standard for the Installation of Centrifugal Fire Pumps*, 1990 edition

NFPA 22, *Standard for Water Tanks for Private Fire Protection*, 1987 edition

NFPA 24, *Standard for the Installation of Private Fire Service Mains and Their Appurtenances*, 1987 edition

NFPA 51B, *Standard for Fire Prevention in Use of Cutting and Welding Processes*, 1989 edition

NFPA 70, *National Electrical Code*, 1990 edition

NFPA 71, *Standard for the Installation, Maintenance, and Use of Signaling Systems for Central Station Service*, 1989 edition

NFPA 72, *Standard for the Installation, Maintenance, and Use of Protective Signaling Systems*, 1990 edition

NFPA 96, *Standard for the Installation of Equipment for the Removal of Smoke and Grease-Laden Vapors from Commercial Cooking Equipment*, 1991 edition

NFPA 231, *Standard for General Storage*, 1990 edition

NFPA 231C, *Standard for Rack Storage of Materials*, 1991 edition

NFPA 251, *Standard Methods of Fire Tests of Building Construction and Materials*, 1990 edition

10-1.2 The following NFPA codes and standards contain specific sprinkler design criteria.

NFPA 15, *Standard for Water Spray Fixed Systems for Fire Protection*, 1990 edition

NFPA 16, *Standard on Deluge Foam-Water Sprinkler and Foam-Water Spray Systems*, 1991 edition

NFPA 30, *Flammable and Combustible Liquids Code*, 1990 edition

NFPA 30B, *Code for the Manufacture and Storage of Aerosol Products*, 1990 edition

NFPA 40, *Standard for the Storage and Handling of Cellulose Nitrate Motion Picture Film*, 1988 edition

NFPA 43A, *Code for the Storage of Liquid and Solid Oxidizers, 1990 edition*

NFPA 45, *Standard on Fire Protection for Laboratories Using Chemicals*, 1991 edition

NFPA 58, *Standard for the Storage and Handling of Liquefied Petroleum Gases*, 1989 edition

NFPA 81, *Standard for Fur Storage, Fumigation and Cleaning*, 1986 edition

NFPA 101,® *Life Safety Code,*® 1991 edition

NFPA 214, *Standard on Water-Cooling Towers*, 1988 edition

NFPA 231, *Standard for General Storage*, 1990 edition

NFPA 231C, *Standard for Rack Storage of Materials*, 1991 edition

NFPA 231D, *Standard for Storage of Rubber Tires*, 1989 edition

NFPA 231E, *Recommended Practice for the Storage of Baled Cotton*, 1989 edition

NFPA 231F, *Standard for Storage of Roll Paper*, 1987 edition

NFPA 232, *Standard for the Protection of Records*, 1991 edition

NFPA 307, *Standard for the Construction and Fire Protection of Marine Terminals, Piers, and Wharves*, 1990 edition

NFPA 409, *Standard on Aircraft Hangars*, 1990 edition

NFPA 423, *Standard for Construction and Protection of Aircraft Engine Test Facilities*, 1989 edition

10-1.3 Other Publications.

10-1.3.1 ANSI Publications. American National Standards Institute, Inc., 1450 Broadway, New York, New York 10018.

ANSI B1.20.1-1983, *Pipe Threads, General Purpose*

ANSI B16.1-1989, *Cast Iron Pipe Flanges and Flanged Fittings, Class 25, 125, 250 and 800*

ANSI B16.3-1985, *Malleable Iron Threaded Fittings, Class 150 and 300*

ANSI B16.4-1985, *Cast Iron Threaded Fittings, Classes 125 and 250*

ANSI B16.5-1988, *Pipe Flanges and Flanged Fittings*

ANSI B16.9-1986, *Factory-Made Wrought Steel Buttwelding Fittings*

ANSI B16.11-1980, *Forged Steel Fittings, Socket-Welding and Threaded*

ANSI B16.18-1984, *Cast Copper Alloy Solder Joint Pressure Fittings*

ANSI B16.22-1989, *Wrought Copper and Copper Alloy Solder Joint Pressure Fittings*

ANSI B16.25-1986, *Buttwelding Ends*

ANSI B36.10M-1985, *Welded and Seamless Wrought Steel Pipe*

10-1.3.2 ASTM Publications. American Society for Testing and Materials, 1916 Race Street, Philadelphia, PA 19105.

ASTM A53-1990, *Standard Specification for Welded Pipe, Steel, Black and Hot-Dipped, Zinc-Coated and Seamless Steel Pipe*

ASTM A135-1989, *Specifications for Electric-Resistance Welded Steel Pipe*

ASTM A234-1990, *Standard Specification for Piping Fittings of Wrought-Carbon Steel and Alloy Steel for Moderate and Elevated Temperatures*

ASTM A795-1990, *Specification for Black and Hot-Dipped Zinc-Coated (Galvanized) Welded and Seamless Steel Pipe for Fire Protection Use*

ASTM B32-1989, *Standard Specification for Solder Metal, 95-5 (Tin-Antimony-Grade 95TA)*

ASTM B75-1986, *Standard Specification for Seamless Copper Tube*

ASTM B88-1989, *Standard Specification for Seamless Copper Water Tube*

ASTM B251-1988, *Standard Specification for General Requirements for Wrought Seamless Copper and Copper-Alloy Tube*

ASTM E136-1982, *Standard Test Method for Behavior of Materials in a Vertical Tube Furnace at 750°C*

ASTM E380-1989, *Standard for Metric Practice*

10-1.3.3 AWS Publications. American Welding Society, 2501 N.W. 7th Street, Miami, FL 33125.

AWS A5.8-1989, *Specification for Brazing Filler Metal*

AWS D10.9-1980, *Specification for Qualification of Welding Procedures and Welders for Piping and Tubing*

Appendix A

This Appendix is not a part of the requirements of this NFPA document, but is included for information purposes only.

A-1-4.2 Miscellaneous Storage. The sprinkler system design criteria for miscellaneous storage at heights below 12 ft (3.7 m) is covered by this standard in Chapters 4 and 5. Section 5-2.3.1.1 describes design criteria and 4-2.2 (Table 4-2.2) describes installation requirements (area limits). These apply to all storage of 12 feet or less in height.

A-1-4.2 Sprinkler System. A sprinkler system is considered to have a single system riser control valve.

A-1-4.4 See Figure A-1-4.4.

A-1-4.5.1 QRES Sprinkler. Research into the development of QRES sprinklers is continuing under the auspices of the National Fire Protection Research Foundation. It is expected that the proposed design criteria will be added to the standard when a thorough analysis of the test data is completed.

A-1-4.5.1 ESFR Sprinkler. It is important to realize that the effectiveness of these highly tested and engineered sprinklers depends on the combination of fast response and the quality and uniformity of the sprinkler discharge. It should also be realized that ESFR sprinklers cannot be relied upon to provide fire control, let alone suppression, if they are used outside the guidelines specified in 5-3.5.

A-1-4.5.3 Dry Sprinkler. Under certain ambient conditions wet pipe systems having dry-pendent (or upright) sprinklers may freeze due to heat loss by conduction. Therefore, due consideration should be given to the amount of heat maintained in the heated space, the length of the nipple in the heated space, and other relevant factors.

A-1-4.6(a) The following are examples of obstructed construction. The definitions are provided as guidance to assist the user in determining the type of construction feature:

(i) *Beam and Girder Construction.* The term *beam and girder construction* as used in this standard includes noncombustible and combustible roof or floor decks supported by wood beams of 4 in. (102 mm) or greater nominal thickness or concrete or steel beams spaced 3 to 7½ ft (0.9 to 2.3 m) on centers and either supported on or framed into girders. [When supporting a wood plank deck, this includes semi-mill and panel construction, and when supporting (with steel framing) gypsum plank, steel deck, concrete, tile, or similar material, this would include much of the so-called noncombustible construction.]

(ii) *Composite Wood Joist Construction.* The term *composite wood joist construction* refers to wood beams of I cross section constructed of wood flanges and solid wood web, supporting a floor or roof deck. Composite wood joists may vary in depth up to 48 in. (1.2 m), may be spaced up to 48 in. (1.2 m) on centers, and may span up to 60 ft (18 m) between supports. Joist channels should be fire-stopped to the full depth of the joists with material equivalent to the web construction so that individual channel areas do not exceed 300 sq ft (27.9 m²). See Figure A-1-4.6(a)(ii) for examples of composite wood joist construction.

(iii) *Panel Construction.* The term *panel construction* as used in this standard includes ceiling panels formed by members capable of trapping heat to aid the operation of sprinklers and limited to a maximum of 300 sq ft (27.9 m²) in area. Beams spaced more than 7½ ft (2.3 m) apart and framed into girders qualify for panel construction provided the 300 sq ft (27.9 m²) area limitation is met.

(iv) *Semi-Mill Construction.* The term *semi-mill construction* as used in this standard refers to a modified standard mill construction, where greater column spacing is used and beams rest on girders.

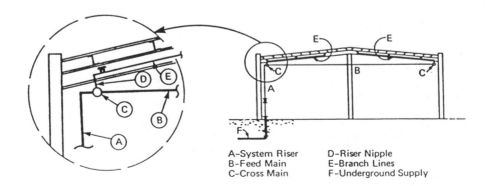

A-System Riser   D-Riser Nipple
B-Feed Main   E-Branch Lines
C-Cross Main   F-Underground Supply

Figure A-1-4.4   Building elevation showing parts of sprinkler piping system.

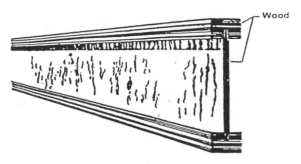

Figure A-1-4.6(a)(ii)   Typical composite wood joist construction.

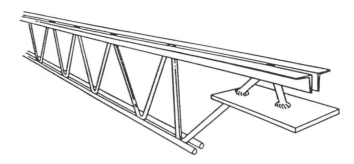

Figure A-1-4.6(b)(i)2   Open-web bar joist construction.

(v) *Wood Joist Construction.*   The term *wood joist construction* refers to solid wood members of rectangular cross section, which may vary from 2 to 4 in. (51 to 102 mm) nominal width and up to 14 in. (356 mm) nominal depth spaced up to 3 ft (0.9 m) on centers, and spanning up to 40 ft (12 m) between supports, supporting a floor or roof deck. Solid wood members less than 4 in. (102 mm) nominal width and up to 14 in. (356 mm) nominal depth, spaced more than 3 ft (0.9 m) on centers are also considered as wood joist construction.

A-1-4.6(b)   The following are examples of unobstructed construction. The definitions are provided as guidance to assist the user in determining the type of construction feature:

(i) *Bar Joist Construction.*   The term *bar joist construction* refers to construction employing joists consisting of steel truss-shaped members. Wood truss-shaped members, which consist of wood top and bottom chord members not exceeding 4 in. (102 mm) in depth with steel tube or bar webs, are also defined as bar joists. Bar joist includes noncombustible or combustible roof or floor decks on bar joist construction. See Figures A-1-4.6(b)(i)1 and A-1-4.6(b)(i)2 for examples of bar joist construction.

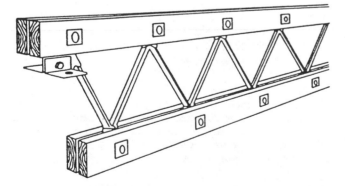

Figure A-1-4.6(b)(i)1   Wood bar joist construction.

(ii) *Open Grid Ceilings.*   Open grid ceilings are ceilings in which the openings are 1/4 in. (6.4 mm) or larger in the least dimension, the thickness of the ceiling material does not exceed the least dimension of the openings, and such openings constitute at least 70 percent of the ceiling area.

(iii) *Smooth Ceiling Construction.*   The term *smooth ceiling construction* as used in this standard includes:

(a)   Flat slab, pan-type reinforced concrete, concrete joist less than 3 ft (0.9 m) on centers.

(b)   Continuous smooth bays formed by wood, concrete, or steel beams spaced more than 7 1/2 ft (2.3 m) on centers — beams supported by columns, girders, or trusses.

(c)   Smooth roof or floor decks supported directly on girders or trusses spaced more than 7 1/2 ft (2.3 m) on centers.

(d)   Smooth monolithic ceilings of at least 3/4 in. (19 mm) of plaster on metal lath or a combination of materials of equivalent fire-resistive rating attached to the underside of wood joists, wood trusses, and bar joists.

(e)   Open web-type steel beams, regardless of spacing.

(f)   Smooth shell-type roofs, such as folded plates, hyperbolic paraboloids, saddles, domes, and long barrel shells.

NOTE: In (b) through (f) above, combustible or noncombustible floor decks are permitted. Item (b) would include standard mill construction.

(g)   Suspended ceilings of combustible or noncombustible construction.

(h)   Smooth monolithic ceilings with fire resistance less than that specified under item (d) attached to the underside of wood joists, wood trusses, and bar joists.

(iv) *Standard Mill Construction.*   The term *standard mill construction* as used in this standard refers to heavy timber construction as defined in NFPA 220, *Standard on Types of Building Construction.*

(v) *Wood Truss Construction.*   The term *wood truss construction* refers to parallel or pitched wood chord members connected by open wood members (webbing) supporting a roof or floor deck. Trusses with steel webbing, similar to bar joist construction, having top and bottom wood chords exceeding 4 in. (102 mm) in depth, should also be considered wood truss construction.

A-1-4.7   Occupancy examples in the listings as shown in the various hazard classifications are intended to represent the norm for those occupancy types. Unusual or abnormal fuel loadings or combustible characteristics and susceptibility for changes in these characteristics, for a particular occupancy, are considerations that should be weighed in the selection and classification.

The Light Hazard classification is intended to encompass residential occupancies; however, this is not intended to preclude the use of listed residential sprinklers in residential occupancies or residential portions of other occupancies.

A-1-4.7.1 Light Hazard Occupancies include occupancies having conditions similar to:

Churches
Clubs
Eaves and overhangs, if combustible construction with
  no combustibles beneath
Educational
Hospitals
Institutional
Libraries, except large stack rooms
Museums
Nursing or convalescent homes
Office, including data processing
Residential
Restaurant seating areas
Theaters and Auditoriums excluding stages and prosceniums
Unused attics.

A-1-4.7.2.1 Ordinary Hazard Occupancies (Group 1) include occupancies having conditions similar to:

Automobile parking and showrooms
Bakeries
Beverage manufacturing
Canneries
Dairy products manufacturing and processing
Electronic plants
Glass and glass products manufacturing
Laundries
Restaurant service areas.

A-1-4.7.2.2 Ordinary Hazard Occupancies (Group 2) include occupancies having conditions similar to:

Cereal mills
Chemical plants — ordinary
Confectionery products
Distilleries
Dry cleaners
Feed mills
Horse stables
Leather goods manufacturing
Libraries — large stack room areas
Machine shops
Metal working
Mercantile
Paper and pulp mills
Paper process plants
Piers and wharves
Post offices
Printing and publishing
Repair garages

Stages
Textile manufacturing
Tire manufacturing
Tobacco products manufacturing
Wood machining
Wood product assembly.

A-1-4.7.3.1 Extra Hazard Occupancies (Group 1) include occupancies having conditions similar to:

Aircraft hangars
Combustible hydraulic fluid use areas
Die casting
Metal extruding
Plywood and particle board manufacturing
Printing [using inks having flash points below 100°F
  (37.9°C)]
Rubber reclaiming, compounding, drying, milling,
  vulcanizing
Saw mills
Textile picking, opening, blending, garnetting, carding,
  combining of cotton, synthetics, wool shoddy, or burlap
Upholstering with plastic foams.

Extra Hazard Occupancies (Group 2) include occupancies having conditions similar to:

Asphalt saturating
Flammable liquids spraying
Flow coating
Mobile home or modular building assemblies (where finished enclosure is present and has combustible interiors)
Open oil quenching
Plastics processing
Solvent cleaning
Varnish and paint dipping.

A-1-4.7.4.1 Other NFPA standards contain design criteria for fire control or fire suppression (*see 1-4.7.4 and Chapter 10*). While these may form the basis of design criteria, this standard describes the methods of design, installation, fabrication, calculation, and evaluation of water supplies that should be used for the specific design of the system.

A-2-1.1 Included among items requiring listing are sprinklers, some pipe and some fittings, hangers, alarm devices, valves controlling flow of water to sprinklers, valve tamper switches, and gauges.

A-2-2.3 Information regarding the highest temperature that may be encountered in any location in a particular installation may be obtained by use of a thermometer that will register the highest temperature encountered; it should be hung for several days in the location in question, with the plant in operation.

A-2-2.4.1 Examples of such locations are paper mills, packing houses, tanneries, alkali plants, organic fertilizer plants, foundries, forge shops, fumigation, pickle and vinegar works, stables, storage battery rooms, electroplating rooms, galvanizing rooms, steam rooms of all descriptions including moist vapor dry kilns, salt storage rooms, locomotive sheds or houses, driveways, areas exposed to outside weather such as piers and wharves exposed to salt air, areas under sidewalks, around bleaching equipment in flour mills, all portions of cold storage buildings where a direct ammonia expansion system is used, and portions of any plant where corrosive vapors prevail.

A-2-2.4.2 Care should be taken in the handling and installation of wax-coated or similar sprinklers to avoid damaging the coating.

A-2-2.4.3 Painting of sprinklers may retard the thermal response of the heat-responsive element, may interfere with the free movement of parts, and may render the sprinkler inoperative. Moreover, painting may invite the application of subsequent coatings, thus increasing the possibility of a malfunction of the sprinkler.

A-2-2.5.2 The use of the wrong type of escutcheon with recessed or flush type sprinklers can result in severe disruption of the spray pattern, which can destroy the effectiveness of the sprinkler.

A-2-2.6 Sprinklers under open gratings should be provided with shields. Shields over automatic sprinklers should not be less, in least dimension, than four times the distance between the shield and fusible element, except special sprinklers incorporating a built-in shield need not comply with this recommendation if listed for the particular application.

A-2-3.2 See Table A-2-3.2.

A-2-3.4 See Table A-2-3.4.

A-2-3.5 Other types of pipe and tube that have been investigated and listed for sprinkler applications include lightweight steel pipe and thermoplastic pipe and fittings. While these products may offer advantages, such as ease of handling and installation, cost effectiveness, reduction of friction losses, and improved corrosion resistance, it is important to recognize that they also have limitations that are to be considered by those contemplating their use or acceptance.

With respect to lightweight steel pipe, corrosion studies have shown that, in comparison to Schedule 40 pipe, its effective life may be reduced, the level of reduction being related to its wall thickness. Further information with respect to corrosion resistance is contained in the individual listings of such products.

With respect to thermoplastic pipe and fittings, exposure of such piping to elevated temperatures in excess of that for which it has been listed may result in distortion or failure. Accordingly, care must be exercised when locating such systems to ensure that the ambient temperature, including seasonal variations, does not exceed the rated value.

Consideration must also be given to the possibility of exposure of the piping to elevated temperatures during a fire. The survival of thermoplastic piping under fire conditions derives primarily from the cooling effect of the discharge from the sprinklers it serves. As this discharge may not occur simultaneously with the rise in ambient temperature and, under some circumstances, may be delayed for periods beyond the tolerance of the piping, protection in the form of a fire resistant membrane is generally required. (Some listings do provide for the use of exposed piping in conjunction with residential or quick-response sprinklers, but only under specific, limited installation criteria.) When protection is required, it is described in the listing information for each individual product, and the requirements given must be followed. Equally important, such protection must be maintained. Removal of, for example, one or more panels in a lay-in ceiling can expose piping in the concealed space to the possibility of failure in the event of a fire. Similarly the relocation of openings through protective ceilings that expose the pipe to heat, inconsistent with the listing, would place the system in jeopardy. The potential for loss of the protective membrane under earthquake conditions should also be considered.

Table A-2-3.2   Steel Pipe Dimensions

Nominal Pipe Size in.	Outside Diameter in.	(mm)	Schedule 10[1] Inside Diameter in.	(mm)	Wall Thickness in.	(mm)	Schedule 30 Inside Diameter in.	(mm)	Wall Thickness in.	(mm)	Schedule 40 Inside Diameter in.	(mm)	Wall Thickness in.	(mm)
1	1.315	(33.4)	1.097	(27.9)	0.109	(2.8)	—	—	—	—	1.049	(26.6)	0.133	(3.4)
1¼	1.660	(42.2)	1.442	(36.6)	0.109	(2.8)	—	—	—	—	1.380	(35.1)	0.140	(3.6)
1½	1.900	(48.3)	1.682	(42.7)	0.109	(2.8)	—	—	—	—	1.610	(40.9)	0.145	(3.7)
2	2.375	(60.3)	2.157	(54.8)	0.109	(2.8)	—	—	—	—	2.067	(52.5)	0.154	(3.9)
2½	2.875	(73.0)	2.635	(66.9)	0.120	(3.0)	—	—	—	—	2.469	(62.7)	0.203	(5.2)
3	3.500	(88.9)	3.260	(82.8)	0.120	(3.0)	—	—	—	—	3.068	(77.9)	0.216	(5.5)
3½	4.000	(101.6)	3.760	(95.5)	0.120	(3.0)	—	—	—	—	3.548	(90.1)	0.226	(5.7)
4	4.500	(114.3)	4.260	(108.2)	0.120	(3.0)	—	—	—	—	4.026	(102.3)	0.237	(6.0)
5	5.563	(141.3)	5.295	(134.5)	0.134	(3.4)	—	—	—	—	5.047	(128.2)	0.258	(6.6)
6	6.625	(168.3)	6.357	(161.5)	0.134[2]	(3.4)	—	—	—	—	6.065	(154.1)	0.280	(7.1)
8	8.625	(219.1)	8.249	(209.5)	0.188[2]	(4.8)	8.071	(205.0)	0.277	(7.0)	—	—	—	—
10	10.75	(273.1)	10.37	(263.4)	0.188[2]	(4.8)	10.14	(257.6)	0.307	(7.8)	—	—	—	—

NOTE 1: Schedule 10 defined to 5 in. (127 mm) nominal pipe size by ASTM A135.
NOTE 2: Wall thickness specified in 2-3.2.

Table A-2-3.4 Copper Tube Dimensions

Nominal Tube Size in.	Outside Diameter in.	(mm)	Type K Inside Diameter in.	(mm)	Wall Thickness in.	(mm)	Type L Inside Diameter in.	(mm)	Wall Thickness in.	(mm)	Type M Inside Diameter in.	(mm)	Wall Thickness in.	(mm)
¾	0.875	(22.2)	0.745	(18.9)	0.065	(1.7)	0.785	(19.9)	0.045	(1.1)	0.811	(20.6)	0.032	(0.8)
1	1.125	(28.6)	0.995	(25.3)	0.065	(1.7)	1.025	(26.0)	0.050	(1.3)	1.055	(26.8)	0.035	(0.9)
1¼	1.375	(34.9)	1.245	(31.6)	0.065	(1.7)	1.265	(32.1)	0.055	(1.4)	1.291	(32.8)	0.042	(1.1)
1½	1.625	(41.3)	1.481	(37.6)	0.072	(1.8)	1.505	(38.2)	0.060	(1.5)	1.527	(38.8)	0.049	(1.2)
2	2.125	(54.0)	1.959	(49.8)	0.083	(2.1)	1.985	(50.4)	0.070	(1.8)	2.009	(51.0)	0.058	(1.5)
2½	2.625	(66.7)	2.435	(61.8)	0.095	(2.4)	2.465	(62.6)	0.080	(2.0)	2.495	(63.4)	0.065	(1.7)
3	3.125	(79.4)	2.907	(73.8)	0.109	(2.8)	2.945	(74.8)	0.090	(2.3)	2.981	(75.7)	0.072	(1.8)
3½	3.625	(92.1)	3.385	(86.0)	0.120	(3.0)	3.425	(87.0)	0.100	(2.5)	3.459	(87.9)	0.083	(2.1)
4	4.125	(104.8)	3.857	(98.0)	0.134	(3.4)	3.905	(99.2)	0.110	(2.8)	3.935	(99.9)	0.095	(2.4)
5	5.125	(130.2)	4.805	(122.0)	0.160	(4.1)	4.875	(123.8)	0.125	(3.2)	4.907	(124.6)	0.109	(2.8)
6	6.125	(155.6)	5.741	(145.8)	0.192	(4.9)	5.845	(148.5)	0.140	(3.6)	5.881	(149.4)	0.122	(3.1)
8	8.125	(206.4)	7.583	(192.6)	0.271	(6.9)	7.725	(196.2)	0.200	(5.1)	7.785	(197.7)	0.170	(4.3)
10	10.13	(257.3)	9.449	(240.0)	0.338	(8.6)	9.625	(244.5)	0.250	(6.4)	9.701	(246.4)	0.212	(5.4)

While the listings of thermoplastic piping do not prohibit its installation in combustible concealed spaces where the provision of sprinkler protection is not required, and while the statistical record of fire originating in such space is low, it should be recognized that the occurrence of a fire in such a space could result in failure of the piping system.

The investigation of pipe and tube other than described in Table 2-3.1 should involve consideration of many factors, including:

(a) Pressure rating.

(b) Beam strength (hangers).

(c) Unsupported vertical stability.

(d) Movement during sprinkler operation (affecting water distribution).

(e) Corrosion (internal and external), chemical and electrolytic.

(f) Resistance to failure when exposed to elevated temperatures.

(g) Methods of joining (strength, permanence, fire hazard).

(h) Physical characteristics related to integrity during earthquakes.

A-2-4.2 Rubber-gasketed pipe fittings and couplings should not be installed where ambient temperatures can be expected to exceed 150°F (66°C) unless listed for this service. If the manufacturer further limits a given gasket compound, those recommendations should be followed.

A-2-4.4 Listed flexible connections are permissible and encouraged for sprinkler installations in racks to reduce the possibility of physical damage. When flexible tubing is used it should be located so that it will be protected against mechanical injury.

A-2-5.1.2 Some steel piping material having lesser wall thickness than specified in 2-5.1.2 has been listed for use in sprinkler systems when joined with threaded connections. The service life of such products may be significantly less than that of Schedule 40 steel pipe, and it should be determined if this service life will be sufficient for the application intended.

All such threads should be checked by the installer using working ring gauges conforming to the Basic Dimensions of Ring Gauges for USA (American) Standard Taper Pipe Threads, NPT, as per ANSI/ASME B1.20.1, Table 8.

A-2-5.2 See Figure A-2-5.2(a) and Figure A-2-5.2(b) on the following page.

A-2-5.2.2 As used in this standard, shop in the term *shop welded* means either:

(a) At the sprinkler contractor's or fabricator's premise.

(b) An approved welding area at the building site.

A-2-5.2.5(a) Listed, shaped, contoured nipples meet the definition of fabricated fittings.

A-2-5.4 The fire hazard of the brazing and soldering processes should be suitably safeguarded.

A-2-5.4.1 Continued corrosive action from self-cleaning fluxes after the soldering or brazing process is completed has resulted in leaks from the seats of sprinklers.

A-2-6.1 See Figure A-2-6.1 on page 79.

A-2-6.1.5 Table 2-6.1.5(a) assumes that the load from 15 ft (5 m) of water-filled pipe, plus 250 lb (114 kg), is located at the midpoint of the span of the trapeze member, with a maximum allowable bending stress of 15 KSI (111 kg). If the load is applied at other than the midpoint, for the purpose of sizing the trapeze member, an equivalent length of trapeze may be used, derived from the formula

$$L = \frac{4\ ab}{a + b}$$

where "L" is the equivalent length, "a" is the distance from one support to the load, and "b" is the distance from the other support to the load.

When multiple mains are to be supported or multiple trapeze hangers are provided in parallel, the required or available section modulus may be added.

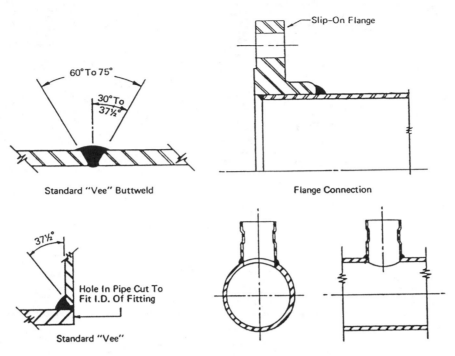

Figure A-2-5.2(a)   Acceptable weld joints.

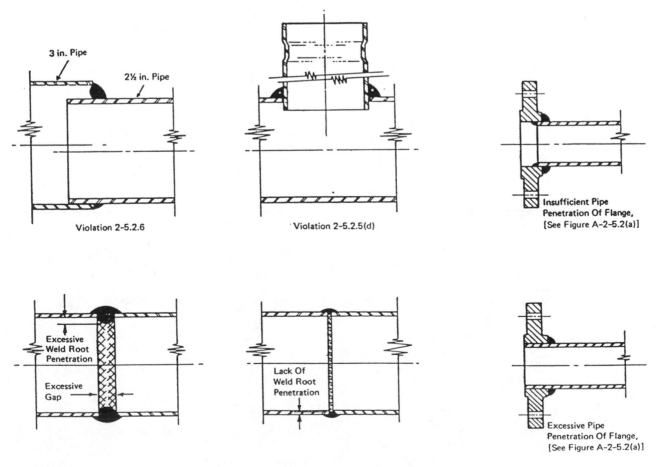

Figure A-2-5.2(b)   Unacceptable weld joints.

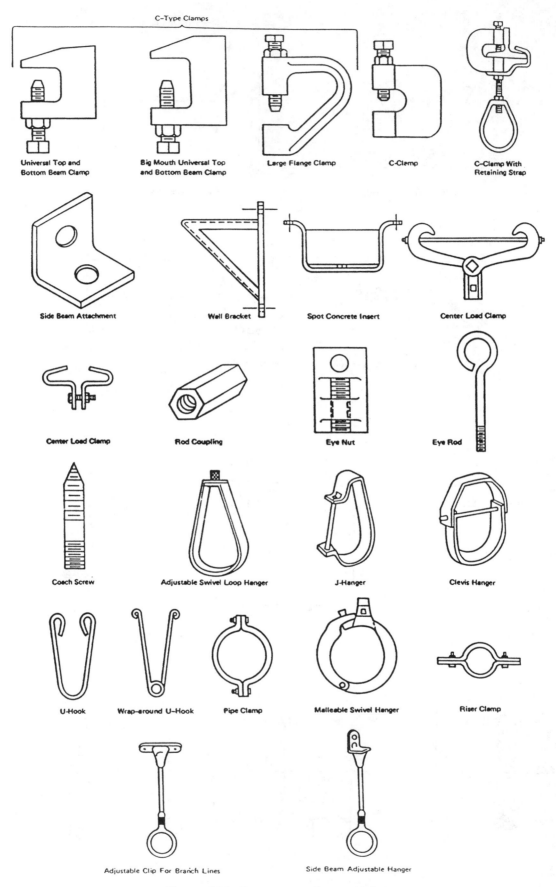

Figure A-2-6.1 Common types of acceptable hangers.

A-2-6.1.7 The rules covering the hanging of sprinkler piping take into consideration the weight of water-filled pipe plus a safety factor. No allowance has been made for the hanging of nonsystem components from sprinkler piping.

A-2-6.3.1 Powder-driven studs should not be used in steel of less than 3/16 in. (4.8 mm) total thickness.

A-2-6.3.2 The ability of concrete to hold the studs varies widely according to type of aggregate, quality of concrete, and proper installation.

A-2-9.2.4 The surge of water when the valve trips may seriously damage the device.

A-2-9.3.1 Audible alarms are normally located on the outside of the building. Listed electric gongs, bells, horns, or sirens inside the building or a combination inside and outside are sometimes advisable.

A-2-9.3.2 All alarm apparatus should be so located and installed that all parts are accessible for inspection, removal, and repair and should be substantially supported.

A-2-9.5.1 Switches that will silence electric alarm sounding devices by interruption of electrical current are not desirable; however, if such means are provided, then the electrical alarm sounding device circuit should be arranged so that when the sounding device is electrically silenced, that fact should be indicated by means of a conspicuous light located in the vicinity of the riser or alarm control panel. This light should remain in operation during the entire period of the electrical circuit interruption.

A-3-2 A dry pipe system should be installed only where heat is not adequate to prevent freezing of water in all or sections of the system. Dry pipe systems should be converted to wet pipe systems when they become unnecessary because adequate heat is provided. Sprinklers should not be shut off in cold weather.

When two or more dry pipe valves are used, systems should preferably be divided horizontally to prevent simultaneous operation of more than one system and the resultant increased time delay in filling systems and discharging water, plus receipt of more than one waterflow alarm signal.

When adequate heat is present in sections of the dry pipe system, consideration should be given to dividing the system into a separate wet pipe system and dry pipe system. Minimized use of dry pipe systems is desirable where speed of operation is of particular concern.

A-3-2.3 The capacities of the various sizes of pipe given in Table A-3-2.3 are for convenience in calculating the capacity of a system.

A-3-2.5 The dry pipe valve should be located in an accessible place near the sprinkler system it controls. When exposed to cold, the dry pipe valve should be located in a valve room or enclosure of adequate size to properly service equipment.

Table A-3-2.3 Capacity of One Foot of Pipe (Based on actual internal pipe diameter)

Nominal Diameter	Gal Sch 40	Gal Sch 10	Nominal Diameter	Gal Sch 40	Gal Sch 10
3/4 in.	0.028	—	3 in.	0.383	0.433
1 in.	0.045	0.049	3 1/2 in.	0.513	0.576
1 1/4 in.	0.078	0.085	4 in.	0.660	0.740
1 1/2 in.	0.106	0.115	5 in.	1.040	1.144
2 in.	0.174	0.190	6 in.	1.501	1.649[1]
2 1/2 in.	0.248	0.283	8 in.	2.66[3]	2.776[2]

For SI Units: 1 in. = 25.4 mm; 1 ft = 0.3048 m; 1 gal = 3.785 L.
[1] 0.134 Wall Pipe
[2] 0.188 Wall Pipe
[3] Schedule 30

A-3-2.6.2 The compressor should draw its air supply from a place where the air is dry and not too warm. Moisture from condensation may cause trouble in the system.

A-3-3.1 Conditions of occupancy or special hazards may require quick application of large quantities of water, and in such cases deluge systems may be needed.

Fire detection devices should be selected to assure operation, yet guard against premature operation of sprinklers, based on normal room temperatures and draft conditions.

In locations where ambient temperature at the ceiling is high from heat sources other than fire conditions, heat-responsive devices that operate at higher than ordinary temperature and are capable of withstanding the normal high temperature for long periods of time should be selected.

When corrosive conditions exist, materials or protective coatings that resist corrosion should be used.

To help avoid ice formation in piping due to accidental tripping of dry pipe valves in cold storage rooms, a deluge automatic water control valve may be used on the supply side of the dry pipe valve. When this combination is employed:

(a) Dry systems may be manifolded to a deluge valve, the protected area not exceeding 40,000 sq ft (3716 m²). The distance between valves should be as short as possible to minimize water hammer.

(b) The dry pipe valves should be pressurized to 50 psi (3.4 bars) to reduce the possibility of dry pipe valve operation from water hammer.

A-3-3.2.1(c) This is sometimes referred to as a double interlock preaction system.

A-3-3.3 When 8-in. (203-mm) piping is employed to reduce friction losses in a system operated by fire detection devices, a 6-in. (152-mm) preaction or deluge valve and 6-in. (152-mm) gate valve between taper reducers should be permitted.

A-3-4.1 Combined dry pipe and preaction systems may be installed when wet pipe systems are impractical. They are intended for use in, but not limited to, structures where a number of dry pipe valves would be required if a dry pipe system were installed.

A-3-4.1.1 See Figure A-3-4.1.1.

A-3-4.3 See Figure A-3-4.3.

A-3-5.1 Antifreeze solutions may be used for maintaining automatic sprinkler protection in small unheated areas. Antifreeze solutions are recommended only for systems not exceeding 40 gal (151 L).

Because of the cost of refilling the system or replenishing small leaks, it is advisable to use small dry valves where more than 40 gal (151 L) are to be supplied.

A-3-5.2 Listed CPVC sprinkler pipe and fittings should be protected from freezing with glycerine only. The use of diethylene, ethylene, or propylene glycols are specifically prohibited. Laboratory testing shows that glycol-based antifreeze solutions present a chemical environment detrimental to CPVC.

A-3-5.2.3 Beyond certain limits, increased proportion of antifreeze does not lower the freezing point of solution. (*See Figure A-3-5.2.3 on the following page.*)

Glycerine, diethylene glycol, ethylene glycol, and propylene glycol should never be used without mixing with water in proper proportions, because these materials tend to thicken near 32°F (0°C).

A-3-5.3 All permitted antifreeze solutions are heavier than water. At the point of contact (interface) the heavier liquid will be below the lighter liquid, preventing diffusion of water into the unheated areas.

A-3-6.1.2 Outlets should be provided at critical points on sprinkler system piping to accommodate attachment of pressure gauges for test purposes.

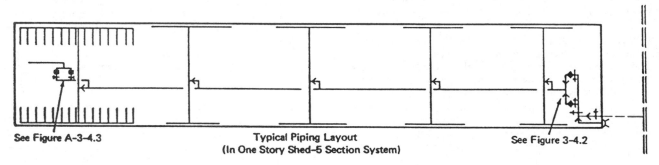

See Figure A-3-4.3

Typical Piping Layout
(In One Story Shed–5 Section System)

See Figure 3-4.2

Figure A-3-4.1.1   Typical piping layout for combined dry pipe and preaction sprinkler system.

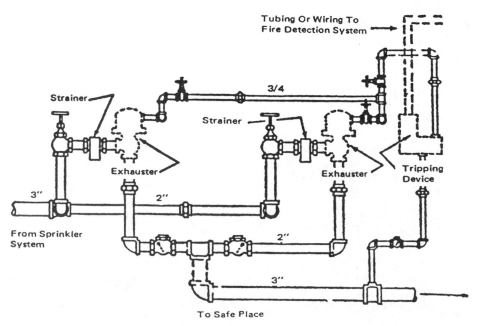

Figure A-3-4.3   Arrangement of air exhaust valves for combined dry pipe and preaction sprinkler system.

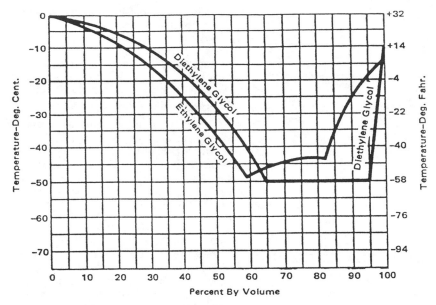

Figure A-3-5.2.3 Freezing points of water solutions of ethylene glycol and diethylene glycol.

A-3-7.2.1 The water supply should be capable of furnishing the total demand for all exposure sprinklers operating simultaneously for protection against the exposure fire under consideration for a duration of not less than 60 minutes.

A-3-8 Careful installation and maintenance, and some special arrangements of piping and devices as outlined in this section, are needed to avoid the formation of ice and frost inside piping in cold storage rooms that will be maintained at or below 32°F (0°C). Conditions are particularly favorable to condensation where pipes enter cold rooms from rooms having temperatures above freezing.

Whenever the opportunity offers, fittings such as those specified in 3-8.1 and illustrated in Figures A-3-8.1(a) and A-3-8.1(b), as well as flushing connections, should be provided in existing systems.

When possible, risers should be located in stair towers or other locations outside of refrigerated areas. This would reduce the probabilities of ice or frost formation within the riser (supply) pipe.

Cross mains should be connected to risers or feed mains with flanges. In general, flanged fittings should be installed at points that would allow easy dismantling of the system. Split ring or other easily removable types of hangers will facilitate the dismantling.

Because it is not practical to allow water to flow into sprinkler piping in spaces that may be constantly subject to freezing, or where temperatures must be maintained at or below 40°F (4.4°C), it is important that means be provided at the time of system installation to conduct trip tests on dry pipe valves that service such systems. NFPA 13A, *Recommended Practice for the Inspection, Testing and Maintenance of Sprinkler Systems*, contains guidance in this matter.

A-3-8.1 Joining of pipe and fittings using split housing couplings may allow separation of pipe for internal inspection.

A-3-8.1(a) This may be accomplished by a blind flange on a fitting (tee or cross) in the riser or cross main or a removable section 24 in. (610 mm) long in the feed main as shown in Figure A-3-8.1(a). Such fittings in conjunction with the flushing connections specified in 9-3.2 permit examination of the entire length of the cross mains. Branch lines may be examined by disconnecting them from cross mains.

A-3-8.1(b) This may be accomplished by means of 2-in. (51-mm) capped nipples or blind flanges on fittings.

A-3-8.1(c) This can be accomplished at floor penetrations by a tee with a blind flange in the cold room and at wall penetrations by a 24-in. (610-mm) flanged removable section in the warm room as shown in Figure A-3-8.1(b).

A-3-8.4 Propylene glycol or other suitable material may be used as a substitute for priming water, to prevent evaporation of the priming fluid and thus reduce ice formation within the system, subject to state and local health regulations.

A-3-9.2 See Figure A-3-9.2 on page 84.

A-4-1 The installation requirements are specific for the normal arrangement of structural members. There will be arrangements of structural members not specifically detailed by the requirements. By applying the basic principles, layouts for such construction can vary from specific illustrations, provided the maximum specified for the spacing and location of sprinklers (Section 4-4) are not exceeded.

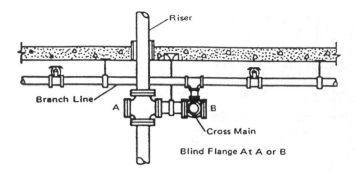

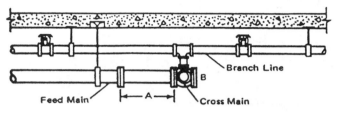

(a) Elevation At Riser And Cross Main

(b) Elevation At Feed Main And Cross Main

For SI Units: 1 in. = 25.4 mm.

Figure A-3-8.1(a) Fittings to facilitate examination of feed mains, risers, and cross mains in freezing areas.

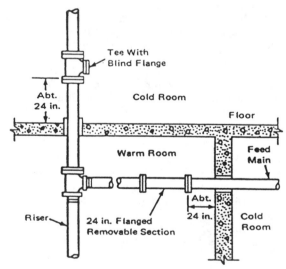

For SI Units: 1 in. = 25.4 mm.

Figure A-3-8.1(b) Fittings in feed main or riser passing through wall or floor from warm room to cold room.

A-4-1.1 This standard contemplates full sprinkler protection for all areas. Other NFPA standards that mandate sprinkler installation may not require sprinklers in certain areas. The requirements of this standard should be used insofar as they are applicable. The authority having jurisdiction should be consulted in each case.

When buildings or portions of buildings are of combustible construction or contain combustible material, standard fire barriers should be provided to separate the areas that are sprinkler protected from adjoining unsprinklered areas. All openings should be protected in accordance with applicable standards, and no sprinkler piping should be placed in an unsprinklered area unless the area is permitted to be unsprinklered by this standard.

Water supplies for partial systems should be designed with consideration to the fact that in a partial system more sprinklers may be opened in a fire that originates in an unprotected area and spreads to the sprinklered area than would be the case in a completely protected building. Fire originating in a non-sprinklered area may overpower the partial sprinkler system.

When sprinklers are installed in corridors only, sprinklers should be spaced up to the maximum of 15 ft (4.5 m) along the corridor, with one sprinkler opposite the center of any door or pair of adjacent doors opening onto the corridor, and with an additional sprinkler installed inside each adjacent room above the door opening. When the sprinkler in the adjacent room provides full protection for that space, an additional sprinkler is not required in the corridor adjacent to the door.

A-4-2.2 Tests involving areas of coverage over 100 sq ft (9.3 m²) for large-drop sprinklers are limited in number, and use of areas of coverage over 100 sq ft (9.3 m²) should be carefully considered.

Joists above Girders or Framed into Girders;
Branch Lines Uniformly Spaced between Girders
Maximum Spacing: 130 sq ft per Sprinkler
L × S = 130 or less

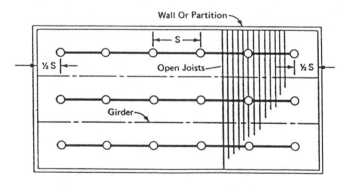

Key

L = Distance between branch lines, limit 15 ft.
S = Distance bewteen sprinklers on branch lines, limit 15 ft.
Y = Maximum distance between girders.

Examples

Y	L	S (Max)	Y	L	S (Max)
10 ft 9 in.	10 ft 9 in.	12 ft 1 in.	10 ft 10 in. 12 ft 1 in.	10 ft 10 in. 12 ft 1 in.	12 ft 0 in. 10 ft 9 in.

For SI Units: 1 in. = 25.4 mm; 1 ft = 0.3048 m; 1 ft² = 0.0929 m².

Figure A-4-2.2 Layout of sprinklers under open wood joist construction—Ordinary Hazard Occupancies.

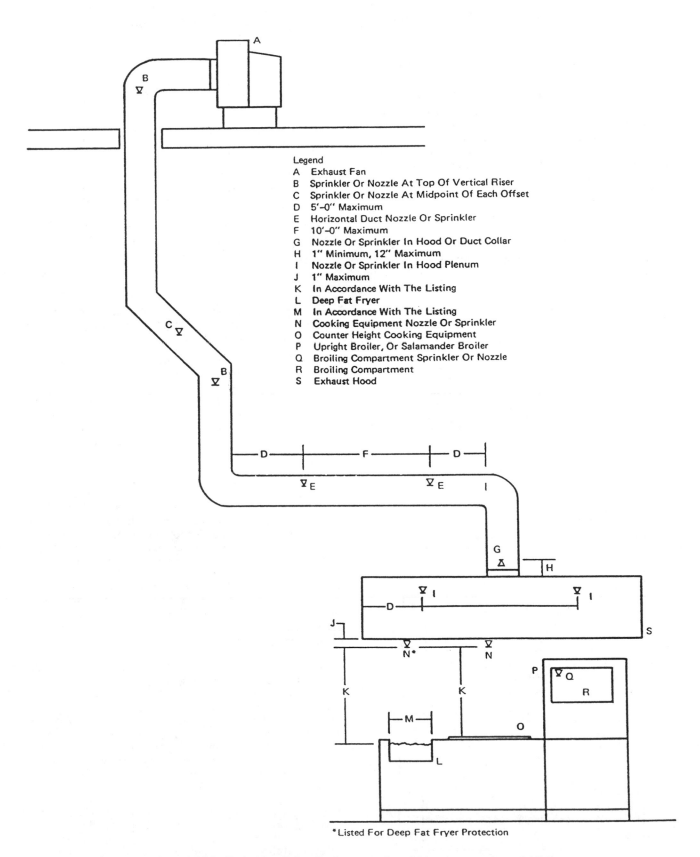

Legend

A   Exhaust Fan
B   Sprinkler Or Nozzle At Top Of Vertical Riser
C   Sprinkler Or Nozzle At Midpoint Of Each Offset
D   5'–0" Maximum
E   Horizontal Duct Nozzle Or Sprinkler
F   10'–0" Maximum
G   Nozzle Or Sprinkler In Hood Or Duct Collar
H   1" Minimum, 12" Maximum
I   Nozzle Or Sprinkler In Hood Plenum
J   1" Maximum
K   In Accordance With The Listing
L   Deep Fat Fryer
M   In Accordance With The Listing
N   Cooking Equipment Nozzle Or Sprinkler
O   Counter Height Cooking Equipment
P   Upright Broiler, Or Salamander Broiler
Q   Broiling Compartment Sprinkler Or Nozzle
R   Broiling Compartment
S   Exhaust Hood

*Listed For Deep Fat Fryer Protection

Figure A-3-9.2   Typical installation showing automatic sprinklers or automatic nozzles being used for the protection of commercial cooking equipment and ventilation systems.

A-4-3.1.1 The evaluation for usage should be based upon a review of available technical data.

A-4-3.1.2 This requirement is to minimize the obstruction of the discharge pattern.

A-4-3.6.1 The response and water distribution pattern of listed residential sprinklers have been shown by extensive fire testing to provide better control than spray sprinklers in residential occupancies. These sprinklers are intended to prevent flashover in the room of fire origin, thus improving the chance for occupants to escape or be evacuated.

A-4-3.8.2 This requirement is to avoid scale accumulation.

A-4-4.1.2.1 Exception An example of sprinklers in small rooms for hydraulically designed and pipe schedule systems is shown in Figure A-4-4.1.2.1(a), and examples for hydraulically designed systems only are shown in Figures A-4-4.1.2.1(b), (c), and (d).

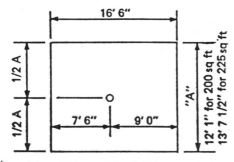

For SI Units: 1 in. = 25.4 mm; 1 ft = 0.3048 m.
Figure A-4-4.1.2.1(a).

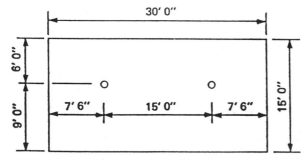

For SI Units: 1 in. = 25.4 mm; 1 ft = 0.3048 m.
Figure A-4-4.1.2.1(b).

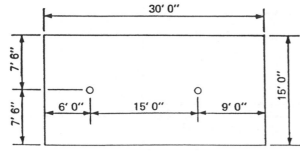

For SI Units: 1 in. = 25.4 mm; 1 ft = 0.3048 m.
Figure A-4-4.1.2.1(c).

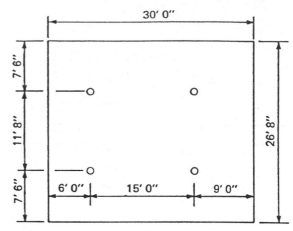

For SI Units: 1 in. = 25.4 mm; 1 ft = 0.3048 m.
Figure A-4-4.1.2.1(d).

A-4-4.1.3.1 When of a depth that will obstruct the spray discharge pattern, girders, beams or trusses forming narrow pockets of combustible construction along walls may require additional sprinklers.

A-4-4.1.3.2.1 Frequently, additional sprinkler equipment can be avoided by reducing the width of decks or galleries and providing proper clearances. Slatting of decks or walkways or the use of open grating as a substitute for automatic sprinklers thereunder is not acceptable. The use of cloth or paper dust tops for rooms forms obstruction to water distribution. If employed, the area below should be sprinklered.

A-4-4.1.3.3 The distances given in Table 4-4.1.3.3 were determined through tests in which privacy curtains with either a solid fabric or close mesh [1/4 in. (6.4 mm)] top panel were installed. For broader-mesh top panels, e.g., 1/2 in. (13 mm), the obstruction of the sprinkler spray is not likely to be severe and the authority having jurisdiction may not need to apply the requirements in 4-4.1.3.3.

A-4-4.1.5 On sprinkler lines larger than 2 in. (51 mm), consideration should be given to the distribution interference caused by the pipe, which can be minimized by installing sprinklers on riser nipples or installing sprinklers in the pendent position.

A-4-4.1.6 The 18 in. (457 mm) dimension is not intended to limit the height of shelving on a wall or shelving against a wall in accordance with 4-4.1.6. When shelving is installed on a wall and is not directly below sprinklers, the shelves, including storage thereon, may extend above the level of a plane located 18 in. (457 mm) below ceiling sprinkler deflectors. Shelving, and any storage thereon, directly below the sprinklers may not extend above a plane located 18 in. (457 mm) below the ceiling sprinkler deflectors.

A-4-4.1.7.1.1 Exceptions No. 1, 2, and 3 do not require sprinkler protection because it is not physically practical to install sprinklers in these spaces. To reduce the possibility of uncontrolled fire spread, consideration should be given in these unsprinklered concealed space situations to using Exceptions No. 5, 8, and 9.

A-4-4.1.7.2.2 When practicable, sprinklers should be staggered at the alternate floor levels, particularly when only one sprinkler is installed at each floor level.

A-4-4.1.7.3.3 See Figures A-4-4.1.7.3.3(a) and (b).

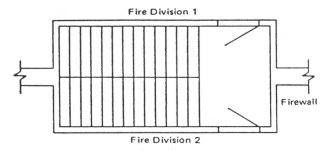

Figure A-4-4.1.7.3.3(a) Noncombustible stair shaft serving two fire sections.

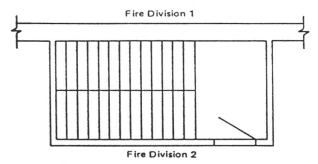

Figure A-4-4.1.7.3.3(b) Noncombustible stair shaft serving one fire section.

A-4-4.1.7.3.4 When sprinklers in the normal ceiling pattern are closer than 6 ft (1.8 m) from the water curtain, it may be preferable to locate the water curtain sprinklers in recessed baffle pockets. (*See Figure A-4-4.1.7.3.4.*)

A-4-4.1.7.4 The installation of sprinklers at floor levels should be arranged so as to protect the sprinklers from mechanical injury and from falling materials and not cause obstruction within the chute. This can usually be accomplished by recessing the sprinkler in the wall of the chute or by providing a protective deflector canopy over the sprinkler. Sprinklers should be placed so that there will be minimum interference of the discharge therefrom. (*See also 1-6.2.*) Sprinklers with special directional discharge characteristics may be advantageous. (*See Figure A-4-4.1.7.4.*)

A-4-4.1.7.6 Small loading docks, covered platforms, ducts, or similar small unheated areas may be protected by dry-pendent sprinklers extending through the wall from wet sprinkler piping in an adjacent heated area. When protecting covered platforms, loading docks, and similar areas, a dry-pendent sprinkler should extend down at a 45 degree angle. The width of the area to be protected should not exceed 7½ ft (2.3 m). Sprinklers should be spaced not over 12 ft (3.7 m) apart. (*See Figure A-4-4.1.7.6.*)

A-4-4.1.7.9.2 Saw-toothed roofs have regularly spaced monitors of saw tooth shape, with the nearly vertical side glazed and usually arranged for venting. Sprinkler placement is limited to a maximum of 3 ft down the slope from the peak because of the effect of venting on sprinkler sensitivity.

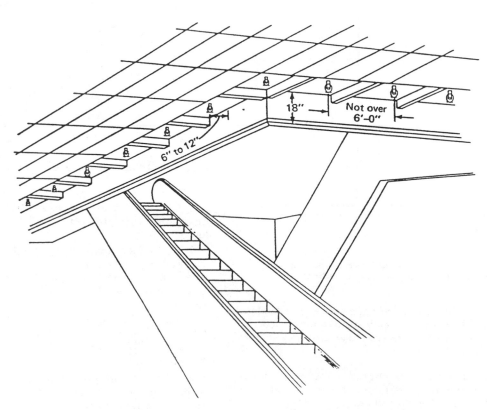

Figure A-4-4.1.7.3.4 Sprinklers around escalators.

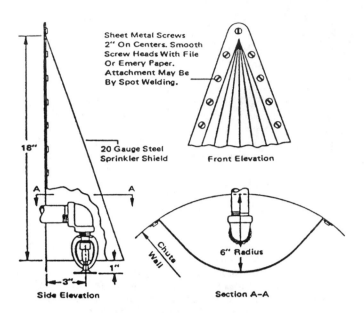

Figure A-4-4.1.7.4 Canopy for protecting sprinklers in building service chutes.

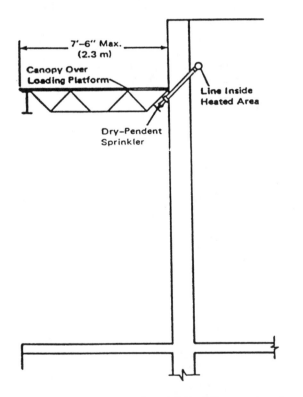

Figure A-4-4.1.7.6 Dry-pendent sprinklers for protection of covered platforms, loading docks, and similar areas.

A-4-4.1.7.13 The installation of open-grid egg crate, louver, or honeycomb ceilings beneath sprinklers restricts the sideways travel of the sprinkler discharge and may change the character of discharge.

A-4-4.1.7.14.3 Drop-out ceilings do not provide the required protection for soft-soldered copper joints or other piping that requires protection.

A-4-4.1.7.14.4 The ceiling tiles may drop before sprinkler operation. Delayed operation may occur because heat must then bank down from the deck above before sprinklers will operate.

A-4-4.1.7.15 See NFPA 81, *Standard on Fur Storage, Fumigation and Cleaning.* For tests of sprinkler performance in fur vaults see Fact Finding Report on Automatic Sprinkler Protection for Fur Storage Vaults of Underwriters Laboratories Inc., dated November 25, 1947.

A-4-4.1.7.23 One and one-half (1½) in. hose connections for use in storage occupancies and other locations where standpipe systems are not required are covered by this standard. When Class II standpipe systems are required, see the appropriate provisions of NFPA 14, *Standard for the Installation of Standpipe and Hose Systems,* with respect to hose stations and water supply for hose connections from sprinkler systems.

A-4-4.1.7.24 Combined automatic sprinkler and standpipe risers should not be interconnected by sprinkler system piping.

A-4-4.1.7.25 See Figure A-4-4.1.7.25.

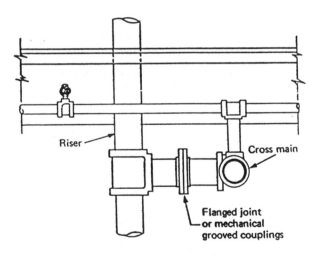

Figure A-4-4.1.7.25 One arrangement of flanged joint at sprinkler riser.

A-4-4.2.2.1 The protection area per sprinkler should be determined using the S x L = Protection Area rule as follows:

1. "S" — Determine distance to the next sprinkler (or to the wall, in case of an end sprinkler on a branch line) upstream and downstream. Choose the larger of either twice the distance to the wall or the distance to the next sprinkler.

2. "L" — The distance to the opposite side of the room will be "L." Where sprinklers are provided on both sides of the room, "L" should be half the distance between the walls.

A-4-4.3.1 It is important that sprinklers in the immediate vicinity of the fire center not skip, and this requirement imposes certain restrictions on the spacing.

A-4-4.3.3 If all other factors are held constant, the operating time of the first sprinkler will vary exponentially with the distance between the ceiling and deflector. At distances greater than 7 in. (178 mm), for other than open wood joist construction, the delayed operating time will permit the fire to gain headway, with the result that substantially more sprinklers operate. At distances less than 7 in. (178 mm), other effects come into play. Changes in distribution, penetration, and cooling nullify the advantage gained by faster operation. The net result is again increased fire damage accompanied by an increase in the number of sprinklers operated. The optimum clearance between deflectors and ceiling is, therefore, 7 in. (178 mm). For open wood joist construction the optimum clearance between deflectors and the bottom of joists is $3\frac{1}{2}$ in. (89 mm).

A-4-4.3.4 To a great extent, large-drop sprinklers rely on direct attack to gain rapid control of both the burning fuel and ceiling temperatures. Therefore, interference with the discharge pattern and obstructions to the distribution should be avoided.

A-4-5.1.1 See Figure A-4-5.1.1.

A-4-5.1.1.1 A water supply connection should not extend into a building or through a building wall unless such connection is under the control of an outside listed indicating valve or an inside listed indicating valve located near the outside wall of the building.

All valves controlling water supplies for sprinkler systems or portions thereof, including floor control valves, should be accessible to authorized persons during emergencies. Permanent ladders, clamped treads on risers, chain-operated hand wheels, or other accepted means should be provided when necessary.

Outside control valves are suggested in the following order of preference:

(a) Listed indicating valves at each connection into the building at least 40 ft (12.2 m) from buildings if space permits.

(b) Control valves installed in a cutoff stair tower or valve room accessible from outside.

(c) Valves located in risers with indicating posts arranged for outside operation.

(d) Key-operated valves in each connection into the building.

A-4-5.1.1.6 When a system having only one dry pipe valve is supplied with city water and fire department connection it will be satisfactory to install the main check valve in water supply connection immediately inside of the building. In instances where there is no outside control valve, the system indicating valve should be placed at the service flange, on the supply side of all fittings.

A-4-5.1.1.7 See Figure A-4-5.1.1.7.

A-4-5.1.2.3 When the relief valve operation would result in water being discharged onto interior walking or working surfaces, consideration should be given to piping the discharge from the valve to a drain connection or other safe location.

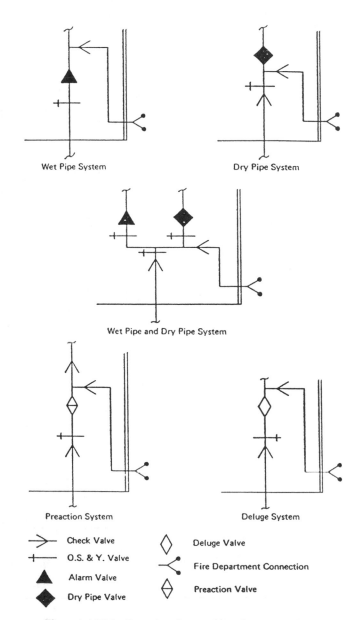

Figure A-4-5.1.1 Examples of acceptable valve arrangements.

A-4-5.2.2.1 When copper tube is to be installed in moist areas or other environments conducive to galvanic corrosion, copper hangers or ferrous hangers with an insulating material should be used.

A-4-5.2.3.1 Exception No. 1 See Figure A-4-5.2.3.1.

A-4-5.2.3.3 Sprinkler piping should be adequately secured to restrict the movement of piping upon sprinkler operation. The reaction forces caused by the flow of water through the sprinkler could result in displacement of the sprinkler, thereby adversely affecting sprinkler discharge. Listed CPVC pipe and listed polybutylene pipe have specific requirements for piping support to include additional pipe bracing of sprinklers. (*See Figure A-4-5.2.3.3.*)

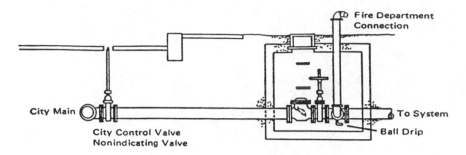

Figure A-4-5.1.1.7   Pit for gate valve, check valve, and fire department connection.

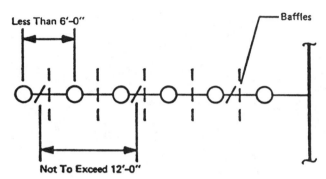

For SI Units: 1 in. = 25.4 mm; 1 ft = 0.3048 m.

Figure A-4-5.2.3.1   Distance between hangers.

A-4-5.2.3.3 Exception No. 1   See Figure A-4-5.2.3.3 Exception No. 1.

A-4-5.2.3.3 Exception No. 2   See Figure A-4-5.2.3.3 Exception No. 2 on the following page.

A-4-5.2.3.4   See Figure A-4-5.2.3.4 on the following page.

A-4-5.2.3.4 Exception   See Figure A-4-5.2.3.4 Exception on the following page.

A-4-5.3.1   All piping should be arranged where practicable to drain to the main drain valve.

A-4-5.3.5.2.3   An example of an accessible location would be a valve located approximately 7 ft (2 m) above the floor level to which a hose could be connected to discharge the water in an acceptable manner.

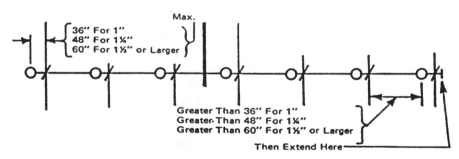

For SI Units: 1 in. = 25.4 mm; 1 ft = 0.3048 m.

Figure A-4-5.2.3.3   Distance from sprinkler to hanger.

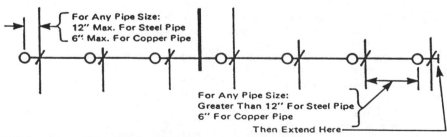

For SI Units: 1 in. = 25.4 mm; 1 ft = 0.3048 m.

Figure A-4-5.2.3.3 Exception No. 1   Distance from sprinkler to hanger where maximum pressure exceeds 100 psi (6.9 bars) and a branch line above a ceiling supplies pendent sprinklers below the ceiling.

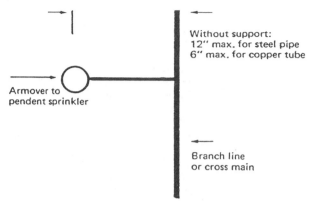

For SI Units: 1 in. = 25.4 mm; 1 ft = 0.3048 m.

NOTE: The pendent sprinkler may be installed either directly in the fitting at the end of the armover or in a fitting at the bottom of a drop nipple.

Figure A-4-5.2.3.4 Exception   Maximum length of unsupported armover when the maximum pressure exceeds 100 psi (6.9 bars) and a branch line above a ceiling supplies pendent sprinklers below the ceiling.

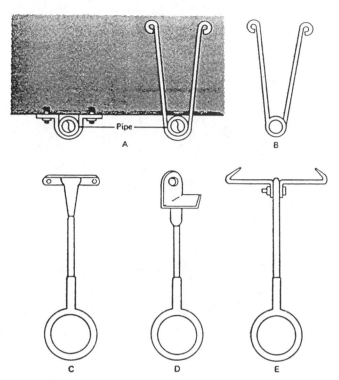

A U-type hangers for branch lines
B Wraparound U-hook
C Adjustable clip for branch lines
D Side beam adjustable hanger
E Adjustable coach screw clip for branch lines

Figure A-4-5.2.3.3 Exception No. 2   Examples of acceptable hangers for end of line (or armover) pendent sprinklers.

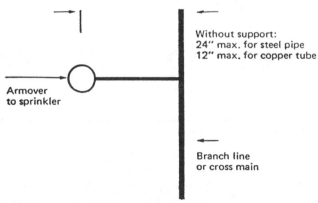

For SI Units: 1 in. = 25.4 mm; 1 ft = 0.3048 m.

Figure A-4-5.2.3.4   Maximum length for unsupported armover.

A-4-5.3.6.1   When possible, the main sprinkler riser drain should discharge outside the building at a point free from the possibility of causing water damage. When it is not possible to discharge outside the building wall, the drain should be piped to a sump, which in turn should discharge by gravity or be pumped to a waste water drain or sewer. The main sprinkler riser drain connection should be of a size sufficient to carry off water from the fully open drain valve while it is discharging under normal water system pressures. When this is not possible, a supplementary

drain of equal size should be provided for test purposes with free discharge, located at or above grade.

A-4-5.4.2.1   Types of locations where corrosive conditions may exist include bleacheries, dye houses, metal plating processes, animal pens, and certain chemical plants.

If corrosive conditions are not of great intensity and humidity is not abnormally high, good results can be obtained by a protective coating of red lead and varnish or by a good grade of commercial acid-resisting paint. The paint manufacturer's instructions should be followed in the preparation of the surface and in the method of application.

Where moisture conditions are severe but corrosive conditions are not of great intensity, copper tube or galvanized steel pipe, fittings, and hangers may be suitable. The exposed threads of steel pipe should be painted.

In instances where the piping is not readily accessible and where the exposure to corrosive fumes is severe, either a protective coating of high quality may be employed or some form of corrosion-resistant material used.

A-4-5.4.3.1   Sprinkler systems are protected against earthquake damage by means of the following:

(a) Stresses that would develop in the piping due to differential building movement are minimized through the use of flexible joints or clearances.

(b) Bracing is used to keep the piping fairly rigid when supported from a building component expected to move as a unit, such as a ceiling.

Areas known to have a potential for earthquakes have been identified in building code and insurance maps. An example of such a map is shown in Figure A-4-5.4.3.1.

A-4-5.4.3.2   Strains on sprinkler piping can be greatly lessened and, in many cases, damage prevented by increasing the flexibility between major parts of the sprinkler system. One part of the piping should never be held rigidly and another part allowed to move freely without provision for relieving the strain. Flexibility can be provided by using listed flexible couplings, by joining grooved end pipe at critical points, and by allowing clearances at walls and floors.

Source—Insurance Services Office

Earthquake Zones

1—Maximum potential for earthquake damage   3—Slight potential
2—Reasonable potential   4 and 5—Earthquake protection not required

Figure A-4-5.4.3.1   Example of seismic map.

Tank or pump risers should be treated the same as sprinkler risers for their portion within a building. The discharge pipe of tanks on buildings should have a control valve above the roof line so any pipe break within the building can be controlled.

Piping 3 in. (76 mm) or smaller in size is pliable enough so that flexible couplings are not usually necessary. A flexible coupling is a mechanical coupling or fitting that permits some angular displacement, axial displacement, and rotation of the piping without failure of the pipe or fitting. "Rigid-type" mechanical couplings that do not permit movement at the grooved connections are not considered flexible couplings [*See Figures A-4-5.4.3.2(a) and (b) on the following page.*]

A-4-5.4.3.2(d)   A building expansion joint is usually a bituminous fiber strip used to separate blocks or units of concrete to prevent cracking due to expansion as a result of temperature changes. In this case, the flexible coupling required on one side by 4-5.4.3.2(d) will suffice.

For seismic separation joints, considerably more flexibility is needed, particularly for piping above the first floor. Figure A-4-5.4.3.3 on page 93 shows a method of providing additional flexibility through the use of swing joints.

A-4-5.4.3.3   Plan and elevation views of a seismic separation assembly assembled with flexible elbows are shown in Figure A-4-5.4.3.3.

A seismic separation assembly is considered to be an assembly of fittings, pipe, and couplings or an assembly of pipe and couplings that permits movement in all directions. The extent of permitted movement should be sufficient to accommodate calculated differential motions during earthquakes. In lieu of calculations, permitted movement can be made at least twice the actual separations, at right angles to the separation as well as parallel to it.

A-4-5.4.3.4   While clearances are necessary around the sprinkler piping to prevent breakage due to building movement, suitable provision should also be made to prevent passage of water, smoke, or fire.

Drains, fire department connections, and other auxiliary piping connected to risers should not be cemented into walls or floors; similarly, pipes that pass horizontally through walls or foundations should not be cemented solidly or strains will accumulate at such points.

When risers or lengths of pipe extend through suspended ceilings, they should not be fastened to the ceiling framing members.

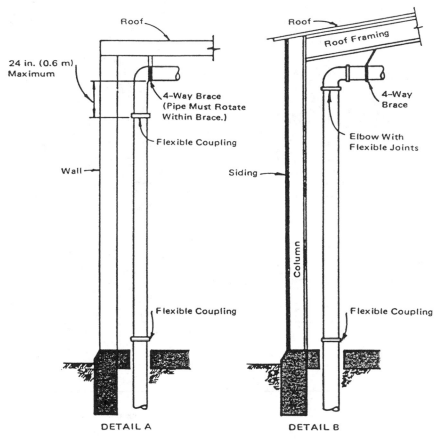

Note to Detail A: The four-way brace should be attached above the upper flexible coupling required for the riser and preferably to the roof structure if suitable. The brace should not be attached directly to a plywood or metal deck.

Figure A-4-5.4.3.2(a)   Riser details.

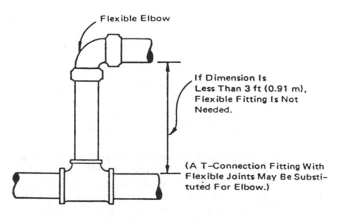

Figure A-4-5.4.3.2(b)   Detail at short riser.

A-4-5.4.3.5.1 Location of Sway Bracing. Two-way braces are either longitudinal or lateral depending on their orientation with the axis of the piping. [*See Figures A-4-5.4.3.5.1(a), (b), (c), and (d) on the following pages.*] The simplest form of two-way brace is a piece of steel pipe or angle. Because the brace must act in both compression and tension, it is necessary to size the brace to prevent buckling.

An important aspect of sway bracing is its location. In Building 1 of Figure A-4-5.4.3.5.1(a), the relatively heavy main will pull on the branch lines when shaking occurs. If the branch lines are held rigidly to the roof or floor above, the fittings can fracture due to the induced stresses.

Bracing should be on the main as indicated at Location B. With shaking in the direction of the arrows, the light branch lines will be held at the fittings. Where necessary, a lateral brace or other restraint should be installed to prevent a branch line from striking against building components or equipment.

A four-way brace is indicated at Location A. This keeps the riser and main lined up and also prevents the main from shifting.

In Building 1, the branch lines are flexible in a direction parallel to the main, regardless of building movement. The heavy main cannot shift under the roof or floor, and it also steadies the branch lines. While the main is braced, the flexible couplings on the riser allow the sprinkler system to move with the floor or roof above, relative to the floor below.

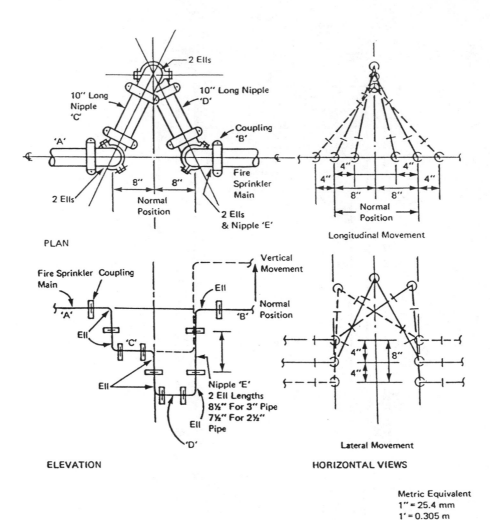

Metric Equivalent
1" = 25.4 mm
1' = 0.305 m

NOTE: The figure illustrates an 8-in. separation crossed by pipes up to 4 in. in nominal diameter. For other
separation distances and pipe sizes, lengths and distances should be modified proportionally.

Figure A-4-5.4.3.3   Seismic separation assembly.

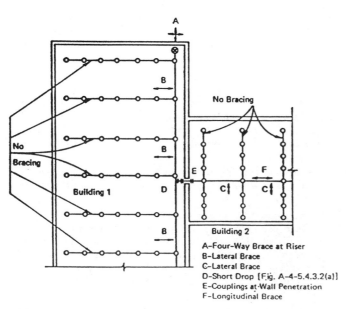

A—Four-Way Brace at Riser
B—Lateral Brace
C—Lateral Brace
D—Short Drop [Fig. A-4-5.4.3.2(a)]
E—Couplings at Wall Penetration
F—Longitudinal Brace

Figure A-4-5.4.3.5.1(a)   Earthquake protection for sprinkler piping.

Figures A-4-5.4.3.5.1(b), (c), and (d) show typical locations of sway bracing.

Listed devices permitting connection of braces to both the pipe and the building structure are available and are recommended. However, alternate means of attachment capable of handling the expected loads are acceptable.

Connection of the brace to the pipe can be made with a pipe clamp or U-bolt. One bolt of the pipe clamp can pass through a flattened end of pipe or one leg of an angle. (The other leg and filet of the angle can be cut away.) Pipe rings should be avoided because they result in a loose fit. Once the pipe is able to vibrate within a loose fitting, the bolts in the ring assembly can be fractured.

The brace can be attached to the structural system directly through a leg of an angle or a flattened portion of pipe. Where dimensions are tight or some play must be allowed, a special fitting can be used. [See Figure A-4-5.4.3.5.1(b).] This threads on an end of pipe. Rotation of the flat around the bolt allows play in the angle of the brace without sacrificing snugness.

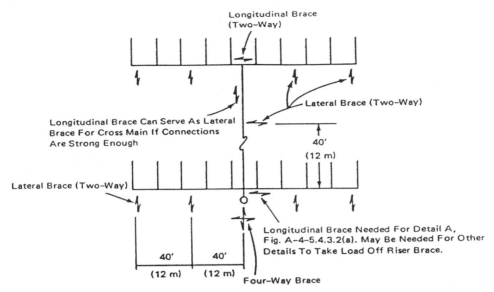

Figure A-4-5.4.3.5.1(b) Typical location of bracing on a tree system.

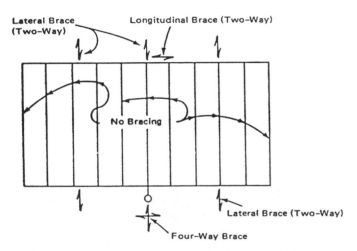

Figure A-4-5.4.3.5.1(c) Typical location of bracing on a gridded system.

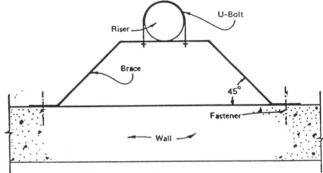

Figure A-4-5.4.3.5.1(e) Detail of four-way brace at riser.

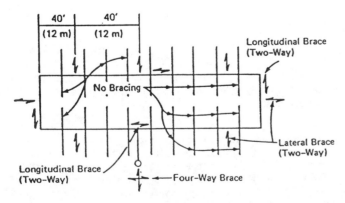

Figure A-4-5.4.3.5.1(d) Typical location of bracing on a looped system.

Some adjustment can be provided in a pipe brace by use of a left-hand/right-hand coupling. For all threaded connections, sight holes or other means should be provided to permit indication that sufficient thread is engaged.

To properly size and space braces, it is necessary to employ the following steps:

(a) Based on the distance of mains from the structural members that will support the braces, choose brace shapes and sizes from Table 4-5.4.3.5.1(b) such that the maximum slenderness ratios l/r do not exceed 200. The angle of the braces from the vertical should be at least 30 degrees and preferably 45 degrees or more.

(b) Tentatively space lateral braces at 40 ft (12 m) maximum distances along mains and tentatively space longitudinal braces at 80 ft (24 m) maximum distances along mains. Lateral braces should meet the piping at right angles, and longitudinal braces should be aligned with the piping.

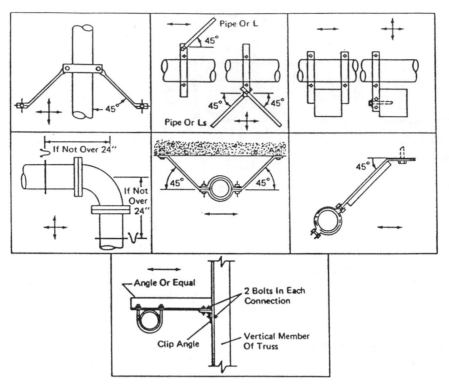

Figure A-4-5.4.3.5.1(f)   Acceptable types of sway bracing.

(c) Determine the total load tentatively applied to each brace in accordance with the examples shown in Figure A-4-5.4.3.5.1(h) and the following:

1. For the loads on lateral braces on cross mains, add one-half the weight of branch to one-half the weight of the portion of the cross main within the zone of influence of the brace. [*See examples 1, 3, 6, and 7 in Figure A-4-5.4.3.5.1(h) on the following page.*]

2. For the loads on longitudinal braces on cross mains, consider only one-half the weight of the cross mains, feed mains, and the first 15 ft of branch line piping within the zone of influence. Branch lines need not be included if piping is provided with lateral sway bracing.

3. For the four-way brace at the riser, add the longitudinal and lateral loads within the zone of influence of the brace. [*See examples 2, 3, 4, 5, 7, and 8 in Figure A-4-5.4.3.5.1(h) on the following page.*]

Use the information on weights of water-filled piping contained within Table A-4-5.4.3.5.1.

(d) If the total expected loads are less than the maximums permitted in Table 4-5.4.3.5.1(b) for the particular brace and orientation, go on to step (e). If not, add additional braces to reduce the zones of influence of overloaded braces.

(e) Check that fasteners connecting the braces to structural supporting members are adequate to support the expected loads on the braces in accordance with Table 4-5.4.3.5.1(c). If not, again add additional braces or additional means of support.

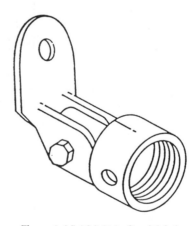

Figure A-4-5.4.3.5.1(g)   Special fitting.

A-4-5.4.3.5.3   The four-way brace provided at the riser may also provide longitudinal and lateral bracing for adjacent mains.

A-4-5.4.3.5.8   Wires used for piping restraints should be attached to the branch line with two tight turns around the pipe, and fastened with four tight turns within 1½ inches, and should be attached to the structure in accordance with the details shown in Figures A-4-5.4.3.5.8(a) through (d) on the following pages or other approved method.

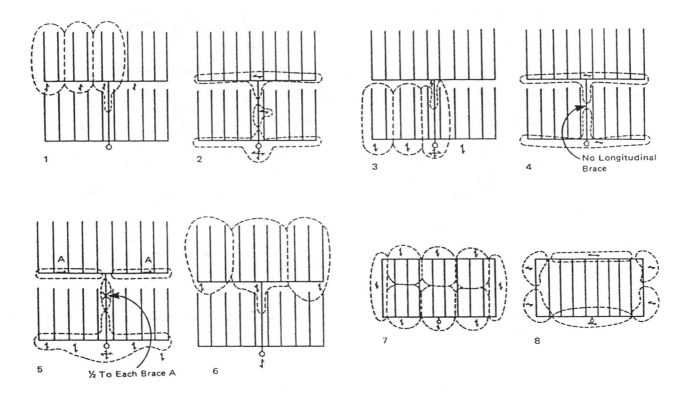

Figure A-4-5.4.3.5.1(h)   Examples of load distribution to bracing.

Table A-4-5.4.3.5.1   Piping Weights for Determining Horizontal Load

Schedule 40 Pipe	Weight of Water-Filled Pipe (lb per ft)	½ Weight of Water-Filled Pipe (lb per ft)
1	2.05	1.03
1¼	2.93	1.47
1½	3.61	1.81
2	5.13	2.57
2½	7.89	3.95
3	10.82	5.41
3½	13.48	6.74
4	16.40	8.20
5	23.47	11.74
6	31.69	15.85
8*	47.70	23.85
Schedule 10 Pipe		
1	1.81	0.91
1¼	2.52	1.26
1½	3.04	1.52
2	4.22	2.11
2½	5.89	2.95
3	7.94	3.97
3½	9.78	4.89
4	11.78	5.89
5	17.30	8.65
6	23.03	11.52
8	40.08	20.04

* Schedule 30

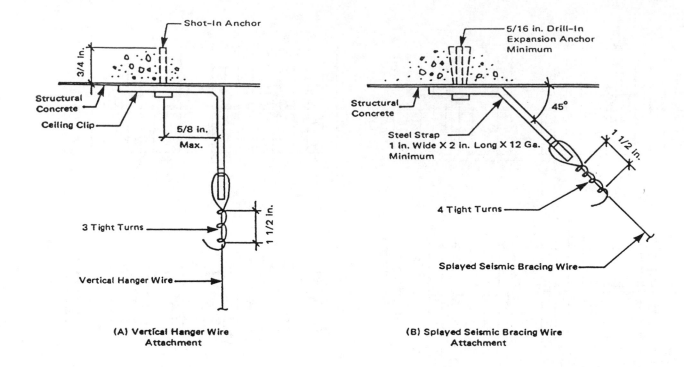

(A) Vertical Hanger Wire Attachment

(B) Splayed Seismic Bracing Wire Attachment

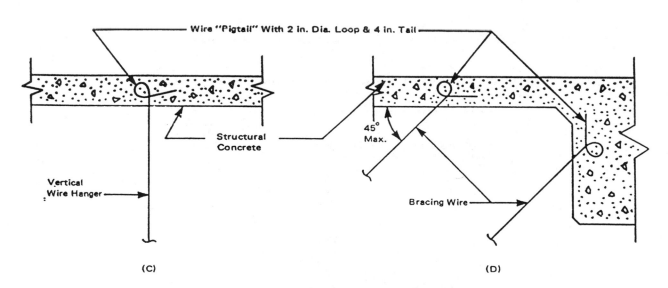

(C)

(D)

Wire Attachment To Cast-In-Place Concrete

Figure A-4-5.4.3.5.8(a).

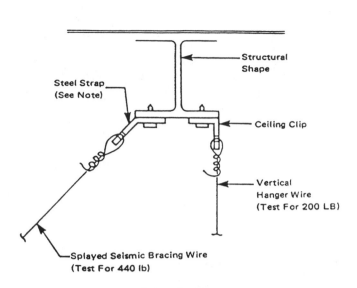

(A) At Steel Beams

Note: See Figure A-4-5.4.3.5.8(a),
Detail B.

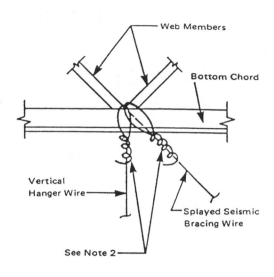

(B) At Open-Web Steel Joist

Note 1: Splay wires parallel to joist.
Splay wires cannot be perpendicular
to joist.
Note 2: See Figure A-4-5.4.3.5.8(a),
Details (A) and (B).

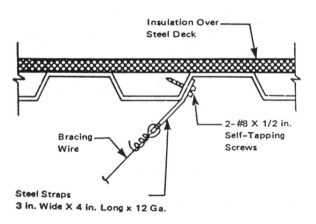

(C) At Steel Roof Deck

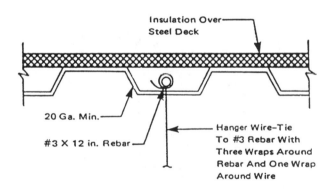

(D) At Steel Roof Deck

Note: If self-tapping screws are used with concrete fill,
set screws before placing concrete.

Acceptable Details—Wire Connections To Steel Framing
Figure A-4-5.4.3.5.8(b).

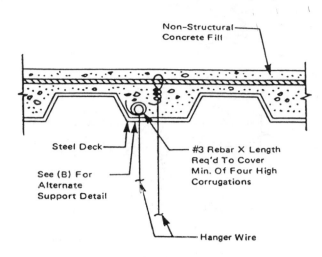

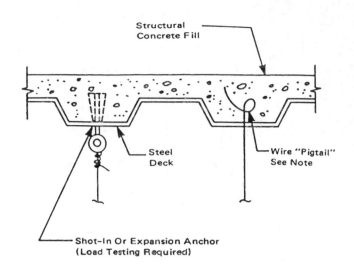

(A) At Steel Deck With
Insulating Fill

Note: Bracing wire detail similar.

(B) At Steel Deck With
Concrete Fill

Note: See Figure A–4–5.4.3.5.8(a),
Detail (C).

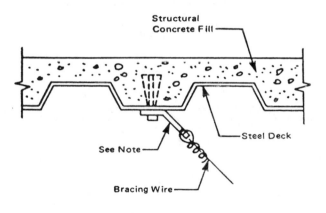

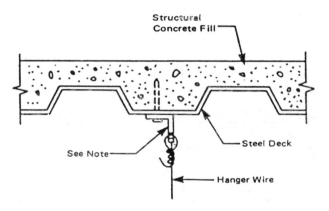

(C) At Steel Deck With
Concrete Fill

Note: See Figure A–4–5.4.3.5.8(a),
Detail (B).

(D) At Steel Deck With
Concrete Fill

Note: See Figure A–4–5.4.3.5.8(a),
Detail (A).

Note: If self-tapping screws are used with concrete fill,
set screws before placing concrete.

Acceptable Details–Wire Connections To Steel Framing

Figure A-4-5.4.3.5.8(c).

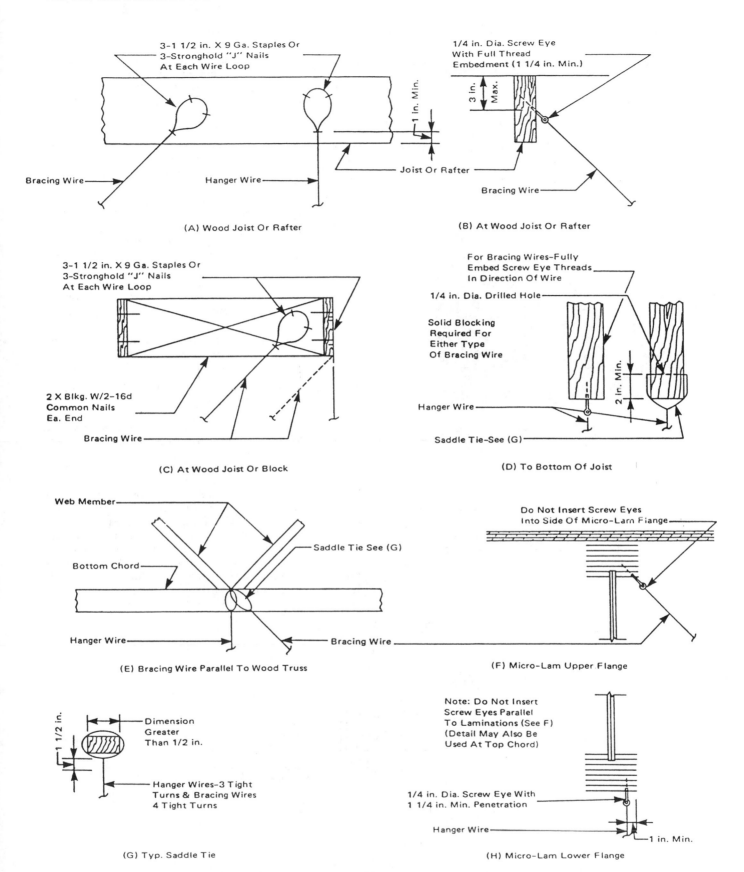

Acceptable Details-Wire Connections To Wood Framing
Figure A-4-5.4.3.5.8(d).

A-4-6.1.1 Central station, auxiliary, remote station, or proprietary protective signaling systems are a highly desirable supplement to local alarms, especially from a safety to life standpoint. (*See 4-6.1.1.6.*)

Identification Signs. Approved identification signs should be provided for outside alarm devices. The sign should be located near the device in a conspicuous position and should be worded as follows:

"SPRINKLER FIRE ALARM — WHEN BELL RINGS CALL FIRE DEPARTMENT OR POLICE."

Figure A-4-6.1.1 Identification sign.

A-4-6.1.1.5 Water-motor-operated devices should be located as near as practicable to the alarm valve, dry pipe valve, or other waterflow detecting device. The total length of the pipe to these devices should not exceed 75 ft (22.9 m) nor should the water-motor-operated device be located over 20 ft (6.1 m) above the alarm device or dry pipe valve.

A-4-6.1.1.6 Monitoring should include but not be limited to control valves, building temperatures, fire pump power supplies and running conditions, and water tank levels and temperatures. Pressure supervision shall also be provided on pressure tanks.

A-4-6.2 The fire department connection should be located not less than 18 in. (457 mm) and not more than 4 ft (1.22 m) above the level of the adjacent grade or access level.

A-4-6.2.1 Fire department connections should be located and arranged so that hose lines can be readily and conveniently attached without interference from nearby objects including buildings, fences, posts, or other fire department connections. When a hydrant is not available, other water supply sources such as a natural body of water, a tank, or reservoir should be utilized. The water authority should be consulted when a nonpotable water supply is proposed as a suction source for the fire department.

A-4-6.2.3 The check valve should be located to maximize accessibility and minimize freezing potential.

A-4-6.4.2 This test connection should be in the upper story, and the connection should preferably be piped from the end of the most remote branch line. The discharge should be at a point where it can be readily observed. In locations where it is not practical to terminate the test connection outside the building, the test connection may terminate into a drain capable of accepting full flow under system pressure. In this event, the test connection should be made using an approved sight test connection containing a smooth bore corrosion-resistant orifice giving a flow equivalent to one sprinkler simulating the least flow from an individual sprinkler in the system. [*See Figures A-4-6.4.2(a) and A-4-6.4.2(b).*] The test valve should be located at an accessible point and preferably not over 7 ft (2.1 m) above the floor. The control valve on the test connection should be located at a point not exposed to freezing.

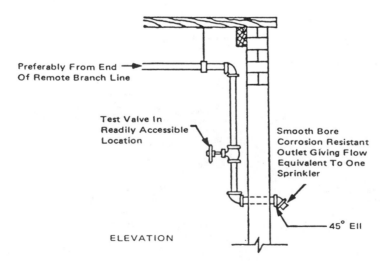

For SI Units: 1 ft = 0.3048 m.

NOTE: Not less than 4 ft (1.2 m) of exposed test pipe in warm room beyond valve when pipe extends through wall to outside.

Figure A-4-6.4.2(a)   System test connection on wet pipe system.

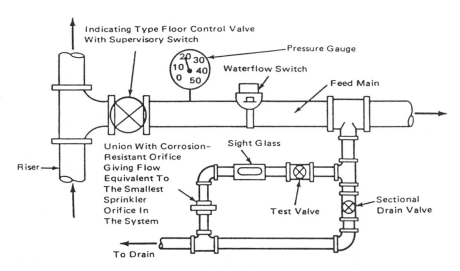

Figure A-4-6.4.2(b) Floor control valve.

A-4-6.4.3 See Figure A-4-6.4.3.

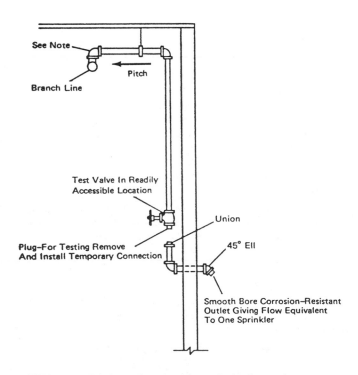

NOTE: To minimize condensation of water in the drop to the test connection, provide a nipple-up off of the branch line.

Figure A-4-6.4.3 System test connection on dry pipe system.

A-5-2.2.3 The additional pressure that is needed at the level of the water supply to account for sprinkler elevation is 0.433 psi per ft (9.8 kPa/m) of elevation above the water supply.

A-5-2.3.1.1 Appropriate area/density, other design criteria, and water supply requirements should be based on scientifically based engineering analyses that may include submitted fire testing, calculations, or results from appropriate computational models.

A-5-2.3.1.3(b) This section is included to compensate for possible delay in operation of sprinklers from fires in combustible concealed spaces found in wood frame, brick veneer, and ordinary construction.

A-5-2.3.1.3(b) Exception No. 3 This exception is intended to apply only when the exposed materials in the space are limited combustible materials or fire retardant treated wood as defined in NFPA 703, *Standard for Fire Retardant Impregnated Wood and Fire Retardant Coatings for Building Materials.*

A-5-2.3.3.1 This section allows for calculation of the sprinklers in the largest room, so long as the calculation produces the greatest hydraulic demand among selection of rooms and communicating spaces. For example, in a case where the largest room has four sprinklers and a smaller room has two sprinklers but communicates through unprotected openings with three other rooms, each having two sprinklers, the smaller room and group of communicating spaces should also be calculated.

Corridors are rooms and should be considered as such.

Walls may terminate at a substantial suspended ceiling and need not be extended to a rated floor slab above for this section to be applied.

A-5-3.2.2 See Figure A-5-3.2.2.

A-5-3.4 See Table A-5-3.4 on pages 104-105.

A-5-3.5 See Table A-5-3.5 on page 106.

A-5-3.6.1 If the system is a deluge type, then all the sprinklers need to be calculated even if they are located on different building faces.

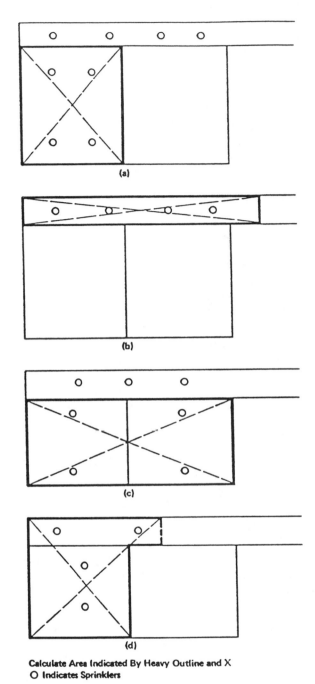

Calculate Area Indicated By Heavy Outline and X
O Indicates Sprinklers

Figure A-5-3.2.2 Examples of design area for dwelling units.

A-6-1 Preliminary layouts should be submitted for review to the authority having jurisdiction before any equipment is installed or remodeled in order to avoid error or subsequent misunderstanding. (*See Figure A-6-1 on page 106.*) Any material deviation from approved plans will require permission of the authority having jurisdiction.

Preliminary layouts should show as much of the following information as is required to provide a clear representation of the system, hazard, and occupancy.

(a) Name of owner and occupant

(b) Location, including street address

(c) Point of compass

(d) Construction and occupancy of each building

NOTE: Data on special hazards should be submitted as they may require special rulings.

(e) Building height in feet

(f) If it is proposed to use a city main as a supply, whether the main is dead-end or circulating, size of main and pressure in psi, and, if dead-end, direction and distance to nearest circulating main

(g) Distance from nearest pumping station or reservoir

(h) In cases where reliable, up-to-date information is not available, a waterflow test of the city main should be conducted in accordance with A-7-2.1. The preliminary plans should specify who conducted the test, date and time, the location of the hydrants where flow was taken, and where static and residual pressure readings were recorded; the size of main supplying these hydrants, and the results of the test, giving size and number of open hydrant butts flowed; also data covering minimum pressure in the connection with the city main should be included.

(i) Data covering waterworks systems in small towns in order to expedite the review of plans

(j) Fire walls, fire doors, unprotected window openings, large unprotected floor openings, and blind spaces

(k) Distance to and construction and occupancy of exposing buildings—e.g., lumber yards, brick mercantiles, fire-resistive office buildings, etc.

(l) Spacing of sprinklers, number of sprinklers in each story or fire area and total number of sprinklers, number of sprinklers on each riser and on each system by floors, total area protected by each system on each floor, total number of sprinklers on each dry pipe system or preaction or deluge system and if extension to present equipment, sprinklers already installed

(m) Capacities of dry pipe systems with bulk pipe included, see Table A-3-2.3; and, if an extension is made to an existing dry pipe system, the total capacity of the existing and also the extended portion of the system

(n) Weight or class, size, and material of any proposed underground pipe

(o) Whether property is located in a flood or earthquake area requiring consideration in the design of sprinkler system

(p) Name and address of party submitting the layout.

A-6-1.1 See Figure A-6-1.1 on page 107.

A-6-1.1.2 See Figures A-6-1.1.2(a) and (b) on page 108.

A-6-2.2 See Figures A-6-2.2(a) through (d) on pages 109 through 112.

A-6-2.3 See Figure A-6-2.3 on page 113.

A-6-2.3(o) See Figure A-6-2.3(o) on page 114.

A-6-2.4 See Figure A-6-2.4 on page 115.

Table A-5-3.4 Large-Drop Sprinkler Data

Pressure and Number of Design Sprinklers Required for Various Hazards for Large Drop Sprinklers

Hazard	Type of System	Minimum Operating Pressure,[1] psi (bar)			Hose Stream Demand gal/min (dm³/min)	Water Supply Duration, Hr
		25 (1.7)	50 (3.4)	75 (5.2)		
		Number Design Sprinklers				
Palletized[2] Storage Class I, II, and III commodities up to 25 ft (7.6 m) with maximum 10 ft (3.0 m) clearance to ceiling	Wet	15	Note 4	Note 4	500 (1900)	2
	Dry	25	Note 4	Note 4		
Class IV commodities up to 20 ft (6.1 m) with maximum 10 ft (3.0 m) clearance to ceiling	Wet	20	15	Note 4	500 (1900)	2
	Dry	Does not apply	Does not apply	Does not apply		
Unexpanded plastics up to 20 ft (6.1 m) with maximum 10 ft (3.0 m) clearance to ceiling	Wet	25	15	Note 4	500 (1900)	2
	Dry	Does not apply	Does not apply	Does not apply		
Expanded plastics commodities up to 18 ft (5.5 m) with maximum 8 ft (2.4 m) clearance to ceiling	Wet	Does not apply	15	Note 4	500 (1900)	2
	Dry	Does not apply	Does not apply	Does not apply		
Idle wood pallets up to 20 ft (6.1 m) with maximum 10 ft (3.0 m) clearance to ceiling	Wet	15	Note 4	Note 4	500 (1900)	1½
	Dry	25	Note 4	Note 4		
Solid Piled[2] Storage Class I, II, and III commodities up to 20 ft (6.1 m) with maximum 10 ft (3.0 m) clearance to ceiling	Wet	15	Note 4	Note 4	500 (1900)	1½
	Dry	25	Note 4	Note 4		
Class IV commodities and unexpanded plastics up to 20 ft (6.1 m) with maximum 10 ft (3.0 m) clearance to ceiling	Wet	Does not apply	15	Note 4	500 (1900)	1½
	Dry	Does not apply	Does not apply	Does not apply		
Double-Row Rack Storage[3] with Minimum 5.5 ft (1.7 m) Aisle Width Class I and II commodities up to 25 ft (7.6 m) with maximum 5 ft (1.5 m) clearance to ceiling	Wet	20	Note 4	Note 4	500 (1900)	1½
	Dry	30	Note 4	Note 4		
Class I and II commodities up to 30 ft (9.2 m) with maximum 5 ft (1.5 m) clearance to ceiling	Wet	20 plus one level of in-rack sprinklers[6]	Note 4	Note 4	500 (1900)	1½
	Dry	30 plus one level of in-rack sprinklers[6]	Note 4	Note 4		
Class I, II, and III commodities up to 20 ft (6.1 m) with maximum 10 ft (3.0 m) clearance to ceiling	Wet	15	Note 4	Note 4	500 (1900)	1½
	Dry	25	Note 4	Note 4		
Class I, II, and III commodities up to 25 ft (7.6 m) with maximum 10 ft (3.0 m) clearance to ceiling	Wet	15 plus one level of in-rack sprinklers[6]	Note 4	Note 4	500 (1900)	1½
	Dry	25 plus one level of in-rack sprinklers[6]	Note 4	Note 4		
Class IV commodities up to 20 ft (6.1 m) with maximum 10 ft (3.0 m) clearance to ceiling	Wet	Does not apply	20	15	500 (1900)	2
	Dry	Does not apply	Does not apply	Does not apply		
Class IV commodities up to 25 ft (7.6 m) with maximum 10 ft clearance to ceiling	Wet	Does not apply	20 plus one level of in-rack sprinklers[6]	15 plus one level of in-rack sprinklers[6]	500 (1900)	2
	Dry	Does not apply	Does not apply	Does not apply		

Table A-5-3.4   (cont.)

Commodity						
Unexpanded plastics up to 20 ft (6.1 m) with maximum 10 ft (3.0 m) clearance to ceiling	Wet	Does not apply	30	20	500 (1900)	2
	Dry	Does not apply	Does not apply	Does not apply		
Unexpanded plastics up to 25 ft (7.6 m) with maximum 10 ft (3.0 m) clearance to ceiling	Wet	Does not apply	30 plus one level of in-rack sprinklers[4]	20 plus one level of in-rack sprinklers[4]	500 (1900)	2
	Dry	Does not apply	Does not apply	Does not apply		
Class IV commodities and unexpanded plastics up to 20 ft (6.1 m) with maximum 5 ft (1.5 m) clearance to ceiling	Wet	Does not apply	15	Note 4	500 (1900)	2
	Dry	Does not apply	Does not apply	Does not apply		
Class IV commodities and unexpanded plastics up to 25 ft (7.6 m) with maximum 5 ft (1.5 m) clearance to ceiling	Wet	Does not apply	15 plus one level of in-rack sprinklers[4]	Note 4	500 (1900)	2
	Dry	Does not apply	Does not apply	Does not apply		
On-end Storage of Roll Paper[2] Heavyweight paper in closed array, banded in open array, or banded or unbanded in a standard array, up to 26 ft (7.9 m) with maximum 34 ft (10.4 m) clearance to ceiling	Wet	Does not apply	15	Note 4		
	Dry	Does not apply	Does not apply	Does not apply	0 (Note 7)	4 (Note 7)
Any grade of paper, except lightweight paper with stacks in closed array, or banded or unbanded in a standard array, up to 20 ft (6.1 m) with maximum 10 ft (3.0 m) clearance to ceiling	Wet	Does not apply	15	Note 4		
	Dry	Does not apply	25	Note 4	0 (Note 7)	4 (Note 7)
Medium weight paper completely wrapped (sides and ends) in one or more layers of heavyweight paper, or lightweight paper in two or more layers of heavyweight paper, with closed array, banded in open array, or unbanded in a standard array, up to 26 ft (7.9 m) with maximum 34 ft (10.4 m) clearance to ceiling	Wet	Does not apply	15	Note 4		
	Dry	Does not apply	Does not apply	Does not apply	0 (Note 7)	4 (Note 7)
Record Storage Paper records and/or computer tapes in multitier steel shelving up to 5 ft (1.5 m) in width and with aisles 30 in. (76 cm) or wider, without catwalks in the aisles, up to 15 ft (4.6 m) with maximum 5 ft (1.5 m) clearance to ceiling	Wet	15	Note 4	Note 4	500 (1900)	1½
	Dry	25	Note 4	Note 4		
Same as above, but with catwalks of expanded metal or metal grid with minimum 50% open area in the aisles	Wet	Does not apply	15	Note 4	500 (1900)	1½
	Dry	Does not apply	15	Note 4		

NOTES:
1. Open wood joist construction. Fully firestop each joist channel to its full depth at intervals not exceeding 20 ft (6.2 m). In unfirestopped open wood joist construction, or if firestops are installed at intervals not exceeding 20 ft (6.1 m), increase the minimum operating pressures of Table A-5-3.4 by 40 percent.
2. See NFPA 231, *Standard for General Storage.*
3. With rack storage, use conventional wood pallets only, no slave pallets.
4. The high pressure may be used, but the required number of design sprinklers may not be reduced from that required for the lower pressure.
5. See NFPA 231F, *Standard for the Storage of Roll Paper.*
6. Install in-rack sprinklers in accordance with NFPA 231C, *Standard for Rack Storage.*
7. Hose stream demands and water supply durations may vary for roll paper storage depending on local conditions. See NFPA 231F, *Standard for the Storage of Roll Paper.*

Table A-5-3.5   ESFR Sprinkler Data

Type of Storage	Commodity	Maximum Height of Storage (ft)	Maximum Height See Note (ft)
Single-, double-, and multiple-row and portable rack storage (no open-top containers or solid-piled or palletized storage)	Cartoned plastics (unexpanded or expanded) and Class I through IV commodities, all either encapsulated or unencapsulated	25	30
Roll paper on end, open/standard closed array, banded or unbanded	Heavyweight paper	20	30
Roll paper on end, open/standard closed array, banded or unbanded	Mediumweight paper	20	30
Aerosol storage	See NFPA 30B		

NOTE: The maximum height is to be measured to the underside of the roof deck or ceiling.

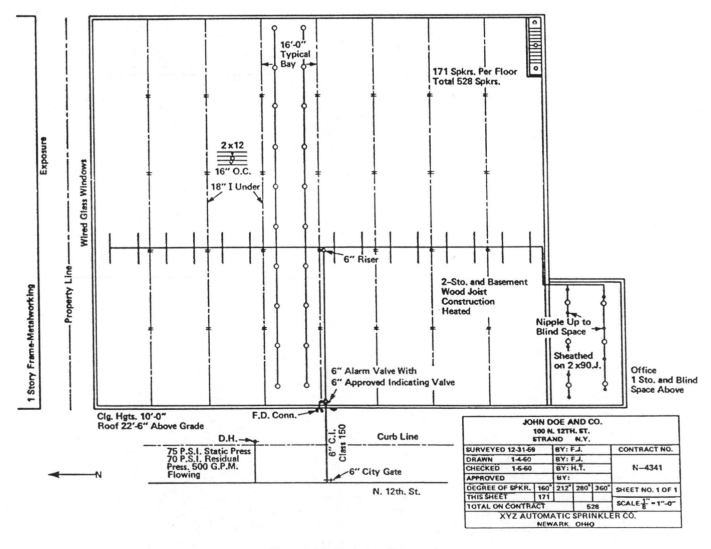

Figure A-6-1   Typical preliminary plan.

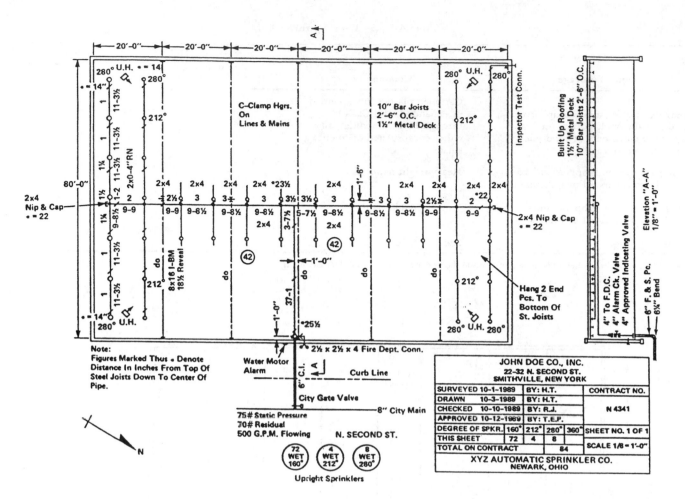

Figure A-6-1.1   Typical working plans.

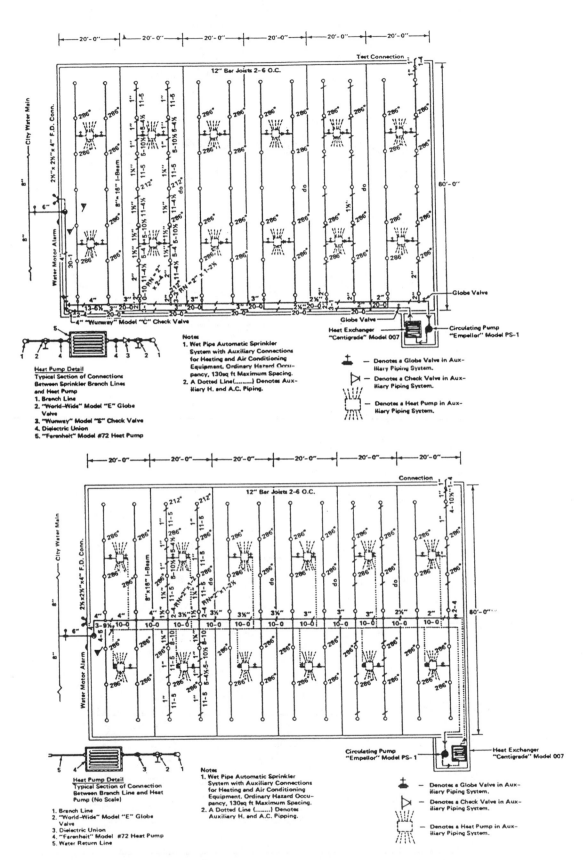

Figure A-6-1.1.2(a) and (b)   Working plans for circulating closed-loop systems.

HYDRAULIC CALCULATIONS

for

ABC Company, Employee Garage

7499 Franklin Road

Charleston, SC

CONTRACT NO. ___4001___

DATE ___1-7-91___

DESIGN DATA:

OCCUPANCY CLASSIFICATION _ORD. GR. 1_

DENSITY __.15__ GPM/SQ. FT.

AREA OF APPLICATION _1500_ SQ. FT.

COVERAGE PER SPRINKLER __130__ SQ. FT.

SPECIAL SPRINKLERS ___—___

NO. OF SPRINKLERS CALCULATED __12__

IN-RACK DEMAND ___—___

HOSE STREAMS __250 GPM.__

TOTAL WATER REQUIRED __510.4__ GPM
INCLUDING HOSE STREAMS

NAME OF CONTRACTOR _____

NAME OF DESIGNER _____

ADDRESS _____

AUTHORITY HAVING JURISDICTION _____

Figure A-6-2.2(a)   Summary sheet.

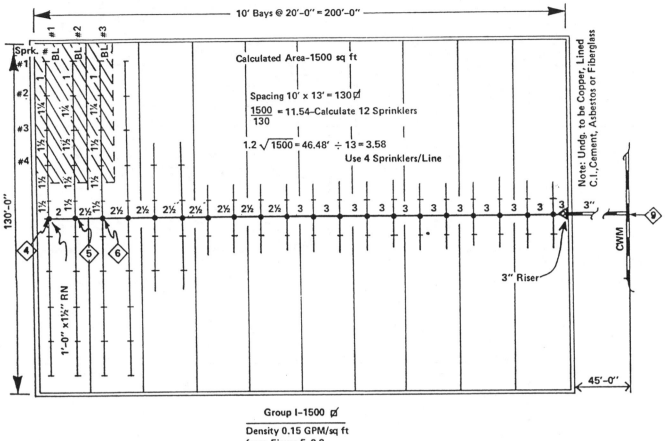

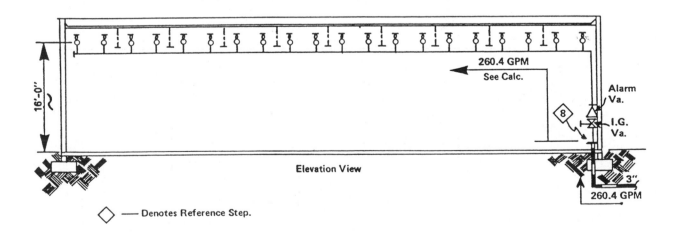

Figure A-6-2.2(b)   Hydraulic calculation example (plan view and elevation view).

CONTRACT NAME __GROUP I 1500 Ø__   SHEET _2_ OF _3_

STEP NO.	NOZZLE IDENT. AND LOCATION	FLOW IN G.P.M.	PIPE SIZE	PIPE FITTINGS AND DEVICES	EQUIV. PIPE LENGTH	FRICTION LOSS P.S.I./FOOT	PRESSURE SUMMARY	NORMAL PRESSURE	NOTES D=0.15 GPM/Ø K=5.65	REF. STEP
1	1 BL-1	q	1		L 13.0	C=120	Pt 11.9	Pt	$q=130 \times .15 = 19.5$	
					F		Pe	Pv		
		Q 19.5			T 13.0	.124	Pf 1.6	Pn		
2	2	q 20.7	1 1/4		L 13.0		Pt 13.5	Pt	$q=5.65\sqrt{13.5}$	
					F		Pe	Pv		
		Q 40.2			T 13.0	.125	Pf 1.6	Pn		
3	3	q 22	1 1/2		L 13.0		Pt 15.1	Pt	$q=5.65\sqrt{15.1}$	
					F		Pe	Pv		
		Q 62.2			T 13.0	.132	Pf 1.7	Pn		
4	4 DN RN	q 23.2	1 1/2	2T-16	L 20.5		Pt 16.8	Pt	$q=5.65\sqrt{16.8}$	4
					F 16.0		Pe	Pv		
		Q 85.4			T 36.5	.237	Pf 8.6	Pn		
5	CM TO BL-2	q	2		L 10.0		Pt 25.4	Pt	$K=\dfrac{85.4}{\sqrt{25.4}}$	5
					F		Pe	Pv	$K=16.95$	
		Q 85.4			T 10.0	.07	Pf .7	Pn		
6	BL-2 CM TO BL-3	q 86.6	2 1/2		L 10.0		Pt 26.1	Pt	$q=16.95\sqrt{26.1}$	6
					F		Pe	Pv		
		Q 172.0			T 10.0	.109	Pf 1.1	Pn		
7	BL-3 CM	q 88.4	2 1/2		L 70.0		Pt 27.2	Pt	$q=16.95\sqrt{27.2}$	
					F		Pe	Pv		
		Q 260.4			T 70.0	.233	Pf 16.3	Pn		
8	CM TO F/S	q	3	E 5	L 119.0		Pt 43.5	Pt	$Pe = 15 \times .433$	8
				AV 15	F		Pe 6.5	Pv		
		Q 260.4		GV 1	T 140.0	.081	Pf 11.3	Pn		
9	THRU UNDER-GROUND TO CITY MAIN	q	3	E 5	L 50.0	C=150	Pt 61.3	Pt	COPPER	9
				GV 1	F 32.0	TYPE "M"	Pe	Pv	$21 \times 1.5' = 32$	
		Q 260.4		T 15	T 82.2	.061	Pf 5.0	Pn		
		q			L		Pt 66.3	Pt		
					F		Pe	Pv		
		Q			T		Pf	Pn		
		q			L		Pt	Pt		
					F		Pe	Pv		
		Q			T		Pf	Pn		
							Pt			

Figure A-6-2.2(c)   Hydraulic calculations.

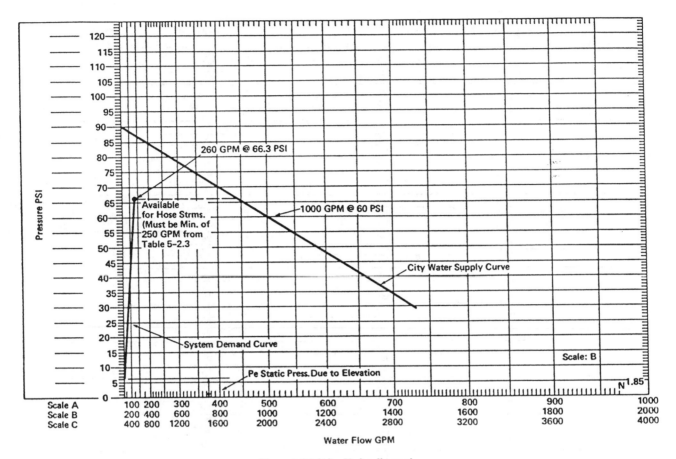

Figure A-6-2.2(d)   Hydraulic graph.

Contract No. _____   Sheet No. _____ of _____

Name & Location _____

Reference	Nozzle Type & Location	Flow in GPM (L/min)	Pipe Size in.	Fitting & Devices	Pipe Eqiv. Length	Friction Loss psi/ft. (bars/m)	Req. Psi. (bars)	Normal Pressure	Notes
		q			lgth.		Pt	Pt	
					ftg.		Pf	Pv	
		Q			tot.		Pe	Pn	
		q			lgth.		Pt	Pt	
					ftg.		Pf	Pv	
		Q			tot.		Pe	Pn	
		q			lgth.		Pt	Pt	
					ftg.		Pf	Pv	
		Q			tot.		Pe	Pn	
		q			lgth.		Pt	Pt	
					ftg.		Pf	Pv	
		Q			tot.		Pe	Pn	
		q			lgth.		Pt	Pt	
					ftg.		Pf	Pv	
		Q			tot.		Pe	Pn	
		q			lgth.		Pt	Pt	
					ftg.		Pf	Pv	
		Q			tot.		Pe	Pn	
		q			lgth.		Pt	Pt	
					ftg.		Pf	Pv	
		Q			tot.		Pe	Pn	
		q			lgth.		Pt	Pt	
					ftg.		Pf	Pv	
		Q			tot.		Pe	Pn	
		q			lgth.		Pt	Pt	
					ftg.		Pf	Pv	
		Q			tot.		Pe	Pn	
		q			lgth.		Pt	Pt	
					ftg.		Pf	Pv	
		Q			tot.		Pe	Pn	
		q			lgth.		Pt	Pt	
					ftg.		Pf	Pv	
		Q			tot.		Pe	Pn	
		q			lgth.		Pt	Pt	
					ftg.		Pf	Pv	
		Q			tot.		Pe	Pn	
		q			lgth.		Pt	Pt	
					ftg.		Pf	Pv	
		Q			tot.		Pe	Pn	
		q			lgth.		Pt	Pt	
					ftg.		Pf	Pv	
		Q			tot.		Pe	Pn	
		q			lgth.		Pt	Pt	
					ftg.		Pf	Pv	
		Q			tot.		Pe	Pn	
		q			lgth.		Pt	Pt	
					ftg.		Pf	Pv	
		Q			tot.		Pe	Pn	
		q			lgth.		Pt	Pt	
					ftg.		Pf	Pv	
		Q			tot.		Pe	Pn	
		q			lgth.		Pt	Pt	
					ftg.		Pf	Pv	
		Q			tot.		Pe	Pn	

Figure A-6-2.3 Sample work sheet.

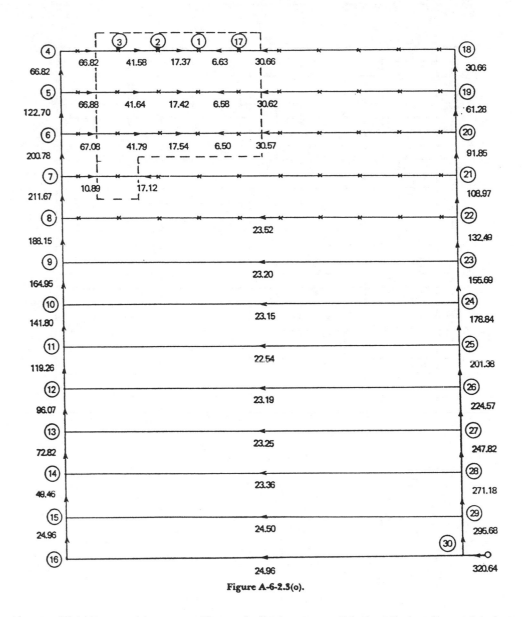

Figure A-6-2.3(o).

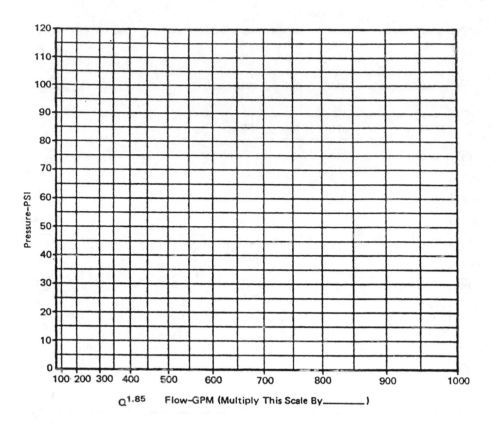

Figure A-6-2.4   Sample graph sheet.

A-6-4.1 When additional sprinkler piping is added to an existing system, the existing piping does not have to be increased in size to compensate for the additional sprinklers, provided the new work is calculated and the calculations include that portion of the existing system as may be required to carry water to the new work.

A-6-4.4 See Figure A-6-4.4.

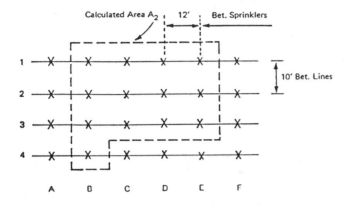

NOTE 1: For gridded systems, the extra sprinkler (or sprinklers) on branch line 4 may be placed in any adjacent location from B to E at the designer's option.

NOTE 2: For tree and looped systems, the extra sprinkler on line 4 should be placed closest to the cross main.

Assume a remote area of 1,500 sq ft with sprinkler coverage of 120 sq ft

$$\text{Total sprinklers to calculate} = \frac{\text{Design Area}}{\text{Area per Sprinkler}}$$

$$= \frac{1500}{120} = 12.5, \text{ calculate } 13$$

$$\text{Number of sprinklers on branch line} = \frac{1.2\sqrt{A}}{S}$$

Where A = Design Area
       S = Distance between Sprinklers on Branch Line

$$\text{Number of sprinklers on branch line} = \frac{1.2\sqrt{1500}}{12} = 3.87.$$

For SI Units: 1 ft = 0.3048 m; 1 sq ft = 0.0929 m^2.

Figure A-6-4.4   **Example of determining the number of sprinklers to be calculated.**

A-6-4.4.1 See Figures A-6-4.4.1(a) and (b).

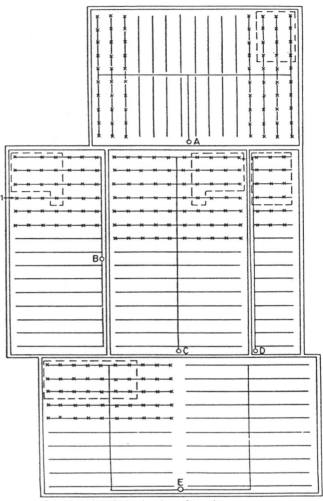

[1] This sprinkler is not in the selected area of operation.

Figure A-6-4.4.1(a)   **Example of hydraulically most demanding area.**

A-6-4.4.2 See Figure A-6-4.4.2.

A-6-4.4.3(a) See Figure A-6-4.4.3(a) on page 118.

A-6-4.4.3(b) This subsection assumes a ceiling constructed so as to reasonably assure that a fire on one side of the ceiling will operate sprinklers on one side only. When a ceiling is sufficiently open, or of such construction that operation of sprinklers above and below the ceiling may be anticipated, the operation of such additional sprinklers should be considered in the calculations.

A-6-4.4.4 When it is not obvious by comparison that the design selected is the hydraulically most remote, additional calculations should be submitted. The most distant area is not necessarily the hydraulically most remote.

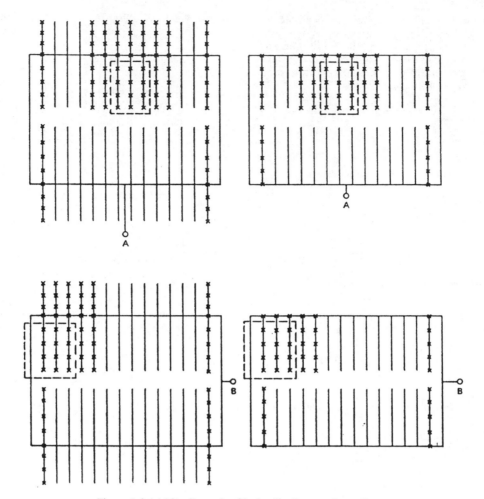

Figure A-6-4.4.1(b)   Example of hydraulically most demanding area.

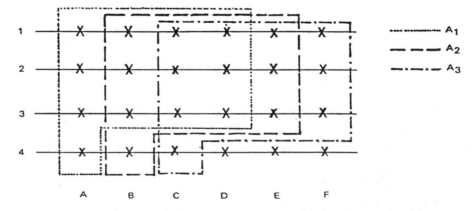

Figure A-6-4.4.2   Example of determining the most remote area for a gridded system.

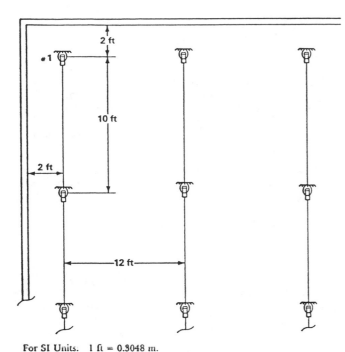

For SI Units.   1 ft = 0.3048 m.

Figure A-6-4.4.3(a)   Sprinkler design area.

A-6-4.4.6 The use of sprinklers with differing orifice sizes in situations where different protection areas are needed is not considered balancing. An example would be a room that could be protected with sprinklers having different orifice size in closet, foyer, and room areas. However, this procedure introduces difficulties when restoring a system to service after operation since it is not always clear which sprinklers go where.

A-6-4.4.7 When velocity pressure is included in the calculations, the following assumptions should be used:

(a) At any flowing outlet along a pipe, except the end outlet, only the normal pressure (P_n) can act on the outlet. At the end outlet the total pressure (P_t) can act. The following should be considered end outlets:

1. The last flowing sprinkler on a dead-end branch line.

2. The last flowing branch line on a dead-end cross main

3. Any sprinkler where a flow split occurs on a gridded branch line

4. Any branch line where a flow split occurs on a looped system.

(b) At any flowing outlet along a pipe, except the end outlet, the pressure acting to cause flow from the outlet is equal to the total pressure (P_t) minus the velocity pressure (P_v) on the upstream (supply) side.

(c) To find the normal pressure (P_n) at any flowing outlet, except the end outlet, assume a flow from the outlet in question and determine the velocity pressure (P_v) for the total flow on the upstream side. Because normal pressure

(P_n) equals total pressure (P_t) minus velocity pressure (P_v), the value of the normal pressure (P_n) so found should result in an outlet flow approximately equal to the assumed flow; if not, a new value should be assumed, and the calculations repeated.

A-6-5.1 The demonstrated effectiveness of pipe schedule systems is limited to their use with $\frac{1}{2}$ in. (13 mm) orifice sprinklers. The use of other size orifices may require hydraulic calculations to prove their ability to deliver the required amount of water within the available water supply.

A-6-5.1.2 Long Runs of Pipe. When the construction or conditions introduce unusually long runs of pipe or many angles in risers or feed or cross mains, an increase in pipe size over that called for in the schedules may be required to compensate for increased friction losses.

A-6-5.2.3.1 For example, a $2\frac{1}{2}$ in. (64 mm) steel pipe, which is permitted to supply 30 sprinklers, may supply a total of 50 sprinklers when not more than 30 sprinklers are above, or below, a ceiling.

A-6-5.3.3.1 For example, a 3 in. (76 mm) steel pipe, which is permitted to supply 40 sprinklers in an Ordinary Hazard area, may supply a total of 60 sprinklers when not more than 40 sprinklers protect the occupied space below the ceiling.

A-6-5.4 Schedule for Extra Hazard Occupancies. This piping schedule is reprinted only as a guide for existing systems. New systems for Extra Hazard Occupancies should be hydraulically calculated as required in 6-5.4.

Table A-6-5.4   Extra Hazard Pipe Schedule

Steel		Copper	
1 in.	1 sprinkler	1 in.	1 sprinkler
1¼ in.	2 sprinklers	1¼ in.	2 sprinklers
1½ in.	5 sprinklers	1½ in.	5 sprinklers
2 in.	8 sprinklers	2 in.	8 sprinklers
2½ in.	15 sprinklers	2½ in.	20 sprinklers
3 in.	27 sprinklers	3 in.	30 sprinklers
3½ in.	40 sprinklers	3½ in.	45 sprinklers
4 in.	55 sprinklers	4 in.	65 sprinklers
5 in.	90 sprinklers	5 in.	100 sprinklers
6 in.	150 sprinklers	6 in.	170 sprinklers

A-6-5.6 In designing an exposure protection system, the flow rate from window and cornice sprinklers is shown in Table 6-5.6. The flow rates are based on the guide numbers selected from Table 2-3 of NFPA 80A, *Recommended Practice for Protection of Buildings from Exterior Fire Exposures*, 1987 edition.

Section A of the Table is for window sprinklers. The orifice size is selected according to the level on which the sprinkler is located.

Section B of the Table is for cornice sprinklers.

A-7-1.2.3 When the system riser is close to an outside wall, underground fittings of proper length should be used in order to avoid pipe joints located in or under the wall. When the connection passes through the foundation wall below grade, a 1- to 3-in. (25- to 76-mm) clearance should be provided around the pipe and the clear space filled with asphalt mastic or similar flexible waterproofing material.

A-7-2.1 Water Supplies. Care should be taken in making water tests to be used in designing or evaluating the capability of sprinkler systems. The water supply tested should be representative of the supply that may be available at the time of a fire. For example, testing of public water supplies should be done at times of normal demand on the system. Public water supplies are likely to fluctuate widely from season to season and even within a 24-hour period. Allowance should be made for seasonal or daily fluctuations, for drought conditions, for possibility of interruption by flood, or for ice conditions in winter. Testing of water supplies also normally used for industrial use should be done while water is being drawn for industrial use. The range of industrial-use demand should be taken into account.

Future changes in water supplies should be considered. For example a large, established, urban supply is not likely to change greatly within a few years. However, the supply in a growing suburban industrial park may deteriorate quite rapidly as greater numbers of plants draw more water.

Testing of Water Supply. To determine the value of public water as a supply for automatic sprinkler systems, it is generally necessary to make a flow test to determine how much water can be discharged at a residual pressure at a rate sufficient to give the required residual pressure under the roof (with the volume flow hydraulically translated to the base of the riser), i.e., a pressure head represented by the height of the building plus the required residual pressure.

The proper method of conducting this test is to use two hydrants in the vicinity of the property. The static pressure should be measured on the hydrant in front of or nearest to the property and the water allowed to flow from the hydrant next nearest the property, preferably the one farthest from the source of supply if the main is fed only one way. The residual pressure will be that indicated at the hydrant where water is not flowing.

Referring to Figure A-7-2.1, the method of conducting the flow tests is as follows:

1. Attach gauge to hydrant (A) and obtain static pressure.

2. Either attach second gauge to hydrant (B) or use pitot tube at outlet. Have hydrant (B) opened wide and read pressure at both hydrants.

3. Use the pressure at (B) to compute the gallons flowing and read the gauge on (A) to determine the residual pressure or that which will be available on the top line of sprinklers in the property.

Water pressure in psi for a given height in feet equals height multiplied by 0.434.

In making flow tests, whether from hydrants or from nozzles attached to hose, always measure the size of the orifice. While hydrant outlets are usually 2½ in. (64 mm) they are sometimes smaller and occasionally larger. The UL play pipe is 1⅛ in. (29 mm) and 1¾ in. (44 mm) with tip removed, but occasionally nozzles will be 1 in. (25 mm) or 1¼ in. (33 mm), and with the tip removed the opening may be only 1½ in. (38 mm).

The Pitot tube should be held approximately one-half the diameter of the hydrant or nozzle opening away from the opening. It should be held in the center of the stream, except that in using hydrant outlets the stream should be explored to get the average pressure.

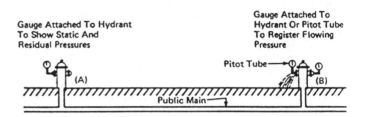

Figure A-7-2.1 Method of conducting flow tests.

A-7-2.2.1 An automatically controlled vertical turbine pump taking suction from a reservoir, pond, lake, river, or well complies with 7-2.2.1.

A-7-2.2.2 See sections dealing with sprinkler equipment supervisory and waterflow alarm services in NFPA 71, *Standard for the Installation, Maintenance, and Use of Signaling Systems for Central Station Service*, or NFPA 72, *Standard for the Installation, Maintenance, and Use of Protective Signaling Systems*.

A-7-2.3.3 The air pressure to be carried and the proper proportion of air in the tank may be determined from the following formulas, in which,

P = Air pressure carried in pressure tank
A = Proportion of air in tank
H = Height of highest sprinkler above tank bottom

When tank is placed above highest sprinkler

$$P = \frac{30}{A} - 15.$$

If A = ⅓ then P = 90 − 15 = 75 lb psi.
If A = ½ then P = 60 − 15 = 45 lb psi.
If A = ⅔ then P = 45 − 15 = 30 lb psi.

When tank is below level of the highest sprinkler

$$P = \frac{30}{A} - 15 + \frac{0.434H}{A}$$

If A = $\frac{1}{3}$ then P = 75 + 1.30H.
If A = $\frac{1}{2}$ then P = 45 + 0.87H.
If A = $\frac{2}{3}$ then P = 30 + 0.65H.

The respective air pressures above are calculated to ensure that the last water will leave the tank at a pressure of 15 psi (1.03 bars) when the base of the tank is on a level with the highest sprinkler, or at such additional pressure as is equivalent to a head corresponding to the distance between the base of the tank and the highest sprinkler when the latter is above the tank.

The final pressure required at the pressure tank for systems designed from Table 5-2.3 will normally be higher than the 15 psi (1.03 bars) anticipated in the previous paragraph. The following formula should be used to determine the tank pressure and ratio of air to water in hydraulically designed systems.

$$P_i = \frac{P_f + 15}{A} - 15$$

where

P_i = Tank pressure
P_f = Pressure required from hydraulic calculations
A = Proportion of air

Example: Hydraulic calculations indicate 75 psi is required to supply the system. What tank pressure will be required?

$$P_i = \frac{75 + 15}{.5} - 15$$

$$P_i = 180 - 15 = 165 \text{ psi}$$

For SI Units: 1ft = 0.3048 m; 1 psi = 0.0689 bar.

In this case the tank would be filled with 50 percent air and 50 percent water and the tank pressure would be 165 psi (11.4 bars). If the pressure is too high, the amount of air carried in the tank will have to be increased.

Location of Pressure Tanks. Pressure tanks should be located above the top level of sprinklers but may be located in the basement or elsewhere.

A-8-2.1 Underground mains and lead-in connections to system risers should be flushed through hydrants at dead ends of the system or through accessible aboveground flushing outlets allowing the water to run until clear. If water is supplied from more than one source or from a looped system, divisional valves should be closed to produce a high-velocity flow through each single line. The flows specified in Table 8-2.1 will produce a velocity of at least 10 ft/sec (3 m/s), which is necessary for cleaning the pipe and for lifting foreign material to an aboveground flushing outlet.

A-8-2.2.1 A sprinkler system has for its water supply a connection to a public water service main. A 100 psi (6.9 bar) rated pump is installed in the connection. With a maximum normal public water supply of 70 psi (4.8 bars) at the low elevation point of the individual system or por-

tion of the system being tested and a 120 psi (8.3 bars) pump (churn) pressure, the hydrostatic test pressure is 70 + 120 + 50 or 240 psi (16.5 bars).

Systems that have been modified or repaired to any appreciable extent should be hydrostatically tested at not less than 50 psi (3.4 bars) in excess of normal static pressure for 2 hours.

To reduce the possibility of serious water damage in case of a break, pressure may be maintained by a small pump, the main controlling gate meanwhile being kept shut during the test.

Polybutylene pipe will undergo expansion during initial pressurization. In this case a reduction in gauge pressure may not necessarily indicate a leak. The pressure reduction should not exceed the manufacturer's specifications and listing criteria.

When pressure testing systems having rigid thermoplastic piping such as CPVC, the sprinkler system should be filled with water. The air should be bled from the highest and farthest sprinklers. Compressed air or compressed gas should never be used to test systems with rigid thermoplastic pipe.

A-8-2.2.7 Valves isolating the section to be tested may not be "drop tight." When such leakage is suspected, test blanks of the type recommended in 8-2.2.7 should be used in a manner that includes the valve in the section being tested.

A-8-5 See Figure A-8-5.

This system as shown on ....company

print no. ....dated............

for ....

at .... contract no.........

is designed to discharge at a rate of ....gpm (L/min) per sq ft of floor area over a maximum area of .... sq ft (m²) when supplied with water at a rate of .... gpm (L/min) at .... psi (bars) at the base of the riser.

Hose stream allowance of .... gpm (L/min) is included in the above.

Figure A-8-5   Sample nameplate.

A-9-1.1 Impairments. Before shutting off a section of the fire service system to make sprinkler system connections, notify the authority having jurisdiction, plan the work carefully, and assemble all materials to enable completion in the shortest possible time. Work started on con-

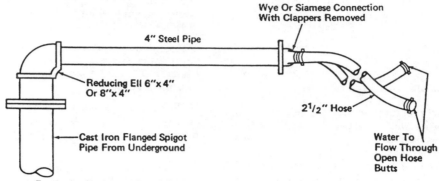

Wye Or Siamese Connection
With Clappers Removed

4" Steel Pipe

Reducing Ell 6"x 4"
Or 8"x 4"

2¹/₂" Hose

Water To
Flow Through
Open Hose
Butts

Cast Iron Flanged Spigot
Pipe From Underground

Employing Horizontal Run Of 4-Inch Pipe And Reducing Fitting Near Base Of Riser.

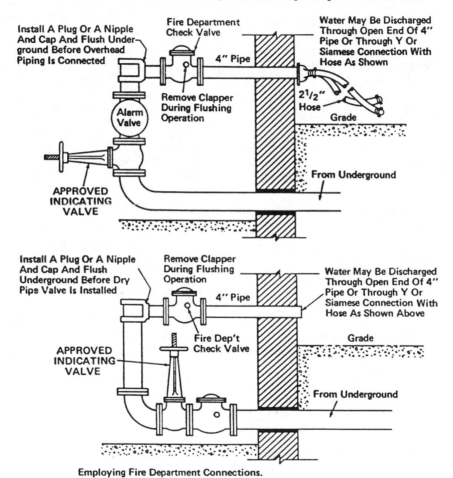

Install A Plug Or A Nipple
And Cap And Flush Under-
ground Before Overhead
Piping Is Connected

Fire Department
Check Valve

Water May Be Discharged
Through Open End Of 4"
Pipe Or Through Y Or
Siamese Connection With
Hose As Shown

4" Pipe

Remove Clapper
During Flushing
Operation

2¹/₂"
Hose

Grade

Alarm
Valve

From Underground

APPROVED
INDICATING
VALVE

Install A Plug Or A Nipple
And Cap And Flush
Underground Before Dry
Pipe Valve Is Installed

Remove Clapper
During Flushing
Operation

Water May Be Discharged
Through Open End Of 4"
Pipe Or Through Y Or
Siamese Connection With
Hose As Shown Above

4" Pipe

Fire Dep't
Check Valve

Grade

APPROVED
INDICATING
VALVE

From Underground

Employing Fire Department Connections.

Figure A-8-2.1 Methods of flushing water supply connections.

nections should be completed without interruption and protection restored as promptly as possible. During the impairment, provide emergency hose lines and extinguishers and maintain extra watch service in the areas affected.

When changes involve shutting off water from any considerable number of sprinklers for more than a few hours, temporary water supply connections should be made to sprinkler systems so that reasonable protection can be maintained. In adding to old systems or revamping them, protection should be restored each night so far as possible. The members of the private fire brigade as well as public fire departments should be notified as to conditions.

Maintenance Schedule. The items shown in Table A-9-1.1 should be checked on a routine basis.

A-9-1.3 When painting sprinkler piping or painting in areas near sprinklers, the sprinklers may be protected by covering them with a biodegradable paper bag that should be removed immediately after the painting has been finished.

A-9-3.3 In the quarterly test, record the static pressure. Then fully open the main drain and record the residual pressure. A significant drop in the recorded residual pressure from the prior test may indicate an obstruction or a partially closed valve. A gradual decrease in pressure over several test intervals may indicate a buildup of corrosion in the supply piping or a decaying water supply.

Table A-9-1.1   Maintenance Schedule

Parts	Activity	Frequency
Flushing Piping	Test	5 years
Fire Department Connections	Inspection	Monthly
Control Valves	Inspection	Weekly—Sealed
	Inspection	Monthly—Locked
	Inspection	Monthly—Tamper Switch
	Maintenance	Yearly
Main Drain	Flow Test	Quarterly
Open Sprinklers	Test	Annual
Pressure Gauge	Calibration Test	
Sprinklers	Test	50 years
Sprinklers—High Temp	Test	5 years
Sprinklers—Residential	Test	20 years
Waterflow Alarms	Test	Quarterly
Preaction/Deluge Detection System	Test	Semiannually
Preaction/Deluge Systems	Test	Annually
Antifreeze Solution	Test	Annually
Cold Weather Valves	Open and Close Valves	Fall, Close; Spring, Open
Dry/Preaction/Deluge Systems Air Pressure and Water Pressure	Inspection	Weekly
Enclosure	Inspection	Daily—Cold Weather
Priming Water Level	Inspection	Quarterly
Low—Point Drains	Test	Fall
Dry Pipe Valves	Trip Test	Annual—Spring
Dry Pipe Valves	Full Flow Trip	3 years—Spring
Quick Opening Devices	Test	Semi-annually

Appendix B

This Appendix is not a part of the requirements of this NFPA document, but is included for information purposes only.

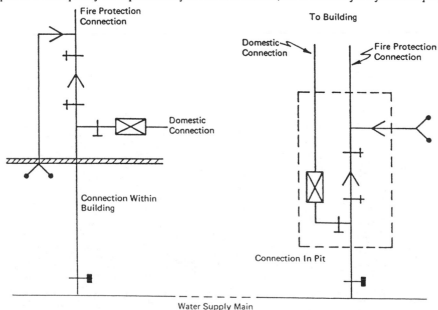

Permitted arrangements between the fire protection water supply and the domestic water supply.

Appendix C   Referenced Publications

This Appendix is not a part of the requirements of this NFPA document, but is included for information purposes only.

C-1   The following documents or portions thereof are referenced within this standard for informational purposes only and thus are not considered part of the requirements of this document. The edition indicated for each reference is the current edition as of the date of the NFPA issuance of this document.

C-1.1 NFPA Publications.   National Fire Protection Association, 1 Batterymarch Park, P.O. Box 9101, Quincy, MA 02269-9101.

NFPA 13A, *Recommended Practice for the Inspection, Testing and Maintenance of Sprinkler Systems*, 1987 edition

NFPA 14, *Standard for the Installation of Standpipe and Hose Systems*, 1990 edition

NFPA 30B, *Code for the Manufacture and Storage of Aerosol Products*, 1990 edition

NFPA 71, *Standard for the Installation, Maintenance, and Use of Signaling Systems for Central Station Service*, 1989 edition

NFPA 72, *Standard for the Installation, Maintenance, and Use of Protective Signaling Systems*, 1990 edition

NFPA 80A, *Recommended Practice for Protection of Buildings from Exterior Fire Exposures*, 1987 edition

NFPA 81, *Standard for Fur Storage, Fumigation and Cleaning*, 1986 edition

NFPA 220, *Standard on Types of Building Construction*, 1985 edition

NFPA 231, *Standard for General Storage*, 1990 edition

NFPA 231C, *Standard for Rack Storage of Materials*, 1991 edition

NFPA 231F, *Standard for the Storage of Roll Paper*, 1987 edition.

NFPA 703, *Standard for Fire Retardant Impregnated Wood and Fire Retardant Coatings for Building Materials*, 1985 edition

C-2   The following NFPA Recommended Practices contain specific sprinkler design criteria on various subjects.

NFPA 16A, *Recommended Practice for the Installation of Closed-Head Foam-Water Sprinkler Systems*, 1988 edition

NFPA 231E, *Recommended Practice for the Storage of Baled Cotton*, 1989 edition

ERRATA

NFPA 13

Installation of Sprinkler Systems

1991 Edition

Reference: 6-4.2.2, Table A-5-3.4, and Table A-5-3.5

The Committee on Automatic Sprinklers notes the following errors in the 1991 edition of NFPA 13, *Standard for the Installation of Sprinkler Systems.*

1. In 6-4.2.2 revise the formula to read:

$$Pv = \frac{0.001123\ Q^2}{D^4}$$

2. In Table A-5-3.4, Large-Drop Sprinkler Criteria, revise the rack storage heading to read as follows:

Double-Row Rack Storage[5] with Minimum 5.5 ft (1.7 m) Aisle Width and Multiple-Row Rack Storage with Minimum 8.0 ft (2.5 m) Aisle Width.

3. In Table A-5-3.5, ESFR Sprinkler Data, revise the first entry under the "Type of Storage" heading as follows:

Single-, double-, and multiple-row and portable rack storage (no open-top containers or solid shelves), and solid-piled or palletized storage.

Issue Date: June 26, 1992
Correction Issued: January, 1993

UNIFORM BUILDING CODE STANDARD 9-2
STANDPIPE SYSTEMS
See Sections 902, 904.1.2 and 904.5.1, *Uniform Building Code*

This standard, with certain exceptions, is based on the National Fire Protection Association Standard for the Installation of Standpipe and Hose Systems, NFPA 14-1993.

Part I of this standard contains exceptions to NFPA 14-1993[1]. Part II of this standard contains NFPA 14-1993[1] reproduced in its entirety with permission of the publisher.

〰〰〰〰 vertically in the margin of Part II indicates there is a revision to the provisions within Part I.

Unless specifically adopted elsewhere, supplemental standards referenced in this primary standard shall only be considered to be guidance material subject to the approval of the building official.

[1]The current edition is NFPA 14-1996.

Part I

SECTION 9.201 — AMENDMENTS

The Standard for Installation of Standpipe and Hose Systems, NFPA 14-1993, applies to the installation of standpipe systems except as follows:

1. Sec. 1-4 is revised by changing the definition of "authority having jurisdiction" as follows:

AUTHORITY HAVING JURISDICTION is the building official.

The definitions of "approved" and "listed" shall be as set forth in Volume I of this code.

The definition of "shall" is deleted.

2. Sec. 2-4.2.5 is revised by substituting "(See NFPA 13)" with "(See UBC Standard 9-1)" in the exception.

3. Sec. 2-7.2 is revised in the third line by deleting the words "not more than."

4. Sec. 4-1.2.5 is revised by substituting "NFPA 13, Standard for the Installation of Sprinkler Systems" with "UBC Standard 9-1."

5. Sec. 5-9.1.3.1 is revised by substituting "NFPA 13, Standard for the Installation of Sprinkler Systems" with "UBC Standard 9-1" in the exception.

6. Sec. 8-7 is revised by substituting "NFPA 72, Standard for the Installation, Maintenance and Use of Protective Signaling Systems" with "UFC Standard 14-1."

7. Sec. 8-8 is revised by deleting Subsection (b).

8. Chapter 10 is deleted.

Part II

Reproduced with permission from the Standard for Installation of Standpipe and Hose Systems, NFPA 14, copyright 1993[1], National Fire Protection Association, 1 Batterymarch Park, Quincy, Massachusetts 02269. Persons desiring to reprint in whole or part any portion of the Standard for Installation of Standpipe Systems, NFPA 14-1993[1], must secure permission from the National Fire Protection Association. The following standard is not necessarily the latest revision used by NFPA. If the reader desires to compare with that latest version, the same is available from NFPA.

[1]The current edition is NFPA 14-1996.

Contents

NFPA 14

Standard for the

Installation of Standpipe and Hose Systems

1993 Edition

NOTICE: An asterisk (*) following the number or letter designating a paragraph indicates explanatory material on that paragraph in Appendix A.

Information on referenced publications can be found in Chapter 10 and Appendix B.

Chapter 1 General Information

1-1 Scope. This standard covers the minimum requirements for the installation of standpipe and hose systems for buildings and structures.

1-2 Purpose. The purpose of this standard is to provide a reasonable degree of protection for life and property from fire through installation requirements for standpipe systems based on sound engineering principles, test data, and field experience. Nothing in this standard is intended to restrict new technologies or alternate arrangements providing the level of safety prescribed by the standard is not lowered.

1-3 Retroactivity. The provisions of this document are considered necessary to provide a reasonable level of protection from loss of life and property from fire. They reflect situations and the state of the art at the time the standard was issued.

Unless otherwise noted, it is not intended that the provisions of this document be applied to facilities, equipment, structures, or installations that were existing or approved for construction or installation prior to the effective date of the document.

Exception: In those cases where it is determined by the authority having jurisdiction that the existing situation involves a distinct hazard to life or property, this standard shall apply.

1-4 Definitions.

Approved. Acceptable to the "authority having jurisdiction."

NOTE: The National Fire Protection Association does not approve, inspect or certify any installations, procedures, equipment, or materials nor does it approve or evaluate testing laboratories. In determining the acceptability of installations or procedures, equipment or materials, the authority having jurisdiction may base acceptance on compliance with NFPA or other appropriate standards. In the absence of such standards, said authority may require evidence of proper installation, procedure or use. The authority having jurisdiction may also refer to the listings or labeling practices of an organization concerned with product evaluations which is in a position to determine compliance with appropriate standards for the current production of listed items.

Authority Having Jurisdiction. The "authority having jurisdiction" is the organization, office or individual responsible for "approving" equipment, an installation or a procedure.

NOTE: The phrase "authority having jurisdiction" is used in NFPA documents in a broad manner since jurisdictions and "approval" agencies vary as do their responsibilities. Where public safety is primary, the "authority having jurisdiction" may be a federal, state, local or other regional department or individual such as a fire chief, fire marshal, chief of a fire prevention bureau, labor department, health department, building official, electrical inspector, or others having statutory authority. For insurance purposes, an insurance inspection department, rating bureau, or other insurance company representative may be the "authority having jurisdiction." In many circumstances the property owner or his designated agent assumes the role of the "authority having jurisdiction"; at government installations, the commanding officer or departmental official may be the "authority having jurisdiction."

Automatic Standpipe System. A standpipe system that is attached to a water supply capable of supplying the system demand at all times and that requires no action other than opening a hose valve to provide water at hose connections. (*See Chapter 3.*)

Branch Line. A piping system, generally in a horizontal plane, connecting one or more hose connections with a standpipe.

Combined System. A standpipe system having piping that supplies both hose connections and automatic sprinklers.

Control Valve. A valve used to control the water supply system of a standpipe system.

Dry Standpipe. A standpipe system designed to have piping contain water only when the system is being utilized. (*See Chapter 3.*)

Feed Main. That portion of a standpipe system that supplies water to one or more standpipes.

Fire Department Connection. A connection through which the fire department can pump water into the standpipe system.

High-Rise Building. A building more than 75 ft (23 m) in height. Building height shall be measured from the lowest level of fire department vehicle access to the floor of the highest occupiable story.

Hose Connection. A combination of equipment provided for connection of a hose to the standpipe system that includes a hose valve with a threaded outlet.

Hose Station. A combination of a hose rack, hose nozzle, hose, and hose connection.

Hose Valve. The valve to an individual hose connection.

Listed. Equipment or materials included in a list published by an organization acceptable to the "authority having jurisdiction" and concerned with product evaluation, that maintains periodic inspection of production of listed equipment or materials and whose listing states either that the equipment or material meets appropriate standards or has been tested and found suitable for use in a specified manner.

NOTE: The means for identifying listed equipment may vary for each organization concerned with product evaluation, some of which do not recognize equipment as listed unless it is also labeled. The "authority having jurisdiction" should utilize the system employed by the listing organization to identify a listed product.

Manual Standpipe System. A standpipe system that relies exclusively on the fire department connection to supply the system demand. (*See Chapter 3.*)

Pressure, Nozzle. Pressure required at the inlet of a nozzle to produce the desired water discharge characteristics.

Pressure, Residual. Pressure acting on a point in the system with a flow being delivered by the system.

Pressure, Static. Pressure acting on a point in the system with no flow from the system.

Pressure Control Valve. A pilot-operated valve designed for the purpose of reducing the downstream water pressure to a specific value under both flowing (residual) and nonflowing (static) conditions.

Pressure Reducing Valve. A valve designed for the purpose of reducing the downstream water pressure under both flowing (residual) and nonflowing (static) conditions.

Pressure Regulating Device. A device designed for the purpose of reducing, regulating, controlling, or restricting water pressure. Examples include pressure reducing valves, pressure control valves, and pressure restricting devices.

Pressure Restricting Device. A valve or device designed for the purpose of reducing the downstream water pressure under flowing (residual) conditions only.

Semiautomatic Standpipe System. A standpipe system that is attached to a water supply capable of supplying the system demand at all times and that requires activation of a control device to provide water at hose connections. See Chapter 3.

Shall.* Indicates a mandatory requirement.

Standpipe. The riser portion of the system piping that delivers the water supply for hose connections, and sprinklers on combined systems, vertically from floor to floor.

Standpipe System. An arrangement of piping, valves, hose connections, and allied equipment installed in a building or structure with the hose connections located in such a manner that water can be discharged in streams or spray patterns through attached hose and nozzles, for the purpose of extinguishing a fire and so protecting a building or structure and its contents in addition to protecting the occupants. This is accomplished by connections to water supply systems or by pumps, tanks, and other equipment necessary to provide an adequate supply of water to the hose connections.

System Demand. The flow rate and residual pressure required from a water supply, measured at the point of connection of a water supply to a standpipe system, to deliver:

(a) The total water flow rate required for a standpipe system established in Section 5-9, and

(b) The minimum residual pressures established by Section 5-7 at the hydraulically most remote hose connection, and

(c) The minimum water flow rate for sprinkler connections, on combined systems.

Type (of System). (*See Chapter 3.*)

Wet Standpipe. A standpipe system having piping containing water at all times. (*See Chapter 3.*)

1-5 Units.

1-5.1 Metric units of measurement in this standard are in accordance with the modernized metric system known as the International System of Units (SI). Two units (liter and bar), outside of but recognized by SI, are commonly used in international fire protection. These units are listed in Table 1-5 with conversion factors.

Table 1-5

Name of Unit	Unit Symbol	Conversion Factor
meter	m	1 ft = 0.3048 m
millimeter	mm	1 in. = 25.4 mm
liter	L	1 gal = 3.785 L
cubic decimeter	dm^3	1 gal = 3.785 dm^3
Pascal	Pa	1 psi = 6894.757 Pa
bar	bar	1 psi = 0.0689 bar
bar	bar	1 bar = 10^5 Pa

For additional conversion and information, see ASTM E380.

1-5.2 If a value for measurement as given in this standard is followed by an equivalent value in other units, the first stated is to be regarded as the requirement. A given equivalent value could be approximate.

Chapter 2   System Components and Hardware

2-1* General. Standpipe system components and hardware shall be in accordance with this chapter. All devices and materials used in standpipe systems shall be of an approved type. System components shall be rated for working pressures not less than the maximum pressure to be developed at that point in the system under any condition including the pressure when a permanently installed fire pump is operating at shutoff pressure.

2-2 Pipe and Tube.

2-2.1 Pipe or tube used in standpipe systems shall meet or exceed one of the standards in Table 2-2.1 or be in accordance with 2-2.2 through 2-2.5.

Table 2-2.1 Pipe or Tube Materials and Dimensions

Material and Dimensions (Specifications)	Standard
Ferrous Piping	
Ductile-Iron Pipe, Centrifugally Cast, in Metal Molds or Sand-Lined Molds for Water or Other Liquids	AWWA C151
Electric-Resistance Welded Steel Pipe Spec. for Black and Hot-Dipped Zinc-Coated (Galvanized)	ASTM A135
Welded and Seamless Steel Pipe for Fire Protection Use	ASTM A795
Welded and Seamless Steel Pipe	ASTM A53
Wrought-Steel and Wrought-Iron Pipe	ANSI B36.10
Copper Tube (Drawn, Seamless)	
Seamless Copper Tube	ASTM B75
Seamless Copper Water Tube	ASTM B88
General Requirements for Wrought Seamless Copper and Copper-Alloy Tube	ASTM B251
Brazing Filler Metal (Classifications BCuP-3 or BCuP-4)	AWS A5.8

2-2.2 Where steel pipe listed in Table 2-2.1 is used and joined by welding as referenced in 2-4.2 or by roll-grooved pipe and fittings as referenced in 2-4.3, the minimum nominal wall thickness for pressures up to 300 psi (20.7 bars) shall be in accordance with Schedule 10 for sizes up to 5 in. (127 mm); 0.134 in. (3.40 mm) for 6 in. (152 mm); and 0.188 in. (4.78 mm) for 8- and 10-in. (203- and 254-mm) pipe.

Exception: Pressure limitations and wall thickness for steel pipe listed in accordance with 2-2.5 shall be in accordance with the listing requirements.

2-2.3 Where steel pipe listed in Table 2-2.1 is joined by threaded fittings referenced in 2-4.1 or by fittings used with pipe having cut grooves, the minimum wall thickness shall be in accordance with Schedule 30 [in sizes 8 in. (203 mm) and larger] or Schedule 40 [in sizes less than 8 in. (203 mm)] pipe for pressures up to 300 psi (20.7 bars).

Exception: Pressure limitations and wall thickness for steel pipe specially listed in accordance with 2-2.5 shall be in accordance with the listing requirements.

2-2.4 Copper tube as specified in the standards listed in Table 2-2.1 shall have a wall thickness of Type K, L, or M where used in standpipe systems.

2-2.5 Other types of pipe or tube investigated for suitability in standpipe installations and listed for this service, including but not limited to steel differing from that provided in Table 2-2.1, shall be permitted where installed in accordance with their listing limitations, including installation instructions. Pipe or tube shall not be listed for portions of an occupancy classification.

2-2.6 Pipe Bending. Bending of Schedule 40 steel pipe and Types K and L copper tube shall be permitted where bends are made with no kinks, ripples, distortions, reductions in diameter, or any noticeable deviations from round. The minimum radius of a bend shall be 6 pipe diameters for pipe sizes 2 in. (51 mm) and smaller, and 5 pipe diameters for pipe sizes 2½ in. (64 mm) and larger.

2-3 Fittings.

2-3.1 Fittings used in sprinkler systems shall meet or exceed the standards in Table 2-3.1 or be in accordance with 2-3.2.

Table 2-3.1 Fittings Materials and Dimensions

Material and Dimensions	Standard
Cast Iron	
Cast-Iron Threaded Fittings, Class 125 and 250	ANSI B16.4
Cast-Iron Pipe Flanges and Flanged Fittings, Class 125 and 250	ANSI B16.1
Malleable Iron	
Malleable Iron Threaded Fittings, Class 150 and 300	ANSI B16.3
Ductile Iron	
Gray-Iron and Ductile-Iron Fittings, 3 in. through 48 in. for Water and Other Liquids	AWWA C110
Steel	
Factory-Made Wrought Steel Buttweld Fittings	ANSI B16.9
Buttwelding Endings for Pipe, Valves, Flanges, and Fittings	ANSI B16.25
Spec. for Piping Fittings of Wrought Carbon Steel and Alloy Steel for Moderate and Elevated Temperatures	ASTM A234
Steel Pipe Flanges and Flanged Fittings	ANSI B16.5
Forged Steel Fittings, Socketed, Welded and Threaded	ANSI B16.11
Copper	
Wrought Copper and Bronze Solder-Joint Pressure Fittings	ANSI B16.22
Cast Bronze Solder Joint Pressure Fittings	ANSI B16.18

2-3.2 Other types of fittings investigated for suitability in standpipe installations and listed for this service, including but not limited to steel differing from that provided in Table 2-3.1, shall be permitted where installed in accordance with their listing limitations, including installation instructions.

2-3.3 Fittings shall be extra-heavy pattern where pressures exceed 175 psi (12.1 bars).

Exception No. 1: Standard weight pattern cast-iron fittings 2 in. (51 mm) in size and smaller shall be permitted where pressures do not exceed 300 psi (20.7 bars).

Exception No. 2: Standard weight pattern malleable iron fittings 6 in. (152 mm) in size and smaller shall be permitted where pressures do not exceed 300 psi (20.7 bars).

Exception No. 3: Fittings shall be permitted for system pressures up to the limits specified in their listings.

2-3.4 Couplings and Unions. Screwed unions shall not be used on pipe larger than 2 in. (51 mm). Couplings and unions of other than screwed-type shall be of types listed specifically for use in sprinkler systems.

2-3.5 Reducers and Bushings. A one-piece reducing fitting shall be used wherever a change is made in the size of the pipe.

Exception: Hexagonal or face bushings shall be permitted in reducing the size of openings of fittings where standard fittings of the required size are not available.

2-4 Joining of Pipe and Fittings.

2-4.1 Threaded Pipe and Fittings.

2-4.1.1 All threaded pipe and fittings shall have threads cut to ANSI/ASME B1.20.1.

2-4.1.2 Steel pipe with wall thicknesses less than Schedule 30 [in sizes 8 in. (203 mm) and larger] or Schedule 40 [in sizes less than 8 in. (203 mm)] shall not be joined by threaded fittings.

Exception: A threaded assembly investigated for suitability in standpipe installations and listed for this service shall be permitted.

2-4.1.3 Joint compound or tape shall be applied only to male threads.

2-4.2 Welded Pipe and Fittings.

2-4.2.1 Welding methods that comply with all of the requirements of AWS D10.9, *Standard Specification for Qualification of Welding Procedures and Welders for Piping and Tubing*, Level AR-3, are acceptable means of joining fire protection piping.

2-4.2.2 Standpipe piping shall be shop welded.

Exception: Welding of standpipe piping in place inside new buildings under construction shall be permitted only where the construction is noncombustible and no combustible contents are present, and when the welding process is performed in accordance with NFPA 51B, Standard for Fire Prevention in Use of Cutting and Welding Processes.

2-4.2.3 Fittings used to join pipe shall be listed fabricated fittings or manufactured in accordance with Table 2-3.1. Such fittings joined in conformance with a qualified welding procedure as set forth in this section are an acceptable product under this standard, provided that materials and wall thickness are compatible with other sections of this standard.

Exception: Fittings are not required where pipe ends are buttwelded.

2-4.2.4 No welding shall be performed if there is impingement of rain, snow, sleet, or high wind on the weld area of the pipe product.

2-4.2.5 When welding is performed:

(a) Holes in piping for outlets shall be cut to the full inside diameter of fittings prior to welding in place of the fittings.

(b) Discs shall be retrieved.

(c) Openings cut into piping shall be smooth bore, and all internal slag and welding residue shall be removed.

(d) Fittings shall not penetrate the internal diameter of the piping.

(e) Steel plates shall not be welded to the ends of piping or fittings.

(f) Fittings shall not be modified.

(g) Nuts, clips, eye rods, angle brackets, or other fasteners shall not be welded to pipe or fittings.

Exception: Only tabs welded to pipe for longitudinal earthquake braces shall be permitted. (See NFPA 13.)

2-4.2.6 When reducing the pipe size in a run of piping, a reducing fitting designed for that purpose shall be used.

2-4.2.7 Torch cutting and welding shall not be permitted as a means of modifying or repairing standpipe systems.

2-4.2.8 Qualifications.

2-4.2.8.1 A welding procedure shall be prepared and qualified by the contractor or fabricator before any welding is done. Qualification of the welding procedure to be used and the performance of all welders and welding operators is required and shall meet or exceed the requirements of American Welding Society Standard AWS D10.9, Level AR-3.

2-4.2.8.2 Contractors or fabricators shall be responsible for all welding they produce. Each contractor or fabricator shall have an established written quality assurance procedure ensuring compliance with the requirements of 2-4.2.5 available to the authority having jurisdiction.

2-4.2.9 Records.

2-4.2.9.1 Welders or welding machine operators shall, upon completion of each weld, stamp an imprint of their identification into the side of the pipe adjacent to the weld.

2-4.2.9.2 Contractors or fabricators shall maintain certified records, which are available to the authority having jurisdiction, of the procedures used and the welders or welding machine operators employed by them along with their welding identification imprints. Records shall show the date and the results of procedure and performance qualifications.

2-4.3 Groove Joining Methods.

2-4.3.1 Pipe joined with grooved fittings shall be joined by a listed combination of fittings, gaskets, and grooves. Grooves cut or rolled on pipe shall be dimensionally compatible with the fittings.

2-4.3.2 Grooved fittings including gaskets used on dry pipe systems shall be listed for dry pipe service.

2-4.4 Brazed and Soldered Joints.

2-4.4.1 Joints for the connection of copper tube shall be brazed.

Exception No. 1: Solder joints shall be permitted for exposed wet standpipe systems in Light Hazard Occupancies.

Exception No. 2: Solder joints shall be permitted for wet standpipe systems in Light Hazard and Ordinary Hazard (Group 1) Occupancies where the piping is concealed.

2-4.4.2 Highly corrosive fluxes shall not be used.

2-4.5 Other Types.
Other joining methods investigated for suitability in standpipe systems and listed for this service shall be permitted where installed in accordance with their listing limitations, including installation instructions.

2-4.6 End Treatment.
After cutting, pipe ends shall have burrs and fins removed.

2-4.6.1 Pipe used with listed fittings and its end treatment shall be in accordance with the fitting manufacturer's installation instructions and the fitting's listing.

2-5 Hangers.

2-5.1* General. Types of hangers shall be in accordance with the requirements of this section.

Exception: Hangers certified by a registered professional engineer to include all of the following shall be acceptable:

(a) Hangers are designed to support 5 times the weight of the water-filled pipe plus 250 lb (114 kg) at each point of piping support.

(b) These points of support are adequate to support the standpipe system.

(c) Hanger components shall be ferrous.

Detailed calculations shall be submitted, where required by the reviewing authority, showing stresses developed both in hangers and piping and safety factors allowed.

2-5.1.1 The components of hanger assemblies that directly attach to the pipe or to the building structure shall be listed.

Exception: Mild steel hangers formed from rods need not be listed.

2-5.1.2 Hangers and their components shall be ferrous.

Exception: Nonferrous components that have been proven by fire tests to be adequate for the hazard application, that are listed for this purpose, and that are in compliance with the other requirements of this section shall be acceptable.

2-5.1.3 Standpipe piping shall be substantially supported from the building structure, which must support the added load of the water-filled pipe plus a minimum of 250 lb (114 kg) applied at the point of hanging.

2-5.1.4 Where standpipe piping is installed below ductwork, piping shall be supported from the building structure or from the ductwork supports, provided such supports are capable of handling both the load of the ductwork and the load specified in 2-5.1.3.

2-5.1.5 For trapeze hangers, the minimum size of steel angle or pipe span between purlins or joists shall be such that the available section modulus of the trapeze member from Table 2-5.1.5(b) equals or exceeds the section modulus required in Table 2-5.1.5(a).

Table 2-5.1.5(a)   Section Modulus Required for Trapeze Member (in^3)

Span of Trapeze	1 in.	1^1/$_4$ in.	1^1/$_2$ in.	2 in.	2^1/$_2$ in.	3 in.	3^1/$_2$ in.	4 in.	5 in.	6 in.	8 in.	10 in.
1 ft 6 in.	.08	.09	.09	.09	.10	.11	.12	.13	.15	.18	.24	.32
	.08	.09	.09	.10	.11	.12	.13	.15	.18	.22	.30	.41
2 ft 0 in.	.11	.12	.12	.13	.13	.15	.16	.17	.20	.24	.32	.43
	.11	.12	.12	.13	.15	.16	.18	.20	.24	.29	.40	.55
2 ft 6 in.	.14	.14	.15	.16	.17	.18	.20	.21	.25	.30	.40	.54
	.14	.15	.15	.16	.18	.21	.22	.25	.30	.36	.50	.68
3 ft 0 in.	.17	.17	.18	.19	.20	.22	.24	.26	.31	.36	.48	.65
	.17	.18	.18	.20	.22	.25	.27	.30	.36	.43	.60	.82
4 ft 0 in.	.22	.23	.24	.25	.27	.29	.32	.34	.41	.48	.64	.87
	.22	.24	.24	.26	.29	.33	.36	.40	.48	.58	.80	1.09
5 ft 0 in.	.28	.29	.30	.31	.34	.37	.40	.43	.51	.59	.80	1.08
	.28	.29	.30	.33	.37	.41	.45	.49	.60	.72	1.00	1.37
6 ft 0 in.	.33	.35	.36	.38	.41	.44	.48	.51	.61	.71	.97	1.30
	.34	.35	.36	.39	.44	.49	.54	.59	.72	.87	1.20	1.64
7 ft 0 in.	.39	.40	.41	.44	.47	.52	.55	.60	.71	.83	1.13	1.52
	.39	.41	.43	.46	.51	.58	.63	.69	.84	1.01	1.41	1.92
8 ft 0 in.	.44	.46	.47	.50	.54	.59	.63	.68	.81	.95	1.29	1.73
	.45	.47	.49	.52	.59	.66	.72	.79	.96	1.16	1.61	2.19
9 ft 0 in.	.50	.52	.53	.56	.61	.66	.71	.77	.92	1.07	1.45	1.95
	.50	.53	.55	.59	.66	.74	.81	.89	1.08	1.30	1.81	2.46
10 ft 0 in.	.56	.58	.59	.63	.68	.74	.79	.85	1.02	1.19	1.61	2.17
	.56	.59	.61	.65	.74	.82	.90	.99	1.20	1.44	2.01	2.74

For SI Units: 1 in. = 25.4 mm; 1 ft = 0.3048 m.

Top values are for Schedule 10 pipe; bottom values are for Schedule 40 pipe.

NOTE: The table is based on a maximum allowable bending stress of 15 KSI and a midspan concentrated load from 15 ft of water-filled pipe, plus 250 lb.

Any other sizes or shapes giving equal or greater section modulus shall be acceptable. All angles shall be used with the longer leg vertical. The trapeze member shall be secured to prevent slippage. Where a pipe is suspended from a pipe trapeze of a diameter less than the diameter of the pipe being supported, ring, strap, or clevis hangers of the size corresponding to the suspended pipe shall be used on both ends.

Table 2-5.1.5(b) Available Section Moduli of Common Trapeze Hangers

Pipe	Modulus	Angles	Modulus
Schedule 10			
1 in.	.12	1 1/2 × 1 1/2 × 3/16	.10
1 1/4 in.	.19	2 × 2 × 1/8	.13
1 1/2 in.	.26	2 × 1 1/2 × 3/16	.18
2 in.	.42	2 × 2 × 3/16	.19
2 1/2 in.	.69	2 × 2 × 1/4	.25
3 in.	1.04	2 1/2 × 1 1/2 × 3/16	.28
3 1/2 in.	1.38	2 1/2 × 2 × 3/16	.29
4 in.	1.76	2 × 2 × 5/16	.30
5 in.	3.03	2 1/2 × 2 1/2 × 3/16	.30
6 in.	4.35	2 × 2 × 3/8	.35
		2 1/2 × 2 1/2 × 1/4	.39
		3 × 2 × 3/16	.41
Schedule 40		3 × 2 1/2 × 3/16	.43
1 in.	.13	3 × 3 × 3/16	.44
1 1/4 in.	.23	2 1/2 × 2 1/2 × 5/16	.48
1 1/2 in.	.33	3 × 2 × 1/4	.54
2 in.	.56	2 1/2 × 2 × 3/8	.55
2 1/2 in.	1.06	2 1/2 × 2 1/2 × 3/8	.57
3 in.	1.72	3 × 3 × 1/4	.58
3 1/2 in.	2.39	3 × 3 × 5/16	.71
4 in.	3.21	2 1/2 × 2 1/2 × 1/2	.72
5 in.	5.45	3 1/2 × 2 1/2 × 1/4	.75
6 in.	8.50	3 × 2 1/2 × 3/8	.81
		3 × 3 × 3/8	.83
		3 1/2 × 2 1/2 × 5/16	.93
		3 × 3 × 7/16	.95
		4 × 4 × 1/4	1.05
		3 × 3 × 1/2	1.07
		4 × 3 × 5/16	1.23
		4 × 4 × 5/16	1.29
		4 × 3 × 3/8	1.46
		4 × 4 × 3/8	1.52
		5 × 3 1/2 × 5/16	1.94
		4 × 4 × 1/2	1.97
		4 × 4 × 5/8	2.40
		4 × 4 × 3/4	2.81
		6 × 4 × 3/8	3.32
		6 × 4 × 1/2	4.33
		6 × 4 × 3/4	6.25
		6 × 6 × 1	8.57

For SI Units: 1 in. = 25.4 mm; 1 ft = 0.30458 m.

2-5.1.6 The size of hanger rods and fasteners required to support the steel angle iron or pipe indicated in Table 2-5.1.5(a) shall comply with 2-5.4.

2-5.1.7 Standpipe piping or hangers shall not be used to support nonsystem components.

2-5.2 Hangers in Concrete.

2-5.2.1 The use of listed inserts set in concrete to support hangers shall be permitted.

2-5.2.2 Listed expansion shields for supporting pipes under concrete construction shall be permitted to be used in a horizontal position in the sides of beams. In concrete having gravel or crushed stone aggregate, expansion shields shall be permitted to be used in the vertical position to support pipes 4 in. (102 mm) or less in diameter.

2-5.2.3 For the support of pipes 5 in. (127 mm) and larger, expansion shields, if used in the vertical position, shall alternate with hangers connected directly to the structural members, such as trusses and girders, or to the sides of concrete beams. In the absence of convenient structural members, pipes 5 in. (127 mm) and larger shall be permitted to be supported entirely by expansion shields in the vertical position, but spaced not more than 10 ft (3 m) apart.

2-5.2.4 Expansion shields shall not be used in ceilings of gypsum or similar soft material. In cinder concrete, expansion shields shall not be used except on branch lines where they shall alternate with through bolts or hangers attached to beams.

2-5.2.5 Where expansion shields are used in the vertical position, the holes shall be drilled to provide uniform contact with the shield over its entire circumference. Depth of the hole shall not be less than specified for the type of shield used.

2-5.2.6 Holes for expansion shields in the side of concrete beams shall be above the center line of the beam or above the bottom reinforcement steel rods.

2-5.3 Powder-Driven Studs and Welding Studs.

2-5.3.1 Powder-driven studs, welding studs, and the tools used for installing these devices shall be listed. Pipe size, installation position, and construction material into which they are installed shall be in accordance with individual listings.

2-5.3.2 Representative samples of concrete into which studs are to be driven shall be tested to determine that the studs will hold a minimum load of 750 lb (341 kg) for 2-in. (51-mm) or smaller pipe, 1000 lb (454 kg) for 2 1/2-, 3-, or 3 1/2-in. (64-, 76-, or 89-mm) pipe, and 1200 lb (545 kg) for 4- or 5-in. (102- or 127-mm) pipe.

2-5.3.3 Increaser couplings shall be attached directly to the powder-driven studs or welding studs.

2-5.3.4 Welding studs or other hanger parts shall not be attached by welding to steel less than U.S. Standard, 12 gauge.

2-5.4 Rods and U-Hooks.

2-5.4.1 Hanger rod size shall be the same as that approved for use with the hanger assembly, and the size of rods shall not be less than that given in Table 2-5.4.1.

Exception: Rods of smaller diameter shall be permitted where the hanger assembly has been tested and listed by a testing laboratory and installed within the limits of pipe sizes expressed in individual listings. For rolled threads, the rod size shall be not less than the root diameter of the thread.

Table 2-5.4.1   Hanger Rod Sizes

Pipe Size	Dia. of Rod	
	in.	mm
Up to and including 4 in.	$3/8$	9.5
5, 6, and 8 in.	$1/2$	12.7
10 and 12 in.	$5/8$	15.9

For SI Units: 1 in. = 25.4 mm.

2-5.4.2 U-Hooks. The size of the rod material of U-hooks shall not be less than that given in Table 2-5.4.2. Drive screws shall be used only in a horizontal position as in the side of a beam in conjunction with U-hangers only.

Table 2-5.4.2   U-Hook Rod Sizes

Pipe Size	Hook Material Diameter	
	in.	mm
Up to 2 in.	$5/16$	7.9
$2\,1/2$ in. to 6 in.	$3/8$	9.5
8 in.	$1/2$	12.7

For SI Units: 1 in. = 25.4 mm.

2-5.4.3 Eye Rods.[1] The size of the rod material for eye rods shall not be less than that specified in Table 2-5.4.3. Where eye rods are fastened to wood structural members, the eye rod shall be backed with a large flat washer bearing directly against the structural member, in addition to the lock washer.

Table 2-5.4.3   Eye Rod Sizes

Pipe Size	Diameter of Rod			
	With Bent Eye		With Welded Eye	
	in.	mm	in.	mm
Up to 4 in.	$3/8$	9.5	$3/8$	9.5
5 to 6 in.	$1/2$	12.7	$1/2$	12.7
8 in.	$3/4$	19.1	$1/2$	12.7

For SI Units: 1 in. = 25.4 mm.

2-5.4.3.1 Eye rods shall be secured with lock washers to prevent lateral motion.

2-5.4.4 Threaded sections of rods shall not be formed or bent.

2-5.4.5 Screws. For ceiling flanges and U-hooks, screw dimensions shall not be less than those given in Table 2-5.4.5.

Exception: Where the thickness of planking and thickness of flange do not permit the use of screws 2 in. (51 mm) long, screws 1 3/4 in. (44 mm) long shall be permitted with hangers spaced not more than 10 ft (3 m) apart. Where the thickness of beams or joists does not permit the use of screws 2 1/2 in. (64 mm) long, screws 2 in. (51 mm) long shall be permitted with hangers spaced not more than 10 ft (3 m) apart.

Table 2-5.4.5   Screw Dimensions for Ceiling Flanges and U-Hooks

Pipe Size	2 Screw Flanges
Up to 2 in.	Wood Screw No. 18 x $1\,1/2$ in.

Pipe Size	3 Screw Flanges
Up to 2 in.	Wood Screw No. 18 x $1\,1/2$ in.
$2\,1/2$ in., 3 in., $3\,1/2$ in.	Lag Screw $3/8$ in. x 2 in.
4 in., 5 in., 6 in.	Lag Screw $1/2$ in. x 2 in.
8 in.	Lag Screw $5/8$ in. x 2 in.

Pipe Size	4 Screw Flanges
Up to 2 in.	Wood Screw No. 18 x $1\,1/2$ in.
$2\,1/2$ in., 3 in., $3\,1/2$ in.	Lag Screw $3/8$ in. x $1\,1/2$ in.
4 in., 5 in., 6 in.	Lag Screw $1/2$ in. x 2 in.
8 in.	Lag Screw $5/8$ in. x 2 in.

Pipe Size	U-Hooks
Up to 2 in.	Drive Screw No. 16 x 2 in.
$2\,1/2$ in., 3 in., $3\,1/2$ in.	Lag Screw $3/8$ in. x $2\,1/2$ in.
4 in., 5 in., 6 in.	Lag Screw $1/2$ in. x 3 in.
8 in.	Lag Screw $5/8$ in. x 3 in.

For SI Units: 1 in. = 25.4 mm.

2-5.4.6 The size bolt or lag (coach) screw used with an eye rod or flange on the side of the beam shall not be less than specified in Table 2-5.4.6.

Table 2-5.4.6   Minimum Bolt or Lag Screw Sizes

Size of Pipe	Size of Bolt or Lag Screw		Length of Lag Screw Used with Wood Beams	
	in.	mm	in.	mm
Up to and including 2 in.	$3/8$	9.5	$2\,1/2$	64
$2\,1/2$ to 6 in. (inclusive)	$1/2$	12.7	3	76
8 in.	$5/8$	15.9	3	76

For SI Units: 1 in. = 25.4 mm.

Exception: Where the thickness of beams or joists does not permit the use of screws 2 1/2 in. (64 mm) long, screws 2 in. (51 mm) long shall be permitted with hangers spaced not more than 10 ft (3 m) apart.

2-5.4.7 Wood screws shall be installed with a screwdriver. Nails are not acceptable for fastening hangers.

2-5.4.8 Screws in the side of a timber or joist shall be not less than $2\,1/2$ in. (64 mm) from the lower edge where supporting branch lines and not less than 3 in. (76 mm) where supporting main lines.

Exception: This requirement shall not apply to 2-in. (51-mm) or thicker nailing strips resting on top of steel beams.

2-5.4.9 The minimum plank thickness and the minimum width of the lower face of beams or joists in which lag screw rods are used shall be as given in Table 2-5.4.9.

Table 2-5.4.9 Minimum Plank Thicknesses and Beam or Joist Widths

Pipe Size	Nominal Plank Thickness		Nominal Width of Beam or Joist Face	
	in.	mm	in.	mm
Up to 2 in.	3	76	2	51
2½ in. to 3½ in.	4	102	2	51
4 in. and 5 in.	4	102	3	76
6 in.	4	102	4	102

For SI Units: 1 in. = 25.4 mm.

2-5.4.10 Lag screw rods shall not be used for support of pipes larger than 6 in. (152 mm). All holes for lag screw rods shall be predrilled ⅛ in. (3.2 mm) less in diameter than the maximum root diameter of the lag screw thread.

2-6 Valves. All valves controlling connections to water supplies and standpipes shall be listed indicating valves.

Such valves shall not close in less than 5 sec when operated at maximum possible speed from the fully open position.

Exception No. 1: A listed underground gate valve equipped with a listed indicator post shall be permitted.

Exception No. 2: A listed water control valve assembly with a reliable position indication connected to a remote supervisory station shall be permitted.

Exception No. 3: A nonindicating valve, such as an underground gate valve with approved roadway box complete with T-wrench, accepted by the authority having jurisdiction, shall be permitted.

2-7 Hose Stations.

2-7.1 Closets and Cabinets.

2-7.1.1 Closets and cabinets used to contain fire hose shall be of sufficient size to permit the installation of the necessary equipment at hose stations and so designed as not to interfere with the prompt use of the hose connection, the hose, and other equipment at the time of fire. Within the cabinet, the hose connections shall be located so that there is at least 1 in. (25 mm) between any part of the cabinet and the handle of the valve when the valve is in any position from fully open to fully closed. The cabinet shall be used for fire equipment only, and each cabinet shall be conspicuously identified.

2-7.1.2 Where a "break glass" type protective cover for a latching device is provided, the device provided to break the glass panel shall be securely attached in the immediate area of the "break glass" panel and shall be so arranged that the device cannot be used to break other glass panels in the cabinet door.

2-7.1.3 Where a fire resistive assembly is penetrated by a cabinet, the fire resistance of the assembly shall be maintained as required by the local building code.

2-7.2* Hose. Each hose connection provided for use by building occupants (Class II and Class III systems) shall be equipped with not more than 100 ft (30.5 m) of listed 1½-in. (38.1-mm) lined, collapsible or noncollapsible fire hose attached and ready for use.

Exception: Where hose less than 1½ in. (38.1 mm) is used for 1½-in. (38.1-mm) hose stations in accordance with 3-3.2 and 3-3.3, listed noncollapsible hose shall be used.

2-7.3 Hose Racks. Each 1½-in. (38.1-mm) hose station provided with 1½-in. (38.1-mm) hose shall be equipped with a listed rack or other approved storage facility.

Each 1½-in. (38.1-mm) hose station provided with hose less than 1½ in. (38.1 mm) in accordance with 3-3.2 and 3-3.3 shall be equipped with a listed continuous flow reel.

2-7.4 Nozzles. Nozzles provided for Class II service shall be listed.

2-7.5 Label. Each rack or storage facility for 1½-in. (38.1-mm) or smaller hose shall be provided with a label that includes "Fire Hose for Use by Occupants" and operating instructions.

2-8 Hose Connections. Hose connections shall have external NH standard threads, for the valve size specified, as specified in NFPA 1963, *Standard for Screw Threads and Gaskets for Fire Hose Connections.* Hose connections shall be equipped with caps to protect hose threads.

Exception: Where local fire department hose threads do not conform to NFPA 1963, the authority having jurisdiction shall designate the hose threads to be used.

2-9* Fire Department Connections.

2-9.1 Fire department connections shall be listed for a working pressure equal to or greater than the pressure requirement of the system demand.

2-9.2* Each fire department connection shall have at least two 2½-in. (63.5-mm) internal threaded swivel fittings having NH standard threads, as specified in NFPA 1963, *Standard for Screw Threads and Gaskets for Fire Hose Connections.* Fire department connections shall be equipped with caps to protect against entry of debris into the system.

Exception: Where the local fire department uses fittings different than those specified, fittings compatible with local fire department equipment shall be used and the minimum size shall be 2½ in. (62 mm).

2-10 Signs. Signs shall be permanently marked and shall be constructed of weather-resistant metal or rigid plastic materials.

Chapter 3 System Requirements

3-1 General.

3-1.1 The number and arrangement of standpipe equipment necessary for proper protection is governed by the local conditions such as occupancy, character, and construction of building and accessibility. The authority having jurisdiction shall be consulted as to the required type of system, class of system, and special requirements.

3-1.2 Spacing and location of standpipes and hose connections shall be in accordance with Chapter 5.

3-1.3 Standpipe and hose systems not required by the authority having jurisdiction and not meeting the requirements of this standard shall be marked with a sign stating "FOR FIRE BRIGADE USE ONLY."

3-2 Types of Standpipe Systems.

3-2.1 Automatic-Dry. An automatic-dry standpipe system shall be a dry standpipe system, normally filled with pressurized air, that is arranged through the use of devices, such as a dry pipe valve, to automatically admit water into system piping upon opening of a hose valve. The water supply for an automatic-dry standpipe system shall be capable of supplying the system demand.

3-2.2 Automatic-Wet. An automatic-wet standpipe system shall be a wet standpipe system that has a water supply that is capable of supplying the system demand automatically.

3-2.3 Semiautomatic-Dry. A semiautomatic-dry standpipe system shall be a dry standpipe system that is arranged through the use of devices, such as a deluge valve, to admit water into system piping upon activation of a remote control device located at a hose connection. A remote control activation device shall be provided at each hose connection. The water supply for a semiautomatic-dry standpipe system shall be capable of supplying the system demand.

3-2.4 Manual-Dry. A manual-dry standpipe system shall be a dry standpipe system that does not have a permanent water supply attached to the system. Manual-dry standpipe systems require water from a fire department pumper (or the like) to be pumped into the system through the fire department connection to supply the system demand.

3-2.5 Manual-Wet. A manual-wet standpipe system shall be a wet standpipe system connected to a small water supply for the purpose of maintaining water within the system, but that does not have a water supply capable of delivering the system demand attached to the system. Manual-wet standpipe systems require water from a fire department pumper (or the like) to be pumped into the system to supply the system demand.

3-3 Classes of Standpipe Systems.

3-3.1 Class I Systems. A Class I standpipe system shall provide 2¹/₂-in. (63.5-mm) hose connections to supply water for use by fire departments and those trained in handling heavy fire streams.

3-3.2 Class II Systems. A Class II standpipe system shall provide 1¹/₂-in. (38.1-mm) hose stations to supply water for use primarily by the building occupants or by the fire department during initial response.

Exception: A minimum 1-in. (25.4-mm) hose shall be permitted to be used for hose stations in Light Hazard Occupancies where investigated and listed for this service and where approved by the authority having jurisdiction.

3-3.3 Class III Systems. A Class III standpipe system shall provide 1¹/₂-in. (38.1-mm) hose stations to supply water for use by building occupants and 2¹/₂-in. (63.5-mm) hose connections to supply a larger volume of water for use by fire departments and those trained in handling heavy fire streams.

Exception No. 1: A minimum 1-in. (25.4-mm) hose shall be permitted to be used for hose stations in Light Hazard Occupancies where investigated and listed for this service and where approved by the authority having jurisdiction.

Exception No. 2: Where the building is protected throughout by an approved automatic sprinkler system, hose stations for use by the building occupants are not required, subject to the approval of the authority having jurisdiction, provided that each hose connection is 2¹/₂ in. (63.5 mm) and is equipped with a 2¹/₂-in. by 1¹/₂-in. (63.5-mm by 38.2-mm) reducer and a cap attached with a chain.

3-4 Requirements for Manual Standpipe Systems.

3-4.1 Manual standpipe systems shall not be used in high-rise buildings.

3-4.2 Each hose connection for manual standpipes shall be provided with a conspicuous sign stating "MANUAL STANDPIPE FOR FIRE DEPARTMENT USE ONLY."

3-4.3 Manual standpipes shall not be used for Class II or Class III systems.

3-5 Requirements for Dry Standpipe Systems.

3-5.1 Dry standpipes shall only be used where piping is subject to freezing.

3-5.2 Dry standpipes shall not be used for Class II or Class III systems.

3-6* Gauges.

3-6.1 A listed 3¹/₂-in. (87-mm) dial spring pressure gauge shall be connected to each discharge pipe from the fire pump and public water works, at the pressure tank, at the air pump supplying the pressure tank, and at the top of each standpipe. Gauges shall be located in a suitable place so water will not freeze. Each gauge shall be controlled by a valve having an arrangement for draining.

Exception: Where several standpipes are interconnected at the top, a single gauge, properly located, shall be permitted to be substituted for a gauge at the top of each standpipe.

3-6.2 A valved outlet for a pressure gauge shall be installed on the upstream side of every pressure regulating device.

3-7* Water Flow Alarms.

3-7.1 Where required by the authority having jurisdiction for automatic or semiautomatic systems, listed water flow alarms shall be provided.

3-7.2 Water flow alarms shall utilize a sensing mechanism appropriate to the type of standpipe.

Chapter 4   Installation Requirements

4-1* Location and Protection of Piping.

4-1.1 Location of Dry Standpipes. Dry standpipes shall not be concealed in building walls or built into pilasters.

4-1.2 Protection of Piping.

4-1.2.1* Standpipe system piping shall not pass through hazardous areas and shall be located so that they are protected from mechanical and fire damage.

4-1.2.2 Standpipes and lateral piping supplied by standpipes shall be located in enclosed exit stairways or shall be protected by a degree of fire resistance equal to that required for enclosed exit stairways in the building in which they are located.

Exception No. 1: In buildings equipped with an approved automatic sprinkler system, lateral piping to 2^1/$_2$-in. (63.5-mm) hose connections shall not be required to be protected.

Exception No. 2: Piping connecting standpipes to 1^1/$_2$-in. (38.1-mm) hose connections.

4-1.2.3 Where a standpipe or lateral pipe that is normally filled with water passes through an area subject to freezing temperatures, it shall be protected by a reliable means to maintain the temperature of the water in the piping between 40°F (4.4°C) and 120°F (48.9°C).

Antifreeze solutions shall not be used to protect standpipe system piping from freezing.

4-1.2.4 Where corrosive conditions exist, or piping is exposed to the weather, corrosion-resistant types of pipe, tube, fittings, and hangers or protective corrosion-resistive coatings shall be used. If steel pipe is to be buried underground, it shall be protected against corrosion before being buried.

4-1.2.5 To minimize or prevent pipe breakage where subject to earthquakes, standpipe systems shall be protected in accordance with the rules contained in NFPA 13, *Standard for the Installation of Sprinkler Systems.*

4-2 Gate Valves and Check Valves.

4-2.1 Connections to each water supply, except the fire department connections, shall be provided with an approved indicating-type valve and check valve located close to the supply, such as at tanks, pumps, and connections from waterworks systems.

Where a backflow prevention device of the reduced pressure type is required by the authority having jurisdiction, the check valve and shutoff shall not be omitted and shall be installed on the discharge side of the reduced pressure backflow device.

4-2.2 Valves shall be provided to permit isolating a standpipe without interrupting the supply to other standpipes from the same source of supply.

4-2.3 Listed indicating type valves shall be provided at the standpipe for controlling branch lines for remote hose stations.

4-2.4 Where wafer-type valve discs are used, they shall be installed in such a manner that they do not interfere with the operation of other system components.

4-2.5 Valves on Combined Systems.

4-2.5.1 Each connection from a standpipe that is part of a combined system to a sprinkler system shall have an individual control valve of the same size as the connection.

4-2.5.2* Each connection from a standpipe that is part of a combined system to a sprinkler system and interconnected with other standpipes shall have an individual control valve and check valve of the same size at the connection.

4-2.6 Connections to public water systems shall be controlled by indicator post valves of an approved type located at least 40 ft (12.2 m) from the building protected. All valves shall be plainly marked to indicate the service that they control.

Exception No. 1: Where the valve cannot be located at least 40 ft (12.2 m) from the building, it shall be placed in an approved location and where it will be readily accessible in case of fire and not subject to damage.

Exception No. 2: Where post indicator valves cannot be used, underground valves shall be permitted. The valve locations, directions to open, and services that they control shall be plainly marked on the buildings served.

4-2.7* Where the standpipes are supplied from a yard main or header in another building, the connection shall be provided with a listed indicating-type valve located outside at a safe distance from the building or at the header.

4-2.8 System water supply valves, isolation control valves, and other valves in feed mains shall be supervised in an approved manner in the open position by one of the following methods:

(a) Central station, proprietary, or remote station signaling service

(b) Local signaling service that will cause the sounding of an audible signal at a constantly attended point

(c) Locking valves open

(d) Sealing of valves and an approved weekly recorded inspection where valves are located within fenced enclosures under the control of the owner.

Exception: Underground gate valves with roadway boxes need not be supervised.

4-2.9 Signs and Room Identification for Valves.

4-2.9.1 All main and sectional system control valves, including water supply control valves, shall have a sign indicating the portion of the system controlled by the valve.

4-2.9.2 All control, drain, and test connection valves shall be provided with signs indicating their purpose.

4-2.9.3 Where sprinkler system piping supplied by a combined system is supplied by more than one standpipe ("loop" or "dual feed" type design), a sign shall be located at each dual or multiple feed connection to the combination system standpipe to identify that to isolate the sprinkler system served by the control valve, an additional control valve or valves at other standpipes must be shut off. The sign shall also identify the location of the additional control valves.

4-2.9.4 Where a main or sectional system control valve is located in a closed room or concealed space, the location of the valve shall be indicated by a sign in an approved location on the outside of the door or near the opening to the concealed space.

4-3* Fire Department Connections.

4-3.1 There shall be no shutoff valve between the fire department connection and the system.

4-3.2 A listed check valve shall be installed in each fire department connection, located as near as practicable to the point where it joins the system.

4-3.3 The fire department connection shall be installed as follows:

(a) Automatic-wet and manual-wet standpipe systems: On the system side of the system control and check valve.

(b) Automatic-dry standpipe systems: On the system side of the control valve and check valve and the supply side of the dry pipe valve.

(c) Semiautomatic-dry standpipe systems: On the system side of the deluge valve.

(d) Manual-dry standpipe systems: Directly connected to system piping.

4-3.4 In areas subject to freezing, a listed automatic drip valve shall be installed in the piping between the check valve and the fire department connection that is arranged to allow drainage without causing water damage.

4-3.5 Location and Identification.

4-3.5.1 Fire department connections shall be on the street side of buildings and shall be located and arranged so that hose lines can be attached to the inlets without interference from nearby objects including buildings, fences, posts, or other fire department connections.

4-3.5.2 Each fire department connection shall be designated by a sign having raised letters, at least 1 in. (25 mm) in size cast on the plate or fitting, reading "STANDPIPE." If automatic sprinklers are also supplied by the fire department connection, the sign or combination of signs shall indicate both designated services, e.g., "STANDPIPE AND AUTOSPKR," or "AUTOSPKR AND STANDPIPE."

A sign shall also indicate the pressure required at the inlets to deliver the system demand.

4-3.5.3 Where a fire department connection services only a portion of a building, a sign shall be attached indicating the portions of the building served.

4-3.5.4* A fire department connection for each standpipe system shall be located not more than 100 ft (30.5 m) from the nearest fire hydrant connected to an approved water supply.

4-3.6 Fire department connections shall be located not less than 18 in. (45.7 cm) nor more than 48 in. (121.9 cm) above the level of the adjoining ground, sidewalk, or grade surface.

4-3.7 Fire department connection piping shall be supported in accordance with Section 4-4.

4-4 Support of Piping.

4-4.1 Support of Standpipes.

4-4.1.1 Standpipes shall be supported by attachments connected directly to the standpipe.

4-4.1.2 Standpipe supports shall be provided at the lowest level, at each alternate level above, and at the top of the standpipe. Supports above the lowest level shall restrain the pipe to prevent movement by an upward thrust where flexible fittings are used.

4-4.1.3 Clamps supporting pipe by means of set screws shall not be used.

4-4.2 Support of Horizontal Piping.

4-4.2.1 Horizontal piping from the standpipe to hose connections that are more than 18 in. (457 mm) in length shall be provided with hangers.

4-4.2.2 Horizontal piping hangers shall be spaced at a maximum separation distance of 15 ft (4.6 m). The piping shall be restrained to prevent movement by horizontal thrust where flexible fittings are used.

4-5 Installation of Signs. Signs shall be secured to a device or the building wall with substantial and corrosion-resistant chains or fasteners.

4-6 Signs for Water Supply Pumps. Where a fire pump is provided, a sign shall be located in the vicinity of the pump indicating the minimum pressure and flow required at the pump discharge flange to meet the system demand.

4-7* Hydraulic Design Information Sign. The installing contractor shall provide a sign identifying the design basis of a system as hydraulic calculations or pipe schedule. The sign shall be located at the water supply control valve for automatic or semiautomatic standpipe systems and at an approved location for manual systems.

The sign shall indicate the following:

(a) The location of the 2 hydraulically most remote hose connections

(b) The design flow rate for the connections identified in (a)

(c) The design residual inlet and outlet pressures for the connections identified in (a)

(d) The design static pressure and the design system demand (flow and residual pressure) at the system control valve, or at the pump discharge flange where a pump is installed, and at each fire department connection.

Chapter 5   Design

5-1* General.   Design of the standpipe system is governed by building height, area per floor occupancy classification, egress system design, required flow rate and residual pressure, and the distance of the hose connection from the source(s) of water supply. See Chapter 3 for general system requirements.

5-2* Pressure Limitation.   The maximum pressure at any point in the system at any time shall not exceed 350 psi.

5-3   Locations of Hose Connections.

5-3.1* General.   Hose connections and hose stations shall be unobstructed and shall be located not less than 3 ft (0.9 m) or more than 5 ft (1.5 m) above the floor.

5-3.2* Class I Systems.   Class I systems shall be provided with 2½-in. (63.5-mm) hose connections in the following locations:

(a) At each intermediate landing between floor levels in every required exit stairway

Exception: Hose connections shall be permitted to be located at main floor landings in exit stairways when approved by the authority having jurisdiction.

(b) On each side of the wall adjacent to exit openings of horizontal exits

(c) In each exit passageway at the entrance from building areas into the passageway

(d) In covered mall buildings, at the entrance to each exit passageway or exit corridor, and at exterior public entrances to the mall

(e) At the highest landing of stairways with stairway access to a roof, and on the roof where stairways do not access the roof

(f)* Where the most remote portion of a nonsprinklered floor or story exceeds 150 ft (45.7 m) of travel distance from a required exit or the most remote portion of a sprinklered floor or story exceeds 200 ft (61 m) of travel distance from a required exit, additional hose connections shall be provided, in approved locations, where required by the local fire department.

5-3.3* Class II Systems.   Class II systems shall be provided with 1½-in. (38.1-mm) hose stations so that all portions of each floor level of the building are within 130 ft (39.7 m) of a hose connection provided with 1½-in. (38.1-mm) hose or within 120 ft (36.6 m) of a hose connection provided with less than 1½-in. (38.1-mm) hose. Distances shall be measured along a path of travel originating at the hose connection.

5-3.4   Class III Systems.   Class III systems shall be provided with hose connections as required for both Class I and Class II systems.

5-4   Number of Standpipes.   Separate standpipes shall be provided in each required exit stairway.

5-5   Interconnection of Standpipes.   Where 2 or more standpipes are installed in the same building or section of building, they shall be interconnected at the bottom.

Where standpipes are supplied by tanks located at the top of the building or zone, they shall also be interconnected at the top; in such cases, check valves shall be installed at the base of each standpipe to prevent circulation.

5-6   Minimum Sizes for Standpipes.

5-6.1   Class I and Class III standpipes shall be at least 4 in. (102 mm) in size.

5-6.2   Standpipes that are part of a combined system shall be at least 6 in. (152 mm) in size.

Exception: In fully sprinklered buildings having a combined standpipe system that is hydraulically calculated, the minimum standpipe size is 4 in (102 mm).

5-7* Minimum Pressure for System Design and Sizing of Pipe.   Standpipe systems shall be designed so that the system demand can be supplied by both the attached water supply, where required, and fire department connections. For the water supply available from a fire department pumper, the authority having jurisdiction shall be consulted. Also see NFPA 1901, *Standard for Pumper Fire Apparatus.* Standpipe systems shall be either:

(a) Hydraulically designed to provide the required water flow rate at a minimum residual pressure of 100 psi (10.3 bars) at the outlet of the hydraulically most remote 2½-in. (63.5-mm) hose connection and 65 psi (4.5 bars) at the outlet of the hydraulically most remote 1½-in. (38.1-mm) hose station.

Exception: Where the authority having jurisdiction permits pressures lower than 100 psi for 2½-in. (63.5-mm) hose connections, based on suppression tactics, the pressure shall be permitted to be reduced but not to less than 65 psi (4.5 bars).

(b) Sized in accordance with the pipe schedule of Table 5-7 to provide the required water flow rate at a minimum residual pressure of 100 psi (10.3 bars) at the topmost 2½-in. (63.5-mm) hose connection and 65 psi (4.5 bars) at the topmost 1½-in. (38.1-mm) hose station. Pipe schedule designs shall be limited to wet standpipes and for buildings that are not defined as high-rise.

Table 5-7   Pipe Schedule – Standpipes and Supply Piping Minimum Nominal Pipe Sizes in Inches

Total Accumulated Flow (gpm)	Total Distance of Piping from Furthest Outlet		
	< 50 ft	50–100 ft	> 100 ft
100	2	2½	3
101–500	4	4	6
501–750	5	5	6
751–1250	6	6	6
1251 and over	8	8	8

For SI Units: 1 gal = 3.785 L/min; 1 ft = 0.3048 m.

5-8* Maximum Pressure for Hose Connections.

5-8.1   Where the residual pressure at a 1½-in. (38.1-mm) outlet on a hose connection available for occupant use exceeds 100 psi (6.9 bars), an approved pressure regulating device shall be provided to limit the residual pressure at the flow required by Section 5-9 to 100 psi (69 bars).

5-8.2 Where the static pressure at a hose connection exceeds 175 psi (12.1 bars), an approved pressure regulating device shall be provided to limit static and residual pressures at the outlet of the hose connection to 100 psi (6.9 bars) for $1^1/_2$-in. (38.1-mm) hose connections available for occupant use and 175 psi (12.1 bars) for other hose connections. The pressure on the inlet side of the pressure regulating device shall not exceed the device's rated working pressure.

5-9 Minimum Flow Rates for Hydraulically Designed Systems.

5.9.1 Class I and Class III Systems.

5-9.1.1* Minimum Flow Rate. For Class I and Class III systems, the minimum flow rate for the hydraulically most remote standpipe shall be 500 gpm (1893 L/min). The minimum flow rate for additional standpipes shall be 250 gpm (946 L/min) per standpipe, the total not to exceed 1250 gpm (4731 L/min).

For combined systems, see 5-9.1.3.

Exception: When the floor area exceeds 80,000 sq ft (7432 m²), the second most remote standpipe shall be designed to accommodate 500 gpm (1893 L/min).

5-9.1.2* Hydraulic Calculation Procedure. Hydraulic calculations and pipe sizes for each standpipe shall be based on providing 250 gpm (946 L/min) at the hydraulically most remote two hose connections on the standpipe and at the top most outlet of each of the other standpipes at the minimum residual pressure required by Section 5-7. Common supply piping shall be calculated and sized to provide the required flow rate for all standpipes connected to such supply piping, the total not to exceed 1250 gpm (4731 L/min).

5-9.1.3 Combined Systems.

5-9.1.3.1* For a building protected throughout by an approved automatic sprinkler system, the system demand established by Section 5-7 and 5-9.1 is also permitted to serve the sprinkler system. Sprinkler demand need not be added.

Exception: Where the sprinkler system water supply requirement, including hose stream allowance as determined in NFPA 13, Standard for the Installation of Sprinkler Systems, exceeds the system demand established by Section 5-7 and 5-9.1, the larger of the two values shall be provided. The flow rate required for the standpipe demand of a combined system in a building protected throughout by an automatic sprinkler system need not exceed 1000 gpm (3785 L/min) unless more supply is required by the authority having jurisdiction.

5-9.1.3.2 For a combined system in a building equipped with partial automatic sprinkler protection, the flow rate required by 5-9.1 shall be increased by an amount equal to the lesser of the hydraulically calculated sprinkler demand or 150 gpm (568 L/min) for Light Hazard Occupancies, or by 500 gpm (1893 L/min) for Ordinary Hazard Occupancies.

5-9.1.3.3 Where an existing standpipe system having standpipes with a minimum diameter of 4 in. (102 mm) is to be utilized to supply a new retrofit sprinkler system, the water supply required by 5-9.1 need not be provided by automatic or semiautomatic means if approved by the authority having jurisdiction, so long as the water supply is adequate to supply the hydraulic demand of the sprinkler system.

5-9.2 Class II Systems.

5-9.2.1 Minimum Flow Rate. For Class II systems, the minimum flow rate for the hydraulically most remote standpipe shall be 100 gpm (379 L/min). Additional flow need not be added when more than 1 standpipe is provided.

5-9.2.2 Hydraulic Calculation Procedure. Hydraulic calculations and pipe sizes for each standpipe shall be based on providing 100 gpm (379 L/min) at the hydraulically most remote hose connection on the standpipe at the minimum residual pressure required by Section 5-7. Common supply piping serving multiple standpipes shall be calculated and sized to provide 100 gpm (379 L/min).

5-10 Equivalent Pipe Lengths of Valves and Fittings for Hydraulically Designed Systems.

5-10.1 General. Table 5-10.1 shall be used to determine the equivalent length of pipe for fittings and devices unless manufacturer's test data indicate that other factors are appropriate. For saddle-type fittings having friction loss greater than that shown in Table 5-10.1, the increased friction loss shall be included in hydraulic calculations.

Table 5-10.1   Equivalent Pipe Length Chart

Fittings and Valves	Fittings and Valves Expressed in Equivalent Feet of Pipe												
	$^3/_4$ in.	1 in.	$1^1/_4$ in.	$1^1/_2$ in.	2 in.	$2^1/_2$ in.	3 in.	$3^1/_2$ in.	4 in.	5 in.	6 in.	8 in.	10 in.	12 in.
45° Elbow	1	1	1	2	2	3	3	3	4	5	7	9	11	13
90° Standard Elbow	2	2	3	4	5	6	7	8	10	12	14	18	22	27
90° Long Turn Elbow	1	2	2	2	3	4	5	5	6	8	9	13	16	18
Tee or Cross (Flow Turned 90°)	3	5	6	8	10	12	15	17	20	25	30	35	50	60
Butterfly Valve	-	-	-	-	6	7	10	-	12	9	10	12	19	21
Gate Valve	-	-	-	-	1	1	1	1	2	2	3	4	5	6
Swing Check*	-	5	7	9	11	14	16	19	22	27	32	45	55	65
Globe Valve	-	-	-	46	-	70	-	-	-	-	-	-	-	-
Angle Valve	-	-	-	20	-	31	-	-	-	-	-	-	-	-

For SI Units: 1 ft = 0.3048 m.
*Due to the variations in design of swing check valves, the pipe equivalents indicated in the above chart are considered average.

5-10.2 Adjustments. Table 5-10.1 shall be used with Hazen-Williams C = 120 only. For other values of C, the values in Table 5-10.1 shall be multiplied by the factors indicated in Table 5-10.2.

Table 5-10.2 Adjustments Chart

Value of C	100	130	140	150
Multiplying Factor	0.713	1.16	1.33	1.51

5-11* Drains and Test Riser.

5-11.1 A permanently installed 3-in. (75-mm) drain riser shall be provided adjacent to each standpipe equipped with pressure regulating devices to facilitate tests of each device. The riser shall be equipped with a 3-in. (76.2-mm) × 2¹/₂-in. (63.5-mm) tee with internal threaded swivel fitting having NH standard threads, as specified in NFPA 1963, *Standard for Screw Threads and Gaskets for Fire Hose Connections*, with plug, located on at least every other floor.

Exception: Where local fire department hose threads do not conform to NFPA 1963, the authority having jurisdiction shall designate the hose threads to be used.

5-11.2 Each standpipe shall be provided with a means of draining. A drain valve and piping, located at the lowest point of the standpipe piping downstream of the isolation valve, shall be arranged to discharge water at an approved location. Sizing shall be as follows:

Standpipe Size	Size of Drain Connection
Up to 2 in.	³/₄ in. or larger
2¹/₂ in., 3 in., or 3¹/₂ in.	1¹/₄ in. or larger
4 in. or larger	2 in. only

5-12* Fire Department Connections.

5-12.1 One or more fire department connections shall be provided for each Class I or Class III standpipe system.

5-12.2 High-rise buildings shall have at least 2 remotely located fire department connections.

Exception: A single connection shall be permitted where acceptable to the fire department.

Chapter 6 Plans and Calculations

6-1* Plans and Specifications. Plans accurately showing the details and arrangement of the standpipe system shall be furnished to the authority having jurisdiction prior to the installation of the system. Such plans shall be clear, readable, and drawn to scale. The drawings shall show the location, arrangement, water supply, equipment, and all other details necessary to show compliance with this standard.

The plans shall include specifications covering the character of materials used and shall describe all system components. Plans shall include an elevation diagram.

6-2 Hydraulic Calculations. Where standpipe system piping is sized by hydraulic calculations, a complete set of calculations shall be submitted with the plans.

Chapter 7 Water Supplies

7-1* Required Water Supply. Automatic and semiautomatic standpipe systems shall be attached to an approved water supply capable of supplying the system demand. Manual standpipe systems shall have an approved water supply accessible to a fire department pumper.

A single automatic or semiautomatic water supply shall be acceptable where it is capable of supplying the system demand for the required duration.

Exception: Where a secondary water supply is required by 7-4.3.

7-1.1* Acceptable water supplies shall be from:

(a) Public waterworks system where pressure and flow rate are adequate

(b) Automatic fire pumps connected to an approved water source

(c) Manually controlled fire pumps in combination with pressure tanks

(d) Pressure tanks installed in accordance with NFPA 22, *Standard for Water Tanks for Private Fire Protection*

(e) Manually controlled fire pumps operated by remote control devices at each hose station

(f) Gravity tanks installed in accordance with NFPA 22, *Standard for Water Tanks for Private Fire Protection*.

7-2 Minimum Supply for Class I and Class III Systems. The water supply shall be sufficient to provide the system demand established by Section 5-7 and 5-9.1 for a period of at least 30 min.

7-3 Minimum Supply for Class II Systems. The minimum supply for Class II systems shall be sufficient to provide the system demand established by Section 5-7 and 5-9.2 for a period of at least 30 min.

7-4 Standpipe System Zones. Each zone requiring pumps shall be provided with a separate pump. This shall not preclude the use of pumps arranged in series.

7-4.1 Where pumps supplying 2 or more zones are located at the same level, each zone shall have separate and direct supply piping of a size not smaller than the standpipe that it serves. Zones with 2 or more standpipes shall have at least 2 direct supply pipes of a size not smaller than the largest standpipe that they serve.

7-4.2 Where supply for each zone is pumped from the next lower zone, and the standpipe or standpipes in the lower zone are used to supply the higher zone, such standpipes shall comply with the provisions for supply lines in 7-4.1. At least 2 lines shall be provided between zones; 1 of these lines shall be arranged so that supply can be automatically delivered from the lower to the higher zone.

7-4.3 For systems with 2 or more zones in which portions of the second and higher zones cannot be supplied with the residual pressure required by Section 5-7 by fire department pumpers through a fire department connection, another auxiliary means of supply shall be provided. This shall be in the form of high-level water storage with additional pumping equipment or other means acceptable to the authority having jurisdiction.

Chapter 8   System Acceptance

8-1* General.

8-1.1 All new systems shall be tested prior to building occupancy. Existing standpipe systems that are to be utilized as standpipes for a combination system in the retrofit of a new sprinkler system shall be tested in accordance with Section 8-4.

8-1.2 The installing contractor shall complete and sign the appropriate Contractors Material and Test Certificate(s). [*See Figures 8-1(a) and 8-1(b).*]

8-2 Flushing of Piping.

8-2.1 Underground piping supplying the system shall be flushed in accordance with NFPA 24, *Standard for the Installation of Private Fire Service Mains and Their Appurtenances.*

8-2.2 Piping between the fire department connection and the check valve in the inlet pipe shall be flushed with a sufficient volume of water so as to remove any construction debris and trash accumulated in this pipe prior to the completion of the system and prior to the installation of the fire department connection.

8-3 Hose Threads. All hose connection and fire department connection threads shall be tested to verify compatibility with threads used by the local fire department. The test shall consist of threading coupling samples, caps, or plugs onto the installed devices.

8-4 Hydrostatic Tests.

8-4.1* General. All new systems, including yard piping and fire department connections, shall be tested hydrostatically at not less than 200 psi (13.8 bars) pressure for 2 hr, or at 50 psi (3.5 bars) in excess of the maximum pressure where the maximum pressure is in excess of 150 psi (10.3 bars). The hydrostatic test pressure shall be measured at the low elevation point of the individual system or zone being tested. The inside standpipe system piping shall show no leakage. Underground pipe shall be tested in accordance with NFPA 24, *Standard for the Installation of Private Fire Service Mains and Their Appurtenances.*

Exception: Where cold weather will not permit testing with water, an interim air test can be conducted prior to the standard hydrostatic test. An air pressure leakage test at 40 psi (2.8 bars) shall be conducted for 24 hr. Any leakage that results in a loss of pressure in excess of $1^{1}/_{2}$ psi (0.1 bars) during a continuous 24-hr period shall be corrected.

8-4.2 Fire Department Connection. Piping between the fire department connection and the check valve in the inlet pipe shall be tested hydrostatically in the same manner as the balance of the system.

8-4.3 Existing Systems. Where an existing standpipe system, including yard piping and fire department connection, is modified, the new piping shall be tested in accordance with 8-4.1.

8-4.4 Protection from Freezing. During testing, care shall be taken to ensure no portion of the piping is subject to freezing during cold weather.

8-4.5 Gauges. During the hydrostatic test, the pressure gauge at the top of each standpipe shall be observed and the pressure recorded.

8-4.6 Water Additives. Additives, corrosive chemicals such as sodium silicate, or derivatives of sodium silicate, brine, or other chemicals shall not be used while hydrostatically testing systems or for stopping leaks.

CONTRACTOR'S MATERIAL & TEST CERTIFICATE FOR ABOVEGROUND PIPING
Standpipe System NFPA 14

PROCEDURE

Upon completion of work, inspection and tests shall be made by the contractor's representative and witnessed by an owner's representative. All defects shall be corrected and system left in service before contractor's personnel finally leave the job.

A certificate shall be filled out and signed by both representatives. Copies shall be prepared for approving authorities, owners, and contractor. It is understood the owner's representative's signature in no way prejudices any claim against contractor for faulty material, poor workmanship, or failure to comply with approving authority's requirements or local ordinances.

PROPERTY NAME _____ DATE_____

PROPERTY ADDRESS _____
_____
_____

PLANS

ACCEPTED BY APPROVING AUTHORITIES (NAMES) _____

ADDRESS _____
_____

INSTALLATION CONFORMS TO ACCEPTED PLANS ☐ YES ☐ NO IF NO, EXPLAIN DEVIATIONS_____
_____

EQUIPMENT USED IS APPROVED OR LISTED ☐ YES ☐ NO IF NO, EXPLAIN DEVIATIONS_____
_____
_____

TYPE OF SYSTEM

AUTOMATIC-DRY ☐ YES
AUTOMATIC-WET ☐ YES
SEMIAUTOMATIC-DRY ☐ YES
MANUAL-DRY ☐ YES
MANUAL-WET ☐ YES
COMBINATION STANDPIPE/SPRINKLER ☐ YES
OTHER ☐ YES EXPLAIN _____

WATER SUPPLY DATA USED FOR DESIGN AND AS SHOWN ON PLANS

FIRE PUMP DATA
MANUFACTURER _____ MODEL _____
TYPE: ☐ ELECTRIC   ☐ DIESEL   ☐ OTHER EXPLAIN _____
RATED GPM _____ RATED PSI _____ SHUT-OFF PSI _____

WATER SUPPLY SOURCE CAPACITY, GALLONS

PUBLIC WATER-WORKS SYSTEM ☐ STORAGE TANK ☐ GRAVITY TANK ☐ OPEN RESERVOIR ☐ OTHER ☐ EXPLAIN
_____
_____

IF PUBLIC WATER-WORKS SYSTEM:
STATIC PSI ☐ RESIDUAL PSI ☐ FLOW IN GPM ☐

HAVE COPIES OF THE FOLLOWING BEEN LEFT ON THE PREMISES?

☐ SYSTEM COMPONENTS INSTRUCTIONS ☐ CARE AND MAINTENANCE OF SYSTEM   ☐ NFPA 25
☐ COPY OF ACCEPTED PLANS   ☐ HYDRAULIC DATA/CALCULATIONS

SUPPLIES BUILDING(S)

MAIN WATER FLOW SHUT-OFF LOCATION _____
NUMBER OF STANDPIPE RISERS _____ DO ALL STANDPIPE RISERS HAVE BASE OF RISER SHUT-OFF VALVES? ☐ YES ☐ NO

VALVE SUPERVISION

LOCKED OPEN ☐ SEALED AND TAG ☐ TAMPER PROOF SWITCH ☐ OTHER ☐ IF OTHER, EXPLAIN
_____

TYPE OF PIPE _____

TYPE OF FITTING_____

BACKFLOW PREVENTER

A) DOUBLE CHECK ASSEMBLY ☐ SIZE _____ MAKE AND MODEL _____
B) REDUCED PRESSURE DEVICE ☐

Figure 8-1(a).

CONTROL VALVE DEVICE

TYPE	SIZE	MAKE	MODEL

TIME TO TRIP THROUGH REMOTE HOSE VALVE _____ MIN ____ SEC WATER PRESSURE _____ AIR PRESSURE _____
TIME WATER REACHED REMOTE HOSE VALVE OUTLET _____ MIN _____ SEC TRIP POINT AIR PRESSURE _____ PSI
ALARM OPERATED PROPERLY ☐ YES ☐ NO IF NO, EXPLAIN _____

TIME WATER REACHED REMOTE HOSE VALVE OUTLET _____ MIN _____ SEC

HYDRAULIC ACTIVATION ☐ YES
ELECTRIC ACTIVATION ☐ YES
PNEUMATIC ACTIVATION ☐ YES
MAKE AND MODEL OF ACTIVATION DEVICE _____
EACH ACTIVATION DEVICE TESTED ☐ YES ☐ NO IF NO, EXPLAIN _____

EACH ACTIVATION DEVICE OPERATED PROPERLY ☐ YES ☐ NO IF NO, EXPLAIN _____

PRESSURE REGULATING DEVICE

LOCATION & FLOOR	MODEL	NON-FLOWING (PSI)		FLOWING (PSI)		GPM
		INLET	OUTLET	INLET	OUTLET	

ALL HOSE VALVES ON SYSTEM OPERATED PROPERLY ☐ YES ☐ NO IF NO, EXPLAIN _____

Figure 8-1(a) (cont.).

TEST DESCRIPTION	HYDROSTATIC: HYDROSTATIC TESTS SHALL BE MADE AT NOT LESS THAN 200 PSI (13.6 BARS) FOR TWO HOURS OR 50 PSI (3.4 BARS) ABOVE STATIC PRESSURE IN EXCESS OF 150 PSI (10.2 BARS) FOR TWO HOURS. DIFFERENTIAL DRY-PIPE VALVE CLAPPERS SHALL BE LEFT OPEN DURING TEST TO PREVENT DAMAGE. ALL ABOVEGROUND PIPING LEAKAGE SHALL BE STOPPED.
	PNEUMATIC: ESTABLISH 40 PSI (2.7 BARS) AIR PRESSURE AND MEASURE DROP WHICH SHALL NOT EXCEED 1-1/2 PSI (0.1 BARS) IN 24 HOURS. TEST PRESSURE TANKS AT NORMAL WATER LEVEL AND AIR PRESSURE AND MEASURE AIR PRESSURE DROP WHICH SHALL NOT EXCEED 1-1/2 PSI (0.1 BARS) IN 24 HOURS.
TESTS	ALL PIPING HYDROSTATICALLY TESTED AT _____ PSI FOR _____ HRS. IF NO, STATE REASON
	DRY PIPING PNEUMATICALLY TESTED ☐ YES ☐ NO
	EQUIPMENT OPERATES PROPERLY ☐ YES ☐ NO
	DO YOU CERTIFY AS THE STANDPIPE CONTRACTOR THAT ADDITIVES AND CORROSIVE CHEMICALS, SODIUM SILICATE OR DERIVATIVES OF SODIUM SILICATE, BRINE, OR OTHER CORROSIVE CHEMICALS WERE NOT USED FOR TESTING SYSTEMS OR STOPPING LEAKS? ☐ YES ☐ NO
	DRAIN TEST — READING OF GAUGE LOCATED NEAR WATER SUPPLY TEST CONNECTION: _____ PSI — RESIDUAL PRESSURE WITH VALVE IN TEST CONNECTION OPEN WIDE _____ PSI
	UNDERGROUND MAINS AND LEAD IN CONNECTIONS TO SYSTEM RISERS FLUSHED BEFORE CONNECTION MADE TO STANDPIPE PIPING.
	VERIFIED BY COPY OF THE U FORM NO. 85B ☐ YES ☐ NO OTHER EXPLAIN
	FLUSHED BY INSTALLER OF UNDER-GROUND STANDPIPE PIPING ☐ YES ☐ NO
BLANK TESTING	NUMBER USED — LOCATIONS — NUMBER REMOVED
WELDING	WELDED PIPING ☐ YES ☐ NO
	IF YES. . .
	DO YOU CERTIFY AS THE STANDPIPE CONTRACTOR THAT WELDING PROCEDURES COMPLY WITH THE REQUIREMENTS OF AT LEAST AWS D10.9, LEVEL AR-3 ☐ YES ☐ NO
	DO YOU CERTIFY THAT THE WELDING WAS PERFORMED BY WELDERS QUALIFIED IN COMPLIANCE WITH THE REQUIREMENTS OF AT LEAST AWS D10.9, LEVEL AR-3 ☐ YES ☐ NO
	DO YOU CERTIFY THAT WELDING WAS CARRIED OUT IN COMPLIANCE WITH A DOCUMENTED QUALITY CONTROL PROCEDURE TO INSURE THAT ALL DISCS ARE RETRIEVED, THAT OPENINGS IN PIPING ARE SMOOTH, THAT SLAG AND OTHER WELDING RESIDUE ARE REMOVED, AND THE THE INTERNAL DIAMETERS OF PIPING ARE NOT PENETRATED ☐ YES ☐ NO
CUTOUTS (DISCS)	DO YOU CERTIFY THAT YOU HAVE A CONTROL FEATURE TO INSURE THAT ALL CUTOUTS (DISCS) ARE RETRIEVED? ☐ YES ☐ NO
HYDRAULIC DATA NAMEPLATE	NAME PLATE PROVIDED IF NO, EXPLAIN
	☐ YES ☐ NO
REMARKS	DATE LEFT IN SERVICE WITH ALL CONTROL VALVES OPEN:

NAME OF SPRINKLER/STANDPIPE CONTRACTOR

NAME OF CONTRACTOR _____
ADDRESS _____
STATE LICENSE NUMBER (IF APPLICABLE) _____

SYSTEM OPERATING TEST WITNESSED BY

FOR PROPERTY OWNER _____ TITLE _____ DATE _____
FOR SPRINKLER/STANDPIPE CONTRACTOR_____ TITLE _____ DATE _____
FOR APPROVING AUTHORITIES _____ TITLE _____ DATE _____

ADDITIONAL EXPLANATION AND NOTES

Figure 8-1(a) (cont.).

CONTRACTOR'S MATERIAL & TEST CERTIFICATE FOR **U**NDERGROUND PIPING

PROCEDURE

Upon completion of work, inspection and tests shall be made by the contractor's representative and witnessed by an owner's representative. All defects shall be corrected and system left in service before contractor's personnel finally leave the job.

A certificate shall be filled out and signed by both representatives. Copies shall be prepared for approving authorities, owners, and contractor. It is understood the owner's representative's signature in no way prejudices any claim against contractor for faulty material, poor workmanship, or failure to comply with approving authority's requirements or local ordinances.

PROPERTY NAME	DATE

PROPERTY ADDRESS

PLANS	ACCEPTED BY APPROVING AUTHORITIES (NAMES)		
	ADDRESS		
	INSTALLATION CONFORMS TO ACCEPTED PLANS	☐ YES	☐ NO
	EQUIPMENT USED IS APPROVED	☐ YES	☐ NO
	IF NO, STATE DEVIATIONS		
INSTRUCTIONS	HAS PERSON IN CHARGE OF FIRE EQUIPMENT BEEN INSTRUCTED AS TO LOCATION OF CONTROL VALVES AND CARE AND MAINTENANCE OF THIS NEW EQUIPMENT? IF NO, EXPLAIN	☐ YES	☐ NO
	HAVE COPIES OF APPROPRIATE INSTRUCTIONS AND CARE AND MAINTENANCE CHARTS BEEN LEFT ON PREMISES? IF NO, EXPLAIN	☐ YES	☐ NO
LOCATION	SUPPLIES BUILDINGS		

		TYPE JOINT		
UNDERGROUND PIPES AND JOINTS	PIPE TYPES AND CLASS			
	PIPE CONFORMS TO _____ STANDARD		☐ YES	☐ NO
	FITTINGS CONFORM TO _____ STANDARD		☐ YES	☐ NO
	IF NO, EXPLAIN			
	JOINTS NEEDING ANCHORAGE CLAMPED, STRAPPED, OR BLOCKED IN		☐ YES	☐ NO
	ACCORDANCE WITH _____ STANDARD			
	IF NO, EXPLAIN			

TEST DESCRIPTION	FLUSHING. Flow the required rate until water is clear as indicated by no collection of foreign material in burlap bags at outlets such as hydrants and blow-offs. Flush at flows not less than 390 GPM (1476 L/min) for 4-inch pipe, 880 GPM (3331 L/min) for 6-inch pipe, 1560 GPM (5905 L/min) for 8-inch pipe, 2440 GPM (9235 L/min) for 10-inch pipe, and 3520 GPM (13323 L/min) for 12-inch pipe. When supply cannot produce stipulated flow rates, obtain maximum available. HYDROSTATIC. Hydrostatic tests shall be made at not less than 200 psi (13.8 bars) for two hours or 50 psi (3.4 bars) above static pressure in excess of 150 psi (10.3 bars) for two hours. LEAKAGE. New pipe laid with rubber gasketed joints shall, if the workmanship is satisfactory, have little or no leakage at the joints. The amount of leakage at the joints shall not exceed 2 qts. per hr. (1.89 L/h) per 100 joints irrespective of pipe diameter. The leakage shall be distributed over all joints. If such leakage occurs at a few joints the installation shall be considered unsatisfactory and necessary repairs made. The amount of allowable leakage specified above may be increased by 1 fl oz per in. valve diameter per hr. (30 mL/25 mm/h) for each metal seated valve isolating the test section. If dry barrel hydrants are tested with the main valve open, so the hydrants are under pressure, an additional 5 oz per minute (150 mL/min) leakage is permitted for each hydrant.

FLUSHING TESTS	NEW UNDERGROUND PIPING FLUSHED ACCORDING TO _____ STANDARD		☐ YES	☐ NO
	BY (COMPANY) IF NO, EXPLAIN			
	HOW FLUSHING FLOW WAS OBTAINED ☐ PUBLIC WATER ☐ TANK OR RESERVOIR ☐ FIRE PUMP	THROUGH WHAT TYPE OPENING ☐ HYDRANT BUTT.	☐ OPEN PIPE	
	LEAD-INS FLUSHED ACCORDING TO _____ STANDARD		☐ YES	☐ NO
	BY (COMPANY) IF NO, EXPLAIN			
	HOW FLUSHING FLOW WAS OBTAINED ☐ PUBLIC WATER ☐ TANK OR RESERVOIR ☐ FIRE PUMP	THROUGH WHAT TYPE OPENING ☐ Y CONN. TO FLANGE & SPIGOT	☐ OPEN PIPE	

85B(10-88)   PRINTED IN USA   (OVER)

Figure 8-1(b).

HYDROSTATIC TEST	ALL NEW UNDERGROUND PIPING HYDROSTATICALLY TESTED AT _____ PSI FOR _____ HOURS	JOINTS COVERED □ YES □ NO	
LEAKAGE TEST	TOTAL AMOUNT OF LEAKAGE MEASURED _____ GALS. _____ HOURS		
	ALLOWABLE LEAKAGE _____ GALS. _____ HOURS		
HYDRANTS	NUMBER INSTALLED	TYPE AND MAKE	ALL OPERATE SATISFACTORILY □ YES □ NO
CONTROL VALVES	WATER CONTROL VALVES LEFT WIDE OPEN IF NO, STATE REASON		□ YES □ NO
	HOSE THREADS OF FIRE DEPARTMENT CONNECTIONS AND HYDRANTS INTERCHANGEABLE WITH THOSE OF FIRE DEPARTMENT ANSWERING ALARM		□ YES □ NO
REMARKS	DATE LEFT IN SERVICE		
SIGNATURES	NAME OF INSTALLING CONTRACTOR		
	TESTS WITNESSED BY		
	FOR PROPERTY OWNER (SIGNED)	TITLE	DATE
	FOR INSTALLING CONTRACTOR (SIGNED)	TITLE	DATE

ADDITIONAL EXPLANATION AND NOTES

Figure 8-1(b) (cont.).

8-5 Flow Tests.

8-5.1* The water supply shall be tested to verify compliance with the design. This test shall be conducted by flowing water from the hydraulically most remote hose connections.

8-5.2 For a manual standpipe, a fire department pumper or portable pump of adequate capacity (required flow and pressure) shall be used, to verify the system design, by pumping into the fire department connection.

8-5.3 A flow test shall be conducted at each roof outlet to verify that the required pressure is available at the required flow.

8-5.4 The filling arrangement for suction tanks shall be verified by shutting down all supplies to the tank, draining the tank to below designated low water level, then opening the supply valve to ensure operation of its automatic features.

8-5.5 Pressure Regulating Devices. Each pressure regulating device shall be tested to verify that the installation is correct, that the device is operating properly, and that the inlet and outlet pressures at the device are in accordance with the design. Static and residual inlet pressure and static and residual outlet pressure and flow shall be recorded on the contractor's test certificate.

8-5.6 Main Drain Flow Test. The main drain valve shall be opened and remain open until the system pressure stabilizes. The static and residual pressure shall be recorded on the contractor's test certificate.

8-5.7 Testing of Automatic and Semiautomatic Dry Systems. Automatic and semiautomatic dry systems shall be tested by initiating a flow of water from the hydraulically most remote hose connection. The system shall deliver a minimum of 250 gpm (946 L/min) at the hose connection within 3 min of opening the hose valve. Each remote control device for operating a semiautomatic system shall be tested in accordance with the manufacturer's instructions.

8-5.8 Systems Having Pumps. Where pumps are part of the water supply for a standpipe system, testing shall be conducted with pumps operating.

8-6 Manual Valve Test. Each valve intended to be manually opened or closed shall be operated by turning the handwheel crank or wrench throughout its range and returned to its normal position. Hose valve caps shall be tightened sufficiently to avoid leaking during the test, then removed after the test to drain water and relieve pressure.

8-7 Alarm and Supervision Tests. Each alarm and supervisory device provided shall be tested in accordance with NFPA 72, *Standard for the Installation, Maintenance, and Use of Protective Signaling Systems.*

8-8 Instructions. The installing contractor shall provide the owner with the following:

(a) All literature and instructions provided by the manufacturer describing proper operation and maintenance of equipment and devices installed

(b) A copy of NFPA 25, *Standard for the Inspection, Testing, and Maintenance of Water-Based Fire Protection Systems*.

8-9 Signs. The installation of signs required by this standard shall be verified.

Chapter 9   Buildings under Construction

9-1 General. Where required by the authority having jurisdiction, in buildings under construction a standpipe system, either temporary or permanent in nature, shall be provided in accordance with this chapter.

9-2 Fire Department Connections. The standpipes shall be provided with conspicuously marked and readily accessible fire department connections on the outside of the building at the street level.

9-3 Other System Features. Pipe sizes, hose connections, hose, water supply, and other details for new construction shall be in accordance with this standard.

9-4 Support of Piping. Standpipes shall be securely supported and restrained at each alternate floor.

9-5* Hose Connections. At each floor level, there shall be provided at least 1 hose connection. Hose valves shall be kept closed at all times and guarded against mechanical injury.

9-6* Extension of System Piping. Standpipes shall be extended up with each floor and securely capped at the top.

9-7 Temporary Installations. Temporary standpipes shall remain in service until the permanent standpipe is complete. Where temporary standpipes normally contain water, the piping shall be protected against freezing.

9-8 Timing of Water Supply Installation. Where construction reaches a height at which public waterworks system pressure is no longer adequate, temporary or permanent fire pumps shall be installed to provide protection to the uppermost level or to the height as required by the authority having jurisdiction.

Exception: Unless local fire department pumping apparatus is acceptable to the authority having jurisdiction as adequate for the standpipe pressure required.

9-9 Protection of Hose Connections and Fire Department Connections. Threaded caps and plugs shall be installed on fire department connections and hose connections. Fire department connections and hose connections shall be protected against physical damage.

Chapter 10   Referenced Publications

10-1 The following documents or portions thereof are referenced within this standard and shall be considered part of the requirements of this document. The edition indicated for each reference is the current edition as of the date of the NFPA issuance of this document.

10-1.1 NFPA Publications. National Fire Protection Association, 1 Batterymarch Park, P.O. Box 9101, Quincy, MA 02269-9101.

NFPA 13, *Standard for the Installation of Sprinkler Systems*, 1991 edition

NFPA 22, *Standard for Water Tanks for Private Fire Protection*, 1993 edition

NFPA 24, *Standard for the Installation of Private Fire Service Mains and Their Appurtenances*, 1992 edition

NFPA 25, *Standard for the Inspection, Testing, and Maintenance of Water-Based Fire Protection Systems*, 1992 edition

NFPA 51B, *Standard for Fire Prevention in Use of Cutting and Welding Processes*, 1989 edition

NFPA 72, *Standard for the Installation, Maintenance, and Use of Protective Signaling Systems*, 1990 edition

NFPA 1901, *Standard for Pumper Fire Apparatus*, 1991 edition

NFPA 1963, *Standard for Screw Threads and Gaskets for Fire Hose Connections*, 1985 edition

10-1.2 ANSI Publications. American National Standards Institute, Inc., 1430 Broadway, New York, NY 10018.

ANSI B16.1-1989, *Cast-Iron Pipe Flanges and Flanged Fittings*

ANSI B16.3-1985, *Malleable Iron Threaded Fittings*, Classes 150 and 300

ANSI B16.4-1985, *Cast-Iron Threaded Fittings*, Classes 125 and 250

ANSI B16.5-1988, *Pipe Flanges and Flanged Fittings*

ANSI B16.9-1986, *Factory-Made Wrought Steel Buttwelding Fittings*

ANSI B16.11-1991, *Forged Fittings, Socket Welding and Threaded*

ANSI B16.18-1984, *Cast Copper Alloy Solder-Joint Pressure Fittings*

ANSI B16.22-1989, *Wrought Copper and Copper Alloy Solder-Joint Pressure Fittings*

ANSI B16.25-1986, *Buttwelding Ends*

ANSI B36.10M-1985, *Welded and Seamless Wrought Steel Pipe*

ANSI B1.20.1-1983, *Pipe Threads, General Purpose (Inch)*

10-1.3 ASTM Publications. American Society for Testing and Materials, 1916 Race Street, Philadelphia, PA 19103.

ASTM A53-1990, *Standard Specification for Pipe, Steel, Black and Hot-Dipped, Zinc-Coated Welded and Seamless Pipe*

ASTM A135-1989, *Standard Specification for Electric-Resistance-Welded Steel Pipe*

ASTM A234-1991, *Standard Specification for Piping Fittings of Wrought Carbon Steel and Alloy Steel for Moderate and Elevated Temperatures*

ASTM A795-1990, *Standard Specification for Black and Hot-Dipped Zinc-Coated (Galvanized) Welded and Seamless Steel Pipe for Fire Protection Use*

ASTM B75-1991, *Standard Specification for Seamless Copper Tube (Metric)*

ASTM B88-1989, *Standard Specification for Seamless Copper Water Tube (Metric)*

ASTM B251-1988, *Standard Specification for General Requirements for Wrought Seamless Copper and Copper-Alloy Tube*

ASTM E380-1991, *Standard Practice for Use of the International System of Units (SI)*

10-1.4 AWS Publications. American Welding Society, 550 N. LeJeune Road, P.O. Box 351040, Miami, FL 33135.

AWS A5.8-1989, *Specification for Filler Metals for Brazing*

AWS D10.9-1980, *Specification for Qualification of Welding Procedures and Welders for Piping and Tubing*

10-1.5 AWWA Publications. American Water Works Association, 6666 W. Quincy Avenue, Denver, CO 80235.

AWWA C110-87, *Ductile-Iron and Gray-Iron Fittings, 3 in. Through 48 in. for Water and Other Liquids*

AWWA C151-80, *Ductile-Iron Pipe, Centrifugally Cast in Metal Molds or Sand-Lined Molds, for Water or Other Liquids*

Appendix A

This Appendix is not a part of the requirements of this NFPA document, but is included for information purposes only.

A-1-4 Should. Indicates a recommendation or that which is advised but not required.

A-2-1 The use of standard-weight valves and fittings should ordinarily be confined to the upper stories of very high buildings and to equipments where the highest available pressures are less than 175 psi (12.1 bars).

A-2-5.1 Many fire departments will lay a hose line from the pumper into the building and connect to an accessible valve outlet using a double female swivel when the building fire department connections are inaccessible or inoperable. To pressurize the standpipe, the hose valve is opened and the engine pumps into the system.

If the standpipe is equipped with pressure reducing hose valves, the valve will act as a check valve prohibiting pumping into the system when the valve is opened.

A supplementary single inlet fire department connection or hose valve with female threads at an accessible location on the standpipe will permit pumping into that system.

A-2-7.2 See NFPA 1961, *Standard for Fire Hose.*

The factors to be considered in selecting a rack or reel for storage of 1½-in. hose are the number of persons likely to be available to place the equipment into operation and the extent to which potential users are trained. With hose racks of the "semiautomatic" or "one-person" type, the hose valve should first be opened wide. The nozzle should then be grasped firmly and the hose lines drawn toward the fire. The water is automatically released as the last few feet of hose are pulled from the rack.

A-2-9 See Figure A-4-3.

A-2-9.2 See Sections 5-7 and 5-12 for design requirements.

A-3-6 Additional pressure gauges at the base of the standpipes may be desirable in some equipment, particularly in large plants and high buildings.

A-3-7 Audible alarms are normally located on the outside of the building. Approved electric gong bells, horns, or sirens inside the building or a combination inside and outside are sometimes advisable.

A-4-1 Connections from fire pumps and sources outside the building should be made at the base of the standpipes.

A-4-1.2.1 Standpipes should not be placed in unsprinklered areas of combustible construction.

A-4-2.5.2 Combined automatic sprinkler and standpipe risers should not be interconnected by sprinkler system piping.

A-4-2.7 See NFPA 24, *Standard for the Installation of Private Fire Service Mains and Their Appurtenances.*

A-4-3 See Figure A-4-3.

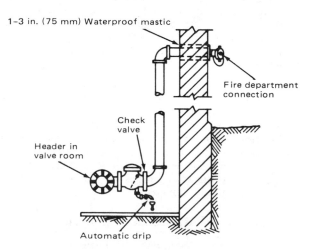

1–3 in. (75 mm) Waterproof mastic

Fire department connection

Check valve

Header in valve room

Automatic drip

Figure A-4-3 Typical fire department connection for wet standpipes.

A-4-3.5.4 The system designer should contact the authority having jurisdiction prior to establishing the location of the fire department connection. The location should be based on the requirements of the fire department.

A-4-7   See Figure A-4-7.

Location of the 2 hydraulically most remote hose connections:_____
Design flow rate for the connections identified above: _____
Design residual inlet and outlet pressures for the connections identified above: _____
Design static pressure and the design system demand (flow and residual pressure) at the system control valve, or at the pump discharge flange when a pump is installed, and at each fire department connection: ____

Figure A-4-7   System hydraulic information.

A-5-1   The building height determines the number of vertical zones. The area of a floor or fire area and exit locations, as well as the occupancy, will determine the number and locations of hose connections. Local building codes influence types of systems, classes of systems, and locations of hose connections. Pipe sizing is dependent on the number of hose connections flowing, quantity of water flowed, the required residual pressure, and vertical and horizontal distance of those hose connections from the water supplies.

For typical elevation drawings, see Figures A-5-1(a), A-5-1(b), and A-5-1(c).

A-5-2   The system pressure units have been implemented to replace the prior height units. Since the issue addressed by the heights units has always been maximum pressure, pressure limitations are a more direct method of regulation and allow flexibility in height units when pumps are used because a pump curve with less excess pressure at churn yields lower maximum system pressures while achieving the required system demand.

The maximum system pressure will normally be at pump churn. The measurement should include both the pump boost and city static pressures. The 350 psi limit was selected because it is the maximum pressure at which most system components are available, and it recognizes the need for a reasonable pressure unit.

A-5-3.1   Hose may be located at one side of the standpipe and supplied by short lateral connections to the standpipe where necessary to avoid obstructions.

Hose connections for Class I systems should be located in a stairway enclosure, and for Class II systems in the corridor or space adjacent to the stairway enclosure and connected through the wall to the standpipe. For Class III systems, the connections for $2^{1}/_{2}$-in. (63.5-mm) hose should be located in a stairway enclosure, and for Class II system hose, located in the corridor or space adjacent to the stairway enclosure. These arrangements make it possible to use Class II system hose streams promptly in case the stairway is filled with people escaping at the time of fire. In buildings having large areas, connections for Class I and Class III systems may be located at interior columns.

A-5-3.2   Hose connections are now specified to be located at intermediate landings between floors to prevent congestion at doorways. Where there are multiple intermediate floor landings between floors, hose connections should be located at the landing approximately midway between floors. It is recognized that fire departments often use the hose connection on the floor below the fire floor, and the location of hose connections at intermediate landings also reduces the hose lay distance in such cases as well.

The approach to locating hose connections with respect to exits is shown in Figure A-5-3.2.

For purposes of this standard, the following definitions will assist the user in locating the hose connections.

Exit Passageways.   Hallways, corridors, passages, or tunnels used as exit components and separated from other parts of the building in accordance with the NFPA *101,® Life Safety Code.®*

Horizontal Exit.   A way of passage from an area in one building to an area in another building on approximately the same level, or a way of passage through or around a fire barrier from one area to another on approximately the same level in the same building that affords safety from fire and smoke originating from the area of incidence and areas communicating therewith.

A-5-3.2(f)   This paragraph is intended to provide authority to local fire departments to require additional hose connections outside of or away from a 2-hr fire-resistive separation. These additional hose connections may be needed to allow fire fighters to attack a fire in a reasonable time frame based on the lengths of hose available on fire department standpipe packs or in carry bags. While it is recognized that outlet spacing limitations provide controls to limit the maximum hose length needed to fight a fire, thereby minimizing the physical demands on fire fighters, it is also recognized that in some cases based on architectural layout, additional outlets may be indicated in open floor areas just to meet spacing requirements. In such cases, it is unlikely that such outlets could be utilized, since there would not be a staging area for fire fighters to use when accessing the hose connection. Therefore, additional hose connections, when provided to meet distance limitations, should be located in 1-hr fire-resistive exit corridors whenever possible to provide a degree of protection for fire fighters accessing the connection. It is also desirable to locate such connections as uniformly as possible from floor to floor for ease of locating connections during a fire.

It is recognized that the 200-ft (61-m) distance allowed for sprinklered buildings may require additional hose lengths to be added to reach the most remote portion of a floor; however, automatic sprinklers should provide adequate control to allow time for fire fighters to extend hoses in those cases where a fire may be located in the most remote area.

A-5-3.3   Hose stations should be so arranged as to permit directing the discharge from the nozzle into all portions of important enclosures such as closets and like enclosures.

A-5-7   When determining the pressure at the outlet of the remote hose connection, the pressure loss in the hose valve should be considered.

It is very important that fire departments choose an appropriate nozzle type for their standpipe fire fighting operations. Constant pressure (automatic) type spray nozzles (*See NFPA 1964*) should not be used for standpipe operations because many of this type require a minimum of 100 psi at the nozzle inlet to produce a reasonably effective fire stream. In standpipe operations, hose friction loss may prevent the delivery of 100 psi to the nozzle.

In high-rise standpipe systems with pressure reducing hose valves, the fire department has little or no control over hose valve outlet pressure.

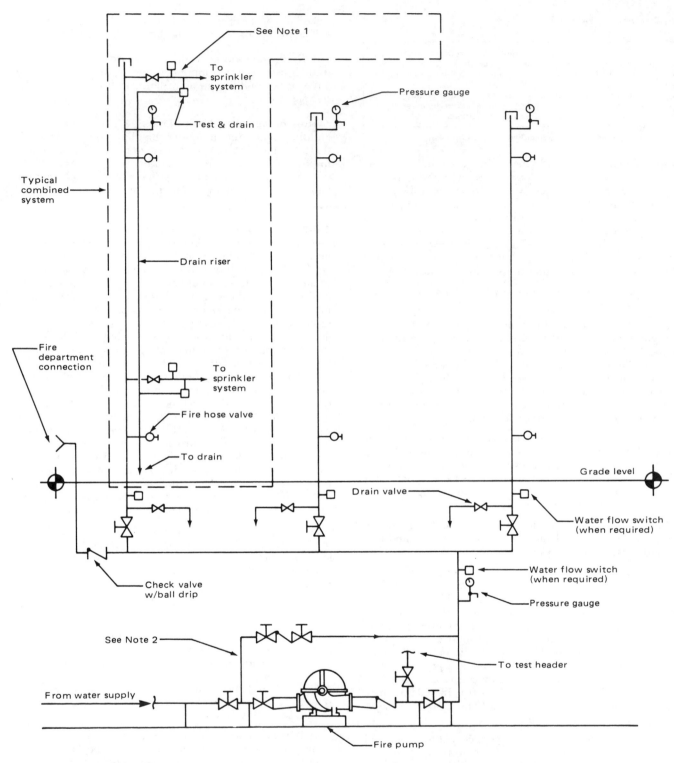

NOTE 1:   Sprinkler floor assembly. NFPA 13.
NOTE 2:   Bypass subject to NFPA 20.

Figure A-5-1(a)   Typical single-zone system.

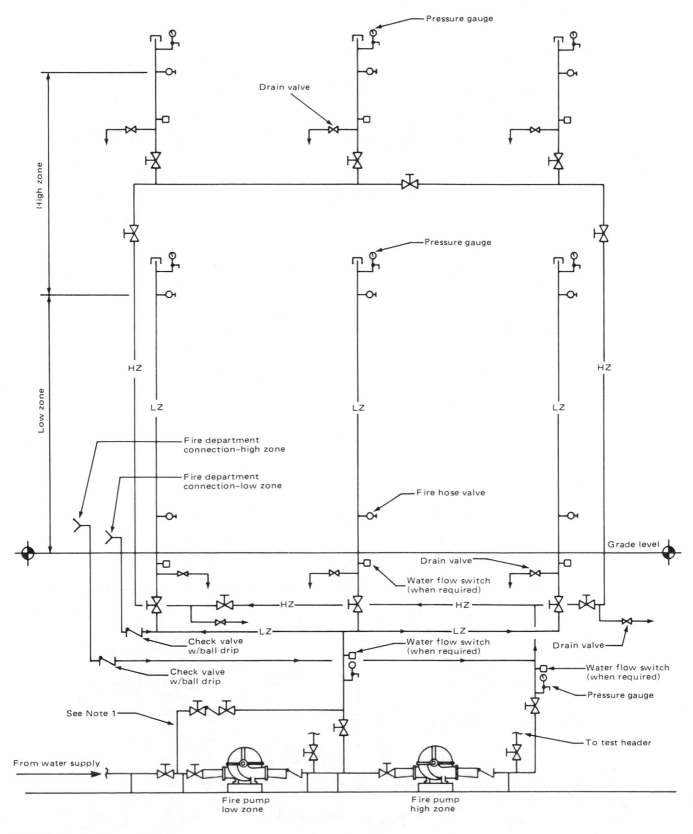

Figure A-5-1(b)   Typical two-zone system.

NOTE 1:   Bypass subject to NFPA 20.
NOTE 2:   High zone pump may be arranged to take suction directly from source of supply.

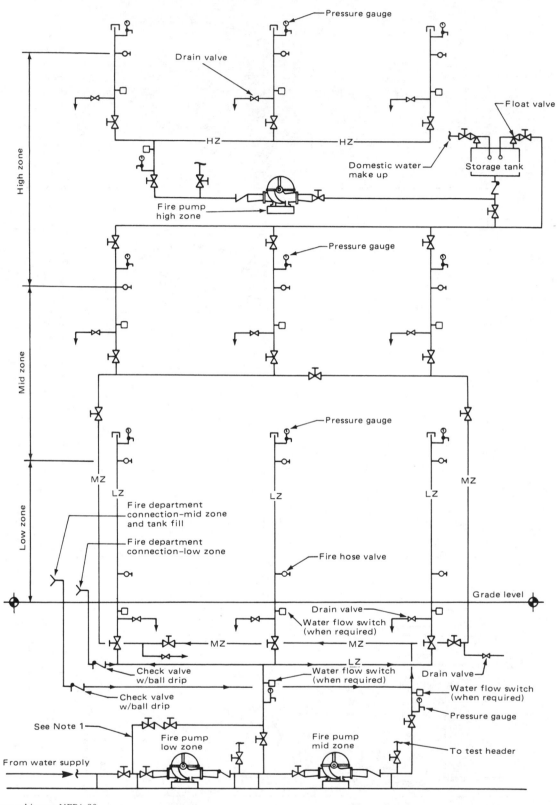

Figure A-5-1(c)   Typical multi-zone system.

NOTE 1:   Bypass subject to NFPA 20.

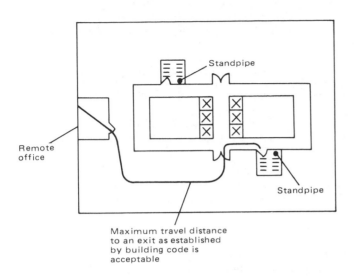

Figure A-5-3.2.

Many fire departments use combination (fog and straight stream) nozzles requiring 100 psi (6.9 bar) residual pressure at the nozzle inlet with 1½-in., 1¾-in., or 2-in. hose in lengths of up to 150 ft. Some use 2½-in. hose with a smooth bore nozzle or a combination nozzle.

The 2½-in. smooth bore with a 1⅛-in. tip will produce a usable stream (250 gpm) at 50 psi inlet pressure requiring 65 psi at the valve outlet with 100 ft of 2½-in. hose or 73 psi at the outlet with 150 ft of hose.

Some departments may use 50 ft of 2½-in. hose to a gated wye, supplying two 100-ft lengths of 1½-in. to 2-in. hose with combination nozzles, requiring 120 psi to 149 psi at the valve outlet. (*See Table A-5-7.*)

Table A-5-7   Hose Stream Friction Losses Summary

Calc #	Nozzle/Hose	Flow (gpm)	psi @ Valve Outlet
1	2½-in. combination nozzle, with 150 ft 2½-in. hose	250	123
2	2½-in. smooth bore with 1⅛-in. tip 150 ft 2½-in. hose	250	73
3	2½-in. combination nozzle with 50 ft 2½-in. hose, 2½-in. gated wye, and 100 ft 1½-in. hose	250	149
4	Same with two 100-ft lengths of 1¾-in. hose	250	139
5	Same with two 100-ft lengths of 2-in. hose	250	120
6	1½-in. combination nozzles with 150 ft 2-in. hose	200	136
7	Same with 1¾-in hose	200	168

A-5-8 Due to the different pressure limitations established in Section 5-8, it may be necessary to arrange piping so that separate pressure regulating devices can be provided on the Class I and Class II hose connections.

A-5-9.1.1 If a water supply system supplies more than one building or more than one fire area, the total supply may be calculated based on the single building or fire area requiring the greatest number of standpipes.

For a discussion of use by the fire department of fire department connections, see NFPA 13E, *Recommendations for Fire Department Operations in Properties Protected by Sprinkler and Standpipe Systems.*

A-5-9.1.2 See Chapter 7 of NFPA 13, *Standard for the Installation of Sprinkler Systems.*

A-5-9.1.3.1 Occupancy examples in the listings as shown in the various hazard classifications are intended to represent the norm for those occupancy types. Unusual or abnormal fuel loadings or combustible characteristics and susceptibility for changes in these characteristics, for a particular occupancy, are considerations that should be weighed in the selection and classification.

The Light Hazard classification is intended to encompass residential occupancies; however, this is not intended to preclude the use of listed residential sprinklers in residential occupancies or residential portions of other occupancies.

Light Hazard Occupancies include occupancies having conditions similar to:

Churches
Clubs
Eaves and overhangs, if combustible construction with no combustibles beneath
Educational
Hospitals
Institutional
Libraries, except large stack rooms
Museums
Nursing or convalescent homes
Office, including data processing
Residential
Restaurant seating areas
Theaters and auditoriums excluding stages and prosceniums
Unused attics.

Ordinary Hazard Occupancies (Group 1) include occupancies having conditions similar to:

Automobile parking and showrooms
Bakeries
Beverage manufacturing
Canneries
Dairy products manufacturing and processing
Electronic plants
Glass and glass products manufacturing
Laundries
Restaurant service areas.

Ordinary Hazard Occupancies (Group 2) include occupancies having conditions similar to:

Cereal mills
Chemical plants — ordinary
Confectionery products
Distilleries
Dry cleaners
Feed mills
Horse stables
Leather goods manufacturing
Libraries — large stack room areas

Machine shops
Metal working
Mercantile
Paper and pulp mills
Paper process plants
Piers and wharves
Post offices
Printing and publishing
Repair garages
Stages
Textile manufacturing
Tire manufacturing
Tobacco products manufacturing
Wood machining
Wood product assembly.

Extra Hazard Occupancies (Group 1) include occupancies having conditions similar to:

Aircraft hangars
Combustible hydraulic fluid use areas
Die casting
Metal extruding
Plywood and particle board manufacturing
Printing [using inks having flash points below 100°F (37.9°C)]
Rubber reclaiming, compounding, drying, milling, vulcanizing
Sawmills
Textile picking, opening, blending, garnetting, carding, combining of cotton, synthetics, wool shoddy, or burlap
Upholstering with plastic foams.

Extra Hazard Occupancies (Group 2) include occupancies having conditions similar to:

Asphalt saturating
Flammable liquids spraying
Flow coating
Mobile home or modular building assemblies (where finished enclosure is present and has combustible interiors)
Open oil quenching
Plastics processing
Solvent cleaning
Varnish and paint dipping.

A-5-11 During flow testing of PRVs, care should be taken in making connections to drain risers. An air gap should be maintained in order to prevent cross connection to nonpotable water sources.

A-5-12 See NFPA 13E, *Recommendations for Fire Department Operations in Properties Protected by Sprinkler and Standpipe Systems.*

The number of $2^1/_2$-in. (63.5-mm) inlets to supply the required water volume and pressure at the fire department connection is dependent on several variables such as the performance of the water supply at the source, the distance from the source to the location of the inlets, the diameter of the hose used, the size of the fire department pumper, and the required water volume and pressure at the base of the standpipe riser(s).

A-6-1 Plans should indicate the type of fire department equipment that the system is designed to serve, including the hose size, hose length, and hose nozzle. Such equipment would be the basis for the pressure selected in accordance with Section 5-7.

A-7-1 The selection of water supplies for each installation should be determined in cooperation with the authority having jurisdiction.

A-7-1.1 See NFPA 22, *Standard for Water Tanks for Private Fire Protection*, and NFPA 20, *Standard for the Installation of Centrifugal Fire Pumps.*

A-8-1 Where standpipe connections are built in the walls or partitions, the hydrostatic tests should be made before they are covered in or permanently sealed.

Example of Required Hydrostatic Test Pressure: A standpipe system has for its water supply the connection to a public water service main. A 100 psi (6.9 bars) rated pump is installed in the connection. With a maximum normal public water supply pressure of 70 psi (4.9 bars) at the low elevation point of the system or zone being tested and a 120 psi (8.3 bars) pump (churn) pressure the hydrostatic test pressure, is 70 + 120 + 50, or 240 psi (16.6 bars). Refer to NFPA 24, *Standard for the Installation of Private Fire Service Mains and Their Appurtenances*, for permissible leakage in underground piping.

A-8-4.1 The testing and flushing of the underground pipe should be in accordance with NFPA 24.

A-8-5.1 The hydraulically most remote hose connections in a building are generally at a roof manifold, if provided, or at the top of a stair leading to the roof. In a multizone system, the testing means is generally at a test header at grade or at a suction tank on higher floors.

Where a flow test at the most hydraulically remote hose connection is not practical, the authority having jurisdiction should be consulted for the appropriate location of the test.

A-9-5 At the highest hose connection there should be maintained a substantial box, preferably of metal, in which should be kept a sufficient amount of hose to reach all parts of the floor, a $1^1/_8$-in. (29-mm) nozzle, spanner wrenches, and hose straps.

A-9-6 Top hose connections should at all times be not more than 1 floor below the highest forms, staging, and like combustibles.

Appendix B   Referenced Publications

B-1 The following documents or portions thereof are referenced within this standard for informational purposes only and thus should not be considered part of the requirements of this document. The edition indicated for each reference is the current edition as of the date of the NFPA issuance of this document.

B-1.1 NFPA Publications. National Fire Protection Association, 1 Batterymarch Park, P.O. Box 9101, Quincy, MA 02269-9101.

NFPA 13, *Standard for the Installation of Sprinkler Systems*, 1991 edition

NFPA 13E, *Recommendations for Fire Department Operations in Properties Protected by Sprinkler and Standpipe Systems*, 1989 edition

NFPA 20, *Standard for the Installation of Centrifugal Fire Pumps*, 1990 edition

NFPA 22, *Standard for Water Tanks for Private Fire Protection*, 1993 edition

NFPA 24, *Standard for the Installation of Private Fire Service Mains and Their Appurtenances*, 1992 edition

NFPA *101*, *Life Safety Code*, 1991 edition

NFPA 1961, *Standard for Fire Hose*, 1992 edition

NFPA 1964, *Standard for Spray Nozzles (Shutoff and Tip)*, 1993 edition.

Fire Protection Handbook, Section 5, Chapter 14

UNIFORM BUILDING CODE STANDARD 9-3
INSTALLATION OF SPRINKLER SYSTEMS IN GROUP R OCCUPANCIES FOUR STORIES OR LESS

See Sections 804.1, 805, 902, 904.1.2, 2603.7.1 and 2603.8.1,
Uniform Building Code

Part I

SECTION 9.301 — ADOPTION OF NFPA STANDARD

Except for the limitations, deletions, modifications and amendments set forth in Section 9.302 of this standard, the installation of sprinkler systems in Group R Occupancies required by this code shall be in accordance with the Standard for the Installation of Sprinkler Systems in Residential Occupancies, NFPA 13R-1989[1], published by the National Fire Protection Association, copyright © 1989, Batterymarch Park, Quincy, Massachusetts 02269, as if set out at length herein, or UBC Standard 9-1.

[1]The current edition is NFPA 13R-1996.

SECTION 9.302 — AMENDMENTS

The National Fire Protection Association standard adopted by Section 9.301 applies to the selection, installation, acceptance inspection and acceptance testing of sprinkler systems in residential occupancies four stories or less, except as follows:

1. Sec. 1-3 is amended as follows:

The definition of "authority having jurisdiction" is revised as follows:

The **"authority having jurisdiction"** is the building official.

The definitions of "approved" and "listed" shall be as set forth in Volume 1 of this code.

The definitions of "should" and "standard" are deleted.

The definition of "residential occupancies" is revised as follows:

RESIDENTIAL OCCUPANCIES are Group R Occupancies.

The definitions of "acceptance" and "building official" are added as follows:

ACCEPTANCE is acceptance by the building official.

BUILDING OFFICIAL is the officer or other designated authority charged with the administration and enforcement of this standard, or the officer's or other designated authority's duly authorized representative.

2. Sec. 1-6.2.1 is revised by changing the reference to "NFPA 13" to "UBC Standard 9-1."

3. Sec. 2-1.3.2 is revised by changing the reference to "NFPA 13" to "UBC Standard 9-1."

4. Sec. 2-3.2 is revised by changing the reference to "NFPA 20 and 22" to "nationally recognized standards" and changing the reference to "NFPA 13" to "UBC Standard 9-1."

5. Sec. 2-3.3.2 is revised by changing the reference to "NFPA 13" to "UBC Standard 9-1."

6. Sec. 2-4.4 is revised by changing the reference to "NFPA 13" to "UBC Standard 9-1."

7. Sec. 2-5.2 is revised by changing the references to "NFPA 13" to "UBC Standard 9-1."

8. Sec. 2-5.3 is revised by changing the reference to "NFPA 13" to "UBC Standard 9-1."

9. Sec. 2-6 is revised by changing the reference to "NFPA 220" to "the Building Code."

10. Secs. 2-7.1 and 2-7.2 are added as follows:

2-7.1. A sprinkler system installed under this standard shall be maintained in accordance with the Fire Code.

2-7.2. The installer of the system shall provide the owner with written instructions and information relating to the care and maintenance of the sprinkler system, with special attention given to the sprinkler system devices.

11. Chapter 3 is deleted in its entirety.

Part II

Reproduced with permission from the Standard for the Installation of Sprinkler Systems in Residential Occupancies up to Four Stories in Height, NFPA 13R, copyright © 1989[1], National Fire Protection Association, Batterymarch Park, Quincy, Massachusetts 02269. Persons desiring to reprint in whole or part any portion of the Standard for Installation of Sprinkler Systems in Residential Occupancies up to Four Stories in Height, NFPA 13R-1989[1], must secure permission from the National Fire Protection Association. The following standard is not necessarily the latest revision used by NFPA. If the reader desires to compare with that version, the same is available from NFPA.

[1]The current edition is NFPA 13R-1996.

Contents

NFPA 13R

Standard for the

Installation of Sprinkler Systems in

Residential Occupancies up to Four Stories

in Height

1989 Edition

NOTICE: An asterisk (*) following the number or letter designating a paragraph indicates explanatory material on that paragraph in Appendix A.

Information on referenced publications can be found in Chapter 3 and Appendix B.

Preface

It is intended that this standard provide a method for those individuals wishing to install a sprinkler system for life safety and property protection. It is not the purpose of this standard to require the installation of an automatic sprinkler system. This standard assumes that one or more smoke detectors will be installed in accordance with NFPA 74, *Standard for the Installation, Maintenance, and Use of Household Fire Warning Equipment.*

Chapter 1   General Information

1-1* Scope. This standard deals with the design and installation of automatic sprinkler systems for protection against fire hazards in residential occupancies up to four stories in height.

1-2* Purpose. The purpose of this standard is to provide design and installation requirements for a sprinkler system to aid in the detection and control of fires in residential occupancies and thus provide improved protection against injury, life loss, and property damage. A sprinkler system designed and installed in accordance with this standard is expected to prevent flashover (total involvement) in the room of fire origin, when sprinklered, and to improve the chance for occupants to escape or be evacuated.

Nothing in this standard is intended to restrict new technologies or alternate arrangements, providing that the level of safety prescribed by the standard is not lowered.

1-3 Definitions.

Approved. Acceptable to the "authority having jurisdiction."

NOTE: The National Fire Protection Association does not approve, inspect or certify any installations, procedures, equipment, or materials nor does it approve or evaluate testing laboratories. In determining the acceptability of installations or procedures, equipment or materials, the authority having jurisdiction may base acceptance on compliance with NFPA or other appropriate standards. In the absence of such standards, said authority may require evidence of proper installation, procedure or use. The authority having jurisdiction may also refer to the listings or labeling practices of an organization concerned with product evaluations which is in a position to determine compliance with appropriate standards for the current production of listed items.

Authority Having Jurisdiction. The "authority having jurisdiction" is the organization, office or individual responsible for "approving" equipment, an installation or a procedure.

NOTE: The phrase "authority having jurisdiction" is used in NFPA documents in a broad manner since jurisdictions and "approval" agencies vary as do their responsibilities. Where public safety is primary, the "authority having jurisdiction" may be a federal, state, local or other regional department or individual such as a fire chief, fire marshal, chief of a fire prevention bureau, labor department, health department, building official, electrical inspector, or others having statutory authority. For insurance purposes, an insurance inspection department, rating bureau, or other insurance company representative may be the "authority having jurisdiction." In many circumstances the property owner or his designated agent assumes the role of the "authority having jurisdiction"; at government installations, the commanding officer or departmental official may be the "authority having jurisdiction."

Check Valve. A valve that allows flow in one direction only.

Control Valve. An indicating valve employed to control (shut) a supply of water to a sprinkler system.

Design Discharge. Rate of water discharged by an automatic sprinkler, expressed in gallons per minute.

Dry System. A system employing automatic sprinklers that are attached to a piping system containing air under atmospheric or higher pressures. Loss of pressure from the opening of a sprinkler or detection of a fire condition causes the release of water into the piping system and out the opened sprinkler.

Dwelling Unit. One or more rooms arranged for the use of one or more individuals living together as in a single housekeeping unit, normally having cooking, living, sanitary, and sleeping facilities.

Labeled. Equipment or materials to which has been attached a label, symbol or other identifying mark of an organization acceptable to the "authority having jurisdiction" and concerned with product evaluation, that maintains periodic inspection of production of labeled equipment or materials and by whose labeling the manufacturer indicates compliance with appropriate standards or performance in a specified manner.

Listed. Equipment or materials included in a list published by an organization acceptable to the "authority having jurisdiction" and concerned with product evaluation, that maintains periodic inspection of production of listed equipment or materials and whose listing states either that the equipment or material meets appropriate standards or has been tested and found suitable for use in a specified manner.

NOTE: The means for identifying listed equipment may vary for each organization concerned with product evaluation, some of which do not recognize equipment as listed unless it is also labeled. The "authority having jurisdiction" should utilize the system employed by the listing organization to identify a listed product.

Multipurpose Piping Systems. Piping systems within residential occupancies intended to serve both domestic and fire protection needs.

Residential Occupancies. Residential occupancies as included in the scope of this standard include the following, as defined in NFPA *101*®, *Life Safety Code*®:

(1) Apartment buildings.

(2) Lodging and rooming houses.

(3) Board and care facilities (slow evacuation type with 16 or less occupants and prompt evacuation type).

(4) Hotels, motels, and dormitories.

Residential Sprinkler. An automatic sprinkler that has been specifically listed for use in residential occupancies.

Shall. Indicates a mandatory requirement.

Should. Indicates a recommendation or that which is advised but not required.

Sprinkler—Automatic. A fire suppression device that operates automatically when its heat-actuated element is heated to or above its thermal rating, allowing water to discharge over a specific area.

Sprinkler System. An integrated system of piping connected to a water supply, with listed sprinklers that will automatically initiate water discharge over a fire area. When required, the sprinkler system also includes a control valve and a device for actuating an alarm when the system operates.

Standard. A document containing only mandatory provisions using the word "shall" to indicate requirements. Explanatory material may be included only in the form of "fine print" notes, in footnotes, or in an appendix.

Waterflow Alarm. A sounding device activated by a waterflow detector or alarm check valve.

Waterflow Detector. An electric signaling indicator or alarm check valve actuated by water flow in one direction only.

Wet System. A system employing automatic sprinklers that are attached to a piping system containing water and connected to a water supply, so that water discharges immediately from sprinklers opened by a fire.

1-4 Units. Metric units of measurement in this standard are in accordance with the modernized metric system known as the International System of Units (SI). Two units (liter and bar), outside of but recognized by SI, are commonly used in international fire protection. These units are listed, with conversion factors, in Table 1-4.

1-4.1 If a value for measurement as given in this standard is followed by an equivalent value in other units, the first

Table 1-4

Name of Unit	Unit Symbol	Conversion Factor
liter	L	1 gal = 3.785 L
pascal	Pa	1 psi = 6894.757 Pa
bar	bar	1 psi = 0.0689 bar
bar	bar	1 bar = 105 Pa

For additional conversions and information see ASTM E380, *Standard for Metric Practice.*

stated is to be regarded as the requirement. A given equivalent value may be approximate.

1-4.2 The conversion procedure for the SI units has been to multiply the quantity by the conversion factor and then round the result to the appropriate number of significant digits.

1-5 Piping.

1-5.1 Pipe or tube used in sprinkler systems shall be of the materials in Table 1-5.1 or in accordance with 1-5.2 through 1-5.5. The chemical properties, physical properties, and dimensions of the materials listed in Table 1-5.1 shall be at least equivalent to the standards cited in the table and designed to withstand a working pressure of not less than 175 psi (12.1 bars).

Table 1-5.1

Materials and Dimensions	Standard
Specification for Black and Hot-Dipped Zinc-Coated (Galvanized) Welded and Seamless Steel Pipe for Fire Protection Use	ASTM A795
Specification for Welded and Seamless Steel Pipe	ASTM A53
Wrought-Steel Pipe	ANSI B36.10M
Specification for Electric-Resistance Welded Steel Pipe	ASTM A135
Copper Tube (Drawn, Seamless) Specification for Seamless Copper Tube	ASTM B88
Specification for General Requirements for Wrought Seamless Copper and Copper-Alloy Tube	ASTM B251
Brazing Filler Metal (Classification BCuP-3 or BCuP-4)	AWS A5.8
Specification for Solder Metal, 95-5 (Tin-Antimony-Grade 95TA)	ASTM B32

1-5.2 Other types of pipe or tube may be used, but only those listed for this service.

1-5.3 Whenever the word pipe is used in this standard, it shall be understood to also mean tube.

1-5.4 Pipe joined with mechanical grooved fittings shall be joined by a listed combination of fittings, gaskets, and grooves. When grooves are cut or rolled on the pipe they shall be dimensionally compatible with the fittings.

Exception: Steel pipe with wall thicknesses less than Schedule 30 [in sizes 8 in. (203 mm) and larger] or Schedule 40 [in sizes less than 8 in. (203 mm)] shall not be joined by fittings used with pipe having cut grooves.

1-5.5 Fittings used in sprinkler systems shall be of the materials listed in Table 1-5.5 or in accordance with 1-5.7. The chemical properties, physical properties, and dimensions of the materials listed in Table 1-5.5 shall be at least equivalent to the standards cited in the table. Fittings used in sprinkler systems shall be designed to withstand the working pressures involved, but not less than 175 psi (12.1 bars) cold water pressure.

Table 1-5.5

Materials and Dimensions	Standard
Cast Iron	
Cast Iron Threaded Fittings, Class 125 and 250	ANSI B16.4
Cast Iron Pipe Flanges and Flanged Fittings	ANSI B16.1
Malleable Iron	
Malleable Iron Threaded Fittings, Class 150 and 300	ANSI B16.3
Steel	
Factory-made Threaded Fittings Class 150 and 300	ANSI B16.9
Buttwelding Ends for Pipe, Valves, Flanges, and Fittings	ANSI B16.25
Spec. for Piping Fittings of Wrought Carbon Steel and Alloy Steel for Moderate and Elevated Temperatures	ASTM A234
Pipe Flanges and Flanged Fittings, Steel Nickel Alloy and Other Special Alloys	ANSI B16.5
Forged Steel Fittings, Socket Welded and Threaded	ANSI B16.11
Copper	
Wrought Copper and Copper Alloy Solder-Joint Pressure Fittings	ANSI B16.22
Cast Copper Alloy Solder-Joint Pressure Fittings	ANSI B16.18

1-5.6 Joints for the connection of copper tube shall be brazed.

Exception: Soldered joints (95-5 solder metal) may be used for wet-pipe copper tube systems.

1-5.7 Other types of fittings may be used, but only those listed for this service.

1-6 System Types.

1-6.1 Wet-Pipe Systems. A wet-pipe system shall be used when all piping is installed in areas not subject to freezing.

1-6.2 Provision shall be made to protect piping from freezing in unheated areas by use of one of the following acceptable methods:

(a) Antifreeze system.

(b) Dry-pipe system.

Exception: Listed standard dry-pendent, dry upright, or dry sidewall sprinklers may be extended into unheated areas not intended for living purposes.

1-6.2.1 Antifreeze solutions shall be installed in accordance with 5-5.3 of NFPA 13, *Standard for the Installation of Sprinkler Systems.*

Chapter 2 Working Plans, Design, Installation, Acceptance Tests, and Maintenance

2-1 Working Plans and Acceptance Tests.

2-1.1 Working Plans.

2-1.1.1 Working plans shall be submitted for approval to the authority having jurisdiction before any equipment is installed or remodeled. Deviations from approved plans will require permission of the authority having jurisdiction.

2-1.1.2 Working plans shall be drawn to an indicated scale, on sheets of uniform size, with a plan of each floor, made so that they can be easily duplicated, and shall show the following data:

(a) Name of owner and occupant.

(b) Location, including street address.

(c) Point of compass.

(d) Ceiling construction.

(e) Full height cross section.

(f) Location of fire walls.

(g) Location of partitions.

(h) Occupancy of each area or room.

(i) Location and size of concealed spaces, attics, closets, and bathrooms.

(j) Any small enclosures in which no sprinklers are to be installed.

(k) Size of city main in street, pressure and whether dead-end or circulating and, if dead-end, direction and distance to nearest circulating main, city main test results including elevation of test hydrant.

(l) Make, manufacturer, type, heat-response element, temperature rating, and nominal orifice size of sprinkler.

(m) Temperature rating and location of high-temperature sprinklers.

(n) Number of sprinklers on each riser, per floor.

(o) Kind and location of alarm bells.

(p) Type of pipe and fittings.

(q) Type of protection for nonmetallic pipe.

(r) Nominal pipe size with lengths shown to scale.

NOTE: Where typical branch lines prevail, it will be necessary to size only one line.

(s) Location and size of riser nipples.

(t) Type of fittings and joints and location of all welds and bends.

(u) Types and locations of hangers, sleeves, braces, and methods of securing sprinklers, where applicable.

(v) All control valves, check valves, drain pipes, and test connections.

(w) Underground pipe size, length, location, weight, material, point of connection to city main; the type of valves, meters, and valve pits; and the depth at which the top of the pipe is laid below grade.

(x) For hydraulically designed systems, the material to be included on the hydraulic data nameplate.

(y) Name and address of contractor.

2-1.2 Approval of Sprinkler Systems.

2-1.2.1 The installer shall perform all required acceptance tests (*see 2-1.3*), complete the Contractor's Material and Test Certificate(s) (*see Figure 2-1.2.1*), and forward the certificate(s) to the authority having jurisdiction, prior to asking for approval of the installation.

2-1.2.2 When the authority having jurisdiction desires to be present during the conducting of acceptance tests, the installer shall give advance notification of the time and date the testing will be performed.

2-1.3 Acceptance Tests.

2-1.3.1 Flushing of Underground Connections.

2-1.3.1.1 Underground mains and lead-in connections to system risers shall be flushed before connection is made to sprinkler piping, in order to remove foreign materials that may have entered the underground piping during the course of the installation. For all systems, the flushing operation shall be continued until water is clear.

2-1.3.1.2 Underground mains and lead-in connections shall be flushed at the hydraulically calculated water demand rate of the system.

CONTRACTOR'S MATERIAL & TEST CERTIFICATE FOR A BOVEGROUND PIPING

PROCEDURE
Upon completion of work, inspection and tests shall be made by the contractor's representative and witnessed by an owner's representative. All defects shall be corrected and system left in service before contractor's personnel finally leave the job.

A certificate shall be filled out and signed by both representatives. Copies shall be prepared for approving authorities, owners, and contractor. It is understood the owner's representative's signature in no way prejudices any claim against contractor for faulty material, poor workmanship, or failure to comply with approving authority's requirements or local ordinances.

PROPERTY NAME		DATE

PROPERTY ADDRESS

PLANS	ACCEPTED BY APPROVING AUTHORITIES (NAMES)		
	ADDRESS		
	INSTALLATION CONFORMS TO ACCEPTED PLANS	☐ YES	☐ NO
	EQUIPMENT USED IS APPROVED	☐ YES	☐ NO
	IF NO, EXPLAIN DEVIATIONS		

INSTRUCTIONS	HAS PERSON IN CHARGE OF FIRE EQUIPMENT BEEN INSTRUCTED AS TO LOCATION OF CONTROL VALVES AND CARE AND MAINTENANCE OF THIS NEW EQUIPMENT?	☐ YES	☐ NO
	IF NO, EXPLAIN		
	HAVE COPIES OF THE FOLLOWING BEEN LEFT ON THE PREMISES:	☐ YES	☐ NO
	1. SYSTEM COMPONENTS INSTRUCTIONS	☐ YES	☐ NO
	2. CARE AND MAINTENANCE INSTRUCTIONS	☐ YES	☐ NO
	3. NFPA 13A	☐ YES	☐ NO

LOCATION OF SYSTEM	SUPPLIES BUILDINGS

SPRINKLERS	MAKE	MODEL	YEAR OF MANUFACTURE	ORIFICE SIZE	QUANTITY	TEMPERATURE RATING

PIPE AND FITTINGS	Type of Pipe _____
	Type of Fittings _____

ALARM VALVE OR FLOW INDICATOR		ALARM DEVICE		MAXIMUM TIME TO OPERATE THROUGH TEST CONNECTION	
	TYPE	MAKE	MODEL	MIN.	SEC.

DRY PIPE OPERATING TEST		DRY VALVE			Q.O.D.		
		MAKE	MODEL	SERIAL NO.	MAKE	MODEL	SERIAL NO.

DRY PIPE OPERATING TEST		TIME TO TRIP THRU TEST CONNECTION*		WATER PRESSURE	AIR PRESSURE	TRIP POINT AIR PRESSURE	TIME WATER REACHED TEST OUTLET*		ALARM OPERATED PROPERLY	
		MIN.	SEC.	PSI	PSI	PSI	MIN.	SEC.	YES	NO
	Without Q.O.D.									
	With Q.O.D.									
	IF NO, EXPLAIN									

* MEASURED FROM TIME INSPECTOR'S TEST CONNECTION IS OPENED.
85A (10-88)   PRINTED IN U.S.A.   (OVER)

Figure 2-1.2.1 Contractor's Material and Test Certificate for Aboveground Piping.

2-1.3.1.3 To avoid property damage, provision shall be made for the disposal of water issuing from test outlets.

2-1.3.2* All systems shall be tested for leakage at 50 psi (3.4 bars) above maximum system design pressure.

Exception: When a fire department connection is provided, hydrostatic pressure tests shall be provided in accordance with NFPA 13, Standard for the Installation of Sprinkler Systems.

2-2 Design and Installation.
2-2.1 Devices and Materials.
2-2.1.1* Only new sprinklers shall be employed in the installation of sprinkler systems.

2-2.1.2 Only listed or approved devices and materials as indicated in this standard shall be used in sprinkler systems.

2-2.1.3 Sprinkler systems shall be designed for a maximum working pressure of 175 psi (12.1 bars).

Exception: Higher design pressures may be used when all system components are rated for pressures higher than 175 psi (12.1 bars).

2-3 Water Supply.
2-3.1 General Provisions.
Every automatic sprinkler system shall have at least one automatic water supply. When stored water is used as the sole source of supply, the minimum quantity shall equal the water demand rate times 30 minutes. (See 2-5.1.3.)

DELUGE & PREACTION VALVES	OPERATION ☐ PNEUMATIC ☐ ELECTRIC ☐ HYDRAULIC						
	PIPING SUPERVISED ☐ YES ☐ NO		DETECTING MEDIA SUPERVISED ☐ YES ☐ NO				
	DOES VALVE OPERATE FROM THE MANUAL TRIP AND/OR REMOTE CONTROL STATIONS ☐ YES ☐ NO						
	IS THERE AN ACCESSIBLE FACILITY IN EACH CIRCUIT FOR TESTING ☐ YES ☐ NO		IF NO, EXPLAIN				
	MAKE	MODEL	DOES EACH CIRCUIT OPERATE SUPERVISION LOSS ALARM YES / NO		DOES EACH CIRCUIT OPERATE VALVE RELEASE YES / NO		MAXIMUM TIME TO OPERATE RELEASE MIN. / SEC.

TEST DESCRIPTION	HYDROSTATIC: Hydrostatic tests shall be made at not less than 50 psi (3.4 bars) above design pressure for two hours. Differential dry-pipe valve clappers shall be left open during test to prevent damage. All aboveground piping leakage shall be stopped. Systems with fire department connections shall be hydrostatically tested in accordance with NFPA 13, paragraph 1-11.2.
	PNEUMATIC: Establish 40 psi (2.7 bars) air pressure and measure drop which shall not exceed 1-1/2 psi (0.1 bars) in 24 hours. Test pressure tanks at normal water level and air pressure and measure air pressure drop which shall not exceed 1-1/2 psi (0.1 bars) in 24 hours.

TESTS	ALL PIPING HYDROSTATICALLY TESTED AT _____ PSI FOR _____ HRS. IF NO, STATE REASON
	DRY PIPING PNEUMATICALLY TESTED ☐ YES ☐ NO
	EQUIPMENT OPERATES PROPERLY ☐ YES ☐ NO
	DO YOU CERTIFY AS THE SPRINKLER CONTRACTOR THAT ADDITIVES AND CORROSIVE CHEMICALS, SODIUM SILICATE OR DERIVATIVES OF SODIUM SILICATE, BRINE, OR OTHER CORROSIVE CHEMICALS WERE NOT USED FOR TESTING SYSTEMS OR STOPPING LEAKS? ☐ YES ☐ NO
	DRAIN TEST READING OF GAGE LOCATED NEAR WATER SUPPLY TEST CONNECTION: _____ PSI RESIDUAL PRESSURE WITH VALVE IN TEST CONNECTION OPEN WIDE _____ PSI
	UNDERGROUND MAINS AND LEAD IN CONNECTIONS TO SYSTEM RISERS FLUSHED BEFORE CONNECTION MADE TO SPRINKLER PIPING. VERIFIED BY COPY OF THE U FORM NO. 85B ☐ YES ☐ NO OTHER EXPLAIN
	FLUSHED BY INSTALLER OF UNDERGROUND SPRINKLER PIPING ☐ YES ☐ NO

BLANK TESTING GASKETS	NUMBER USED LOCATIONS	NUMBER REMOVED

WELDING	WELDED PIPING ☐ YES ☐ NO
	IF YES...
	DO YOU CERTIFY AS THE SPRINKLER CONTRACTOR THAT WELDING PROCEDURES COMPLY WITH THE REQUIREMENTS OF AT LEAST AWS D10.9, LEVEL AR-3 ☐ YES ☐ NO
	DO YOU CERTIFY THAT THE WELDING WAS PERFORMED BY WELDERS QUALIFIED IN COMPLIANCE WITH THE REQUIREMENTS OF AT LEAST AWS D10.9, LEVEL AR-3 ☐ YES ☐ NO
	DO YOU CERTIFY THAT WELDING WAS CARRIED OUT IN COMPLIANCE WITH A DOCUMENTED QUALITY CONTROL PROCEDURE TO INSURE THAT ALL DISCS ARE RETRIEVED, THAT OPENINGS IN PIPING ARE SMOOTH, THAT SLAG AND OTHER WELDING RESIDUE ARE REMOVED, AND THAT THE INTERNAL DIAMETERS OF PIPING ARE NOT PENETRATED ☐ YES ☐ NO

CUTOUTS (DISCS)	DO YOU CERTIFY THAT YOU HAVE A CONTROL FEATURE TO ENSURE THAT ALL CUTOUTS (DISCS) ARE RETRIEVED? ☐ YES ☐ NO

HYDRAULIC DATA NAMEPLATE	NAME PLATE PROVIDED ☐ YES ☐ NO IF NO, EXPLAIN

REMARKS	DATE LEFT IN SERVICE WITH ALL CONTROL VALVES OPEN:

SIGNATURES	NAME OF SPRINKLER CONTRACTOR		
	TESTS WITNESSED BY		
	FOR PROPERTY OWNER (SIGNED)	TITLE	DATE
	FOR SPRINKLER CONTRACTOR (SIGNED)	TITLE	DATE

ADDITIONAL EXPLANATION AND NOTES

85A BACK

Figure 2-1.2.1 (Continued)   Contractor's Material and Test Certificate for Aboveground Piping.

2-3.2* Water Supply Sources. The following water supply sources are acceptable:

(a) A connection to a reliable water works system with or without a booster pump, as required.

(b) An elevated tank.

(c) A pressure tank installed in accordance with NFPA 13, *Standard for the Installation of Sprinkler Systems*, and NFPA 22, *Standard for Water Tanks for Private Fire Protection*.

(d) A stored water source with an automatically operated pump, installed in accordance with NFPA 20, *Standard for the Installation of Centrifugal Fire Pumps*.

2-3.3 Multipurpose Piping System.

2-3.3.1* A common supply main to the building, serving both sprinklers and domestic uses, shall be acceptable when the domestic design demand is added to the sprinkler system demand.

Exception: Domestic design demand need not be added if provision is made to prevent flow on the domestic water system upon operation of sprinklers.

2-3.3.2 Sprinkler systems with nonfire protection connections shall comply with Section 5-6 of NFPA 13, *Standard for the Installation of Sprinkler Systems*.

2-4 System Components.

2-4.1 Valve and Drains.

2-4.1.1 When a common supply main is used to supply both domestic and sprinkler systems, a single listed control valve shall be provided to shut off both the domestic and sprinkler systems, and a separate shutoff valve shall be provided for the domestic system only. [*See Figure A-2-3.2(a).*]

Exception: The sprinkler system piping may have a separate control valve when supervised by one of the following methods:

(a) Central station, proprietary, or remote station alarm service,

(b) Local alarm service that will cause the sounding of an audible signal at a constantly attended point, or

(c) Locking the valves open.

2-4.1.2 Each sprinkler system shall have a 1-in. (25.4-mm) or larger drain and test connection with valve on the system side of the control valve.

2-4.1.3 Additional ½-in. (13-mm) drains shall be installed for each trapped portion of a dry system that is subject to freezing temperatures.

2-4.2 At least one 1½ in. (38 mm) or 2½ in. (64 mm) fire department connection shall be provided when the sprinkler system has 20 sprinklers or more.

2-4.3 Pressure Gages. Pressure gages shall be provided to indicate pressures on the supply and system sides of main check valves and dry-pipe valves, and to indicate pressure on water supply pressure tanks.

2-4.4 Piping Support. Piping hanging and bracing methods shall comply with NFPA 13, *Standard for the Installation of Sprinkler Systems*.

2-4.5 Sprinklers.

2-4.5.1 Listed residential sprinklers shall be used inside dwelling units. The basis of such a listing shall consist of tests to establish the ability of the sprinklers to control residential fires under standardized fire test conditions. The standardized room fires shall be based on a residential array of furnishings and finishes.

Exception No. 1: Residential sprinklers shall not be used in dry systems unless specifically listed for that purpose.

Exception No. 2: Other types of listed sprinklers may be installed in accordance with their listing in dwelling units meeting the definition of a compartment (as defined in 2-5.1.2.2) provided no more than four sprinklers are located in the dwelling unit and at least one smoke detector is provided in each sleeping room.

2-4.5.2 Ordinary temperature rated sprinklers [135 to 170°F (57 to 77°C)] shall be installed where maximum ambient ceiling temperatures do not exceed 100°F (38°C).

2-4.5.3 Intermediate temperature rated residential sprinklers [175 to 225°F (79 to 107°C)] shall be installed where maximum ambient ceiling temperatures are between 101 and 150°F (38 and 66°C).

2-4.5.4 The following practices shall be observed when installing residential sprinklers, unless maximum expected ambient temperatures are otherwise determined.

(a) Sprinklers under glass or plastic skylights exposed to direct rays of the sun shall be of intermediate temperature classification.

(b) Sprinklers in an unventilated concealed space under an uninsulated roof, or in an unventilated attic, shall be of intermediate temperature classification.

2-4.5.5 When residential sprinklers are installed within a compartment, as defined in 2-5.1.2.2, all sprinklers shall be from the same manufacturer and have the same heat-response element, including temperature rating.

Exception: Different temperature ratings are permitted when required by 2-4.5.4.

2-4.5.6 Standard sprinklers shall be used in areas outside the dwelling unit.

Exception No. 1: Residential sprinklers may be used in adjoining corridors or lobbies with flat, smooth ceilings and a height not exceeding 10 ft (3.0 m).

Exception No. 2: Quick-response sprinklers may be used in accordance with 2-5.2, Exception No. 1.

2-4.5.7 Operated or damaged sprinklers shall be replaced with sprinklers having the same performance characteristics as original equipment.

2-4.5.8 When nonmetallic ceiling plates (escutcheons) are used, they shall be listed. Escutcheon plates used to create a recessed or flush-type sprinkler shall be part of a listed sprinkler assembly.

2-4.5.9 Painting and Ornamental Finishes.

2-4.5.9.1 Sprinkler frames may be factory painted or enameled as ornamental finish in accordance with 2-4.5.9.2; otherwise, sprinklers shall not be painted and any sprinklers that have been painted, except those with factory applied coatings, shall be replaced with new listed sprinklers.

2-4.5.9.2* Ornamental finishes shall not be applied to sprinklers by anyone other than the sprinkler manufacturer, and only sprinklers listed with such finishes shall be used.

2-4.6 Alarms. Local waterflow alarms shall be provided on all sprinkler systems and shall be connected to the building fire alarm system, when provided.

2-5 System Design.

2-5.1 Design Criteria—Inside Dwelling Unit.

2-5.1.1 Design Discharge. The system shall provide a discharge of not less than 18 gpm (68 L/min) to any single operating sprinkler and not less than 13 gpm (49 L/min) per sprinkler to the number of design sprinklers, but not less than the listing of the sprinkler(s).

Exception: Design discharge for sprinklers installed in accordance with Exception No. 2 of 2-4.5.1 shall be in accordance with sprinkler listing criteria.

2-5.1.2* Number of Design Sprinklers.

2-5.1.2.1 The number of design sprinklers shall include all sprinklers within a compartment to a maximum of four sprinklers.

2-5.1.2.2 The definition of compartment for use in 2-5.1.2.1 to determine the number of design sprinklers is a space that is completely enclosed by walls and a ceiling. The compartment enclosure may have openings to an adjoining space if the openings have a minimum lintel depth of 8 in. (203 mm) from the ceiling.

2-5.1.3 Water Demand. The water demand for the system shall be determined by multiplying the design discharge of 2-5.1.1 by the number of design sprinklers of 2-5.1.2.

2-5.1.4 Sprinkler Coverage.

2-5.1.4.1 Residential sprinklers shall be spaced so that the maximum area protected by a single sprinkler does not exceed 144 sq ft (13.4 m²).

2-5.1.4.2 The maximum distance between sprinklers shall not exceed 12 ft (3.7 m) and the maximum distance to a wall or partition shall not exceed 6 ft (1.8 m).

2-5.1.4.3 The minimum distance between sprinklers within a compartment shall be 8 ft (2.4 m).

2-5.1.5 The minimum operating pressure of any sprinkler shall be in accordance with the listing information of the sprinkler and shall provide the minimum flow rates specified in 2-5.1.1.

2-5.1.6 Application rates, design areas, areas of coverage, and minimum design pressures other than those specified in 2-5.1.1, 2-5.1.2, 2-5.1.4, and 2-5.1.5 may be used with special sprinklers that have been listed for such specific residential installation conditions.

2-5.1.7 Position of Residential Sprinklers.

2-5.1.7.1 Pendent and upright sprinklers shall be positioned so that the deflectors are within 1 to 4 in. (25.4 to 102 mm) from the ceiling.

Exception: Special residential sprinklers shall be installed in accordance with the listing limitations.

2-5.1.7.2 Sidewall sprinklers shall be positioned so that the deflectors are within 4 to 6 in. (102 to 152 mm) from the ceiling.

Exception: Special residential sprinklers shall be installed in accordance with the listing limitations.

2-5.1.7.3* Sprinklers shall be positioned so that the response time and discharge are not unduly affected by obstructions such as ceiling slope, beams, or light fixtures.

2-5.2 Design Criteria—Outside Dwelling Unit. The design discharge, number of design sprinklers, water demand of the system, sprinkler coverage, and position of sprinklers for areas to be sprinklered outside the dwelling unit shall comply with specifications in NFPA 13, *Standard for the Installation of Sprinkler Systems.*

Exception No. 1: When compartmented into areas of 500 sq ft (46 m²) or less by 30-minute fire-rated construction, and the area is protected by standard or quick-response sprinklers not exceeding 130 sq ft (12 m²) per sprinkler, the system demand may be limited to the number of sprinklers in the compartment area, but not less than a total of four sprinklers. Openings from the compartments need not be protected provided such openings are provided with a lintel at least 8 in. (203 mm) in depth and the total area of such openings does not exceed 50 sq ft (4.6 m²) for each compartment. Discharge density shall be appropriate for the hazard classification as determined by NFPA 13.

Exception No. 2: Lobbies, in other than hotels and motels, foyers, corridors, and halls outside the dwelling unit, with flat, smooth ceilings and not exceeding 10 ft (3.0 m) in height, may be protected with residential sprinklers, with a maximum system demand of four sprinklers.

2-5.3 Pipe Sizing. Piping shall be sized in accordance with hydraulic calculation procedures to comply with NFPA 13, *Standard for the Installation of Sprinkler Systems.*

2-6 Location of Sprinklers. Sprinklers shall be installed in all areas.

Exception No. 1: Sprinklers may be omitted from bathrooms not exceeding 55 sq ft (5.1 m²) with noncombustible plumbing fixtures.

Exception No. 2: Sprinklers may be omitted from small clothes closets where the least dimension does not exceed 3 ft (0.9 m) and the area does not exceed 24 sq ft (2.2 m²) and the walls and ceiling are surfaced with noncombustible or limited combustible materials as defined by NFPA 220, Standard on Types of Building Construction.

Exception No. 3: Sprinklers may be omitted from open attached: porches, balconies, corridors, and stairs.

Exception No. 4: Sprinklers may be omitted from attics, penthouse equipment rooms, crawl spaces, floor/ceiling spaces, elevator shafts, and other concealed spaces that are not used or intended for living purposes or storage.

2-7* Maintenance. The owner is responsible for the condition of a sprinkler system and shall keep the system in normal operating condition.

Chapter 3   Referenced Publications

3-1 The following documents or portions thereof are referenced within this standard and shall be considered part of the requirements of this document. The edition indicated for each reference is the current edition as of the date of the NFPA issuance of this document.

3-1.1 NFPA Publications. National Fire Protection Association, Batterymarch Park, Quincy, MA 02269.

NFPA 13-1989, *Standard for the Installation of Sprinkler Systems*

NFPA 20-1987, *Standard for the Installation of Centrifugal Fire Pumps*

NFPA 22-1987, *Standard for Water Tanks for Private Fire Protection*

NFPA 74-1989, *Standard for the Installation, Maintenance, and Use of Household Fire Warning Equipment*

NFPA 101®-1988, *Life Safety Code®*

NFPA 220-1985, *Standard on Types of Building Construction.*

3-1.2 Other Publications.

3-1.2.1 ANSI Publications. American National Standards Institute, Inc., 1430 Broadway, New York, NY 10018.

ANSI B16.1-1975, *Cast Iron Pipe Flanges and Flanged Fittings, Class 25, 125, 250 and 800*

ANSI B16.3-1985, *Malleable Iron Threaded Fittings, Class 150 and 300*

ANSI B16.4-1985, *Cast Iron Threaded Fittings, Classes 125 and 250*

ANSI B16.5-1981, *Pipe Flanges and Flanged Fittings*

ANSI B16.9-1986, *Factory-Made Wrought Steel Buttwelding Fittings*

ANSI B16.11-1980, *Forged Steel Fittings, Socket-Welding and Threaded*

ANSI B16.18-1984, *Cast Copper Alloy Solder Joint Pressure Fittings*

ANSI B16.22-1980, *Wrought Copper and Copper Alloy Solder Joint Pressure Fittings*

ANSI B16.25-1986, *Buttwelding Ends*

ANSI B36.10M-1985, *Welded and Seamless Wrought Steel Pipe.*

3-1.2.2 ASTM Publications. American Society for Testing and Materials, 1916 Race Street, Philadelphia, PA 19103.

ASTM A53-1987, *Standard Specification for Pipe, Steel, Black and Hot-Dipped, Zinc-Coated Welded and Seamless Steel Pipe*

ASTM A135-1986, *Standard Specification for Electric-Resistance-Welded Steel Pipe*

ASTM A234-1987, *Standard Specification for Piping Fittings of Wrought-Carbon Steel and Alloy Steel for Moderate and Elevated Temperatures*

ASTM A795-1985, *Specification for Black and Hot-Dipped Zinc-Coated (Galvanized) Welded and Seamless Steel Pipe for Fire Protection Use*

ASTM B32-1987, *Standard Specification for Solder Metal, 95-5 (Tin-Antimony-Grade 95TA)*

ASTM B88-1986, *Standard Specification for Seamless Copper Water Tube*

ASTM B251-1987, *Standard Specification for General Requirements for Wrought Seamless Copper and Copper-Alloy Tube*

ASTM E380-1986, *Standard for Metric Practice.*

3-1.2.3 AWS Publication. American Welding Society, 2501 N.W. 7th Street, Miami, FL 33125.

AWS A5.8-1981, *Specification for Brazing Filler Metal.*

Appendix A

This Appendix is not a part of the requirements of this NFPA document, but is included for information purposes only.

A-1-1 NFPA 13R is appropriate for use only in residential occupancies, as an option to NFPA 13, *Standard for the Installation of Sprinkler Systems*, as defined in this standard, up to four stories in height. Residential portions of any other building may be protected with residential sprinklers in accordance with 3-11.2.9 of NFPA 13, *Standard for the Installation of Sprinkler Systems*. Other portions of such sections should be protected in accordance with NFPA 13.

The criteria in this standard are based on full-scale fire tests of rooms containing typical furnishings found in residential living rooms, kitchens, and bedrooms. The furnishings were arranged as typically found in dwelling units in a manner similar to that shown in Figures A-1-1(a), (b), and (c). Sixty full-scale fire tests were conducted in a two-story dwelling in Los Angeles, California, and 16 tests were conducted in a 14-ft (4.3-m) wide mobile home in Charlotte, North Carolina. Sprinkler systems designed and installed according to this standard are expected to prevent flashover within the compartment of origin if sprinklers are installed in the compartment. A sprinkler system designed and installed according to this standard may not, however, be expected to control a fire involving unusually higher average fuel loads than typical for dwelling units [10 psi (0.7 bar)], configurations of fuels other than those with typical residential occupancies, or conditions where the interior finish has an unusually high flame spread rating (greater than 225).

To be effective, sprinkler systems installed in accordance with this standard must have the sprinklers closest to the fire open before the fire exceeds the ability of the sprinkler discharge to extinguish or control that fire. Conditions that allow the fire to grow beyond that point before sprinkler activation or that interfere with the quality of water distribution can produce conditions beyond the capabilities of the sprinkler system described in this standard. Unusually high ceilings or ceiling configurations that tend to divert the rising hot gases from sprinkler locations or change the sprinkler discharge pattern from its standard pattern can produce fire conditions that cannot be extinguished or controlled by the systems described in this standard.

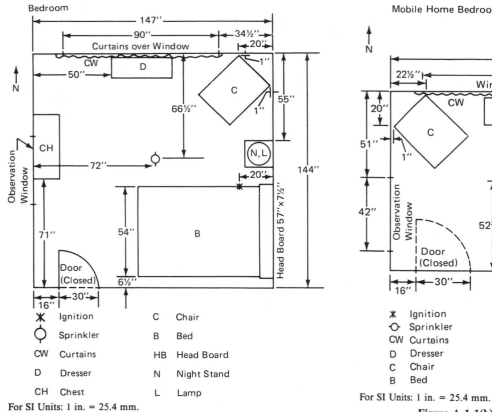

For SI Units: 1 in. = 25.4 mm.

Figure A-1-1(a) Bedroom.

✳ Ignition   C Chair
○ Sprinkler   B Bed
CW Curtains   HB Head Board
D Dresser   N Night Stand
CH Chest   L Lamp

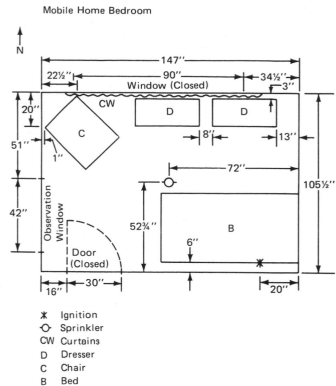

For SI Units: 1 in. = 25.4 mm.

Figure A-1-1(b) Mobile Home Bedroom.

✳ Ignition
○ Sprinkler
CW Curtains
D Dresser
C Chair
B Bed

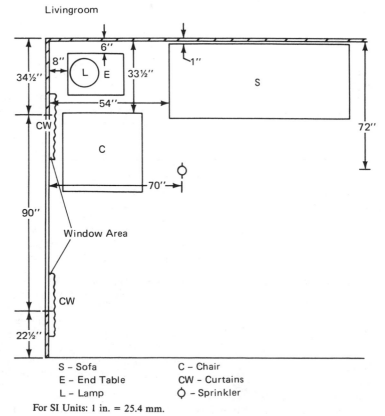

S – Sofa   C – Chair
E – End Table   CW – Curtains
L – Lamp   ○ – Sprinkler

For SI Units: 1 in. = 25.4 mm.

Figure A-1-1(c) Living Room.

Table A-1-2
Annual Averages of Deaths and Injuries in Apartments
1980-1984

Fires–123,000	Civilian Deaths–930		Civilian Injuries–5,470
	Percentages by Area of Origin		
Area of Origin (901 Code)	**Civilian Deaths (Used for Ranking)**	**Fires**	**Civilian Injuries**
Living room, den, lounge (14)	38.5	11.3	23.2
Bedroom (21-22)	28.7	17.4	27.1
Kitchen (24)	9.8	35.3	27.2
Hallway corridor (101)	4.3	3.2	3.4
Interior stairway (03)	3.2	1.0	1.1
Structural Area (70-79)	3.1	8.1	3.5
[Balcony, porch (72)]	(1.2)	(1.3)	(0.7)
[Unspecified (79)]	(1.0)	(0.5)	(0.2)
[Ceiling/Roof assembly (74)]	(0.3)	(0.7)	(0.3)
Lobby (05)	1.3	0.6	0.7
Dining room (23)	1.2	0.8	1.0
Closet (42)	1.2	1.9	1.9
Balcony, porch (72)	1.2	1.3	0.7
Other known single area	4.1	17.8	8.8
[Bathroom (25)]	(0.6)	(2.1)	(1.3)
Multiple areas (97)	1.6	0.7	0.9
Unclassified, not applicable (98-99)	1.8	0.6	0.5
Total:	100.0	100.0	100.0

A-1-2 Levels of Protection. Various levels of sprinkler protection are available to provide life safety and property protection. The standard is designed to provide a high, but not absolute, level of life safety and a lesser level of property protection. Greater protection to both life and property could be achieved by sprinklering all areas in accordance with NFPA 13, *Standard for the Installation of Sprinkler Systems*, which permits the use of residential sprinklers in residential areas.

This standard recommends, but does not require, sprinklering of all areas in the building; it permits sprinklers to be omitted in certain areas. These areas are the ones shown by NFPA statistics to be ones where the incidence of life loss from fires in residential occupancies is low. Such an approach provides a reasonable degree of fire safety to life. (*See Table A-1-2 for Deaths and Injuries in Multifamily Residential Buildings.*)

It should be recognized that the omission of sprinklers from certain areas could result in the development of untenable conditions in adjacent spaces. Where evacuation times may be delayed, additional sprinkler protection and other fire protection features, such as detection and compartmentation, may be necessary.

A-2-1.3.2 Testing of a system can be accomplished by filling the system with water and checking visually for leakage at each joint or coupling.

Fire department connections are not required for all systems covered by this standard, but may be installed at the discretion of the owner. In these cases, hydrostatic tests in accordance with NFPA 13, *Standard for the Installation of Sprinkler Systems*, are required.

Dry systems should also be tested by placing the system under air pressure. Any leak that results in a drop in system pressure greater than 2 psi (0.14 bar) in 24 hours should be corrected. Check for leaks using soapy water brushed on each joint or coupling. Leaks will be shown by the presence of bubbles. This test should be made prior to concealing of piping.

A-2-2.1.1 At least three spare sprinklers of each type, temperature rating, and orifice size used in the system should be kept on the premises. When fused sprinklers are replaced by the owner, fire department, or others, care should be taken to assure that the replacement sprinkler has the same operating characteristics.

A-2-3.2 Connection for fire protection to city mains is often subject to local regulation concerning metering and backflow prevention requirements. Preferred and acceptable water supply arrangements are shown in Figures A-2-3.2(a), (b), and (c). When a meter must be used between the city water main and the sprinkler system supply, an acceptable arrangement is shown in Figure A-2-3.2(c). Under these circumstances, the flow characteristics of the meter must be included in the hydraulic calculation of the system. When a tank is used for both domestic and fire protection purposes, a low water alarm acuated when the water level falls below 110 percent of the minimum quantity specified in 2-3.1 should be provided.

A-2-3.3.1 The tables on the following page can be used to determine a domestic design demand. Using Table A-2-3.3.1(a), determine the total number of water supply fixture units downstream of any point in the piping serving both sprinkler and domestic needs. Using Table A-2-3.3.1(b), determine the appropriate total flow allowance, and add this flow to the sprinkler demand at the total pressure required for the sprinkler system at that point.

A-2-4.5.9.2 Decorative painting of a residential sprinkler is not to be confused with the temperature identification

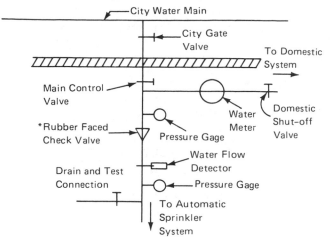

Figure A-2-3.2(a) Preferable Arrangement.

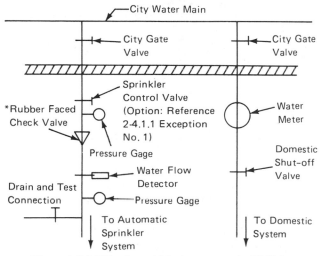

Figure A-2-3.2(b) Acceptable Arrangement with Valve Supervision. (*See 2-4.1.1 Exception.*)

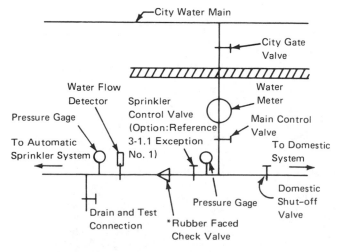

*Rubber Faced Check Valves Optional.

Figure A-2-3.2(c) Acceptable Arrangement with Valve Supervision. (*See 2-4.1.1 Exception.*)

Table A-2-3.3.1(a)   Fixture Load Values

Private facilities (within individual dwelling units)	Unit
Bathroom group with flush tank (including lavatory, water closet, and bathtub with shower)	6
Bathroom group with flush valve	8
Bathtub	2
Dishwasher	1
Kitchen sink	2
Laundry trays	3
Lavatory	1
Shower stall	2
Washing machine	2
Water closet with flush valve	6
Water closet with flush tank	3

Public Facilities	
Bathtub	4
Drinking fountain	0
Kitchen sink	4
Lavatory	2
Service sink	3
Shower head	4
Urinal with 1 in. flush valve	10
Urinal with ¾ in. flush valve	5
Urinal with flush tank	3
Washing machine (8 lb)	3
Washing machine (16 lb)	4
Water closet with flush valve	10
Water closet with flush tank	5

Table A-2-3.3.1(b)   Total Estimated Domestic Demand

Total Fixture Load Units [from Table A-2-3.3.1(a)]	Total Demand in Gallons Per Minute For Systems with Predominantly Flush Tanks	For Systems with Predominantly Flush Valves
1	3 gpm	
2	5	
5	10	15 gpm
10	15	25
20	20	35
35	25	45
50	30	50
70	35	60
100	45	70
150	55	80
200	65	90
250	75	100
350	100	125
500	125	150
750	175	175
1000	200	200
1500	275	275
2000	325	325
3500	500	500

colors as referenced in 3-11.6 of NFPA 13, *Standard for the Installation of Sprinkler Systems.*

A-2-5.1.2   It is intended that the design area is to include up to four adjacent sprinklers producing the greatest water demand within the compartment.

A-2-5.1.7.3   Fire testing has indicated the need to wet walls in the area protected by residential sprinklers at a level

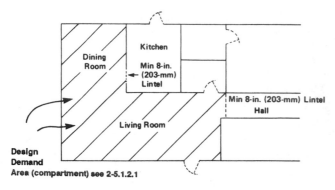

Figure A-2-5.1.2(a) Sprinkler Design Areas for Typical Residential Occupancy.

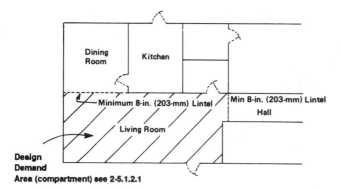

Figure A-2-5.1.2(b) Sprinkler Design Areas for Typical Residential Occupancy.

closer to the ceiling than that accomplished by standard sprinkler distribution. Where beams, light fixtures, sloped ceilings, and other obstructions occur, additional residential sprinklers may be necessary to achieve proper response and distribution, and a greater water supply may be necessary.

Table A-2-5.1.7.3 and Figure A-2-5.1.7.3 provide guidance for location of sprinklers near ceiling obstructions.

Table A-2-5.1.7.3   Maximum Distance from Sprinkler Deflector to Bottom of Ceiling Obstruction

Distance from Sprinkler to Side of Ceiling Obstruction	Maximum Distance from Sprinkler Deflector to Bottom of Ceiling Obstruction
Less than 6 in.	Not permitted
6 in. to less than 1 ft	0 in.
1 ft to less than 2 ft	1 in.
2 ft to less than 2 ft 6 in.	2 in.
2 ft 6 in. to less than 3 ft	3 in.
3 ft to less than 3 ft 6 in.	4 in.
3 ft 6 in. to less than 4 ft	6 in.
4 ft to less than 4 ft 6 in.	7 in.
4 ft 6 in. to less than 5 ft	9 in.
5 ft to less than 5 ft 6 in.	11 in.
5 ft 6 in. to less than 6 ft	14 in.

For SI Units: 1 in. = 25.4 mm; 1 ft = 0.3048 m.

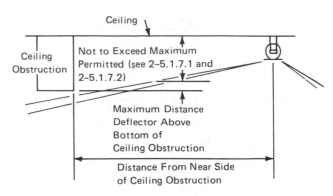

Figure A-2-5.1.7.3 Position of Deflector, Upright or Pendent, When Located Above Bottom of Ceiling Obstruction.

A-2-7   The responsibility for properly maintaining a sprinkler system is the obligation of the owner or manager, who should understand the sprinkler system operation. A minimum monthly maintenance program should include the following:

(a) Visual inspection of all sprinklers to ensure against obstruction of spray.

(b) Inspection of all valves to assure that they are open.

(c) Testing of all waterflow devices.

(d) Testing of the alarm system, if installed.

NOTE: When it appears likely that the test will result in a response of the fire department, notification to the fire department should be made prior to the test.

(e) Operation of pumps, where employed, should be operated. See NFPA 20, *Standard for the Installation of Centrifugal Fire Pumps.*

(f) Checking of the pressure of air used with dry systems.

(g) Checking of water level in tanks.

Table A-2-7
Inspection, Testing, and Maintenance Requirements

Component	Activity	Frequency	Reference
Control Valve	Inspection	Monthly	
	Maintenance	Annually	NFPA 13A, 2-7.1.4
Main Drain Valve	Flow Test	Annually	NFPA 13A, 2-6.1
Inspectors' Test Valve	Flow Test	Annually	
Waterflow Alarm	Flow Test	Annually	NFPA 13A, 4-5.3, 4-7.1
Sprinklers	Test	50 Yrs.	NFPA 13A, 3-3.3
Sprinklers, Res/QR	Test	20 Yrs.	NFPA 13A, 3-3.4
Pump	Flow Test	Annually	NFPA 13A, 2-4.2.5
Antifreeze Solutions	Test	Annually	NFPA 13A, 4-7.3

(h) Care should be taken to see that sprinklers are not painted either at the time of installation or during subsequent redecoration. When painting sprinkler piping or painting in areas next to sprinklers, the sprinklers may be protected by covering with a bag, which should be removed immediately after painting is finished.

For further information see NFPA 13A, *Recommended Practice for the Inspection, Testing and Maintenance of Sprinkler Systems.*

Appendix B   Referenced Publications

B-1 The following documents or portions thereof are referenced within this standard for informational purposes only and thus are not considered part of the requirements of this document. The edition indicated for each reference is the current edition as of the date of the NFPA issuance of this document.

B-1.1 NFPA Publications.   National Fire Protection Association, Batterymarch Park, Quincy, MA 02269.

NFPA 13-1989, *Standard for the Installation of Sprinkler Systems*

NFPA 13A-1987, *Recommended Practice for the Inspection, Testing and Maintenance of Sprinkler Systems*

NFPA 20-1987, *Standard for the Installation of Centrifugal Fire Pumps.*

UNIFORM BUILDING CODE STANDARD 10-1
POWER-OPERATED EGRESS DOORS
Test Standard of the International Conference of Building Officials
See Sections 1001.2 and 1003.3.1.2, *Uniform Building Code*

SECTION 10.101 — SCOPE

10.101.1 General. These requirements and methods of test apply to power-operated swinging doors and combination sliding and swinging doors intended for installation in locations where conforming exits are required by Chapter 10.

10.101.2 Operators and Activators. Power-operated doors may be provided with air, hydraulic or electric operators actuated from a floor, activating carpet, photoelectric device or other approved signaling device.

10.101.3 Fire Door Assemblies. Power-operated doors intended for installation in openings where fire door assemblies are required shall, in addition to the requirements of this standard, be tested in accordance with Fire Tests of Door Assemblies, UBC Standard 7-2.

SECTION 10.102 — GENERAL

10.102.1 Panic Hardware. Power-operated doors intended for installation in openings where panic hardware is required shall be tested with panic hardware on the doors.

10.102.2 Opening Degree. When manually operated in the direction of egress, leaves of swinging doors or swing-out sections of sliding doors shall swing open to not less than 90 degrees from the closed position.

10.102.3 Locking Mechanisms. Locking mechanisms on doors intended for locations which do not require panic hardware shall be of a type readily identified as locked, and the doors shall be posted with durable, permanent signs reading THESE DOORS MUST REMAIN UNLOCKED DURING BUSINESS HOURS. Signs shall be 1-inch-high (25.4 mm) block letters on a contrasting background. Signs shall be located on the header framing.

10.102.4 Swinging and Sliding Doors. Each swing-out leaf of swinging or sliding doors with swinging sections shall be provided with durable signs in not less than 1-inch (25.4 mm) block letters on a contrasting background reading, IN EMERGENCY PUSH TO OPEN, or other approved wording. The sign shall be located at the closing edge of the door not less than 36 inches (914 mm) nor more than 60 inches (1524 mm) above the floor. The sign shall read horizontally and may be in two lines.

10.102.5 Electrical Wiring and Devices. Electrical wiring, electrical devices and controls shall be of a type tested and approved by the building official.

10.102.6 Testing. Doors with power operators shall be examined and tested by an approved testing agency.

10.102.7 Test Report. The test report shall contain engineering data and drawings, size and weight of door tested, wiring diagrams of electrical control systems, schematic drawings of mechanical controls and operating manuals. The report shall describe the mechanical operation of the power operator in sequence as the door opens and closes under normal and emergency conditions. The report shall set forth the tests performed in accordance with the provisions of this standard and the results thereof. Additionally, the report shall contain an analysis comparing each feature of the design against the performance test procedures contained herein.

10.102.8 Simulated Installation and Test Equipment. Doors with power operators shall be installed in a simulated wall and door framing assembly in accordance with the manufacturer's instructions. The test specimen shall not be less than 3 feet wide (914 mm) by 7 feet high (2134 mm). A motor-driven or suitable mechanism shall be used to actuate the activating carpet. The rate of operation or number of cycles shall be three to five per minute. On sliding doors with a swing-out section, additional operating endurance tests shall be conducted. A motor-driven mechanism or other approved means shall be used to push the swinging door section open and pull the swinging section closed at a rate of three to five cycles per minute, so that the latching mechanism and disconnect switches operate as in service. During the test the door specimen shall have only the lubrication which is provided by the manufacturer at the factory, or as may be recommended in the manufacturer's installation instructions.

10.102.9 Endurance Tests. The power operator shall function as intended to open and close the door for 100,000 cycles of operation without failure or excessive wear of parts. The release mechanisms and disconnect switches of the swinging section in sliding doors shall function as intended for 250 cycles of operation without failure or excessive wear of parts. The opening and closing forces, and the speed of opening and closing, shall be recorded at the start of the endurance tests and shall again be recorded at the end of the endurance tests. Opening and closing forces at the beginning and at the end of the endurance test shall not exceed the maximum forces prescribed in these test procedures.

SECTION 10.103 — SWINGING DOORS

10.103.1 Opening Size. Each door opening, when the door is in the 90-degree open position, shall provide a clear opening width of not less than 32 inches (813 mm), with no single leaf less than 24 inches (610 mm) in width.

10.103.2 Doors in Pairs. Doors in pairs shall be equipped with a separate operator for each leaf unless tests with a tandem operator with one leaf jammed in a closed and in a partially open position indicates that the second leaf continues to operate or is free to swing into the open position without exceeding the maximum permitted manual opening pressures. On doors with mechanical controls, one mechanism shall be subjected to fault conditions; during the fault condition, the second leaf shall be openable manually without exceeding the maximum permitted opening pressure.

10.103.3 Closing Mechanism. Normal closing of doors shall be by spring action, pressure-operated mechanism or electrically driven mechanism. The closing force measured at the closing stile shall not exceed 40 pounds (178 N) at any point in the closing arc. The time of final 10 degrees of closing shall not be less than one and one-half seconds.

10.103.4 Operation. Each possible fault condition that affects the power supply shall be introduced into the door and power operator assembly. Under each fault condition, single doors and each leaf of doors in pairs shall open to the 90-degree position with an applied pressure at the normal location of the push plate not exceeding 40 pounds (178 N).

10.103.5 In-swinging Doors. Power-operated in-swinging doors are not recognized for determining exit width opening required to swing in the direction of egress.

10.103.6 Activating Carpets and Safety Mats. Activating carpets and safety mats shall comply with the following provisions:

1. When carpets are used as the activating device, they shall have a width not less than 10 inches (254 mm) less than the clear width of the door opening with the center line of the carpet in the center line of the door opening. The width shall be measured between the exposed edges of the carpet tread surface excluding molded edge bevels or edge trim.

2. The length of activating carpets shall not be less than 42 inches (1067 mm). The length of activating carpets for doors exceeding 42 inches (1067 mm) in width shall not be less than 56 inches (1422 mm). The length shall be measured from the center line of the door pivot to the exposed edge of the carpet tread surface excluding molded edge bevels or edge trim.

3. Doors serving one-way traffic only shall be provided with a safety mat having a length not less than the width of the widest leaf. A safety mat is one that will prevent the door from opening if there is pressure on the safety mat before pressure is applied to the activating mat, and one that will prevent the door from closing following normal door actuation until pressure on the safety mat is removed.

4. Doors serving both egress and ingress shall have a series of joined carpets on the swing side of the door arranged as follows:

   4.1 One safety carpet or mat nearest to the door at least as long as the width of the door leaf;

   4.2 One or more activating carpets to provide a total carpet length on the swing side of not less than two and one-half times the width of the widest door leaf.

SECTION 10.104 — SLIDING DOORS

10.104.1 General. Sliding doors shall comply with the following provisions:

1. Sliding leaves of sliding doors shall be provided with swinging sections arranged to swing in the direction of egress when pressure is applied at the location of normal push plates or on the crossbar of panic hardware on doors where panic hardware is required.

2. Operation of the swinging section shall disconnect the sliding door power operator.

3. Permanent stops shall be provided to prevent double swing.

4. Location of the breakaway tension adjustment, opening and closing speed adjustment, opening and closing snub speed adjustments, opening and closing power pressure adjustments, and similar controls shall be concealed and not readily accessible where they may be subject to tampering.

5. Doors shall be suspended from an overhead track. Operators and control levers or mechanisms shall be guarded.

10.104.2 Closing Mechanism. The closing force of sliding doors at 24 inches (610 mm) of opening shall not exceed 30 pounds (133 N) with a closing speed not in excess of 1.5 feet (457 mm) per second.

10.104.3 Opening Width. The minimum clear width of the door opening with the swinging section or sections in the 90-degree open position shall not be less than 32 inches (813 mm) with no single leaf less than 24 inches (610 mm) in width.

10.104.4 Opening Forces. The swinging section in sliding doors shall swing open into the full open position when an opening force not exceeding 40 pounds (178 N) is applied at the normal push plate location or on the crossbar of panic hardware.

10.104.5 Fault Condition Introduced. Under each possible fault condition that affects the power supply and with the sliding leaf or leaves retracted one half the leaf width into its or their pocket, each swinging section shall open to the 90-degree position with an applied pressure at the normal location of the push plate not exceeding 40 pounds (178 N).

10.104.6 Sliding Doors without Swing-out Section. Power-operated sliding doors which are not provided with a swing-out section may be evaluated for conformance to the mechanical requirements and endurance tests provided in this standard. Power-operated sliding doors which are not provided with a swing-out section shall not be listed for use in locations where required exits are specified by this code.

10.104.7 Activating Carpets and Safety Mats. Activating carpets and safety mats shall conform to Section 10.103.5.

SECTION 10.105 — MARKING

The name of the manufacturer, or trademark by which the manufacturer can be readily identified, shall be legibly marked on the operating equipment where it can be seen after installation. The type, model number or letter designation identifying the product as a listed device shall be provided on a label attached in a location as indicated in its listing.

UNIFORM BUILDING CODE STANDARD 10-2
STAIRWAY IDENTIFICATION
Specification Standard of the International Conference of Building Officials
See Sections 1001.2 and 1003.3.3.13, *Uniform Building Code*

SECTION 10.201 — SCOPE

Signs to provide information to the occupants and fire department personnel to ensure that they do not become confused during emergencies shall be installed in accordance with this standard.

SECTION 10.202 — GENERAL

Standardized signs shall be installed in stairways when the building is four or more stories in height. The signs shall identify each stair landing and indicate the upper and lower termination of the stairway.

SECTION 10.203 — SIGN DETAILS

10.203.1 Size. Signs shall be a minimum 12 inches (305 mm) by 12 inches (305 mm).

10.203.2 Stairway Location. The stairway location, such as STAIR NO. 1 or WEST STAIR, shall be placed at the top of the sign in 1-inch-high (25.4 mm) block lettering with $1/4$-inch (6.4 mm) strokes.

10.203.3 Upper Terminus. The stairway's upper terminus, such as ROOF ACCESS or NO ROOF ACCESS, shall be placed under the stairway identification in 1-inch-high (25.4 mm) block lettering with $1/4$-inch (6.4 mm) strokes.

10.203.4 Floor Level Number. The floor level number shall be placed in the middle of the sign in 5-inch-high (127 mm) lettering with $3/4$-inch (19 mm) strokes. The mezzanine levels shall have the letter "M" preceding the floor number. Basement levels shall have the letter "B" preceding the floor number.

10.203.5 Lower Terminus. The lower and upper terminus of the stairway shall be placed at the bottom of the sign in 1-inch-high (25.4 mm) block lettering with $1/4$-inch (6.4 mm) strokes.

Examples:

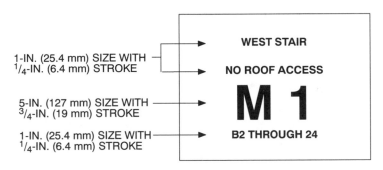

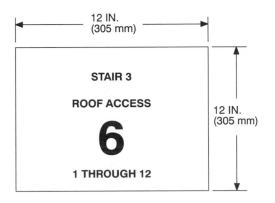

UNIFORM BUILDING CODE STANDARD 10-3

EXIT LADDER DEVICE

Test Standard of the International Conference of Building Officials

See Appendix Section 3407.1, *Uniform Building Code*

SECTION 10.301 — SCOPE

This standard for exit ladder devices is applicable where such devices are permitted by the building official for installation on existing apartment houses and hotels in conformance with Appendix Section 3412.1 of this code.

SECTION 10.302 — INSTRUCTIONS

Installation shall be in accordance with the manufacturer's instructions. Instructions shall be illustrated and shall include directions and information adequate for attaining proper and safe installation of the product. Where exit ladder devices are intended for mounting on different support surfaces, specific installation instructions shall be provided for each surface.

SECTION 10.303 — GENERAL DESIGN

All load-bearing surfaces and supporting hardware shall be of noncombustible materials. Exit ladder devices shall have a minimum width of 12 inches (305 mm) when in the position intended for use. The design load shall not be less than 400 pounds (1780 N) for 16-foot (4877 mm) length and 600 pounds (2669 N) for 25-foot (7620 mm) length.

SECTION 10.304 — PERFORMANCE

10.304.1 Exit ladder devices shall be capable of withstanding an applied load of four times the design load when installed in the manner intended for use. Test loads shall be applied for a period of one hour.

10.304.2 Exit ladder devices of the retractable type shall, in addition to the static load requirements of Section 10.304.1, be capable of withstanding the following tests:

1. Rung strength.
2. Rung-to-side-rail shear strength.
3. Release mechanism.
4. Low temperature.

SECTION 10.305 — RUNG-STRENGTH TEST

Rungs of retractable exit ladder devices shall be capable of withstanding a load of 1,000 pounds (4448 N) when applied to a $3^1/_2$-inch-wide (89 mm) block resting at the center of the rung. The test load shall be applied for a period of one hour. The ladder shall remain operational following this test.

SECTION 10.306 — RUNG-TO-SIDE-RAIL SHEAR TEST

Rungs of retractable exit ladder devices shall be capable of withstanding a load of 1,000 pounds (4448 N) when applied to a $3^1/_2$-inch-wide (89 mm) block resting on the center rung as near the side rail as possible. The test load shall be applied for a period of one hour. Upon removal of the test load the fasteners attaching the rung to the side rail shall show no evidence of failure. The ladder shall remain operational following this test.

SECTION 10.307 — RELEASE MECHANISM TEST

The release mechanism of retractable exit ladder devices shall operate with an average applied force of not more than 5 pounds (22.2 N) for hand-operated releasing mechanisms and an average applied force of not more than 25 pounds (111 N) for foot-pedal types of releasing mechanisms. For these tests, a force gauge shall be applied to the release mechanism, and the average of three consecutive readings shall be computed.

SECTION 10.308 — LOW TEMPERATURE OPERATION TEST

Representative samples of the exit ladder device shall be subjected to a temperature of –40°C in an environmental chamber for a period of 24 hours. The release mechanism shall be operated immediately upon removal from the chamber. The ladder device shall function as intended without any restriction of operation.

UNIFORM BUILDING CODE STANDARD 10-4
PANIC HARDWARE

Based on Standard 305, July 30, 1979, of the Underwriters Laboratories Inc.

See Sections 1001.2 and 1003.3.1.9, *Uniform Building Code*

SECTION 10.401 — SCOPE

10.401.1 General. These requirements cover releasing devices actuated by a crossbar for outward-opening doors designed to facilitate the safe egress of persons from buildings in the event of panic or other emergency.

10.401.2 Installation. A copy of the operating and installation instructions or equivalent information is to be furnished with the samples submitted for investigation for use as a guide in the examination and test of the mechanism. For this purpose a printed edition is not required.

SECTION 10.402 — CONSTRUCTION

10.402.1 Assembly. The mechanism shall be of a type which can be readily maintained in proper operating condition.

The mechanism shall be designed so as to release the door latch or latches when pressure is applied to the release bar in the direction of exit travel.

The ends of the release bar shall be curved, guarded or otherwise designed to prevent them from catching on the clothing of persons during exit.

The release mechanism shall not depend on springs to open the door latch or latches.

A locking or dogging device provided as part of the mechanism shall not prevent release of the door latch or latches when pressure is applied to the release bar in the direction of exit travel.

A dead-locking bolt shall not be employed unless it is released by the action of the release bar.

The projection of the release bar when in the depressed position shall not unduly restrict the exit opening.

10.402.2 Materials. The materials employed shall have adequate mechanical strength to perform their intended function. A metal or alloy shall have a solidus point not less than 1,000°F (538°C).

The materials employed shall minimize the likelihood of the release mechanism becoming inoperative due to corrosion.

SECTION 10.403 — PERFORMANCE

10.403.1 Endurance Test. The release mechanism and latches shall function as intended for 100,000 cycles of operation without failure or excessive wear of the parts.

The assembly is to be installed on a simulated door and frame assembly in accordance with the manufacturer's instructions. A motor-driven mechanism is to actuate the release bar so as to release the latches and push the door open, as in service. The rate of operation is to be approximately 30 cycles of operation per minute. For this test, the assembly is to have the lubrication which is provided at the factory or recommended by the manufacturer.

10.403.2 Emergency Operation Test. The release mechanism shall be so designed that a horizontal force of 15 pounds (67 N) or less will actuate the release bar and latches. When the latched door is subjected to outward pressure as described below, a force of 50 pounds (222 N) or less shall actuate the release bar.

The sample is to be subjected to the 15-pound (67 N) test before and after the endurance test and subjected to the 50-pound (222 N) test after the endurance test.

A horizontal force of 250 pounds (1112 N) is to be applied against the latching edge adjacent to the latch in the direction in which the door opens. A spring scale or similar means is to be used to measure the horizontal force which is applied against the center of the release bar.

For double doors, a horizontal force of 250 pounds (1112 N) is to be applied against the midpoint of the outer stile of each door.

The release bar is not to be deformed by the test, and a spacing of at least 1 inch (25.4 mm) is to be provided between the release bar and the door face when the horizontal force is applied against the center of the release bar.

SECTION 10.404 — MARKING

The manufacturer's or vendor's name and a distinctive type of model designation shall be plainly marked on the release-bar assembly.

If a manufacturer produces panic hardware assemblies at more than one factory, each such assembly shall have a distinctive marking or identifying symbol to identify it as the product of a particular factory.

UNIFORM BUILDING CODE STANDARD 14-1
KRAFT WATERPROOF BUILDING PAPER
Based on Federal Specification UU-B-790a (February 5, 1968)
See Sections 601.3, 711.1, 1401.2 and 1402.1, *Uniform Building Code*

SECTION 14.101 — SCOPE

This standard covers building papers composed predominantly of sulfate pulp fibers intended for use as a weather-resistive barrier.

SECTION 14.102 — CLASSIFICATION

The building papers shall be of Type I and not less than the following grades:

Grade A—High water-vapor resistance.

Grade B—Moderate water-vapor resistance.

Grade C—Water resistant.

Grade D—Water-vapor permeable.

Style 1a—Uncreped, not reinforced.

Style 1b—Uncreped, not reinforced, red rosin sized.

Style 2—Uncreped, not reinforced, saturated.

Style 3—Creped one direction, not reinforced.

Style 4—Uncreped, reinforced.

SECTION 14.103 — GENERAL REQUIREMENTS

14.103.1 Description. The paper shall be either a single-ply or a multi-ply lamination.

14.103.2 Paper. The paper shall consist of 100 percent sulfate pulp fibers, free of ground wood pulp, except as permitted in Section 14.104.8.

14.103.3 Construction. Lapped papers shall be securely cemented together throughout the seam area and shall have a minimum lap of 4 inches (102 mm). Laminated paper shall contain no area of more than $^1/_2$ inch (13 mm), measured from the longitudinal edge of the combined sheet, which is devoid of the laminating agent. The paper shall not stick together to such an extent as to cause tearing when unrolled.

14.103.4 Treatment. The paper shall be treated by the addition of asphalt, asphalt waxes, wax blends, wet-strength resins, rosins, fire-retarding salts or any combining agent, to impart the necessary characteristics to the paper.

14.103.5 Reinforcing. When reinforcing is provided, the paper shall be reinforced by imbedding cords or strands of vegetable or inorganic fibers in the combining agent of the lamination.

SECTION 14.104 — SPECIFIC REQUIREMENTS

14.104.1 General. Except for Style 2, the paper shall not crack when bent over a $^1/_{16}$-inch (1.6 mm) mandrel at the temperature of 32°F (0°C). If reinforced, the cords or strands shall average not less than 10 per foot (305 mm) in each direction.

14.104.2 Grade A, High Water-Vapor Resistant. Grade A paper shall have the dry tensile strength, water-resistance and water-vapor transmission properties shown in Table 14-1-A.

14.104.3 Grade B, Moderate Water-Vapor Resistant. Grade B paper shall have the dry tensile strength, water-resistance and water-vapor transmission properties shown in Table 14-1-A.

14.104.4 Grade C, Water Resistant. Grade C paper shall have the dry tensile strength and water-resistance properties shown in Table 14-1-A.

14.104.5 Grade D, Water-Vapor Permeable. Grade D paper shall have the dry tensile strength, water-resistance and water-vapor transmission properties shown in Table 14-1-A.

14.104.6 Style 1a, Uncreped, Unreinforced. Style 1a paper shall be uncreped and shall not be reinforced.

14.104.7 Style 1b, Uncreped, Unreinforced, Red Rosin Sized. Style 1b paper shall be uncreped, not reinforced, and shall be coated with red rosin sizing.

14.104.8 Style 2, Uncreped, Unreinforced, Saturated. Style 2 paper shall be uncreped, not reinforced, and shall be saturated or infused with asphalt on both sides. Ground wood pulp may be included in the paper.

14.104.9 Style 3, Creped One Direction, Unreinforced. Style 3 paper shall be creped in one direction, not reinforced, and shall have a minimum elongation (stretch) of 15 percent.

14.104.10 Style 4, Uncreped, Reinforced. Style 4 paper shall be uncreped and reinforced.

SECTION 14.105 — TEST SPECIMENS

14.105.1 General. Test specimens shall be of the size designated by the applicable test or as otherwise provided herein.

The specimens shall be cut from the interior of the sample roll so that no specimen edge is nearer than 3 inches (76 mm) to the original sample edge. A minimum of 10 specimens, five in each direction of the paper, shall be cut from each sample for fire-resistance tests. Five specimens, each 5 inches square (127 mm by 127 mm), shall be cut from each sample for water-repellency tests. One specimen, 6 inches by 1 inch (153 mm by 25 mm) in the machine direction of the paper, shall be cut from each sample for the pliability test.

14.105.2 Grade Requirement. Grade requirement tests shall be made. Nonconformance to grade requirements of Table 14-1-A shall constitute failure of this test.

TABLE 14-1-A—GRADE REQUIREMENTS[1]

PHYSICAL PROPERTY REQUIREMENT	GRADE			
	A	B	C	D
Dry tensile strength: minimum, pounds per inch width, both directions	20 (3500 N/m)	20 (3500 N/m)	20 (3500 N/m)	20 (3500 N/m)
Water resistance: permeation of water through papers, hours minimum	24	16	8	$^1/_6$
Water-vapor transmission: grams per sq. meter per 24 hours Maximum Minimum	4 —	6 —	— —	— 35

[1]Approved test methods shall be used.

UNIFORM BUILDING CODE STANDARD 14-2
VINYL SIDING

Based on Standard Specification D 3679-91 for Rigid Polyvinyl Chloride (PVC) of the American Society for Testing and Materials

See Sections 1401.2 and 1404, *Uniform Building Code*

SECTION 14.201 — SCOPE

This standard establishes requirements and test methods for the materials, dimensions, warp, impact strength, weatherability, expansion and appearance of extruded single-wall siding manufactured from rigid PVC compound.

Unless specifically adopted elsewhere, supplemental standards referenced in this primary standard shall only be considered as guidance subject to the approval of the building official.

SECTION 14.202 — CONDITIONING

Specimens shall be preconditioned and tested in accordance with Procedure A of the ASTM D 618-61 (Reapproved 1990) for Method of Conditioning Plastics and Electrical Insulating Materials for Testing.

SECTION 14.203 — PHYSICAL REQUIREMENTS

The siding shall be made principally of polyvinyl chloride compound prepared from polyvinyl chloride homopolymer resin. The compound shall conform to the requirements of Table 14-2-A. The siding made from the resin shall conform to the requirements of Table 14-2-B.

14.203.1 Warp. A full length of siding shall not have a warp greater than $1/8$ inch (3.2 mm).

14.203.2 Surface Distortion. The siding shall be free of bulges, waves and ripples.

SECTION 14.204 — WEATHERABILITY

14.204.1 General. The purpose of this test is to determine whether the siding will successfully retain its appearance after exposure to weather conditions for an extended period of time.

14.204.2 Procedure. Extruded specimens 6 inches (153 mm) long shall be exposed to the following climates:

1. Hot, dry climate (example: Phoenix, Arizona).

2. Hot, humid climate (example: Miami, Florida).

3. Temperature, northern, industrial climate (example: Cincinnati, Ohio).

Specimen exposures shall be in accordance with ASTM D 1435-85. Samples shall face south either at a 45-degree angle of elevation for a minimum of one year or at an angle of elevation representative of the manufacturer's normal installation requirements for the siding for at least two years.

14.204.3 Conditions of Acceptance. Following exposure, the siding shall maintain a uniform color and be free of any visual surface or structural changes such as peeling, chipping, cracking, flaking and pitting.

SECTION 14.205 — MARKING

Each carton shall be labeled "Conforms to UBC Standard 14-2."

TABLE 14-2-A—MINIMUM PROPERTIES FOR PVC COMPOUNDS USED FOR SIDING

Impact strength: (ft. lb./in. of notch)	1.5 (0.08 N•m/mm of notch)
Tensile strength (psi)	5,510 (37.99 MPa)
Modulus of elasticity (psi)	290,000 (1999 MPa)
Deflection temperature under load, (°F, at 264 psi)	158 (70°C, at 1.82 MPa)

TABLE 14-2-B—MINIMUM PROPERTIES FOR PVC SIDING

Thickness (in.)	0.035 (0.89 mm)
Impact Resist. (in./lb./mil) Embossed Siding Unembossed	1.74 (391 mm/N/mm) 2.0 (450 mm/N/mm)
Coefficient of Lineal Expansion (max.) (in./in./°F)	4.5×10^{-5} (2.5×10^{-5} m/m/°C)

UNIFORM BUILDING CODE STANDARD 15-1
ROOFING AGGREGATES
Material Standard of the International Conference of Building Officials
See Section 1501.1 and Table 15-E, *Uniform Building Code*

SECTION 15.101 — SCOPE

This standard covers the quality, grading and amounts to be applied of mineral roofing aggregate.

SECTION 15.102 — CHARACTERISTICS

The mineral aggregate at the time of application shall be hard, durable, opaque, chemically inert, free of clay, loam, sand or foreign substances, and surface dry to 0.5 percent by weight moisture content.

SECTION 15.103 — GRADING

The mineral aggregate shall conform to the sieve analysis requirements prescribed in Table 15-1-A.

SECTION 15.104 — WATER ABSORPTION

Aggregate shall not absorb more than 5 percent of the dry weight of the aggregate when tested using any nationally recognized standard.

SECTION 15.105 — TRANSLUCENCY

Aggregate shall have a translucency intensity of not more than "slight" when visually inspected.

SECTION 15.106 — HARDNESS

Aggregate shall have a hardness factor of not more than 20 percent.

SECTION 15.107 — APPLICATION

If the unit weight (loose) of the aggregate is 60 pounds per cubic foot (960 kg/m^3), or more, the amount applied per roofing square shall be as specified in this code.

If the unit weight (loose) is less than 60 pounds per cubic foot (960 kg/m^3), the amount applied shall be as follows:

1. For an embedment coat of 60 pounds of asphalt per roofing square (3.0 kg/m^2), not less than 5 cubic feet of aggregate per roofing square (0.015 m^3/m^2) shall be applied.

2. For an embedment coat of 50 pounds of asphalt per roofing square (2.5 kg/m^2), not less than 4 cubic feet of aggregate per roofing square (0.012 m^3/m^2) shall be applied.

TABLE 15-1-A—MINERAL AGGREGATE SIEVE ANALYSIS REQUIREMENTS

SIEVE SIZE	FOR USE WITH EMBEDMENT COAT OF 60 POUNDS PER ROOFING SQUARE (3.0 kg/m^2) (percentage)	FOR USE WITH EMBEDMENT COAT OF 50 POUNDS PER ROOFING SQUARE (2.5 kg/m^2) (percentage)
$^5/_8''$ (16 mm)	100	100
$^1/_2''$ (12.5 mm)	90-100	100
$^3/_8''$ (9.5 mm)	25-60	90-100
$^1/_4''$ (6.3 mm)	0-10	30-70
No. 4 (4.75 mm)	0-2	0-10
No. 8 (2.36 mm)		0-4
No. 10 (2 mm)		0-1
No. 20 (850 mm)	0-0.5	0-0.5

UNIFORM BUILDING CODE STANDARD 15-2

TEST STANDARD FOR DETERMINING THE
FIRE RETARDANCY OF ROOF ASSEMBLIES

Based on Standard Specification 790 October 5, 1983,
of the Underwriters Laboratories Inc.

See Sections 601.3; 1501.1; 1502; 2602.5.2; 2603.1.6; 2603.7.1, Item 2;
Table 15-A, *Uniform Building Code*

SECTION 15.201 — GENERAL

15.201.1 Scope. These requirements cover the performance of roof-covering materials exposed to fire conditions, and are intended to indicate the characteristics of roof coverings when exposed to fire originating from sources outside a building on which the coverings may be installed. They are applicable to roof coverings intended for installation on either combustible or noncombustible decks when the roof coverings are applied as intended.

Class A roofing assemblies are effective against severe fire test exposures. Under such exposures, roofing assemblies of this class are not readily flammable, afford a fairly high degree of fire protection to the roof deck, do not slip from position, and are not expected to produce flying brands.

Class B roofing assemblies are effective against moderate fire test exposures. Under such exposures, roofing assemblies of this class are not readily flammable, afford a moderate degree of fire protection to the roof deck, do not slip from position, and are not expected to produce flying brands.

Class C roofing assemblies are effective against light fire test exposures. Under such exposures, roofing assemblies of this class are not readily flammable, afford a measurable degree of fire protection to the roof deck, do not slip from position and are not expected to produce flying brands.

Tests conducted in accordance with these requirements are intended to demonstrate the performance of roof coverings during the types and periods of exposure involved, but are not intended to determine the acceptability of roof coverings for use after exposure to fire.

Roof-covering materials are also required to comply with the requirements for construction, material specifications and performance as applicable to specific types, designs, sizes and arrangements. All such applicable additional requirements are not considered to be within the scope of these requirements for fire tests.

The terms "combustible" and "noncombustible" as used in the standard apply to decks as follows:

1. Combustible is a deck formed of wood (sheathing boards or plywood).

2. Noncombustible is a deck formed of metal, concrete or poured gypsum.

15.201.2 Test Apparatus. As illustrated in Figure 15-2-1, the apparatus used for the tests described in Section 15.202 is to consist of the following:

1. A test deck to which the roof-covering materials to be tested are applied, mounted on a framework. The pitch of the framework is to be adjustable.

2. A construction of noncombustible boards, mounted on the front of the framework to simulate eaves and cornices.

3. A gas burner (for intermittent-flame, spread-of-flame and flying-brand tests) consisting of a 44-inch (1120 mm) length of nominal 2-inch (51 mm) [2.38-inch (60.3 mm) outside diameter] pipe having a $^1/_2$-inch-wide (12.7 mm), 36-inch-long (910 mm) slot in the side toward the test deck. The burner is to be supplied with gas at both ends through nominal 1-inch (25 mm) [1.32-inch (33.4 mm) outside diameter] pipe to provide uniform gas pressure at the burner assembly.

4. A blower and air duct for providing the required wind conditions. The air introduced by the blower is to be taken from outside the test room.

5. Adjustable fins mounted inside the air duct to straighten the airstream and reduce turbulence.

6. A baffle mounted on the back edge of the test deck to prevent backfiring under the deck.

7. Noncombustible boards extending from the sides and bottom of the air duct to the simulated-eaves-and-cornice construction mentioned in Item 2 (not used during burning-brand test).

The tests are to be conducted in a room vented to the outer air to relieve the air pressure created by the blower. During these tests, all doors and windows in the room are to be closed, and the room otherwise controlled as necessary to prevent outside wind and weather conditions from affecting the test results. Tests are not to be conducted if the room temperature is less than 50°F (10°C) or more than 90°F (32°C).

Figure 15-2-2 illustrates the essential elements of the rain test apparatus.

15.201.3 Preparation of Samples.

15.201.3.1 Deck construction. Except for treated wood shingles or shakes for the intermittent-flame and the burning-brand tests, the test deck is to be $3^1/_3$ feet (1016 mm) wide by $4^1/_3$ feet (1320 mm) long and is to be made of kiln-dried No. 1 white pine or ponderosa pine lumber with not less than 8 percent or more than 12 percent moisture content. The lumber is to be free from large or loose knots, sapwood, rot or pitch pockets, and is to contain no edge knots. Individual deck boards are to be of nominal 1-inch-by-8-inch (25 mm by 203 mm) lumber (dressed on four sides). If used for the Class C burning-brand test, the width of the deck board is to be such that the brands will be located directly over the spaces between the boards. The deck boards are to be laid across the shorter dimension of the test deck, spaced $^1/_4$ inch (6.4 mm) apart, and securely nailed to two nominal 2-inch-by-4-inch (51 mm by 102 mm) wood battens located under and flush with the outer edges of the deck. Decks so constructed are to be even and uniform.

For the intermittent-flame, burning-brand and flying-brand tests on treated wood shingles and shakes, the test decks are to be constructed of nominal 1-inch-by-4-inch (25 mm by 102 mm) lumber (dressed on four sides), spaced $^1/_2$ inch (13 mm) apart and securely nailed to two nominal 2-inch-by-4-inch (51 mm by 102 mm) wood battens. The lumber is to be of the quality specified in the above paragraph.

At the manufacturer's option, the roof covering may be investigated when applied to plywood decks of the minimum thickness recommended by the manufacturer. The plywood (A-C grade,

Group 1, exterior) is to have face and back veneers of Douglas fir. A plywood deck is to have $^1/_8$-inch (3.2 mm) vertical and horizontal joints, and all vertical joints are to be centered on nominal 2-inch-by-4-inch (51 mm by 102 mm) wood battens. If the manufacturer specifies that the battens are also to be used for horizontal joints, the classification shall be so restricted.

A plywood deck to be used for the intermittent-flame test is to have a horizontal joint 8 inches (229 mm) from and parallel to the $3^1/_3$-foot-long (1020 mm) leading edge. In addition, a vertical joint that is centered on the deck and extends from the leading edge of the deck to the horizontal joint is to be provided. As the lower $1^1/_2$ inches (38 mm) of this joint is not protected by the nominal 2-inch-by-4-inch (51 mm by 102 mm) batten, due to the mounting arrangement of the carriage, the underside of this joint from the end of the 2 by 4 (51 mm by 102 mm) to the leading edge of the deck is to be covered by a piece of sheet steel 2 inches (51 mm) wide.

A plywood deck to be used for a Class A or Class B burning-brand test is to be provided with a horizontal joint that is $22^1/_2$ inches (572 mm) from and parallel to the leading edge of the deck. A deck to be used for a Class A test is to have a vertical joint centered on the deck and extending above the horizontal joint. A deck to be used for a Class B test is to be provided with two vertical joints, extending above the horizontal joint, and each located 10 inches (254 mm) from and parallel to the side edges of the deck. A plywood deck to be used for a Class C burning-brand test is to have five horizontal joints with at least $^1/_8$-inch (3.2 mm) spacing between joints in the plywood.

Unless the material to be tested is intended for use on noncombustible decks only, the test deck for the spread-of-flame test, on material other than wood shingles and shakes, is to be constructed in accordance with either the intermittent-flame test or the manufacturer's option above, except that (1) the vertical and horizontal joints need not be provided and (2) the length of the deck is to be 13 feet (3962 mm) for Class C tests; 9 feet (2743 mm) for Class B tests; and 8 feet (2438 mm) for Class A tests. For tests on materials intended for use on noncombustible decks only, a noncombustible deck of the applicable length may be used. The test deck for wood shingles and shakes is to be constructed of nominal 1-inch-by-4-inch (25 mm by 102 mm) lumber (dressed on four sides) spaced $1^1/_2$ inches (38 mm) apart, and securely nailed to two nominal 2-inch-by-4-inch (51 mm by 102 mm) wood battens, except that the length of the deck is to be as specified above.

15.201.3.2 Roofing assembly application. Representative samples of roofing assemblies or roof-covering material are to be applied to test decks constructed in accordance with the applicable requirements described. The assemblies are to be conditioned in accordance with Section 15.201.3.3. The material to be tested is to be applied, in accordance with the manufacturer's instructions, to the applicable number of test decks as specified in Table 15-2-A. The material is to extend to, and be flush with, the edges of the deck, except for a 1-inch (25 mm) overhang at the leading edge.

15.201.3.3 Conditioning. The completed test assemblies are to be stored indoors at temperatures not lower than 60°F (16°C) or higher than 90°F (32°C) for the period of time necessary to cure the material, but not more than 60 days. Should storage conditions vary from those specified, the decks are to be stored until moisture determinations indicate that the deck lumber has no less than 8 percent or more than 12 percent moisture content. Test decks are to be stored so that each will be surrounded by freely circulating air.

SECTION 15.202 — PERFORMANCE

15.202.1 General. The intermittent-flame test, the spread-of-flame test and the burning-brand test are applicable to all roof coverings. The flying-brand test, the rain test and the weathering test are conducted only on treated wood shingles and shakes.

> **EXCEPTION:** When the roof covering is limited to installation on noncombustible decks, the penetration tests, that is, the intermittent-flame test and the burning-brand test, need not be conducted.

For these tests, mortar (cementitious mixture, lime and water) is to be troweled into the joint formed by the leading edge of the roof-covering material and the framework of the carriage, to prevent air or the test flame from traveling under the material being tested.

During the tests, the test decks are to be subjected to an air current that flows uniformly over the top surface of the roof-covering material, as determined by a pretest calibration of the equipment using a bare $3^1/_3$-foot-by-$3^1/_4$-foot (1016 mm by 991 mm) plywood deck. At points midway up the slope of the bare deck, with the deck positioned at an incline of 5 inches to the horizontal foot (127 mm per 0.3 m), the velocity of the air current is to be 12 ± $^1/_2$ miles per hour (19 ± 0.8 km/h), as measured at the center and edges of the deck, with each measurement being $3^{11}/_{16}$ inches (94 mm) above the surface of the deck.

For these tests, the test decks are to be at an incline of 5 inches per horizontal foot (127 mm per 0.3 m); except that built-up roof coverings are to be tested at the maximum incline recommended by the manufacturer, but not more than 5 inches per horizontal foot (127 mm per 0.3 m).

15.202.2 Intermittent-flame Test. A test deck is to be mounted on the framework at the required incline, and subjected to the specified air current. The test deck is then to be subjected to a luminous gas flame approximately triangular in shape, approximately 3 feet (914 mm) wide at the leading edge of the deck, and gradually narrowing to a width of approximately 6 inches (151 mm) at the top of the deck. Licks of flame may extend approximately an additional 1 to 2 feet (300 mm to 600 mm). The gas supply is to be regulated so that the flame, if not augmented by combustion of the roof covering, develops a temperature of 1,400°F ± 50°F (760°C ± 28°C) for a Class A or Class B test, and 1,300°F ± 50°F (704°C ± 28°C) for a Class C test. The temperature is to be determined by a No. 14 B.&S. gage (0.064 inches) (1.63 mm) chromel-alumel wire thermocouple located 1 inch (25.4 mm) toward the source of flame from the lower edge of the first board of a bare deck formed of noncombustible material.

The flame is to be intermittently applied at intervals as specified in Table 15-2-B.

Following the last application of flame, air current is to be maintained until all evidence of flame, glow and smoke has disappeared from the exposed surface of the material being tested or until unacceptable results occur, but in no case is the air current to be maintained for more than one hour for a Class A or Class B test or one-half hour for a Class C test.

During the intermittent-flame test, including the on and off periods of flame application and the subsequent period of maintained airflow, the test deck is to be observed for the appearance of sustained flaming on the underside, production of flaming or glowing brands, displacement of portions of the test sample, and exposure or falling away of portions of the roof deck.

15.202.3 Spread-of-flame Test. A test deck is to be mounted and luminous gas flame applied, as described in Section 15.202.2, second paragraph, for the intermittent-flame tests.

For a Class A or Class B test, the gas flame is to be applied continuously for 10 minutes or until the spread of flame (flaming of the material being tested) permanently recedes from a point of maximum spread, whichever is the shorter duration. For a Class C test, the gas flame is to be applied for four minutes and then removed.

During and after the application of the test flame, the test sample is to be observed for the distance to which flaming of the material has spread, production of flaming or glowing brands, and displacement of portions of the test sample. The observation is to continue until the flame has permanently receded from a point of maximum spread.

15.202.4 Burning-brand Test.

15.202.4.1 General. A test deck is to be mounted as described in Section 15.202.2, second paragraph, for the intermittent-flame test, except that the framework is to be 60 inches (1524 mm) from the air duct outlet (see Figure 15-2-1), and the gas piping and burner are to be removed so as not to obstruct the airflow.

15.202.4.2 Size and construction of brands. The brands to be used in these tests are to be as shown in Figure 15-2-3 and are to be constructed as follows. Prior to the test, the brands are to be conditioned in an oven at 105°F to 120°F (40°C to 49°C) for at least 24 hours.

The Class A brand is to consist of a grid, 12 inches (305 mm) square and approximately $2^1/_4$ inches (57 mm) thick, made of kiln-dried Douglas fir lumber that is free from knots and pitch pockets. The brand is to be made of 36 strips of lumber each $3/_4$ inch by $3/_4$ inch (19.1 mm by 19.1 mm) square by 12 inches (305 mm) long, placed in three layers of 12 strips each, with strips placed $1/_4$ inch (6.4 mm) apart. These strips are to be placed at right angles to those in adjoining layers and are to be nailed, using $1^1/_2$-inch (38.1 mm) long No. 16 gage nails, or stapled using No. 16 gage steel wire staples having a $7/_32$-inch (5.6 mm) crown and $1^1/_4$-inch (31.8 mm) legs, at each end of each strip on one face, and in a diagonal pattern as shown in Figure 15-2-3 on the other face. The dry weight of the finished brand is to be 2,000 grams ± 150 grams at the time of the test.

The Class B brand is to consist of a grid, 6 inches (153 mm) square and approximately $2^1/_4$ inches (57 mm) thick, made of kiln-dried Douglas fir lumber that is free from knots and pitch pockets. The brand is to be made of 18 strips of lumber $3/_4$ inch by $3/_4$ inch (19.1 mm by 19.1 mm) square and 6 inches (153 mm) long, placed in three layers of six strips each, with strips spaced $1/_4$ inch (6.4 mm) apart. The strips are to be placed at right angles to those in adjoining layers and are to be nailed, using $1^1/_2$-inch-long (38.1 mm) No. 16 gage nails, or stapled using No. 16 gage steel wire staples having a $7/_32$-inch (5.6 mm) crown and $1^1/_4$-inch (31.8 mm) legs, at each end of each strip on one face, and in a diagonal pattern as shown in Figure 15-2-3 on the other face. The dry weight of the finished brand is to be 500 grams ± 50 grams at the time of the test.

The Class C brand is to consist of a piece of kiln-dried nonresinous white pine lumber that is free from knots and pitch pockets. The brand is to measure $1^1/_2$ inches by $1^1/_2$ inches by $25/_32$ inch (38.1 mm by 38.1 mm by 19.8 mm) and a saw kerf $1/_8$ inch (3.2 mm) wide is to be cut across the center of both the top and bottom faces to a depth of one half the thickness of the brand, and at right angles to each other. The dry weight of the finished brand is to be $9^1/_4$ grams ± $1^1/_4$ grams at the time of the test.

15.202.4.3 Ignition of brands. Before application to the test deck, the brands are to be ignited so as to burn freely in still air as described below. The flame of the gas burner used to ignite the brands is to essentially envelop the brands during the process of ignition. The temperature of the igniting flame is to be 1,630°F ±

50°F (888°C ± 10°C) measured $2^5/_16$ inches (58.7 mm) above the top of the burner. The burner is to be shielded from drafts.

Class A brands are to be exposed to the flame for five minutes, during which time they are to be rotated to present each surface to the flame as follows:

Each 12-inch-by-12-inch (305 mm by 305 mm) face for 30 seconds.

Each $2^1/_4$-inch-by-12-inch (57.2 mm by 305 mm) face for 45 seconds.

Each 12-inch-by-12-inch (305 mm by 305 mm) face again for 30 seconds.

Class B brands are to be exposed to the flame for four minutes, during which time they are to be rotated to present each surface to the flame as follows:

Each 6-inch-by-6-inch (152 mm by 152 mm) face for 30 seconds.

Each $2^1/_4$-inch-by-6-inch (57.2 mm by 152 mm) face for 30 seconds.

Each 6-inch-by-6-inch (152 mm by 152 mm) face again for 30 seconds.

Class C brands are to be exposed to the flame for two minutes, during which time they are to be rotated to present each of the $1^1/_2$-inch-by-$1^1/_2$-inch (38.1 mm by 38.1 mm) faces to the flame for one minute.

15.202.4.4 Test conditions.

15.202.4.4.1 Class A. A brand is to be placed on the surface of each test deck at the location considered most vulnerable (point of minimum coverage over deck joint) with respect to ignition of the deck, but in no case closer than 4 inches (102 mm) from either side or 12 inches (305 mm) from the top or bottom edge of the deck. The brand is to be placed so that the strips in both the upper and lower layers are parallel to the direction of airflow. The brand is to be secured to the deck by a No. 18 B.&S. gage (0.040 inches) (1.02 mm) soft iron wire.

If the roofing assembly is applied to a pine board deck, the brand ordinarily will be in the most vulnerable location when the upper edge of the brand is located 3 inches (76 mm) above a horizontal joint in the test deck. If the roofing assembly is applied to a plywood deck, the brand ordinarily will be in the most vulnerable location when the brand is placed so that it is centered laterally with respect to the vertical joint in the test deck, and the upper edge of the brand is located 3 inches (76 mm) above the horizontal joint.

15.202.4.4.2 Class B. A brand is to be placed on the surface of the test deck at each of the two locations considered most vulnerable (point of minimum coverage over deck joint) with respect to ignition of the deck. Each brand is to be positioned with its upper edge $1^1/_2$ inches (38.1 mm) above the selected joint in the deck boards, but in no case closer than 6 inches (152 mm) from each side or 12 inches (305 mm) from the top or bottom edge of the deck. The brands are to be placed so that the strips in both the upper and lower layers are parallel to the direction of airflow. They are to be secured to the deck by a No. 18 B.&S. gage (0.040 inch) (1.02 mm) soft iron wire. The second brand is not to be applied until all burning resulting from the first brand has ceased.

If the roofing assembly is applied to a pine board deck, the brands ordinarily will be in the most vulnerable location when the upper edge of each brand is located 3 inches (76 mm) above a horizontal joint in the test deck. If the roofing assembly is applied to a plywood deck, the brands ordinarily will be in the most vulnerable location when they are placed so that they are centered laterally with respect to a vertical joint in the test deck, and the upper edge of each brand is located $1^1/2$ inches (38.1 mm) above the horizontal joint.

15.202.4.4.3 Class C asphalt shingles. Loose or unfastened portions of the shingles that can be bent up to 90 degrees without injury to the fastenings are to be cut away. Twenty ignited brands are then to be placed at one- or two-minute intervals in the areas of minimum coverage $1/2$ inch (12.7 mm) away from any cut edge of shingles in the course above that course on which the brand is placed. No brand is to be placed closer than 4 inches (102 mm) to the point where the previous brand was located.

Brands are to be located not closer than 2 inches (50.8 mm) to the joints between adjacent shingles on the same course. All brands are to be placed so that the center of each brand is directly over the space between the deck boards. Brands are to be held in position throughout the test by a No. 18 B.&S. gage (0.040 inches) (1.02 mm) soft iron wire stretched across the width of the deck. The saw kerf on the deck side of the brand is to be parallel to the direction of the airflow. The wire is to be placed in the other saw kerf.

If the roofing assembly is applied to plywood decks, the brands are to be placed centrally over the joints in the plywood deck.

15.202.4.4.4 Class C sheet roofing or built-up covering assemblies. Twenty ignited brands are to be placed at one- or two-minute intervals in the areas of minimum coverage. No brand is to be placed closer than 4 inches (102 mm) to the joint where a previous brand was located. All brands are to be placed so that the center of each brand is directly over the space between the deck boards. See "asphalt shingles" for securing of brands in place and relative positioning of brand saw kerfs.

15.202.4.4.5 Class C treated wood shingles and shakes. Twenty ignited brands are to be placed on each treated wood shingle deck at one- or two-minute intervals. For treated wood shakes, 20 ignited brands are to be distributed at one- or two-minute intervals on each pair of decks. Each brand is to be centered over the $1/4$-inch (6.4 mm) joint between shakes or shingles so that the top edge of the brand is approximately $1/2$ inch (12.7 mm) below the butt of the shake or shingle in the course above. No brand is to be placed closer than 4 inches (102 mm) to the point where a previous brand was located. See "asphalt shingles" for securing of brands in place and relative positioning of brand saw kerfs.

15.202.4.4.6 Duration of tests. Each individual test, whether Class A, Class B or Class C, is to be continued until the brand is consumed and until all evidence of flame, glow and smoke has disappeared from both the exposed surface of the material being tested and the underside of the test deck, or until unacceptable results occur, but not for more than $1^1/2$ hours for a Class A or Class B test. The results of tests in which the brands do not show progressive and substantially complete consumption after application to the test deck are to be disregarded.

15.202.4.4.7 Observations. During the tests, observations are to be made for the appearance of sustained flaming on the underside of the test deck, production of flaming or glowing brands of roof-covering material, displacement of the test sample and the exposure or falling away of portions of the roof deck.

15.202.5 Flying-brand Test. This test applies to Class B and Class C treated wood shingles and shakes. If a Class A rating is desired, appropriate tests of increased severity are to be conducted.

A test deck is to be mounted and a luminous gas flame applied as described in Section 15.202.2, second paragraph, for the intermittent-flame test.

The gas flame is to be applied continuously for (1) 10 minutes for a Class B test and (2) four minutes for a Class C test. The air current is to be maintained until all evidence of flame, glow and smoke has disappeared from the exposed surface of the material being tested to determine if flying brands will be developed. For treated wood shakes, the velocity of the air current is to be increased to 18 miles per hour (29 km/h) after the gas flame is extinguished.

15.202.6 Rain Test. The test decks are to be mounted in a framework at 4 units vertical in 12 units horizontal (33.3% slope). Spray nozzles that deliver an average of 0.7 inch (18 mm) of water per hour at a temperature of 35°F to 60°F (2°C to 15°C) are to be mounted approximately 7 feet (2134 mm) above the test decks. The test decks are to be exposed to 12 one-week conditioning cycles. Each cycle is to consist of 96 hours of water exposure followed by 72 hours of drying time at 140°F (60°C). The final drying cycle is to be controlled so that the moisture content of the deck lumber is between 8 and 12 percent. The conditioned decks are then to be tested in accordance with Table 15-2-A.

An alternative test cycle may be utilized at the manufacturer's option whereby two sets of six decks are to be alternately exposed to seven days (168 hours) of water exposures, followed by two days' (48 hours) draining and five days' (120 hours) curing at 140°F (60°C). This cycle is to be repeated seven times, except that the seventh water exposure is to be reduced to six days (144 hours).

15.202.7 Weathering Test. The test decks are to be mounted outdoors at an incline of 5 units vertical in 12 units horizontal (41.7% slope), facing south. After each of one, two, three, five and 10 years of exposure, three test decks are to be brought indoors and conditioned until the deck lumber attains a moisture content between 8 and 12 percent. From each set of decks, one deck is to be subjected to the intermittent-flame test, one to the burning-brand test and one to the flying-brand test.

SECTION 15.203 — CONDITIONS OF ACCEPTANCE FOR CLASSIFICATION

At no time during the intermittent-flame, spread-of-flame or burning-brand tests shall:

1. Any portion of the roof-covering material be blown or fall off the test deck in the form of flaming or glowing brands, or

2. The roof deck be exposed by breaking, sliding, cracking or warping of the roof covering, or

3. Portions of the roof deck fall away in the form of glowing particles.

For the purpose of the requirements, any piece of roof covering that continues to glow or flame upon landing on the test room floor is considered to be a glowing or flaming brand, respectively.

At no time during the Class A, Class B or Class C intermittent-flame or burning-brand tests shall there be sustained flaming of the underside of the deck.

> **EXCEPTION:** If flaming does occur, another series of tests may be conducted and the results accepted provided no additional sustained flaming occurs.

For the spread-of-flame test, the flaming of the material shall not have spread beyond 6 feet (1829 mm) for Class A, 8 feet (2438 mm) for Class B and 13 feet (3962 mm) (the top of the deck) for Class C. There shall have been no significant lateral spread of flame from the path directly exposed to the test flame.

For the flying-brand test on treated wood shingles and shakes, flying, flaming or glowing brands shall not be produced.

TABLE 15-2-A—REQUIRED TESTS AND TEST ASSEMBLIES

MATERIAL TO BE TESTED	REQUIRED NUMBER OF TEST ASSEMBLIES					
	Intermittent-flame Test	Spread-of-flame Test	Burning-brand Test	Flying-brand Test	Rain Test	Weathering Test
Other than wood shakes or shingles, for installation on:						
A. Combustible decks:						
1. Class A	2	2	4	NA	NA	NA
2. Class B or C	2	2	2	NA	NA	NA
B. Noncombustible decks only	NA	2	NA	NA	NA	NA
Wood shakes and shingles:						
A. Class A	3 (2) [5]	3	6 (2) [5]	3 (2) [5]	6	15
B. Class B or C	3 (2) [5]	3	3 (2) [5]	3 (2) [5]	6	15

NOTES:
NA—Test is not required.
The number in parentheses is the number of samples from the rain test.
The number in brackets is the number of samples from the weathering test.

TABLE 15-2-B—FLAME APPLICATION

CLASS	FLAME ON (minutes)	FLAME OFF (minutes)	NUMBER OF TEST CYCLES
A	2	2	15
B	2	2	8
C	1	2	3

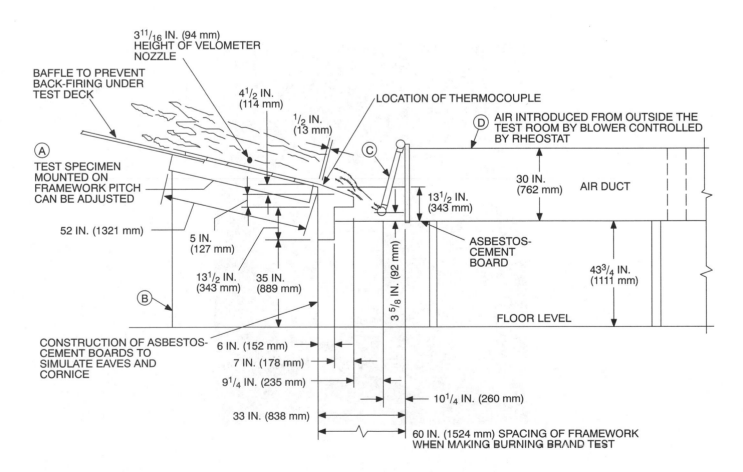

FIGURE 15-2-1—FIRE TEST APPARATUS

SECTION SHOWING IMPORTANT SPACE RELATIONS

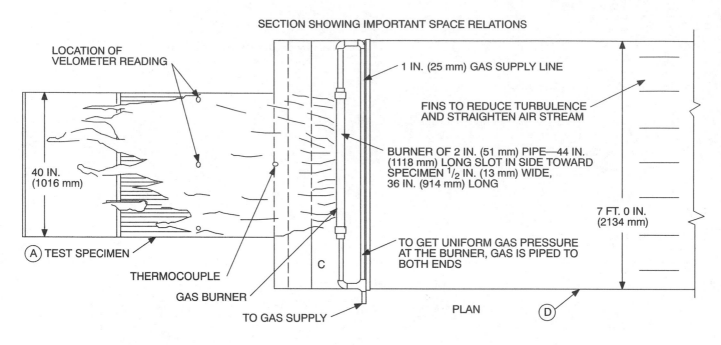

LOCATION OF VELOMETER READING

40 IN. (1016 mm)

Ⓐ TEST SPECIMEN

THERMOCOUPLE

GAS BURNER

TO GAS SUPPLY

1 IN. (25 mm) GAS SUPPLY LINE

FINS TO REDUCE TURBULENCE AND STRAIGHTEN AIR STREAM

BURNER OF 2 IN. (51 mm) PIPE—44 IN. (1118 mm) LONG SLOT IN SIDE TOWARD SPECIMEN 1/2 IN. (13 mm) WIDE, 36 IN. (914 mm) LONG

TO GET UNIFORM GAS PRESSURE AT THE BURNER, GAS IS PIPED TO BOTH ENDS

PLAN

7 FT. 0 IN. (2134 mm)

Ⓓ

Free outlet to be provided to relieve air pressure created by blower. Doors and windows in the room that houses the apparatus to be kept closed at all times during tests to prevent turbulence which would otherwise distort flame and prevent adequate control thereof.

FIGURE 15-2-1—FIRE TEST APPARATUS—(Continued)

FIGURE 15-2-2—RAIN-TEST APPARATUS

FIGURE 15-2-3—A, B AND C BRANDS

UNIFORM BUILDING CODE STANDARD 15-3
WOOD SHAKES

**Based on Grading and Packing Rules for Red Cedar Shakes of the
Cedar Shake and Shingle Bureau, 1975**

See Sections 1501.1, 1502, 1507.2 and 1507.12, *Uniform Building Code*

Part I—Wood Shakes (Nonpreservative Treated)

SECTION 15.301 — SCOPE

Wood shakes regulated under this part shall be of an approved durable wood and shall be manufactured and graded No. 1 shakes or No. 1 or 2 taper-sawn shakes in accordance with this standard, and their use shall be governed by the provisions of Chapter 15 of this code.

SECTION 15.302 — DEFINITIONS

15.302.1 General. For the purposes of this part, certain words and phrases are defined as follows:

BEST FACE is the side of a shake or shingle which is graded and contains the least amount of defects as described within this standard.

BREAKAGE is damage caused after manufacture and subsequent to packing.

BUNDLE is a unit or package comprising sufficient material of the same grade and length to cover a specified area at recommended exposures.

BUTT is the thicker end of the shake.

BUTT CHECK (SUN CHECK) is a condition caused by heat or excessively dry temperature and usually occurs while the raw material is in block form. It is considered a defect when it extends more than $^3/_8$ inch (9 mm) upward from the butt of the shake.

CHECK is any separation of the wood. A check that causes an obvious, readily identifiable section that is easily separated during the grading process shall not be considered defective unless the separated sections are less than the minimum required width.

CLEAR LINE is an imaginary line across the width of a shake which marks the "clear zone."

CLEAR ZONE is that portion of the shake between the butt and the "clear line" involving both the face and the reverse.

COURSE is a horizontal layer forming one of a series of layers on a roof or wall or in the packed bundle.

CRIMPS is a breaking down or collapse of wood cells during drying, characterized by a caved-in or corrugated appearance.

DECAY (ROT) is the decomposition of wood substance caused by action of wood-destroying fungi, resulting in softening, loss of strength and weight, and change of texture and color.

EDGE is the long side of a shake.

EXPOSURE is the portion which, when applied, is exposed to the weather.

EXPOSURE LINE is an imaginary line drawn across the shake at the same distance above the butt that is equal to the weather exposure.

FEATHER TIP or shim is a condition of manufacture found on the thin ends (tips) of some shakes where the saw came out of the piece prematurely, producing a thin, flimsy, feather-like tip that is uneven or has corners sawn off.

GRAIN is the direction, size, arrangement, appearance or quality of the fibers in wood. To have a specific meaning, the term must be qualified:

Cross Grain is a condition that should not be confused with the terms "flat grain" or "edge grain," and that might better be termed "cross fiber," since it is a deviation of the wood fibers from the true parallel of the face of the taper-sawn shake. It is a defect when it runs from one face of the taper-sawn shake to the other within a longitudinal distance of 3 inches (75 mm) or less in that portion measured $5^1/_2$ inches (140 mm), $7^1/_2$ inches (190 mm) and 10 inches (255 mm) from the butt on 15-inch (380 mm), 18-inch (455 mm) and 24-inch (610 mm) shakes. There is to be no excessive cross grain in the remainder of the shake.

Diagonal Grain is a condition where the grain of the wood does not run parallel to the edges of the shake. It is considered a defect when the grain diverges or slants 2 inches (50 mm) or more in width in 12 inches (305 mm) of length measured from the butt.

Edge Grain or Vertical Grain is wood cut in a plane approximately at right angles to the annual rings. A condition in which the rings form an angle of 45 degrees or more with the face of the piece.

Flat Grain is wood cut in a plane approximately tangential to the annual rings and means a condition in which the rings form an angle of less than 45 degrees with the face of the piece.

Mixed Grain is the condition in which edge and flat grain are present in the same piece of wood.

Torn Grain (Torn Fiber) is a fuzzy or whiskered appearance in the face of the shake. Usually caused by a dull saw or grain deviations.

HEARTWOOD (HEART) is the inner layer of a woody stem wholly composed of nonliving cells and usually differentiated from the outer enveloping layer (sapwood) by its darker color.

KNOT is that portion of a branch or limb which has been surrounded by subsequent growth of wood of the tree.

KNOT, DIAMETER, shall be measured by average facial dimensions.

LINEAL INCHES are the total width of any given number of shakes when laid edge to edge.

PLY is the minimum number of thicknesses, when applied, of shakes or at any point on the covered surface. This term is relative to exposure.

REVERSE FACE refers to the entire reverse side of a shake or shingle, which would be expected to be installed down.

SAPWOOD is wood containing some living cells and forming the initial wood layer beneath the bark of the log. Sapwood may be lighter in color than heartwood.

SHIM. See "feather tip."

SQUARE PACK is a unit providing sufficient shakes for the coverage of a given area when the shakes are laid at the required exposure to the weather. (See Tables 15-3-A and 15-3-B.)

TIP is the thinner end of the shake.

TIP ZONE refers to that area 22 inches (560 mm) or more from the butt in 24-inch (610 mm) shakes, 17 inches (430 mm) or more from the butt in 18-inch (455 mm) shakes and 14 inches (355 mm) or more from the butt in 15-inch (380 mm) shakes.

WARPAGE refers to facial curvature (bow), or twist, or both. Warpage is measured from a level plane, with the shake convex to the highest point at the butt. The shake is held firmly 4 inches (102 mm) down from the tip.

WAVES are the washboard-like irregularities on the face of a shake.

WORMHOLE is a hole or passage burrowed by a worm or insect.

15.302.2 Shake Types. Shake types shall be one of the following types:

1. **Handsplit-and-resawn** have split faces and sawn backs, and are produced by running split wood blanks or boards of proper thickness diagonally through a bandsaw to produce two tapered shakes from each blank.

2. **Straight-split** are manufactured by splitting from only one end of a block of wood, producing shakes which are the same thickness throughout.

3. **Taper-sawn** are tapered pieces sawn both sides.

4. **Taper-split** are split both sides. A natural taper, from butt to tip, is achieved by reversing the block, end for end, with each split.

SECTION 15.303 — QUALITY STANDARDS

15.303.1 No. 1 Grade Shake. Shakes shall be 100 percent clear, graded from the split face in the case of handsplit-and-resawn shakes and from the best face in the case of taper-split, taper-sawn and straight-split shakes.

Shakes shall be 100 percent heartwood, free of bark and sapwood, except that up to $^1/_8$ inch (3 mm) of sapwood is permitted on one edge from the butt to the maximum recommended exposure line on the graded face. Additional sapwood shall be permitted above the exposure line provided the sapwood is contained within a diagonally drawn line from the outside edge at the butt to a point 1 inch (25 mm) inward from the tip edge on handsplit and resawn shakes and $^5/_8$ inch (16 mm) on tapersawn shakes.

Taper-split shakes and straight-split shakes shall be 100 percent edge-grain. Handsplit-and-resawn shakes and taper-sawn shakes may average up to 20 percent of flat-grain in the lineal inches (mm) of any bundle.

Curvature in the sawed face of handsplit-and-resawn shakes shall not exceed 1 inch (25 mm) from a level plane in the length of the shake. Excessive grain sweep on the face shall not be permitted. Knots, wormholes, decay, checks, crimps, waves and torn fiber are not permitted.

15.303.2 No. 2 Grade Taper-sawn Shakes. No. 2 grade taper-sawn shakes shall be of sound and serviceable material, graded from the best face. Flat grain is allowed in the No. 2; sapwood is restricted to 1 inch (25 mm) in width in the first 10 inches (255 mm) above the butt. Defects such as knots, wormholes, decay, crimps, cross grain, waves or torn fiber are not allowed in the first $7^1/_2$ inches, 9 inches and 12 inches (190 mm, 230 mm and 305 mm) from the butt in the 15-inch, 18-inch and 24-inch (380 mm, 455 mm and 610 mm) lengths, respectively, of the No. 2 grade taper-sawn shakes. In the same product, grain characteristics, other than excessive cross grain, are not considered defects; defects may be up to $1^1/_2$ (38 mm) inches in diameter, but aggregate defects must not exceed one half the width of the shakes.

15.303.3 Standard Grade Shakes. Shakes shall be handsplit-and-resawn taper-sawn. Shakes shall be edge grain or flat grain or any combination of edge and flat grain. Shakes shall be graded from the split or best face. Grain characteristics other than excessive cross grain are not considered defects. Curvature shall not exceed 1 inch (25 mm) from a level plane in the length of the shake.

SECTION 15.304 — SIZE

15.304.1 Length.

15.304.1.1 No. 1 grade shakes. Nominal shake lengths shall be 15 inches, 18 inches or 24 inches (380 mm, 455 mm or 610 mm), with a minus tolerance of 1 inch (25 mm) and a plus tolerance of 2 inches (50 mm) for 18-inch (455 mm) shakes. A variation, including shims or feather tips, of 1 inch (25 mm) from these nominal lengths of 18-inch (455 mm) shakes shall be permitted in any bundle. A variation of 2 inches (50 mm) below the nominal length shall be permitted in 24-inch (610 mm) shakes and may contain, but is not limited to, shims or feather tips within the specified variation and shall have a plus tolerance of 3 inches (75 mm). See Table 15-3-A. The 15-inch (380 mm) starter-finish course grade shall permit a tolerance of 1 inch (25 mm) over and under the nominal 15-inch (380 mm) length.

15.304.1.2 No. 2 taper-sawn grade shakes. For No. 2 grade taper-sawn shakes, minimum lengths of 15-inch, 18-inch and 24-inch (380 mm, 455 mm and 610 mm) shakes shall be 14, 16 and 22 inches (355, 405 and 560 mm), respectively.

15.304.1.3 Standard grade shakes. For standard grade shakes, the minimum length of 18-inch (455 mm) and 24-inch (610 mm) shakes shall be 17 inches (430 mm) and 22 inches (560 mm), respectively.

15.304.2 Thickness.

15.304.2.1 No. 1 grade shakes. Shake thickness shall be determined by measurement of the butt within $^1/_2$ inch (13 mm) from each edge. If corrugations or valleys exceed $^1/_2$ inch (13 mm) in depth, a minus tolerance of $^1/_8$ inch (3 mm) is permitted in the minimum specified thickness. [Providing the required minimum shake thickness is maintained within $^1/_2$ inch (13 mm) of each edge at the butt, a minus tolerance of $^1/_{16}$ inch (1.5 mm) less than the nominal thickness shall be permitted on the remaining width of the shake.] No minus tolerance shall be permitted for 24-inch-by-$^3/_8$-inch (610 mm by 9 mm) shakes. The thickness at the exposure line shall be a minimum of one half the butt thickness, except that $^3/_8$-inch (9 mm) shakes shall have a minimum thickness of $^1/_4$ inch (6 mm) at the exposure line.

15.304.2.2 No. 1 and No. 2 grade taper-sawn shakes. No. 1 and No. 2 grade taper-sawn shakes shall have one of two thicknesses at the butt, $^5/_8$ inch (16 mm) or $^3/_4$ inch (19 mm) with a minus tolerance of $^1/_{16}$ inch (1.5 mm) in 10 percent of a bundle.

15.304.2.3 Standard grade shakes. Standard grade shakes shall have one thickness. Eighteen-inch (455 mm) and 24-inch (610 mm) shakes shall have a minimum butt thickness of $^3/_4$-inch (19 mm). Thickness at the exposure line shall be a minimum of one half the minimum specified butt thickness.

15.304.3 Width.

15.304.3.1 No. 1 grade shake. Shakes shall be of random widths, none narrower than 4 inches (100 mm). Minimum width for taper-sawn shakes shall be $3^1/_2$ inches (90 mm). Taper-sawn shakes less than 4 inches (100 mm) in width shall not constitute more than 5 percent of the running inches (mm) of each bundle.

15.304.3.2 No. 2 grade taper-sawn shake. No. 2 grade taper-sawn shakes shall have a minimum width of 3 inches (75 mm).

Taper-sawn shakes less than 4 inches (100 mm) in width shall not constitute more than 10 percent of the running inches of each bundle. Edges shall be parallel within $^1/_2$ inch (13 mm).

15.304.3.3 Standard grade shakes. Standard grade shakes shall be of random widths no narrower than 4 inches (100 mm) and none wider than 8 inches (200 mm).

15.304.4 Edges. Edges of shakes shall be parallel within 1 inch (25 mm). Edges of taper-sawn shakes shall be parallel within $^5/_8$ inch (16 mm).

SECTION 15.305 — PACKING

15.305.1 General. Shakes shall be packed in straight courses in regular frames 18 to 20 inches (457 to 508 mm) wide. See Tables 15-3-A and 15-3-B.

15.305.2 Identification. Each bundle of wood shakes graded under this standard shall bear the label of an approved inspection bureau or agency. The label shall be white base stock printed with predominately blue ink and shall clearly indicate No. 1 grade. For No. 2 grade taper-sawn shakes, the label shall be white base stock printed with predominately red ink and shall clearly indicate the No. 2 grade. For standard grade shakes, the label shall be white base stock printed with predominately brown ink and shall clearly indicate standard grade.

SECTION 15.306 — INSPECTION

Shakes packed in a five-bundle square shall be judged off grade if the total lineal inches of on-grade shakes is less than 268 inches (6807 mm) per bundle.

SECTION 15.307 — REINSPECTION

In case of reinspection, 10 or more bundles selected at random shall constitute a fair sampling of the shipment. The criteria for inspection of shakes specified in Section 15.306 shall also apply for reinspection.

Part II—Grading Rules for Shake Hip and Ridge Based on the Standards of the Cedar Shake and Shingle Bureau

SECTION 15.308 — DEFINITION

Shake hip and ridge are two shakes that have one edge, each sawn on a bevel and fastened together to produce the cap for the hip or ridge of the roof.

SECTION 15.309 — QUALITY STANDARDS

No. 1 hip and ridge units shall be produced from material that meets the standard for No. 1 shakes; No. 2 units shall be produced from material that meets the standard for No. 2 taper-sawn shakes. Lower grade material is not permitted.

SECTION 15.310 — SIZE

At the time of manufacture, the shake hip and ridge assembly width shall be 9 inches (230 mm), measured on the underneath side of the assembly at the butt end. A minus tolerance of $^1/_8$ inch (3 mm) is allowed. Butt misalignment of assemblies in excess of $^1/_4$ inch (6 mm) is not permitted. The narrow component shall have a minimum width of $4^1/_2$ inches (115 mm) at the butt end. For

taper-sawn ridge, top corners at the outer edge of the units shall not be more than a 90-degree angle.

SECTION 15.311 — PACKING

Individual shake hip and ridge units are made up of one wide and one narrow component. They shall be packed 20 units per bundle with an equal number of right-hand and left-hand units (for alternating laps). Units shall be manufactured to a 4 units vertical in 12 units horizontal (33.3% slope) pitch or steeper. Units shall be joined with not less than two fasteners applied between 1 inch and 8 inches (25 mm and 200 mm) from the butt. Either staples or nails are acceptable. Fasteners shall be corrosion resistant, spaced approximately 4 inches (100 mm) apart.

SECTION 15.312 — INSPECTION

Each off-grade unit counts as 5 percent of the grade; more than two off-grade units per bundle shall preclude a passing grade.

Part III—Wood Shakes Preservatively Treated

SECTION 15.313 — SCOPE

Wood shakes regulated by this part shall be manufactured, preservative treated and graded in accordance with this standard, and their use shall be governed by the provisions of Chapter 15 of this code.

SECTION 15.314 — DEFINITIONS

For the purpose of this section, certain words and phrases are defined as follows:

COVERED AREA refers specifically to that portion of the face which will be covered in place.

EXPOSED FACE refers specifically to that 10-inch (250 mm) or $7^1/_2$-inch (190 mm) section which will be exposed to the elements.

FACE refers to the entire best side of the shake, which would be expected to be installed facing up.

REVERSE refers to the entire reverse side which would be expected to be installed facing down.

TAPER-SAWN SHAKES are sawn both sides with edges sawn and are 18 inches or 24 inches (455 mm or 610 mm) in length.

TIP ZONE refers to the final 4 inches (100 mm) or 3 inches (75 mm) [of a 24-inch (610 mm) or 18-inch (455 mm) shake, respectively] adjacent to the tip.

SECTION 15.315 — QUALITY STANDARDS

15.315.1 Manufacture.

15.315.1.1 Length. The length of shakes shall be 24 inches (610 mm) and 18 inches (455 mm), allowing for a minus tolerance of $^1/_2$ inch (13 mm) and a plus tolerance of 2 inches (50 mm).

A variation of a minus 1 inch (25 mm), including shims and feathertips, would be permitted in 5 percent of lineal inches (mm) of shakes per bundle, provided that the shake thickness on both edges at the 22-inch (560 mm) and 16-inch (405 mm) lengths is at least $^1/_8$ inch (3 mm).

Angled end trim at butt shall not exceed approximately $^1/_2$ inch (13 mm) per 4 inches (100 mm) of width.

15.315.1.2 Thickness. The green butt thickness of shakes shall be $^{13}/_{16}$ inch (21 mm), with a minus tolerance of $^{1}/_{8}$ inch (3 mm) allowed in 10 percent of lineal inches (mm) of shakes per bundle. The maximum thickness shall not exceed $1^{1}/_{16}$ inches (25 mm).

Tip thickness shall be $^{1}/_{8}$ inch to $^{1}/_{4}$ inch (3 mm to 6 mm).

Thickness variation across the width limited by the above-stated maximums and minimums.

"Dish out" of thickness along length is allowed if it does not reduce the thickness more than $^{1}/_{4}$ inch (6 mm) on the exposed face and is not less than one half the standard thickness in the covered area.

15.315.1.3 Width. Minimum green width shall be 4 inches (100 mm); maximum shall be 8 inches (200 mm). When checking dry material, a maximum shrinkage allowance of $^{1}/_{4}$ inch (6 mm) under the 4-inch (100 mm) minimum will be considered.

Shakes shall be parallel within $^{1}/_{2}$ inch (13 mm).

15.315.1.4 Treatment. Southern pine and red pine taper-sawn shakes shall be preservative treated in accordance with approved nationally recognized standards.

15.315.2 Grade Defects Limited throughout Each Shake.

15.315.2.1 Compression wood. Compression wood is prohibited if in readily identifiable and damaging form. Damaging form includes, but is not limited to, bands of compression wood exceeding $^{1}/_{2}$ inch (13 mm) in width, or bands running along an edge, or solid blocks of compression wood.

15.315.2.2 Density. Medium to dense grain is required measured across the entire butt. Not less than four complete annual rings per inch are permitted at any location.

15.315.2.3 Heart or ring shakes. Heart or ring shakes are prohibited.

15.315.2.4 Slope of grain. Diagonal or spiral grain shall not exceed 1 inch (25 mm) in 10 inches (255 mm). Abnormal grain distortions on face are not permitted.

15.315.2.5 Stain. Medium blue stain is permitted.

15.315.2.6 Unsound wood. Unsound wood is prohibited on either face.

15.315.2.7 Warp. Facial curvature (bow), twist, or both, shall not exceed $^{1}/_{4}$ inch (6.4 mm) from a level plane.

15.315.3 Grade Defects Limited by Location.

15.315.3.1 General. The shake shall be graded from the best face.

15.315.3.2 Holes. Well-scattered ambrosia beetle pin holes up to $^{1}/_{16}$ inch (1 mm) in diameter are allowed if not through the thickness and if limited to six per 10 inches (255 mm) of length on the face. All other types of knot, insect or mechanical holes are prohibited, except an occasional $^{1}/_{2}$-inch (13 mm) hole or encased pith knot is allowed along an edge of the covered area if not extending more than $^{1}/_{2}$ inch (13 mm) into the shake width.

15.315.3.3 Knots. Knots shall be measured by average facial dimensions.

Pith knots are prohibited on the face. They are allowed on reverse side only if the pith hole is not through the thickness.

Generally, no knots are permitted on the exposed face. However, 5 percent of the lineal inches (mm) of shakes per bundle may have up to a $1^{1}/_{2}$-inch (38 mm) cumulative area of sound or firm and tight knots.

Sound or firm and tight knots are limited to a 2-inch (50 mm) cumulative size located in the top one half of the shake at the tapered end.

Individual knots of any quality are limited to a maximum size of $1^{1}/_{2}$ inches (38 mm) on the reverse face. A No. 2 shake may contain up to a $1^{1}/_{2}$-inch (38 mm) cumulative area of sound or firm and tight knots in the exposed $7^{1}/_{2}$- or $5^{1}/_{2}$-inch (190 mm or 140 mm) face.

15.315.3.4 Grain. Generally, vertical grain is required. On the exposed face, flat grain is allowed only along an edge of the face. Center of flat grain not permitted within $1^{1}/_{2}$ inches (38 mm) of center of shake. For No. 2 grade shakes, there are no restrictions on amount or location of flat grain in shake.

15.315.3.5 Pitch pockets. Pitch pockets are prohibited on the exposed face. They are allowed if not through in the covered area and on the reverse side, with the exception that through pitch pockets are allowed in the tip zone.

15.315.3.6 Pith. Pith is not allowed if contained within the thickness of a shake, or if along the surface of the exposed face. A superficial (split) pith is allowed in the covered area or on the reverse side.

15.315.3.7 Wane. Pencil wane is only allowed on the face. Wane on the reverse side is allowed, not to exceed one half the thickness by one sixth the width if located within one half the shake length from the butt; otherwise, wane in occasional pieces may be through the thickness if not reducing the face width by more than $^{1}/_{2}$ inch (13 mm).

15.315.3.8 Reverse Face. Other than the limitations described, the reverse face shall be free of defects which might prevent normal use.

SECTION 15.316 — INSPECTION

Shakes shall be adjudged off grade if the total lineal inches (mm) of defective shakes exceeds 5 percent of the total lineal inches (mm) per bundle. See Table 15-3-A.

SECTION 15.317 — REINSPECTION

In case of reinspection, 10 or more bundles selected at random shall constitute a fair sampling of the shipment. The 5 percent tolerance for defective materials per bundle specified in Section 15.316 shall also apply for reinspection.

Part IV—Southern Yellow Pine, Red Pine, Black Gum/Sweetgum Taper-sawn Shake Hip and Ridge Units

SECTION 15.318 — SCOPE

Southern yellow pine, red pine, black gum/sweetgum taper-sawn shake hip and ridge units regulated by this part shall be manufactured, treated and graded in accordance with this standard and their use shall be governed by the provisions of Chapter 15 of this code.

SECTION 15.319 — QUALITY STANDARDS

Shake hip and ridge units shall be manufactured from only No. 1 grade taper-sawn shakes.

Units shall be fabricated at point of attachment with alternating laps, and shall be correspondingly packed 12/12 inches (12/30 mm) per bundle.

Inner surface of units at the butt shall measure not less than 9 inches (230 mm), with the width of the narrower pieces not less than $4^1/_2$ inches (115 mm).

Units shall be joined with not less than two fasteners applied within 8 inches (203 mm) of the butt. Fasteners shall be a minimum of approximately 3 inches (75 mm) apart and shall be corrosion resistant. Either staples or nails are acceptable. Fasteners shall hold the assembly together until applied properly on the roof.

TABLE 15-3-A—HANDSPLIT SHAKES SUMMARY OF SIZES, PACKING REGULATIONS AND COVERAGE

LENGTH AND THICKNESS × 25.4 for mm	20-INCH (508 mm) PACK No. of Courses per Bdl. × 25.4 for mm	No. of Bdls. per Sq. (9.29 m²)	18-INCH (457 mm) PACK No. of Courses per Bdl. × 25.4 for mm	No. of Bdls. per Sq. (9.29 m²)	5½" (140 mm)	6½" (165 mm)	7" (178 mm)	7½" (191 mm)	8" (203 mm)	8½" (216 mm)	10" (254 mm)	11½" (292 mm)	13" (330 mm)	14" (356 mm)	15" (381 mm)	16" (406 mm)
18" × ½" handsplit and resawn	10/10	4	9/9	5	55	65	70	75	80	85						
18" × ¾" handsplit and resawn	8/8	5	9/9	5	55	65	70	75	80	85						
24" × ⅜" handsplit	10/10	4	9/9	5	—	65	70	75	80	85	100	115				
24" × ½" handsplit and resawn	10/10	4	9/9	5	—	65	70	75	80	85	100	115				
24" × ¾" handsplit and resawn	8/8	5	9/9	5	—	65	70	75	80	85	100	115				
24" × ½" taper split	10/10	4	9/9	5	—	65	70	75	80	85	100	115				
18" × ⅜" true edge straight split	14 Straight	4	—	—	—	—	—	—	—	—	—	—	—	100	106	112
18" × ⅜" straight split	19 Straight	5	—	—	65	75	80	90	95	100						
24" × ⅜" straight split	16 Straight	5	—	—	—	65	70	75	80	85	100	115				
15" starter finish course	8/8 / 10/10	5 / 4	9/9	5	Use supplementary with shakes applied not over 10" (254 mm) weather exposure											
18" × ⅝" taper sawn	—	—	9/9	5	55	65	70	75	—	85	100					
24" × ⅝" taper sawn	—	—	9/9	5	—	65	70	75	—	85	100	115				

[1]For maximum weather exposure on wall construction, see Table 23-L; on roof construction, see Table 15-3-B of the *Uniform Building Code*.

TABLE 15-3-B—MAXIMUM WEATHER EXPOSURE

GRADE LENGTH	3 INCHES TO LESS THAN 4 INCHES IN 12 INCHES (25% to less than 33%)	4 INCHES IN 12 INCHES AND STEEPER (33% and steeper)
	× 25.4 for mm	
Wood Shakes[1]		
No. 1 18-inch	7½	7½
No. 1 24-inch	10	10
No. 2 18-inch taper-sawn shakes	—	5½
No. 2 24-inch taper-sawn shakes	—	7½

[1]Exposure of 24-inch by ⅜-inch (610 by 10 mm) handsplit resawn shakes shall not exceed 5 inches (127 mm) regardless of the roof slope.

UNIFORM BUILDING CODE STANDARD 15-4

WOOD SHINGLES

See Sections 1501.1, 1502, 1507.2 and 1507.13, *Uniform Building Code*

**Part I—Based on the Standards of the
Red Cedar Shingle and Handsplit Shake Bureau and
Material Product Standards of the
International Conference of Building Officials**

SECTION 15.401 — SCOPE

This standard provides a minimum specification for sawn wood shingles of No. 1 grade, No. 2 grade and No. 3 grade. It covers length, width, thickness, and grain characteristics for these requirements, plus definitions and specifications.

SECTION 15.402 — DEFINITIONS

For the purposes of this standard, the following terms shall be construed as herein specified.

BEST FACE is the side of a shingle which is graded and contains the least amount of defects.

BREAKAGE is damage caused after manufacture and subsequent to packing.

BUNDLE is a unit or package comprising sufficient material of the same grade and length to cover a specified area at recommended exposures.

BUTT is the thicker end of the shingle.

BUTT CHECK (SUN CHECK) is a condition caused by heat or excessively dry temperature and usually occurs while the raw material is in block form. It is considered a defect when it extends more than $^3/_8$ inch (9 mm) upward from the butt of the shake.

CHECK is any separation of the wood.

CLEAR LINE is an imaginary line across the width of a shingle which marks the "clear zone."

CLEAR ZONE is that portion of the shingle between the butt and the "clear line," involving both the face and the reverse.

COURSE is a horizontal layer forming one of a series of layers on a roof or wall or in the packed bundle.

CRIMPS are a breaking down or collapse of wood cells during drying, characterized by a caved-in or corrugated appearance.

DECAY (ROT) is the decomposition of wood substance caused by action of wood-destroying fungi, resulting in softening, loss of strength and weight, and change of texture and color.

EDGE is the long side of a shingle.

EXPOSURE is the portion which, when applied, is exposed to the weather.

EXPOSURE LINE is an imaginary line drawn across the shake or shingle at the same distance above the butt that is equal to the weather exposure.

GRAIN is the direction, size, arrangement, appearance or quality of the fibers in wood. To have a specific meaning, the term must be qualified:

Cross Grain is a condition that should not be confused with the terms "flat" or "edge" grain, and that might better be termed "cross fiber," since it is a deviation of the wood fibers from the true parallel of the face of the shingle. It is a defect when it runs from one face of the shingle to the other within a longitudinal distance of 3 inches (75 mm) or less in that portion measured 6 inches (150 mm) from the butt. Excessive cross grain must not be present in the remainder of the shingle.

Diagonal Grain is a condition where the grain of the wood does not run parallel to the edges of the shingle. It is considered a defect when the grain diverges or slants 2 inches (50 mm) or more in width in 12 inches (305 mm) of length.

Edge Grain or Vertical Grain is wood cut in a plane approximately at right angles to the annual rings. A condition in which the rings form an angle of 45 degrees or more with the face of the piece.

Flat Grain is a condition in shingles or lumber where the growth rings are flat or horizontal, as opposed to edge-grained or quartered material where the growth rings are on edge, or vertical to the surface. Wood cut in a plane approximately tangential to the annual rings and means a condition in which the rings form an angle of less than 45 degrees with the face of the piece.

FEATHER TIPS (or shims) is a condition of manufacture found on the thin ends (tips) of some shingles where the saw came out of the piece prematurely, producing a thin, flimsy, feather-like tip that is uneven or has corners sawn off.

HEARTWOOD (HEART) is the inner layer of a woody stem wholly composed of nonliving cells and usually differentiated from the outer enveloping layer (sapwood) by its darker color.

KNOT is that portion of a branch or limb which has been surrounded by subsequent growth of wood of the tree.

KNOT DIAMETER shall be measured by average facial dimensions.

LINEAL INCHES are the total width of any given number of shingles when laid edge to edge.

PLY is the minimum number of thicknesses, when applied, of shingles at any point on the covered surface. This term is related to exposure.

REVERSE FACE refers to the entire reverse side of a shake or shingle, which would be expected to be installed down.

SAPWOOD is wood containing some living cells and forming the initial wood layer beneath the bark of the log. Sapwood may be lighter in color than heartwood.

SHIM. See "feather tips."

SQUARE PACK is a unit providing sufficient shingles for the coverage of a given area when the shingles are laid at the specified exposure to the weather in Tables 15-C and 23-II-K of this code.

TIP is the thinner end of the shingle.

TIP ZONE refers to that area 23 inches (585 mm) or more from the butt in 24-inch (610 mm) shingles, 17 inches (430 mm) or more from the butt in 18-inch (455 mm) shingles, and 15 inches (380 mm) or more from the butt in 16-inch (405 mm) shingles.

TORN FIBER (TORN GRAIN) is a fuzzy or whiskered appearance on the face of the shingle usually caused by a dull saw or grain deviations.

WAVES are the washboard-like irregularities on the face of a shingle.

WORMHOLE is a hole or passage burrowed by a worm or insect.

SECTION 15.403 — GRADING AND LABELING

15.403.1 General. Each bundle of No. 1 grade, No. 2 grade and No. 3 grade wood shingles graded under this standard shall bear the label of an approved inspection bureau or agency. For No. 1 grade, the label shall be of white base stock printed with predominantly blue ink and shall clearly indicate the No. 1 grade. For No. 2 grade, the label shall be of white base stock printed with predominantly red ink and shall clearly indicate the No. 2 grade. For No. 3 grade, the label shall be of white base stock printed with predominantly black ink and shall clearly indicate the No. 3 grade. All grades shall be well manufactured and neatly packed; they shall comply with or exceed the specifications herein established for quality. All shingles shall be graded from their best face. Wormholes, decay and crimps are not allowed on either face of No. 1 shingles and below the clear line to the butts on either face of No. 2 and No. 3 grade shingles.

15.403.2 Characteristics.

15.403.2.1 General. Shingles characteristics shall be in accordance with the provisions of this section:

15.403.2.2 No. 1 grade. No. 1 grade shall be vertical grain or edge grain, be clear of defects on the graded face and be 100 percent heartwood. Knots, knotholes, wormholes, decay and crimps are not allowed on either face. Flat grain, cross grain and sapwood constitute natural characteristics that are not admissible. Defects in manufacturing, including shims, excessive feather tips, diagonal grain, and cross grain are likewise not admissible. Manufacturing defects such as checks, waves or torn fiber are permitted on the ungraded face.

15.403.2.3 No. 2 grade. In No. 2 grade, sapwood is restricted to 1 inch (25 mm) in width in the first 10 inches (255 mm) above the butt. Grain characteristics, other than cross grain, are not considered defects. Defects such as knots, knotholes, wormholes, decay and crimps are not allowed on either face in the first 10 inches, 11 inches and 16 inches (255 mm, 280 mm and 405 mm) from the butt in the 16-inch, 18-inch and 24-inch (405 mm, 455 mm and 610 mm) lengths, respectively. Manufacturing defects such as checks, waves or torn fiber are permitted on the ungraded face. Defects may be up to 3 inches (75 mm) in diameter, but aggregate defects shall not exceed one half the width of the shingle.

15.403.2.4 No. 3 Grade. In No. 3 grade, sapwood is permitted. Other grain deviations are not considered defects. Other defects, as listed above for No. 2 grade, are not allowed in the first 6 inches (150 mm) from the butt for 16-inch (405 mm) and 18-inch (455 mm) lengths and 10 inches (255 mm) for 24-inch (610 mm) lengths. Defects may be up to 3 inches (75 mm) in diameter, but aggregate defects shall not exceed two-thirds the width of the shingle.

SECTION 15.404 — LENGTH, WIDTH, THICKNESS

15.404.1 Length.

15.404.1.1 No. 1 Grade. Shingles are usually manufactured in 16-inch, 18-inch and 24-inch (405 mm, 455 mm and 610 mm) lengths. A minus tolerance of 1 inch (25 mm) below the nominal length is allowed.

15.404.1.2 No. 2 Grade. For No. 2 grade the minimum lengths, including shims or feather tips for 16-inch, 18-inch and 24-inch (405 mm, 455 mm and 610 mm) shingles, shall be 15 inches (381 mm), 16 inches (406 mm) and 20 inches (510 mm), respectively.

15.404.1.3 No. 3 Grade. For No. 3 grade the minimum lengths, including shims or feather tips for 16-inch, 18-inch and 24-inch

(405 mm, 455 mm and 610 mm) shingles, shall be 14 inches (355 mm), 16 inches (406 mm) and 18 inches (455 mm), respectively.

15.404.2 Width.

15.404.2.1 No. 1 Grade. Minimum width up to but not including 24-inch lengths (610 mm), shall be 3 inches (75 mm). Minimum width for shingles 24 inches (610 mm) and longer shall be 4 inches (100 mm). In 16-inch and 18-inch (405 mm and 455 mm) shingles those less than 4 inches (100 mm) in width shall not constitute more than 10 percent of the running inches per bundle. Shingles shall be uniform in width; that is, with parallel sides. Edges shall be parallel within a tolerance of $^1/_4$ inch (6 mm) on 16-inch (405 mm) and 18-inch (455 mm) shingles and $^3/_8$ inch (9 mm) on 24-inch (610 mm) shingles.

15.404.2.2 No. 2 Grade. Minimum width shall be 3 inches (75 mm). Not more than 20 percent of the running inches (mm) in each bundle shall be less than 4 inches (100 mm) wide. Edges shall be parallel within a tolerance of $^1/_4$ inch (6 mm) in the 16-inch (405 mm) and $^3/_8$ inch (9 mm), 18-inch and 24-inch (455 mm and 610 mm) lengths.

15.404.2.3 No. 3 Grade. Minimum width shall be 3 inches (75 mm) except it may be $2^1/_2$ inches (65 mm) for the 16-inch (405 mm) length. Not more than 30 percent of the running inches in each bundle shall be less than 4 inches (100 mm) wide. Edges shall be parallel within a tolerance of $^3/_8$ inch (9 mm).

15.404.3 Thickness. Shingles are measured for thickness at the butt ends and designated according to the number of pieces necessary to constitute a specific unit of thickness. At the time of manufacture, 16-inch (405 mm) shingles shall be nominally 5/2 [the thickness of five butts will be 2 inches (50 mm)], 18 inches (455 mm) shall be nominally $5/2^1/_4$ [five butts measure $2^1/_4$ inches (55 mm)] and 24 inches (610 mm) shall be nominally 4/2 [four butts measure 2 inches (50 mm)]. Shingles shall be uniform in thickness, with a plus or minus tolerance of 3 percent permitted to compensate for variations in saw movement. A further plus or minus tolerance of 3 percent is allowable to compensate for the difference in shrinkage due to seasoning or kiln drying. This tolerance is based on the total thickness of the bundle.

SECTION 15.405 — INSPECTION

Shingles packed as a four-bundle square shall be judged off grade if the total lineal inches (mm) of on-grade shingles is less than 695 inches (17 653 mm), 635 inches (16 129 mm) and 465 inches (11 811 mm) per bundle for 16-inch (405 mm), 18-inch (455 mm) and 24-inch (610 mm) shingles, respectively.

SECTION 15.406 — REINSPECTION

In case of reinspection, 10 or more bundles selected at random shall constitute a fair sampling of the shipment. The 4 percent tolerance for defective shingles specified in Section 15.405 shall also apply for reinspection.

Part II—Grading Rules for Shingle Hip and Ridge Units Based on the Standards of the Cedar Shake and Shingle Bureau

SECTION 15.407 — DEFINITION

Hip and ridge shingles are two shingles that have one edge of each sawn on a bevel and fastened together to produce the cap for the hip or ridge of the roof. Hip and ridge units are manufactured from No. 1 or No. 2 grade shingles.

SECTION 15.408 — QUALITY STANDARDS

No. 1 hip and ridge units shall be produced from material that meets the standard for No. 1 shingles; No. 2 hip and ridge units shall be produced from material that meets the standard for No. 2 shingles. Lower-grade material is not permitted.

SECTION 15.409 — SIZE

At the time of manufacture, the shingle hip and ridge assembly width shall be 7 inches (180 mm), measured over the top of the assembly at the butt end. A minus tolerance of $1/8$ inch (3 mm) is allowed. Butt misalignment of assemblies in excess of $1/8$ inch (3 mm) is not permitted. On the outer edge of the units, top corners shall not be more than a 90-degree angle. The narrow component shall have a minimum width of $3^5/_{16}$ (85 mm) inches at the butt end.

SECTION 15.410 — PACKING

Individual shingle and ridge units are made up of one wide and one narrow component. Sixteen-inch (405 mm) shingles shall be packed 40 units per bundle; 18-inch (455 mm) shingles shall be packed 36 units per bundle, with an equal number of right-hand and left-hand units (for alternating laps). Units shall be manufactured to a 4 units vertical to 12 units horizontal (33.3%) pitch or steeper. Units shall be joined with not less than two fasteners applied between $1/2$ inch and $5^1/2$ inches (13 mm and 140 mm) from the butt. Either staples or nails are acceptable. Fasteners shall be corrosion resistant, spaced approximately 3 inches (75 mm) apart.

SECTION 15.411 — INSPECTION

Each off-grade unit shall count for $2^1/2$ percent of the grade; more than four off-grade units per bundle shall preclude a passing grade.

UNIFORM BUILDING CODE STANDARD 15-5
ROOF TILE

Recommended Standard of the International Conference of Building Officials

See Sections 1501.1, 1502 and 1507.7, *Uniform Building Code*

SECTION 15.501 — SCOPE

This standard applies to all clay, concrete and other cement-based tiles. Supplementary tests justifying adequacy under loads prescribed in Chapter 16 shall be provided.

SECTION 15.502 — BASIC INFORMATION

The following basic information shall be submitted:

1. Manufacturing data as applicable such as mix design, density, protective coatings, mixing, forming, extruding, firing, curing, coloring and glazing.

2. Dimensioned scale drawings and details noting thicknesses, lugs, lips, contours, water diverters, size and location of all fasteners.

3. Method of packaging and identification of components.

SECTION 15.503 — REPORT OF TESTS

A qualified representative of the independent testing agency shall witness the production, fabrication and installation of test specimens.

The test report must be in sufficient detail to identify specimen properties that could affect performance as a roof covering. The testing agency must verify and report dimensions, weight, density, moisture content and other relevant physical properties of the major components.

SECTION 15.504 — REQUIRED TESTS

Tiles shall be tested for strength and water absorption as set forth in this standard.

SECTION 15.505 — SAMPLES

A total of 10 representative samples shall be selected by the independent laboratory from the production line. The laboratory shall document production procedures as specified in Section 15.503. Cement-based products shall be conditioned at a temperature of $73°F \pm 5°F$ ($23°C \pm 2.8°C$) and 50 percent relative humidity for a period of 28 days. At the end of the conditioning period, the size and weight for each specimen shall be recorded.

SECTION 15.506 — TEST PROCEDURES

15.506.1 Strength Test.

15.506.1.1 Sample. Five samples conditioned as specified in Section 15.505 shall be subjected to the strength test.

15.506.1.2 Procedure.

15.506.1.2.1 Barrel-shaped ("Spanish") tile. The supports for the sample shall be two knife edges of the rocker type with edges at least as long as the width of the sample. The loading knife edge may be either the fixed or the rocker type and shall be at least as long as the width of the sample.

Place the sample on the knife edges with the open side or turned-down edges down, so that the sample is supported by the knife edges at a span of 12 inches (305 mm) centered on the length of the sample. Apply the load at center of the span and sample width through the loading knife edge. Apply loads at rates not to exceed 10 pounds (4.45 N) per second until failure and record the breaking load to the nearest 5 pounds (2.2 N).

15.506.1.2.2 Other tile. The test span shall be the maximum unsupported span specified for field installation. The sample shall be tested as shown in Figure 15-5-1 with the load applied at a uniform rate not exceeding 10 pounds (4.45 N) per second until failure, which shall be recorded to the nearest pound (5 N). The test shall be repeated on the other specimens and the average breaking load determined.

15.506.1.3 Conditions of acceptance.

15.506.1.3.1 Barrel-shaped tile. Barrel-shaped tiles are tiles having a minimum rise-to-width ratio of 1:4. The average breaking load shall be not less than 400 pounds (1780 N) with no single load less than 350 pounds (1560 N).

15.506.1.3.2 Other tiles. The average breaking load shall not be less than 300 pounds (1335 N) for five consecutively tested samples or 250 pounds (1110 N) for any individual sample.

15.506.2 Water Absorption Test.

15.506.2.1 Sample. A minimum of five samples from the tile fractured in the strength test shall be tested for water absorption. The sum of the dry weight for five samples at room temperature shall not be less than 12 pounds (5.4 kg). A total of five or more samples of the ridge and other accessory tile not subjected to the strength test shall also be tested. The aggregate dry weight at room temperature of these samples shall not be less than 5 pounds (2.2 N).

15.506.2.2 Procedure. Loose particles shall be removed by scrubbing with a fiber brush and clean water. Samples shall be dried in a well-ventilated oven for 24 hours at a temperature of $221°F$ ($105°C$) varying not more than $3.6°F$ ($2.0°C$). After drying, the samples may be cooled at room temperature for 15 minutes after identifying and weighing to the nearest 0.01 gram. The samples shall then be immersed in filtered or distilled water for 48 hours at a temperature of $68°F$ ($20°C$), varying not more than $9°F$ ($5°C$). One sample shall be removed, surfaces wiped dry and weighed immediately. The process shall be repeated for each sample.

15.506.2.3 Condition of acceptance. No sample shall absorb more than 15 percent water of its dry weight.

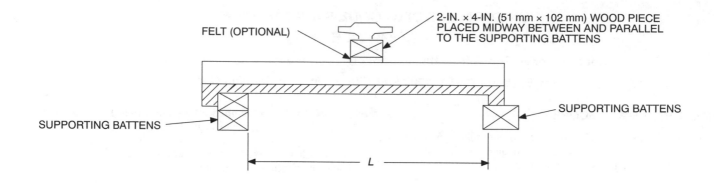

L = maximum unsupported span specified for field installation.

NOTE: The load shall be applied with a 2-in. × 4-in. (51 mm by 102 mm) (nominal size) wood piece laid flat and continuous from edge to edge of the tile. Where the effective width of tile exceeds 16 inches (406 mm), the loads specified in Section 15.506.1.2 shall be increased in proportion to the tile width.

FIGURE 15-5-1—TRANSVERSE BREAKING STRENGTH

UNIFORM BUILDING CODE STANDARD 15-6
MODIFIED BITUMEN, THERMOPLASTIC AND THERMOSET MEMBRANES USED FOR ROOF COVERINGS

Based on Standard Specifications D 412-87, D 471-79, D 570-81, D 624-86, D 638-84, D 751-79, D 816-82, D 1004-66 (1981), D 1204-84, D 2136-84 and D 2137-83 of the American Society for Testing and Materials

See Sections 1501.1 and 1502, *Uniform Building Code*

SECTION 15.601 — SCOPE

15.601.1 General. This standard covers the following membranes used for roof coverings.

15.601.2 Modified Bitumen Membranes. Composite sheets consisting of bitumen modifiers and reinforcements. The material shall be of the following types of classes:

Type I—APP modified bitumen reinforced membrane composed primarily of asphalt blended with atactic polypropylene.

Type II—SBS modified bitumen reinforced membrane composed primarily of asphalt blended with styrene-butadiene-styrene.

Type III—Self-adhesive modified bitumen membrane composed primarily of asphalt blended with styrene-butadiene-styrene.

15.601.3 Thermoplastic Membranes. Sheets composed of polymers and other proprietary ingredients whose chemical composition allows the sheet to be welded together by either heat or solvent throughout its service life.

15.601.4 Thermoset Membranes. Sheets composed of polymers and other proprietary ingredients whose chemical composition vulcanizes or cross-links during its service life.

SECTION 15.602 — PHYSICAL PROPERTIES

The materials shall conform to the physical properties prescribed in Tables 15-6-A, 15-6-B, 15-6-C, 15-6-D and 15-6-E.

TABLE 15-6-A—PROPERTIES OF THERMOSET REINFORCED MEMBRANES USED FOR ROOF COVERINGS

MATERIALS' PROPERTIES	TEST METHODS[1]	UNITS	PHYSICAL PROPERTIES
Thickness	ASTM D 751-79	inches ($\times$ 25.4 for mm)	≥ 0.030
Breaking strength[2]	ASTM D 751-79	lb./inch ($\times$ 0.175 for N/mm)	≥ 90
Elongation at fabric break[3]	ASTM D 751-79	Percentage	≥ 15
Tear resistance	ASTM D 751-79	lb. ($\times$ 4.45 for N)	≥ 25
Water absorption	ASTM D 471-79 166 hours at 73°F	Weight change percentage	≤ 10
Dimensional stability	ASTM D 1204-84 24 hours at 130°F	Percentage	≤ 2
Low temperature flexibility	ASTM D 2137-83	°F ($-32 \div 1.8$ for °C)	≤ -30
Factory seam strength	ASTM D 751-79	lb./inch ($\times$ 0.175 for N/mm)	≥ 50[4]

[1]The test to be used shall be a method approved by the building official.
[2]Results of tensile strength after heat aging at 212°F (100°C) for 166 hours will remain at $\geq$ 90 pounds (400 N). Accelerated weathering in xenon, carbon arc or QUV with water spray for 2,000 hours at 176°F (80°C) will not reduce the breaking strength to less than 90 pounds (400 N).
[3]Elongation at break shall not be reduced by heat aging or accelerated weathering by more than 20 percent.
[4]Or membrane rupture.

TABLE 15-6-B—PROPERTIES OF THERMOSET NONREINFORCED MEMBRANES USED FOR ROOF COVERINGS

MATERIALS' PROPERTIES	TEST METHODS[1]	UNITS	PHYSICAL PROPERTIES
Thickness	ASTM D 412-87	inches ($\times$ 25.4 for mm)	≥ 0.040
Tensile strength[2]	ASTM D 412-87	psi ($\times$ 6.89 for kPa)	$\geq 1,000$
Elongation[3]	ASTM D 412-87	Percentage	≥ 300
Tear resistance	ASTM D 624-86	lb./inch ($\times$ 0.175 for N/mm)	≥ 120
Water absorption	ASTM D 471-79 166 hours at 158°F	Weight change percentage	≤ 10
Dimensional stability	ASTM D 1204-84 70 hours at 212°F	Percentage	≤ 2.0
Low temperature flexibility	ASTM D 2137-83	°F ($-32 \div 1.8$ for °C)	≤ -30
Factory seam strength	ASTM D 816-82	lb./inch ($\times$ 0.175 for N/mm)	≥ 30[4]

[1]The test to be used shall be a method approved by the building official.
[2]Results of tensile strength after heat aging at 212°F (100°C) for 166 hours will remain at $\geq$ 1,000 psi (6890 kPa). Accelerated weathering in xenon, carbon arc or QUV with water spray for 2,000 hours at 176°F (80°C) will not reduce the tensile strength to less than 1,000 pounds (6890 kPa).
[3]Elongation shall not be reduced by heat aging or accelerated weathering to less than 200 percent.
[4]Or membrane rupture.

TABLE 15-6-C—PROPERTIES OF THERMOPLASTIC REINFORCED MEMBRANES USED FOR ROOF COVERINGS

MATERIALS' PROPERTIES	TEST METHODS[1]	UNITS	PHYSICAL PROPERTIES
Thickness	ASTM D 751-79	inches (× 25.4 for mm)	≥ 0.030
Breaking strength[2]	ASTM D 751-79	lb. (× 4.45 for N)	≥ 90
Elongation at fabric break[3]	ASTM D 751-79	Percentage	≥ 15
Tear resistance	ASTM D 751-79	lb. (× 4.45 for N)	≥ 20
Water absorption	ASTM D 570-81 166 hours at 158°F	Weight change percentage	≤ 5.0
Dimensional stability	ASTM D 1204-84 6 hours at 176°F	Percentage	≤ 1.0
Low temperature flexibility	ASTM D 2136-84	°F (−32 ÷ 1.8 for °C)	≤ −30
Factory seam strength	ASTM D 751-79	lb./inch (× 0.175 for N/mm)	≥ 50[4]

[1]The test to be used shall be a method approved by the building official.

[2]Results of tensile strength after heat aging at 158°F (70°C) for 30 days will remain at ≥ 90 pounds (400 N). Accelerated weathering in xenon, carbon arc or QUV with water spray for 2,000 hours at 145°F (63°C) will not reduce the breaking strength to less than 90 pounds (400 N).

[3]Elongation at break shall not be reduced by heat aging or accelerated weathering by more than 20 percent.

[4]Or membrane rupture.

TABLE 15-6-D—PROPERTIES OF THERMOPLASTIC NONREINFORCED MEMBRANES USED FOR ROOF COVERINGS

MATERIALS' PROPERTIES	TEST METHODS[1]	UNITS	PHYSICAL PROPERTIES
Thickness	ASTM D 638-84	inches (× 25.4 for mm)	≥ 0.045
Tensile strength[2]	ASTM D 638-84	psi (× 6.89 for kPa)	≥ 1,500
Elongation[3]	ASTM D 638-84	Percentage	≥ 250
Tear resistance	ASTM D 1004-66 (1981)	lb. (× 4.45 for N)	≥ 10
Water absorption	ASTM D 570-81 166 hours at 158°F	Weight change percentage	≤ 3.0
Dimensional stability	ASTM D 1204-84 6 hours at 176°F	Percentage	≤ 2.0
Low temperature flexibility	ASTM D 2136-84	°F (−32 ÷ 1.8 for °C)	≤ −30
Factory seam strength	ASTM D 638-84	psi (× 6.89 for kPa)	≥ 1,300[4]

[1]The test to be used shall be a method approved by the building official.

[2]Results of tensile strength after heat aging at 194°F (90°C) for 168 hours will remain at ≥ 1,000 psi (6890 kPa). Accelerated weathering in xenon, carbon arc or QUV with water spray for 2,000 hours at 145°F (63°C) will not reduce the tensile strength to less than 1,000 psi (6890 kPa).

[3]Elongation at break shall not be reduced by heat aging or accelerated weathering to less than 200 percent.

[4]Or membrane rupture.

TABLE 15-6-E—PROPERTIES OF MODIFIED BITUMEN MEMBRANES USED FOR ROOF COVERINGS

MATERIALS' PROPERTIES	UNITS	PHYSICAL PROPERTIES[1]		
		Type I Membrane	Type II Membrane	Type III Membrane
Thickness	mils (× 0.0254 for mm)	≥ 120	≥ 120	≥ 40
Weight	lb./100 ft.[2] (× 0.05 for kg/m[2])	≥ 60	≥ 60	≥ 30
Tensile strength at 0°F[2,3] machine or cross-machine direction	lb./in. (× 0.175 for N/mm)	≥ 100	≥ 100	≥ 50
Elongation at 0°F[2,3] machine or cross-machine direction	Percentage	≥ 4	≥ 4	≥ 50
Strain energy at 0°F[3]	lb. in./in. (× 4.45 for N mm/mm)	≥ 2	≥ 2	N/A
Water absorption	Percentage	≤ 5	≤ 5	≤ 5
Low temperature flexibility[2]	°F (−32 ÷ 1.8°C)	≤ 32	≤ 5	≤ 5
Dimensional stability	Percentage	≤ 1	≤ 1	≤ 1
Compound stability	°F (−32 ÷ 1.8°C)	≥ 250	≥ 220	N/A

[1]Tests shall be approved methods of evaluating the properties of roofing materials.

[2]Stated property is before and after heat conditioninng at 158°F (70°C) for 2,000 hours. Accelerated weathering in xenon, carbon arc or QUV with water spray for 2,000 hours at 145°F (63°C) will not reduce the tensile strength by more than 5 percent or the elongation by more than 10 percent.

[3]Strain energy is the area under the load elongation curve obtained from the machine chart or computer system converted to units of pounds per inch per inch (N per mm per mm). This is required if one of the minimum values for tensile strength or elongation is not met. Ultimate elongation for this calculation shall be the elongation to the point the load is 5 percent of the tensile strength of the membrane after the maximum load has been reached.

UNIFORM BUILDING CODE STANDARD 15-7
AUTOMATIC SMOKE AND HEAT VENTS
Standard of the International Conference of Building Officials
See Sections 906.1, 906.4 and 1501.1, *Uniform Building Code*

SECTION 15.701 — SCOPE

15.701.1 General. This standard applies to thermally activated, automatic smoke and heat vents designed for installation on the roof of buildings as required by Section 906 of the Building Code.

15.701.2 Instructions. A copy of the installation and operating instructions shall be supplied with each unit. The instructions shall prescribe construction representative of that used in the examination and testing of the product.

SECTION 15.702 — CONSTRUCTION AND MATERIALS

The critical operating components of vents, such as heat sensors, hinges, latches, linkages and other mechanical parts, shall be constructed of corrosion-resistant materials.

Plastics shall be approved plastics as defined in the Building Code.

Vent design for minimum roof live load shall be of adequate strength and durability to withstand the design loads as prescribed in the Building Code.

SECTION 15.703 — METHOD OF ACTIVATION

Releasing devices for vents shall be activated by heat. The heat-activated device shall be one of the following:

1. A fixed-temperature device having a melting temperature rating at least 30°F (17°C) above the maximum expected ambient temperatures at the intended location.

2. A rate-of-rise device.

3. Approved, heat-sensitive glazing designed to shrink and drop out of the vent opening.

SECTION 15.704 — TEST PROCEDURES

15.704.1 General. Recognized and accepted testing procedures and testing equipment shall be used.

15.704.2 Samples. Samples submitted for acceptance tests shall be production units whose materials, design and specifications are representative of the models for which acceptance is sought. Written specifications shall be submitted for each model. Tests for multiple-sized models shall utilize the largest size unit for evaluations.

15.704.3 Heat Sensors. Heat-sensing devices shall be capable of activation in accordance with the requirements of the simulated fire test.

15.704.4 Load Performance. Vents shall be tested to open freely and fully against a live load of 10 pounds per square foot (495 N/m^2). Vents intended for installation in areas subject to snow loads shall be tested to open freely and fully against snow loads as determined by the building official.

15.704.5 Simulated Fire Test.

15.704.5.1 Requirements. Vents shall be tested to open fully to operational position in five minutes when subjected to a precalibrated time-temperature gradient that heats the air within the vent cavity to 500°F (260°C) within the five-minute period. Where vents are operated by fixed-temperature fusible devices, the device shall be located in the expected flow pattern of hot gases and not shielded from fire temperatures. The actual load on the device shall not exceed its greatest load capacity.

15.704.5.2 Calibration. Correction of the test calibration may be accomplished by varying the height of the vent being tested or the height of the test-fuel pan.

15.704.5.3 Test method. Test units shall be end-supported 35 inches (890 mm) above the fire test floor. Two Type K, chrome lus. alumel 18-gage thermocouples shall be attached to the inside of the vent, 1 inch (25.4 mm) below the highest point of the cavity. The leads shall be connected to a recording potentiometer, 0°F to 2,000°F (−18°C to 1093°C) range multipoint.

A one-square-foot (305 mm by 305 mm) steel test-fuel pan shall be centered under the test unit on the floor. Isopropyl alcohol shall be poured into the pan to a depth of $^1/_2$ inch (13 mm). The alcohol shall be ignited and a determination made as to the ability of the test unit to meet the test requirements.

During the test there shall not be any flame impingment on the test unit lid or dropout glazing.

15.704.5.4 Repetitions. Each unit tested shall successfully pass five simulated fire tests per mode of operation without mechanical or structural failure. Modes of operation tested shall include (i) activation of the manual release mechanism on units so equipped, and (ii) activation of the heat-sensing device.

> **EXCEPTION:** Drop-out glazing vents need be tested only once per unit. Release of the glazing is a normal test response.

Necessary resetting or replacement of the heat-sensing device shall not be considered a mechanical or structural failure.

SECTION 15.705 — MARKING

Each unit shall bear a durable, visible label stating the name and location of the manufacturer, the model designation and the year of manufacture.

UNIFORM BUILDING CODE STANDARD 18-1
SOILS CLASSIFICATION

Based on Standard Method D 2487-69 of the American Society for Testing and Materials.
Extracted, with permission, from the *Annual Book of ASTM Standards,* copyright American Society for
Testing and Materials, 100 Barr Harbor Drive, West Conshohocken, PA 19428

See Sections 1801.2 and 1803.1, *Uniform Building Code*

SECTION 18.101 — SCOPE

This standard describes a system for classifying mineral and organomineral soils for engineering purposes based on laboratory determination of particle-size characteristics, liquid limit and plasticity index.

SECTION 18.102 — APPARATUS

Apparatus of an approved type shall be used to perform the following tests and procedures: Preparation of soil samples, liquid limit test, plastic limit test and particle-size analysis.

SECTION 18.103 — SAMPLING

Sampling shall be conducted in accordance with approved methods for soil investigation and sampling by auger borings, for Penetration Test and Split-barrel Sampling of Soils, and for Thin-walled Tube Sampling of Soils.

The sample shall be carefully identified as to origin by a boring number and sample number in conjunction with a job number, a geologic stratum, a pedologic horizon or a location description with respect to a permanent monument, a grid system or a station number and offset with respect to a stated center line.

The sample should also be described in accordance with an approved visual-manual procedure. (A soil which is composed primarily of undecayed or partially decayed organic matter and has a fibrous texture, dark brown to black color, and organic odor should be designated as a highly organic soil, PT, and not subjected to the classification procedures described hereafter.)

SECTION 18.104 — TEST SAMPLE

Test samples shall represent that portion of the field sample finer than the 3-inch (76 mm) sieve and shall be obtained as follows:

Air dry the field sample; weigh the field sample; and separate the field sample into two fractions on a 3-inch (76 mm) sieve. Weigh the fraction retained on the 3-inch (76 mm) sieve. Compute the percentage of plus 3-inch (76 mm) material in the field sample and note this percentage as auxiliary information. Thoroughly mix the fraction passing the 3-inch (76 mm) sieve and select test samples.

SECTION 18.105 — PRELIMINARY CLASSIFICATION PROCEDURE

Procedure for the determination of percentage finer than the No. 200 (75 μm) sieve is as follows:

1. From the material passing the 3-inch (76 mm) sieve, select a test sample and determine the percentage of the test sample finer than the No. 200 (75 μm) sieve. (This step may be omitted if the soil can obviously be classified as fine-grained by visual inspection.)

2. Classify the soil as coarse-grained if more than 50 percent of the test sample is retained on the No. 200 (75 μm) sieve.

3. Classify the soil as fine-grained if 50 percent or more of the test sample passes the No. 200 (75 μm) sieve.

SECTION 18.106 — PROCEDURE FOR CLASSIFICATION OF COARSE-GRAINED SOILS (MORE THAN 50 PERCENT RETAINED)

Select test samples from the material passing the 3-inch (76 mm) sieve for the determination of particle-size characteristics, liquid limit and plasticity index. Determine the cumulative particle-size distribution of the fraction coarser than the No. 200 (75 μm) sieve.

Classify the sample as *gravel,* G, if 50 percent or more of the coarse fraction [plus No. 200 (75 μm) sieve] is retained on the No. 4 (4.75 mm) sieve. Classify the sample as *sand,* S, if more than 50 percent of the coarse fraction [plus No. 200 (75 μm) sieve] passes the No. 4 (75 mm) sieve.

If less than 5 percent of the test sample passed the No. 200 (75 μm) sieve, compute the coefficient of uniformity, C_u, and coefficient of curvature, C_z, as given in Formulas 18-1-1 and 18-1-2:

$$C_u = \frac{D_{60}}{D_{10}} \qquad (18\text{-}1\text{-}1)$$

$$C_z = \frac{(D_{30})^2}{D_{10} \times D_{60}} \qquad (18\text{-}1\text{-}2)$$

in which D_{10}, D_{30} and D_{60} are the particle size diameters corresponding respectively to 10, 30 and 60 percent passing on the cumulative particle size distribution curve.

Classify the sample as well-graded gravel, GW, or well-graded sand, SW, if C_u is greater than 4 for gravel and 6 for sand, and C_z is between 1 and 3. Classify the sample as poorly graded gravel, GP, or poorly graded sand, SP, if either the C_u or the C_z criteria for well-graded soils are not satisfied.

If more than 12 percent of the test sample passed the No. 200 (75 μm) sieve, determine the liquid limit and the plasticity index of a portion of the test sample passing the No. 40 (425 μm) sieve in accordance with approved methods.

Classify the sample as silty gravel, GM, or silty sand, SM, if the results of the limits tests show that the fines are silty, that is, the plot of the liquid limit versus plasticity index falls below the "A" line (see Plasticity Table 18-1-A) or the plasticity index is less than 4.

Classify the sample as clayey gravel, GC, or clayey sand, SC, if the fines are clayey, that is, the plot of liquid limit versus plasticity index falls above the "A" line and the plasticity index is greater than 7.

If the fines are intermediate between silt and clay, that is, the plot of liquid limit versus plasticity index falls on or practically on the "A" line or falls above the "A" line but the plasticity index is in the range of 4 to 7, the soil should be given a borderline classification, such as GM-GC or SM-SC.

If 5 to 12 percent of the test sample passed the No. 200 (75 μm) sieve, the soil should be given a borderline classification based on both its gradation and limit test characteristics, such as GW-GC or SP-SM. (In doubtful cases the rule is to favor the less plastic classification. Example: A gravel with 10 percent fines, a C_u of 20, a C_z of 2.0, and a plasticity index of 6 would be classified as GW-GM rather than GW-GC.)

SECTION 18.107 — PROCEDURE FOR CLASSIFICATION OF FINE-GRAINED SOILS (50 PERCENT OR MORE PASSING)

From the material passing the 3-inch (76 mm) sieve, select a test sample for the determination of the liquid limit and plasticity index. The method for wet preparation shall be used for soils containing organic matter or irreversible mineral colloids.

Determine the liquid limit and the plasticity index of a portion of the test sample passing the No. 40 (425 µm) sieve.

Classify the soil as inorganic clay, C, if the plot of liquid limit versus plasticity index falls above the "A" line and the plasticity index is greater than 7.

Classify the soil as inorganic clay of low to medium plasticity, CL, if the liquid limit is less than 50 and the plot of liquid limit versus plasticity index falls above the "A" line and the plasticity index is greater than 7. See area identified as CL on the Plasticity Chart of Table 18-1-A.

Classify the soil as inorganic clay of high plasticity, CH, if the liquid limit is greater than 50 and the plot of liquid limit versus plasticity index falls above the "A" line. In cases where the liquid limit exceeds 100 or the plasticity index exceeds 60, the plasticity chart may be expanded by maintaining the same scales on both axes and extending the "A" line at the indicated slope. See areas identified as CH on the Plasticity Chart, Table 18-1-A.

Classify the soil as inorganic silt, M, if the plot of liquid limit versus plasticity index falls below the "A" line or if the plasticity index is less than 4, unless it is suspected that organic matter is present in sufficient amounts to influence the soil properties, then tentatively classify the soil as organic silt or clay, O.

If the soil has a dark color and an organic odor when moist and warm, a second liquid limit test should be performed on a test sample which has been oven dried at 110°C ± 5°C for 24 hours.

Classify the soil as organic silt or clay, O, if the liquid limit after oven drying is less than three fourths of the liquid limit of the original sample determined before drying.

Classify the soil as inorganic silt of low plasticity, ML, or as organic silt of low plasticity, ML, or as organic silt or silt-clay of low plasticity, OL, if the liquid limit is less than 50 and the plot of liquid limit versus plasticity index falls below the "A" line or the plasticity index is less than 4. See area identified as ML and OL on the Plasticity Chart, Table 18-1-A.

Classify the soil as inorganic silt of medium to high plasticity, MH, or as organic clay or silt-clay of medium to high plasticity, OH, if the liquid limit is more than 50 and the plot of liquid limit versus plasticity index falls below the "A" line. See area identified as MH and OH on the Plasticity Chart of Table 18-1-A.

In order to indicate their borderline characteristics, some fine-grained soils should be classified by dual symbols.

If the plot of liquid limit versus plasticity index falls on or practically on the "A" line or above the "A" line where the plasticity index is in the range of 4 to 7, the soil should be given an appropriate borderline classification such as CL-ML or CH-OH.

If the plot of liquid limit versus plasticity index falls on or practically on the line liquid limit = 50, the soil should be given an appropriate borderline classification such as CL-CH or ML-MH. (In doubtful cases the rule for classification is to favor the more plastic classification. Example: a fine-grained soil with a liquid limit of 50 and a plasticity index of 22 would be classified as CH-MH rather than CL-ML.)

TABLE 18-1-A—SOIL CLASSIFICATION CHART

	MAJOR DIVISIONS		GROUP SYMBOLS	TYPICAL NAMES
COARSE-GRAINED SOILS More than 50% retained on No. 200 (75 µm) sieve*	GRAVELS 50% or more of coarse fraction retained on No. 4 (4.75 mm) sieve	CLEAN GRAVELS	GW	Well-graded gravels and gravel-sand mixtures, little or no fines
			GP	Poorly graded gravels and gravel-sand mixtures, little or no fines
		GRAVELS WITH FINES	GM	Silty gravels, gravel-sand-silt mixtures
			GC	Clayey gravels, gravel-sand-clay mixtures
	SANDS More than 50% of coarse fraction passes No. 4 (4.75 mm) sieve	CLEAN SANDS	SW	Well-graded sands and gravelly sands, little or no fines
			SP	Poorly graded sands and gravelly and sands, little or no fines
		SANDS WITH FINES	SM	Silty sands, sand-silt mixtures
			SC	Clayey sands, sand-clay mixtures
FINE-GRAINED SOILS 50% or more passes No. 200 (75 µm) sieve[1]	SILTS AND CLAYS Liquid limit 50% or less		ML	Inorganic silts, very fine sands, rock flour, silty or clayey fine sands
			CL	Inorganic clays of low to medium plasticity, gravelly clays, sandy clays, silty clays, lean clays
			OL	Organic silts and organic silty clays of low plasticity
	SILTS AND CLAYS Liquid limit greater than 50%		MH	Inorganic silts, micaceous or diatomaceous fine sands or silts, elastic silts
			CH	Inorganic clays of high plasticity, fat clays
			OH	Organic clays of medium to high plasticity
	Highly Organic Soils		PT	Peat, muck and other highly organic soils

[1]Based on the material passing the 3-inch (76 mm) sieve.

TABLE 18-1-A—SOIL CLASSIFICATION CHART—(Continued)

CLASSIFICATION CRITERIA		
	$C_u = D_{60}/D_{10}$ Greater than 4	
	$C_z = \dfrac{(D_{30})^3}{D_{10} \times D_{60}}$ Between 1 and 3	
	Not meeting both criteria for GW	
	Atterberg limits plot below "A" line or plasticity index less than 4	Atterberg limits plotting in hatched area are borderline classifications requiring use of dual symbols
CLASSIFICATION ON BASIS OF PERCENTAGE OF FINES	Atterberg limits plot below "A" line and plasticity index greater than 7	
Less than 5%, Pass No. 200 (75 µm) sieve GW, GP, SW, SP More than 12% Pass N. 200 (75 µm) sieve GM, GC, SM, SC 5% to 12% Pass No. 200 (75 µm) sieve **Borderline Classification** **requiring use of dual symbols**	$C_u = D_{60}/D_{10}$ Greater than 6	
	$C_z = \dfrac{(D_{30})^3}{D_{10} \times D_{60}}$ Between 1 and 3	
	Not meeting both criteria for SW	
	Atterberg limits plot below "A" line or plasticity index less than 4	Atterberg limits plotting in hatched area are borderline classifications requiring use of dual symbols
	Atterberg limits plot above "A" line and plasticity index greater than 7	

PLASTICITY CHART

For classification of fine-grained soils and fine fraction of coarse-grained soils

Atterberg limits plotting in hatched area are borderline classifications requiring use of dual symbols.

Equation of A-line:

$PI = 0.73 (LL - 20)$

Plasticity Index

Liquid Limit

Visual-Manual Identification

UNIFORM BUILDING CODE STANDARD 18-2
EXPANSION INDEX TEST
Based on Recommendations of the Los Angeles Section ASCE Soil Committee
See Sections 1801.2 and 1803.1, *Uniform Building Code*

SECTION 18.201 — SCOPE

The expansion index test is designed to measure a basic index property of the soil and in this respect is comparable to other index tests such as the Atterberg limits. In formulating the test procedures no attempt has been made to duplicate any particular moisture or loading conditions which may occur in the field. Rather, an attempt has been made to control all variables which influence the expansive characteristics of a particular soil and still retain a practical test for general engineering usage.

SECTION 18.202 — APPARATUS

18.202.1 Mold. The mold shall be cylindrical in shape, made of metal and have the capacity and dimensions indicated in Figure 18-2-1. It shall have a detachable collar inscribed with a mark 2.00 inches (50.8 mm) above the base. The lower section of the mold is designed to retain a removable stainless steel ring 1.00 inch (25.4 mm) in height, 4.01-inch (101.85 mm) internal diameter and 0.120-inch (3.048 mm) wall thickness.

18.202.2 Tamper. A metal tamper having a 2-inch-diameter (50.8 mm) circular face and weighing 5.5 pounds (2.5 kg) shall be equipped with a suitable arrangement to control height of drop to a free fall of 12 inches (305 mm) above the top of the soil.

18.202.3 Balance. A balance or scale of at least 1,000-gram capacity sensitive to 0.1 gram.

18.202.4 Drying Oven. A thermostatically controlled drying oven capable of maintaining a temperature of 230°F ± 9°F (110°C ± 5°C), for drying moisture samples.

18.202.5 Straight Edge. Steel straight edge 12 inches (305 mm) in length and having one bevelled edge.

18.202.6 Sieves. A No. 4 (4.75 mm) sieve conforming to the requirements of the specifications for sieves for testing purposes.

18.202.7 Mixing Tools. Miscellaneous tools such as mixing pans, spoons, trowels, spatula, etc., or a suitable mechanical device for thoroughly mixing the sample of soil with increments of water.

SECTION 18.203 — SAMPLE PREPARATION

18.203.1 Preparation for Sieving. If the soil sample is damp when received from the field, dry it until it becomes friable under a trowel. Drying may be in air or by use of drying apparatus such that the temperature of the sample does not exceed 140°F (60°C). Then thoroughly break up the aggregations in such a manner as to avoid reducing the natural size of the individual particles. If particles larger than $^1/_4$ inch (6.4 mm) are possibly expansive, such as claystone, shale or weathered volcanic rock, they should be broken down so as to pass the No. 4 (4.75 mm) sieve.

18.203.2 Sieving. Sieve an adequate quantity of the representative pulverized soil over the No. 4 (4.75 mm) sieve. Record the percentage of coarse material retained on the No. 4 (4.75 mm) sieve and discard.

18.203.3 Sample. Select a representative sample, weighing approximately 2 pounds (0.91 kg) or more, of the soil prepared as described in Sections 18.203.1 and 18.203.2 above.

SECTION 18.204 — SPECIMEN PREPARATION

18.204.1 Moisture Determination. Thoroughly mix the selected representative sample with sufficient distilled water to bring the soil to approximately optimum moisture content. After mixing, take a representative sample of the material for moisture determination and seal the remainder of the soil in a close-fitting airtight container for a period of at least six hours.

Weigh the moisture sample immediately and dry in an oven at 230° ± 9°F (110°C ± 5°C), for at least 12 hours or to a constant weight to determine the moisture content. Moisture sample shall not weigh less than 300 grams.

18.204.2 Specimen Molding. Form a specimen by compacting the cured soil in the 4-inch-diameter (102 mm) mold in two equal layers to give a total compacted depth of approximately 2 inches (51 mm). Compact each layer by 15 uniformly distributed blows of the tamper dropping free from a height of 12 inches (305 mm) above the top of the soil, when a sleeve-type rammer is used, or from 12 inches (305 mm) above the approximate elevation of each finally compacted layer when a stationary mounted type of tamper is used. During the compaction the mold shall rest on a uniform, rigid foundation, such as provided by a cube of concrete weighing at least 200 pounds (90.72 kg).

18.204.3 Trim Specimen. Following compaction, remove the upper and lower portions of the mold from the inner ring and carefully trim the top and bottom of the ring by means of the straight edge.

18.204.4 Saturation. Weigh the compacted sample and determine the percent saturation. Adjust the moisture content to achieve 50 percent saturation by the addition of water or air drying the sample. Repeat Sections 18.204.2 and 18.204.3 above.

18.204.5 Specific Gravity. Repeat Section 18.204.4 until the saturation of the compacted sample is between 49 percent and 51 percent for a specific gravity of 2.7.

SECTION 18.205 — EXPANSION MEASUREMENT

18.205.1 Consolidometer. Place the soil specimen in a consolidometer or equivalent loading device with porous stones at the top and bottom. Place on the specimen a total load of 12.63 pounds (56.2 N), including the weight of the upper porous stone and any unbalanced weight of the loading machine. Allow the specimen to consolidate under this load for a period of 10 minutes, after which time make the initial reading on the consolidometer dial indicator to an accuracy of 0.0005 inch (0.010 mm).

18.205.2 Sample Submersion. Submerge the sample in distilled water, making periodic readings on the dial indicator for a period of 24 hours or until the rate of expansion becomes less than 0.0002 inch (0.0051 mm) per hour but not less than three hours submerged time.

18.205.3 Weighing. Remove the sample from the loading machine after the final reading and weigh the specimen to the nearest 0.1 gram.

SECTION 18.206 — CALCULATIONS AND REPORT

18.206.1 Expansion Index. Calculate the expansion index as follows:

$$E.I. = \frac{(\text{final thickness} - \text{initial thickness})}{\text{initial thickness}} \times 1,000$$

Report the expansion index to the nearest whole number. If the initial sample thickness is greater than the final sample thickness, report the expansion index as 0. The molding moisture content and initial dry density of the specimen should accompany the expansion index in the complete presentation of results.

18.206.2 Weighted Expansion Index. The weighted expansion index for a particular soil profile shall be determined as the summation of the products obtained by multiplying the expansion index by the factor appropriate to its elevation.

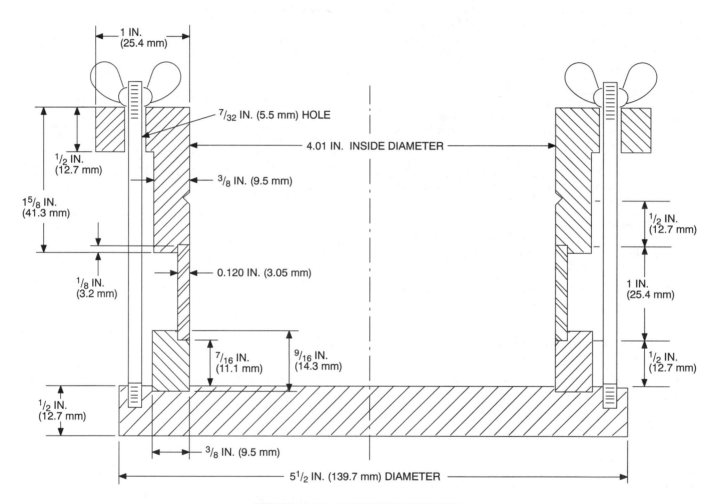

FIGURE 18-2-1—EXPANSION TEST MOLD

UNIFORM BUILDING CODE STANDARD 19-1
WELDING REINFORCING STEEL, METAL INSERTS AND CONNECTIONS IN REINFORCED CONCRETE CONSTRUCTION
See Sections 1903.5.2, 1903.10, and 1912.14,
Uniform Building Code

SECTION 19.101 — ADOPTION OF AWS CODE

19.101.1 Except for the limitations, deletions, modifications or amendments set forth in Section 19.102 of this standard, the welding of concrete reinforcing steel for splices (prestressing steel excepted), steel connection devices, inserts, anchors and anchorage details, as well as any other welding required in reinforced concrete construction, shall be in accordance with the *Structural Welding Code—Reinforcing Steel,* ANSI/AWS D1.4-92, published by the American Welding Society, Inc., Copyright 1992, 550 North LeJeune Road, Miami, Florida 33135, as if set out at length herein.

SECTION 19.102 — DELETIONS AND AMENDMENTS

19.102.1 General. The American Welding Society, Inc., code adopted by Section 19.101 applies to all materials, processes, design, workmanship and testing of welding performed as a part of reinforced concrete construction, except as set forth in this section.

19.102.2 Deletions. The following sections and chapters are deleted:

Section 1.6

Section 1.7

Section 3.7

Section 5.6.3

Chapter 7

19.102.3 Amendments

1. **Sec. 1.2.1** is amended by changing the last sentence to read as follows:

When reinforcing steel is welded to primary structural steel members, welding procedures, welder qualification requirements and welding electrodes shall be in accordance with Chapter 22, Divisions II, III and VI or VII, of this code and approved national standards.

2. **Sec. 1.2.3** is amended to read as follows:

1.2.3. All references to the need for approval shall be interpreted to mean approval by the building official.

3. **Sec. 1.2.4** is amended to read as follows:

1.2.4 When structural steel base metals make up the entire weld joint, the engineer may select the use of welding procedures and welder qualifications in accordance with Chapter 22, Divisions II, III and VI or VII, of this code and approved national standards to perform that weld, provided other relevant provisions of UBC Standard 19-1 are considered.

4. **Sec. 1.3.3** is amended to read as follows:

1.3.3 Base metal, other than those previously listed, shall be one of the structural steels listed in Chapter 22, Divisions II, III and VI or VII, of this code.

5. **Sec. 1.5** is amended to read as follows:

1.5 Definitions

The welding terms used in this code shall be interpreted in accordance with the definitions given in Chapter 22, Divisions V, VIII and IX or X, of this code and approved national standards.

6. **Sec. 2.1** is amended to read as follows:

2.1 Base Metal Stresses. The allowable base metal stresses shall be those specified in this code for reinforced concrete construction.

UNIFORM BUILDING CODE STANDARD 19-2

MILL-MIXED GYPSUM CONCRETE AND
POURED GYPSUM ROOF DIAPHRAGMS

Based on Reports of Test Programs by S. B. Barnes and Associates dated February 1955, November 1956, January 1958, and February 1962, and Standard Specification C 317-70 of the American Society for Testing and Materials. Extracted, with permission, from the _Annual Book of ASTM Standards,_ copyright American Society for Testing and Materials, 100 Barr Harbor Drive, West Conshohocken, PA 19428

See Sections 1903.9 and 1925.3, _Uniform Building Code_

Part I—Mill-mixed Gypsum Concrete

SECTION 19.201 — SCOPE

This part covers mill-mixed gypsum concrete. Gypsum concrete supplied under this standard shall be mill-mixed gypsum concrete, consisting essentially of calcined gypsum and suitable aggregate, requiring the addition of water only at the job. Gypsum concrete is intended for use in construction of poured-in-place roof decks or slabs. Two classes, based on the compressive strength and density, are covered.

SECTION 19.202 — COMPOSITION

Gypsum concrete shall consist essentially of calcined gypsum and wood chips or wood shavings, proportioned to meet the applicable requirements of this standard. Calcined gypsum used in the mill mixed gypsum concrete shall conform to the requirements of ASTM C 28-76a. Wood chips or wood shavings shall be of dry wood, uniform and clean in appearance, shall pass a 1-inch (25 mm) sieve, and shall not be more than $1/16$ inch (1.6 mm) in thickness.

SECTION 19.203 — TIME OF SETTING

Gypsum concrete shall not set in less than 20 minutes nor more than 90 minutes.

SECTION 19.204 — COMPRESSIVE STRENGTH AND DENSITY

Gypsum concrete shall have the following compressive strength and density for the respective classes:

	COMPRESSIVE STRENGTH MINIMUM psi (MPa)	DENSITY POUNDS PER CUBIC FOOT (kg/m³)
Class A	500 (3.5)	60 (960)
Class B	1,000 (6.9)	—

SECTION 19.205 — METHODS OF TESTING

The physical properties of gypsum concrete shall be determined in accordance with approved methods.

Part II—Poured-in-place Reinforced Gypsum Concrete

SECTION 19.206 — SCOPE

This part covers the design of poured-in-place reinforced gypsum concrete roof decks when used as a horizontal diaphragm.

SECTION 19.207 — DESIGN

19.207.1 General. The gypsum roof diaphragm shall consist of sub-purlins welded transversely to primary purlins. Formboard is then placed on the flanges of the subpurlins. Wire mesh reinforcement is then placed over the subpurlins and formboard and lapped at least 4 inches (102 mm) or one mesh on ends and edges, whichever is greater. Gypsum concrete meeting the requirements of Part I of this standard is then placed to a minimum thickness of 2 inches (51 mm) over the formboard and $5/8$ inch (16 mm) over the subpurlins and doweling elements. The bulb section or top flange of the subpurlin shall be fully embedded in the gypsum concrete.

19.207.2 Diaphragm Shear. Shear in poured gypsum concrete diaphragms shall be determined by the formula:

$$Q = .16f_g \, t \, C_l + 1,000 \, (k_1 \, d_1 + k_2 \, d_2)$$

For **SI:** $\quad Q = 1.36f_g \, t \, C_l + 17.86 \, (k_1 \, d_1 + k_2 \, d_2)$

WHERE:

C_l = 1.0 for Class A gypsum; 1.5 for Class B gypsum.

d_1 = diameter of mesh wires passing over subpurlins, in inches (mm), except hexagonal mesh.

d_2 = diameter, in inches (mm), of mesh wires parallel to subpurlins or of hexagonal wires.

f_g = oven-dry compressive strength of gypsum in pounds per square inch (MPa) as determined by tests conforming to this standard.

k_1 = number of mesh wires per foot (m) passing over subpurlins.

k_2 = number of mesh wires per foot (m) parallel to subpurlins or .7 times the number of hexagonal wires. Note: k_2 = 8.5 (27.9) for 2-inch (51 mm) hexagonal mesh woven of No. 19 gage galvanized wire with additional longitudinal No. 16 gage galvanized wires spaced every 3 inches (76 mm) across the width of the mesh.

Q = allowable shear on diaphragm in pounds per linear foot (kg/m), which includes a one-third increase for short-time loading.

t = thickness of gypsum concrete between subpurlins, in inches (mm). For the purpose of computing diaphragm shear values, t shall not exceed 4 inches (102 mm).

The solution of the above equation for commonly used thickness and mesh types for each class of gypsum would give the values set forth in Table 19-2-A.

19.207.3 Shear Transfer. Bolts, dowels or other approved elements may be used to transfer diaphragm shears to perimeter or other structural members. Allowable bolt and dowel stresses shall comply with Table 19-G and Section 1603 of this code.

TABLE 19-2-A—ALLOWABLE SHEAR VALUES IN POUNDS PER FOOT USING BULB TEE SUBPURLINS[1]

CLASS OF GYPSUM CONCRETE	CONCRETE THICKNESS (inches)	MESH TYPE[2]		
		4″ × 8″ (102 mm × 203 mm) No. 12-No. 14 (Galvanized)	6″ × 6″ (152 mm × 152 mm) No. 10-No. 10	Hexagonal[3] (Galvanized)
× 6.89 for kPa	× 25.4 for mm	× 14.59 for N/m		
A (500 psi)	2 $2^1/_2$	600 640	700 740	760 800
B (1,000 psi)	2 $2^1/_2$	920 1,040	1,020 1,140	1,080 1,200

[1]The tabulated shear values are for short-time loads due to wind or earthquake forces and are not permitted a one-third increase for duration of load.

[2]Mesh shall be lapped at least 4 inches (102 mm) or one mesh on ends and edges, whichever is greater.

[3]Two-inch (51 mm) hexagonal mesh woven of No. 19 gage galvanized wire with additional longitudinal No. 16 gage galvanized wires spaced every 3 inches (76 mm) across the width of the mesh.

UNIFORM BUILDING CODE STANDARD 21-1
BUILDING BRICK, FACING BRICK AND HOLLOW BRICK
(MADE FROM CLAY OR SHALE)

Based on Standard Specifications C 62-94a, C 216-92c, and C 652-94 of the American Society for Testing and Materials. Extracted, with permission, from the *Annual Book of ASTM Standards,* copyright American Society for Testing and Materials, 100 Barr Harbor Drive, West Conshohocken, PA 19428

See Section 2102.2, Item 4, *Uniform Building Code*

SECTION 21.101 — SCOPE

21.101.1 General. This standard covers brick made from clay or shale and subjected to heat treatment at elevated temperatures (firing), and intended for use in brick masonry. In addition, this standard covers dimension and distortion tolerances for facing brick and hollow brick to be used in masonry construction.

21.101.2 Definition.

BRICK is a solid clay masonry unit whose net cross-sectional area in any plane parallel to the surface containing the cores or cells is at least 75 percent of the gross cross-sectional area measured in the same plane.

21.101.3 Grades. Three grades of brick are covered.

Grade SW. Brick intended for use where a high and uniform resistance to damage caused by cyclic freezing is desired and the exposure is such that the brick may be frozen when saturated with water.

Grade MW. Brick intended for use where moderate resistance to cyclic freezing damage is permissible or where brick may be damp but not saturated with water when freezing occurs.

Grade NW. Brick with little resistance to cyclic freezing damage but which may be acceptable for applications protected from water absorption and freezing.

21.101.4 Grade Requirements for Face Exposure. The selection of the grade of brick for face exposure of vertical or horizontal surfaces shall conform to Table 21-1-A and Figure 21-1-1.

SECTION 21.102 — PHYSICAL PROPERTIES

21.102.1 Durability. The brick shall conform to the physical requirements for the grade specified, as prescribed in Table 21-1-B.

21.102.2 Substitution of Grades. Grades SW and MW may be used in lieu of Grade NW, and Grade SW in lieu of Grade MW.

21.102.3 Waiver of Saturation Coefficient. The saturation coefficient shall be waived provided the average cold-water absorption of a random sample of five bricks does not exceed 8 percent, no more than one brick of the sample exceeds 8 percent and its cold-water absorption must be less than 10 percent.

21.102.4 Freezing and Thawing. The requirements specified in this standard for water absorption (five-hour boiling) and saturation coefficient shall be waived, provided a sample of five bricks, meeting all other requirements, complies with the following requirements when subjected to 50 cycles of the freezing-and-thawing test:

Grade SW — No breakage and not greater than 0.5 percent loss in dry weight of any individual brick.

Brick is not required to conform to the provisions of this section, and these do not apply unless the sample fails to conform to the requirements for absorption and saturation coefficient prescribed in Table 21-1-B or the absorption requirements in Section 21.102.3.

A particular lot or shipment shall be given the same grading as a previously tested lot, without repeating the freezing-and-thawing test, provided the brick is made by the same manufacturer from similar raw materials and by the same method of forming; and provided also that a sample of five bricks selected from the particular lot has an average and individual minimum strength not less than a previously graded sample, and has average and individual maximum water absorption and saturation coefficient not greater than those of the previously tested sample graded according to the freezing-and-thawing test.

21.102.5 Waiver of Durability Requirements. If brick is intended for use exposed to weather where the weathering index is less than 50 (see Figure 21-1-1), unless otherwise specified, the requirements given in Section 21.102.1 for water absorption (five-hour boiling) and for saturation coefficient shall be waived and a minimum average strength of 2,500 pounds per square inch (17 200 kPa) shall apply.

SECTION 21.103 — SIZE, CORING AND FROGGING

21.103.1 Tolerances on Dimensions. The maximum permissible variation in dimensions of individual units shall not exceed those given in Table 21-1-C.

21.103.2 Coring. The net cross-sectional area of cored brick in any plane parallel to the surface containing the cores or cells shall be at least 75 percent of the gross cross-sectional area measured in the same plane. No part of any hole shall be less than $3/4$ inch (19.1 mm) from any edge of the brick.

21.103.3 Frogging. One bearing face of each brick may have a recess or panel frog and deep frogs. The recess or panel frog shall not exceed $3/8$ inch (9.5 mm) in depth and no part of the recess or panel frog shall be less than $3/4$ inch (19.1 mm) from any edge of the brick. In brick containing deep frogs, frogs deeper than $3/8$ inch (9.5 mm), any cross section through the deep frogs parallel to the surface containing the deep frogs shall conform to the requirements of Section 21.103.2.

SECTION 21.104 — VISUAL INSPECTION

21.104.1 General. The brick shall be free of defects, deficiencies and surface treatments, including coatings, that would interfere with the proper setting of the brick or significantly impair the strength or performance of the construction.

Minor indentations or surface cracks incidental to the usual method of manufacture, or the chipping resulting from the customary methods of handling in shipment and delivery should not be deemed grounds for rejection.

SECTION 21.105 — SAMPLING AND TESTING

21.105.1 Sampling and Testing. Brick shall be sampled and tested in accordance with ASTM C 67.

SECTION 21.106 — FACING BRICK

21.106.1 General. Facing brick shall be of Grade SW or MW and shall comply with the degree of mechanical perfection and size variations specified in this section. Grade SW may be used in lieu of Grade MW.

21.106.2 Types. Three types of facing brick are covered:

Type FBS. Brick for general use in exposed exterior and interior masonry walls and partitions where greater variation in sizes are permitted than are specified for Type FBX.

Type FBX. Brick for general use in exposed exterior and interior masonry walls and partitions where a high degree of mechanical perfection and minimum permissible variation in size are required.

Type FBA. Brick manufactured and selected to produce characteristic architectural effects resulting from nonuniformity in size and texture of individual units.

When the type is not specified, the requirements for Type FBS shall govern.

21.106.3 Tolerances on Dimensions. The brick shall not depart from the specified size to be used by more than the individual tolerance for the type specified set forth in Table 21-1-D. Tolerances on dimensions for Type FBA shall be as specified by the purchaser, but not more restrictive than Type FBS.

21.106.4 Warpage. Tolerances for distortion or warpage of face or edges of indivi-dual brick from a plane surface and from a straight line, respectively, shall not exceed the maximum for the type specified as set forth in Table 21-1-E. Tolerances on distortion for Type FBA shall be as specified by the purchaser.

21.106.5 Coring. Brick may be cored. The net cross-sectional area of cored brick in any plane parallel to the surface containing the cores or cells shall be at least 75 percent of the gross cross-sectional area measured in the same plane. No part of any hole shall be less than $^3/_4$ inch (19.1 mm) from any edge of the brick.

21.106.6 Frogging. One bearing face of each brick may have a recess or panel frog and deep frogs. The recess or panel frog shall not exceed $^3/_8$ inch (9.5 mm) in depth and no part of the recess or panel frog shall be less than $^3/_4$ inch (19.1 mm) from any edge of the brick. In brick containing deep frogs, frogs deeper than $^3/_8$ inch (9.5 mm), any cross section through the deep frogs parallel to the surface containing the deep frogs shall conform to the requirements of Section 21.106.5.

21.106.7 Visual Inspection. In addition to the requirements of Section 21.104, brick used in exposed wall construction shall have faces which are free of cracks or other imperfections detracting from the appearance of the designated sample when viewed from a distance of 15 feet (4600 mm) for Type FBX and a distance of 20 feet (6100 mm) for Types FBS and FBA.

SECTION 21.107 — HOLLOW BRICK

21.107.1 General. Hollow brick shall be of Grade SW or MW and comply with the physical requirements in Table 21-1-B and other requirements of this section. Grade SW may be used in lieu of Grade MW.

21.107.2 Definitions.

HOLLOW BRICK is a clay masonry unit whose net cross-sectional area (solid area) in any plane parallel to the surface, containing the cores, cells or deep frogs is less than 75 percent of its gross cross-sectional area measured in the same plane.

CORES are void spaces having a gross cross-sectional area equal to or less than $1^1/_2$ square inches (968 mm²).

CELLS are void spaces having a gross cross-sectional area greater than $1^1/_2$ square inches (968 mm²).

21.107.3 Types. Four types of hollow brick are covered:

Type HBS. Hollow brick for general use in exposed exterior and interior masonry walls and partitions greater variation in size are permitted than is specified for Type HBX.

Type HBX. Hollow brick for general use in exposed exterior and interior masonry walls and partitions where a high degree of mechanical perfection and minimum permissible variation in size are required.

Type HBA. Hollow brick manufactured and selected to produce characteristic architectural effects resulting from nonuniformity in size and texture of the individual units.

Type HBB. Hollow brick for general use in masonry walls and partitions where a particular color, texture, finish, uniformity, or limits on cracks, warpage, or other imperfections detracting from the appearance are not a consideration.

When the type is not specified, the requirements for Type HBS shall govern.

21.107.4 Class. Two classes of hollow brick are covered:

Class H40V. Hollow brick intended for use where void areas or hollow spaces greater than 25 percent, but not greater than 40 percent, of the gross cross-sectional area of the unit measured in any plane parallel to the surface containing the cores, cells or deep frogs are desired. The void spaces, web thicknesses and shell thicknesses shall comply with the requirements of Sections 21.107.5, 21.107.6 and 21.107.7.

Class H60V. Hollow brick intended for use where larger void areas are desired. The sum of these void areas shall be greater than 40 percent, but not greater than 60 percent, of the gross cross-sectional area of the unit measured in any plane parallel to the surface containing the cores, cells or deep frogs. The void spaces, web thicknesses and shell thicknesses shall comply with the requirements of Sections 21.107.5, 21.107.6 and 21.107.7 and to the minimum requirements of Table 21-1-F.

When the class is not specified, the requirements for Class H40V shall govern.

21.107.5 Hollow Spaces. Core holes shall not be less than $^5/_8$ inch (15.9 mm) from any edge of the brick, except for cored-shell hollow brick. Cored-shell hollow brick shall have a minimum shell thickness of $1^1/_2$ inches (38 mm). Cores greater than 1 square inch (645 mm²) in cored shells shall not be less than $^1/_2$ inch (13 mm) from any edge. Cores not greater than 1 inch square (645 mm²) in shells cored not more than 35 percent shall not be less than $^3/_8$ inch (9.5 mm) from any edge.

Cells shall not be less than $^3/_4$ inch (19.1 mm) from any edge of the brick except for double-shell hollow brick.

Double-shell hollow brick with inner and outer shells not less than $^1/_2$ inch (13 mm) thick may not have cells greater than $^5/_8$ inch (15.9 mm) in width or 5 inches (127 mm) in length between the inner and outer shell.

21.107.6 Webs. The thickness for webs between cells shall not be less than $^1/_2$ inch (13 mm), $^3/_8$ inch (9.5 mm) between cells and cores or $^1/_4$ inch (6 mm) between cores. The distance of voids from unexposed edges, which are recessed not less than $^1/_2$ inch (13 mm), shall not be less than $^1/_2$ inch (13 mm).

21.107.7 Frogging. One bearing face of each brick may have a recess or panel frog and deep frogs. The recess or panel frog shall not exceed $3/8$ inch (9.5 mm) in depth and no part of the recess or panel frog shall be less than $5/8$ inch (15.9 mm) from any edge of the brick. In brick containing deep frogs, frogs deeper than $3/8$ inch (9.5 mm), any cross section through the deep frogs parallel to the bearing surface shall conform to other requirements of Sections 21.107.2 and 21.107.4 for void area and Section 21.107.5 for hollow spaces.

21.107.8 Tolerances on Dimensions. The hollow brick shall not depart from the specified size by more than the individual tolerance for specified size by more than individual tolerances for the type specified as set forth in Table 21-1-G. Tolerances and dimensions for Type HBA shall be as specified by the purchaser.

21.107.9 Warpage. Tolerances for distortion or warpage of face or edges of individual hollow brick from a plane surface and from a straight line, respectively, shall not exceed the maximum for the type specified in Table 21-1-H. Tolerances on distortion for Type HBA shall be as specified by the purchaser.

21.107.10 Visual Inspection. In addition to the requirements of Section 21.104, brick used in exposed wall construction shall have faces which are free of cracks or other imperfections detracting from the appearance of a sample wall when viewed from a distance of 15 feet (4600 mm) for Type HBX and a distance of 20 feet (6100 mm) for Types HBS and HBA.

TABLE 21-1-A—GRADE REQUIREMENTS FOR FACE EXPOSURE

EXPOSURE	WEATHERING INDEX		
	Less than 50	50 to 500	500 and greater
In vertical surfaces: In contact with earth Not in contact with earth	MW MW	SW SW	SW SW
In other than vertical surfaces. In contact with earth Not in contact with earth	SW MW	SW SW	SW SW

TABLE 21-1-B—PHYSICAL REQUIREMENTS FOR TYPES OF UNIT MASONRY[5]

TYPE OF MASONRY	GRADE	MINIMUM FACE SHELL THICKNESS (inches)	MINIMUM[1] COMPRESSIVE STRENGTH PSI AVERAGE GROSS AREA × 6.89 for kPa — Average of Five Tests	Individual	MAXIMUM WATER ABSORPTION By Five-hour Boiling (percent) Average of Five Tests	Individual	MAXIMUM SATURATION COEFFICIENT[2] Average of Five Test	Individual	WATER ABSORPTION Maximum Pounds per Cubic Foot × 16 for kg/m³	MOISTURE CONTENT Maximum Percentage of Total Absorption	MINIMUM MODULUS OF RUPTURE Average of Five Tests	Individual
24-1. Building brick made from clay or shale[3]	SW		(brick flatwise) 3,000	2,500	17	20	.78	.80			(brick flatwise) psi Average Gross Area × 6.89 for kPa	
	MW		2,500	2,200	22	25	.88	.90				
	NW		1,500	1,250	no limit							
Hollow Brick[3]	SW	See Table 21-1-F	(net area)[4] 3,000	2,500	17	20	.78	.80				
	MW		2,500	2,000	22	25	.88	.90				
24-2. Sand-lime building brick	SW		4,500	3,500							600	400
	MW		2,500	2,000							450	300
24-14. Unburned clay masonry units			Based on Net Area (psi)[4] × 6.89 for kPa 300	250					Based on % of Dry Wt. 2.5%	4.0%	50	35

[1]Gross area of a unit shall be determined by multiplying the horizontal face dimension of the unit as placed in the wall by its thickness.

[2]The saturation coefficient is the ratio of absorption by 24-hour submersion in cold water to that after five-hour submersion in boiling water.

[3]If the average cold-water absorption of a random sample of five bricks does not exceed 8.0 percent, when no more than one brick unit of the sample exceeds 8.0 percent and its cold-water absorption must be less than 10.0 percent, the saturation coefficient shall be waived.

[4]Based on net area of a unit which shall be taken as the area of solid material in shells and webs actually carrying stresses in a direction parallel to the direction of loading.

[5]For the compressive strength requirements, test the unit with the compressive force perpendicular to the bed surface of the unit, with the unit in the stretcher position.

TABLE 21-1-C—TOLERANCES ON DIMENSIONS

SPECIFIED DIMENSION (inches)	MAXIMUM PERMISSIBLE VARIATION FROM SPECIFIED DIMENSION, PLUS OR MINUS (inch)
× 25.4 for mm	
Up to 3, incl.	$3/32$
Over 3 to 4, incl.	$1/8$
Over 4 to 6, incl.	$3/16$
Over 6 to 8, incl.	$1/4$
Over 8 to 12, incl.	$5/16$
Over 12 to 16, incl.	$3/8$

TABLE 21-1-D—TOLERANCES ON DIMENSIONS

SPECIFIED DIMENSION (inches)	MAXIMUM PERMISSIBLE VARIATION FROM SPECIFIED DIMENSION, PLUS OR MINUS (inch)	
	Type FBX	Type FBS
× 25.4 for mm		
3 and under	$1/16$	$3/32$
Over 3 to 4, incl.	$3/32$	$1/8$
Over 4 to 6, incl.	$1/8$	$3/16$
Over 6 to 8, incl.	$5/32$	$1/4$
Over 8 to 12, incl.	$7/32$	$5/16$
Over 12 to 16, incl.	$9/32$	$3/8$

TABLE 21-1-E—TOLERANCES ON DISTORTION

MAXIMUM FACE DIMENSION (inches)	MAXIMUM PERMISSIBLE DISTORTION (inch)	
	Type FBX	Type FBS
× 25.4 for mm		
8 and under	$1/16$	$3/32$
Over 8 to 12, incl.	$3/32$	$1/8$
Over 12 to 16, incl.	$1/8$	$5/32$

TABLE 21-1-F—HOLLOW BRICK (Class H60V) MINIMUM THICKNESS OF FACE SHELLS AND WEBS

NOMINAL WIDTH OF UNIT (inches)	FACE SHELL THICKNESS (inches)		END SHELLS OR WEBS (inches)	WEB THICKNESS PER FOOT, TOTAL (inches per foot)[1]
	Solid	Cored or Double Shell		
× 25.4 for mm				× 83 for mm per m
3 and 4	$3/4$	—	$3/4$	$1 5/8$
6	1	$1 1/2$	1	$2 1/4$
8	$1 1/4$	$1 1/2$	1	$2 1/4$
10	$1 3/8$	$1 5/8$	$1 1/8$	$2 1/2$
12	$1 1/2$	2	$1 1/8$	$2 1/2$

[1]The sum of the measured thickness of all webs in the unit, multiplied by 12 (305 when using metric), and divided by the length of the unit. In the case of open-ended units where the open-end portion is solid grouted, the length of that open-ended portion shall be deducted from the overall length of the unit.

TABLE 21-1-G—TOLERANCES ON DIMENSIONS

SPECIFIED DIMENSION (inches)	MAXIMUM PERMISSIBLE VARIATION FROM SPECIFIED DIMENSION, PLUS OR MINUS (inch)	
	Type HBX	Types HBS and HBB
	× 25.4 for mm	
3 and under	$1/16$	$3/32$
Over 3 to 4, incl.	$3/32$	$1/8$
Over 4 to 6, incl.	$1/8$	$3/16$
Over 6 to 8, incl.	$5/32$	$1/4$
Over 8 to 12, incl.	$7/32$	$5/16$
Over 12 to 16, incl.	$9/32$	$3/8$

TABLE 21-1-H—TOLERANCES ON DISTORTION

MAXIMUM FACE DIMENSION (inches)	MAXIMUM PERMISSIBLE DISTORTION (inch)	
	Type HBX	Types HBS and HBB
	× 25.4 for mm	
8 and under	$1/16$	$3/32$
Over 8 to 12, incl.	$3/32$	$1/8$
Over 12 to 16, incl.	$1/8$	$5/32$

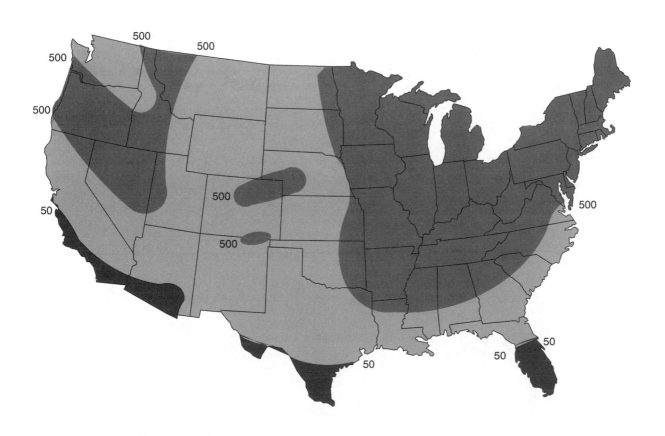

WEATHERING REGIONS

- NEGLIGIBLE WEATHERING
- MODERATE WEATHERING
- SEVERE WEATHERING

FIGURE 21-1-1—WEATHERING INDEXES IN THE UNITED STATES

UNIFORM BUILDING CODE STANDARD 21-2
CALCIUM SILICATE FACE BRICK
(SAND-LIME BRICK)

**Based on Standard Specification C 73-95 of the American Society for Testing and Materials.
Extracted, with permission, from the *Annual Book of ASTM Standards,* copyright American Society for
Testing and Materials, 100 Barr Harbor Drive, West Conshohocken, PA 19428**

See Section 2102.2, Item 6, *Uniform Building Code*

SECTION 21.201 — SCOPE

21.201.1 Grades. This standard covers brick made from sand and lime and intended for use in brick masonry. Two grades of brick are covered:

21.201.1.1 Grade SW. Brick intended for use where exposed to temperatures below freezing in the presence of moisture.

21.201.1.2 Grade MW. Brick intended for use where exposed to temperature below freezing but unlikely to be saturated with water.

21.201.2 Definition. The term "brick" used in this standard shall mean brick or a solid sand-lime masonry unit.

SECTION 21.202 — PHYSICAL PROPERTIES

21.202.1 Durability. The brick shall conform to the physical requirements for the grade specified as prescribed in Table 21-2-A.

21.202.2 Substitution of Grades. Unless otherwise specified, brick of Grade SW shall be accepted in lieu of Grade MW.

SECTION 21.203 — SIZE

The size of the brick shall be as specified by the purchaser, and the average size of brick furnished shall approximate the size specified in the invitation for bids.

No overall dimension (width, height and length) shall differ by more than $1/8$ inch (3.2 mm) from the specified standard dimension. Standard dimensions of units are the manufacturer's designated dimensions.

SECTION 21.204 — VISUAL INSPECTION

Brick shall pass a visual inspection for soundness, compact structure, reasonably uniform shape, and freedom from the following: cracks, warpage, large pebbles, balls of clay, or particles of lime that would affect the serviceability or strength of the brick.

SECTION 21.205 — METHODS OF SAMPLING AND TESTING

The purchaser or the purchaser's authorized representative shall be accorded proper facilities to inspect and sample the units at the place of manufacture from the lots ready for delivery. At least 10 days should be allowed for completion of the tests.

Sample and test units in accordance with ASTM C 140.

TABLE 21-2-A—PHYSICAL REQUIREMENTS FOR SAND-LIME BUILDING BRICK

TYPE OF MASONRY	GRADE	MINIMUM COMPRESSIVE STRENGTH PSI AVERAGE GROSS AREA		MINIMUM MODULUS OF RUPTURE		WATER ABSORPTION MAX. lb./ft.³ (kg/m³)
		Average of Five Tests	Individual	Average of Five Tests	Individual	
		× 6.89 for kPa		(Brick Flatwise) psi Average Gross Area		
Sand-lime	SW	4500	3500	600	400	10 (160)
Building brick	MW	2500	2000	450	300	13 (208)

Gross area of a unit shall be determined by multiplying the horizontal face dimension of the unit as placed in the wall by its thickness.

UNIFORM BUILDING CODE STANDARD 21-3
CONCRETE BUILDING BRICK

**Based on Standard Specification C 55-95 of the American Society for Testing and Materials.
Extracted, with permission, from the *Annual Book of ASTM Standards,* copyright American Society for
Testing and Materials, 100 Barr Harbor Drive, West Conshohocken, PA 19428**

See Section 2102.2, Item 5, *Uniform Building Code*

SECTION 21.301 — SCOPE

This standard covers concrete building brick and similar solid units made from portland cement, water and suitable mineral aggregates with or without the inclusion of other materials.

SECTION 21.302 — CLASSIFICATION

21.302.1 Types. Two types of concrete brick in each of two grades are covered, as follows:

21.302.1.1 Type I, moisture-controlled units. Concrete brick designated as Type I (Grades N-I and S-I) shall conform to all requirements of this standard, including the requirements of Table 21-3-A.

21.302.1.2 Type II, nonmoisture-controlled units. Concrete brick designated as Type II (Grades N-II and S-II) shall conform to all requirements of this standard except the requirements of Table 21-3-A.

21.302.2 Grades. Concrete brick manufactured in accordance with this standard shall conform to two grades as follows:

21.302.2.1 Grade N. For use as architectural veneer and facing units in exterior walls and for use where high strength and resistance to moisture penetration and severe frost action are desired.

21.302.2.2 Grade S. For general use where moderate strength and resistance to frost action and moisture penetration are required.

SECTION 21.303 — MATERIALS

21.303.1 Cementitious Materials. Materials shall conform to the following applicable standards:

1. Portland Cement—ASTM C 150 modified as follows:

   Limitation on insoluble residue—1.5 percent.
   Limitation on air content of mortar,
      Volume percent—22 percent maximum.
   Limitation on loss on ignition—7 percent maximum.
   Limestone with a minimum 85 percent calcium carbonate ($CaCO_3$) content may be added to the cement, provided the requirements of ASTM C 150 as modified above are met.

2. Blended Cements—ASTM C 595.

3. Hydrated Lime, Type S—UBC Standard 21-13.

21.303.2 Other Constituents. Air-entraining agents, coloring pigments, integral water repellents, finely ground silica, etc., shall be previously established as suitable for use in concrete or shall be shown by test or experience not to be detrimental to the durability of the concrete.

SECTION 21.304 — PHYSICAL REQUIREMENTS

At the time of delivery to the work site, the concrete brick shall conform to the physical requirements prescribed in Table 21-3-B.

At the time of delivery to the purchaser, the total linear drying shrinkage of Type II units shall not exceed 0.065 percent when tested in accordance with ASTM C 426.

The moisture content of Type I concrete brick at the time of delivery shall conform to the requirements prescribed in Table 21-3-A.

SECTION 21.305 — DIMENSIONS AND PERMISSIBLE VARIATIONS

Overall dimensions (width, height, or length) shall not differ by more than $1/8$ inch (3.2 mm) from the specified standard dimensions.

> **NOTE:** Standard dimensions of concrete brick are the manufacturer's designated dimensions. Nominal dimensions of modular-size concrete brick are equal to the standard dimensions plus $3/8$ inch (9.5 mm), the thickness of one standard mortar joint. Nominal dimensions of nonmodular size concrete brick usually exceed the standard dimensions by $1/8$ inch to $1/4$ inch (3.2 mm to 6.4 mm).

Variations in thickness of architectural units such as split-faced or slumped units will usually vary from the specified tolerances.

SECTION 21.306 — VISUAL INSPECTION

21.306.1 General. All concrete brick shall be sound and free of cracks or other defects that would interfere with the proper placing of the unit or impair the strength or permanence of the construction. Minor cracks incidental to the usual method of manufacture, or minor chipping resulting from customary methods of handling in shipment and delivery, shall not be deemed grounds for rejection.

21.306.2 Brick in Exposed Walls. Where concrete brick is to be used in exposed wall construction, the face or faces that are to be exposed shall be free of chips, cracks or other imperfections when viewed from 20 feet (6100 mm), except that if not more than 5 percent of a shipment contains slight cracks or small chips not larger than $1/2$ inch (13 mm), this shall not be deemed grounds for rejection.

SECTION 21.307 — METHODS OF SAMPLING AND TESTING

The purchaser or authorized representative shall be accorded proper facilities to inspect and sample the concrete brick at the place of manufacture from the lots ready for delivery. At least 10 days shall be allowed for completion of the test.

Sample and test concrete brick in accordance with ASTM C 140 and C 426, when applicable.

Total linear drying shrinkage shall be based on tests of concrete brick made with the same materials, concrete mix design, manufacturing process and curing method, conducted in accordance with ASTM C 426 not more than 24 months prior to delivery.

SECTION 21.308 — REJECTION

If the shipment fails to conform to the specific requirements, the manufacturer may sort it, and new specimens shall be selected by the purchaser from the retained lot and tested at the expense of the manufacturer. If the second set of specimens fails to conform to the test requirements, the entire lot shall be rejected.

TABLE 21-3-A—MOISTURE CONTENT REQUIREMENTS FOR TYPE I CONCRETE BRICK

LINEAR SHRINKAGE, PERCENT	MOISTURE CONTENT, MAX. PERCENT OF TOTAL ABSORPTION (Average of 3 Concrete Brick)		
	Humidity[1] Conditions at Jobsite or Point of Use		
	Humid	Intermediate	Arid
0.03 or less	45	40	35
From 0.03 to 0.045	40	35	30
0.045 to 0.065, max.	35	30	25

[1]Arid—Average annual relative humidity less than 50 percent.
  Intermediate—Average annual relative humidity 50 to 75 percent.
  Humid—Average annual relative humidity above 75 percent.

TABLE 21-3-B—STRENGTH AND ABSORPTION REQUIREMENTS

	COMPRESSIVE STRENGTH, MIN., psi (Concrete Brick Tested Flatwise)		WATER ABSORPTION, MAX., (Avg. of 3 Brick) WITH OVEN-DRY WEIGHT OF CONCRETE Lb./Ft.^{3}		
	× 6.89 for kPa		× 16 for kg/m^3		
	Average Gross Area		Weight Classification		
Grade	Avg. of 3 Concrete Brick	Individual Concrete Brick	Lightweight Less Than 105	Medium Weight Less Than 125 to 105	Normal Weight 125 or More
N-I	3,500	3,000	15	13	10
N-II	3,500	3,000	15	13	10
S-I	2,500	2,000	18	15	13
S-II	2,500	2,000	18	15	13

UNIFORM BUILDING CODE STANDARD 21-4

HOLLOW AND SOLID LOAD-BEARING CONCRETE MASONRY UNITS

Based on Standard Specification C 90-95 of the American Society for Testing and Materials. Extracted, with permission, from the *Annual Book of ASTM Standards,* copyright American Society for Testing and Materials, 100 Barr Harbor Drive, West Conshohocken, PA 19428

SECTION 21.401 — SCOPE

This standard covers solid (units with 75 percent or more net area) and hollow load-bearing concrete masonry units made from portland cement, water and mineral aggregates with or without the inclusion of other materials.

SECTION 21.402 — CLASSIFICATION

21.402.1 Types. Two types of concrete masonry units in each of two grades are covered as follows:

21.402.1.1 Type I, moisture-controlled units. Units designated as Type I shall conform to all requirements of this standard including the moisture content requirements of Table 21-4-A.

21.402.1.2 Type II, nonmoisture-controlled units. Units designated as Type II shall conform to all requirements of this standard except the moisture content requirements of Table 21-4-A.

21.402.2 Grades. Concrete masonry units manufactured in accordance with this standard shall conform to two grades as follows:

21.402.2.1 Grade N. Units having a weight classification of 85 pcf (1360 kg/m³) or greater, for general use such as in exterior walls below and above grade that may or may not be exposed to moisture penetration or the weather and for interior walls and backup.

21.402.2.2 Grade S. Units having a weight classification of less than 85 pcf (1360 kg/m³), for uses limited to above-grade installation in exterior walls with weather-protective coatings and in walls not exposed to the weather.

SECTION 21.403 — MATERIALS

21.403.1 Cementitious Materials. Materials shall conform to the following applicable standards:

1. Portland Cement—ASTM C 150 modified as follows:

   Limitation on insoluble residue—1.5 percent maximum.
   Limitation on air content of mortar,
     Volume percent—22 percent maximum.
   Limitation on loss on ignition—7 percent maximum.
   Limestone with a minimum 85 percent calcium carbonate (C_aCO_3) content may be added to the cement, provided the requirements of ASTM C 150 as modified above are met.

2. Blended Cements—ASTM C 595.

3. Hydrated Lime, Type S—UBC Standard 21-13.

21.403.2 Other Constituents and Aggregates. Air-entraining agents, coloring pigments, integral water repellents, finely ground silica, aggregates, and other constituents, shall be previously established as suitable for use in concrete or shall be shown by test or experience to not be detrimental to the durability of the concrete.

SECTION 21.404 — PHYSICAL REQUIREMENTS

At the time of delivery to the work site, the units shall conform to the physical requirements prescribed in Table 21-4-B. The moisture content of Type I concrete masonry units at time of delivery shall conform to the requirements prescribed in Table 21-4-A.

At the time of delivery to the purchaser, the linear shrinkage of Type II units shall not exceed 0.065 percent.

SECTION 21.405 — MINIMUM FACE-SHELL AND WEB THICKNESSES

Face-shell (FST) and web (WT) thicknesses shall conform to the requirements listed in Table 21-4-C.

SECTION 21.406 — PERMISSIBLE VARIATIONS IN DIMENSIONS

21.406.1 Precision Units. For precision units, no overall dimension (width, height and length) shall differ by more than $^1/_8$ inch (3.2 mm) from the specified standard dimensions.

21.406.2 Particular Feature Units. For particular feature units, dimensions shall be in accordance with the following:

1. For molded face units, no overall dimension (width, height and length) shall differ by more than $^1/_8$ inch (3.2 mm) from the specified standard dimension. Dimensions of molded features (ribs, scores, hex-shapes, patterns, etc.) shall be within $^1/_{16}$ inch (1.6 mm) of the specified standard dimensions and shall be within $^1/_{16}$ inch (1.6 mm) of the specified placement of the unit.

2. For split-faced units, all non-split overall dimensions (width, height and length) shall differ by no more than $^1/_8$ inch (3.2 mm) from the specified standard dimensions. On faces that are split, overall dimensions will vary. Local suppliers should be consulted to determine dimensional tolerances achievable.

3. For slumped units, no overall height dimension shall differ by more than $^1/_8$ inch (3.2 mm) from the specified standard dimension. On faces that are slumped, overall dimensions will vary. Local suppliers should be consulted to determine dimension tolerances achievable.

> **NOTE:** Standard dimensions of units are the manufacturer's designated dimensions. Nominal dimensions of modular size units, except slumped units, are equal to the standard dimensions plus $^3/_8$ inch (9.5 mm), the thickness of one standard mortar joint. Slumped units are equal to the standard dimensions plus $^1/_2$ inch (13 mm), the thickness of one standard mortar joint. Nominal dimensions of nonmodular size units usually exceed the standard dimensions by $^1/_8$ inch to $^1/_4$ inch (3.2 mm to 6.4 mm).

SECTION 21.407 — VISUAL INSPECTION

All units shall be sound and free of cracks or other defects that would interfere with the proper placing of the unit or impair the strength or perm-anence of the construction. Units may have minor cracks incidental to the usual method of manufacture, or minor chipping resulting from customary methods of handling in shipment and delivery.

Units that are intended to serve as a base for plaster or stucco shall have a sufficiently rough surface to afford a good bond.

Where units are to be used in exposed wall construction, the face or faces that are to be exposed shall be free of chips, cracks or other imperfections when viewed from 20 feet (6100 mm), except that not more than 5 percent of a shipment may have slight cracks or small chips not larger than 1 inch (25.4 mm).

SECTION 21.408 — METHODS OF SAMPLING AND TESTING

The purchaser or authorized representative shall be accorded proper facilities to inspect and sample the units at the place of manufacture from the lots ready for delivery.

Sample and test units in accordance with ASTM C 140.

Total linear drying shrinkage shall be based on tests of concrete masonry units made with the same materials, concrete mix design, manufacturing process and curing method, conducted in accordance with ASTM C 426 and not more than 24 months prior to delivery.

SECTION 21.409 — REJECTION

If the samples tested from a shipment fail to conform to the specified requirements, the manufacturer may sort it, and new specimens shall be selected by the purchaser from the retained lot and tested at the expense of the manufacturer. If the second set of specimens fails to conform to the specified requirements, the entire lot shall be rejected.

TABLE 21-4-A—MOISTURE CONTENT REQUIREMENTS FOR TYPE I UNITS

LINEAR SHRINKAGE, PERCENT	MOISTURE CONTENT, MAX. PERCENT OF TOTAL ABSORPTION (Average of 3 Units)		
	Humidity Conditions at Jobsite or Point of Use		
	Humid[1]	Intermediate[2]	Arid[3]
0.03 or less	45	40	35
From 0.03 to 0.045	40	35	30
0.045 to 0.065, max.	35	30	25

[1]Average annual relative humidity above 75 percent.

[2]Average annual relative humidity 50 to 75 percent.

[3]Average annual relative humidity less than 50 percent.

TABLE 21-4-B—STRENGTH AND ABSORPTION REQUIREMENTS

COMPRESSIVE STRENGTH, MIN, psi (MPa)		WATER ABSORPTION, MAX, lb./ft. (kg/m) (Average of 3 Units)		
Average Net Area		Weight Classification—Oven-dry Weight of Concrete, lb./ft. (kg/m)		
Average of 3 Units	Individual Unit	Lightweight, Less than 105 (1680)	Medium Weight, 105 to less than 125 (1680-2000)	Normal Weight, 125 (2000) or more
1900 (13.1)	1700 (11.7)	18 (288)	15 (240)	13 (208)

TABLE 21-4-C—MINIMUM THICKNESS OF FACE-SHELLS AND WEBS

NOMINAL WIDTH (W) OF UNIT (inches)	FACE-SHELL THICKNESS (FST) MIN., (inches)[1, 4]	WEB THICKNESS (WT)	
		Webs[1] Min., (inches)	Equivalent Web Thickness, Min., In./Lin. Ft.[2]
	× 25.4 for mm		× 83 for mm/lin. m
3 and 4	$3/4$	$3/4$	$1^5/8$
6	1	1	$2^1/4$
8	$1^1/4$	1	$2^1/4$
10	$1^3/8$ $1^1/4^3$	$1^1/8$	$2^1/2$
12	$1^1/2$ $1^1/4^3$	$1^1/8$	$2^1/2$

[1]Average of measurements on three units taken at the thinnest point.

[2]Sum of the measured thickness of all webs in the unit, multiplied by 12 (305 when using metric), and divided by the length of the unit. In the case of open-ended units where the open-ended portion is solid grouted, the length of that open-ended portion shall be deducted from the overall length of the unit.

[3]This face-shell thickness (FST) is applicable where allowable design load is reduced in proportion to the reduction in thicknesses shown, except that allowable design load on solid-grouted units shall not be reduced.

[4]For split-faced units, a maximum of 10 percent of a shipment may have face-shell thicknesses less than those shown, but in no case less than $3/4$ inch (19 mm).

UNIFORM BUILDING CODE STANDARD 21-5
NONLOAD-BEARING CONCRETE MASONRY UNITS

Based on Standard Specification C 129-95 (1980) of the American Society for Testing and Materials.
Extracted, with permission, from the *Annual Book of ASTM Standards,* copyright American Society for
Testing and Materials, 100 Barr Harbor Drive, West Conshohocken, PA 19428

See Section 2102.2, Item 5, *Uniform Building Code*

SECTION 21.501 — SCOPE

This standard covers hollow and solid nonload-bearing concrete masonry units made from portland cement, water, and mineral aggregates with or without the inclusion of other materials. Such units are intended for use in nonload-bearing partitions but under certain conditions may be suitable for use in nonload-bearing exterior walls above grade, where effectively protected from the weather.

SECTION 21.502 — CLASSIFICATION

21.502.1 Weight Classifications. Nonload-bearing concrete masonry units manufactured in accordance with this standard shall conform to one of three weight classifications and two types as follows:

WEIGHT CLASSIFICATION	OVEN-DRY WEIGHT OF CONCRETE lb./cu.ft.
Lightweight	105 (1680 kg/m^3) max.
Medium weight	105 - 125 (1680 - 2000 kg/m^3)
Normal weight	125 (2000 kg/m^3) min.

21.502.2 Types. Nonload-bearing concrete masonry units shall be of two types as follows:

21.502.2.1 Type I, moisture-controlled units. Type I units shall conform to all requirements of this standard, including the requirements of Table 21-5-A.

21.502.2.2 Type II, nonmoisture-controlled units. Type II units shall conform to all requirements of this standard, except the requirements listed in Table 21-5-A.

SECTION 21.503 — MATERIALS

21.503.1 Cementitious Materials. Cementitious materials shall conform to the following applicable standards:

1. Portland Cement—ASTM C 150 modified as follows:

    Limitation on insoluble residue—1.5 percent.
    Limitation on air content of mortar,
        Volume percent—22 percent maximum.
    Limitation on loss on ignition—7 percent maximum.
    Limestone with a minimum 85 percent calcium carbonate (CaCO$_3$) content may be added to the cement, provided the requirements of ASTM C 150 as modified above are met.

2. Blended Cements—ASTM C 595.

3. Hydrated Lime, Type S—UBC Standard 21-13.

21.503.2 Other Constituents. Air-entraining agents, coloring pigments, integral water repellents, finely ground silica, etc., shall be previously established as suitable for use in concrete or shall be shown by test or experience not to be detrimental to the durability of the concrete.

SECTION 21.504 — PHYSICAL REQUIREMENTS

At the time of delivery to the work site, the units shall conform to the strength requirements prescribed in Table 21-5-B.

The moisture content of Type I concrete masonry units at the time of delivery shall conform to the requirements prescribed in Table 21-5-A.

At the time of delivery to the purchaser, the total linear drying of Type II units shall not exceed 0.065 percent.

SECTION 21.505 — DIMENSIONS AND PERMISSIBLE VARIATIONS

Minimum face-shell thickness shall not be less than $^1/_2$ inch (13 mm).

No overall dimension (width, height or length) shall differ by more than $^1/_8$ inch (3.2 mm) from the specified standard dimensions.

> **NOTE:** Standard dimensions of units are the manufacturer's designated dimensions. Nominal dimensions of modular-size units are equal to the standard dimensions plus $^3/_8$ inch (9.5 mm), the thickness of one standard mortar joint. Nominal dimensions of nonmodular size units usually exceed the standard dimensions by $^1/_8$ inch to $^1/_4$ inch (3.2 mm to 6.4 mm).

Variations in thickness of architectural units such as split-faced or slumped units will usually exceed the specified tolerances.

SECTION 21.506 — VISUAL INSPECTION

21.506.1 General. All units shall be sound and free of cracks or other defects that would interfere with the proper placing of the units or impair the strength or permanence of the construction. Units may have minor cracks incidental to the usual method of manufacture, or minor chipping resulting from customary methods of handling in shipment and delivery.

21.506.2 Exposed Units. Where units are to be used in exposed wall construction, the face or faces that are to be exposed shall be free of chips, cracks or other imperfections when viewed from 20 feet (6100 mm), except that not more than 5 percent of a shipment may have slight cracks or small chips not larger than 1 inch (25 mm).

21.506.3 Identification. Nonloading concrete masonry units shall be clearly marked in a manner to preclude their use as load-bearing units.

SECTION 21.507 — METHODS OF SAMPLING AND TESTING

The purchaser or authorized representative shall be accorded proper facilities to inspect and sample the units at the place of manufacture from the lots ready for delivery. At least 10 days shall be allowed for the completion of the tests.

Sample and test units in accordance with ASTM C 140 and ASTM C 426 when applicable.

Total linear drying shrinkage shall be based on tests of concrete masonry units made with the same materials, concrete mix design, manufacturing process and curing method, conducted in accordance with ASTM C 426 and not more than 24 months prior to delivery.

SECTION 21.508 — REJECTION

If the shipment fails to conform to the specified requirements, the manufacturer may sort it, and new specimens shall be selected by the purchaser from the retained lot and tested at the expense of the manufacturer. If the second set of specimens fails to conform to the specified requirements, the entire lot shall be rejected.

TABLE 21-5-A—MOISTURE CONTENT REQUIREMENTS FOR TYPE I UNITS

LINEAR SHRINKAGE, PERCENT	MOISTURE CONTENT, MAX. PERCENT OF TOTAL ABSORPTION (Average of 3 Units)		
	Humidity[1] Conditions at Jobsite or Point of Use		
	Humid	Intermediate	Arid
0.03 or less	45	40	35
From 0.03 to 0.045	40	35	30
0.045 to 0.065, max.	35	30	25

[1]Arid—Average annual relative humidity less than 50 percent.

Intermediate—Average annual relative humidity 50 to 75 percent.

Humid—Average annual relative humidity above 75 percent.

TABLE 21-5-B—STRENGTH REQUIREMENTS

	COMPRESSIVE STRENGTH (Average Net Area) Min., psi
	× 6.89 for kPa
Average of 3 units	600
Individual units	500

UNIFORM BUILDING CODE STANDARD 21-6
IN-PLACE MASONRY SHEAR TESTS
Test Standard of the International Conference of Building Officials
See Appendix Chapter 1, Sections A106.3.3 and A107.2,
Uniform Code for Building Conservation

SECTION 21.601 — SCOPE

This standard applies when the *Uniform Code for Building Conservation* requires in-place testing of the quality of masonry mortar.

SECTION 21.602 — PREPARATION OF SAMPLE

The bed joints of the outer wythe of the masonry shall be tested in shear by laterally displacing a single brick relative to the adjacent bricks in the same wythe. The head joint opposite the loaded end of the test brick shall be carefully excavated and cleared. The brick adjacent to the loaded end of the test brick shall be carefully removed by sawing or drilling and excavating to provide space for a hydraulic ram and steel loading blocks.

SECTION 21.603 — APPLICATION OF LOAD AND DETERMINATION OF RESULTS

Steel blocks, the size of the end of the brick, shall be used on each end of the ram to distribute the load to the brick. The blocks shall not contact the mortar joints. The load shall be applied horizontally, in the plane of the wythe, until either a crack can be seen or slip occurs. The strength of the mortar shall be calculated by dividing the load at the first cracking or movement of the test brick by the nominal gross area of the sum of the two bed joints.

UNIFORM BUILDING CODE STANDARD 21-7
TESTS OF ANCHORS IN UNREINFORCED MASONRY WALLS
Test Standard of the International Conference of Building Officials
See Appendix Chapter 1, Section A107.3 and A107.4,
Uniform Code for Building Conservation

SECTION 21.701 — SCOPE

Shear and tension anchors in existing masonry construction shall be tested in accordance with this standard when required by the *Uniform Code for Building Conservation.*

SECTION 21.702 — DIRECT TENSION TESTING OF EXISTING ANCHORS AND NEW BOLTS

The test apparatus shall be supported by the masonry wall. The distance between the anchor and the test apparatus support shall not be less than one half the wall thickness for existing anchors and 75 percent of the embedment for new embedded bolts. Existing wall anchors shall be given a preload of 300 pounds (1335 N) prior to establishing a datum for recording elongation. The tension test load reported shall be recorded at $1/8$ inch (3.2 mm) relative movement of the existing anchor and the adjacent masonry surface. New embedded tension bolts shall be subject to a direct tension load of not less than 2.5 times the design load but not less than 1,500 pounds (6672 N) for five minutes (10 percent deviation).

SECTION 21.703 — TORQUE TESTING OF NEW BOLTS

Bolts embedded in unreinforced masonry walls shall be tested using a torque-calibrated wrench to the following minimum torques:

$1/2$-inch-diameter (13 mm) bolts—40 foot pounds (54.2 N·m)

$5/8$-inch-diameter (16 mm) bolts—50 foot pounds (67.8 N·m)

$3/4$-inch-diameter (19 mm) bolts—60 foot pounds (81.3 N·m)

SECTION 21.704 — PREQUALIFICATION TEST FOR BOLTS AND OTHER TYPES OF ANCHORS

This section is applicable when it is desired to use tension or shear values for anchors greater than those permitted by Table A-1-E of the *Uniform Code for Building Conservation.* The direct-tension test procedure set forth in Section 21.702 for existing anchors may be used to determine the allowable tension values for new embedded or through bolts, except that no preload is required. Bolts shall be installed in the same manner and using the same materials as will be used in the actual construction. A minimum of five tests for each bolt size and type shall be performed for each class of masonry in which they are proposed to be used. The allowable tension values for such anchors shall be the lesser of the average ultimate load divided by a factor of safety of 5.0 or the average load of which $1/8$ inch (3.2 mm) elongation occurs for each size and type of bolt and class of masonry.

Shear bolts may be similarly prequalified. The test procedure shall comply with ASTM E 488-90 or another approved procedure.

The allowable values determined in this manner may exceed those set forth in Table A-1-E of the *Uniform Code for Building Conservation.*

SECTION 21.705 — REPORTS

Results of all tests shall be reported. The report shall include the test results as related to anchor size and type, orientation of loading, details of the anchor installation and embedment, wall thickness, and joist orientation.

UNIFORM BUILDING CODE STANDARD 21-8
POINTING OF UNREINFORCED MASONRY WALLS
Construction Specification of the International Conference of Building Officials
See Appendix Chapter 1, Section A106.3.3.2,
Uniform Code for Building Conservation

SECTION 21.801 — SCOPE

Pointing of deteriorated mortar joints when required by the *Uniform Code for Building Conservation* shall be in accordance with this standard.

SECTION 21.802 — JOINT PREPARATION

The old or deteriorated mortar joint shall be cut out, by means of a toothing chisel or nonimpact power tool, to a uniform depth of $3/4$ inch (19 mm) until sound mortar is reached. Care shall be taken not to damage the brick edges. After cutting is complete, all loose material shall be removed with a brush, air or water stream.

SECTION 21.803 — MORTAR PREPARATION

The mortar mix shall be Type N or Type S proportioned as required by the construction specifications. The pointing mortar shall be prehydrated by first thoroughly mixing all ingredients dry and then mixing again, adding only enough water to produce a damp unworkable mix which will retain its form when pressed into a ball. The mortar shall be kept in a damp condition for one and one-half hours; then sufficient water shall be added to bring it to a consistency that is somewhat drier than conventional masonry mortar.

SECTION 21.804 — PACKING

The joint into which the mortar is to be packed shall be damp but without freestanding water. The mortar shall be tightly packed into the joint in layers not exceeding $1/4$ inch (6.4 mm) in depth until it is filled; then it shall be tooled to a smooth surface to match the original profile.

UNIFORM BUILDING CODE STANDARD 21-9
UNBURNED CLAY MASONRY UNITS AND STANDARD METHODS OF SAMPLING AND TESTING UNBURNED CLAY MASONRY UNITS

Test Standard of the International Conference of Building Officials

See Section 2102.2, Item 6, *Uniform Building Code*

Part I—Unburned Clay Masonry

SECTION 21.901 — SCOPE

This standard covers unburned clay masonry units made from a suitable mixture of soil, clay and stabilizing agent, and intended for use in brick masonry.

SECTION 21.902 — COMPOSITION OF UNITS

21.902.1 Soil. The soil used shall contain not less than 25 percent and not more than 45 percent of material passing a No. 200 mesh (75 μm) sieve. The soil shall contain sufficient clay to bind the particles together, but shall contain not more than 0.2 percent of water-soluble salts.

21.902.2 Stabilizer. The stabilizing agent shall be emulsified asphalt. The stabilizing agent shall be uniformly mixed with the soil in amounts sufficient to provide the required resistance to absorption.

SECTION 21.903 — PHYSICAL REQUIREMENTS

The units shall conform to the physical requirements prescribed in Table 21-1-B of UBC Standard 21-1.

SECTION 21.904 — SHRINKAGE CRACKS

No units shall contain more than three shrinkage cracks, and no shrinkage crack shall exceed 3 inches (76 mm) in length or $^1/_8$ inch (3.2 mm) in width.

Part II—Sampling and Testing of Unburned Clay Masonry Units

SECTION 21.905 — SCOPE

These methods cover procedures for the sampling and testing of unburned clay masonry units for compressive strength, modulus of rupture, absorption and moisture content.

Sampling

SECTION 21.906 — TEST SPECIMENS

For each of the tests prescribed in this standard, five sample units shall be selected at random from each lot of 5,000 units or fraction thereof.

SECTION 21.907 — IDENTIFICATION

Each specimen shall be marked so that it may be identified at any time. Markings shall not cover more than 5 percent of the superficial area of the specimen.

Compressive Strength

SECTION 21.908 — PROCEDURE

Five full-size specimens shall be tested for compressive strength according to the following procedure:

1. Dry the specimens at a temperature of 85°F ± 15°F (29°C ± 9°C) in an atmosphere having a relative humidity of not more than 50 percent. Weigh the specimens at one-day intervals until constant weight is attained.

2. Test the specimens in the position in which the unburned clay masonry unit is designed to be used, and bed on and cap with a felt pad not less than $^1/_8$ inch (3.2 mm) nor more than $^1/_4$ inch (6.4 mm) in thickness.

3. The specimens may be suitably capped with calcined gypsum mortar or the bearing surfaces of the tile may be planed or rubbed smooth and true. When calcined gypsum is used for capping, conduct the test after the capping has set and the specimen has been dried to constant weight in accordance with Item 1 of this section.

4. The loading head shall completely cover the bearing area of the specimen and the applied load shall be transmitted through a spherical bearing block of proper design. The speed of the moving head of the testing machine shall not be more than 0.05 inch (1.27 mm) per minute.

5. Calculate the average compressive strength of the specimens tested and report this as the compressive strength of the block.

Modulus of Rupture

SECTION 21.909 — PROCEDURE

Five full-size specimens shall be tested for modulus of rupture according to the following procedure:

1. Cured specimen shall be positioned on cylindrical supports 2 inches (51 mm) in diameter, located 2 inches (51 mm) from each end, and extending across the full width of the specimen.

2. A cylinder 2 inches (51 mm) in diameter shall be positioned on the specimen midway between and parallel to the cylindrical supports.

3. Load shall be applied to the cylinder at the rate of 500 pounds (2224 N) per minute until failure occurs.

4. Calculate modulus of rupture from the formula

$$S = \frac{3WL}{2Bd^2}$$

WHERE:

B = width of specimen.

d = thickness of specimen.

L = distance between supports.

S = modulus of rupture, psi (kPa).

W = load at failure.

Absorption

SECTION 21.910 — PROCEDURE

A 4-inch (102 mm) cube cut from a sample unit shall be tested for absorption according to the following procedure:

1. Dry specimen to a constant weight in a ventilated oven at 212°F to 239°F (100°C to 115°C).

2. Place specimen on a constantly water-saturated porous surface for seven days. Weigh specimen.

3. Calculate absorption as a percentage of the initial dry weight.

Moisture Content

SECTION 21.911 — PROCEDURE

Five representative specimens shall be tested for moisture content according to the following procedure:

1. Obtain weight of each specimen immediately upon receiving.

2. Dry all specimens to constant weight in a ventilated oven at 212°F to 239°F (100°C to 115°C) and obtain dry weight.

3. Calculate moisture content as a percentage of the initial dry weight.

UNIFORM BUILDING CODE STANDARD 21-10
JOINT REINFORCEMENT FOR MASONRY
Specification Standard of the International Conference of Building Officials
See Sections 2102.2; 2104 and 2106.1.12.4, Item 2, *Uniform Building Code*

Part I—Joint Reinforcement for Masonry

SECTION 21.1001 — SCOPE

This standard covers joint reinforcement fabricated from cold-drawn steel wire for reinforcing masonry.

SECTION 21.1002 — DESCRIPTION

Joint reinforcement consists of deformed longitudinal wires welded to cross wires (Figure 21-10-1) in sizes suitable for placing in mortar joints between masonry courses.

SECTION 21.1003 — CONFIGURATION AND SIZE OF LONGITUDINAL AND CROSS WIRES

21.1003.1 General. The distance between longitudinal wires and the configuration of cross wires connecting the longitudinal wires shall conform to the design and the requirements of Figure 21-10-1.

21.1003.2 Longitudinal Wires. The diameter of longitudinal wires shall not be less than 0.148 inch (3.76 mm) or more than one half the mortar joint thickness.

21.1003.3 Cross Wires. The diameter of cross wires shall not be less than (No. 9 gage) 0.148-inch (3.76 mm) diameter nor more than the diameter of the longitudinal wires. Cross wires shall not project beyond the outside longitudinal wires by more than $1/8$ inch (3.2 mm).

21.1003.4 Width. The width of joint reinforcement shall be the out-to-out distance between outside longitudinal wires. Variation in the width shall not exceed $1/8$ inch (3.2 mm).

21.1003.5 Length. The length of pieces of joint reinforcement shall not vary more than $1/2$ inch (13 mm) or 1.0 percent of the specified length, whichever is less.

SECTION 21.1004 — MATERIAL REQUIREMENTS

21.1004.1 Tensile Properties. Wire of the finished product shall meet the following requirements:

Tensile strength, minimum	75,000 psi (517 MPa)
Yield strength, minimum	60,000 psi (414 MPa)
Reduction of area, minimum	30 percent

For wire testing over 100,000 psi (689 MPa), the reduction of area shall not be less than 25 percent.

21.1004.2 Bend Properties. Wire shall not break or crack along the outside diameter of the bend when tested in accordance with Section 21.1008.

21.1004.3 Weld Shear Properties. The least weld shear strength in pounds shall not be less than 25,000 (11.3 Mg) multiplied by the specified area of the smaller wire in square inches.

SECTION 21.1005 — FABRICATION

Wire shall be fabricated and finished in a workmanlike manner, shall be free from injurious imperfections and shall conform to this standard.

The wires shall be assembled by automatic machines or by other suitable mechanical means which will assure accurate spacing and alignment of all members of the finished product.

Longitudinal and cross wires shall be securely connected at every intersection by a process of electric-resistance welding.

Longitudinal wires shall be deformed. One set of four deformations shall occur around the perimeter of the wire at a maximum spacing of 0.7 times the diameter of the wire but not less than eight sets per inch (25.4 mm) of length. The overall length of each deformation within the set shall be such that the summation of gaps between the ends of the deformations shall not exceed 25 percent of the perimeter of the wire. The height or depth of the deformations shall be 0.012 inch (0.305 mm) for $3/16$ inch (4.76 mm) diameter or larger wire, 0.011 (0.28 mm) for 0.162-inch (4.11 mm) diameter wire and 0.009 inch (0.23 mm) for 0.148-inch (3.76 mm) diameter wire.

SECTION 21.1006 — TENSION TESTS

Tension tests shall be made on individual wires cut from the finished product across the welds.

Tension tests across a weld shall have the welded joint located approximately at the center of the wire being tested.

Tensile strength shall be the average of four test values determined by dividing the maximum test load by the specified cross-sectional area of the wire.

Reduction of area shall be determined by measuring the ruptured section of a specimen which has been tested.

SECTION 21.1007 — WELD SHEAR STRENGTH TESTS

Test specimens shall be obtained from the finished product by cutting a section of wire which includes one weld.

Weld shear strength tests shall be conducted using a fixture of such design as to prevent rotation of the cross wire. The cross wire shall be placed in the anvil of the testing device which is secured in the tensile machine and the load then applied to the longitudinal wire.

Weld shear strength shall be the average test load in pounds of four tests.

SECTION 21.1008 — BEND TESTS

Test specimens shall be obtained from the finished product by cutting a section of wire without welds.

The test specimens shall be bent cold through 180 degrees around a pin, the diameter of which is equal to the diameter of the specimen.

The specimen shall not break nor shall there be visual cracks on the outside diameter of the bend.

SECTION 21.1009 — FREQUENCY OF TESTS

One set of tension tests, weld strength shear tests and bend tests shall be performed for each 2,000,000 lineal feet (610 000 m) of joint reinforcement, but not less than monthly.

SECTION 21.1010 — CORROSION PROTECTION

When corrosion protection of joint reinforcement is provided, it shall be in accordance with one of the following:

21.1010.1 Brite Basic. No coating.

21.1010.2 Mill Galvanized. Zinc coated, by the hot-dipped method, with no minimum thickness of zinc coating. The coating may be applied before fabrication.

21.1010.3 Class I Mill Galvanized. Zinc coated, by the hot-dipped method, with a minimum of 0.40 ounce of zinc per square foot (0.12 kg/m^2) of surface area. The coating may be applied before fabrication.

21.1010.4 Class III Mill Galvanized. Zinc coated, by the hot-dipped method, with a minimum of 0.80 ounce of zinc per square foot (0.24 kg/m^2) of surface area. The coating may be applied before fabrication.

21.1010.5 Hot-dipped Galvanized. Zinc coated, by the hot-dipped method, with a minimum of 1.50 ounces of zinc per square foot (0.45 kg/m^2) of surface area. The coating shall be applied after fabrication.

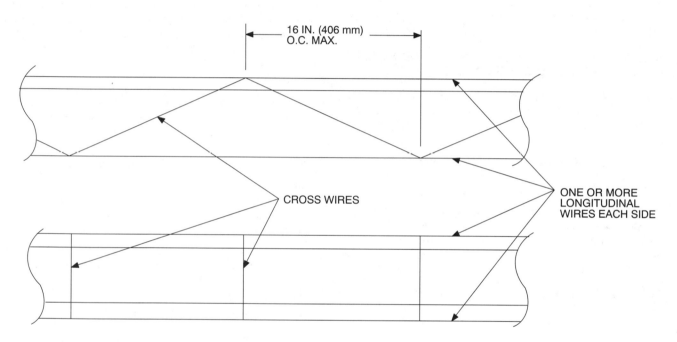

FIGURE 21-10-1—JOINT REINFORCEMENT

Part II—Cold-drawn Steel Wire for Concrete Reinforcement

Based on Standard Specification A 82-90a of the American Society for Testing and Materials. Extracted, with permission, from the *Annual Book of ASTM Standards,* copyright American Society for Testing and Materials, 100 Barr Harbor Drive, West Conshohocken, PA 19428

See Sections 2101.3; 2104 and 2106.1.12.4, Item 2, *Uniform Building Code*

SECTION 21.1011 — SCOPE

This standard covers cold-drawn steel wire to be used as such or in fabricated form, for the reinforcement as follows:

SIZE NUMBER	NOMINAL DIAMETER (inch) (× 25.4 for mm)	NOMINAL AREA (square inch) (× 645 for mm²)
W 31	0.628	0.310
W 30	0.618	0.300
W 28	0.597	0.280
W 26	0.575	0.260
W 24	0.553	0.240
W 22	0.529	0.220
W 20	0.505	0.200
W 18	0.479	0.180
W 16	0.451	0.160
W 14	0.422	0.140
W 12	0.391	0.120
W 10	0.357	0.100
W 8	0.319	0.080
W 6	0.276	0.060
W 5.5	0.265	0.055
W 5	0.252	0.050
W 4.5	0.239	0.045
W 4	0.226	0.040
W 3.5	0.211	0.035
W 2.9	0.192	0.029
W 2.5	0.178	0.025
W 2	0.160	0.020
W 1.4	0.134	0.014
W 1.2	0.124	0.012
W 0.5	0.080	0.005

SECTION 21.1012 — PROCESS

The steel shall be made by one or more of the following processes: open hearth, electric furnace or basic oxygen.

The wire shall be cold drawn from rods that have been hot rolled from billets.

Unless otherwise specified, the wire shall be "as cold drawn," except wire smaller than size number W 1.2 for welded fabric, which shall be galvanized at finish size.

SECTION 21.1013 — TENSILE PROPERTIES

The material, except as specified in this section, shall conform to the following tensile property requirements based on nominal area of wire:

Tensile strength, minimum, psi	80,000 (552 MPa)
Yield strength, minimum, psi	70,000 (483 MPa)
Reduction of area, minimum, percent	30

For material testing over 100,000 pounds per square inch (689 MPa) tensile strength, the reduction of area shall not be less than 25 percent.

For material to be used in the fabrication of welded fabric, the following tensile and yield strength properties based on nominal area of wire shall apply:

	SIZE W. 1.2 AND LARGER	SMALLER THAN SIZE W 1.2
Tensile strength, minimum, psi	75,000 (517 MPa)	70,000 (483 MPa)
Yield strength, minimum, psi	65,000 (448 MPa)	56,000 (386 MPa)

The yield strength shall be determined at an extension of 0.005 inch per inch (0.005 mm per mm) of gage length.

The material shall not exhibit a definite yield point as evidenced by a distinct drop of the beam or halt in the gage of the testing machine prior to reaching ultimate tensile load.

SECTION 21.1014 — BENDING PROPERTIES

The bend test specimen shall stand being bent cold through 180 degrees without cracking on the outside of the bent portion, as follows:

SIZE NUMBER OF WIRE	BEND TEST
W 7 and smaller	Bend around a pin, the diameter of which is equal to the diameter of the specimen.
Larger than W 7	Bend around a pin, the diameter of which is equal to twice the diameter of the specimen.

SECTION 21.1015 — TEST SPECIMENS

Tension and bend test specimens shall be of the full section of the wire and shall be obtained from ends of wire coils.

SECTION 21.1016 — NUMBER OF TESTS

One tension test and one bend test shall be made from each 10 tons (89 kN) or less of each size of wire or fraction thereof in a lot, or a total of seven samples, whichever is less. A lot shall consist of all the coils of a single size offered for delivery at the same time.

If any test specimen shows imperfections or develops flaws, it may be discarded and another specimen substituted.

SECTION 21.1017 — PERMISSIBLE VARIATIONS IN WIRE DIAMETER

The permissible variation in the diameter of the wire shall conform to the following:

SIZE NUMBER	PERMISSIBLE VARIATION PLUS AND MINUS (inch) (× 25.4 for mm)
Smaller than W 5	0.003
W 5 to W 12, inclusive	0.004
Over W 12 to W 20, inclusive	0.006
Over W 20	0.008

The difference between the maximum and minimum diameter, as measured on any given cross section of the wire, shall be more than the tolerances shown above for the given wire size.

SECTION 21.1018 — FINISH

The wire shall be free from injurious imperfections and shall have a workmanlike finish with smooth surface.

Galvanized wire shall be completely covered in a workmanlike manner with a zinc coating.

UNIFORM BUILDING CODE STANDARD 21-11
CEMENT, MASONRY

Based on Standard Specification C 91-93 of the American Society for Testing and Materials.
Extracted, with permission, from the *Annual Book of ASTM Standards,* copyright American Society for
Testing and Materials, 100 Barr Harbor Drive, West Conshohocken, PA 19428

See Section 2102.2, Item 2 and Table 21-A, *Uniform Building Code*

SECTION 21.1101 — SCOPE

This standard covers three types of masonry cement for use in masonry mortars.

SECTION 21.1102 — CLASSIFICATIONS

21.1102.1 General. Masonry cement complying with this standard shall be classified as one of the types set forth in this section.

21.1102.2 Type N. Type N cement is for use as the cementitious material in the prep-aration of UBC Standard 21-15 Type N and Type O mortars. It is for use in combination with portland or blended hydraulic cements in the preparation of Type S or Type M mortars.

21.1102.3 Type S. Type S cement is for use as the cementitious material in the preparation of UBC Standard 21-15 Type S mortar.

21.1102.4 Type M. Type M cement is for use as the cementitious material in the preparation of UBC Standard 21-15 Type M mortar.

SECTION 21.1103 — PHYSICAL REQUIREMENTS

Masonry cement shall conform to the requirements set forth in Table 21-11-A for its classifications.

SECTION 21.1104 — PACKAGE LABELING

Masonry cement packages shall carry a statement indicating that the product conforms to requirements of this standard and shall include the brand, name of manufacturer, type of masonry cement and net weight of the package in pounds.

SECTION 21.1105 — CERTIFICATION

Certification shall be submitted upon request of the building official and shall certify compliance with the requirements of this standard.

SECTION 21.1106 — SAMPLING AND TESTING

Every 90 days, each masonry cement producer shall retain an approved agency to obtain a random sample from a local point of supply in the market area served by the producer.

The agency shall test the masonry cement for compliance with the physical requirements of Table 21-11-A.

Upon request of the building official, the producer shall furnish (at no cost) test results to the building official, architect, structural engineer, general contractor and masonry contractor.

SECTION 21.1107 — TEMPERATURE AND HUMIDITY

The temperature of the air in the vicinity of the mixing slab and dry materials, molds, base plates and mixing bowl shall be maintained between 68°F and 81.5°F (20°C and 27.5°C). The temperature of the mixing water, moist cabinet or moist room, and water in the storage tank shall not vary from 73.4°F (23°C) by more than 3°F (1.7°C).

The relative humidity of the laboratory air shall not be less than 50 percent. The moist cabinet or moist room atmosphere shall have a relative humidity of not less than 90 percent.

The moist cabinet or moist room shall conform to applicable standards.

SECTION 21.1108 — FINENESS

The fineness of the cement shall be determined from the residue on the No. 325 (45 μm) sieve.

SECTION 21.1109 — NORMAL CONSISTENCY

Determine normal consistency by the Vicat apparatus.

SECTION 21.1110 — AUTOCLAVE EXPANSION

The autoclave expansion shall be determined. After molding, store the bars in the moist cabinet or room for 48 hours ± 30 minutes before removal from the molds for measurement and test in the autoclave. Calculate the difference in the lengths of the test specimen before and after autoclaving to the nearest 0.01 percent of the effective gage length and report as the autoclave expansion of the masonry cement.

SECTION 21.1111 — TIME OF SETTING

The time of setting shall be determined by the Gillmore needle method.

SECTION 21.1112 — DENSITY

The density of the masonry cement shall be determined by using kerosene as the liquid. Use the density so determined in the calculation of the air content of the mortars.

SECTION 21.1113 — APPARATUS FOR MORTAR TESTS

The apparatus for mortar tests shall be in accordance with applicable standards.

SECTION 21.1114 — BLENDED SAND

The sand shall be a blend of equal parts by weight of graded standard sand and Standard 20-30 sand.

SECTION 21.1115 — PREPARATION OF MORTAR

21.1115.1 Proportions for Mortar. Mortar for air entrainment, compressive strength and water-retention tests shall be proportioned to contain the weight of cement, in grams, equal to six times the printed bag weight in pounds (13.228 times the printed bag weight in kilograms) and 1,440 grams of sand. The sand shall consist of 720 grams of graded Ottawa sand and 720 grams of Standard 20-30 sand. The quantity of water, measured in milliliters, shall be such as to produce a flow of 110 ± 5 as determined by the flow table.

21.1115.2 Mixing of Mortars. The mortar shall be mixed in accordance with the applicable standards.

21.1115.3 Determination of Flow. The flow shall be determined in accordance with applicable standards.

SECTION 21.1116 — AIR ENTRAINMENT

21.1116.1 Procedure. If the mortar has the correct flow, use a separate portion of the mortar for the determination of entrained air. Determine the mass of 400 ml of the mortar.

21.1116.2 Calculation. Calculate the air content of the mortar and report it to the nearest 0.1 percent as follows:

$$D = (W_1 + W_2 + V_w) [(W_1/S_1) + (W_2/S_2) + V_w]$$

$$A = 100 - (w_m/4D)$$

WHERE:

A = volume percent of entrained air.

D = density of air-free mortar, g/ml.

S_1 = density of cement, g/ml.

S_2 = density of standard sand, 2.65 g/ml.

V_w = milliliters-grams of water used.

W_m = mass of 400 ml.

W_1 = mass of cement, g.

W_2 = mass of sand, g.

SECTION 21.1117 — COMPRESSIVE STRENGTH

21.1117.1 Test Specimens.

21.1117.1.1 Molding. Immediately after determining the flow and the mass of 400 ml of mortar, return all the mortar to the mixing bowl and remix for 15 seconds at the medium speed. Then mold test specimens in accordance with applicable standards, except that elapsed time for mixing mortar, determining flow, determining air entrainment and starting the molding of cubes shall be within eight minutes.

21.1117.1.2 Storage. Store all test specimens immediately after molding in the molds on plane plates in a moist cabinet or moist room for 48 to 52 hours, in such a manner that the upper surfaces shall be exposed to the moist air. Then remove the cubes from the molds and place in the moist cabinet or moist room for five days in such a manner as to allow free circulation of air around at least five faces of the specimens. At the age of seven days, immerse the cubes for the 28-day tests in saturated lime water in storage tanks of noncorrodible materials.

21.1117.2 Procedure. Test the cube specimens immediately after their removal from the moist cabinet or moist room for seven-day specimens, and immediately after their removal from storage water for all other specimens. If more than one specimen at a time is removed from the moist cabinet or moist room for seven-day tests, cover these cubes with a damp cloth until time of testing. If more than one specimen at a time is removed from the storage water for testing, place these cubes in a pan of water at a temperature

of 73.4°F ± 3°F (23°C ± 1.7°C), and of sufficient depth to completely immerse each cube until time of testing.

The remainder of the testing procedure shall conform to applicable standards.

SECTION 21.1118 — WATER RETENTION

21.1118.1 Apparatus. The water-retention test shall conform to applicable standards.

21.1118.2 Procedure. Adjust the mercury relief column to maintain a vacuum of 51 ± 3 mm as indicated by the manometer. Seat the perforated dish on the greased gasket or greased rim of the funnel. Place a wetted filter paper in the bottom of the dish. Turn the stopcock to apply the vacuum to the funnel and check the apparatus for leaks and to determine that the required vacuum is obtained. Then turn the stopcock to shut off the vacuum from the funnel.

Mix the mortar to a flow of 110 ± 5 percent in accordance with applicable standards. Immediately after making the flow test, return the mortar on the flow table to the mixing bowl and remix the entire batch for 15 seconds at medium speed. Immediately after remixing the mortar, fill the perforated dish with the mortar to slightly above the rim. Tamp the mortar 15 times with the tamper. Apply 10 of the tamping strokes at approximately uniform spacing adjacent to the rim of the dish and with the long axis of the tamping face held at right angles to the radius of the dish. Apply the remaining five tamping strokes at random points distributed over the central area of the dish. The tamping pressure shall be just sufficient to ensure filling of the dish. On completion of the tamping, the top of the mortar will extend slightly above the rim of the dish. Smooth off the mortar by drawing the flat side of the straightedge (with the leading edge slightly raised) across the top of the dish. Then cut off the mortar to a plane surface flush with the rim of the dish by drawing the straightedge with a sawing motion across the top of the dish in two cutting strokes, starting each cut from near the center of the dish. If the mortar is pulled away from the side of the dish during the process of drawing the straightedge across the dish, gently press the mortar back into contact with the side of the dish using the tamper.

Turn the stopcock to apply the vacuum to the funnel. The time elapsed from the start of mixing the cement and water to the time of applying the vacuum shall not exceed eight minutes. After suction for 60 seconds, quickly turn the stopcock to expose the funnel to atmospheric pressure. Immediately slide the perforated dish off from the funnel, touch it momentarily on a damp cloth to remove droplets of water, and set the dish on the table. Then, using the bowl scraper, plow and mix the mortar in the dish for 15 seconds. Upon completion of mixing, place the mortar in the flow mold and determine the flow. The entire operation shall be carried out without interruption and as quickly as possible, and shall be completed within an elapsed time of 11 minutes after the start of mixing the cement and water for the first flow determination. Both flow determinations shall be made in accordance with applicable standards.

21.1118.3 Calculation. Calculate the water-retention value for the mortar as follows:

$$\text{Water-retention value} = (A/B) \times 100$$

WHERE:

A = flow after suction.

B = flow immediately after mixing.

TABLE 21-11-A—PHYSICAL REQUIREMENTS

MASONRY CEMENT TYPE	N	S	M
Fineness, residue on a No. 325 (45 μm) sieve, maximum percent	24	24	24
Soundness: Autoclave expansion, maximum, percent	1.0	1.0	1.0
Time of setting, Gilmore method: Initial set, minimum, hour . . . . Final set, maximum, hour	2 24	$1^1/_2$ 24	$1^1/_2$ 24
Compressive strength (average of 3 cubes): Initial compressive strength of mortar cubes, composed of 1 part cement and 3 parts blended sand (half Graded Ottawa sand, and half Standard 20-30 Ottawa sand) by volume, prepared and tested in accordance with this specification shall be equal to or higher than the values specified for the ages indicated below: 7 days, psi. . . . . 28 days, psi.	500 (3445 kPa) 900 (6201 kPa)	1,300 (8957 kPa) 2,100 (14 469 kPa)	1,800 (12 402 kPa) 2,900 (19 981 kPa)
Air content of mortar: Minimum percent by volume . . . . Maximum percent by volume	8 21	8 19	8 19
Water retention, flow after suction, minimum, percent of original flow	70	70	70

UNIFORM BUILDING CODE STANDARD 21-12
QUICKLIME FOR STRUCTURAL PURPOSES

Based on Standard Specification C 5-79 (Reapproved 1992) of the American Society for Testing and Materials. Extracted, with permission, from the *Annual Book of ASTM Standards,* copyright American Society for Testing and Materials, 100 Barr Harbor Drive, West Conshohocken, PA 19428

See Section 2102.2, Item 3, *Uniform Building Code*

SECTION 21.1201 — SCOPE

This standard covers all classes of quicklime, such as crushed lime, granular lime, ground lime, lump lime, pebble lime and pulverized lime, used for structural purposes.

SECTION 21.1202 — GENERAL REQUIREMENTS

Quicklime shall be slaked and aged in accordance with the printed directions of the manufacturer. The resulting lime putty shall be stored until cool.

SECTION 21.1203 — CHEMICAL COMPOSITION

The quicklime shall conform to the following requirements as to chemical composition, calculated to the nonvolatile basis:

	CALCIUM LIME	MAGNESIUM LIME
Calcium oxide, minimum, percent	75	—
Magnesium oxide, minimum, percent	—	20
Calcium and magnesium oxides, minimum, percent	95	95
Silica, alumina, and oxide of iron, maximum, percent	5	5
Carbon dioxide, maximum, percent:		
If sample is taken at the place of manufacture	3	3
If sample is taken at any other place	10	10

SECTION 21.1204 — RESIDUE

The quicklime shall not contain more than 15 percent by weight of residue.

SECTION 21.1205 — QUALITY CONTROL

Every 90 days, each lime producer shall retain an approved agency to obtain a random sample from a local point of supply in the market area served by the producer.

The agency shall test the lime for compliance with the physical requirements of Section 21.1204.

Upon request of the building official, the producer shall furnish (at no cost) test results to the building official, architect, structural engineer, general contractor and masonry contractor.

UNIFORM BUILDING CODE STANDARD 21-13
HYDRATED LIME FOR MASONRY PURPOSES

**Based on Standard Specification C 207-91 (Reapproved 1992) of the American Society for Testing and Materials.
Extracted, with permission, from the *Annual Book of ASTM Standards,* copyright American Society for
Testing and Materials, 100 Barr Harbor Drive, West Conshohocken, PA 19428**

See Section 2102.2, Item 3, *Uniform Building Code*

SECTION 21.1301 — SCOPE

This standard covers four types of hydrated lime. Types N and S are suitable for use in mortar, in the scratch and brown coats of cement plaster, for stucco, and for addition to portland-cement concrete. Types NA and SA are air-entrained hydrated limes that are suitable for use in any of the above uses where the inherent properties of lime and air entrainment are desired. The four types of lime sold under this specification shall be designated as follows:

Type N—Normal hydrated lime for masonry purposes.

Type S—Special hydrated lime for masonry purposes.

Type NA—Normal air-entraining hydrated lime for masonry purposes.

Type SA—Special air-entraining hydrated lime for masonry purposes.

> **NOTE:** Type S, special hydrated lime, and Type SA, special air-entraining hydrated lime, are differentiated from Type N, normal hydrated lime, and Type NA, normal air-entraining hydrated lime, principally by their ability to develop high, early plasticity and higher water retentivity and by a limitation on their unhydrated oxide content.

SECTION 21.1302 — DEFINITION

HYDRATED LIME. The hydrated lime covered by Type N or S in this standard shall contain no additives for the purpose of entraining air. The air content of cement-lime mortars made with Type N or S shall not exceed 7 percent. Types NA and SA shall contain an air-entraining additive as specified by Section 21.1305. The air content of cement-lime mortars made with Type NA or SA shall have a minimum of 7 percent and a maximum of 14 percent.

SECTION 21.1303 — ADDITIONS

Types NA and SA hydrated lime covered by this standard shall contain additives for the purpose of entraining air.

SECTION 21.1304 — MANUFACTURER'S STATEMENT

Where required, the nature, amount and identity of the air-entraining agent used and of any processing addition that may have been used shall be provided, as well as test data showing compliance of such air-entraining addition.

SECTION 21.1305 — CHEMICAL REQUIREMENTS COMPOSITION

Hydrated lime for masonry purposes shall conform to the requirements as to chemical composition set forth in Table 21-13-A.

SECTION 21.1306 — RESIDUE, POPPING AND PITTING

The four types of hydrated lime for masonry purposes shall conform to one of the following requirements:

1. The residue retained on a No. 30 (600 µm) sieve shall not be more than 0.5 percent, or

2. If the residue retained on a No. 30 (600 µm) sieve is over 0.5 percent, the lime shall show no pops and pits when tested.

SECTION 21.1307 — PLASTICITY

The putty made from Type S, special hydrate, or Type SA, special air-entraining hydrate, shall have a plasticity figure of not less than 200 within 30 minutes after mixing with water, when tested.

SECTION 21.1308 — WATER RETENTION

Hydrated lime mortar made with Type N, normal hydrated lime, or Type NA, normal air-entraining hydrated lime, after suction for 60 seconds, shall have a water-retention value of not less than 75 percent when tested in a standard mortar made from the dry hydrate or from putty made from the hydrate which has been soaked for a period of 16 to 24 hours.

Hydrated lime mortar made with Type S, special hydrated lime, or Type SA, special air-entraining hydrated lime, after suction for 60 seconds, shall have a water-retention value of not less than 85 percent when tested in a standard mortar made from the dry hydrate.

SECTION 21.1309 — SPECIAL MARKING

When Type NA or SA air-entraining hydrated lime is delivered in packages, the type under this standard and the words "air-entraining" shall be plainly indicated thereon or, in case of bulk shipments, so indicated on shipping notices.

SECTION 21.1310 — QUALITY CONTROL

Every 90 days, each lime producer shall retain an approved agency to obtain a random sample from a local point of supply in the market area served by the producer.

The agency shall test the lime for compliance with the physical requirements of Sections 21.1306, 21.1307 and 21.1308.

Upon request of the building official, the producer shall furnish (at no cost) test results to the building official, architect, structural engineer, general contractor and masonry contractor.

TABLE 21-13-A—CHEMICAL REQUIREMENTS

	HYDRATE TYPES			
	N	**NA**	**S**	**SA**
Calcium and magnesium oxides (nonvolatile basis), min. percent	95	95	95	95
Carbon dioxide (as-received basis), max. percent				
If sample is taken at place of manufacture	5	5	5	5
If sample is taken at any other place	7	7	7	7
Unhydrated oxides (as-received basis), max. percent	—	—	8	8

UNIFORM BUILDING CODE STANDARD 21-14
MORTAR CEMENT
Test Standard of the International Conference of Building Officials
See Section 2102.2, Item 2, *Uniform Building Code*

SECTION 21.1401 — SCOPE

This standard covers mortar cement for use in masonry mortars.

SECTION 21.1402 — CLASSIFICATIONS

There are three types of mortar cement:

1. **Type N.** For use as the cementitious material in the preparation of UBC Standard 21-15 Type N and Type O mortars. For use in combination with portland or blended hydraulic cements in the preparation of Type S or Type M mortars.

2. **Type S.** For use as the cementitious material in the preparation of UBC Standard 21-15 Type S mortar.

3. **Type M.** For use as the cementitious material in the preparation of UBC Standard 21-15 Type M mortar.

SECTION 21.1403 — PHYSICAL REQUIREMENTS

Mortar cement shall conform to the requirements set forth in Table 21-14-A for its classifications.

SECTION 21.1404 — CONSTITUENT MATERIALS

Upon request of the building official, the constituent materials shall be provided to the building official and engineer of record.

SECTION 21.1405 — RESTRICTED MATERIALS

Materials used in mortar cement shall conform to the requirements set forth in Table 21-14-B.

SECTION 21.1406 — DELETERIOUS MATERIAL

Materials listed in Table 21-14-C shall not be used in mortar cement.

SECTION 21.1407 — PACKAGE LABELING

Mortar cement packages shall carry a statement indicating that the product conforms to requirements of this standard and shall include the brand, name of manufacturer, type of mortar cement and net weight of the package in pounds.

SECTION 21.1408 — CERTIFICATION

Certification shall be submitted upon request of the building official and shall certify compliance with the requirements of this standard.

SECTION 21.1409 — SAMPLING AND TESTING

Every 90 days, each mortar cement producer shall retain an approved agency to obtain a random sample from a local point of supply in the market area served by the producer.

The agency shall test the mortar cement for compliance with the physical requirements of Table 21-14-A.

Upon request of the building official, the producer shall furnish (at no cost) test results to the building official, architect, structural engineer, general contractor and masonry contractor.

SECTION 21.1410 — TEMPERATURE AND HUMIDITY

The temperature of the air in the vicinity of the mixing slab and dry materials, molds, base plates and mixing bowl shall be maintained between 68°F and 81.5°F (20°C and 27.5°C). The temperature of the mixing water, moist cabinet or moist room, and water in the storage tank shall not vary from 73.4°F (23°C) by more than 3°F (1.7°C).

The relative humidity of the laboratory air shall not be less than 50 percent. The moist cabinet or moist room atmosphere shall have a relative humidity of not less than 90 percent.

The moist cabinet or moist room shall conform to applicable standards.

SECTION 21.1411 — FINENESS

Determine the residue on the No. 325 (45 μm) sieve.

SECTION 21.1412 — NORMAL CONSISTENCY

Determine normal consistency by the Vicat apparatus.

SECTION 21.1413 — AUTOCLAVE EXPANSION

Determine autoclave expansion. After molding, store bars in the moist cabinet or room for 48 hours, plus or minus 30 minutes, before removal from the molds for measurement and test in the autoclave. Calculate the difference in length of the test specimen before and after autoclaving to the nearest 0.01 percent of the effective gauge length and report as the autoclave expansion of the mortar cement.

SECTION 21.1414 — TIME OF SETTING

Determine the time of setting by the Gillmore needle method.

SECTION 21.1415 — DENSITY

Determine the density of the mortar cement using kerosene as the liquid. Use the density so determined in the calculation of the air content of the mortars.

SECTION 21.1416 — APPARATUS FOR MORTAR TESTS

Apparatus shall be in accordance with applicable standards.

SECTION 21.1417 — BLENDED SAND

The sand shall be a blend of equal parts by weight of graded Ottawa sand and Standard 20-30 Ottawa sand.

SECTION 21.1418 — PREPARATION OF MORTAR

21.1418.1 Proportions for Mortar. Mortar for air entrainment, compressive strength and water-retention tests shall be proportioned to contain the weight of cement, in grams, equal to six times the printed bag weight in pounds (13.228 times the printed bag weight in kilograms) and 1,440 grams of sand. The sand shall consist of 720 grams of graded Ottawa sand and 720 grams of Standard 20-30 sand. The quantity of water, measured in milliliters, shall be such as to produce a flow of 110 ± 5 as determined by the flow table.

21.1418.2 Mixing of Mortars. Mix the mortar in accordance with applicable standards.

21.1418.3 Determination of Flow. Determine the flow in accordance with applicable standards.

SECTION 21.1419 — AIR ENTRAINMENT

21.1419.1 Procedure. If the mortar has the correct flow, use a separate portion of the mortar for the determination of entrained air. Determine the weight of 400 cm^3 of mortar.

21.1419.2 Calculation. Calculate the air content of the mortar and report it to the nearest 0.1 percent as follows:

$$D = (W_1 + W_2 + V_w)/[(W_1/S_1) + (W_2/S_2) + V_w]$$
$$A = 100 - (W_m/4D)$$

WHERE:

A = volume percent of entrained air.

D = density of air-free mortar, g/cm^3.

S_1 = density of cement, g/cm^3.

S_2 = density of standard sand, 2.65 g/cm^3.

V_w = milliliters-grams of water used.

W_m = mass of 400 ml of mortar, g.

W_1 = weight of cement, g.

W_2 = weight of sand, g.

SECTION 21.1420 — COMPRESSIVE STRENGTH OF TEST SPECIMENS

21.1420.1 Molding. Immediately after determining the flow and the weight of 400 cm^3 or mortar, return all the mortar to the mixing bowl and remix for 15 seconds at the medium speed. Then mold test specimens in accordance with applicable standards, except that the elapsed time for mixing mortar, determining flow, determining air entrainment and starting the molding of cubes shall be within eight minutes.

21.1420.2 Storage. Store all test specimens immediately after molding in the molds on plane plates in a moist cabinet maintained at a relative humidity of 90 percent or more for 48 to 52 hours in such a manner that the upper surfaces shall be exposed to the moist air. Then remove the cubes from the molds and place in the moist cabinet for five days in such a manner as to allow free circulation of air around at least five faces of the specimens. At the age of seven days, immerse the cubes for the 28-day tests in saturated lime water in storage tanks of noncorrodible materials.

SECTION 21.1421 — PROCEDURE

Test the cube specimens immediately after their removal from the moist cabinet for seven-day specimens, and immediately after their removal from storage water for all other specimens. If more than one specimen at a time is removed from the moist closet for seven-day tests, cover these cubes with a damp cloth until time of testing. If more than one specimen at a time is removed from the storage water for testing, place these cubes in a pan of water at a temperature of 73.4°F ± 3°F (23°C ± 1.7°C), and of sufficient depth to completely immerse each cube until time of testing.

The remainder of the testing procedure shall conform to applicable standards.

SECTION 21.1422 — WATER RETENTION

21.1422.1 Water-retention Apparatus. For the water-retention test, and apparatus essentially the same as that shown in Figure 21-14-1 shall be used. This apparatus consists of a water aspirator or other source of vacuum controlled by a mercury-relief column and connected by way of a three-way stopcock to a funnel upon which rests a perforated dish. The perforated dish shall be made of metal not attacked by masonry mortar. The metal in the base of the dish shall have a thickness of 1.7 to 1.9 mm and shall conform to the requirements given in Figure 21-14-1. The bore of the stopcock shall have a 4 mm plus or minus 0.5 mm diameter, and the connecting glass tubing shall have a minimum inside diameter of 4 mm. A mercury manometer, connected as shown in Figure 21-14-1, indicates the vacuum. The contact surface of the funnel and perforated dish shall be plane and shall be lapped to ensure intimate contact. An airtight seal shall be maintained between the funnel and the dish during a test. This shall be accomplished by either of the following procedures: (1) a synthetic (grease-resistant) rubber gasket may be permanently sealed to the top of the funnel, using petrolatum or light grease to ensure a seal between the funnel and dish, or (2) the top of the funnel may be lightly coated with petrolatum or light grease to ensure a seal between the funnel and dish. Care should be taken to ensure that none of the holes in the perforated dish are clogged from the grease. Hardened, very smooth, not rapid filter paper shall be used. It shall be of such diameter that it will lie flat and completely cover the bottom of the dish.

A steel straightedge not less than 8 inches (203 mm) long and not less than $^1/_{16}$ inch (1.6 mm) nor more than $^1/_8$-inch (3.2 mm) thickness shall be used.

Other apparatus required for the water-retention tests shall conform to the applicable requirements of Section 21.1416.

21.1422.2 Procedure. Adjust the mercury-relief column to maintain a vacuum of 50.8 mm as measured on the manometer. Seat the perforated dish on the greased gasket of the funnel. Place a wetted filter paper in the bottom of the dish. Turn the stopcock to apply the vacuum to the funnel and check the apparatus for leaks and to determine that the required vacuum is obtained. Then turn the stopcock to shut off the vacuum from the funnel.

Mix the mortar to a flow of 110 plus or minus 5 percent in accordance with applicable standards. Immediately after making the flow test, return the mortar on the flow table to the mixing bowl and remix the entire batch for 15 seconds at medium speed. Immediately after remixing the mortar, fill the perforated dish with the mortar to slightly above the rim. Tamp the mortar 15 times with the tamper. Apply 10 of the tamping strokes at approximately uniform spacing adjacent to the rim of the dish and with the long axis of the tamping face held at right angles to the radius of the dish. Apply the remaining five tamping strokes at random points distributed over the central area of the dish. The tamping pressure shall be just sufficient to ensure filling of the dish. On completion of the tamping, the top of the mortar should extend slightly above the rim of the dish. Smooth off the mortar by drawing the flat side of the straightedge (with the leading edge slightly raised) across the top of the dish. Then cut off the mortar to a plane surface flush with the rim of the dish by drawing the straightedge with a sawing motion across the top of the dish in two cutting strokes, starting each cut from near the center of the dish. If the mortar is pulled away from the side of the dish during the process of drawing the straightedge across the dish, gently press the mortar back into contact with the side of the dish using the tamper.

Turn the stopcock to apply the vacuum to the funnel. The time elapsed from the start of mixing the cement and water to the time of applying the vacuum shall not exceed eight minutes. After suction for 60 seconds, quickly turn the stopcock to expose the funnel to atmospheric pressure. Immediately slide the perforated dish off from the funnel, touch it momentarily on a damp cloth to remove droplets of water, and set the dish on the table. Then, using the bowl scraper, in accordance with applicable standards, plow and mix the mortar in the dish for 15 seconds. Upon completion of mixing, place the mortar in the flow mold and determine the flow.

The entire operation shall be carried out without interruption and as quickly as possible, and shall be completed within an elapsed time of 11 minutes after the start of mixing the cement and water for the first flow determination. Both flow determinations shall be made in accordance with applicable standards.

21.1422.3 Calculation. Calculate the water-retention value for the mortar as follows:

$$\text{Water-retention value} = (a/b) \times 100$$

WHERE:

a = flow after suction.

b = flow immediately after mixing.

TABLE 21-14-A—PHYSICAL REQUIREMENTS

MORTAR CEMENT TYPE	N	S	M
Fineness, residue on a No. 325 (45 µm) sieve Maximum percent	24	24	24
Autoclave expansion Maximum, percent	1.0	1.0	1.0

Time of setting, Gillmore method:
    Initial set, minimum, hour
    Final set, maximum, hour
	2
	24
		$1^1/_2$
		24
			$1^1/_2$
			24

Compressive strength[1]
    7 days, minimum psi
    28 days, minimum psi
	500 (3445 kPa)
	900 (6201 kPa)
		1300 (8957 kPa)
		2100 (14 469 kPa)
			1800 (12 402 kPa)
			2900 (19 981 kPa)

Flexural bond strength[2] 28 days, minimum psi	71 (489 kPa)	104 (717 kPa)	116 (799 kPa)

Air content of mortar
    Minimum percent by volume
    Maximum percent by volume
	8
	16
		8
		14
			8
			14

Water retention Minimum, percent	70	70	70

[1]Compressive strength shall be based on the average of three mortar cubes composed of one part mortar cement and three parts blended sand (one half graded Ottawa sand, and one half Standard 20-30 Ottawa sand) by volume and tested in accordance with this standard.

[2]Flexural bond strength shall be determined in accordance with UBC Standard 21-20.

TABLE 21-14-B—RESTRICTED MATERIALS

MATERIAL	MAXIMUM LIMIT (percentage)
Chloride salts	0.06
Carboxylic acids	0.25
Sugars	1.00
Glycols	1.00
Lignin and derivatives	0.50
Stearates	0.50
Fly ash	No limit
Clay (except fireclay)	5.00

TABLE 21-14-C—DELETERIOUS MATERIALS NOT PERMITTED IN MORTAR CEMENT

Epoxy resins and derivatives Phenols Asbestos fiber Fireclays

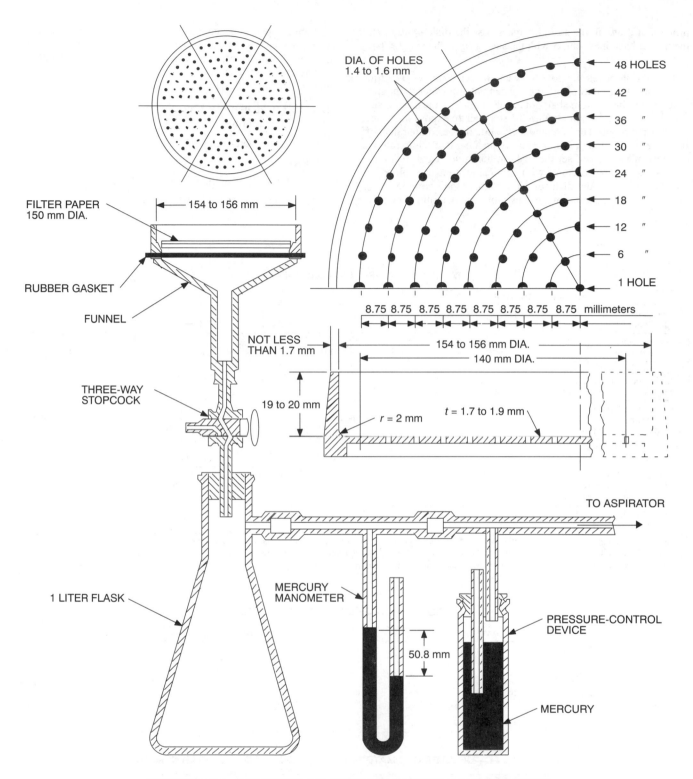

FIGURE 21-14-1—APPARATUS ASSEMBLY FOR THE WATER-RETENTION TEST

UNIFORM BUILDING CODE STANDARD 21-15
MORTAR FOR UNIT MASONRY AND REINFORCED MASONRY OTHER THAN GYPSUM

Based on Standard Specification C 270-95 of the American Society for Testing and Materials. Extracted, with permission, from the *Annual Book of ASTM Standards,* copyright American Society for Testing and Materials, 100 Barr Harbor Drive, West Conshohocken, PA 19428

See Section 2102.2, Item 8, *Uniform Building Code*

SECTION 21.1501 — SCOPE

These specifications cover the required properties of mortars determined by laboratory tests for use in the construction of reinforced brick masonry structures and unit masonry structures. Two alternative specifications are covered as follows:

21.1501.1 Property specifications. Property specifications are those in which the acceptability of the mortar is based on the properties of the ingredients (materials) and the properties (water retention and compressive strength) of samples of the mortar mixed and tested in the laboratory.

21.1501.2 Proportion specifications. Proportion specifications are those in which the acceptability of the mortar is based on the properties of the ingredients (materials) and a definite composition of the mortar consisting of fixed proportions of these ingredients.

Unless data are presented to show that the mortar meets the requirements of the physical property specifications, the proportion specifications shall govern. For field tests of grout and mortars see UBC Standard 21-16.

Property Specifications

SECTION 21.1502 — MATERIALS

21.1502.1 General. Materials used as ingredients in the mortar shall conform to the requirements specified in the pertinent UBC Standards.

21.1502.2 Cementitious Materials. Cementitious materials shall conform to the following specifications:

1. **Portland cement.** Type I, IA, II, IIA, III or IIIA of ASTM C 150.

2. **Blended hydraulic cement.** Type IS, IS-A, S, S-A, IP, IP-A, I(PM) or I(PM)-A of ASTM C 1157.

3. **Plastic cement.** Plastic cement conforming to the requirements of UBC Standard 25-1 and UBC Standard 21-11, when used in lieu of masonry cement.

4. **Mortar cement.** UBC Standard 21-14.

5. **Masonry cements.** UBC Standard 21-11.

6. **Quicklime.** UBC Standard 21-12.

7. **Hydrated lime.** UBC Standard 21-13.

21.1502.3 Water. Water shall be clean and free of deleterious amounts of acids, alkalies or organic materials.

21.1502.4 Admixtures or Mortar Colors. Admixtures or mortar colors shall not be added to the mortar at the time of mixing unless provided for in the contract specifications and, after the material is so added, the mortar shall conform to the requirements of the property specifications.

Only pure mineral mortar colors shall be used.

21.1502.5 Antifreeze Compounds. No antifreeze liquid, salts or other substances shall be used in the mortar to lower the freezing point.

21.1502.6 Storage of Materials. Cementitious materials and aggregates shall be stored in such a manner as to prevent deterioration or intrusion of foreign material. Any material that has become unsuitable for good construction shall not be used.

SECTION 21.1503 — MIXING MORTAR

Mortar blended on the jobsite shall be mixed for a minimum period of three minutes, with the amount of water required to produce the desired workability, in a drum-type batch mixer. Factory-dry blended mortar shall be mixed with water in a mechanical mixer until workable but not to exceed 10 minutes.

SECTION 21.1504 — MORTAR

21.1504.1 Mortar for Unit Masonry. Mortar conforming to the proportion specifications shall consist of a mixture of cementitious material and aggregate conforming to the requirements of Section 21.1502, and the measurement and mixing requirements of Section 21.1503, and shall be proportioned within the limits given in Table 21-15-B for each mortar type specified.

21.1504.2 Mortar for Reinforced Masonry. In mortar used for reinforced masonry the following special requirements shall be met: Sufficient water has been added to bring the mixture to a plastic state. The volume of aggregate in mortar shall be at least two and one-fourth times but not more than three times the volume of cementitious materials.

21.1504.3 Aggregate Ratio. The volume of damp, loose aggregate in mortar used in brick masonry shall be not less than two and one-fourth times or more than three times the total separate volumes of cementitious materials used.

21.1504.4 Water Retention. Mortar shall conform to the water retention requirements of Table 21-15-A.

21.1504.5 Air Content. Mortar shall conform to the air content requirements of Table 21-15-A.

SECTION 21.1505 — COMPRESSIVE STRENGTH

The average compressive strength of three 2-inch (51 mm) cubes of mortar (before thinning) shall not be less than the strength given in Table 21-15-A for the mortar type specified.

Proportion Specifications

SECTION 21.1506 — MATERIALS

21.1506.1 General. Materials used as ingredients in the mortar shall conform to the requirements of Section 21.1502 and to the requirements of this section.

21.1506.2 Portland Cement. Portland cement shall conform to the requirements of ASTM C 150.

21.1506.3 Blended Hydraulic Cements. Blended hydraulic cements of Type IS, IS-A, IP, IP-A, I(PM) or I(PM)-A shall conform to the requirements of ASTM C 595, when used in lieu of masonry cement.

21.1506.4 Plastic Cement. Plastic cement conforming to the requirements of UBC Standard 25-1 and UBC Standard 21-11.

21.1506.5 Mortar Cement. Mortar cement shall conform to the requirements of UBC Standard 21-14.

21.1506.6 Masonry Cement. Masonry cement shall conform to the requirements of UBC Standard 21-11.

21.1506.7 Hydrated Lime. Hydrated lime shall conform to either of the two following requirements:

1. The total free (unhydrated) calcium oxide (CaO) and magnesium oxide (MgO) shall not be more than 8 percent by weight (calculated on the as-received basis for hydrates).

2. When the hydrated lime is mixed with portland cement in the proportion set forth in Table 21-15-B, the mixture shall give an autoclave expansion of not more than 0.50 percent.

Hydrated lime intended for use when mixed dry with other mortar ingredients shall have a plasticity figure of not less than 200 when tested 15 minutes after adding water.

21.1506.8 Lime Putty. Lime putty made from either quicklime or hydrated lime shall be soaked for a period sufficient to produce a plasticity figure of not less than 200 and shall conform to either the requirements for limitation on total free oxides of calcium and magnesium or the autoclave test specified for hydrated lime in Section 21.1506.5.

SECTION 21.1507 — MORTAR

Mortar shall consist of a mixture of cementitious materials and aggregate conforming to the requirements specified in Section 21.1504, mixed in one of the proportions shown in Table 21-15-B, to which sufficient water has been added to reduce the mixture to a plastic state.

TABLE 21-15-A—PROPERTY SPECIFICATIONS FOR MORTAR[1]

MORTAR	TYPE	AVERAGE COMPRESSIVE STRENGTH OF 2-INCH (51 mm) CUBES AT 28 DAYS (Min., psi) × 6.89 for kPa	WATER RETENTION (Min., percent)	AIR CONTENT (Max., percent)[2]	AGGREGATE MEASURED IN A DAMP, LOOSE CONDITION
Cement-lime or mortar cement	M	2,500	75	12	Not less than $2^1/_4$ and not more than $3^1/_2$ times the sum of the separate volumes of cementitious materials
	S	1,800	75	12	
	N	750	75	14[3]	
	O	350	75	14[3]	
Masonry cement	M	2,500	75	18	
	S	1,800	75	18	
	N	750	75	18	
	O	350	75	18	

[1]Laboratory-prepared mortar only.

[2]Determined in accordance with applicable standards.

[3]When structural reinforcement is incorporated in cement-lime mortar or mortar-cement mortar, the maximum air content shall be 12 percent.

TABLE 21-15-B—MORTAR PROPORTIONS FOR UNIT MASONRY

MORTAR	TYPE	Portland Cement or Blended Cement[1]	Masonry Cement[2] M	Masonry Cement[2] S	Masonry Cement[2] N	Mortar Cement[3] M	Mortar Cement[3] S	Mortar Cement[3] N	Hydrated Lime or Lime Putty[1]	AGGREGATE MEASURED IN A DAMP, LOOSE CONDITION
Cement-lime	M	1	—	—	—	—	—	—	$^1/_4$	Not less than $2^1/_4$ and not more than 3 times the sum of the separate volumes of cementitious materials
	S	1	—	—	—	—	—	—	over $^1/_4$ to $^1/_2$	
	N	1	—	—	—	—	—	—	over $^1/_2$ to $1^1/_4$	
	O	1	—	—	—	—	—	—	over $1^1/_4$ to $2^1/_2$	
Mortar cement	M	1	—	—	—	—	—	1	—	
	M	—	—	—	—	1	—	—	—	
	S	$^1/_2$	—	—	—	—	—	1	—	
	S	—	—	—	—	—	1	—	—	
	N	—	—	—	—	—	—	1	—	
Masonry cement	M	1	—	—	1	—	—	—	—	
	M	—	1	—	—	—	—	—	—	
	S	$^1/_2$	—	—	1	—	—	—	—	
	S	—	—	1	—	—	—	—	—	
	N	—	—	—	1	—	—	—	—	
	O	—	—	—	1	—	—	—	—	

[1]When plastic cement is used in lieu of portland cement, hydrated lime or putty may be added, but not in excess of one tenth of the volume of cement.

[2]Masonry cement conforming to the requirements of UBC Standard 21-11.

[3]Mortar cement conforming to the requirements of UBC Standard 21-14.

UNIFORM BUILDING CODE STANDARD 21-16
FIELD TESTS SPECIMENS FOR MORTAR
Test Standard of the International Conference of Building Officials
See Section 2102.2, Item 8, *Uniform Building Code*

SECTION 21.1601 — FIELD COMPRESSIVE TEST SPECIMEN FOR MORTAR

Spread mortar on the masonry units $1/2$ inch to $5/8$ inch (13 mm to 16 mm) thick, and allow to stand for one minute, then remove mortar and place in a 2-inch by 4-inch (51 mm by 102 mm) cylinder in two layers, compressing the mortar into the cylinder using a flat-end stick or fingers. Lightly tap mold on opposite sides, level off and immediately cover molds and keep them damp until taken to the laboratory. After 48 hours' set, have the laboratory remove molds and place them in the fog room until tested in damp condition.

SECTION 21.1602 — REQUIREMENTS

Each such mortar test specimen shall exhibit a minimum ultimate compressive strength of 1,500 pounds per square inch (10 304 kPa).

UNIFORM BUILDING CODE STANDARD 21-17
TEST METHOD FOR COMPRESSIVE
STRENGTH OF MASONRY PRISMS

Based on Standard Test Method E 447-92 of the American Society for Testing and Materials.
Extracted, with permission, from the *Annual Book of ASTM Standards,* copyright American Society for
Testing and Materials, 100 Barr Harbor Drive, West Conshohocken, PA 19428

See Sections 2102.2, Item 6.4; 2105.3.2; and 2105.3.3, *Uniform Building Code*

SECTION 21.1701 — SCOPE

This standard covers procedures for masonry prism construction, testing and procedures for determining the compressive strength of masonry.

SECTION 21.1702 — CONSTRUCTION OF PRISMS

Prisms shall be constructed on a flat, level base. Masonry units used in the prism shall be representative of the units used in the corresponding construction. Each prism shall be built in an opened moisture-tight bag which is large enough to enclose and seal the completed prism. The orientation of units, where top and bottom cross sections vary due to taper of the cells, or where the architectural surface of either side of the unit varies, shall be the same orientation as used in the corresponding construction. Prisms shall be a single wythe in thickness and laid up in stack bond (see Figure 21-17-1).

The length of masonry prisms may be reduced by saw cutting; however, prisms composed of regular shaped hollow units shall have at least one complete cell with one full-width cross web on either end. Prisms composed of irregular-shaped units shall be cut to obtain as symmetrical a cross section as possible. The minimum length of saw-cut prisms shall be 4 inches (102 mm).

Masonry prisms shall be laid in a full mortar bed (mortar bed both webs and face shells). Mortar shall be representative of that used in the corresponding construction. Mortar joint thickness, the tooling of joints and the method of positioning and aligning units shall be representative of the corresponding construction.

Prisms shall be a minimum of two units in height, but the total height shall not be less than 1.3 times the least actual thickness or more than 5.0 times the least actual thickness. Immediately following the construction of the prism, the moisture-tight bag shall be drawn around the prism and sealed.

Where the corresponding construction is to be solid grouted, prisms shall be solid grouted. Grout shall be representative of that used in the corresponding construction. Grout shall be placed not less than one day nor more than two days following the construction of the prism. Grout consolidation shall be representative of that used in the construction. Additional grout shall be placed in the prism after reconsolidation and settlement due to water loss, but prior to the grout setting. Excess grout shall be screeded off level with the top of the prism. Where open-end units are used, additional masonry units shall be used as forms to confine the grout during placement. Masonry unit forms shall be sufficiently braced to prevent displacement during grouting. Immediately following the grouting operation, the moisture-tight bag shall be drawn around the prism and resealed.

Where the corresponding construction is to be partially grouted, two sets of prisms shall be constructed; one set shall be grouted solid and the other set shall not be grouted.

Where the corresponding construction is of multiwythe composite masonry, masonry prisms representative of each wythe shall be built and tested separately.

Prisms shall be left undisturbed for at least two days after construction.

SECTION 21.1703 — TRANSPORTING MASONRY PRISMS

Prior to transporting each prism, strap or clamp the prism together to prevent damage during handling and transportation. Secure prism to prevent jarring, bouncing or falling over during transporting.

SECTION 21.1704 — CURING

Prisms shall remain sealed in the moisture-tight bag until two days prior to testing; the moisture-tight bag shall then be removed and curing continued in laboratory air maintained at a temperature of 75°F ± 15°F (24°C ± 8°C). Prisms shall be tested at 28 days after constructing the prism or at test age designated.

SECTION 21.1705 — PREPARATION FOR TESTING

21.1705.1 Capping the Prism. Cap top and bottom of the prism prior to testing with sulfur-filled capping or with high-strength gypsum plaster capping (such as "Hydrostone" or "Hyprocal White"). Sulfur-filled capping material shall be 40 to 60 percent by weight sulfur, the remainder being ground fireclay or other suitable inert material passing a No. 100 (150 μm) sieve, with or without a plasticizer. Spread the capping material over a level surface which is plane within 0.003 inch (0.076 mm) in 16 inches (406 mm). Bring the surface to be capped into contact with the capping paste; firmly press down the specimen, holding it so that its axis is at right angles to the capping surfaces. The average thickness of the cap shall not exceed $^1/_8$ inch (3.2 mm). Allow caps to age at least two hours before testing.

21.1705.2 Measurement of the Prism. Measure the length and thickness of the prism to the nearest 0.01 inch (0.25 mm) by averaging three measurements taken at the center and quarter points of the height of the specimen. Measure the height of the prism, including caps, to the nearest 0.1 inch (2.54 mm).

SECTION 21.1706 — TEST PROCEDURE

21.1706.1 Test Apparatus. The test machine shall have an accuracy of plus or minus 1.0 percent over the load range. The upper bearing shall be spherically seated, hardened metal block firmly attached at the center of the upper head of the machine. The center of the sphere shall lie at the center of the surface held in its spherical seat, but shall be free to turn in any direction, and its perimeter shall have at least $^1/_4$-inch (6.4 mm) clearance from the head to allow for specimens whose bearing surfaces are not exactly parallel. The diameter of the bearing surface shall be at least 5 inches (127 mm). A hardened metal bearing block may be used beneath the specimen to minimize wear of the lower platen of the machine. The bearing block surfaces intended for contact with the specimen shall have a hardness not less than 60 HRC (620 HB). These surfaces shall not depart from plane surfaces by more than

0.001 inch (0.0254 mm) in any 6-inch (153 mm) dimension. When the bearing area of the spherical bearing block is not sufficient to cover the area of the specimen, a steel plate with surfaces machined to true planes within plus or minus 0.001 inch (0.0254 mm) in any 6-inch (153 mm) dimension, and with a thickness equal to at least the distance from the edge of the spherical bearings to the most distant corner, shall be placed between the spherical bearing block and the capped specimen.

21.1706.2 Installing the Prism in the Test Machine. Wipe clean the bearing faces of the upper and lower platens or bearing blocks and of the test specimen and place the test specimen on the lower platen or bearing block. Align both centroidal axes of the specimen with the center of thrust of the test machine. As the spherically seated block is brought to bear on the specimen, rotate its movable portion gently by hand so that uniform seating is obtained.

21.1706.3 Loading. Apply the load, up one half of the expected minimum load, at any convenient rate, after which adjust the controls of the machine so that the remaining load is applied at a uniform rate in not less than one or more than two minutes.

21.1706.4 Observations. Describe the mode of failure as fully as possible or illustrate crack patterns, spalling, etc., on a sketch, or both. Note whether failure occurred on one side or one end of the prism prior to failure of the opposing side or end of the prism.

SECTION 21.1707 — CALCULATIONS

Calculations of test results shall be as follows:

21.1707.1 Net cross-sectional area. Determine the net cross-sectional area [square inches (mm^2)] of solid grouted prisms by multiplying the average measured width dimension [inches (mm)] by the average measured length dimension [inches (mm)]. The net cross-sectional area of ungrouted prisms shall be taken as the net cross-sectional area of masonry units determined from a representative sample of units.

21.1707.2 Masonry prism strength. Determine the compressive strength of each prism [psi (kPa)] by dividing the maximum compressive load sustained [pounds (N)] by the net cross-sectional area of the prism [square inches (mm^2 × 1,000,000)].

21.1707.3 Compressive strength of masonry. The compressive strength of masonry [psi (kPa)] for each set of prisms shall be the lesser of the average strength of the prisms in the set, or 1.25 times the least prism strength multiplied by the prism height-to-thickness correction factor from Table 21-17-A. Where a set of grouted and nongrouted prisms are tested, the compressive strength of masonry shall be determined for the grouted set and for the nongrouted set separately. Where a set of prisms is tested for each wythe of a multiwythe wall, the compressive strength of masonry shall be determined for each wythe separately.

SECTION 21.1708 — MASONRY PRISM TEST REPORT

The test report shall include the following:

1. Name of testing laboratory and name of professional engineer responsible for the tests.

2. Designation of each prism tested and description of prism, including width, height and length dimensions, mortar type, grout and masonry unit used in the construction.

3. Age of prism at time of test.

4. Maximum compressive load sustained by each prism, net cross-sectional area of each prism and net area compressive strength of each prism.

5. Test observations for each prism in accordance with Section 21.1706.

6. Compressive strength of masonry for each set of prisms.

TABLE 21-17-A—PRISM HEIGHT-TO-THICKNESS CORRECTION FACTORS

Prisms h/t_p[1]	1.30	1.50	2.00	2.50	3.00	4.00	5.00
Correction factor	0.75	0.86	1.00	1.04	1.07	1.15	1.22

[1]h/t_p—ratio of prism height to least actual lateral dimension of prism.

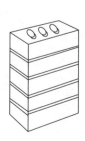
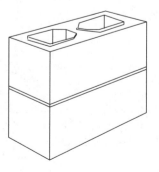

FIGURE 21-17-1—CONSTRUCTION OF PRISMS

UNIFORM BUILDING CODE STANDARD 21-18
METHOD OF SAMPLING AND TESTING GROUT

**Based on Standard Method C 1019-89a (93) of the American Society for Testing and Materials.
Extracted, with permission, from the *Annual Book of ASTM Standards,* copyright American Society for Testing
and Materials, 100 Barr Harbor Drive, West Conshohocken, PA 19428**

See Section 2102.2, Item 9; and Table 21-B, *Uniform Building Code*

SECTION 21.1801 — SCOPE

This method covers procedures for both field and laboratory sampling and compression testing of grout used in masonry construction.

SECTION 21.1802 — APPARATUS

21.1802.1 Maximum-Minimum Thermometer.

21.1802.2 Straightedge. A steel straightedge not less than 6 inches (152.4 mm) long and not less than $^{1}/_{16}$ inch (1.6 mm) in thickness.

21.1802.3 Tamping Rod. A nonabsorbent smooth rod, either round or square in cross section nominally $^{5}/_{8}$ inch (15.9 mm) in dimension with ends rounded to hemispherical tips of the same diameter. The rod shall be a minimum length of 12 inches (304.8 mm).

21.1802.4 Wooden Blocks. Wooden squares with side dimensions equal to one-half the desired grout specimen height, within a tolerance of 5 percent, and of sufficient quantity or thickness to yield the desired grout specimen height, as shown in Figures 21-18-1 and 21-18-2.

Wooden blocks shall be soaked in limewater for 24 hours, sealed with varnish or wax, or covered with an impermeable material prior to use.

SECTION 21.1803 — SAMPLING

21.1803.1 Size of Sample. Grout samples to be used for slump and compressive strength tests shall be a minimum of $^{1}/_{2}$ ft.^{3} (0.014 m^{3}).

21.1803.2 Field Sample. Take grout samples as the grout is being placed into the wall. Field samples may be taken at any time except for the first and last 10 percent of the batch volume.

SECTION 21.1804 — TEST SPECIMEN AND SAMPLE

21.1804.1 Each grout specimen shall be a square prism, nominally 3 inches (76.2 mm) or larger on the sides and twice as high as its width. Dimensional tolerances shall be within 5 percent of the nominal width selected.

21.1804.2 Three specimens constitute one sample.

SECTION 21.1805 — PROCEDURE

21.1805.1 Select a level location where the molds can remain undisturbed for 48 hours.

21.1805.2 Mold Construction.

21.1805.2.1 The mold space should simulate the grout location in the wall. If the grout is placed between two different types of masonry units, both types should be used to construct the mold.

21.1805.2.2 Form a square prism space, nominally 3 inches (76.2 mm) or larger on each side and twice as high as its width, by stacking masonry units of the same type and moisture condition as those being used in the construction. Place wooden blocks, cut to proper size and of the proper thickness or quantity, at the bottom of the space to achieve the necessary height of specimen. Tolerance on space and specimen dimensions shall be within 5 percent of the specimen width. See Figures 21-18-1 and 21-18-2.

21.1805.2.3 Line the masonry surfaces that will be in contact with the grout specimen with a permeable material, such as paper towel, to prevent bond to the masonry units.

21.1805.3 Measure and record the slump of the grout.

21.1805.4 Fill the mold with grout in two layers. Rod each layer 15 times with the tamping rod penetrating $^{1}/_{2}$ inch (12.7 mm) into the lower layer. Distribute the strokes uniformly over the cross section of the mold.

21.1805.5 Level the top surface of the specimen with a straightedge and cover immediately with a damp absorbent material such as cloth or paper towel. Keep the top surface of the sample damp by wetting the absorbent material and do not disturb the specimen for 48 hours.

21.1805.6 Protect the sample from freezing and variations in temperature. Store an indicating maximum-minimum thermometer with the sample and record the maximum and minimum temperatures experienced prior to the time the specimens are placed in the moist room.

21.1805.7 Remove the masonry units after 48 hours. Transport field specimens to the laboratory, keeping the specimens damp and in a protective container.

21.1805.8 Store in a moist room conforming to nationally recognized standards.

21.1805.9 Cap the specimens in accordance with the applicable requirements of UBC Standard 21-17.

21.1805.10 Measure and record the width of each face at midheight. Measure and record the height of each face at midwidth. Measure and record the amount out of plumb at midwidth of each face.

21.1805.11 Test the specimens in a damp condition in accordance with applicable requirements of UBC Standard 21-17.

SECTION 21.1806 — CALCULATIONS

The report shall include the following:

1. Mix design.

2. Slump of the grout.

3. Type and number of units used to form mold for specimens.

4. Description of the specimens—dimensions, amount out of plumb—in percent.

5. Curing history, including maximum and minimum temperatures and age of specimen, when transported to laboratory and when tested.

6. Maximum load and compressive strength of the sample.

7. Description of failure.

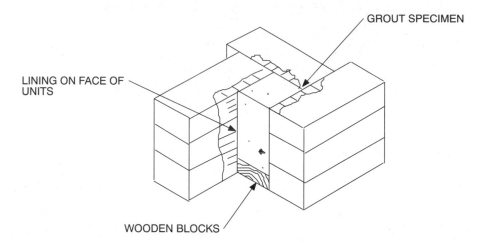

FIGURE 21-18-1—GROUT MOLD [UNITS 6 INCHES (152 mm) OR LESS IN HEIGHT, 2^1/$_2$-INCH-HIGH (63.5 mm) BRICK SHOWN]

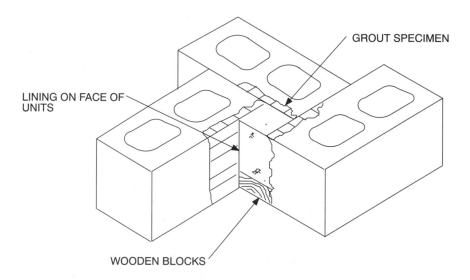

FIGURE 21-18-2—GROUT MOLD [UNITS GREATER THAN 6 INCHES (152 mm) IN HEIGHT, 8-INCH-HIGH (203 mm) CONCRETE MASONRY UNIT SHOWN]

UNIFORM BUILDING CODE STANDARD 21-19
GROUT FOR MASONRY

**Based on Standard Specification C 476-91 of the American Society for Testing and Materials.
Extracted, with permission, from the *Annual Book of ASTM Standards*, copyright American Society for
Testing and Materials, 100 Barr Harbor Drive, West Conshohocken, PA 19428**

See Section 2102.2, Item 9, *Uniform Building Code*

SECTION 21.1901 — SCOPE

This standard covers grout for use in the construction of reinforced and nonreinforced masonry structures.

SECTION 21.1902 — MATERIALS

Materials used as ingredients in grout shall conform to the following:

21.1902.1 Cementitious Materials. Cementitious materials shall conform to one of the following standards:

    A. Portland Cement—Types I, II and III of ASTM C 150.

    B. Blended Cement—Type IS, IS(MS) or IP of ASTM C 595.

    C. Quicklime—UBC Standard 21-12.

    D. Hydrated lime—Type S of UBC Standard 21-13.

21.1902.2 Water. Water shall be clean and potable.

21.1902.3 Admixtures. Additives and admixtures to grout shall not be used unless approved by the building official.

21.1902.4 Antifreeze Compounds. No antifreeze liquids, chloride salts or other substances shall be used in grout.

21.1902.5 Storage of Materials. Cementitious materials and aggregates shall be stored in such a manner as to prevent deterioration or intrusion of foreign material or moisture. Any material that has become unsuitable for good construction shall not be used.

SECTION 21.1903 — MEASUREMENT OF MATERIALS

The method of measuring materials for the grout used in construction shall be such that the specified proportions of the grout materials can be controlled and accurately maintained.

SECTION 21.1904 — GROUT

Grout shall consist of cementitious material and aggregate that have been mixed thoroughly for a minimum of five minutes in a mechanical mixer with sufficient water to bring the mixture to the desired consistency. The grout proportions and any additives shall be based on laboratory or field experience considering the grout ingredients and the masonry units to be used, or the grout shall be proportioned within the limits given in Table 21-B of this code, or the grout shall have a minimum compressive strength when tested in accordance with UBC Standard 21-18 equal to its specified strength, but not less than 2,000 psi (13 800 kPa).

> **EXCEPTION:** Dry mixes for grout which are blended in the factory and mixed at the jobsite shall be mixed in mechanical mixers until workable, but not to exceed 10 minutes.

UNIFORM BUILDING CODE STANDARD 21-20
STANDARD TEST METHOD FOR FLEXURAL BOND STRENGTH OF MORTAR CEMENT
Test Standard of the International Conference of Building Officials

**See Section 2102.2, Item 8, _Uniform Building Code_, and
UBC Standard 21-14, Table 21-14-A**

SECTION 21.2001 — SCOPE

This method covers the laboratory evaluation of the flexural bond strength of a standardized mortar and a standardized masonry unit.

SECTION 21.2002 — APPARATUS

The test apparatus consists of a metal frame designed to support a prism as shown in Figures 21-20-1 and 21-20-2. The prism support system shall be adjustable to support prisms ranging in height from two to seven masonry units. The upper clamping bracket that is clamped to the top masonry unit of the prism shall not come into contact with the lower clamping bracket during the test. An alignment jig, mortar template, and drop hammer as shown in Figures 21-20-3, 21-20-4 and 21-20-5 are used in the fabrication of prism specimens for testing.

SECTION 21.2003 — MATERIALS

21.2003.1 Masonry units used shall be standard masonry units selected for the purpose of determining the flexural bond strength properties of mortar cement mortars. The standard unit shall be in accordance with the following requirements:

1. Dimensions of units shall be $3^5/_8$ inches (92 mm) wide by $2^1/_4$ inches (57 mm) high by $7^5/_8$ inches (194 mm) long within a tolerance of plus or minus $^1/_8$ inch (3.2 mm) and shall be 100 percent solid.

2. The unit material shall be concrete masonry manufactured with the following material proportions by volume:

   One part portland cement to eight parts aggregate

3. Aggregate used in the manufacture of the unit shall be as follows:

Bulk Specific Gravity Gradation	2.6 to 2.7 Percent Retained by Weight
$^3/_8$-inch (9.5 mm) sieve	0
No. 4 (4.75 mm) sieve	0 to 5
No. 8 (2.36 mm) sieve	20 to 30
No. 16 (1.18 mm) sieve	20 to 30
No. 30 (600 µm) sieve	15 to 25
No. 50 (300 µm) sieve	5 to 15
No. 100 (150 µm) sieve	5 to 10
Pan	5 to 10

4. Density of the unit shall be 125 to 135 pounds per cubic foot (2000 to 2160 kg/m³).

5. Unit shall be cured in a 100 percent relative humidity environment at 140°F ± 10°F (60°C ± 5.6°C) at atmospheric pressure for 10 to 20 hours. Additional curing, under covered atmospheric conditions, shall continue for at least 28 days. Unit shall be loose stacked in the cube (separated by a $^1/_4$-inch (6.4 mm) gap) to allow air to circulate during drying.

6. At the time of fabricating the prisms, units shall have a moisture content in the range of 25 percent to 35 percent.

7. Upon delivery units shall be stored in the laboratory at normal temperature and humidity. Units shall not be wetted or surface treated prior to or during prism fabrication.

21.2003.2 Mortar. Mortar shall be prepared in accordance with the following:

1. Mortar proportions shall be in accordance with Table 21-20-A. The aggregate shall consist of a blend of one-half graded Ottawa sand and one-half Standard 20-30 Ottawa sand.

2. Mortar materials shall be mixed in a drum-type batch mixer for five minutes.

3. Determine mortar flow in accordance with applicable standards and adjust water until a flow of 125 ± 5 is achieved.

4. Determine mortar density, air content and initial cone penetration immediately after mixing the mortar in accordance with applicable standards. Mortar shall not be used when cone penetration is less than 80 percent of the initial cone penetration value.

SECTION 21.2004 — TEST SPECIMENS

21.2004.1 Number. Test specimens shall consist of one set of six prisms constructed with the mortar cement mortar. Each prism shall be six units in height.

21.2004.2 Prism Construction. (1) Each prism shall be built in an opened moisture-tight bag which is large enough to enclose and seal the completed prism. Set the first unit on a $^1/_2$-inch (13 mm) plywood pallet in an alignment jig as shown in Figure 21-20-3. (2) Place the mortar template shown in Figure 21-20-4 on the unit such that the mortar bed depth prior to compaction is $^1/_2$ inch (13 mm). Place mortar in template and strike off excess mortar with straight edge. (3) Remove template and immediately place the next unit on the mortar bed in contact with the three alignment bolts for that course using a bulls-eye level to assure uniform initial contact of the unit surface and bed mortar. Carefully position drop hammer apparatus shown in Figure 21-20-5 on top of unit and drop its 4-pound (1.81 kg) weight, round end down, once from a height of 1.5 inches (38 mm). (4) Repeat (2) and (3) until the prisms are complete. (5) Joints shall be cut flush after the prism is completely built. Joints shall not be tooled. (6) One hour, ± 15 minutes after completion of construction, place two masonry units of the type used to construct the prism upon the top course. (7) Identify all prisms using a water-resistant marker. (8) Draw and seal the moisture-tight bag around the prism. (9) All prisms should be cured for 28 days. Two days prior to testing remove the moisture-tight bag and continue curing in the laboratory air, maintained at a temperature of 75°F ± 15°F (23.9°C ± 8.3°C), with a relative humidity between 30 to 70 percent.

SECTION 21.2005 — TEST PROCEDURE

Place the prism vertically in the support frame as shown in Figure 21-20-1 and clamp firmly into a locked position using the lower clamping bracket. Orient the prism so that the face of the joint intended to be subjected to flexural tension is on the same side of the specimen as the clamping screws. The prism shall be positioned at the required elevation that results in a single unit projecting above the lower clamping bracket. A soft bearing material (for example, polystyrene) at least $^1/_2$-inch (13 mm) thick shall be placed between the bottom of the prism and the adjustable prism base support.

Attach the upper clamping bracket to the top unit as shown in Figure 21-20-1. Tighten each clamping bolt using a torque not greater than 20 inch-pounds (2.26 N·m).

Apply the load at a uniform rate so that the total load is applied in not less than one minute or more than three minutes. Measure load to an accuracy of ± 2 percent with maximum error of five pounds (22.2 N).

SECTION 21.2006 — CALCULATIONS

Calculate the modulus of rupture of each mortar joint as follows:

$$f_r = \frac{6(PL + P_1 L_1)}{bd^2} - \frac{(P + P_1)}{bd}$$

For **SI:**

$$f_r = \frac{6(PL + P_1 L_1)}{1000\, bd^2} - \frac{(P + P_1)}{1000\, bd}$$

WHERE:

b = average width of cross section of failure surface, inches (mm).

d = average thickness of cross section of failure surface, inches (mm).

f_r = modulus of rupture, psi (kPa).

L = distance from center of prism to loading point, inches (mm).

L_1 = distance from center of prism to centroid of loading arm, inches (mm).

P = maximum applied load, pounds (N).

P_1 = weight of loading arm, pounds (N).

The flexural bond strength of mortar shall be determined as the average modulus of rupture of 30 joints minus 1.28 times the standard deviation of the sample which yields a value that a mortar joint's modulus of rupture will equal or exceed nine out of 10 times.

SECTION 21.2007 — REPORT

The report shall include the manufacturer of the mortar cement being evaluated, the source of manufacture, type of mortar cement, date of testing, laboratory name and laboratory personnel.

Report mortar density, air content, flow and cone penetration test data. Report the following data for the mortar cement mortar being evaluated:

PRISM NO.	PRISM WEIGHT (lbs.) (kg)	JOINT NO.	TEST LOAD (lbs.) (N)	MOMENT (in.-lbs.) (N·m)	MODULUS OF RUPTURE			
					f_r psi (kPa)	Mean psi (kPa)	Std. Dev. psi[1] (kPa)	COV %
1	—	1	—	—	—	—	—	—
		2	—	—	—			
		3	—	—	—			
		4	—	—	—			
		5	—	—	—			

[1]Also, report the standard deviation for all six prisms (30 joints).

Report the flexural bond strength (determined in accordance with Section 21.2006) of the mortar cement mortar.

TABLE 21-20-A—MORTAR PROPORTIONS BY VOLUME FOR EVALUATING FLEXURAL BOND

MORTAR	MORTAR CEMENT TYPE	PROPORTIONS	
		Mortar Cement	Aggregate
Type N	N	1	3
Type S	S	1	3
Type M	M	1	3

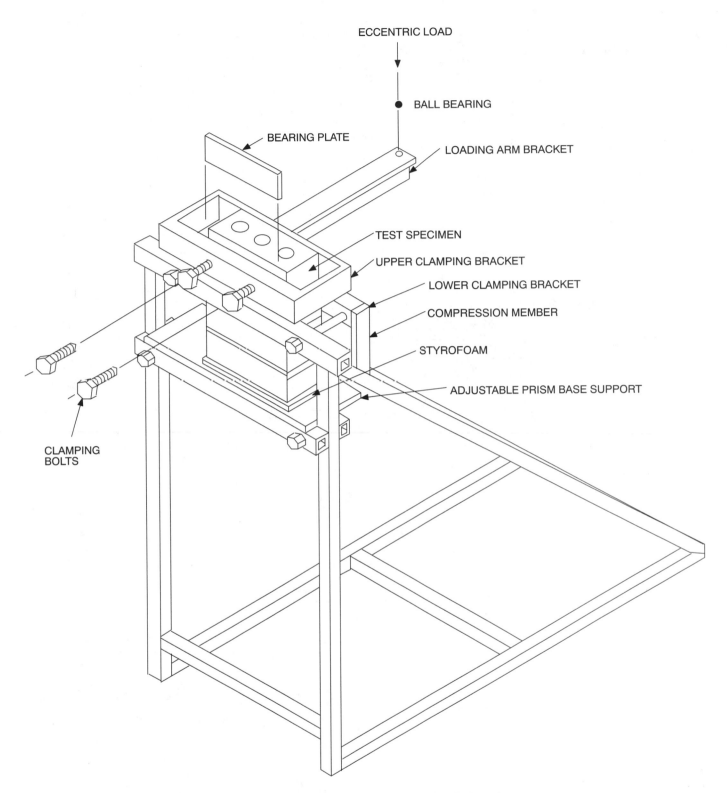

ECCENTRIC LOAD

BALL BEARING

BEARING PLATE

LOADING ARM BRACKET

TEST SPECIMEN

UPPER CLAMPING BRACKET

LOWER CLAMPING BRACKET

COMPRESSION MEMBER

STYROFOAM

ADJUSTABLE PRISM BASE SUPPORT

CLAMPING BOLTS

FIGURE 21-20-1—BOND WRENCH TEST APPARATUS

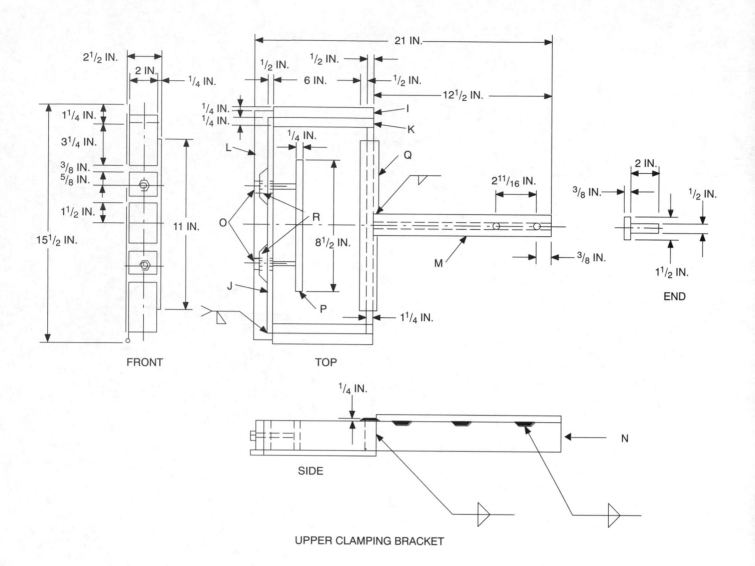

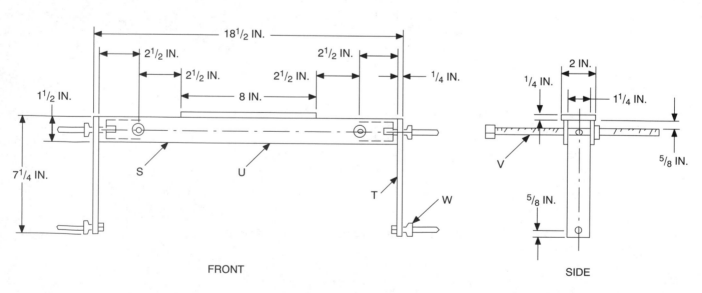

For **SI**: 1 inch = 25.4 mm.

LOWER CLAMPING BRACKET

FIGURE 21-20-2—DETAIL DRAWINGS OF BOND WRENCH

(Continued)

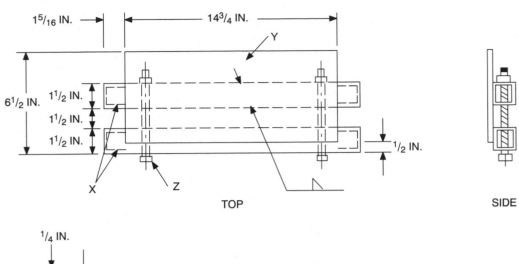

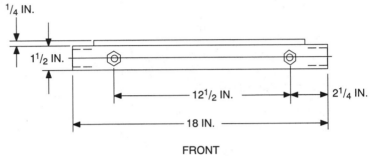

TOP

SIDE

FRONT

PRISM BASE SUPPORT

For **SI**: 1 inch = 25.4 mm.

FIGURE 21-20-2—DETAIL DRAWINGS OF BOND WRENCH—(Continued)

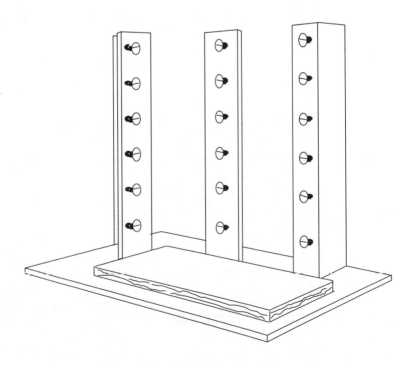

FIGURE 21-20-3—BOND WRENCH JIG WITH PALLET

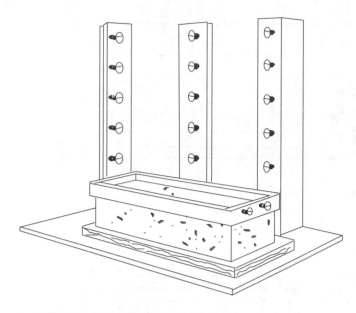

FIGURE 21-20-4—FIRST BRICK WITH MORTAR TEMPLATE

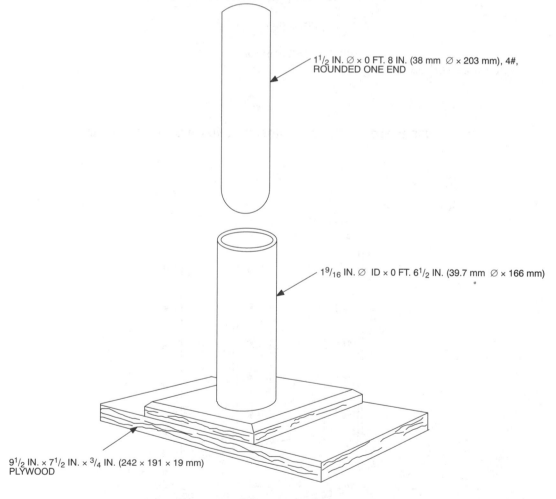

$1^{1}/_{2}$ IN. $\varnothing \times$ 0 FT. 8 IN. (38 mm $\varnothing \times$ 203 mm), 4#,
ROUNDED ONE END

$1^{9}/_{16}$ IN. $\varnothing$ ID $\times$ 0 FT. $6^{1}/_{2}$ IN. (39.7 mm $\varnothing \times$ 166 mm)

$9^{1}/_{2}$ IN. $\times 7^{1}/_{2}$ IN. $\times {}^{3}/_{4}$ IN. (242 $\times$ 191 $\times$ 19 mm)
PLYWOOD

FIGURE 21-20-5—DROP HAMMER AND GUIDE

UNIFORM BUILDING CODE STANDARD 22-1
MATERIAL SPECIFICATIONS FOR STRUCTURAL STEEL

Based on Standard Specifications A 27, A 36, A 48, A 53, A 148, A 242, A 252, A 283, A 307, A 325, A 366, A 446, A 449, A 490, A 500, A 501, A 514, A 529, A 563, A 569, A 570, A 572, A 588, A 606, A 607, A 611, A 618, A 666, A 690 and A 715 of the American Society for Testing and Materials. Extracted, with permission, from the *Annual Book of ASTM Standards,* copyright American Society for Testing and Materials, 100 Barr Harbor Drive, West Conshohocken, PA 19428

See Sections 1808.6.1, 1808.7 and 2202, *Uniform Building Code,* and Section 402.2, *Uniform Sign Code*

SECTION 22.101 — SCOPE

This standard covers steel and iron shapes, plates, sheet, strip, connectors and bars for use in the construction of buildings and for general structural purposes.

SECTION 22.102 — MATERIAL REQUIREMENTS

The material shall conform to the requirements as to the tensile properties set forth in Table 22-1-A.

TABLE 22-1-A—TENSILE REQUIREMENTS

MATERIAL	GRADE	SPECIFICATION TITLE	SIZE AND PRODUCT LIMITATIONS × 25.4 for mm	TENSILE STRENGTH (ksi) × 6.89 for MPa	YIELD POINT (ksi)	REFERENCED ELSEWHERE
A27-81a	60-30	Mild- to medium-strength carbon steel castings		60	30	
	65-35			65	35	
	70-36			70	36	
	70-40			70	40	
A36-81a		Structural steel		58-80	36	UBC Chapter 22, Divisions VII and IX
A48-76	**Class No.** 20 A, B, C and S	Gray iron castings		20	—	
	25 ″			25	—	
	30 ″			30	—	
	35 ″			35	—	
	40 ″			40	—	
	45 ″			45	—	
	50 ″			50	—	
	55 ″			55	—	
	60 ″			60	—	
A53-82	Type F	Steel pipe, black and hot-dipped, zinc-coated; welded and seamless	Furnace—butt welded	45	25	UMC Standard 11-1
	A (Types E and S)		Electric—resistance welded and seamless	48	30	
	B (Types E and S)		Electric—resistance welded and seamless	60	35	
A148-81	80-40	High-strength steel casting for structural purposes		80	40	
	80-50			80	50	
	90-60			90	60	
	105-85			105	85	
	120-95			120	95	
	150-125			150	125	
	175-145			175	145	
A242-81		High-strength Low-alloy Structural steel	$3/4''$ thick and under	70	50	UBC Chapter 22, Divisions VII and IX
			Over $3/4''$ to $1 1/2''$, inclusive	67	46	
			Over $1 1/2''$ to $4''$ thick	63	42	
A252-82	1	Welded and seamless steel pipe piles		50	30	
	2			60	35	
	3			66	45	
A283-81	A	Low and intermediate strength carbon steel plates shapes and bars		45-55	24	
	B			50-60	27	
	C			55-65	30	
	D			60-72	33	
A307-82a	A and B	Bolts		60 (min)	—	
	B	Bolts with cast-iron flanges		100 (max)		
A325-83c		High-strength bolts for structural steel joints	$1/2''$ to $1''$ diameter, inclusive	105	92	
			$1 1/8''$ to $1 1/2''$ diameter, inclusive	120	81	

(Continued)

TABLE 22-1-A—TENSILE REQUIREMENTS—(Continued)

MATERIAL	GRADE	SPECIFICATION TITLE	SIZE AND PRODUCT LIMITATIONS × 25.4 for mm	TENSILE STRENGTH (ksi) × 6.89 for MPa	YIELD POINT (ksi) × 6.89 for MPa	REFERENCED ELSEWHERE
A366-72 (79)		Carbon steel cold-rolled sheet, commercial quality		—	—	
A446-76 (81)	A B C D E F	Steel sheet zinc-coated (galvanized) by hot-dip process structural quality		45 52 55 65 82 70	33 37 40 50 80 50	UBC Chapter 22, Division VII
A449-83a		Quenched and tempered steel bolts and studs	$^1/_4''$ to 1", inclusive Over 1" to $1^1/_2''$, inclusive Over $1^1/_2''$ to 3", inclusive	120 105 90	92 81 58	
A490-83a		Quenched and tempered alloy steel bolts for structural steel connections	$^1/_2''$ to $1^1/_2''$, inclusive	150 (min) 170 (max)	130	
A500-82a	A B C A B C	Cold-formed welded and seamless carbon steel structural tubing in rounds and shapes	Rounds Shapes	45 58 62 45 58 62	33 42 46 39 46 50	
A501-83		Hot-formed welded and seamless carbon steel structural tubing		58	36	
A514-82a		High-yield strength quenched and tempered alloy steel plate	$2^1/_2''$ Over $2^1/_2''$ to 6", inclusive	110-130 100-130	100 90	
A529-82		Structural steel with 42,000 psi minimum yield point	$^1/_2''$ maximum thickness	60-85	42	UBC Chapter 22, Division VII
A563-88a	O A B C D DH	Carbon and alloy steel nuts				UBC Chapter 22, Division III
A569-72 (79)		Steel, carbon hot-rolled sheet and strip, commercial quality		—	—	
A570-79	30 33 36 40 45 50	Hot-rolled carbon steel sheets and strip, structural quality	Maximum thickness of 0.2299"	49 52 53 55 60 65	30 33 36 40 45 50	UBC Chapter 22, Divisions VII and IX
A572-82	42 50 60 65	High-strength low-alloy columbium-vanadium steel, structural quality	Shapes, plates, piling and bars	60 65 75 80	42 50 60 65	UBC Chapter 22, Divisions VII and IX
A588-82		High-strength low-alloy structural steel with a 50 ksi minimum yield point to 4 inches thick	Plate and bars to 4", inclusive Over 4" to 5", inclusive Over 5" to 8", inclusive Structural shapes—all grades	70 67 63 70	50 46 42 50	UBC Chapter 22, Divisions VII and IX
A606-75		Steel sheet and strip hot-rolled and cold-rolled high-strength low-alloy improved atmospheric corrosion resistance	Hot-rolled cut lengths Hot-rolled coils, Annealed or normalized cut lengths and coils	70 65 65	50 45 45	UBC Chapter 22, Divisions VII and IX
A607-75 (81)	45 50 55 60 65 70	Steel sheet and strip hot-rolled and cold-rolled high-strength low-alloy columbium and/or vanadium	Cut lengths or coils	60 65 70 75 80 85	45 50 55 60 65 70	UBC Chapter 22, Divisions VII and IX
A611-82	A B C D E	Types I and II cold-rolled sheet carbon steel, structural		42 45 48 52 82	25 30 33 40 80	UBC Chapter 22, Divisions VII and IX

(Continued)

TABLE 22-1-A—TENSILE REQUIREMENTS—(Continued)

MATERIAL	GRADE	SPECIFICATION TITLE	SIZE AND PRODUCT LIMITATIONS	TENSILE STRENGTH (ksi)	YIELD POINT (ksi)	REFERENCED ELSEWHERE
			× 25.4 for mm	× 6.89 for MPa		
A618-81	Ia, Ib, II Ia, Ib, II III	Hot-formed welded and seamless high-strength low-alloy structural tubing	Walls $3/4''$ and under Walls over $3/4''$ to $1^1/_2''$, inclusive Walls over $3/4''$ to $1^1/_2''$, inclusive	70 67 65	50 46 50	UBC Chapter 22, Division VII
A666-82	A B C D	Austenitic stainless steel, sheet strip, plate and flat bar for structural applications		75 75-95 115-125 125-150	30 40-4 75 100-110	
A668-85a	A B C D E F G H J K L M N	Steel forgings, carbon and alloy for general industrial use		47 60 66 75 85-83 90-82 80 90 95-105 105-100 125-110 145-135 170-160	— 30 33 37 44-43 55-48 50 60-58 65-80 80-75 105-85 120-110 140-130	UBC Chapter 22, Division III
A690-81a		Sheet piling for marine environment		70	50	
A715-81	50 60 70 80	Steel sheet and strip hot-rolled high-strength low-alloy		60 70 80 90	50 60 70 80	UBC Chapter 22, Division VII
A792-85	33 37 40 50B 50A	Steel sheet, aluminum-zinc alloy coated by the hot-dip process	Coils and lengths	45 52 55 65 —	33 37 40 50 50	
A852-88a		Quenched and tempered low-alloy structural steel plate with 70 ksi minimum yield strength	Maximum 4″ thick	90-110	70	UBC Chapter 22, Division III

UNIFORM BUILDING CODE STANDARD 23-1
CLASSIFICATION, DEFINITION, METHODS OF GRADING AND DEVELOPMENT OF DESIGN VALUES FOR ALL SPECIES OF LUMBER

See Sections 2302.1 and 2303, *Uniform Building Code*

SECTION 23.101 — ADOPTION OF ASTM D 1990, ASTM D 245 AND ASTM D 2555, THE WOOD HANDBOOK NO. 72, PS20-94 AND THE NATIONAL GRADING RULE FOR DIMENSION LUMBER

Classification, definition, methods of grading and development of design values for all species of lumber shall be in accordance with ASTM D 1990-91, ASTM D 245-88 and ASTM D 2555-95 published by the American Society for Testing and Materials, Wood Handbook No. 72 published by the U.S. Department of Agriculture, Voluntary Product Standard PS20-94 published by the U.S. Department of Commerce and the National Grading Rule for Dimension Lumber promulgated by the National Grading Rule Committee, Post Office Box 210, Germantown, Maryland 20875-0210, and published in the American Lumber Standard Committee certified grading rules, as if set out at length herein.

The grade mark on lumber or end-jointed lumber shall include an approved, easily distinguished mark, or insignia of the grading agency which has been accredited by an accreditation body which complies with the requirements of U.S. Department of Commerce PS20-94, or equivalent.

UNIFORM BUILDING CODE STANDARD 23-2
CONSTRUCTION AND INDUSTRIAL PLYWOOD

Based on Product Standard PS 1-95 (for Construction and Industrial Plywood) of the United States Department of Commerce, and National Institute of Science and Technology Calculation of Diaphragm Action, an Engineering Standard of the International Conference of Building Officials

See Sections 1404.1, 2302.1, 2303 and 2304, and Tables 23-III-A, 23-II-H, 23-II-I-1 and 23-II-E-2, *Uniform Building Code*

SECTION 23.201 — SCOPE

23.201.1 General. This standard covers construction and industrial plywood for both Exterior and Interior types. This standard also covers construction and industrial hardwood plywood of red and white lauan (Philippine mahogany), tanoak, red alder and western poplar.

23.201.2 Wood Species. Plywood produced under this standard considers four species classifications: Groups 1, 2, 3 and 4. The species used for the face and back plies are at the option of the manufacturer. When face and back veneers are of the same species group, the panels shall be identified as being of that species group. The species covered in each group are set forth in Table 23-2-A. In addition, other softwood or hardwood species having an average specific gravity of 0.41 or more, based on green volume and oven dry weight, may be used for inner plies except as required for premium grades in Section 23.205.

SECTION 23.202 — DEFINITIONS

General definitions not included in the following section are to be interpreted as defined in UBC Standard 23-1.

BACK is the side of a panel that is of lower veneer quality on any panel whose outer plies are of different veneer grades.

BORER HOLES are voids made by wood-boring insects, such as grubs or worms.

BROKEN GRAIN is a (leafing, shelling, grain separation) separation on veneer surface between annual rings.

CENTERS are inner plies whose grain direction runs parallel to that of the outer plies. May be of parallel laminated plies.

CHECK is a lengthwise separation of wood fibers, usually extending across the rings of annual growth caused chiefly by strains produced in seasoning.

CLASS I, CLASS II are terms used to identify different species group combinations of B-B concrete form panels. The standard provides for two classes, Class I and Class II, as described in Section 23.205.3.

CORE is sometimes referred to as a crossband.

CROSSBAND GAP and CENTER GAP are open joints extending through or partially through a panel, which results when crossband or center veneers are not tightly butted.

CROSSBANDS are inner layers whose grain direction runs perpendicular to that of the outer plies. They may be of parallel laminated plies and are sometimes referred to as core.

DEFECTS, OPEN, are irregularities such as splits, open joints, knotholes, or loose knots, that interrupt the smooth continuity of the veneer.

DELAMINATION is a visible separation between plies that would normally receive glue at their interface and be firmly contacted in the pressing operation. Wood characteristics, such as checking, leafing, splitting and broken grain, are not to be construed as delamination. See corresponding definition for those terms.

1. For purposes of reinspection, areas coinciding with open knotholes, pitch pockets, splits and gaps and other voids or characteristics permitted in the panel grade are not considered in evaluating ply separation of Interior-type panels bonded with interior or intermediate glue.

2. In evaluating Interior panels bonded with exterior glue, delamination in any glueline shall not exceed 3 square inches (1935 mm^2) except where directly attributable to defects permitted in the grade as follows:

Delamination associated with:

2.1 Knots and knotholes—shall not exceed the size of the defect plus a surrounding band not wider than $3/4$ inch (19 mm).

2.2 All other forms of permissible defects—shall not exceed the size of the defect.

3. In evaluating Exterior-type panels for ply separation, the area coinciding with the grade characteristics noted in Item 1 are considered, and a panel is considered delaminated if visible ply separation at a single glueline in such area exceeds 3 square inches (1935 mm^2).

EDGE SPLITS are wedge-shaped openings in the inner plies caused by splitting of the veneer before pressing.

FACE is the better side of any panel whose outer plies are of different veneer grades; also either side of a panel where the grading rules draw no distinction between faces.

GROUP is the term used to classify species covered by this standard in an order that provides a basis for simplified marketing and efficient utilization. Species covered by the standard are classified as Groups 1, 2, 3 and 4. See Table 23-2-A for listing of species in individual groups.

HEARTWOOD is the nonactive core of a log generally distinguishable from the outer portion (sapwood) by its darker color.

INNER PLIES are other than exposed face and back plies in a panel construction.

JOINTED INNER PLIES are crossband and center veneer that have had edges machine-squared to permit tightest possible layup.

KNOT is a natural characteristic of wood that occurs where a branch base is embedded in the trunk of a tree. Generally the size of a knot is distinguishable by (1) a difference in color of limbwood and surrounding trunkwood; (2) abrupt change in growth ring width between knot and bordering trunkwood; and (3) diameter of circular or oval shape described by points where checks on the face of a knot that extend radially from its center to its side experience abrupt change in direction.

KNOTHOLES are voids produced by the dropping of knots from the wood in which they are originally embedded.

LAP is a condition where the veneers are so placed that one piece overlaps the other.

LAYER is a single veneer ply or two or more plies laminated with grain direction parallel. Two or more plies laminated with grain direction parallel is a parallel laminated layer.

NOMINAL THICKNESS is full "designated" thickness. For example, $^1/_{10}$-inch (2.5 mm) nominal veneer is 0.10 inch (2.5 mm) thick. Nominal $^1/_2$-inch-thick (13 mm) panel is 0.50 inch (13 mm) thick. Also, commercial size designations are subject to acceptable tolerances.

PATCHES are insertions of sound wood or synthetic material in veneers or panels for replacing defects. "Boat" patches are oval shaped with sides tapering in each direction to a point or to a small rounded end. "Router" patches have parallel sides and rounded ends. "Sled" patches are rectangular with feathered ends.

PITCH POCKET is a well-defined opening between rings of annual growth, usually containing, or which has contained, pitch, either solid or liquid.

PITCH STREAK is a localized accumulation of resin in coniferous woods which permeates the cells forming resin soaks, patches or streaks.

PLUGS are sound wood of various shapes, including, among others, circular and dogbone, for replacing defective portions of veneer used to fill openings and provide a smooth, level, durable surface. Plugs usually are held in veneer by friction until veneers are bonded into plywood.

PLY is a single veneer lamina in a glued plywood panel. (See also "layer.")

PLYWOOD is a flat panel, built up of sheets of veneer called plies, united under pressure by a bonding agent to create a panel with an adhesive bond between plies as strong as or stronger than the wood. Plywood is constructed of an odd number of layers with grain of adjacent layers perpendicular. Layers may consist of a single ply or two or more plies laminated with grain direction parallel. Outer layers and all odd-numbered layers generally have the grain direction oriented parallel to the long dimension of the panel. The odd number of layers with alternating grain direction equalizes strains, prevents splitting and minimizes dimensional change and warping of the panel.

Exterior type—Plywood of this type is produced with a C grade veneer or better throughout and is bonded with completely waterproof adhesives. It is a plywood that will retain its glue bond when repeatedly wetted and dried or otherwise subjected to the weather, and is therefore intended for permanent exterior exposure. Table 23-2-E lists the grades within this type. Adhesive performance requirements are provided in Section 23.207.

Interior type—Plywood of this type is moisture resistant. It is intended for all interior applications as well as applications where it may be temporarily exposed to the elements. Table 23-2-D lists the grades within this type. Adhesive performance requirements are provided in Section 23.207.

Intermediate glue (IMG) type—Plywood of this type is bonded with adhesives that possess high-level bacteria, mold and moisture resistance. It is plywood suitable for protected construction and industrial uses where delays in providing protection may be expected. Adhesive performance requirements are provided in Section 23.207. (The grades of IMG-type plywood generally available are given in Table 23-2-D.)

Overlaid plywood is Exterior-type plywood to which has been added a resin-treated fiber surfacing material on one or both sides. It is made in two standard categories, "High Density" and "Medium Density," and a "Special" category, all of which refer to the surfacing materials. The overlay surfaces are permanently fused to the base panel under heat and pressure. Although designed for all types of moisture exposure and service, all overlaid plywood is made only in the Exterior type. This refers to the base panel and to the overlay itself.

REPAIR is any patch, plug or shim.

SAPWOOD is the living wood of lighter color occurring in the outer portion of a log. Sapwood is sometimes referred to as "sap."

SHIM is a long narrow repair of wood or suitable synthetic not more than $^3/_{16}$ inch (4.8 mm) wide.

SHOP CUTTING PANELS are panels which have been rejected as not conforming to grade requirements of standard grades in this standard. Identification of these panels shall be with a separate mark that makes no reference to this standard and contains the notation, "Shop Cutting Panel—All Other Marks Void." Blistered panels are not considered as coming within the category covered by this stamp.

SPAN RATING is a set of numbers used in marking sheathing and combination subfloor underlayment (single floor) grades of plywood as described in Section 23.209.

SPLIT is lengthwise separation of wood fibers completely through the veneer caused chiefly by manufacturing process or handling.

STREAKS are synonymous with "pitch streaks."

STRUCTURAL I is a name used to identify panels that provide for greatest refinement of engineering properties which may be important in the use of plywood for structural components and other sophisticated engineered applications. Manufacturing requirements include special provisions for species, panel construction and veneer grade characteristics as described in Section 23.205.4.

TORN GRAIN. See "broken grain."

TOUCH-SANDING is a sizing operation consisting of a light surface sanding in a sander. Sander skips to any degree are admissible.

VENEER consists of thin sheets of wood of which plywood is made. Veneer is also referred to as plies in the glued panel.

WATERPROOF ADHESIVE is glue capable of bonding plywood in a manner to satisfy the exterior performance requirements given herein.

WHITE POCKET is a form of decay (*Fomes pini*) that attacks most conifers but has never been known to develop in wood in service. In plywood manufacture, routine drying of veneer effectively removes any possibility of decay surviving.

Heavy white pockets may contain a great number of pockets, in dense concentrations, running together and at times appearing continuous. Holes may extend through the veneer but wood between pockets appears firm. At any cross section extending across the width of the affected area, sufficient wood fiber shall be present to develop not less than 40 percent of the strength of clear veneer. Brown cubical and similar forms of decay which have caused the wood to crumble are prohibited.

Light white pockets are advanced beyond incipient or stain stage to the point where the pockets are present and plainly visible, mostly small and filled with white cellulose and generally distributed with no heavy concentrations. Pockets for the most part are separate and distinct with few to no holes through the veneer.

WOOD FAILURE (PERCENT) is the area of wood fiber remaining at the glueline following completion of the specified shear test. Determination is by means of visual examination and expressed as a percent of the 1-square-inch (645 mm^2) test area. (See Section 23.214 for test.)

SECTION 23.203 — REQUIREMENTS

23.203.1 Workmanship. Unless otherwise specified, sanded plywood shall be surfaced on two sides. Faces and backs of panels shall be full width and full length except that C grade and D grade backs may be narrow on one edge or short on one end only, but by not more than $^1/_8$ inch (3.2 mm) for half the panel length or width, respectively. Inner plies shall be full width and length except that one edge or end void not exceeding $^1/_8$ inch (3.2 mm) in depth or 8 inches (203 mm) in length per panel will be acceptable. Crossband veneers not exceeding $^1/_8$ inch (3.2 mm) in thickness may be lapped but by not more than $^3/_{16}$ inch (4.8 mm) when adjacent to faces, or $^1/_2$ inch (13 mm) when adjacent to backs, and provided such laps create no adjacent visible opening. Sanding defects resulting from crossband laps shall not be permitted in panel faces.

C or D grade veneers may be lapped by not more than $^1/_2$ inch (13 mm), provided such laps create no adjacent visible opening. All plies of CD panels only shall be full length and full width except that no more than half the length of one edge nor half the width of one end may contain short or narrow plies. This is contingent on such plies not being short or narrow by more than $^3/_{16}$ inch (4.8 mm), the aggregate area in the plane of the plies of such edge characteristics not exceeding 6 square inches (3871 mm^2) in the entire panel, and such edge characteristics not occurring in more than one ply at any panel cross section.

In grades other than CD, backs may be narrow on one edge or short on one end only, but by not more than $^1/_8$ inch (3.2 mm) for half the panel length or width, respectively; inner plies shall be full width and length, except that one edge or end void not exceeding $^1/_8$ inch (3.2 mm) in depth or 8 inches (203 mm) in length per panel will be acceptable.

Crossband gaps or center gaps, except as noted for plugged crossband and jointed crossband shall not exceed 1 inch (25 mm) in width for a depth of 8 inches (203 mm) (measured from panel edge) and the average of all gaps occurring in a panel shall not exceed $^1/_2$ inch (13 mm). Every effort shall be made to produce closely butted core joints.

Where plugged inner plies are specified, inner plies shall be of C-Plugged veneer and gaps between adjacent pieces of inner plies shall not exceed $^1/_2$ inch (13 mm). Where jointed inner plies are specified, gaps between pieces of inner plies shall not exceed $^3/_8$ inch (9.5 mm), and the average of all gaps occurring in a panel shall not exceed $^3/_{16}$ inch (4.8 mm).

Unless otherwise specified, plugged core (also referred to as solid core) shall be core and center construction of C-Plugged veneer, and gaps between adjacent pieces of core shall not exceed $^1/_2$ inch (13 mm). When jointed core is specified, gaps between pieces of core shall not exceed $^3/_8$ inch (9.5 mm), and the average of all gaps occurring in a panel shall not exceed $^3/_{16}$ inch (4.8 mm).

Plywood shall be clean, well manufactured, and free from blisters, laps and other defects, except as expressly permitted herein. Panels shall have no continuous holes or through openings from face to back.

End butt joints may be used only under the following conditions:

1. Decorative grades as provided in Section 23.205.2.

2. Butt joints having a total aggregate width not exceeding the width of the panel may occur in the center ply of five-ply, five-layer panels. The butt joints must be perpendicular to the grain of the panel face and back plies. The use of butt-jointed centers is allowed in Interior sanded grades in thicknesses up to and including $^1/_2$ inch (13 mm), and in C-D and C-D Plugged thicknesses up to and including $^3/_4$ inch (19 mm). End butt joints shall not be used

in Structural I panels. Panels with butt joints in center plies shall be marked "butt-jointed center."

Plywood panels shall be constructed in the grades and veneer combinations as set forth in Tables 23-2-D and 23-2-E. All terms used herein shall be interpreted as described in Section 23.202. Constructions for all panels shall conform to the minimum number of plies and layers as set forth in Table 23-2-C. The proportion of wood with grain perpendicular to panel face grain shall not be less than 33 percent or more than 70 percent of the total panel thickness. The combined thickness of inner layers in panels having four or more plies shall not be less than 45 percent of the total panel thickness. For application of the above requirements, the panel thickness shall be the actual finished panel thickness and veneer thickness shall be the dry veneer thickness before layup. The grain of all layers shall be at right angles to the grain of adjacent layers and to the ends or edges of the panels. The entire area of each contacting surface of the adjacent veneer plies including repairs shall be bonded with an adhesive in a manner to assure satisfactory compliance with the performance requirements for its type as set forth in the tests described in this standard. Where face or back plies consist of more than one piece of edge-joined veneer, gaps between adjacent pieces shall be graded as splits. Any adhesive or bonding system that causes degradation of the wood or latent failure of bond will not be permitted.

For the purpose of veneer repairing or edge joining, strings, ribbons or tapes up to $^3/_8$-inch (9.5 mm) maximum width can occur in a glueline and shall be considered as allowable localized defects in the evaluation of glueline test specimens. Wider strings, ribbons or tapes may be used for veneer repairing or joining if they are prequalified to show bonding equal to the required bonding for that panel. Glueline test specimens cut to include the strings, ribbons or tapes wider than $^3/_8$ inch (9.5 mm) shall not be discarded because of the presence of these materials.

Veneer strips may be joined by string stitching, provided the punch for making holes prior to stitching has a dimension across the grain of 0.095 inch (2.4 mm) or less and the holes are spaced $^1/_2$ inch (13 mm) center-to-center or greater. All veneer used for inner plies may be stitched. Stitched veneer used for outer plies is limited to panels with C or D grade faces or backs, except stitched C veneer may not be used for faces in decorative panels. Panels may have face or back plies stitched but not both.

Shims or strips of veneer shall not be used to repair panel edge voids. However, filling of permissible edge voids with approved synthetic fillers neatly applied will be admitted. Staples or pins of metal or synthetic material are prohibited. Face and back plies of exposed N, A and B veneer panels shall have the bark or tight surface out. Plies directly under surfaces of overlaid panels are not considered exposed veneers.

23.203.2 Tolerance. A tolerance of + 0.0 inch − $^1/_{16}$ inch (0.0625) (+ 0.0 mm − 1.6 mm) shall be allowed on the specified length and/or width. Sanded panels shall have a thickness tolerance of $^1/_{64}$ inch (0.0156) (0.4 mm) of the specified panel thickness of $^3/_4$ inch (19 mm) and less, and ± 3.0 percent of the specified thickness for panels thicker than $^3/_4$ inch (19 mm). Unsanded, touch-sanded, and overlaid panels shall fall within a plus or minus tolerance of $^1/_{32}$ inch (0.0312) (0.8 mm) of the specified panel thickness for all thicknesses through $^{13}/_{16}$ inch (21 mm), and such panels greater than $^{13}/_{16}$ inch (21 mm) shall have a thickness tolerance of 5 percent over or under the specified thickness. Panel thickness shall be based on a moisture content of 9 percent.

Panels shall be square within $^1/_{64}$ inch per lineal foot (1.3 mm per m) for panels of 4-foot by 4-foot (1219 mm by 1219 mm) size or larger. Panels less than 4 feet (1219 mm) in length or width shall be square within $^1/_{16}$ inch (1.6 mm) measured along the short dimension. All panels shall be sawn so that a straight line drawn from one corner to the adjacent corner shall fall within $^1/_{16}$ inch (1.6 mm) of panel edge.

23.203.3 Moisture Content. Moisture content of panels at time of shipment shall not exceed 18 percent of oven-dry weight as determined by the oven-dry test specified in Section 23.217.

SECTION 23.204 — VENEER

23.204.1 General. Except as noted, veneers shall be $^1/_{10}$ inch (2.5 mm) or thicker in panels $^3/_8$ inch (9.5 mm) rough (unsanded) thickness or over; $^1/_{12}$ inch (2.1 mm) or thicker in panels of lesser thickness. In no case shall veneers used in face or back layers be thicker than $^1/_4$ inch (6.4 mm), or veneers used in inner layers thicker than $^5/_{16}$ inch (7.9 mm).

One-twelfth-inch (2.1 mm) veneer may be used as crossbands in five-ply, five-layer, $^1/_2$-inch (13 mm) panels and in parallel laminated layers.

One-sixteenth-inch (1.6 mm) veneer may be used for any ply in five-ply Exterior-type panels less than $^1/_2$ inch (13 mm) in thickness, as the center only in other five-ply panels, and may be included in a parallel laminated layer.

Face and back veneers must be $^1/_8$-inch (3.2 mm) minimum thickness for $^{19}/_{32}$ inch and $^5/_8$ inch (15.1 mm and 15.9 mm), three-, four- and five-ply, three-layer panels of C-D, C-D Plugged, C-C, C-C Plugged and Underlayment grades.

For further limitations on panel layup, refer to Table 23-2-C panel constructions and workmanship.

The average veneer thickness shall conform to the limitations given in this standard within a tolerance of 5 percent of the specified nominal thickness measured dry before layup.

Parallel laminated outer layers may be used only in C-C, C-D, Structural I C-C and C-D grades. Such layers shall consist of veneers $^1/_{10}$ inch (2.5 mm) or thicker in any thickness combination not exceeding $^1/_4$-inch (6.4 mm) total layer thickness. The face and back plies or exposed plies of outer layers shall conform to the species group and grade requirements for faces and backs, respectively, of the panel grade. The unexposed plies of outer layers, or subface and subback plies, shall conform to the species group and grade requirements for inner plies of the panel grade as specified in Sections 23.204.3 and 23.204.4.

The maximum split or gap in subfaces and subbacks shall be $^1/_4$ inch (6.4 mm) under the faces of Structural I C-C and C-D panels, $^1/_2$ inch (13 mm) under the faces of C-C and C-D grades, and $^1/_2$ inch (13 mm) under D backs.

Parallel laminated inner layers in any grade shall consist of veneers $^1/_{16}$ inch (1.6 mm) or thicker in any thickness combination not exceeding $^7/_{16}$-inch (11 mm) total layer thickness. Individual plies in such layers shall conform to the species group and grade requirements for inner plies of the panel grade.

The veneers used in each ply of each panel and the completed panel shall conform with the applicable veneer grade and with the construction and workmanship requirements given herein. Additionally, the type and frequency of the characteristics shall be further limited as set forth for the grades listed in Table 23-2-B.

23.204.2 Number of Plies. For a given thickness, the number of plies used in the panel makeup shall not be less than as provided in Table 23-2-C.

23.204.3 Species for Faces and Backs. For purposes of this standard, veneer species are classified into the four groups given in Table 23-2-A. The species of face and back plies may be from any group; however, when a face or back is made of more than one

piece, the entire ply shall be of the same species. Panels, other than unsanded and touch-sanded panels, with span ratings which are produced with face and back veneers of the same species group shall be classified as being of that species group. Touch-sanded panels without span ratings that are manufactured with face and back plies of different species groups shall be identified by the larger numbered species group (i.e., Group 4 is larger numbered than Group 1). Sanded panels $^3/_8$ inch (9.5 mm) or less in thickness and decorative panels of any thickness that are manufactured with face and back plies of different species groups shall be identified by the face species group number. Sanded panels greater than $^3/_8$ inch (9.5 mm) that are manufactured with face and back plies of different species groups shall be identified by the larger numbered species group, except that sanded panels with C or D grade backs may be identified by the face species group number if backs are no more than one species group larger in number than the face and are $^1/_8$ inch (3.2 mm) or thicker before sanding. The species classification group (except for unsanded and touch-sanded panels with span ratings) shall be set forth in the grade mark on each panel. See Section 23.209 for identification requirements for unsanded and touch-sanded panels with span ratings. Where intermixing between species groups occurs in the faces and backs of unsanded or touch-sanded panels with span ratings, provisions of Table 23-2-G shall be followed. (Douglas fir for the purpose . . . and loblolly *[Pinus taeda] pines.*) Because black, white and Engelmann spruce cannot be separated in veneer form by gross structure or minute anatomy, these species shall be classed as Engelmann spruce unless procedures are established for identification prior to peeling.

23.204.4 Species for Inner Plies. Inner plies may be of any species or of any softwood species or any hardwood species having a published average specific gravity value of 0.41 or more, based on green volume and oven-dry weight, except as required for premium panels in Section 23.205.

23.204.5 Scarfed Veneers. Scarfed veneer may be used for any face, back or inner ply except as provided in Section 23.211. Scarfed joints shall not have a slope steeper than 1 in 8, but may be specified at less than 1 in 8. Veneer in the scarf area shall not contain defects which reduce its effective cross section by more than 20 percent. Veneer scarfed joints shall be glued with a waterproof adhesive.

23.204.6 Classification. All veneers used in the construction of the plywood panels shall conform to one of the following grade requirements of which N grade is the highest classification:

23.204.6.1 Grade N veneer. Grade N veneer (intended for natural finish) shall be smoothly cut 100 percent heartwood or 100 percent sapwood, free from knots, knotholes, pitch pockets, open splits, other open defects, and stain; limited to not more than two pieces in a 48-inch (1219 mm) width; not more than three pieces in wider panels; and well matched for color and grain.

Suitable synthetic fillers may be used to fill small cracks or checks not more than $^1/_{32}$ inch (0.8 mm) wide; small splits or openings up to $^1/_{16}$ inch (1.6 mm) wide if not exceeding 2 inches (51 mm) in length; and small chipped areas or openings not more than $^1/_8$ inch (3.2 mm) wide by $^1/_4$ inch (6.4 mm) long. Pitch streaks averaging not more than $^3/_8$ inch (9.5 mm) in width and blending with color of wood are permitted.

Repairs shall be neatly made and parallel to grain and are limited to a total of six in number in any 4-foot by 8-foot (1219 mm by 2438 mm) face, with proportional limits for other sizes. They shall also be well matched for color and grain.

Patches are limited to three "router" patches not exceeding 1 inch (25 mm) in width and $3^1/_2$ inches (89 mm) in length.

No overlapping is permitted.

Wood shims not exceeding $^3/_{16}$ inch (4.8 mm) in width and 12 inches (305 mm) in length that occur only at the ends of the panel are permitted.

23.204.6.2 Grade A veneer. Grade A veneer (suitable for painting) shall be firm, smoothly cut and free from knots, pitch pockets, open splits and other open defects. It shall be well joined when of more than one piece.

Suitable synthetic fillers may be used to fill, in Exterior-type panels, small cracks or checks not more than $^1/_{32}$ inch (0.8 mm) wide; small splits or openings up to $^1/_{16}$ inch (1.6 mm) wide, if not exceeding 2 inches (51 mm) in length; and small chipped areas or openings not more than $^1/_8$ inch (3.2 mm) wide by $^1/_4$ inch (6.4 mm) long. In Interior-type panels: small cracks or checks not more than $^3/_{16}$ inch (4.8 mm) wide; openings or depressions up to $^1/_2$ inch (13 mm) wide by 2 inches (51 mm) long or equivalent area.

Pitch streaks averaging not more than $^3/_8$ inch (9.5 mm) in width, blending with color of wood, are permitted.

Sapwood and discolorations are also permitted.

Repairs shall be wood or of synthetic patching material neatly made and parallel to grain, limited to a total of 18 in number, excluding shims, in any 4-foot by 8-foot (1219 mm by 2438 mm) face and shall have proportional limits on other sizes.

Patches are limited to the boat, router and sled types. Radius of ends of boat patches shall not exceed $^1/_8$ inch (3.2 mm). Patches shall not exceed $2^1/_4$ inches (57 mm) in width singly. Multiple patches consisting of not more than two patches, neither of which may exceed 7 inches (178 mm) in length if either is wider than 1 inch (25 mm) are permitted, except that there may be one multiple repair consisting of three die-cut veneer patches. Synthetic repairs shall not exceed $2^1/_4$ inches (57 mm) in width. Shims are permitted except over or around patches or as multiple repairs.

23.204.6.3 Grade B veneer. Grade B veneer shall be solid and free from open defects and broken grain except as noted. Slightly rough grain and minor sanding and patching defects, including sander skips not exceeding 5 percent of panel area are permitted.

Suitable synthetic filler may be used to fill, in Exterior-type panels, small splits or openings up to $^1/_{16}$ inch (1.6 mm) wide if not exceeding 2 inches (51 mm) in length and small chipped areas or openings not more than $^1/_8$ inch (3.2 mm) wide by $^1/_4$ inch (6.4 mm) long. In Interior-type panels: small cracks or checks not more than $^3/_{16}$ inch (4.8 mm) wide; openings or depressions up to $^1/_2$ inch (13 mm) wide by 2 inches (51 mm) long or equivalent area.

Knots up to 1 inch (25 mm) measured across the grain if both sound and tight, pitch streaks averaging not more than 1 inch (25 mm) in width, and discolorations are permitted.

Splits not wider than $^1/_{32}$ inch (0.8 mm) and vertical holes not exceeding $^1/_{16}$ inch (1.6 mm) in diameter if not exceeding an average of one per square foot in number are permitted. Horizontal or surface tunnels limited to $^1/_{16}$ inch (1.6 mm) across, 1 inch (25 mm) in length, and 12 in number in a 4-foot by 8-foot (1219 mm by 2438 mm) panel or proportionately in panels of other dimensions are also permitted.

Repairs shall be neatly made of wood or synthetic patching material. Repairs permitted are patches ("boat," "router" and "sled") not exceeding 3 inches (76 mm) in width individually where occurring in multiple repairs, or 4 inches (102 mm) in width where occurring singly. Synthetic veneer repairs shall not exceed 4 inches (102 mm) in width. Synthetic panel repairs shall not exceed $2^1/_4$ inches (57 mm) in width. Shims are permitted. Synthetic shims shall completely fill kerfs or voids; shall present a smooth level surface; and shall not crack, shrink or lose their bond under Exterior-type plywood test exposures described in Sections 23.215.2 and 23.215.3. Performance of synthetic shims under normal conditions of service shall be comparable to that of wood shims.

Synthetic plugs not exceeding dimensions specified previously which present solid, level, hard surfaces and whose performances under normal conditions of service are comparable to that of wood plugs are permitted.

23.204.6.4 Grade C veneer. Grade C veneer permits sanding defects that will not impair the strength or serviceability of the panel, knots if tight and not more than $1^1/_2$ inches (38 mm) across the grain, and knotholes up to 1 inch (25 mm) measured across the grain. An occasional knothole more than 1 inch (25 mm) but not more than $1^1/_2$ inches (38 mm) measured across the grain, occurring in any section 12 inches (305 mm) along the grain in which the aggregate width of all knots and knotholes occurring wholly within the section does not exceed 6 inches (152 mm) in a 48-inch (1219 mm) width, and proportionately for other widths is also permitted.

Splits tapering to a point and limited to $^1/_2$ inch (13 mm) by one-half panel length, $^3/_8$ inch (9.5 mm) by any panel length are permitted, provided separation at one end does not exceed $^1/_{16}$ inch (1.6 mm) where split runs full panel length, or $^1/_4$ inch (6.4 mm) maximum width where located within 1 inch (25 mm) of parallel panel edge.

Voids due to missing wood on panel faces and backs not otherwise specified above shall not exceed the maximum width of knotholes permitted in the grade and the length of such voids shall not exceed 6 inches (152 mm).

Repairs shall be wood or synthetic material, neatly made. Wood veneer repairs shall be die cut, and wood panel repairs shall be router or sled type. Wood repairs shall not exceed 3 inches (76 mm) in width individually where occurring in multiple repairs, or 4 inches (102 mm) in width where occurring singly; plugs (circular or "dog bone") not exceeding 3 inches (76 mm) in width individually where occurring in multiple repairs or 4 inches (102 mm) in width where occurring singly; and shims including synthetic as provided for in B grade.

Synthetic veneer repairs shall not exceed 4 inches (102 mm) in width.

Synthetic panel repairs shall not exceed $2^1/_4$ inches (57 mm) in width.

Shims are permitted.

C-Plugged veneer (veneer used for faces of underlayment, C-D Plugged and C-C Plugged grades, and inner plies of overlaid panels and other products if specified) may contain knotholes, worm and borer holes, and other open defects not larger than $^1/_4$ inch by $^1/_2$ inch (6.4 mm by 13 mm), sound and tight knots up to $1^1/_2$ inches (38 mm) measured across the grain, splits up to $^1/_8$ inch (3.2 mm) wide, broken grain, pitch pockets, if solid and tight, plugs, patches and shims. Synthetic repairs in veneer shall not exceed 4 inches (102 mm) in width. Synthetic panel repairs shall not exceed $2^1/_4$ inches (57 mm) in width. Where grades having C-Plugged face veneer are specified as fully sanded, sanding defects shall be the same as admitted under B grade. Sander skips to any degree shall be admissible in C-Plugged veneer.

23.204.6.5 Grade D veneer. Grade D veneer permits any number of plugs, patches, shims, worm or borer holes, sanding defects and other characteristics, provided they do not seriously impair the strength or serviceability of the panels. See also Section 23.203.

Tight knots are permitted in inner plies; and in D grade backs where limited to $2^1/_2$ inches (64 mm) measured across the grain.

In D grade backs, an occasional tight knot larger than $2^{1}/_{2}$ inches (64 mm) but not larger than 3 inches (76 mm) measured across the grain, occurring in any section 12 inches (305 mm) along the grain in which the aggregate width of all knots and knotholes occurring wholly within the section does not exceed 10 inches (254 mm) in a 48-inch (1219 mm) width and proportionately for other widths is also permitted.

Knotholes up to $2^{1}/_{2}$ inches (64 mm) across the grain, an occasional knothole larger than $2^{1}/_{2}$ inches (64 mm) but not larger than 3-inch (76 mm) dimension occurring in any section 12 inches (305 mm) along the grain in which the aggregate width of all knots and knotholes occurring wholly within the section does not exceed 10 inches (254 mm) in a 48-inch (1219 mm) width, and proportionately for other widths; in sanded panels, knotholes not exceeding $2^{1}/_{2}$ inches (64 mm) across the grain in veneer thicker than $1/_{8}$ inch (3.2 mm); and knotholes not exceeding $3^{1}/_{2}$ inches (89 mm) across the grain are permitted in veneers at least two plies removed from the face and back plies of C-D and C-D Plugged grades having five or more plies.

Splits measured at a point 8 inches (203 mm) from their end shall not exceed 1 inch (25 mm) in width, tapering to not more than $1/_{16}$ inch (1.6 mm) where split runs full panel length; how-ever, the maximum width within 8 inches (203 mm) of the end of the split shall not exceed the maximum width of knotholes permitted within the grade.

Splits on panel faces and backs shall not exceed $1/_{4}$ inch (6.4 mm) where located within 1 inch (25 mm) of parallel panel edge.

Voids due to missing wood on panel backs not otherwise specified above shall not exceed the maximum width of knotholes permitted in the grade and the length of such voids shall not exceed 6 inches (152 mm).

Any area 24 inches (610 mm) wide across the grain and 12 inches (305 mm) long, in which light or heavy white pocket occurs, shall not contain more than three of the following characteristics, in any combination: 6-inch (152 mm) width of heavy white pocket; 12-inch (305 mm) width of light white pocket. One knot or knothole, $1^{1}/_{2}$ inches to $2^{1}/_{2}$ inches (38 mm to 64 mm), or two knots or knotholes, 1 inch to $1^{1}/_{2}$ inches (25 mm to 38 mm); knots or knotholes less than 1 inch (25 mm) shall not be considered. Size of any knot or knothole shall be measured in greatest dimension. Any repair in white pocket area shall be treated for grading purposes as a knothole.

23.204.6.6 Synthetic repairs. Synthetic fillers shall be limited to the repair of minor defects as specified in this standard. Synthetic fillers shall be of an approved type.

23.204.6.7 Synthetic shims, patches and plugs. These repairs shall completely fill kerfs or voids; shall present a smooth, level surface; and shall not crack, shrink, or lose their bond. Performance of synthetic shims, patches and plugs under normal conditions of service shall be comparable to that of wood repairs. The equivalency shall be established by testing and evaluation in accordance with approved procedures.

SECTION 23.205 — PREMIUM GRADES

23.205.1 Marine Plywood. Marine grade shall be of Exterior-type meeting applicable requirements of this standard, and of one of the following grades: A-A, A-B, B-B, High Density Overlay, or Medium Density Overlay, all as modified below for "Marine" plywood.

Only Douglas fir 1 and western larch veneer shall be used.

"A" faces shall be limited to a total of nine single repairs in a 4-foot by 8-foot (1219 mm by 2438 mm) sheet, or to a proportionate number in any other size as manufactured. "B" faces or backs where specified, and all inner plies, shall conform to "B" quality veneer requirements and shall be full length and width.

All patches shall be glued with an adhesive meeting Exterior-type performance requirements of this standard and, in addition, shall be set in the panel using a technique involving both heat and pressure.

When the inner ply veneers consist of two or more pieces of veneer, the edges shall be straight and square without lapping.

Neither edge of a panel shall have any crossband gap or edge-split in excess of $1/_{8}$ inch (3.2 mm) wide. Crossband gaps and edge-splits per 8 feet (2438 mm) of crossband ply shall not exceed four in number. End splits and gaps on either end of a panel shall not exceed $1/_{8}$ inch (3.2 mm) in aggregate width. Filling of crossband gaps and edge-splits with crossband gaps and edge-split materials that serve to conceal the gaps or splits is prohibited.

23.205.2 Decorative Panels. Specialty panels with decorative face veneer treatments in the form of striations, grooving, embossing, brushing, etc., which, except for the special face treatment, meet all of the requirements of this standard, including veneer qualities, glue bond performance and workmanship, shall be considered as conforming to the standard.

An occasional butt joint up to 6 inches (152 mm) in width shall be permitted for decorative effect in veneer on one panel face only. Where butt joints occur, the aggregate width of all knots and knotholes and two thirds the aggregate width of all repairs, including butt joints, shall not exceed 6 inches (152 mm) in any area 12 inches (305 mm) along the grain by 48 inches (1219 mm) wide or proportionately for other widths.

23.205.3 Exterior B-B (Concrete Form) Panels. A panel especially made for general concrete form use. Face veneers shall not be less than B grade and shall always be from the same species group. Inner plies shall not be less than C grade. (See Table 23-2-E for veneer grade limitations of High Density overlaid concrete form panels.) This grade of plywood is produced in two classes and panels of each class shall be identified accordingly. Panels shall be sanded two sides, edge-sealed and, unless otherwise specified, mill-oiled. Species shall be limited as follows and are applicable also to High Density overlaid exterior concrete form panels.

Class I—Faces of any Group 1 species, crossband of any Group 1 or 2 species, and centers of any Group 1, 2, 3 or 4 species.

Class II—Faces of any Group 1 or 2 species, and crossband and centers of any Group 1, 2, 3 or 4 species, or faces of Group 3 species of $1/_{8}$-inch (3.2 mm) minimum thickness before sanding, crossband of any Group 1, 2 or 3 species, and centers of any Group 1, 2, 3 or 4 species.

23.205.4 Structural Grade Panels. Panels especially designed for engineered applications such as structural components where design properties including tension, compression, shear, cross-panel flexural properties and nail bearing may be of significant importance. In addition to the special species, grade and glue bond requirements set forth in Table 23-2-F, all other provisions of this standard for the specific types and grades form a part of the specifications for Structural grade panels.

23.205.5 Special Exterior. A premium panel of Exterior type that may be produced of any specified species covered by this standard. It shall otherwise meet all of the requirements for Marine Exterior and be produced in one of the following grades: A-A, A-B, B-B, High Density Overlay, or Medium Density Overlay.

23.205.6 Underlayment, C-C Plugged. Face veneer shall be $1/10$ inch (2.5 mm) or thicker before sanding. The veneer immediately adjacent to the face ply of C-C Plugged and Underlayment shall be C grade or better with no knotholes over 1 inch (25 mm) across the grain, except that (1) veneer immediately adjacent to the face ply of Underlayment may be D grade with open defects up to $2^1/2$ inches (64 mm) across the grain or (2) veneer immediately adjacent to the face ply of C-C Plugged may be C grade with open defects up to $1^1/2$ inches (38 mm) across the grain, provided the face veneer is Group 1 or Group 2 species of $1/6$-inch (4.2 mm) minimum thickness before sanding. Also see requirements set forth in Table 23-2-B.

SECTION 23.206 — OVERLAYS

23.206.1 General. The standard grades of overlaid plywood are listed in Table 23-2-E.

23.206.2 High Density. The surfacing on the finished product shall be hard, smooth and of such character that further finishing by paint or varnish is not necessary. It shall consist of a cellulose-fiber sheet or sheets, containing not less than 45 percent resin solids based on a volatile-free weight of fiber and resin. The resin shall be a thermosetting phenol or melamine type. The total resin-impregnated materials for each face shall not be less than 0.012 inch (0.3 mm) thick before pressing and shall weigh not less than 60 pounds per 1,000 square feet (0.29 kg/m^2), including both resin and fiber. The resin impregnation shall be sufficient to make a continuous bond without voids or blisters between the surfacing material and the plywood. The overlay face is usually produced in natural translucent color, but certain other colors may be used by manufacturers for identification.

Other resin-cellulose fiber overlay systems having a weight of not less than 60 pounds per 1,000 square feet (0.29 kg/m^2) of single surface exclusive of glueline, and which possess performance capabilities of the above phenol system, may be identified as High Density Overlay. Determination of equivalent performance shall be based on approved tests.

23.206.3 Medium Density. The resin-treated facing on the finished product shall present a smooth, uniform surface intended for high-quality paint finishes. It shall consist of a cellulose-fiber sheet containing not less than 17 percent resin solids for a beater loaded sheet, or 22 percent for an impregnated sheet, both based on the volatile-free weight of resin and fiber exclusive of glueline. The resin shall be a thermosetting phenol or melamine type. The resin-treated material shall not weigh less than 58 pounds per 1,000 square feet (0.28 kg/m^2) of single face including both resin and fiber but exclusive of glueline. After application, the material shall not measure less than 0.012 inch (0.3 mm) thick. Some evidence of the underlying grain may appear. The overlay face is produced in a natural color and certain other colors.

Other resin-cellulose fiber overlay systems having a weight of 58 pounds per 1,000 square feet (0.28 kg/m^2) of single surface exclusive of glueline, and which possess performance capabilities of the above phenol system, may be identified as Medium Density Overlay. Determination of equivalent performance shall be based on approved test methods.

23.206.4 Special Overlays. Surfacing materials having special characteristics which do not fit the exact description of High Density or Medium Density types as outlined previously. These must meet the test requirements for overlaid plywood and have a durable surface material. Panels shall be identified as "Special Overlay."

SECTION 23.207 — ADHESIVE BOND REQUIREMENTS

23.207.1 General. Lots represented by test panels shall be considered as meeting the requirements of this standard if all of the following minimum requirements are met.

23.207.2 Interior-type Bonded with Interior Glue (Underlayment, C-D Plugged and C-D). A panel shall be considered as meeting the requirements of the standard if three or more of the five test specimens pass. The material represented by the sampling shall be considered as meeting the requirements of this standard if 90 percent or more of the panels pass the test described in Section 23.213.

23.207.3 Interior-type Bonded with Exterior Glue (Structural C-D). When tested in accordance with Section 23.213, the average wood failure of all test specimens, regardless of the number of panels tested, shall not be less than 80 percent.

When more than one panel is tested:

1. At least 90 percent of the panels represented by the test pieces shall have 60 percent wood failure or better.

2. At least 95 percent of the panels represented by the test pieces shall have 30 percent wood failure or better.

These requirements are applicable separately and independently to the results obtained from the vacuum-pressure test and the boiling test. Specimens cut through localized defects permitted in the grade shall be discarded. Test specimens showing delamination in excess of $1/8$ inch (3.2 mm) deep and 1 inch (25 mm) long shall be rated as 0 percent wood failure.

23.207.4 All Other Grades of Interior-type Plywood. A panel shall be classed as failing if more than two of the five test specimens fail. The material represented by the sampling shall be considered as meeting the requirements of this standard if 85 percent or more of the panels pass, when tested in accordance with Section 23.213.

23.207.5 Mold Resistance. Underlayment, C-D Plugged, and Standard shall be made with an adhesive possessing a mold resistance equivalent to that created by adding, to plain protein glue, 5 pounds (2.27 kg) of pentachlorophenol or its sodium salt per 100 pounds (45.36 kg) of dry glue base.

IMG-type plywood shall be made with an adhesive possessing a high degree of resistance to attack by bacteria and mold organisms. Adhesives, in order to qualify for use in the manufacture of IMG-type panels, must meet the "bacteria test" requirements published by the American Plywood Association. This procedure is specifically designed for adhesive qualification and is not applicable to inspection and testing, as covered in Section 23.212.

23.207.6 Resistance to Elevated Temperature. Underlayment, C-D Plugged shall be made with an adhesive possessing resistance to temperatures up to 160°F (71°C) at least equal to that of plain protein glue. Urea resin glue shall not be used in these grades unless evidence is submitted indicating performance equivalent to plain protein glues.

23.207.7 Interior-type Bonded with Intermediate Glue (IMG-type). When tested in accordance with Section 23.214, IMG-type plywood shall be considered as meeting the requirements of the standard if all of the following minimum conditions are met:

1. The average wood failure of all test specimens, regardless of the number of panels tested, shall not be less than 45 percent.

2. When more than one panel is tested, at least 90 percent of the panels represented by the test pieces shall have 30 percent wood failure or better.

Specimens cut through localized defects permitted in the grade shall be discarded. Test specimens showing delamination in excess of $^1/_8$ inch (3.2 mm) deep and 1 inch (25 mm) long shall be rated as 0 percent wood failure.

23.207.8 Exterior Type. When tested in accordance with Section 23.215, Exterior-type plywood shall be considered as meeting the requirements of this standard if all of the following minimum conditions are met:

1. The average wood failure of all test specimens, regardless of the number of panels tested, shall not be less than 85 percent.

2. When more than one panel is tested:

    2.1 At least 75 percent of the panels represented by the test pieces shall have 80 percent wood failure or better.

    2.2 At least 90 percent of the panels represented by the test pieces shall have 60 percent wood failure or better.

    2.3 At least 95 percent of the panels represented by the test pieces shall have 30 percent wood failure or better.

These requirements are applicable separately and independently to the results obtained from the vacuum-pressure test and the boiling test. Specimens cut through localized defects permitted in the grade shall be discarded. Test specimens showing delamination in excess of $^1/_8$ inch (3.2 mm) deep and 1 inch (25 mm) long shall be rated as 0 percent wood failure.

Plywood shall be tested for heat durability as described in Section 23.215. Any delamination due to combustion shall be considered as failure, except when occurring at a localized defect permitted in the grade. When testing overlaid plywood. blisters or bubbles in the surface caused by combustion shall not be considered delamination.

The bond between veneers of overlaid plywood as well as the bond between the overlay and the base panel shall meet the wood failure requirements described above for exterior. In evaluating specimens for separation of resin-treated face from the plywood, fiber failure shall be considered the same as wood failure.

SECTION 23.208 — GRADE MARKING

All plywood shall be grade marked in accordance with Section 2303 of this code. No reference shall be made to this standard in the certification or trademarking or grade marking of panels not conforming to all provisions of the standard. Each panel shall be identified with the mark of a qualified inspection and testing agency that shall designate the species group classification or span rating, glue bond type (Interior or Exterior), grade name or the grade of face and back veneers, and a symbol signifying conformance with the standard.

Panels not fully satisfying Exterior veneer requirements shall be identified as "Interior." However, the additional notation "Exterior Glue" or "Intermediate" (IMG) may be used where applicable to supplement the designation of Interior grades bonded with Exterior glue or Intermediate glue. Any further reference to adhesive bond, including those which imply premium performance or special warranty by the manufacturer, as well as manufacturer's proprietary designations, shall be separated from the grade marks or trademarks of the testing agency by not less than 6 inches (152 mm).

SECTION 23.209 — SPAN RATING FOR UNSANDED AND TOUCH-SANDED PANELS

Grade marking or trademarking of C-C, C-D, Structural C-C and Structural C-D, and of C-C Plugged and Underlayment to be used as combination subfloor underlayment (single floor) shall include a span rating for the thickness shown in Table 23-2-G. The numbers are presented as a fraction in the marking of sheathing grades of plywood, and as a single number for C-C Plugged and Underlayment. They describe the recommended maximum spans in inches (mm) under normal use conditions and correspond with commonly accepted criteria. For sheathing, the left-hand number refers to spacing of roof framing, and the right-hand number relates to spacing of the floor framing. The single number for Underlayment and C-C Plugged refers to spacing of the floor framing in single floor applications. The span rating number is related to species and thickness of the panel face and back veneers and panel thickness. It is established by either one of the following procedures:

1. By specification as detailed in Table 23-2-G.

2. By performance testing to satisfy the strength, stiffness and durability criteria as detailed in Section 23.210. Such performance testing is to be performed by a qualified testing agency.

Panels manufactured as C-C, C-D, Structural C-C and Structural C-D shall not be sanded, touch-sanded, surface textured or thickness sized by any mechanical means. However, sanded or touch-sanded panels which do not meet the grades for which they were intended may be reclassified and marked as C-C or C-D, provided the panels meet all applicable requirements for C-C or C-D and the finished face and back veneers after sanding each have a minimum net thickness equal to 90 percent of the applicable thickness in Table 23-2-G.

SECTION 23.210 — PERFORMANCE TESTING QUALIFICATION REQUIREMENTS

23.210.1 General. Acceptance of performance-tested plywood under this standard is based upon testing of panel strength, stiffness and durability. Panels selected for testing shall be of near-minimum grade and near-minimum thickness. All provisions of veneer grade and panel workmanship are applicable.

23.210.2 Performance Testing. Panels qualified for performance testing shall satisfy the criteria called for in this section when tested as required in Sections 23.210.3 and 23.210.4.

23.210.3 Structural Performance.

23.210.3.1 Concentrated loads. A minimum of 10 tests (specimens taken from at least five panels) shall be conducted for both concentrated static and impact loads according to Section 23.216. The tests shall be conducted for each exposure condition specified in Table 23-2-L or 23-2-N (wet, dry and/or wet/redry).

23.210.3.1.1 Deflection. At least 90 percent of tests shall deflect no more than the specified maximum.

23.210.3.1.2 Retest. If no more than two tests in a lot of 10 fail to meet the deflection requirements, another lot of 10 may be tested for that requirement. If no more than one test fails in this second round of testing, the requirements shall be considered satisfied.

23.210.3.1.3 Ultimate load. For each lot, 100 percent of tests shall support the specified minimum ultimate load.

23.210.3.1.4 Retest. If no more than one test in a lot of ten fails to meet the minimum ultimate load requirement, another lot of 10 may be tested for that requirement. If all pass the retest, the requirements shall be considered satisfied.

23.210.3.2 Uniform loads. A minimum of 10 tests (specimens taken from at least five panels) shall be conducted for uniform load capacity according to Section 23.217. The tests shall be conducted for each exposure condition specified in Table 23-2-M or 23-2-O.

23.210.3.2.1 Deflection. The average deflection shall not be greater than that specified.

23.210.3.2.2 Retest. If the average deflection is greater than specified, but does not exceed the requirement by 20 percent, another lot of 10 may be tested for that requirement. If the average of the first and second lot taken together does not exceed that specified, the requirement shall be considered satisfied.

23.210.3.2.3 Ultimate load. For each lot, 100 percent of tests shall support the specified minimum ultimate load.

23.210.3.2.4 Retest. If no more than one test in a lot of 10 fails to meet the ultimate load requirement, another lot of 10 may be tested for that requirement. If all specimens pass this retest, the requirements shall be completely satisfied.

23.210.4 Bond Durability. Panels shall be classed as Exposure 1 or Exterior.

23.210.4.1 Exposure Panels rated as Exposure 1 shall be so identified and shall satisfy the bond requirements for Interior panels bonded with exterior glue as specified in Section 23.207.3.

23.210.4.2 Exterior. Panels rated as Exterior shall be so identified and shall satisfy the bond requirements as specified in Section 23.207.8.

23.210.5 Product Evaluation. Upon satisfactory completion of the appropriate requirements of Sections 23.210.3 and 23.210.4, a manufacturing specification will be written based on product evaluation under this section. This specification is to be used for quality assurance purposes by the manufacturer and the manufacturer's qualified testing agency. Product evaluation will be made on the same lot supplied by the manufacturer for qualification testing. Control values established during product evaluation will be the basis for quality evaluation of future production. The mill specification shall contain the following information.

23.210.5.1 Panel construction. Panels shall be defined as to veneer species and construction.

23.210.5.2 Mechanical properties. Twenty tests (specimens taken from at least 10 panels) shall be evaluated for bending stiffness both along and across the major panel axis according to the procedures of Section 23.218. The control value for each panel direction will be the sample mean and the minimum will be the lower value of a 90 percent confidence interval established on the mean.

Ten tests (specimens taken from at least 10 different panels) shall be tested for maximum bending moment both along and across the major panel axis according to the procedures of Section 23.218. The control value for each panel direction will be the minimum observed value, or the sample mean less 1.8 times the sample standard deviation, whichever is the higher value.

23.210.6 Reexamination.

23.210.6.1 Quarterly reexamination. A product qualified by performance testing shall be subjected to quarterly reexamination by the manufacturer's qualified testing agency. Panels shall be tested according to the procedures of Section 23.210.5.2.

23.210.6.2 Resampling. Failure to meet established control values shall result in an immediate intensive resampling of current production which will be tested for the failing property. This resampling shall consist of 20 panels.

23.210.6.3 Requalification. When results of the resampling fail to meet the applicable test requirements, a requalification for structural properties under Section 23.210.3 shall be required.

SECTION 23.211 — SCARF- AND FINGER-JOINTED PANELS

23.211.1 General. Neither panels with N faces nor the faces of such panels, unless longer than 10 feet (3048 mm), shall be scarfed or finger jointed except when specifically so ordered. Panels of other grades may be scarfed or finger jointed. Panels longer than 12 feet (3658 mm) are necessarily scarfed. Scarf joints shall not have a slope greater than 1 to 8, but may be specified as less than 1 to 8. Joints shall be glued with a waterproof adhesive and meet the test requirements specified in this section as applicable. In addition, the adhesive shall not show creep or flow characteristics greater than unjointed wood when subject to load under any conditions of temperature and moisture.

23.211.2 Strength Requirements (Interior, IMG and Exterior) Scarfed and Finger-jointed Panels. Panels shall be tested in accordance with Section 23.216.1. If the average ultimate stress of the three test specimens of any one panel is less than 4,000 psi (27.58 N/mm^2) for panels of Group 1 species, or less than 2,800 psi (19.3 N/mm^2) for panels of Group 2 or Group 3 species, or 2,400 psi (16.55 N/mm^2) for panels of Group 4 species, then that panel fails. The jointed panels represented by the sampling are acceptable if not more than one of the panels fails.

23.211.3 Scarf- and Finger-joint Durability for Interior and IMG Panels. Panels shall be tested as outlined in Section 23.216.2. Test specimens showing continuous delamination in excess of $^1/_{16}$ inch (1.6 mm) deep and $^1/_2$ inch (13 mm) long at the joint glueline shall be considered as failing. More than one failing specimen in a panel shall constitute failure of that panel. The jointed panels represented by the sampling are acceptable if not more than one of the panels fails.

23.211.4 Scarf-joint Durability for Exterior and Interior Panel Bonded with Exterior and Intermediate Glue. Panels shall be tested in accordance with Section 23.219.3. The material represented by the sampling shall be evaluated in accordance with Sections 23.207.2 and 23.207.3.

23.211.5 Finger-joint Durability for Exterior-type Panels and Interior-type Panels Bonded with Exterior or Intermediate Glue. Panels shall be tested in accordance with Section 23.216. The joints shall meet the following minimum conditions:

23.211.5.1 The average wood failure rating of all specimens from each panel when tested in accordance with Section 23.216 shall not be less than 85 percent.

23.211.5.2 No single specimen from a panel (average of face and back gluelines) shall rate less than 60 percent wood failure.

23.211.5.3 No single face or back glueline in any specimen shall rate less than 30 percent wood failure.

SECTION 23.212 — INSPECTION AND TESTING

23.212.1 General. The tests specified in this section shall be used to determine the glue bond quality of plywood produced under this standard.

23.212.2 Inspections. All plywood designated as complying with this standard shall be subject to inspection prior to coating or finishing, except that concrete form material may have a priming coat of oil or other clear preparation before inspection. The above requirement does not apply to Interior-type plywood bonded with exterior glue or to Exterior-type plywood when tested for glue bond quality.

23.212.3 Plywood Panel Grade, Size and Thickness Reinspections. If reinspection establishes that an item is more than 5 percent below grade or out of dimensional tolerance according to the grade description, that item fails to pass the reinspection. The below-grade panels shall not be accepted. If reinspection establishes that a disputed item is 5 percent or less below grade or out of dimensional tolerance, it passes the reinspection. In addition to the above 5 percent grade and dimensional tolerance, a 5 percent tolerance shall apply separately to the inner-ply gap limitations, including the limitations applicable to the plugged crossband and jointed crossband, as specified in Section 23.203.

23.212.4 Plywood Glue Bond Quality Reinspections. Reinspection of the unused panels shall be carried out following the procedures specified in Sections 23.212, 23.213, 23.214 and 23.215. If the reinspection tests establish that the glue bond quality does not meet the requirements of Section 23.207, as applicable, the panels fail to pass the reinspection. If the glue bond quality requirements are met, panels pass the reinspection. Any delaminated Exterior-type or overlaid panels are not acceptable.

23.212.5 Sampling for Panel Grade, Size and Thickness Reinspections. Grade, size and thickness may include all panels of an item in dispute. However, when approved, a reduced basis for sampling consisting of at least 20 percent or 300 panels, whichever is smaller, shall be inspected for conformance to grade. For reduced sampling, the quantity of panels selected from each disputed item shall be prorated according to the number of panels. Panels found to be below grade or out of tolerance for size and thickness shall have improper grademarks obliterated and shall be remarked for appropriate classification with a special inspection mark registered by the qualified agency conducting the reinspection and applied by this agency's authorized representative.

23.212.6 Sampling for Glue Bond Reinspections. For test purposes, 20 panels, or 5 percent of the panels, whichever is less, shall be selected at random from the item which is in dispute. The number of panels required shall be calculated by applying the "percent panels" to the lot size and converting part panels to whole panels by using a rounding procedure where 0.01 to 0.49 parts are considered to be the smaller whole number, while 0.50 to 0.99 parts are considered to be the larger whole number. These panels shall be selected from locations distributed as widely as practicable throughout the material being sampled. When an item, lot, or shipment involves panels with different adhesive bond requirements as provided for in Section 23.207, testing and evaluation shall apply separately to each category.

Sampling shall include no less than 20 panels of Interior-type Underlayment, C-D Plugged, and C-D. Sampling of Interior-type (including the different adhesive qualities) or Exterior-type shall be prorated on the basis of ratio of their volume to total volume (i.e., for shipments containing 50 percent Exterior, 10 Exterior panels shall be selected), but in no case shall less than 10 panels of each type or adhesive quality be selected. Shipments of Interior-type plywood bonded with exterior glue shall be sampled in the same manner as Exterior plywood.

23.212.7 Specimen Preparation. One piece shall be cut from each Interior panel selected and from that piece five test specimens shall be cut. Each specimen shall be 2 inches wide by 5 inches (51 mm wide by 127 mm) along the grain. From each Exterior panel selected, one piece shall be cut from the panel and from that piece 10 test specimens shall be cut as described in Section 23.215.1. Of the 10 specimens cut from each test piece, five

shall be for vacuum pressure test, and five shall be for the boil test. From each overlaid panel selected, 10 specimens shall be cut as described for Exterior plywood. These shall be for testing the bond between veneers. A second set of 10 specimens shall be cut to test the bond between the overlay and the base panel as described in Section 23.215.1.

From five of the Exterior test panels and five of the overlaid test panels, $5^1/_2$-inch by 8-inch (140 mm by 203 mm) specimens shall be cut and tested as described in Section 23.215.4.

SECTION 23.213 — TEST FOR INTERIOR-TYPE PLYWOOD

The test specimens prepared as described in Section 23.219.3 shall be placed in a pressure vessel and completely submerged in 110°F (43.3°C) water. A vacuum of 15 inches of mercury (50.7 kPa) shall be drawn, maintained for 30 minutes and released. Specimens shall then be allowed to soak in the same water at atmospheric pressure for four and one half hours with no additional heating. They shall be removed and dried for 15 hours at 150°F (65.6°C) in an oven with fan-forced air circulation of 45 to 50 air changes per minute. Specimens shall then be examined for delamination and evaluated in accordance with requirements given in the following paragraph.

Total continuous visible delamination of $^1/_4$ inch (6.4 mm) or more in depth and 2 inches (51 mm) in length along the edges of a 2-inch by 5-inch (51 mm by 127 mm) test specimen shall be considered as failure. Where required, this shall be determined by probing with a suitable feeler gage not greater than 0.013 inch (0.3 mm) in thickness. When delamination occurs by reason of a localized defect permitted in the grade, other than white pocket, that test specimen shall be discarded.

SECTION 23.214 — TESTS FOR IMG-TYPE PLYWOOD

23.214.1 Preparation of Test Specimens. Test specimens, taken as described in Section 23.219.3, shall be cut $3^1/_4$ inches (83 mm) long and 1 inch (25 mm) wide, and kerfed one third of the length of the specimen from each end, as illustrated in Figure 23-2-1, so that a 1-inch (25 mm) square test area in the center results. Specimens shall be oriented so that the grain direction of the ply under test runs at a 90-degree angle to the length of the specimen. Kerfing shall extend two thirds of the way through the ply under test, and shall not penetrate the next glueline.

If the number of plies exceeds three, the cuts shall be made so as to test any two of the joints, but the additional plies need not be stripped except as demanded by the limitations of the width of the retaining jaws on the testing device. When desired, special jaws may be constructed to accommodate the thicker plywood. If the number of plies exceeds three, the choice of joints to be tested shall be left to the discretion of the approved inspection and testing agency, but at least one half of the tests shall include the innermost joints.

23.214.2 Vacuum Soak Test. The test specimens shall be placed in a pressure vessel and submerged in water 120°F (48.9°C). A vacuum of 15 inches of mercury (50.7 kPa) shall be drawn and maintained for 30 minutes. Following release of vacuum, specimens shall continue soaking for 15 hours at atmospheric pressure. The temperature of the water shall not drop below 75°F (23.9°C) at any time during the 15-hour soaking period. Specimens shall then be removed from the vessel and tested while wet by tension loading to failure in a shear testing machine operated at a maximum head travel of 16 inches per minute (406 mm per minute). Jaws of the machine shall securely grip the specimen so there is no slippage. The percentage of wood failure of the specimens shall be determined with specimens in a dry condition and evaluated as described in Section 23.207.7.

SECTION 23.215 — TESTS FOR EXTERIOR- AND INTERIOR-TYPE BONDED EXTERIOR GLUE (INCLUDES STRUCTURAL C-D AND C-D WITH EXTERIOR GLUE)

23.215.1 Preparation of Test Specimens. Test specimens, taken as described in Section 23.212.4 shall be cut $3^1/_4$ inches (83 mm) long and 1 inch (25 mm) wide, and kerfed one third of the length of the specimen from each end, as illustrated in Figure 23-2-1, so that a 1-inch (25 mm) square test area in the center results. Specimens shall be oriented so that the grain direction of the ply under test runs at a 90-degree angle to the length of the specimen. Kerfing shall extend two thirds of the way through the ply under test, and shall not penetrate the next glueline. Overlaid plywood specimens, taken as described in Section 23.212.3 for testing of bond between veneers, shall be cut as described above for Exterior specimens. Overlaid specimens for testing the bond between the overlay and the base panel, shall be cut 1 inch (25 mm) wide and long enough for handling (3 inches [76 mm] is a convenient length) and kerfed just through the overlay 1 inch (25 mm) from the end, on each overlay face.

If the number of plies exceeds three, the cuts shall be made so as to test any two of the joints, but the additional plies need not be stripped except as demanded by the limitations of the width of the retaining jaws on the testing device. When desired, special jaws may be constructed to accommodate the thicker plywood. If the number of plies exceeds three, the choice of joints to be tested shall be left to the discretion of the approved inspection and testing agency, but at least one half of the tests shall include the innermost joints.

23.215.2 Vacuum-pressure Test. The test specimen shall be placed in a pressure vessel and submerged in cold tap water. A vacuum of 25 inches of mercury (84.4. kPa) shall be drawn and maintained for 30 minutes, followed immediately with application of 65-70 psi (448-483 kPa) of pressure for 30 minutes duration. Specimens shall then be removed from the vessel and tested while wet by tension loading to failure in a shear testing machine operated at a maximum head travel of 16 inches per minute (406 mm per minute). Jaws of the machine shall securely grip the specimens so there is no slippage. The percentage of wood failure of the specimens shall be determined with specimens in a dry condition and evaluated as described in Section 23.207.8.

The bond between veneers in overlaid plywood shall be tested in an identical manner and evaluated as described in Section 23.207.8. Specimens for testing the bond between the overlay and the base panel shall be subjected to the same test cycle described above. The bond between the overlay and the base panel shall be tested by inserting a sharp, thin blade of adequate stiffness into the corner of the 1-inch (25 mm) test area at the overlay-veneer interface, taking care not to cut into the overlay, and attempting to peel off the overlay. It may be necessary to reinsert the blade several times in order to remove the overlay from the 1-square-inch (645 mm^2) area. The percentage of wood and/or fiber failure shall then be estimated with specimens in a dry condition and evaluated as described in Section 23.207.8. The value for each specimen shall be the average of the test areas on each face.

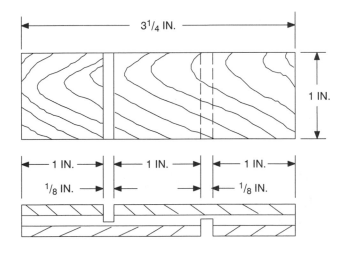

(a) THREE-PLY SPECIMEN

(b) FIVE-PLY SPECIMEN

For **SI:** 1 inch = 25.4 mm.

NOTE: Orient grain direction across specimens to test inner two joints.

FIGURE 23-2-1—SHEAR TEST SPECIMENS

23.215.3 Boiling Test. Test specimens shall be boiled in water for four hours and then dried for 20 hours at a temperature of 145°F ± 5°F (62.8°C ± 2.8°C) with sufficient air circulation to lower moisture content of the specimens to a maximum of 8 percent, based on oven-dry weight. The specimens shall be boiled again for a period of four hours, cooled in water, and tested while wet by tension loading for failure in a shear testing machine operated at a maximum head travel of 16 inches per minute (406 mm per minute). Jaws of the machine shall securely grip the specimens so there is no slippage. The percentage of wood failure of the specimens shall be determined with specimens in a dry condition and evaluated as described in Section 23.207.8. The bond between veneers in overlaid plywood shall be tested and evaluated in an identical manner. Specimens to test the bond between the overlay and the base panels shall be subjected to the same test cycle described above. The bond between the overlay and the base panel shall be tested by inserting a sharp, thin blade of adequate stiffness into the corner of the 1-inch (25 mm) test area at the overlay-veneer interface, taking care not to cut into the overlay, and attempting to peel off the overlay. It may be necessary to reinsert the blade several times in order to remove the overlay from the 1-square-inch (645 mm²) area. The percentage of wood and/or fiber failure shall then be estimated with specimens in a dry condition and evaluated as described in Section 23.207.8. The value for each specimen shall be the average of the test areas on each face.

23.215.4 Heat Durability Test. Specimens cut as described in Section 23.212.3 shall be placed on a stand as illustrated in Figure 23-2-1. It shall then be subjected to a 1,472°F to 1,652°F (800°C to 900°C) flame from a Bunsen-type burner for a period of 10 minutes or, in the case of a thin specimen, until a brown char area appears on the backside. The burner shall be equipped with a wing top to envelop the entire width of the specimen in flame. The top of the burner shall be 1 inch (25 mm) from the specimen face and the flame 1¹⁄₂ inches (38 mm) high. The flame shall impinge on the face of the specimen 2 inches (51 mm) from the bottom end. After the test, the sample shall be removed from the stand and the gluelines examined for delamination by separating the charred plies with a sharp, chisel-like instrument. Specimens shall be evaluated in accordance with Section 23.207.8.

SECTION 23.216 — TESTS FOR PERFORMANCE UNDER CONCENTRATED STATIC AND IMPACT LOADS

23.216.1 Preparation of Test Specimens. Samples shall be selected representative of the plywood product being evaluated. Length, L, of panels shall conform to the maximum center-to-center support spacing, S, anticipated in service, continuous over the minimum number of spans recommended for its use. See Figures 23-2-7 and 23-2-8. Width, W, of individual pieces shall be 24 inches (610 mm) or greater for span ratings up to 24 inches (610 mm) on center and 48 inches (1219 mm) for greater span ratings.

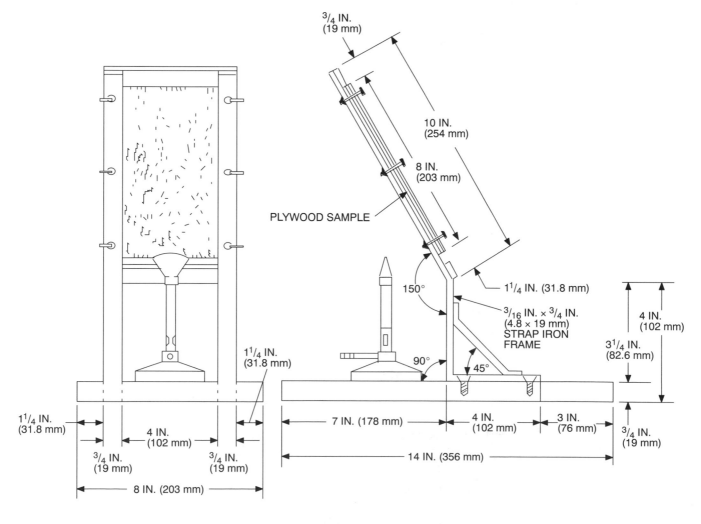

FIGURE 23-2-2—APPARATUS FOR HEAT DURABILITY TEST

23.216.2 Test Procedure.

23.216.2.1 Concentrated static. Specimens shall be loaded at locations shown in Figure 23-2-7 using a 3-inch-diameter (76 mm) loading disc, except a 1-inch-diameter (25 mm) loading disc shall be used to determine strength of single-layer floor panels in the dry or redried condition.

Stiffness shall be determined by measuring deflection in 50-pound (222 N) increments to 200 pounds (890 N). Strength shall be determined by loading to failure.

23.216.2.2 Concentrated impact. Specimens shall be loaded at locations shown in Figure 23-2-8 using an impact device 9 to $10^1/_2$ inches (229 to 267 mm) in diameter and weighing 30 pounds (13.6 kg), except that for span ratings greater than 24 inches (610 mm) on center, the impact device shall weigh 60 pounds (27.2 kg).

Strength shall be determined by impacting the specimen from the specified height at increments of 6 inches (152 mm). Deflection under a 200-pound (890 N) concentrated load, using a 3-inch-diameter (76 mm) disc, shall be measured before the test and after each impact. After the specified impact load has been reached, the concentrated load shall be applied to failure.

SECTION 23.217 — TEST FOR PERFORMANCE UNDER UNIFORM LOADS

23.217.1 Apparatus. A vacuum chamber is used consisting of a sealed box with the panel to be tested forming the top. See Figure 23-2-9. A 6-mil (0.15 mm) polyethylene sheet or equivalent is securely taped at the perimeter to seal the top surface. A vacuum pump reduces air pressure under the specimen such that load is measured.

23.217.2 Preparation of Test Specimens. Samples shall be selected representative of the plywood product being evaluated. The specimen length perpendicular to framing shall be equal to twice the maximum center-to-center support spacing, S, anticipated in service. See Figure 23-2-10. The specimen width is at least $23^1/_2$ inches (597 mm).

23.217.3 Test Procedure. The specimen is mounted in the vacuum box following anticipated joist spacing and recommended nail size and spacing and sealed. The panel is loaded to the specified level. Deflections are measured at locations shown in Figure 23-2-10 sufficient to develop the straight-line portion of the load-deflection curve, but in no case shall the number of data points be less than six.

SECTION 23.218 — TEST FOR PANEL BENDING

23.218.1 Apparatus. A testing machine shall be used capable of applying pure moments to opposite ends of the test panel through loading frames and measurement of moment and deformation.

23.218.2 Preparation of Test Specimens. Samples shall be selected representative of the plywood product being evaluated. Specimens shall measure 4 feet by 4 feet (1219 mm by 1219 mm).

23.218.3 Test Procedure. Separate specimens are subjected to pure moment along and across the major axis. Deformation or curvature is measured in a manner adequate to calculate bending stiffness. Test is carried on to failure to evaluate maximum moment.

SECTION 23.219 — SCARF- AND FINGER-JOINT TESTS

23.219.1 Strength. Three test specimens shall be cut at random along each joint from panels selected as directed in Section 23.219.3. Type, grade and species of the panels shall be recorded. The specimens shall be cut so as to include the joint and shall be prepared as illustrated in Figure 23-2-3.

Insofar as possible, the joint test area shall contain no localized natural defects permitted within the grade. At the joint, the maximum thickness and width of plies parallel with the load shall be recorded. Each specimen shall then be placed in the tension grips of a testing machine and loaded continuously at a rate of cross-head travel of 0.030 to 0.040 inch per minute (0.76 to 1.02 mm per minute) until failure, and the ultimate load recorded. The ultimate stress in pounds per square inch shall be computed using the ultimate load and area of those plies whose grain is parallel with direction of load. Moisture content of specimens at the time of testing shall not exceed 16 percent.

23.219.2 Scarf-joint Durability of Interior-type Panels Bonded with Interior Glue. Ten test specimens shall be cut at random along each scarf joint from panels selected as directed in Section 23.219.3, and shall be prepared following the general procedure in the same subsection, but shall be cut so that the scarf joint occurring on one surface of the panel runs across the middle of five specimens and the joint occurring on the opposite surface runs across the middle of the other five specimens. The specimens shall be subjected to the same test procedure as outlined in Section 23.212.

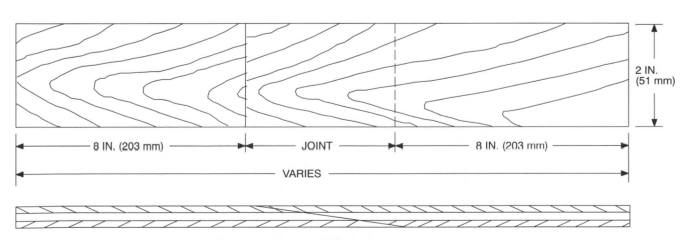

FIGURE 23-2-3—TENSION SPECIMEN FOR SCARF-JOINTED PANELS

23.219.3 Scarf-joint Durability of Exterior-type Panels and Interior-type Panels Bonded with Exterior or Intermediate Glue. Ten test specimens shall be cut at random along each joint from panels selected as directed in Section 23.219.3. The specimens shall be prepared following the general procedure described in Section 23.221.1, but, in addition, shall be cut so that the joints run through the test specimens as shown in Figure 23-2-4. For Exterior-type panels and Interior-type bonded with exterior glue, five specimens shall be subjected to the vacuum-pressure test described in Section 23.215.2, and five to the boiling test of Section 23.215.3. The panels shall be evaluated as described in Section 23.207.

For Interior-type panels bonded with intermediate glue (IMG), the 10 specimens shall be subjected to the vacuum soak test outlined in Section 23.214.2. The panels shall be evaluated as described in Section 23.207.

23.219.4 Finger-joint Durability of Interior-type Panels Bonded with Interior Glue. Five specimens shall be cut at random along the finger joint from each panel selected and shall be prepared following the general procedure in Section 23.211 so that the middle of the joint coincides with the middle of the five specimens. The specimens shall be subjected to the same test procedure as outlined in Section 23.219.

23.219.5 Finger-joint Durability of Exterior-type Panels and Interior-type Panels Bonded with Exterior or Intermediate-type Glue. Ten specimens shall be cut at random along the finger joint from each panel selected according to Section 23.211. These specimens shall be cut so as to include the joint and shall be prepared as illustrated in Figure 23-2-5.

For Exterior-type panels and Interior-type panels bonded with exterior glue, five of the specimens shall be subjected to the vacuum pressure test of Section 23.215.2 and five to the boiling test of Section 23.215.1.

For Interior-type panels bonded with intermediate glue, the 10 specimens shall be subjected to the vacuum soak test of Section 23.214.

Upon completion of the vacuum pressure and boil tests, or vacuum soak tests, as applicable, a wedge or chisel (see Figure 23-2-6) shall be inserted in locations shown in Figure 23-2-5 in such a manner as to pry apart the scarfed portions of the joint without directly contacting the glued area. Test specimens shall be dried and percent wood failure in the test area estimated and applied separately for both the boil and vacuum pressure treatments. The panels shall be evaluated as described in Section 23.207.

SECTION 23.220 — TEST FOR DETERMINATION OF MOISTURE CONTENT (OVEN-DRYING METHOD)

The moisture content of the plywood shall be determined as follows: a small test specimen shall be cut from each sample panel; the test specimen shall measure not less than 9 square inches (5806 mm^2) in area and shall weigh not less than 20 grams (approximately $^3/_4$ ounce). All loose splinters shall be removed from the specimen. The specimen shall be immediately weighed on a scale that is accurate to 0.5 percent, and the weight shall be recorded as original weight. The specimen shall then be dried in an oven at 212°F to 221°F (100°C to 105°C) until constant weight is attained. After drying, the specimen shall be reweighed immediately, and this weight shall be recorded as the oven-dry weight. The moisture content shall be calculated as follows:

$$\frac{\text{Original weight} - \text{Oven-dry weight}}{\text{Oven-dry weight}} \times 100 = \text{Moisture content (percent)}$$

SECTION 23.221 — PLYWOOD SECTION PROPERTIES

23.221.1 General. Section properties set forth in Tables 23-2-H and 23-2-I shall be used with all species and grades of plywood in this standard. The section properties shall be used in determining compliance with allowable stresses set forth in Table 23-III-A of this code. The properties have been adjusted to reflect "effective" section properties in each of two directions, assuming a homogenous material. As a result of these adjusted values, moment of inertia "I" shall be used only in stiffness calculations, with section modulus "S" used in bending stress calculations.

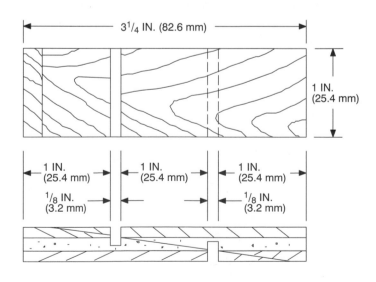

(a) THREE-PLY SPECIMEN

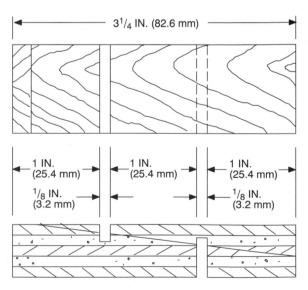

(b) FIVE-PLY SPECIMEN

FIGURE 23-2-4—SCARF-JOINT SPECIMENS FOR VACUUM SOAK, VACUUM PRESSURE AND BOILING TESTS

23.221.2 Veneer Lay-up. Section properties listed are adjusted to allow for variations in panel veneer constructions. Properties parallel to the face grain of the plywood are based on a panel construction giving minimum values in that direction. Properties perpendicular to the face grain are based on a different panel construction, giving minimum values in that direction. Properties for the two directions, however, cannot be added to achieve properties of the full panel.

SECTION 23.222 — CALCULATION OF DIAPHRAGM DEFLECTION

Calculations for diaphragm deflection shall account for the usual bending and shear components as well as any other factors, such as nail deformation, which will contribute to the deflection.

The deflection (Δ) of a blocked plywood diaphragm uniformly nailed throughout may be calculated by use of the following formula. If not uniformly nailed, the constant 0.188 (0.614) in the third term must be modified accordingly.

$$\Delta = \frac{5vL^3}{8EAb} + \frac{vL}{4Gt} + 0.188\, Le_n + \frac{\Sigma(\Delta_c X)}{2b}$$

For **SI**:
$$\Delta = \frac{52vL^3}{EAb} + \frac{vL}{4Gt} + 0.614\, Le_n + \frac{\Sigma(\Delta_c X)}{2b}$$

WHERE:

A = area of chord cross section, in square inches (mm²).

b = diaphragm width, in feet (m).

E = elastic modulus of chords, in pounds per square inch (N/mm²).

e_n = nail deformation, in inches (mm) (see Table 23-2-K).

G = modulus of rigidity of plywood, in pounds per square inch (N/mm²) (see Table 23-2-J).

L = diaphragm length, in feet (m).

t = effective thickness of plywood for shear, in inches (mm) (see Tables 23-2-H and 23-2-I).

v = maximum shear due to design loads in the direction under consideration, in pounds per lineal foot (N/m).

Δ = the calculated deflection, in inches (mm).

$\Sigma(\Delta_c X)$ = sum of individual chord-splice slip values on both sides of the diaphragm, each multiplied by its distance to the nearest support.

SECTION 23.223 — CALCULATION OF SHEAR WALL DEFLECTION

The deflection (Δ) of a blocked shear wall uniformly nailed throughout may be calculated by use of the following formula:

$$\Delta = \frac{8vh^3}{EAb} + \frac{vh}{Gt} + 0.75he_n + \frac{h}{b}\, d_a$$

For **SI**:
$$\Delta = \frac{2000\, vh^3}{3EAb} + \frac{vh}{Gt} + 2.46\, he_n + \frac{h}{b}\, d_a$$

WHERE:

A = area of boundary element cross section in square inches (mm²) (vertical member at shear wall boundary).

b = wall width, in feet (m).

d_a = deflection due to anchorage details (rotation and slip at tie-down bolts).

E = elastic modulus of boundary element (vertical member at shear wall boundary), in pounds per square inch (N/mm²).

e_n = nail deformation, in inches (mm) (see Table 23-2-K).

G = modulus of rigidity of plywood, in pounds per square inch (N/mm²) (see Table 23-2-J).

h = wall height, in feet (m).

t = effective thickness of plywood for shear, in inches (mm) (see Tables 23-2-H and 23-2-I).

v = maximum shear due to design loads at the top of the wall, in pounds per lineal foot (N/m).

Δ = the calculated deflection, in inches (mm).

SECTION 23.224 — ALLOWABLE STRESSES FOR SHEAR THROUGH THE THICKNESS

Shear-through-the-thickness stresses in Table 23-III-A of this code are based on the most common structural applications, as where plywood is mechanically fastened to framing. If the plywood is rigidly glued to full-length, continuous (unjointed) framing around all panel edges, increase allowable shear-through-the-thickness stresses by 33 percent. If the continuous framing is glued to only two edges parallel to the face grain, increase stresses by 19 percent. When continuous framing is only at edges perpendicular to the face grain, no increase in stresses shall be taken.

In lieu of the increase in shear-through-the-thickness stresses given above for continuous glued framing, a 33 percent increase may be taken when panels are regraded to limit core gap width and placement. Contiguous core gaps in adjacent plies within a layer shall be measured as a single gap from the outermost edge of one to the opposite edge of the other. Noncontiguous core gaps in any parallel ply of the panel shall be offset by at least 1 inch (25 mm), measured from innermost edges of the gaps. Gap width limitations are as follows:

1. For all three-layer panels (including three-ply and four-ply), core gaps shall not be wider than $^1/_4$ inch (6.4 mm).

2. For panels with five or more layers, core gaps shall be limited to 1 inch (25 mm) in $^1/_2$-inch-thick (13 mm) panels and to $^1/_2$ inch (13 mm) in thicker panels.

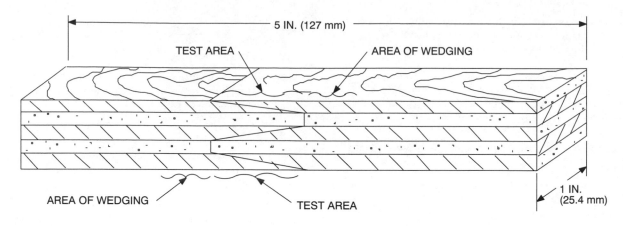

FIGURE 23-2-5—CLEAVAGE TEST, TYPICAL TEST SPECIMEN

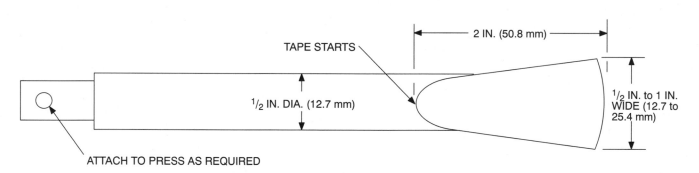

FIGURE 23-2-6—WEDGE OR CHISEL FOR CLEAVAGE TEST

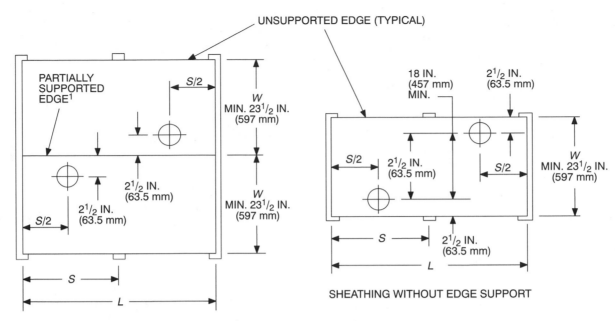

SHEATHING WITH PARTIAL EDGE SUPPORT[1]

SHEATHING WITHOUT EDGE SUPPORT

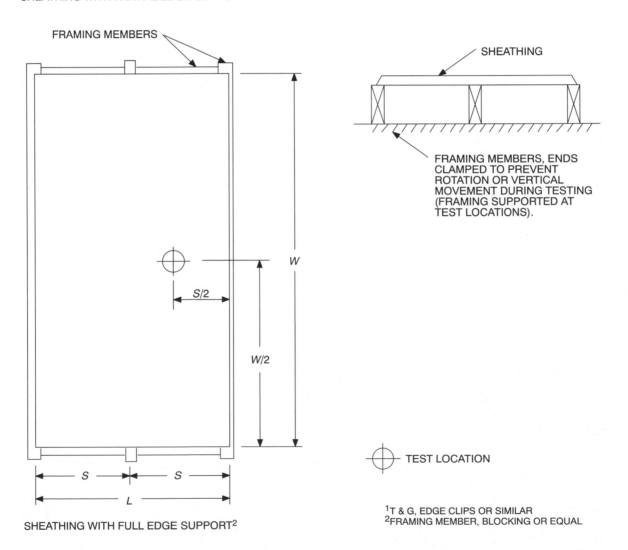

SHEATHING WITH FULL EDGE SUPPORT[2]

[1]T & G, EDGE CLIPS OR SIMILAR
[2]FRAMING MEMBER, BLOCKING OR EQUAL

FIGURE 23-2-7—CONCENTRATED STATIC LOAD TEST SPECIMENS

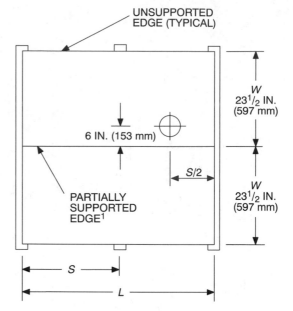

SHEATHING WITH PARTIAL EDGE SUPPORT[1]

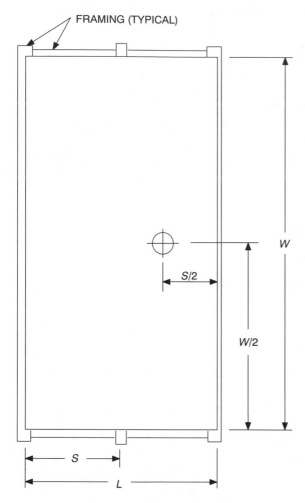

SHEATHING WITH FULL EDGE SUPPORT[2]

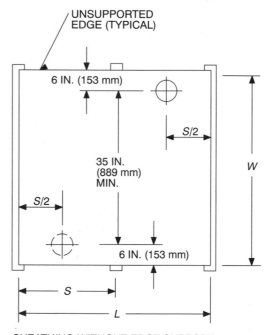

SHEATHING WITHOUT EDGE SUPPORT

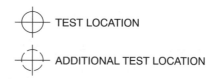

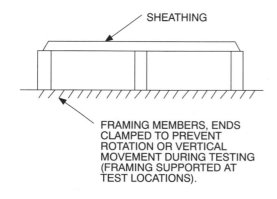

[1]T & G, edge clips or similar.
[2]Framing member, blocking or equal.

FIGURE 23-2-8—IMPACT LOAD TEST SPECIMENS

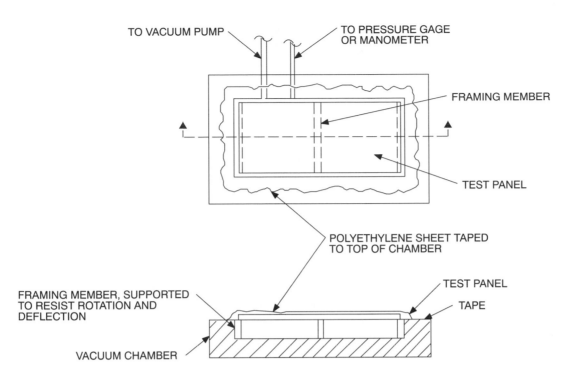

FIGURE 23-2-9—VACUUM CHAMBER TEST EQUIPMENT

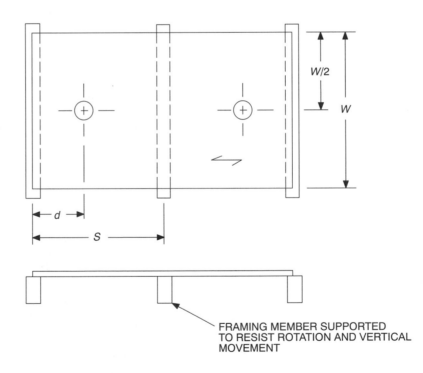

S = Center-to-center support spacing.
d = 0.4215(S) for two span.
W = Panel width, minimum = 23.5 inches (597 mm).
$\oplus$ = Location of deflection measurement.

FIGURE 23-2-10—UNIFORM LOAD TEST SPECIMENS

TABLE 23-2-A—CLASSIFICATION OF SPECIES

GROUP 1	GROUP 2		GROUP 3	GROUP 4

Aptiong[1, 2]
Beech, American
Birch
   Sweet
   Yellow
Douglas fir 1[3]
Kapur[1]
Keruing[1, 2]
Larch, western
Maple, sugar
Pine
   Caribbean
   Ocote
Pine, southern
   Loblolly
   Longleaf
   Shortleaf
   Slash
Tanoak
	Cedar, Port Oxford
	Cypress
	Douglas fir 2[3]
	Fir
	   Balsam
	   California red
	   Grand
	   Noble
	   Pacific silver
	   White
	Hemlock, western
	Lauan
	   Almon
	   Bagtikan
	   Mayapis
	   Red lauan
	   Tangile
		White lauan
		Maple, black
		Mengkulang[1]
		Meranti, red[1, 4]
		Mersawa[1]
		Pine
		   Pond
		   Red
		   Virginia
		   Western White
		Spruce
		   Black
		   Red
		   Sitka
		Sweetgum
		Tamarack
		Yellow-poplar
			Alder, red
			Birch, paper
			Cedar, Alaska
			Fir, subalpine
			Hemlock, eastern
			Maple, bigleaf
			Pine
			   Jack
			   Lodgepole
			   Ponderosa
			   Spruce
			Redwood
			Spruce
			   Engelmann
			   White
				Aspen
				   Bigtooth
				   Quaking
				Cativo
				Cedar
				   Incense
				   Western red
				Cottonwood
				   Eastern
				   Black (western poplar)
				Pine
				   Eastern white
				   Sugar

[1]Each of these names represents a trade group of woods consisting of a number of closely related species.

[2]Species from the genus Dipterocarpus are marked collectively: Aptiong if originating in the Philippines; Keruing if originating in Malaysia or Indonesia.

[3]Douglas fir from trees grown in the states of Washington, Oregon, California, Idaho, Montana, Wyoming, and the Canadian provinces of Alberta and British Columbia shall be classed as Douglas fir No. 1. Douglas fir from trees grown in the states of Nevada, Utah, Colorado, Arizona and New Mexico shall be classed as Douglas fir No. 2.

[4]Red meranti shall be limited to species having a specific gravity of 0.41 or more based on green volume and oven-dry weight.

TABLE 23-2-B—CHARACTERISTICS PROHIBITED OR RESTRICTED IN CERTAIN PANEL GRADES

PANEL GRADE DESIGNATION	DESCRIPTION AND NUMBER OF CHARACTERISTICS PER PANEL
N-N, N-A	No crossband laps adjacent to faces and backs
N-B	No crossband laps adjacent to N faces No more than 2 crossband laps adjacent to B grade side Laps are limited to $^3/_{16}$ inch (4.8 mm)

N-D	No crossband laps adjacent to faces
	No more than a total of 2 of any combination of the following:
	  — Knothole in D veneer over $2^1/_2$ inches (64 mm) but not over 3 inches (76 mm)
	  — Split in D veneer over $^1/_2$ inch (13 mm) [not over 1 inch (25 mm)]
	  — Crossband lap adjacent to backs

Underlayment and C-C Plugged	No knotholes in veneer adjacent to face over 1 inch (25 mm) across the grain where C grade is required per Tables 23-2-D and 23-2-E No knotholes in veneer adjacent to face over $2^1/_2$ inches (64 mm) where D grade is permitted or $1^1/_2$ inches (38 mm) where C grade is permitted per Section 23.205.6 No laps adjacent to face

Structural I C-D	No splits in faces over $^1/_4$ inch (6.4 mm)
	No splits in backs over $^1/_2$ inch (13 mm)
	No more than a total of 2 of any combination of the following:
	  — Knothole in C veneer over 1 inch (25 mm) but not over $1^1/_2$ inches (38 mm)
	  — Knot in D backs over $2^1/_2$ inches (64 mm) but not over 3 inches (76 mm)
	  — Knothole in D veneer over $2^1/_2$ inches (64 mm) but not over 3 inches (76 mm)
	  — Crossband lap adjacent to faces per Section 23.205.4
	  — Crossband lap adjacent to backs per Section 23.205.4

Structural I C-D Plugged	No splits in backs over $^1/_2$ inch (13 mm)
	No more than a total of 2 of any combination of the following:
	  — Knot in D backs over $2^1/_2$ inches (64 mm) but not over 3 inches (76 mm)
	  — Knothole in D veneer over $2^1/_2$ inches (64 mm) but not over 3 inches (76 mm)
	  — Crossband lap adjacent to faces per Section 23.205.4
	  — Crossband lap adjacent to backs per Section 23.205.4

Structural I Underlayment	No knotholes in core veneer next to face over 1 inch (25 mm)
	No crossband laps adjacent to faces
	No splits in backs over $^1/_2$ inch (13 mm)
	No more than a total of 2 of any combination of the following:
	  — Knot in D backs over $2^1/_2$ inches (64 mm) but not over 3 inches (76 mm)
	  — Knothole in D veneer over $2^1/_2$ inches (64 mm) but not over 3 inches (76 mm)
	  — Crossband lap adjacent to backs per Section 23.205.4

TABLE 23-2-C—PANEL CONSTRUCTIONS

PANEL GRADES	FINISHED PANEL NOMINAL THICKNESS RANGE (inch) × 25.4 for mm	MINIMUM NUMBER OF PLIES	MINIMUM NUMBER OF LAYERS

Exterior
Marine
Special Exterior
  (See Section 23.205.4)
  B-B concrete form
  High Density Overlay
  High Density concrete form overlay
	Through $3/8$
	Over $3/8$, through $3/4$
	Over $3/4$
		3
		5
		7
			3
			5
			7

Interior
N-N, N-A, N-B, N-D, A-A, A-B, A-D, B-B, B-D
Structural I (C-D, C-D Plugged and Underlayment)
Exterior
  A-A, A-B, A-C, B-B, B-C
  Structural I C-C and C-C Plugged
  (See Section 23.205.4)
  Medium Density and Special Overlays
	Through $3/8$
	Over $3/8$, through $1/2$
	Over $1/2$, through $7/8$
	Over $7/8$
		3
		4
		5
		6
			3
			3
			5
			5

Interior
  (including grades with Exterior glue)
  Underlayment
Exterior
  C-C Plugged
	Through $1/2$
	Over $1/2$, through $3/4$
	Over $3/4$
		3
		4
		5
			3
			3
			5

Interior
  (including grades with Exterior glue)
  C-D
  C-D Plugged
Exterior
  C-C
	Through $5/8$
	Over $5/8$, through $3/4$
	Over $3/4$
		3
		4
		5
			3
			3
			5

TABLE 23-2-D—INTERIOR-TYPE GRADES

PANEL GRADES DESIGNATIONS	MINIMUM VENEER QUALITY			SURFACE
	Face	Back	Inner Plies	
N-N	N	N	C	Sanded 2 sides
N-A	N	A	C	Sanded 2 sides
N-B	N	B	C	Sanded 2 sides
N-D	N	D	D	Sanded 2 sides
A-A	A	A	D	Sanded 2 sides
A-B	A	B	D	Sanded 2 sides
A-D	A	D	D	Sanded 2 sides
B-B	B	B	D	Sanded 2 sides
B-D	B	D	D	Sanded 2 sides
Underlayment[1]	C Plugged	D	C and D	Touch-sanded
C-D Plugged	C Plugged	D	D	Touch-sanded
Structural I C-D	See Section 23.205.4			Unsanded[2]
Structural I C-D Plugged, Underlayment	See Section 23.205.4			Touch-sanded
C-D	C	D	D	Unsanded[2]
C-D with Exterior glue (See Section 23.215)	C	D	D	Unsanded[2]

[1]See Section 23.205.6 for special limitations.

[2]Except for decorative grades, panels shall not be sanded, touch-sanded, surface textured or thickness sized by any mechanical means.

TABLE 23-2-E—EXTERIOR-TYPE GRADES[1]

PANEL GRADES DESIGNATIONS	MINIMUM VENEER QUALITY			SURFACE
	Face	Back	Inner Plies	
Marine, A-A, A-B, B-B, HDO, MDO		Section 23.205.1		See regular grades
Special Exterior, A-A,				See regular grades
A-B, B-B, HDO, MDO		Section 23.205.5		Sanded 2 sides
A-A				Sanded 2 sides
A-B	A	A	C	Sanded 2 sides
A-C	A	B	C	
B-B (concrete form)	A	C	C	
B-B		Section 23.205.3		Sanded 2 sides
B-C	B	B	C	Sanded 2 sides
C-C Plugged[2]	B	C	C	Touch-sanded
C-C	C Plugged	C	C	Unsanded[3]
A-A High Density	C	C	C	
Overlay				
B-B High Density	A	A	C Plugged	
Overlay				
B-B High Density	B	B	C Plugged[4]	
Concrete Form Overlay				
(See Section 23.205.3)				
B-B Medium Density	B	B	C Plugged	
Overlay				
Special Overlays	B	B	C	
	C	C	C	

[1]Available also in Structural I classification as provided in Section 23.205.4.

[2]See Section 23.205.6 for special limitations.

[3]Except for decorative grades, panels shall not be sanded, touch-sanded, surface textured or thickness sized by any mechanical means.

[4]C centers may be used in panels of five or more plies.

TABLE 23-2-F—PREMIUM GRADES

GRADE	GLUE BOND	SPECIES
Structural I C-D[1.1] C-D Plugged[1] Underlayment[1]	Shall meet the requirements of Section 23.215	Face, back and all inner plies limited to Group 1 species
Structural I All Exterior grades (see Table 23-2-E)	Exterior	Face, back and all inner plies limited to Group 1 species

[1]Special limitations applying to Structural (C-D, C-D Plugged, Underlayment) grade panels are:

[1.1] In D grade veneers white pocket in any area larger than the size of the largest knot hole, pitchpocket or split specifically permitted in D grade shall not be permitted in any ply.

[1.2] Sound tight knots in D grade shall not exceed $2^1/_2$ inches (64 mm) measured across the grain, except as provided in Table 23-2-B.

[1.3] Plugs, including multiple repairs, shall not exceed 4 inches (102 mm) in width.

[1.4] Panel construction shall be as specified in Section 23.203.1.

TABLE 23-2-G—SPAN RATINGS FOR SHEATHING AND SINGLE-FLOOR PANELS
(For special ply-layer and species requirements applicable to STRUCTURAL panels, see Section 23.205.4 and Tables 23-2-C and 23-2-F. For crossband and total inner-ply thickness proportion requirements, see Section 23.203.1.)

SPAN RATING[1]	NOMINAL PANEL THICKNESS (inch)[2] ×25.4 for mm	MINIMUM NUMBER OF PLIES-LAYERS	MINIMUM FACE AND BACK VENEER THICKNESS BEFORE PRESSING, FOR SPECIES GROUP[3] (inches) ×25.4 for mm				INNER-PLY SPECIES GROUP
			1	2	3	4	
SHEATHING PANELS (C-D, C-C)							
12/0	5/16	3-3	1/12	1/12	1/12	1/12	1, 2, 3 or 4
16/0	5/16	3-3	1/12	1/12	1/12	4	1, 2, 3 or 4
	11/32	3-3	1/12	1/12	1/12	1/12	1, 2, 3 or 4
20/0	5/16	3-3	1/12	4	4	4	1, 2, 3 or 4
	11/32	3-3	1/12	1/12	1/10	4	1, 2, 3 or 4
	3/8	3-3	1/10	1/10	1/10	1/10	1, 2, 3 or 4
24/0	3/8	3-3	1/10	4	4	4	1, 2, 3 or 4
	13/32	3-3	1/10	1/10	4	4	1, 2, 3 or 4
	1/2	3-3	1/10	1/10	1/10	1/10	1, 2, 3 or 4
32/16	1/2	3-3	1/10	1/6	4	4	1, 2, 3 or 4
	17/32	3-3	1/10	1/10	1/6	4	1, 2, 3 or 4
	5/8	3-3	5	5	5	5	1, 2, 3 or 4
40/20	5/8	3-3	5	1/6	4	4	1, 2, 3 or 4
	21/32	3-3	1/10	1/8	1/6	4	1, 2, 3 or 4
	3/4	4-3	1/10	1/10	1/10	1/8	1, 2, 3 or 4
	25/32	4-3	1/10	1/10	1/10	1/10	1, 2, 3 or 4
48/24	3/4	4-3	1/10	1/6	4	4	1, 2, 3 or 4
	25/32	4-3	1/10	1/8	1/6	4	1, 2, 3 or 4
	7/8	5-5	1/10	1/10	1/10	4	1, 2, 3 or 4
	29/32	5-5	1/10	1/10	1/10	1/8	1, 2, 3 or 4
SINGLE-FLOOR PANELS (UNDERLAYMENT, C-C PLUGGED)							
16 o.c.	1/2	3-3	1/10	4	4	4	1, 2, 3 or 4
	19/32	4-3	5	5	5	1/6	1, 2, 3 or 4
	5/8	4-3	5	5	5	5	1, 2, 3 or 4
20 o.c.	19/32	4-3	5	1/6	4	4	1, 2, 3 or 4
	5/8	4-3	5	1/8	1/6	4	1, 2, 3 or 4
	23/32	4-3	1/10	1/10	1/10	1/8	1, 2, 3 or 4
	3/4	4-3	1/10	1/10	1/10	1/10	1, 2, 3 or 4
24 o.c.	23/32	4-3	1/10	1/6	3/16	4	1, 2, 3 or 4
	3/4	4-3	1/10	1/8	1/6	4	1, 2, 3 or 4
	7/8	5-5	1/10	1/10	1/10	1/8	1, 2, 3 or 4
48 o.c.	1 1/8	7-5	1/8	1/6	4	4	1 or 2
	1 1/8	7-5	1/7	1/6	4	4	1, 2 or 3
	1 1/8	7-7	1/10	1/6	3/16	4	1
	1 1/8	7-7	1/8	1/6	3/16	4	1, 2 or 3

[1]See Section 23.209 for description.

[2]Panels for which there is no span rating shall be identified by largest species group number of the face and back, or by the span rating of the next thinner comparable panel. Sheathing panels manufactured 1/32-inch (0.8 mm) over standard thickness may be identified as the standard thickness.

[3]Intermixing between species groups and/or thicknesses in the faces and backs of panel is permitted. Use the lowest applicable span rating to identify the panel.

[4]Not permitted.

[5]One-eighth-inch minimum for 3-, 4- and 5-ply three-layer panels per Section 23.204.1. May be 1/10 inch (2.5 mm) minimum for five-ply, five-layer panels.

TABLE 23-2-H—FACE PLIES OF DIFFERENT SPECIES GROUP THAN INNER PLIES
(Includes all standard grades except those noted in Table 23-2-I)

NOMINAL THICKNESS (inches)	APPROXIMATE WEIGHT (psf)	EFFECTIVE THICKNESS FOR SHEAR (inches)	STRESS APPLIED PARALLEL TO FACE GRAIN				STRESS APPLIED PERPENDICULAR TO FACE GRAIN			
			A Area (in.^{2}/ft.)	I Moment of Inertia (in.^{4}/ft.)	KS Eff. Section Modulus (in.^{3}/ft.)	Ib/Q Rolling Shear Constant (in.^{2}/ft.)	A Area (in.^{2}/ft.)	I Moment of Inertia (in.^{4}/ft.)	KS Eff. Section Modulus (in.^{3}/ft.)	Ib/Q Rolling Shear Constant (in.^{2}/ft.)
× 25.4 for mm	× 4.882 for kg/m^2	× 25.4 for mm	× 2.117 for mm^2/mm	× 1365.6 for mm^4/mm	× 53.76 for mm^3/mm	× 2.117 for mm^2/mm	× 2.117 for mm^2/mm	× 1365.6 for mm^4/mm	× 53.76 for mm^3/mm	× 2.117 for mm^2/mm
Unsanded Panels										
$^5/_{16}$-U	1.0	0.268	1.491	0.022	0.112	2.569	0.660	0.001	0.023	4.497
$^3/_8$-U	1.1	0.278	1.866	0.037	0.154	3.110	0.799	0.002	0.031	5.444
$^{15}/_{32}$ and $^1/_2$-U	1.5	0.298	2.292	0.074	0.247	3.921	1.007	0.004	0.051	2.450
$^{19}/_{32}$ and $^5/_8$-U	1.8	0.319	2.330	0.146	0.355	5.273	1.354	0.010	0.091	3.126
$^{23}/_{32}$ and $^3/_4$-U	2.2	0.445	3.247	0.227	0.496	6.544	1.563	0.033	0.208	3.613
$^7/_8$-U	2.6	0.607	3.509	0.340	0.678	7.175	1.950	0.112	0.397	5.097
1-U	3.0	0.842	3.916	0.493	0.859	9.244	3.611	0.210	0.660	7.115
$1^1/_8$-U	3.3	0.859	4.725	0.676	1.047	9.960	3.079	0.288	0.768	8.821
Sanded Panels										
$^1/_4$-S	0.8	0.267	0.996	0.008	0.059	2.010	0.348	0.001	0.009	2.019
$^{11}/_{32}$-S	1.0	0.284	0.996	0.019	0.093	2.765	0.417	0.001	0.016	2.589
$^3/_8$-S	1.1	0.288	1.307	0.027	0.125	3.088	0.626	0.002	0.023	3.510
$^{15}/_{32}$-S	1.4	0.421	1.947	0.066	0.214	4.113	1.251	0.006	0.067	2.832
$^1/_2$-S	1.5	0.425	1.947	0.077	0.236	4.466	1.409	0.009	0.087	3.099
$^{19}/_{32}$-S	1.7	0.546	2.423	0.115	0.315	5.471	1.389	0.021	0.137	2.861
$^5/_8$-S	1.8	0.550	2.475	0.129	0.339	5.824	1.528	0.027	0.164	3.119
$^{23}/_{32}$-S	2.1	0.563	2.822	0.179	0.389	6.717	1.737	0.050	0.231	3.818
$^3/_4$-S	2.2	0.568	2.884	0.197	0.412	7.121	2.084	0.063	0.285	4.079
$^7/_8$-S	2.6	0.586	2.942	0.278	0.515	8.182	2.841	0.122	0.470	5.078
1-S	3.0	0.817	3.721	0.423	0.664	8.882	3.163	0.185	0.591	7.031
$1^1/_8$-S	3.3	0.836	3.854	0.548	0.820	9.883	3.180	0.271	0.744	8.428
Touch-sanded Panels										
$^1/_2$-T	1.5	0.342	2.698	0.083	0.271	4.252	1.159	0.006	0.061	2.746
$^{19}/_{32}$ and $^5/_8$-T	1.8	0.408	2.354	0.122	0.291	5.350	1.555	0.017	0.138	3.220
$^{23}/_{32}$ and $^3/_4$-T	2.2	0.439	2.715	0.196	0.398	6.589	2.014	0.032	0.219	3.635
$1^1/_8$-T	3.3	0.839	4.548	0.633	0.977	11.258	4.067	0.272	0.743	8.535

TABLE 23-2-I—STRUCTURAL I AND MARINE WITH ALL PLIES FROM SAME SPECIES GROUP

NOMINAL THICKNESS (inches)	APPROXIMATE WEIGHT (psf)	EFFECTIVE THICKNESS FOR SHEAR (inches)	STRESS APPLIED PARALLEL TO FACE GRAIN				STRESS APPLIED PERPENDICULAR TO FACE GRAIN			
			A Area (in.²/ft.)	I Moment of Inertia (in.⁴/ft.)	KS Eff. Section Modulus (in.³/ft.)	Ib/Q Rolling Shear Constant (in.²/ft.)	A Area (in.²/ft.)	I Moment of Inertia (in.⁴/ft.)	KS Eff. Section Modulus (in.³/ft.)	Ib/Q Rolling Shear Constant (in.²/ft.)
× 25.4 for mm	× 4.882 for kg/m²	× 25.4 for mm	× 2.117 for mm²/mm	× 1365.6 for mm⁴/mm	× 53.76 for mm³/mm	× 2.117 for mm²/mm	× 2.117 for mm²/mm	× 1365.6 for mm⁴/mm	× 53.76 for mm³/mm	× 2.117 for mm²/mm
Unsanded Panels										
⁵/₁₆-U	1.0	0.356	1.619	0.022	0.126	2.567	1.188	0.002	0.029	6.037
³/₈-U	1.1	0.371	2.226	0.041	0.195	3.107	1.438	0.003	0.043	7.307
¹⁵/₃₂ and ¹/₂-U	1.5	0.535	2.719	0.074	0.279	4.206	2.175	0.014	0.127	2.408
¹⁹/₃₂ and ⁵/₈-U	1.8	0.707	3.464	0.154	0.437	5.685	2.742	0.045	0.240	3.072
²³/₃₂ and ³/₄-U	2.2	0.739	4.219	0.241	0.572	6.148	2.813	0.064	0.299	3.540
⁷/₈-U	2.6	0.776	4.388	0.346	0.690	6.948	3.510	0.192	0.584	5.086
1-U	3.0	1.088	5.200	0.529	0.922	8.512	6.500	0.366	0.970	7.052
1¹/₈-U	3.3	1.118	6.654	0.751	1.164	9.061	5.542	0.503	1.131	8.755
Sanded Panels										
¹/₄-S	0.8	0.342	1.280	0.012	0.083	2.009	0.626	0.001	0.013	2.723
¹¹/₃₂-S	1.0	0.365	1.280	0.026	0.133	2.764	0.751	0.001	0.023	3.397
³/₈-S	1.1	0.373	1.680	0.038	0.177	3.086	1.126	0.002	0.033	4.927
¹⁵/₃₂-S	1.4	0.537	1.947	0.067	0.247	4.107	2.251	0.009	0.093	2.807
¹/₂-S	1.5	0.545	1.947	0.078	0.271	4.457	2.536	0.014	0.123	3.076
¹⁹/₃₂-S	1.7	0.709	3.018	0.116	0.338	5.566	2.501	0.034	0.199	2.811
⁵/₈-S	1.8	0.717	3.112	0.131	0.361	5.934	2.751	0.045	0.238	3.073
²³/₃₂-S	2.1	0.741	3.735	0.183	0.439	6.707	3.126	0.085	0.338	3.780
³/₄-S	2.2	0.748	3.848	0.202	0.464	7.146	3.751	0.108	0.418	4.047
⁷/₈-S	2.6	0.778	3.952	0.288	0.569	7.539	5.114	0.212	0.692	5.046
1-S	3.0	1.091	5.215	0.479	0.827	7.978	5.693	0.321	0.870	6.981
1¹/₈-S	3.3	1.121	5.593	0.623	0.955	8.841	5.724	0.474	1.098	8.377
Touch-sanded Panels										
¹/₂-T	1.5	0.543	2.698	0.084	0.282	4.511	2.486	0.020	0.162	2.720
¹⁹/₃₂ and ⁵/₈-T	1.8	0.707	3.127	0.124	0.349	5.500	2.799	0.050	0.259	3.183
²³/₃₂ and ³/₄-T	2.2	0.739	4.059	0.201	0.469	6.592	3.625	0.078	0.350	3.596

TABLE 23-2-J—VALUES OF G FOR USE WITH EFFECTIVE THICKNESS FOR SHEAR (TABLES 23-2-H AND 23-2-I) IN CALCULATING DEFLECTION OF PLYWOOD DIAPHRAGMS

PLYWOOD GRADES OR SPECIES GROUP NOS.	G—(MODULUS OF RIGIDITY—psi)[1]
	× 0.00689 for N/mm²
Group 1	90,000
Group 2	75,000
Group 3	60,000
Group 4	50,000
Structural I	90,000
Exterior C-C and C-D with Exterior glue	
The combination of Identification Index designation and panel thickness determines the minimum species group and, therefore, the modulus of rigidity to be used: ⁵/₁₆ (7.9 mm)—20/0; ³/₈ (9.5 mm)—24/0; ¹⁵/₃₂, ¹/₂ (12, 13 mm)—32/16; ¹⁹/₃₂, ⁵/₈ (16 mm)—42/20; ²³/₃₂, ³/₄ (18, 19 mm)—48/24	90,000
All other combinations of C-C and C-D with Exterior glue	50,000

[1]Values of "G" shown apply to plywood bonded with Exterior glue. For plywood bonded with Interior glue, multiply by 0.91.

TABLE 23-2-K—"e_n" VALUES (INCHES) FOR USE IN CALCULATING DIAPHRAGM DEFLECTION DUE TO NAIL SLIP (STRUCTURAL I)[1]

LOAD PER NAIL (pounds)	NAIL DESIGNATION		
	6d	8d	10d
× 4.448 for N	× 25.4 for mm		
60	0.012	0.008	0.006
80	0.020	0.012	0.010
100	0.030	0.018	0.013
120	0.045	0.023	0.018
140	0.068	0.031	0.023
160	0.102	0.041	0.029
180	—	0.056	0.037
200	—	0.074	0.047
220	—	0.096	0.060
240	—	—	0.077

[1]Increase "e_n" values 20 percent for plywood grades other than Structural I.

Values apply to common wire nails.

Load per nail = maximum shear per foot divided by the number of nails per foot at interior panel edges.

Decrease values 50 percent for seasoned lumber.

TABLE 23-2-L—CONCENTRATED STATIC AND IMPACT TEST PERFORMANCE CRITERIA FOR PANELS TESTED ACCORDING TO SECTION 23.216—SHEATHING

END USE—SPAN RATING	TEST EXPOSURE CONDITIONS[1]	PERFORMANCE REQUIREMENTS		Maximum Deflection (in.) under 200-Lb. (890 N) Load[3]
		Minimum Ultimate Load (lb.)		
		× 4.448 for N		× 25.4 for mm
		Static	Following Impact[2]	
Roof—16	Dry	400	300	7/16 (0.438)[4]
	Wet	400	300	
Roof—20	Dry	400	300	15/32 (0.469)[4]
	Wet	400	300	
Roof—24	Dry	400	300	1/2 (0.500)[4]
	Wet	400	300	
Roof—32	Dry	400	300	1/2 (0.500)[4]
	Wet	400	300	
Roof—40	Dry	400	300	1/2 (0.500)[4]
	Wet	400	300	
Roof—48	Dry	400	300	1/2 (0.500)[4]
	Wet	400	300	
Subfloor—16	Dry	400	400	3/16 (0.188)
	Wet/redry	400	400	3/16 (0.188)
Subfloor—20	Dry	400	400	7/32 (0.219)
	Wet/redry	400	400	7/32 (0.219)
Subfloor—24	Dry	400	400	1/4 (0.250)
	Wet/redry	400	400	1/4 (0.250)

[1]Wet/redry is exposure to three days continuous wetting followed by testing dry. Wet conditioning is exposure to three days continuous wetting and tested wet.

[2]Impact shall be 75 foot-pounds (102 N·m) for span ratings up to 24 on center (610 mm), 90 foot-pounds (122 N·m) for 32 on center (813 mm), 120 foot-pounds (163 N·m) for 40 on center (1016 mm), and 150 foot-pounds (203 N·m) for 48 on center (1219 mm).

[3]Criteria apply under static concentrated load according to Section 23.216. They do not apply following impact.

[4]Not applicable.

TABLE 23-2-M—UNIFORM LOAD PERFORMANCE CRITERIA FOR PANELS TESTED ACCORDING TO SECTION 23.217—SHEATHING

END USE—SPAN RATING	TEST EXPOSURE CONDITIONS[1]	PERFORMANCE REQUIREMENTS	Minimum Ultimate Uniform Load (psf)
		Average Deflection (in.) under Load (psf)	
		× 25.4 for mm × 0.0000479 for N/mm²	× 0.0000479 for N/mm²
Roof—16	Dry	0.067 at 35 psf	150
Roof—20	Dry	0.080 at 35 psf	150
Roof—24	Dry	0.100 at 35 psf	150
Roof—32	Dry	0.133 at 35 psf	150
Roof—40	Dry	0.167 at 35 psf	150
Roof—48	Dry	0.200 at 35 psf	150
Subfloor—16	Dry	0.044 at 100 psf	330
	Wet/Redry	0.044 at 100 psf	330
Subfloor—20	Dry	0.053 at 100 psf	330
	Wet/Redry	0.053 at 100 psf	330
Subfloor—24	Dry	0.067 at 100 psf	330
	Wet/Redry	0.067 at 100 psf	330

[1]Wet/redry is exposure to three days continuous wetting followed by testing dry.

**TABLE 23-2-N—CONCENTRATED STATIC AND IMPACT TEST PERFORMANCE CRITERIA
FOR PANELS TESTED ACCORDING TO SECTION 23.216—SINGLE FLOOR**

		PERFORMANCE REQUIREMENTS		
		Minimum Ultimate Load (lb.)		Maximum Deflection (in.) (mm) Under 200-Lb. (890 N) Load[2]
		× 4.45 for N		
SPAN RATING	TEST EXPOSURE CONDITIONS[1]	Static	Following 75 Ft.·Lb. (102 N·m) Impact	× 25.4 for mm
16	Dry	550	400	$\frac{5}{64}$ (0.078)
	Wet/redry	550	400	$\frac{5}{64}$ (0.078)
20	Dry	550	400	$\frac{6}{64}$ (0.094)
	Wet/redry	550	400	$\frac{6}{64}$ (0.094)
24	Dry	550	400	$\frac{7}{64}$ (0.108)
	Wet/redry	550	400	$\frac{7}{64}$ (0.108)

[1]Wet/redry is exposure to three days continuous wetting followed by testing dry.
[2]Criteria apply under static concentrated load and following a 75 foot-pounds (102 N·m) impact according to Section 23.216.

**TABLE 23-2-O—UNIFORM LOAD PERFORMANCE CRITERIA FOR PANELS
TESTED ACCORDING TO SECTION 23.217—SINGLE FLOOR**

		PERFORMANCE REQUIREMENTS	
		Average Deflection (in.) (mm) under Load (psf) (N/mm²)	Minimum Ultimate Uniform Load (psf)
SPAN RATING	TEST EXPOSURE CONDITIONS[1]	× 25.4 for mm × 0.00689 for N/mm²	× 0.00689 for N/mm²
16	Dry or wet/redry	0.044 at 100 psf	330
20	Dry or wet/redry	0.053 at 100 psf	330
24	Dry or wet/redry	0.067 at 100 psf	330

[1]Wet/redry is exposure to three days continuous wetting followed by testing dry.

UNIFORM BUILDING CODE STANDARD 23-3
PERFORMANCE STANDARD FOR WOOD-BASED STRUCTURAL-USE PANELS
See Sections 2302.1, 2303, 2304.2 and 2502, and
Tables 23-II-H, 23-II-I-1 and 23-II-E-2, *Uniform Building Code*

SECTION 23.301 — ADOPTION OF USVPS CODE

Wood-based structural-use panels shall be in accordance with United States Voluntary Product Standard PS 2-92, "Performance Standard for Wood-Based Structural-Use Panels," published by the Department of Commerce, the American Plywood Association, copyright 1992, Post Office Box 11700, Tacoma, Washington 98411 and TECO, 2401 Daniels Street, Madison, Wisconsin 53704, as if set out at length herein.

UNIFORM BUILDING CODE STANDARD 23-4

FIRE-RETARDANT-TREATED WOOD TESTS ON DURABILITY AND HYGROSCOPIC PROPERTIES

Based on American Society for Testing and Materials Standard Test Methods ASTM D 2898-81 and D 3201-79. Extracted, with permission, from the *Annual Book of ASTM Standards,* copyright American Society for Testing and Materials, 100 Barr Harbor Drive, West Conshohocken, PA 19428, and American Wood Preservers Association Standards C 20-83 and C 27-83

See Sections 201, 207 and 2303, *Uniform Building Code*

SECTION 23.401 — SCOPE

These methods cover the (1) durability of a fire-retardant treatment of wood and wood-base products under exposure to accelerated weathering, (2) measurement of the hygroscopic properties of fire-retardant-treated wood, and (3) identification classifications for material having qualified under these tests. The fire-retardant treatment for lumber and plywood is by pressure impregnation.

SECTION 23.402 — ACCELERATED WEATHERING

23.402.1 Scope. This section describes the conditioning method for a test specimen prior to subjecting that specimen to an appropriate fire test. The condition simulates effects of leaching, drying and temperature such as might reasonably be anticipated on a wood element exposed to the weather over a long term.

23.402.2 Apparatus. The test apparatus shall be capable of subjecting the specimen uniformly to the test conditions described in Section 23.402.4.

No special means of protecting the specimen back and edges are required, but water shall not impinge directly on those surfaces which are not exposed either to the weather in the assembled form, or to fire in the subsequent test. Water spray nozzles shall be provided and arranged so as to distribute water evenly over the exposed specimen surface.

Heating shall be thermostatically controlled. Forced-air movement shall be uniform across the specimen surface, with provisions made for adequate air changes to assure thorough drying.

23.402.3 Test Specimen. The test specimen shall include all those essential parts of the corresponding fire test specimen that may be subjected to weather exposure in normal use.

Specimens may be mounted in sections which can be reassembled subsequently without trimming into the appropriate fire test specimen.

The specimen surface shall have a slope of 4 in 12.

23.402.4 Exposure Cycle. Subject the specimens to an exposure cycle consisting of twelve one-week cycles. Each cycle is to consist of 96 hours of water exposure and 72 hours of drying.

Apply water in a moderately fine spray uniformly over the exposed specimen surfaces by spray nozzles that deliver an average of 0.7 inch of water (174 Pa) per hour [0.0073 gallons per minute per square foot (0.000307 m³/minute/m²) of specimen surface] at a temperature between 35°F and 60°F (1.7°C to 15.6°C). Do not recirculate the water.

Dry at a thermostatically controlled temperature of 135°F to 140°F (57.2°C to 60.0°C) in a room or cell. The controlling temperature shall be the air temperature measured 1 inch (25.4 mm) above the specimen surface. Accompany drying with the air

movement directed across the face of the specimens at a rate of at least 25 feet (7620 mm) per minute.

At the end of each cycle, change the position of each specimen within the apparatus so that each specimen or segment occupies approximately an equal number of cycles in each location used.

23.402.5 Conditioning. Upon completion of the prescribed exposure, the specimen shall be conditioned to a moisture content specified by the applicable fire test standard.

SECTION 23.403 — HYGROSCOPIC PROPERTIES OF FIRE-RETARDANT WOOD

23.403.1 Scope. This section prescribes the method for determining the moisture content of fire-retardant-treated wood samples after exposure to a standard high relative humidity condition of 92 ± 2 percent at 27°C ± 2°C.

23.403.2 Apparatus. Conditioning room or chamber with air circulation and controlling instruments capable of being maintained at 27°C ± 2°C and a relative humidity of 92 ± 2 percent. Other suitable means of maintaining these conditions are also acceptable.

Oven, air-circulated and vented, capable of maintaining a temperature of 103°C ± 2°C.

A weighing scale or balance that will weigh a specimen within an accuracy of ± 0.2 percent.

23.403.3 Test Specimens. Specimens shall be selected that represent the lot. Unless otherwise specified, specimens shall be full cross sections, no less than 25.4 millimeters along the grain, but longer as needed to provide a minimum volume of 33 cubic centimeters.

The specimens shall be penetrated by the chemical to be representative for the treated product.

The specimens shall be in moisture equilibrium with a laboratory ambient condition of 30 to 65 percent relative humidity or shall be exposed for at least seven days at such a condition prior to high-humidity exposure.

Untreated specimens, when available, of the same species or wood-base product and of the same size, shall be exposed to the preconditioning, high-humidity exposure, and drying along with the treated specimens.

23.403.4 Procedure. Weigh each specimen to an accuracy of ± 0.2 percent.

Expose all specimens under constant humidity conditions of 92 ± 2 percent at 27°C ± 2°C for seven days. Specimens shall be suitably suspended so that all surfaces are exposed.

Weigh each specimen immediately to an accuracy of ± 0.2 percent one at a time as they are removed from the conditioning chamber. Observe and record the general appearance of the specimens.

Dry each specimen in an oven at 103°C ± 2°C until approximately constant weight is attained, and reweigh. Constant weight can be assumed when two consecutive readings taken two hours apart agree within 0.2 percent. Avoid drying for periods longer than necessary to achieve constant weight, since thermal decomposition of chemical or wood might occur reflecting a higher than actual moisture content.

23.403.5 Calculations. Calculate the "apparent" moisture content of each sample prior to high-humidity exposure as follows:

$$\text{Moisture content: percent} = [(A - B)/B] \times 100$$

WHERE:

A = weight prior to high-humidity exposure.

B = oven-dry weight.

Calculate the "apparent" moisture content of each sample after high-humidity exposure as follows:

$$\text{Moisture content: percent} = [(C - B)/B] \times 100$$

WHERE:

B = oven-dry weight.

C = weight after high-humidity exposure.

The change in the "apparent" moisture content of the specimens shall be calculated as the difference between the average moisture content for the treated and untreated specimens as calculated in this section.

23.403.6 Report. The report shall include the following:

Complete identification of the fire-retardant product as to species of wood, wood product, and treatment.

Description of sampling procedure and number and dimensions of test specimens.

General description of humidity chamber and controls used for the test.

The average moisture content of the untreated specimens shall be reported.

The average "apparent" moisture content for the treated specimens, both before and after high-humidity exposure, including the basis of the computation; treated specimen (wood and chemical) or wood-only basis, shall be reported. The change in the average moisture content after high-humidity exposure compared to the moisture content of untreated specimens shall also be reported.

Report any change in the appearance of the specimen during exposure, including surface wetness, chemical exudation, or crystals on surface.

SECTION 23.404 — CLASSIFICATION

23.404.1 Scope. This part establishes the classification of fire-retardant-treated wood.

23.404.2 Classifications.

23.404.2.1 Interior Type A. Material that has been fire tested in accordance with Section 207 of the code to qualify as fire-retardant-treated wood and has an equilibrium moisture content of not over 28 percent when tested at 92 ± 2 percent relative humidity when conditioned as specified in Section 23.403.

23.404.2.2 Interior Type B. Material that has been fire tested in accordance with Section 207 of the code to qualify as fire-retardant-treated wood, but does not qualify as Interior Type A when conditioned as specified in Section 23.403.

23.404.2.3 Exterior type. Material that has been subjected to the weathering test of Section 23.402 and then fire tested in accordance with Section 207 of the Building Code to qualify as fire-retardant-treated wood.

UNIFORM BUILDING CODE STANDARD 23-5
FIRE-RETARDANT-TREATED WOOD
Design Values for Fire-retardant-treated Lumber
See Sections 207 and 2303, *Uniform Building Code*

SECTION 23.501 — SCOPE

This standard establishes the test protocol, acceptance criteria, and quality control procedure for assuring that fire-retardant treatments qualify for the design values assigned and that appropriate treating and redrying methods are used. Only lumber pressure impregnated with fire-retardant chemicals that is identified by the quality mark of an approved inspection agency shall be eligible for the design values specified in the Building Code.

Part I—Test Protocol

SECTION 23.502 — TYPE OF MATERIAL

The effects of fire-retardant treatment shall be determined on the basis of tests on matched samples of clear, straight-grain material. This is consistent with procedures presently used to establish design values and modifications for condition of use for visually graded sawn lumber.

SECTION 23.503 — NUMBER OF SPECIES

The effects of fire-retardant treatment may vary depending upon species. Because evaluation of such treatment for all species and properties is considered prohibitive, testing of three species representative of a range of wood density and treating characteristics is recommended. A specific treatment may be evaluated for only one of these species, but testing of three species representative of a range of wood density and treated characteristics is recommended.

Qualification may be obtained for any one species by evaluation of that species.

SECTION 23.504 — IDENTIFICATION

Each fire-retardant treatment shall be identified by the commercial name assigned by the developer of the treatment and each specimen shall be marked to identify the drying temperatures and relative humidity schedules used.

SECTION 23.505 — STRENGTH TESTING

Material to be subjected to strength testing shall be treated to the penetration and retention level required for that treatment and species to meet the definition of fire-retardant-treated wood given in Section 207.

To allow for variability in treatment especially for species classified as moderate to difficult to treat, it may be necessary to treat up to twice the number of samples required for test. Equal numbers of samples of low and high treatability may be excluded from strength testing to ensure that material of average treatability is evaluated.

Following treatment, strength test material shall be dried at a maximum temperature of 160°F (71.1°C) with relative humidity schedules and air velocities that will simulate commercial conditions. A record of the operating conditions of the kiln shall be kept for the entire run and shall include humidity conditions and temperature in the hottest part of the kiln.

SECTION 23.506 — SAMPLING AND TREATMENT

23.506.1 Species. For each fire-retardant treatment to be evaluated for general qualification, strength test material shall be selected from each of the following species:

Southern pine (*Pinus taeda or echinata*)

Coast Douglas fir

White spruce (*Picea glauca*)

The southern pine material shall be all sapwood. Where a treatment is to be evaluated only for a particular species, strength test material shall be selected from each such species.

23.506.2 Number of Samples, Size and Quality. For each species to be evaluated, 25 essentially clear, straight-grained 2 by 4s (51 by 102), 8 feet (2438 mm) or longer shall be selected from the production of one or more mills. All pieces shall be identified as being Surfaced Dry and shall have an average specific gravity within ± 10 percent of the average specific gravity (green volume basis) of the species.

23.506.3 Sample Identification. From each 2-inch-by-4-inch (51 mm by 102 mm) member selected for sampling, two end-matched 4-foot (1219 mm) blanks shall be cut for strength testing. One blank shall be designated for treatment and the other as control. All blanks shall be coded as to member number and treatment or control.

23.506.4 Pressure Treatment of Samples. All blanks to be fire-retardant treated shall be processed in accordance with the specific procedures established for the treatment being evaluated. Blanks shall be pressure treated and dried to a maximum moisture content of 19 percent in 2-inch by 4-inch (51 mm by 102 mm) by 4-foot (1219 mm) size. The same treatment and drying times, stickering practices, and other procedures to be employed in commercial charges shall be used.

23.506.5 Conditioning of Blanks. After redrying to a maximum moisture content of 19 percent, treated blanks and untreated controls shall be conditioned at 68°F ± 6°F (20°C ± 3.3°C) and 65 percent ± 1 percent relative humidity until approximate equilibrium weight is attained.

SECTION 23.507 — STRENGTH TESTS

23.507.1 Type and Number of Specimens. One- and one-half-inch-by-$1^1/_2$-inch-by-23-inch (38 mm by 38 mm by 584 mm) static bending specimen, two 1-inch-by-$^1/_4$-inch-by-16-inch (25 mm by 6.4 mm by 406 mm) tension specimens, one $1^1/_2$-inch-by-$1^1/_2$-inch-by-6-inch (38 mm by 38 mm by 152 mm) compression specimen, one $1^1/_2$-inch-by-$1^1/_2$-inch-by-$2^1/_2$-inch (38 mm by 38 mm by 64 mm) shear specimen, and $1^1/_2$-inch-by-$1^1/_2$-inch-by-2-inch (38 mm by 38 mm by 51 mm) specific gravity specimen shall be cut from each treated and untreated blank. Bending and compression specimens from both treated and control blanks shall be cut such that three sides of the specimen represent the original surfaces or edge of the 2-inch-by-4-inch (51 mm by 102 mm) member. Two sides of the shear and specific gravity specimens shall represent original surfaces. One of the 1-inch-wide (25 mm) faces of one of the tension specimens shall represent one original surface of the blank and one of the wide surfaces of the other specimen shall represent the opposite original blank surface.

One method of selecting specimens to obtain the required placement of original surfaces is shown in Figure 23-5-3. Any orientation of growth rings relative to the edge of the specimens shall be acceptable.

Tension specimens shall be further machined to the size and shape shown in Figure 23-5-2. Shear specimens shall be notched as shown in Figure 23-5-1.

23.507.2 Slope of Grain. The slope of grain in all bending specimens and in the critical section of tension specimens shall be 1 in 20 or less. Compression and shear specimens shall have a slope of grain of 1 in 16 or less.

23.507.3 Identification and Conditioning. The blank identification of each treated and control specimen shall be retained. After final machining, test specimens shall be reconditioned to constant weight before test.

SECTION 23.508 — TESTING PROCEDURE

23.508.1 General. Testing procedures of an approved nationally recognized test standard shall be used. Load deformation curves shall be taken for static bending tests only. Maximum load shall be observed in all tests.

23.508.2 Order of Testing. The treated specimen and the matching untreated control from each blank shall be tested consecutively.

23.508.3 Measurement. The dimensions of the critical cross-sectional area, or in the case of the shear specimen the area of the shear plane of each specimen, shall be measured to an accuracy of at least 0.01 inch (0.254 mm).

23.508.4 Static Bending. Bending specimens shall be center loaded at span of 21 inches (533 mm). A machine cross-head speed of 0.075 inch per minute (1.9 mm per minute) shall be used. Bending specimens shall be positioned in the testing machine such that two opposite original surfaces represent the compression and tension faces of the beam.

23.508.5 Moisture Samples. All moisture samples selected from each specimen after test shall be oven dried at 103°C ± 2°C until approximately constant weight of the untreated control is reached.

23.508.6 Specific Gravity. Dimensions of the specific gravity samples shall be measured after final conditioning to determine volume at 65 percent relative humidity. Samples shall be dried at 103°C ± 2°C until approximate constant weight of the untreated control is reached.

SECTION 23.509 — REPORT

The treatment and redrying procedures shall be described in accordance with Section 23.505.

The species evaluated and testing procedures followed shall be fully described.

Individual values of treated and control specimens shall be reported for specific gravity, moisture content, modulus of elasticity, modulus of rupture, maximum tensile stress, maximum compression stress, and maximum shear stress. Average values, standard deviations, average ratios of treated to control values, and median ratios of treated to control values shall be reported for each strength and stiffness property and each species.

Part II—Acceptance Criteria

SECTION 23.510 — MINIMUM PROPERTY RATIO

A fire-retardant treatment evaluated for a particular species under this standard shall qualify for the design value adjustments in Section 2304.3 of the Building Code if the median ratio of treated to untreated strength or stiffness for each of the following properties equals or exceeds the specified adjustment factor for that property:

Extreme fiber in bending

Modulus of elasticity

Maximum stress in tension parallel to grain

Maximum stress in compression parallel to grain

Maximum stress in horizontal shear

Qualification of the adjustment factor for compression perpendicular to grain shall be based on the median factor for maximum stress in compression parallel to grain. Qualification of the adjustment factor for fastener loads shall be based on the lower of the median ratio for maximum stress in compression parallel to grain and the median ratio for maximum stress in horizontal shear.

SECTION 23.511 — RESAMPLING

Where marginal results occur for one property, a second 25-piece sample may be taken for that property and the combined results of the first and second samples be used to determine qualification.

SECTION 23.512 — GENERAL QUALIFICATION

A treatment meeting the requirements of Section 23.510 for each of the three species identified in Section 23.506 of this standard shall be considered qualifying for the design value adjustments in Section 2304.3 of the Building Code for all species.

Part III—Identification

SECTION 23.513 — PRODUCT ELIGIBILITY

Only lumber pressure impregnated with fire-retardant chemicals that is identified by the quality mark of an approved inspection agency shall be eligible for the design value adjustments given in Section 2304.3 of the Building Code. Such agency shall maintain continuing supervision, testing and inspection over the quality of the treated product as necessary to (1) ensure compliance with the fire performance requirements for fire-retardant-treated wood in Section 207 and (2) ensure eligibility for strength classification under the provisions of this standard.

SECTION 23.514 — QUALIFICATION COMPLIANCE

The approved agency shall review and analyze the test data developed in accordance with Part I of this standard and shall attest to the following:

1. Competency of the personnel and the adequacy of the facilities of the testing laboratory.

2. Conformance of reported sampling and testing procedures to Part I of this standard.

3. Compliance of test results with acceptance criteria in Part II of this standard.

SECTION 23.515 — QUALITY MARK

The quality symbol shall indicate that the treated lumber bearing the mark has been treated and redried in conformance with the procedures established by the manufacturer of the treatment which were used in the evaluation and qualification of that treatment under Parts I and II of this standard.

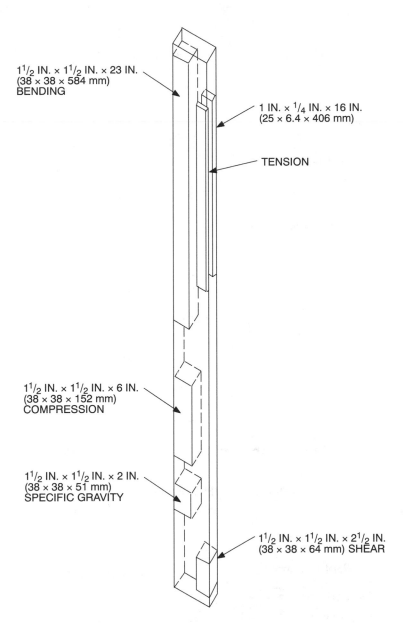

$1^1/_2$ IN. × $1^1/_2$ IN. × 23 IN.
(38 × 38 × 584 mm)
BENDING

1 IN. × $^1/_4$ IN. × 16 IN.
(25 × 6.4 × 406 mm)

TENSION

$1^1/_2$ IN. × $1^1/_2$ IN. × 6 IN.
(38 × 38 × 152 mm)
COMPRESSION

$1^1/_2$ IN. × $1^1/_2$ IN. × 2 IN.
(38 × 38 × 51 mm)
SPECIFIC GRAVITY

$1^1/_2$ IN. × $1^1/_2$ IN. × $2^1/_2$ IN.
(38 × 38 × 64 mm) SHEAR

FIGURE 23-5-1—MATCHING DIAGRAM

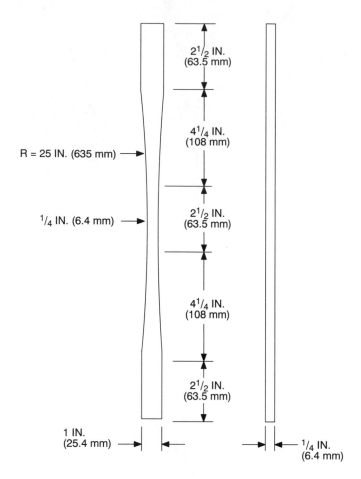

FIGURE 23-5-2—TENSION SPECIMEN

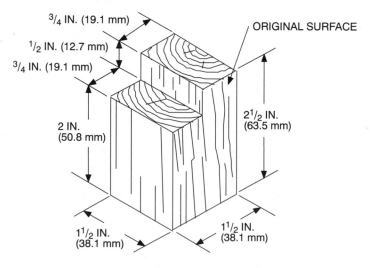

FIGURE 23-5-3—SHEAR SPECIMEN

UNIFORM BUILDING CODE STANDARD 24-1
FLAT GLASS

Based on ASTM Standard C 1036-85, Standard Specification for Flat Glass. Extracted, with permission,
from the *Annual Book of ASTM Standards,* copyright American Society for Testing and Materials,
100 Barr Harbor Drive, West Conshohocken, PA 19428

See Sections 2401.2 and 2401.4, *Uniform Building Code*

SECTION 24.101 — SCOPE

This standard provides general material requirements for glass regulated by the Building Code.

SECTION 24.102 — DEFINITIONS

For the purpose of this standard, certain terms are defined as follows:

FLOAT GLASS is glass formed in a continuous ribbon by floating molten glass on a bath of molten tin in a controlled atmosphere; the glass is smooth with parallel surfaces and requires no further treatment.

FULLY TEMPERED GLASS is regular glass that has been heated and quenched in a controlled operation to provide a high level of surface compression; its strength is roughly four times that of regular glass for most types of loads; when fractured, it breaks into small, relatively harmless particles; it is a safety glazing material.

HEAT-STRENGTHENED GLASS is regular glass that has been heated and quenched in a controlled operation to provide a degree of surface compression; its strength is roughly two times that of regular glass; when fractured, this glass breaks into large fragments, much like regular glass; it is not a safety glazing material.

INSULATING GLASS is factory-fabricated double glazing with the periphery of the air space sealed to minimize infiltration of water vapor.

LAMINATED GLASS is a sandwich of two or more glass plies bonded together with a resilient plastic interlayer, normally polyvinyl butyral; when this glass breaks, the fragments are held together by the plastic interlayer.

PATTERNED GLASS is rolled glass with a pattern or texture impressed on one or both surfaces; some glasses with shallow patterns can be tempered or heat strengthened.

REGULAR (ANNEALED) GLASS is sheet (window) glass and plate glass with smooth surfaces that have not been modified after manufacture; it breaks into large pieces; although the terms "sheet" and "plate glass" are commonly used, they are misnomers since virtually all glass is made by the float process; this glass may be clear or tinted.

SAFETY GLASS is glass designed to minimize cutting and piercing injuries when impacted by people; fully tempered glass, laminated glass and wired glass are recognized safety glazing materials.

TEMPERED GLASS. See "fully tempered glass."

WIRED GLASS is a single sheet of glass which has had a wire mesh embedded in roughly the thickness center during production; this glass, coupled with a suitable framing system, is fire rated; for low levels of impact, the wire in the glass will retain the broken fragments.

SECTION 24.103 — DESIGN CRITERIA

The maximum allowable areas of glass subjected to wind loads, snow loads and dead loads shall not be greater than those determined from Table 24-A of this code.

Table 24-1-A lists the coefficients of variation for various glass types. These values are used as part of the basis for Table 24-A of this code. Each value applies for all glass products using each glass type. For example, the value for annealed glass would apply for laminated annealed glass and insulating glass units using annealed glass panes, as well as for single annealed glass.

In cases where more than one glass type is used in a fabricated glass product (e.g., laminated glass, insulating glass), the more conservative values from Table 24-1-A apply.

SECTION 24.104 — FLOAT GLASS

24.104.1 Thickness. For each nominal thickness, the furnished glass thickness shall not be less than that listed in Table 24-1-B.

24.104.2 Allowable Imperfections. Imperfections shall not exceed those allowed in Table 24-1-C.

SECTION 24.105 — WIRED GLASS

24.105.1 Wire. The diameter of wires shall be from 0.017 inch to 0.025 inch (0.43 mm to 0.64 mm). Discoloration and slight distortion of wire is permissible.

24.105.2 Mesh. Diamond mesh shall be welded and the opening in mesh shall not exceed $1^1/_4$ inches (31.8 mm) measured across diagonals of the diamond; square mesh shall be welded and the openings in mesh shall not exceed $5/_8$ inch (15.9 mm) measured along a side of the square; parallel stand—spacing as specified.

24.105.3 Thickness. The minimum thickness shall not be less than that listed in Table 24-1-D.

SECTION 24.106 — PATTERNED GLASS

24.106.1 Thickness. The thickness shall not be less than that listed in Table 24-1-E for each nominal thickness.

24.106.2 Fire Cracks and Stones. Glass shall not have continuous fire cracks and stones that can cause spontaneous breakage in annealed glass.

SECTION 24.107 — A GLOSSARY OF TERMS FOR GLASS IMPERFECTIONS

For the purpose of this standard, certain terms are defined as follows:

CRUSH is a lightly pitted area resulting in a dull gray appearance over the region.

DIGS are deep, short scratches.

DIRT is a small particle of foreign matter embedded in the glass surface.

GASEOUS INCLUSIONS are round or elongated bubbles in the glass.

KNOT is a transparent area of incompletely assimilated glass having an irregular knotty or tangled appearance.

LINES are fine cords or strings, usually on the surface of sheet glass.

OPEN GASEOUS INCLUSIONS are bubbles at the surface of glass which are open, leaving a cavity in the finished surface.

PROCESS SURFACE DEFECTS. The surfaces of plate glass have very fine surface defects remaining from the grinding and polishing process, consisting of fine pits and cracks which are denoted as "finish." When this condition is visible it is called "short finish." Float glass can also have some slight surface defects which originate in the process. These can be small particles of foreign materials on either surface or slight defects in the bottom (float) surface.

REAM is inclusions within the glass or layers or strings of glass which are not homogeneous with the main body of the glass.

RUBS are abrasions of the glass surface producing a frosted appearance. A rub differs from a scratch in having appreciable width.

SCRATCHES are any marking or tearing of the surface produced in manufacturing or handling which appear as though they were done by a sharp or rough instrument.

SMOKE is streaked areas appearing as slight discoloration.

STONES are any crystalline inclusions embedded in the glass.

STRINGS are transparent lines appearing as though a thread of glass had been incorporated into the sheets.

WAVES are defects resulting from irregularities of the surface of the glass, making objects viewed at varying angles appear wavy or bent.

TABLE 24-1-A—COEFFICIENTS OF VARIATION FOR GLASS STRENGTH

GLASS TYPE	COEFFICIENT OF VARIATION
Regular (annealed)	0.25
Heat-strengthened	0.15
Fully tempered	0.10

TABLE 24-1-B—MINIMUM ALLOWABLE THICKNESSES FOR FLOAT GLASS

NOMINAL THICKNESS OR DESIGNATION (inch)	MINIMUM ALLOWABLE THICKNESS (inch)
× 25.4 for mm	
Single	0.085
Lami	0.102
Double-$^1/_8$ in.	0.115
$^5/_{32}$ in.	0.149
$^3/_{16}$ in	0.180
$^7/_{32}$ in.	0.200
$^1/_4$ in.	0.219
$^5/_{16}$ in.	0.292
$^3/_8$ in.	0.355
$^1/_2$ in.	0.469
$^5/_8$ in.	0.595
$^3/_4$ in.	0.719
$^7/_8$ in.	0.844

TABLE 24-1-C—MAXIMUM ALLOWABLE IMPERFECTIONS FOR THICKNESSES OF $^1/_4$ INCH (6.4 mm) OR LESS[1]

IMPERFECTIONS	UP TO 2.5 m²		2.5 TO 7.0 m²		OVER 7.0 m²	
	Central[2]	Outer[2]	Central[2]	Outer[2]	Central[2]	Outer[2]
Gaseous inclusions, maximum size[3]	1.6 mm[4,5]	2.4 mm[4,5]	3.2 mm[4,5]	4.8 mm[4,5]	6.4 mm[4,5]	6.4 mm[4,5]
Open or translucent gaseous inclusions, maximum size[3]	1.2 mm[4,5]	1.6 mm[4,5]	1.2 mm[4,5]	1.6 mm[4,5]	6.4 mm[4,5]	6.4 mm[4,5]
Knots, dirt and stones, maximum size[3]	0.4 mm[4]	0.8 mm[4]	1.6 mm[4]	1.6 mm[4]	3.2 mm[4]	3.2 mm[4]
Scratches and rubs (intensity)	medium[6]	medium[6]	medium[6]	heavy[6]	heavy[6]	heavy[6]
Crush (intensity, maximum length)	medium[6] <1.6 mm	medium[6] <2.4 mm	medium[6] <3.2 mm	heavy[6] <4.8 mm	heavy[6] <6.4 mm	heavy[6] <6.4 mm
Digs, maximum length	1.6 mm[7]	2.4 mm[7]	3.2 mm[4]	4.8 mm[4]	6.4 mm[4]	6.4 mm[4]
Ream, strings, lines and other linear distortion (maximum angle or intensity)	45°[8] or medium[9]		90°[8] or heavy		90°[8] or heavy	
Wave (intensity)	medium[10]	medium[10]	medium[10]	heavy[10]	heavy[10]	heavy[10]
Process surface imperfections (intensity)	medium[11]	medium[11]	medium[11]	heavy[11]	heavy[11]	heavy[11]

[1]Glass greater than 6.0 mm ($^1/_4$ in.) in thickness may contain proportionally more and larger imperfections.

[2]The central area is considered to form an oval or circle centered on the light whose axes or diameters do not exceed 80 percent of the overall dimension. The remaining area is considered the outer area.

[3]Gaseous inclusions, knots, dirt and stones may be round or elongated. For elongated imperfections of this type(s) the maximum size specified shall be determined by adding the length and width of the imperfection and dividing by two, for example $(l + 11)/2$.

[4]Separated by at least 305 mm (12 in.).

[5]For imperfections of a smaller size or of less intensity, the minimum separation shall be proportionately less. The larger of the two imperfections shall govern the separation. Imperfections not specifically mentioned shall be compared to the imperfection they most closely resemble.

[6]*Intensity (scratches, rubs and crush)*—When looking through the glass and perpendicular to it, using daylight without direct sunlight or with background light suitable for observing each type of imperfection, the imperfection shall not be detectable at distances greater than the following, except for heavy intensity (see Note 3).

Intensity	Distance
Faint	203 mm
Light	914 mm
Medium	3.3 m
Heavy	detected at distances greater than 3.3 m

[7]Separated by at least 610 mm (24 in.).

[8]Vision interference angle (see Note 1).

[9]*Intensity (ream, strings, lines and other linear distortion)*—When evaluated using the shadowgraph, the intensities of these imperfections are defined as having a shadowgraph readout at distances greater than or equal to the following (see Note 2).

Intensity	Minimum Distance, mm
Light	76
Medium	51
Heavy	25

[10]*Intensity (wave)*—When evaluated using the shadowgraph, the intensities of wave are defined as having shadowgraph readouts at distances greater than or equal to the following (see Note 2).

Intensity	Minimum Distance, mm
Medium	254
Heavy	152

[11]*Intensity (process surface imperfections)*—When viewed in normal reflected light, the imperfections are classified as follows: faint—visible only to the trained eye; light—just noticeable; medium—visible as a slight grayish haze; and heavy—readily visible as a cloudy surface.

NOTE 1: *Ream, Strings and Distortion (Method A)*—Place specimen in a vertical position at a distance of approximately 914 mm from a brick wall or similar background showing straight lines. The viewer shall look through the sample at a distance of 914 mm from the sample using daylight without direct sunlight or with background light suitable for observing each type of imperfection. View the sample at an angle to the surface of not less than vision interference angle in Table 24-1-C, for the applicable glass. The line of vision shall be perpendicular to the wall.

NOTE 2: *Ream, Strings, Lines and Wave (Method B, Shadowgraph)*—Focus a light projector with a 500-W lamp, or equivalent, and an objective lens with an approximate 51-mm aperture and an approximate 305-mm focal length on a flat white projection screen positioned 8 m from the light source in a dark room. Place the glass in a vertical position parallel to the screen between the light and the screen. Move the glass slowly toward the screen with a circular motion in the plane perpendicular to the light beam. The shadowgraph readout is the distance at which the distortion just blends with the general shadow of the glass on the screen.

NOTE 3: *Scratches, Rubs, Stones and Gaseous Inclusions*—Place samples in a vertical position approximately 914 mm from the viewer's position. The viewer shall look through the sample using daylight without direct sunlight or with background light suitable for observing each type of imperfection.

TABLE 24-1-D—MINIMUM ALLOWABLE THICKNESSES FOR WIRED GLASS

NOMINAL THICKNESS (inch)	MINIMUM ALLOWABLE THICKNESS (inch)
× 25.4 for mm	
$7/32$	0.203
$1/4$	0.250
$3/8$	0.328

TABLE 24-1-E—MINIMUM ALLOWABLE THICKNESSES FOR PATTERNED GLASS

NOMINAL THICKNESS OR DESIGNATION (inch)	MINIMUM ALLOWABLE THICKNESS (inch)
× 25.4 for mm	
SS	0.085
DS	0.110
$1/8$	0.110
$5/32$	0.142
$3/16$	0.172
$7/32$	0.203
$1/4$	0.234
$5/16$	0.281
$3/8$	0.344

UNIFORM BUILDING CODE STANDARD 24-2
SAFETY GLAZING

Part I—Based on Safety Standard for Architectural Glazing Materials (16 C.F.R., Part 1201) of the United States Consumer Product Safety Commission

See Sections 2401.2, 2401.4, 2406.2, 2406.3, 2406.5 and 2408.1, *Uniform Building Code*

SECTION 24.201 — SCOPE

Part I of this standard covers safety glazing materials for use in areas subject to human impact as specified in this code. Part I is applicable to safety glazing material other than polished wired glass or glazing in wardrobe doors.

SECTION 24.202 — DEFINITIONS

For the purpose of this part, the definitions in Section 24.102 of UBC Standard 24-1 are applicable.

SECTION 24.203 — IDENTIFICATION

Each light of safety glazing material shall be identified in accordance with Sections 2402 and 2406.2 of this code and in addition with the following:

1. The category class as noted in Table 24-2-A shall be specified as part of a permanent label.

2. Safety plastic that only meets the requirements of Section 24.206.4 entitled "Aging Tests (for plastic used in indoor applications only)" shall bear a statement INDOOR USE ONLY as part of a permanent label.

3. Organic-coated glass that meets the requirements of Section 24.206.3.2, entitled "Specimen weathering and test—organic-coated glass" and tested for exposure from one side only, shall bear a permanent label on the coating stating GLAZE THIS SIDE IN and shall bear in the central 50 percent of the surface area the following message in letters at least $^{1}/_{4}$ inch (6.4 mm) high: SEE PERMANENT LABEL FOR IMPORTANT MOUNTING INSTRUCTION. The latter message shall be attached to either side of the glazing by any means which shall ensure the message will remain in place until installation.

SECTION 24.204 — CATEGORY CLASSIFICATION

Glazing required to conform with Part I of this standard shall be classified as Category I or II glazing in accordance with the impact test requirements in Section 24.206.1. Glass classified as Category I glazing shall not be used where Category II glass is required by Table 24-2-A. The categories noted in the table are based on the maximum size in square feet of the largest single glazing in the unit and the intended use of the unit.

SECTION 24.205 — SPECIMENS TO BE TESTED

24.205.1 Thickness. The thickness of the samples to be tested shall be recorded as a nominal thickness for glass as set forth in UBC Standard 24-1.

24.205.2 Specimens.

24.205.2.1 Classification. Safety glazing panels shall be classed in accordance with their size as "limited" or "unlimited" as set forth in Table 24-2-B.

24.205.2.2 Condition of specimens. All specimens shall be tested as supplied by the manufacturer following removal of any temporary protective masking materials. Tests shall not commence before the specimens have been stored in the laboratory for four hours. Specimens shall be arranged to permit free circulation of air to all surfaces during this period.

24.205.2.3 Number of specimens. For impact test of any safety glazing material, four specimens of the thickness and size described in Section 24.205.2.1 shall be provided.

For impact test after aging of plastic used in indoor applications, four specimens of the thickness and size described in Section 24.205.2.1 shall be provided.

For boil test, three specimens 12 inches by 12 inches (305 mm by 305 mm), manufactured in a manner identical to the impact specimens and of like thickness, shall be provided.

For weathering test, the number of test specimens shall comply with the following and be of identical manufacture as the impact specimens and of like thickness: For plastic, 10 specimens, $^{1}/_{2}$ inch by 5 inches (13 mm by 127 mm); for orientation specified, six organic-coated glass specimens, 2 inches by 6 inches (51 mm by 152.4 mm); for orientation unspecified, nine organic-coated glass specimens, 2 inches by 6 inches (51 mm by 152.4 mm), except that when the glazing material is symmetric across its thickness, six specimens may be used.

Samples for boil and weathering tests shall be cut from production samples of the size and thickness submitted for impact testing.

SECTION 24.206 — TEST SPECIFICATIONS

24.206.1 Impact Test.

24.206.1.1 General. Unless it has been established that specimens have a modulus of elasticity less than 750,000 psi (5171 MPa) and a Rockwell hardness less than 140 M or R scale, four specimens shall be impact tested in accordance with this section.

24.206.1.2 Apparatus. The test apparatus consists of two basic parts: (1) the test frame, and (2) the impactor.

24.206.1.2.1 Test frame. The test frame shall be designed to minimize movement and deflection of its members during testing. For this purpose, the structural framing and bracing members shall be steel angles [L5 × 3 × $^{1}/_{4}$ (L127 × 76 × 6.4)] or channels [C4 × 7.25 (C100 × 11)], or other sections and materials of equal or greater rigidity, as shown in Figure 24-2-1.

This structural framing shall be welded or securely bolted at the corners to minimize racking or twisting during testing. Also, it shall be securely bolted to the floor and braced by one of the alternate methods shown in Figure 24-2-1.

The clamping frame for securing the test specimen on all four edges shall be reinforced at the corners. See Detail A of Figure 24-2-1. Other materials may be used, provided there is positive assurance that the test specimen will contact only the neoprene strips.

Pressures on the test specimen shall be controlled, and the compression of the neoprene strips shall be between 10 and 15 percent of the original thickness of the neoprene. Securing methods such as wing bolts as shown in Detail A of Figure 24-2-1 and clamps shall be uniformly spaced no greater than 18 inches (457.2 mm) apart with no fewer than two on any edge. To limit the compression of the neoprene and prevent distortion of the clamping frame, metal shims of an appropriate thickness shall be used as shown in Detail A of Figure 24-2-1.

Any reasonable means may be used to secure the clamping frame to the test frame so long as the mounting is secure and the pressure on the glazing in the clamping frame is not significantly altered when the clamping frame is removed.

24.206.1.2.2 Impactor. The impactor shall be a standard leather punching bag modified as shown in Figure 24-2-3. The bag shall be filled with No. $7^1/_2$ [0.095 inch (2.4 mm) diameter] chilled lead shot to a total weight of completed assembly of 100 pounds ± 4 ounces (45.4 kg ± 0.11 kg). The rubber bladder shall be left in place and filled through a hole cut into the upper part. After filling the rubber bladder, the top shall either be twisted around the threaded metal rod below the metal sleeve or pulled over the metal sleeve and tied with a cord or leather thong. Note that the hanging strap shall be removed. The bag shall be laced in the normal manner. The exterior of the bag shall be completely covered with $1/_2$-inch (12.7 mm) tape as indicated in Figure 24-2-3.

24.206.1.3 Procedure. The impacting object (shot bag), constructed in accordance with Figure 24-2-3, shall be suspended from an overhead support so located that the impacting object, when at rest will, at its maximum diameter, be no more than $1/_2$ inch (13 mm) from the surface of the specimen and no more than 2 inches (50.8 mm) from the center of the specimen (see Figure 24-2-1).

Each specimen shall be centered within the neoprene mounting strips before impacting, such that approximately $3/_8$-inch (9.53 mm) grip is provided on each edge of the specimen.

Specimens for Category I shall be impacted one time from a drop height of 18 inches to $18^1/_2$ inches (457 mm to 469.9 mm). Specimens for Category II shall be impacted one time from a drop height of 48 inches to $48^1/_2$ inches (1219 mm to 1231.9 mm). For all specimens that are not symmetric from surface to surface, an equal number of specimens shall be impacted on each side. The drop height is to be measured from the maximum diameter of the impacting object to the horizontal center line of the specimen (see Figure 24-2-1). The impacting object shall be stabilized before release.

24.206.1.4 Interpretation of results. A glazing material shall be judged to pass the impact test if each of the four specimens tested meets any one of the following criteria:

1. When breakage occurs (numerous cracks and fissures may occur), no opening shall develop in the test sample through which a 3-inch-diameter (76.2 mm) solid steel sphere, weighing 4 pounds ± 3 ounces (18.14 kg ± 0.085 kg), passes when placed (not dropped) in the opening and permitted to remain for a period of one second. For this criterion, the sample, after being impacted, shall be placed, while remaining in the clamping frame, in a horizontal, impact side-up position with a minimum of 1 foot (305 mm) of free space immediately beneath the specimen.

2. When breakage occurs, what appear to be the 10 largest particles shall be selected within five minutes subsequent to the test and shall weigh no more than the equivalent weight of 10 square inches (6452 mm²) of the original specimen. For the purposes of this section, "particle" means a portion of a broken test specimen which is determined by identifying the smallest possible

perimeter around all points in the portion of the broken test specimen, always passing along cracks or exposed surfaces.

3. The specimen remains intact after the drop test, though not necessarily remaining within the clamping frame.

24.206.2 Boil Test (for laminated glass only).

24.206.2.1 General. The test is made to determine the probable effect of exposure to high temperature and humidity conditions for a long period of time.

24.206.2.2 Procedure. Three 12- by 12-inch (305 mm by 305 mm) flat specimens, as submitted, shall be immersed vertically on edge in water at 150°F ± 5°F (65.5°C ± 3°C) for three minutes and then quickly transferred to and similarly immersed in boiling water. The rack shall be positioned so that each specimen is surrounded by at least 1 inch (25.4 mm) of water. The specimen shall be kept in the boiling water for two hours and then removed.

24.206.2.3 Interpretation of results. The glass itself may crack in this test, but bubbles or other defects shall not develop more than $1/_2$ inch (12.7 mm) from the outer edge of the specimen or from any cracks that may develop. Any specimen in which the glass cracks to such an extent that the results are confused shall be discarded without prejudice and another specimen shall be tested in its stead.

24.206.3 Weathering Tests (for organic-coated glass used in exterior exposure applications only).

24.206.3.1 Purpose. The purpose of these tests is to determine whether these safety glazing materials will successfully retain their safety characteristics after exposure to weathering conditions for an extended period of time. Specimens shall be exposed to weathering and then tested in accordance with this subsection.

24.206.3.2 Specimen weathering and tests—organic-coated glass.

24.206.3.2.1 Weathering.

24.206.3.2.1.1 Apparatus. The specimens shall be subject to exposure in a xenon arc (water-cooled) Weather-Ometer employing a lamp rated at 6,500 watts and automatic light-monitoring and control systems. Borosilicate inner and outer filters shall be used. An appropriate water-spray cycle shall be used. Operating procedures shall be in accordance with ASTM Recommended Practice for Operating Light- and Water-exposure Apparatus (Xenon-arc Type) for Exposure of Nonmetallic Materials.

24.206.3.2.1.2 Procedure. The specimens shall be retained in the Weather-Ometer for a period of 1,200 ± 1 hour, and exposed to a radiant flux of 50 microwatts per square centimeter (12 calories per second per square centimeter) while monitoring at a wavelength of 340 nanometers.

For organic-coated glass having orientation specified, three specimens shall be mounted with the surface that is intended to be oriented indoors faced away from the radiation source; the other three specimens shall be kept in darkness at 73°F (23°C) for use as controls.

For organic-coated glass having orientation unspecified, three specimens shall be mounted with one of the surfaces toward the radiation, three specimens shall be mounted with the other surface toward the radiation, and three specimens shall be kept in darkness at 73°F (23°C) for use as controls. When the glazing material is symmetric across its thickness, three specimens shall be irradiated.

24.206.3.2.2 Interpretation of results. Specimens shall be judged satisfactory if they pass the adhesion test and the tensile strength test.

24.206.3.2.2.1 Adhesion test. The specimens for this test are the six 2-inch by 6-inch (51 mm by 152.4 mm) specimens prepared for the weathering test. The specimens shall be conditioned just prior to the performance of the adhesion test at 73.5°F ± 3.5°F (23°C ± 2°C) and 50 percent ± 2 percent relative humidity for 24 hours.

The test apparatus shall consist of a constant rate of extension (CRE)-type tensile tester with the moving crosshead set to move at 12 inches per minute (305 mm/min.) and load range such that the average peel force will fall at 30 percent to 50 percent of full scale, and a cutter containing new razor blades for cutting 1-inch-wide (25.4 mm) specimens (use blades one time only).

Using the 1-inch (25.4 mm) razor cutter, cut a straight strip of the organic coating in the lengthwise direction of the glass sample. Peel back about 2 inches (51 mm) of one end of the 1-inch-wide (25.4 mm) organic strip. Attach a strip of pressure-sensitive tape to the side of the organic strip opposite the adhesive to extend this free end to about 8 inches (203.2 mm) in length. Place the end of the glass panel from which the organic strip was removed in the lower clamp of the tensile tester and the free end of the tape in the upper clamp. Peel the remainder of the organic strip from the glass mechanically and obtain a record of the peel value. Determine the average pull for each specimen from the chart record.

The organic-coated glass adhesion shall be judged satisfactory if the average adhesion value of the three exposed specimens is no less than 90 percent of the average of the adhesion value of the three control specimens.

24.206.3.2.2.2 Tensile strength test. The samples for this test are the same six 2-inch by 6-inch (50.8 mm by 152.4 mm) specimens used in the adhesion test and conditioned as in Section 24.206.3.2.1.

The CRE tensile tester shall be set as follows: gage length— 2 inches (50.8 mm); crosshead speed—2 inches per minute (50.8 mm/min.); load range—set full-scale load so that specimens will break at 30 percent to 60 percent of full scale.

Using a $^1/_2$-inch (13 mm) razor cutter (use blade one time only), cut a straight strip of the organic coating in the lengthwise direction of the glass sample for the full 6-inch (152.4 mm) length. Carefully peel this strip from the glass panel and test it for breaking strength in the tensile tester.

The organic coating tensile strength shall be judged satisfactory if the average tensile value of the three exposed specimens is no less than 75 percent of the average of the three control specimens.

24.206.4 Aging Tests (for plastics used in indoor applications only.)

24.206.4.1 Purpose. The purpose of this test is to determine whether plastic for indoor use only will successfully retain its safety characteristics after exposure to simulated aging conditions for an extended period of time.

24.206.4.2 Apparatus. The safety glazing materials shall be subjected to exposure to warm, humid and dry cycles, using the following apparatus:

24.206.4.2.1 Balance. A balance capable of weighing accurately of 0.05 percent for a test specimen weighing 0.250 pound (0.113 kg) or less, and to 0.1 percent for a test specimen weighing over 0.250 pound (0.113 kg).

24.206.4.2.2 Oven. A circulating-air oven capable of maintaining the required temperature of test within ± 1.8°F (± 1°C).

24.206.4.2.3 Containers. Noncorroding containers with a shelf to support the test specimen above the solution used for maintaining the required humidity. The container shall be tightly sealed ex-

cept for a small capillary which permits release of vapor pressure that might otherwise lift the top off the container. Each test specimen shall be tested, preferably in a separate container.

24.206.4.2.4 Desiccator. A clean, dry, uncharged desiccator or equivalent closed container in which to bring test specimens to room temperature.

24.206.4.2.5 Absorbent cloth. Clean, nonlinting absorbent cloth for use in wiping exudation or condensed moisture from test specimens.

24.206.4.2.6 Micrometer. A micrometer capable of measuring dimensions of test specimens to 0.001 inch (0.0254 mm).

24.206.4.2.7 Cold box. A cold box capable of maintaining the required temperature of test within ± 5.4°F (± 3°C).

24.206.4.3 Procedure. The four plastic specimens shall be subjected to 10 complete humid/dry test cycles (480 hours) in accordance with the following:

1. The test cycle shall be as follows: 24 hours at 140°F (60°C) and 95 percent humidity, followed by 24 hours at 140°F (60°C) in the oven.

2. Condition the specimen, weigh and measure dimensions as follows. One additional specimen shall be retained unexposed as a control for the effects of the exposure cycling.

   2.1 **Conditioning.** Condition the test specimens at 73.4°F ± 3.6°F (23°C ± 2°C) and 50 ± 5 percent relative humidity for not less than 40 hours prior to test.

   2.2 **Test conditions.** Conduct tests in the Standard Laboratory Atmosphere of 73.4°F ± 3.6°F (23°C ± 2°C) and 50 ± 5 percent relative humidity, unless otherwise specified in the test methods or in this specification. In cases of disagreement, the tolerances shall be 1.8°F (1°C) and ± 2 percent relative humidity.

   2.3 **Measurements of test specimens.** The following measurements shall be made on conditioned test specimens prior to testing, after reconditioning at the end of a test procedure, and at any intermediate stage as prescribed in the test procedures:

      Weight—The weight within 0.05 percent if the specimen weighs 0.250 pound (0.113 kg) or less, and within 0.1 percent if the specimen exceeds 0.250 pound (0.113 kg) in weight.

      Dimensions—The thickness to 0.001 inch (0.03 mm), the plane dimension in the direction of injection or transfer to 0.001 inch (0.03 mm), and the plane dimension across the direction of injection or transfer to 0.001 inch (0.03 mm).

      Dimensions of compression-molded specimen—The thickness to 0.001 inch (0.03 mm), and the perpendicular dimensions in the plane at right angles to the direction of molding to 0.001 inch (0.03 mm).

3. Expose the specimen for 24 hours on the shelf of a container maintained at 140°F ± 1.8°F (60°C ± 1°C) in the oven, and containing a saturated solution of sodium sulfate to maintain a relative humidity of 95 percent.

4. Remove the specimen from the container, place it in the uncharged desiccator and bring to room temperature.

5. Wipe the specimen with the absorbent cloth, then weigh, measure dimensions and examine visually. Noticeable qualitative changes in surfaces, outline and general appearance of the test specimen shall be recorded after each stage of the testing procedure. These changes include color, surface irregularities, odor and

splits. Changes shall also be noted as they occur, especially those which alter the shape so that intended dimensions are no longer significant.

6. Within two hours after completion of the operation described in Item 3, expose the specimen for 24 hours in the oven at 140°F ± 1.8°F (60°C ± 1°C).

7. Place the specimen in the uncharged desiccator and bring to room temperature.

24.206.4.4 Interpretation of results. Specimens shall be judged satisfactory if, after the indoor aging test, they again pass the impact test in Section 24.206.1.

Part II—Based on Performance Specifications and Methods of Test for Transparent Safety Glazing Material Used in Buildings, ANSI Z97.1-1975 of the American National Standards Institute, Inc.

See Sections 2401.2, 2401.4, 2406.3 and 2406.5, *Uniform Building Code*

SECTION 24.207 — SCOPE

Part II of this standard covers safety glazing materials for use in areas subject to human impact as specified in this code. Part II is applicable to polished wired glass and glazing in wardrobe doors.

SECTION 24.208 — DEFINITIONS

For the purpose of this part, the definitions in Section 24.102 of UBC Standard 24-1 are applicable.

SECTION 24.209 — IDENTIFICATION

Each light of safety glazing material shall be identified in accordance with Sections 2402 and 2406.2 of this code and, in addition, safety plastic that only meets the requirements of Section 24.211.4 entitled "Aging Tests (for plastics used in indoor applications only)" shall bear the statement INDOOR USE ONLY as part of a permanent label.

SECTION 24.210 — SPECIMENS TO BE TESTED

The specimens, size and number shall be in accordance with the requirements of Section 24.205.

SECTION 24.211 — TEST SPECIFICATIONS

24.211.1 Impact Test.

24.211.1.1 General. The specimens tested shall be in accordance with the requirements of Section 24.206.1.1

24.211.1.2 Apparatus. The test apparatus requirements for the impact test shall be in accordance with Section 24.206.1.2.

24.211.1.3 Procedure. The test procedure requirements for the impact test shall be in accordance with Section 24.206.1.3, except the specimen shall be struck with the impactor object swinging in a pendulum arc from a drop height of 12 inches (305 mm). When no breakage occurs, the same specimen shall again be impacted at a drop of 18 inches (457 mm), and if no breakage occurs, again at 48 inches (1219 mm).

24.211.1.4 Interpretation of results. The impact test shall be judged to have been satisfactorily completed if any one of the fol-

lowing safety criteria shall be met by each of the four specimens tested:

1. When breakage occurs at 12 inches (305 mm), 18 inches (457 mm) or 48 inches (1219 mm), numerous cracks and fissures may occur, but a 3-inch-diameter (76 mm) sphere shall not be freely passed.

2. When disintegration occurs at 12 inches (305 mm), 18 inches (457 mm) or 48 inches (1291 mm), the 10 largest crack-free particles selected five minutes subsequent to the test shall weigh no more than the equivalent weight of 10 square inches (6452 mm²) of the original test specimen.

NOTE: Breakage by other means could produce particles exceeding this weight.

3. When breakage occurs at 12 inches (305 mm), 18 inches (457 mm) or 48 inches (1291 mm), the stiffness and hardness of the specimen shall be determined. A modulus of elasticity less than 750,000 psi (5171 MPa) and a Rockwell hardness less than 140 M or R scale shall indicate satisfactory compliance.

4. The specimen remains intact after one 48-inch (1219 mm) drop test, though not necessarily remaining within the clamping frame.

24.211.2 Boil Test (for laminated glass only). The boil test shall be in accordance with the requirements of Section 24.206.2.

24.211.3 Weathering Tests (for plastic and organic-coated glass used in exterior exposure applications only).

24.211.3.1 General. The purpose of these tests is to determine whether these safety glazing materials will successfully retain their safety characteristics after exposure to weathering conditions for an extended period of time. Specimens shall be exposed to simulated weathering and then tested in accordance with this subsection.

24.211.3.2 Specimen weathering and tests—organic-coated glass.

24.211.3.2.1 Weathering.

24.211.3.2.1.1 Apparatus. The specimens shall be subject to exposure in a twin enclosed carbon-arc lamp apparatus, such as specified as Type D or DH in ASTM Recommended Practice for Operating Light- and Water-exposure Apparatus (Carbon-arc Type) for exposure of nonmetallic materials, or equivalent.

24.211.3.2.1.2 Procedure. The specimens shall be exposed for 2,000 hours in accordance with ASTM Recommended Practice for Operating Light- and Water-exposure Apparatus (Carbon-arc Type). For the organic-coated glass, three specimens with the side marked for exterior exposure shall be exposed to the energy source. The other three specimens of organic-coated glass are controls and shall be held in darkness at 73.5°F ± 3.5°F (23°C ± 2°C) until needed.

24.211.3.2.2 Interpretation of results. The specimen test after weathering shall be in accordance with the requirements of Section 24.206.3.2.2.

24.211.3.3 Specimen weathering and test—plastic material.

24.211.3.3.1 Weathering.

24.211.3.3.1.1 Apparatus. The specimen shall be subjected to exposure by any one of the following methods:

1. Twin enclosed carbon-arc such as specified as Type D or DH in ASTM G23-69 (1975).

2. 6,000 or 6,500 watt xenon-arc light exposure apparatus as specified as Type B or BH in ASTM G26-77.

3. Fixed-rack outdoor exposure in south Florida.

24.211.3.3.1.2 Procedure. Depending upon the exposure method chosen in Section 24.211.3.3.1.1, the appropriate procedure from the following shall apply:

1. **Twin-carbon arc.** The panel shall be exposed for 2,000 hours in accordance with ASTM D1499-64.

2. **Xenon-arc apparatus.** The panel shall be exposed for 2,900 hours in accordance with ASTM G 26-77 using method A with 102 minutes of light-only exposure and 18 minutes of water spray and light exposure.

3. **Outdoor exposure.** The unbacked panel shall be exposed for one year on a fixed rack at station latitude in south Florida.

24.211.3.3.2 Tests after weathering. Specimens shall be evaluated before and after exposure in accordance with the Charpy un-notched impact test. The exposed specimen shall be tested with the exposed surface subjected to tension. In the case of thin materials, the span of the specimen shall be reduced to 2 inches (51 mm) to avoid having the specimen bend enough to slip between the supports without breaking. The average of five specimens shall be reported. Plastic material shall be acceptable for safety glazing if the impact strength is not reduced by more than 25 percent after exposure. Some discoloration may develop, but defects other than this discoloration shall not develop. Bubbles or other noticeable decomposition shall not develop in the irradiated portion.

24.211.4 Aging Tests (for plastic used in indoor applications only). The aging tests shall be in accordance with the requirements of Section 24.206.4.3, Item 3, except that the humidity shall be 88 percent in Section 24.206.4.3, Item 3 and 85 to 95 percent in Section 24.206.4.3, Item 3.

TABLE 24-2-A—MINIMUM CATEGORY CLASSIFICATION OF GLAZING

SURFACE AREA OF ONE SIDE OF SINGLE GLAZING IN THE UNIT	GLAZING IN STORM OR COMBINATION DOORS (Category Class)	GLAZING IN DOORS (Category Class)	FIXED GLAZED PANELS (Category Class)	GLAZING IN DOORS AND ENCLOSURES FOR BATHTUBS AND SHOWERS (Category Class)	SLIDING GLASS DOORS PATIO TYPE) (Category Class)
9 square feet (0.837 m^2) or less of surface area	I	I	I	II	II
More than 9 square feet (0.837 m^2) of surface area	II	II	II		

TABLE 24-2-B—DESCRIPTION OF SPECIMENS

CLASSIFICATION	DIMENSIONS OF SPECIMEN
Limited (for all sizes up to and including dimensions of specimens tested)	Largest size commercially produced by the manufacturer up to 34 inches by 76 inches (864 mm by 1930 mm)
Unlimited (for all sizes)	34 inches by 76 inches (864 mm by 1930 mm)

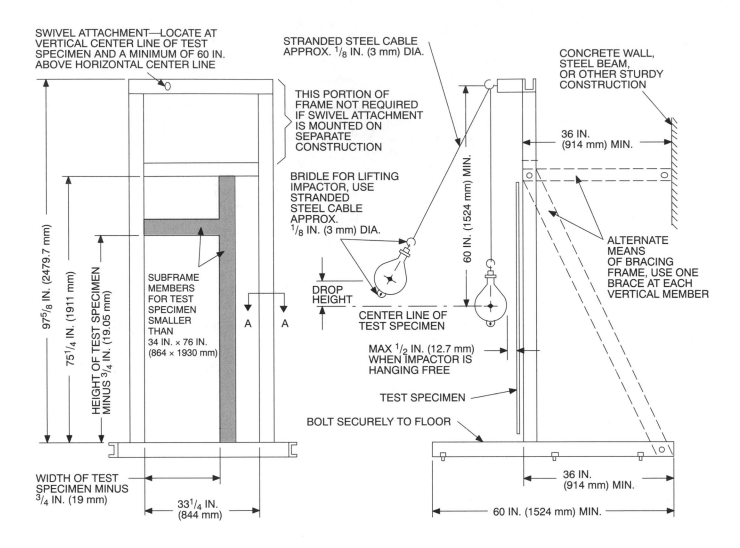

NOTE: Clamping frame for holding test specimen not shown.

FIGURE 24-2-1—TEST FRAME

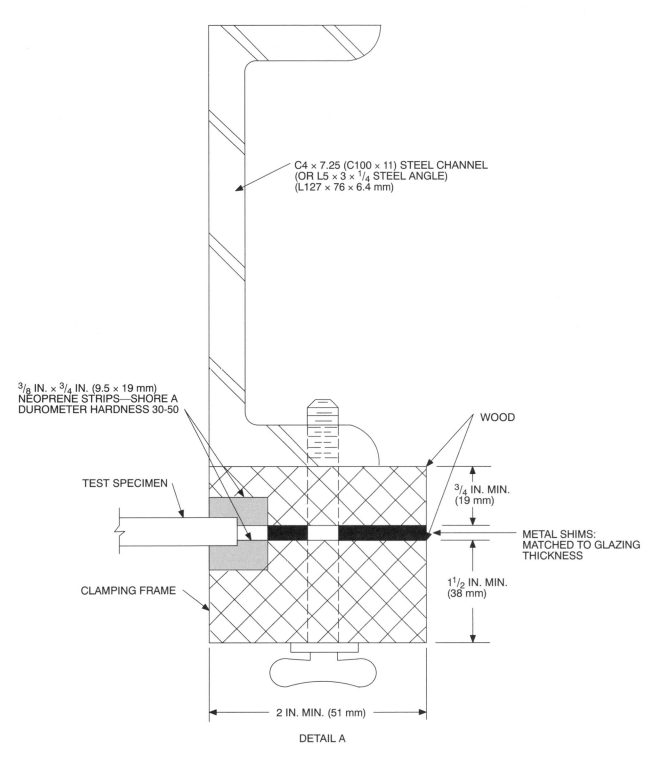

C4 × 7.25 (C100 × 11) STEEL CHANNEL
(OR L5 × 3 × $^1/_4$ STEEL ANGLE)
(L127 × 76 × 6.4 mm)

$^3/_8$ IN. × $^3/_4$ IN. (9.5 × 19 mm)
NEOPRENE STRIPS—SHORE A
DUROMETER HARDNESS 30-50

WOOD

TEST SPECIMEN

$^3/_4$ IN. MIN.
(19 mm)

METAL SHIMS:
MATCHED TO GLAZING
THICKNESS

CLAMPING FRAME

$1^1/_2$ IN. MIN.
(38 mm)

2 IN. MIN. (51 mm)

DETAIL A

SECTION A-A OF FIGURE 24-2-1

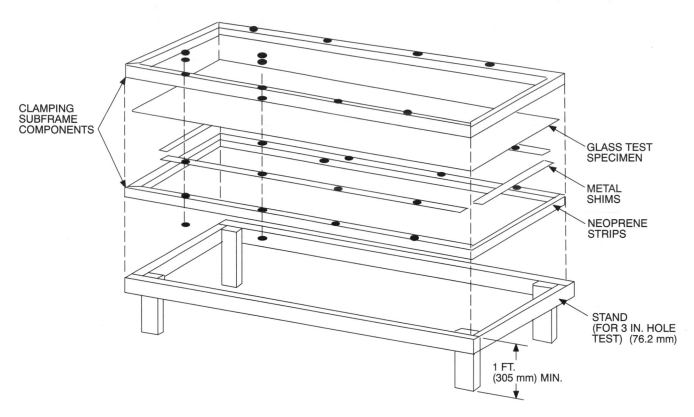

**FIGURE 24-2-2—GLASS TEST SPECIMEN CLAMPING FRAME
(EXPLODED) AND STAND**

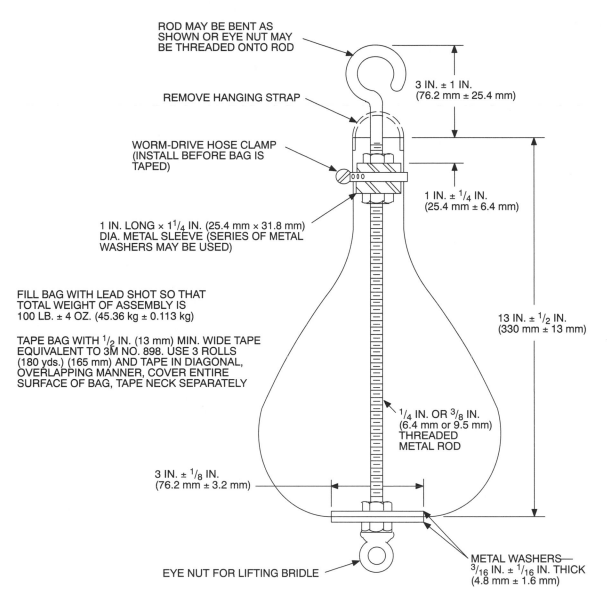

ROD MAY BE BENT AS
SHOWN OR EYE NUT MAY
BE THREADED ONTO ROD

3 IN. ± 1 IN.
(76.2 mm ± 25.4 mm)

REMOVE HANGING STRAP

WORM-DRIVE HOSE CLAMP
(INSTALL BEFORE BAG IS
TAPED)

1 IN. ± $\frac{1}{4}$ IN.
(25.4 mm ± 6.4 mm)

1 IN. LONG × 1$\frac{1}{4}$ IN. (25.4 mm × 31.8 mm)
DIA. METAL SLEEVE (SERIES OF METAL
WASHERS MAY BE USED)

FILL BAG WITH LEAD SHOT SO THAT
TOTAL WEIGHT OF ASSEMBLY IS
100 LB. ± 4 OZ. (45.36 kg ± 0.113 kg)

TAPE BAG WITH $\frac{1}{2}$ IN. (13 mm) MIN. WIDE TAPE
EQUIVALENT TO 3M NO. 898. USE 3 ROLLS
(180 yds.) (165 mm) AND TAPE IN DIAGONAL,
OVERLAPPING MANNER, COVER ENTIRE
SURFACE OF BAG, TAPE NECK SEPARATELY

13 IN. ± $\frac{1}{2}$ IN.
(330 mm ± 13 mm)

$\frac{1}{4}$ IN. OR $\frac{3}{8}$ IN.
(6.4 mm or 9.5 mm)
THREADED
METAL ROD

3 IN. ± $\frac{1}{8}$ IN.
(76.2 mm ± 3.2 mm)

EYE NUT FOR LIFTING BRIDLE

METAL WASHERS—
$\frac{3}{16}$ IN. ± $\frac{1}{16}$ IN. THICK
(4.8 mm ± 1.6 mm)

FIGURE 24-2-3—IMPACTOR

UNIFORM BUILDING CODE STANDARD 25-1
PLASTIC CEMENT
See Sections 2102.2, Item 2, and 2508.1, *Uniform Building Code*

SECTION 25.101 — SCOPE

This standard covers plastic cement for use in plastering.

SECTION 25.102 — PHYSICAL REQUIREMENTS

Plastic cement shall conform to the requirements set forth in Table 25-1-A.

SECTION 25.103 — PACKAGE LABELING

Plastic cement packages shall carry a statement indicating that the product conforms to requirements of this standard and shall include the brand, name of manufacturer and net weight of the package in pounds.

SECTION 25.104 — CERTIFICATION

Certification shall be submitted upon request of the building official and shall certify compliance with the requirements of this standard.

SECTION 25.105 — TEMPERATURE AND HUMIDITY

The temperature of the air in the vicinity of the mixing slab and dry materials, molds, base plates and mixing bowl shall be maintained between 68°F and 81.5°F (20°C and 27.5°C). The temperature of the mixing water, moist cabinet or moist room, and water in the storage tank shall not vary from 73.4°F by more than 3°F (23°C ± 1.7°C).

The relative humidity of the laboratory air shall not be less than 50 percent. The moist cabinet or moist room atmosphere shall have a relative humidity of not less than 90 percent.

The moist cabinet or moist room shall conform to applicable standards.

SECTION 25.106 — FINENESS

The fineness of the cement shall be determined from the residue on the No. 325 sieve (45 μm).

SECTION 25.107 — NORMAL CONSISTENCY

Determine normal consistency by the Vicat apparatus.

SECTION 25.108 — AUTOCLAVE EXPANSION

The autoclave expansion of plastic cement shall be determined. After molding, the specimens shall be stored in the moist cabinet or moist room for 48 hours ± 30 minutes before removal.

SECTION 25.109 — TIME OF SETTING

The time of setting shall be determined by the Gillmore needle method.

SECTION 25.110 — DENSITY

The density of the plastic cement shall be determined by using kerosene as the liquid. Use the density so determined in the calculation of the air content of the specimens.

SECTION 25.111 — APPARATUS FOR MORTAR TESTS

The apparatus for mortar tests shall be in accordance with applicable standards.

SECTION 25.112 — BLENDED SAND

The sand shall be a blend of equal parts by weight of graded standard sand and Standard 20-30 sand.

SECTION 25.113 — PREPARATION OF MORTAR

25.113.1 Proportions for Mortar. Mortar for air entrainment, compressive strength, and water retention tests shall be proportioned to contain a mass of cement, in grams, equal to six times the net bag weight in pounds, representing a nominal 1 cubic foot (0.0283 m^3) of plastic cement and 1,440 grams of sand. The sand shall consist of 720 grams of graded standard sand and 720 grams of 20-30 standard sand. The quantity of water measured in millimeters shall be such as to produce a flow of 110 ± 5 as determined by the flow table.

25.113.2 Mixing of Mortars. The mortar shall be mixed in accordance with applicable standards.

25.113.3 Determination of Flow. The flow shall be determined in accordance with applicable standards.

SECTION 25.114 — AIR ENTRAINMENT

25.114.1 Procedure. If the mortar has the correct flow, use a separate portion of the mortar for the determination of entrained air. Determine the mass of the 400 milliliters of the mortar.

25.114.2 Calculation. Calculate the air content of the mortar and report it to the nearest 0.1 percent as follows:

$$D = (W_1 + W_2 + V_w)/[(W_1/S_1) + (W_2/S_2) + V_w]$$
$$A = 100 - (W_m/4D)$$

WHERE:

A = volume percent of entrained air.

D = density of air-free mortar, g/ml.

S_1 = density of cement, g/ml.

S_2 = density of standard sand, 2.65 g/ml.

V_w = milliliters-grams of water used.

W_1 = mass of cement, g.

W_2 = mass of sand, g.

W_m = mass of 400 ml.

SECTION 25.115 — COMPRESSIVE STRENGTH

25.115.1 Test Specimens.

25.115.1.1 Molding. Immediately after determining the flow and the mass of 400 milliliters of mortar, return all the mortar to the mixing bowl and remix for 15 seconds at the medium speed. Then mold test specimens, except that elapsed time for mixing mortar, determining flow, determining air entrainment and starting the molding of cubes shall be within eight minutes.

25.115.1.2 Storage. Store all test specimens immediately after molding in the molds on plane plates in a moist cabinet or moist room for 48 to 52 hours, in such a manner that the upper surfaces shall be exposed to the moist air. Then remove the cubes from the molds and place in the moist cabinet or moist room for five days in such a manner as to allow free circulation of air around at least five faces of the specimens. At the age of seven days, immerse the cubes for the 28-day tests in saturated lime water in storage tanks of noncorrodible materials.

25.115.2 Procedure. Test the cube specimens immediately after their removal from the moist cabinet or moist room for seven-day specimens and immediately after their removal from storage water for all other specimens. If more than one specimen at a time is removed from the moist cabinet or moist room for seven-day tests, cover these cubes with a damp cloth until time of testing. If more than one specimen at a time is removed from the storage water for testing, place these cubes in a pan of water at a temperature of 73.4°F ± 3°F (23°C ± 1.7°C) and of sufficient depth to completely immerse each cube until time of testing.

The remainder of the testing procedure shall conform to applicable standards.

SECTION 25.116 — WATER RETENTION

25.116.1 Apparatus. For the water-retention test, an apparatus essentially the same as that shown in Figure 25-1-1 shall be used. This apparatus consists of a water-aspirator or other source of vacuum controlled by a mercury-relief column and connected by way of a three-way stopcock to a funnel upon which rests a perforated dish. The perforated dish shall be made of metal not attacked by plastic mortar. The metal in the base of the dish shall have a thickness of 1.7 mm to 1.9 mm and shall conform to the requirements given in Figure 25-1-1. The stopcock bore shall have a 4.0 mm ± 0.5 mm diameter, and the connecting glass tubing shall have a minimum inside diameter of 4 mm. A mercury manometer, connected as shown in Figure 25-1-1, indicates the vacuum. The contact surfaces of the funnel and perforated dish shall be placed and may need to be lapped to ensure intimate contact. An airtight seal shall be maintained between the funnel and the dish during a test. This shall be accomplished by either of the following procedures:

A. A synthetic (grease-resistant) rubber gasket may be permanently sealed to the top of the funnel using petrolatum or light grease to ensure a seal between the basket and dish.

B. The top of the funnel may be lightly coated with petrolatum or light grease to ensure a seal between the funnel and dish.

Care shall be taken to ensure that none of the holes in the perforated dish are clogged. Hardened, very smooth, not rapid, filter paper shall be used. It shall be 150 mm in diameter and be placed so as to completely cover the perforations in the dish.

A steel straightedge not less than 8 inches (203 mm) long and not less than $1/16$ inch (1.6 mm) or more than $1/8$ inch (3.2 mm) in thickness.

Other apparatus required for the water-retention test shall conform to the requirements of Section 25.111.

25.116.2 Procedure. Adjust the mercury-relief column to maintain a vacuum of 51 mm ± 3 mm as indicated by the manometer. Seat the perforated dish on the greased gasket or greased rim of the funnel. Place a wetted filter paper in the bottom of the dish. Turn the stopcock to apply the vacuum to the funnel and check the apparatus for leaks and to determine that the required vacuum is obtained. Then turn the stopcock to shut off the vacuum from the funnel.

Mix the mortar to a flow of 110 ± 5 percent in accordance with applicable standards. Immediately after making the flow test, return the mortar on the flow table to the mixing bowl and remix the entire batch for 15 seconds at medium speed. Immediately after remixing the mortar, fill the perforated dish with the mortar to slightly above the rim. Tamp the mortar 15 times with the tamper. Apply 10 of the tamping strokes at approximately uniform spacing adjacent to the rim of the dish and with the long axis of the tamping face held at right angles to the radius of the dish. Apply the remaining five tamping strokes at random points distributed over the central area of the dish. The tamping pressure shall be just sufficient to ensure filling of the dish. Upon completion of the tamping, the top of the mortar will extend slightly above the rim of the dish. Smooth off the mortar by drawing the flat side of the straightedge (with leading edge slightly raised) across the top of the dish. Then cut off the mortar to a plane surface flush with the rim of the dish by drawing the straightedge with a sawing motion across the top of the dish in two cutting strokes, starting each cut from near the center of the dish. If the mortar is pulled away from the side of the dish during the process of drawing the straightedge across the dish, gently press the mortar back into contact with the side of the dish using the tamper.

Turn the stopcock to apply the vacuum to the funnel. The time elapsed from the start of mixing the cement and water to the time of applying the vacuum shall not exceed eight minutes. After suction for 60 seconds, quickly turn the stopcock to expose the funnel to atmospheric pressure. Immediately slide the perforated dish off from the funnel, touch it momentarily on a damp cloth to remove droplets of water, and set the dish on the table. Then, using the bowl scraper, plow and mix the mortar in the dish for 15 seconds. Upon completion of mixing, place the mortar in the flow mold and determine the flow. The entire operation shall be carried out without interruption and as quickly as possible, and shall be completed within an elapsed time of 11 minutes after the start of mixing the cement and water for the first flow determination. Both flow determinations shall be made in accordance with applicable standards.

25.116.3 Calculation. Calculate the water-retention value for the mortar as follows:

$$\text{Water-retention value} = (A/B) \times 100$$

WHERE:

A = flow after suction.

B = flow immediately after mixing.

TABLE 25-1-A—PHYSICAL REQUIREMENTS

Fineness, residue on a No. 325 sieve (45 μm), maximum, percentage	24
Soundness: Autoclave expansion, maximum, percentage	1.0

Time of setting, Gillmore method:
  Initial set, minimum, hour
  Final set, maximum, hour
	$1^1/_2$
	24

Compressive strength (average of three cubes):
Initial compressive strength of mortar cubes, composed of one part cement and three parts blended sand (half graded Ottawa sand, and half Standard 20-30 Ottawa sand) by volume, prepared and tested in accordance with this specification shall be equal to or higher than the values specified for the ages indicated below:
  seven days, psi (kPa)
  28 days, psi (kPa)
	1,800 (12 402 kPa)
	2,900 (19 981 kPa)

Air content of mortar: Minimum percentage by volume	8
Maximum percentage by volume	20
Water retention, flow after suction, minimum, percentage of original flow	70

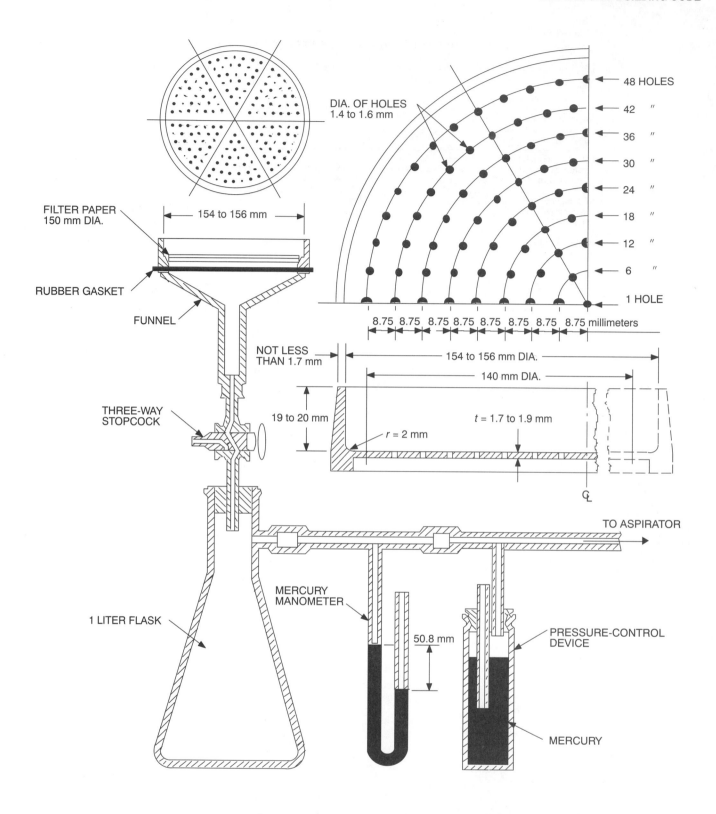

NOTE: The gasket is to be synthetic rubber. The stopcock and the bore of the tubing should measure at least 4 mm. A check valve or water trap, or both, are suggested for the connection to the aspirator.

FIGURE 25-1-1—APPARATUS ASSEMBLY FOR THE WATER-RETENTION TEST

UNIFORM BUILDING CODE STANDARD 25-2
METAL SUSPENSION SYSTEMS FOR ACOUSTICAL TILE AND FOR LAY-IN PANEL CEILINGS

Based on Standard Specification C 635-69 and Standard Recommended Practice C 636-69 of the American Society for Testing and Materials. Extracted, with permission, from the *Annual Book of ASTM Standards,* **copyright American Society for Testing and Materials, 100 Barr Harbor Drive, West Conshohocken, PA 19428**

See Table 25-A, *Uniform Building Code*

Part I—General

SECTION 25.201 — SCOPE

This standard covers metal ceiling suspension systems used primarily to support acoustical tile or acoustical lay-in panels.

SECTION 25.202 — CLASSIFICATION

The structural performance required from a ceiling suspension system shall be in accordance with its structural classification.

The load-carrying capacity shall be the maximum uniformly distributed load (pounds per linear foot) that a simply supported main runner section having a span length of 4 feet 0 inch (1219 mm) is capable of supporting without a midspan deflection exceeding 0.133 inch (3.4 mm) or $1/_{360}$ of the 4-foot 0-inch (1219 mm) span length.

The structural classification listed in Table 25-2-A shall be determined by the capability of main runners or nailing bars to support a uniformly distributed load. These classifications shall be:

1. **Light-duty systems.** Used primarily for residential and light commercial structures where ceiling loads other than acoustical tile or lay-in panels are not anticipated.

2. **Intermediate-duty systems.** Used primarily for ordinary commercial structures where some ceiling loads, due to light fixtures and air diffusers, are anticipated.

3. **Heavy-duty systems.** Used primarily for commercial structures in which the quantities and weights of ceiling fixtures (lights, air diffusers, etc.) are greater than those for an ordinary commercial structure.

Cross runners shall be capable of carrying the design load as dictated by job conditions without exceeding the maximum allowable deflection equal to $1/_{360}$ of its span. A cross runner that supports another cross runner is a main runner for the purpose of structural classification and shall be capable of supporting a uniformly distributed load at least equal to the intermediate classification.

SECTION 25.203 — DIMENSIONAL TOLERANCE

25.203.1 Straightness. The amount of bow, camber or twist in main runners, cross runners, wall molding, splines or nailing bars of various lengths shall not exceed the values shown in Table 25-2-B.

Main runners, cross runners, wall moldings, splines or nailing bars of ceiling suspension systems shall not contain local kinks or bends.

Straightness of structural members shall be measured with the member suspended vertically from one end.

25.203.2 Length. The variation in the specified length of main runner sections or cross runner sections that are part of an interlocking grid system shall not exceed ± 0.010 inch/4 feet (± 0.25 mm/1219 mm).

The variation in the specified spacing of slots or other cutouts in the webs of main runners or cross runners that are employed in assembling a ceiling suspension grid system shall not exceed 0.010 inch (0.25 mm).

25.203.3 Overall Cross-section Dimensions. For steel systems, the overall height of the cross section of main runners, cross runners, wall molding or nailing bar shall be the specified dimensions ± 0.030 inch (0.76 mm). The width of the cross section of exposed main runners or cross runners shall be the specified dimension ± 0.008 inch (0.20 mm).

25.203.4 Section Squareness. Intersecting webs and flanges of structural members (I, T, or Z sections) shall form angles between them of 90 degrees ± 2 degrees. If deviations from squareness at more than one such intersection are additive with respect to their use in a ceiling, the total angle shall be not greater than 2 degrees.

The ends of structural members that abut or intersect other members in exposed grid systems shall be cut perpendicular to the exposed face, 90 degrees +0, -2 degrees.

25.203.5 Suspension System Devices. Suspension system assembly devices shall satisfy the following requirements and tolerances:

A joint connection shall be judged suitable both before and after ceiling loads are imposed if the joint provides sufficient alignment so that:

The horizontal and the vertical displacements of the exposed surfaces of two abutting main runners do not exceed 0.015 inch (0.38 mm).

There shall be no visually apparent angular displacement of the longitudinal axis of one runner with respect to the other.

Assembly devices shall provide sufficient spacing control so that horizontal gaps between exposed surfaces of either abutting or intersecting members shall not exceed 0.020 inch (0.5 mm).

Spring wire clips used for supporting main runners shall maintain tight contact between the main runners and the carrying channels when the ceiling loads are imposed on the runners.

SECTION 25.204 — COATINGS AND FINISHES FOR SUSPENSION SYSTEM COMPONENTS

25.204.1 Protective Coatings for Normal Environments. Component materials that oxidize or corrode when exposed to normal-use environments shall be provided with protective coatings except for cut or punched edges fabricated after the coating is applied.

Components fabricated from sheet steel shall be given an electrogalvanized, hot-dipped galvanized, cadmium or equal protective coating.

Components fabricated from aluminum alloys shall be anodized or protected by other approved techniques.

Components formed from other materials shall be provided with an approved protective coating.

25.204.2 Adhesion and Resilience. Finishes shall exhibit good adhesion properties and resilience so that chipping or flaking does not occur as a result of the manufacturing process.

25.204.3 Protective Coatings for Severe Environment. Protected components for acoustical ceilings shall be suitable for their environment. When they are subject to the severe environmental conditions of high humidity and salt spray (fog), or both, they shall be ranked according to their ability to protect the components of suspension systems from deterioration. A salt spray (fog) test conducted in accordance with the following test conditions shall be performed:

1. **Salt solution.** Five parts by weight NaCl to 95 parts distilled water.

2. **Humidity in chamber.** Ninety percent relative humidity.

3. **Temperature in chamber.** 90°F (32°C).

4. **Exposure period.** Ninety-six hours continuous.

5. **Report.** Upon request, the photographs shall be provided showing worst corrosion conditions on components and shall provide comments regarding corrosion that occurs on cut metal edges, on galvanized surfaces without paint, on galvanized and painted surfaces, at edges rolled after being painted, and on any change of paint color or gloss that is apparent at the conclusion of the test. Color and gloss inspection of the component shall be made after washing in a mild soap solution.

25.204.4 High-humidity Test. The test and inspection shall be identical to that of the salt spray test, except that distilled water instead of salt solution shall be used.

SECTION 25.205 — STRUCTURAL MEMBERS

The manufacturer shall determine the load-deflection performance. The structural members tested shall be identical to the sections used in the final system design. All cutouts, slots, etc., as exist in the system component shall be included in the sections evaluated.

Load-deflection studies of structural members shall utilize sections fabricated in accordance with the system manufacturers' published metal thicknesses and dimensions.

SECTION 25.206 — SECTION PERFORMANCE

The performance of structural members of suspension systems shall be represented by individual load-deflection plots obtained from tests performed at each different span length used in service.

The results of replicate tests of three individual sections, each tested on the same span length, shall be plotted and averaged to obtain a characteristic load-deflection curve for the structural member.

The average load-deflection curve shall be used to establish the maximum uniformly distributed load that the structural member can successfully sustain prior to reaching the deflection limit of $1/360$ of the span length in inches.

The load-deflection curve shall be used to establish the maximum loading intensity beyond which the structural member begins to yield.

SECTION 25.207 — SUSPENSION SYSTEM PERFORMANCE

Published performance data for individual suspension systems shall be developed by the manufacturer on the basis of results obtained from load-deflection tests of its principal structural members. Where a ceiling design incorporates a number of components, each of which experiences some deflection as used in the system, the additive nature of these displacements shall be recognized in setting an allowable system deflection criteria.

Part II—Installation

SECTION 25.208 — SCOPE

This part describes procedures for the installation of suspension systems for acoustical tile and lay-in panels.

SECTION 25.209 — INSTALLATION OF COMPONENTS

25.209.1 Hangers. Hangers shall be attached to the bottom edge of the wood joists or to the vertical face of the wood joists near the bottom edge. Bottom edge attachment devices shall be an approved type.

In concrete construction, mount hangers using cast-in-place hanger wires, hanger inserts, or other hanger attachment devices shall be an approved type. If greater center-to-center distances than 4 feet 0 inch (1219 mm) are used for the hangers, the load-carrying capacity of the ceiling suspension system shall be reduced commensurate with the actual center-to-center hanger distances.

Hangers shall be plumb and shall not press against insulation covering ducts or pipes. If some hangers must be splayed, countersplaying or other approved means shall be used to offset the horizontal force.

Hangers formed from galvanized sheet metal shall be suitable for suspending carrying channels or main runners from an existing structure provided that the hangers do not yield, twist or undergo other objectionable movement.

Wire hangers for suspending carrying channels or main runners from an existing structure shall be a minimum of No. 12 gage (2.7 mm), galvanized, soft annealed, mild steel wire.

Special attachment devices that support the carrying channels or main runners shall be approved to support five times the design load.

25.209.2 Carrying Channels. The carrying channels shall be installed so that they are level to within $1/8$ inch in 12 feet (3.2 m in 3660 mm). Leveling shall be performed with the supporting hangers taut. Local kinks or bends shall not be made in hanger wires as a means of leveling carrying channels. In installations where hanger wires are wrapped around carrying channels, the wire loops shall be tightly formed to prevent any vertical movement or rotation of the member within the loop.

25.209.3 Main Runners. Main runners shall be installed so that they are all level to within $1/8$ inch in 12 feet (3.2 mm in 3660 mm). Where main runners are supported directly by hangers, leveling shall be performed with the supporting hanger taut. Local kinks or bends shall not be made in hanger wires as a means of leveling main runners. In installations where hanger wires are wrapped through or around main runners, the wire loops shall be tightly wrapped and sharply bent.

25.209.4 Cross Runners. Cross runners shall be supported by either main runners or by other cross runners to within $1/32$ inch

(0.79 mm) of the required center distances. This tolerance shall be noncumulative beyond 12 feet (3528 mm). Intersecting runners shall form a right angle. The exposed surfaces of two intersecting runners shall lie within a vertical distance of 0.015 inch (0.38 mm) of each other with the abutting (cross) member always above the continuous (main) member.

25.209.5 Splines. Splines used to form a concealed mechanical joint seal between adjacent tiles shall be compatible with the tile kerf design so that the adjacent tile will be horizontal when installed. Where splines are longer than the dimension between edges of supporting members running perpendicular to the splines, place the splines so that they rest either all above or all below the main running members.

25.209.6 Assembly Devices. Abutting sections of main runner shall be joined by means of suitable connections such as splices, interlocking ends, tab locks, pin locks, etc. A joint connection shall be judged suitable both before and after ceiling loads are imposed if the joint provides sufficient alignment so that the exposed surfaces of two abutting main runners lie within a vertical distance of 0.015 inch (0.38 mm) of each other and within a horizontal distance of 0.015 inch (0.38 mm) of each other.

There shall be no visually apparent angular displacement of the longitudinal axis of one runner with respect to the other.

Assembly devices shall provide sufficient spacing control so that horizontal gaps between exposed surfaces of either abutting or intersecting members shall not exceed 0.020 inch (0.51 mm).

Spring wire clips used for supporting main runners shall maintain tight contact between the main runners and the carrying channels when the ceiling loads are imposed on the runners.

25.209.7 Ceiling Fixtures. Fixtures installed in acoustical tile or lay-in panel ceilings shall be mounted in a manner that will not compromise ceiling performance.

Fixtures shall not be supported from main runners or cross runners if the weight of the fixtures causes the total dead load to exceed the deflection capability of the ceiling suspension system. In such cases, the fixture load shall be supported by supplemental hangers within 6 inches (152.4 mm) of each corner, or the fixture shall be separately supported.

Fixtures shall not be installed so that main runners or cross runners will be eccentrically loaded except where provision is inherent in the system (or is separately provided for) to prevent undesirable section rotation or displacement, or both. In any case, runners supporting ceiling fixtures shall not rotate more than 2 degrees after the fixture loads are imposed.

Where fixture installation would produce rotation of runners in excess of 2 degrees, the fixtures shall be with the use of suitable accessory devices. These devices shall support the fixture in such a manner that the main runners and cross runners will be loaded symmetrically rather than eccentrically.

Part III—Lateral Design Requirements

SECTION 25.210 — SCOPE

Suspended ceilings which are designed and constructed to support ceiling panels or tiles, with or without lighting fixtures, ceiling-mounted air terminals or other ceiling-mounted services shall comply with the requirements of this standard.

EXCEPTIONS: 1. Ceiling area of 144 square feet (13.38 m²) or less surrounded by walls which connect directly to the structure above are exempt from the lateral load design requirements of this standard.

2. Ceilings constructed of lath and plaster or gypsum board, screw or nail attached to suspended members that support a ceiling on one level extending from wall to wall are exempt from this standard.

SECTION 25.211 — MINIMUM DESIGN LOADS

25.211.1 Lateral Forces. Ceiling systems and their connections to the building structure shall be designed and constructed to resist the lateral force specified in Chapter 16, Part III of the Building Code.

Where the ceiling system provides lateral support for nonbearing partitions, it shall be designed for the prescribed lateral force reaction from the partitions as specified in Section 25.215.

Connection of lighting fixtures to the ceiling system shall be designed for a lateral force of 100 percent of the weight of the fixture in addition to the prescribed vertical loading as specified in Section 25.213.

25.211.2 Grid Members, Connectors and Expansion Devices. The main runners and cross runners of the ceiling system and their splices, intersection connectors and expansion devices shall be designed and constructed to carry a mean ultimate test load of not less than 180 pounds (801 N) or twice the actual load, whichever is greater, in tension with a 5-degree misalignment of the members in any direction, and in compression. In lieu of 5-degree misalignment, the load may be applied with a 1-inch (25.4 mm) eccentricity on a sample not more than 24 inches (610 mm) long on each side of the splice. The connections at splices and intersections shall all be of the mechanical interlocking type.

When the composition or configuration of ceiling systems members or assemblies and their connections are such that calculations of their allowable load-carrying capacity cannot be made in accordance with established methods of analysis, their performance shall be established by test.

Evaluation of test results shall be made on the basis of the mean values resulting from tests of three or more identical specimens, provided the deviation of any individual test result from the mean value does not exceed plus or minus 10 percent. The allowable load-carrying capacity as determined by test shall not exceed one half of the mean ultimate test value.

25.211.3 Substantiation. The ceiling systems manufacturer shall furnish lateral loading capacity and displacement or elongation characteristics, indicating the following:

1. Maximum bracing pattern and minimum wire sizes.

2. Tension and compression force capabilities of main runner splices, cross runner connections and expansion devices.

Tests shall be conducted by an approved testing agency.

SECTION 25.212 — INSTALLATION

25.212.1 Vertical Hangers. Suspension wires shall not be smaller than No. 12 gage (2.7 mm) spaced at 4 feet (1219 mm) on center or No. 10 gage (3.4 mm) at 5 feet (1524 mm) on center along each main runner unless calculations justifying the increased spacing are provided.

Each vertical wire shall be attached to the ceiling suspension member and to the support above with a minimum of three turns. Connection devices at the supporting construction shall be capable of carrying not less than 100 pounds (445 N).

Suspension wires shall not hang more than 1 in 6 out-of-plumb unless countersloping wires are provided.

Wires shall not attach to or bend around interfering material or equipment. A trapeze or equivalent device shall be used where obstructions preclude direct suspension. Trapeze suspensions shall be a minimum of back-to-back $1^1/_4$-inch (31.75 mm) cold-rolled channels for spans exceeding 48 inches (1219 mm).

25.212.2 Perimeter Hangers. The terminal ends of each cross runner and main runner shall be supported independently a maximum of 8 inches (203.2 mm) from each wall or ceiling discontinuity with No. 12 gage (2.7 mm) wire or approved wall support.

25.212.3 Lateral Force Bracing. Where substantiating design calculations are not provided, horizontal restraints shall be effected by four No. 12 gage (2.7 mm) wires secured to the main runner within 2 inches (50.8 mm) of the cross runner intersection and splayed 90 degrees from each other at an angle not exceeding 45 degrees from the plane of the ceiling. A strut fastened to the main runner shall be extended to and fastened to the structural members supporting the roof or floor above. The strut shall be adequate to resist the vertical component induced by the bracing wires. These horizontal restraint points shall be placed not more than 12 feet (3658 mm) on center in both directions with the first point within 6 feet (1829 mm) from each wall. Attachment of the restraint wires to the structure above shall be adequate for the load imposed.

Lateral-force bracing members shall be spaced a minimum of 6 inches (154 mm) from all horizontal piping or ductwork that is not provided with bracing restraints for horizontal forces. Bracing wires shall be attached to the grid and to the structure in such a manner that they can support a design load of not less than 200 pounds (890 N) or the actual design load, whichever is greater, with a safety factor of 2.

25.212.4 Perimeter Members. Unless perimeter members are a structural part of the approved system, wall angles or channels shall be considered as aesthetic closures and with no structural value. Ends of main runners and cross members shall be tied together to prevent their spreading.

25.212.5 Attachment of Members to the Perimeter. To facilitate installation, main runners and cross runners may be attached to the perimeter member at two adjacent walls with clearance between the wall and the runners maintained at the other two walls or as otherwise shown or described for the approved system.

SECTION 25.213 — LIGHTING FIXTURES

Intermediate or heavy-duty ceiling systems as defined in Section 25.202 shall be used for the support of lighting fixtures.

All lighting fixtures shall be positively attached to the suspended ceiling system. The attachment device shall have a capacity of 100 percent of the lighting fixture weight acting in any direction.

When intermediate systems are used, No. 12 gage (2.7 mm) hangers shall be attached to the grid members within 3 inches (76 mm) of each corner of each fixture. Tandem fixtures may utilize common wires.

When heavy-duty systems are used, supplemental hangers are not required if a 48-inch (1219 mm) modular hanger pattern is followed. When cross runners are used without supplemental hangers to support lighting fixtures, these cross runners shall provide the same carrying capacity as the main runner.

Lighting fixtures weighing less than 56 pounds (25.4 kg) shall have, in addition to the requirements outlined above, two No. 12 gage (2.7 mm) hangers connected from the fixture housing to the structure above. These wires may be slack.

Lighting fixtures weighing 56 pounds (25.4 kg) or more shall be supported directly from the structure above by approved hangers.

Pendant-hung lighting fixtures shall be supported directly from the structure above with No. 9 gage (3.8 mm) wire or approved alternate support without using the ceiling suspension system for direct support.

SECTION 25.214 — MECHANICAL SERVICES

Ceiling-mounted air terminals or services weighing less than 20 pounds (9.07 kg) shall be positively attached to the ceiling suspension main runners or to cross runners with the same carrying capacity as the main runners.

Terminals or services weighing 20 pounds (9.07 kg), but not more than 56 pounds (25.4 kg), in addition to the above, shall have two No. 12 gage (2.7 mm) hangers connected from the terminal or service to the ceiling system hangers or to the structure above. These wires may be slack.

Terminals or services weighing more than 56 pounds (25.4 kg) shall be supported directly from the structure above by approved hangers.

SECTION 25.215 — PARTITIONS

Where the suspended ceiling system is required to provide lateral support for permanent or relocatable partitions, the connection of the partition to the ceiling system, the ceiling system members and their connections, and the lateral force bracing shall be designed to support the reaction force of the partition from prescribed loads applied perpendicular to the face of the partition. These partition reaction forces shall be in addition to the loads described in Section 25.211. Partition connectors, the suspended ceiling system and the lateral-force bracing shall be engineered to suit the individual partition application and shall be shown or defined in the drawings or specifications.

SECTION 25.216 — DRAWINGS AND SPECIFICATIONS

The drawings shall clearly identify all systems and shall define or show all supporting details, lighting fixture attachment, lateral-force bracing, partition bracing, etc. Such definition may be by reference to this standard, or approved system, in whole or in part. Deviations or variations shall be shown or defined in detail.

TABLE 25-2-A—MINIMUM LOAD-CARRYING CAPABILITIES OF MAIN RUNNER MEMBERS

	SUSPENSION SYSTEM (pounds per linear foot)		
	× 14.59 for N/m		
MAIN RUNNER MEMBERS	Direct-hung	Indirect-hung	Furring Bar
Light-duty	5.0	2.0	4.5
Intermediate-duty	12.0	3.5	6.5
Heavy-duty	16.0	8.0	—

**TABLE 25-2-B—STRAIGHTNESS TOLERANCES
OF STRUCTURAL MEMBERS OF SUSPENSION SYSTEMS**

DEFORMATION	STRAIGHTNESS TOLERANCES
Bow	$^{1}/_{32}$ in. in any 2 ft. (1.3 mm in any 1 m), or $^{1}/_{32}$ in. × (total length, ft.)/2 [1.3 mm × (total length, m)/2]
Camber	$^{1}/_{32}$ in. in any 2 ft. (1.3 mm in any 1 m), or $^{1}/_{32}$ in. × (total length, ft.)/2 [1.3 mm × (total length, m)/2]
Twist	1 degree in any 2 ft. (610 mm), or 1 degree × [total length, ft. (m)]/2

UNIFORM BUILDING CODE STANDARD 26-1
TEST METHOD TO DETERMINE POTENTIAL HEAT OF BUILDING MATERIALS

Test Standard of the International Conference of Building Officials

See Sections 601.3, 2602.4 and 2602.5.2, *Uniform Building Code*

SECTION 26.101 — SCOPE

26.101.1 General. This method of test defines a means of determining the potential release of heat of materials (typically involved in building fires) under specified conditions. The method is applicable to a variety of materials including metals and especially materials with low combustible content. Determinations may be made on simple materials or on composite assemblies of materials from a which a representative sample can be taken and pulverized into a homogeneous mixture.

26.101.2 Definition of Potential Heat. Potential heat of a material is the difference between the heat of combustion of a representative specimen of the material and the heat of combustion of any residue remaining after exposure to a specified standard fire using combustion, calorimetric techniques.

SECTION 26.102 — TEST PROCEDURES

26.102.1 General. One of two specimens removed from the material to be tested shall be pulverized, pelleted and burned in a high-pressure-oxygen atmosphere in accordance with approved standard procedures for determination of the heat of combustion. Caution should be observed when performing bomb calorimetric measurements on materials containing significant proportions of metallic ingredients. Apart from the high reaction temperatures which may occur with the resulting possible involvement of portions of the bomb, consideration should be given to the possibility of electrical shorts in the ignition system.

26.102.2 Test Specimens. Two air-dry specimens representative of the material or assembly involved are required for each determination. A specimen is considered "air dry" when it has reached constant weight in an atmosphere maintained at 73°F ± 2°F (23°C ± 1°C) and 50 ± 5 percent relative humidity. The two specimens are subject to separate test procedures as set forth in Sections 26.102.3 and 26.102.4.

26.102.3 Procedure for Direct Bomb Test. The following steps shall be used for the direct bomb test:

Step 1. All or a representative portion of this specimen shall be pulverized into a form suitable to pass a No. 60 sieve (250 μm).

Step 2. A 1-gram pellet of a representative sample of the powder formed in Step 1 is prepared.

Step 3. The pellet formed in Step 2 shall be used as the test specimen following the procedures described in Section 26.102.1. The usual sulfur and acid corrections shall be made. These take into account the oxidation of sulfur and nitrogen, if present, which would not normally occur during fire exposure.

Step 4. If after being fired in the oxygen bomb the pellet is found to have burned completely or to have left no significant amount of residue or ash, the heat of combustion on an air-dry basis shall be computed, and Steps 5, 6 and 7 shall be omitted.

Step 5. If the pellet does not burn or a residue remains after the firing, another 1-gram pellet shall be prepared with a mixture of the powdered sample and a standard sample of benzoic acid combustion promoter in approximately equal weight proportions.

Step 6. The pellet prepared in Step 5 shall be used as a test specimen following the same procedures as for the original specimen.

Step 7. A correction for the heat of combustion of the benzoic acid present in the pellet is supplied to the measured heat release by the specimen. The heat of combustion of the specimen material on an air-dry basis is then computed.

26.102.4 Procedure for Muffle Furnace and Bomb Test. The following steps shall be used for the muffle furnace and bomb test:

Step 1. An air-dry specimen representative of the test material or assembly shall be cut in the form of a rectangular prism $1/2$ inch by $3/4$ inch by 3 inches (13 mm by 19 mm by 76 mm). Sheet materials may be folded or laminated to these dimensions.

Step 2. The muffle furnace is preheated to 1,382°F ± 18°F (750°C ± 10°C) The weighed specimen is supported in a fused silica or ceramic container of $1^1/4$-inch (32 mm) inside diameter by 4 inches (102 mm) in length. The specimen, container cap and the tube for supply air to the bottom of the container are assembled. The assembly is then placed on a firebrick support within the electric muffle furnace. Firing is continued for two hours with a regulated air flow of $1/10$ cubic foot per minute (0.47 L/s) measured under laboratory conditions to assist in oxidation of the specimen. In cases where ignition occurs immediately, application of air is delayed until initial flaming has stopped.

Step 3. The container with the specimen shall be cooled in a desiccator, after which the weight of the residue is determined.

Step 4. If the residue from the muffle-firing procedure is less than 5 percent of the initial weight of the specimen, Steps 5 through 7 following shall be omitted, and the heat of combustion previously determined under the direct bomb test shall be reported as the potential heat of the material.

Step 5. If the residue after the muffle firing is in excess of 5 percent of the original specimen weight, the residue shall be pulverized, mixed with an equal weight of benzoic acid and treated as specified in the procedure for direct bomb test. The resulting heat of combustion is reported as that of the residue.

Step 6. The heat of combustion of the residue is multiplied by the ratio of the residue weight to the original specimen weight.

Step 7. The resulting difference in the heats of combustion is a measure of the gross heat released during the firing process in the muffle furnace and is reported as the potential heat.

26.102.5 Reporting Potential Heat. The potential heat determined either as a result of Step 4 or 7 of Section 26.102.4 shall be reported as the potential heat of the material. The potential heat shall be reported in either Btu per pound (kJ/kg) or Btu per cubic foot (kJ/kg).

UNIFORM BUILDING CODE STANDARD 26-2
TEST METHOD FOR THE EVALUATION
OF THERMAL BARRIERS

Standard of the International Conference of Building Officials

See Sections 601.3 and 2602.4, *Uniform Building Code*

SECTION 26.201 — SCOPE

This method of test for thermal barriers is applicable to building construction assemblies which incorporate foamed plastics which are required to be covered by a protective membrane.

The purpose of the test is to evaluate the temperature use or thermal transmission performance of the thermal barrier when the assembly is subjected to a standard fire exposure condition. This method does not evaluate the performance of the thermal barrier material with respect to its ability to remain in place under all actual fire exposure conditions.

SECTION 26.202 — TEST SPECIMEN

The thermal barrier material and method of securing the thermal barrier shall be representative of the construction for which the thermal barrier index rating is required.

If the thermal barrier material incorporates joints, at least one such joint shall be incorporated in the test specimen.

SECTION 26.203 — SPECIMEN CONDITIONING

Prior to fire test, assemblies shall be conditioned so as to provide a moisture conditioning within the specimen approximately representative of that likely to exist in similar construction in buildings. For that purpose of standardization, this condition is to be considered as that which would be established at equilibrium resulting from conditioning in an ambient atmosphere of 50 ± 5 percent relative humidity and $73.4°F \pm 5°F$ ($23°C \pm 3°C$).

SECTION 26.204 — TEST CONDITIONS

26.204.1 General. The dimensions of the furnace shall be as shown in Figure 26-2-1 entitled "Small-scale Horizontal Exposure Furnace."

The thermal barrier shall be installed in a manner representative of the construction for which the thermal barrier index rating is required. The specimen exposed to the fire shall have minimum horizontal dimensions of 28 inches by 28 inches (711 mm by 711 mm).

The calcium-silicate board shall be installed as shown in Figure 26-2-2, shall have a thickness of $1/2$ inch (13 mm) and a density of 46 pounds per cubic foot (736 kg/m³).

26.204.2 Furnace Temperature. The furnace temperature, as recorded by the thermocouples specified in Section 26.204.3, shall follow the standard time-temperature curve specified in UBC Standard 7-1 for which the temperatures at 5, 10 and 15 minutes following the commencement of the test are as given in Table 26-2-A.

26.204.3 Accuracy of Furnace Control. The accuracy of the furnace control shall be such that the area under the time-temperature curve given by the average of the specified thermocouples shall be within 10 percent of the corresponding area under the standard time-temperature curve specified in Section 26.204.2.

26.204.4 Thermocouple Location. The furnace temperature shall be registered by three or more thermocouples located so as to monitor the uniformity of the exposure to the thermal barrier. They shall be located 12 inches (305 mm) away from the face of the specimen and shall have a length of lead exposed within the furnace of not less than 12 inches (305 mm). They shall be enclosed in sealed porcelain tubes $3/4$ inch (19 mm) in outside diameter and $1/8$ inch (3.2 mm) in wall thickness or, as an alternative in the case of base metal thermocouples, enclosed in sealed, standard-weight, $1/2$-inch (13 mm) black wrought-steel or black wrought-iron pipe.

The temperature of the interface of the thermal barrier and the calcium-silicate board shall be sensed by at least nine thermocouples as shown in Figure 26-2-2 located at the center of the specimen, at the center of each quarter of the specimen and at potentially critical locations such as joints in the material. The leads to each thermocouple shall be in the plane of this interface for a length of not less than $1^1/2$ inches (38 mm). The wires for the thermocouples shall not be heavier than No. 20 AWG (0.032 inch) (0.81 mm).

26.204.5 Furnace Pressures. Furnace pressures shall be kept as close to atmospheric pressure as possible during the test.

26.204.6 Duration of Test. The test shall be continued for 15 minutes or until the thermal barrier has fallen away or disintegrated.

26.204.7 Recording Temperatures. Throughout the period of test, the temperature registered at each of the thermocouples required by Section 26.204.4 shall be recorded at intervals not exceeding one minute.

SECTION 26.205 — DETERMINATION OF THERMAL BARRIER INDEX

The thermal barrier index shall be determined as the number of minutes at which the temperature rises above initial temperature at the interface of the thermal barrier and the calcium-silicate board has not exceeded $250°F$ ($121°C$) average or $325°F$ ($163°C$) at any one of the thermocouples specified in Section 26.204.4.

TABLE 26-2-A—FURNACE TEMPERATURES

TIME	TEMPERATURE	
	°F	°C
5 minutes	1000	538
10 minutes	1300	704
15 minutes	1399	760

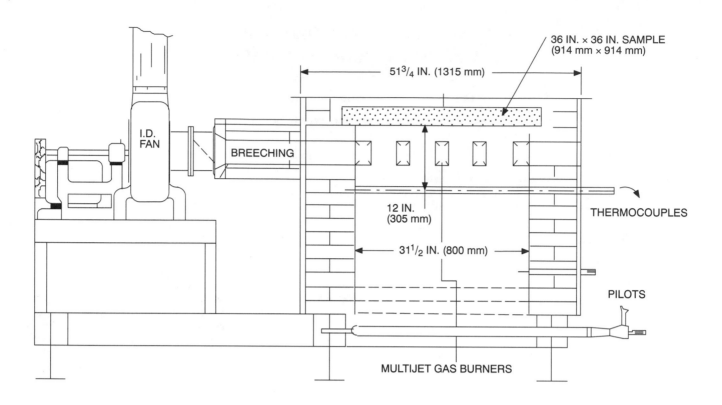

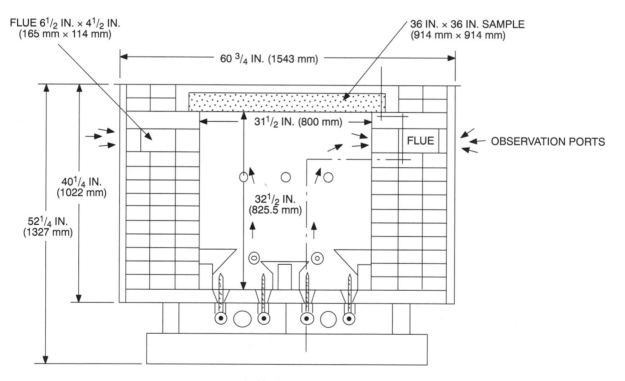

FIGURE 26-2-1—SMALL-SCALE HORIZONTAL EXPOSURE FURNACE

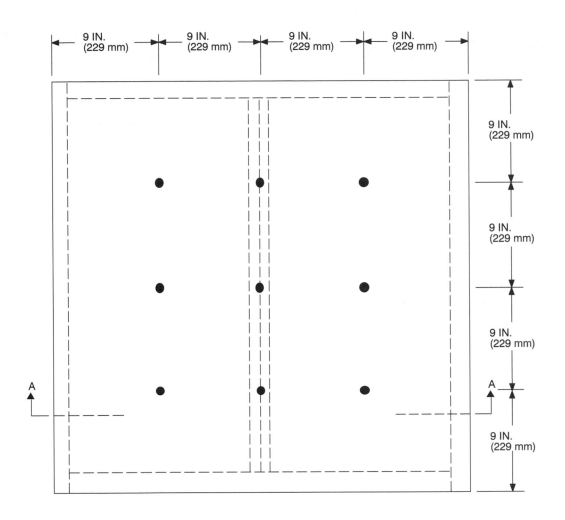

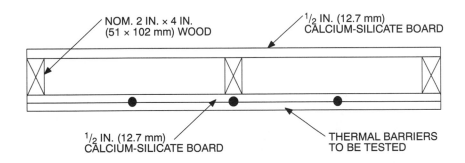

● THERMOCOUPLE

SECTION A–A

FIGURE 26-2-2—THERMOCOUPLE LOCATIONS

UNIFORM BUILDING CODE STANDARD 26-3
ROOM FIRE TEST STANDARD FOR INTERIOR
OF FOAM PLASTIC SYSTEMS

Test Standard of the International Conference of Building Officials

See Sections 601.3 and 2602.6, *Uniform Building Code*

SECTION 26.301 — SCOPE

This standard details a test method to evaluate the burning characteristics of foam plastic assemblies in a standard room configuration. It is intended to be a test for use under Section 2602.6 of this code.

SECTION 26.302 — FIRE TEST STRUCTURE

The fire test structure shall consist of a room with interior dimensions of 8 feet ± 1 inch (2438 mm ± 25 mm) by 12 feet ± 1 inch (3658 mm ± 25 mm) having a ceiling height of 8 feet ± 0.5 inch (2438 mm ± 13 mm) located in an enclosed building. A doorway 2 feet 6 inches ± 0.5 inch (762 mm ± 13 mm) by 7 feet 0 inches ± 0.5 inch (2134 mm ± 13 mm) shall be centered in one of the 8-foot-long (2438 mm) walls of the test structure. See Figure 26-3-1.

The wall test area shall consist of wall sections 8 feet (2438 mm) square intersecting at the corner opposite the doorway. Ceiling specimens shall cover an area 8 feet (2438 mm) square with two edges resting on or adjoining the intersecting wall test sections. Vertical and horizontal joints shall be included in the test wall and ceiling specimens to represent field conditions.

Except for composite panels, the construction of the walls and ceiling beyond the test area which serve as a substrate for foam plastic shall consist of $^1/_2$-inch (13 mm) glass-reinforced cement board or $^1/_2$-inch (13 mm) gypsum wallboard supported by suitable framing.

Composite wall and ceiling or roof panels with structural foam plastic cores shall be installed without a substrate and in the manner intended for use, including connections along all joints and perimeters. Panels intended to support superimposed loads shall be fire tested with the panels loaded in a manner resulting in conditions of maximum allowable stress.

EXCEPTION: Testing under loaded conditions may be waived in Type V construction when the panels need not be fire resistive.

When the test concerns nonstructural protective material, the foam plastic base shall be applied to the maximum thickness anticipated and have a minimum flame-spread rating of 75.

Material and fabrication of test assemblies must be certified by the testing agency as complying with descriptions or details that are a part of the report of tests.

The building containing the test structure shall have a temperature between 60°F and 90°F (15.6°C and 32.2°C) at the start of the fire test and shall be free of excessive drafts.

SECTION 26.303 — TEST PROCEDURE

26.303.1 Cribs. The fuel for the room test shall be a wood crib constructed of $1^1/_2$-inch (38 mm) square white fir, Douglas fir or spruce-pine fir fire sticks cut to 15-inch (381 mm) lengths. The equivalency of other types of wood shall be based on comparative full-scale tests. At a 12 percent moisture content, the crib shall weigh 30 pounds (13.6 kg) and be 15 inches (381 mm) square in

plan. One 8d nail shall be driven at each corner of each tier. Each interior stick shall be attached at each end to a perimeter stick with one 8d nail. Approximately 45 to 50 sticks will be involved and must be assembled in nine or 10 tiers with five sticks in each tier. The placement of sticks in each tier shall be oriented at 90 degrees to sticks in adjacent tiers. After fabrication the crib shall be conditioned to a maximum constant moisture content of 8 percent. Standard bricks cut in half and placed at each corner of the crib shall be used to support the crib not less than 3 inches (76 mm) above the floor located as described in Section 26.303.3.

26.303.2 Starter Material. One pound of shredded, fluffed wood excelsior is distributed around the bricks with the excelsior extending from the wall surfaces and covering an area approximately 21 inches by 21 inches (533 mm by 533 mm). To start the test, the wood excelsior is soaked with 4 ounces (0.12 L) of reagent ethyl alcohol or absolute ethyl alcohol, except for a triangular area approximately 6 inches by 6 inches (153 mm by 153 mm) diametrically opposite the intersection of the walls. The crib is then located 1 inch (25 mm) from the intersecting wall surfaces on the bricks.

26.303.3 Ignition. A match is placed in the excelsior to initiate burning. Under proper conditions for ignition, flames typically progress slowly through the dry excelsior for only 10 seconds until the soaked alcohol portion is reached, whereupon flames flash through the entire excelsior, providing uniform application of the ignition flame beneath the entire crib.

26.303.4 Extinguishment. Fire extinguishment is permitted 15 minutes after crib ignition. Charring of the test panels must not be affected by the extinguishing procedures.

26.303.5 Temperature Readings. Temperature readings at locations shown in Figure 26-3-2 shall be taken at maximum two-minute intervals and at 15 minutes from crib ignition with properly calibrated thermocouples of the type described in UBC Standard 7-1.

26.303.6 Smoke Measurement. Smoke generated during the 15-minute test period shall be measured by photoelectric instrumentation if there is sufficient available data to establish a basis of acceptance. In lieu of this, the test report shall include films taken during the test.

SECTION 26.304 — CONDITIONS OF ACCEPTANCE

A foam plastic wall or ceiling assembly shall be considered as meeting the requirements for acceptable performance within the following conditions:

1. Charring of the foam plastic shall not extend to the outer extremities of the test area within a 15-minute period after ignition of the excelsior. Discoloration extending not more than $^1/_4$ inch (6 mm) into the foam plastic shall not be considered as charring.

2. Smoke levels generated during the test period shall not be excessive.

3. Structural panels shall sustain the applied load during the test period.

SECTION 26.305 — REPORT OF TEST

The report of test shall include the following:

1. A detailed description of the foam plastic assembly including specifications on all components and manner of fabrication and installation.

2. A statement by the testing agency that preparation, fabrication and installation of the foam plastic assembly was in accordance with Item 1 and this standard.

3. A statement of compliance or specific points of deviation from test procedures set forth in this standard.

4. An account of visual observation of the foam plastic assemblies during the test.

5. Location and extent of charring in the foam plastic assemblies at the conclusion of the test.

6. Temperature readings during the test as set forth in Section 26.303.5.

7. Smoke measurement during the test or films of the test.

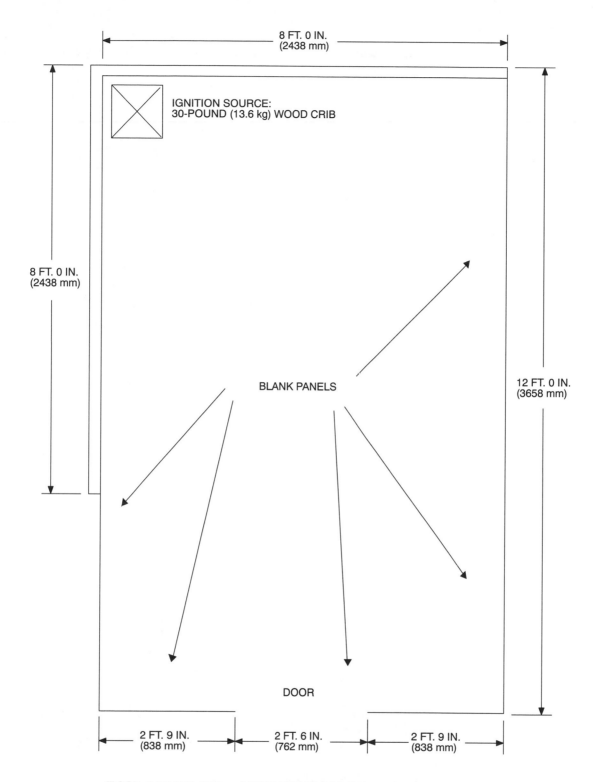

8 FT. 0 IN.
(2438 mm)

IGNITION SOURCE:
30-POUND (13.6 kg) WOOD CRIB

8 FT. 0 IN.
(2438 mm)

12 FT. 0 IN.
(3658 mm)

BLANK PANELS

DOOR

2 FT. 9 IN.
(838 mm)

2 FT. 6 IN.
(762 mm)

2 FT. 9 IN.
(838 mm)

[DOOR: 2 FT. 6 IN. (762 mm) WIDE BY 7 FT. 0 IN. (2134 mm) HIGH]

FIGURE 26-3-1—ROOM TEST CONFIGURATION

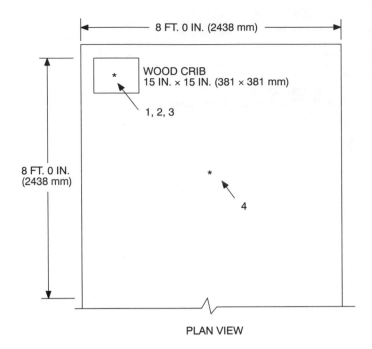

PLAN VIEW

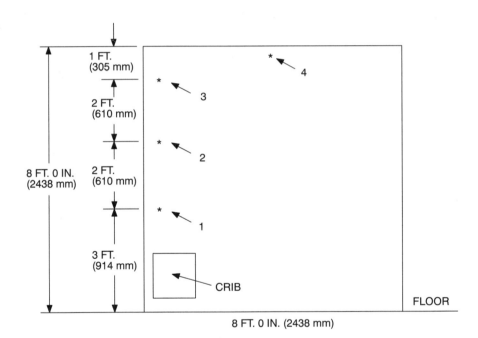

* THERMOCOUPLE LOCATIONS   ELEVATION

NOTES:
1. Thermocouples 1, 2 and 3 located 3 inches (76 mm) from adjacent wall surfaces.
2. Thermocouple 4 located 1 inch (25 mm) below the ceiling, 4 feet (1219 mm) from each of three walls.

FIGURE 26-3-2—THERMOCOUPLE LOCATIONS

UNIFORM BUILDING CODE STANDARD 26-4
METHOD OF TEST FOR THE EVALUATION OF
FLAMMABILITY CHARACTERISTICS OF EXTERIOR, NONLOAD-BEARING
WALL PANEL ASSEMBLIES USING FOAM PLASTIC INSULATION

Test Standard of the International Conference of Building Officials

See Sections 601.3 and 2602.5.2, *Uniform Building Code*

SECTION 26.401 — SCOPE

This test provides a method of determining the flammability characteristics of foam plastic insulated, exterior, nonload-bearing wall panel assemblies. The test structure is intended to simulate a "full-scale" multistory building installation. Test assemblies are evaluated on a "full-scale" basis.

The primary performance characteristics to be evaluated are:

1. Capability of the test panels to resist vertical spread of flame within the core of the panel from one story to the next;

2. Capability to resist flame propagation over the exterior face of the panels;

3. Capability to resist vertical spread of flame over the interior (room side) surface of the panels from one story to the next; and

4. Capability to resist lateral spread of flame from the compartment of fire origin to adjacent spaces.

SECTION 26.402 — FIRE TEST STRUCTURE

The fire test structure shall consist of a two-story, 24-foot-high (7315 mm) building having unfinished/unprotected inside room dimensions of (edge of slab to concrete block) 15 feet ± 2 inches (4572 mm ± 51 mm) wide by 15 feet ± 2 inches (4572 mm ± 51 mm) deep. See Figures 26-4-1A through 26-4-1D. Floor-to-floor height (unfinished/unprotected) shall be 12 feet ± 2 inches (3658 mm ± 51 mm). Floors and roof shall be of reinforced concrete or similar construction supported with columns. The first-floor slab shall be 12 inches ± 1 inch (305 mm ± 25 mm) thick, whereas the second floor and roof shall be 8 inches ± 0.5 inch (203 mm ± 13 mm) thick. Permanent walls of the structure shall be of 8-inch-thick (200 mm) concrete block or similar construction. The concrete block shall completely close two walls of the test structure, except for a 3-foot, 4-inch ± 3 inches (1016 mm ± 76 mm) wide by 6-foot, 8-inch ± 3 inches (2032 mm ± 76 mm) high access opening at the first- and second-floor levels. Additional access openings in the second-floor area are permitted, but must be closed off prior to test.

Spandrel beams on the underside of the second floor shall be designed to be replaceable and are required only when the mounting of the test sample requires them to be present. When used, the spandrel beams shall be of W10 by 12 (W250 by 18) and shall be installed as shown in Figures 26-4-1A through 26-4-1D.

Test panels shall be secured to the test structure using a girt system of replaceable 4-inch-by-4-inch-by-$^3/_{16}$-inch (102 mm by 102 mm by 4.8 mm) steel angles. The test panels shall completely close the two walls of the test structure, except for a window opening in one of the test walls. One of the test walls shall be fabricated with a 4-foot ± 0.5 inch (1219 mm ± 13 mm) high by 8-foot ± 0.5 inch (2438 ± 13 mm) long window opening in the first story. The window opening shall have a sill height of 3 feet ± 1 inch (914 mm ± 25 mm). The window opening shall be the only opening in the first-story burn room enclosure at the time of test.

Test panels shall be secured to the test structure using a method of fastening including all joints and perimeters to represent actual field conditions. Details of erection shall follow the manufacturer's instructions and shall be typical of actual product use. When a product may have vertical or horizontal joints, joints typical of normal construction, including caulking, backing and other details as appropriate, shall be incorporated in the test panels.

Prior to the start of a test, the access opening in the burn room shall be closed using an assembly having a minimum of three layers of $^5/_8$-inch-thick (15.9 mm) Type X gypsum wallboard on the burn room side of any supports. The access door opening in the second story may remain open during testing, but any additional access openings shall be closed.

In the first-floor burn room prior to each test, the two concrete block walls and the ceiling are to be protected with three layers of $^5/_8$-inch (15.9 mm) Type X gypsum wallboard. A framing/attachment system may be used between the concrete block/Type X gypsum wallboard and the concrete ceiling/Type X gypsum wallboard with the provision that the framing/attachment system not be thicker than 1.5 inches (38 mm). The floor is protected with at least one layer of $^5/_8$-inch (15.9 mm) Type X gypsum wallboard. The column located within the burn room shall be protected with appropriate fireproofing and boxed in with a single layer of $^5/_8$-inch (15.9 mm) Type X gypsum wallboard. Spandrel beams if used may or may not be protected at the discretion of the testing laboratory or client. The outriggers and the girt angles are not protected.

In the second story, prior to each test, the concrete block walls and ceiling are protected by one layer of Marinite board or $^5/_8$-inch (15.9 mm) Type X gypsum wallboard. The floor is protected by one layer of $^5/_8$-inch-thick (15.9 mm) Type X gypsum wallboard. The interior steel column shall be appropriately protected and boxed with one layer of $^5/_8$-inch (15.9 mm), Type X gypsum wallboard. Girt angles are left unprotected.

Material and fabrication of test assemblies must be certified by the testing agency as complying with the description or details that are a part of the report of test. The test laboratory shall retain a 1-foot-by-1-foot-square (305 mm by 305 mm) sample of the test system.

For outdoor facilities a windshield shall be utilized (see Figure 26-4-2) to minimize wind action across the face of the test structure.

SECTION 26.403 — INSTRUMENTATION AND DOCUMENTATION

26.403.1 Instrumentation. In this procedure, test instrumentation consists primarily of temperature measurements placed in the following locations:

1. Inside room of fire origin—underside of second-story floor and underside of structural steel members.

2. Window opening—6 inches (153 mm) below top of window opening.

3. On exterior face of wall panels.

4. On interior face of wall panels—at floors and in panel cores at second-floor level and above.

Temperature measurements are made using 20-gage Type K thermocouples.

Specific thermocouple locations are provided in Figures 26-4-3 through 26-4-7. Temperatures shall be recorded at intervals not to exceed 15 seconds.

26.403.2 Documentation. Documentation of tests is provided by:

1. Color videotape of exterior, and

2. Color 35 mm slides of exterior.

In order to facilitate documentation of flame penetration (if any) into the second-floor level, a video camera is placed looking inside the second floor. The camera is aimed at the test wall/floor intersection and observations relating to flame penetration and/or smoke development are made.

After the test is terminated by extinguishment of the fire in the wood crib, special note shall be made of the extent and duration of any residual burning in the test panel.

After a cool-down period, the interior and exterior sides of the test walls shall be described as to visual appearance and shall be photographed. The test walls shall then be dismantled and dissected to determine height and depth of char damage within the cavity and condition of panel facings.

SECTION 26.404 — TEST PROCEDURE

26.404.1 Crib Fire Exposure. The burn room shall be provided with a 1,285-pound (583 kg) wood crib fuel load which, when burned, produces the standard time/temperature curve described in Sections 7.102 and 7.103 of UBC Standard 7-1 as measured using the average of thermocouples (see Figure 26-4-3) inside the burn room for a period of not less than 30 minutes. The crib shall generate a fire exposure producing an intermittent flame plume similar to that generated in an actual fire discharging out of the burn room window. During the test the plume shall periodically attach itself to and shall expose the face of the test panel for a minimum of 5 feet (1524 mm) above the top of the burn room window. Makeup air for combustion of the crib shall be supplied solely through the 4-foot-by-8-foot (1219 mm by 2438 mm) window opening. No other ventilation is provided. Control temperatures are measured at the underside of the second floor and at the underside of the spandrel beams if used.

The fuel for the fire exposure shall be a 1,285-pound (583 kg) wood crib. The crib shall be constructed of dried 2-inch-by-4-inch (51 by 102 mm) No. 1 select grade Douglas fir members having a moisture content of 11 percent plus or minus 1 percent. Crib members are cut into 4-foot and 8-foot (1219 and 2438 mm) lengths. The 2-inch-by-4-inch (51 by 102 mm) members shall be nailed into a lattice-type crib consisting of full tiers and one partial tier of three 8-foot (2438 mm) 2 by 4's (51 mm by 102 mm). Overall crib dimensions shall be 48 inches deep (1219 mm), 96 inches (2438 mm) wide and $28^1/_2$ inches (724 mm) high. See Figure 26-4-9. The determining factor in the crib construction shall be the weight; however, in no case shall less than 18 tiers be used.

The crib shall be centered on the burn room window but located off center toward the window. See Figure 26-4-9.

The crib shall be supported above floor level by 8-inch concrete blocks. A layer of $5/_8$-inch-thick (15.9 mm) Type X gypsum wallboard is placed between the crib and the concrete block support. See Figure 26-4-10.

26.404.2 Starter Material. Prior to ignition, 1 gallon (3.8 L) of kerosene is equally divided into eight pans ($7^1/_4$ inches in diameter, $^{15}/_{16}$ inch deep) (184 mm in diameter, 24 mm deep) and the

pans are placed under the crib. The pans are interconnected using kerosene-soaked rags that have been soaked sufficiently to facilitate ignition. Additionally, 2 pints (1 L) of kerosene are poured over the crib just prior to ignition. The kerosene is to provide quick ignition of the crib and also cause an initial rapid increase in temperature within the burn room.

26.404.3 Ignition. After proper operation of all instrumentation and documentation equipment is verified, the pans containing kerosene are placed under the crib.

A match or torch is used to ignite a kerosene-soaked rag which, in turn, causes flames to spread to the kerosene in the eight pans located under the crib. The start of the test is ignition of the kerosene in one of the pans. The fire develops quickly with flames reaching the ceiling of the burn room within several minutes. Flames begin to emerge from the burn room window in three to five minutes.

26.404.4 Control. During the last several minutes of the test, the crib fire may produce higher temperatures than those described in UBC Standard 7-1. Should the average temperature in the burn room as measured by the thermocouples described in Figure 26-4-3 exceed 1,800°F (982°C) for a period greater than one minute, then a control measure may be used at the discretion of the testing laboratory or the client to maintain the temperatures within the room in accordance with Section 26.404.1. One example of a control measure is the use of water fog such that approximately 1 gallon (3.8 L) of water is applied directly to the wood crib.

26.404.5 Duration. The test is continued for 30 minutes. At the conclusion of the test, the crib fire is extinguished using a hose line. Any residual burning in or on the surface of the test panels shall be noted and panels shall be allowed to burn freely until self-extinguishment occurs or fire spreads to the limits of the test panels.

26.404.6 Weather Conditions. Outdoor tests shall not be conducted if, at the start of the test, the average wind velocity exceeds 10 miles per hour (16 km/h), if the relative humidity is 100 percent or if there is fog or precipitation present at the test site.

SECTION 26.405 — CONDITIONS OF ACCEPTANCE

The performance of a test assembly shall be judged on the basis of visual observations both during and after the test in conjunction with temperature data. An exterior wall assembly shall be considered as meeting the requirements for acceptable performance if during the 30-minute test period:

1. Flames do not propagate over the surface of the test walls beyond the immediate area of crib flame impingement on the exterior face of the wall panels.

2. Flame propagation does not occur vertically or laterally through the core insulation. Flame propagation may be judged to occur within the test panels when temperatures within the insulation core as measured by Thermocouples 28, 29, 30, 42, 18, 46, 56, 55, 54, 38, 20, 53, 73, 65, 74, 66, 78 and 64, as shown in Figures 26-4-4 and 26-4-5, exceed 750°F (400°C) above ambient.

3. Flame propagation shall not occur to the first-floor wall panels extending beyond the concrete block walls of the test fixture either through core insulation or over the exterior or interior panel surfaces. Where the flame cannot be directly observed, flame propagation shall be assumed to occur where the temperatures as measured by Thermocouples 58, 57, 79 and 80 within the insulation core exceed 750°F (400°C) above ambient.

4. Temperatures measured 1 inch (25 mm) from the interior surfaces of the wall assembly within the second story do not exceed 350°F (180°C) above ambient.

5. Flames do not enter the second-story room.

SECTION 26.406 — REPORT OF TEST

The report of test shall contain the following:

1. Description of test wall assembly to include:

   1.1 Drawings showing structural design, plan, elevation, principal cross section plus other sections as needed for clarity and joint locations and details.

   1.2 Details of attachment of walls to test facility.

   1.3 Flame-spread and smoke-developed values of foam plastic per UBC Standard 8-1.

   1.4 Ignition temperature of foam plastic.

2. Location of thermocouples.

3. General ambient condition at test time.

4. Temperature data obtained during the test for all thermocouple locations.

5. Visual observations made during the test.

6. Photographs of the following:

   6.1 Test walls prior to test.

   6.2 Test in progress.

   6.3 Test walls exterior—posttest.

   6.4 Test walls interior—posttest.

   6.5 Core insulation of both walls—posttest.

7. Performance of wall system with respect to:

   7.1 Damage to the walls and core.

   7.2 Flame advance over exterior faces.

   7.3 Flame advance over interior faces.

   7.4 Flame penetration into second floor.

   7.5 Smoke accumulation inside the second-story room.

   7.6 Extent of residual burning.

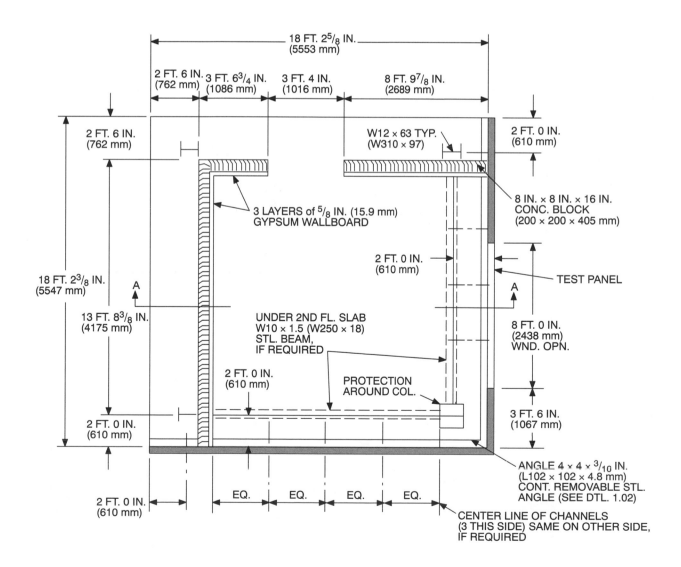

FIGURE 26-4-1A—FIRST/SECOND FLOOR PLAN

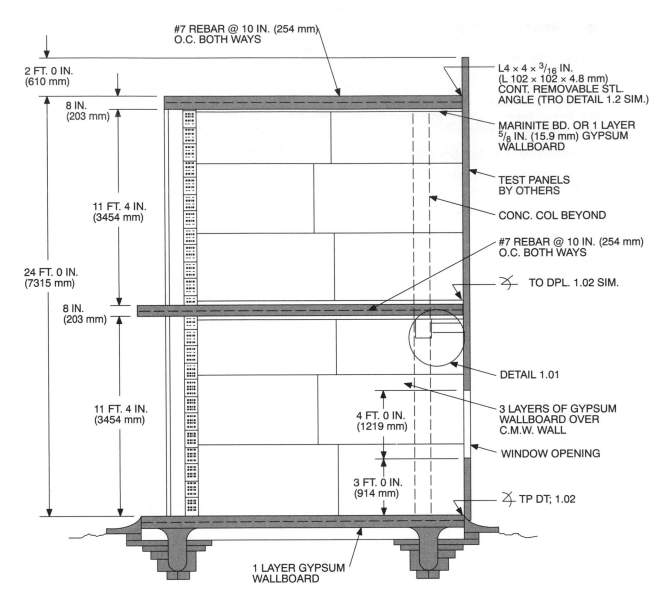

FIGURE 26-4-1B—SECTION A–A

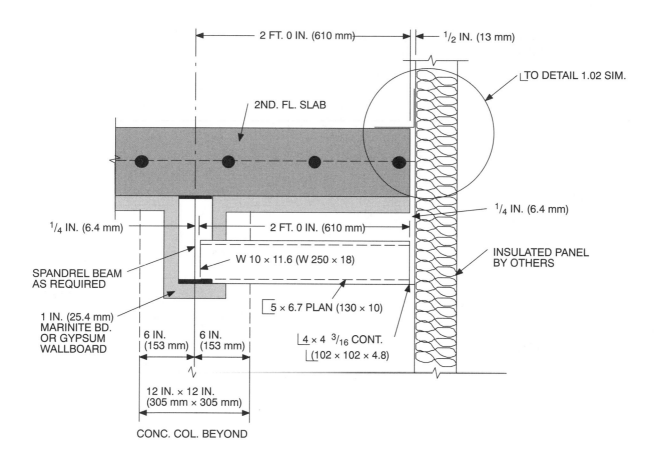

2 FT. 0 IN. (610 mm)

¹/₂ IN. (13 mm)

TO DETAIL 1.02 SIM.

2ND. FL. SLAB

¹/₄ IN. (6.4 mm)

INSULATED PANEL BY OTHERS

¹/₄ IN. (6.4 mm)

2 FT. 0 IN. (610 mm)

W 10 × 11.6 (W 250 × 18)

SPANDREL BEAM AS REQUIRED

└ 5 × 6.7 PLAN (130 × 10)

1 IN. (25.4 mm) MARINITE BD. OR GYPSUM WALLBOARD

└ 4 × 4 ³/₁₆ CONT.
(102 × 102 × 4.8)

6 IN. (153 mm)

6 IN. (153 mm)

12 IN. × 12 IN. (305 mm × 305 mm)

CONC. COL. BEYOND

FIGURE 26-4-1C—1.01 SECTION DETAIL

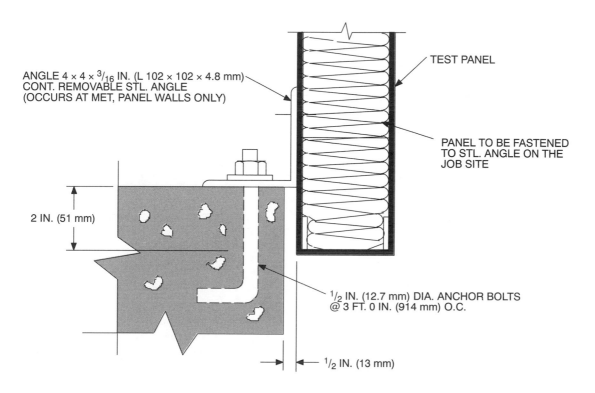

ANGLE 4 × 4 × ³/₁₆ IN. (L 102 × 102 × 4.8 mm) CONT. REMOVABLE STL. ANGLE (OCCURS AT MET, PANEL WALLS ONLY)

TEST PANEL

PANEL TO BE FASTENED TO STL. ANGLE ON THE JOB SITE

2 IN. (51 mm)

¹/₂ IN. (12.7 mm) DIA. ANCHOR BOLTS @ 3 FT. 0 IN. (914 mm) O.C.

¹/₂ IN. (13 mm)

FIGURE 26-4-1D—1.02 SECTION DETAIL

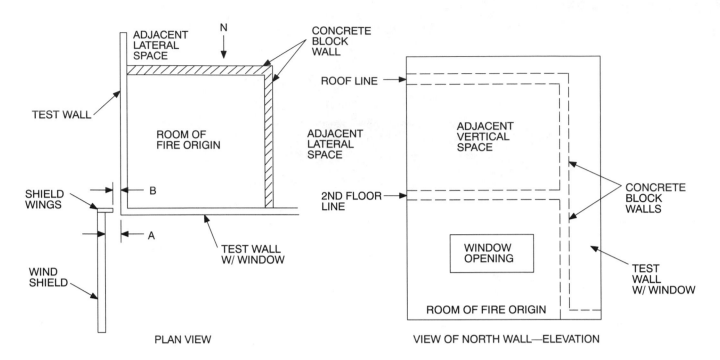

FIGURE 26-4-2—TEST ARRANGEMENT

BURN ROOM—PLAN VIEW

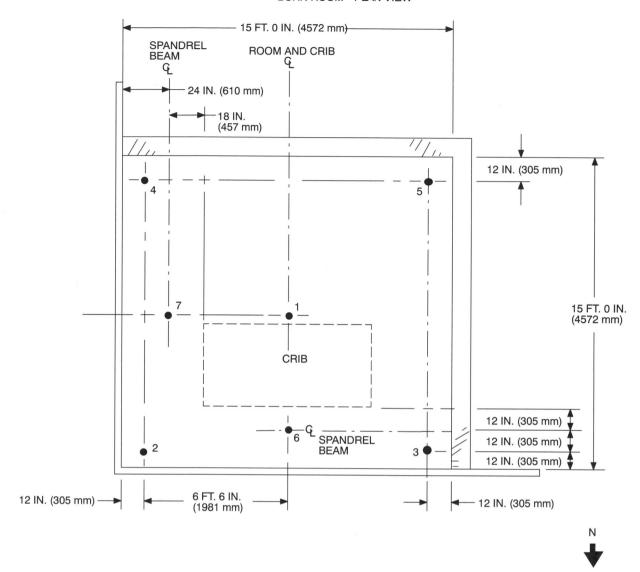

Thermocouples 1 and 5 are 6 in. (153 mm) below ceiling

Thermocouples 2, 3 and 4 are 2 in. (51 mm) below spandrel
beam and centered between wall and beam

Thermocouples 6 and 7 are 1 in. (25 mm) below bottom
surface of spandrel beam

NOTE: If no spandrel beam is used, then Thermocouples 2, 3, 4, 6 and 7 are to be
6 inches (153 mm) below ceiling.

FIGURE 26-4-3—THERMOCOUPLE LAYOUT

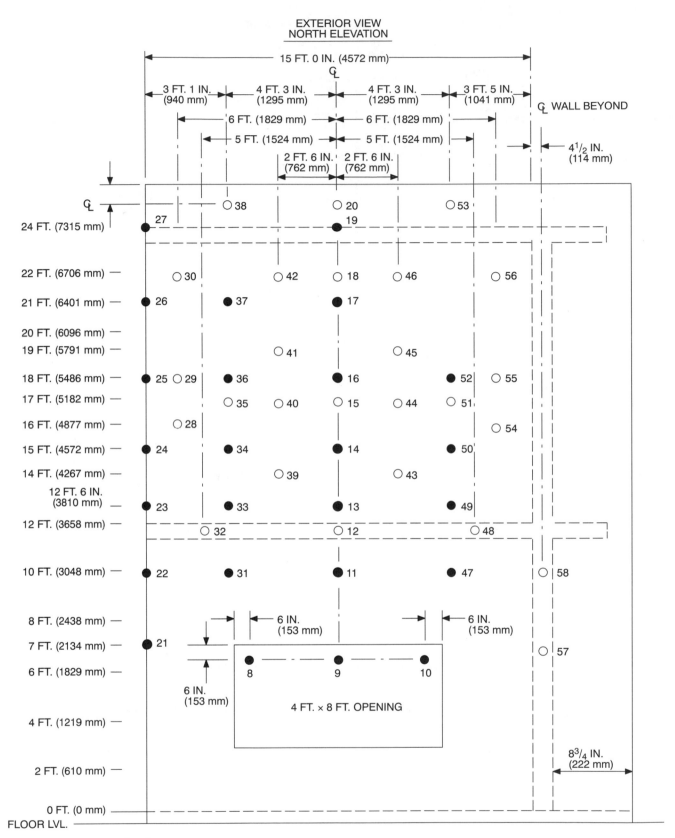

FIGURE 26-4-4—THERMOCOUPLE LAYOUT

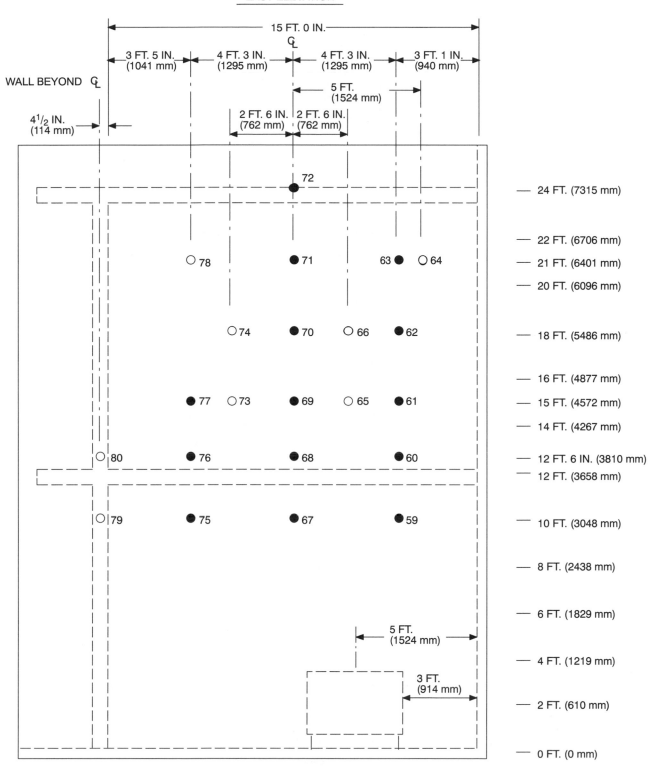

FIGURE 26-4-5—THERMOCOUPLE LAYOUT

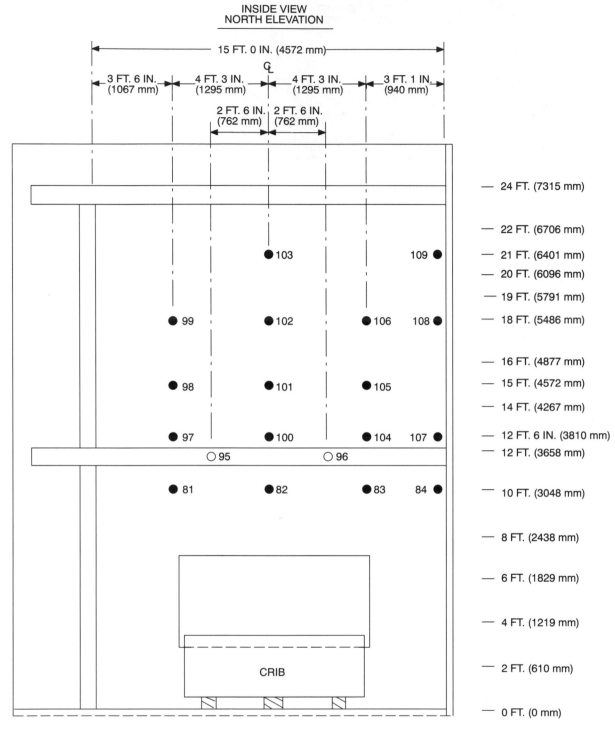

INSIDE VIEW
NORTH ELEVATION

NOTES:

● Thermocouples placed 1 in. (25 mm) from wall surfaces.

○ Thermocouples placed in safing material—center of floor level.

FIGURE 26-4-6—THERMOCOUPLE LAYOUT

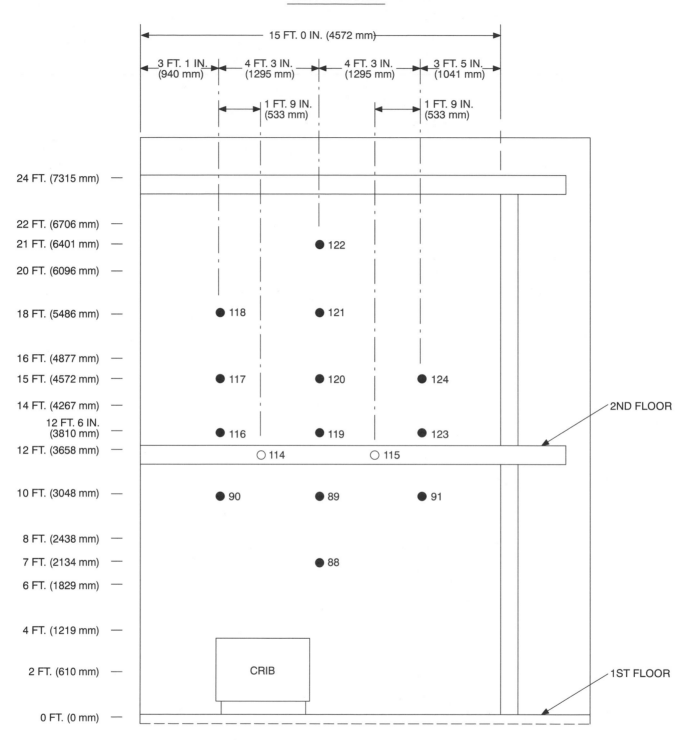

FIGURE 26-4-7—THERMOCOUPLE LAYOUT

NOTES:

● Thermocouples placed 1 in. (25 mm) from wall surfaces.

○ Thermocouples placed in safing material—center of floor level.

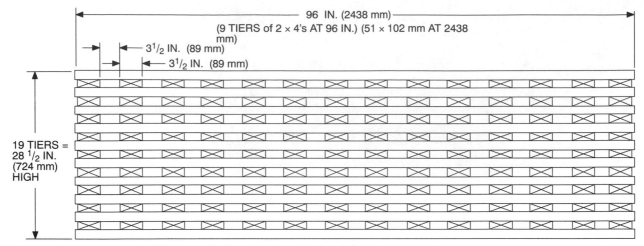

FRONT VIEW OF CRIB

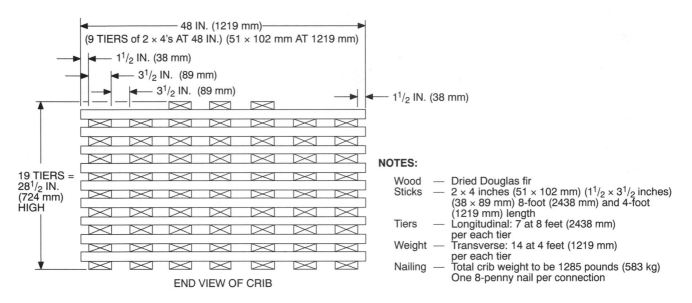

END VIEW OF CRIB

NOTES:

Wood	—	Dried Douglas fir
Sticks	—	2 × 4 inches (51 × 102 mm) ($1^1/_2$ × $3^1/_2$ inches) (38 × 89 mm) 8-foot (2438 mm) and 4-foot (1219 mm) length
Tiers	—	Longitudinal: 7 at 8 feet (2438 mm) per each tier
Weight	—	Transverse: 14 at 4 feet (1219 mm) per each tier
Nailing	—	Total crib weight to be 1285 pounds (583 kg) One 8-penny nail per connection

FIGURE 26-4-8—CRIB CONSTRUCTION

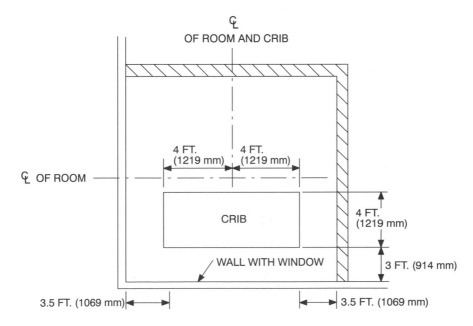

FIGURE 26-4-9—PLACEMENT OF CRIB IN ROOM

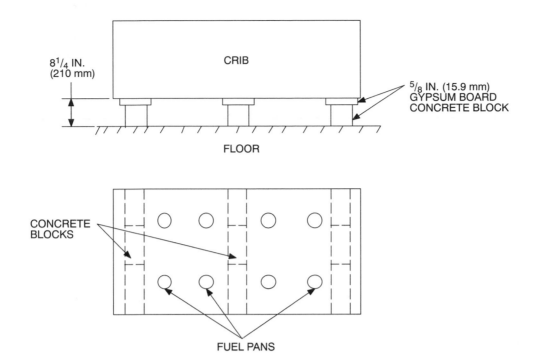

FIGURE 26-4-10—CRIB ARRANGEMENT

UNIFORM BUILDING CODE STANDARD 26-5

CHAMBER METHOD OF TEST FOR MEASURING THE DENSITY OF SMOKE FROM THE BURNING OR DECOMPOSITION OF PLASTIC MATERIALS

**Based on Standard Test Method D 2843-70 of the American Society for Testing and Materials.
Extracted, with permission, from the *Annual Book of ASTM Standards,* copyright American Society for
Testing and Materials, 100 Barr Harbor Drive, West Conshohocken, PA 19428**

**See Sections 217 and 2603.1.6, *Uniform Building Code;* and
Section 212, *Uniform Sign Code***

SECTION 26.501 — SCOPE

This test method covers a procedure for measuring and observing the relative amounts of smoke produced by the burning or decomposition of plastics. It is intended to be used for measuring the smoke-producing characteristics of plastics under controlled conditions of combustion or decomposition. The measurements are made in terms of the loss of light transmission through a collected volume of smoke produced under controlled, standardized conditions. The apparatus is constructed so that the flame and smoke can be observed during the test.

SECTION 26.502 — SUMMARY OF METHOD

A 1-inch-by-1-inch (25 mm by 25 mm) specimen of the thickness intended for use is placed on a supporting metal screen and is burned in a laboratory test chamber (see Figure 26-5-1) under active flame conditions using a propane burner operating at a pressure of 40 psi (276 kPa). The 12-inch-by-12-inch-by-31-inch (300 mm by 300 mm by 791 mm) test chamber is instrumented with a light source, a photoelectric cell, and a meter to measure light absorption horizontally across the 12-inch (300 mm) light beam path. The chamber is closed during the four-minute test period except for the 1-inch-high (25 mm) ventilation openings around the bottom.

The light absorption data are plotted versus time. A typical plot is shown in Figure 26-5-2.

SECTION 26.503 — SIGNIFICANCE

This test method is designed to permit the measurement of smoke generation and its visibility-obscuring effects (density). Results of tests made on a plastic material under conditions herein prescribed can be used to evaluate the smoke-production characteristics by determining the smoke density rating of the material. The smoke density rating shall represent the total amount of smoke present in the chamber for the four-minute time interval. It is the area under the curve of light absorption versus time divided by the total area of the graph times 100.

The visual and instrumental observations from this test compare well with the visual observations of the smoke generated by plastic materials when added to a freely burning, large outdoor fire (burning conditions that are favorable to minimum smoke production). Hence, this method serves as a reliable method of identifying materials which could be expected to smoke excessively under almost all conditions of burning and decomposition.

The basic assumption underlying this procedure is that the hazard associated with smoke in human occupancies will be significant only if a material is burning or decomposing in the presence of flame. Therefore, the test specimen is exposed to flame for the duration of the test, and the smoke is substantially trapped in the chamber in which combustion occurs. The usefulness of this test procedure is in its ability to measure the amount of smoke produced, which is done in a simple, direct and meaningful manner.

SECTION 26.504 — APPARATUS

26.504.1 Chamber. The chamber shall consist of a 0.064-inch (1.63 mm) (No. 14 B.&S. gage) 12-inch-by-12-inch-by-31-inch (300 mm by 300 mm by 790 mm) aluminum box to which is hinged a heat-resistant glazed glass door. This box shall be mounted on a 14-inch-by-16-inch-by-$2^1/_4$-inch (350 mm by 400 mm by 57 mm) base which houses the controls. Depending on the materials tested, the metal may require protection from corrosion.

The chamber shall be sealed except for 1-inch-by-9-inch (25.4 mm by 229 mm) openings on the four sides of the bottom of the chamber. A 60 cfm (1700 L/min.) blower shall be mounted on one side of the chamber. The inlet duct to the blower shall be equipped with a close-fitting damper. The outlet of the blower shall be connected through a duct to the laboratory exhaust system.

The two sides adjacent to the door shall be fitted with $2^3/_4$-inch-diameter (70 mm) smoketight glazed areas centered $19^3/_4$ inches (502 mm) above the base. Boxes containing the optical equipment and additional controls shall be attached at these locations and outside the chamber.

A removable white plastic plate shall be attached to the back of the chamber. There shall be a $3^1/_2$-inch-by-6-inch (90 mm by 150 mm) clear area centered about $19^3/_4$ inches (502 mm) above the bottom of the chamber through which is seen an illuminated white-on-red exit sign. The white background permits observation of the flame, smoke and burning characteristics of the material. The viewing of the exit sign helps to correlate visibility and measured values.

26.504.2 Specimen Holder. The specimen shall be supported on a $2^1/_2$-inch (64 mm) square of $1/_4$-inch-by-$1/_4$-inch (6 mm by 6 mm), 0.035-inch-gage (0.9 mm) stainless steel wire cloth 8 inches (203.2 mm) above the base and equidistant from all sides of the chamber. This screen shall lie in stainless steel bezel supported by a rod through the right side of the chamber. From the same rod, a similar bezel shall be located 3 inches (76 mm) below and it shall support a square of asbestos paper which catches any particles that may drip from the specimen during the test. By rotating the specimen holder rod, the burning specimen can be quenched in a shallow pan of water positioned below the specimen holder.

26.504.3 Ignition System. The specimen shall be ignited by a propane flame from a burner operating at a pressure of 40 psi (276 kPa). The fuel shall be mixed with air which has been propelled through the burner by the venturi effect of the propane [commercial grade 85.0 percent minimum, gross heating value 2,590 Btu per cubic foot (23 000 cal/L) propane meets the requirements] as it passes from a 0.006-inch-diameter (0.152 mm) orifice. The burner shall be assembled as shown in the exploded view of the burner in Figure 26-5-3. The burner must be designed to provide adequate outside air. Since the orifice provides the metering effect proportionate to the supply pressure, care must be taken that the orifice is the only means of fuel egress.

The burner shall be capable of being quickly positioned under the specimen so that the axis of the burner falls on a line passing through a point $3/10$ inch (8 mm) above the base at one back corner of the chamber, extending diagonally across the chamber and sloping upward at an angle of 45 degrees with the base. The exit opening of the burner shall be $10^7/32$ inches (259.56 mm) from the reference point at the rear of the chamber.

A duct at least 6 inches (150 mm) outside of the chamber shall provide the air piped to the burner.

Propane pressure shall be adjustable and preferably automatically regulated. Propane pressure shall be indicated by means of a Bourdon tube gage.

26.504.4 Photometric System. A light source, a barrier-layer photoelectric cell and a temperature-compensated meter shall be used to measure the proportion of a light beam which penetrates a 12-inch (300 mm) path through the smoke. The light path shall be arranged horizontally as shown in Figure 26-5-4.

A light source shall be mounted in a box (4 B1 in Figure 26-5-1) extending from the left side of the chamber at the mean height of $19^3/4$ (502 mm) inches above the base. The light source shall be a compact filament microscope lamp No. 1493 operated at 5.8 volts and a spherical reflector, with power supplied by a voltage-regulating transformer. (Microscope lamps No. 1493 are manufactured by General Electric Company, Westinghouse and others.) A $2^1/2$-inch (63.5 mm) focal length lens shall focus a spot of light on the photocell in the right-hand instrument panel.

Another box containing the photometer (4 B2 in Figure 26-5-1) shall be attached to the right-hand side of the chamber. The barrier-layer photoelectric cell shall have standard observer spectral response. An egg-crate grid in front of the photocell shall be used to protect the cell from stray light. The grid shall be finished in dull black and have openings at least twice as deep as they are wide. The current produced by the photocell is indicated in terms of percent light absorption on a meter. The photocell linearity decreases as the temperature increases; compensations shall therefore be made.

The meter may have two ranges. The range change shall be accomplished by shunting the meter to one-tenth its sensitivity. When enough smoke accumulates to absorb 90 percent of the light beam, a momentary switch shall be depressed returning the meter to its basic sensitivity. By doing this, the meter scale now reads 90 to 100 percent instead of 0 to 100 percent.

26.504.5 Timing Device. A clock to indicate 15-second intervals shall be used. If the time intervals are audible, it will be convenient for the operator to record observations.

26.504.6 Planimeter. A planimeter or other suitable means shall be used for measuring the area under the light absorption curve.

SECTION 26.505 — TEST SPECIMENS

The specimen shall be 1 inch by 1 inch (25.4 mm by 25.4 mm) by the thickness intended for use. Thicknesses other than those intended for use may be tested, and the thickness should be reported with the smoke density values.

The specimens shall be sanded, machined or die cut in a manner that produces a cut surface that is free from projecting fibers, chips and ridges.

The test sample shall consist of three specimens.

SECTION 26.506 — CONDITIONING

Specimens shall be preconditioned and tested in accordance with Procedure A of the ASTM Method D618-61 for Method of Conditioning Plastics and Electrical Insulating Materials for Testing, unless otherwise specified.

Tests shall be conducted in a hood which has a window for observing the test.

SECTION 26.507 — PROCEDURE

Turn on photometer lamp, exit sign, and exhaust blower.

Turn on propane, ignite burner and adjust the propane pressure to 40 psi (276 kPa). Caution: Do not fail to light burner immediately.

Set temperature compensation.

Adjust lamp control to zero percent light absorption.

Lay the test specimen flat on the screen in such a position that the burner flame will be directly under the specimen when the burner is swung into position.

Set the timer to zero.

Shut off the exhaust blower, close the smoke chamber door, and immediately position the burner under the specimen and start the timer.

Close the hood door to within 2 inches (50 mm) of the bottom of the hood.

Record the percent light absorbed at 15-second intervals for four minutes.

Record observations during the conduct of the test. Include the time it takes for the sample to burst into flame, time for flame extinguishment or specimen consumption, obscuration of the exit sign by smoke accumulation and any general or usual burning characteristics noted, such as melting, dripping, foaming or charring.

Upon completion of the test, turn on exhaust blower to ventilate the combustion products from the chamber. (It should be noted that for some materials the product of burning may be toxic, and care should be taken to guard the operator from the effects of these gases. The ventilating fan in the hood should be turned on and the damper opened immediately after the test is completed and before opening the hood door in order to remove any irritating products of the test. The exhaust fan is turned off and the hood damper closed during the test to prevent backdraft.)

Open the door and clean the combustion deposits from the photometer, exit sign and door glass with detergent and water. Burn off any material remaining on the screen or replace the screen and asbestos square for the next test.

Run all tests in triplicate.

SECTION 26.508 — OPTIONAL PROCEDURES

The output of the photocell may be recorded versus time on an appropriate graphic recorder.

With a suitably sensitive meter, more than one decade change may be used to separate readings in the very dense smoke range.

SECTION 26.509 — TREATMENT OF DATA

The readings of 15-second intervals of light absorption for the three specimens per group shall be averaged. The average light absorption shall be plotted against time on linear paper. Figure 26-5-2 is a sample curve.

The total smoke produced shall be determined by measuring the area under the curve. The smoke density rating shall represent the total amount of smoke present in the chamber for the four-minute time interval. It is the area under the curve of light absorption versus time, divided by the total area of the graph times 100.

SECTION 26.510 — REPORT

The report shall include the following:

Identification of the material.

Thickness of the specimen.

Readings of light absorption at 15-second intervals for each test and average.

Plots of average light absorption versus time.

Area in percent under the light absorption-time curve (smoke density rating).

Observations on behavior of material.

Observations on obscurement of exit sign.

The details of any departure from the specifications of the method of testing.

EXAMPLE: In the light absorption-time plot in Figure 26-5-2, the plot has been made using 1 inch (25.4 mm) equal to 30 percent as the ordinate and 1 inch (25.4 mm) equal to 0.75 minute as the abscissa. The graph area for four minutes is found to be 17.78 square inches (11 470.94 mm^2). The area under the curve is found to be 14.02 square inches (9045.14 mm^2). The smoke density rating is then computed as follows:

$$\text{Smoke Density Rating} = \frac{14.02}{17.78} \times 100$$

$$\text{in percent} = 78.8$$

For **SI:**

$$\text{Smoke Density Rating} = \frac{9045.14}{11\,470.94} \times 100$$

$$\text{in percent} = 78.8$$

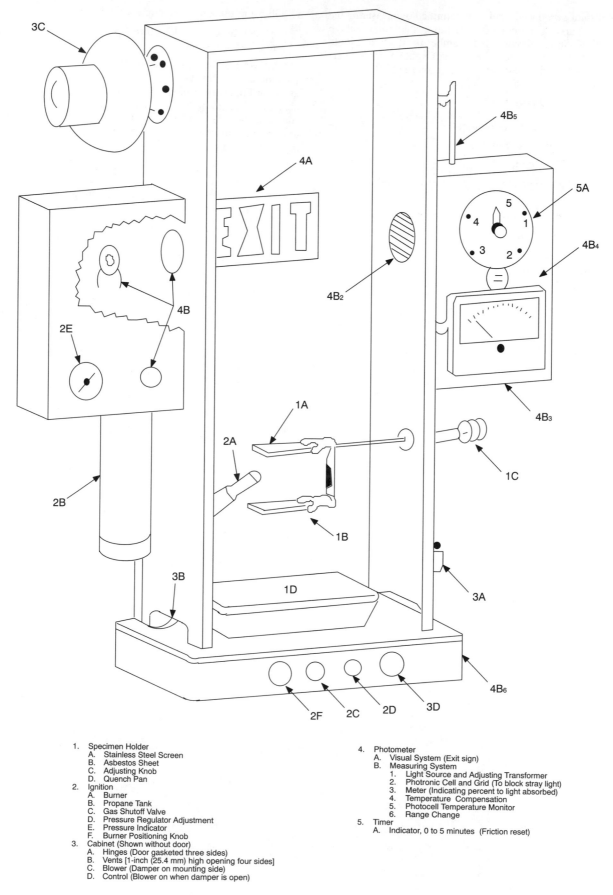

1. Specimen Holder
   A. Stainless Steel Screen
   B. Asbestos Sheet
   C. Adjusting Knob
   D. Quench Pan
2. Ignition
   A. Burner
   B. Propane Tank
   C. Gas Shutoff Valve
   D. Pressure Regulator Adjustment
   E. Pressure Indicator
   F. Burner Positioning Knob
3. Cabinet (Shown without door)
   A. Hinges (Door gasketed three sides)
   B. Vents [1-inch (25.4 mm) high opening four sides]
   C. Blower (Damper on mounting side)
   D. Control (Blower on when damper is open)

4. Photometer
   A. Visual System (Exit sign)
   B. Measuring System
      1. Light Source and Adjusting Transformer
      2. Photronic Cell and Grid (To block stray light)
      3. Meter (Indicating percent to light absorbed)
      4. Temperature Compensation
      5. Photocell Temperature Monitor
      6. Range Change
5. Timer
   A. Indicator, 0 to 5 minutes (Friction reset)

FIGURE 26-5-1—SCHEMATIC DIAGRAM OF SMOKE CHAMBER

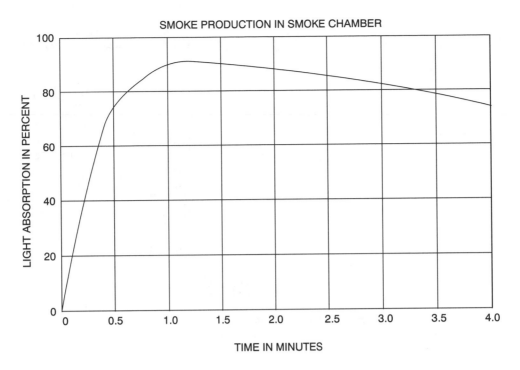

FIGURE 26-5-2—LIGHT ABSORPTION VERSUS TIME

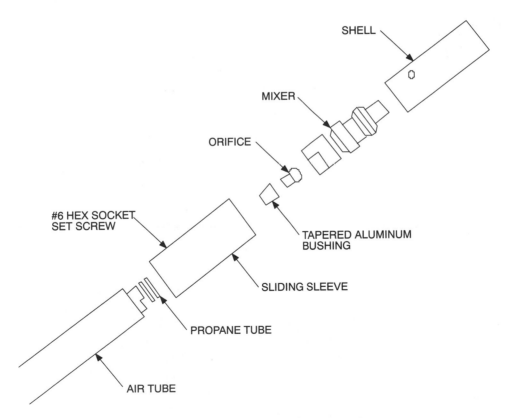

FIGURE 26-5-3—EXPLODED VIEW OF THE BURNER

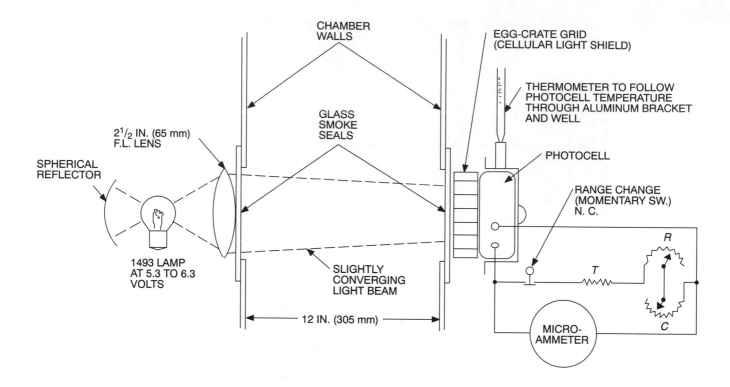

$T =$ Temperature sensitive winding in or on meter case to increase in resistance in proportion to increase in meter resistance with temperature.

$R =$ Potentiometer with calibrated scale to reduce resistance in proportion to decrease in photocell output with rise in temperature.

$C =$ Potentiometer to calibrate total resistance of shunt to change meter sensitivity exactly by 10:1 ratio.

FIGURE 26-5-4—SMOKE DENSITY TEST CHAMBER PHOTOMETER

UNIFORM BUILDING CODE STANDARD 26-6

IGNITION PROPERTIES OF PLASTICS

Based on Standard Test Method D 1929-68 (1975) of the American Society for Testing and Materials. Extracted, with permission, from the *Annual Book of ASTM Standards,* copyright American Society for Testing and Materials, 100 Barr Harbor Drive, West Conshohocken, PA 19428

See Sections 217, 2602.6 and 2603.8.1, Item 1, *Uniform Building Code;* and Section 212, *Uniform Sign Code*

SECTION 26.601 — SCOPE

This method of test covers a laboratory procedure for determining the self-ignition and flash-ignition temperatures of plastics using a hot-air ignition furnace.

SECTION 26.602— SIGNIFICANCE

Tests made under conditions herein prescribed can be of considerable value in comparing the relative ignition characteristics of different materials. Values obtained represent the lowest ambient air temperature that will cause ignition of the material under the conditions of this test. Test values are expected to rank materials according to ignition susceptibility under actual use conditions.

This test is not intended to be the sole criterion for fire hazard. In addition to ignition temperatures, fire hazard includes such other factors as burning rate or flame spread, intensity of burning, fuel contribution, products of combustion and others.

SECTION 26.603 — DEFINITIONS

FLASH-IGNITION TEMPERATURE is the lowest initial temperature of air passing around the specimen at which a sufficient amount of combustible gas is evolved to be ignited by a small external pilot flame.

SELF-IGNITION BY TEMPORARY GLOW. In some cases slow decomposition and carbonization of the plastic result only in glow of short duration at various points in the specimen without general ignition actually taking place. This is a special case of self-ignition temperature defined as "self-ignition by temporary glow."

SELF-IGNITION TEMPERATURE is the lowest initial temperature of air passing around the specimen at which, in the absence of an ignition source, the self-heating properties of the specimen lead to ignition or ignition occurs of itself as indicated by an explosion flame or sustained glow.

SECTION 26.604 — APPARATUS

The apparatus shall be a hot-air ignition furnace as shown in Figure 26-6-1 and shall consist primarily of the following parts:

26.604.1 Furnace Tube. A vertical tube with an inside diameter of 4 inches (102 mm) and a length of $8^1/_2$ inches to 10 inches (216 mm to 254 mm) made of a ceramic that will withstand 1382°F (750°C) and with an opening at the bottom fitted with a plug for the removal of accumulated residue.

26.604.2 Inner Ceramic Tube. A ceramic tube with inside diameter of 3 inches (76 mm), length of $8^1/_2$ inches to 10 inches (216 mm to 254 mm) and thickness of about 0.125 inch (76 mm) placed inside the furnace tube and positioned $^3/_4$ inch (19 mm) above the furnace floor on three small spacer blocks. The top shall be covered by a disk of heat-resistant material with a 1-inch (25 mm) diameter opening which is used to insert thermocouple leads for observation and for passage of smoke and gases. The pilot flame shall be located immediately above the opening.

26.604.3 Air Source. An outside air source to admit clean air tangentially near the top of the annular space between the ceramic tubes through a copper tube at a steady and controllable rate. Air shall be heated and circulated in the space between the two tubes and enter the inner furnace tube at the bottom. Air shall be metered by a rotameter or other suitable device; refer to air calibration curves (Figure 26-6-2) for proper furnace air velocities.

26.604.4 Heating Unit. An electrical heating unit made of 50 turns of No. 16 B.&S. (1.3 mm) wire. (Nichrome V alloy wire.) The wires, contained within an asbestos sleeve, shall be wound around the furnace tube and shall be embedded in cement.

26.604.5 Insulation. Consisting of a layer of asbestos wool approximately $2^1/_2$ inches (64 mm) thick and covered by a sheet iron jacket.

26.604.6 Pilot Flame. Consisting of $^1/_{16}$-inch (1.6 mm) diameter copper tubing attached to a gas supply and placed horizontally $^1/_4$ inch (6.4 mm) above the top surface of the divided disk. The pilot flame shall be adjusted to $^3/_4$ inch (19 mm) in length and centered above the opening in the disk.

26.604.7 Specimen Support and Holder. A convenient specimen holder, measuring $1^1/_2$ inches (38 mm) in diameter by $^1/_2$ inch (13 mm) in depth, is a $^1/_2$-ounce (14.2 g) metal container of approximately 5-mil (0.13 mm) thick steel. One-half of the container shall be used as a specimen holder and shall be held in a ring of $^1/_{16}$-inch (1.6 mm) stainless steel welding rod. The ring shall be welded to a length of the same type rod extending through the cover of the furnace as shown in Figure 26-6-1. The specimen holder shall be located 7 inches to $7^1/_2$ inches (178 mm to 191 mm) down from the top of the furnace.

26.604.8 Thermocouples. Chromel-alumel or iron-constantan [0.020-inch (0.51 mm)] thermocouples for temperature measurement. These shall be conveniently connected to a multiple-point recorder and each thermocouple temperature shall be recorded at least every 15 seconds. Thermocouple 1 (T_1) measures the temperature of the specimen. It should be located as near the center of the specimen as possible when the specimen is in place in the furnace. Thermocouple 2 (T_2) measures the temperature of the air traveling past the specimen. It shall be located slightly below and to the side of the specimen holder. Thermocouple 3 (T_3) measures the temperature of the heating coil. Thermocouple 1 is used also for measuring initial air temperature in constant-temperature runs before insertion of the specimen.

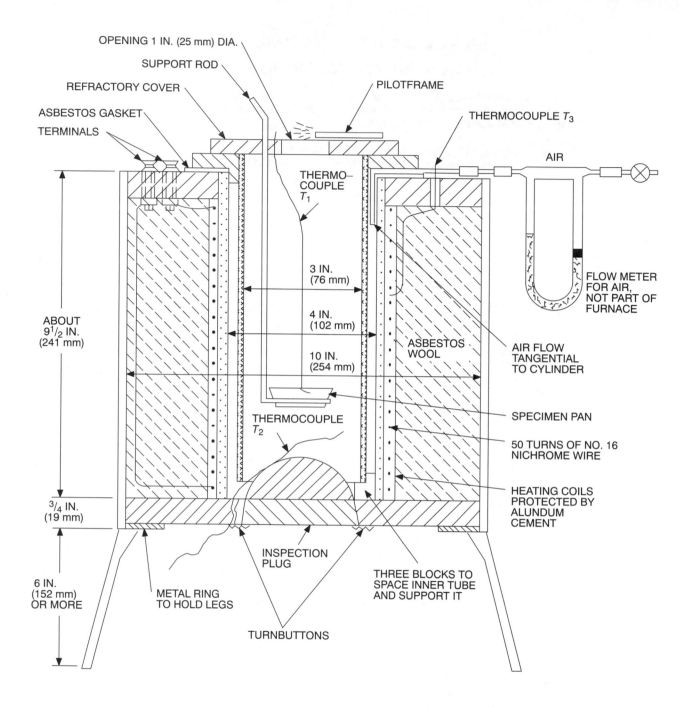

FIGURE 26-6-1—CROSS SECTION OF HOT-AIR IGNITION FURNACE ASSEMBLY

SECTION 26.605 — TEST SPECIMENS

Thermoplastic materials may be tested in pellet form normally supplied for molding. Where only sheet samples are available or for thermosetting materials $^3/_4$-inch-by-$^3/_4$-inch (19 mm by 19 mm) squares of the available sheet or film shall be bound together with fine wire. A specimen weight of 3 grams ± 0.5 gram is required.

SECTION 26.606 — CONDITIONING

26.606.1 General. Measurements of temperature and relative humidity during conditioning and testing of specimens shall be recorded and such measurement shall be taken within 2 feet (610 mm) of the specimen.

26.606.2 Conditioning. Condition test specimens at 73.4°F ± 1.8°F (23°C ± 1°C) and 50 ± 2 percent relative humidity. Specimens 0.25 (6.4 mm) or less in thickness shall be conditioned for 40 hours immediately prior to testing. Specimens with a thickness greater than 0.25 (6.4 mm) shall be conditioned for 88 hours immediately prior to testing.

Adequate air circulation on all sides of the test specimen shall be provided by placing them in suitable racks, hanging them from metal clips, or laying them on wiremesh, wire screen frames with at least 1 inch (25 mm) between the screen and the surface of the bench.

26.606.3 Test Conditions. Conduct tests in the standard laboratory atmosphere of 73.4°F ± 1.8°F (23°C ± 1°C) and 50 ± 2 percent relative humidity.

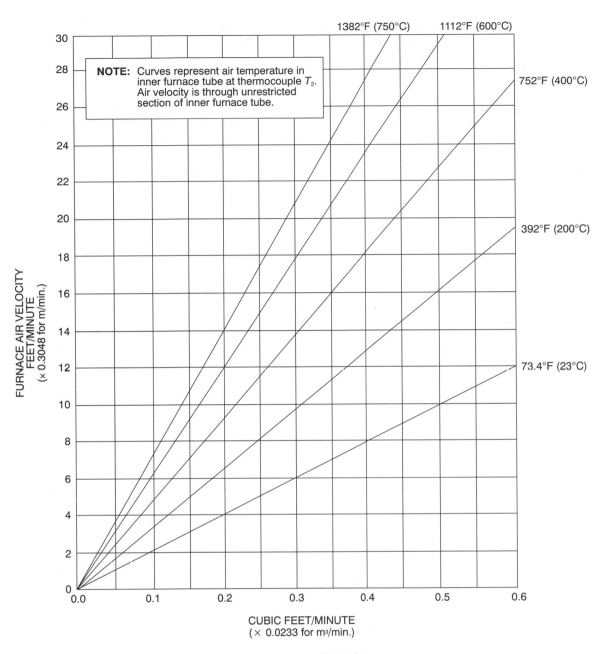

FIGURE 26-6-2—AIR CALIBRATION CURVES FOR HOT-AIR IGNITION FURNACE

SECTION 26.607 — PROCEDURE A

26.607.1 First Approximation of Flash-ignition Temperature (Effect of Airflow Rate).

26.607.1.1 Low airflow determination. Raise the cup to the cover opening and place the specimen in the furnace. Set the airflow at 5 feet per minute (1.5 m/min). Adjust the transformer controlling current to the furnace coils to provide a rise in the temperature (T_2) of approximately 1080°F (582°C) per hour (± 10 percent). Light the gas pilot flame and place it across the hole in the top of the furnace. Note the air temperature (T_2) at which the combustible gases are ignited. This point is evidenced by a rapid rise in the specimen temperature (T_1). This is an approximation of the flash-ignition temperature.

26.607.1.2 Medium airflow determination. Repeat paragraph 1, but with an air setting of 10 feet per minute (3.0 m/min).

26.607.1.3 High airflow determination. Repeat paragraph 1, but with an air setting at 20 feet per minute.

26.607.2 First Approximation of Self-ignition Temperature (Effect of Airflow Rate). Repeat Section 26.607.1.1, but without the pilot flame. Note the recorded air temperature (T_2) at which the specimen flames, explodes or glows.

Repeat Section 26.607.1.2, but without the pilot flame. Note the recorded air temperature (T_2) at which the specimen flames explodes or glows.

Repeat Section 26.607.1.3, but without the pilot flame. Note the recorded air temperature (T_2) at which the specimen flames, explodes or glows.

26.607.3 Second Approximation of Flash-ignition Temperature. Choose the air setting from Section 26.607.1 that gives the lowest flash temperature, and repeat the appropriate determination, Sections 26.607.1.1, 26.607.1.2 or 26.607.1.3, using a temperature rise of 540°F (282°C) per hour (± 10 percent).

26.607.4 Second Approximation of Self-ignition Temperature. Choose the air setting from Section 26.607.2 that gives the lowest self-ignition temperature, and repeat the appropriate determination, Section 26.607.1.1, 26.607.1.2 or 26.607.1.3, using a temperature rise of 540°F (282°C) per hour (± 10 percent).

26.607.5 Constant-temperature Tests to Determine Minimum Ignition Temperatures.

26.607.5.1 Minimum flash-ignition temperature. Start the furnace with the air setting user in Section 26.607.3. Adjust the transformer setting until the initial air temperature (T_1) stays constant as indicated by the recorded temperature reading for a 15-minute period. The initial temperature should be maintained not more than 18°F (10°C) below the flash temperature found in Section 26.607.3. Place the specimen in the furnace, ignite the pilot flame and watch for ignition of gases from the specimen. If ignition occurs, repeat this run with temperature (T_1) maintained at an 18°F (10°C) lower setting. Repeat at successively lower temperatures until there is not ignition in 30 minutes. When temperature (T_1) is reached at which no ignition occurs, it is suggested that a second run be made to ensure that this is truly below the self-ignition temperature. Report the lowest air temperature (T_1) setting at which ignition occurred as the minimum flash-ignition temperature.

26.607.5.2 Minimum self-ignition temperature. Repeat paragraph 1 but without the pilot flame. Start with an air temperature 18°F (10°C) lower than the ignition temperature found in Section 26.607.4.

SECTION 26.608 — PROCEDURE B (SHORT METHOD)

26.608.1 Minimum Flash-ignition Temperature. Set the air-flow rate to provide a velocity of 5 feet/minute (1.5 m/min) at 752°F (400°C) in the test chamber of the furnace. Adjust the current to the heating coil until the initial air temperature (T_2) remains constant at 752°F for 15 minutes.

> **NOTE:** The temperature of 752°F (400°C) is used when no prior knowledge of the probable ignition temperature range is available.

Other starting temperature may be selected if information about the material indicates better choice.

Locate thermocouple T_1 centrally in the specimen holder intimately surrounded by the test material and lower the unit into the furnace. Start a timer, ignite the gas pilot flame and watch for ignition. Flash ignition will be evidenced by a flash or mild explosion of combustible gases which may be followed by continuous burning of the specimen. If the specimen burns, by flaming or glowing, a rapid rise will be observed in the temperature at thermocouple T_1 above that at T_2.

If at the end of five minutes ignition has or has not occurred, lower or raise the temperature (T_1) 122°F (68°C) as required and repeat the test with a fresh specimen. When the minimum ignition temperature has been bracketed, tests are begun 50°F (28°C) below the lowest ignition temperature observed and repeated, dropping the temperature in 50°F (28°C) intervals until the temperature is reached at which there is no ignition during 13 minutes. A repeat run may be desirable at this temperature using an air velocity of 10 feet/minute (3.0 m/min) to verify the use of 5 feet/minute (1.5 m/min) as optimum.

The lowest air temperature (T_2) at which a flash is observed is recorded as the minimum flash-ignition temperature.

26.608.2 Minimum Self-ignition Temperature. Follow the same procedure as in Section 26.608.1 but without the gas pilot flame.

Self-ignition will be evidenced by flaming or glowing of the specimen. It may be difficult, with some materials, to detect self-ignition visually when burning is by glowing rather than flaming. In such cases, the rapid rise in temperature at thermocouple T_1 above that at T_2 is the more reliable reference.

The lowest air temperature (T_2) at which the specimen burns is recorded as the minimum self-ignition temperature.

SECTION 26.609 — REPORT

The report shall include the following:

1. Designation of material, including name of manufacturer, composition and state of subdivision (granules, sheet, etc.).

2. Air velocities used. If air velocity is not critical, this should be noted.

3. Flash-ignition temperature.

4. Self-ignition temperature.

5. Visual observation (melting, bubbling, smoking, etc.).

UNIFORM BUILDING CODE STANDARD 26-7
METHOD OF TEST FOR DETERMINING CLASSIFICATION OF APPROVED LIGHT-TRANSMITTING PLASTICS

Based on Standard Test Method D635-74 of the American Society for Testing and Materials.
Extracted, with permission, from the *Annual Book of ASTM Standards,* copyright American Society
for Testing and Materials, 100 Barr Harbor Drive, West Conshohocken, PA 19428

See Sections 217 and 2603.1.3, *Uniform Building Code,*
and Section 212, *Uniform Sign Code*

SECTION 26.701 — SCOPE

This method of test covers a small scale laboratory test for the purpose of classifying approved light-transmitting plastics in the form of bars, molded or cut from sheets, plates or panels tested in the horizontal position. This method should be used to establish the proper classification of approved light-transmitting plastics and should not be used as a fire hazard test method.

SECTION 26.702 — SUMMARY OF METHOD

A bar of the material to be tested is supported horizontally at one end; the free end is exposed to a specified gas flame for 30 seconds. The time and extent of burning are measured and reported if the specimen does not burn more than 4 inches (102 mm). An average burning rate is reported for a material if it burns beyond the 4-inch (102 mm) mark from the ignited end.

SECTION 26.703 — APPARATUS

26.703.1 Test Chamber. The test chamber is to be a laboratory hood totally enclosed with a heat-resistant glass window for observing the test. A mirror is to be provided within the chamber to provide a rear view of the specimen during the test. The exhaust fan is turned off during the test and turned on immediately following the test in order to remove products of combustion which may be toxic when testing some materials. Alternatively, the test may be made in a metal cabinet placed inside the hood leaving the hood exhaust fan turned on. The cabinet must have air holes on the bottom and top. The holes must allow ample passage of air for characteristic burning but must not allow drafts across the burning specimen.

26.703.2 Specimen Holder. The specimen shall be supported in the proper position by laboratory ring stands with two small clamps adjustable, by means of a check nut, to any angle.

26.703.3 Ignition Source. The ignition source shall be a standard $^3/_8$-inch (9.5 mm) diameter Bunsen burner with a laboratory gas supply.

SECTION 26.704 — TEST SPECIMEN

At least 10 test specimens 5 inches (127 mm), plus or minus $^1/_4$ inch (6.4 mm) in length, by $^1/_2$ inch (13 mm), plus or minus 0.008 inch (0.20 mm) in width and of the thickness of material normally supplied, shall be cut from sheets or molded from each of the samples to be tested.

The specimens shall normally be tested in the as-received condition unless otherwise specified.

Each test specimen shall be marked by scribing a line 4 inches (102 mm) from end of the specimen.

The edges of the test specimen shall be smooth. Sawed edges should be fine sanded to a smooth finish.

SECTION 26.705 — PROCEDURE

Clamp the specimen at the marked end in a support with its longitudinal axis horizontal and its transverse axis inclined at 45 degrees to the horizontal. Under the test specimen, clamp a screen of 20-mesh wire gauze, about 4 inches (102 mm) square, in a horizontal position $^3/_8$ inch (9.5 mm) below the edge of the specimen and with about $^1/_2$ inch (13 mm) of the specimen extending beyond the edge of the wire gauze (see Figure 26-7-1). Any material remaining on the screen from the previous test must be burned off on a new screen used for each test. A pan of water should be placed on the floor of the hood in a position to catch any burning particles that may drop during the test.

Adjust a standard $^3/_8$-inch (9.5 mm) diameter Bunsen burner, with air ports open, to produce a blue flame approximately 1 inch (25 mm) high. Place the burner so that the tip of the outer cone of the flame contacts the end of the test specimen starting the stopwatch simultaneously. Apply the flame for 30 seconds. If the specimen warps, melts or shrinks away from the flame, move the flame to keep it in contact with the specimen. Excessive distortion of the specimen during the test may invalidate the results. At the end of 30 seconds, remove the flame and place it at least 18 inches (457 mm) from the specimen to reduce the effects of draft in the hood while the specimen is allowed to burn.

Stop the watch when burning (flame) or glowing combustion (visible glow without flame) ceases, or when it has proceeded to the mark 4 inches (102 mm) from the free end. Record the time in seconds on the watch as burning time, *t*.

If the burning has not reached the mark, measure the unburned length to the nearest 0.04 inch (1.0 mm) along the lower edge of the specimen from the mark. The extent of burning is defined as 4 inches (102 mm) minus the unburned length in the same units.

If specimen has burned to or beyond the mark, calculate the burning rate as 240/*t* [inches/minute (6096/*t* mm/min)].

Repeat the procedure above until three specimens have burned to or beyond the mark or 10 specimens have been tested. If only one of 10 specimens tested burns to the mark or beyond, repeat the procedure above with 10 additional specimens.

SECTION 26.706 — REPORT

26.706.1 Burning Rate. If two or more specimens have burned to the gage mark, average burning rate (inches/minute) (mm/min) shall be reported as the average of the burning rates of all specimens which have burned to the mark.

26.706.2 Average Time of Burning and Average Extent of Burning. The average time of burning and average extent of burning of the samples shall be reported if none of 10 or no more than one of 20 specimens has burned to the mark.

26.706.3 Average Time of Burning. The average time of burning shall be equal the sum of *t* minus 30 seconds divided by the number of specimens [Σ (*t* – 30)/number of specimens] rounded (after averaging) to the nearest multiple of five seconds; that is, "less than five seconds" would be reported if burning or flowing continued less than three seconds after removal of flame. In no case is an average time of burning of "zero" to be recorded.

26.706.4 Average Extent of Burning. The average extent of burning is equal to the summation of the quantity of 4 inches (102 mm) minutes the unburned length divided by the number of specimens [Σ (4 inches (102 mm) – unburned length/number of specimens)] rounded (after averaging) to the nearest 0.2 of an inch (5.1 mm); extent of burning less that $1/8$ of an inch (3.2 mm), report as "less than 0.2 of an inch (5.1 mm)," in no case reporting "zero." Extent of burning of a single specimen that burns to the mark is counted as 4 inches (102 mm).

26.706.5 Classification. Approved light-transmitting plastic materials shall be classified as either CC1 or CC2 in accordance with the following requirements:

CC1: Plastic materials which have a burning extent of 1 inch (25 mm) or less when tested in nominal 0.060-inch (1.5 mm) thickness (or in the thickness intended for use) by this test.

CC2: Plastic materials which have a burning rate of 2.5 inches per minute (64 mm/min) or less when tested in nominal 0.060-inch (1.5 mm) thickness (or in the thickness intended for use) by this test.

26.706.6 Items to be Reported. The complete report shall include the following:

1. Identification of the sample including method of preparation and condition.

2. Average thickness of the specimen to ± 1 percent.

3. Number of specimens tested.

4. Range of time of burning values.

5. Range of extent of burning values.

6. If a specimen does not burn to the mark because of dripping, flowing or falling burning particles, the report must so indicate.

7. If a specimens reignited by burning material on the wire gauze, the report must so state.

8. Classification of material in accordance with Section 26.706.5.

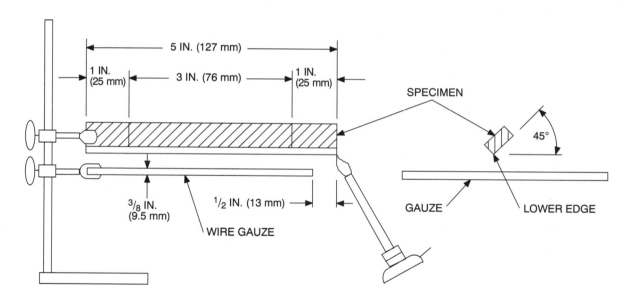

FIGURE 26-7-1—TEST APPARATUS

UNIFORM BUILDING CODE STANDARD 26-8
ROOM FIRE TEST STANDARD FOR GARAGE DOORS
USING FOAM PLASTIC INSULATION
Test Standard of the International Conference of Building Officials
See Sections 601.3 and 2602.5.5, *Uniform Building Code*
NOTE: This is a new standard.

SECTION 26.801 — SCOPE

This standard is a test method designed to evaluate the contribution of garage doors using foam plastic insulation to the creation of fire hazard under specified fire exposure conditions. The method is conducted in a standard room configuration. This standard determines compliance of garage doors in accordance with Section 2602.5.5 of the *Uniform Building Code.*

This standard is to be used to evaluate the flammability characteristics of garage door assemblies using foam plastic insulation when the foam plastic is not separated from occupied spaces by a facing of minimum 0.3 mm (0.010 in.) steel or 3.2 mm ($^1/_8$ in.) wood in accordance with Section 2602.5.5 of the *Uniform Building Code.*

This standard is not intended to evaluate the fire endurance of assemblies, nor does it provide full information concerning the toxicity of combustion gases.

SECTION 26.802 — SIGNIFICANCE AND USE

This fire test measures fire performance characteristics of foam plastic insulated garage doors in an enclosure when the test specimen is subjected to a specified flaming ignition source under well-ventilated conditions. The method determines the extent to which foam plastic insulated garage doors contribute to the creation of fire hazard in a room under the conditions specified. The method also assesses the potential for fire spread beyond the room under the particular conditions simulated.

The test indicates the maximum extent of fire growth in a room, the rate of heat release, smoke obscuration, flame propagation tendencies, and, if they occur, the time to flashover and the time for flame extension beyond the doorway.

The effect of the fire on objects in or near the room, but remote from the ignition source, is evaluated by measurements of:

1. The total heat flux incident on the center of the floor.

2. The upper level gas temperature in the room.

3. The instantaneous peak rate of heat release.

The effects of the fire on areas remote from the room of origin are evaluated mainly by the measurement of total heat release of the fire.

Rate of heat release is measured by the principle of oxygen consumption. Measurements of the rate of production of carbon monoxide and carbon dioxide are normally taken. Where carbon dioxide or carbon monoxide is "scrubbed" and, therefore, not measured, Section 26.813 provides alternative calculation methods for rate of heat release.

Smoke obscuration is measured by an optical system within the fire room exhaust duct. Smoke obscuration measurement (as the rate of smoke release, total smoke released or the optical density of the smoke) is used to estimate the reduction in visibility caused by the smoke released during a test.

SECTION 26.803 — SUMMARY OF METHOD

A 2.13 m (7 ft.) high by 2.4 m (8 ft.) wide foam plastic insulated garage door is mounted adjacent to the rear wall of a 2.4 m (8 ft.) wide, 3.6 m (12 ft.) long by 2.4 m (8 ft.) high room enclosure. The test specimen covers the rear wall from floor level to 2.13 m (7 ft.) high.

This method uses a gas burner to produce a diffusion flame. The burner is located in the corner of the test room adjacent to the test specimen. The burner produces a prescribed rate of heat release output of 40 kW (38 Btu/s) for five minutes followed by 150 kW (142 Btu/s) for 10 minutes, for a total exposure period of 15 minutes. The contribution of the test specimen to room fire hazard is measured via constant monitoring of the rate of heat release, smoke release rate, the temperature of the gases in the upper part of the room, temperature rise in the core of the test sample, incident heat flux on the center of the floor and time to flashover. The test is conducted with natural ventilation to the room provided by a single doorway 0.76 m (30 in.) wide by 2.03 m (80 in.) high.

The combustion products are collected in a hood feeding into a plenum connected to an exhaust duct in which measurements are made of the gas velocity, temperature, percent light transmission and concentration of selected gases.

SECTION 26.804 — DEFINITIONS

For purposes of this standard, the following terms shall be defined as indicated:

AVERAGE UPPER GAS LAYER TEMPERATURE shall be based on the average of the four ceiling quadrant thermocouples and the center of the room ceiling thermocouple.

FLASHOVER shall be determined to have occurred when any two of the following conditions have been attained:

1. Heat flux at floor reaches 25 kW/m^2 (2.2 Btu/ft.^{2}·s).

2. Average upper air temperature exceeds 650°C (1200°F).

3. Flames exit doorway.

4. Spontaneous ignition of paper target on floor occurs.

SECTION 26.805 — IGNITION SOURCE

26.805.1 Burner Dimensions. The ignition source for the test shall be a gas burner with a nominal 0.3 m by 0.3 m (12 in. by 12 in.) porous top surface of refractory material. See Figure 26-8-1. A burner shall be constructed with a 25.4 mm (1 in.) thick porous ceramic fiberboard over a 152 mm (6 in.) plenum, or a minimum 102 mm (4 in.) layer of Ottawa sand shall be permitted to be used to provide the horizontal surface through which the gas is supplied.

26.805.2 Burner Location. The top surface of the burner through which the gas is applied shall be 0.3 m (12 in.) above the floor in the left rear corner of the room as viewed from the door. The burner enclosure shall be located such that the edge of the diffusion surface is located 51 mm (2 in.) from the left side wall and 51 mm (2 in.) from the facing over the foam plastic core of the test specimen. See Figure 26-8-2.

26.805.3 Burner Gas Supply. The gas supply to the burner shall be of C.P. grade propane (99 percent purity) or methane. The burner shall be capable of producing a gross heat output of 40 kW ± 1 kW (38 Btu/s ± 1 Btu/s) for five minutes followed by a gross heat output of 150 kW ± 5 kW (142 Btu/s ± 5 Btu/s) for 10 minutes. Heat release rates shall be calculated using propane's net heat of combustion, which is 46.5 MJ/kg (0.020 Btu/lb.) or methane's net heat of combustion, which is 50.0 MJ/kg (0.0215 Btu/lb.). The burner design shall allow switching from 40 kW (38 Btu/s) to 150 kW (142 Btu/s) within 10 seconds. Burner controls are permitted for automatic shutoff of the gas supply if flameout occurs. Two acceptable arrangements for a gas supply are illustrated by Figure 26-8-3.

26.805.4 Burner Ignition. The burner shall be ignited by a pilot burner or a remotely controlled ignitor.

SECTION 26.806 — COMPARTMENT GEOMETRY AND CONSTRUCTION

26.806.1 Fire Room Dimensions. The interior dimensions of the floor of the fire room, when the specimens are in place, shall measure 2.44 m ± 0.1 m by 3.66 m ± 0.1 m (8 ft. ± 3.9 in. by 12 ft. ± 3.9 in.). The finished ceiling shall be 2.44 ± 0.1 m (8 ft. ± 3.9 in.) above the floor. There shall be four walls at right angles defining the compartments. See Figure 26-8-4.

26.806.2 Doorway. There shall be a 0.76 m ± 6.4 mm by 2.03 m ± 6.4 mm (30 in. ± 0.25 in. by 80 in. ± 0.25 in.) doorway in the center of one of the 2.44 m by 2.44 m (8 ft. by 8 ft.) walls, and there shall be no other wall, floor or ceiling openings that allow ventilation. The door frame shall be constructed to remain unchanged during the test period to a tolerance of ± 1 percent in height and width.

26.806.3 Fire Room Construction. The fire room shall be permitted to be a framed or a masonry structure. The floor, ceiling, and walls of the test compartment shall be covered by calcium-silicate board or by gypsum wallboard. The inside surface of the wall containing the door shall be of calcium-silicate board of 736 kg/m^3 (46 lb./ft.^{3}) density and 12 mm (0.5 in.) in nominal thickness or 12 mm (0.5 in.) gypsum wallboard.

SECTION 26.807 — SPECIMEN MOUNTING

Specimen mounting details shall be comparable to that intended for actual product use. Specimens shall consist of full garage door assemblies incorporating inside and outside facings, gaskets, framing members, insulation, air gaps, and other details, as appropriate to the product being evaluated, and as follows:

1. A minimum 2.4 m (8 ft.) wide by 2.13 m (7 ft.) high test specimen shall be mounted adjacent to the gypsum wallboard rear wall of the fire room enclosure, as shown in Figure 26-8-2.

2. The garage door shall be mounted in the fire room so that the bottom of the door rests on the floor of the fire room and the top of the door is not more than 305 mm (12 in.) below the underside of the ceiling. Where a garage door in an actual installation may be installed with less than 305 mm (12 in.) separation between the top of the door and the underside of the ceiling, the door shall be mounted in the fire room using the minimum separation contemplated for the actual installation.

3. Test specimens are attached to the gypsum wallboard fire room enclosure using metal stud screws and fender washers at the edges of panels as indicated on Figure 26-8-2. Angle brackets are located at panel edges, so that one bracket attaches to, and secures, two panels in place. See Figure 26-8-5. The screws and angle

brackets located directly above the burner are tightened to hold the test specimen securely in place. The angle bracket and metal stud screws placed in the slots of the angle bracket on the end of the panels remote from the burner are lightly tightened, allowing the specimen to expand during tests. The right side of the test specimen, as viewed from the room door, is to be separated up to a maximum of 38.1 mm (1^1/$_2$ in.) from the right side wall of the test room enclosure to allow for thermal expansion.

4. Test specimens are oriented such that the normally inside face of the garage door assembly faces the burner.

SECTION 26.808 — SPECIMEN CONDITIONING

Prior to testing, specimens shall be conditioned for a minimum of seven days or until the sample reaches a rate of weight change of less than 0.1 percent per day at a temperature of 49°C ± 2.8°C (70°F ± 5°F) and a relative humidity of 50 percent ± 5 percent.

SECTION 26.809 — ENVIRONMENTAL CONDITIONS

26.809.1 Fire Room Air Supply. The building in which the fire room is located shall have vents for the discharge of combustion products and have provision for fresh air intake, so that no oxygen deficient air is introduced into the fire room during the test. Prior to the start of the test, the ambient air at the mid-height entrance to the fire room shall have a velocity of less than 0.5 m/sec (100 ft./min.) in any direction. The building shall be of adequate size so that there shall be no smoke accumulation in the building below the level of the top of the fire room.

26.809.2 Ambient Temperature. The ambient temperature in the test building around the fire room shall be above 4°C (40°F) and the relative humidity shall be less than 75 percent for the duration of the test.

26.809.3 Ambient Conditions. If test samples are installed within the fire room for two or more hours prior to the test, the following ambient conditions shall be maintained:

1. The ambient temperature in the fire room measured by one of the thermocouples specified in Section 26.810.2.3 shall be 18°C to 24°C (65°F to 75°F).

2. The ambient relative humidity in the fire room shall be 50 percent ± 5 percent.

SECTION 26.810 — INSTRUMENTATION

The following instrumentation shall be provided for this test.

26.810.1 Total Heat Flux Gage.

26.810.1.1 Location. A gage shall be mounted a maximum of 51 mm (2 in.) above the floor surface, facing upward in the geometric center of the fire room. See Figure 26-8-6.

26.810.1.2 Specification. The gage shall be of the Gardon or Schmidt-Boelter type, with a circular flat black surface of 13 mm (^{1}/$_2$ in.) diameter and a 180-degree view angle. In operation, it shall be maintained at a constant temperature within 2.8°C (± 5 percent °F) above the dewpoint by water supplies at a temperature of 50°C to 65°C (120°F to 150°F). This will normally require a flow rate of at least 0.38 L/min. (0.1 gal./min.). The full scale output range shall be 50 kW/m^2 [4.4 Btu/(ft.^{2}·s)] for the gage.

26.810.2 Thermocouples.

26.810.2.1 Specification. Bare Type K thermocouples, 0.5 mm (20 mil) in diameter, shall be used at each required location. The thermocouple wire within 13 mm (0.5 in.) of the bead shall be run along expected isotherms to minimize conduction errors. The insulation between the chromel and alumel wires shall be stable to at least 1100°C (2000°F), or the wires shall be separated.

26.810.2.2 Location in doorway. A thermocouple shall be located in the interior plane of the door opening on the door centerline, 100 mm (4 in.) from the top. See Figure 26-8-6.

26.810.2.3 Location in room. Thermocouples shall be located 100 mm (4 in.) below the ceiling, at the center of the ceiling, at the center of each of the four ceiling quadrants and directly over the center of the ignition burner. The thermocouples shall be mounted on supports or penetrate through the ceiling with their junctions 100 mm (4 in.) away from a solid surface. See Figure 26-8-6. Any ceiling penetration shall be just large enough to permit passage of the thermocouples. Spackling compound or ceramic fiber insulation shall be used to backfill the holes around the thermocouple wire.

26.810.2.4 Location in canopy and exhaust duct. One pair of thermocouples shall be placed a minimum of 8.25 duct diameters downstream of the entrance to the horizontal duct. The pair of thermocouples shall straddle the center of the duct and be separated 50 mm (2 in.) from each other. See Figure 26-8-7.

26.810.2.5 Location in specimen foam core. One thermocouple shall be placed near the center of the foam plastic core, approximately 76.2 mm (3 in.) from the right side and 330 mm (13 in.) below the ceiling of the fire room. See Figure 26-8-2.

26.810.3 Canopy Hood and Exhaust Duct.

26.810.3.1 Location and design. A hood shall be installed immediately adjacent to the door of the fire room. The bottom of the hood shall be level with the top surface of the room. The face dimensions of the hood shall be a minimum of 2.44 m by 2.44 m (8 ft. by 8 ft.) and the minimum depth shall be 1.1 m (3.5 ft.). The hood shall feed into a plenum having a minimum 0.92 m by 0.92 m (3 ft. by 3 ft.) cross-section. The plenum shall have a minimum height of 0.92 m (3 ft.). This height shall be permitted to be increased to a maximum of 1.8 m (6 ft.) to satisfy building constraints. The exhaust duct connected to the plenum shall be a minimum of 0.4 m (16 in.) in diameter, horizontal and shall be permitted to have a circular aperture of at least 0.3 m (12 in.) at its entrance or mixing vanes in the duct. See Figures 26-8-7 and 26-8-8 for additional details.

26.810.3.2 Exhaust flow rate. The hood shall have sufficient draft to collect all of the combustion products leaving the room. This draft shall be capable of moving up to 3.4 m³/sec (7,000 standard ft.³/min.) equivalent to 7.25 m³/s (16,100 cfm) at 399°C (750°F) during the test. Provision shall be made so that the draft can operate at 0.47 to 3.4 m³/sec (1,000 to 7,000 standard ft.³/min.). Mixing vanes shall be provided in the duct if concentration gradients are found to exist.

26.810.3.3 Alternative exhaust design. An alternative exhaust system design shall be permitted to be used if it meets the requirements of Section 26.811.

26.810.4 Duct Gas Velocity.

26.810.4.1 Specification. A bidirectional probe or an equivalent measuring system shall be used to measure gas velocity in the duct. The probe shall consist of a short, stainless steel cylinder 44 mm (1.75 in.) long and of 22 mm (0.875 in.) inside diameter with a solid diaphragm in the center or other design shown capable of measuring gas velocity in the duct. See Figure 26-8-9. The pressure taps on either side of the diaphragm support the probe. The axis of the probe shall run along the centerline of the duct a minimum of 8.25 duct diameters downstream from the entrance. See

Figure 26-8-7. The taps shall be connected to a pressure transfuser that shall be able to resolve pressure differences of 0.25 Pa (0.001 in. water).

26.810.5 Oxygen Depletion Measurements.

26.810.5.1 Determination of rate of heat release. A stainless steel gas sampling tube shall be located a minimum of 8.63 duct diameters downstream from the entrance to the duct at the geometric center of the duct, ± 13 mm (± $^1/_2$ in.), to obtain a continuously flowing sample for determining the oxygen concentration of the exhaust gas as a function of time. See Figure 26-8-7. A suitable filter and cold trap shall be placed in the line ahead of the analyzer to remove particulates and water. The oxygen analyzer shall be of the paramagnetic or polarographic type and shall be capable of measuring oxygen concentration in a range of 21 percent to 15 percent, with a relative accuracy of 50 parts per million (ppm) in this concentration range. The signal from the oxygen analyzer shall be within 5 percent of its final value and occur within 30 seconds of introducing a step change in composition of the gas stream flowing past the inlet to the sampling tube.

26.810.5.2 Duct carbon dioxide concentration. The gas sampling tube, described in Section 26.810.5.l, shall be used to provide a continuous sample for the measurement of the carbon dioxide concentration using an analyzer with a range not more than 0 to 6 percent (vol.), with a maximum relative error of 2 percent of full scale. The total system response time between the sampling inlet and the meter shall be no longer than 30 seconds.

26.810.5.3 Duct carbon monoxide concentration. The gas sampling tube, defined in Section 26.810.5.1, shall be used to provide a continuous sample for the measurement of the carbon monoxide concentration using an analyzer with a range not more than 0 to 1 percent (vol.), with a maximum relative error of 2 percent of full scale. The signal from the analyzer shall be within 5 percent of its final value and occur within 30 seconds after introducing a step change in composition of the gas stream flowing past the inlet to the sampling tube.

26.810.6 Smoke Obscuration Measurement.

26.810.6.1 Optical system. An optical system for measurement of light obscuration across the centerline of the exhaust duct shall be provided and shall be located a minimum of 9 duct diameters downstream from the entrance to the duct. See Figure 26-8-7. The optical density of the smoke shall be determined by measuring the light transmitted across the centerline of the exhaust duct with a photometer system consisting of a white light source and a photocell/detector or a laser system.

26.810.6.2 Specifications. The optical system shall consist of a lamp, plano convex lenses, an aperture, a photocell and an appropriate power supply. The lenses, lamp and photocell shall be mounted inside two housings, located on the exhaust duct, diametrically opposite each other. The system shall be constructed such that soot deposits on the optics during a test do not reduce the light transmission by more than 5 percent.

26.810.6.3 Lamp. A lamp of the incandescent filament type, which operates at a color temperature of 2900 ± 100 K (2627°C ± 100°C), shall be used. Supply the lamp with stabilized direct current, stable within ± 0.2 percent (including temperature, short-term and long-term stability). Center the resultant light beam on the photocell.

26.810.6.4 Lens system. Select the lens system such that lens L_2 has a diameter, d, chosen with regard to the focal length, f, of L_2 so that $d/f \geq 0.04$. Place the aperture in the focus of lens L_2. See Figure 26-8-10.

26.810.6.5 Detector. Use a detector with a spectrally distributed response according to the CIE photopic curve and linear within

5 percent over an output range of at least 3.5 decades. Check this linearity over the entire range of the instrument periodically with calibrated optical filters.

26.810.6.6 Optical system. Optical system design shall be one that is purged easily against soot deposits. Holes shall be provided in the periphery of the two housings as a means of achieving this objective.

26.810.6.7 Paper targets. Two paper target flashover indicators shall be placed on the floor of the test room. See Figure 26-8-12. The targets shall consist of a single piece of newsprint crumpled into an approximate 152 mm (6 in.) diameter ball.

26.810.6.8 Photographic documentation. Photographic or video equipment shall be used to record the fire spread in the fire room and the fire projection from the door of the room. The location of the cameras shall avoid interference with airflow. The interior wall surfaces of the fire room adjacent to the corner in which the burner is located shall be clearly marked. A clock shall appear in all photographic records, showing the time to at least the nearest one second from the start of the test. This clock shall be accurately synchronized with all other measurements, or other provision shall be made to correlate the photo record with time. Color slides or photographs shall be taken at intervals for the duration of the test, or a continuous video recording shall be made.

SECTION 26.811 — CALIBRATION

26.811.1 Heat Release, Temperature and Velocity. A calibration test shall be performed prior to and within 30 days of any fire test. The calibration test shall last for a minimum of 10 minutes. Take measurements a minimum of once every six seconds. The standard ignition source shall be used with inert wall and ceiling materials—calcium-silicate board of 736 kg/m^3 (56 lb./ft.^{3}) density, 13 mm (0.50 in.) thickness or gypsum wallboard.

26.811.1.1 Calibration factor. The data resulting from a calibration test shall provide:

1. The output as a function of time, after the burner is activated, of all instruments normally used for the standard fire test.

2. The maximum extension of the burner flame, as recorded by still photographs taken at approximately 30-second intervals or continuous video recording.

3. Calculation of C factor when either an orifice plate or bidirectional probe is used: The C factor in Formula (13-4) shall be determined in accordance with the following. Place the sand burner in the room/corner. Set the methane or propane flow to provide a constant heat release rate of 150 kW. Ignite the gas, and continue the burner for 10 minutes, and then switch off the gas. Then calculate the C factor as follows:

    3.1 Estimate the initial calibration constant for C using the product 22.1 A, where "A" is the area of the duct (m^2). This gives a good estimation (generally within about 20 percent) of the final value one can expect for "C."

    3.2 Burn either propane or methane fuel at 150 kW for a 10-minute interval. Measure the heat-release rate using oxygen consumption calorimetry, and Formula (13-3) using E and α values appropriate to the fuel. See E and α values contained within the list of defined symbols.

    3.3 Calculate the total heat released (THR) from the mass loss of fuel and its heat of combustion, as specified in the standard (e.g., 1.8 kg of methane consumed = 90,000 kJ).

    3.4 Adjust the calibration constant "C" so that the total rate of heat released, as determined by the oxygen consumption calculation, agrees with that from the mass of fuel consumed to within 5 percent.

$$C_{new} = \left[\cfrac{\cfrac{A * B * 1,000}{t}}{\displaystyle\int_o q(t)dt} \right] * C_{old}$$

WHERE:

    A = the fuel value of the fuel being used (MJ/kg).

    B = the total weight of fuel burned in the period T (kg).

$\displaystyle\int_o^t q(t)dt$ is in (kJ) and 1,000 is the conversion (kJ/MJ).

    3.5 Use the new constant for subsequent tests for calculation of heat release rate and volumetric flow rate as noted in the example.

Example: An initial value of 6.6 is assigned to C. A 10-minute calibration burn uses 1.8 kg of methane (50 MJ/kg) at a fuel flow rate that corresponds to 150 kW. The oxygen consumption calculations reveal an average heat release rate of 160 kW during the burn period. Integrating the heat release rate curve over the 10-minute burn period shows that the total heat measured is 96 000 kJ. Applying the formula above, one finds:

$$C_{new} = [0.94] * C_{old}$$

The new calibration constant is 6.2. This will adjust the measured heat release rate (and THR) so that it agrees with the heat released from the fuel burned. Use the new calibration constant in all subsequent tests up until a new calibration burn is performed.

26.811.1.2 Calculated heat release. The total rate of heat production as determined by the oxygen consumption calculation, independent measurement of the volumetric flow rate, and weight loss of propane or methane supply shall agree to within 5 percent. The net heat of combustion is 46.5 MJ/kg (0.020 Btu/lb.) for propane and 50.0 MJ/kg (0.0215 Btu/lb.) for methane. This value shall be used for this calculation.

26.811.1.3 Smoke obscuration. The smoke meter shall be calibrated to read correctly for two neutral density filters at 0.5 and 1.0 values of optical density and at 100 percent transmission. The 0 value of extinction coefficient (100 percent transmission) shall be verified each day prior to testing.

26.811.1.4 Gas analysis. Gas analyzers shall be calibrated daily prior to testing, in accordance with ASTM E 800-88, Standard Guide for Measurement of Gases Present or Generated During Fires.

SECTION 26.812 — TEST PROCEDURE

The test procedure shall consist of the following:

1. Establish an initial volumetric flow rate of at least 0.47 m^3/sec (1,000 ft.^{3}/min.) through the duct and increase the volume flow rate of 3.4 m^3/sec (7,000 ft.^{3}/min.) as required to keep the oxygen content above 14 percent and to capture all effluents from the fire room.

2. Turn on all sampling and recording devices and take measurements a minimum of once every six seconds. Establish steady-state baseline readings for a minimum of one minute prior to starting a test.

3. Ignite the gas burner and simultaneously start the clock and increase flow rate to provide a rate of heat release of 40 kW ± 1 kW (38 Btu/s ± 1 Btu/s) by the burner. Continue the exposure at the 40 kW ± 1 kW (38 Btu/s ± 1 Btu/s) level for five minutes. Within 10 seconds following the five-minute exposure, increase the gas flow to provide a rate of heat release by the burner of 150 kW ± 5 kW (142 Btu/s ± 4.74 Btu/s) exposure for 10 minutes.

4. Take 35-mm color photographs at approximately 30-second intervals, or provide a continuous video recording to document the growth of the fire.

5. Provide a voice or written record of the fire, which documents the times of all significant events, such as time of ignition, escape of flames through the doorway, flashover, etc.

6. The ignition burner shall be shut off 15 minutes after start of the test and the test terminated at that time, unless safety considerations dictate an earlier termination.

7. Document damage after the test, using words, pictures and drawings.

SECTION 26.813 — CALCULATIONS

26.813.1 Heat Release. The calculation methods to determine the gross (total) rate of heat release (burner and specimen) shall be as follows:

Calculate mass flow rate using Formula (13-1):

$$\dot{m}_e = C * (\Delta p/T_e)^{1/2} \tag{13-1}$$

Case 1: Only O_2 concentration measurements are used.

Calculate the mass flow rate according to Formula (13-1) and the oxygen depletion factor according to Formula (13-2):

$$\Phi = \frac{X^{Ao}{}_{O_2} - X^A{}_{O_2}}{\left[1 - X^A{}_{O_2}\right] * X^{Ao}{}_{O_2}} \tag{13-2}$$

Then calculate the rate of heat release (q) according to Formula (13-3):

$$\dot{q} = E * \frac{M_{O_2}}{M_a} * \frac{\Phi}{1 + \Phi * (a-1)} * \dot{m}_e * X^{Ao}{}_{O_2} \tag{13-3}$$

If only O_2 is measured, Formula (13-3) simplifies to Formula (13-4):

$$\dot{q} = E * 1.10 * C\sqrt{\frac{\Delta p}{T_e}} * \left[\frac{X^{Ao}{}_{O_2} - X^A{}_{O_2}}{1.105 - 1.5 * X^A{}_{O_2}}\right] \tag{13-4}$$

Case 2: Only O_2 and CO_2 concentration measurements are used. Calculate the mass flow rate according to Formula (13-1) and the oxygen depletion factor according to Formula (13-5).

$$\Phi = \frac{X^{Ao}{}_{O_2} * \left[1 - X^A{}_{CO_2}\right] - X^A{}_{O_2} * \left[1 - X^{Ao}{}_{CO_2}\right]}{X^{Ao}{}_{O_2} * \left[1 - X^A{}_{O_2} - X^A{}_{CO_2}\right]} \tag{13-5}$$

and the rate of heat release according to the same Formula (13-3).

Case 3: O_2 and CO_2 and CO concentration measurements are used:

Calculate the mass flow rate according to Formula (13-1), the moisture content of the incoming atmosphere according to Formula (13-3) and the oxygen depletion factor according to Formula (13-6):

$$\Phi = \frac{X^{Ao}{}_{O_2} * \left[1 - X^A{}_{CO_2} - X^A{}_{CO}\right] - X^A{}_{O_2} * \left[1 - X^{Ao}{}_{CO_2}\right]}{X^{Ao}{}_{O_2} * \left[1 - X^A{}_{O_2} - X^A{}_{CO_2} - X^A{}_{CO}\right]} \tag{13-6}$$

Finally, calculate the rate of heat release according to Formula (13-7).

$$\dot{q} = \left[E * \Phi - \left[E_{CO} - E\right] * \frac{1 - \Phi}{2} * \frac{X^A{}_{CO}}{X^A{}_{O_2}}\right] * \frac{M_{O_2}}{M_e} * \frac{\dot{m}_e}{1 + \Phi * (a-1)} * X^{Ao}{}_{O_2} \tag{13-7}$$

26.813.2 Smoke Release Rate. Smoke measurement calculation methods shall be as follows:

Optical density (*OD*) [Formula (13-8)]:

$$OD = \log\left[I_o/I\right] \tag{13-8}$$

The volumetric flow rate is calculated as the product of the mass flow rate and the density of air, at the corresponding temperature. Both the volumetric flow and the density of air undergo temperature corrections. The volumetric duct flow rate (*V*) is adjusted because it is measured in the exhaust duct, but required at the temperature near the photodetector, as shown in Formula (13-9):

$$\dot{V}_s = V_e * \left(\frac{T_s}{T_e}\right) \tag{13-9}$$

The density of air is adjusted between the literature value, measured at 273.15 K, and the value at the temperature in the exhaust duct, as shown in Formula (13-10):

$$\rho = \rho_o * 273.15/T_e \tag{13-10}$$

Then the final formula for the volumetric flow rate is Formula (13-11):

$$\dot{V}_s = (\dot{m}_e/\rho_o) * (T_e/273.15) \tag{13-11}$$

Rate of smoke release (*RSR*) is defined by Formula (13-12):

$$RSR = \dot{V}_s * OD * 1/L_p \tag{13-12}$$

Total smoke released (*TSR*) is defined by Formula (13-13):

$$TSR = \int RSR\, dt \tag{13-13}$$

WHERE:

A = cross-sectional area of duct (m^2).

C = orifice plate coefficient ($kg^{1/2}\, m^{1/2}\, K^{1/2}$).

E_{CO} = net heat released for complete combustion per unit of oxygen consumed, for CO (17 600 kJ/kg O_2).

E_m = net heat released for complete combustion of methane per unit of oxygen consumed (12 500 kJ/kg O_2).

E_P = net heat released for complete combustion of propane per unit of oxygen consumed (12 800 KJ/kg O_2).

E_{ts} = net heat released for complete combustion of test specimens, per unit of oxygen consumed (13 100 kJ/kg O_2).

$f(R_e)$ = Reynolds number correction (nondimensional).

I = light intensity for a parallel light beam having traversed a certain length of smoky environment and reaching photodetector (nondimensional).

I_o = light intensity for a beam of parallel light rays, measured in a smoke-free environment, with a detector having the same spectral sensitivity as the human eye and reaching the photodetector (nondimensional).

k_c = velocity profile shape factor (nondimensional).

L_p = light path length of beam through smoke environment (m).

M_a = molecular weight of incoming and exhaust air (29 kg/kmol).

M_{co} = molecular weight of carbon monoxide (28 kg/kmol).

M_{CO_2} = molecular weight of carbon dioxide (44 kg/kmol).

M_{H_2O} = molecular weight of water (18 kg/kmol).

M_{n_2} = molecular weight of nitrogen (28 kg/kmol).

M_{O_2} = molecular weight of oxygen (32 kg/kmol).

m_e = $C(\Delta p/T_e)^{1/2}$ [mass flow rate, by measurement of pressure drop, in kg/s, according to Formula (13-1)].

OD = optical density (nondimensional).

q = rate of heat release (kW).

RSR = rate of smoke release (m^2/s).

TSR = total smoke released (m^2).

T_e = combustion gas temperature at the orifice plate (K).

T_s = combustion gas temperature (near photodetector) (K).

V_e = volumetric flow rate in exhaust duct (at measuring location of mass flow rate) (m^3/s).

V_s = volumetric flow rate at location of smoke meter (value adjusted for smoke measurement calculations) (m^3/s).

X_{CO}^A = measured mole fraction of CO in exhaust flow (nondimensional).

$X_{CO_2}^A$ = measured mole fraction of CO_2 in exhaust flow (nondimensional).

$X_{O_2}^A$ = measured mole fraction of O_2 in exhaust flow (nondimensional).

$X_{CO_2}^{Ao}$ = measured mole fraction of CO_2 in incoming air (nondimensional).

$X_{O_2}^{Ao}$ = measured mole fraction of O_2 in incoming air (nondimensional).

α_m = combustion expansion factor for methane (nondimensional; normally a value of 1.105).

α_p = combustion expansion factor for propane (nondimensional; normally a value of 1.084).

α_{ts} = combustion expansion factor for test specimens (nondimensional; normally a value of 1.105).

Δp = pressure drop across the orifice plate or bidirectional probe (Pa).

ρ = density of air at the temperature in exhaust duct (kg/m^3).

ρ_o = density of air at 273.15 K (1.293 kg/m^3).

Φ = oxygen depletion factor (nondimensional).

SECTION 26.814 — TEST REPORT

The test report shall include the following:

1. Name and address of testing laboratory.

2. Date and identification number of the report number.

3. Name and address of the test sponsor.

4. Materials:

    4.1 Product description. Identification of the product; foam plastic thickness, type and density; door facing materials, type and thickness; all other details of door construction necessary to accurately describe the product being tested.

    4.2 Mounting details. Product mounting details, including the height of the door tested.

    4.3 Conditioning. Product conditioning and time between removal of the specimen from the conditioning room and the start of testing.

    4.4 Room conditions. Relative humidity and temperature of the room and the test building prior to, and during, the test.

5. **Burner gas flow.** The burner gas flow is the fuel gas flow to the ignition burner and its calculated rate of heat output.

6. **Time history of the total heat flux to floor.** The time history of the total heat flux to floor is the total incident heat flux at the center of the floor for the heat flux gauge as a function of time starting a minimum of one minute prior to the test.

7. **Time history of the gas temperature.** The time history of the gas temperature is the temperature of gases in the room, in the doorway, and in the exhaust duct for each thermocouple; as a function of time starting a minimum of one minute prior to the test.

8. **Time history of the total rate of heat production of the fire, including burner output and specimen burning.** The total rate of heat production is calculated from the measured oxygen and carbon monoxide concentrations or measured oxygen, carbon monoxide, and carbon dioxide concentrations and the temperature and volumetric flow rate of the gas in the duct.

9. **Time history of the net rate of heat release from burning of the test specimen.** The net rate of heat release is calculated by subtracting the burner output from the total rate of heat production computed in accordance with Item 8.

10. **Time history of the smoke release rate.** The time history of the smoke release rate is calculated from the measured reduction in light transmission in the exhaust duct as a function of time starting a minimum of one minute prior to the test.

11. **Time history of the specimen core temperature.** The time history of the specimen core temperature is the temperature measured by the thermocouple in the specimen foam core as specified in Section 26.810.2.5, as a function of time starting a minimum of one minute prior to the test.

12. **Time history of the fire growth.** The time history of the fire growth is a transcription of the visual, photographic, audio and written records of the fire test. The records shall indicate the time of ignition of the test specimen, the approximate location of the flame front most distant from the ignition source at approximately 30-second intervals during the fire test and, if they occur, the time of flashover, and the time at which flames extend outside the doorway. In addition, still photographs taken at approximately 30-second intervals or continuous video recording shall be supplied.

13. Drawings and photographs or video recording shall be supplied to show the extent of the damage of the materials after the test.

14. Table of numerical results containing the following:

    14.1 Peak total rate of heat release (kW) and the time a which it occurred.

14.2 Peak net (specimen only) rate of heat release (kW) and the time at which it occurred.

14.3 Total heat released (MJ).

14.4 Maximum heat flux at floor level (kW/m^2) and the time at which it occurred.

14.5 Peak rate of smoke release (m^2/s) and the time at which it occurred.

14.6 Total smoke released (m^2).

14.7 Total smoke released at five minutes and at 7.5 minutes (m^2).

14.8 Peak specimen core temperature and the time at which it occurred.

14.9 Peak fire room temperatures (°C) and the time at which they occurred.

14.10 Formula used to calculate rate of heat release. Formula used to calculate rate of heat release.

SECTION 26.815 — ACCEPTANCE CRITERIA

Foam plastic insulated garage doors shall be considered as demonstrating satisfactory performance if the following conditions are met:

1. The maximum instantaneous net peak rate of heat release of the test sample shall not exceed 250 kW (237 Btu/s).

2. Flames shall not propagate for the full width of the test specimen. Propagation for the full width of the specimen shall be judged to occur:

If flames are visually observed to spread for the full width of the specimen, or

If the test specimen core temperature rise, determined by the thermocouple specified in Section 26.810.2.5, exceeds 400°C (750°F).

3. The total smoke released shall not exceed 60 m^2 (670 ft.^{2}) five minutes after the start of the test, nor shall the total smoke release exceed 150 m^2 (1,670 ft.^{2}) 7.5 minutes after the start of the test.

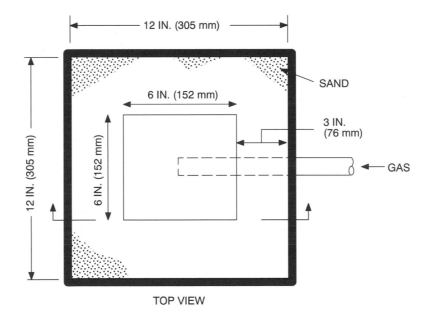

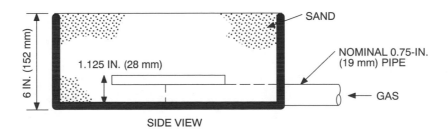

FIGURE 26-8-1—GAS BURNER

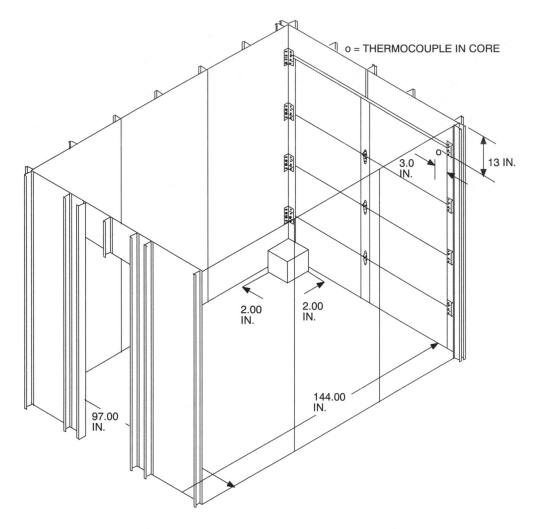

For **SI:** 1 inch = 25.4 mm.

FIGURE 26-8-2—BURNER LOCATION AND SPECIMEN MOUNTING DETAILS

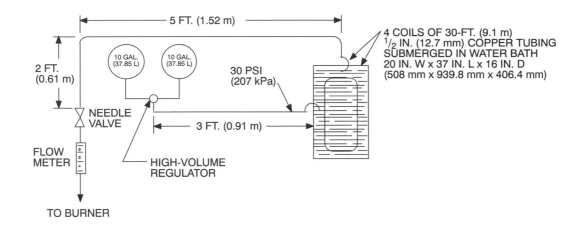

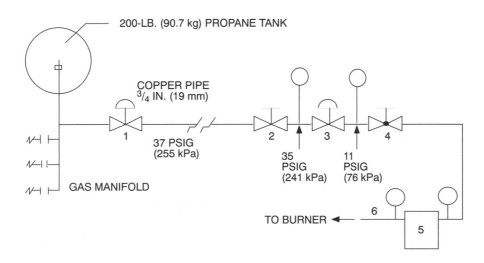

1. Propane gas regulator (high pressure) (main gas supply)
2. Shutoff valve
3. Regular (low pressure)
4. Adjustable valve for flow impedance
5. Volume meter
6. Steel braid over tubing to burner
Line pressures are shown.

FIGURE 26-8-3—GAS FLOW REGULATION SYSTEMS

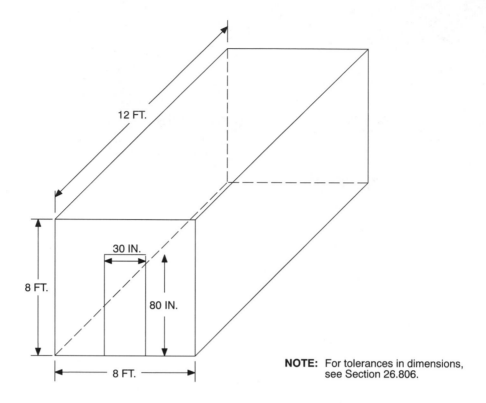

NOTE: For tolerances in dimensions, see Section 26.806.

For **SI:** 1 inch = 25.4 mm, 1 foot = 304.8 mm.

FIGURE 26-8-4—INTERIOR ROOM AND DOORWAY DIMENSIONS

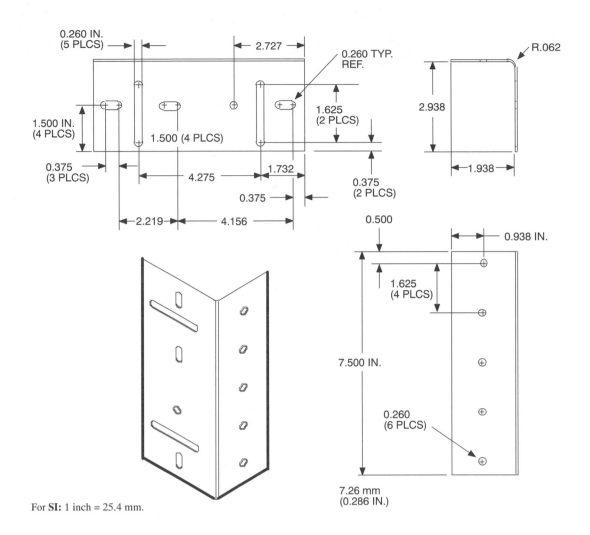

For **SI:** 1 inch = 25.4 mm.

FIGURE 26-8-5—ANGLE BRACKETS

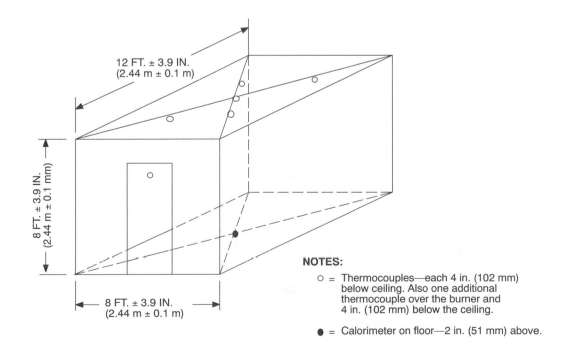

NOTES:

○ = Thermocouples—each 4 in. (102 mm) below ceiling. Also one additional thermocouple over the burner and 4 in. (102 mm) below the ceiling.

● = Calorimeter on floor—2 in. (51 mm) above.

FIGURE 26-8-6—THERMOCOUPLE AND CALORIMETER PLACEMENT

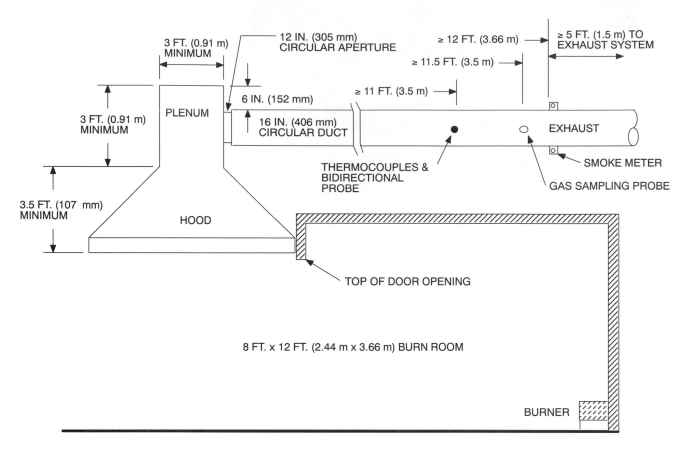

FIGURE 26-8-7—CANOPY HOOD AND EXHAUST DUCT

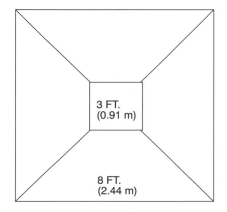

FIGURE 26-8-8—PLAN VIEW OF CANOPY HOOD

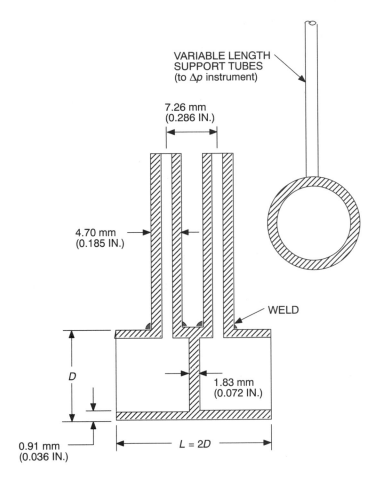

FIGURE 26-8-9—BIDIRECTIONAL PROBE

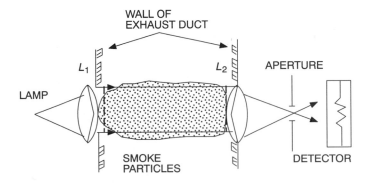

FIGURE 26-8-10—OPTICAL SYSTEM, USING A WHITE LIGHT

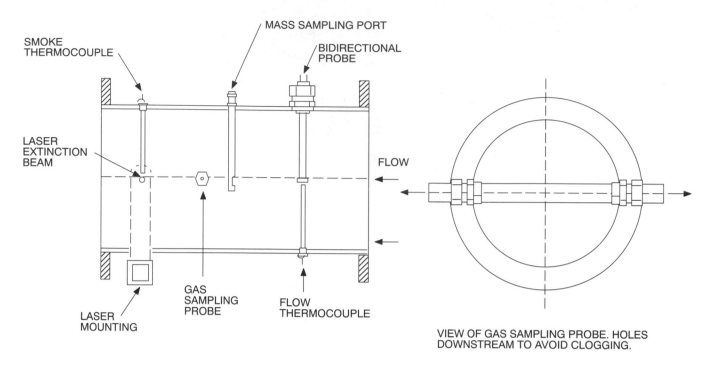

FIGURE 26-8-11—MOUNTING DETAILS FOR INSTRUMENTATION IN DUCT

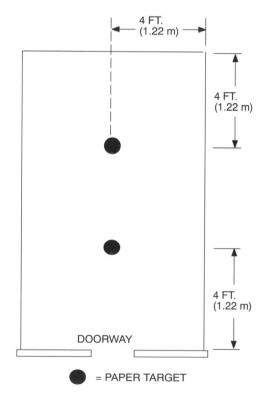

FIGURE 26-8-12—PAPER TARGET ARRANGEMENT—PLAN VIEW

UNIFORM BUILDING CODE STANDARD 26-9

METHOD OF TEST FOR THE EVALUATION OF FLAMMABILITY CHARACTERISTICS OF EXTERIOR, NONLOAD-BEARING WALL ASSEMBLIES CONTAINING COMBUSTIBLE COMPONENTS USING THE INTERMEDIATE-SCALE, MULTISTORY TEST APPARATUS

Test Standard of the International Conference of Building Officials

See Section 2602.5.2.2, *Uniform Building Code*

NOTE: This is a new standard.

SECTION 26.901 — SCOPE

This test provides a method of determining the flammability characteristics of exterior, nonload-bearing wall assemblies/panels which contain combustible components. The test structure used in this test is the intermediate-scale, multistory test apparatus. It is intended to simulate the tested wall assemblies' "full-scale" fire performance.

The primary performance characteristics to be evaluated in this test are as follows:

1. The capability of the test wall assembly to resist flame propagation over the exterior face of the system,

2. The capability of the test wall assembly to resist vertical spread of flame within the combustible core/component of the panel from one story to the next,

3. The capability of the test wall assembly to resist vertical spread of flame over the interior (room side) surface of the panels from one story to the next, and

4. The capability of the test wall assembly to resist lateral spread of flame from the compartment of fire origin to adjacent spaces.

The ability of the test wall assembly to meet these performance characteristics is determined by visual observations along with temperature data obtained during the test.

This test method is to be applied to wall assemblies/panels which contain combustible components such as those that contain foam plastic insulation or to wall assemblies/panels that contain plastic core materials. This method is not intended to apply to wall assemblies that contain, as the only combustible, insulation materials such as glass fiber and mineral wool.

This test is not an evaluation of the methods used to seal voids at the floor/wall intersection per se. While this test requires the use of materials to seal voids at the floor/wall intersection, the results of the test should not be restricted to the sealing method used but rather should encompass any approved sealing method suitable for the type of wall assembly tested.

SECTION 26.902 — TEST APPARATUS

26.902.1 Test Facility. The test apparatus described in Section 26.902.2 shall be located inside a test facility. The facility shall be a minimum of 40 feet by 40 feet by 25 feet high (12 192 mm by 12 192 mm by 7620 mm). The facility shall have provisions for supplying fresh combustion makeup air during the test. The facility shall also be constructed so as to allow for the exhaust of the combustion by-products during the test while not inducing an air flow on the exterior face of the test panels. The test facility shall protect the test apparatus and test samples from weather conditions such as wind and rain.

26.902.2 Test Apparatus. The intermediate-scale, multistory test apparatus (ISMA) consists of a two-story test structure having floor to top dimensions of 15 feet, 4 inches ± 1 inch (4674 mm ± 25 mm). Each room has inside dimensions (unfinished/unprotected) of 10 feet ± 0.5 inch by 10 feet ± 0.5 inch (3048 mm ± 13 mm by 3048 mm ± 13 mm) with floor to ceiling height (unfinished/unprotected) of 7 feet ± 0.5 inch (2134 mm ± 13 mm). See Figures 26-9-1 through 26-9-4 for diagrams of the test fixture.

The floors are constructed of reinforced concrete and are supported by steel columns of an appropriate size. The columns shall not be inside either the first- or second-story test rooms. The first floor slab shall be a minimum of 18 inches (457 mm) thick, and the second floor and third floor slabs shall be 8 inches ± 0.5 inch (203 mm ± 13 mm) thick.

The three permanent walls that form each room shall be constructed of 8 inches ± 0.5 inch (203 mm ± 13 mm) concrete block or similar construction.

The interior surfaces of the first floor burn room shall be insulated as follows:

1. Walls and ceiling—one layer of $^5/_8$ inch (15.9 mm) thick, Type X gypsum wallboard and one layer of $1^1/_2$ inches (38 mm) thick, 8 lb./ft.^{3} (128 kg/m^3) ceramic fiber insulation on the interior face. The insulation thickness on each individual wall or the ceiling shall not exceed $2^1/_2$ inches (64 mm).

2. Floor—two layers of $^5/_8$-inch (15.9 mm) thick, Type X gypsum wallboard.

No insulation is required in the second floor area.

Each floor level shall have one access opening approximately 3.5 feet wide by 6.75 feet high (1067 mm by 2057 mm). The access door opening on the first floor shall be capable of being closed during tests while the access opening on the second floor shall remain open during tests.

Additional access openings may be made in the second floor area for instrumentation and video; however, they shall be closed during tests.

Test wall assemblies may be built directly onto the test apparatus or they can be built into a movable frame system that is in turn fastened to the test apparatus.

26.902.3 Movable Test Frame. Figure 26-9-5 provides a sketch of the movable test frame. The frame is designed such that the 4 inches by 4 inches by $^3/_{16}$ inch (102 mm by 102 mm by 4.8 mm) angles will meet at the top of the respective floor lines on the test apparatus. The frame shall be sufficiently rugged so that no racking or movement will occur in the test wall assembly during movement and/or fastening. The frame system shown in Figure 26-9-5 will serve the minimum size test wall assembly. Larger frame assemblies are permitted.

26.902.4 Burners. The burner arrangement shall consist of two gas-fired burners. The first burner is positioned inside the first floor burn room while the second burner is positioned inside the window opening of the test wall assembly.

The burn room burner is constructed of 2 inch (51 mm) O.D. steel pipe with $^1/_8$-inch (3.2 mm) diameter holes placed 1 inch (25 mm) on center. The holes are positioned such that they face upward. The holes start at 3.5 feet (1067 mm) from the back wall on both sides of the gas supply pipes and continue across the front gas supply pipe.The entire gas supply pipe system is wrapped with a single layer of nominally 1 inch (25 mm) thick, 8 lb./ft.^{3} (128 kg/m^3) ceramic fiber blanket. The burner is supported such that its centerline is 2.5 feet ± 1.0 inch (762 mm ± 25 mm) above the floor. Figures 26-9-6 and 26-9-7 provide sketches of the burn room burner.

The window burner is similar to the burner used in the "Spread of Flame Test" portion of UBC Standard 15-2. The gas burner shall consist of a 60 inches ± 0.5 inch (1524 mm ± 13 mm) length of nominal 2-inch (51 mm) O.D. pipe having a 0.5 inch ± 0.06 inch (13 mm ± 1.5 mm) wide by 44 inches ± 0.5 inch (1118 mm ± 13 mm) long slot. The burner is to be supplied with gas at both ends through nominal 1-inch (25 mm) O.D. pipe to provide uniform gas pressure at the burner slot. Figures 26-9-7 and 26-9-8 provide sketches of the window burner.

The burner is wrapped with a layer of nominally 1 inch (25 mm) thick, 8 lb./ft.^{3} (128 kg/m^3) ceramic fiber insulation. The burner is mounted on a movable trolley, positioned such that the slot is facing upward, and it is centered horizontally in the window opening. The horizontal centerline of the burner is 9 inches ± 0.5 inch (229 mm ± 13 mm) below the window header. The vertical centerline of the burner shall be placed such that it is 0 to 5 inches (127 mm) from the exterior face of the test wall assembly. The exact placement (inches from the exterior face) shall be based on information developed during the calibration procedure.

The burners shall be fired during the test according to the burner regime shown in Table 26-9-A. Each burner shall attain its assigned flow rate within 15 seconds of each change. If during the calibration procedure it is demonstrated that the burners need to follow slightly different flow rates to attain the prescribed burn room and/or exterior temperatures and heat fluxes, then the flows derived from the calibration tests shall be used.

SECTION 26.903 — TEST WALL ASSEMBLIES

The test wall assemblies shall be either built on the test apparatus or shall be built in a movable test frame. Figures 26-9-9 through 26-9-11 provide sketches of the test wall assembly mounting methods.

As a minimum, the test wall assembly shall be 17.5 feet high by 13.33 feet wide (5334 mm by 4064 mm). Larger wall assemblies are permitted.

The test wall assembly shall extend to the following:

1. Below the first floor a minimum of 2 inches (51 mm),

2. Above the top of the test apparatus a minimum of 2 feet (610 mm), and

3. Past the outside edges of both of the concrete block sidewalls a minimum of 1 foot (305 mm).

The test wall assembly shall completely close the front face of the test apparatus except for a simulated window opening in the first floor area. The window shall be 30 inches ± 0.5 inch high by 78 inches ± 0.5 inch wide (76 mm ± 13 mm by 1981 mm ± 13 mm) with a sill height of 30 inches ± 0.5 inch (76 mm ± 13 mm). It shall be centered horizontally with respect to the burn room. The window opening shall be the only opening in the first-story burn room area during the test.

The test wall assembly shall be secured to the test apparatus using a girt system of replaceable nominal 4 inches by 4 inches by $^3/_{16}$ inch (102 mm by 102 mm by 4.8 mm) steel angles.

A replaceable spandrel beam shall be mounted on the underside of the second floor when the attachment of the test wall assembly requires it to be present. The spandrel beam shall be W8 by 21 (W200 by 31) and shall be installed as shown in Figures 26-9-3 and 26-9-4. The spandrel beam shall extend across the burn room compartment from one protected interior wall surface to the opposite protected interior wall surface.

The spandrel beam, when used, shall be permitted to be either protected or unprotected at the discretion of the test laboratory or the client. If the spandrel beam is to be protected, then one layer of nominal 1 inch (25 mm) thick, 6 lb./ft.^{3} (96 kg/m^3) ceramic fiber shall be used. All outriggers and additional connections shall not be protected.

The test wall assembly shall be constructed and secured to the test apparatus using fastening and construction details representative of actual field conditions. Details of the erection shall follow the manufacturer's instructions and shall be typical of actual product use. When a product has vertical or horizontal joints/seams, joints/seams typical of normal construction including caulking, backing and other details as appropriate shall be incorporated into the test assembly.

Prior to test, the test wall assembly and its components shall be cured as required by the manufacturer. In the case of cementitious coatings/materials, a minimum of 28 days shall elapse from completion of construction to testing. During the cure time, the wall assemblies shall be protected from weather.

SECTION 26.904 — INSTRUMENTATION

The test instrumentation shall consist of the following:

1. Temperature measurements at the following locations:

   1.1 Exterior face of test wall assembly as shown in Figure 26-9-12,

   1.2 Core of the test wall assembly as shown in Figures 26-9-12 and 26-9-15,

   1.3 Interior surface of test wall system as shown in Figure 26-9-13, and

   1.4 Burn room ceiling area as shown in Figure 26-9-14.

The temperature measurements shall be made using 20 gage, Type K thermocouples except that those used to measure the temperatures shown in Figure 26-9-14 shall be 18 gage, Type K thermocouples.

2. Flow rate of gas to each of the burners shall be monitored and recorded.

All data shall be recorded at intervals not to exceed 15 seconds.

SECTION 26.905 — DOCUMENTATION

Documentation shall consist of the following:

1. Thirty-five mm color slides/photographs during construction of the test wall assembly, during actual test (at least once every minute), and posttest to include dissection of the test assembly;

2. Color videotape of the exterior face of the test wall assembly prior to, during and posttest;

3. Immediately prior to the start of the test, the exterior face of the assembly, the laboratory test report identification number and test date shall be filmed;

4. Color videotape of the test wall/floor intersection in the second floor level during the test period. This camera is used to assist in determination of flame penetration and/or smoke development; and

5. A clock or timer depicting "real time" shall be included in all videos. The timer may be integral to the video camera or a clock/timer may be used provided it can be clearly viewed throughout the test.

SECTION 26.906 — TEST PROCEDURE

The following test procedure shall be used:

1. Instrumentation on the completed test wall assembly shall be verified for operation;

2. Placement of window burner shall be verified;

3. Ambient conditions prior to test shall be as follows:

   3.1 Temperature: 50°F to 90°F (10°C to 32°C)

   3.2 Relative humidity: 20 percent to 80 percent

   3.3 Airflow across the exterior face of the test assembly shall be less than 4.4 ft./sec. (1.3 m/s) as determined by an anemometer placed at right angles to the exterior face;

4. Start video and data collection one minute prior to ignition of room burner;

5. Ignition of burn room burner;

6. Follow flow regime for burners;

7. Record visual observation of the performance of the wall assembly during the test period;

8. At 30 minutes after ignition of room burner, shut-off gas supply to both burners;

9. Continue data collection until residual burning has stopped or 10 minutes has elapsed after gas flow was shut off;

10. Allow any residual burning on the wall assembly to continue until extinguishment or until 10 minutes has elapsed after gas flow was shut off; and

11. The interior and exterior walls shall be photographed and visual observations taken. The test wall assembly shall be dismantled and dissected to determine height and depth of damage within the combustible core and the condition of the panel facings.

SECTION 26.907 — CALIBRATION PROCEDURE

An initial calibration test shall be performed to evaluate the flow rates of the gas burners and it shall be conducted prior to product testing.

The test wall assembly for the calibration test shall be constructed of two layers of $5/8$ inch (15.9 mm) thick, Type X gypsum wallboard applied to both sides of 18 gage steel studs that are at 24 inch (610 mm) centers. All joints shall be taped or caulked. Figure 26-9-16 provides a sketch of this construction. The test wall assembly shall extend 18 feet (5486 mm) above the first floor level and shall be 14 feet (4267 mm) wide.

The interior surface of the window opening shall be gypsum wallboard.

No spandrel beam shall be used.

Calibration instrumentation shall consist of the following:

1. As a minimum, temperature measurements at the locations shown in Figures 26-9-17 through 26-9-19 shall be made. The temperature measurements shall be made using 20 gage, Type K thermocouples except that those used to measure the temperatures shown in Figure 26-9-18 shall be 18 gage, Type K thermocouples.

2. A minimum of three 0-5 watt/cm^2 circular foil total heat flux gauges. Figure 26-9-17 provides the locations for these instruments; and

3. Flow rate measurements for each of the burners.

Prior to the conduct of the calibration test, the paper facing of the gypsum wallboard on the exterior face of the calibration wall assembly shall be burned away. This is accomplished by igniting both the room burner and the window burner and immediately adjusting the burners to their maximum flow rates as prescribed in Table 26-9-A. The burners shall be run for five minutes at these flows.

The calibration test shall be conducted such that the burners are fired during the test according to the burner regime shown in Table 26-9-A. Each burner shall be at its assigned flow rate within 15 seconds of each change.

The initial calibration test shall be conducted with the window burner positioned such that the vertical centerline of the burner is flush with the exterior face of the wall assembly.

At the conclusion of the test, the data obtained shall be compared to the specified values in Table 26-9-B. To prevent burner changes from affecting the data, determine the average values for each time period, using data from 15 seconds into the period through 15 seconds short of the end of the period. For example, if the average for the 5-10 minute time interval is being processed, use the data from the actual times of 5:15 through 9:45 for the average.

The allowable tolerances for the comparison of determined average values to the specified average values shall be ± 10 percent for temperatures and as shown in Table 26-9-B for the heat flux measurements. All of the determined average values for the locations shown in Table 26-9-B shall fall within the tolerances of those specified in Table 26-9-B. The values for Thermocouples 1 and 8 through 14, as shown in Figure 26-9-17, shall be reported, but they are not used in the calibration determination.

If the actual test values are not within the allowable tolerances, then the calibration shall be repeated and the gas flows or window burner position adjusted until the determined values are within the allowable tolerances.

If it is demonstrated that the burners must follow different flow rates to attain the prescribed burn room and/or exterior temperatures and heat fluxes, then the flows derived from the calibration test shall be used.

If it is demonstrated that the window burner must be repositioned within 0 to 5 inches (127 mm) of the exterior face of the calibration wall to attain the prescribed exterior temperatures and heat fluxes, then the position derived from the calibration shall be used in all subsequent testing.

The following calibrations shall be performed:

1. Initially, prior to the first wall assembly test,

2. When significant changes (i.e., new flow meters, etc.) to the gas flow systems are made, and

3. Within one year prior to the test of an actual product wall assembly.

SECTION 26.908 — CONDITIONS OF ACCEPTANCE

The performance of the test wall assembly shall be judged on the basis of visual observations both during and after the test in conjunction with the temperature data obtained during the test. An exterior nonload-bearing wall assembly shall be considered as meeting the requirements for acceptable performance if during the 30-minute test period:

1. Flame propagation does not occur either vertically or laterally beyond the area of flame plume impingement on the exterior face of the wall assembly. Propagation is judged to occur if

   1.1 Temperatures of 1000°F (538°C) are attained at any of Thermocouples 11, 14, 15, 16 and 17 (Refer to Figure 26-9-12), or

   1.2 Flames emitting from the surface of the exterior face reach a vertical elevation of 10 feet (3048 mm) above the top of the window opening, or

   1.3 Flames emitting from the surface of the exterior face reach a lateral distance of 5 feet (1524 mm) from the vertical centerline of the window opening. Figure 26-9-20 provides a sketch showing these limits.

2. Flame propagation does not occur either vertically or laterally through the core components as determined by the following:

   2.1 For wall systems constructed of exterior wall panels greater than $1/4$ inch (6.4 mm) thick having combustible components (refer to Figures 26-9-12 and 26-9-15, Details A and B), temperatures in the combustible components shall not exceed 750°F (399°C) above ambient as measured by Thermocouples 28, 34, 35, 39, 40, 31, 32, 33, 36, 37 and 38.

   2.2 For wall systems constructed of exterior wall panels $1/4$ inch (6.4 mm) thick or less having combustible components and utilizing a wall cavity with an air space (refer to Figures 26-9-12 and 26-9-15, Detail C),

   2.2.1 Temperatures in the air cavity shall not exceed 1000°F (538°C) as measured by Thermocouples 28, 34, 35, 39, 40, 31, 32, 33, 36, 37 and 38 and

   2.2.2 Temperatures in the wall cavity insulation shall not exceed 750°F (399°C) above ambient as measured by Thermocouples 55, 56, 57, 58, 59, 60, 61, 62, 63, 64 and 65.

   2.3 For wall systems constructed of exterior wall panels $1/4$ inch (6.4 mm) thick or less having combustible components and utilizing a wall cavity without an air space (refer to Figures 26-9-12 and 26-9-15, Detail D), temperatures in the cavity insulation shall not exceed 750°F (399°C) above ambient as measured by Thermocouples 28, 34, 35, 39, 40, 31, 32, 33, 36, 37 and 38.

3. Flame propagation does not occur laterally beyond the limits of the burn room. This determination shall be made based on

   3.1 Flames do not occur over the surfaces of the exterior face beyond the concrete block fixture walls.

   3.2 Flames do not occur beyond the intersection of the test wall assembly and the concrete block fixture walls.

   3.3 Flame propagation does not occur laterally through the core components in the first floor area based on

   3.3.1 For wall systems constructed of exterior wall panels greater than $1/4$ inch (6.4 mm) thick having combustible components (refer to Figures 26-9-12 and 26-9-15, Details A and B), temperatures in the combustible components shall not

exceed 750°F (399°C) above ambient as measured by Thermocouples 18 and 19.

   3.3.2 For wall systems constructed of exterior wall panels $1/4$ inch (6.4 mm) thick or less having combustible components and utilizing a wall cavity with an air space (refer to Figures 26-9-12 and 26-9-15, Detail C).

   3.3.2.1 Temperatures in the air cavity shall not exceed 1000°F (538°C) as measured by Thermocouples 18 and 19, and

   3.3.2.2 Temperatures in the wall cavity insulation shall not exceed 750°F (399°C) above ambient as measured by Thermocouples 66 and 67.

   3.3.3 For wall systems constructed of exterior wall panels $1/4$ inch (6.4 mm) thick or less having combustible components and utilizing a wall cavity without an air space (refer to Figures 26-9-12 and 26-9-15, Detail D), temperatures in the cavity insulation shall not exceed 750°F (399°C) above ambient as measured by Thermocouples 18 and 19.

4. Temperatures 1 inch (25 mm) from the interior surface of the test wall assembly within the second floor area shall not exceed 500°F (260°C) above their initial ambient temperature. This criteria is based on Thermocouples 49, 50, 51, 52, 53 and 54 (refer to Figure 26-9-13).

5. Flames shall not occur in the second floor room.

SECTION 26.909 — TEST REPORT

The test report shall contain as a minimum the following:

1. Description of the test wall assembly to include the following:

   1.1 Drawings showing structural design, plan, elevation, principal cross section plus other sections as needed for clarity and joint locations and details;

   1.2 Details of attachment of walls to the test apparatus;

   1.3 Flame spread and smoke developed values per UBC Standard 8-1 as required;

   1.4 Self-ignition temperature of plastic materials per UBC Standard 26-6;

   1.5 Potential heat value of plastic materials per UBC Standard 26-1 converted to Btu/ft.^{2} (MJ/m^2) for the assembly tested; and

   1.6 Location of thermocouples.

2. Ambient conditions at the start of the test;

3. Temperature and burner flow data obtained during the test to include total gas flow of both burners for duration of test;

4. Comparison of burner flow data obtained during the test to the burner flow data obtained during the latest calibration test;

5. Position of vertical centerline of burner with respect to the exterior face of the wall assembly for both the actual test and the previous calibration test;

6. Visual observations made during the test;

7. Photographs of the following:

   7.1 Test wall—prior to test—exterior face

   7.2 Test wall—test in progress—exterior face

   7.3 Test wall—posttest—exterior face

7.4 Test wall—posttest—interior face—both floors

7.5 Core insulation of wall—posttest

8. Damage sketch(es) of the wall assembly;

9. Extent of residual burning;

10. Smoke accumulation inside the second-story room; and

11. Performance of the wall assembly with respect to each of the Conditions of Acceptance.

TABLE 26-9-A—CALIBRATION FLOW RATES

TIME INTERVAL	ROOM BURNER SCFM (m³/min)	ROOM BURNER kW (Btu/min.)	WINDOW BURNER SCFM (m³/min)	WINDOW BURNER kW (Btu/min.)
0:00 - 5:00	38.0 (1.08)	687 (39,064)	0.0 (0.00)	0 (0)
5:00 - 10:00	38.0 (1.08)	687 (39,064)	9.0 (0.25)	163 (9,252)
10:00 - 15:00	43.0 (1.22)	777 (44,204)	12.0 (0.34)	217 (12,336)
15:00 - 20:00	46.0 (1.30)	831 (47,288)	16.0 (0.45)	289 (16,448)
20:00 - 25:00	46.0 (1.30)	831 (47,288)	19.0 (0.54)	343 (19,532)
25:00 - 30:00	50.0 (1.42)	904 (51,400)	22.0 (0.62)	398 (22,616)

TABLE 26-9-B—CALIBRATION AVERAGE VALUES ($\overline{X}$ values for time period indicated)

TIME	0-5	5-10	10-15	15-20	20-25	25-30
Burn Room $\overline{X}$ Temperature [°F (°C)]	1151 (622)	1346 (730)	1482 (806)	1600 (871)	1597 (869)	1648 (898)
Interior Wall Surface $\overline{X}$ of 3 [°F (°C)]	1065 (574)	1298 (703)	1433 (778)	1578 (859)	1576 (858)	1655 (902)
1 foot (305 mm) above Window [°F (°C)]	602 (317)	870 (466)	952 (511)	992 (533)	1046 (563)	1078 (581)
2 feet (610 mm) above Window [°F (°C)]	679 (359)	1015 (546)	1121 (605)	1183 (639)	1245 (674)	1296 (702)
3 feet (914 mm) above Window [°F (°C)]	646 (341)	971 (521)	1096 (591)	1174 (634)	1245 (674)	1314 (712)
4 feet (1219 mm) above Window [°F (°C)]	577 (302)	858 (459)	982 (528)	1063 (573)	1135 (613)	1224 (662)
5 feet (1524 mm) above Window [°F (°C)]	521 (272)	765 (407)	875 (469)	949 (509)	1007 (542)	1106 (597)
6 feet (1829 mm) above Window [°F (°C)]	472 (244)	690 (366)	787 (419)	856 (458)	913 (489)	1010 (543)
Calorimeter 2 feet (610 mm) above Window (W/cm²)	0.9 ± 0.2	1.9 ± 0.4	2.5 ± 0.5	2.9 ± 0.6	3.4 ± 0.7	3.8 ± 0.8
Calorimeter 3 feet (914 mm) above Window (W/cm²)	1.0 ± 0.2	2.0 ± 0.4	2.6 ± 0.5	3.2 ± 0.6	3.7 ± 0.7	4.0 ± 0.8
Calorimeter 4 feet (1219 mm) above Window (W/cm²)	0.8 ± 0.2	1.5 ± 0.3	2.0 ± 0.4	2.5 ± 0.5	3.0 ± 0.6	3.4 ± 0.7

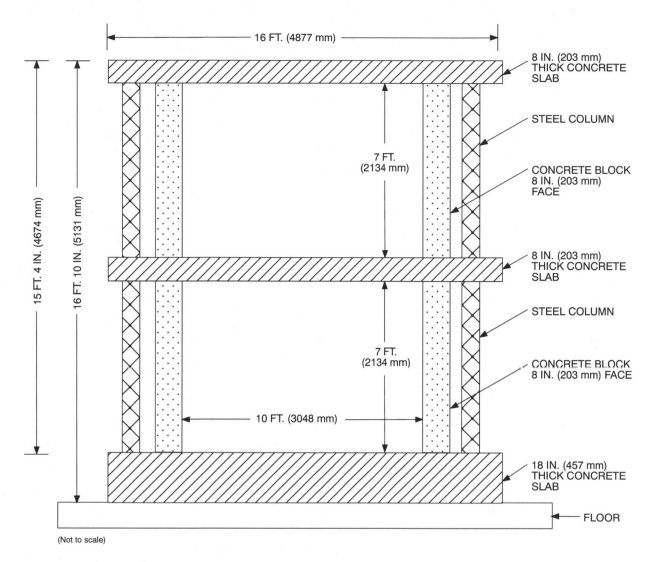

FIGURE 26-9-1—FRONT VIEW OF TEST STRUCTURE

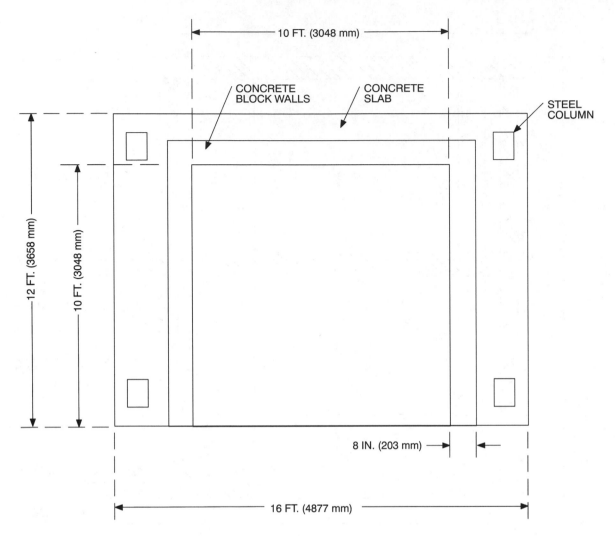

FIGURE 26-9-2—PLAN VIEW—BOTH FLOORS

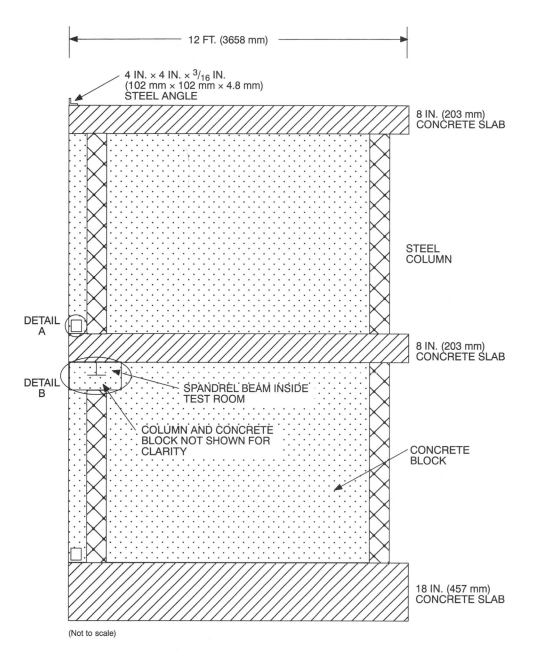

(Not to scale)

FIGURE 26-9-3—SIDE VIEW

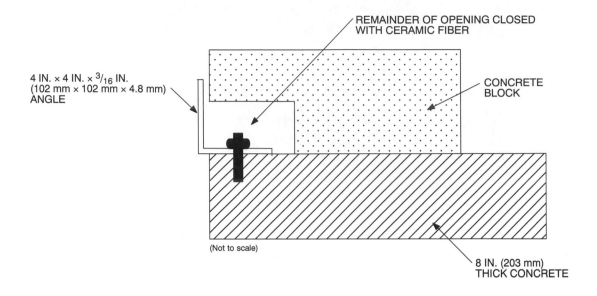

DETAIL A

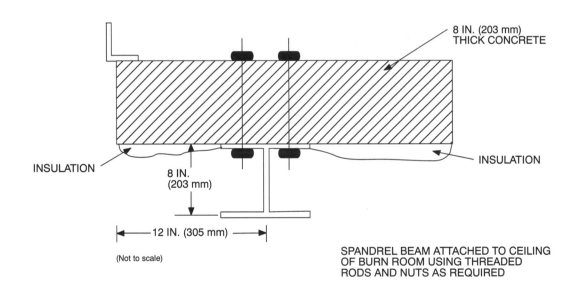

DETAIL B

FIGURE 26-9-4—TEST FIXTURE DETAILS

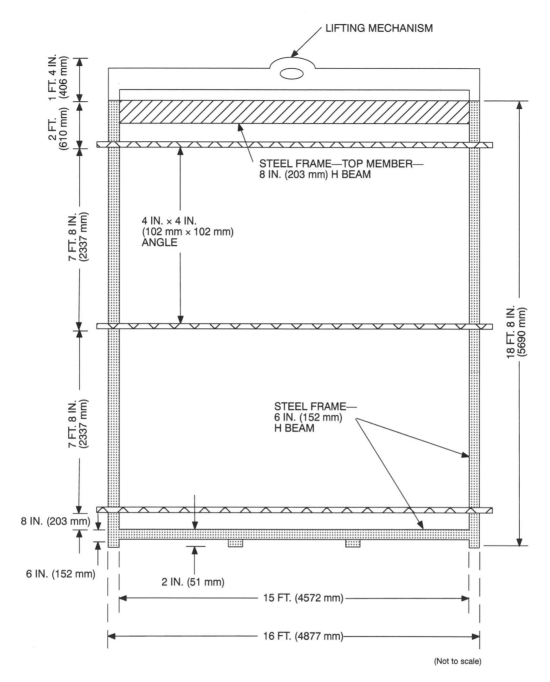

LIFTING MECHANISM

STEEL FRAME—TOP MEMBER— 8 IN. (203 mm) H BEAM

4 IN. × 4 IN. (102 mm × 102 mm) ANGLE

STEEL FRAME— 6 IN. (152 mm) H BEAM

1 FT. 4 IN. (406 mm)

2 FT. (610 mm)

7 FT. 8 IN. (2337 mm)

7 FT. 8 IN. (2337 mm)

8 IN. (203 mm)

6 IN. (152 mm)

2 IN. (51 mm)

18 FT. 8 IN. (5690 mm)

15 FT. (4572 mm)

16 FT. (4877 mm)

(Not to scale)

FIGURE 26-9-5—FRONT VIEW OF WALL FRAME

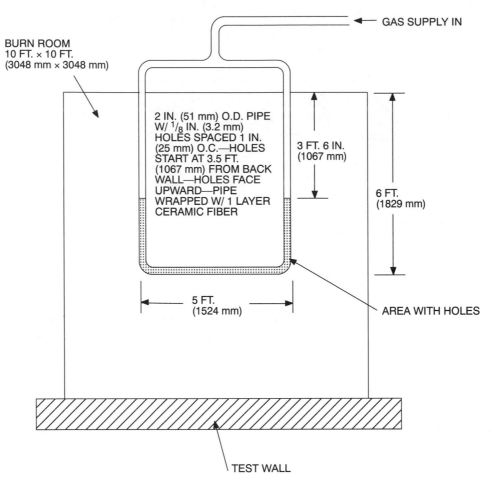

FIGURE 26-9-6—BURN ROOM BURNER—PLAN VIEW

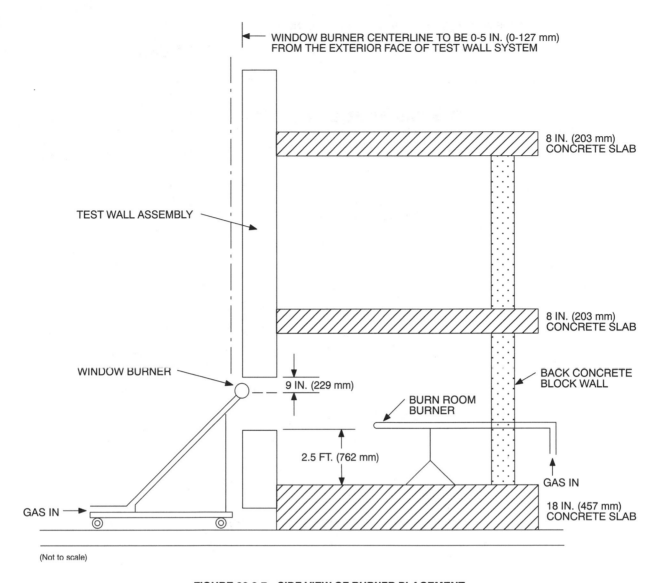

FIGURE 26-9-7—SIDE VIEW OF BURNER PLACEMENT

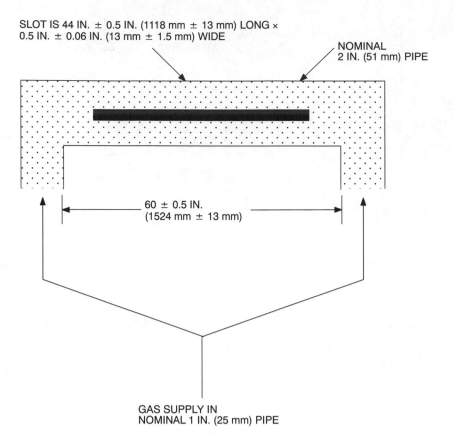

SLOT IS 44 IN. ± 0.5 IN. (1118 mm ± 13 mm) LONG ×
0.5 IN. ± 0.06 IN. (13 mm ± 1.5 mm) WIDE

NOMINAL
2 IN. (51 mm) PIPE

60 ± 0.5 IN.
(1524 mm ± 13 mm)

GAS SUPPLY IN
NOMINAL 1 IN. (25 mm) PIPE

BURNER WRAPPED WITH 1 LAYER OF CERAMIC
INSULATION AND CENTERED HORIZONTALLY IN
WINDOW OPENING

FIGURE 26-9-8—PLAN VIEW OF WINDOW BURNER

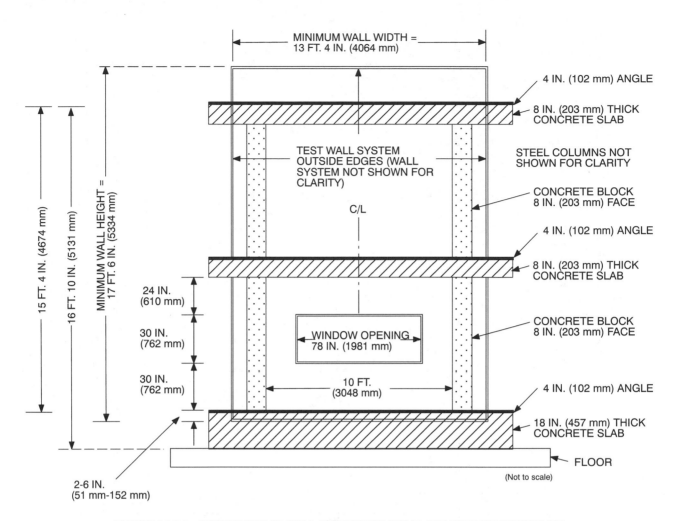

FIGURE 26-9-9—FRONT VIEW OF WALL SYSTEM BUILT IN PLACE ON TEST STRUCTURE

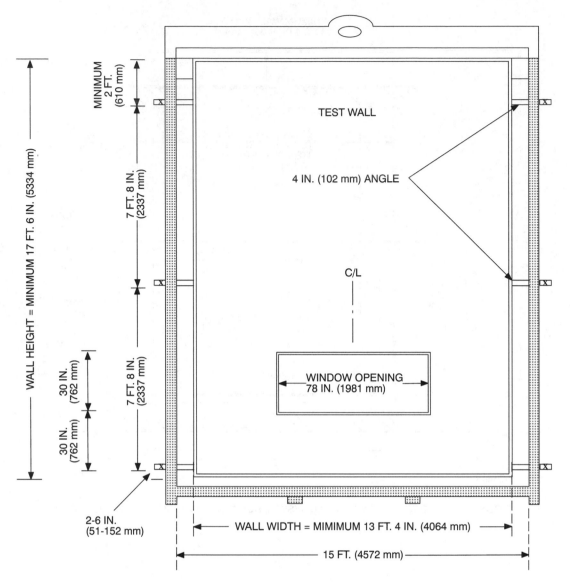

FIGURE 26-9-10—FRONT VIEW OF WALL SYSTEM IN FRAME

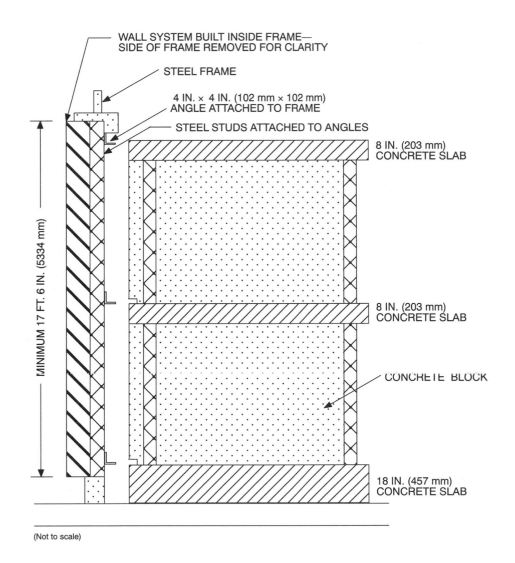

(Not to scale)

FIGURE 26-9-11—SIDE VIEW OF WALL SYSTEM IN FRAME

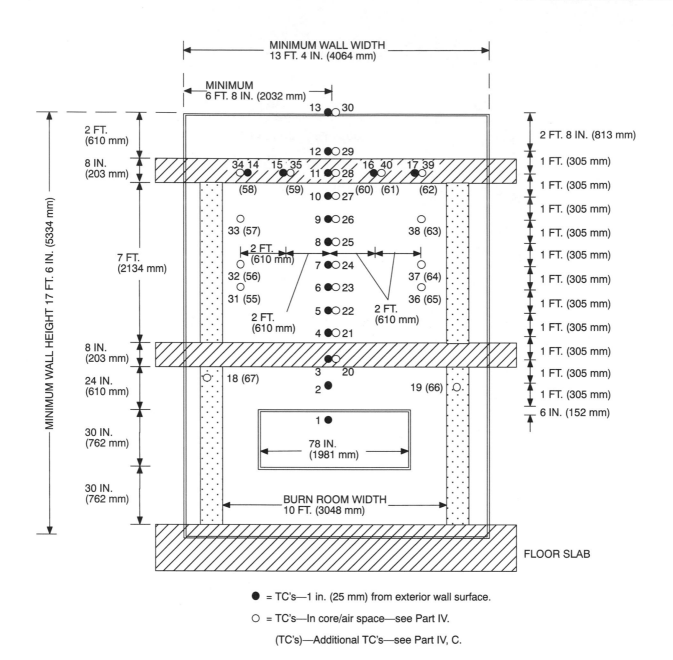

● = TC's—1 in. (25 mm) from exterior wall surface.

○ = TC's—In core/air space—see Part IV.

(TC's)—Additional TC's—see Part IV, C.

EXTERIOR VIEW OF EXTERIOR WALL

FIGURE 26-9-12—INSTRUMENTATION ARRANGEMENT—PART I

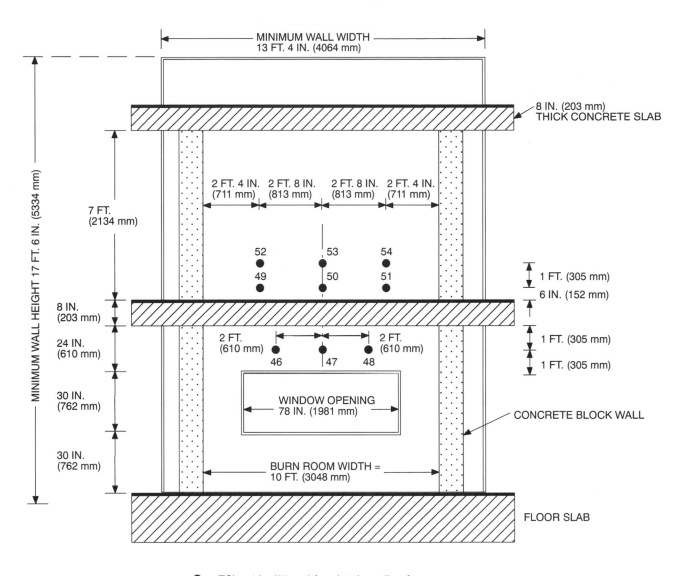

● = TC's—1 in. (25 mm) from interior wall surface.

INTERIOR VIEW OF EXTERIOR WALL

FIGURE 26-9-13—INSTRUMENTATION ARRANGEMENT—PART II

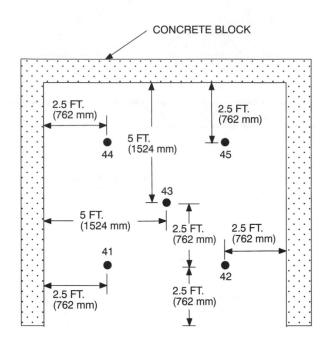

● = Thermocouples (5) inside burn room 6 in. (152 mm) below ceiling.

PLAN VIEW LOOKING DOWN – BURN ROOM

FIGURE 26-9-14—INSTRUMENTATION ARRANGEMENT—PART III

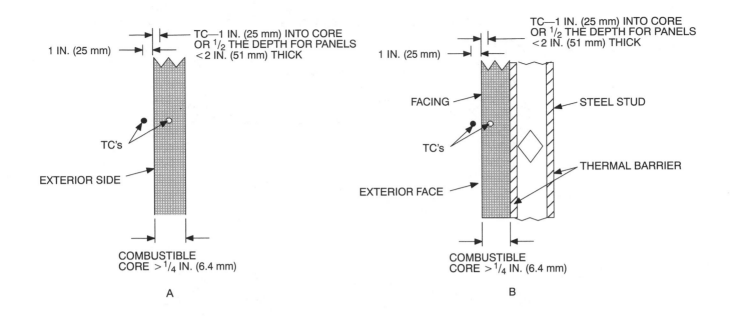

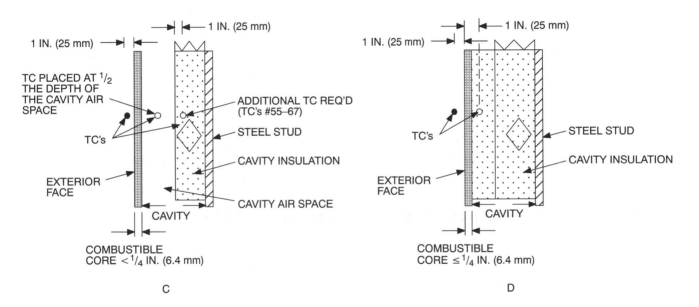

FIGURE 26-9-15—INSTRUMENTATION ARRANGEMENT—PART IV

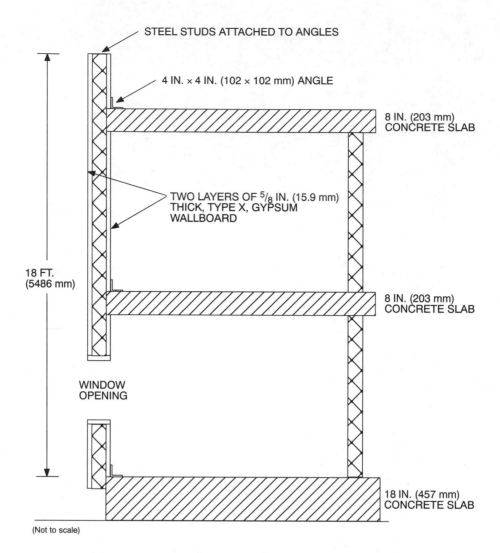

FIGURE 26-9-16—SIDE VIEW OF CALIBRATION WALL SYSTEM

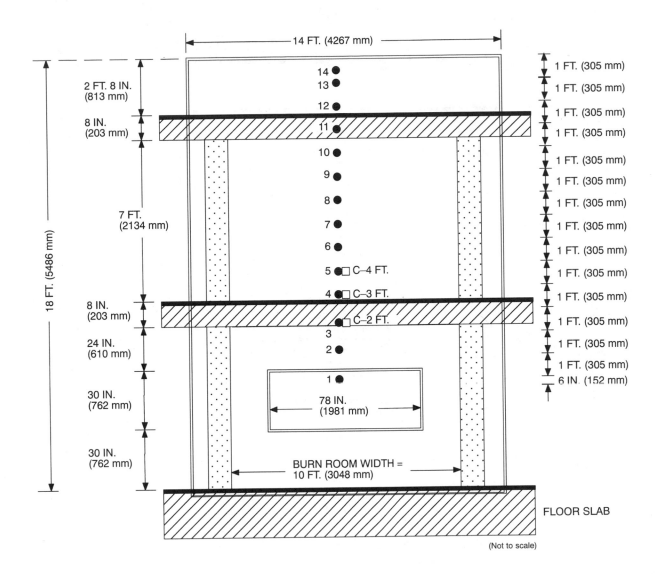

● = TC's—1 in. (25 mm) from exterior wall surface.

□ = Calorimeters in wall—flush w/ exterior wall surface.

FRONT VIEW OF EXTERIOR WALL

FIGURE 26-9-17—CALIBRATION INSTRUMENTATION—PART I

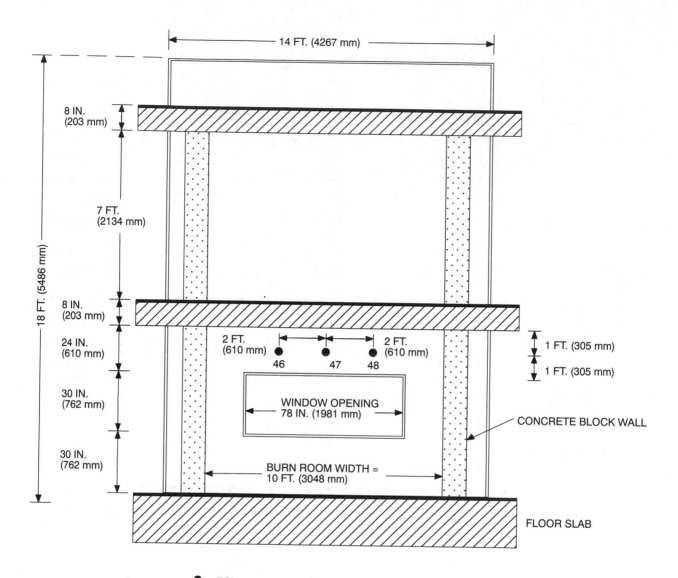

● = TC's—1 in. (25 mm) from exterior wall surface.

INTERIOR VIEW OF EXTERIOR WALL

FIGURE 26-9-18—CALIBRATION INSTRUMENTATION—PART II

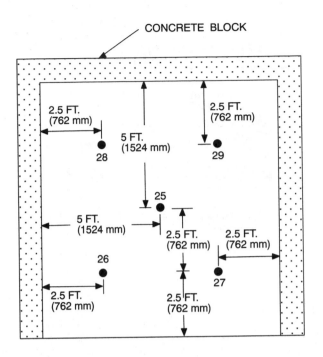

CONCRETE BLOCK

● = Thermocouples (5) inside burn room 6 in. (152 mm) below ceiling.

PLAN VIEW LOOKING DOWN—BURN ROOM

FIGURE 26-9-19—CALIBRATION INSTRUMENTATION—PART III

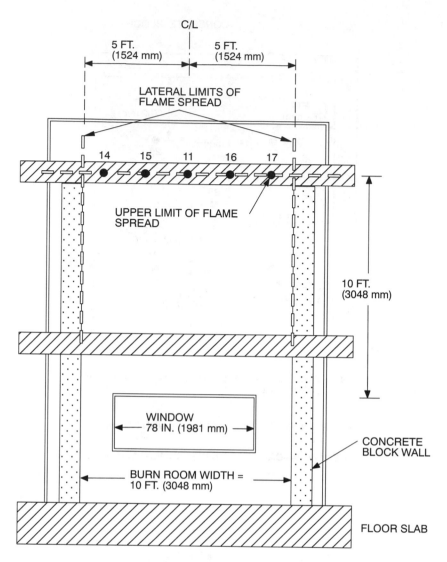

FIGURE 26-9-20—LIMITS OF FLAME PROPAGATION

UNIFORM BUILDING CODE STANDARD 31-1
FLAME-RETARDANT MEMBRANES

Test Standard of the International Conference of Building Officials

See Appendix Section 3112.2, *Uniform Building Code*

SECTION 31.101 — SCOPE

This standard covers requirements for flame-retardant membranes which are not noncombustible, intended for use in membrane structures as defined in this code.

SECTION 31.102 — TEST APPARATUS

The apparatus for conducting the flame test shall consist of a sheet-iron stack 12 inches (305 mm) square transversely, 7 feet (2134 mm) high and supported 1 foot (305 mm) above the floor on legs. The stack shall be open only at top and bottom and shall be provided with an observation window of wired glass extending the full length of the front.

The stack is to be arranged so that the specimen can be suspended vertically in the stack with its full width facing the observer with the bottom of the specimen 4 inches (101.6 mm) above the top of a Bunsen burner having $^3/_8$-inch-diameter (9.5 mm) tube and placed on the floor below the stack. The gas supply to the burner is to be natural gas or a mixture of natural and manufactured gases having a heat value of approximately 800 Btu to 1,000 Btu per cubic foot (29 807.1 kJ/m^3 to 37 258.9 kJ/m^3). With a gas pressure of $4^1/_4$ inches of water (1058 Pa), the burner is to be adjusted to produce an 11-inch (279 mm) oxidizing flame having an indistinct inner cone. Guide wire and clamps are to be provided to lightly restrain the edges of the specimen.

SECTION 31.103 — SPECIMENS

At least 10 specimens 5 inches by 7 feet (127 mm by 2134 mm) shall be tested. Specimens shall be taken from as widely separated and symmetrically located sections as possible over the entire area of representative sample of the membrane. Where there is a grain to the sample, one-half of the specimen for each conditioning shall be taken parallel to the grain and the other one-half perpendicular to the grain. At least six of the specimens shall be conditioned as specified in Section 31.104.1 and at least four of the specimens shall be conditioned as specified in Section 31.104.2.

SECTION 31.104 — CONDITIONING

31.104.1 Accelerated Weathering. One of the two procedures described below shall be followed for at least six of the test specimens:

1. The apparatus shall consist of a vertical carbon arc with solid electrodes 0.5 inch (12.7 mm) in diameter (one cored electrode is used if the arc operates on alternating current) and uniform in composition throughout, mounted at the center of a vertical metal cylinder. The arc shall be surrounded by a clear globe of optical heat-resistant glass with a cutoff at 2750A, with an increase in transmission of 91 percent at 3700A, or other enclosure having equivalent absorbing and transmitting properties. The electrodes shall be renewed at intervals sufficiently frequent to insure full operative conditions of the lamp. The globe shall be cleaned when carbons are removed or at least once in each 36 hours of operation. The arc shall be operated on 13 amperes direct current or 17 amperes, 60 cycles alternating current with the voltage at the arc of

140 volts. The specimens for test shall be mounted on the inside of the cylinder facing the arc. The diameter of the cylinder shall be such that the distance of the face of the specimen holder from the center of the arc is $14^3/_4$ inches (374.7 mm). The cylinder shall rotate about the arc at a uniform speed of approximately three revolutions per hour. A water spray discharging about 0.7 gallon per minute (2.7 L/min.) shall strike each specimen in turn for about one minute during each revolution of the cylinder. Specimens shall be subjected to this exposure for 360 hours. They shall then be allowed to dry thoroughly at a temperature between 70°F and 100°F (21°C and 38°C).

2. The apparatus shall consist of a vertical carbon arc mounted at the center of a vertical cylinder. The arc is designed to accommodate two pairs of carbons, No. 22, upper carbons, and No. 13, lower carbons; however, the arc burns between only one pair of carbons at a time. The arc shall be operated on 60 amperes and 50 volts across the arc for alternating current or 50 amperes and 60 volts across the arc for direct current. The specimens for test shall be mounted on a rotating rack inside the cylinder and facing the arc. The diameter of the rotating rack shall be such that the distance from the center of the arc to the face of the specimen is $18^3/_4$ inches (476.3 mm). The rack shall rotate about the arc at a uniform speed of about one revolution in two hours. No filters or enclosures shall be used between the arc and the specimens. Spray nozzles shall be mounted in the cylinder so that the specimens shall be exposed to wetting once during each revolution of the rack. Specimens shall be subjected to this exposure for 100 hours. They shall then be allowed to dry thoroughly at a temperature between 70°F and 100°F (21°C and 38°C).

31.104.2 Unweathered Samples. At least four of the test specimens shall be conditioned in an oven having forced air circulation with free airflow around each specimen at temperatures of 140°F to 145°F (60°C to 63°C) for durations of not less than one hour nor more than one and one-half hours before testing. Materials which distort or melt at the above indicated oven exposure are to be conditioned at 60°F to 80°F (15.5°C to 26.7°C) and 25 to 50 percent relative humidity for not less than 24 hours. Specimens shall be removed from the oven one at a time and immediately subjected to the flame test described in Section 31.105.

SECTION 31.105 — TESTING

Suspend the specimen in the apparatus attaching clamps to the edges to retain the specimen in position. Position the burner so that the flame will be applied near the middle of the lower end of the specimen and fix the barrel of the burner at an angle of 25 degrees.

The test flame shall be applied to the specimen for two minutes, then withdrawn, and the duration of flaming combustion on the specimen recorded. After all flaming and afterglow on the specimen has ceased, the length of char shall be determined. For purposes of this test, the length of char is defined as the vertical distance on the specimen from the tip of the test flame to the top of the charred area resulting from spread of flame and afterglow. For synthetic membranes, the length of char is defined as the vertical distance from the tip of the test flame to a horizontal line, above which all material is sound and in essentially original condition.

SECTION 31.106 — CONDITION OF ACCEPTANCE

When subjected to the test described in Section 31.105, material shall not continue flaming for more than two seconds after the test flame is removed from contact with the specimen. The vertical spread of burning on the material shall not exceed 10 inches (254 mm) above the tip of the test flame. This vertical spread shall be measured as the distance from the tip of the test flame to a horizontal line above which all material is sound and in original condition, except for possible smoke deposits.

Portions or residues of textiles or films which break or drip from the test specimens shall not continue to flame after they reach the floor of the tester.

UNIT CONVERSION TABLES

SI SYMBOLS AND PREFIXES

BASE UNITS		
Quantity	**Unit**	**Symbol**
Length	Meter	m
Mass	Kilogram	kg
Time	Second	s
Electric current	Ampere	A
Thermodynamic temperature	Kelvin	K
Amount of substance	Mole	mol
Luminous intensity	Candela	cd

SI SUPPLEMENTARY UNITS		
Quantity	**Unit**	**Symbol**
Plane angle	Radian	rad
Solid angle	Steradian	sr

SI PREFIXES		
Multiplication Factor	**Prefix**	**Symbol**
$1\ 000\ 000\ 000\ 000\ 000\ 000 = 10^{18}$	exa	E
$1\ 000\ 000\ 000\ 000\ 000 = 10^{15}$	peta	P
$1\ 000\ 000\ 000\ 000 = 10^{12}$	tera	T
$1\ 000\ 000\ 000 = 10^{9}$	giga	G
$1\ 000\ 000 = 10^{6}$	mega	M
$1\ 000 = 10^{3}$	kilo	k
$100 = 10^{2}$	hecto	h
$10 = 10^{1}$	deka	da
$0.1 = 10^{-1}$	deci	d
$0.01 = 10^{-2}$	centi	c
$0.001 = 10^{-3}$	milli	m
$0.000\ 001 = 10^{-6}$	micro	μ
$0.000\ 000\ 001 = 10^{-9}$	nano	n
$0.000\ 000\ 000\ 001 = 10^{-12}$	pico	p
$0.000\ 000\ 000\ 000\ 001 = 10^{-15}$	femto	f
$0.000\ 000\ 000\ 000\ 000\ 001 = 10^{-18}$	atto	a

SI DERIVED UNIT WITH SPECIAL NAMES			
Quantity	**Unit**	**Symbol**	**Formula**
Frequency (of a periodic phenomenon)	hertz	Hz	$1/s$
Force	newton	N	$kg \cdot m/s^2$
Pressure, stress	pascal	Pa	N/m^2
Energy, work, quantity of heat	joule	J	$N \cdot m$
Power, radiant flux	watt	W	J/s
Quantity of electricity, electric charge	coulomb	C	$A \cdot s$
Electric potential, potential difference, electromotive force	volt	V	W/A
Capacitance	farad	F	C/V
Electric resistance	ohm	Ω	V/A
Conductance	siemens	S	A/V
Magnetic flux	weber	Wb	$V \cdot s$
Magnetic flux density	tesla	T	Wb/m^2
Inductance	henry	H	Wb/A
Luminous flux	lumen	lm	$cd \cdot sr$
Illuminance	lux	lx	lm/m^2
Activity (of radionuclides)	becquerel	Bq	$1/s$
Absorbed dose	gray	Gy	J/kg

CONVERSION FACTORS

To convert	to	multiply by
LENGTH		
1 mile (U.S. statute)	km	1.609 344
1 yd	m	0.9144
1 ft	m	0.3048
	mm	304.8
1 in	mm	25.4
AREA		
1 mile^2 (U.S. statute)	km^2	2.589 998
1 acre (U.S. survey)	ha	0.404 6873
	m^2	4046.873
1 yd^2	m^2	0.836 1274
1 ft^2	m^2	0.092 903 04
1 in^2	mm^2	645.16
VOLUME, MODULUS OF SECTION		
1 acre ft	m^3	1233.489
1 yd^3	m^3	0.764 5549
100 board ft	m^3	0.235 9737
1 ft^3	m^3	0.028 316 85
	L(dm^3)	28.3168
1 in^3	mm^3	16 387.06
	mL (cm^3)	16.3871
1 barrel (42 U.S. gallons)	m^3	0.158 9873
(FLUID) CAPACITY		
1 gal (U.S. liquid)*	L**	3.785 412
1 qt (U.S. liquid)	mL	946.3529
1 pt (U.S. liquid)	mL	473.1765
1 fl oz (U.S.)	mL	29.5735
1 gal (U.S. liquid)	m^3	0.003 785 412
*1 gallon (UK) approx. 1.2 gal (U.S.)	**1 liter approx. 0.001 cubic meter	
SECOND MOMENT OF AREA		
1 in^4	mm^4	416 231 4
	m^4	416 231 4 $\times$ 10^{-7}
PLANE ANGLE		
1° (degree)	rad	0.017 453 29
	mrad	17.453 29
1' (minute)	urad	290.8882
1" (second)	urad	4.848 137
VELOCITY, SPEED		
1 ft/s	m/s	0.3048
1 mile/h	km/h	1.609 344
	m/s	0.447 04
VOLUME RATE OF FLOW		
1 ft^3/s	m^3/s	0.028 316 85
1 ft^3/min	L/s	0.471 9474
1 gal/min	L/s	0.063 0902
1 gal/min	m^3/min	0.0038
1 gal/h	mL/s	1.051 50
1 million gal/d	L/s	43.8126
1 acre ft/s	m^3/s	1233.49
TEMPERATURE INTERVAL		
1°F	°C or K	0.555 556 $^5/_9$°C = $^5/_9$K
EQUIVALENT TEMPERATURE ($t_{°C} = T_K - 273.15$)		
$t_{°F}$	$t_{°C}$	$t_{°F} = {}^9/_5 t_{°C} + 32$

(Continued)

CONVERSION FACTORS—(Continued)

To convert	to	multiply by
MASS		
1 ton (short ***)	metric ton	0.907 185
	kg	907.1847
1 lb	kg	0.453 5924
1 oz	g	28.349 52
***1 long ton (2,240 lb)	kg	1016.047
MASS PER UNIT AREA		
1 lb/ft^2	kg/m^2	4.882 428
1 oz/yd^2	g/m^2	33.905 75
1 oz/ft^2	g/m^2	305.1517
DENSITY (MASS PER UNIT VOLUME)		
1 lb/ft^3	kg/m^3	16.01846
1 lb/yd^3	kg/m^3	0.593 2764
1 ton/yd^3	t/m^3	1.186 553
FORCE		
1 tonf (ton-force)	kN	8.896 44
1 kip (1,000 lbf)	kN	4.448 22
1 lbf (pound-force)	N	4.448 22
MOMENT OF FORCE, TORQUE		
1 lbf·ft	N·m	1.355 818
1 lbf·in	N·m	0.112 9848
1 tonf·ft	kN·m	2.711 64
1 kip·ft	kN·m	1.355 82
FORCE PER UNIT LENGTH		
1 lbf/ft	N/m	14.5939
1 lbf/in	N/m	175.1268
1 tonf/ft	kN/m	29.1878
PRESSURE, STRESS, MODULUS OF ELASTICITY (FORCE PER UNIT AREA) (1 Pa = 1 N/m^2)		
1 tonf/in^2	MPa	13.7895
1 tonf/ft^2	kPa	95.7605
1 kip/in^2	MPa	6.894 757
1 lbf/in^2	kPa	6.894 757
1 lbf/ft^2	Pa	47.8803
Atmosphere	kPa	101.3250
1 inch mercury	kPa	3.376 85
1 foot (water column at 32°F)	kPa	2.988 98
WORK, ENERGY, HEAT(1J = 1N·m = 1W·s)		
1 kWh (550 ft·lbf/s)	MJ	3.6
1 Btu (Int. Table)	kJ	1.055 056
	J	1055.056
1 ft·lbf	J	1.355 818
COEFFICIENT OF HEAT TRANSFER		
1 Btu/(ft^2·h·°F)	W/(m^2·K)	5.678 263
THERMAL CONDUCTIVITY		
1 Btu/(ft·h·°F)	W/(m·K)	1.730 735
ILLUMINANCE		
1 lm/ft^2 (footcandle)	lx (lux)	10.763 91
LUMINANCE		
1 cd/ft^2	cd/m^2	10.7639
1 foot lambert	cd/m^2	3.426 259
1 lambert	kcd/m^2	3.183 099

GAGE CONVERSION TABLE

APPROXIMATE MINIMUM THICKNESS (inch/mm) FOR CARBON SHEET STEEL CORRESPONDING TO MANUFACTURER'S STANDARD GAGE AND GALVANIZED SHEET GAGE NUMBERS

Manufacturer's Standard Gage No.	CARBON SHEET STEEL				Galvanized Sheet Gage No.	GALVANIZED SHEET			
	Decimal and Nominal Thickness Equivalent		Recommended Minimum Thickness Equivalent[1]			Decimal and Nominal Thickness Equivalent		Recommended Minimum Thickness Equivalent[1]	
	(inch)	(mm)[2]	(inch)	(mm)[2]		(inch)	(mm)[2]	(inch)	(mm)[2]
8	0.1644	4.17	0.156	3.46	8	0.1681	4.27	0.159	4.04
9	0.1495	3.80	0.142	3.61	9	0.1532	3.89	0.144	3.66
10	0.1345	3.42	0.127	3.23	10	0.1382	3.51	0.129	3.23
11	0.1196	3.04	0.112	2.84	11	0.1233	3.13	0.114	2.90
12	0.1046	2.66	0.097	2.46	12	0.1084	2.75	0.099	2.51
13	0.0897	2.28	0.083	2.11	13	0.0934	2.37	0.084	2.13
14	0.0747	1.90	0.068	1.73	14	0.0785	1.97	0.070	1.78
15	0.0673	1.71	0.062	1.57	15	0.0710	1.80	0.065	1.65
16	0.0598	1.52	0.055	1.40	16	0.0635	1.61	0.058	1.47
17	0.0538	1.37	0.050	1.27	17	0.0575	1.46	0.053	1.35
18	0.0478	1.21	0.044	1.12	18	0.0516	1.31	0.047	1.19
19	0.0418	1.06	0.038	0.97	19	0.0456	1.16	0.041	1.04
20	0.0359	0.91	0.033	0.84	20	0.0396	1.01	0.036	0.91
21	0.0329	0.84	0.030	0.76	21	0.0366	0.93	0.033	0.84
22	0.0299	0.76	0.027	0.69	22	0.0336	0.85	0.030	0.76
23	0.0269	0.68	0.024	0.61	23	0.0306	0.78	0.027	0.69
24	0.0239	0.61	0.021	0.53	24	0.0276	0.70	0.024	0.61
25	0.0209	0.53	0.018	0.46	25	0.0247	0.63	0.021	0.53
26	0.0179	0.45	0.016	0.41	26	0.0217	0.55	0.019	0.48
27	0.0164	0.42	0.014	0.36	27	0.0202	0.51	0.017	0.43
28	0.0149	0.38	0.013	0.33	28	0.0187	0.47	0.016	0.41
					29	0.0172	0.44	0.014	0.36
					30	0.0157	0.40	0.013	0.33

[1]The thickness of the sheets set forth in the code correspond to the thickness shown under these columns. They are the approximate minimum thicknesses and are based on the following references:

Carbon sheet steel—Thickness 0.071 inch and over:
ASTM A 568-74, Table 3, Thickness Tolerances of Hot-Rolled Sheet
(Carbon Steel).

Carbon sheet steel—Thickness less than 0.071 inch:
ASTM A 568-74, Table 23, Thickness Tolerances of Cold-Rolled Sheet
(Carbon and High Strength Low Alloy).

Galvanized sheet steel—All thicknesses:
ASTM A 525-79, Table 4, Thickness Tolerances of Hot-Dip Galvanized Sheet.

Minimum thickness is the difference between the thickness equivalent of each gage and the maximum negative tolerance for the widest rolled width.

[2]The SI equivalents are calculated and rounded to two significant figures following the decimal point.